Annual Review of
Psychology

Production Editor: Caitlin Barbera
Managing Editors: Linley E. Hall, Nina G. Perry, Maria Duncan
Electronic Content Coordinators: Suzanne Moses, Erin H. Lee
Illustration Editor: Carin Cain

Annual Review of Psychology

Volume 69, 2018

Susan T. Fiske, *Editor*
Princeton University

Daniel L. Schacter, *Associate Editor*
Harvard University

Shelley E. Taylor, *Associate Editor*
University of California, Los Angeles

www.annualreviews.org • science@annualreviews.org • 650-493-4400

Annual Reviews
4139 El Camino Way • P.O. Box 10139 • Palo Alto, California 94303-0139

Annual Reviews
Palo Alto, California, USA

International Standard Serial Number: 0066-4308
International Standard Book Number: 978-0-8243-0269-6
Library of Congress Control Number: 50013143

TYPESET BY APTARA
PRINTED AND BOUND BY SHERIDAN BOOKS, INC., CHELSEA, MICHIGAN

Introduction

As I write, the *Annual Review of Psychology* has just spun off another new journal, the *Annual Review of Developmental Psychology*, under the founding Co-Editors Susan Gelman and Sandy Waxman. The Co-Editors will gather their Editorial Committee in 2018 to identify topics and authors to invite for their inaugural volume. They plan a lifespan approach to cognitive and social development—a much-needed series. The Co-Editors note that, due to theoretical, methodological, and technological advances over the past several decades, developmental scientists are rapidly making important new discoveries. The research findings are exciting and broadly relevant beyond psychology in fields including education, cognitive science, economics, public health, and public policy.

The *Annual Review of Psychology* generated the *Annual Review of Clinical Psychology* and the *Annual Review of Organizational Psychology and Organizational Behavior*, as well as participating in the creation of the *Annual Review of Vision Science*, not to mention the long-standing *Annual Review of Neuroscience*.

We continue to publish review articles in each of these areas, but a richer collection appears in each of these journals. Meanwhile, we will concentrate more on brain mechanisms of behavior, cognitive psychology and cognitive neuroscience, sensory sciences in general, judgment and decision making, social psychology and social neuroscience, personality psychology, health psychology, educational psychology, and methods in psychological science. As always, we still offer an array of pithy overviews aimed at students and colleagues. Relish the science!

Susan T. Fiske
Princeton, New Jersey

Daniel L. Schacter
Cambridge, Massachusetts

Shelley E. Taylor
Los Angeles, California

Annual Review of
Psychology

Volume 69, 2018

Contents

Indexes

Errata

An online log of corrections to *Annual Review of Psychology* articles may be found at
http://www.annualreviews.org/errata/psych

Related Articles

From the *Annual Review of Organizational Psychology and Organizational Behavior*, Volume 5 (2018)

From the *Annual Review of Statistics and Its Application*, Volume 5 (2018)

The Properties and Antecedents of Hedonic Decline

Jeff Galak[1] and Joseph P. Redden[2]

[1] Tepper School of Business, Carnegie Mellon University, Pittsburgh, Pennsylvania 15213; email: jgalak@cmu.edu

[2] Carlson School of Management, University of Minnesota, Minneapolis, Minnesota 55455

Annu. Rev. Psychol. 2018. 69:1–25

First published as a Review in Advance on August 30, 2017

The *Annual Review of Psychology* is online at psych.annualreviews.org

https://doi.org/10.1146/annurev-psych-122216-011542

Keywords

hedonic decline, satiation, satiety, habituation, hedonic adaptation, enjoyment

Abstract

We review the phenomenon of hedonic decline, whereby repeated exposure to a stimulus typically reduces the hedonic response (e.g., enjoyment). We first discuss the typical trajectory of hedonic decline and the common research paradigms used to study it. We next discuss the most popular theories regarding general mechanisms widely believed to underlie hedonic decline. We then propose a taxonomy to organize these various general theories and to incorporate more recent work on top-down, self-reflective theories. This taxonomy identifies three general classes of antecedents to hedonic decline: physiological feedback, perceptual changes, and self-reflection. For each class, we review the supporting evidence for specifically identified antecedents and recent developments on how each antecedent influences hedonic decline. Our review focuses especially on more recent work in the growing area of self-reflection.

Contents

INTRODUCTION

The field of psychology has long been interested in understanding the dynamics of how individuals respond to repeated exposure to a stimulus. This is especially true for liked stimuli that people most often seek out and consume. With a few exceptions, research in this area has shown that repetition of most affectively relevant stimuli eventually leads to a prominent attenuation of response (and sometimes a small initial increase). That is, at some point, people respond less and less to every additional exposure to a stimulus. We focus our review on this attenuating response, given that it is more ubiquitous than any fleeting increase in response, and review the current understanding of this phenomenon of hedonic decline.

The topic of hedonic decline is important for a variety of reasons. First, it creates a so-called hedonic treadmill (Brickman & Campbell 1971), whereby people must continually find new and better experiences merely to maintain their current level of satisfaction. Thus, a diminished hedonic response has clear implications for general well-being. Second, a core tenet of economics is that people try to maximize the utility of their experiences. Obviously, a changing hedonic response presents a dynamic aspect that makes maximizing enjoyment more difficult. Third, a diminishing hedonic response also creates difficulties for those trying to encourage behavioral change. These could include policy makers hoping for continued compliance, marketers trying to sustain satisfaction with a product, or educators struggling to maintain student interest in a topic. In sum, the ubiquitous and consequential nature of hedonic decline makes it an important phenomenon to understand.

This diminished response has typically been characterized with two particular manifestations: the desire to reconsume a stimulus and the continued enjoyment of that stimulus. Specifically, with repetition, an individual's willingness to reconsume an affectively relevant stimulus and their subsequent enjoyment of that stimulus typically decreases. Various literatures have used different terms to describe this reduction, but it has most commonly been described as homeostasis (or physiological set points), satiation, habituation, or adaptation. Although the physiological and psychological mechanisms that underlie each of these various accounts differ somewhat, the conclusions are the same: Repetition ultimately leads to a decreased hedonic response in the form of less desire and less ongoing enjoyment. To unify the literature, we call this general phenomenon hedonic decline without regard to any particular underlying mechanism.

In this review, we synthesize multiple literatures to develop a coherent understanding of how humans respond to repeated exposure to affectively relevant stimuli. We do this by first fleshing out the typical properties of hedonic decline, the common research paradigms used to investigate it, and the widely accepted general mechanisms that underlie it. We then provide a taxonomy that organizes these broad theories to incorporate both long-established findings and recent developments. Specifically, we identify three classes of antecedents to hedonic decline: physiological feedback, perceptual changes, and self-reflection. By doing so, we are able to span several siloed literatures to provide a unifying view that we hope will fuel future research in the general area of hedonic decline.

TYPICAL TRAJECTORY OF HEDONIC DECLINE

Although changes in hedonic response tend to vary considerably when viewed at the individual level, in aggregate, there are three common patterns for hedonic changes with repeated exposure to a stimulus (**Figure 1**). These are (*a*) steady decline in response (**Figure 1*a***), (*b*) protracted increased response (**Figure 1*b***), and (*c*) increased response followed by greater decline (**Figure 1*c***). The decrease in response is typically attributed to satiation (Raynor & Epstein 1999, Rolls et al. 1981, Sorensen et al. 2003), habituation (Groves & Thompson 1970, McSweeney 2004), or hedonic adaptation (Diener et al. 2006, Frederick & Loewenstein 1999, Kahneman & Snell 1992, Nelson & Meyvis 2008, Nelson et al. 2009). Any increase in response is typically attributed to arousal (Bizo et al. 1998, Killeen 1995), familiarity (Zajonc 1968), or sensitization (Crolic & Janiszewski 2016, McSweeney & Murphy 2009). The existence of the two offsetting effects of decreased and increased response, sometimes referred to as the dual process theory (Groves & Thompson 1970) or opponent process theory (Soloman & Corbit 1974), can then lead to a wide-ranging variety of patterns over time for any individual.

The most prominent response, however, is the ongoing decline observed with sufficient exposure to a stimulus. Whereas an increased response is only occasionally observed, sufficient

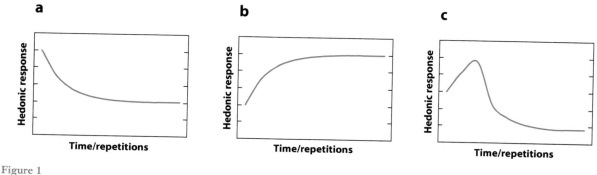

Figure 1

Three typical trajectories of hedonic response. (*a*) Steady decline in response. (*b*) Protracted increased response. (*c*) Increased response followed by greater decline.

exposure nearly always makes a decline in hedonic response inevitable. It should be noted that hedonic decline means that an initially liked stimulus becomes less pleasant with repetition, whereas an initially disliked stimulus becomes less unpleasant. For example, people derive less pleasure after repeated exposure to their favorite food (Epstein et al. 2009), music (Schellenberg et al. 2008), art (Redden 2008), or even close others (Galak et al. 2009). Likewise, participants report declines in their aversion to tart yogurt over 8 days (Kahneman & Snell 1992), decreases in irritation with an unpleasant sound after a few minutes (Nelson & Meyvis 2008), increases in manageability of incarceration over the years (Zamble 1992), and largely unchanged life satisfaction years after becoming paraplegic or quadriplegic (Schulz & Decker 1985, Wortman & Silver 1987). Although exceptions may exist (Zajonc 1968), the strong initial hedonic response from either a positive or negative stimulus eventually fades. Therefore, as a general rule, regardless of the valence, response to a stimulus inevitably diminishes with prolonged repeated exposures (i.e., hedonic decline).

Following this hedonic decline, in the absence of stimulus exposure, spontaneous recovery, or the return of hedonic response, typically occurs (Groves & Thompson 1970, Thompson & Spencer 1966). We know of no work directly examining any factors that influence the speed of spontaneous recovery following protracted hedonic decline. There is work in physiology showing that reaction recovers more quickly for responses that declined faster in the first place, often due to the rate of exposure (Rankin et al. 2009). Work on significant life events (such as the death of a loved one) indicates that recovery happens more quickly when one can more easily explain and understand the event (Wilson & Gilbert 2008). However, it is notable that none of this work explores ongoing hedonic decline specifically. More generally, little is known about either the rate of recovery from hedonic decline or the factors driving it.

COMMON RESEARCH PARADIGMS

Given that hedonic decline manifests with repeated exposure, any study of it will necessarily consider the roles of exposure quantity and time. However, the manners in which these two dimensions are manipulated greatly vary. We discuss the most common paradigms in the next sections, as well as some examples of research within each paradigm. These paradigms primarily differ on two dimensions: (*a*) whether the timing of the stimulus exposure is within a single session or across multiple sessions and (*b*) whether the hedonic response is measured once or repeatedly. We detail some of the differences among these methodologies below. However, in spite of these differences, all of these paradigms ultimately share the same goal of measuring hedonic decline (albeit in different ways).

Within-Session Paradigms

In within-session settings, there are typically two methodological approaches. First, a stimulus is repeatedly experienced to the point where consumption is typically no longer pleasurable or desired. Then, following this preload, participants are exposed to both similar and dissimilar stimuli, and either their subjective hedonic evaluations or their desire to reconsume are assessed. When subjective evaluations and desire are lower for similar stimuli than for dissimilar stimuli, one concludes that a decline in response has occurred. Alternatively, different preloads can be administered across different participants, and desire to consume a focal stimulus can be measured. If desire is lower for one of the preloaded stimuli but not the other, then decline in hedonic response is once again inferred.

For instance, in a recent study, participants were asked to consume either sweet or savory rice meal equivalent to about 10% of their daily energy needs. Following this, they were exposed to both sweet and savory snacks. Whether measured in terms of subjective evaluations, willingness to work for more snacks, or ad libitum consumption of the snacks, the same pattern of results emerged: When participants first ate the sweet rice meal, their evaluation of and desire to reconsume sweet snacks declined, whereas their evaluation of and desire to reconsume savory snacks was unaffected. In contrast, when participants first ate the savory rice meal, the opposite was true (Griffioen-Roose et al. 2010). When exposed to sufficient quantities of a stimulus, enjoyment of and desire to consume stimuli of the same type declines, and this decline is taken as a measure of decline in hedonic response.

In general, this methodology and this type of result are ubiquitous primarily in the food literature (Havermans et al. 2009, Johnson & Vickers 1993, Rolls et al. 1981, Weijzen et al. 2009). Importantly, in this paradigm, decline in hedonic response is inferred from a reduction in desire to consume the preloaded stimulus. When desire for consumption of a similar item is observed, it is inferred that this is due to a decline in hedonic response, even though this decline is only sometimes actually directly observed.

In contrast to the preload approach, the second-most-common within-session approach is to repeatedly expose participants to a stimulus. Explicit measures of the change in response are then taken using subjective ratings either after each instance or at the beginning and end of the consumption session. The decline in subjective ratings over time is taken as a measure of the decline in hedonic response.

Whereas the previous methodology is primarily observed in the context of food, this approach is prevalent in a range of contexts. For instance, in the domain of food, participants' salivation in response to and hedonic ratings of lemon and lime juice declined across 10 repetitions (Epstein et al. 1992). In the domain of music, when focused on listening to a happy song, participants initially increased their hedonic ratings, but their ratings sharply decline after sufficient exposures (Schellenberg et al. 2008). In the domain of art, participants' enjoyment of attractive photographs declined across 16 repetitions (Redden 2008). In the domain of video games, participants' hedonic ratings of a pleasurable video game declined across six rounds of play when pacing of play was sufficiently fast (Galak et al. 2013). In all of these cases, a decline in response to an affectively relevant stimulus was assessed as a function of the change in response from the first encounter to the last encounter with that stimulus. Thus, rather than exposing participants to a stimulus and then using a measure of future consumption intent as a proxy for decline in response, these studies (and many others) directly measured the change in response either via subjective ratings or through measurable physiological changes (e.g., salivation).

Across-Session Paradigms

In across-session paradigms, there are, again, two typical approaches taken. The first involves observing response decline in a relatively short testing period and then remeasuring response to the target stimulus some time later. For instance, in the context of food, women's consumption of an oil high in linoleic acid decreased following a two-week consumption period (Kamphuis et al. 2001). In a slightly different food-related context, Ethiopian refugees reported decreased pleasantness for three foods that they had been consuming for the previous 6 months compared to three novel foods (Rolls & de Waal 1985). In the context of music, participants exposed to 20 repetitions of a favorite song showed strong decline in enjoyment over these 20 within-session iterations and also showed continued suppression of enjoyment following a two-week period (Galak et al. 2009, study 1). In the context of sexual arousal, men showed decreased sexual arousal in response to sexually explicit audio recordings across six sessions spaced one week apart (O'Donohue & Plaud 1991). In all of these cases, there was an initial decrease in hedonic response that was observed to last for a long period of time. Importantly, hedonic responses were always assessed at least twice, allowing for direct observation of hedonic decline.

In contrast, the second approach involves comparing the subjective evaluations of individuals who have experienced a long-lasting stimulus to individuals who have not. If a decline in response has occurred, then one would expect those individuals to have different hedonic responses over time. For example, lottery winners were shown to be no happier than non–lottery winners after sufficient time had elapsed (Brickman et al. 1978). In other words, although the lottery winners were likely much happier immediately after winning the lottery, as time passed, their happiness returned to a lower baseline level, and thus, their response to the lottery itself declined. In most cases, it is difficult (if not impossible) to obtain a measure of hedonic response at the onset of such an affectively relevant life event. Therefore, the lack of difference between those who experienced the event and a reasonable control sample is typically taken as evidence of a decline in response. For instance, in the above example, it is quite difficult to measure hedonic response immediately following the fateful moment when an individual wins the lottery (e.g., they are unlikely to fill out a questionnaire). However, it is reasonable to believe that their affective state is likely quite elevated (at least temporarily) as compared to someone who did not recently win the lottery. The fact that, following sufficient passage of time, their affective response is no different from individuals who did not win the lottery is quite telling in regards to how fleeting the influence of even extreme life events are on hedonic responses.

This type of observation is not limited to lottery winners. For instance, academic recipients of tenure were no happier than their untenured counterparts following sufficient passage of time (Gilbert et al. 1998, study 2). Again, the inference is that individuals were likely quite happy immediately after receiving tenure, but their hedonic response declined with time. Similarly, despite a likely strong hedonic response immediately following the election of a favored politician, after as little as 1 month, participants were just as happy whether their favored politician won or lost, suggesting that decline in response had occurred (Gilbert et al. 1998, study 3). Another example that, in fact, does allow for direct assessment of both initial response and eventual decline is that of the influence of marriage on hedonic response. Although marriage initially results in an increase in hedonic response, longitudinal data from 24,000 individuals demonstrates that, within as little as 2 years, individuals' hedonic response tends to revert to premarriage levels (Lucas & Clark 2006, Lucas et al. 2003). In other words, despite an observed initial increase in hedonic response following marriage, this major life event seemingly has little impact in the long run. Of course, a more robust measurement approach (more frequent measurements, longer time frames, different constructs) could find some evidence of a larger continuing benefit, but we would still expect this benefit to decline somewhat as the years pass.

The same type of evidence has been used to show that hedonic response to a voluntary job change is not long lived. Although researchers initially observed a boost in hedonic response following such a job change, with enough time, there was no evidence of any lasting hedonic influences on the individuals making the change (Boswell et al. 2005). In other words, hedonic response declined with time. Importantly, none of the studies discussed in this section directly assessed the decline in hedonic response; they, rather, inferred it from a comparison between a measured response to a stimulus and a control population.

GENERAL MECHANISMS OF HEDONIC DECLINE

Given the breadth of research on hedonic decline, it is no surprise that a number of general theories have been proposed as potential mechanisms. Historically, these general theories have developed within siloed research programs with slightly different methods, terminology, and mechanistic explanations. These include approaches rooted in physiology (e.g., homeostasis, negative alliesthesia), the senses (e.g., sensory-specific satiety, adaptation), and attention (e.g., habituation, monitoring). Going forward, we first provide descriptions of the most prominent theories to provide an overview of how each can underlie hedonic decline. We later present a general taxonomy for these mechanisms to help organize them to reveal common patterns and properties and to provide a structure for reviewing the breadth of recent (and future) findings.

Homeostasis

The defining characteristic of the mechanism of homeostasis is the maintenance of an ideal point through physiological feedback. This idea of satiation, which comes from the Latin word satis, meaning having enough, has long been used for feeding behaviors in nonhuman animals (Glanzer 1953). The term was appropriated for use in the study of food consumption in humans to describe the cessation of consumption following satiety factors. These factors typically take the form of physiological feedback cues such as oral stimulation, stomach filling and distension, and cellular hydration (Mook & Votaw 1992). These feedback cues are then translated into a reduced sensation, which some researchers have termed negative alliesthesia (Cabanac & Duclaux 1970). We present a more detailed account of these considerations in the section titled Physiological Feedback Factors.

The homeostasis approach holds that hedonic decline represents an excess relative to some desired physiological state (e.g., eating until one no longer has nutritional deficiencies or hunger pangs). Beyond specific physiological needs, set point theory proposes that each person also has a relatively stable overall level of subjective well-being that serves to mute deviations (Fujita & Diener 2005). That is, people seem to have limits on how long they can feel particularly happy or sad (versus an inherent baseline level). As a result, repeated exposure to a stimulus will lead to hedonic decline.

Sensory-Specific Satiety

Whereas original theories of satiation were focused on explaining the influence of physiological considerations (e.g., macronutrients such as calories), sensory-specific satiety posits that hedonic decline is also a function of sensory properties (e.g., color or flavor). In other words, hedonic decline for a given food is primarily a function of past consumption of that specific food, rather than the macronutritional accumulation of all previously consumed foods.

The seminal work on this account was developed in the food sciences by Rolls and colleagues (1981), and their core result is that ratings of pleasantness decrease considerably more for a food just eaten than for uneaten foods. More specifically, after eating a particular food, hedonic decline extends largely to other foods sharing the same flavor, rather than to foods sharing the same macronutritional content (Johnson & Vickers 1993) or the same brand name (Inman 2001).

Similar sensory-specific satiety has also been found to extend to color, saltiness, sweetness, and shape (Hetherington & Rolls 1996). In addition, using the effects of eating on ratings of food odors, researchers have neurologically traced sensory-specific satiety to the orbitofrontal cortex (Kringelbach et al. 2000), an area linked to sensory integration and affective value.

Perhaps the best illustration that macronutritional content does not drive satiation is the example of sham feeding. In this case, participants are asked to simply hold food in their mouths for a fixed period of time but never actually ingest the food. In this way, they experience only the sensory properties of the food (taste, smell, appearance) without receiving any of the nutritional benefits. Following this sham consumption procedure, preference for the food held in the mouth versus food not held in the mouth is assessed. As the theory predicts, even though no consumption has taken place, merely experiencing the food through a sham feeding procedure produces hedonic decline for that food but not other foods (Nolan & Hetherington 2009). Therefore, across all of these findings, hedonic decline clearly has a sensory component, reflected in the notion of sensory-specific satiety.

Adaptation

In addition to effects related to food consumption, more general perceptual effects have also been linked to hedonic decline. One of the earliest proposed mechanisms was adaptation (Helson 1947), which led to a wealth of further exploration and applications (Frederick & Loewenstein 1999, Parducci 1995). The core notion of this mechanism is that stimuli are perceived relative to an adaptation level that reflects past exposures. For instance, eating a sweet chocolate bar now makes every other food seem a little less sweet by comparison. However, this adaptation goes beyond sensory aspects and can include virtually any stimulus, such as the number of dots in a pattern or the weight of a barbell (Helson 1971).

According to the theory of adaptation level, repeated exposure to a stimulus will necessarily diminish the ongoing response. For example, returning to the chocolate bar, the first bite will typically taste quite sweet and bring enjoyment. However, with each additional bite, the reference point that defines what is perceived as sweet is rising. As this adaptation level keeps increasing, the constant level of sweetness in the chocolate bar will necessarily seem less and less sweet by comparison. The net result is eventual hedonic decline.

Hedonic Adaptation

Leveraging the concept of the reference point that lies at the core of the theory of general adaptation, the theory of hedonic adaptation considers the long-term influences of large life events on overall well-being (Brickman & Campbell 1971, Frederick & Loewenstein 1999). There are a few unique aspects to this work. First, hedonic adaptation emphasizes the shifting importance of different reference points. For instance, a new relationship may be quite enjoyable if one regularly notices how one's new mate improves on dimensions that a previous partner lacked. Of course, the salience of this reference point will fade over time, and the focus may even eventually shift to attributes lacking in the new mate. Second, hedonic adaptation also considers that one may dynamically alter their behavior in response to repeated exposures. For instance, if a person starts regularly drinking an afternoon smoothie, then they may compensate by reducing how much they eat at lunch each day. The result of this could be greater hunger in the afternoon, which could slow down the hedonic decline with the smoothie. Third, hedonic adaptation typically focuses on overall well-being rather than on a momentary response to a stimulus. For instance, in the case of marriage, the central question is typically not how much one enjoys marriage per se, but rather how much being married influences well-being and life satisfaction. In this case, as with most experiences, considerable evidence shows that the influence of marriage on well-being declines with time (Lucas & Clark 2006). In fact, although not the primary interest of this review, much research on well-being focuses on the hedonic decline (or occasional lack thereof) over time in response to negative life events. Work in this area shows that people seemingly come to understand these events and explain them away, leading to a lessening impact over time (Wilson & Gilbert 2008).

Habituation

Habituation captures the decreased responsiveness to a stimulus after repeated exposure (Groves & Thompson 1970). Habituation does not involve sensory adaptation or fatigue; rather, it has been characterized as a learned suppression (Kandel 1991). The core notion of habituation is that a repeated stimulus elicits a lessening response as one learns that the stimulus is not critical and does not require much attention. This learned suppression then extends beyond the stimulus to other stimuli that are highly similar.

It is critical to note that this learning can apply to any stimulus, and that it is not tied to any particular physiological feedback or sensory aspect. As a result, habituation can readily account for long-lasting effects of hedonic decline for virtually any type of stimulus. In fact, the mechanism of sensory-specific satiety has been referred to as a particular application of habituation (Epstein et al. 2009, Higgs et al. 2008).

The seminal work on habituation studied cat leg muscles and sea slugs (e.g., Thompson & Spencer 1966), but habituation has proven just as instrumental to understanding hedonic decline for humans. For instance, habituation has been used to explain a wide range of eating behaviors and disorders such as obesity and bulimia nervosa (Epstein et al. 2009). Likewise, habituation was enlisted to explain why participants experienced spontaneous recovery from hedonic decline with the presentation of a novel food (Temple et al. 2008b). Broadly speaking, the general nature of habituation suggests that it likely plays some role in most settings with hedonic decline.

One of the most interesting properties of habituation is the degree of specificity, as laid out over 50 years ago by Thomson & Spencer (1966). This specificity helps researchers separate habituation from adaptation, as has been done in limited instances (Bernhard & van der Kooy 2000, Schifferstein & Kuiper 1997). For example, more intense stimuli should have slower habituation but faster adaptation. Of course, in many other cases, habituation and adaptation would both simultaneously contribute to hedonic decline in a similar fashion.

The notion of habituation has been expanded over time to now include 14 empirical characteristics (see **Table 1**; McSweeney & Murphy 2000). These essential properties that define habituation have been repeatedly demonstrated in countless studies. Habituation theory has remained relatively stable and powerful in its ability to predict hedonic response to repeated exposure to a myriad of stimuli across a myriad of organisms.

Self-Reflection

In addition to these well-established literatures, a relatively recent body of work has focused on self-reflection as a contributor to hedonic decline. The core notion of this work is that simply reflecting on past consumption can lead to the sense of having more exposure, which lessens the future response (Redden 2015). This reflection can arise in a variety of ways, including better initial encoding (Higgs & Donohoe 2011) and easier retrieval (Galak et al. 2014), cues of past consumption (Robinson et al. 2013, Wansink et al. 2005), cues of past variety (Galak et al. 2009),

Table 1　Empirical characteristics of habituation

Characteristic	Description
Spontaneous recovery	Responsiveness to an habituated stimulus recovers when that stimulus is not presented for an extended period of time.
Stimulus specificity	Habituation is disrupted by changes in the presented stimulus.
Variety effects	Habituation occurs more slowly to stimuli that are presented in a variable, rather than a fixed, manner (e.g., after variable, rather than fixed, interstimulus intervals).
Dishabituation	Presenting a strong, different, or extra stimulus restores responsiveness to an habituated stimulus.
Dishabituation habituates	Repeated presentation of dishabituators reduces their ability to restore habituated responding.
Stimulus rate	Faster rates of stimulus presentation yield faster and more pronounced habituation than slower rates.
Stimulus rate and recovery	Spontaneous recovery may be faster after faster rates of stimulus presentation than after slower rates.
Stimulus exposure	Responsiveness to a repeatedly presented stimulus decreases with increases in stimulus exposure.
Long-term habituation	Some habituation is learned and persists over time.
Repeated habituations	Habituation may become more rapid with repeated habituations.
Stimulus intensity	Habituation is sometimes, but not always, faster and more pronounced for less intense stimuli than for more intense stimuli.
Generality	Habituation occurs for most, if not all, stimuli and species of animals. The exact rate of habituation depends on the species, the stimulus, the response, and the individual subject.
Sensitization by early stimulus presentations	An increase (sensitization), rather than a decrease (habituation), in responsiveness may occur during the first few presentations of a repeatedly presented stimulus.
Sensitization by stimuli from another modality	An increase in responsiveness to a stimulus may be produced by the introduction of a stimulus from another modality (e.g., a light or noise). Both sensitization and dishabituation may involve the introduction of a stimulus from another modality. Results are conventionally described as dishabituation if the added stimulus restores responsiveness to an already habituated stimulus and as sensitization if the added stimulus increases response before substantial habituation occurs to the other stimulus.

Table adapted from McSweeney & Murphy (2000).

and comparing exposure levels to those of other people (Redden & Galak 2013). All of this work shows that, as past consumption is more easily recalled or framed as more recent or greater, hedonic decline will likewise increase.

It is notable that this self-reflection is likely a much higher-order cognition than all of the previously discussed mechanisms. Whereas other mechanisms may operate spontaneously and automatically, self-reflection is likely very sensitive to the context and individual. Thus, we expect that a great deal of the work showing differences in the rate of hedonic decline across people (as measured by the rate of change in rated enjoyment) likely results from changes in this self-reflection. We review some of this recent work in the section titled Self-Reflection Factors.

A TAXONOMY OF ANTECEDENTS OF HEDONIC DECLINE

The previous section provided a summary of the most popular theories contributing to research on hedonic decline. These various theories have often been cited as competing accounts that operate independently with unique predictions. We propose instead that these theories describe processes that often jointly contribute to hedonic decline and that, in some cases, they may even simply represent multiple ways of describing a single underlying mechanism. To deal with this inherent ambiguity, we present a limited set of classes of factors that drive hedonic decline. As a result,

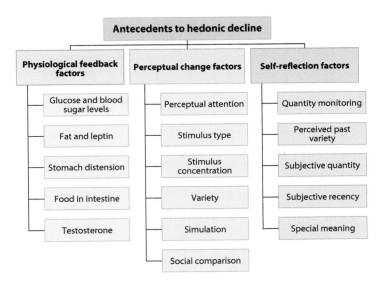

Figure 2

Taxonomy of antecedents to hedonic decline. Individual factors are representative of the antecedent category; we have outlined only the major antecedents in each category. Additionally, there are likely other antecedents within each category that have yet to be discovered and studied.

we can span these highly related yet relatively siloed literatures and provide a comprehensive account focused on the various antecedents of hedonic decline. We distinguish between three general types of factors affecting hedonic decline: physiological feedback, perceptual changes, and self-reflection (**Figure 2**). This approach and taxonomy then lets us synthesize the predictions and findings of these numerous literatures into a single comprehensive collection of factors driving hedonic decline.

Past work on hedonic decline has typically not explicitly demonstrated the presence of a particular mechanism. Given this, rather than add to any growing debates, we instead treat a set of related phenomena as a class of factors serving as an antecedent to hedonic decline. For instance, we do not try to distinguish between habituation and adaptation; rather, we treat both as perceptual change factors. Of course, realizing that many findings likely involve multiple mechanisms, we have discussed each finding in the section dealing with the mechanism that we expect was likely the primary contributor. We base this classification largely on whether the finding referred to bodily processing, set points, or ingestion (physiological feedback); adaptation, general attention, or sensory experiences (perceptual changes); or memory, metacognitions, or delayed effects (self-reflection).

PHYSIOLOGICAL FEEDBACK FACTORS

Most research examining physiological influences on hedonic decline involves nonhuman subjects, as the direct observation of physiological change in humans is quite difficult. Moreover, because most of this work deals with nonhuman subjects, hedonic measures are nearly impossible to obtain. Instead, most of this work deals with motivational responses that take the form of goal-directed behavior, such as the decision to continue consuming. In order to make the conceptual leap to hedonic response, we must necessarily make the following assumption: Motivational response, such as desire to consume, is at least somewhat correlated with hedonic response, such as pleasure derived from consumption. This assumption accords with general intuition as well as with past findings, such as a study indicating that the time an individual takes before eating again is predicted by the most recent rating of enjoyment (Garbinsky et al. 2014). However, it is worth noting that divergences between liking and wanting have been intermittently demonstrated (Berridge 2009), both in common contexts such as eating and in abnormal behaviors such as drug addictions. Regardless, in most instances, we expect behavior will be at least somewhat affected by the hedonic response.

Under this assumption, there are a host of physiological inputs in observed hedonic decline, the majority of which deal with food consumption. Because there have been several recent reviews of these physiological factors (e.g., Benelam 2009, Berthoud 2011), we only briefly detail the more prominent physiological inputs, and instead focus our review on the other two primary inputs to hedonic decline: perceptual changes and self-reflection. We also note that much of the research on physiological feedback has been in the food domain, perhaps because food is essential to health and ingestion is an inherently physiological process.

Glucose and Blood Sugar Levels

One of the primary physiological inputs determining when to consume food is blood glucose levels. When these levels decline, desire to consume increases (Grossman 1986). For instance, when the amount of energy derived from glucose is decreased by the exogenous introduction of insulin, desire to consume food dramatically increases (Lotter & Woods 1997). Conversely, as the body processes glucose from consumed food, the desire to consume, and presumably hedonic response, declines (Woods et al. 2000).

Fat and Leptin

Glucose, although central to the regulation of food intake, is only one source of energy for the body. Fatty acids are also critically important to food regulation. As the body accumulates adipose tissue, a store for excess fat, a hypothalamic signal is released to indicate that consumption should decrease (Zhang et al. 1994, 2005). This is accomplished via the leptin hormone. As the body accumulates fat reserves, leptin is introduced into the blood stream, resulting in decreased desire to consume (Peters et al. 2005). Whether this decline in motivation to consume then results in a decrease in experienced enjoyment, however, is an open question.

Stomach Distension

Independent of the glucose or fat content of food, merely filling the stomach results in decreased desire to consume more food (Geliebter 1988, Wang et al. 2008). This filling can take the form of water, food, or even an inflated balloon. When a balloon is inserted into the stomach, the volume of the balloon acts as a signal that inhibits consumption (Kissileff et al. 2003). Similarly, in the case of the decline in hedonic response, there is suggestive evidence that stomach distension not only influences the desire to consume food, but also the enjoyment of that food. In one study, sensory-specific satiety was observed for the olfactory properties of food to a larger extent when the food was consumed as compared to when it was merely smelled (Rolls & Rolls 1997). Although it is difficult to dissociate the influence of nutrition from that of the volume of food consumed because the pleasantness ratings for the food were measured relatively shortly after consumption, it is more likely that distension contributed to the decline in hedonic response, as nutritional factors take longer (perhaps 30 minutes) to manifest.

Food in the Intestine

Like stomach distension, presentation of food directly to the duodenum, the portion of the small intestine closest to the stomach, results in decreased desire to consume food (Liebling et al. 1975, Moran & Dailey 2011). The hormone cholecystokinin (CCK) is primarily responsible for this decline in desire (Gibbs et al. 1973), although the additional distension of the stomach by food or drink is required for CCK to have an influence on food consumption in humans (Lieverse et al. 1995; see Benelam 2009 for a more detailed discussion of other hormones that play a role in the decline in response to food). This decline has yet to be linked to a decline in any form of hedonic response, but when cessation of consumption occurs due to food entering the intestine, a decline in the palatability of food presumably follows.

Testosterone

Moving away from food consumption, there is evidence that testosterone levels are a predictor of male sexual arousal and interest (Rupp & Wallen 2007). Specifically, in one study, although hedonic decline to sexual images occurred in all participants, the degree of endogenous testosterone moderated this decline such that those men who had high levels of testosterone exhibited a much slower hedonic decline (Rupp & Wallen 2007). In other words, the presence of higher levels of testosterone slows the decline in hedonic responses, suggesting that it is a principal physiological input in sexual arousal. Interestingly, testosterone also plays a role in female sexual arousal, but its influence on the hedonic decline that women experience with repeated exposure to sexual stimuli has yet to be documented (Tuiten et al. 2000).

PERCEPTUAL CHANGE FACTORS

A wide variety of research has demonstrated that, beyond physiological processes, the ongoing perception of a stimulus also affects the rate of hedonic decline. This nondigestive antecedent to hedonic decline has proven both important and prevalent. Whereas physiological antecedents to the decline in hedonic response are relatively slow processes, often taking tens of minutes to take effect, perceptual-based antecedents are rather quick, often influencing hedonic decline almost immediately as part of the subjective experience itself. In the next sections, we detail several examples of how these perceptually based antecedents influence the rate of hedonic decline. As is the case with physiological antecedents, hedonic response is not always directly measured, requiring us to infer, in some cases, that a decline in desire to consume translates to a decline in the hedonic response.

Perceptual Attention

Much of the work showing the influence of attention to the stimulus on hedonic decline has again focused on food consumption. For instance, in one study, participants consumed either pizza or macaroni and cheese ad libitum while either watching television (a highly involved experience) or listening to classical music (a less involved experience). While watching television, when their attention was presumably averted more from eating, participants ate 36% more pizza and 71% more macaroni and cheese (Blass et al. 2006). Participants conversely reported both a lower desire to consume and lower ratings of the pleasantness of Jaffa Cakes when their attention was not diverted from consumption (Brunstrom & Mitchell 2006). However, when attention was diverted via an involving video game, no such decline was observed. In other words, perceptual attention to the stimulus being consumed was an antecedent to hedonic decline. However, the notion of perceptual attention may be multifaceted, as a recent study found an exception: Having knowledge of the duration of the stimulus (versus not having this knowledge) increased attention to the final exposure and led to greater hedonic savoring toward the end (Zhao & Tsai 2011). This suggests that numerous factors may moderate the effect of attention on hedonic decline, making different types of attention and their effects potentially fruitful areas for future research.

Stimulus Type

The type of stimulus being consumed can also lead to perceptual changes that affect hedonic decline. For example, hedonic decline tends to happen more rapidly for simple versus complex stimuli (Berlyne 1971, Cox & Cox 2002). Researchers have also documented that the rate of satiety systematically, and sometimes quite dramatically, differs across a range of common food types (Holt et al. 1995). Beyond food, other recent work has found that material goods cause a greater hedonic decline than experiences (Nicolao et al. 2009). In this case, experiences presumably possess more unique aspects, ongoing memories, group consumption, etc. Similarly, Yang & Galak (2015) showed that gifts imbued with sentimental meaning (versus items bought for oneself) are more resistant to hedonic decline, even over long periods of time. These findings suggest, more generally, that stimuli tapping into higher-order cognitive functions may serve to slow hedonic decline.

Stimulus Concentration

Past research on hedonic decline has explored the construct of concentration along two dimensions. The first dimension is the dosage level for each exposure of a stimulus and has led to mixed results for hedonic decline. In some cases, more intense stimuli can lead to greater decline. For example, a well-liked beer led to lower local evaluations of the next beer but higher overall ratings of the global experience (Ghosal et al. 2014). People were similarly less satiated with a lower-calorie version of spaghetti Bolognese (O'Sullivan et al. 2010), yet caloric content had no effect on salivation to repeated exposures of a lemon gelatin (Epstein et al. 1993). Perhaps not surprisingly, two of the core theories of hedonic decline even make opposing predictions. Adaptation predicts that increasing the intensity of the stimuli would increase hedonic decline by raising the adaptation level to which everything is subsequently compared. In contrast, one of the properties that define habituation is that hedonic response declines less for a more intense stimulus (see **Table 1**, stimulus intensity). Future work (and theories) will need to tease out under what conditions each outcome emerges and dominates.

The second dimension examines the frequency or rate of consumption, with the clear finding that more concentrated consumption leads to faster hedonic decline. For example, when eating six chocolate candies, people became satiated faster when eating them at their own pace over 20 minutes versus being forced to space them out at the maximal 200-second intervals (Galak et al. 2013). Hedonic adaptation similarly slowed when breaks were inserted into a consumption experience, whether the breaks were empty time (Nelson & Meyvis 2008) or television commercials (Nelson et al. 2009). Likewise, when participants ate chocolate in two sessions a week apart, those told to abstain from chocolate in the intervening period experienced less hedonic decline than those given no instructions or those told to eat as much as possible during the intervening week (Quoidbach & Dunn 2013). These findings all show that hedonic decline accelerates as consumption is more concentrated over time.

Variety

The introduction of nonfocal stimuli (i.e., variety) reduces the rate of hedonic decline, which has been shown in a myriad of studies and contexts (Brondel et al. 2009, Epstein et al. 2009, Galak et al. 2011, Havermans & Brondel 2013, Inman 2001, Sorensen et al. 2003, Temple et al. 2008a). In fact, even eating varied foods beforehand can reduce the subsequent rate of satiation when eating a different food later (Hetherington et al. 2006). The fact that variety reduces hedonic decline is intuitive and directly follows from the property of dishabituation (see **Table 1**, dishabituation). Given this, more recent research has tended to focus on the question of what qualifies as variety and to what extent it reduces hedonic decline.

The ability of variety to slow hedonic decline has been shown to increase as people subcategorize the stimuli more (Raghunathan & Irwin 2001, Redden 2008) and as people are asked to explicitly recall past variety that they have experienced (Galak et al. 2009). It seems that people must view variety as different from, yet somewhat related to, the stimulus on which they have previously experienced hedonic decline. Variety also does more to counter hedonic decline when people consume the stimuli at a faster rate, which leads to more satiation (Galak et al. 2011). The effect of variety on hedonic decline also depends on the attribute being varied. For example, consumers became satiated more quickly on a particular flavor than on a particular brand name of chip (Inman 2001). More generally, it could be that any sensory aspect is more prone to perceptual changes (and hence hedonic decline) than more abstract attributes. In fact, once a food undergoes sensory-specific satiety after an individual repeatedly eats it, the hedonic decline for this food persists even after the individual eats another food (Havermans 2012).

Within the context of perceptual changes, we also offer a different interpretation of why variety slows hedonic decline. A new stimulus may act as a distractor from the focal stimulus and divert attention away from consumption, which could then reduce the resulting hedonic decline. Interestingly, the same logic could also apply to the previously noted effect of more frequent exposure accelerating hedonic decline. That is, as interconsumption intervals increase, there is more opportunity for one to attend to other stimuli in the environment (not just other somewhat related stimuli, as is the case with variety). This shift in attention may then be responsible for the observed hedonic decline.

Simulation

Recent work has also shown that hedonic decline can occur even without any actual consumption. For example, people had a lower desire to earn a cheese reward after imagining eating a cheese cube 20 times in a row (Morewedge et al. 2010). Subsequent work further established that simply viewing advertisements with salty (versus sweet) foods lowered the subsequent enjoyment of eating salted peanuts (Larson et al. 2014). Alternatively, the knowledge that future consumption would offer an opportunity for a novel food served to slow the current rate of hedonic decline (Sevilla et al. 2016). These findings show that the mere perceptual experience of consumption can mimic the hedonic decline (and recovery) found with actual consumption.

Social Comparison

One area of research that has garnered a great deal of attention is the influence of a change in social status on well-being. For example, does an increase in income (a temporary shock or a permanent change) result in a lasting change in happiness and well-being, or does such a change instead yield a temporary increase followed by the typically observed hedonic decline over time? Past research has generally found mixed results, mostly suggesting that life changes do not have a strong (if any) lasting influence on well-being.

Past research has found little gain in national well-being with increased national real income (Campbell 1981, Diener & Biswas-Diener 2002, Easterlin 1995), little lasting effect for lottery winners (compared to nonwinners) 1 to 18 months later (Brickman et al. 1978), and only a mild correlation between income and well-being in the United States (Diener et al. 1993). In contrast, other research has found a log linear (i.e., diminishing) relationship for well-being as income increases (Stevenson & Wolfers 2013) and some evidence of longer-lasting gains in well-being with increased income for the very poor (Diener & Biswas-Diener 2002) as basic needs (e.g., shelter) are met.

Overall, though, the more common finding seems to be the lack of a lasting relationship. These diminishing effects of greater income (and the benefits it could potentially provide) are often attributed to the mechanisms underlying hedonic decline, as well as rising aspirations to which the current circumstances are compared (Sheldon & Lyubomirsky 2012).

SELF-REFLECTION FACTORS

Both physiological and perceptual antecedents to hedonic decline occur as a direct response to consumption itself. In contrast, a third class of antecedents to hedonic decline emerges from top-down processes that occur only upon reflection on present or past consumption. Specifically, people seemingly apply their lay beliefs about what should influence the trajectory of hedonic response in order to inform actual hedonic response, absent any change in actual consumption. These top-down beliefs then act alongside the many other signals (often low-level, bottom-up signals) that also contribute to hedonic decline. In many ways, reflecting on past consumption can produce and mimic the effects of hedonic decline in much the same way as actual consumption.

Given that this notion of self-reflection is relatively recent in the literature, these lay beliefs and antecedents have not yet been well explored and clearly defined. In the next sections, we provide a taxonomy and organization for those identified so far. This review also focuses on more detailed descriptions of the few initial studies providing evidence for these self-reflection effects. It is also noteworthy that many of these studies demonstrate these self-reflection factors for hedonic decline across a broad range of domains (music, art, food, social interactions), but we maintain our focus on just one prototypical example from any given paper.

Quantity Monitoring

In a seminal piece demonstrating that hedonic decline is not directly linked to ingestion, Wansink (2005) had participants eat soup from either a regular bowl or a bowl that was surreptitiously connected to a vat of soup that automatically and imperceptibly refilled the soup bowl as participants ate. Participants consumed 73% more soup when the bowl was refilled unbeknownst to them, even though they did not realize that they had consumed more than those who ate a fixed amount of soup from a regular bowl. Conversely, people ate fewer potato chips when special red chips were interspersed at regular intervals to act as a cue of the quantity eaten (Geier et al. 2012) and reduced their subsequent intake after first completing a brief mindfulness training to attune them to their physiological feedback (Van De Veer et al. 2015).

In another, more direct, assessment of hedonic decline, participants cued to attend to the number of times they swallowed reported greater decreases in enjoyment while eating cereal or candy bars than those not cued (Redden & Haws 2013). Similarly, people experienced greater hedonic decline when explicitly choosing from three songs to hear prior to hearing them as compared to having the songs chosen for them at random by a computer (Redden et al. 2017). People also experience greater hedonic decline when regularly asked how many chocolate pieces they had eaten throughout a consumption experience as compared to when they are not asked (Sevilla & Redden 2014). In the latter case, it was shown that attention to the quantity being consumed increased the sense of how much had been consumed, which presumably triggered the lay belief that this should increase the hedonic decline (which it did).

Perceived Past Variety

Another class of self-reflective antecedents is belief about how much variety has been consumed. As previously discussed, there is ample evidence that greater variety slows hedonic decline (Brondel et al. 2009, Galak et al. 2011, Havermans & Brondel 2013). However, the belief of how much variety has been consumed may also affect hedonic decline, in addition to the objective variety in and of itself.

In one study (Galak et al. 2009), similar to a preload in food research, participants were exposed to the chorus of a favorite song 20 times to induce hedonic decline (45 points on 101-point scale). Two weeks later, the same participants were instructed to think of either all other musical artists they had listened to during the past two weeks (treatment) or all television programs they had watched during that time (control). Importantly, the actual variety of songs listened to during this two-week period did not vary across conditions. Participants in the treatment condition were instead merely reminded that they had consumed a variety of songs during this period of time. Participants who were not reminded of the variety of songs they listened to still exhibited hedonic decline (33 scale points) that had recovered little over the intervening two weeks. However, when merely reminded of the fact that they listened to other songs during the intervening period, these participants' enjoyment of the song returned nearly to their initial enjoyment level, and they showed little hedonic decline (9 scale points).

It seems that these participants engaged in a self-reflective thought process that incorporated their belief that if they did consume variety, then they should be able to once again enjoy their favorite song. In other words, these participants used their belief that variety reduces hedonic decline (Read & Loewenstein 1995, Simonson 1990) to actually influence their hedonic response when listening again to their favorite song. Likewise, people not cued to recall past variety seemingly engaged in a form of focalism that leads them to primarily focus on the stimulus at hand and neglect thoughts of alternative related stimuli (Kahneman & Miller 1986, Klayman & Ha 1987). That is, the mere consumption of variety, in and of itself, does not seem in all cases to be enough to spontaneously influence hedonic response.

Subjective Quantity

Another self-reflective antecedent to hedonic decline is subjective assessment of the quantity of past consumption. Actual quantity consumed clearly drives the extent of hedonic decline, with more consumption producing greater hedonic decline (Groves & Thompson 1970, Rolls et al. 1981). However, much like the case of variety, recent work has shown that the subjective assessment of consumption quantity may matter as much as the actual quantity.

Indeed, in one experiment (Redden & Galak 2013, study 3), participants were first exposed to an aesthetically pleasing photograph 20 times to produce a sizable hedonic decline (30 points on 101-point scale). Importantly, participants were never explicitly made aware of how many times they were exposed to the photograph, but rather were told only that they would view it "several times." Following the final iteration, participants were led to believe that they either saw the photo many times or saw it only a few times, using a scale-based manipulation adapted from Shwarz et al. (1985). Upon subsequently seeing the photograph again, participants made to feel that they saw the photograph only a few times showed half as much hedonic decline (13 scale points) as those made to feel that they had seen it many times (25 scale points). In other words, merely changing how much these participants felt that they were exposed to the photograph influenced their actual level of subsequent enjoyment. Presumably, people believe that when one is exposed to a stimulus only a few times, hedonic decline should be less, and so their actual enjoyment, indeed, does not decline much at all.

Importantly, one reason that this type of intervention can influence the rate of hedonic decline is because perceived quantity of consumption is something that is, itself, quite malleable (Blair & Burton 1987, Menon et al. 1995). Given that people do not always keep running tabs on how much of a stimulus they have consumed, their lay beliefs play a key role in determining their hedonic response to subsequent exposures to the same stimulus. They reflect on what they believe to have been their level of past consumption, and this self-reflection ultimately acts as an antecedent to hedonic decline.

Subjective Recency

Another antecedent to hedonic decline is subjective assessment of the time that has passed since the last consumption episode. Generally speaking, the more time that passes between consumption episodes, the smaller is the hedonic decline (Groves & Thompson 1970, Hetherington et al. 1989). In addition, to the extent that people hold a lay belief that longer passages of time result in less hedonic decline (Galak et al. 2013), the perception of how much time has passed may matter just as much as the actual passage of time.

For instance, in one experiment (Galak et al. 2014), participants were first shown a photograph of a beach 12 times to induce hedonic decline (25 points on 101-point scale). Participants then watched a 10-minute video, but during the video, they were made to believe that either much time or little time had actually elapsed. By adapting a prior methodology (Sackett et al. 2010), an on-screen timer was sped up (or slowed down) to make participants feel that the video they watched was particularly short (or long). Upon subsequently viewing the beach photo again, those made to feel that little time had passed since they last saw the photograph showed more hedonic decline (15 scale points) than those made to feel that more time had elapsed (2 scale points). In other words, the mere belief about how much time had passed since a previous exposure to a pleasing photograph influenced actual enjoyment during a subsequent consumption episode. This same paper also conceptually replicated this effect, as restaurant patrons who were made to feel that their last meal was quite recent ate less food than those made to feel that their last meal was quite temporally distant.

In these findings, people seemingly self-reflected on the fact that either little or much time had passed and then applied their belief that hedonic decline should be smaller when more time has passed between consumption episodes. Importantly, one of the key reasons that such an effect is possible is that people's perception of time is generally quite malleable (Kyung et al. 2010, Semin & Smith 1999, Zauberman et al. 2010). That is, people do not always have a good sense of how much time has passed, and so they use external cues, such as those in the above-described experiments, to inform their subjective assessment of the passage of time. Coupled with the lay belief that the length of interconsumption intervals influences the rate of hedonic decline, it is clear how such a self-reflective antecedent can be influential.

Special Meaning

The final antecedent of hedonic decline related to self-reflection is the imbuing of consumption experiences with some special meaning. The general lay belief operating in this case is that some stimuli hold a special place in an individual's mind that slows the hedonic decline resulting from consumption. For instance, Yang & Galak (2015) showed, in one study, that people showed less hedonic decline for items they received as gifts (which are frequently sentimental) versus items they bought for themselves. Special meaning can also come from a rare opportunity to consume, as people told that a chocolate was only available at certain times of the year showed less hedonic decline while eating it than those told that the same chocolate was always available (Sevilla & Redden 2014). Finally, another study showed that hedonic decline slowed when it threatened an important self-identity (Chugani et al. 2015). Undergraduates continued enjoying chocolates longer and ate more of them when the chocolates were in their university's school colors versus when they were in other, nonimportant colors. Participants seemingly resolved the cognitive dissonance that arises from the conflict between hedonic decline and a stimulus that one's identity dictates should be liked. More generally, it is likely that any stimulus imbued with a property suggesting it should be permanently liked will similarly prove more resistant to hedonic decline.

CONCLUSIONS

Over the many decades of research trying to understand how both human and nonhuman animals respond to repeated exposure to hedonic stimuli, the core finding has been that hedonic responses decline with repetition. However, this conclusion has been spread across a number of siloed literatures, making it difficult for researchers to produce a single coherent understanding of what drives such decline. Indeed, work rooted in explanations such as homeostasis, satiation, habituation, and adaptation have all tackled the same basic problems yet have largely treated each differing approach as idiosyncratic rather than related. In this review, we have summarized the main findings of these varied literatures and provided a taxonomy of what factors influence hedonic decline. Specifically, we have demonstrated that all of these diverse research streams can fit within just three categories of antecedents to hedonic decline: physiological feedback, perceptual change, and self-reflection. These three categories comprehensively organize the drivers of hedonic decline, as well as past and potential future findings in this rich area.

The intent of this review is to provide a taxonomy to not only synthesize previous work but also to provide direction for future research. To that end, we have several specific recommendations for researchers interested in studying hedonic decline. First, the phenomenology of hedonic decline is poorly understood. That is, across all the literature that we cite, the results are shallow with regard to its explanations of how humans actually experience hedonic decline with stimuli. The literature clearly observes that hedonic decline occurs for many different stimuli and under many different contexts, but it is mute as to how people actually experience this decline. For example, is hedonic decline explicitly felt? Is it below conscious awareness? Does it operate more on emotions or cognitions? Generally, we know little about the actual experience of hedonic decline. We speculate that feelings of boredom and irritation are likely candidates in some cases, but hedonic decline likely involves a much larger range of experiences. Second, there are clearly differences in the underlying psychological explanations provided by the myriad of theories that attempt to explain not just hedonic decline, but response decline more generally. As mentioned above, it is unlikely that these mechanisms operate independently and in isolation. Rather, it seems far more plausible that all forms of response decline are multidetermined and should be studied as such. By focusing on the similarities between these approaches rather than their differences, future research may develop better models to both understand and predict hedonic decline. Third, several of our conclusions are based on assumptions that the decline in response to hedonic stimuli likely mirrors a decline in response to nonhedonic stimuli. There is plenty of evidence to believe that this is so, but such a core assumption must be empirically tested in a thorough fashion. To that end, future research should examine cases in which the principles outlined by the various theories that explain response decline apply differentially to hedonic versus nonhedonic stimuli. Such an understanding will not only allow for more precision in prediction but will also allow for a deeper understanding of the core psychological processes that govern human behavior. Finally, we document a host of antecedents to hedonic decline but do not, in any way, suggest that we have been exhaustive. Indeed, there are likely many other antecedents to hedonic decline that have yet to be systematically investigated. Future research should continue to expand on our taxonomy in hopes of documenting the full breadth of influence on hedonic decline.

SUMMARY POINTS

1. Hedonic decline is the phenomenon whereby continued and repeated exposure to a stimulus typically leads to a reduced hedonic response.

2. The effects of hedonic decline can be studied using a variety of measurements across different time periods (within a single session versus across multiple sessions) and measurement occasions (single measurement versus repeated measurement).

3. Hedonic decline has been attributed to myriad mechanisms that include homeostasis (set points), sensory-specific satiety, adaptation, habituation, and self-reflection.

4. We provide a taxonomy of three classes of antecedents of hedonic decline: physiological feedback, perceptual changes, and self-reflection.

5. Physiological antecedents largely result from bodily feedback that reflects the extent of consumption (e.g., leptin levels or stomach distension).

6. Perceptual change antecedents alter the rate of hedonic decline by changing the ongoing experience itself (e.g., through attention redirection or shifting reference levels).

7. Self-reflection antecedents influence hedonic decline by incorporating lay beliefs (e.g., subjective quantity of past consumption) about what hedonic decline should be, which shapes the subsequent hedonic decline actually experienced.

DISCLOSURE STATEMENT

The authors are not aware of any affiliations, memberships, funding, or financial holdings that might be perceived as affecting the objectivity of this review.

LITERATURE CITED

Benelam B. 2009. Satiation, satiety and their effects on eating behaviour. *Nutr. Bull.* 34:126–73

Berlyne DE. 1971. *Aesthetics and Psychobiology*. East Norwalk, CT: Appleton-Century-Crofts

Bernhard N, van der Kooy D. 2000. A behavioral and genetic dissection of two forms of olfactory plasticity in *Caenorhabditis elegans*: adaptation and habituation. *Learn. Mem.* 7:199–212

Berridge KC. 2009. "Liking" and "wanting" food rewards: brain substrates and roles in eating disorders. *Physiol. Behav.* 97:537–50

Berthoud HR. 2011. Metabolic and hedonic drives in the neural control of appetite: Who is the boss? *Curr. Opin. Neurobiol.* 21:888–96

Bizo LA, Bogdanov SV, Killeen PR. 1998. Satiation causes within-session decreases in instrumental responding. *J. Exp. Psychol. Anim. Behav. Process.* 24:439–52

Blair E, Burton S. 1987. Cognitive processes used by survey respondents to answer behavioral frequency questions. *J. Consum. Res.* 14:280–88

Blass EM, Anderson DR, Kirkorian HL, Pempek TA, Price I, Koleini MF. 2006. On the road to obesity: Television viewing increases intake of high-density foods. *Physiol. Behav.* 88:597–604

Boswell W, Boudreau J, Tichy J. 2005. The relationship between employee job change and job satisfaction: the honeymoon-hangover effect. *J. Appl. Psychol.* 90:882–92

Brickman P, Campbell DT. 1971. Hedonic relativism and planning the good society. In *Adaptation-Level Theory*, ed. MH Appley, pp. 287–302. New York: Academic

Brickman P, Coates D, Janoff-Bulman R. 1978. Lottery winners and accident victims: Is happiness relative? *J. Personal. Soc. Psychol.* 36:917–27

Brondel L, Romer M, Van Wymelbeke V, Pineau N, Jiang T, et al. 2009. Variety enhances food intake in humans: role of sensory-specific satiety. *Physiol. Behav.* 97:44–51

Brunstrom JM, Mitchell GL. 2006. Effects of distraction on the development of satiety. *Br. J. Nutr.* 96:761–69

Cabanac M, Duclaux R. 1970. Physiological role of pleasure. *Nature* 227:966–67

Campbell A. 1981. *The Sense of Well-Being in America*. New York: McGraw-Hill

Chugani SK, Irwin JR, Redden JP. 2015. Happily ever after: the effect of identity-consistency on product satiation. *J. Consum. Res.* 42:564–77

Cox D, Cox AD. 2002. Beyond first impressions: the effects of repeated exposure on consumer liking of visually complex and simple product designs. *J. Acad. Mark. Sci.* 30:119–30

Crolic C, Janiszewski C. 2016. Hedonic escalation: when food just tastes better and better. *J. Consum. Res.* 43(3):388–406

Diener E, Biswas-Diener R. 2002. Will money increase subjective well-being? *Soc. Indic. Res.* 57:119–69

Diener E, Lucas RE, Scollon CN. 2006. Beyond the hedonic treadmill: revising the adaptation theory of well-being. *Am. Psychol.* 61:305–14

Diener E, Sandvik E, Seidlitz L, Diener M. 1993. The relationship between income and subjective well-being: relative or absolute? *Soc. Indic. Res.* 28:195–223

Easterlin RA. 1995. Will raising the incomes of all increase the happiness of all? *J. Econ. Behav. Organ.* 27:35–47

Epstein LH, Caggiula AR, Rodefer JS, Wisneiwski L, Mitchell SL. 1993. The effects of calories and taste on habituation of the human salivary response. *Addict. Behav.* 18:179–85

Epstein LH, Rodefer JS, Wisniewski L, Caggiula AR. 1992. Habituation and dishabituation of human salivary response. *Physiol. Behav.* 51:945–50

Epstein LH, Temple JL, Roemmich JN, Bouton ME. 2009. Habituation as a determinant of human food intake. *Psychol. Rev.* 116:384–407

Frederick S, Loewenstein G. 1999. Hedonic adaptation. In *Well-Being: The Foundations of Hedonic Psychology*, ed. E Diener, N Shwarz, pp. 302–29. New York: Russell Sage

Fujita F, Diener E. 2005. Life satisfaction set point: stability and change. *J. Personal. Soc. Psychol.* 88:158–64

Galak J, Kruger J, Loewenstein G. 2011. Is variety the spice of life? It all depends on the rate of consumption. *Judgm. Decis. Mak.* 6:230–38

Galak J, Kruger J, Loewenstein G. 2013. Slow down! Insensitivity to rate of consumption leads to avoidable satiation. *J. Consum. Res.* 39:993–1009

Galak J, Redden JP, Kruger J. 2009. Variety amnesia: Recalling past variety can accelerate recovery from satiation. *J. Consum. Res.* 36:575–84

Galak J, Redden JP, Yang Y, Kyung EJ. 2014. How perceptions of temporal distance influence satiation. *J. Exp. Soc. Psychol.* 52:118–23

Garbinsky EN, Morewedge CK, Shiv B. 2014. Interference of the end: why recency bias in memory determines when a food is consumed again. *Psychol. Sci.* 25:1466–74

Geier A, Wansink B, Rozin P. 2012. Red potato chips: Segmentation cues can substantially decrease food intake. *Health Psychol.* 31:398–401

Geliebter A. 1988. Gastric distension and gastric capacity in relation to food intake in humans. *Physiol. Behav.* 44:665–68

Ghosal T, Yorkston E, Nunes JC, Boatwright P. 2014. Multiple reference points in sequential hedonic evaluation: an empirical analysis. *J. Mark. Res.* 51(5):563–77

Gibbs J, Young RC, Smith GP. 1973. Cholecystokinin decreases food intake in rats. *J. Comp. Physiol. Psychol.* 84:488–95

Gilbert DT, Pinel EC, Wilson TD, Blumberg SJ, Wheatley TP. 1998. Immune neglect: a source of durability bias in affective forecasting. *J. Personal. Soc. Psychol.* 75:617–38

Glanzer M. 1953. Stimulus satiation: an explanation of spontaneous alternation and related phenomena. *Psychol. Rev.* 60:247–68

Griffioen-Roose S, Finlayson G, Mars M, Blundell JE, de Graaf C. 2010. Measuring food reward and the transfer effect of sensory specific satiety. *Appetite* 55:648–55

Grossman SP. 1986. The role of glucose, insulin and glucagon in the regulation of food intake and body weight. *Neurosci. Biobehav. Rev.* 10:295–315

Groves PM, Thompson RF. 1970. Habituation: a dual-process theory. *Psychol. Rev.* 77:419–50

Havermans RC. 2012. Stimulus specificity but no dishabituation of sensory-specific satiety. *Appetite* 58:852–55

Havermans RC, Brondel L. 2013. Satiety in face of variety: on sensory-specific satiety and perceived food variety. *Food Qual. Preference* 28:161–63

Havermans RC, Janssen T, Giesen JC, Roefs A, Jansen A. 2009. Food liking, food wanting, and sensory-specific satiety. *Appetite* 52:222–25

Helson H. 1947. Adaptation-level as frame of reference for prediction of psychophysical data. *Am. J. Psychol.* 60:1–29

Helson H. 1971. Adaptation-level theory: 1970 and after. In *Adaptation-Level Theory*, ed. MH Appley, pp. 5–17. New York: Academic

Hetherington MM, Foster R, Newman T, Anderson AS, Norton G. 2006. Understanding variety: Tasting different foods delays satiation. *Physiol. Behav.* 87:263–71

Hetherington MM, Rolls BJ. 1996. Sensory-specific satiety: theoretical frameworks and central characteristics. In *Why We Eat What We Eat: The Psychology of Eating*, ed. ED Capaldi, pp. 267–90. Washington, DC: Am. Psychol. Assoc.

Hetherington MM, Rolls BJ, Burley VJ. 1989. The time course of sensory-specific satiety. *Appetite* 12:57–68

Higgs S, Donohoe JE. 2011. Focusing on food during lunch enhances lunch memory and decreases later snack intake. *Appetite* 57:202–6

Higgs S, Williamson AC, Rotshtein P, Humphreys GW. 2008. Sensory-specific satiety is intact in amnesics who eat multiple meals. *Psychol. Sci.* 19:623–26

Holt S, Miller J, Petocz P, Farmakalidis E. 1995. A satiety index of common foods. *Eur. J. Clin. Nutr.* 49:675–90

Inman JJ. 2001. The role of sensory-specific satiety in attribute-level variety seeking. *J. Consum. Res.* 28:105–20

Johnson J, Vickers Z. 1993. Effect of flavor and macronutrient composition of food servings on liking, hunger and subsequent intake. *Appetite* 21:25–39

Kahneman D, Miller DT. 1986. Norm theory: comparing reality to its alternatives. *Psychol. Rev.* 93:136–53

Kahneman D, Snell J. 1992. Predicting a changing taste: Do people know what they will like? *J. Behav. Decis. Mak.* 5:187–200

Kamphuis M, Westerterp-Plantenga M, Saris W. 2001. Fat-specific satiety in humans for fat high in linoleic acid versus fat high in oleic acid. *Eur. J. Clin. Nutr.* 55:499–508

Kandel ER. 1991. Cellular mechanisms of learning and the biological basis of individuality. In *Principles of Neural Science*, ed. ER Kandel, JH Schwartz, TM Jessell, pp. 1009–31. New York: Elsevier

Killeen PR. 1995. Economics, ecologics, and mechanics: the dynamics of responding under conditions of varying motivation. *J. Exp. Anal. Behav.* 64:405–31

Kissileff HR, Carretta JC, Geliebter A, Pi-Sunyer XF. 2003. Cholecystokinin and stomach distension combine to reduce food intake in humans. *Am. J. Phsyiol.* 285:R992–98

Klayman J, Ha Y-W. 1987. Confirmation, disconfirmation, and information in hypothesis testing. *Psychol. Rev.* 94:211–28

Kringelbach ML, O'Doherty J, Rolls ET, Andrews C. 2000. Sensory-specific satiety for the flavour of food is represented in the orbitofrontal cortex. *NeuroImage* 11:S767

Kyung EJ, Menon G, Trope Y. 2010. Reconstruction of things past: Why do some memories feel so close and others so far away? *J. Exp. Soc. Psychol.* 46:217–20

Larson JS, Redden JP, Elder RS. 2014. Satiation from sensory simulation: Evaluating foods decreases enjoyment of similar foods. *J. Consum. Psychol.* 24:188–94

Liebling DS, Eisner JD, Gibbs J, Smith GP. 1975. Intestinal satiety in rats. *J. Comp. Physiol. Psychol.* 89:955–65

Lieverse R, Jansen J, Masclee A, Lamers C. 1995. Satiety effects of a physiological dose of cholecystokinin in humans. *Gut* 36:176–79

Lotter EC, Woods SC. 1997. Injections of insulin and changes of body weight. *Physiol. Behav.* 18:293–97

Lucas RE, Clark AE. 2006. Do people really adapt to marriage? *J. Happiness Stud.* 7:405–26

Lucas RE, Clark AE, Georgellis Y, Diener E. 2003. Reexamining adaptation and the set point model of happiness: reactions to changes in marital status. *J. Personal. Soc. Psychol.* 84:527–39

McSweeney FK. 2004. Dynamic changes in reinforcer effectiveness: satiation and habituation have different implications for theory and practice. *Behav. Anal.* 27:171–88

McSweeney FK, Murphy ES. 2000. Criticisms of the satiety hypothesis as an explanation for within-session decreases in responding. *J. Exp. Anal. Behav.* 74:347–61

McSweeney FK, Murphy ES. 2009. Sensitization and habituation regulate reinforcer effectiveness. *Neurobiol. Learn. Mem.* 92:189–98

Menon G, Raghubir P, Schwarz N. 1995. Behavioral frequency judgments: an accessibility-diagnosticity framework. *J. Consum. Res.* 22:212–28

Mook DG, Votaw MC. 1992. How important is hedonism? Reasons given by college students for ending a meal. *Appetite* 18:69–75

Moran TH, Dailey MJ. 2011. Intestinal feedback signaling and satiety. *Physiol. Behav.* 105:77–81

Morewedge CK, Huh YE, Vosgerau J. 2010. Thought for food: Imagined consumption reduces actual consumption. *Science* 330:1530–33

Nelson LD, Meyvis T. 2008. Disrupting adaptation to hedonic experiences. *J. Mark. Res.* 45:654–64

Nelson LD, Meyvis T, Galak J. 2009. Enhancing the television viewing experience through commercial interruptions. *J. Consum. Res.* 36:160–72

Nicolao L, Irwin JR, Goodman JK. 2009. Happiness for sale: Do experiential purchases make consumers happier than material purchases? *J. Consum. Res.* 36:188–98

Nolan LJ, Hetherington MM. 2009. The effects of sham feeding-induced sensory specific satiation and food variety on subsequent food intake in humans. *Appetite* 52:720–25

O'Donohue W, Plaud JJ. 1991. The long-term habituation of sexual arousal in the human male. *J. Behav. Ther. Exp. Psychiatry* 22:87–96

O'Sullivan HL, Alexander E, Ferriday D, Brunstrom JM. 2010. Effects of repeated exposure on liking for a reduced-energy-dense food. *Am. J. Clin. Nutr.* 91:1584–89

Parducci A. 1995. *Happiness, Pleasure, and Judgment: The Contextual Theory and Its Applications*. Hillsdale, NJ: Lawrence Erlbaum Assoc.

Peters JH, McKay BM, Simasko SM, Ritter RC. 2005. Leptin-induced satiation mediated by abdominal vagal afferents. *Am. J. Physiol. Regul. Integr. Comp. Physiol.* 288:R879–84

Quoidbach J, Dunn EW. 2013. Give it up: a strategy for combating hedonic adaptation. *Soc. Psychol. Personal. Sci.* 4:563–68

Raghunathan R, Irwin JR. 2001. Walking the hedonic product treadmill: default contrast and mood-based assimilation in judgments of predicted happiness with a target product. *J. Consum. Res.* 28:355–68

Rankin CH, Abrams T, Barry RJ, Bhatnagar S, Clayton DF, et al. 2009. Habituation revisited: an updated and revised description of the behavioral characteristics of habituation. *Neurobiol. Learn. Mem.* 92:135–38

Raynor HA, Epstein LH. 1999. Effects of sensory stimulation and post-ingestive consequences on satiation. *Physiol. Behav.* 70:465–70

Read D, Loewenstein G. 1995. Diversification bias: explaining the discrepancy in variety seeking between combined and separated choices. *J. Exp. Psychol. Appl.* 1:34–49

Redden JP. 2008. Reducing satiation: the role of categorization level. *J. Consum. Res.* 34:624–34

Redden JP. 2015. Desire over time: the multi-faceted nature of satiation. In *The Psychology of Desire*, ed. W Hofmann, LF Nordgren, pp. 82–103. New York: Guilford Press

Redden JP, Galak J. 2013. The subjective sense of feeling satiated. *J. Exp. Psychol. Gen.* 142:209–17

Redden JP, Haws KL. 2013. Healthy satiation: the role of decreasing desire in effective self-control. *J. Consum. Res.* 39:1100–14

Redden JP, Haws KL, Chen J. 2017. The ability to choose can increase satiation. *J. Personal. Soc. Psychol.* 112(2):186–200

Robinson E, Aveyard P, Daley A, Jolly K, Lewis A, et al. 2013. Eating attentively: a systematic review and meta-analysis of the effect of food intake memory and awareness on eating. *Am. J. Clin. Nutr.* 97(4):728–42

Rolls BJ, Rolls ET, Rowe EA, Sweeney K. 1981. Sensory specific satiety in man. *Physiol. Behav.* 27:137–42

Rolls ET, de Waal AWL. 1985. Long-term sensory-specific satiety: evidence from an Ethiopian refugee camp. *Physiol. Behav.* 34:1017–20

Rolls ET, Rolls JH. 1997. Olfactory sensory-specific satiety in humans. *Physiol. Behav.* 61:467–73

Rupp HA, Wallen K. 2007. Relationship between testosterone and interest in sexual stimuli: the effect of experience. *Horm. Behav.* 52:581–89

Sackett AM, Meyvis T, Nelson LD, Converse BA, Sackett AL. 2010. You're having fun when time flies: the hedonic consequences of subjective time progression. *Psychol. Sci.* 21:111–17

Schellenberg EG, Peretz I, Vieillard S. 2008. Liking for happy- and sad-sounding music: effects of exposure. *Cogn. Emot.* 22:218–37

Schifferstein HNJ, Kuiper WE. 1997. Sequence effects in hedonic judgments of taste stimuli. *Percept. Psychophys.* 59:900–12

Schulz R, Decker S. 1985. Long-term adjustment to physical disability: the role of social support, perceived control, and self-blame. *J. Personal. Soc. Psychol.* 48:1162–72

Semin GR, Smith ER. 1999. Revisiting the past and back to the future: memory systems and the linguistic representation of social events. *J. Personal. Soc. Psychol.* 76:877–92

Sevilla J, Redden JP. 2014. Perceived scarcity reduces the rate of satiation. *J. Mark. Res.* 51:205–17

Sevilla J, Zhang J, Kahn BE. 2016. Anticipation of future variety reduces satiation from current experiences. *J. Mark. Res.* 53(6):954–68

Sheldon KM, Lyubomirsky S. 2012. The challenge of staying happier: testing the hedonic adaptation prevention model. *Personal. Soc. Psychol. Bull.* 38:670–80

Shwarz N, Hippler H-J, Deutsch B, Strack F. 1985. Effects of category range on reported behavior and comparative judgments. *Public Opin. Q.* 49:388–95

Simonson I. 1990. The effect of purchase quantity and timing on variety-seeking behavior. *J. Mark. Res.* 27:150–62

Soloman RL, Corbit JD. 1974. An opponent-process theory of motivation: I. Temporal dynamics of affect. *Psychol. Rev.* 81:119–45

Sorensen LB, Moller P, Flint A, Martens M, Raben A. 2003. Effect of sensory perception of foods on appetite and food intake: a review of studies on humans. *Int. J. Obes. Relat. Metab. Disord.* 27:1152–66

Stevenson B, Wolfers J. 2013. Subjective well-being and income: Is there any evidence of satiation? *Am. Econ. Rev.* 103:598–604

Temple JL, Giacomelli AM, Roemmich JN, Epstein LH. 2008a. Dietary variety impairs habituation in children. *Health Psychol.* 27:S10–19

Temple JL, Giacomelli AM, Roemmich JN, Epstein LH. 2008b. Habituation and within session changes in motivated responding for food in children. *Appetite* 50:390–96

Thompson RF, Spencer WA. 1966. Habituation: a model phenomenon for the study of neuronal substrates of behavior. *Psychol. Rev.* 73:16–43

Tuiten A, van Hok J, Koppeschaar H, Bernaards C, Thijssen J, Verbaten R. 2000. Time course of effects of testosterone administration on sexual arousal in women. *Arch. Gen. Psychiatry* 57:149–53

Van De Veer E, Van Herpen E, Van Trijp HC. 2015. Body and mind: Mindfulness helps consumers to compensate for prior food intake by enhancing the responsiveness to physiological cues. *J. Consum. Res.* 42(5):783–803

Wang GJ, Tomasi D, Backus W, Wang R, Telang F, et al. 2008. Gastric distention activates satiety circuitry in the human brain. *NeuroImage* 39:1824–31

Wansink B. 2005. Bottomless bowls: why visual cues of portion size may influence intake. *Obes. Res.* 13:93–100

Wansink B, Rozin P, Geiger A. 2005. *Consumption interruption and the red potato chip: packaging ideas that help control consumption*. Work. Pap. 05–110, Cornell Food Brand Lab, Cornell Univ., Ithaca, NY

Weijzen PL, Smeets PA, de Graaf C. 2009. Sip size of orangeade: effects on intake and sensory-specific satiation. *Br. J. Nutr.* 102:1091–97

Wilson TD, Gilbert DT. 2008. Explaining away: a model of affective adaptation. *Perspect. Psychol. Sci.* 3(5):370–86

Woods SC, Schwartz MW, Baskin DG, Seeley RJ. 2000. Food intake and the regulation of body weight. *Annu. Rev. Psychol.* 51:255–77

Wortman CB, Silver RC. 1987. *Coping with irrevocable loss*. Presented at Am. Psychol. Assoc. Conv., Aug., Washington, DC

Yang Y, Galak J. 2015. Sentimental value and its influence on hedonic adaptation. *J. Personal. Soc. Psychol.* 109:767–90

Zajonc RB. 1968. Attitudinal effects of mere exposure. *J. Personal. Soc. Psychol.* 9:1–27

Zamble E. 1992. Behavior and adaptation in long-term prison inmates. Descriptive longitudinal results. *Crim. Justice Behav.* 19:409–25

Zauberman G, Levav J, Diehl K, Bhargave R. 2010. 1995 feels so close yet so far: the effect of event markers on subjective feelings of elapsed time. *Psychol. Sci.* 21:133–39

Zhang F, Chen Y, Heiman M, DiMarchi R. 2005. Leptin: structure, function and biology. *Vitam. Horm.* 71:345–72

Zhang Y, Proenca R, Maffei M, Barone M, Leopold L, Friedman JM. 1994. Positional cloning of the mouse obese gene and its human homologue. *Nature* 372:425–32

Zhao M, Tsai C. 2011. The effects of duration knowledge on forecasted versus actual affective experiences. *J. Consum. Res.* 38:525–34

How We Hear: The Perception and Neural Coding of Sound

Andrew J. Oxenham

Department of Psychology, University of Minnesota, Minneapolis, Minnesota 55455;
email: oxenham@umn.edu

Annu. Rev. Psychol. 2018. 69:27–50

First published as a Review in Advance on October 16, 2017

The *Annual Review of Psychology* is online at psych.annualreviews.org

https://doi.org/10.1146/annurev-psych-122216-011635

Keywords

auditory perception, frequency selectivity, pitch, auditory scene analysis, hearing loss

Abstract

Auditory perception is our main gateway to communication with others via speech and music, and it also plays an important role in alerting and orienting us to new events. This review provides an overview of selected topics pertaining to the perception and neural coding of sound, starting with the first stage of filtering in the cochlea and its profound impact on perception. The next topic, pitch, has been debated for millennia, but recent technical and theoretical developments continue to provide us with new insights. Cochlear filtering and pitch both play key roles in our ability to parse the auditory scene, enabling us to attend to one auditory object or stream while ignoring others. An improved understanding of the basic mechanisms of auditory perception will aid us in the quest to tackle the increasingly important problem of hearing loss in our aging population.

Contents

INTRODUCTION

Hearing provides us with access to the acoustic world, including the fall of raindrops on the roof, the chirping of crickets on a summer evening, and the cry of a newborn baby. It is the primary mode of human connection and communication via speech and music. Our ability to detect, localize, and identify sounds is astounding given the seemingly limited sensory input: Our eardrums move to and fro with tiny and rapid changes in air pressure, providing us only with a continuous measure of change in sound pressure at two locations in space, about 20 cm apart, on either side of the head. From this simple motion arises our rich perception of the acoustic environment around us. The feat is even more impressive when one considers that sounds are rarely presented in isolation: The sound wave that reaches each ear is often a complex mixture of many sound sources, such as the conversations at surrounding tables of a restaurant, mixed with background music and the clatter of plates. All that reaches each eardrum is a single sound wave, and yet, in most cases, we are able to extract from that single waveform sufficient information to identify the different sound sources and direct our attention to the ones that currently interest us.

Deconstructing a waveform into its original sources is no simple matter; in fact, the problem is mathematically ill posed, meaning that there is no unique solution. Similar to solutions in the visual domain (e.g., Kersten et al. 2004), our auditory system is thought to use a combination of information learned during development and more hardwired solutions developed over evolutionary time to solve this problem. Decades of psychological, physiological, and computational research have gone into unraveling the processes underlying auditory perception. Understanding basic auditory processing, auditory scene analysis (Bregman 1990), and the ways in which humans solve the "cocktail party problem" (Cherry 1953) has implications not only for furthering fundamental scientific progress but also for audio technology applications. Such applications include low-bit-rate audio coding (e.g., MP3) for music storage, broadcast and cell phone technology, automatic speech recognition, and the mitigation of the effects of hearing loss through hearing aids and cochlear implants.

This review focuses on recent trends and developments in the area of auditory perception, as well as on relevant computational and neuroscientific studies that shed light on the processes involved. The areas of focus include the peripheral mechanisms that enable the rich analysis of the auditory scene, the perception and coding of pitch, and the interactions between attention and auditory scene analysis. The review concludes with a discussion of hearing loss and the efforts underway to understand and alleviate its potentially devastating effects.

EARLY STAGES: PERCEPTION AND THE COCHLEA

Frequency Range of Hearing

Just as the visual system is sensitive to oscillations in the electromagnetic spectrum, the auditory system is sensitive to oscillations in the acoustic spectrum. There are, however, interesting quantitative differences in the ranges of sensitivity. For instance, the human visual system is sensitive to light wavelengths between approximately 380 and 750 nm (or frequencies between 400 and 790 THz), spanning just under 1 octave (a doubling in frequency), which we perceive as the spectrum of colors. In contrast, the human auditory system is sensitive to sound frequencies between 20 Hz and 20,000 Hz, or approximately 10 octaves, which we perceive along the dimension of pitch. Just as important as the ability to hear a wide range of frequencies is the ability to analyze the frequency content of sounds. Both our sensitivity and our selectivity with respect to frequency originate in the cochlea of the inner ear.

Cochlear Tuning and Frequency Selectivity

The basilar membrane runs along the length of the cochlea and vibrates in response to the sounds that enter the cochlea via the vibrations of the eardrum and the middle ear bones. The action of the basilar membrane can be compared to that of a prism—the wide range of frequencies within a typical sound are dispersed to different locations along the basilar membrane within the cochlea. Every point along the basilar membrane responds best to a certain frequency, known as the best frequency or characteristic frequency (CF). In this way, the frequency content of a sound is represented along the length of the basilar membrane in a frequency-to-place map, providing tonotopic organization with a gradient from low to high frequencies from the apex to the base of the cochlea. This organization is maintained from the cochlea via the inner hair cells and the auditory nerve, through the brainstem and midbrain, to the primary auditory cortex. Place coding thus represents a primary organizational principle for both neural coding and perception.

Although the passive properties of the basilar membrane (e.g., its mass and stiffness gradients) provide the foundations for the tonotopic organization (von Békésy 1960), the separation of frequencies along the basilar membrane is enhanced by sharp tuning that is mediated by the action of the outer hair cells within the cochlea (Dallos et al. 2006). This sharp tuning has a profound impact on our perception of sound. There are many ways to measure our perceptual ability to separate sounds of different frequencies, or our frequency selectivity. One of the most common perceptual measures involves the masking of one sound by another. By parametrically varying the frequency relationship between the masking sound and a target and measuring the level of the masker and target sounds at the detection threshold, it is possible to determine the sharpness of tuning (Patterson 1976). It has often been assumed that cochlear tuning determines the frequency selectivity measured behaviorally, so that the first stages of auditory processing limit the degree to which we are able to hear out different frequencies within a mixture. However, because of the inability to make direct measurements of the cochlea in humans, and because of the difficulty of deriving behavioral measures in animals, this assumption has rarely been tested. Another difficulty is posed by the highly nonlinear nature of cochlear processing, as shown directly through physiological measures in animals (Ruggero 1992) and indirectly through behavioral measures in humans (Oxenham & Plack 1997). The nonlinearity means that estimates of frequency selectivity will differ depending on the precise measurement technique used and the stimulus level at which the measurements are made.

One study measured both cochlear tuning and behavioral frequency selectivity in guinea pigs and found reasonably good correspondence between the two (Evans 2001). Because it has generally been assumed that the cochleae of humans and of mammals commonly used in laboratory experiments (such as guinea pigs, cats, and chinchillas) are similar, it has also been assumed that human cochlear tuning is similar to that of other mammals and that, therefore, human perceptual frequency selectivity is also limited by cochlear tuning. Indeed, a number of physiological studies have examined the representation of speech sounds in the auditory nerves of other species, making the explicit assumption that cochlear tuning is similar across species (Delgutte 1984, Young & Sachs 1979). As our understanding of otoacoustic emissions (OAEs)—sounds generated by the ear—has improved, it has been possible to probe the tuning properties of the human cochlea in a noninvasive manner (e.g., Bentsen et al. 2011). The combination of OAE measurements and behavioral masking studies in humans has led to confirmation of the idea that behavioral frequency selectivity reflects cochlear tuning, but also (and more surprisingly), that human tuning may be considerably sharper than that found in common laboratory animals, such as cats and guinea pigs (Shera et al. 2002). This conclusion was based on the fact that the latencies (or delays) of stimulus-frequency OAEs (SFOAEs) in humans are longer than those measured in other mammals and that latency is related to the sharpness of cochlear tuning (Shera et al. 2010).

The claim that human cochlear tuning is sharper than that in many other species has generated some controversy (Lopez-Poveda & Eustaquio-Martin 2013, Ruggero & Temchin 2005). Nevertheless, the initial claims have been supported by further studies in different rodent species (Shera et al. 2010), as well as in a species of old-world monkey, where cochlear tuning appears to be intermediate between that of rodent and human, suggesting a progression from small nonprimate mammals to small primates to humans (Joris et al. 2011). All of these studies have used a combination of (a) OAE measurements, (b) direct measurements of tuning in the auditory nerve, and (c) behavioral measurements of frequency selectivity. However, none of the earlier studies used all three methods in the same species; the auditory nerve measurements are too invasive to be carried out in humans, and the behavioral measurements have posed challenges in terms of animal training. More recently, a study was carried out in ferrets that included all three measurements. The results from this study reveal a good correspondence between all three types of measurement and confirm that tuning is, indeed, broader in ferrets than in humans (Sumner et al. 2014).

In summary, our current thinking is that the frequency tuning established in the cochlea determines our perceptual ability to separate sounds of different frequencies. In some ways, this is a remarkable finding, given the extensive and complex processing of neural signals between the cochlea and the auditory cortex: These multiple stages of neural processing neither enhance nor degrade the basic tuning patterns that are established in the cochlea. Another main conclusion is that human frequency tuning is sharper than that of many other mammals. This finding has important, and not yet fully explored, implications for understanding human hearing and acoustic communication in general. It may be that sharp tuning is a prerequisite for developing the fine acoustic communication skills necessary for speech. However, this speculation is rendered less likely by the fact that speech is highly robust to spectral degradation and remains intelligible even under conditions of very poor spectral resolution (Shannon et al. 1995). It currently appears more likely that our sharp cochlear tuning underlies our fine pitch perception and discrimination abilities. As discussed in the next section, there appear to be some fundamental and qualitative differences in the way pitch is perceived by humans and by other species, which, in turn, may be related to the differences in frequency tuning found in the very first stages of auditory processing.

PITCH PERCEPTION AND NEURAL CODING

Pitch is a perceptual quality that relates most closely to the physical variable of frequency or repetition rate of a sound. Its technical definition, provided by the American National Standards Institute, is "that attribute of auditory sensation by which sounds are ordered on the scale used for melody in music" (ANSI 2013, p. 58). Pitch plays a crucial role in auditory perception. In music, sequences of pitch define melody, and simultaneous combinations of pitch define harmony and tonality. In speech, pitch contours provide information about prosody and speaker identity; in tone languages, such as Mandarin or Cantonese, pitch contours also provide lexical information. In addition, differences in pitch between sounds enable us to segregate competing sources, thereby helping solve the cocktail party problem (Darwin 2005).

Place and Time Theories

The questions of how pitch is extracted from acoustic waveforms and how it is represented in the auditory system have been debated for well over a century but remain topics of current investigation and some controversy. Two broad categories of theories addressing these questions can be identified, both of which have long histories: place theories and timing theories. As outlined in the previous section, the cochlea establishes a tonotopic representation that is maintained throughout the early auditory pathways. Broadly speaking, the premise of place theories is that the brain is able to extract the frequency content of sounds from this tonotopic representation to derive the percept of pitch. Timing theories, on the other hand, are based on the observation that action potentials, or spikes, in the auditory nerve tend to occur at a given phase in the cycle of a stimulating waveform, producing a precise relationship between the waveform and the timing of the spikes, known as phase locking (Rose et al. 1967). Auditory nerve phase locking enables the auditory system to extract timing differences between a sound arriving at each of the two ears, enabling us to localize sounds in space (Blauert 1997). The fact that humans can discriminate interaural time differences as small as 20 μs attests to the exquisite sensitivity of the auditory system to timing information. Timing theories of pitch postulate that the same exquisite sensitivity to timing can be harnessed by the auditory system to measure the time intervals between spikes, which are related to the period (i.e., the duration of one repetition) of the waveform.

A third category of theories could be termed place-time theories. According to these approaches, spike timing information is used by the auditory system not by comparing time intervals between successive spikes but rather by using the phase dispersion along the basilar membrane and utilizing coincident spikes from different cochlear locations to extract information about the frequency of a tone (Loeb et al. 1983, Shamma 1985). Various place, timing, and place-time theories have been postulated over the decades to account for pitch of both pure and complex tones. Some background and recent findings are reviewed in the following sections for both classes of stimuli.

Pitch of Pure Tones

Pure tones—sinusoidal variations in air pressure—produce a salient pitch sensation over a wide range of frequencies. In the range of greatest sensitivity to frequency changes (between approximately 1 and 2 kHz), humans can discriminate between two frequencies that differ by as little as 0.2% (Micheyl et al. 2012). At the low and high ends of the frequency spectrum (below approximately 500 Hz and above approximately 4,000 Hz), sensitivity deteriorates. At high frequencies, the deterioration is particularly dramatic, with increases in frequency discrimination thresholds by an order of magnitude between 2 and 8 kHz (Moore & Ernst 2012). Indeed, our ability to recognize musical intervals (such as an octave or a fifth), or even familiar melodies, essentially disappears at frequencies above 4–5 kHz (Attneave & Olson 1971).

There is reasonably good correspondence between the deterioration in our ability to discriminate between frequencies and the deterioration in the accuracy of auditory nerve phase locking in small mammals that occurs as frequency increases: The synchronization index for phase locking degrades to about half its maximum value by approximately 2–3 kHz, and significant phase locking is no longer observed above approximately 4–5 kHz, depending somewhat on the species (Heil & Peterson 2015). Phase locking has not been measured directly in the human auditory nerve due to the invasive nature of the measurements. On the one hand, usable phase locking may only extend up to approximately 1.5 kHz, as indicated by the fact that we cease to be able to detect timing differences between the two ears for pure tones above 1.5 kHz (Blauert 1997). On the other hand, the fact that frequency discrimination thresholds (as a proportion of the center frequency) continue to increase up to approximately 8 kHz and then remain roughly constant at even higher frequencies has been proposed as evidence for some residual phase locking up to 8 kHz (Moore & Ernst 2012). Thus, if it is agreed that human phase locking is at least qualitatively similar to that observed in other mammals, it seems reasonable to assume that its effects begin to degrade above 1 kHz and are no longer perceptually relevant above 8 kHz, placing the highest frequency at which phase locking is used at least within the range of the 4–5 kHz limit for musical pitch (Attneave & Olson 1971).

The fact that the breakdown in phase locking seems to occur at around the same frequency as the breakdown in musical pitch perception has led to the proposal that timing information from the auditory nerve is necessary for musical pitch perception; indeed, it is tempting to speculate that the highest note on current musical instruments (e.g., C_8 on the grand piano, with a frequency of 4,186 Hz) is determined by the coding limitations imposed at the earliest stages of the auditory system (Oxenham et al. 2011). In contrast, place theory provides no explanation for the fact that frequency discrimination and pitch perception both degrade at high frequencies—if anything, cochlear filters become sharper at high frequencies, suggesting more accurate place coding (Shera et al. 2010).

Another argument in favor of a timing theory of pitch for pure tones is the fact that our ability to discriminate between two frequencies is much finer than would be predicted by basic place theories of pitch. According to place theories, an increase in frequency is detected by a shift in the peak of response from a more apical to a more basal cochlear location, which, in turn, produces a decrease in response from cochlear locations apical to the peak and an increase in response from locations basal to the peak (**Figure 1a**). Place theories have contended that the frequency increase becomes detectable when the change in response at any given cochlear location exceeds some threshold. In this way, changes in frequency can be coded as changes in amplitude (Zwicker 1970; **Figure 1a**). The challenge for the place theory is that a just-detectable change in frequency produces a predicted change in cochlear response that is much smaller than that needed to detect a change in the amplitude of a tone (Heinz et al. 2001).

Although the current weight of evidence seems to favor timing theories of pure-tone pitch, some recent studies have led to a reconsideration of these earlier ideas (Micheyl et al. 2013b, Whiteford

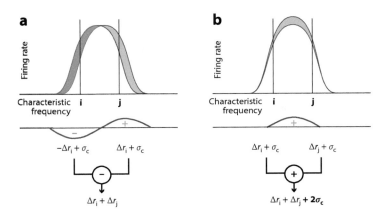

Figure 1

(*a*) Schematic of response (excitation pattern) for two tones close together in frequency. An increase in frequency leads to a shift in the peak of the response to the right, which, in turn, leads to a response decrease below the peak (r_i) and a response increase above the peak (r_j). If some of the neuronal noise is correlated, then the correlated portion of the noise (σ_c) will be canceled out when the two responses are compared by subtraction, leading to improved discrimination. (*b*) For intensity discrimination, correlated neuronal noise between i and j has a different effect because the increment in intensity is detected by adding (not subtracting) the neuronal responses, leading to an increased effect of the correlated noise and, thus, poorer discrimination. Overall, smaller differences in response (or excitation) patterns are required for the detection of a change in frequency than a change in intensity, in line with human perceptual data (Micheyl et al. 2013b).

& Oxenham 2015). One question is whether frequency discrimination, and pitch perception more generally, is really limited by peripheral constraints. In contrast to frequency selectivity (tuning), discussed in the section titled Cochlear Tuning and Frequency Selectivity, frequency discrimination is highly susceptible to training, with dramatic improvements often observed over fairly short periods of time. For instance, professional musicians have been found to have lower (better) frequency discrimination thresholds than nonmusicians by a factor of approximately 6, but nonmusicians can reach levels of performance similar to those of the professional musicians after only 4–8 hours of training (Micheyl et al. 2006). One interpretation of this extended perceptual learning is that discrimination is limited not by peripheral coding constraints (e.g., auditory nerve phase locking), but rather by more central, possibly cortical, coding constraints that are more likely to demonstrate rapid plasticity (e.g., Yin et al. 2014). If so, we may not expect perceptual performance to mirror peripheral limitations, such as auditory nerve phase locking; instead, performance may reflect higher-level constraints, perhaps shaped by passive exposure, with high-frequency tones being sparsely represented and poorly perceived due to the lack of exposure to them in everyday listening conditions. Indeed, the fact that some people have been reported to perceive musical intervals for pure tones of approximately 10 kHz (Burns & Feth 1983) suggests that the more usual limit of 4–5 kHz is not imposed by immutable peripheral coding constraints.

Another line of evidence suggesting that frequency discrimination is not limited by peripheral constraints comes from studies of frequency modulation (FM) and amplitude modulation (AM). According to timing-based theories, the detection of FM at slow modulation rates is mediated by phase locking to the temporal fine structure of the pure tone, whereas the detection of FM at fast modulation rates is mediated via the transformations of the FM to AM via cochlear filtering (Moore & Sek 1996). A recent study of individual differences in 100 young normal-hearing listeners found that slow-rate FM thresholds were significantly correlated with slow-rate changes in interaural time differences, which are known to be mediated by phase locking. However, slow-rate FM detection thresholds were just as strongly correlated with fast-rate FM and AM detection thresholds, suggesting that the individual differences were not mediated by the peripheral coding constraints of phase locking, but rather by more central constraints (Whiteford & Oxenham 2015).

One remaining problem for the place theories of pure-tone pitch is the apparently large difference in sensitivity between frequency discrimination and intensity discrimination. A computational modeling study of cortical neural coding has provided one solution to this problem. Using simple assumptions about the properties of cortical neurons with tuning similar to that observed in the auditory nerve and in the cortex of primate species, Micheyl et al. (2013b) were able to resolve the apparent discrepancy between frequency and intensity discrimination abilities within a unified place-based code. They assumed some underlying correlation between the firing rates of neurons with similar CFs that is independent of the stimulus. The effect of this noise correlation (e.g., Cohen & Kohn 2011) is to limit the usefulness of integrating information across multiple neurons in the case of intensity discrimination, where the correlation decreases the independence of the information in each neuron. However, in the case of frequency discrimination, the effect of the noise correlation is less detrimental because it can be reduced by subtracting the responses of neurons with CFs above the stimulus frequency from the responses of neurons with CFs below the stimulus frequency, thereby enhancing the effects of a shift in frequency. In this way, the same model, with the same sensitivity, can account for observed human performance in both frequency and intensity discrimination tasks (Micheyl et al. 2013b; **Figure 1**).

Regardless of how pitch is extracted from information in the auditory nerve, these representations clearly involve some transformations between the cochlea and the cortex. Timing information becomes increasingly coarse at higher stages of the auditory pathways. In the cochlear nucleus (the first stage of processing beyond the cochlea), phase-locked information is maintained via primary-like neurons that seem to maintain the temporal properties of auditory nerve fibers (Rhode et al. 1983). However, already in the inferior colliculus of the midbrain, phase-locked responses are not normally observed above 1,000 Hz (Liu et al. 2006), and in the auditory cortex, phase locking is generally not observed above 100 Hz (e.g., Lu & Wang 2000). Therefore, any timing-based code in the auditory periphery must be transformed into a population rate or place code at higher stages of processing. In contrast, the place-based, or tonotopic, representation in the auditory periphery is maintained at least up to the primary auditory cortex (e.g., Moerel et al. 2014).

In summary, some aspects of pure-tone pitch perception and frequency discrimination are well accounted for by a timing theory. However, in most cases, a place-based or tonotopic theory can also be used to account for the available perceptual data. Questions surrounding the coding of pure tones in the auditory periphery are not only of basic scientific interest; they also have important implications for attempts to restore hearing via auditory prostheses, such as cochlear implants. This topic is addressed below (see the section titled Perceptual Consequences of Hearing Loss and Cochlear Implants). In any case, pure tones are a special case and are not a particularly ecologically relevant class of stimuli. For a more general case, we turn to harmonic complex tones, such as those we encounter in speech and music.

Pitch of Complex Tones

A complex tone is defined as any sound composed of more than one sinusoid or pure tone. Harmonic complex tones consist of a fundamental frequency (F0) and harmonics (also known as upper partials or overtones) with frequencies at integer multiples of the F0. For instance, a violin playing a note with a pitch corresponding to an orchestral A (440 Hz) produces a waveform that repeats 440 times per second (**Figure 2a**) but has energy not only at 440 Hz but also at

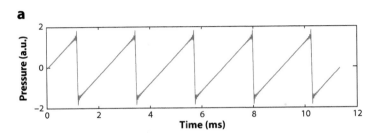

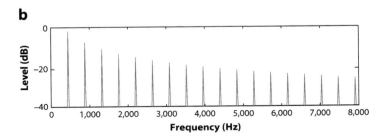

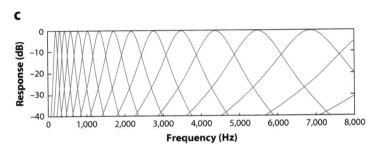

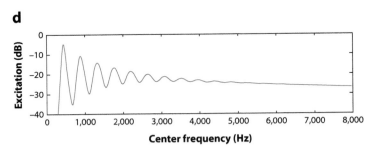

Figure 2

Representations of a harmonic complex tone with a fundamental frequency (F0) of 440 Hz. (*a*) Time waveform. (*b*) Power spectrum of the same waveform. (*c*) Auditory filter bank representing the filtering that occurs in the cochlea. (*d*) Excitation pattern, or the time-averaged output of the auditory filter bank. (*e*) Sample time waveforms at the output of the filter bank, simulating basilar membrane (BM) vibration, including filters centered at the F0 (440 Hz) and the fourth harmonic (1,760 Hz), illustrating resolved harmonics, and filters centered at the eighth (3,520 Hz) and twelfth (5,280 Hz) harmonics of the complex, illustrating harmonics that are less well resolved and show amplitude modulations at a rate corresponding to the F0. Figure modified with permission from Oxenham (2012).

880 Hz, 1,320 Hz, 1,760 Hz, etc. (**Figure 2b**). Interestingly, we tend to hear a single sound with a single pitch, corresponding to the F0, despite the presence of many other frequencies. Indeed, the pitch continues to be heard at the F0 even if the energy at the F0 is removed or masked. This phenomenon is known as residue pitch, periodicity pitch, or the pitch of the missing fundamental. The constancy of the pitch in the presence of masking makes sense from an ecological perspective: We would expect the primary perceptual properties of a sound to remain invariant in the presence of other competing sounds in the environment, just as we expect perceptual constancy of visual objects under different lighting conditions, perspectives, and occlusions. But if it is not derived from the component at the F0 itself, how is pitch extracted from a complex waveform?

To better understand how pitch is extracted from a complex tone, it is useful to consider first how the tone is represented in the auditory periphery. **Figure 2c** illustrates the filtering process of the cochlea, represented as a bank of bandpass filters. Although the filters tend to sharpen somewhat with increasing CF in terms of their bandwidth relative to the CF (known as quality factor, or Q, in filter theory; Shera et al. 2010), their absolute bandwidths in Hz increase with increasing CF, as shown in **Figure 2c**. This means that the filters are narrow, relative to the spacing of the harmonics, for the low-numbered harmonics but become broader with increasing harmonic number. The implications of the relationship between filter bandwidth and harmonic spacing are illustrated in **Figure 2d**, which shows the excitation pattern produced when the harmonic complex is passed through the filter bank illustrated in **Figure 2c**: Low-numbered harmonics each produce distinct peaks in the excitation pattern and are, therefore, spectrally resolved, whereas multiple higher harmonics fall within the bandwidth of a single filter, meaning that they are no longer resolved. The putative time waveforms produced by the complex at different locations along the basilar membrane are shown in **Figure 2e**. For the resolved harmonics, the output resembles a pure tone, whereas for the higher, unresolved harmonics, the output of each filter is itself a complex waveform that repeats at a rate corresponding to the F0.

Numerous studies have shown that the overall pitch of a complex tone is dominated by the lower, resolved harmonics (Plomp 1967). These harmonics could be represented by their place (**Figure 2d**) or their time (**Figure 2e**) representations. In contrast, the unresolved harmonics do not produce clear place cues. Indeed, the fact that any pitch information can be transmitted via unresolved harmonics provides strong evidence that the auditory system is able to use timing information to extract pitch. However, the pitch strength of unresolved harmonics is much weaker than that produced by resolved harmonics, and F0 discrimination thresholds are generally much poorer (by up to an order of magnitude) than thresholds for complexes with resolved harmonics (Bernstein & Oxenham 2003, Houtsma & Smurzynski 1990, Shackleton & Carlyon 1994). The reliance on low-numbered harmonics for pitch may be due to the greater robustness of these harmonics to interference. For instance, the lower-numbered harmonics tend to be more intense and, therefore, less likely to be masked. Also, room acoustics and reverberation can scramble the phase relationships between harmonics. This has no effect on resolved harmonics, but it can severely degrade the temporal envelope information carried by the unresolved harmonics (Qin & Oxenham 2005, Sayles & Winter 2008). The most important question for natural pitch perception, therefore, is how pitch is extracted from the low-numbered resolved harmonics.

As with pure tones, the pitch of harmonic complex tones has been explained in terms of place, timing, and place-time information (Cedolin & Delgutte 2010, Shamma & Klein 2000). Most recent perceptual work has been based on the premise that timing information is extracted, and there has been a plethora of studies concentrating on the perceptual effects of temporal fine structure (TFS), a term that usually refers to the timing information extracted from resolved harmonics or similarly narrowband sounds (Lorenzi et al. 2006, Smith et al. 2002). However, for the same reasons that it is difficult to distinguish place and time codes for pure tones, it is difficult to determine whether the TFS of resolved harmonics is being coded via an auditory nerve timing code or a via a place-based mechanism. Two studies have suggested that timing information from individual harmonics presented to the wrong locations in the cochlea cannot be used to extract pitch information corresponding to the missing F0 (Deeks et al. 2013, Oxenham et al. 2004), suggesting that timing information is not sufficient for the extraction of pitch information. In addition, one study has demonstrated that the pitch of the missing F0 can be extracted from resolved harmonics even when all the harmonics are above approximately 7.5 kHz (Oxenham et al. 2011). If one accepts that phase locking is unlikely to be effective at frequencies of 8 kHz and above, this result suggests that timing information is also not necessary for the perception of complex pitch. Finally, a recent study has found that the F0 discrimination found for these very high-frequency complexes is better than predicted based on optimal integration of the information from each individual harmonic, suggesting that performance is not limited by peripheral coding constraints, such as limited phase locking, and is instead limited at a more central processing stage, where the information from the individual harmonics has already been combined (Lau et al. 2017).

Some studies have attempted to limit place information by presenting stimuli at high levels, where frequency selectivity is poorer, and have found results that do not seem consistent with a purely place-based code (e.g., Marmel et al. 2015). In particular, the discrimination of harmonic from inharmonic complex tones was possible in situations where the changes in the frequencies of the tones produced no measurable change in the place of stimulation based on masking patterns. However, as discussed above (see **Figure 1**), relatively small changes in excitation may be sufficient to code changes in pitch even if they are too small to measure in a masking paradigm (Micheyl et al. 2013b).

Studies of pitch perception in other species have generally concluded that animals can perceive a pitch corresponding to the missing F0. However, some important differences between humans and other species have been identified. First, absolute pitch, or simply spectral similarity, seems to be particularly salient for other species, including other mammals (Yin et al. 2010) and songbirds (Bregman et al. 2016), whereas humans tend to focus on relative pitch relations. Second, the few studies that have attempted to determine the mechanisms of pitch perception in other species have found that judgments seem to be based on temporal envelope cues from unresolved harmonics rather than resolved harmonics, perhaps because the poorer frequency selectivity of other species means that fewer harmonics are resolved than in humans (Shofner & Chaney 2013).

As with pure tones, no matter how complex tones are represented in the auditory nerve, it seems likely that the code is transformed into some form of rate or rate-place population-based code at higher levels of the auditory system. Some behavioral studies have demonstrated that perceptual grouping effects (which are thought to be relatively high-level phenomena) can affect the perception of pitch; conversely, pitch and harmonicity can strongly affect perceptual grouping, suggesting that pitch itself is a relatively high-level, possibly cortical, phenomenon (Darwin 2005). Studies in nonhuman primates (marmosets) have identified small regions of the auditory cortex that seem to respond selectively to harmonic stimuli in ways that are either independent of or dependent on the harmonic numbers presented. Neurons in the former category have been termed pitch neurons (Bendor & Wang 2005), whereas the neurons in the latter category have been termed harmonic template neurons (Feng & Wang 2017). Such fine-grained analysis has not been possible in human neuroimaging studies, including positron emission tomography, functional magnetic resonance imaging, and, more recently, electrocorticography (ECoG); however, there exist a number of reports of anterolateral regions of the human auditory cortex, potentially homologous to the regions identified in marmoset monkeys, that seem to respond selectively to harmonic stimuli in ways that suggest that they are responsive to perceived pitch strength, rather than just stimulus regularity (e.g., Norman-Haignere et al. 2013, Penagos et al. 2004).

Despite these encouraging findings, it remains unclear to what extent such neurons extract pitch without regard to other aspects of the stimulus. For instance, a study in ferrets used stimuli that varied along three dimensions, F0 (corresponding to the perception of pitch), location, and spectral centroid (corresponding to the timbral dimension of brightness), and failed to find evidence for neurons that were sensitive to changes in one dimension but not the others (Walker et al. 2011). In particular, neurons that were modulated by changes in F0 were generally also sensitive to changes in spectral centroid. Interestingly, a human neuroimaging study that also covaried F0 and spectral centroid came to a similar conclusion (Allen et al. 2017). In fact, the failure to find a clear neural separation between dimensions relating to pitch and timbre is consistent with results from perceptual experiments that have demonstrated strong interactions and interference between the two dimensions (e.g., Allen & Oxenham 2014).

Combinations of Pitches: Consonance and Dissonance

Some combinations of pitches sound good or pleasing together (consonant), whereas other do not (dissonant). In this section, we consider only the very simple case of tones presented simultaneously in isolation from any surrounding musical context. The question of which combinations are consonant and why has intrigued scientists, musicians, and music theorists for over two millennia. Pythagoreans attributed the pleasing nature of some consonant musical intervals, such as the octave (2:1 frequency ratio) or the fifth (3:2 frequency ratio), to the inherent mathematical beauty of low-numbered ratios. Indeed, some combinations, such as the octave and the fifth, do seem to occur across multiple cultures and time periods, suggesting explanations that are more universal than simple acculturation (McDermott & Oxenham 2008). More recently, consonance has been attributed to an absence of acoustic beats—the amplitude fluctuations that occur when two tones are close but not identical in frequency (e.g., Fishman et al. 2001, Plomp & Levelt 1965). Another alternative is that a combination of harmonic tones is judged as being most consonant when the combined harmonics most closely resemble a single harmonic series (e.g., Tramo et al. 2001). It has been difficult to distinguish between theories based on acoustic beats and those based on harmonicity because the two properties generally covary: The less a combination of tones resembles a single harmonic series, the more likely it is to contain beating pairs of harmonics.

The question has recently been addressed by exploiting individual differences in preferences. McDermott et al. (2010) used artificial diagnostic stimuli to independently test preference ratings for stimuli in which acoustic beats were either present or absent and for stimuli that were either harmonic or inharmonic. They then correlated individual preference ratings for the diagnostic stimuli with preferences for consonant and dissonant musical intervals and chords using real musical sounds. The outcome was surprisingly clear cut: Preferences for harmonicity correlated strongly with preferences for consonant versus dissonant musical intervals, whereas preferences for (or antipathy to) acoustic beats did not. In addition, the number of years of musical training was found to correlate with harmonicity and musical consonance preferences but not with acoustic beat preferences. From this study, it seems that harmonicity, rather than acoustic beats, determines preferences for consonance, and that these preferences may be learned to some extent.

The suggestion that preferences for consonance may be learned was somewhat surprising at the time given the fact that some earlier studies in infants had suggested that a preference for consonance may be innate (Trainor & Heinmiller 1998, Zentner & Kagan 1996). However, a more recent study in infants questioned the findings from these earlier studies and found no preference for consonant over dissonant intervals (Plantinga & Trehub 2014); instead, this study found only a preference for music to which the infants had previously been exposed. The lack of any innate aspect of consonance judgments was supported by a recent cross-cultural study that compared the judgments of members of a native Amazonian society with little or no exposure to Western culture or music to those of urban residents in Bolivia and the United States (McDermott et al. 2016). That study found that the members of the Amazonian society exhibited no clear distinctions in preference between musical intervals that are deemed consonant and those that are deemed dissonant in Western music.

In summary, studies in adults and infants, as well as studies across cultures, seem to be converging on the conclusion that Western judgments of consonance and dissonance for isolated simultaneous combinations of tones are driven by the harmonicity of the combined tones, rather than the presence of acoustic beats, and that these preferences are primarily learned through active or passive exposure to Western music.

SURVEYING THE AUDITORY SCENE

Acoustic Cues to Solve the Cocktail Party Problem

The auditory system makes use of regularities in the acoustic structure of sounds from individual sources to assist in parsing the auditory scene (Bregman 1990). The first stage of parsing occurs in the cochlea, where sounds are mapped along the basilar membrane according to their frequency content or spectrum. Thus, two sounds with very different spectra will activate different portions of the basilar membrane and will, therefore, stimulate different populations of auditory nerve fibers. In such cases, the perceptual segregation of sounds has a clear basis in the cochlea itself. This phenomenon forms the core of the peripheral channeling theory of stream segregation— sequences of sounds can be perceptually segregated only if they stimulate different populations of peripheral neurons (Hartmann & Johnson 1991). Although peripheral channeling remains the most robust form of perceptual segregation of competing sources, there have since been several instances reported in which streaming occurs even in the absence of peripheral channeling. For instance, by using harmonic complex tones containing only unresolved harmonics, Vliegen & Oxenham (1999) showed that differences in F0 or pitch could lead to perceptual segregation even when the complexes occupied exactly the same spectral region. Similar results have been reported using differences in wave shape, even when the same harmonic spectrum was used (Roberts et al. 2002). Indeed, it has been proposed that perceptual segregation can occur with differences along any perceptual dimension that can be discriminated (Moore & Gockel 2002).

One aspect of ongoing sound sequences (such as speech or music) that is important in binding together elements and features of sound is temporal coherence, i.e., a repeated synchronous relationship between elements. In addition to differences in features such as spectral content or F0, which are necessary to induce stream segregation of two sound sequences, another necessary component is some form of temporal incoherence between the two sequences. If the sequences are presented coherently and synchronously, they will tend to form a single stream, even if they differ along other dimensions (Micheyl et al. 2013a). Note that temporal coherence goes beyond simple synchrony: Although sound elements are generally perceived as belonging to a single source if they are gated synchronously (e.g., Bregman 1990), when synchronous sound elements are embedded in a longer sequence of similar sounds that are not presented synchronously or coherently, no grouping occurs, even between the elements that are synchronous (Christiansen & Oxenham 2014, Elhilali et al. 2009).

Some attempts have been made to identify the neural correlates of sensitivity to temporal coherence. Despite the perceptual difference between synchronous and alternating tones, an initial study found that responses to sequences of tone pairs in the primary auditory cortex of awake but passive ferrets did not depend on whether the two tones were synchronous or alternating

(Elhilali et al. 2009). This outcome led the authors to conclude that the neural correlates of the differences in perception elicited by synchronous and alternating tone sequences must emerge at a level higher than the primary auditory cortex. However, another study that compared the neural responses of ferrets when they were either passively listening or actively attending to the sounds found evidence supporting the theory of temporal coherence, with alternating tones producing suppression relative to the responses elicited by synchronous tones, but only when the ferrets were actively attending to the stimuli (Lu et al. 2017).

In addition to using differences in acoustic properties, the auditory system is able to make use of the regularities and repetitive natures of many natural sounds to help in the task of segregating competing sources. McDermott et al. (2011) found that listeners were able to segregate a repeating target sound from a background of varying sounds even when there were no acoustic cues with which to segregate the target sound. It seems that the repetitions themselves, against a varying background, allow the auditory system to extract the stable aspects of the sound. The authors proposed that this may be one way in which we are able to learn new sounds, even when they are never presented to us in complete isolation (McDermott et al. 2011).

Perceptual Multistability, Informational Masking, and the Neural Correlates of Auditory Attention and Awareness

As is the case with visual stimuli, the same acoustic stimulus can be perceived in more than one way, leading to perceptual ambiguity and, in some cases, multistability (Mehta et al. 2016). Alternating sound sequences provide one common example of such ambiguity: A rapidly alternating sequence of two tones is perceived as a single auditory stream if the frequency separation is small. However, the same sequence will be perceived as two separate streams (one high and one low) if the frequency separation between the two tones is large. In between, there exists a gray region where the percept can alternate between the two states and can depend on the attentional state of the listener. Studies comparing the dynamics of this bistability have found that it has a similar time course as analogous conditions in the visual domain but that the times at which switching occurs within each sensory modality are independent of the others even when the auditory and visual stimuli are presented at the same time (Pressnitzer & Hupe 2006). Neural correlates of such bistability have been identified in both auditory (Gutschalk et al. 2005) and nonauditory (Cusack 2005) regions of the cortex. Such stimuli are useful because they can, in principle, be used to distinguish between neural responses to the stimuli and neural correlates of perception.

Another approach to elucidating the neural correlates of auditory perception, attention, and awareness has been to use a phenomenon known as informational masking (Durlach et al. 2003). Informational masking is a term used to describe most kinds of masking that cannot be explained in terms of interactions or interference within the cochlea. Such peripherally based masking is known as energetic masking. Informational masking tends to occur when the masker and the target share some similarities (e.g., they both consist of pure tones and both emanate from the same spatial location) and when there is some uncertainty associated with the spectrotemporal properties of the masker or the target sound. Uncertainty can be produced by using randomly selected frequencies for tones within the masker. Informational masking shares some similarities with a visual phenomenon known as visual crowding (Whitney & Levi 2011) in that it, too, cannot be explained in terms of the limits of peripheral resolution. The term informational masking has been applied to both nonspeech sounds (Oxenham et al. 2003) and speech (Kidd et al. 2016), although it is not clear if the same mechanisms underlie both types of masking.

Because informational masking occurs when stimuli that are clearly represented in the auditory periphery are not heard, it provides an opportunity to probe the neural correlates of auditory awareness or consciousness. An early study into the neural correlates of auditory awareness using informational masking in combination with magnetoencephalography found that the earliest cortical responses to sound, measured via the steady-state response to a 40-Hz modulation, provided a robust representation of the target sound that did not depend on whether the target was heard or not. In contrast, a later response (peaking approximately 100–150 ms after stimulus onset) was highly dependent on whether the target was heard, with no measurable response recorded when the target remained undetected (Gutschalk et al. 2008). This outcome suggests that informational masking does not occur in subcortical processing but already affects responses in the auditory cortex itself. However, it seems clear that the effects are not limited to the auditory cortex. For instance, the fact that visual stimuli can influence these responses suggests a feedback mechanism based on supramodal processing (Hausfeld et al. 2017).

Several recent studies have reported strong attentional modulation of auditory cortical responses using both speech (O'Sullivan et al. 2015) and nonspeech sounds (Chait et al. 2010). A study in patients using ECoG was able to accurately determine which of two talkers was attended based on cortical responses, to the extent that the neural response was wholly dominated by the sound of the attended talker (Mesgarani & Chang 2012).

PERCEPTUAL CONSEQUENCES OF HEARING LOSS AND COCHLEAR IMPLANTS

Importance of Hearing Loss

Hearing loss is a very common problem in industrial societies. In the United States alone, it is estimated that approximately 38 million adults have some form of bilateral hearing loss (Goman & Lin 2016). The problem worsens dramatically with age, so that more than 25% of people in their 60s suffer from hearing loss; for people in their 80s, the incidence rises to nearly 80% (Lin et al. 2011). If we take a stricter definition of a substantial or disabling hearing loss, meaning greater than 40 dB average loss between 500 and 4,000 Hz, the numbers are still very high, incorporating approximately one third of the world's adults aged 65 or older (WHO 2012). Hearing loss is defined as a loss of sensitivity to quiet sounds, but one of the most pressing problems associated with hearing loss is a reduced ability to hear out or segregate sounds, such as someone talking against a background of other sounds. This difficulty in understanding, and thus taking part in, conversations leads many people with hearing loss to avoid crowded situations, which, in turn, can lead to more social isolation, potential cognitive decline, and more general health problems (Kamil et al. 2016, Sung et al. 2016, Wayne & Johnsrude 2015). Understanding how hearing loss occurs, and how best to treat it, is a challenge of growing importance in our aging societies.

Cochlear Hearing Loss

By far the most common form of hearing loss is cochlear in origin. As discussed in the section titled Cochlear Tuning and Frequency Selectivity, the outer hair cells provide the cochlea with amplification of low-level sounds and sharp tuning. Strong amplification at low levels and little or no amplification at high levels produce a compressive input–output function, where a 100-dB range of sound levels is fitted into a much smaller range of vibration amplitudes in the cochlea (Ruggero 1992). A loss of function of the outer hair cells results in (*a*) a loss of sensitivity, (*b*) a loss of dynamic range compression, and (*c*) poorer frequency tuning. Each of these three factors has perceptual consequences for people with cochlear hearing loss (Oxenham & Bacon 2003). The loss of sensitivity is the classic symptom of hearing loss and the symptom that is measured most frequently in clinical tests of hearing via the audiogram. Although the audibility of quiet sounds can be restored by amplification (e.g., with a hearing aid), simple linear amplification does not restore normal hearing because it does not address the remaining two factors of dynamic range and frequency tuning. The loss of dynamic range means that low-level sounds are no longer audible, but high-level sounds seem just as loud, leading to a smaller range of audible but tolerable sound levels. This phenomenon of loudness recruitment (Moore 2007) was known long before it was discovered that it could be explained by changes in the mechanics of the cochlea caused by a linearization of the basilar membrane response to sound in the absence of functioning outer hair cells (Ruggero 1992). Some aspects of loudness recruitment can be compensated for by introducing a compression circuit, which amplifies low-level sounds more than high-level sounds, into a hearing aid. However, this still leaves the consequences of poorer frequency tuning untreated.

The effects of poor cochlear frequency tuning can be measured behaviorally using the same masking methods that are employed to measure frequency selectivity in people with normal hearing, and such methods generally show poorer-than-normal frequency selectivity in people with hearing loss (Moore 2007). The loss of frequency selectivity may explain some of the difficulties faced by people with hearing loss in noisy environments: Poorer selectivity implies a reduced ability to segregate competing sounds.

Pitch perception is also generally poorer than normal in people with cochlear hearing loss. Again, this may be due in part to poorer frequency selectivity and a loss of spectrally resolved harmonics (Bernstein & Oxenham 2006, Bianchi et al. 2016). Relatively few studies have explored auditory stream segregation in hearing-impaired listeners, but those studies that exist also indicate that poorer frequency selectivity affects segregation abilities, which, in turn, is likely to explain some of the difficulties experienced by hearing-impaired listeners when trying to understand speech in complex acoustic environments (Mackersie 2003).

Unfortunately, hearing aids cannot restore sharp cochlear tuning. Because damage to the outer hair cells is currently irreversible, and because the consequences of hearing loss can be severe and wide ranging, it is particularly important to protect our hearing from overexposure to loud sounds. As outlined in the next section, even avoiding damage to the outer hair cells may not be sufficient to maintain acute hearing over the lifespan.

Hidden Hearing Loss

Most of us have experienced temporary threshold shift (TTS) at some time or other, such as after a very loud sporting event or rock concert. The phenomenon is often accompanied by a feeling of wooliness and, possibly, a sensation of ringing, but it usually resolves itself within 24 to 48 hours. However, recent physiological studies have suggested that the long-term consequences of TTS may not be as benign as previously thought. A landmark study by Kujawa & Liberman (2009) in mice revealed that noise exposure sufficient to cause TTS, but not sufficient to cause permanent threshold shifts, can result in a significant loss of the synapses between the inner hair cells in the cochlea and the auditory nerve. These synapses effectively connect the ear to the brain, so a 50% loss of synapses (as reported in many recent animal studies; e.g., Kujawa & Liberman 2009) is likely to have some important perceptual consequences. The surprising aspect of these results is that a 50% loss of synapses does not produce a measurable change in absolute thresholds, meaning that it would not be detected in a clinical hearing test, leading to the term hidden hearing loss (Schaette & McAlpine 2011).

The questions currently in need of urgent answers are: (*a*) Do humans suffer from hidden hearing loss? (*b*) If so, how prevalent is it? (*c*) What are the perceptual consequences in everyday life? Finally, (*d*) how can it best be diagnosed? A number of studies are currently under way to provide answers to these questions. Indeed, studies have already suggested that some of the difficulties encountered by middle-aged and older people in understanding speech in noise may be related to hidden hearing loss (Bharadwaj et al. 2015, Ruggles et al. 2011). In addition, some consideration has gone into developing either behavioral or noninvasive physiological tests as indirect diagnostic tools to detect hidden hearing loss (Liberman et al. 2016, Plack et al. 2016, Stamper & Johnson 2015). Although it seems likely that people with more noise exposure would suffer from greater hidden hearing loss, the results from the first study with a larger sample of younger listeners (>100) have not yet revealed clear associations (Prendergast et al. 2017).

It may appear puzzling that a 50% loss of fibers leads to no measurable change in absolute thresholds for sound. There are at least three possible reasons for this, which are not mutually exclusive. First, further physiological studies have shown that the synapses most affected are those that connect to auditory nerve fibers with high thresholds and low spontaneous firing rates (Furman et al. 2013). These fibers are thought to be responsible for coding the features of sound that are well above absolute threshold, so a loss of these fibers may not affect sensitivity to very quiet sounds near absolute threshold. Second, higher levels of auditory processing, from the brainstem to the cortex, may compensate for the loss of stimulation by increasing neural gain (Chambers et al. 2016, Schaette & McAlpine 2011). Third, theoretical considerations based on signal detection theory have suggested that the perceptual consequences of synaptic loss may not be very dramatic until a large proportion of the synapses are lost (Oxenham 2016). In fact, with fairly simple and reasonable assumptions, it can be predicted that a 50% loss of synapses would result in only a 1.5-dB worsening of thresholds, which would be unmeasurable. Taken further, a 90% loss of fibers would be required to produce a 5-dB worsening of thresholds—still well below the 20-dB loss required for a diagnosis of hearing loss (Oxenham 2016). However, if the loss of fibers is concentrated in the small population of fibers with high thresholds and low spontaneous rates, then a loss of 90% or more is feasible, and may result in severe deficits for the processing of sounds that are well above absolute threshold—precisely the deficits that cause middle-aged and elderly people to have difficulty understanding speech in noisy backgrounds. In summary, hidden hearing loss remains a topic of considerable interest that has the potential to dramatically change the way hearing loss is diagnosed and treated.

Cochlear Implants

Cochlear implants represent by far the most successful sensory–neural prosthetic. They have enabled hundreds of thousands of people who would otherwise be deaf or severely hearing impaired to regain some auditory and speech capacities. Cochlear implants consist of an array of tiny electrodes that are surgically inserted into the turns of the cochlea with the aim of bypassing the ear and electrically stimulating the auditory nerve. Placing electrodes along the length of the array and stimulating them with different parts of the audio frequency spectrum are intended to recreate an approximation of the tonotopic mapping that occurs in the normal cochlea. Given that a crude array of 12–24 electrodes is used to replace the functioning of around 3,500 inner hair cells, perhaps the most surprising aspect of cochlear implants is that they work at all. However, many people with cochlear implants can understand speech in quiet conditions, even without the aid of lip reading.

One reason why cochlear implants have been so successful in transmitting speech information to their recipients is that speech is extremely robust to noise and distortion and requires very little in terms of spectral resolution (Shannon et al. 1995). Thus, even the limited number of spectral channels provided by a cochlear implant can be sufficient to convey speech. Pitch, on the other hand, requires much finer spectral resolution and, thus, remains a major challenge for cochlear implants. Two main dimensions of pitch have been explored in cochlear implants. The first is referred to as place pitch and varies with the location of the stimulating electrode, with lower pitches reported as the place of stimulation moves further in toward the apex of the cochlea. The second is referred to as temporal, or rate, pitch and increases with an increasing rate of electrical pulses, at least up to approximately 300 Hz (McDermott 2004). It has generally been found that place pitch and temporal pitch in cochlear implant users are represented along independent dimensions (McKay et al. 2000) in much the same way as pitch and brightness are considered different dimensions (despite some interference) in acoustic hearing (Allen & Oxenham 2014). Thus, the place pitch in cochlear implant users may be more accurately described as a dimension of timbre (McDermott 2004).

In general, the pitch extracted from the pulse rate or envelope modulation rate by cochlear implant users is weak and inaccurate, with average thresholds often between 5% and 10%, or nearly 1–2 semitones (Kreft et al. 2013). Interestingly, similar thresholds are found in normal hearing listeners when they are restricted to just the temporal envelope cues provided by unresolved harmonics (Kreft et al. 2013, Shackleton & Carlyon 1994).

To restore accurate pitch sensations via cochlear implants would require the transmission of the information normally carried by resolved harmonics. Can this be achieved? A number of factors suggest that this may be challenging. First, the number of electrodes in current devices is limited to between 12 and 24, depending on the manufacturer. This would likely to be too few to provide an accurate representation of harmonic pitch. Second, even with a large number of channels, resolution is limited by the spread and interaction of current between adjacent electrodes and by possibly uneven neural survival along the length of the cochlea. For instance, in speech perception, the performance of cochlear implant users as the number of electrodes increases typically reaches a plateau at approximately 8 electrodes (Friesen et al. 2001) because the interference or crosstalk between electrodes limits the number of effectively independent channels (Bingabr et al. 2008). Third, the depth of insertion of an implant is limited by surgical constraints, meaning the implants generally do not reach the most apical portions of the cochlea, which, in turn, means that the auditory nerve fibers tuned to the lowest frequencies (and the ones most relevant for pitch) are not reached by the implant.

Some studies have used acoustic simulations to estimate the number of channels that might be needed to transmit accurate pitch information via cochlear implants (Crew et al. 2012, Kong et al. 2004). However, these studies allowed the use of temporal pitch cues, as well as cues based on the lowest frequency present in the stimulus, and so did not test the ability of listeners to extract information from resolved harmonics. A recent study limited listeners' access to the temporal envelope and spectral edge cues and found that at least 32 channels would be needed but, less encouragingly, that extremely narrow stimulation would be required from each channel. Simulating current spread with attenuation slopes as steep as 72 dB per octave was still not sufficient to elicit accurate pitch (Mehta & Oxenham 2017). To put that into context, current cochlear implants deal with spread that is equivalent to closer to 12–24 dB per octave (Bingabr et al. 2008, Oxenham & Kreft 2014). Even with recent developments in current focusing (Bierer & Litvak 2016), it is highly unlikely that sufficiently focused stimulation can be achieved using today's devices. This result suggests that novel interventions may be needed; these interventions may include neurotrophic agents that encourage neuronal growth toward the electrodes (Pinyon et al. 2014), optogenetic approaches that provide greater specificity of stimulation (Hight et al. 2015), or a different location of implantation, such as in the auditory nerve itself, where electrodes can achieve more direct contact with the targeted neurons (Middlebrooks & Snyder 2010).

Improving pitch perception via cochlear implants will not only provide the users with improved music perception, but should also improve many aspects of speech perception, especially for tone languages, as well as the ability of cochlear implant recipients to hear out target sounds in the presence of interferers.

CONCLUSIONS

Auditory perception provides us with access to the acoustic environment and enables communication via speech and music. Some of the fundamental characteristics of auditory perception, such as frequency selectivity, are determined in the cochlea of the inner ear. Other aspects, such as pitch, are derived from higher-level representations, which are nonetheless affected by cochlear processing. More than 60 years since Cherry (1953) posed the famous cocktail party problem, work on human and animal behavior, work on human neuroimaging, and work on animal neurophysiology are being combined to answer the question of how the auditory brain is able to parse information in complex acoustic environments. The furthering of our knowledge of basic auditory processes has helped us to understand the causes of many types of hearing loss, but new findings on hidden hearing loss may signal a dramatic shift in how hearing loss is diagnosed and treated. Cochlear implants represent a highly successful intervention that provides speech understanding to many recipients, but they also highlight current limitations in technology and in our understanding of the underlying auditory processes.

FUTURE ISSUES

1. Is human frequency selectivity really much sharper than that found in other animals, and, if so, what differences in auditory perception between humans and other species can this variation explain?

2. Can we harness the knowledge gained from perceptual and neural studies of auditory scene analysis and source segregation to enhance automatic speech recognition and sound identification by computers?

3. Is cochlear synaptopathy, or hidden hearing loss, a common phenomenon in humans? If so, what are its consequences, and how can it best be diagnosed and treated?

4. How can we best restore pitch perception to recipients of cochlear implants? Will this restoration require a new electrode–neural interface or a completely different site of implantation?

DISCLOSURE STATEMENT

The author is not aware of any affiliations, memberships, funding, or financial holdings that might be perceived as affecting the objectivity of this review.

ACKNOWLEDGMENTS

The National Institute on Deafness and Other Communication Disorders at the National Institutes of Health provided support through grants R01 DC005216, R01 DC007657, and R01 DC012262. Emily Allen provided assistance with figure preparation. Emily Allen, Gordon Legge, Anahita Mehta, and Kelly Whiteford provided helpful comments on earlier versions of this review.

LITERATURE CITED

Allen EJ, Burton PC, Olman CA, Oxenham AJ. 2017. Representations of pitch and timbre variation in human auditory cortex. *J. Neurosci.* 37:1284–93

Allen EJ, Oxenham AJ. 2014. Symmetric interactions and interference between pitch and timbre. *J. Acoust. Soc. Am.* 135:1371–79

ANSI (Am. Nat. Stand. Inst.). 2013. *American National Standard: acoustical terminology.* Rep. S1.1-2013, Am. Nat. Stand. Inst./Accredit. Stand. Comm. Acoust., Acoust. Soc. Am., Washington, DC/Melville, NY

Attneave F, Olson RK. 1971. Pitch as a medium: a new approach to psychophysical scaling. *Am. J. Psychol.* 84:147–66

Bendor D, Wang X. 2005. The neuronal representation of pitch in primate auditory cortex. *Nature* 436:1161–65

Bentsen T, Harte JM, Dau T. 2011. Human cochlear tuning estimates from stimulus-frequency otoacoustic emissions. *J. Acoust. Soc. Am.* 129:3797–807

Bernstein JG, Oxenham AJ. 2003. Pitch discrimination of diotic and dichotic tone complexes: harmonic resolvability or harmonic number? *J. Acoust. Soc. Am.* 113:3323–34

Bernstein JG, Oxenham AJ. 2006. The relationship between frequency selectivity and pitch discrimination: sensorineural hearing loss. *J. Acoust. Soc. Am.* 120:3929–45

Bharadwaj HM, Masud S, Mehraei G, Verhulst S, Shinn-Cunningham BG. 2015. Individual differences reveal correlates of hidden hearing deficits. *J. Neurosci.* 35:2161–72

Bianchi F, Fereczkowski M, Zaar J, Santurette S, Dau T. 2016. Complex-tone pitch discrimination in listeners with sensorineural hearing loss. *Trends Hear.* 20:2331216516655793

Bierer JA, Litvak L. 2016. Reducing channel interaction through cochlear implant programming may improve speech perception: current focusing and channel deactivation. *Trends Hear.* 20:2331216516653389

Bingabr M, Espinoza-Varas B, Loizou PC. 2008. Simulating the effect of spread of excitation in cochlear implants. *Hear. Res.* 241:73–79

Blauert J. 1997. *Spatial Hearing: The Psychophysics of Human Sound Localization.* Cambridge, MA: MIT Press

Bregman AS. 1990. *Auditory Scene Analysis: The Perceptual Organisation of Sound.* Cambridge, MA: MIT Press

Bregman MR, Patel AD, Gentner TQ. 2016. Songbirds use spectral shape, not pitch, for sound pattern recognition. *PNAS* 113:1666–71

Burns EM, Feth LL. 1983. Pitch of sinusoids and complex tones above 10 kHz. In *Hearing—Physiological Bases and Psychophysics*, ed. R Klinke, R Hartmann, pp. 327–33. Berlin: Springer Verlag

Cedolin L, Delgutte B. 2010. Spatiotemporal representation of the pitch of harmonic complex tones in the auditory nerve. *J. Neurosci.* 30:12712–24

Chait M, de Cheveigne A, Poeppel D, Simon JZ. 2010. Neural dynamics of attending and ignoring in human auditory cortex. *Neuropsychologia* 48:3262–71

Chambers AR, Resnik J, Yuan Y, Whitton JP, Edge AS, et al. 2016. Central gain restores auditory processing following near-complete cochlear denervation. *Neuron* 89:867–79

Cherry EC. 1953. Some experiments on the recognition of speech, with one and two ears. *J. Acoust. Soc. Am.* 25:975–79

Christiansen SK, Oxenham AJ. 2014. Assessing the effects of temporal coherence on auditory stream formation through comodulation masking release. *J. Acoust. Soc. Am.* 135:3520–29

Cohen MR, Kohn A. 2011. Measuring and interpreting neuronal correlations. *Nat. Neurosci.* 14:811–19

Crew JD, Galvin JJ III, Fu QJ. 2012. Channel interaction limits melodic pitch perception in simulated cochlear implants. *J. Acoust. Soc. Am.* 132:EL429–35

Cusack R. 2005. The intraparietal sulcus and perceptual organization. *J. Cogn. Neurosci.* 17:641–51

Dallos P, Zheng J, Cheatham MA. 2006. Prestin and the cochlear amplifier. *J. Physiol.* 576:37–42

Darwin CJ. 2005. Pitch and auditory grouping. In *Pitch: Neural Coding and Perception*, ed. CJ Plack, AJ Oxenham, R Fay, AN Popper, pp. 278–305. Berlin: Springer Verlag

Deeks JM, Gockel HE, Carlyon RP. 2013. Further examination of complex pitch perception in the absence of a place-rate match. *J. Acoust. Soc. Am.* 133:377–88

Delgutte B. 1984. Speech coding in the auditory nerve: II. Processing schemes for vowel-like sounds. *J. Acoust. Soc. Am.* 75:879–86

Durlach NI, Mason CR, Kidd G Jr., Arbogast TL, Colburn HS, Shinn-Cunningham BG. 2003. Note on informational masking. *J. Acoust. Soc. Am.* 113:2984–87

Elhilali M, Ma L, Micheyl C, Oxenham AJ, Shamma SA. 2009. Temporal coherence in the perceptual organization and cortical representation of auditory scenes. *Neuron* 61:317–29

Evans EF. 2001. Latest comparisons between physiological and behavioural frequency selectivity. In *Physiological and Psychophysical Bases of Auditory Function*, ed. J Breebaart, AJM Houtsma, A Kohlrausch, VF Prijs, R Schoonhoven, pp. 382–87. Maastricht: Shaker

Feng L, Wang X. 2017. Harmonic template neurons in primate auditory cortex underlying complex sound processing. *PNAS* 114:E840–48

Fishman YI, Volkov IO, Noh MD, Garell PC, Bakken H, et al. 2001. Consonance and dissonance of musical chords: neural correlates in auditory cortex of monkeys and humans. *J. Neurophysiol.* 86:2761–88

Friesen LM, Shannon RV, Baskent D, Wang X. 2001. Speech recognition in noise as a function of the number of spectral channels: comparison of acoustic hearing and cochlear implants. *J. Acoust. Soc. Am.* 110:1150–63

Furman AC, Kujawa SG, Liberman MC. 2013. Noise-induced cochlear neuropathy is selective for fibers with low spontaneous rates. *J. Neurophysiol.* 110:577–86

Goman AM, Lin FR. 2016. Prevalence of hearing loss by severity in the United States. *Am. J. Public Health* 106:1820–22

Gutschalk A, Micheyl C, Melcher JR, Rupp A, Scherg M, Oxenham AJ. 2005. Neuromagnetic correlates of streaming in human auditory cortex. *J. Neurosci.* 25:5382–88

Gutschalk A, Micheyl C, Oxenham AJ. 2008. Neural correlates of auditory perceptual awareness under informational masking. *PLOS Biol.* 6:1156–65

Hartmann WM, Johnson D. 1991. Stream segregation and peripheral channeling. *Music Percept.* 9:155–84

Hausfeld L, Gutschalk A, Formisano E, Riecke L. 2017. Effects of cross-modal asynchrony on informational masking in human cortex. *J. Cogn. Neurosci.* 29(6):980–90

Heil P, Peterson AJ. 2015. Basic response properties of auditory nerve fibers: a review. *Cell Tissue Res.* 361:129–58

Heinz MG, Colburn HS, Carney LH. 2001. Evaluating auditory performance limits: I. One-parameter discrimination using a computational model for the auditory nerve. *Neural Comput.* 13:2273–316

Hight AE, Kozin ED, Darrow K, Lehmann A, Boyden E, et al. 2015. Superior temporal resolution of Chronos versus channelrhodopsin-2 in an optogenetic model of the auditory brainstem implant. *Hear Res.* 322:235–41

Houtsma AJM, Smurzynski J. 1990. Pitch identification and discrimination for complex tones with many harmonics. *J. Acoust. Soc. Am.* 87:304–10

Joris P, Bergevin C, Kalluri R, McLaughlin M, Michelet P, et al. 2011. Frequency selectivity in Old-World monkeys corroborates sharp cochlear tuning in humans. *PNAS* 108:17516–20

Kamil RJ, Betz J, Powers BB, Pratt S, Kritchevsky S, et al. 2016. Association of hearing impairment with incident frailty and falls in older adults. *J. Aging Health* 28:644–60

Kersten D, Mamassian P, Yuille A. 2004. Object perception as Bayesian inference. *Annu. Rev. Psychol.* 55:271–304

Kidd G Jr., Mason CR, Swaminathan J, Roverud E, Clayton KK, Best V. 2016. Determining the energetic and informational components of speech-on-speech masking. *J. Acoust. Soc. Am.* 140:132–44

Kong YY, Cruz R, Jones JA, Zeng FG. 2004. Music perception with temporal cues in acoustic and electric hearing. *Ear Hear.* 25:173–85

Kreft HA, Nelson DA, Oxenham AJ. 2013. Modulation frequency discrimination with modulated and unmodulated interference in normal hearing and in cochlear-implant users. *J. Assoc. Res. Otolaryngol.* 14:591–601

Kujawa SG, Liberman MC. 2009. Adding insult to injury: cochlear nerve degeneration after "temporary" noise-induced hearing loss. *J. Neurosci.* 29:14077–85

Lau BK, Mehta AH, Oxenham AJ. 2017. Superoptimal perceptual integration suggests a place-based representation of pitch at high frequencies. *J. Neurosci.* 37:9013–21

Liberman MC, Epstein MJ, Cleveland SS, Wang H, Maison SF. 2016. Toward a differential diagnosis of hidden hearing loss in humans. *PLOS ONE* 11:e0162726

Lin FR, Niparko JK, Ferrucci L. 2011. Hearing loss prevalence in the United States. *Arch. Intern. Med.* 171:1851–52

Liu LF, Palmer AR, Wallace MN. 2006. Phase-locked responses to pure tones in the inferior colliculus. *J. Neurophysiol.* 95:1926–35

Loeb GE, White MW, Merzenich MM. 1983. Spatial cross correlation: a proposed mechanism for acoustic pitch perception. *Biol. Cybern.* 47:149–63

Lopez-Poveda EA, Eustaquio-Martin A. 2013. On the controversy about the sharpness of human cochlear tuning. *J. Assoc. Res. Otolaryngol.* 14:673–86

Lorenzi C, Gilbert G, Carn H, Garnier S, Moore BCJ. 2006. Speech perception problems of the hearing impaired reflect inability to use temporal fine structure. *PNAS* 103:18866–69

Lu K, Xu Y, Yin P, Oxenham AJ, Fritz JB, Shamma SA. 2017. Temporal coherence structure rapidly shapes neuronal interactions. *Nat. Commun.* 8:13900

Lu T, Wang X. 2000. Temporal discharge patterns evoked by rapid sequences of wide-and narrowband clicks in the primary auditory cortex of cat. *J. Neurophysiol.* 84(1):236–46

Mackersie CL. 2003. Talker separation and sequential stream segregation in listeners with hearing loss: patterns associated with talker gender. *J. Speech Lang. Hear. Res.* 46:912–18

Marmel F, Plack CJ, Hopkins K, Carlyon RP, Gockel HE, Moore BC. 2015. The role of excitation-pattern cues in the detection of frequency shifts in bandpass-filtered complex tones. *J. Acoust. Soc. Am.* 137:2687–97

McDermott HJ. 2004. Music perception with cochlear implants: a review. *Trends Amplif.* 8:49–82

McDermott JH, Lehr AJ, Oxenham AJ. 2010. Individual differences reveal the basis of consonance. *Curr. Biol.* 20:1035–41

McDermott JH, Oxenham AJ. 2008. Music perception, pitch, and the auditory system. *Curr. Opin. Neurobiol.* 18:452–63

McDermott JH, Schultz AF, Undurraga EA, Godoy RA. 2016. Indifference to dissonance in native Amazonians reveals cultural variation in music perception. *Nature* 535:547–50

McDermott JH, Wrobleski D, Oxenham AJ. 2011. Recovering sound sources from embedded repetition. *PNAS* 108:1188–93

McKay CM, McDermott HJ, Carlyon RP. 2000. Place and temporal cues in pitch perception: Are they truly independent? *Acoust. Res. Lett. Online* 1:25–30

Mehta AH, Oxenham AJ. 2017. Vocoder simulations explain complex pitch perception limitations experienced by cochlear implant users. *J. Assoc. Res. Otolaryngol.* In press

Mehta AH, Yasin I, Oxenham AJ, Shamma S. 2016. Neural correlates of attention and streaming in a perceptually multistable auditory illusion. *J. Acoust. Soc. Am.* 140:2225

Mesgarani N, Chang EF. 2012. Selective cortical representation of attended speaker in multi-talker speech perception. *Nature* 485:233–36

Micheyl C, Delhommeau K, Perrot X, Oxenham AJ. 2006. Influence of musical and psychoacoustical training on pitch discrimination. *Hear. Res.* 219:36–47

Micheyl C, Hanson C, Demany L, Shamma S, Oxenham AJ. 2013a. Auditory stream segregation for alternating and synchronous tones. *J. Exp. Psychol. Hum. Percept. Perform.* 39:1568–80

Micheyl C, Schrater PR, Oxenham AJ. 2013b. Auditory frequency and intensity discrimination explained using a cortical population rate code. *PLOS Comput. Biol.* 9:e1003336

Micheyl C, Xiao L, Oxenham AJ. 2012. Characterizing the dependence of pure-tone frequency difference limens on frequency, duration, and level. *Hear. Res.* 292:1–13

Middlebrooks JC, Snyder RL. 2010. Selective electrical stimulation of the auditory nerve activates a pathway specialized for high temporal acuity. *J. Neurosci.* 30:1937–46

Moerel M, De Martino F, Formisano E. 2014. An anatomical and functional topography of human auditory cortical areas. *Front. Neurosci.* 8:225

Moore BCJ. 2007. *Cochlear Hearing Loss: Physiological, Psychological and Technical Issues.* Chichester, UK: Wiley

Moore BCJ, Ernst SM. 2012. Frequency difference limens at high frequencies: evidence for a transition from a temporal to a place code. *J. Acoust. Soc. Am.* 132:1542–47

Moore BCJ, Gockel H. 2002. Factors influencing sequential stream segregation. *Acta Acust. Unit. Acust.* 88:320–33

Moore BCJ, Sek A. 1996. Detection of frequency modulation at low modulation rates: evidence for a mechanism based on phase locking. *J. Acoust. Soc. Am.* 100:2320–31

Norman-Haignere S, Kanwisher N, McDermott JH. 2013. Cortical pitch regions in humans respond primarily to resolved harmonics and are located in specific tonotopic regions of anterior auditory cortex. *J. Neurosci.* 33:19451–69

O'Sullivan JA, Power AJ, Mesgarani N, Rajaram S, Foxe JJ, et al. 2015. Attentional selection in a cocktail party environment can be decoded from single-trial EEG. *Cereb. Cortex* 25:1697–706

Oxenham AJ. 2012. Pitch perception. *J. Neurosci.* 32:13335–38

Oxenham AJ. 2016. Predicting the perceptual consequences of hidden hearing loss. *Trends Hear.* 20:2331216516686768

Oxenham AJ, Bacon SP. 2003. Cochlear compression: perceptual measures and implications for normal and impaired hearing. *Ear Hear.* 24:352–66

Oxenham AJ, Bernstein JGW, Penagos H. 2004. Correct tonotopic representation is necessary for complex pitch perception. *PNAS* 101:1421–25

Oxenham AJ, Fligor BJ, Mason CR, Kidd G Jr. 2003. Informational masking and musical training. *J. Acoust. Soc. Am.* 114:1543–49

Oxenham AJ, Kreft HA. 2014. Speech perception in tones and noise via cochlear implants reveals influence of spectral resolution on temporal processing. *Trends Hear.* 18:2331216514553783

Oxenham AJ, Micheyl C, Keebler MV, Loper A, Santurette S. 2011. Pitch perception beyond the traditional existence region of pitch. *PNAS* 108:7629–34

Oxenham AJ, Plack CJ. 1997. A behavioral measure of basilar-membrane nonlinearity in listeners with normal and impaired hearing. *J. Acoust. Soc. Am.* 101:3666–75

Patterson RD. 1976. Auditory filter shapes derived with noise stimuli. *J. Acoust. Soc. Am.* 59:640–54

Penagos H, Melcher JR, Oxenham AJ. 2004. A neural representation of pitch salience in non-primary human auditory cortex revealed with fMRI. *J. Neurosci.* 24:6810–15

Pinyon JL, Tadros SF, Froud KE, Wong ACY, Tompson IT, et al. 2014. Close-field electroporation gene delivery using the cochlear implant electrode array enhances the bionic ear. *Sci. Transl. Med.* 6:233ra54

Plack CJ, Leger A, Prendergast G, Kluk K, Guest H, Munro KJ. 2016. Toward a diagnostic test for hidden hearing loss. *Trends Hear.* 20:2331216516657466

Plantinga J, Trehub SE. 2014. Revisiting the innate preference for consonance. *J. Exp. Psychol. Hum. Percept. Perf.* 40:40–49

Plomp R. 1967. Pitch of complex tones. *J. Acoust. Soc. Am.* 41:1526–33

Plomp R, Levelt WJM. 1965. Tonal consonance and critical bandwidth. *J. Acoust. Soc. Am.* 38:548–60

Prendergast G, Guest H, Munro KJ, Kluk K, Leger A, et al. 2017. Effects of noise exposure on young adults with normal audiograms: I. Electrophysiology. *Hear. Res.* 344:68–81

Pressnitzer D, Hupe JM. 2006. Temporal dynamics of auditory and visual bistability reveal common principles of perceptual organization. *Curr. Biol.* 16:1351–57

Qin MK, Oxenham AJ. 2005. Effects of envelope-vocoder processing on F0 discrimination and concurrent-vowel identification. *Ear Hear.* 26:451–60

Rhode WS, Oertel D, Smith PH. 1983. Physiological response properties of cells labeled intracellularly with horseradish peroxidase in cat ventral cochlear nucleus. *J. Comp. Neurol.* 213:448–63

Roberts B, Glasberg BR, Moore BCJ. 2002. Primitive stream segregation of tone sequences without differences in fundamental frequency or passband. *J. Acoust. Soc. Am.* 112:2074–85

Rose JE, Brugge JF, Anderson DJ, Hind JE. 1967. Phase-locked response to low-frequency tones in single auditory nerve fibers of the squirrel monkey. *J. Neurophysiol.* 30:769–93

Ruggero MA. 1992. Responses to sound of the basilar membrane of the mammalian cochlea. *Curr. Opin. Neurobiol.* 2:449–56

Ruggero MA, Temchin AN. 2005. Unexceptional sharpness of frequency tuning in the human cochlea. *PNAS* 102:18614–19

Ruggles D, Bharadwaj H, Shinn-Cunningham BG. 2011. Normal hearing is not enough to guarantee robust encoding of suprathreshold features important in everyday communication. *PNAS* 108:15516–21

Sayles M, Winter IM. 2008. Reverberation challenges the temporal representation of the pitch of complex sounds. *Neuron* 58:789–801

Schaette R, McAlpine D. 2011. Tinnitus with a normal audiogram: physiological evidence for hidden hearing loss and computational model. *J. Neurosci.* 31:13452–57

Shackleton TM, Carlyon RP. 1994. The role of resolved and unresolved harmonics in pitch perception and frequency modulation discrimination. *J. Acoust. Soc. Am.* 95:3529–40

Shamma S, Klein D. 2000. The case of the missing pitch templates: how harmonic templates emerge in the early auditory system. *J. Acoust. Soc. Am.* 107:2631–44

Shamma SA. 1985. Speech processing in the auditory system: II. Lateral inhibition and the central processing of speech evoked activity in the auditory nerve. *J. Acoust. Soc. Am.* 78:1622–32

Shannon RV, Zeng FG, Kamath V, Wygonski J, Ekelid M. 1995. Speech recognition with primarily temporal cues. *Science* 270:303–4

Shera CA, Guinan JJ, Oxenham AJ. 2002. Revised estimates of human cochlear tuning from otoacoustic and behavioral measurements. *PNAS* 99:3318–23

Shera CA, Guinan JJ Jr., Oxenham AJ. 2010. Otoacoustic estimation of cochlear tuning: validation in the chinchilla. *J. Assoc. Res. Otolaryngol.* 11:343–65

Shofner WP, Chaney M. 2013. Processing pitch in a nonhuman mammal (*Chinchilla laniger*). *J. Comp. Psychol.* 127:142–53

Smith ZM, Delgutte B, Oxenham AJ. 2002. Chimaeric sounds reveal dichotomies in auditory perception. *Nature* 416:87–90

Stamper GC, Johnson TA. 2015. Auditory function in normal-hearing, noise-exposed human ears. *Ear Hear.* 36:172–84

Sumner CJ, Wells T, Bergevin C, Palmer AR, Oxenham AJ, Shera CA. 2014. Comparing otoacoustic, auditory-nerve, and behavioral estimates of cochlear tuning in the ferret. *Proc. Midwinter Meet. Assoc. Res. Otolaryngol., San Diego, CA*, p. 123. San Diego, CA: Assoc. Res. Otolaryngol.

Sung YK, Li L, Blake C, Betz J, Lin FR. 2016. Association of hearing loss and loneliness in older adults. *J. Aging Health* 28:979–94

Trainor LJ, Heinmiller BM. 1998. The development of evaluative responses to music: Infants prefer to listen to consonance over dissonance. *Infant Behav. Dev.* 21:77–88

Tramo MJ, Cariani PA, Delgutte B, Braida LD. 2001. Neurobiological foundations for the theory of harmony in Western tonal music. *Ann. N. Y. Acad. Sci.* 930:92–116

Vliegen J, Oxenham AJ. 1999. Sequential stream segregation in the absence of spectral cues. *J. Acoust. Soc. Am.* 105:339–46

von Békésy G. 1960. *Experiments in Hearing*. New York: McGraw-Hill

Walker KM, Bizley JK, King AJ, Schnupp JW. 2011. Multiplexed and robust representations of sound features in auditory cortex. *J. Neurosci.* 31:14565–76

Wayne RV, Johnsrude IS. 2015. A review of causal mechanisms underlying the link between age-related hearing loss and cognitive decline. *Aging Res. Rev.* 23:154–66

Whiteford KL, Oxenham AJ. 2015. Using individual differences to test the role of temporal and place cues in coding frequency modulation. *J. Acoust. Soc. Am.* 138:3093–104

Whitney D, Levi DM. 2011. Visual crowding: a fundamental limit on conscious perception and object recognition. *Trends Cogn. Sci.* 15:160–68

WHO (World Health Organ.). 2012. *Hearing loss in persons 65 years and older based on WHO global estimates on prevalence of hearing loss: mortality and burden of diseases and prevention of blindness and deafness*. Rep., World Health Organ., Geneva. **http://www.who.int/pbd/deafness/news/GE_65years.pdf**

Yin P, Fritz JB, Shamma SA. 2010. Do ferrets perceive relative pitch? *J. Acoust. Soc. Am.* 127:1673–80

Yin P, Fritz JB, Shamma SA. 2014. Rapid spectrotemporal plasticity in primary auditory cortex during behavior. *J. Neurosci.* 34:4396–408

Young ED, Sachs MB. 1979. Representation of steady-state vowels in the temporal aspects of the discharge patterns of populations of auditory-nerve fibres. *J. Acoust. Soc. Am.* 66:1381–403

Zentner MR, Kagan J. 1996. Perception of music by infants. *Nature* 383:29

Zwicker E. 1970. Masking and psychological excitation as consequences of the ear's frequency analysis. In *Frequency Analysis and Periodicity Detection in Hearing*, ed. R Plomp, GF Smoorenburg, pp. 376–94. Leiden: Sijthoff

The Psychology of Music: Rhythm and Movement

Daniel J. Levitin,[1] Jessica A. Grahn,[2]
and Justin London[3]

[1]Department of Psychology, McGill University, Montreal, QC H3A 1G1, Canada;
email: daniel.levitin@mcgill.ca

[2]Department of Psychology and Brain and Mind Institute, Western University, London,
Ontario N6A 5B7, Canada; email: jgrahn@uwo.ca

[3]Departments of Music and Cognitive Science, Carleton College, Northfield, Minnesota 55057;
email: jlondon@carleton.edu

Annu. Rev. Psychol. 2018. 69:51–75

First published as a Review in Advance on October 16, 2017

The *Annual Review of Psychology* is online at psych.annualreviews.org

https://doi.org/10.1146/annurev-psych-122216-011740

Keywords

music perception, tempo, timing, rhythm, entrainment, movement

Abstract

The urge to move to music is universal among humans. Unlike visual art, which is manifest across space, music is manifest across time. When listeners get carried away by the music, either through movement (such as dancing) or through reverie (such as trance), it is usually the temporal qualities of the music—its pulse, tempo, and rhythmic patterns—that put them in this state. In this article, we review studies addressing rhythm, meter, movement, synchronization, entrainment, the perception of groove, and other temporal factors that constitute a first step to understanding how and why music literally moves us. The experiments we review span a range of methodological techniques, including neuroimaging, psychophysics, and traditional behavioral experiments, and we also summarize the current studies of animal synchronization, engaging an evolutionary perspective on human rhythmic perception and cognition.

Contents

1. INTRODUCTION

The field of music cognition traces its origins to the fourth century BCE, 2,000 years before the establishment of experimental psychology itself. Aristoxenus, an Aristotelian philosopher, went against the Pythagoreans, arguing that musical intervals should be classified by their effects on listeners, rather than merely examined in terms of their mathematical ratios (Griffiths et al. 2004, Levitin 1999). This argument focused the scientific study of music on the brain, followed (20 centuries later) by the first psychophysics experiments, which sought to map changes in the physical world onto changes in the psychological (mental) world [e.g., von Helmholtz 1954 (1863), Fechner 1860]. Many of the earliest studies in experimental psychology dealt with music, and the Gestalt psychology movement was formed to address questions about part–whole relationships in music and melody [von Ehrenfels 1988 (1890)].

Music has been defined as sound organized across time [Varèse & Wen-Chung 1966, Cage 2011 (1961)]. One of the most common human responses to music is to move to it, and many languages do not have separate words for music and dance (Besson & Schön 2001, Thompson 2014). Synchronizing our movements to music appears to be important for both listening and performing (Cross 2005). We focus in this review on studies of music psychology that address rhythm, movement, synchronization, and temporal factors.

2. TEMPO AND TEMPORAL STRUCTURE

2.1. Definitions: Rhythm, Meter, Tactus, and Tempo

Rhythm is "the serial pattern of variable note durations in a melody" (Schulkind 1999, p. 896). Consider the song "Happy Birthday"—you can probably imagine the song in your head. Now tap out the rhythm: long-short-long-long-long-looong (pause); long-short-long-long-long-looong (pause). Rhythm consists of the relative durations of tones (or, more precisely, the relative timing of the intervals between note onsets). If you speed up or slow down Happy Birthday, the relative rhythmic proportions remain the same—the long notes are still longer than the short ones and by the same percentage.

At the same time that you hear the rhythm of Happy Birthday, you also feel a sense of pulse or beat, and, moreover, you hear those pulses in recurring groups of three (with implied rests before the singing begins):

```
(rest) (rest) Hap-py |birth day to |you, (rest) Hap-py |birth day to |you
   1      2     3      1   2   3    1    2      3      1    2   3    1.
```

This recurring pattern of pulses or beats defines the meter, the timing framework under which a given pattern of rhythmic durations is understood (as discussed in Section 2.4.1, meter entails entrainment). Meter organizes the perceived series of beats into regularly repeating patterns of stressed and unstressed beats; a musician would say that Happy Birthday is in 3/4 or waltz time, indicating that every third beat is stressed, starting with the first one, indicated by boldface type above. The rhythm–meter distinction is fundamental to a proper understanding of the psychology of rhythm and movement (McAuley 2010, London 2012).

Tactus refers to the most natural rate at which a listener might tap or clap their hands to a musical piece and is generally synonymous with the beat. However, individuals may disagree about the rate of the tactus (Martens 2011) because they extract different perceptual groupings from the musical signal—for example, some listeners may feel the beat at twice the rate of others in the same music (and thus clap their hands twice as often as others). Beat perception is typically strongest for tempos of approximately 100–120 beats per minute; this is believed to be related to a general shift from beat-based to interval processing at slow tempi in striato-thalamo-cortical networks (McAuley et al. 2012). This shift may be evolutionarily related to synchronized running behaviors among groups of early humans.

Tempo refers to the pace of music, or the rate at which musical events unfold over time (McAuley 2010). Although tempo is most strongly associated with beat rate [i.e., beats per minute (bpm)], multiple factors influence the perception of tempo, including event density, register, and loudness (Drake et al. 1999, London 2011). Musical tempos generally range from 40 to 200 bpm. As points of reference, Chopin's Funeral March (Chopin 1839, movement 3) is typically performed at approximately 48 bpm, Adele's "Hello" (Adkins & Kurstin 2015) is at 79 bpm, Michael Jackson's "Beat It" (Jackson 1983) is at 132 bpm, and Charlie Parker's "Bird Gets the Worm" (Parker 1949) is at 340 bpm.

Tempo plays a role in emotional interpretation. Generally speaking across cultures, slower tempos are associated with sadness or reflection, and faster tempos are associated with activity and happiness. Even 5-year-olds can make these associations (Poon & Schutz 2015, Swaminathan & Schellenberg 2015). Musical events span a timeline that runs from less than a millisecond in the

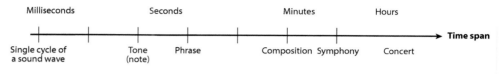

Musical events and time

Milliseconds   Seconds   Minutes   Hours

Time span

Single cycle of   Tone   Phrase   Composition   Symphony   Concert
a sound wave   (note)

Figure 1

Timeline of typical durations for different musical events.

case of a single cycle of a high-pitched sound wave, to 2–3 seconds in the case of the duration of a tone, to minutes or hours in the case of the duration of a composition (see **Figure 1**) (Levitin et al. 2002). However, when we discuss musical rhythm, we are most concerned with our perception of and interaction with sounds and sound patterns in the range of 100 ms to 5–6 s.

2.2. Discrimination

The just noticeable difference (JND) is the smallest discriminable change in a stimulus. Temporal JNDs can be expressed in terms of absolute durations or as tempo. Extradurational factors, particularly pitch and loudness, affect temporal JNDs (Jeon & Fricke 1997, Scharf & Buus 1986). For example, a 200 Hz tone must be presented for longer than a 1,000 Hz tone for the two to be considered equivalent durations (Burghardt 1973).

JNDs for musical duration have been shown to follow a modified version of Weber's law: The JND is approximately 2.5% for note lengths between 240 and 1,000 ms but becomes constant, rather than proportional, at 5–6 ms for note lengths below 240 ms (Abel 1972, Friberg & Sundberg 1995). For absolute duration of individual tones, JNDs as low as 10 ms have been reported (Friberg & Sundströöm 2002).

The JND for tempo discrimination varies according to the measurement method. In a listening task in which participants judged which of two tone sequences was faster, the JND was found to be 6.2–8.8% (Drake & Botte 1993, Miller & McAuley 2005). Using the psychophysical method of adjustment (the listener adjusts the difference between two stimuli until they are perceived to be equal), the JND was 4.5% (Friberg & Sundberg 1993). When participants judged the displacement of a single element in a continuous sequence, the JND for tempo was found to be approximately 6% (Hibi 1983). In discrimination of a swing rhythm from a march rhythm, JNDs as high as 20% have been reported (Friberg & Sundströöm 2002).

In related work on timing discrimination using actual musical performances, listeners rated performances of Chopin piano pieces that varied in timing and amplitude variability from 0% (deadpan) to 175% of normal performance values. The 100% version was more expressive than, for example, the 75% version, but less expressive than the 125% version, creating a natural ranking of expressivity in the excerpts presented. Participants effectively recreated the rank ordering of versions from most to least expressive, even though excerpts were presented at random and listeners were blind as to the manipulation. Listeners also rated how much they liked the different versions and showed a peak preference in the 100–120% range. Taken together, these findings suggest that there exists an optimal amount of timing and amplitude variability and that performers typically create within that range without prompting (Bhatara et al. 2011). Previously unreported in that research is the fact that the timing information that listeners based their judgments on was an average note length deviation of 68 ms (14%) and note onset variation of 153 ms (30%), representing a kind of temporal JND using real-world, ecologically valid stimuli.

In synchronization–continuation tasks, participants tap along with a pulse at a certain tempo (synchronization) or continue tapping at that tempo after the stimulus stops (continuation). By introducing perturbations (i.e., early or late stimulus onsets), researchers can measure the difference that is required for participants to notice and adjust their tapping to account for the error and stay synchronized. Corrections to differences of 3–4% have been reported for synchronization (Collyer et al. 1994, Povel 1981) and 7–11% for continuation (Allen 1975). Even better sensitivity, of 1–2%, is evident in the subliminal corrections we are able to make in maintaining synchrony with perturbed sequences (Repp 2000). As Repp has noted,

> . . . the temporal information available to the timekeeping and feedback mechanisms in sensorimotor coordination is different from the one that enables a listener to explicitly detect deviations from temporal regularity or judge the temporal order of two events. There appears to be a level of highly accurate temporal perception subserving motor control which precedes the level of conscious perception and judgment. (Repp 2000, p. 139)

This observation is consistent with the literature on judgements of cross-modal synchrony, which concludes that temporal order judgements ("Which came first?") are served by separate neural mechanisms than judgements of simultaneity ("Did they occur at the same time?"), with thresholds that differ accordingly (Cohen 1954, Hirsh & Sherrick 1961, Mitrani et al. 1986).

2.3. Memory

Memory for tempo has been shown to be robust and precise. This forms a parallel in the time domain to absolute pitch memory (Levitin & Rogers 2005). When nonmusicians sang their favorite popular songs from memory, their productions tended to occur within 4% of the JND for the original tempo (Levitin & Cook 1996), a finding that has been extended to labeling tempo markings (Gratton et al. 2016). Absolute tempo has also been found in mothers' production of songs for their infants (Bergeson & Trehub 2002). It is well known that professional drummers remember tempos with high accuracy, although this has not been studied experimentally. In contrast, changing the tempo of an unfamiliar musical piece has been shown to impair subsequent recognition (Halpern & Müllensiefen 2008), as the tempo appears to be encoded as an integral part of the song's identity, at least upon first hearing.

People can generally recognize familiar melodies when they fall within a range of 0.8 to 6 notes per second, but when they are sped up or slowed down beyond this range, recognition degrades considerably (Halpern & Andrews 2008, Warren et al. 1991). There are some styles of minimalist music, however, that involve very long, sustained durations, perhaps the most extreme example being John Cage's 1987 composition "Organ/ASLSP (As Slow as Possible)," the performance of which has lasted from 20 min to nearly 15 h; a version currently underway is planned to last 639 years (Judkis 2011). A novel application of the idea was released by the singer Publio Delgado, who performed Bach's "Cello Suite No. 1" by singing two notes per day for nearly a year (**https://www.youtube.com/watch?v=r4rc92Uoj74**).

Memory for rhythm, as distinct from tempo, is also robust under certain circumstances. One recent study sought to discover if certain songs are widely identifiable based on rhythmic information alone, presumably as a function of their underlying compositional features (Rosch 1978). That is, some songs may have rhythms with high cue validity. Participants heard 30 familiar songs and had to name the songs without receiving a list of possible song names. Three songs, when presented as click trains that therefore lacked pitch information, yielded uniformly high identification rates: "Jingle Bells," Mendelssohn's "Wedding March," and "Deck the Halls" (Houlihan & Levitin 2011).

2.4. Beat Processing and Entrainment

The degree to which rhythms and beats induce corresponding movements falls along a continuum. Some rhythms (within a given musical culture or subculture) are easily ignored, whereas others can get an entire crowd on their feet. In 1989 America, the latter category might have included "Love Shack" by the B-52s, and in 2017, "You, I & the Music" by Junior Sanchez. Other pieces of music lead to unwanted movement: an audience taking to the exits, as happened at the premier of Igor Stravinsky's "Rite of Spring" and Bob Dylan's 1966 tour. In this section, we look at what is currently known about how musical beats are processed and how movement and auditory perception are linked. We revisit this topic in Section 6.

2.4.1. Entrainment and musical meter.
Entrainment occurs when our bodily movements lock in to and synchronize with music. This process can be manifest as handclapping, playing a musical instrument, or dancing, for example. A self-sustaining oscillatory process in the brain becomes phase locked to the periodic input or stimulus (Glass & Mackey 1988). With music as the input, our internal neural firings and body movements are said to be driven by the external musical cues, especially those related to our sensorimotor system. These internal rhythmic processes are usually characterized as hierarchical oscillators tuned to particular temporal frequencies. Humans can entrain their movements to regular stimuli with almost perfect tempo matching (movement rate matching the beat rate) and phase matching (movements occurring at the beat onset time) (Repp & Su 2013). To achieve entrainment, an internal representation of the beat must exist, so that the individual can initiate their movements in synchrony with the beat rather than reacting to each beat (as would happen if the individual had to wait to hear the beat before initiating the movement). These processes are believed to be governed by a network that includes the cerebellum, the supplementary motor area (SMA), and the premotor cortex (PMC), as neurons fire in synchrony with the music (Cameron & Grahn 2014, Chen et al. 2006), with the temporal anticipation additionally involving Brodmann Area (BA) 47 (Levitin & Menon 2003).

Some of the earliest studies of entrainment measured the accuracy and variability of tapping to an auditory or visual sequence of events. Musical training can reduce the variability of tapping from approximately 4% down to 0.5–2% of the intertap interval. Taps tend to precede the target sequence tones by a few tens of milliseconds, rather than being distributed evenly before and after the tone onsets. This negative mean asynchrony is an indication that the regularity of the tone sequence has been perceived and that individuals are anticipating the timing of future tones. Although some studies have suggested a shift from anticipatory to reactive tapping as sequences slow down (the transition occurring at approximately 26 bpm; Mates et al. 1994), more comprehensive studies do not find any evidence for this shift, even when the interval between tone onsets is as long as 3.5 s (Repp & Doggett 2007).

Current models of rhythmic entrainment (Eck 2002, Large & Kolen 1994, Large & Palmer 2002, Toiviainen & Snyder 2003) posit that multiple internal oscillators phase lock to periodicities in a rhythm—most often to the beat, or tactus, but also to other levels of the metric hierarchy, such as the downbeats of successive measures. This phase locking is what allows a musician to keep track of multiple musical events simultaneously and to recover from errors while staying in time. The hierarchical oscillators are even more important for musicians who want to play rubato or before or behind the beat—they need to know exactly when various levels of beat are being experienced (by themselves, by listeners, and by other ensemble players) in order to expressively alter their own timing. Musicians often use these techniques. Frank Sinatra famously sang behind the beat (giving the performance a cool quality), and Kendrick Lamar tends to sing ahead of the beat (giving the performance urgency).

Oscillator models reproduce features of human perception: They can resonate at frequencies that are not present in the input but that humans perceive (Large 2008, Large et al. 2010), allowing one to fill in missing beats or perceive loud rests (London 1993). When The Rascals stop playing completely during "Good Lovin'" and then start up again after a silent gap, we hear a loud rest and anticipate the re-entrance (Clark & Resnick 1966).

2.4.2. Rhythmic entrainment in the brain. An important component of beat perception is the perception of accents, by which certain events in a rhythmic sequence are perceived as more salient than others. Accents often emphasize the beat periodicity itself or certain beats relative to others. Syncopation (defined below) can create a sense of accent; for example, Herbie Hancock's song "Chameleon" (Hancock 1973) has a characteristic six-note riff that begins with three short pickup notes, and then the following three notes are on the beat, off the beat, and off the beat, creating a double syncopation.

Some accents are acoustically marked (e.g., by differences in the intensity of a tone), whereas others arise from top-down intentions or the expectations of the listener. For example, even in isochronous sequences (i.e., sequences in which the duration of every note is the same), and with tones that do not vary in pitch, listeners may spontaneously perceive some tones (e.g., every second or every third tone) as accented (Brochard et al. 2003).

The perception of accents relates to changes in oscillatory power in the delta band (1–4 Hz, which is the range for beat and meter perception) as well as in the beta band (15–30 Hz). For example, listening to an isochronous rhythm that has alternating accented and unaccented tones leads to increases in beta power on the accented tones (Iversen et al. 2009). Even simply imagining an accent on every second or third tone (that is, imposing a march or waltz meter on the perception of unaccented tones) enhances oscillatory power at the frequency of the imagined meter (Nozaradan et al. 2011, 2012). Imagined accents also alter oscillations in the beta frequency band, with greater beta power being measured for tones that are imagined to be accented than for those imagined to be unaccented (Iversen et al. 2009, Fujioka et al. 2015). More broadly, beta oscillations have been linked to movement and motor brain areas (Salmelin & Hari 1994), and their modulation during rhythm and beat perception provides evidence for the link between rhythm and the motor system. A causal link, however, between oscillatory power and beat perception remains to be conclusively demonstrated (Henry et al. 2017).

A key part of entrainment to the beat involves accurate prediction of upcoming events. Imagined or implied accents are a staple of composition in which the composer sets up an expectation for where the beat is but contradicts that expectation with the introduction of other instruments. Two contemporary examples are the songs "Hypnotized" (Welch 1973) and "Bodhisattva" (Becker & Fagen 1973): Both begin with a drum part that implies that the first tone sounded was on the downbeat (the one), but as other instruments are added, it becomes apparent that the drum pattern was, in fact, syncopated and did not start on the downbeat. More recent examples of this include Radiohead's (1997) "Paranoid Android" and Mbongwana Star's (2015) "Malukayi"; CSNY's "Woodstock" (Mitchell 1970) is a textbook example.

During beat perception and synchronization, sensory and motor brain areas are active. Functional magnetic resonance imaging (fMRI) studies have identified brain areas that are key for entrainment, including the basal ganglia (e.g., putamen), the SMA, and the PMC, as well as the auditory cortex and anterior insula (implicated in auditory memory) (Chen et al. 2008a,b, 2006; Grahn & Rowe 2009, 2012; Grahn & Brett 2007; Teki et al. 2011; Vuust et al. 2006). These motor areas are active in response to simply hearing a rhythm, even if no movement is made. The basal ganglia and SMA appear to be particularly important for beat perception (Cameron et al. 2016, Grahn & Brett 2009), which alters communication within motor networks and between auditory and motor areas. During beat perception, greater connectivity is observed between the basal ganglia and cortical motor areas, such as the SMA and PMC (Grahn & Rowe 2009), as well as between the basal ganglia and auditory memory areas, such as the anterior insula (Kung et al. 2013). Finally, connectivity between the PMC and the auditory cortex increases as the salience of the beat in isochronous sequences increases (Chen et al. 2006).

2.4.3. Developmental research on entrainment.
Synchronized movement to music emerges with no specific training and at a very young age. For example, in the first 2 years of life, and even prior to full control over their motor system (Martin 2005), infants move their bodies rhythmically in response to music (Zentner & Eerola 2010). Although these early movements are spontaneous and occur without any prompting, there is no evidence that they are accurately entrained to the beat. In some children, accurate entrainment ability emerges by age 3 or 4, but many children are not accurate until they are older (Eerola et al. 2006, McAuley et al. 2006). In addition, individuals vary in their preferred rates of entrainment, and these preferred rates (often measured with spontaneous tapping) change with age (Drake et al. 2000, McAuley et al. 2006). Younger children show a faster spontaneous tapping rate (approximately 400 ms; 150 bpm) than older children and adults (approximately 600 ms; 100 bpm), and young children are also more accurate when synchronizing with faster tempos. Although older children and adults have a slower preferred tempo, they are also more flexible and accurate and, thus, able to entrain well to both slow and fast tempos.

The perception of a regular beat in music has also been studied in newborns (Winkler et al. 2009) using the mismatch negativity (MMN). The MMN is a brain response reflecting cortical processing of rare, unexpected events in a series of ongoing standard events (Näätänen et al. 2007). It occurs rapidly after stimulus onset (and can occur even in response to stimuli that the participant is not paying attention to) and is characterized by a negative electrical component in an electroencephalogram (EEG). In adults, when notes that are on the beat, as opposed to off the beat, are omitted, the MMN is larger, suggesting that, in some cases, the beat is perceived preattentively. Similar results were found in newborn infants, although the stimuli in that study confounded beat changes with changes in the number of instruments sounding (Winkler et al. 2009).

Several studies have demonstrated a developmental link between rhythmic abilities and language. Children who are better able to entrain to a metronome also have better language skills, including phonological awareness and verbal memory (Carr et al. 2014, 2016). Reading skills in adults are also correlated with entrainment accuracy (Tierney & Kraus 2013), and both children and adults with reading disabilities often have difficulty entraining taps to a metronome (Thomson & Goswami 2008, Thomson et al. 2006). Tapping steadily in silence is less associated with language skills than entraining to an external metronome (Thomson & Goswami 2008, Thomson et al. 2006, Tierney & Kraus 2013), suggesting that the ability to integrate auditory input with motor output is a key factor in the relationship between rhythm and language.

2.5. Evolutionary Approaches: Entrainment in Nonhuman Species

Although beat perception was long thought to be unique to humans, investigations have recently turned to nonhuman animals (Cook et al. 2013, Patel et al. 2009, Schachner et al. 2009). Snowball, the dancing cockatiel and YouTube sensation (**https://www.youtube.com/watch?v=cJOZp2ZftCw**), can bob his head to music (Patel et al. 2009, Schachner et al. 2009), but when recorded and analyzed under controlled conditions, Snowball showed only brief periods of synchronization and only around a narrow range of tempos, and he performed better when he could see his human handler. Humans, in contrast, can flexibly synchronize across a wide tempo range and without visual cues. There is also preliminary evidence that budgerigars, bonobos, chimpanzees, and elephants may be able to spontaneously synchronize to simple stimuli, such as metronome tones (Hasegawa et al. 2011, Hattori et al. 2013, Large & Gray 2015, Schachner et al. 2009). Currently, the best nonhuman example of complex entrainment is a California sea lion named Ronan. Ronan accurately bobs her head in synchrony with isochronous sequences as well as with music, and can generalize this ability in response to music she has never heard before (Cook et al. 2013, Rouse et al. 2016). Moreover, her behavior matches the predictions of oscillator models that display coupling between auditory and motor oscillators, suggesting Ronan's behavior is similar to that of humans (Rouse et al. 2016).

Entrainment behavior has been directly compared between human and nonhuman primates with synchronization–continuation tapping tasks (in which tapping is synchronized with an isochronous sequence and then continues at the same rate after the sequence stops). Rhesus macaques and humans are similarly accurate when reproducing single time intervals, but humans are far superior when synchronizing with metronome sequences (Zarco et al. 2009) and performing continuation tapping. Moreover, macaques tap 100–250 ms after stimulus onset, whereas humans tend to tap ahead of the beat, indicating that the macaques are not employing prediction processes.

EEG studies with macaques have shown that unexpected tone omissions from isochronous tone sequences elicit an MMN similar to that of humans. Unlike humans, however, macaques did not show different MMN responses for on- and off-beat omissions, suggesting that they are unable to detect the beat (or syncopation) in rhythm. Monkeys can extract temporal information from isochronous metronome sequences but not from more complex rhythms. In one study, macaques showed changes of gaze and facial expressions in response to deviations in isochronous but not irregular sequences, whereas humans accurately detected deviations in both types of sequences (Selezneva et al. 2013). Overall, these findings suggest that monkeys have some capabilities for beat perception, particularly when the stimuli are isochronous. Thus, macaques may possess some, but not all, of the brain machinery used in humans for beat perception and entrained movement (Merchant & Honing 2014, Patel & Iversen 2014). Crucial evolutionary changes in the human brain that allowed for music included mechanisms for extracting structure from an acoustic stream, mental representation, and prediction. A key region in humans for music, BA 44, is far less developed in macaques (Petrides & Pandya 2002). Moreover, the human brain has far more folds and convolutions than the macaque brain, making it possible to squeeze millions more neurons into a relatively confined space. These differences in fine structure (BA 44) and gross structure (folds) may be the reason why monkeys lack the musical abilities of humans.

Studies of nonhuman animals have led to two theories regarding the capacity for beat perception. One suggests that beat perception occurs only in species that are capable of vocal learning (the ability to alter vocalizations in response to environmental input), as supported by neural connections that link auditory input with vocal motor control (Patel 2006). Snowball, as a cockatiel, is a vocal learner, as are budgerigars (Patel et al. 2009). The second account suggests that timing abilities in primates correlate with greater anatomical connections between auditory and motor areas (Merchant & Honing 2014). Rhesus macaques have limited connections between auditory and motor areas and can perform only basic timing tasks such as producing single time intervals (Merchant et al. 2013), whereas chimpanzees—who developed roughly 13 million years later than macaques—have more connections and have shown some ability to spontaneously synchronize (Hattori et al. 2013). However, neither account explains the existence of beat perception in all of the nonhuman species (including animals that are neither primates nor vocal learners) that demonstrate it, such as sea lions like Ronan (Cook et al. 2013).

3. SYNCHRONIZATION

3.1. Tapping

Tapping studies have revealed much about auditory–motor entrainment. We distinguish two adaptive processes, one predictive, the other reactive. One way to test these processes is to introduce various perturbations to a sequence as participants tap along with it and observe how they adapt to the perturbation(s). Changing the timing of a single note creates a large tap-to-target asynchrony, which requires adjustment of the timing of the following tap (e.g., Repp 2002, Repp & Keller 2004). This reactive adjustment is automatic and is called the phase correction response (Repp 2005). Phase correction occurs even when the perturbation is not consciously detected (Repp 2005). Moreover, the kinematics of the tapping movement change as quickly as 100 ms after the perturbation (Hove et al. 2014), which is sufficiently fast to indicate that phase correction is likely subcortical.

In music, many expressive timing variations or alterations in tempo tend to occur globally and in largely predictable ways (Bhatara et al. 2011). Anticipatory processes are more important for remaining synchronized during these types of changes (van der Steen et al. 2015), and individuals are more able to remain synchronized when the changes are larger, perhaps because they are more perceptible.

3.2. Walking

Synchronization and its effects on movement have also been investigated with respect to walking (Leow et al. 2014, 2015; Leman et al. 2013; Styns et al. 2007). One question of interest is whether people spontaneously synchronize their footsteps to music. In both laboratory and naturalistic settings, people generally perform this synchronization only when they are specifically instructed to do so (Franěk et al. 2014, Mendonça et al. 2014). Thus, although spontaneous synchronization can occur during certain physical activities, it is not common during walking. This may be why, for thousands of years, groups of humans who march (such as military units) have made an effort to practice such synchronization (McNeill 1995).

People walk faster to music than to metronomes (Styns et al. 2007), and it is not simply the beat that drives movement. When individuals are asked to walk to a variety of music that has the same beat rate (130 bpm), some songs cause faster walking, but others cause slower walking (Leman et al. 2013). Thus, expressive factors in the music are important and can explain up to 60% of the variance in walking speed. Perceived groove and familiarity also increase walking speed (Leow et al. 2014, 2015), with the effects of groove being much larger than the effects of familiarity.

3.3. Dyads and Larger Groups

When groups of people synchronize their movements, such as during group music performance, the interactions between sound and movement can be highly complex. Group performance requires generation of an internal beat through the collectively produced auditory rhythms and the simultaneous individual tracking of that beat. Individual musicians must adjust the timing of their movements to the subtle errors and asynchronies among other musicians, as well as between other musicians and themselves, to maintain the ongoing, predictable temporal structure of music.

The ability to synchronize with others in dyadic tapping is related to individual differences in the ability to predictively track, or anticipate, a regular beat (Pecenka & Keller 2011). In addition, successful adjustment of timing requires adaptation to unexpected timing changes, and these two skills—anticipation and adjustment—predict synchronization success independently and in interaction (Mills et al. 2015). In dyadic, synchronized tapping, individuals benefit from mutual adaptation, adjusting to one another's subtle deviations and corrections in real time to maintain stable synchronization and minimize asynchronies between taps (Himberg 2014, Konvalinka et al. 2010, Nowicki et al. 2013). Interestingly, humans engaging in dyadic tapping demonstrate greater synchronization than one human tapping with a regular, computer-generated rhythm (Himberg 2014). Interpersonal synchronization in larger groups requires more complex interactions. String quartets, for example, can display autocratic and democratic behaviors, when, respectively, "following" musicians adjust their timing in response to the "leader" (autocratic) versus when all musicians mutually adjust their timings (democratic; see Wing et al. 2014).

Music listening, as shown by fMRI, synchronizes brain responses across listeners in networks spanning a wide range of regions: the brain stem, the bilateral auditory midbrain and thalamus, the primary auditory and auditory association cortices, right-lateralized structures in the frontal and parietal cortices, and the PMC (Abrams et al. 2013). These effects are greater for natural music than for quasi-musical control stimuli. Remarkably, intersubject synchronization in the midbrain (inferior colliculus) and thalamus (medial geniculate nucleus) was also found to be greater for natural music. This indicates that synchronization at these early stages of auditory processing is not simply driven by spectro-temporal features of the stimulus, which are processed in higher cortical structures. Increased synchronization was also evident in a right-hemisphere frontoparietal attention network and bilateral cortical regions involved in motor planning.

4. EMBODIED COGNITION OF RHYTHM AND MOVEMENT

4.1. Metrical Embodiment

Spontaneous movement in adults is generally synchronized to the beat, but it is also influenced by metrical levels other than the beat (Burger et al. 2013). The movements selected during dancing, for example, differ depending on the metrical level that the movement is synchronized to. For example, arm movements from the body out to the side are at the beat rate or slower, whereas vertical hand and torso movements occur at the beat rate (Toiviainen et al. 2010). Rotation of the torso and swaying of the body from side to side occur at even slower rates (e.g., four times the beat rate). The movement rates may relate to the amount of energy expended to move, and, thus, we select slower rates for parts that require more energy (Toiviainen et al. 2010). Timbral features of music also affect movement (Burger et al. 2013). The length, overall size and stiffness of a limb also constrain the natural harmonic oscillation rate and variability for movement (Lametti & Ostry 2010). Head movements tend to be synchronized to low-frequency sounds (e.g., the kick drum or bass guitar in popular music and jazz), whereas hand movements tend to be synchronized to high-frequency sounds (e.g., hi-hat or cymbal), perhaps because the freedom of movement of the hands enables them to synchronize to the faster rates presented in the higher-frequency percussion sounds. Finally, when there is a clear, strong beat in the music, overall body movements tend to be more regular and stable in their timing; when the beat is weaker or less regular, body movements are also less temporally regular (Burger et al. 2013).

Movement to the beat can alter meter perception. In one study, babies were bounced to an ambiguous rhythm—one group was bounced every other beat, whereas another group was bounced every third beat. Babies in each group were subsequently biased in their recognition of a binary or ternary accented version of the rhythm, respectively, as familiar, even though they had only ever heard an ambiguous unaccented rhythm (Phillips-Silver & Trainor 2005). A neural correlate of this result has also been shown by EEG (Chemin et al. 2014). Participants listened to a rhythm while an EEG was recorded; they then moved their body (e.g., nodding or clapping) in either a binary or ternary fashion to the rhythm, and the EEG was recorded after this movement (when participants were still). The oscillatory power at either binary or ternary frequencies was enhanced based on the way that they had previously moved to the rhythm. Thus, moving to rhythm alters subsequent perception of that rhythm, as well as neural entrainment.

4.2. Bodily Movement and Timing Sensitivity

Moving to the beat can influence beat perception and timing accuracy. Tapping along to auditory rhythms enhances beat finding for complex rhythms (Su & Pöppel 2012). Tapping may direct attention to the beat, improving the ability to detect it and synchronize to it. In another study, participants tapped in time with an isochronous sequence and then judged whether a final probe tone heard after the sequence stopped was on time (Manning & Schutz 2013). When people tapped during the initial sequence, they were more accurate than when they did not. Importantly, this did not depend on producing a tap along with the probe tone: Timing was better even when tapping ended before the probe tone, indicating that participants were not simply comparing the probe tone position with their final tap. When percussionists completed the task, moving along helped them even more than it did musical novices, although, interestingly, novices and percussionists performed similarly when just listening (Manning & Schutz 2016). Thus, engaging in movement appears to alter both beat perception and timing accuracy and produces greater benefits in those with extensive training.

Musicians and nonmusicians who tapped in synchrony with progressively more complex and less metrically structured auditory rhythms showed, in fMRI, a functionally connected network involving the dorsal PMC, possibly involved in extracting higher-order features of the rhythm's temporal structure (Chen et al. 2008b). Musicians recruited the prefrontal cortex to a greater degree than did nonmusicians, whereas secondary motor regions were recruited to the same extent. The superior ability of musicians to deconstruct and organize a rhythm's temporal structure may relate to the greater involvement of the prefrontal cortex in mediating working memory and may possibly involve the documented leftward shift as musical expertise increases (Bhattacharya & Petsche 2005, Kuchenbuch et al. 2012).

4.3. Rhythm Perception and Production and Theories of Embodied Cognition

The intimate relationship between music and movement has led researchers to examine how music perception is influenced by the physical properties of the human body, a process known as embodied music cognition (Leman & Maes 2015). Embodied cognition suggests that many higher cognitive functions are grounded in lower-level sensorimotor functioning. The reciprocal influence between movement and perception, as well as the activation of motor brain areas during rhythm perception (both detailed above), are often taken as indirect support for embodied music cognition. Leman & Maes propose that our acquired associations between motor output and the consequent sensory input creates an integrated network underlying both music production and music perception.

An additional line of evidence is the fact that we are able to distinguish who is producing actions based on sound alone (Sevdalis & Keller 2014). Even very simple auditory information, such as clapping or taps, can enable identification, and the tempo and variations in timing seem to be among the most important cues. This identification also occurs when expert music listeners identify, say, a favorite saxophone player based on subtle differences in parameters of timing and timbre. Allocating agency to an auditory action recruits mental simulations that relies on motor systems (Jeannerod 2006, Sevdalis & Keller 2014), and these systems are used to predict the auditory properties of our own movements, as well as those of others. These findings are consistent with claims that music has an evolutionary basis in signaling and sharing information, including an individual's identity, among conspecifics.

5. RHYTHMIC PATHOLOGIES AS MOVEMENT DEFICITS

5.1. Beat Deafness

Beat perception is a universal human capacity, yet a few reported cases of beat deafness—a type of amusia—exist, in which individuals show severe limitations in their capacity to perceive and synchronize to a musical beat despite having no rhythmic deficits in other domains, such as motor coordination and speech (Levitin 1999, Phillips-Silver et al. 2011). One reported individual, Mathieu, could neither bounce up and down to the beat of music nor accurately judge whether a video of a dancer was synchronized with the perceived music (Phillips-Silver et al. 2011). Yet Mathieu was able to synchronize his bouncing with a metronome. Mathieu and another beat deaf individual, Marjorie, were also asked to synchronize tapping with a metronome that was occasionally perturbed. Although both showed some ability to readjust their tapping following a perturbation, they took abnormally long to do so compared to controls (Palmer et al. 2014). Moreover, their tapping performance was assessed using a harmonic oscillator model, which found that Mathieu and Marjorie had different underlying deficits (involving intrinsic oscillator frequency and relaxation time, respectively).

Heterogeneity in deficits of beat perception and synchronization was further suggested in a tapping study in which seven individuals out of a sample of 99 showed abnormally poor synchronization (Sowiński & Dalla Bella 2013). Two of the poor synchronizers met the criteria to be considered beat deaf (presenting deficits in beat perception and synchronization but not in pitch perception), and two others showed selective deficits in synchronizing to real music but normal sensitivity to changes in durations and rhythms.

5.2. Brain Lesions and Disorders

Damage to or dysfunction in motor brain areas can produce timing and rhythm problems that cannot be attributable solely to motor problems. One example is seen in Parkinson's disease, a neurological disorder that impairs basal ganglia function and movement. The ability of Parkinson's patients to perceive changes in rhythmic patterns is significantly impaired compared to healthy controls (Cameron et al. 2016, Grahn & Brett 2009), even though no movement is required for the task. Similarly, patients with other basal ganglia disorders, such as Huntington's disease or multiple system atrophy, show deficits on a battery of rhythm and timing tasks (Cope et al. 2014). Finally, when basal ganglia lesion patients are asked to synchronize to a sequence with gradual tempo changes, they show higher timing variability than controls (Schwartze et al. 2011, van der Steen 2015). Modeling of the variability suggests that internal timekeeping processes are noisy in these patients and that their ability to accurately predict tempo changes has been reduced.

6. GROOVE

6.1. Definition of Groove

It is one thing to be able to tap your toe along with a drumbeat or melody—it is something else when the music compels you to move along with it. This compulsion is the essence of groove (also called pocket). Groove is defined as "the urge to move in response to music, combined with the positive affect associated with the coupling of sensory and motor processes while engaging with music" (Janata et al. 2012, p. 54). In jazz, groove is associated with the swing rhythm applied in performance, one in which a series of notes with the same notated duration are performed with a "forward propelling directionality" (Schuller 1968, p. 7). This is typically accomplished by dividing a beat unevenly, with the first subdivision about twice as long as the second. The sense of swing or groove is not experienced analytically, but rather through our bodily engagement with the music (Iyer 2002, Roholt 2014). In moving to groovy music, we become aware of its rhythmic flow, and groove is manifested as the kinematic feeling arising from one's embodied experience of entrainment to the music. Groove, then, is a pleasurable response to certain musical rhythms that not only compel us to move, but also make us aware of the way that our bodies are moving with the music.

What is it in the music that gives rise to a sense of groove? Madison (2006) presented listeners with music from a wide range of musical styles and genres, including music from Africa, India, Latin America, and Southern Europe. Listeners rated each example on a number of descriptive terms, including groove. Listeners were able to make ratings of amount of groove (grooviness) just as readily as other factors, and groove was associated with music that was also "driving, intensive, and somewhat rapid and bouncing" (Madison 2006, p. 206). Moreover, grooviness was associated with more than one musical style and genre, and it was consistently recognized (i.e., there was good intersubjective agreement as to what was groovy). Janata et al. (2012) had listeners rate the grooviness of a large sample of North American popular music. They found that, whereas R&B music (that is, Motown and Soul but not Hip-Hop or Rap), was rated higher for groove than were other genres (Rock, Folk, and Jazz), there were no significant differences among other genres, at least in their sample of university students. Faster music (>100 bpm) tended to be rated higher for groove than slower music, as was music that was familiar or enjoyed by participants. Janata et al. also had participants move in various ways, including (*a*) tapping along to an isochronous beat, (*b*) freely tapping in any rhythm along with the music, and (*c*) not tapping. Participants felt that it was easier to tap along with high- than with low-groove music and felt more in the groove with high-groove stimuli. Analysis of video data from the nontapping condition found that higher-groove music gave rise to spontaneous body movements (e.g., of the head, torso, or foot) to a significantly greater degree than did low-groove music. Music with high groove gives rise to robust sensorimotor entrainment, and groove strength is correlated with beat strength and pulse strength.

6.2. Groovy Structural Factors: Swing and Syncopation

What are the structural factors of the music that give rise to a sense of groove? Given that groove is correlated with a strong sense of felt beat, groove is sensitive to tempo, as is beat induction more generally (van Noorden & Moelants 1999); as noted above, groovy music tends to fall within a moderate to quick tempo range (100–130 bpm; Janata et al. 2012).

Various studies have examined two other structural factors: rhythmic complexity and expressive timing, or rather, swing. Both are thought to influence groove because the listener must make a greater effort to follow the rhythmic flow than would be the case with a simple and wholly predictable series of durations performed with a deadpan timing. The working hypothesis is that syncopations and expressive timing deviations optimize the listener's predictive engagement with the unfolding rhythm, making listening an active rather than passive activity. This was the basis of Keil's (1987) theory of participatory discrepancies in jazz, which was adopted by Iyer (2002), who posited that fine-grained timing variations are an essential aspect of groove. In many styles associated with groove (e.g., jazz, R&B), rhythms are swung to varying degrees and, thus, systematically deviate from deadpan timing. Other studies have found that microtiming deviations were not required to give a sense of groove (Butterfield 2010, Fruhauf et al. 2013, Madison 2006, Senn et al. 2016), and in some cases, deadpan timings were preferred. These results make some sense, as Repp (2005) has noted that the phase corrections one makes in following fine-grained timing variations are often subliminal and involuntary, whereas only larger shifts in tempo (i.e., period corrections) involve conscious awareness and volitional control.

Empirical evidence for optimization of predictive engagement comes from studies of syncopation and groove. Defining syncopation is difficult, as it can manifest in different ways in different rhythmic contexts, depending on the number of beats in the measure and the ways in which the beats themselves are divided. Syncopation most typically occurs in 4-beat meters in which the beats are divided into eighth-note duplets. In this example, the integers represent the beats proper (the first eighth note of each duplet), and the word *and* represents the offbeat position (the second eighth note of each duplet): 1 *and* 2 *and* 3 *and* 4 *and* etc. A syncopation occurs when a note is articulated on one of the *ands* and is then held through the following eighth note. The characteristic bump one feels from syncopation occurs because the listener fills in the missing beat (see Huron 2006). Amounts of syncopation vary, but too much syncopation effaces the sense of beat, essentially creating an unsyncopated rhythm that has been phase shifted. Moderate amounts of syncopation result in the highest groove responses (Witek et al. 2014). In addition to syncopation, higher rhythmic density—more subdivisions of the beat—and rhythmic complexity also contribute to a sense of groove: Once a passage is composed with a certain amount of rhythmic density and syncopation, it is difficult to remove the sense of groove that results (Madison & Sioros 2014). This may explain why deadpan timings did not hurt the perceived groove of the stimuli used in previous experiments.

6.3. Groovy Listeners and Groovy Music

The operational definition of groove used in the studies given above—"the urge to move with the music and take pleasure in doing so" (Janata et al. 2012, p. 54)—is clearly dependent on the listener's receptiveness and mental and physical responses. Even music that was found to be highly rated for groove in some studies [e.g., Stevie Wonder's Superstition, which had the highest overall rating in the study by Janata et al. (2012)] may leave some listeners unmoved. An open question is how devotees of marches, folk dances, or historical dance styles would respond to music from these respective repertoires, as well as to contemporary music with high groove ratings in previous studies. Experts show greater sensitivity to changes in microtiming than do nonexperts (Bhatara et al. 2011, Senn et al. 2016). Complicating the scientific study of groove, participants sometimes report that a musical excerpt gives them the urge to move but do not move to it, and participants also sometimes move to music that did not give them a reported urge to move. "It seems that the groove experience is not that easy to measure. It will take considerable effort to develop reliable methods to assess a listeners' groove experience and bodily entrainment" (Senn et al. 2016, p. 12).

7. CROSS-MODAL CORRESPONDENCES IN RHYTHM PERCEPTION

7.1. Cross-Modal Correspondences: Perception, Integration, and Synesthesia

We usually think of rhythm as an auditory parameter arising from repetitive behaviors that create periodic sound patterns (as in, "He tapped out a staccato rhythm as he hammered the shingles on his roof"). However, rhythms can also be perceived via other sensory modalities, including our haptic, proprioceptive, visual, and vestibular systems (Kosonen & Raisamo 2006, Phillips-Silver & Trainor 2008, Trainor et al. 2009). After audition, vision plays the greatest role in our temporal processes and perception of events in the world. The McGurk effect (McGurk & MacDonald 1976), in which the phonetic articulation we see influences what phonemes we hear, is just one of many examples of the influence of vision in auditory perception (e.g., Colavita 1974, Posner et al. 1976). Visual cues can alter musical experiences (Vines et al. 2011), and the influence of vision can change with age (Diaconescu et al. 2013).

Repeated elements in static images and sculptures may be described in terms of their visual rhythm, or an impression of coherence and movement created by pattern, repetition, and regularity in the arrangement of objects in the visual field. Although this is an important aspect of visual perception (as are the temporal aspects of vision, such as the saccades of the eye), in this section, we focus on the visual apprehension of dynamic processes and arrays and its relation to temporal perception in music. We distinguish among the following factors:

- cross-modal perception, in which perceptions in two modalities remain distinct but are mutually influencing;
- multisensory integration, in which sensations from two sensory modalities are fused into a single percept; and
- synesthesia, in which vivid percepts arise in one modality due to stimulation in another modality (Talsma et al. 2009). There are at least 35 types of documented synesthesia (Day 2005), including tone–color synesthesia, in which individuals report seeing colors in their visual field in response to hearing particular pitches. These tone–color associations do not appear to be systematic across individuals.

7.2. Rhythm and Motion in Vision and Audition

Perceiving a visual rhythm depends on either (*a*) a periodic change in the appearance of a stationary object, such as a flashing light or rotating multicolored ball, or (*b*) a periodic movement of an object, such as a bouncing ball or the steps of a dancer. It is also possible for an array of static objects, such as a series of flashing lights, to produce the illusion of motion. Such apparent motions depend on the sequential presentation of visual information, governed by the time and distance between successive events according to Korte's third law of apparent motion (Korte 1915, Shiffrar 2005). Although we hear a similar type of motion when we listen to music, this perception is also illusory, a kind of virtual motion in a virtual space of pitch or rhythm (Gjerdingen 1994, Langer 1953). Similar temporal constraints in neural processing appear to operate across the two sensory modalities.

Tests of our visual perception of rhythm have long used many of the same approaches and methods as those of auditory perception, replacing the clicks of a metronome or the sustained sine tones of a durational sequence with flashing lights. Initial experiments using these discrete visual stimuli indicated that vision seemed to be an order of magnitude slower and less accurate for tasks such as synchronization, durational discrimination, and perturbation detection (Grahn 2012, Grondin & McAuley 2009, Repp & Penel 2002). However, more recent studies using continuous visual stimuli, such as a bouncing ball, a light that continuously varies in intensity, or a rotating disc, found that, under these circumstances, differences between the two modalities largely disappeared (Grahn 2012, Hove et al. 2013, Iversen et al. 2015, Varlet et al. 2012), especially if the stimulus presented a physically realistic motion trajectory (Iversen et al. 2015). Moreover, when an individual tracks a periodically moving object, such as a conductor's baton, the absolute acceleration along the object's movement trajectory is the main cue for rhythmic periodicity and temporal location, although beat clarity and tempo are also important (Luck & Sloboda 2009).

Moreover, although one may associate discontinuous or discrete events with beat-based timing and continuous events with interval timing, continuously varying visual stimuli can also give rise to beat-based timing (Grahn 2012, Su & Salazar-López 2016). In addition, a beat may be perceived in visual stimuli when an individual is primed by hearing an auditory version of the rhythm before seeing it (Grahn et al. 2011).

Differences in temporal continuity across different modalities may inhibit perceptual integration, either because different neural systems are used to sense and encode discrete and continuous stimuli in each modality (a failure of structural correspondence) or simply because paired stimuli with continuity mismatches simply do not occur as part of our natural experience and, thus, give rise to a failure of statistical correspondence. Moreover, statistical correspondences are normally grounded in causal relationships that are understood to exist between auditory and visual stimuli, i.e., when one observes the action that gives rise to a sound (Schutz & Kubovy 2009). For example, one typically observes continuous motion, such as the movement of a violin bow, co-occurring with the production a continuous sound (the sustained violin tone). Similarly, discrete motions, such as the impact of a drumstick, co-occur with discontinuous sounds (a sharp, short drumbeat). Yet even this association is not consistent. Schutz & Lipscomb (2007) found that modifying the continuity of a visually presented marimba stroke—a short and jerky impact motion versus a longer sweeping impact motion—gave rise to illusory differences in the perceived tone duration (see also Varlet et al. 2012). Schutz & Kubovy (2009) further noted that the causal link between observed action and resultant sound could not be violated; when the impact motion (a marimba stroke) was paired with a different impact sound (a piano note), the illusion was weaker, and when it was paired with a nonimpact sound, the illusion did not occur. They took this to be support for the binding by causality hypothesis: There needs to be not only a statistical correspondence between what one sees and hears, but also a causal link when one is appropriate (Schutz & Kubovy 2009).

7.3. Cross-Modal Perception of Duration, Beat, Tempo, and Rhythmic Grouping

Music involves more than just the perception of single durations; the ability to extract beat and tempo from the acoustic stream is a prerequisite to grasping rhythmic and melodic shape, as well as the music's expressive character. A sense of beat can be extracted from a continuous visual stimulus (Grahn 2012), and a bouncing point-light figure paired with a simple auditory beat can influence the perceived location of on-beat versus off-beat accents, that is, the metrical structure of the beat sequence (Su 2014). Similarly, patterns of bodily movement can bias the perceptual organization of an ambiguous rhythm, and this bias is retained when the rhythm is subsequently heard in a nonmovement condition. Phillips-Silver & Trainor (2007, p. 533) hypothesized that "the movement-sound interaction develops early and is fundamental to music processing throughout life." Thus, movement—whether observed, felt, or both—can affect the perception of beats, as well as their metric organization. This may be a fairly subtle effect: As Brochard et al. (2003) have shown, we tend to impose a sense of strong and weak alteration on a series of beats in the absence of any other cues (what they call the tick-tock phenomenon), and thus visual arrays may serve to bias our pre-existing tendency to impose a subjective sense of meter on an otherwise undifferentiated series of pulses.

The perceived rate at which pulses occur can also be influenced by visual information. Observing an accelerating or decelerating pattern of moving dots (which give rise to a sense of optic flow) can bias our sense of the tempo of a concurrent auditory sequence (Su & Jonikaitis 2011). In a somewhat more ecologically valid context, when participants listened to classic rhythm-and-blues songs and watched a stick figure animation (created from motion capture data of a human dancer), a vigorous dance interpretation led to faster tempo ratings for the music than did a relaxed dance interpretation or the music alone (London et al. 2016). Both dance interpretations were synchronized with the musical beat, and the vigorous dance interpretations were characterized by greater total acceleration, adding support to Luck & Sloboda's (2009) findings regarding the salience of acceleration in a continuous visual display as a rhythmic cue.

Research in the cognitive neuroscience of music in general and in rhythm and movement in particular has grown exponentially over the past two decades. Questions that originated within the domains of philosophy and music theory can now be investigated using modern experimental approaches. The advent of digital recording, which allows for the easy creation, manipulation, and preservation of musical stimuli, has enabled far more rigorous experimentation than had been possible 20 years ago. Coupling advances in neuroimaging techniques with the continuing application of methods from psychophysics and social psychology has created a golden age of music psychology research.

Over the next 10 years, we anticipate major advances in our understanding of the neurophysiological underpinnings of musical behaviors, especially from converging methods in the time domain (EEG, magnetoencephalography) and the spatial domain (positron emission tomography, fMRI). An especially promising area is the neurochemistry of music (e.g., Chanda & Levitin 2013, Mallik et al. 2017), and we hope that more researchers will undertake experiments that selectively target specific neurochemical systems. If we look farther into the future, mapping the connectome of human brains will help to map the connections between neurons and promises to inform a deeper understanding of musical behaviors than chemistry or anatomy alone can reveal. Perhaps chief among the major unanswered questions are what the evolutionary basis of music may be, what the connection between music and health outcomes is, and what makes some musical compositions more memorable and enjoyable than others. We believe that the answers to these questions may be on the horizon, as evidenced by the broad range of disciplinary backgrounds represented at scientific meetings and in the journals devoted to music perception and cognition—psychologists are collaborating with music theorists, economists, archeologists, biologists, chemists, radiologists, anthropologists, nurses, psychiatrists, otolaryngologists, and professional musicians, to name just a few. Many of the unanswered questions that linger will benefit from this type of collaborative, team-based approach, and we look forward to the results of these richly interdisciplinary studies.

DISCLOSURE STATEMENT

The authors are not aware of any affiliations, memberships, funding, or financial holdings that might be perceived as affecting the objectivity of this review.

LITERATURE CITED

Abel SM. 1972. Duration discrimination of noise and tone bursts. *J. Acoust. Soc. Am.* 51(4B):1219–23

Abrams DA, Ryali S, Chen T, Chordia P, Khouzam A, et al. 2013. Inter-subject synchronization of brain responses during natural music listening. *Eur. J. Neurosci.* 37(9):1458–69

Adkins A, Kurstin G. 2015. Hello. Recorded by Adele, *25*. London: XL Recordings

Allen GD. 1975. Speech rhythms: its relation to performance universals and articulatory timing. *J. Phon.* 3(2):75–86

Becker W, Fagen D. 1973. Bodhisattva. Recorded by Steely Dan, *Countdown to Ecstasy*. Los Angeles: ABC Records

Bergeson TR, Trehub SE. 2002. Absolute pitch and tempo in mothers' songs to infants. *Psychol. Sci.* 13:72–75

Besson M, Schön D. 2001. Comparison between language and music. *Ann. N. Y. Acad. Sci.* 930(1):232–58

Bhatara A, Tirovolas AK, Duan LM, Levy B, Levitin DJ. 2011. Perception of emotional expression in musical performance. *J. Exp. Psychol. Hum. Percept. Perform.* 37(3):921–34

Bhattacharya J, Petsche H. 2005. Phase synchrony analysis of EEG during music perception reveals changes in functional connectivity due to musical expertise. *Signal Process.* 85(11):2161–77

Brochard R, Abecasis D, Potter D, Ragot R, Drake C. 2003. The "ticktock" of our internal clock: direct brain evidence of subjective accents in isochronous sequences. *Psychol. Sci.* 14(4):362–66

Burger B, Thompson MR, Luck G, Saarikallio S, Toiviainen P. 2013. Influences of rhythm- and timbre-related musical features on characteristics of music-induced movement. *Front. Psychol.* 4:183

Burghardt H. 1973. Die subjektive Dauer schmalbandiger Schalle bei verschiedenen Frequenzlagen. *Acustica* 28:278–84

Butterfield MW. 2010. Participatory discrepancies and the perception of beats in jazz. *Music Percept.* 27:157–76

Cage J. 2011 (1961). *Silence: Lectures and Writings*. Middletown, CT: Wesleyan Univ. Press

Cameron DJ, Grahn JA. 2014. Neuroscientific investigations of musical rhythm. *Acoust. Aust.* 42(2):111

Cameron DJ, Pickett KA, Earhart GM, Grahn JA. 2016. The effect of dopaminergic medication on beat-based auditory timing in Parkinson's disease. *Front. Neurol.* 7:19

Carr KW, Tierney A, White-Schwoch T, Kraus N. 2016. Intertrial auditory neural stability supports beat synchronization in preschoolers. *Dev. Cogn. Neurosci.* 17:76–82

Carr KW, White-Schwoch T, Tierney A, Strait DL, Kraus N. 2014. Beat synchronization predicts neural speech encoding and reading readiness in preschoolers. *PNAS* 111(40):14559–64

Chanda ML, Levitin DJ. 2013. The neurochemistry of music. *Trends Cogn. Sci.* 17(4):79–93

Chemin B, Mouraux A, Nozaradan S. 2014. Body movement selectively shapes the neural representation of musical rhythms. *Psychol. Sci.* 25:2147–59

Chen JL, Penhune VB, Zatorre RJ. 2008a. Listening to musical rhythms recruits motor regions of the brain. *Cereb. Cortex* 18(12):2844–54

Chen JL, Penhune VB, Zatorre RJ. 2008b. Moving on time: brain network for auditory-motor synchronization is modulated by rhythm complexity and musical training. *J. Cogn. Neurosci.* 20(2):226–39

Chen JL, Zatorre RJ, Penhune VB. 2006. Interactions between auditory and dorsal premotor cortex during synchronization to musical rhythms. *NeuroImage* 32:1771–81

Chopin F. 1839. Piano Sonata No. 2, Op. 35

Clark R, Resnick A. 1966. Good Lovin'. Recorded by The Rascals, *The Young Rascals*. New York: Atlantic Records

Cohen J. 1954. The experience of time. *Acta. Psychol.* 10:207–19

Colavita FB. 1974. Human sensory dominance. *Atten. Percept. Psychophys.* 16(2):409–12

Collyer CE, Broadbent HA, Church RM. 1994. Preferred rates of repetitive tapping and categorical time production. *Atten. Percept. Psychophys.* 55(4):443–53

Cook P, Rouse A, Wilson M, Reichmuth CJ. 2013. A California sea lion (*Zalophus californianus*) can keep the beat: motor entrainment to rhythmic auditory stimuli in a non vocal mimic. *J. Comp. Psychol.* 127:1–16

Cope TE, Grube M, Singh B, Burn DJ, Griffiths TD. 2014. The basal ganglia in perceptual timing: timing performance in multiple system atrophy and Huntington's disease. *Neuropsychologia* 52(100):73–81

Cross I. 2005. Music and meaning, ambiguity and evolution. In *Musical Communication*, ed. D Miell, R MacDonald, DJ Hargreaves, pp. 27–43. Oxford, UK: Oxford Univ. Press

Day S. 2005. Some demographic and socio-cultural aspects of synesthesia. In *Synesthesia: Perspectives from Cognitive Neuroscience*, ed. L Robertson, N Sagiv, pp. 11–33. Oxford, UK: Oxford Univ. Press

Diaconescu AO, Hasher L, McIntosh AR. 2013. Visual dominance and multisensory integration changes with age. *NeuroImage* 65:152–66

Drake C, Botte MC. 1993. Tempo sensitivity in auditory sequences: evidence for a multiple-look model. *Atten. Percept. Psychophys.* 54(3):277–86

Drake C, Gros L, Penel A. 1999. How fast is that music? The relation between physical and perceived tempo. In *Music, Mind, and Science*, ed. SW Yi, pp. 190–203. Seoul, South Korea: Seoul Univ. Press

Drake C, Jones MR, Baruch C. 2000. The development of rhythmic attending in auditory sequences: attunement, referent period, focal attending. *Cognition* 77:251–88

Eck D. 2002. Finding downbeats with a relaxation oscillator. *Psychol. Res.* 66(1):18–25

Eerola T, Luck G, Toiviainen P. 2006. An investigation of pre-schoolers' corporeal synchronization with music. *Proc. Int. Conf. Music Percept. Cogn., 9th, Bologna, Italy*, pp. 472–76. Bologna, Italy: Soc. Music Percept. Cogn./Eur. Soc. Cogn. Sci. Music

Fechner GT. 1860. *Elemente der Psychophysik*. Leipzig, Ger.: Breitkopf und Härtel

Franěk M, Van Noorden L, Režný L. 2014. Tempo and walking speed with music in the urban context. *Front. Psychol.* 5:1361

Friberg A, Sundberg J. 1993. Perception of just noticeable time displacement of a tone presented in a metrical sequence at different tempos. In *Quarterly Progress and Status Report*, ed. Kunglinga Tek. Högsk. Speech Transm. Lab., pp. 49–55. Stockholm: R. Inst. Technol.

Friberg A, Sundberg J. 1995. Time discrimination in a monotonic, isochronous sequence. *J. Acoust. Soc. Am.* 98(5):2524–31

Friberg A, Sundströöm A. 2002. Swing ratios and ensemble timing in jazz performance: evidence for a common rhythmic pattern. *Music Percept.* 19(3):333–49

Fruhauf J, Kopiez R, Platz F. 2013. Music on the timing grid: the influence of microtiming on the perceived groove quality of a simple drum pattern performance. *Music Sci.* 17(2):246–60

Fujioka T, Ross B, Trainor LJ. 2015. Beta-band oscillations represent auditory beat and its metrical hierarchy in perception and imagery. *J. Neurosci.* 35:15187–98

Gjerdingen RO. 1994. Apparent motion in music? *Music Percept.* 11(4):335–70

Glass L, Mackey MC. 1988. *From Clocks to Chaos: The Rhythms of Life*. Princeton, NJ: Princeton Univ. Press

Grahn JA. 2012. See what I hear? Beat perception in auditory and visual rhythms. *Exp. Brain Res.* 220(1):51–61

Grahn JA, Brett M. 2007. Rhythm perception in motor areas of the brain. *J. Cogn. Neurosci.* 19(5):893–906

Grahn JA, Brett M. 2009. Impairment of beat-based rhythm discrimination in Parkinson's disease. *Cortex* 45(1):54–61

Grahn JA, Henry MJ, McAuley JD. 2011. FMRI investigation of cross-modal interactions in beat perception: Audition primes vision, but not vice versa. *NeuroImage* 54:1231–43

Grahn JA, Rowe JB. 2009. Feeling the beat: premotor and striatal interactions in musicians and non-musicians during beat processing. *J. Neurosci.* 29(23):7540–48

Grahn JA, Rowe JB. 2012. Finding and feeling the musical beat: striatal dissociations between detection and prediction of regularity. *Cereb Cortex* 23(4):913–21

Gratton I, Brandimonte MA, Bruno N. 2016. Absolute memory for tempo in musicians and non-musicians. *PLOS ONE* 11(10):e0163558

Griffiths TD, Warren JD, Scott SK, Nelken I, King AJ. 2004. Cortical processing of complex sound: a way forward? *Trends Neurosci.* 27(4):181–85

Grondin S, McAuley JD. 2009. Duration discrimination in crossmodal sequences. *Perception* 38(10):1542–59

Halpern AR, Andrews MW. 2008. Melody recognition at fast and slow tempos: effects of age, experience, and familiarity. *Atten. Percept. Psychophys.* 70:496–502

Halpern AR, Müllensiefen D. 2008. Effects of timbre and tempo change on memory for music. *Q. J. Exp. Psychol.* 61(9):1371–84

Hancock H. 1973. Chameleon. Recorded by Herbie Hancock, *Headhunters*. New York: Columbia Records

Hasegawa A, Okanoya K, Hasegawa T, Seki Y. 2011. Rhythmic synchronization tapping to an audio-visual metronome in budgerigars. *Sci. Rep.* 1:120

Hattori Y, Tomonaga M, Matsuzawa T. 2013. Spontaneous synchronized tapping to an auditory rhythm in a chimpanzee. *Sci. Rep.* 3:1566

Henry MJ, Herrmann B, Grahn JA. 2017. What can we learn about beat perception by comparing brain signals and stimulus envelopes? *PLOS ONE* 12(2):e0172454

Hibi S. 1983. Rhythm perception in repetitive sound sequence. *J. Acoust. Soc. Jpn.* 4:83–95

Himberg T. 2014. *Interaction in Musical Time*. PhD Thesis, Univ. Cambridge, UK

Hirsh I, Sherrick C. 1961. Perceived order in difference sense modalities. *J. Exp. Psychol.* 62:423–32

Houlihan K, Levitin DJ. 2011. *Recognition of melodies from rhythm and pitch*. Presented at Bi-Annu. Meet. Soc. Music Percept. Cogn., Rochester, NY

Hove MJ, Balasubramaniam R, Keller PE. 2014. The time course of phase correction: a kinematic investigation of motor adjustment to timing perturbations during sensorimotor synchronization. *J. Exp. Psychol. Hum. Percept. Perform.* 40:2243–51

Hove MJ, Iversen JR, Zhang A, Repp BH. 2013. Synchronization with competing visual and auditory rhythms: Bouncing ball meets metronome. *Psychol. Res.* 77(4):388–98

Huron D. 2006. *Sweet Anticipation: Music and the Psychology of Expectation*. Cambridge, MA: MIT Press

Iversen JR, Patel AD, Nicodemus B, Emmorey K. 2015. Synchronization to auditory and visual rhythms in hearing and deaf individuals. *Cognition* 134:232–44

Iversen JR, Repp BH, Patel AD. 2009. Top-down control of rhythm perception modulates early auditory responses. *Ann. N. Y. Acad. Sci.* 1169:58–73

Iyer V. 2002. Embodied mind, situated cognition, and expressive microtiming in African-American music. *Music Percept.* 19(3):387–414

Jackson M. 1983. Beat It. Recorded by Michael Jackson, *Thriller*. New York: Epic Records

Janata P, Tomic ST, Haberman J. 2012. Sensorimotor coupling in music and the psychology of the groove. *J. Exp. Psychol. Gen.* 141(1):54–75

Jeannerod M. 2006. *Motor Cognition: What Actions Tell to the Self*. Oxford, UK: Oxford Univ. Press

Jeon JY, Fricke FR. 1997. Duration of perceived and performed sounds. *Psychol. Music* 25(1):70–83

Judkis M. 2011. World's longest concert will last 639 years. *The Washington Post*, November 21. **https://www.washingtonpost.com/blogs/arts-post/post/worlds-longest-concert-will-last-639-years/2011/11/21/gIQAWrdXiN_blog.html**

Keil C. 1987. Participatory discrepancies and the power of music. *Cult. Anthropol.* 2:275–83

Konvalinka I, Vuust P, Roepstorff A, Frith CD. 2010. Follow you, follow me: continuous mutual prediction and adaptation in joint tapping. *Q. J. Exp. Psychol.* 63:2220–30

Korte A. 1915. Kinematoskopische Untersuchungen [Cinematoscopic investigations]. *Z. Psychol.* 72:193–296

Kosonen K, Raisamo R. 2006. Rhythm perception through different modalities. *Proc. Eurohaptics, July 3–6, Paris*, pp. 365–70. Aarhus, Den.: Interact. Des. Found.

Kuchenbuch A, Paraskevopoulos E, Herholz SC, Pantev C. 2012. Electromagnetic correlates of musical expertise in processing of tone patterns. *PLOS ONE* 7(1):e30171

Kung SJ, Chen JL, Zatorre RJ, Penhune VB. 2013. Interacting cortical and basal ganglia networks underlying finding and tapping to the musical beat. *J. Cogn. Neurosci.* 25(3):401–20

Lametti DR, Ostry DJ. 2010. Postural constraints on movement variability. *J. Neurophys.* 104(2):1061–67

Langer S. 1953. *Feeling and Form*. New York: Scribners

Large EW. 2008. Resonating to musical rhythm: theory and experiment. In *Psychology of Time*, ed. S Grondin, pp. 189–232. Bingley, UK: Emerald

Large EW, Almonte F, Velasco M. 2010. A canonical model for gradient frequency neural networks. *Physica D* 239:905–11

Large EW, Gray PM. 2015. Spontaneous tempo and rhythmic entrainment in a bonobo (*Pan paniscus*). *J. Comp. Psychol.* 129(4):317–28

Large EW, Kolen JF. 1994. Accent structures in music performance. *Connect. Sci.* 6:177–208

Large EW, Palmer C. 2002. Perceiving temporal regularity in music. *Cogn. Sci.* 26:1–37

Leman M, Maes PJ. 2015. The role of embodiment in the perception of music. *Empir. Music. Rev.* 9(3–4):236–46

Leman M, Moelants D, Varewyck M, Styns F, van Noorden L, Martens JP. 2013. Activating and relaxing music entrains the speed of beat synchronized walking. *PLOS ONE* 8(7):e67932

Leow LA, Parrott T, Grahn JA. 2014. Individual differences in beat perception affect gait responses to low- and high-groove music. *Front. Hum. Neurosci.* 8:811

Leow LA, Rinchon VE, Grahn JA. 2015. Familiarity with music increases walking speed in rhythmic auditory cueing. *Ann. N. Y. Acad. Sci.* 1337:53–61

Levitin DJ. 1999. Tone deafness: failures of musical anticipation and self-reference. *Int. J. Comput. Anticip. Syst.* 4:243–54

Levitin DJ, Cook PR. 1996. Memory for musical tempo: additional evidence that auditory memory is absolute. *Atten. Percept. Psychophys.* 58(6):927–35

Levitin DJ, McAdams S, Adams RL. 2002. Control parameters for musical instruments: a foundation for new mappings of gesture to sound. *Organ. Sound* 7(2):171–89

Levitin DJ, Menon V. 2003. Musical structure is processed in "language" areas of the brain: a possible role for Brodmann Area 47 in temporal coherence. *NeuroImage* 20(4):2142–52

Levitin DJ, Rogers SE. 2005. Absolute pitch: perception, coding, and controversies. *Trends Cogn. Sci.* 9(1):26–33

London J. 2011. Tactus ≠ tempo: some dissociations between attentional focus, motor behavior. *Empir. Musicol. Rev.* 6(1):43–55

London J, Burger B, Thompson M, Toiviainen P. 2016. Speed on the dance floor: auditory and visual cues for musical tempo. *Acta Psychol.* 164:70–80

London JM. 1993. Loud rests and other strange metric phenomena (or, meter as heard). *Music Theory Online* 0(2):1067–3040

London JM. 2012. *Hearing in Time: Psychological Aspects of Musical Meter.* Oxford, UK: Oxford Univ. Press. 2nd ed.

Luck G, Sloboda JA. 2009. Spatio-temporal cues for visually mediated synchronization. *Music Percept.* 26(5):465–73

Madison G. 2006. Experiencing groove induced by music: consistency and phenomenology. *Music Percept.* 24(2):201–8

Madison G, Sioros G. 2014. What musicians do to induce the sensation of groove in simple and complex melodies, and how listeners perceive it. *Front. Psychol.* 5:894

Mallik A, Chanda ML, Levitin DJ. 2017. Anhedonia to music and mu-opioids: evidence from the administration of naltrexone. *Sci. Rep.* 7:41952

Manning F, Schutz M. 2013. "Moving to the beat" improves timing perception. *Psychon. B* 20:1133–39

Manning FC, Schutz M. 2016. Trained to keep a beat: movement-related enhancements to timing perception in percussionists and non-percussionists. *Psychol. Res.* 80(4):532–42

Martens PA. 2011. The ambiguous tactus: tempo, subdivision, benefits, and three listener strategies. *Music Percept.* 28(5):433–48

Martin JH. 2005. The corticospinal system: from development to motor control. *Neuroscientist* 11(2):161–73

Mates J, Muller U, Radil T, Poppel E. 1994. Temporal integration in sensorimotor synchronization. *J. Cogn. Neurosci.* 6(4):332–40

Mbongwana Star. 2015. Malukayi. Recorded by Mbongwana Star, *From Kinshasa.* London: World Circuit

McAuley JD. 2010. Tempo and rhythm. In *Music Perception*, ed. MR Jones, pp. 165–99. New York: Springer

McAuley JD, Henry MJ, Tkach J. 2012. Tempo mediates the involvement of motor areas in beat perception. *Ann. N. Y. Acad. Sci.* 1252(1):77–84

McAuley JD, Jones MR, Holub S, Johnston HM, Miller NS. 2006. The time of our lives: life span development of timing and event tracking. *J. Exp. Psychol. Gen.* 135(3):348–67

McGurk H, MacDonald J. 1976. Hearing lips and seeing voices. *Nature* 264:746–48

McNeill W. 1995. *Keeping Together in Time: Dance and Drill in Human History.* Cambridge, MA: Harvard Univ. Press

Mendonça C, Oliveira M, Fontes L, Santos J. 2014. The effect of instruction to synchronize over step frequency while walking with auditory cues on a treadmill. *Hum. Mov. Sci.* 33:33–42

Merchant H, Honing H. 2014. Are non-human primates capable of rhythmic entrainment? Evidence for the gradual audiomotor evolution hypothesis. *Front. Neurosci.* 7:274

Merchant H, Pérez O, Zarco W, Gámez J. 2013. Interval tuning in the primate medial premotor cortex as a general timing mechanism. *J. Neurosci.* 33(21):9082–96

Miller NS, McAuley JD. 2005. Tempo sensitivity in isochronous tone sequences: the multiple-look model revisited. *Percept. Psychophys.* 67(7):1150–60

Mills PF, van der Steen MC, Schultz BG, Keller PE. 2015. Individual differences in temporal anticipation and adaptation during sensorimotor synchronization. *Timing Time Percept.* 3(1–2):13–31

Mitchell J. 1970. Woodstock. Recorded by Crosby, Stills, Nash & Young, *Déjà Vu.* New York: Atlantic Records

Mitrani L, Shekerdijiiski S, Yakimoff N. 1986. Mechanisms and asymmetries in visual perception of simultaneity and temporal order. *Biol. Cybernet.* 54:159–65

Näätänen R, Paavilainen P, Rinne T, Alho K. 2007. The mismatch negativity (MMN) in basic research of central auditory processing: a review. *Clin. Neurophysiol.* 118(12):2544–90

Nowicki L, Prinz W, Grosjean M, Repp BH, Keller PE. 2013. Mutual adaptive timing in interpersonal action coordination. *Psychomusicol. Music Mind Brain* 23:6–20

Nozaradan S, Peretz I, Missal M, Mouraux A. 2011. Tagging the neuronal entrainment to beat and meter. *J. Neurosci.* 31:10234–40

Nozaradan S, Peretz I, Mouraux A. 2012. Selective neuronal entrainment to the beat and meter embedded in a musical rhythm. *J. Neurosci.* 32:17572–81

Palmer C, Lidji P, Peretz I. 2014. Losing the beat: deficits in temporal coordination. *Philos. Trans. R. Soc. B* 369:20130405

Parker C. 1949. Bird Gets the Worm. Recorded by Charlie "Bird" Parker, *Bird Gets the Worm*. Newark, NJ: Savoy Records

Patel AD. 2006. Musical rhythm, linguistic rhythm, and human evolution. *Music Percept.* 24:99–104

Patel AD, Iversen JR. 2014. The evolutionary neuroscience of musical beat perception: the Action Simulation for Auditory Prediction (ASAP) hypothesis. *Front. Sys. Neurosci.* 8:57

Patel AD, Iversen JR, Bregman MR, Schulz I. 2009. Experimental evidence for synchronization to a musical beat in a nonhuman animal. *Curr. Biol.* 19(10):827–30

Pecenka N, Keller PE. 2011. The role of temporal prediction abilities in interpersonal sensorimotor synchronization. *Exp. Brain. Res.* 211(3):505–15

Petrides M, Pandya DN. 2002. Comparative cytoarchitectonic analysis of the human and the macaque ventrolateral prefrontal cortex and corticocortical connection patterns in the monkey. *Eur. J. Neurosci.* 16(2):291–310

Phillips-Silver J, Toiviainen P, Gosselin N, Piché O, Nozaradan S, et al. 2011. Born to dance but beat deaf: a new form of congenital amusia. *Neuropsychologia* 49:961–69

Phillips-Silver J, Trainor LJ. 2005. Feeling the beat: Movement influences infant rhythm perception. *Science* 308:1430

Phillips-Silver J, Trainor LJ. 2007. Hearing what the body feels: auditory encoding of rhythmic movement. *Cognition* 105:533–46

Phillips-Silver J, Trainor LJ. 2008. Vestibular influence on auditory metrical interpretation. *Brain Cogn.* 67(1):94–102

Poon M, Schutz M. 2015. Cueing musical emotions: An empirical analysis of 24-piece sets by Bach and Chopin documents parallels with emotional speech. *Front. Psychol.* 6:1419

Posner MI, Nissen MJ, Klein RM. 1976. Visual dominance: an information-processing account of its origins and significance. *Psychol. Rev.* 83(2):157–71

Povel DJ. 1981. Internal representation of simple temporal patterns. *J. Exp. Psychol. Hum. Percept. Perform.* 7(1):3–18

Radiohead. 1997. Paranoid Android. Recorded by Radiohead, *OK Computer*. London: Parlophone

Repp BH. 2000. Subliminal temporal discrimination revealed in sensorimotor coordination. In *Rhythm Perception and Production*, ed. P Desain, WL Windsor, pp. 129–42. Lisse: Swets & Zeitlinger

Repp BH. 2002. Phase correction following a perturbation in sensorimotor synchronization depends on sensory information. *J. Mot. Behav.* 34(3):291–98

Repp BH. 2005. Sensorimotor synchronization: a review of the tapping literature. *Psychon. Bull. Rev.* 12:969–92

Repp BH, Doggett R. 2007. Tapping to a very slow beat: a comparison of musicians and non-musicians. *Music Percept.* 24:367–76

Repp BH, Keller PE. 2004. Adaptation to tempo changes in sensorimotor synchronization: effects of intention, attention, and awareness. *Q. J. Exp. Psychol.* 57(3):499–521

Repp BH, Penel A. 2002. Auditory dominance in temporal processing: new evidence from synchronization with simultaneous visual and auditory sequences. *J. Exp. Psychol. Hum. Percept. Perform.* 28(5):1085–99

Repp BH, Su YH. 2013. Sensorimotor synchronization: a review of recent research (2006–2012). *Psychon. Bull. Rev.* 20:403–52

Roholt T. 2014. *Groove: A Phenomenology of Musical Nuance*. New York: Bloomsbury

Rosch E. 1978. Principles of categorization. In *Cognition and Categorization*, Vol. 1, ed. E Rosch, BB Lloyd, pp. 27–48. Hillsdale, NJ: Lawrence Erlbaum Assoc.

Rouse AA, Cook PF, Large EW, Reichmuth C. 2016. Beat keeping in a sea lion as coupled oscillation: implications for comparative understanding of human rhythm. *Front. Neurosci.* 10:257

Salmelin R, Hari R. 1994. Spatiotemporal characteristics of sensorimotor neuromagnetic rhythms related to thumb movements. *Neuroscience* 60:537–50

Schachner A, Brady TF, Pepperberg IM, Hauser MD. 2009. Spontaneous motor entrainment to music in multiple vocal mimicking species. *Curr. Biol.* 19(10):831–36

Scharf B, Buus S. 1986. Audition. In *Handbook of Perception and Human Performance*, Vol. 1, ed. KR Boff, L Kaufman, JP Thomas, pp. 14-1–14-71. Hoboken, NJ: Wiley

Schulkind MD. 1999. Long-term memory for temporal structure: evidence from the identification of well-known and novel songs. *Mem. Cogn.* 27(5):896–906

Schuller G. 1968. *Early Jazz: Its Roots and Musical Development*. Oxford, UK: Oxford Univ. Press

Schutz M, Kubovy M. 2009. Causality and cross-modal integration. *J. Exp. Psychol. Hum. Percept. Perform.* 35(6):1791–810

Schutz M, Lipscomb S. 2007. Hearing gestures, seeing music: Vision influences perceived tone duration. *Perception* 36(6):888–97

Schwartze M, Keller PE, Patel AD, Kotz SA. 2011. The impact of basal ganglia lesions on sensorimotor synchronization, spontaneous motor tempo, and the detection of tempo changes. *Behav. Brain Res.* 216(2):685–91

Selezneva E, Deike S, Knyazeva S, Scheich H, Brechmann A, Brosch M. 2013. Rhythm sensitivity in macaque monkeys. *Front. Syst. Neurosci.* 7:49

Senn O, Kilchenmann L, Von Georgi R, Bullerjahn C. 2016. The effect of expert performance microtiming on listeners' experience of groove in swing or funk music. *Front. Psychol.* 7:1487

Sevdalis V, Keller PE. 2014. Know thy sound: perceiving self and others in musical contexts. *Acta Psychol.* 152:67–74

Shiffrar M. 2005. Movement and event perception. In *The Blackwell Handbook of Perception and Cognition*, ed. EB Goldstein, pp. 237–71. Hoboken, NJ: Wiley

Sowiński J, Dalla Bella S. 2013. Poor synchronization to the beat may result from deficient auditory-motor mapping. *Neuropsychologia* 51(10):1952–63

Styns F, van Noorden L, Moelants D, Leman M. 2007. Walking on music. *Hum. Mov. Sci.* 26(5):769–85

Su YH. 2014. Audiovisual beat induction in complex auditory rhythms: point-light figure movement as an effective visual beat. *Acta Psychol.* 151:40–50

Su YH, Jonikaitis D. 2011. Hearing the speed: Visual motion biases the perception of auditory tempo. *Exp. Brain Res.* 214(3):357–71

Su YH, Pöppel E. 2012. Body movement enhances the extraction of temporal structures in auditory sequences. *Psychol. Res.* 76(3):373–82

Su YH, Salazar-López E. 2016. Visual timing of structured dance movements resembles auditory rhythm perception. *Neural Plast.* 2016:1678390

Swaminathan S, Schellenberg EG. 2015. Current emotion research in music psychology. *Emot. Rev.* 7(2):189–97

Talsma D, Senkowski D, Woldorff MG. 2009. Intermodal attention affects the processing of the temporal alignment of audiovisual stimuli. *Exp. Brain Res.* 198(2–3):313–28

Teki S, Grube M, Kumar S, Griffiths TD. 2011. Distinct neural substrates of duration-based and beat-based auditory timing. *J. Neurosci.* 31:3805–12

Thomson JM, Fryer B, Maltby J, Goswami U. 2006. Auditory and motor rhythm awareness in adults with dyslexia. *J. Res. Read.* 29:334–48

Thomson JM, Goswami U. 2008. Rhythmic processing in children with developmental dyslexia: Auditory and motor rhythms link to reading and spelling. *J. Physiol. Paris* 102:120–29

Thompson WF. 2014. *Music in the Social and Behavioral Sciences: An Encyclopedia*. Thousand Oaks, CA: SAGE Publ.

Tierney A, Kraus N. 2013. The ability to tap to a beat relates to cognitive, linguistic, and perceptual skills. *Brain Lang.* 124:225–31

Toiviainen P, Luck G, Thompson MR. 2010. Embodied meter: hierarchical eigenmodes in music-induced movement. *Music Percept.* 28:59–70

Toiviainen P, Snyder JS. 2003. Tapping to Bach: resonance-based model of pulse. *Music Percept.* 21(1):43–80

Trainor LJ, Gao X, Lei JJ, Lehtovaara K, Harris LR. 2009. The primal role of the vestibular system in determining musical rhythm. *Cortex* 45(1):35–43

van der Steen MC, Schwartze M, Kotz SA, Keller PE. 2015. Modeling effects of cerebellar and basal ganglia lesions on adaptation and anticipation during sensorimotor synchronization. *Ann. N. Y. Acad. Sci.* 1337(1):101–10

van Noorden L, Moelants D. 1999. Resonance in the perception of musical pulse. *J. New Music Res.* 28(1):43–66

Varèse E, Wen-Chung C. 1966. The liberation of sound. *Perspect. New Music* 5(1):11–19

Varlet M, Marin L, Issartel J, Schmidt RC, Bardy BG. 2012. Continuity of visual and auditory rhythms influences sensorimotor coordination. *PLOS ONE* 7(9):e44082

Vines BW, Krumhansl CL, Wanderley MM, Dalca IM, Levitin DJ. 2011. Music to my eyes: cross-modal interactions in the perception of emotions in musical performance. *Cognition* 118(2):157–70

Von Ehrenfels CF. 1988 (1890). On "gestalt qualities". In *Foundations of Gestalt Theory*, ed. B Smith, pp. 14–17. Munich: Philosophia Verlag

von Helmholtz H. 1954 (1863). *On the Sensations of Tone.* New York: Dover

Vuust P, Roepstorff A, Wallentin M, Mouridsen K, Ostergaard L. 2006. It don't mean a thing. . . Keeping the rhythm during polyrhythmic tension activates language areas (BA47). *NeuroImage* 31:832–41

Warren RM, Gardner DA, Brubaker BS, Bashford JA Jr. 1991. Melodic and nonmelodic sequences of tones: effects of duration on perception. *Music Percept.* 8:277–90

Welch B. 1973. Hypnotized. Recorded by Fleetwood Mac, *Mystery to Me.* Burbank: Reprise Records

Wing AM, Endo S, Bradbury A, Vorberg D. 2014. Optimal feedback correction in string quartet synchronization. *J. R. Soc.* 11(93):20131125

Winkler I, Háden GP, Ladinig O, Sziller I, Honing H. 2009. Newborn infants detect the beat in music. *PNAS* 106:2468–71

Witek MA, Clarke EF, Wallentin M, Kringelbach ML, Vuust P. 2014. Syncopation, body-movement and pleasure in groove music. *PLOS ONE* 9(4):e94446

Zarco W, Merchant H, Prado L, Mendez JC. 2009. Subsecond timing in primates: comparison of interval production between human subjects and rhesus monkeys. *J. Neurophysiol.* 102(6):3191–202

Zentner M, Eerola T. 2010. Rhythmic engagement with music in infancy. *PNAS* 107(13):5768–73

Multistable Perception and the Role of the Frontoparietal Cortex in Perceptual Inference

Jan Brascamp,[1,*] Philipp Sterzer,[2,*] Randolph Blake,[3,4,*] and Tomas Knapen[5,*]

[1]Department of Psychology, Michigan State University, East Lansing, Michigan 48824

[2]Department of Psychiatry and Psychotherapy, Campus Charité Mitte, Charité–Universitätsmedizin, 10117 Berlin, Germany

[3]Department of Psychology, Vanderbilt University, Nashville, Tennessee 37240; email: randolph.blake@vanderbilt.edu

[4]Vanderbilt Vision Research Center, Vanderbilt University, Nashville, Tennessee 37240

[5]Department of Cognitive Psychology, Vrije Universiteit Amsterdam, 1081BT Amsterdam, Netherlands

Annu. Rev. Psychol. 2018. 69:77–103

First published as a Review in Advance on September 11, 2017

The *Annual Review of Psychology* is online at psych.annualreviews.org

https://doi.org/10.1146/annurev-psych-010417-085944

*All authors contributed equally to this work

Keywords

multistable perception, binocular rivalry, perceptual inference, predictive coding, functional magnetic resonance imaging, transcranial magnetic stimulation

Abstract

A given pattern of optical stimulation can arise from countless possible real-world sources, creating a dilemma for vision: What in the world actually gives rise to the current pattern? This dilemma was pointed out centuries ago by the astronomer and mathematician Ibn Al-Haytham and was forcefully restated 150 years ago when von Helmholtz characterized perception as unconscious inference. To buttress his contention, von Helmholtz cited multistable perception: recurring changes in perception despite unchanging sensory input. Recent neuroscientific studies have exploited multistable perception to identify brain areas uniquely activated in association with these perceptual changes, but the specific roles of those activations remain controversial. This article provides an overview of theoretical models of multistable perception, a review of recent neuroimaging and brain stimulation studies focused on mechanisms associated with these perceptual changes, and a synthesis of available evidence within the context of current notions about Bayesian inference that find their historical roots in von Helmholtz's work.

Contents

INTRODUCTION

The year 2017 marks the 150th anniversary of the publication of the third volume of Herrmann von Helmholtz's monumental three-volume *Handbuch der physiologischen Optik* (von Helmholtz 1867), one of the most important, comprehensive books in the history of sensory physiology. Among the book's many credits is von Helmholtz's explication of the idea that perception entails unconscious inference. The origin of this idea can be traced back almost 1,000 years to the polymath Ibn Al-Haytham, also known as Alhazen (Al-Haytham 1989, Cavanagh 2011, Howard 1996). Centuries later, as pointed out by Wade & Ono (1985), intimations of that idea resurfaced in Wheatstone's famous essay on binocular stereopsis (Wheatstone 1838). But it is von Helmholtz who is credited with resurrecting the idea of unconscious inference with a clarity that ensured its endurance to this day. Specifically, visual perception perforce comprises an inferential process carried out at an unconscious level, the aim being to identify what in the world one is looking at (a challenge dubbed inverse optics in contemporary parlance). This process of "unconscious inference" is essential, so goes the argument, because optical images formed on the retina provide ambiguous information about the specific objects and events that constitute the sources of those retinal images. To resolve those ambiguities, the nervous system must rely on information embodied in prior experience, in expectations, in context, and in the motor activities of the person faced with the challenge of seeing. In other words, the nervous system must make a perceptual decision regarding the most likely state of the world given the evidence from these different sources of information.

The notion that vision entails inference has continued to reverberate throughout the century and a half since von Helmholtz gave new life to Alhazen's idea. Thus, one encounters an appeal to inference-like processes in the writings of Brunswik (1943), Gregory (1980), MacKay (1956), Rock (1983), Neisser (1967), Barlow (Barlow et al. 1972), and Knill & Richards (1996), to name just a few. Besides unconscious inference, various other terms have been used to characterize this process, including analysis by synthesis, hypothesis testing, probabilistic functionalism, cognitive agency, and Bayesian inference. In recent years, the idea has gained substantial traction within computational neuroscience (e.g., Friston 2005, Petrovici et al. 2016, Summerfield & de Lange 2014) with the development of so-called predictive coding models that frame perception as the culmination of dynamical neural activity within a hierarchical predictive system (an idea we return to in our Discussion).

Not only did von Helmholtz champion Alhazen's idea that perception must be an inference-based decision-making process, he also buttressed his conviction with reference to viewing situations where the culmination of this inferential process is laid bare in the viewer's experience. As von Helmholtz (1867, pp. 15–16) put it:

SFM:
structure-from-motion

> Without any change of the retinal images, the same observer [in these situations] may see in front of him various perceptual images in succession, in which case the variation is easy to recognize ... in a case of this sort various perceptual images may be developed; and we should seek ... to discover what circumstances are responsible for the decision one way or the other.

In this quote, von Helmholtz discusses viewing situations that give rise to multistable perception: situations where what an individual is looking at remains invariant but what the individual sees fluctuates over time between alternative, incompatible perceptual interpretations. Von Helmholtz may have been primed for this line of reasoning by reading section 10 of Wheatstone's (1838, pp. 381–82) essay on binocular vision, where Wheatstone comments on viewing situations where "indetermination" of perceptual judgment arises in viewing situations permitting "double interpretation." As one such example, Wheatstone explicitly points to the reversible figure popularly known as the Necker cube. An example of that figure and other classic examples of viewing situations that promote multistable perception are shown in **Figure 1**.

At face value, multistable perception does indeed seem to provide an excellent means for testing theories built around the notion of perception as inference: Metaphorically speaking, when faced with ambiguity or visual conflict, the brain weighs evidence favoring different, alternative hypotheses about what is being viewed, and when that evidence is insufficiently compelling to reject all but one interpretation, the brain vacillates between the alternatives (**Figure 1**, *bottom row*). Indeed, several characteristics of multistable perception comport well with the idea of perception as inference based on multiple information sources. To give some examples:

- When the fidelity of the evidence that favors one interpretation during multistable perception is higher than that of the evidence that favors another, perception is biased toward that former interpretation. Thus during binocular rivalry, a form of multistable perception evoked when the two eyes view dissimilar monocular stimuli (**Figure 1c**), a well-focused monocular stimulus enjoys greater predominance in the observer's perceptual experience than does a blurred one (Arnold et al. 2007, Levelt 1966). Similarly, an ambiguous structure-from-motion (SFM) animation (**Figure 1d**) is more frequently seen to rotate in a given direction when supplementary visual information (e.g., luminance disparity) consistent with that direction is added to the display (Dosher et al. 1986).

- When the ecological likelihood of one perceptual outcome is higher than that of a competing outcome, the more plausible interpretation predominates. Thus, when viewing an ambiguous SFM stimulus, perceived rotational motion tends to be resolved in favor of the rotational direction implied by friction, in obedience to physical principles (Gilroy & Blake 2004). In a similar vein, a visual stimulus portraying a ground surface dominates in binocular rivalry over a stimulus portraying a ceiling surface, presumably reflecting the ground-plane perspective's salience for humans, who spend nearly all our time navigating on ground surfaces (Ozkan & Braunstein 2009).

- When stimulus information from another, nonvisual sensory modality accompanies viewing of a multistable display, that auxiliary information can boost predominance in favor of the visual interpretation that is consistent with the nonvisual input. These kinds of ancillary multisensory interactions have been reported for multistability elicited by an ambiguous face picture (i.e., old woman/young girl figure) accompanied by unambiguous voices (Hsiao

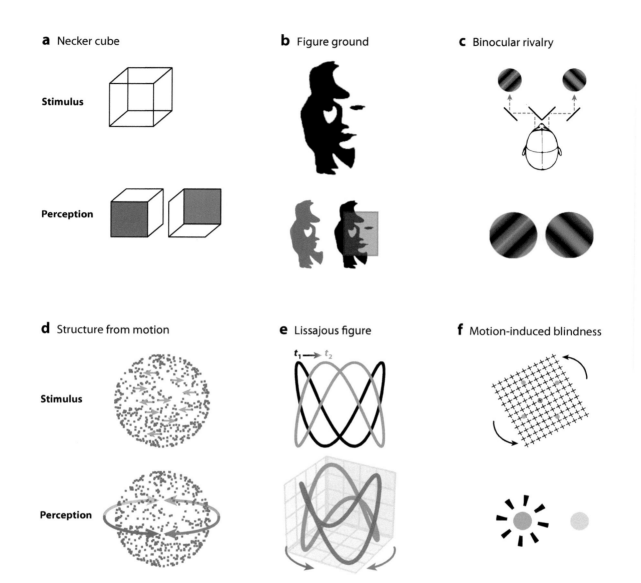

a Necker cube

Stimulus

Perception

b Figure ground

c Binocular rivalry

d Structure from motion

Stimulus

Perception

e Lissajous figure

$t_1 \rightarrow t_2$

f Motion-induced blindness

Figure 1

Examples of multistable stimuli (*top rows*) and their associated perceptual interpretations, schematically indicated in red and blue (*bottom rows*). (*a*) The Necker cube is ambiguous in terms of the three-dimensional geometry it pictorially represents. Two different cube faces can be perceived as the forward-facing side of the cube. (*b*) Ambiguities in figure–ground assignment promote alternative interpretations of the pictorial content, which, in this stimulus, can correspond to either a saxophone player or a woman's face. (*c*) Binocular rivalry takes place when the two eyes view dissimilar monocular images, presented in this case through a stereoscope. At any given moment, the dominant percept corresponds to one of the two eyes' images. (*d*) Motion is a potent visual cue to spatial structure, leading to the perceptual phenomenon of structure-from-motion or the kinetic depth effect. When the projection of a sphere of dots is presented orthographically, depth order is ambiguous, and the sphere can be seen to rotate with the front-surface dots moving either leftward or rightward. (*e*) Lissajous figures are also ambiguous structure-from-motion stimuli. When viewing this stimulus, transitions between the perceptual interpretations of the nearest line segment moving left or right are temporally confined to moments of self-occlusion. (*f*) Motion-induced blindness occurs when static stimuli (*yellow circles*) are presented near a moving surface. The static stimuli periodically disappear from the viewer's awareness. Panel *b* is reproduced with the kind permission of Roger Shepard, the copyright holder of this image (Shepard 1990).

et al. 2012) and by ambiguous apparent motion stimuli paired with tactile motion (Conrad et al. 2012). In the case of binocular rivalry, there are multiple examples of auxiliary, nonvisual influences, such as rivalry involving visual musical notation accompanied by melodic sound (Lee et al. 2015), visual gratings paired with tactile stimulation by a grooved surface (Lunghi et al. 2010), or pictures of familiar objects accompanied by distinct odors (Zhou et al. 2012).

- When a given visual interpretation is more consistent than a competing interpretation with the current behavioral context, perceptual dominance favors the interpretation implied by the context (Sundareswara & Schrater 2008). Thus, for example, a self-controlled, rotating globe dominates in binocular rivalry compared to the same globe rotating in the same manner but not under the viewer's control (Maruya et al. 2007).

- Multistable perception is influenced by prior experience and expectations. When observers are repeatedly exposed to the same ambiguous stimulus, perception upon each new stimulus presentation strongly tends to be the same as the percept during the preceding presentation (Leopold et al. 2002, Orbach et al. 1963, Pearson & Brascamp 2008). Similarly, perception of ambiguous stimuli can also be strongly biased by prior exposure to an unambiguous stimulus (priming) (Pearson et al. 2008, Schmack et al. 2016). Moreover, it is also well documented that learned expectations—both implicit and explicit—can bias the interpretation of perceptually ambiguous stimuli (Di Luca et al. 2010; Schmack et al. 2013a, 2016; Sterzer et al. 2008).

fMRI: functional magnetic resonance imaging

TMS: transcranial magnetic stimulation

EEG: electroencephalography

Scientific interest in multistable perception has endured since the time of von Helmholtz, but different eras have had different emphases and angles on the subject. During the past few decades, much research has been concerned with the search for neural processes that bring about the spontaneous perceptual alternations that characterize multistable perception. For instance, functional magnetic resonance imaging (fMRI) research has focused on neural events that specifically accompany the transitions between perceptual states, hoping that those events could provide insights into the inference processes that govern the dynamics of multistable perception. In this article, we review this body of work and evaluate it in the light of von Helmholtz's and Alhazen's ideas. In particular, we first give an overview of theoretical models of multistable perception and their implications for perceptual inference. We then review recent neuroimaging and brain stimulation work that has focused on the mechanisms underlying transitions in multistable perception, also touching on an ongoing controversy regarding the involvement of frontal and parietal brain regions in this context. Finally, we attempt to provide a synthesis of the available empirical evidence within current models of perceptual inference.

Methodologically, the focus of our review is primarily psychophysical observations combined with transcranial magnetic stimulation (TMS) and fMRI—these are the approaches that, in our view, have promoted the substantial progress witnessed in recent years. This means that our discussions do not touch on related work involving approaches such as electroencephalography (EEG; reviewed in Kornmeier & Bach 2012) or assessment of multistable perception in lesion patients (e.g., Ricci & Blundo 1990, Valle-Inclan & Gallego 2006). Nevertheless, some of our more general points are likely to be relevant to that work as well.

MECHANISMS CAUSING PERCEPTUAL TRANSITIONS IN MULTISTABLE PERCEPTION

Although it makes sense to focus on the time period surrounding perceptual transitions when trying to understand their cause, the neural processes that lead to transitions are not necessarily confined to this time period alone. Existing attempts to model the dynamics of multistable perception posit rapid neural changes at the time of the transition, as well as gradual changes during quiescent periods when perception remains stable between transitions. In this section, we review and link two dominant classes of such models and illustrate the relevant concepts in **Figure 2**.

Traditionally, dynamical systems accounts of multistable perception assume three neurally plausible ingredients shaping the time course of multistable perception: inhibition, adaptation, and neural noise (Hock et al. 2003, Kalarickal & Marshall 2000, Laing & Chow 2002, McDougall 1903). Under such accounts, separate pools of neurons, each representing the information pertaining to one of the two perceptual interpretations, exert mutual inhibition on one another. It is this inhibition that allows one interpretation's neuronal pool to suppress activity in the neuronal pool representing the other interpretation, thus temporarily promoting coherent perceptual dominance of one of the two alternatives (**Figure 2a**). During these dominance periods, activity in the dominant pool diminishes as a result of adaptation (**Figure 2b**, *top*); the dominant pool thereby slowly relinquishes its suppressive grip on the other until the balance of power tips and a rapid transition

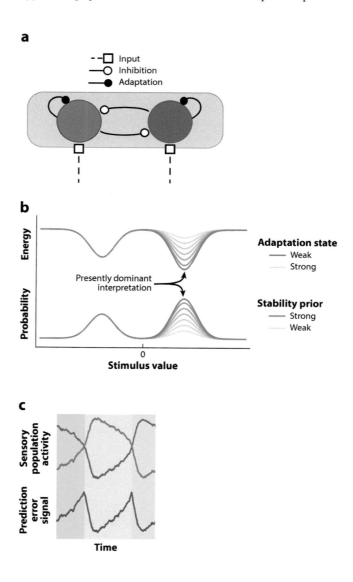

occurs (**Figure 2c**, *top*). When multiple cycles of alternating dominance are allowed, the process will further involve recovery from adaptation of the now-suppressed pool. Thus, in this view, the relative activations of the perceptual interpretations are continually modulated by adaptation and those activations change rapidly during the transition. Additionally, various sources of noise combine to introduce variability in the time elapsing between successive transitions (Kang & Blake 2011, Moreno-Bote et al. 2007). Evidence from psychophysics, brain imaging, and neuropharmacology supports the involvement of each of these three ingredients (Alais et al. 2010, Blake et al. 2003, Pastukhov & Braun 2011, van Loon et al. 2013; although see Sandberg et al. 2016), and simulations of dynamical systems models that employ these ingredients capture hallmark temporal characteristics of multistability (Brascamp et al. 2006, Noest et al. 2007, Wilson 2007).

This traditional conceptualization has recently been supplemented by conceptualizations that frame perceptual multistability in terms of the Bayesian principle of predictive coding (Gershman et al. 2012, Hohwy et al. 2008, Kanai et al. 2011, Megumi et al. 2015, Schmack et al. 2016, Schrater & Sundareswara 2006, Weilnhammer et al. 2017). On the face of it, predictive coding theories are more closely related to von Helmholtz's and Alhazen's ideas, in the sense that they are explicitly phrased in terms of inference. In particular, under these theories, perception results from hierarchical Bayesian inference, in which each level of the processing hierarchy forms a hypothesis to predict, in a feedback fashion, the input received by the level below it. This lower level, in turn, sends upward a so-called prediction-error signal that codes the discrepancy between this prediction and the actual input, and the predictive model is then adjusted on the basis of this discrepancy (Friston 2005, Hohwy 2012, Lee & Mumford 2003). Perception, in this framework, is the result of iterative adjustments across all levels of the hierarchy, mirroring von Helmholtz's conceptual notion that perception would involve a neural reconstruction of the hypothesized cause of input. According to one model of multistable perception that conforms to this predictive coding view (Hohwy et al. 2008), a stimulus that gives rise to multistable perception provides equally strong sensory evidence (Bayesian likelihood) for two (or more) different percepts, but the currently dominant percept establishes an implicit prediction (prior) that perception will remain similar in the near future. This stabilizing prediction would be implemented as feedback from higher to lower hierarchical levels. The application of Bayes' rule combines the sensory evidence

---

Figure 2

Mechanisms of multistable perception. (*a*) In the dynamical systems account, multistable perception results from mutual inhibition between, and adaptation of, distinct neural populations that correspond to the alternative perceptual states. (*b*) (*top*) The dynamical system can be represented by means of an energy landscape in which the system state tends to occupy the lowest point in the landscape (the bottom of a so-called well). During the dominance period of a perceptual interpretation, adaptation decreases the depth of the presently occupied well and leads to the occurrence of a transition to the other, now deeper, well. (*b*) (*bottom*) In the predictive coding account of multistable perception, the presently dominant state remains dominant as a result of a stability prior, thought to reflect learned temporal characteristics of the world. The fact that sensory input of the suppressed interpretation is unexplained leads to prediction errors that gradually decrease the strength of the stability prior, eventually ushering in a transition between perceptual interpretations. (*c*) Results of a simulation using a dynamical systems model. Red and blue shaded regions indicate periods of perceptual dominance of the two alternative interpretations. The top part of the panel depicts neural activations of two sensory neuronal pools evolving antagonistically (each color corresponds to one neuronal pool). The bottom part of the panel depicts one potential component of the predictive coding account, i.e., a prediction error–type signal, which can be modeled as the relative amount of suppressed sensory activation at different points in time. This signal, in this case constructed by taking the negative value of the square of the difference between sensory activations, slowly builds up during a perceptual dominance period and peaks at the time of the transition.

with the stability prior into a posterior that represents stronger evidence for the dominant percept but still contains residual evidence for the suppressed percept. This residual evidence, in turn, is tantamount to a prediction error that percolates through the hierarchy in a feed-forward fashion, and this leads to the update of the stability prior. This progressive updating of the prior based on the unexplained sensory information draws the posterior toward the suppressed percept and eventually results in a perceptual transition (**Figure 2b**, *bottom*).

Conceptual differences notwithstanding, the dynamical systems and predictive coding accounts of multistable perception are strikingly similar in terms of the dynamics of the processes they portray, as illustrated by **Figures 2b** (*bottom*) and **2c** (*bottom*). For example, accumulation of unexplained prediction error in the predictive coding account parallels the buildup of adaptation in the traditional dynamical systems account (**Figure 2c**, *bottom*), and one might consider whether adaptation is simply a description, in the context of dynamical systems, of the changing stability prior of the predictive coding account. Of note, conceptual connections between adaptation and predictions have been drawn by researchers working on problems quite different from multistable perception (Grotheer & Kovács 2016, Srinivasan et al. 1982, Stefanics et al. 2014). Even though both accounts of multistable perception suggest similar dynamic properties, a potentially important difference is that dynamical systems models are usually interpreted in terms of local neural circuits at sensory processing stages, whereas the inherent hierarchical structure of predictive coding models can naturally incorporate higher levels of processing such as those putatively mediated by frontal and parietal brain regions. This difference becomes particularly relevant as our review of the literature on perceptual transitions unfolds because much debate regarding that topic centers on the putative involvement of frontal and parietal brain regions.

It should be noted that there are other theories about perceptual alternations that have little to do with inference or with low-level neural adaptation, a prime example being the interhemispheric switching hypothesis. Advocates of this position, like many theorists, focus on the paradigm of binocular rivalry (Miller et al. 2000, Pettigrew & Miller 1998); according to them, binocular rivalry involves competition between alternative perceptual representations embodied in neural activity within the separate brain hemispheres, and the switching itself is governed by signals originating in bistable, subcortical oscillators. This provocative idea puts a very different twist on the account of transition-related neural activity, and it seems incompatible with the empirical evidence as presented in the following sections. Still, the oscillator model has parsimony on its side when it comes to explaining the correlation in alternation frequencies for different kinds of multistable phenomena (Carter & Pettigrew 2003; see also the sidebar titled Varieties of Multistable Perception: Different yet Fundamentally the Same?).

PERCEPTUAL STATE TRANSITIONS AS A WINDOW ONTO PERCEPTUAL INFERENCE

As previewed in the Introduction, multistable perception provides a potentially revealing means for studying the inferential processes implicated in perception. Our aim is to review work that centers on the perceptual transitions during multistable perception, events that provide clearly demarcated, measurable time stamps signifying a neural state change in the putative inference process. Specifically, our emphasis is on neural events, identified through neuroimaging, that accompany transitions, as well as on changes in alternation frequency that are brought about by neurostimulation. In recent years, considerable empirical evidence on both of these topics has emerged, and our review identifies the common findings across studies. In addition, uncertainty and controversy exist regarding the interpretation of the empirical data, and we also provide a tentative synthesis that ties multistability to the more general notion of perceptual inference.

VARIETIES OF MULTISTABLE PERCEPTION: DIFFERENT YET FUNDAMENTALLY THE SAME?

Do various instances of multistable perception arise from a single neural network or mechanism, or from neural events implemented within different networks varying not only in anatomical location but also in the underlying mechanism? Consider the configurations in **Figure 1**. The source of conflict in these configurations varies: Conflict arises from ambiguity about border ownership in **Figure 1b**, from eye-of-origin competition in **Figure 1c**, and from underspecification of 3D structure in **Figure 1d**. Moreover, multistability perceptually manifests itself in diverse ways: In some instances, perceived stimulus organization fluctuates (**Figure 1a,b,d,e**), whereas in others, salient stimulus components perceptually disappear and then reappear (**Figure 1c,f**). Still, these distinct forms of multistable perception share common properties, including statistical characteristics of the durations of perceptual dominance and dependence on stimulus characteristics such as salience (Brascamp et al. 2015b, Klink et al. 2008). Moreover, the rate at which perception fluctuates [a stable trait within a given individual (Schmack et al. 2013b)] correlates significantly across different stimuli (Carter & Pettigrew 2003). Perhaps, then, fluctuations in perceptual state result from canonical computations performed by different neural substrates. For that matter, the neural substrates promoting multistability may vary depending on an observer's task and the larger behavioral context in which that task is performed, an idea explored in this review.

The chapter of scientific history reviewed in this article starts in 1998. In one of the first, highly influential fMRI studies on multistable perception, Lumer et al. (1998) measured blood-oxygen-level dependent (BOLD) signals associated with perceptual transitions during binocular rivalry. To dissociate the specific neural processes involved in spontaneous perceptual transitions from those evoked by actual changes in visual stimulation, they used a version of the replay condition devised by Blake & Fox (1974) (see also the sidebar titled Replaying Multistable Perception). To implement this replay condition, Lumer and colleagues first recorded the sequence of perceptual transitions indicated by the participants during binocular rivalry and then mimicked this sequence by physically presenting two stimuli in alternation. Lumer et al. found that activity in a number of brain regions was greater during spontaneous perceptual transitions than during these re-played transitions. These regions included a right-lateralized network of brain areas in the frontal and parietal cortices, and several of these regions overlapped with those identified in a second study performed in the same year, in which multistability was elicited using ambiguous images (Kleinschmidt et al. 1998). The apparent involvement of this frontoparietal brain network could be construed to imply a literal relation between reasoning and perceptual inference, as regions in this network are thought to be involved in high-level, cognitive operations such as visual working memory (Todd & Marois 2004), perceptual decision making (Heekeren et al. 2004), and inhibitory control (Aron et al. 2004), as well as in shifting spatial attention (Silver et al. 2006, Yantis et al. 2002) and guiding eye movements (Corbetta et al. 1998). Moreover, the right hemisphere lateralization bias is reminiscent of the dominant role of right hemisphere parietal regions in spatial attention (Corbetta & Shulman 2002, Sheremata & Silver 2015, Sheremata et al. 2010), and rightward lateralization is also observed in the distribution of noradrenergic locus coeruleus terminals to frontoparietal regions (Corbetta et al. 2008) that change the dynamics of the cognitive processes these brain regions perform (Aston-Jones & Cohen 2005, Eldar et al. 2013). Lumer et al. (1998, p. 1933) themselves proposed a close association between multistable perception and attention (fully concordant with von Helmholtz's views on that matter, incidentally) and suggested that both "call upon a common neural machinery in frontoparietal cortex, involved in the selection of neuronal events leading to visual awareness."

BOLD:
blood-oxygen-level dependent

REPLAYING MULTISTABLE PERCEPTION

To isolate the unique neural source of endogenous perceptual transitions, some neuroimaging studies have contrasted transition-related activations with those associated with on-screen, animated, replay transitions. However, any perceptual difference between these two event types could also contribute to the signal revealed by this contrast (Knapen et al. 2011). Formal analyses of perceptual equivalence are rare and, when performed, confined to certain aspects of the transition, such as its duration (Weilnhammer et al. 2013). It is, furthermore, our personal impression that replay transitions are often easily perceptually distinguishable from endogenous transitions, at least for trained observers. Perhaps, then, analysis contrasts involving conventional replay conditions do not effectively isolate the inferential neural processes of interest in the present context. Thus, researchers would have to create replay transitions that better approximate the real perceptual experience (Knapen et al. 2011, Weilnhammer et al. 2013), so that, in the limit of perceptual indistinguishability, this type of replay contrast finds the neural processes genuinely involved in the perceptual inference process. Interestingly, recent paradigms that render transitions perceptually indistinct (Brascamp et al. 2015a, Zou et al. 2016) can thus also be thought of as involving replay: Any successful attempt to render transitions perceptually indistinguishable from periods during which no transition happens makes those periods a perfect replay of sorts.

The putative link with high-level cognition was subsequently elaborated in an influential review article by Leopold & Logothetis (1999). In that article, the authors endorsed a causal role for frontoparietal activations in perceptual multistability by proposing an "iterative and random system of 'checks and balances', whereby higher integrative centers periodically force perception to reorganize or 'refresh'" (Leopold & Logothetis 1999, p. 261). In the decades following these seminal papers, a number of brain imaging studies have, by and large, replicated the finding of greater right-lateralized frontoparietal activations during spontaneous than during stimulus-induced perceptual transitions (as reviewed in more detail in the section Functional Neuroimaging of Multistable Perception), regardless of the stimulus paradigm used to evoke multistability. Lumer et al.'s (1998) interpretation of the data, however, remains just one of several proposed alternatives, which are reviewed in the Discussion section.

Around the same time, there began to appear studies using transcranial magnetic stimulation (TMS) to transiently influence neural processing in areas of the right parietal and frontal cortices and, then, to assess resulting changes in the cycle of perceptual transitions. Although both categories of studies—fMRI and TMS—tended to highlight the right frontal and parietal cortices, upon closer inspection, there are differences in the functional anatomies implicated by results derived from these two different methodologies. To make explicit which frontoparietal regions are most relevant to this review, we first provide a meta-analysis that shows which brain areas have been implicated most commonly, without reference to interpretation. After that, we provide a historical overview that also touches on potential interpretations that have competed in the literature.

META-ANALYSIS OF CORTICAL TOPOGRAPHY OF FUNCTIONAL MAGNETIC RESONANCE IMAGING AND TRANSCRANIAL MAGNETIC STIMULATION FINDINGS

Figure 3 shows the results of a meta-analysis across 10 neuroimaging studies, as well as the two loci targeted in the majority of relevant TMS studies. Although methodologies varied across the neuroimaging studies summarized in this section, in each case the included analysis derived something akin to the difference maps between spontaneous perceptual transitions and replayed transitions produced by Lumer et al. (1998). Our meta-analysis confirms that the areas showing differential BOLD activations in such comparisons are located predominantly in the right hemisphere. Focusing on this hemisphere, several hotspots that consistently crop up are highlighted using a color scale that ranges from red to yellow. The most consistently reported region is located in the inferior frontal cortex (IFC) and encompasses the anterior insula and the inferior frontal gyrus (sometimes termed the inferior frontal junction or inferior precentral sulcus, which forms the posterior boundary of the inferior frontal gyrus). Another focus of activation in the frontal cortex is in the superior precentral sulcus [also termed the frontal eye field (FEF)]. There are also activations in a more anterior lateral region, which we refer to as the dorsolateral prefrontal cortex (DLPFC), but these are less consistent than those in the other two loci. In the parietal lobe, the main locus of transition-related activation straddles the intraparietal sulcus (IPS), extending more extensively into the superior parts of the anterior parietal lobe (i.e., into the superior parietal lobule) than into the inferior parts (inferior parietal lobule). The second focus of parietal activation lies in a more anterior and lateral direction, in the temporoparietal junction (TPJ). Interestingly, most if not all of these regions are known to be organized retinotopically: Within these regions, the anatomical distances between neurons that respond to stimulation of different visual field locations mirror those locations' relative positions in visual space, resulting in orderly representations of visual space along the cortical surface, known as retinotopic maps (Jerde et al. 2012, Silver & Kastner 2009, Silver et al. 2005, Swisher et al. 2007).

The blue disks in **Figure 3** mark the two parietal loci that are most commonly targeted in TMS studies. Although imaging and neurostimulation results can be conveniently construed as two sides of the same coin when it comes to parietal involvement in multistability, it is noteworthy that the main locus of parietal BOLD activation in this meta-analysis does not coincide with either of the TMS loci. We discuss this in detail when reviewing TMS results in the section Brain Stimulation.

In the Discussion, we speculate about the roles played in multistability by the five areas identified by this meta-analysis. For now, we want to reiterate what others have noted (e.g., Leopold & Logothetis 1999, Sterzer et al. 2009), namely, the extensive overlap between this set of areas and those that compose the dorsal and ventral attention-related networks identified by Corbetta and colleagues (Corbetta & Shulman 2002, Corbetta et al. 2008). The dorsal attention system includes the anterior IPS and FEF bilaterally and is thought to be involved in preparing and applying goal-directed (top-down) selection for stimuli and responses. The ventral attention system comprises the right TPJ and IFC and is thought to be specialized for the detection of behaviorally relevant stimuli, particularly when they are salient or unexpected. This ventral system has been hypothesized to work as a circuit breaker for the dorsal system, directing attention to salient events. Such a division of labor between ventral and dorsal regions may also play a role in the context of multistable perception, subserving different aspects of the perceptual inference process.

Having identified the overall anatomical pattern that emerges from the body of work reviewed in this section, we proceed in the next section to an overview, organized roughly chronologically, of the specific questions asked by various authors and of the interpretations and discussions that have emerged. We start with work using fMRI and then turn to studies that have used TMS.

FUNCTIONAL NEUROIMAGING OF MULTISTABLE PERCEPTION

The central question running throughout this literature is not whether the frontoparietal areas highlighted in **Figure 3** show transition-related, endogenous BOLD activations, as this pattern of activations is consistent across studies. Rather, the question is what function those activations reflect. Although the BOLD activations may reflect inferential processes that give rise to the new

IFC: inferior frontal cortex

FEF: frontal eye field

DLPFC: dorsolateral prefrontal cortex

IPS: intraparietal sulcus

TPJ: temporoparietal junction

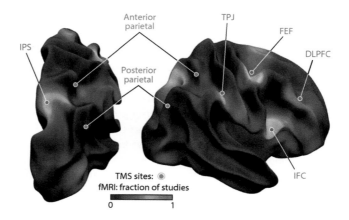

Figure 3

Results of fMRI and TMS meta-analysis. Posterior (*left*) and lateral (*right*) views on the inflated standard-brain right cortical hemisphere. For each included fMRI study, we took the MNI locations of peak activations from reported analyses that were conceptually similar to the "endogenous transitions > replay" contrast in Lumer et al. (1998). In other words, these analyses were designed to incorporate a basic control for nonspecific activations such as those associated with key presses. Studies without such analyses were not included, nor were some recent analyses that were designed to be more restrictive. In cases where Talairach coordinates were reported, these were converted to MNI coordinates using the transform proposed by Lancaster et al. (2007; see also **http://sdmproject.com/utilities/?show=Coordinates**). MNI coordinates were converted to vertex locations on an average surface using FreeSurfer, after which we smoothed these locations with a 15 mm Gaussian window on the surface. Thus, for the fMRI results, the red and yellow shading represents, for each vertex, the fraction of evaluated fMRI studies on multistable perception that report a peak activation in an approximately 15 mm vicinity on the surface. For the TMS data, the markers correspond to the MNI coordinates of the two locations most commonly targeted by TMS studies: (36, −45, 51) and (38, −64, 32) (Kanai et al. 2011). The included literature for the fMRI data, along with the analysis used in each case, is as follows: Brascamp et al. (2015a), transition without key press > no transition, "different colors" condition; Frässle et al. (2014), transition with key press > replay transition with key press; Kleinschmidt et al. (1998), transition with key press > key press without transition; Knapen et al. (2011), transition with key press > "instantaneous" replay transition with key press; Lumer et al. (1998), transition with key press > replay transition with key press; Lumer & Rees (1999), time-series correlation with Brodmann area 18/19 during rivalry without key presses > during replay without key presses; Megumi et al. (2015), transition with key press > replay transition with key press; Sterzer & Kleinschmidt (2007), transition with key press > replay transition with key press; Weilnhammer et al. (2013), transition with key press > replay transition with key press; Zaretskaya et al. (2010), transition with key press > replay transition with key press. Abbreviations: DLPFC, dorsolateral prefrontal cortex; FEF, frontal eye field; fMRI, functional magnetic resonance imaging; IFC, inferior frontal cortex; IPS, intraparietal sulcus; MNI, Montreal Neurological Institute; TMS, transcranial magnetic stimulation; TPJ, temporoparietal junction.

perceptual interpretation, the broad range of cognitive functions supported by these areas (Todd & Marois 2004) suggests a second, alternative interpretation: Perhaps the activations in these areas reflect elevated cognitive demands that result from the occurrence of a perceptual transition. For instance, the unpredictable transitions may capture an observer's attention or may require heightened scrutiny when the observer is required to report them. This ambiguity in interpreting the origins of these activations has been acknowledged from the beginning: It motivated Lumer and colleagues (1998) to employ the replay condition and has since motivated other design choices in this field.

One of the earliest studies to follow up on Lumer and colleagues' work was performed by Sterzer & Kleinschmidt (2007). In an experiment involving ambiguous apparent motion, these investigators confirmed that activation in IFC was greater during spontaneous perceptual transitions than during replay. As noted above, the IFC in the right hemisphere is also the region that most consistently appears in the studies covered in our meta-analysis (**Figure 3**). To explore whether this IFC activation reflects a causal role or an ancillary consequence of perceptual transitions, Sterzer & Kleinschmidt performed chronometric analyses of the transition-related BOLD signal time courses. They found an earlier onset of the BOLD response in the right IFC associated with spontaneous transitions, as compared to replayed transitions, and no such onset difference in any other brain region, including occipital and parietal regions. The earlier onset of transition-related activation in the right IFC was interpreted as indicating a role for this brain region in inducing perceptual reorganizations, an idea advanced earlier by Leopold & Logothetis (1999). However, it should be noted that conclusions from such chronometric analyses of fMRI signals—even when appropriately grounded in demonstrating a region-by-condition interaction that removes effects of local variations in neurovascular coupling (Sterzer & Kleinschmidt 2007)—are still limited by our incomplete understanding of the relationship between neural activity and hemodynamic responses.

Knapen et al. (2011) raised concerns regarding the approaches of Lumer et al. and Sterzer & Kleinschmidt. These authors focused on the unique character of perceptual transitions originating endogenously, noting that such transitions are often not instantaneous and, instead, take time to unfold, unlike the exogenously created transitions used in studies up until that time, i.e., transitions involving instantaneous changes from one on-screen stimulus to the other. This difference between endogenous and exogenous transitions introduces two potential concerns. First, the subtle but real timing differences between these two conditions are relevant for chronometric analyses, which rely on small temporal differences. Second, any imperfection in the perceptual match between spontaneous and replayed transitions can contribute to a BOLD signal difference between the two types of transitions. To quantify the duration of perceptual transitions, Knapen and colleagues required participants to report both the onset and the offset of transitions during binocular rivalry, as well as during ambiguous motion perception. They then devised two distinct replay conditions: a traditional one with near-instantaneous transitions and a modified replay condition, in which on-screen simulations of transitions were matched in visual complexity and duration to those recorded during rivalry. In the condition with traditional replay, this study replicated the finding of greater transition-related activations during multistable perception in much the same regions as had been implicated in previous studies (Lumer et al. 1998, Sterzer & Kleinschmidt 2007), but, when using the duration-matched replay, no difference between conditions was observed. This observation suggested that greater transition-related activation during multistable perception may be explained by a mismatch in perceptual properties between multistable perception and replay, rather than by neural activity that corresponds to the causal origin of perceptual transitions (see also the sidebar titled Replaying Multistable Perception).

The role of transition duration was also addressed by Weilnhammer et al. (2013) using a type of SFM stimulus called a Lissajous figure (**Figure 1e**). Using careful behavioral assessment, Weilnhammer and colleagues established that perceptual transitions generated by this stimulus are reliably abrupt and are thus equivalent temporally to those in an unambiguous replay version. In other words, when comparing brain activation associated with the two conditions, transition duration can be ruled out as a confounding factor. Still, Weilnhammer and colleagues observed greater activation in a right-lateralized frontoparietal network resembling the network identified in earlier studies, which rendered it unlikely that differences in transition duration were the sole explanation for these activations. Moreover, analyses of effective connectivity using dynamic causal modeling (Friston et al. 2003) showed that enhanced activity accompanying perceptual transitions was associated with a modulation of connectivity from the IFC to the visual cortex, arguing for a top-down effect of the IFC on visual processing in association with perceptual transitions.

Another question arises when interpreting the traditional frontoparietal activations accompanying perceptual transitions: Are these activations dependent on the task being performed by the participant (Knapen et al. 2011)? One possibility is that frontal and parietal regions play a role in the act of reporting perceptual events. In a recent study, Frässle et al. (2014) directly addressed this question by inferring participants' perceptual transitions from objective ocular-motor data rather than relying on manual report (see also Tsuchiya et al. 2015; see the sidebar titled No-Report Paradigms). In this study, binocular rivalry was induced between two gratings that had a particularly large spatial extent and that differed in either mean luminance or motion direction, thus allowing the investigators to distinguish between the two possible perceptual states by analyzing pupil size and optokinetic nystagmus, respectively. In this no-report condition, as compared to the traditional condition, the contrast between spontaneous and replayed perceptual transitions yielded a weaker signal in some frontoparietal regions. The result was most pronounced in the right DLPFC, where any remaining signal did not reach statistical significance in the no-report condition. The FEF and IFC, however, still showed significant activations even without report, echoing earlier findings (Weilnhammer et al. 2013). This suggests differential functional roles for frontal subregions in multistable perception, with the right DLPFC being specifically involved in registering and reporting perceptual transitions, but with responses in the other regions also reflecting additional aspects that are unrelated to active report. The notion that some frontoparietal signals persist even without manual report is consistent with results from an early study that also involved a no-report paradigm (Lumer & Rees 1999).

Brascamp et al. (2015a) recently employed a different tactic to distinguish various influences on frontoparietal involvement around the time of transitions. Given that factors such as task relevance and salience of the perceptual transition play a role in the work reviewed above, Brascamp and colleagues asked whether frontoparietal regions still show elevated BOLD responses when perceptual transitions go unnoticed. They developed a binocular rivalry procedure in which the two eyes were presented with different visual motion stimuli and perception demonstrably switched between these two inputs. However, the stimuli were designed in such a way that the transitions were so inconspicuous as to become unreportable. Interestingly, transition-related frontoparietal activations were minimized by this procedure. This suggests that frontoparietal regions may not be involved in rivalry transitions that are not consciously registered, implying that transitions prompted by conflicting input do not necessarily require the involvement of higher-level brain circuits, at least in situations where the transitions are not consciously registered.

This tentative interpretation received further support from a study by Zou et al. (2016), who induced binocular rivalry between two color-modulated gratings that were rendered invisible by means of rapid counter-phase flicker and the onset of which produced no detectable BOLD activations in frontal and parietal areas. These invisible gratings produced rivalry dynamics similar to those of visible gratings, further strengthening the notion that higher-level brain circuits are unnecessary for eliciting transitions during binocular rivalry (see also Giles et al. 2016).

Studies such as those by Brascamp et al. (2015a) and Zou et al. (2016) contribute to the incremental deconstruction of the cascade of perceptual and cognitive events that surround transitions in multistable perception and thereby help elucidate the functional nature of frontal and parietal involvement. However, this type of result, which pivots on invisibility or unreportability, cannot easily be translated from binocular rivalry to other forms of multistable perception, such as that arising from ambiguous figures (**Figure 1**), which inherently and inevitably involve transitions between perceptually distinct states. Thus, the role of certain brain areas in perceptual transitions may vary depending on the nature of the sensory conflict and perceptual experience. Although the visual system may be able to resolve the conflict between competing monocular inputs at a local level (see also Xu et al. 2016), integration of a broader range of information, coded by a broader set of brain areas, may be involved when the alternating states evoke distinguishable perceptual experiences and when transitions between these states are behaviorally relevant.

The studies reviewed above were all designed to disambiguate the specifics of the role of frontoparietal involvement in perceptual transitions. Several other fMRI studies have also replicated Lumer and colleagues' empirical result, yet without the specific aim of arbitrating between alternative hypotheses. In particular, in a study investigating the effect of TMS on the transition rate in binocular rivalry, Zaretskaya et al. (2010) performed an fMRI experiment to determine, in each participant, the regions that showed greater activation in association with perceptual transitions during standard reported binocular rivalry relative to a conventional replay condition; this experiment replicated Lumer and colleagues' result. A further replication using ambiguous SFM was provided by Megumi et al. (2015) (as discussed in more detail in the section Functional Roles of Frontal and Parietal Subregions). Other studies have performed more advanced analyses on patterns of frontoparietal BOLD data collected during multistable perception, again without the specific objective of disambiguating various causal explanations (e.g., Wang et al. 2013, Watanabe et al. 2014).

Rather than having to rely on particular design features of an fMRI study, a more direct strategy to infer causal involvement of particular brain regions in perceptual transitions is via TMS. In particular, several studies have used TMS to interfere temporarily with the function of various brain regions during perceptual multistability and, thus, to assess the effect of such virtual lesions on perceptual transitions. This work has focused mostly on the parietal cortex, so when thinking roughly in terms of frontoparietal involvement, such work would seem to address the same questions as the fMRI studies discussed above. But the links between results from these two types of methods deserve closer examination, and in the next section, we review existing TMS work with a special focus on these links (see Ngo et al. 2013 for a review with a different focus).

BRAIN STIMULATION

The earliest work using brain stimulation in the context of perceptual multistability was not explicitly guided by functional imaging results. In a pioneering study, Miller et al. (2000) found that single TMS pulses applied to the left hemisphere of observers experiencing binocular rivalry hastened a transition in dominance from the currently dominant stimulus to the other, currently suppressed monocular stimulus. This finding was interpreted as supporting the interhemispheric switching hypothesis mentioned above (Miller et al. 2000, Pettigrew & Miller 1998). Follow-up work showed a similar effect during motion-induced blindness (**Figure 1f**), this time with single pulses delivered to either the left or the right hemisphere (Funk & Pettigrew 2003). TMS coil placement in both of these studies was guided by scalp landmarks and, consequently, the specific brain structures receiving maximal TMS are unknown, but it is plausible that the parietal cortex was among the brain areas impacted by TMS in both cases. A later study observed that TMS to the occipital cortex also can prompt the occurrence of a perceptual transition in binocular rivalry (Pearson et al. 2007).

In a number of more recent TMS studies, coil placement was guided by high-resolution anatomical images obtained using MRI, making it easier to draw explicit parallels between those results and fMRI data. Arguably the most-established finding in this context is that the dynamics of perceptual multistability can be influenced by TMS applied to a locus quite anterior along the IPS [anterior parietal in **Figure 3**; its location in standard coordinates would place this locus in or near retinotopic maps IPS4–5 (Konen & Kastner 2008)]. Even though this locus does not coincide exactly with the parietal hotspot identified in our meta-analysis (**Figure 3**), it does regularly show up in the BOLD contrast between spontaneous and replayed transitions, and some TMS studies have specifically targeted this location on the basis of transition-related BOLD signals in binocular rivalry (Carmel et al. 2010, Zaretskaya et al. 2010). One study that involved offline (i.e., prior to stimulus presentation) TMS to this area observed an increased incidence of transitions (i.e., shorter percept durations) during subsequent binocular rivalry for right-hemisphere stimulation (Carmel et al. 2010). This finding was later replicated using an ambiguous SFM stimulus (Kanai et al. 2011). Although the two studies used different TMS protocols, both protocols are thought to cause reduced neural excitability in the targeted region. A study that targeted essentially the same parietal locus using an altogether different TMS protocol with online stimulation (i.e., during stimulus presentation) observed a decreased incidence of binocular rivalry transitions (Zaretskaya et al. 2010). This study stimulated the locus in both hemispheres and, although confirming an overall stronger TMS effect in the right hemisphere, demonstrated that the degree of lateralization in individual participants correlated with the degree of lateralization of the transition-related BOLD responses. Another study provided evidence that TMS of that parietal area can also affect perceptual transitions for intermittently presented ambiguous stimuli (Vernet et al. 2015). It seems reasonable to assume that differences in TMS protocol can explain the differences in effect direction reported in various studies, and, taken together, there is a compelling body of work implicating this anterior IPS region in perceptual multistability. The case is further supported by structural imaging findings showing that high gray matter density in this region correlates with longer percept durations (Kanai et al. 2011, Watanabe et al. 2014).

In several TMS studies, this anterior locus was examined in combination with a site more posterior along the IPS [posterior parietal in **Figure 3**; based on standard coordinates, this site is about 2.7 cm removed from the anterior one and would lie near retinotopic map IPS1 (Konen & Kastner 2008, Szczepanski et al. 2010)]. Using an ambiguous SFM stimulus, one study provided evidence that an offline TMS protocol that accelerates the alternation cycle when applied over the anterior locus (Kanai et al. 2011) instead decelerates the cycle when applied over this posterior locus, regardless of hemisphere (Kanai et al. 2010). Similarly, this study found that gray matter density in this posterior region was positively correlated with shorter dominance durations (see also Watanabe et al. 2014), again the opposite of what was found for the anterior region. With regard to fMRI findings, there is relatively little evidence that the posterior locus falls within the areas that typically show enhanced transition-related BOLD responses [one region-of-interest analysis centered on the locus demonstrated such a response (Megumi et al. 2015)].

Taken together, these results provide compelling evidence that different regions along the IPS, especially in the right hemisphere, play distinct roles in perceptual multistability. Evidence for a role in multistability is not as strong for the posterior locus as it is for the anterior locus, and a recent replication study provided further support for involvement of the anterior locus but did not corroborate involvement of the posterior locus (Sandberg et al. 2016). Regardless of the status of the posterior locus, however, there is reason to believe that the effects found for the anterior coordinates are localized to that particular region along the IPS. For instance, one study found an effect on perceptual multistability when stimulating the anterior locus but not when stimulating a region only slightly more posterior (Zaretskaya et al. 2010).

The possibility that different regions along the IPS differ in their function during perceptual multistability makes it more difficult to interpret results from studies that positioned their TMS coils using less precise methods. In particular, several studies stimulated the right parietal cortex by targeting electrode P4 of the international 10–20 EEG system, the location of which varies considerably among participants (de Graaf et al. 2011, Sack et al. 2009), although it appears closer, on average, to the posterior locus than to the anterior one (de Graaf et al. 2011). This might explain why some such studies observed a reduced frequency of perceptual transitions for an ambiguous apparent motion stimulus following inhibitory TMS and an increased frequency following facilitatory TMS (Ge et al. 2008, Nojima et al. 2010; see VanRullen et al. 2008 for a potentially related finding), whereas a different study found no effect for an ambiguous SFM stimulus (de Graaf et al. 2011).

Very little TMS evidence is available for frontal regions. De Graaf et al. (2011) observed no influence of right frontal TMS on the perceptual cycle, although the same manipulation did influence participants' ability to volitionally control this cycle. A double-coil experiment, furthermore, led to the suggestion that TMS to this same frontal locus might interact with the effects of parietal TMS on multistable perception (Vernet et al. 2015). The implications of these findings in relation to functional imaging results are not entirely clear because the specific frontal area targeted in these studies does not seem to fall within the set of areas indicated by our meta-analysis (it appears to lie somewhat anterior to the FEF hotspot shown in **Figure 3**).

FUNCTIONAL ROLES OF FRONTAL AND PARIETAL SUBREGIONS

What can we conclude regarding the functional involvement of the frontal and parietal cortices in multistable perception? Can we differentiate among putative, distinct roles played by various subregions? We can say that the transition-related BOLD signal in these regions is diminished in paradigms that preserve perceptual transitions but reduce associated cognitive demands by manipulating perceptual salience or behavioral relevance. These regions' involvement, then, may be partly in evaluating and acting on a perceptual event in its wake. At the same time, it is also conceivable that involvement of a given brain region in perceptual inference itself may depend on whether the underlying sensory conflict is relevant perceptually or behaviorally.

Among the implicated frontal regions, the right IFC stands out as the strongest candidate for playing a directive role in perceptual transitions. It is the area most consistently implicated by fMRI BOLD contrasts (**Figure 3**), and analyses of chronometry and functional connectivity also support this notion. The weakest candidate, in turn, appears to be the right anterior DLPFC, given its lack of consistent activation in our meta-analysis and the observation by Frässle et al. (2014) that activation of this region was linked to manual report. By suggesting that the right IFC might be more closely associated with perception and the DLPFC with action, these results bring to mind a posterior-to-anterior gradient in frontal cortical function that has been suggested in other contexts (Azuar et al. 2014, Badre et al. 2009). More anterior regions along this gradient would be involved in more abstract representations and in later stages of the perception–action cycle (Fuster & Bressler 2012). Supporting this view, recent work investigating the functional roles of frontal cortical subregions in perceptual decision making shows that distinct frontal regions along a posterior-to-anterior gradient support the control of progressively later stages of the perceptual decision-making process (Rahnev et al. 2016, Sterzer 2016). During a demanding perceptual decision-making task, the FEF was engaged in perceptual selection processes, whereas the DLPFC supported criterion-setting processes. Finally, a particular anterior region within the right DLPFC was involved in the metacognitive evaluation of perceptual decisions (Rahnev et al. 2016). In the context of perceptual decisions in situations of multistable perception, a similar functional subdivision of the frontal cortex may apply, with more posterior regions such as the right IFC playing a role in the process of perceptual interpretation and more anterior regions being involved in metacognitive processes, such as introspection, that are required for active report (Frässle et al. 2014). In the context of perceptual inference, one potential role of the right IFC might be to respond to prediction errors arising in the sensory cortex, a suggestion elaborated in the Discussion. One footnote to the overall relatively strong evidence regarding the right IFC comes from the study that provided the first structural imaging evidence for parietal involvement in multistable perception (see the section Brain Stimulation; Kanai et al. 2010). This same study also specifically examined a frontal cortex region extremely close to the right IFC locus of our meta-analysis (**Figure 3**), yet found no structural correlates with multistable perception in that region.

Regarding the parietal cortex, the most compelling evidence for a causal role in perceptual transitions is associated with the right anterior IPS region (discussed above). Although the transition-related BOLD signal in this region is not spared from the dependence on task relevance, as discussed above for frontal regions, this is the only specific brain region that has been implicated by both fMRI and TMS work, and, moreover, it is the sole region where TMS and structural MRI findings have been replicated multiple times.

TMS researchers have speculated about the functional nature of parietal involvement in multistable perception. Although it is reasonable to point to right parietal involvement in attention function (Carmel et al. 2010, Kanai et al. 2011, Zaretskaya et al. 2010), given plausible relations between attention and perceptual multistability (Bressler et al. 2008, Leopold & Logothetis 1999), the available evidence does not favor any specific attention-related account. For instance, an account that likens perceptual transitions to attention shifts would have to accommodate the fact that fMRI BOLD correlates of attention shifts are typically located in considerably more medial regions than either of the TMS sites discussed above (Serences 2004, Yantis et al. 2002). More generally, the functional anatomy of the parietal cortex in terms of attention does not provide clear clues as to why TMS influences on multistable perception would be so specifically localized to these particular loci along the IPS. One study attempted to address this issue by investigating the influence on attention tasks of the specific TMS manipulations previously used in studies of perceptual multistability but found no evidence for altered attention function (Schauer et al. 2016). An alternative functional account of the parietal TMS results was inspired by the hierarchical predictive coding ideas we discuss at the beginning of this review (Clark 2013, Friston 2005, Hohwy et al. 2008) and is, in that sense, more directly related to our present theme. This account holds that the anterior locus and the posterior locus play complementary roles in perception, with the anterior locus providing a top-down hypothesis as to the interpretation of sensory input and the posterior locus coding the discrepancy between this hypothesis and the present sensory signal (Kanai et al. 2011, Megumi et al. 2015). An additional piece of the puzzle regarding parietal involvement is provided by the finding that the anterior parietal locus has strong functional connectivity with large parts of the transition-related frontoparietal network, whereas the posterior locus has strong functional connectivity with a different network that includes areas in the temporal cortex and on the medial wall (Baker et al. 2015). This latter network overlaps substantially with areas where BOLD signals are reduced, rather than enhanced, in association with perceptual alternations (Brascamp et al. 2015a), corroborating the idea that studies using parietal TMS have tapped into two genuinely complementary networks involved in resolving perceptual ambiguity.

DISCUSSION

Von Helmholtz's work is seminal in a rich tradition of thought stating that perception can be usefully understood as the process of inference based on both current sensory input and contextual information such as that provided by past experience and generic world knowledge. A principal motive for this line of thought is the notion that current sensory signals alone cannot unambiguously stipulate the real-world source of those signals. Perceptual multistability, with its plain separation between sensation and perception, was recognized by Wheatstone and developed later by von Helmholtz as a prime illustration of this notion that perception requires added ingredients besides sensory evidence. But how are these sources of contextual information integrated in the computations that generate our perceptual experiences? In this final section, we attempt to coalesce the findings reviewed above by evaluating how the empirical work relates to hypothesized mechanisms of multistable perception, focusing in particular on the ways in which top-down mechanisms, which may provide contextual information, can impact perception during perceptual multistability.

Both of the theoretical accounts described at the beginning of this review, i.e., the traditional dynamical systems account of adaptation and inhibition and the predictive coding account, posit a relative diminution of the dominant perceptual state's neural representation during the period leading up to the perceptual transition (**Figure 2**). The functional properties of the right IFC would suggest that it is exquisitely sensitive to such reduced fidelity of the current sensory signal (Haynes et al. 2005, Heekeren et al. 2004, Sunaert et al. 2000), and it is tempting to speculate that this characteristic is perhaps shared by other regions such as the anterior parietal lobe and TPJ (see Sterzer et al. 2009 for a similar suggestion). This suggests a first possible conceptualization of the nature of top-down influences during multistable perception. Transition-related activation in these regions may be related to the rising prediction error or falling fidelity of the sensory signal during a process that culminates in a switch to the previously suppressed perceptual state. Direct empirical support for this idea comes from a recent fMRI study that estimated the time course of prediction errors during multistable motion perception using a Bayesian predictive-coding model (Weilnhammer et al. 2017). Concordant with the IFC's known role in sensory decision making (Baldauf & Desimone 2014, Heekeren et al. 2004) and inhibitory control (Aron et al. 2014), this region's response to the gradual change in sensory regions could be to provide feedback to these sensory regions, peaking around the time of the perceptual transitions. In the context of perceptual inference, one might think of this feedback in terms of top-down hypotheses, a reading that would certainly be consistent with one proposed role of the anterior parietal lobe during multistability (Kanai et al. 2011).

Under this first conceptualization, then, top-down signals would be most strongly associated with destabilization of sensory representations and might be expected to start rising before the actual perceptual transition. However, a second potential role that top-down signals might play, not mutually exclusive with the first, would associate those signals more strongly with stabilization of sensory representations and with the period that follows the transition. In this view, top-down signals would play a reinforcing role in the process of settling into a new perceptual state after the temporary neural instability signified by a perceptual alternation. One could liken such a top-down role to the roles suggested in perceptual decision making, where making and committing to a perceptual decision can impact the content of the concomitant perceptual experience (Jazayeri & Movshon 2006, 2007) and the neural activity underlying it (Nienborg & Cumming 2009). Such a post hoc stabilizing role would be consistent with the observation that neural events around the time of transitions, reflected in magnetoencephalography signals, prolong subsequent perceptual phases in motion-induced blindness (Kloosterman et al. 2015). There is, furthermore, a close mutual tie between the act of reporting a perceptual decision and the perceptual decision process itself (Cisek & Pastor-Bernier 2014, Lepora & Pezzulo 2015), suggesting a natural explanation for the observed contribution of perceptual report on transition-related frontal activity in multistable perception (Frässle et al. 2014).

Regardless of the precise role of top-down signals in multistable perception, predictive coding accounts of perception have the benefit of entailing back-and-forth interactions between successive levels, in a process that repeats many times and reverberates throughout an extended hierarchy. As such, accounts that fall along these lines might naturally encompass both bottom-up and top-down factors involved in multistable perception, and they might also fit with the observation that the involvement of many regions can evidently be eliminated by stripping away various perceptual and cognitive aspects of the sensory conflict. The right IFC, for instance, may register in a bottom-up fashion prediction errors that are generated at sensory processing levels, but it may also send a prediction-based signal down to sensory processing levels, and its involvement may depend on the extent to which the competing sensory solutions correspond in fact to distinguishable perceptual states, an extent that is minimized in recent studies of binocular rivalry (Brascamp et al. 2015a, Zou et al. 2016). At the same time, even if higher-level factors can be stripped away in certain conditions, the associated brain areas might nevertheless influence the perceptual cycle in other conditions where those factors remain in play.

Although many of the ideas discussed in this section are tentative, we anticipate that crucial information regarding the specific mechanisms underlying multistable perception will become available thanks to recent methodological advances. For instance, top-down and bottom-up streams of information processing should become more clearly separable using methods such as band-limited encephalography (Bastos et al. 2015, Donner & Siegel 2011, Siegel et al. 2012), high-resolution fMRI acquisition techniques that allow the independent imaging of the different cortical layers (Fracasso et al. 2016, Kok et al. 2016), and methods for inferring effective connectivity from neuroimaging data (Friston et al. 2003). Similarly, a recent increase in sophistication in pupillometric methods (Cheadle et al. 2014, de Gee et al. 2014, Knapen et al. 2016) should help elucidate decision-related and action-related changes in cortical state (Harris & Thiele 2011; McGinley et al. 2015a,b) that might accompany perceptual transitions and that are likely reflected in pupil size fluctuations (Hupé et al. 2009, Naber et al. 2011, Sara 2009).

To conclude, it has been 150 years since von Helmholtz elaborated on Alhazen's ideas about perceptual inference and highlighted multistable perception as prima facie evidence for a central role of inference in perception. The findings surveyed in this review—derived from psychophysics, brain imaging, and TMS—attest to the validity of his view and the prescience of von Helmholtz's realization of the illuminating quality of perceptual multistability on the inferential nature of perception. Those of us actively involved in researching the details of those inference-like processes are indebted to his insight, and although we may disagree on the details of those processes, we are united in our respect for the unifying power of his ideas.

FUTURE ISSUES

1. Future studies will need to distinguish the specific roles that individual frontal subregions play in multistable perception. This research can be guided by the hypothesis, discussed in this review, of a functional gradient within the frontal cortex from perceptual interpretation in posterior regions to deliberative mental activity in anterior regions (see also Sterzer 2016). A related, but more specific, guiding hypothesis is that the DLPFC is not involved in the generation, but only in the report, of perceptual alternations (see also Frässle et al. 2014).

2. If it is true that the neural substrate of perceptual switching depends to a great extent on the nature of the conflict and the perceptual experience, it will be necessary to identify what determines this substrate and how this relates to the functional roles played by the neural components involved.

3. Research should continue working toward a unified picture of the effects of right IPS TMS on the rate of alternations in multistable perception. Work in this direction should focus on clarifying the dependence on stimulation protocol and on examining the extent to which the effects found for stimulation of the posterior locus can be replicated.

4. Future research should determine the extent to which candidate accounts of multistable perception can explain the pronounced individual differences in rates of perceptual fluctuations and whether those differences are associated with individual differences in other cognitive functions, such as perceptual decision making and metacognitive efficiency, subserved by the brain areas putatively involved in perceptual switching.

5. How do top-down signals arising from (the report of) a transition impact the representation of ambiguous information in the visual cortex? Recent methodological advances that allow the separation of top-down and bottom-up information flows could elucidate this issue.

6. Assuming that predictive coding is a homeostatic process, what are the time scales for inducing biases in perceptual state based on learning, reward, or context, and how are those instantiated neurally?

7. Given that many parallels exist between accounts of multistability that focus on factors such as adaptation and inhibition and accounts phrased in terms of predictive coding, future studies should establish whether the two are, in fact, distinguishable and, if so, arbitrate between the two classes of accounts.

8. More generally, the enduring popularity of the metaphor of perception as inference could be construed as evidence for its validity, but also as a sign that the idea seamlessly blends in with a wide range of scientific viewpoints and empirical findings. To express this thought in a contemporary voice, how would one go about disproving that perception entails predictive coding?

DISCLOSURE STATEMENT

The authors are not aware of any affiliations, memberships, funding, or financial holdings that might be perceived as affecting the objectivity of this review.

ACKNOWLEDGMENTS

P.S. is supported by the German Research Foundation (grants STE1430/6-2 and STE1430/7-1), R.B. is supported by a Centennial Research Award from Vanderbilt University, and T.K. is supported by CAS-NWO Joint Research Project 012.200.012. We thank Patrick Cavanagh and Nicholas Wade for helpful pointers concerning historical roots of the concept of perceptual inference.

LITERATURE CITED

Al-Haytham I. 1989. *The Optics of Ibn Al-Haytham: On Direct Vision*, Books I–III, ed. AI Sabra, transl. AI Sabra. London: Warburg Inst.

Alais D, Cass J, O'Shea RP, Blake R. 2010. Visual sensitivity underlying changes in visual consciousness. *Curr. Biol.* 20(15):1362–67

Alais D, Keetels M, Freeman AW. 2014. Measuring perception without introspection. *J. Vis.* 14(11):1

Arnold DH, Grove PM, Wallis TSA. 2007. Staying focused: a functional account of perceptual suppression during binocular rivalry. *J. Vis.* 7(7):7.1–8

Aron AR, Robbins TW, Poldrack RA. 2004. Inhibition and the right inferior frontal cortex. *Trends Cogn. Sci.* 8(4):170–77

Aron AR, Robbins TW, Poldrack RA. 2014. Inhibition and the right inferior frontal cortex: one decade on. *Trends Cogn. Sci.* 18(4):177–85

Aston-Jones G, Cohen JD. 2005. An integrative theory of locus coeruleus-norepinephrine function: adaptive gain and optimal performance. *Annu. Rev. Neurosci.* 28:403–50

Azuar C, Reyes P, Slachevsky A, Volle E, Kinkingnehun S, et al. 2014. Testing the model of caudo-rostral organization of cognitive control in the human with frontal lesions. *NeuroImage* 84:1053–60

Badre D, Hoffman J, Cooney JW, D'Esposito M. 2009. Hierarchical cognitive control deficits following damage to the human frontal lobe. *Nat. Neurosci.* 12(4):515–22

Baker DH, Karapanagiotidis T, Coggan DD, Wailes-Newson K, Smallwood J. 2015. Brain networks underlying bistable perception. *NeuroImage* 119:229–34

Baldauf D, Desimone R. 2014. Neural mechanisms of object-based attention. *Science* 344(6182):424–27

Barlow HB, Narasimhan R, Rosenfeld A. 1972. Visual pattern analysis in machines and animals. *Science* 177(49):567–75

Bastos AM, Vezoli J, Bosman CA, Schoffelen J-M, Oostenveld R, et al. 2015. Visual areas exert feedforward and feedback influences through distinct frequency channels. *Neuron* 85(2):390–401

Blake R, Fox R. 1974. Adaptation to invisible gratings and the site of binocular rivalry suppression. *Nature* 249(456):488–90

Blake R, Sobel KV, Gilroy LA. 2003. Visual motion retards alternations between conflicting perceptual interpretations. *Neuron* 39(5):869–78

Brascamp JW, Brascamp J, Blake R, Knapen T. 2015a. Negligible fronto-parietal BOLD activity accompanying unreportable switches in bistable perception. *Nat. Neurosci.* 18(11):1672–78

Brascamp JW, Klink PC, Levelt W. 2015b. The 'laws' of binocular rivalry: 50 years of Levelt's propositions. *Vis. Res.* 109:20–37

Brascamp JW, van Ee R, Noest AJ, Jacobs RHAH, van den Berg AV. 2006. The time course of binocular rivalry reveals a fundamental role of noise. *J. Vis.* 6(11):1244–56

Bressler SL, Tang W, Sylvester CM, Shulman GL, Corbetta M. 2008. Top-down control of human visual cortex by frontal and parietal cortex in anticipatory visual spatial attention. *J. Neurosci.* 28(40):10056–61

Brouwer GJ, van Ee R. 2007. Visual cortex allows prediction of perceptual states during ambiguous structure-from-motion. *J. Neurosci.* 27(5):1015–23

Brown RJ, Norcia AM. 1997. A method for investigating binocular rivalry in real-time with the steady-state VEP. *Vis. Res.* 37(17):2401–8

Brunswik E. 1943. Organismic achievement and environmental probability. *Psychol. Rev.* 50(3):255–72

Carmel D, Walsh V, Lavie N, Rees G. 2010. Right parietal TMS shortens dominance durations in binocular rivalry. *Curr. Biol.* 20(18):R799–800

Carter OL, Pettigrew JD. 2003. A common oscillator for perceptual rivalries? *Perception* 32(3):295–305

Cavanagh P. 2011. Visual cognition. *Vis. Res.* 51(13):1538–51

Cheadle S, Wyart V, Tsetsos K, Myers N, de Gardelle V, et al. 2014. Adaptive gain control during human perceptual choice. *Neuron* 81(6):1429–41

Cisek P, Pastor-Bernier A. 2014. On the challenges and mechanisms of embodied decisions. *Philos. Trans. R. Soc. Lond. Biol. Sci.* 369(1655):20130479

Clark A. 2013. Whatever next? Predictive brains, situated agents, and the future of cognitive science. *Behav. Brain Sci.* 36(3):181–204

Conrad V, Vitello MP, Noppeney U. 2012. Interactions between apparent motion rivalry in vision and touch. *Psychol. Sci.* 23(8):940–48

Corbetta M, Akbudak E, Conturo TE, Snyder AZ, Ollinger JM, et al. 1998. A common network of functional areas for attention and eye movements. *Neuron* 21(4):761–73

Corbetta M, Patel G, Shulman GL. 2008. The reorienting system of the human brain: from environment to theory of mind. *Neuron* 58(3):306–24

Corbetta M, Shulman GL. 2002. Control of goal-directed and stimulus-driven attention in the brain. *Nat. Rev. Neurosci.* 3(3):201–15

de Gee JW, Knapen T, Donner TH. 2014. Decision-related pupil dilation reflects upcoming choice and individual bias. *PNAS* 111(5):E618–25

de Graaf TA, de Jong MC, Goebel R, van Ee R, Sack AT. 2011. On the functional relevance of frontal cortex for passive and voluntarily controlled bistable vision. *Cereb. Cortex* 21(10):2322–31

Di Luca M, Ernst MO, Backus BT. 2010. Learning to use an invisible visual signal for perception. *Curr. Biol.* 20(20):1860–63

Donner TH, Siegel M. 2011. A framework for local cortical oscillation patterns. *Trends Cogn. Sci.* 15(5):191–99

Dosher BA, Sperling G, Wurst SA. 1986. Tradeoffs between stereopsis and proximity luminance covariance as determinants of perceived 3D structure. *Vis. Res.* 26(6):973–90

Eldar E, Cohen JD, Niv Y. 2013. The effects of neural gain on attention and learning. *Nat. Neurosci.* 16(8):1146–53

Fox R, Todd S, Bettinger LA. 1975. Optokinetic nystagmus as an objective indicator of binocular rivalry. *Vis. Res.* 15(7):849–53

Fracasso A, Petridou N, Dumoulin SO. 2016. Systematic variation of population receptive field properties across cortical depth in human visual cortex. *NeuroImage* 139:427–38

Frässle S, Sommer J, Jansen A, Naber M, Einhäuser W. 2014. Binocular rivalry: frontal activity relates to introspection and action but not to perception. *J. Neurosci.* 34(5):1738–47

Friston K. 2005. A theory of cortical responses. *Philos. Trans. R. Soc. Lond. Biol. Sci.* 360(1456):815–36

Friston KJ, Harrison LM, Harrison L, Penny W. 2003. Dynamic causal modelling. *NeuroImage* 19(4):1273–302

Funk AP, Pettigrew JD. 2003. Does interhemispheric competition mediate motion-induced blindness? A transcranial magnetic stimulation study. *Perception* 32(11):1325–38

Fuster JM, Bressler SL. 2012. Cognit activation: a mechanism enabling temporal integration in working memory. *Trends Cogn. Sci.* 16(4):207–18

Ge S, Ueno S, Iramina K. 2008. Effects of repetitive transcranial magnetic stimulation on perceptual reversal. *J. Magnet. Soc. Jpn.* 32(4):458–61

Gershman SJ, Vul E, Tenenbaum JB. 2012. Multistability and perceptual inference. *Neural Comput.* 24(1):1–24

Giles N, Lau H, Odegaard B. 2016. What type of awareness does binocular rivalry assess? *Trends Cogn. Sci.* 20(10):719–20

Gilroy LA, Blake R. 2004. Physics embedded in visual perception of three-dimensional shape from motion. *Nat. Neurosci.* 7(9):921–22

Gregory RL. 1980. Perceptions as hypotheses. *Philos. Trans. R. Soc. Lond. Biol. Sci.* 290(1038):181–97

Grotheer M, Kovács G. 2016. Can predictive coding explain repetition suppression? *Cortex* 80:113–24

Harris KD, Thiele A. 2011. Cortical state and attention. *Nat. Rev. Neurosci.* 12(9):509–23

Haynes J-D, Driver J, Rees G. 2005. Visibility reflects dynamic changes of effective connectivity between V1 and fusiform cortex. *Neuron* 46(5):811–21

Haynes J-D, Rees G. 2005. Predicting the stream of consciousness from activity in human visual cortex. *Curr. Biol.* 15(14):1301–7

Heekeren HR, Marrett S, Bandettini PA, Ungerleider LG. 2004. A general mechanism for perceptual decision-making in the human brain. *Nature* 431(7010):859–62

Hock HS, Schöner G, Giese M. 2003. The dynamical foundations of motion pattern formation: stability, selective adaptation, and perceptual continuity. *Percept. Psychophys.* 65(3):429–57

Hohwy J. 2012. Attention and conscious perception in the hypothesis testing brain. *Front. Psychol.* 3:96

Hohwy J, Roepstorff A, Friston K. 2008. Predictive coding explains binocular rivalry: an epistemological review. *Cognition* 108(3):687–701

Howard IP. 1996. Alhazen's neglected discoveries of visual phenomena. *Perception* 25(10):1203–17

Hsiao J-Y, Chen Y-C, Spence C, Yeh S-L. 2012. Assessing the effects of audiovisual semantic congruency on the perception of a bistable figure. *Conscious. Cogn.* 21(2):775–87

Hupé J-M, Lamirel C, Lorenceau J. 2009. Pupil dynamics during bistable motion perception. *J. Vis.* 9(7):10

Jazayeri M, Movshon JA. 2006. Optimal representation of sensory information by neural populations. *Nat. Neurosci.* 9(5):690–96

Jazayeri M, Movshon JA. 2007. A new perceptual illusion reveals mechanisms of sensory decoding. *Nature* 446(7138):912–15

Jerde TA, Merriam EP, Riggall AC, Hedges JH, Curtis CE. 2012. Prioritized maps of space in human frontoparietal cortex. *J. Neurosci.* 32(48):17382–90

Kalarickal GJ, Marshall JA. 2000. Neural model of temporal and stochastic properties of binocular rivalry. *Neurocomputing* 32–33:843–53

Kanai R, Bahrami B, Rees G. 2010. Human parietal cortex structure predicts individual differences in perceptual rivalry. *Curr. Biol.* 20(18):1626–30

Kanai R, Carmel D, Bahrami B, Rees G. 2011. Structural and functional fractionation of right superior parietal cortex in bistable perception. *Curr. Biol.* 21(3):R106–7

Kang M-S, Blake R. 2011. An integrated framework of spatiotemporal dynamics of binocular rivalry. *Front. Hum. Neurosci.* 5:88

Kleinschmidt A, Büchel C, Zeki S, Frackowiak RSJ. 1998. Human brain activity during spontaneously reversing perception of ambiguous figures. *Proc. Biol. Sci.* 265(1413):2427–33

Klink PC, van Ee R, van Wezel RJA. 2008. General validity of Levelt's propositions reveals common computational mechanisms for visual rivalry. *PLOS ONE* 3(10):e3473

Kloosterman NA, Meindertsma T, Hillebrand A, van Dijk BW, Lamme VAF, Donner TH. 2015. Top-down modulation in human visual cortex predicts the stability of a perceptual illusion. *J. Neurophysiol.* 113(4):1063–76

Knapen T, Brascamp J, Pearson J, van Ee R, Blake R. 2011. The role of frontal and parietal brain areas in bistable perception. *J. Neurosci.* 31(28):10293–301

Knapen T, de Gee JW, Brascamp J, Nuiten S, Hoppenbrouwers S, Theeuwes J. 2016. Cognitive and ocular factors jointly determine pupil responses under equiluminance. *PLOS ONE* 11(5):e0155574

Knill DC, Richards W. 1996. *Perception as Bayesian Inference*. Cambridge, UK: Cambridge Univ. Press

Kok P, Bains LJ, van Mourik T, Norris DG, de Lange FP. 2016. Selective activation of the deep layers of the human primary visual cortex by top-down feedback. *Curr. Biol.* 26(3):371–76

Konen CS, Kastner S. 2008. Representation of eye movements and stimulus motion in topographically organized areas of human posterior parietal cortex. *J. Neurosci.* 28(33):8361–75

Kornmeier J, Bach M. 2012. Ambiguous figures—what happens in the brain when perception changes but not the stimulus. *Front. Hum. Neurosci.* 6:51

Laing CR, Chow CC. 2002. A spiking neuron model for binocular rivalry. *J. Comput. Neurosci.* 12(1):39–53

Lancaster JL, Tordesillas-Gutiérrez D, Martinez M, Salinas F, Evans A, et al. 2007. Bias between MNI and Talairach coordinates analyzed using the ICBM-152 brain template. *Hum. Brain Mapp.* 28(11):1194–205

Lee M, Blake R, Kim S, Kim C-Y. 2015. Melodic sound enhances visual awareness of congruent musical notes, but only if you can read music. *PNAS* 112(27):8493–98

Lee TS, Mumford D. 2003. Hierarchical Bayesian inference in the visual cortex. *J. Opt. Soc. Am. Opt. Image Sci. Vis.* 20(7):1434–48

Leopold DA, Logothetis NK. 1999. Multistable phenomena: changing views in perception. *Trends Cogn. Sci.* 3(7):254–64

Leopold DA, Wilke M, Maier A, Logothetis NK. 2002. Stable perception of visually ambiguous patterns. *Nat. Neurosci.* 5(6):605–9

Lepora NF, Pezzulo G. 2015. Embodied choice: how action influences perceptual decision making. *PLOS Comput. Biol.* 11(4):e1004110

Levelt WJM. 1966. The alternation process in binocular rivalry. *Br. J. Psychol.* 57(3–4):225–38

Lumer ED, Friston KJ, Rees G. 1998. Neural correlates of perceptual rivalry in the human brain. *Science* 280(5371):1930–34

Lumer ED, Rees G. 1999. Covariation of activity in visual and prefrontal cortex associated with subjective visual perception. *PNAS* 96(4):1669–73

Lunghi C, Binda P, Morrone MC. 2010. Touch disambiguates rivalrous perception at early stages of visual analysis. *Curr. Biol.* 20(4):R143–44

MacKay DM. 1956. Towards an information-flow model of human behaviour. *Br. J. Psychol.* 47(1):30–43

Mamassian P, Goutcher R. 2005. Temporal dynamics in bistable perception. *J. Vis.* 5(4):7–15

Maruya K, Yang E, Blake R. 2007. Voluntary action influences visual competition. *Psychol. Sci.* 18(12):1090–98

McDougall W. 1903. The nature of inhibitory processes within the nervous system. *Brain* 26(2):153–91

McGinley MJ, David SV, McCormick DA. 2015a. Cortical membrane potential signature of optimal states for sensory signal detection. *Neuron* 87(1):179–92

McGinley MJ, Vinck M, Reimer J, Batista-Brito R, Zagha E, et al. 2015b. Waking state: rapid variations modulate neural and behavioral responses. *Neuron* 87(6):1143–61

Megumi F, Bahrami B, Kanai R, Rees G. 2015. Brain activity dynamics in human parietal regions during spontaneous switches in bistable perception. *NeuroImage* 107:190–97

Miller SM, Liu GB, Liu GB, Ngo TT, Hooper G, et al. 2000. Interhemispheric switching mediates perceptual rivalry. *Curr. Biol.* 10(7):383–92

Moreno-Bote R, Rinzel J, Rubin N. 2007. Noise-induced alternations in an attractor network model of perceptual bistability. *J. Neurophysiol.* 98(3):1125–39

Naber M, Frässle S, Einhäuser W. 2011. Perceptual rivalry: reflexes reveal the gradual nature of visual awareness. *PLOS ONE* 6(6):e20910

Neisser U. 1967. *Cognitive Psychology*. New York: Appleton-Century-Crofts

Ngo TT, Barsdell WN, Law PCF, Miller SM. 2013. Binocular rivalry, brain stimulation and bipolar disorder. In *The Constitution of Visual Consciousness*, ed. SM Miller, pp. 211–52. Amsterdam: John Benjamins

Nienborg H, Cumming BG. 2009. Decision-related activity in sensory neurons reflects more than a neuron's causal effect. *Nature* 459(7243):89–92

Noest AJ, van Ee R, Nijs MM, van Wezel RJA. 2007. Percept-choice sequences driven by interrupted ambiguous stimuli: a low-level neural model. *J. Vis.* 7(8):10

Nojima K, Ge S, Katayama Y, Iramina K. 2010. Time change of perceptual reversal of ambiguous figures by rTMS. *Conf. Proc. IEEE Eng. Med. Biol. Soc.* 2010:6579–82

Orbach J, Ehrlich D, Heath HA. 1963. Reversibility of the Necker cube. I. An examination of the concept of "satiation of orientation." *Percept. Mot. Skills* 17:439–58

Ozkan K, Braunstein ML. 2009. Predominance of ground over ceiling surfaces in binocular rivalry. *Atten. Percept. Psychophys.* 71(6):1305–12

Pastukhov A, Braun J. 2011. Cumulative history quantifies the role of neural adaptation in multistable perception. *J. Vis.* 11(10):12

Pearson J, Brascamp JW. 2008. Sensory memory for ambiguous vision. *Trends Cogn. Sci.* 12(9):334–41

Pearson J, Clifford CWG, Tong F. 2008. The functional impact of mental imagery on conscious perception. *Curr. Biol.* 18(13):982–86

Pearson J, Tadin D, Blake R. 2007. The effects of transcranial magnetic stimulation on visual rivalry. *J. Vis.* 7(7):2.1–11

Petrovici MA, Bill J, Bytschok I, Schemmel J, Meier K. 2016. Stochastic inference with spiking neurons in the high-conductance state. *Phys. Rev. E* 94(4):042312

Pettigrew JD, Miller SM. 1998. A "sticky" interhemispheric switch in bipolar disorder? *Proc. Biol. Sci.* 265(1411):2141–48

Rahnev D, Nee DE, Riddle J, Larson AS, D'Esposito M. 2016. Causal evidence for frontal cortex organization for perceptual decision making. *PNAS* 113(21):6059–64

Ricci C, Blundo C. 1990. Perception of ambiguous figures after focal brain lesions. *Neuropsychologia* 28(11):1163–73

Rock I. 1983. *The Logic of Perception*. Cambridge, MA: MIT Press

Sack AT, Cohen Kadosh R, Schuhmann T, Moerel M, Walsh V, Goebel R. 2009. Optimizing functional accuracy of TMS in cognitive studies: a comparison of methods. *J. Cogn. Neurosci.* 21(2):207–21

Sandberg K, Blicher JU, Del Pin SH, Andersen LM. 2016. Improved estimates for the role of grey matter volume and GABA in bistable perception. *Cortex* 83:292–305

Sara SJ. 2009. The locus coeruleus and noradrenergic modulation of cognition. *Nat. Rev. Neurosci.* 10(3):211–23

Schauer G, Kanai R, Brascamp JW. 2016. Parietal theta burst TMS: functional fractionation observed during bistable perception not evident in attention tasks. *Conscious. Cogn.* 40:105–15

Schmack K, de Castro A, Rothkirch M, Sekutowicz M, Rössler H, et al. 2013a. Delusions and the role of beliefs in perceptual inference. *J. Neurosci.* 33(34):13701–12

Schmack K, Sekutowicz M, Rössler H, Brandl EJ, Müller DJ, Sterzer P. 2013b. The influence of dopamine-related genes on perceptual stability. *Eur. J. Neurosci.* 38(9):3378–83

Schmack K, Weilnhammer V, Heinzle J, Stephan KE, Sterzer P. 2016. Learning what to see in a changing world. *Front. Hum. Neurosci.* 10(39):263

Schrater PR, Sundareswara R. 2006. Theory and dynamics of perceptual bistability. In *Advances in Neural Information Processing Systems 19*, ed. B Schölkopf, JC Platt, T Hoffman, pp. 1217–24. Cambridge, MA: MIT Press

Serences JT. 2004. Control of object-based attention in human cortex. *Cereb. Cortex* 14(12):1346–57

Shepard RN. 1990. *Mind Sights: Original Visual Illusions, Ambiguities, and Other Anomalies, with a Commentary on the Play of Mind in Perception and Art*. New York: W.H. Freeman

Sheremata SL, Bettencourt KC, Somers DC. 2010. Hemispheric asymmetry in visuotopic posterior parietal cortex emerges with visual short-term memory load. *J. Neurosci.* 30(38):12581–88

Sheremata SL, Silver MA. 2015. Hemisphere-dependent attentional modulation of human parietal visual field representations. *J. Neurosci.* 35(2):508–17

Siegel M, Donner TH, Engel AK. 2012. Spectral fingerprints of large-scale neuronal interactions. *Nat. Rev. Neurosci.* 13(2):121–34

Silver MA, Kastner S. 2009. Topographic maps in human frontal and parietal cortex. *Trends Cogn. Sci.* 13(11):488–95

Silver MA, Ress D, Heeger DJ. 2005. Topographic maps of visual spatial attention in human parietal cortex. *J. Neurophysiol.* 94(2):1358–71

Silver MA, Ress D, Heeger DJ. 2006. Neural correlates of sustained spatial attention in human early visual cortex. *J. Neurophysiol.* 97(1):229–37

Srinivasan MV, Laughlin SB, Dubs A. 1982. Predictive coding: a fresh view of inhibition in the retina. *Proc. R. Soc. Lond. Biol. Sci.* 216(1205):427–59

Stefanics G, Kremláček J, Czigler I. 2014. Visual mismatch negativity: a predictive coding view. *Front. Hum. Neurosci.* 8(47):666

Sterzer P. 2016. Moving forward in perceptual decision making. *PNAS* 113(21):5771–73

Sterzer P, Frith C, Petrovic P. 2008. Believing is seeing: Expectations alter visual awareness. *Curr. Biol.* 18(16):R697–98

Sterzer P, Kleinschmidt A. 2007. A neural basis for inference in perceptual ambiguity. *PNAS* 104(1):323–28

Sterzer P, Kleinschmidt A, Rees G. 2009. The neural bases of multistable perception. *Trends Cogn. Sci.* 13(7):310–18

Summerfield C, de Lange FP. 2014. Expectation in perceptual decision making: neural and computational mechanisms. *Nat. Rev. Neurosci.* 15(11):745–56

Sunaert S, Van Hecke P, Marchal G, Orban GA. 2000. Attention to speed of motion, speed discrimination, and task difficulty: an fMRI study. *NeuroImage* 11:612–23

Sundareswara R, Schrater PR. 2008. Perceptual multistability predicted by search model for Bayesian decisions. *J. Vis.* 8(5):12.1–19

Swisher JD, Halko MA, Merabet LB, McMains SA, Somers DC. 2007. Visual topography of human intra-parietal sulcus. *J. Neurosci.* 27(20):5326–37

Szczepanski SM, Konen CS, Kastner S. 2010. Mechanisms of spatial attention control in frontal and parietal cortex. *J. Neurosci.* 30(1):148–60

Todd JJ, Marois R. 2004. Capacity limit of visual short-term memory in human posterior parietal cortex. *Nature* 428(6984):751–54

Tsuchiya N, Wilke M, Frässle S, Lamme V. 2015. No-report paradigms: extracting the true neural correlates of consciousness. *Trends Cogn. Sci.* 19(12):757–70

Valle-Inclan F, Gallego E. 2006. Bilateral frontal leucotomy does not alter perceptual alternation during binocular rivalry. *Prog. Brain Res.* 155:235–39

van Loon AM, Knapen T, Scholte HS, St John-Saaltink E, Donner TH, Lamme VAF. 2013. GABA shapes the dynamics of bistable perception. *Curr. Biol.* 23(9):823–27

VanRullen R, Pascual-Leone A, Battelli L. 2008. The continuous Wagon wheel illusion and the "when" pathway of the right parietal lobe: a repetitive transcranial magnetic stimulation study. *PLOS ONE* 3(8):e2911

Vernet M, Brem A-K, Farzan F, Pascual-Leone A. 2015. Synchronous and opposite roles of the parietal and prefrontal cortices in bistable perception: a double-coil TMS-EEG study. *Cortex* 64:78–88

von Helmholtz H. 1867. *Handbuch Der Physiologischen Optik.* Leipzig: Leopold Voss

Wade NJ, Ono H. 1985. The stereoscopic views of Wheatstone and Brewster. *Psychol. Res.* 47(3):125–33

Wang M, Arteaga D, He BJ. 2013. Brain mechanisms for simple perception and bistable perception. *PNAS* 110(35):E3350–59

Watanabe T, Masuda N, Megumi F, Kanai R, Rees G. 2014. Energy landscape and dynamics of brain activity during human bistable perception. *Nat. Commun.* 5:4765

Weilnhammer VA, Ludwig K, Hesselmann G, Sterzer P. 2013. Frontoparietal cortex mediates perceptual transitions in bistable perception. *J. Neurosci.* 33(40):16009–15

Weilnhammer VA, Stuke H, Hesselmann G, Sterzer P, Schmack K. 2017. A predictive coding account of bistable perception—a model-based fMRI study. *PLOS Comput. Biol.* 13(5):e1005536

Wheatstone C. 1838. Contributions to the physiology of vision. Part the first. On some remarkable, and hitherto unobserved, phenomena of binocular vision. *Philos. Trans. R. Soc. Lond.* 128:371–94

Wilbertz G, van Slooten J, Sterzer P. 2014. Reinforcement of perceptual inference: Reward and punishment alter conscious visual perception during binocular rivalry. *Front. Psychol.* 5(7):495

Wilson HR. 2007. Minimal physiological conditions for binocular rivalry and rivalry memory. *Vis. Res.* 47(21):2741–50

Xu H, Han C, Chen M, Li P, Zhu S, et al. 2016. Rivalry-like neural activity in primary visual cortex in anesthetized monkeys. *J. Neurosci.* 36(11):3231–42

Yantis S, Schwarzbach J, Serences JT, Carlson RL, Steinmetz MA, et al. 2002. Transient neural activity in human parietal cortex during spatial attention shifts. *Nat. Neurosci.* 5(10):995–1002

Yu K, Blake R. 1992. Do recognizable figures enjoy an advantage in binocular rivalry? *J. Exp. Psychol. Hum. Percept. Perform.* 18(4):1158–73

Zaretskaya N, Thielscher A, Logothetis NK, Bartels A. 2010. Disrupting parietal function prolongs dominance durations in binocular rivalry. *Curr. Biol.* 20(23):2106–11

Zhang P, Jamison K, Engel S, He B, He S. 2011. Binocular rivalry requires visual attention. *Neuron* 71(2):362–69

Zhou W, Zhang X, Chen J, Wang L, Chen D. 2012. Nostril-specific olfactory modulation of visual perception in binocular rivalry. *J. Neurosci.* 32(48):17225–29

Zou J, He S, Zhang P. 2016. Binocular rivalry from invisible patterns. *PNAS* 113(30):8408–13

Ensemble Perception

David Whitney[1,2,3] and Allison Yamanashi Leib[1]

[1]Department of Psychology, University of California, Berkeley, California 94720;
email: dwhitney@berkeley.edu

[2]Vision Science Program, University of California, Berkeley, California 94720

[3]Helen Wills Neuroscience Institute, University of California, Berkeley, California 94720

Annu. Rev. Psychol. 2018. 69:105–29

First published as a Review in Advance on September 11, 2017

The *Annual Review of Psychology* is online at psych.annualreviews.org

https://doi.org/10.1146/annurev-psych-010416-044232

Keywords

vision, summary statistics, consciousness, crowding, texture, scene, object recognition

Abstract

To understand visual consciousness, we must understand how the brain represents ensembles of objects at many levels of perceptual analysis. Ensemble perception refers to the visual system's ability to extract summary statistical information from groups of similar objects—often in a brief glance. It defines foundational limits on cognition, memory, and behavior. In this review, we provide an operational definition of ensemble perception and demonstrate that ensemble perception spans across multiple levels of visual analysis, incorporating both low-level visual features and high-level social information. Further, we investigate the functional usefulness of ensemble perception and its efficiency, and we consider possible physiological and cognitive mechanisms that underlie an individual's ability to make accurate and rapid assessments of crowds of objects.

Contents

1. INTRODUCTION

We process the vibrant complexity of natural scenes using the relatively limited capacity of the visual system. The fidelity with which we can perceive any complex scene at a glance is restricted by finite attentional resources (Cavanagh & Alvarez 2005, Dux & Marois 2009, Simons & Levin 1997), limits of eye movements and scanning (Kowler 2011, Wolfe 1994), and minimal visual working memory capacity (Luck & Vogel 2013). Human visual processing is further constrained by coarse peripheral resolution (Anstis 1974, Virsu & Rovamo 1979) and the fundamental limits set by visual crowding (Pelli 2008, Strasburger et al. 2011, Whitney & Levi 2011). Fortunately, although natural scenes are dense with information, this clutter is not completely random. Instead, natural scenes are filled with similar or redundant groups of objects, features, and textures. The visual system is sensitive to these similarities in both natural (e.g., stand of trees, crowd of faces) and artificial (e.g., car lot, bike rack) groups in the form of ensemble or summary statistical information (Alvarez 2011, Haberman & Whitney 2012, Whitney et al. 2014). For example, in **Figure 1**, we can extract summary statistics along many dimensions, including the average hue of the tree leaves, average facial expression of the bystanders, and average speed of the cyclists. In this review, we address the types of visual information that are represented as ensembles, what perceptual and cognitive benefits ensemble perception affords, how attention is involved in representing ensembles, and which proposed mechanisms may account for many aspects of ensemble perception.

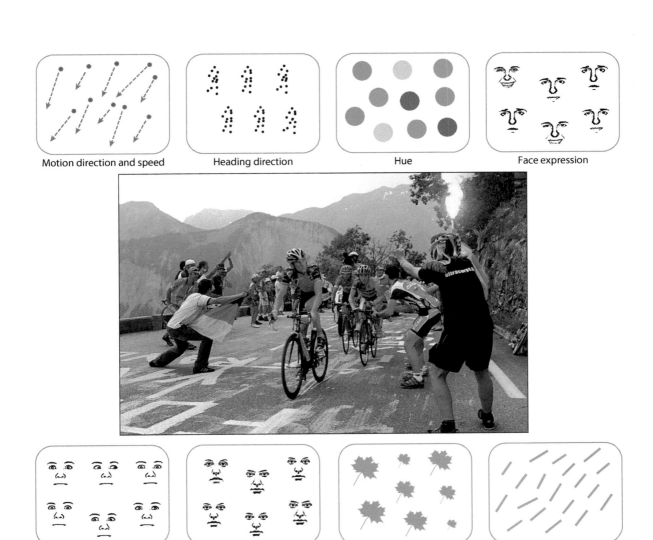

Figure 1

Multiple ensembles are present in natural scenes. Natural scenes contain numerous groups of similar and redundant stimuli. Observers perceive these groups in the form of summary statistics, such as the average orientation, size, and hue of the foliage; the average speed, motion direction, and heading of the bikers; and the average emotional expression, gaze direction, and family resemblance of the bystanders. Ensemble perception is hierarchical and occurs at many levels of visual processing. Photo credit: Max Pixel, available for reuse under the Creative Commons Zero (CC0 1.0).

2. ENSEMBLE PERCEPTS ACROSS MULTIPLE LEVELS OF VISUAL ANALYSIS

2.1. Low-Level Ensemble Perception

Ensemble perception has been reported for many low-level features, including motion, orientation, brightness, hue, and spatial position. It has been examined using a variety of psychophysical techniques (**Figure 2**). Of the low-level stimuli that have been studied, visual motion provides a canonical example of ensemble perception (Watamaniuk & McKee 1998, Watamaniuk et al. 1989).

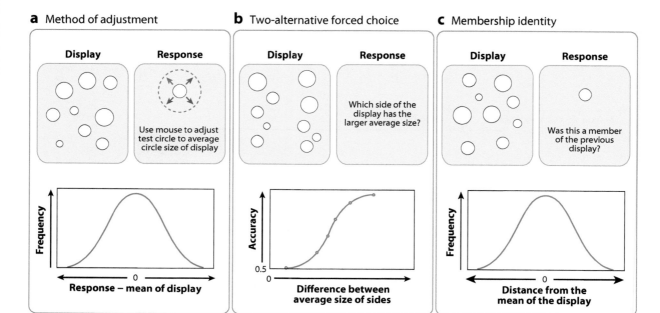

a Method of adjustment

Display

Response

Use mouse to adjust test circle to average circle size of display

Frequency

← Response − mean of display →
0

b Two-alternative forced choice

Display

Response

Which side of the display has the larger average size?

Accuracy

0.5
0

Difference between average size of sides

c Membership identity

Display

Response

Was this a member of the previous display?

Frequency

← Distance from the mean of the display →
0

Figure 2

Methods of testing ensemble perception. (*a*) Participants match the average size of a test circle to a set of displayed circles. The spread or variance of the resulting distribution (e.g., Gaussian, Von Mises, Cauchy, etc.) reflects the matching performance. Robust sensitivity to summary statistical performance will yield a narrow distribution centered at 0. (*b*) Observers make a two-alternative forced-choice judgment about which display (left/right or which of two intervals) contains the larger average size. A psychometric function fitted to the data reveals the sensitivity to the summary statistic (e.g., discrimination threshold). (*c*) In the implicit membership identity task, observers report whether the test circle was present in the previous display. When the test circle is the average of the displayed set, participants false alarm at a high rate. The shape and location of the resulting histogram reflects sensitivity to the ensemble (average size).

Watamaniuk and colleagues (1989; Watamaniuk & McKee 1998) asked observers to judge the average motion direction of random-dot cinematograms that resembled blowing snow and found that observers accurately reported the average motion direction of the drifting dots. Similarly, observers easily estimated the average speed of random dots moving at diverse speeds with a precision comparable to their estimations of dots moving at a homogeneous speed (Watamaniuk & Duchon 1992). In addition to motion, observers can accurately discriminate, report, and reproduce the average orientation of stimuli (Dakin & Watt 1997, Miller & Sheldon 1969, Parkes et al. 2001). Further, observers can also perceive the average brightness (Bauer 2009), average hue (Demeyere et al. 2008, Webster et al. 2014), and average spatial position of a cloud of random stimuli (Alvarez & Oliva 2008, Melcher & Kowler 1999, Vishwanath & Kowler 2003). These low-level visual summary statistical representations of spatial frequency, color, and orientation may form the basis of texture recognition and discrimination (Landy 2014) as well as of scene gist impressions (Oliva & Torralba 2006).

2.2. Mid-Level Ensembles

Mid-level features and objects are also perceived as ensembles. For example, observers perceive the average size in an array of circles, even for very brief displays of less than one-tenth of a second (Ariely 2001, Chong & Treisman 2003). Ensemble size perception is somewhat controversial

(Myczek & Simons 2008), in part because, unlike perception of average motion, position, or orientation, the existence of low-level size detectors is less clear. In contrast, the size and scale of single circles could be represented as early as V1 (Schwarzkopf et al. 2011). If we consider size to be a mid-level feature, then summary statistical information about groups of circles may be associated with surface or depth perception. Consistent with this possibility, observers can perceive the average depth of a crowd of objects that have varying binocular disparity (Wardle et al. 2017), suggesting that ensemble information contributes to depth and scene perception and, perhaps, to Gestalt grouping, as well (Wagemans et al. 2012). It remains an intriguing question whether the visual system extracts ensemble information about other depth cues such as average height in field, average atmospheric perspective, and average texture gradients. Average depth information from any of these sources could facilitate recognition not only of the depth of individual objects but also of their identity and size in scenes. Ensemble percepts of average cast shadows (Koenderink et al. 2004, Sanders et al. 2010), if present, could assist in recovering global lighting in scenes and inform depth assignments of objects throughout the scene. While these are still open questions, future work on ensemble surface and mid-level visual information will be important for documenting the extent to which summary statistical representations contribute to the fundamental building blocks of surface, object, and scene perception.

2.3. High-Level Ensembles

Recent work on summary statistical perception highlights its significant role in high-level object, scene, and social perception. Most of this work has documented how ensemble perception operates on groups of face stimuli, allowing observers to rapidly access the emotional tenor or intent of a crowd. Haberman & Whitney (2007, 2009) found that observers can evaluate and discriminate the average emotional expression and gender in a crowd of faces. Observers can also accurately evaluate average facial identity (e.g., family resemblance; see Bai et al. 2015, de Fockert & Wolfenstein 2009, Neumann et al. 2013, Yamanashi Leib et al. 2012b). These studies emphasize the fact that humans can rapidly extract important social information from crowds during a brief glance, perhaps as short as 100 ms or less (Haberman & Whitney 2009, Li et al. 2016, Yamanashi Leib et al. 2016). Observers are not as sensitive to crowds of inverted or scrambled faces (Haberman & Whitney 2009, Yamanashi Leib et al. 2012b), which suggests that observers extract summary statistical information based on configural or holistic face representations. Different images of the same face and multiple viewpoints of faces can also be incorporated into a unified ensemble percept (Neumann et al. 2013, Yamanashi Leib et al. 2014), indicating that summary statistics are computed over viewpoint-invariant representations, not just two-dimensional image-level information. In addition to facial expression and identity, observers can also judge the average gaze direction and mean head rotation of the crowd (Florey et al. 2016, Sweeny & Whitney 2014), which could be useful in guiding attention and behavior. In addition to face crowds, the visual system extracts ensemble information about dynamic objects as well. Sweeny and colleagues (2013) discovered that observers viewing a crowd of point-light walkers can accurately match and discriminate their average direction. An intriguing implication of the high-level ensemble work is that complex perceptual interpretations, such as the perception of crowd panic, may be subserved by ensemble representations (see Section 5).

2.4. Multiple Ensembles

Most ensemble research focuses on the perception of one specific ensemble characteristic from a particular group of stimuli (e.g., average size or expression). However, a few studies have investigated whether participants can extract multiple ensemble characteristics from one or more groups of stimuli. For example, Chong & Treisman (2005b) asked participants to view a group of disks containing stimuli of two different colors and found that observers were sensitive to the average size of both sets of colored disks even though their attention was divided between the two colors (Chong & Treisman 2005b). Other studies have shown that observers can successfully extract multiple ensembles from up to four groups of stimuli (Attarha & Moore 2015, Attarha et al. 2014). However, Attarha and colleagues (2014; Attarha & Moore 2015) found that undivided attention enhanced performance, suggesting that extracting multiple ensembles is not entirely capacity free (see Section 4 for the role of attention in ensemble perception).

Whereas the aforementioned studies of multiple groups of stimuli examined participants' ability to extract the same characteristic (size), other studies have investigated sensitivity to simultaneous but different ensemble characteristics. For example, Emmanouil & Treisman (2008) found that observers could perceive the average speed and size of a group of circles. Although accuracy was lower in the multiple-ensemble conditions than in the single-ensemble conditions, this result suggests that observers can perceive multiple ensemble features. Future studies should continue to explore the perceptual interactions between multiple ensembles and the capacity limits of multiple-ensemble processing.

The studies described above were restricted to visual stimuli, but it has been hypothesized that ensemble perception may be a general mechanism that operates across several sensory domains, and researchers have documented that ensemble percepts can incorporate auditory as well as visual stimuli. Listeners can perceive the average in a sequence of pure tones (Piazza et al. 2013) and can efficiently discriminate sound textures, such as those present in auditory scenes (McDermott et al. 2013). Moreover, although there is some cost when perceiving multiple ensembles within one modality (e.g., Emmanouil & Treisman 2008), there is relatively little cost in perceiving ensemble information across different modalities. For example, participants can recognize ensemble tone and visual size simultaneously, and there is little evidence of a cost associated with simultaneous displays (Albrecht et al. 2012).

2.5. Beyond Average

The most commonly measured form of ensemble representation is the perceived average of a group of items. However, the diversity or variance in a set of stimuli is also very important (**Figure 3**). For example, when walking through a crowd of people, the average emotion is informative, but equally critical is the variation of emotion present in the crowd. Haberman et al. (2015b) found that observers who viewed a crowd of up to 16 faces for 1 s successfully matched and discriminated the variance of the crowd, and subsequent tests confirmed that observers distinguished among numerous levels of variance, not merely between homogeneous and heterogeneous crowds (Haberman et al. 2015b). Variance information is useful in several respects. First, it signals the reliability of the estimated average: A homogeneous group of angry faces implies something very different than a set of faces that varies in expression. Second, ensemble variance might provide direct information about the diversity, mixture, or ambivalence of a crowd. Third, variance information might be useful to identify statistical outliers, such as deviant expressions in a crowd (Whitney et al. 2014). Ensemble variance is not available at the level of any single individual; it is an emergent property only accessible by encoding summary statistical information. Ensemble variance information is extracted for high-level (e.g., facial expression, age, and gender and racial diversity), low-level (e.g., orientation) (Dakin & Watt 1997, Morgan et al. 2008, Norman et al. 2015), and mid-level (e.g., size) features (Solomon et al. 2011). Whether third-order statistics, such as kurtosis, are extracted remains unclear. Interpreting variance in the crowd seems to be as ubiquitous a calculation as extracting summary statistical information about the average.

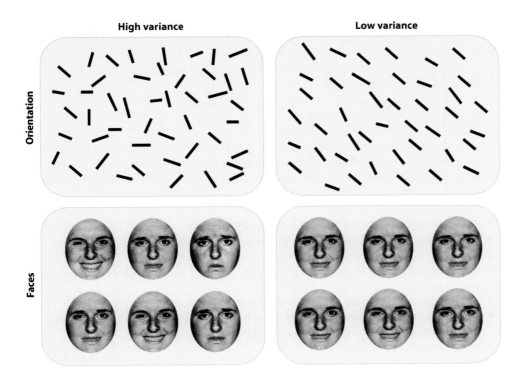

High variance **Low variance**

Orientation

Faces

Figure 3

Extracting variance from groups of stimuli. Extracting the mean, or average, characteristic from a group of stimuli is the most commonly reported ensemble percept. However, ensemble perception may include extracting diverse statistical information, such as variance, range, or even kurtosis. In this figure, we show examples from research documenting the fact that participants can accurately evaluate the variance within groups of redundant stimuli (Haberman et al. 2015b, Solomon 2010).

2.6. Ensemble Cognition

Summary statistical representations exist at the highest levels of perceptual and cognitive processing—what we will refer to as ensemble cognition. The perceptual and cognitive evaluations we once thought required conscious scrutiny and deliberation are actually rapidly extracted as ensemble percepts. For example, subjective percepts like attractiveness can be estimated via ensemble perception (Anderson et al. 1973, Post et al. 2012, Walker & Vul 2013). In natural scenes, abstract percepts such as liveliness or animacy are also rapidly represented in the form of an ensemble (Yamanashi Leib et al. 2016). In one recent study, observers rated random crowds of animals, insects, plants, and household objects on their average lifelikeness (Yamanashi Leib et al. 2016). Observers' ratings of the crowds' lifelikeness were highly correlated with the mathematical mean of the items rated individually, even though the individual items were rated by independent observers. This indicates that observers agree about the lifelikeness of objects and crowds. Ensemble liveliness is extracted for displays as brief as 250 ms, even when observers cannot recall individual stimuli in the crowd (Yamanashi Leib et al. 2016). This suggests that ensemble information underlies observers' first impressions of the liveliness of natural scenes (Yamanashi Leib et al. 2016).

The fact that perceived liveliness can be extracted so quickly and efficiently suggests that other high-level perceptual, cognitive, and inferential processes may also rely on ensemble representations. For example, early research hints that social labels may be evaluated through an averaging process (Leon et al. 1973), and there are intriguing findings that long-term memory consolidation may resemble ensemble representations (Richards et al. 2014). Thus, cognitive processes beyond perception may also rely on averaging mechanisms, perhaps even the same ensemble mechanisms discussed in this review.

3. OPERATIONALLY DEFINING ENSEMBLE PERCEPTION

From the discussion in the previous section, it may seem that anything—any arbitrary set of features, objects, or configurations—can be perceived as an ensemble. However, this is not the case. Ensemble perception has unique features that can help establish the foundation for an operational definition to distinguish what ensemble perception is not, identify how ensemble perception is related to other seemingly similar phenomena, and isolate the underlying neural mechanisms. A flexible operational definition of ensemble coding should include the following five concepts:

- Ensemble perception is the ability to discriminate or reproduce a statistical moment.
- Ensemble perception requires the integration of multiple items.
- Ensemble information at each level of representation can be precise relative to the processing of single objects at that level.
- Single-item recognition is not a prerequisite for ensemble coding.
- Ensemble representations can be extracted with a temporal resolution at or beyond the temporal resolution of individual object recognition.

3.1. Ensemble Perception Is the Ability to Discriminate or Reproduce a Statistical Moment

Not every group or set of things is perceived as an ensemble. We can perceive groups of random objects or interactions between features and objects that have no meaningful or consistent relationship to each other, have no underlying statistical distribution, and cannot be reported or discriminated as a set. We can also recognize Gestalt or holistic grouping cues, but these need not involve the perception of a statistical moment and, thus, are not diagnostic of ensemble processing. Gestalt grouping may interact with ensemble perception, either by constraining ensemble representations or by being generated by them. In contrast to other phenomena, sensitivity to ensemble information—to a statistical moment—depends on the variance of the underlying distribution, such that increasing variance in the dimension of interest reduces sensitivity to the summary statistic (Dakin 2001, Fouriezos et al. 2008, Haberman et al. 2015b, Im & Halberda 2013, Morgan et al. 2008, Solomon et al. 2011). However, for sets with constant variance, the shape of the underlying statistical distribution (e.g., normal, rectangular, bimodal) is less critical (Allik et al. 2013, Chong & Treisman 2003, Haberman & Whitney 2009).

3.2. Ensemble Perception Requires the Integration of Multiple Items

In terms of an operational definition for what counts as an ensemble representation for perception, the only requirement is an integration of two or more stimuli. Technically, integrating (sampling) two items is sufficient evidence for an ensemble representation, and this happens in some cases (Allik et al. 2013, Maule & Franklin 2016). However, beyond that, there is no particular quantity of items (or minimum subset of items) that is required to meet the criteria for an ensemble or summary statistical representation. In many studies, the number of features or objects integrated is greater than two (**Figure 4**; see also **Table 1**). For instance, when discriminating the average size

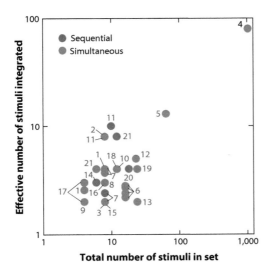

Figure 4

Efficiency of integration in ensemble perception. The number of stimuli integrated (ordinate) is plotted against the number of items in the display (abscissa) for a variety of published studies. Red circles represent experiments that displayed sequential objects in a set. Blue circles represent experiments that displayed objects simultaneously in a spatial array. The best-fitting power function for these data is $f(x) = x^{0.58}$, which suggests that, across a variety of studies, observers integrate approximately the square root of the number of displayed objects. Gray numbers denote the associated references (see **Table 1**).

or variance in a set of circles, observers performed at 60–75% efficiency, integrating at least three circles (Allik et al. 2013, Solomon et al. 2011). Observers in other studies of basic visual features incorporated information ranging from approximately 3 to 5 items per display (Im & Halberda 2013, Solomon 2010); in another study, observers incorporated information from approximately four items with replacement at approximately 5 Hz (Gorea et al. 2014). At the higher end of the range, some studies report that observers sample approximately the square root of the number of display items, even for very large set sizes (Dakin 2001). Higher-level ensemble perception studies, such as those using face crowds, biological motion, and other stimuli, indicate that observers can often integrate more than 4–8 objects (Haberman & Whitney 2010; Sweeny et al. 2013; Yamanashi Leib et al. 2014, 2016).

The estimates of efficiency or number of items integrated in ensemble representations clearly vary and are sometimes debated (Chong et al. 2008, Dakin 2001, Marchant et al. 2013, Myczek & Simons 2008, Solomon et al. 2011). This is, in part, because efficiency depends on several factors, including the stimulus type, methods used (e.g., ideal observer or equivalent noise modeling versus empirical set size manipulations), and assumptions of those methods (Solomon et al. 2011). Attention seems to influence efficiency, as well (Dakin et al. 2009), opening up the possibility of variations in estimated efficiency depending on task design, observer goals, and attentional demands (see Section 4). Further, individual differences can significantly impact how much information observers integrate (Bai et al. 2015, Haberman & Whitney 2010, Haberman et al. 2015a, Solomon 2010).

Despite the variations in methods and modeling approaches, however, there is general agreement across ensemble tasks that multiple features or objects are integrated. In fact, when a large sample of experimental estimates of efficiency are plotted together, a striking pattern emerges (**Figure 4**), suggesting that observers integrate approximately the square root of the number of

Table 1   References for Figures 4 and 6

Reference number	Reference
1	Allik et al. (2013)
2	Alvarez & Oliva (2008)
3	Chong et al. (2008)
4	Dakin (2001)
5	Dakin et al. (2005)
6	Florey et al. (2016)
7	Florey et al. (2017)
8	Gorea et al. (2014)
9	Haberman & Whitney (2009)
10	Haberman & Whitney (2010)
11	Hubert-Wallander & Boynton (2015)
12	Im & Halberda (2013)
13	Myczek & Simons (2008)
14	Piazza et al. (2013)
15	Solomon (2010)
16	Solomon et al. (2011)
17	Sweeny & Whitney (2014)
18	Sweeny et al. (2013)
19	Wolfe et al. (2015)
20	Yamanashi Leib et al. (2014)
21	Yamanashi Leib et al. (2016)

The following approach was used to estimate the approximate number integrated for each point on the graphs. If the researcher reported a range of stimuli integrated (e.g., 3–4 stimuli were integrated), we plotted the lower estimate. In some cases, the difference was minimal. In other cases the difference was substantially larger (Yamanashi Leib et al. 2014). Thus, the ordinate on the graph represents a conservative estimate, or lower bound, of effective integration across multiple ensemble perception studies. This list is not exhaustive; many studies have not estimated the efficiency or number of integrated samples, or have done so indirectly. The methods used in each study vary: Some used empirical manipulations and some used ideal observer modeling, regression approaches, or equivalent noise analysis.

objects in their summary statistical representations. Notwithstanding the individual differences and multiple factors that modulate integration efficiency, the general rule that observers effectively integrate approximately the square root of the number of stimuli thus appears reasonable under many circumstances (**Figure 4**).

Most ensemble perception research emphasizes spatial integration, but summary statistics are perceived in temporal sequences, as well. Observers successfully estimate summary statistics, including average object location, facial expression, object size, tone, and animacy, from sequentially presented objects (Albrecht & Scholl 2010, Chong & Treisman 2003, Haberman et al. 2009, Whiting & Oriet 2011, Yamanashi Leib et al. 2014). Thus, summary statistical information can be extracted flexibly over time from spatially local or global scales, in contrast to Navon figures (Navon 1977). In fact, it appears that the integration efficiency for temporally presented sets is as high as or higher than that for spatial arrays (Florey et al. 2017, Gorea et al. 2014).

Although multiple items are integrated in ensemble representations, not all items need to be weighted equally. For example, statistical outliers (deviants) are downplayed, or filtered, in the cases of color (Michael et al. 2014) and faces (Haberman & Whitney 2010). Summary statistical perception in temporal arrays also reveals a type of weighting, in the form of primacy and recency effects, such that the first- or last-seen object can bias the estimated ensemble property (Hubert-Wallander & Boynton 2015). In addition to order- and outlier-based weighting, there is also the potential for weighting based on attention (de Fockert & Marchant 2008), eccentricity (Ji et al. 2014), and expectancy (Cheadle et al. 2014). For example, a study investigating ensemble circle size provided some evidence that attending to items biases the reported mean (de Fockert & Marchant 2008). Foveally viewed stimuli may also pull or bias estimates of the summary statistic, such as average expression (Ji et al. 2014, Wolfe et al. 2015), but foveally viewed objects are not necessary, as other studies have demonstrated integration of multiple peripheral objects without any foveal stimulation (Haberman et al. 2009, Wolfe et al. 2015).

Although **Figure 4** shows that there is little debate about the criterion that ensemble perception must involve two or more items being integrated, there is an ongoing debate about whether ensemble perception is automatic, obligatory, unconscious, parallel, or outside the focus of attention. Because these issues are not diagnostic of ensemble coding and because arguments about efficiency—the number of objects integrated into the ensemble representation—do not address these debates, we reserve discussion of these issues to Section 4, where we explore the role of attention in ensemble perception.

3.3. Ensemble Information at Each Level of Representation Can Be Precise Relative to Processing of Single Objects at That Level

Averaging cancels uncorrelated noise associated with individual items (Alvarez 2011, Galton 1907, Surowiecki 2004). As such, one might expect that sensitivity will increase with increasing sample size, and this result is sometimes found (Robitaille & Harris 2011). When individual object representations are especially noisy (e.g., brief), observers can be more sensitive to the ensemble as a whole, compared to the single item (Gorea et al. 2014, Li et al. 2016, Sweeny et al. 2013, Yamanashi Leib et al. 2014). These enhancements are not required for ensemble perception, however. Indeed, several authors have reported relatively constant sensitivity with increasing set size (Allik et al. 2013, Alvarez 2011, Ariely 2001, Chong & Treisman 2005b). The benefit of averaging across larger sample sizes may be offset by factors such as increased correlated noise and positional uncertainty, potentially yielding a pattern of results that appears as if there is constant sensitivity across set sizes. Moreover, late-stage noise may limit the apparent benefit of averaging. Nonetheless, ensemble sensitivity is generally better than would be predicted if discrimination thresholds were set by single-object discrimination. For example, there is compulsory averaging of orientation (Parkes et al. 2001), size (Allik et al. 2014), and facial expression (Fischer & Whitney 2011), and objects that are crowded and, therefore, unrecognizable nonetheless contribute to the perceived ensemble (Fischer & Whitney 2011, Ikeda et al. 2013, Parkes et al. 2001).

3.4. Single-Item Recognition Is Not a Prerequisite for Ensemble Coding

An ensemble can be perceived even if the individuals that comprise the ensemble cannot be reliably reported. Observers accurately report ensemble size and expression information during rapid serial visual presentation (RSVP) paradigms (Haberman et al. 2009, Oriet & Corbett 2008). In these tasks, the individual items are presented too quickly for observers to accurately register each one, yet the ensemble percept still incorporates them. Similarly, studies employing a change blindness paradigm found that observers extracted summary statistical information about color variance (Ward et al. 2016) or average expression from the same stimuli they were attentionally blind to (**Figure 5b**; Haberman & Whitney 2011). Ensemble perception remains robust even

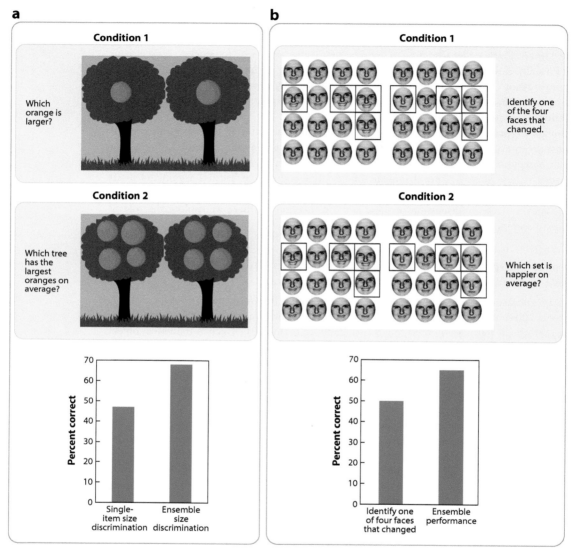

Figure 5

Ensemble perception does not require recognition of individual constituents. (*a*) Two conditions in a size discrimination task from Sweeny et al.'s (2015) study on the development of ensemble perception. In Condition 1, children chose which tree contained the largest orange. In Condition 2, children chose which tree contained the larger oranges on average. Although single-item discrimination was poor, ensemble sensitivity was robust. (*b*) Two conditions from a change localization task (Haberman & Whitney 2011). In Condition 1, participants were asked to localize any one of the four locations where the facial expression changed between the first (*left*) and second (*right*) display of faces. In Condition 2, participants were asked to report which display, on average, contained happier faces. Observers were at chance during the change localization task but nonetheless exhibited above chance ensemble perception sensitivity. Together, these and other experiments suggest that individual set members can influence ensemble percepts even when those objects go unrecognized or unnoticed.

when single-item perception is impeded by crowding, at least for orientation and faces (Fischer & Whitney 2011, Parkes et al. 2001; cf. Banno & Saiki 2012). Moreover, ensemble perception of circle size may be possible during object substitution masking, which greatly reduces the visibility of individual circles (Choo & Franconeri 2010, Jacoby et al. 2012). Further supporting this idea, studies of children, who are still developing individual object recognition, show evidence of ensemble perception (Rhodes et al. 2015, Sweeny et al. 2015). In addition, patients with simultanagnosia, unilateral visual neglect, and congenital prosopagnosia all show some evidence of ensemble perception, even when their single-item discrimination is impaired (Demeyere et al. 2008; Hochstein et al. 2015; Yamanashi Leib et al. 2012a,b). Moreover, individual differences reveal that sensitivity to ensemble information is not perfectly correlated with single-object discrimination (Haberman et al. 2015a, Sweeny et al. 2015). Taken together, a broad range of experiments suggests that ensemble coding does not depend on the recognition or memory of individual objects.

Of course, there are caveats to each example given above. For example, noise limits the conclusions that can be drawn from developing children and patients. Independent noise sources may produce a pattern where ensemble performance and single-item discrimination seem artificially disparate. Finally, although the correlation of individual differences is not perfect, ensemble discrimination and single-item discrimination are correlated to some degree (Haberman et al. 2015a). Nevertheless, the variety of ensemble perception studies using different methods and stimuli provide converging evidence that single-object representations can be lost, neglected, forgotten, unrecognized, or noisy while they are still preserved in the ensemble representation. This does not mean that ensembles are extracted outside of the focus of attention (see Section 4), but it does inform and limit the sorts of models that can be proposed to underlie ensemble perception (see Section 6).

3.5. Ensemble Representations Can Be Extracted with a Temporal Resolution at or Beyond the Temporal Resolution of Individual Object Recognition

Ensemble perception can operate at very brief durations and for fast temporal sequences (**Figure 6**). Our perception of ensemble or gist information from groups of objects can be faster than locating any particular object, such as an extreme one or one closest to the average (Haberman et al. 2009, Yamanashi Leib et al. 2014). As examples, observers perceive average facial expression (Haberman & Whitney 2009), average size (Gorea et al. 2014), average gaze (Florey et al. 2017), and average crowd animacy (Yamanashi Leib et al. 2016) even when set images are displayed as frequently as 20 per s (Haberman et al. 2009), which is beyond the limit of attentional resolution or the dwell time required to scrutinize or find individual faces in the sequence (Nothdurft 1993, Tong & Nakayama 1999, Verstraten et al. 2000). Spatial ensemble information is perceived in crowds of objects displayed for as little as 50 ms (Ariely 2001, Chong & Treisman 2003, Haberman & Whitney 2009, Li et al. 2016, Yamanashi Leib et al. 2016). In addition, ensemble information is extracted from RSVP sequences before individual objects are registered in short-term memory (Joo et al. 2009, McNair et al. 2016).

There is a distinction between the temporal resolution and integration period of ensemble coding. The temporal resolution of ensemble perception is high (and diagnostic): Stimuli in a set can be integrated even when the individuals are not recognized or recalled. However, individual stimuli are not simply blurred (Neumann et al. 2013; Yamanashi Leib et al. 2014, 2016); the individual objects must be registered before integration. Ensemble perception, therefore, resolves individual objects that cannot be uniquely resolved in memory encoding, maintenance, or retrieval.

The accuracy of ensemble estimates often improves with increasing exposure duration (Haberman et al. 2009, Li et al. 2016, Whiting & Oriet 2011), suggesting a temporal integration

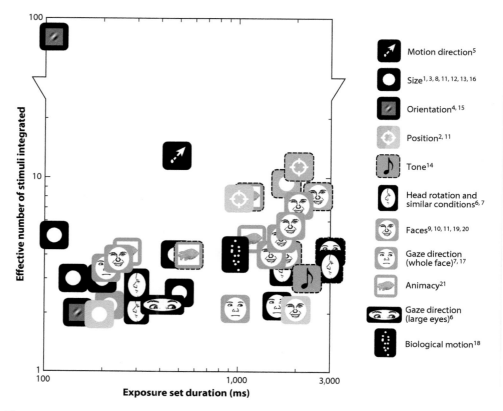

Figure 6

Ensemble perception as a function of set duration. The number of items integrated (ordinate) is plotted as a function of stimulus duration (abscissa). Data points bordered by dashed lines represent sequentially displayed set members. Published studies used different methods to estimate efficiency, indicated by different colored backgrounds. Superscript numbers in the legend denote the associated study (see **Table 1**). Overlapping data points were jittered slightly for visual clarity.

mechanism with a time constant of several hundred ms, at least for mid- and high-level stimuli (Chong & Treisman 2003, Haberman et al. 2009, Whiting & Oriet 2011). Beyond a few hundred ms, the number of integrated objects is fairly constant (**Figure 6**). Thus, there is some degree of duration invariance, at least when considering a large sample of studies that tested a range of different stimuli. Whether there are unique integration periods for different types of stimuli remains unclear [low-level features may have shorter temporal integration periods (e.g., Watamaniuk et al. 1989)], but, given the fact that ensembles are extracted more or less independently from different levels of visual analysis (**Figure 1**), it seems reasonable that there may be distinct time courses for different forms of ensemble coding.

The fact that ensemble properties like average size or expression are represented quickly, or are derived from sets of stimuli presented too fast to individuate or recall, does not mean that ensembles are necessarily unaffected by, isolated from, or calculated before attentional processes. On the contrary, attention sometimes plays an important role in ensemble perception, as will be reviewed in the following section. Therefore, attention (or lack thereof) should not be used as a diagnostic criterion for the purposes of operationally defining what counts as summary statistical or ensemble coding.

Likewise, memory is not a diagnostic criterion for ensemble perception because ensembles can be formed on sets whose objects are not accurately encoded or recalled (Ariely 2001, Alvarez & Oliva 2008, Haberman & Whitney 2007, Haberman et al. 2009). Similarly, although ensemble representations may inform statistical learning (Fiser & Aslin 2001, Solso & McCarthy 1981), summary statistical perception occurs at first sight for novel stimuli and dimensions (Haberman & Whitney 2007, Yamanashi Leib et al. 2016) and without training or learning (Haberman & Whitney 2012).

4. WHAT IS THE ROLE OF ATTENTION IN PERCEIVING ENSEMBLES?

There remains some debate regarding whether ensemble coding requires attention, whether serial or parallel mechanisms are involved, and whether this is even a valid distinction. Some experiments suggest that directed attention is not necessary for ensemble perception. For example, using a divided attention task, Alvarez & Oliva (2008) found that observers could report the centroid or average final position of clouds of dots with comparable accuracy whether they were attended or ignored. Other studies have also demonstrated that attention directed to individual set members is not necessary to obtain ensemble estimates of color variance (Bronfman et al. 2014), circle size (Chong & Treisman 2005b), and orientation (Alvarez & Oliva 2009). Consistent with these results, ensemble motion perception (Allik 1992, Allik & Dzhafarov 1984, Watamaniuk et al. 1989) and adaptation (Harp et al. 2007) occur even when crowding makes it impossible to individuate each item (Whitney & Levi 2011). Finally, obligatory averaging reported in some domains (Fischer & Whitney 2011, Parkes et al. 2001) could suggest that ensemble percepts are extracted when and where attention cannot be deployed (Joo et al. 2009, Oriet & Brand 2013; but see also McNair et al. 2016).

Although attention may not be necessary for ensemble perception, it may strongly modulate ensemble perception. For example, attention may bias estimates of average set size (Chong & Treisman 2005a, de Fockert & Marchant 2008). Moreover, some studies have shown that dividing attention between two sets of stimuli incurs a cost in performance accuracy (Brand et al. 2012, Huang 2015). Another study showed that diverting attention reduced efficiency—the number of integrated samples—in an ensemble orientation discrimination task (Dakin et al. 2009). Consistent with this finding, limiting attentional resources may reduce the number of faces sampled to estimate average expression (McNair et al. 2016), perhaps by modulating the spatial distribution of integration. Indeed, observers who were primed with a task requiring global attention prior to performing an ensemble perception task performed significantly better than those who were primed with local attention tasks (Chong & Treisman 2005a). Finally, it is possible that attention could limit other processes like the spatial resolution of perception (e.g., crowding), working memory, decision processes, and motor control—which may make ensemble perception appear attention dependent even if it is not directly dependent on attention (Attarha & Moore 2015, de Fockert & Marchant 2008). Thus, although focused attention may not be strictly necessary for ensemble perception to occur, there is ample evidence that attention facilitates it.

Thus, the concepts of directed attention and ensemble perception are not at odds (Allik et al. 2013), and the black-and-white dichotomy between serial and parallel ensemble processing is not especially useful. Taken together, these findings reveal that ensemble perception can be valuable in situations that allow directed attention to a crowd and similarly useful in situations where attention is limited. Instead of exploring an oversimplified dichotomy, future work should attempt to characterize the interactions between attention and ensemble perception at multiple levels of visual processing to identify the mechanism through which attention facilitates summary statistical representations.

For example, it is worth considering attention's interaction with the hierarchical nature of ensemble perception. Attention may operate at the level of the ensemble even if it does not operate at the level of the individual components within the ensemble. There is substantial evidence for gist representations without explicit knowledge of the individual components, including ensemble orientation discrimination (Parkes et al. 2001), ensemble face recognition (Haberman & Whitney 2007), ensemble change detection (Haberman & Whitney 2011), and ensemble size discrimination (Allik et al. 2013, Chong & Treisman 2005b, Choo & Franconeri 2010, Oriet & Brand 2013). In each of these cases, task demands required observers to attend to the ensemble characteristic as a whole, so attention to the relevant ensemble dimension may have been necessary even if awareness of the individual member was not (see Section 3.4). A promising recent approach to addressing this issue is to measure aftereffects following adaptation to summary statistical information. In such an experiment, observers' attention (and awareness) can be controlled during the adaptation period. Prior adaptation studies have investigated adaptation to an ensemble statistic, such as average size or motion direction (Anstis et al. 1998, Corbett et al. 2012, Harp et al. 2007), without rigorously controlling for attention. One recent study that did control for attention found adaptation to the average facial expression in a rapid sequence of faces (Ying & Xu 2017). Future studies can use this and related adaptation paradigms to isolate the particular role of attention in ensemble representations.

5. USEFULNESS OF ENSEMBLE REPRESENTATIONS

Ensemble representations might be the basis of some of our fastest and richest perceptual experiences (Intraub 1981, Potter 1975, Thorpe et al. 1996), which do not rely on explicitly or consciously representing all of the individual members of the scene (see Section 3.4). For example, we can perceive the average liveliness of a scene in the briefest of glances (Yamanashi Leib et al. 2016). A face that is crowded such that it is unrecognizable nonetheless influences the ensemble expression perceived in the crowd (Fischer & Whitney 2011), and a changing object that goes unnoticed or unrecognized can still alter the perceived ensemble property of the scene as a whole (Haberman & Whitney 2011, Ward et al. 2016). One interpretation of these and similar findings is that the individual objects are phenomenally available to consciousness but unreportable (Block 2011, McClelland & Bayne 2016, Shea & Bayne 2010). Alternatively, the visual system might encode summary statistical information in crowds of objects by unconsciously processing individual object identities (Chaney et al. 2014, Cohen et al. 2016). In either case, the resulting percept is richer than would be expected when faced with the limits of visual short-term memory, cognition, language, or attention (Cohen et al. 2016). Therefore, much of what counts as our rich visual experience may take the form of ensemble representations (Block 2011, Cohen et al. 2016, McClelland & Bayne 2016).

Ensemble representations may be especially useful at the highest levels of perceptual processing because they carry emergent and social information—unique characteristics of crowds, environments, and social interactions that can only be specified at the level of the group. For example, observers are sensitive to the ambivalence, mixture of emotion, or racial diversity of a crowd, but these cannot be conveyed at the level of individual faces (Haberman et al. 2015b). Other emergent ensemble percepts may include the overall threat of a crowd, its gaze direction (Mareschal et al. 2016, Sweeny & Whitney 2014), and its heading direction (Sweeny et al. 2013). For example, the perception of crowd panic is probably based on summary statistical information involving a calculation of heading direction (Sweeny et al. 2013) as well as variance in direction and speed. Visuosocial summary statistical information not only is important for recognition and awareness but also serves as an important cue to guide action: Crucial behavioral decisions in crowd navigation (where to walk next, speed of walking, etc.) may be driven by summary statistical information. Finally, ensemble information may be constructive, amplifying the perception of summary statistical dimensions (Price et al. 2014). For example, the perceived attractiveness of faces in a crowd may be exaggerated (van Osch et al. 2015, Walker & Vul 2013).

Ensemble representations may be a critical component of visual working and long-term memory. Recent research suggests that the average circle size in scenes biases subsequent estimates of individual object size in memory tasks (Brady & Alvarez 2011), and that recalled locations of individual objects in a cluster are pulled toward the ensemble centroid location (Lew & Vul 2015). Thus, individual objects in memory are not treated simply as independent entities but as part of a hierarchy that includes information about individual details and ensembles (Brady & Alvarez 2011). This is advantageous because statistical structure or ensemble information affords more information than would be available from only encoding independent individual objects. For example, grouping proximate sets of circles by ensemble characteristics increases the capacity of visual working memory (VWM) (Im & Chong 2014), and ensemble representations might also facilitate statistical learning and category boundary formation (Oriet & Hozempa 2016). Insofar as memory consolidation results in summary statistical-like representations (Richards et al. 2014), an intriguing possibility is that ensemble coding might also facilitate long-term memory for outliers, just as summary statistical perception improves deviance detection and pop-out in visual search (Whitney et al. 2014). More broadly, we can better model and understand the mechanisms of memory if we incorporate the important role of ensemble representations into theories of memory encoding and consolidation (Brady & Tenenbaum 2013).

6. POSSIBLE PHYSIOLOGICAL AND COGNITIVE MECHANISMS OF ENSEMBLE PERCEPTION

The relationship between ensemble perception and other visual phenomena has raised the possibility that they result from shared mechanisms. One of the most common associations we can examine for insight on these mechanisms is that between ensemble coding and visual crowding. Visual crowding is the deleterious effect of clutter on object recognition and awareness in the peripheral visual field (Pelli 2008, Whitney & Levi 2011). Traditional models of visual perception and crowding argue that the visual system lacks the bandwidth to encode detailed information outside of the fovea, so peripheral high-fidelity visual information is irreversibly lost. Instead, what might emerge from crowded scenes is summary statistical information. In that sense, crowding and ensemble percepts might be thought of as two sides of the same coin (Parkes et al. 2001) or caused by similar pooling processes (Balas et al. 2009, Freeman & Simoncelli 2011). However, ensemble perception can occur with or without crowding (Bulakowski et al. 2011, Dakin et al. 2009), so ensemble representations do not require crowding.

Models of crowding also face challenges in describing ensemble perception. Pooling models, which often use variations of texture synthesis algorithms (Portilla & Simoncelli 2000), may help account for some aspects of low-level texture perception in crowding (Balas et al. 2009, Freeman & Simoncelli 2011; but see also Wallis et al. 2016). However, these models do not operate at the level of object representations and, thus, cannot explain object-level crowding (Farzin et al. 2009, Ikeda et al. 2013, Kimchi & Pirkner 2015, Louie et al. 2007, Manassi et al. 2012) or high-level ensemble perception (Whitney et al. 2014). Nor can these models explain how crowded and unrecognized faces can prime subsequent valence judgments (Faivre et al. 2012, Kouider et al. 2011) or how these faces can influence ensemble expression perception (Fischer & Whitney 2011). Current pooling and texture synthesis models (Balas et al. 2009, Freeman & Simoncelli 2011, Pelli 2008, Rosenholtz et al. 2012) would not generate these effects. Likewise, scene gist (Oliva & Torralba 2006) and texture models stop short of describing object-level processing and cannot explain higher-level ensemble percepts, such as average identity, expression, and animacy or the perceived variance of these properties (de Fockert & Wolfenstein 2009, Haberman & Whitney 2007, Haberman et al. 2015a, Neumann et al. 2013, Yamanashi Leib et al. 2016).

The research discussed above challenges any model of ensemble coding to explain how object information can be unrecognizable due to crowding but retained for subsequent ensemble perception (Faivre et al. 2012, Fischer & Whitney 2011, Ikeda et al. 2013, Parkes et al. 2001). One way in which this problem could be reconciled is if the visual system maintains and passes high-fidelity representations through each level of visual analysis but these representations cannot be selected with sufficient resolution to recognize particular objects (Chaney et al. 2014). According to this hierarchical sparse selection model, when observers attempt to select a feature or object in a crowd, they may not be able to resolve that feature or object, although they can extract an ensemble of that feature or object dimension. Thus, we see that crowding occurs, and ensembles can be extracted, at multiple levels of visual processing (Whitney & Levi 2011). Modified versions of the pooling models mentioned above could be implemented hierarchically at multiple levels of visual processing along these lines to explain the multiple levels of crowding and ensemble perception. An updated reverse hierarchy visual model (Hochstein et al. 2015) may also be invoked to help explain how high-fidelity individual object information contributes to ensemble percepts even when crowding severely impedes recognition of that object.

The neural mechanism(s) of ensemble perception remain unknown, but it is unlikely that there is a single unified mechanism. Psychophysical evidence suggests that ensemble representations are distributed, or available at multiple levels of visual processing. For example, the individual differences in ensemble perception for low- and high-level objects do not correlate well, suggesting that there may be independent mechanisms for different types of ensembles (Haberman et al. 2015a, Sweeny et al. 2015). This interpretation also potentially explains the lack of patients who exhibit a unique deficit in ensemble processing. Many patients do not have impaired ensemble discrimination or exhibit less difficulty than would be predicted based on their single-item impairments alone (Demeyere et al. 2008; Hochstein et al. 2015; Karaminis et al. 2017; Yamanashi Leib et al. 2012a,b, 2014; cf. Rhodes et al. 2015). There is also physiological and neuroimaging evidence for multiple stages of ensemble representation, including motion, color, and textures, in occipital visual areas (e.g., Okazawa et al. 2015), MT+ (Born & Bradley 2005) and the anterior-medial ventral visual cortex (Cant & Xu 2012). The neural loci and mechanisms involved in coding crowds of faces, biological motion, and animacy remain to be explored. Because ensemble representations can be easily calculated from population codes that occur at nearly every level of visual processing, a distinct possibility is that ensemble representations will be found at virtually any stage examined (Chaney et al. 2014).

7. CONCLUSIONS

Ensemble perception is ubiquitous. It occurs at multiple levels of visual analysis, ranging from low-level orientation processing to high-level social impressions (e.g., the emotional tenor or the liveliness of a crowd). In this review, we have proposed an operational definition of perceptual ensemble coding, which includes five factors: the perception of a statistical moment in a crowd, the integration of multiple stimuli (approximately the square root of the number of stimuli in the scene), precise representation of the ensemble property, lack of a requirement for sensitivity to particular individual set members, and high temporal resolution. This operational definition helps distinguish ensemble perception from other phenomena. Ensemble perception provides an efficient way to access group-level information in a quick glance without the need to scrutinize or recall individual objects. Even in circumstances when single-item analysis may be possible, ensemble perception of the integrated group provides emergent, functionally useful information that cannot be attained from any single group member. The accumulating evidence reviewed above suggests that summary statistical perception is a significant contributing factor to visual perception and may generate much of what contributes to a rich conscious experience during rapid, first-glance assessments of visual scenes.

FUTURE ISSUES

1. How stable are the individual differences in ensemble perception? How do group differences such as culture, gender, and (typical and atypical) cognitive development influence ensemble perception?

2. How does ensemble perception interact with visual search functions, such as outlier detection or pop-out? For example, are individual differences in visual search performance predicted by or correlated with the fidelity of summary statistical representations?

3. What is the capacity limit for multiple parallel ensembles? Do multiple-ensemble representations interact with each other, and how do multiple ensembles inform fast scene recognition?

4. How is ensemble information integrated across modalities within scenes? For example, is the perception of ensemble biological motion in the whole scene (e.g., an orchestra) independent from or integrated with ensemble auditory information from the parts of the scene (e.g., the collection of instruments in the orchestra)?

5. Can ensemble perception be trained and improved? What cognitive, social, and developmental benefits are conferred by enhanced ensemble perception? Does it enhance emotional intelligence? Does it improve interactions with the world, such as driving? Does it improve scene recognition or the fidelity of memory and richness of conscious experience?

DISCLOSURE STATEMENT

The authors are not aware of any affiliations, memberships, funding, or financial holdings that might be perceived as affecting the objectivity of this review.

ACKNOWLEDGMENTS

Thanks to Jason Haberman, Mauro Manassi, and Tim Sweeny for helpful discussions. Thanks to Zixuan Wang for editorial assistance. This work was supported by National Science Foundation grant 074689 and National Institutes of Health grant EY018216.

LITERATURE CITED

Albrecht AR, Scholl BJ. 2010. Perceptually averaging in a continuous visual world: extracting statistical summary representations over time. *Psychol. Sci.* 21(4):560–67

Albrecht AR, Scholl BJ, Chun MM. 2012. Perceptual averaging by eye and ear: computing summary statistics from multimodal stimuli. *Atten. Percept. Psychophys.* 74(5):810–15

Allik J. 1992. Competing motion paths in sequence of random dot patterns. *Vis. Res.* 32(1):157–65

Allik J, Dzhafarov EN. 1984. Motion direction identification in random cinematograms: a general model. *J. Exp. Psychol. Hum. Percept. Perform.* 10(3):378–93

Allik J, Toom M, Raidvee A, Averin K, Kreegipuu K. 2013. An almost general theory of mean size perception. *Vis. Res.* 83:25–39

Allik J, Toom M, Raidvee A, Averin K, Kreegipuu K. 2014. Obligatory averaging in mean size perception. *Vis. Res.* 101:34–40

Alvarez GA. 2011. Representing multiple objects as an ensemble enhances visual cognition. *Trends Cogn. Sci.* 15(3):122–31

Alvarez GA, Oliva A. 2008. The representation of simple ensemble visual features outside the focus of attention. *Psychol. Sci.* 19(4):392–98

Alvarez GA, Oliva A. 2009. Spatial ensemble statistics are efficient codes that can be represented with reduced attention. *PNAS* 106(18):7345–50

Anderson NH, Lindner R, Lopes LL. 1973. Integration theory applied to judgments of group attractiveness. *J. Personal. Soc. Psychol.* 26(3):400–8

Anstis S. 1974. A chart demonstrating variations in acuity with retinal position. *Vis. Res.* 14:589–92

Anstis S, Verstraten FAJ, Mather G. 1998. The motion aftereffect. *Trends Cogn. Sci.* 2(3):111–17

Ariely D. 2001. Seeing sets: representation by statistical properties. *Psychol. Sci.* 12(2):157–62

Attarha M, Moore CM. 2015. The capacity limitations of orientation summary statistics. *Atten. Percept. Psychophys.* 7(4):1116–31

Attarha M, Moore CM, Vecera SP. 2014. Summary statistics of size: fixed processing capacity for multiple ensembles but unlimited processing capacity for single ensembles. *J. Exp. Psychol. Hum. Percept. Perform.* 40(4):1440–49

Bai Y, Yamanashi Leib A, Puri AM, Whitney D, Peng K. 2015. Gender differences in crowd perception. *Front. Psychol.* 6:1300

Balas B, Nakano L, Rosenholtz R. 2009. A summary-statistic representation in peripheral vision explains visual crowding. *J. Vis.* 9(12):13

Banno H, Saiki J. 2012. Calculation of the mean circle size does not circumvent the bottleneck of crowding. *J. Vis.* 12(11):13

Bauer B. 2009. Does Stevens's power law for brightness extend to perceptual brightness averaging? *Psychol. Res.* 59:171–86

Block N. 2011. Perceptual consciousness overflows cognitive access. *Trends Cogn. Sci.* 15(12):567–75

Born RT, Bradley DC. 2005. Structure and function of visual area MT. *Annu. Rev. Neurosci.* 28:157–89

Brady TF, Alvarez GA. 2011. Hierarchical encoding in visual working memory: Ensemble statistics bias memory for individual items. *Psychol. Sci.* 22(3):384–92

Brady TF, Tenenbaum JB. 2013. A probabilistic model of visual working memory: incorporating higher order regularities into working memory capacity estimates. *Psychol. Rev.* 120(1):85–109

Brand J, Oriet C, Tottenham LS. 2012. Size and emotion averaging: costs of dividing attention after all. *Can. J. Exp. Psychol.* 66(1):63–69

Bronfman ZZ, Brezis N, Jacobson H, Usher M. 2014. We see more than we can report: "cost free" color phenomenality outside focal attention. *Psychol. Sci.* 25(7):1394–403

Bulakowski PF, Post RB, Whitney D. 2011. Dissociating crowding from ensemble percepts. *Atten. Percept. Psychophys.* 73(4):1003–9

Cant JS, Xu Y. 2012. Object ensemble processing in human anterior-medial ventral visual cortex. *J. Neurosci.* 32(22):7685–700

Cavanagh P, Alvarez GA. 2005. Tracking multiple targets with multifocal attention. *Trends Cogn. Sci.* 9(7):349–54

Chaney W, Fischer J, Whitney D. 2014. The hierarchical sparse selection model of visual crowding. *Front. Integr. Neurosci.* 8:73

Cheadle S, Wyart V, Tsetsos K, Myers N, de Gardelle V, et al. 2014. Adaptive gain control during human perceptual choice. *Neuron* 81(6):1429–41

Chong SC, Joo SJ, Emmanouil TA, Treisman A. 2008. Statistical processing: not so implausible after all. *Percept. Psychophys.* 70(7):1327–34

Chong SC, Treisman A. 2003. Representation of statistical properties. *Vis. Res.* 43(4):393–404

Chong SC, Treisman A. 2005a. Attentional spread in the statistical processing of visual displays. *Percept. Psychophys.* 67(1):1–13

Chong SC, Treisman A. 2005b. Statistical processing: computing the average size in perceptual groups. *Vis. Res.* 45(7):891–900

Choo H, Franconeri SL. 2010. Objects with reduced visibility still contribute to size averaging. *Atten. Percept. Psychophys.* 72(1):86–99

Cohen MA, Dennett DC, Kanwisher N. 2016. What is the bandwidth of perceptual experience? *Trends Cogn. Sci.* 20(5):324–35

Corbett JE, Wurnitsch N, Schwartz A, Whitney D. 2012. An aftereffect of adaptation to mean size. *Vis. Cogn.* 20(2):211–31

Dakin SC. 2001. Information limit on the spatial integration of local orientation signals. *J. Opt. Soc. Am. A* 18(5):1016–26

Dakin SC, Bex PJ, Cass JR, Watt RJ. 2009. Dissociable effects of attention and crowding on orientation averaging. *J. Vis.* 9(11):28

Dakin SC, Mareschal I, Bex PJ. 2005. Local and global limitations on direction integration assessed using equivalent noise analysis. *Vis. Res.* 45(24):3027–49

Dakin SC, Watt RJ. 1997. The computation of orientation statistics from visual texture. *Vis. Res.* 37(22):3181–92

de Fockert JW, Marchant AP. 2008. Attention modulates set representation by statistical properties. *Percept. Psychophys.* 70(5):789–94

de Fockert JW, Wolfenstein C. 2009. Rapid extraction of mean identity from sets of faces. *Q. J. Exp. Psychol.* 62(9):1716–22

Demeyere N, Rzeskiewicz A, Humphreys KA, Humphreys GW. 2008. Automatic statistical processing of visual properties in simultanagnosia. *Neuropsychologia* 46(11):2861–64

Dux PE, Marois R. 2009. How humans search for targets through time: a review of data and theory from the attentional blink. *Atten. Percept. Psychophys.* 71(8):1683–700

Emmanouil TA, Treisman A. 2008. Dividing attention across feature dimensions in statistical processing of perceptual groups. *Percept. Psychophys.* 70(6):946–54

Faivre N, Berthet V, Kouider S. 2012. Nonconscious influences from emotional faces: a comparison of visual crowding, masking, and continuous flash suppression. *Front. Psychol.* 3:129

Farzin F, Rivera SM, Whitney D. 2009. Holistic crowding of Mooney faces. *J. Vis.* 9(6):18

Fischer J, Whitney D. 2011. Object-level visual information gets through the bottleneck of crowding. *J. Neurophysiol.* 106(3):1389–98

Fiser J, Aslin RN. 2001. Unsupervised statistical learning of higher-order spatial structures from visual scenes. *Psychol. Sci.* 12(6):499–504

Florey J, Clifford CWG, Dakin S, Mareschal I. 2016. Spatial limitations in averaging social cues. *Sci. Rep.* 6:32210

Florey J, Dakin SC, Mareschal I. 2017. Comparing averaging limits for social cues over space and time. *J. Vis.* 17(9):17

Fouriezos G, Rubenfeld S, Capstick G. 2008. Visual statistical decisions. *Percept. Psychophys.* 70(3):456–64

Freeman J, Simoncelli EP. 2011. Metamers of the ventral stream. *Nat. Neurosci.* 14(9):1195–201

Galton F. 1907. Vox populi (the wisdom of crowds). *Nature* 75:450–51

Gorea A, Belkoura S, Solomon JA. 2014. Summary statistics for size over space and time. *J. Vis.* 14(9):22

Haberman J, Brady TF, Alvarez GA. 2015a. Individual differences in ensemble perception reveal multiple, independent levels of ensemble representation. *J. Exp. Psychol. Gen.* 144(2):432–46

Haberman J, Harp T, Whitney D. 2009. Averaging facial expression over time. *J. Vis.* 9(11):1

Haberman J, Lee P, Whitney D. 2015b. Mixed emotions: sensitivity to facial variance in a crowd of faces. *J. Vis.* 15(4):16

Haberman J, Whitney D. 2007. Rapid extraction of mean emotion and gender from sets of faces. *Curr. Biol.* 17(7):751–53

Haberman J, Whitney D. 2009. Seeing the mean: ensemble coding for sets of faces. *J. Exp. Psychol. Hum. Percept. Perform.* 35(3):718–34

Haberman J, Whitney D. 2010. The visual system discounts emotional deviants when extracting average expression. *Atten. Percept. Psychophys.* 72(7):1825–38

Haberman J, Whitney D. 2011. Efficient summary statistical representation when change localization fails. *Psychon. Bull. Rev.* 18(5):855–59

Haberman J, Whitney D. 2012. Ensemble perception: summarizing the scene and broadening the limits of visual processing. In *From Perception to Consciousness: Searching with Anne Treisman*, ed. J Wolfe, L Robinson, pp. 1–21. Oxford, UK: Oxford Univ. Press

Harp TD, Bressler DW, Whitney D. 2007. Position shifts following crowded second-order motion adaptation reveal processing of local and global motion without awareness. *J. Vis.* 7(2):15

Hochstein S, Pavlovskaya M, Bonneh YS, Soroker N. 2015. Global statistics are not neglected. *J. Vis.* 15(4):7

Huang L. 2015. Statistical properties demand as much attention as object features. *PLOS ONE* 10(8):e0131191

Hubert-Wallander B, Boynton GM. 2015. Not all summary statistics are made equal: evidence from extracting summaries across time. *J. Vis.* 15(4):5

Ikeda H, Watanabe K, Cavanagh P. 2013. Crowding of biological motion stimuli. *J. Vis.* 13(4):20

Im HY, Chong SC. 2014. Mean size as a unit of visual working memory. *Perception* 43(7):663–76

Im HY, Halberda J. 2013. The effects of sampling and internal noise on the representation of ensemble average size. *Atten. Percept. Psychophys.* 75(2):278–86

Intraub H. 1981. Rapid conceptual identification of sequentially presented pictures. *J. Exp. Psychol. Hum. Percept. Perform.* 7(3):604–10

Jacoby O, Kamke MR, Mattingley JB. 2012. Is the whole really more than the sum of its parts? Estimates of average size and orientation are susceptible to object substitution masking. *J. Exp. Psychol. Hum. Percept. Perform.* 39(1):233–44

Ji L, Chen W, Fu X. 2014. Different roles of foveal and extrafoveal vision in ensemble representation for facial expressions. In *Engineering Psychology and Cognitive Ergonomics*, ed. D Harris, pp. 164–73. Berlin: Springer

Joo SJ, Shin K, Chong SC, Blake R. 2009. On the nature of the stimulus information necessary for estimating mean size of visual arrays. *J. Vis.* 9(9):7

Karaminis T, Neil L, Manning C, Turi M, Fiorentini C, et al. 2017. Investigating ensemble perception of emotions in autistic and typical children and adolescents. *Dev. Cogn. Neurosci.* 24:51–62

Kimchi R, Pirkner Y. 2015. Multiple level crowding: crowding at the object parts level and at the object configural level. *Perception* 44(11):1275–92

Koenderink JJ, Van Doorn AJ, Pont SC. 2004. Light direction from shad(ow)ed random Gaussian surfaces. *Perception* 33(12):1405–20

Kouider S, Berthet V, Faivre N. 2011. Preference is biased by crowded facial expressions. *Psychol. Sci.* 22(2):184–89

Kowler E. 2011. Eye movements: the past 25 years. *Vis. Res.* 51(13):1457–83

Landy MS. 2014. Texture analysis and perception. In *The New Visual Neurosciences*, ed. JS Werner, LM Chalupa, pp. 639–52. Cambridge, MA: MIT Press

Leon M, Oden GC, Anderson NH. 1973. Functional measurement of social values. *J. Personal. Soc. Psychol.* 27(3):301–10

Lew TF, Vul E. 2015. Ensemble clustering in visual working memory biases location memories and reduces the Weber noise of relative positions. *J. Vis.* 15(4):10

Li H, Ji L, Tong K, Ren N, Chen W, et al. 2016. Processing of individual items during ensemble coding of facial expressions. *Front. Psychol.* 7:1332

Louie EG, Bressler DW, Whitney D. 2007. Holistic crowding: selective interference between configural representations of faces in crowded scenes. *J. Vis.* 7(2):24

Luck SJ, Vogel EK. 2013. Visual working memory capacity: from psychophysics and neurobiology to individual differences. *Trends Cogn. Sci.* 17(8):391–400

Manassi M, Sayim B, Herzog MH. 2012. Grouping, pooling, and when bigger is better in visual crowding. *J. Vis.* 12(10):13

Marchant AP, Simons DJ, de Fockert JW. 2013. Ensemble representations: effects of set size and item heterogeneity on average size perception. *Acta Psychol.* 142(2):245–50

Mareschal I, Otsuka Y, Clifford MD. 2016. "Are you looking at me?" How children's gaze judgments improve with age. *Dev. Psychol.* 52:695–703

Maule J, Franklin A. 2016. Accurate rapid averaging of multihue ensembles is due to a limited capacity subsampling mechanism. *J. Opt. Soc. Am. A.* 33:A22–29

McClelland T, Bayne T. 2016. Ensemble coding and two conceptions of perceptual sparsity. *Trends Cogn. Sci.* 20(9):641–42

McDermott J, Schemitsch M, Simoncelli EP. 2013. Summary statistics in auditory perception. *Nat. Neurosci.* 16(4):493–98

McNair NA, Goodbourn PT, Shone LT, Harris IM. 2016. Summary statistics in the attentional blink. *Atten. Percept. Psychophys.* 79:100–16

Melcher D, Kowler E. 1999. Shapes, surfaces and saccades. *Vis. Res.* 39(17):2929–46

Michael E, de Gardelle V, Summerfield C. 2014. Priming by the variability of visual information. *PNAS* 111(21):7873–78

Miller AL, Sheldon R. 1969. Magnitude estimation of average length and average inclination. *J. Exp. Psychol.* 81(1):16–21

Morgan MJ, Chubb C, Solomon JA. 2008. A "dipper" function for texture discrimination based on orientation variance. *J. Vis.* 8(11):9

Myczek K, Simons DJ. 2008. Better than average: alternatives to statistical summary representations for rapid judgments of average size. *Percept. Psychophys.* 70(5):772–88

Navon D. 1977. Forest before trees: the precedence of global features in visual perception. *Cogn. Psychol.* 9:353–83

Neumann MF, Schweinberger SR, Burton AM. 2013. Viewers extract mean and individual identity from sets of famous faces. *Cognition* 128(1):56–63

Norman LJ, Heywood CA, Kentridge RW. 2015. Direct encoding of orientation variance in the visual system. *J. Vis.* 15:3

Nothdurft HC. 1993. Faces and facial expressions do not pop out. *Perception* 22(11):1287–98

Okazawa G, Tajima S, Komatsu H. 2015. Image statistics underlying natural texture selectivity of neurons in macaque V4. *PNAS* 112(4):E351–60

Oliva A, Torralba A. 2006. Building the gist of a scene: the role of global image features in recognition. *Prog. Brain Res.* 155:23–36

Oriet C, Brand J. 2013. Size averaging of irrelevant stimuli cannot be prevented. *Vis. Res.* 79:8–16

Oriet C, Corbett JE. 2008. Evidence for rapid extraction of average size in RSVP displays of circles. *J. Vis.* 8(6):13

Oriet C, Hozempa K. 2016. Incidental statistical summary representation over time. *J. Vis.* 16(3):3

Parkes L, Lund J, Angelucci A. 2001. Compulsory averaging of crowded orientation signals in human vision. *Nat. Neurosci.* 4(7):739–44

Pelli DG. 2008. Crowding: a cortical constraint on object recognition. *Curr. Opin. Neurobiol.* 18(4):445–51

Piazza EA, Sweeny TD, Wessel D, Silver MA, Whitney D. 2013. Humans use summary statistics to perceive auditory sequences. *Psychol. Sci.* 24(8):1389–97

Portilla J, Simoncelli EP. 2000. A parametric texture model based on joint statistics of complex wavelet coefficients. *Int. J. Comput. Vis.* 40(1):49–71

Post RB, Haberman J, Iwaki L, Whitney D. 2012. The frozen face effect: why static photographs may not do you justice. *Front. Psychol.* 3:22

Potter M. 1975. Meaning in visual search. *Science* 187(4180):965–66

Price PC, Kimura NM, Smith AR, Marshall LD. 2014. Sample size bias in judgments of perceptual averages. *J. Exp. Psychol. Learn.* 40(5):1321–31

Rhodes G, Neumann MF, Ewing L, Palermo R. 2015. Reduced set averaging of face identity in children and adolescents with autism. *Q. J. Exp. Psychol.* 68(7):1391–403

Richards BA, Xia F, Santoro A, Husse J, Woodin MA, et al. 2014. Patterns across multiple memories are identified over time. *Nat. Neurosci.* 17(7):981–86

Robitaille N, Harris IM. 2011. When more is less: extraction of summary statistics benefits from larger sets. *J. Vis.* 11(12):18

Rosenholtz R, Huang J, Ehinger KA. 2012. Rethinking the role of top-down attention in vision: effects attributable to a lossy representation in peripheral vision. *Front. Psychol.* 3:13

Sanders K, Haberman J, Whitney D. 2010. Mean representation beyond a shadow of a doubt: summary statistical representation of shadows and lighting direction. *J. Vis.* 8(6):334

Schwarzkopf DS, Song C, Rees G. 2011. The surface area of human V1 predicts the subjective experience of object size. *Nat. Neurosci.* 14(1):28–30

Shea N, Bayne T. 2010. The vegetative state and the science of consciousness. *Br. J. Philos. Sci.* 61(3):459–84

Simons DJ, Levin DT. 1997. Change blindness. *Trends Cogn. Sci.* 1(7):261–67

Solomon JA. 2010. Visual discrimination of orientation statistics in crowded and uncrowded arrays. *J. Vis.* 10(14):19

Solomon JA, Morgan MJ, Chubb C. 2011. Efficiencies for the statistics of size discrimination. *J. Vis.* 11(12):13

Solso RL, McCarthy JE. 1981. Prototype formation of faces: a case of pseudo-memory. *Br. J. Psychol.* 72(4):499–503

Strasburger H, Rentschler I, Jüttner M. 2011. Peripheral vision and pattern recognition: a review. *J. Vis.* 11(5):13

Surowiecki J. 2004. *The Wisdom of Crowds.* New York: Random House

Sweeny TD, Haroz S, Whitney D. 2013. Perceiving group behavior: sensitive ensemble coding mechanisms for biological motion of human crowds. *J. Exp. Psychol. Hum. Percept. Perform.* 39(2):329–37

Sweeny TD, Whitney D. 2014. Perceiving crowd attention: ensemble perception of a crowd's gaze. *Psychol. Sci.* 25(10):1903–13

Sweeny TD, Wurnitsch N, Gopnik A, Whitney D. 2015. Ensemble perception of size in 4–5-year-old children. *Dev. Sci.* 18(4):556–68

Thorpe S, Fize D, Marlot C. 1996. Speed of processing in the human visual system. *Nature* 381(6582):520–22

Tong F, Nakayama K. 1999. Robust representation for faces: evidence from visual search. *J. Exp. Psychol. Hum. Percept. Perform.* 25(4):1016–35

van Osch Y, Blanken I, Meijs MHJ, van Wolferen J. 2015. A group's physical attractiveness is greater than the average attractiveness of its members: the group attractiveness effect. *Personal. Soc. Psychol. Bull.* 41(4):559–74

Verstraten FAJ, Cavanagh P, Labianca A. 2000. Limits of attentive tracking reveal temporal properties of attention. *Vis. Res.* 40(26):3651–64

Virsu V, Rovamo J. 1979. Visual resolution, contrast sensitivity, and the cortical magnification factor. *Exp. Brain Res.* 37(3):475–94

Vishwanath D, Kowler E. 2003. Localization of shapes: eye movements and perception compared. *Vis. Res.* 43(15):1637–53

Wagemans J, Elder JH, Kubovy M, Palmer SE, Peterson MA, et al. 2012. A century of Gestalt psychology in visual perception: I. Perceptual grouping and figure-ground organization. *Psychol. Bull.* 138(6):1172–217

Walker D, Vul E. 2013. Hierarchical encoding makes individuals in a group seem more attractive. *Psychol. Sci.* 25(1):230–35

Wallis TSA, Bethge M, Wichmann FA. 2016. Testing models of peripheral encoding using metamerism in an oddity paradigm. *J. Vis.* 16(2):4

Ward EJ, Bear A, Scholl BJ. 2016. Can you perceive ensembles without perceiving individuals? The role of statistical perception in determining whether awareness overflows access. *Cognition* 152:78–86

Wardle SG, Bex PJ, Alais D. 2017. Stereoacuity in the periphery is limited by internal noise. *J. Vis.* 12(6):12

Watamaniuk SN, Duchon A. 1992. The human visual system averages speed information. *Vis. Res.* 32(5):931–41

Watamaniuk SN, McKee SP. 1998. Simultaneous encoding of direction at a local and global scale. *Percept. Psychophys.* 60(2):191–200

Watamaniuk SN, Sekuler R, Williams DW. 1989. Direction perception in complex dynamic displays: the integration of direction information. *Vis. Res.* 29(1):47–59

Webster J, Kay P, Webster MA. 2014. Perceiving the average hue of color arrays. *J. Opt. Soc. Am. A* 31(4):A283–92

Whiting BF, Oriet C. 2011. Rapid averaging? Not so fast! *Psychon. Bull. Rev.* 18(3):484–89

Whitney D, Haberman J, Sweeny T. 2014. From textures to crowds: multiple levels of summary statistical perception. In *The New Visual Neuroscience*, ed. JS Werner, LM Chalupa, pp. 695–710. Cambridge, MA: MIT Press

Whitney D, Levi DM. 2011. Visual crowding: a fundamental limit on conscious perception and object recognition. *Trends Cogn. Sci.* 15(4):160–68

Wolfe BA, Kosovicheva AA, Yamanashi Leib A, Wood K, Whitney D. 2015. Foveal input is not required for perception of crowd facial expression. *J. Vis.* 15(4):11

Wolfe JM. 1994. Guided Search 2.0: a revised model of visual search. *Psychon. Bull. Rev.* 1(2):202–38

Yamanashi Leib A, Fischer J, Liu Y, Qiu S, Robertson L, et al. 2014. Ensemble crowd perception: a viewpoint-invariant mechanism to represent average crowd identity. *J. Vis.* 14(8):26

Yamanashi Leib A, Kosovicheva A, Whitney D. 2016. Fast ensemble representations for abstract visual impressions. *Nat. Commun.* 7:13186

Yamanashi Leib A, Landau AN, Baek Y, Chong SC, Robertson L. 2012a. Extracting the mean size across the visual field in patients with mild, chronic unilateral neglect. *Front. Hum. Neurosci.* 6:267

Yamanashi Leib A, Puri AM, Fischer J, Bentin S, Whitney D, Robertson L. 2012b. Crowd perception in prosopagnosia. *Neuropsychologia* 50(7):1698–707

Ying H, Xu H. 2017. Adaptation reveals that facial expression averaging occurs during rapid serial presentation. *J. Vis.* 17(1):15

Neuro-, Cardio-, and Immunoplasticity: Effects of Early Adversity

Eric Pakulak,[1] Courtney Stevens,[2] and Helen Neville[1]

[1] Brain Development Lab, Department of Psychology, University of Oregon, Eugene, Oregon, 97403; email: pak@uoregon.edu, neville@uoregon.edu

[2] Department of Psychology, Willamette University, Salem, Oregon 97301; email: cstevens@willamette.edu

Annu. Rev. Psychol. 2018. 69:131–56

First published as a Review in Advance on August 28, 2017

The *Annual Review of Psychology* is online at psych.annualreviews.org

https://doi.org/10.1146/annurev-psych-010416-044115

Keywords

neuroplasticity, early adversity, HPA axis, autonomic nervous system, immune system

Abstract

The relationship between early adversity and outcomes across the lifespan is apparent in a striking range of measures. Evidence suggests that many of these outcomes can be traced to the impacts of early adversity on multiple and integrated biological systems mediated by the brain. In this review, we integrate empirical and theoretical advances in the understanding of relationships among the brain and the functions of the endocrine, autonomic, and immune systems. We emphasize the effects of environmental experiences related to caregiver relationships because it is these experiences, in particular, that shape regulatory and threat response systems in ways that increase vulnerability and may underlie the wide range of poor outcomes associated with early adversity. Thus, we metaphorically extend the concept of plasticity to highlight our goal of a broader consideration of these interconnected mechanisms. We conclude by discussing implications for neurobiologically informed interventions that can potentially ameliorate the broad and costly effects of early adversity.

Contents

INTRODUCTION

Levels of societal inequality are rising in many developed and developing countries, including the United States (e.g., Hoffmann et al. 2016, Saez & Zucman 2016). At the same time, awareness of the costs of inequality—including those related to health outcomes, economic productivity, and crime victimization—is also increasing, both among the general public and within political circles (Caspi et al. 2016, Holzer et al. 2008). However, beyond identifying probabilistic relationships between early experience and later life outcomes, research across multiple disciplines is increasingly making progress toward identifying the mechanisms that underlie the long-term, biological embedding of early adversity (e.g., Brito & Noble 2014, Bruce et al. 2013, Fisher et al. 2016, Hackman et al. 2010, Lipina & Posner 2012, Loman & Gunnar 2010, McEwen & Gianaros 2010, Nusslock & Miller 2016, Propper & Holochwost 2013, Shonkoff et al. 2012, Ursache & Noble 2016). By providing mechanistic links between early experiences and distal outcomes, this research is identifying how early experiences get under the skin in ways that have lasting impacts. Such research has begun to address the complex interplay among biological and environmental factors in development and spans a wide range of disciplines.

Although the term early adversity encompasses a range of negative early experiences, our focus in this review is primarily on socioeconomic background, with an emphasis on the adverse effects of growing up in poverty or in households with lower socioeconomic status (SES). We seek to broaden the scope of previous reviews by integrating recent empirical and theoretical advances in several overlapping literatures. Specifically, we focus on the association between early adversity and brain function for self-regulation and attention, stress regulation via both the endocrine and autonomic nervous systems, and immune system function. In taking this approach, we join other recent calls for continued and increased interdisciplinary collaboration and novel approaches to the identification of neurobiological targets for interventions that can potentially ameliorate the broad and costly effects of early adversity.

The relationship between early adversity and outcomes throughout the lifespan is apparent across a striking range of outcome measures. Among the longest-studied effects of early adversity are those that span physical and mental health problems and that can occur immediately following or decades after adverse experiences, even in the absence of subsequent risky behaviors. These effects include greater risks of mortality, cardiovascular disease, asthma, obesity, pulmonary disease, and autoimmune disease, as well as dysregulation in immune, metabolic, cardiovascular, and behavioral functions and heightened risk for a range of mental illnesses, including anxiety, depression, and substance abuse (for reviews, see e.g., McEwen & Gianaros 2010, Miller et al. 2011a, Sapolsky 2004, Schickedanz et al. 2015, Shonkoff et al. 2012). Beyond health outcomes, early adversity is also associated with poorer cognitive and educational outcomes, and, as in the case of health, these disparities begin early, widen with age, and are evident across the educational trajectory and into adulthood (e.g., Bradbury et al. 2015, Hackman et al. 2010, Ursache & Noble 2016).

These gradient relationships are also evident across an increasingly wide range of societies and cultures. Relationships between early adversity and numerous health and life outcomes have been documented across a wide range of countries (Marmot 2015), and gradient relationships with early adversity have also been documented in specific cognitive and socioemotional domains of early childhood development in a wide range of cultural contexts. Recent examples of these contexts include Vietnam (Duc 2016); Turkey (Baydar & Akcinar 2015); Colombia (Rubio-Codina et al. 2015); Bangladesh (Hamadani et al. 2014); Chile, Colombia, Ecuador, Nicaragua, and Peru (Schady et al. 2015); Madagascar (Fernald et al. 2011); and India, Indonesia, Peru, and Senegal (Fernald et al. 2012).

Because these gradient patterns between early adversity and life outcomes are observed in both poorer and richer societies, the associations likely reflect effects that result not from absolute or material deprivation but, rather, from relative deprivation. As Marmot (2015) notes, whereas a poor person in Glasgow is rich compared to an average person in India, that individual's health is nonetheless worse. Such relative differences also have broader implications, as a wide range of socially relevant outcomes, particularly social and health problems, vary as a function of the level of economic inequality across developed countries, as well as across states in the United States (Wilkinson & Pickett 2009). Across multiple disciplines studying gradient relationships, including pediatrics, epidemiology, economics, and public health, there is an increasing recognition of the importance of social and psychosocial factors in explaining these relationships and a recognition that an increased understanding of the biological mechanisms underlying such patterns is crucial to ameliorating the effects of early adversity (Heckman 2006, Marmot 2015, Schickedanz et al. 2015, Shonkoff 2012, Wilkinson & Pickett 2009). In this review, we limit our focus to specific aspects of neurocognitive function and environmental experience that are common themes across literatures and are central to theoretical discussions of early adversity and outcomes (e.g., Loman & Gunnar 2010, McEwen & Gianaros 2010, Nusslock & Miller 2016, Propper & Holochwost 2013, Shonkoff et al. 2012, Ursache & Noble 2016). We focus on neural systems that support self-regulation and attention as well as threat appraisal, specifically the prefrontal cortex (PFC), amygdala, and hippocampus. These systems are among those most affected by early adversity and, because of their central role in the regulation of endocrine, autonomic, and immune systems, are also key to the theoretical advances we discuss.

Early adversity also has profound effects on multiple neurocognitive systems, in particular those important for language; however, these are beyond the scope of the current review. In addition, numerous factors contribute to differential outcomes associated with early adversity, including genetic factors important to individual differences in trait characteristics such as temperament, as well as a myriad of environmental factors, e.g., exposure to toxins and pollutants, poor nutrition, and lack of exercise. We limit our focus to environmental experiences related to caregiver relationships, parenting, and parental nurturance because these experiences, in particular, shape regulatory and threat response systems in ways that increase vulnerability and underlie the wide range of poor outcomes associated with early adversity. Thus, we metaphorically extend the concept of plasticity to highlight our goal of a broader consideration of these interconnected mechanisms.

We have characterized the unique sensitivity of the brain to experience, i.e., neuroplasticity, as a double-edged sword (e.g., Stevens & Neville 2006) because the systems that are most vulnerable to environmental differences, such as those associated with poverty, are also likely to be the most amenable to enhancement under different environmental conditions. Although our focus is on mechanisms underlying vulnerability, one primary goal of research on these mechanisms is to provide and inform evidence-based approaches to targeting environments that give rise to these effects, so we conclude by highlighting several among the many promising directions in this effort.

This article begins with a brief review of evidence on environmental experiences related to caregiver relationships, after which we discuss the brain systems central to self-regulation and threat appraisal and the effects of early adversity on these systems. We then turn to relationships between these brain systems and systems important for stress regulation, particularly endocrine and autonomic systems, and the effects of early adversity. Next, we discuss interactions between the brain and the immune system, how early adversity affects these interactions, and a model that emphasizes multiple pathways by which early adversity might affect these interacting systems in ways that potentially underlie associated poor health outcomes. Finally, we discuss implications for neurobiologically informed interventions that can potentially ameliorate effects of early adversity and consider future directions in this research.

CAREGIVING, PARENTAL NURTURANCE, AND EARLY ADVERSITY

Abundant evidence from animal and human studies indicates that early caregiving experience influences the development of systems important for stress regulation and threat appraisal and that developmental shaping of these systems can, in turn, impact the function of systems important for self-regulation and attention. Important to the development of regulatory and appraisal systems is the establishment of a relationship, early in development, with a consistently responsive caregiver (Loman & Gunnar 2010). As discussed in the section titled Stress Regulation, studies of rodents demonstrate how differences in early parental nurturance (i.e., licking and grooming behavior) influence the developing brain and, in particular, brain regions important for stress regulation and threat appraisal in ways that shape the way an animal interacts with potential threats in the environment. In humans, parental sensitivity and responsiveness are critical for the development of a secure attachment relationship, which is, in turn, important for the development of regulatory and appraisal function (e.g., Gunnar et al. 1996). A high level of caregiver nurturance is a potential buffer against the long-term health problems associated with early adversity (Miller et al. 2011b); as discussed throughout this review, parenting behavior interacts with multiple systems to confer both vulnerability and potential resilience.

Early experiences with caregivers interact with individual differences in physiological sensitivity to environmental stimulation in important ways to shape development (Blair & Raver 2012). Depending upon a child's natural tendency to be more or less reactive, these profiles can respond differently to variation in the caregiving environment in ways that lead to recursive feedback processes. For example, the development of self-regulation is shaped by this feedback between the environment and differences in emotional reactivity, higher-order attention, and executive control processes; in contexts of early adversity, this relationship can result in the development of reactivity profiles that have consequences for school readiness and broader effects (Blair & Raver 2012, 2015). Individual differences in reactivity also interact with the degree of environmental adversity such that biological sensitivity to context can be adaptive in more supportive caregiving environments but less so in more adverse environments (Ellis & Boyce 2008).

In this review, we primarily focus on early adversity associated with differences in SES, typically measured as parental education, occupation, and/or income during a child's early development.

There are many important considerations in the measurement of SES, including which components to measure, how and whether to aggregate them, and to what degree they might assess different aspects of the environment, as well as the need to consider duration of exposure (e.g., Raver et al. 2013, Ursache & Noble 2016); however, a detailed discussion of these considerations is beyond the scope of this review. Relevant to the current discussion, SES as a proxy variable broadly captures aspects of the environment associated with differences in caregiving. For example, lower SES environments are more likely to be characterized by more chaotic living conditions (e.g., crowding, noise, family instability), inconsistent parenting, lack of routines, and higher levels of unpredictability; such characteristics have been shown to account for up to half of the disparities in academic outcomes associated with SES (Brooks-Gunn & Duncan 1997, Evans 2004, Evans et al. 2005, Farah et al. 2008). As discussed in the next section, these factors impact the development of neurobiological systems important for regulatory and threat appraisal functions.

BRAIN SYSTEMS SUPPORTING REGULATION AND THREAT APPRAISAL

Neurobiological pathways supporting self-regulation and attention, stress regulation, and threat appraisal constitute a distributed network of cortical and subcortical regions with different profiles of development and neuroplasticity. The PFC, amygdala, and hippocampus are neural structures at the heart of this network and, therefore, are also key to characterizations of how early adversity gets under the skin (for more extensive reviews, see e.g., Arnsten 2009, Brito & Noble 2014, Hertzman & Boyce 2010, McEwen & Gianaros 2010). We begin with an overview of these neural structures before considering the effects of early adversity on their development and function.

The PFC is important for many aspects of top-down regulation, including the inhibition of inappropriate responses and the promotion of task-relevant actions, and, as such, is crucial for the flexible regulation of behavior and adaptation in an ever-changing environment (e.g., Arnsten 2009). The PFC has functional subdivisions, organized in a topographical manner, with extensive connections to cortical and subcortical areas. More dorsal and lateral regions of the PFC are involved in the regulation of attention, thought, and action and have extensive connections to sensory and motor cortices, whereas more ventral and medial regions mediate emotional regulation and have extensive connections to subcortical areas including the amygdala, striatum, and hypothalamus. In addition, the PFC has connections to areas in the brainstem that produce catecholamines, such as dopamine, epinephrine, and norepinephrine, that underlie physiological changes associated with the stress response, particularly the fight-or-flight response mediated by the sympathetic nervous system (SNS). Also important for top-down regulation is the anterior cingulate cortex (ACC), involved in error monitoring (dorsal ACC) and assessment of emotional salience and motivation (ventral ACC).

The amygdala, located deep in the medial temporal lobe, is involved in the detection of biologically relevant stimuli with both positive and negative valence; however, amygdala reactivity appears biased toward negatively valenced information in the environment. This is consistent with the general tendency of the brain to prioritize negative information, known as the negativity bias (Cacioppo et al. 1999), which is hypothesized to relate to the mobilization of the SNS as a default response to uncertainty and novelty and, thus, to a potential threat in the environment (e.g., Thayer & Lane 2009). The amygdala is thought to be central to this response, serving as a rapid detector of potential threats and mediator of adaptive responses to them. Upon encountering a potential threat, the amygdala, via connections to the brainstem and hypothalamus, stimulates the release of the catecholamines and glucocorticoids that underlie the SNS and neuroendocrine responses to stress.

Crucial to the relationship between early adversity and poor outcomes is the regulation of the amygdala by the PFC, particularly the ventromedial PFC (vmPFC). Default inhibition of amygdala activity by the vmPFC is thought to reflect an integration of the external context (potential threat) with the internal context (perceptions of control over the potential threat) (e.g., Maier et al. 2006, Thayer et al. 2012). Under conditions of uncertainty and potential threat, the vmPFC becomes hypoactive, and this disinhibition leads to increased amygdala activity and energy mobilization in response to the potential threat and a shift from slower, more thoughtful PFC-regulated action to more reflexive and rapid emotional action (e.g., Arnsten 2009). As discussed in the section titled Threat Appraisal, early adversity influences the development of both the PFC and the amygdala in ways that can lead to more reactive physiological profiles.

The hippocampus, also located in the medial temporal lobe, is closely connected to the amygdala as well as to the PFC. The hippocampus is important for many aspects of learning and memory, particularly the consolidation of information into long-term episodic, declarative, and spatial memory. Although less involved in self-regulation than the PFC, the hippocampus also plays an important regulatory role in the stress response. The hippocampus contributes to the perception of potential threats via contextual memory of the environmental conditions associated with events related to potential threat. This connectivity is adaptive, as events with more emotional salience are better remembered.

Finally, connections between these brain systems and subcortical areas, including the hypothalamus and brainstem, are important for stress regulation, as well as the regulation of cardiac function via both parasympathetic nervous system (PNS) and SNS afferents (e.g., Thayer & Lane 2009). The PFC, amygdala, and hippocampus are all connected to the ventral striatum in the basal ganglia, which is important for sensitivity to rewarding environmental stimuli and motivation, including aspects of drug sensitivity and risky behavior (Haber & Knutson 2010). The degrees to which these systems are interconnected, sensitive to glucocorticoids and catecholamines associated with stress, and connected to more peripheral physiological systems are central to theories that provide a more mechanistic understanding of the effects of early adversity.

VULNERABILITY OF BRAIN SYSTEMS FOR SELF-REGULATION AND STRESS REGULATION

Self-Regulation

Consistent with the effects on brain systems discussed below, the relationship between early adversity and behavioral outcomes associated with self-regulation constitutes one of the more reliably documented relationships between early adversity and cognitive outcomes. Several studies have shown that early adversity is associated with poorer performance on specific aspects of executive function (EF), including working memory, inhibitory control, and attention shifting (e.g., Blair et al. 2011; Farah et al. 2006; Noble et al. 2005, 2007; Sarsour et al. 2011). For systems such as working memory and inhibitory control, these differences emerge as early as infancy (Lipina et al. 2005). Children with higher temperamental reactivity exhibit lower EF in families facing greater economic adversity but higher EF in families facing less adversity (Raver et al. 2013). This is consistent with the theory that children with more reactive profiles display more sensitivity to context, for better or worse (Ellis & Boyce 2008). These effects of early adversity on self-regulation persist into early adolescence (Farah et al. 2006), and some evidence suggests that they endure into adulthood (Evans & Schamberg 2009). Longer exposure to poverty is also associated with greater deficits in EF in both children and young adults (Evans & Schamberg 2009, Raver et al. 2013).

Brain systems underlying aspects of self-regulation are also vulnerable to early adversity. Neuroimaging studies of EF suggest that early adversity is associated with poorer performance and less efficient recruitment of PFC resources during a novel rule-learning task (Sheridan et al. 2012), as well as reduced PFC activation during EF tasks (Bruce et al. 2013). These effects are evident in adults after as little as one month of chronic psychosocial stress, which results in poorer performance on an attention-shifting task and disrupted functional connectivity between the PFC and a frontoparietal network underlying attention; interestingly, these effects were reversed after one month of reduced stress (Liston et al. 2009). Several event-related potential (ERP) studies also suggest that neural systems important for specific aspects of attention are particularly vulnerable to early adversity. In performance-monitoring tasks, children who had experienced institutionalized or foster care early in development show a reduced brain response to errors and feedback (Bruce et al. 2009b, McDermott et al. 2012). Differences have also been found in selective attention, with children from lower SES backgrounds showing differential early responses associated with selectively attending visual and auditory stimuli (e.g., D'Angiulli et al. 2008, Kishiyama et al. 2009, Stevens et al. 2009). We have further documented specific deficits in mechanisms related to suppressing distracting information, as opposed to enhancing task-relevant information, in the environment (Hampton Wray et al. 2017, Stevens et al. 2009). This is consistent with the hypothesis that differences in self-regulation associated with early adversity may be one of the primary mechanisms by which poverty affects academic outcomes, as reduced suppression of environmental information might be adaptive in more chaotic environments associated with early adversity but maladaptive in a classroom environment (Blair & Raver 2012, 2015).

Early adversity is also associated with other aspects of prefrontal regulatory function. Adults from lower SES backgrounds show atypical behavioral responses to reward and reduced activation to reward cues in regions of the basal ganglia important for reward and motivation (Dillon et al. 2009), as well as reduced dorsomedial PFC and ACC activation and decreased functional connectivity between prefrontal and striatal regions important for reward processing and impulse control (Gianaros et al. 2011). In addition, as discussed below, sickness behaviors associated with blunted reward sensitivity may interact with biomarkers of inflammation to affect the functioning of this system in ways that impact health.

Stress Regulation

The brain is the central organ of the stress response, making it key to understanding how early adversity is associated with lifespan outcomes. It is the brain that decides what is threatening to the organism and regulates the response to stressors. The same brain systems that are important for self-regulation are also the primary neural components of the stress regulation system, which involves neuroendocrine, autonomic, metabolic, and immune systems with diverse biomediators. These systems interact spatially and temporally on multiple timescales as a nonlinear and interactive network that enables a coordinated, adaptive response to a diverse range of stressors (for more comprehensive reviews, see, e.g., Lupien et al. 2009, McEwen & Gianaros 2010). Given this complexity, the stress response system has aptly been characterized as a neuro-symphony (Joëls & Baram 2009). Although a detailed overview is beyond the scope of this paper, we focus in this section on two interconnected systems that operate on different timescales and are vulnerable to experiences associated with early adversity: the hypothalamic-pituitary-adrenal (HPA) axis and the autonomic nervous system (ANS). Whereas the HPA axis is the most well-studied stress response system in the context of early adversity, the ANS is one focus of studies of neurobiological flexibility related to multiple outcomes, as well as of models of reactivity and sensitivity to the environment in the context of early adversity.

An important concept with regard to outcomes associated with early adversity, particularly health outcomes, is allostatic load. Allostasis is an active process of dynamic adaptation to changing environmental demands as an organism encounters physical and behavioral stressors; this adaptation is mediated by changes in the physiological responses of multiple neurobiological systems involved in stress regulation, including both the HPA axis and the ANS, as well as immune systems (McEwen & Gianaros 2010). In the context of adversity, this adaptation can be costly, and McEwen & Stellar (1993) have called this cost allostatic load. Allostatic load refers to the wear and tear on the brain and peripheral systems as a consequence of chronic exposure to stress, as well as to changes in lifestyle that can result from this exposure, such as substance use and abuse and changes to diet, sleep, and level of exercise. Within this framework, four types of physiological response are associated with allostatic load: the frequency and intensity of stressors; the failure to habituate to repetition of stressors, leading to persistently elevated levels of biomediators such as cortisol; the failure to effectively terminate otherwise adaptive regulatory responses to stress; and the failure to mount an adequate response to acute stressors.

The hypothalamic-pituitary-adrenal axis. In conjunction with the SNS, the HPA axis plays a key role in mounting and coordinating the physiological response to stressors. Whereas the SNS initiates a faster, fight-or-flight response via the release of catecholamines, the HPA axis mounts a slower response. When a potential stressor is detected or perceived, the hypothalamus releases corticotrophin-releasing hormone (CRH), which, in turn, stimulates the release of adrenocorticotrophin hormone (ACTH) in the pituitary gland; ACTH then stimulates the release of cortisol from the adrenal cortex. Cortisol can be measured in saliva approximately 20 minutes after the perception of an acute stressor, which is one reason why this system has been better studied in the context of early adversity. Cortisol acts via corticosteroid receptors in the peripheral nervous system and in the brain, with corticosteroid receptors in the PFC, amygdala, and hippocampus mediating both fast and slow effects of this system on brain function. Importantly, there are two types of corticosteroid receptors that have different levels of affinity for cortisol: glucocorticoid receptors (GRs) and mineralocorticoid receptors (MRs), with the latter exhibiting a higher affinity for cortisol. In areas of the brain with both types of receptors, such as the amygdala and hippocampus, GRs are only occupied with higher levels of cortisol. Because the PFC has much higher concentrations of GRs, it is more sensitive to even mild stress that can improve amygdala and hippocampus function (Arnsten 2009). Whereas acute elevation of glucocorticoids helps terminate physiological and behavioral responses to stress, chronic elevation can adversely impact the structure and function of brain regions important for stress regulation and have longer-term effects (e.g., Loman & Gunnar 2010).

The development of the HPA axis is highly dependent on experience and, therefore, vulnerable to early adversity. Studies using animal models provided some of the first evidence of this vulnerability (for reviews, see Gunnar & Quevedo 2007, Hackman et al. 2010, Lupien et al. 2009), including epigenetic mechanisms mediating these effects. Rats who experience lower levels of maternal sensitivity early in development (e.g., reduced licking and grooming following a stressor such as brief separation) exhibit elevated levels of corticosterone accompanied by elevated levels of anxiety in response to a stressor as adults. This programmed response of the HPA axis is mediated by epigenetic alterations of GR expression in the hippocampus.

Studies in humans also reveal that early adversity is associated with dysregulation of the HPA axis, although there is some inconsistency to date in the results concerning directionality of effects. Several studies have found that early adversity is associated with higher levels of diurnal (daytime variability in) cortisol (Blair et al. 2011, Cicchetti & Rogosch 2001) or higher cortisol levels either in the morning (e.g., Lupien et al. 2001) or overnight (Evans & English 2002). Other studies have reported that early adversity is associated with lower levels of cortisol (e.g., Badanes et al. 2011, Chen & Paterson 2006), and studies of children experiencing early adversity that is more extreme than that typically associated with socioeconomic differences also report a blunted HPA response. Institutionalized children raised in orphanages show lower levels of diurnal cortisol (for a review, see Gunnar & Vazquez 2001), and the degree to which this response is blunted is associated with both longer time in institutional care (Gunnar et al. 2001) and lower levels of social care and more problem behaviors postadoption (Koss et al. 2014). Children from lower SES backgrounds in foster care are more likely to have low morning cortisol levels than their peers who are not in foster care (Bruce et al. 2009a), and other studies of children in foster care have also reported reduced diurnal cortisol levels (Dozier et al. 2006). This inconsistency with regard to cortisol and dysregulation is likely related to multiple factors, including the age of the participants; the type, degree, and timing of the stressor(s) experienced; and the length of time since the occurrence of the stressor (e.g., Bruce et al. 2013, Miller et al. 2007, Ursache et al. 2015).

In addition to dysregulation of HPA activity, early and chronic exposure to stress is also associated with structural differences in the neural network involved in stress regulation. Evidence from studies using animal models shows that chronic stress is associated with structural differences, including in volume, neurogenesis, and dendritic branching, in the PFC, hippocampus, and amygdala, and that these structural differences are associated with differences in behavior, such as fear responses and learning (McEwen & Gianaros 2010). Studies of humans show a similar pattern of results for macrostructure: Structural differences, including differences in both cortical volume and cortical surface area, have been found in the PFC (Noble et al. 2012, 2015; Raizada et al. 2008), hippocampus (Hanson et al. 2011; Jednoróg et al. 2012; Noble et al. 2012, 2015), and amygdala (Gianaros et al. 2008, Luby et al. 2013, Noble et al. 2012; for an extensive review, see Brito & Noble 2014). In results underscoring the importance of caregiver relationships, parental nurturance at age four has been found to predict hippocampal volume in a sample of adolescents from lower SES backgrounds (Rao et al. 2010), and caregiver support has been shown to mediate the effects of early adversity on hippocampal volume (Luby et al. 2013). Although there is some degree of inconsistency in the results, which likely depends both on the timing of the stressor and on the time of measurement (for a discussion, see Tottenham & Sheridan 2010), there is generally convergence between human studies and animal studies in that early adversity is associated with structural atrophy in the PFC and hippocampus but hypertrophy of the amygdala structure. As discussed in the next section, this pattern is likely associated with heightened threat sensitivity via increased amygdala reactivity and reduced inhibition of the amygdala by the vmPFC.

Threat appraisal. An important function of the stress regulation system is the identification and processing of socially relevant stimuli that are potentially threatening. Importantly for allostatic effects, it is the brain that decides what is perceived as threatening, and therefore stressful, to an individual (McEwen & Gianaros 2010). This decision making initially involves rapid assignment of the emotional salience of environmental events by the amygdala, which can initiate a rapid response with little cortical processing (Loman & Gunnar 2010, Phelps & LeDoux 2005). The amygdala has bidirectional connections with the PFC and ACC, which play important roles in both the regulation of the response to threat and aspects of self-regulation and attention that are sensitive to early adversity.

Differences in the functioning of the threat appraisal system are thought to play a major role in the effects of early adversity on health, particularly mental health outcomes such as depression and anxiety. In addition, as discussed in the section titled Vulnerability of Immune System Function, this system is a major part of emerging theories linking early adversity to diverse poor health outcomes via compromised neuroimmune function. Importantly, anticipatory responses to perceived threat (e.g., including perceptions related to social standing and status) can lead to activation of allostatic biomediators such as ACTH and cortisol. This activation can contribute to wear and tear associated with prolonged anxiety resulting from dysregulation of systems important for sensing and responding to potential threats in the environment (McEwen & Gianaros 2010). Thus, perceptions of threat shaped by the environment can lead to prolonged states of vigilance, with deleterious effects on health.

Relationships among early adversity, threat sensitivity, and related aspects of socioemotional processing, as well as the corticoamygdala network underlying this sensitivity, represent another of the more robust findings in the literature. Children from lower SES backgrounds show higher rates of internalizing and externalizing behaviors and conduct disorders, as well as higher rates of depression and anxiety (e.g., Duncan et al. 1994, Goodman et al. 2003, McLoyd 1998, Merikangas et al. 2010, Tracy et al. 2008) and lower self- and parent-reported psychological well-being (Evans & English 2002). Adolescents from lower SES backgrounds are also more likely to judge ambiguous scenarios as threatening (Chen & Matthews 2003). Moreover, heightened threat perception mediates relationships between childhood SES and immune processes in children with asthma (Chen et al. 2006) and partially mediates the relationship between childhood SES and increases in daily cortisol output over a 2-year period (Chen et al. 2010). As discussed in the section titled Vulnerability of Immune System Function, this suggests that threat sensitivity is one mechanism by which early adversity has broader effects on health.

In addition to the amygdala's critical role in the perception of and response to potential threat, the vmPFC also plays an important role in the regulation of the HPA axis via connections to the hypothalamus and the SNS response. The PFC has connections to areas in the brainstem that produce catecholamines, such as dopamine, epinephrine, and norepinephrine, that underlie physiological changes associated with the stress response, particularly the fight-or-flight response mediated by the sympathetic nervous system. Under conditions of moderate stress, the sensitivity of the PFC to catecholamines and cortisol leads to arousal and improved attention and effortful regulation (Blair & Raver 2015). However, at higher levels of stress, PFC activity is reduced as amygdala activity increases, resulting in a shift from more reflective, top-down processing to more reactive, bottom-up processing (Arnsten 2009). As discussed in the section titled Vulnerability of Immune System Function, the balance between PFC regulation and amygdala reactivity interacts with experiences associated with early adversity in ways that contribute to increased allostatic load, as activity from enhanced reactivity mobilizes downstream stress systems (the SNS, the HPA axis) that contribute to allostatic load and modulate inflammation.

Increasingly, evidence suggests that chronic stress associated with early adversity affects PFC and amygdala function across development. Adolescents who have faced more extreme early adversity in the form of institutionalization show greater amygdala reactivity to emotional stimuli (Gee et al. 2013, Tottenham et al. 2011), and young adults from lower SES backgrounds show greater amygdala activity in response to threatening facial expressions (Gianaros et al. 2008). This increased reactivity may result from insufficient top-down regulation by the PFC. Young adults from lower SES backgrounds show both greater amygdala activity and reduced PFC activity during effortful regulation of negative emotion, and chronic stress exposure across development mediates the relationship between early adversity and PFC activation (Kim et al. 2013).

Systems important for both self-regulation and reactivity to threat are shaped by interactions with the environment in a complex and dynamic process characterized as canalization, or channeling, of development (Blair & Raver 2012, 2015; Raver et al. 2013). In contexts of early adversity, this may not result in consistent levels of arousal over time, which are important for more reflective self-regulation processes that facilitate learning. As Blair & Raver (2012, 2015) have noted, heightened vigilance to emotionally negative stimuli (e.g., Cicchetti & Rogosch 2009, Pollak et al. 2005) may lead to a response profile that is more reactive to experience, which may be beneficial in the short term in certain environments associated with early adversity but maladaptive in educational environments (Blair & Raver 2012). These interactions thus shape individual differences in self-regulation at least in part via the stress response system, and evidence suggests that early adversity affects self-regulation via both emotional regulation and dysregulation of the HPA axis. Emotional regulation profiles in infancy predict self-regulation skills later in development such that children from lower SES backgrounds with high levels of emotional reactivity in a fear-eliciting task and low levels of emotional regulation have poor EF performance; however, children with high reactivity but also high levels of emotional regulation have better EF performance, and positive parenting is associated with better emotional regulation (Ursache et al. 2013). Early adversity is associated with poorer EF, and this relationship is mediated by caregiving and HPA function such that lower parental sensitivity is associated with higher basal cortisol levels that, in turn, predict poorer EF performance in 3-year-olds (Blair et al. 2011). In adults, poorer EF performance is associated with a greater amount of time spent in childhood poverty, and this relationship is mediated by allostatic load associated with elevated chronic stress during childhood (Evans & Schamberg 2009). Thus, a more reactive response profile is associated with several poor outcomes related to early adversity. In the next section, we consider another stress response system that may index the prefrontal hypoactivity and amygdala hyperreactivity associated with this profile.

Autonomic nervous system function. The dynamic interaction between the heart and brain in response to changing environmental demands constitutes another important aspect of stress regulation that is also shaped by early adversity in ways that likely increase allostatic load (e.g., Porges 2007, Thayer & Lane 2009). Central to this interaction is the autonomic nervous system (ANS), which plays a prominent role in the determination of heart rate via inputs from the brainstem from both SNS and PNS branches. Whereas the SNS initiates physiological arousal when a real or perceived threat arises, the PNS modulates SNS input to the heart and other peripheral systems, serving a regulatory function that restores and contributes to the maintenance of homeostasis. Because the cardiovascular system is one of the systems most vulnerable to stress (McEwen & Gianaros 2010), and because of the important role of the ANS in aspects of self-regulation, the ANS is also central to theories of how early adversity gets under the skin. In addition, responses to stress take place at different timescales ranging from milliseconds to days (Joëls & Baram 2009), and examinations of the ANS provide the opportunity to examine stress at the timescale of milliseconds. Recent methodological developments also present the opportunity to integrate measures of brain function and stress regulation on a trial-by-trial basis at this timescale (e.g., Mueller et al. 2010), which could prove fruitful in future investigations of early adversity and neurobiology.

One influential model of adaptation to environmental stressors emphasizes the importance of flexibility in the face of changing environmental demands to successful adaptation and proposes that this flexibility is achieved via a system that integrates input from internal and external systems to generate adaptive responses (Thayer & Lane 2009). In this model of neurovisceral integration, Thayer & Lane propose that high-frequency heart rate variability (HRV) may index this system. High-frequency HRV (0.15 to 0.4 Hz) reflects the influence of the vagus nerve, a cranial nerve that provides a bidirectional link between the heart and brain structures (Thayer & Lane 2009) and that is thought to be analogous to a central executive in the PNS that lowers heart rate and overall levels of arousal. There are ongoing methodological issues surrounding the measurement of vagal function (e.g., Graziano & Derefinko 2013) and, thus, varying methods and terminology used in the literature (e.g., vagal tone, respiratory sinus arrhythmia); however, this debate is beyond the scope of this review, and, following Thayer & Lane (2009), we use HRV for ease of comparison across studies.

Increases in HRV reflect increased activation of the vagus nerve, often co-occurring with decreased heart rate and arousal akin to a vagal brake (Berntson et al. 1993). Because the vagally mediated PNS provides a more rapid and flexible response, resting cardiac balance is characterized by PNS dominance over SNS influences. When a stressor is encountered, the vagal brake is withdrawn to facilitate an increase in heart rate, and this brake can then be reengaged to facilitate a return to a calm state after a stressor. A large body of literature has found associations between vagal function (lower baseline HRV) and poor cardiovascular health outcomes (e.g., Thayer & Lane 2007), as well as a broader range of poor physical and mental health outcomes across development and into adulthood that include many outcomes associated with early adversity. This has led Beauchaine & Thayer (2015) to identify HRV as a transdiagnostic biomarker of psychopathology such that lower HRV may index vulnerability to a wide range of disorders.

Interestingly, vagally mediated cardiac activity is modulated by the same prefrontal systems that are involved in the regulation of the HPA axis. Evidence suggests a preferential role for the right PFC in aspects of inhibitory control of both cognition and affective behavior (e.g., Aron et al. 2004), as well as for modulation of cardiac activity via the vagus nerve (Thayer & Lane 2009). Central to this role is the tonic inhibition of the amygdala by the PFC, most prominently the medial and orbitofrontal PFC (Thayer et al. 2012). Tonic default inhibition of amygdala activity by the vmPFC is thought to reflect an integration of the external context (potential threat) with the internal context (perceptions of control over the potential threat) (Maier et al. 2006, Thayer et al. 2012). As discussed above, PFC hypoactivity leads to increased amygdala activation and SNS- and HPA-mediated mobilization of resources in response to a potential threat. Thayer and colleagues (2012) hypothesized that a prolonged state of PFC hypoactivity associated with chronic stress, as indexed by HRV, produces increases in allostatic load that likely contribute to the range of poor health outcomes associated with HRV. Moreover, some longitudinal evidence suggests that chronic stress associated with exposure to parents' marital conflict in childhood results in lower resting HRV in adolescence (El-Sheikh et al. 2011) and that lower educational attainment in young adulthood is associated with lower resting HRV (Sloan et al. 2005).

As discussed above, early adversity is associated with a more reactive response profile characterized by heightened vigilance to emotionally negative stimuli, and the neurovisceral integration model posits that both tonic and reactive HRV provide an index of this prefrontal hypoactive state associated with disinhibition of SNS activity. Consistent with this hypothesis, neuroimaging studies document a consistent association between HRV and both vmPFC and amygdala activity (Thayer et al. 2012). Differences in PNS function, as assessed by HRV, are related to emotional regulation and threat sensitivity, as well as cognition. Both higher levels of resting HRV and increases in HRV during emotional regulation tasks (i.e., removal of the vagal brake) are associated with more effective emotional regulation across development, from early childhood (Porges 1996) into adulthood (e.g., Park & Thayer 2014, Thayer & Brosschot 2005), as well as less sensitivity to potential threats (Shook et al. 2007) and inhibition of threat responses to nonthreatening stimuli (Thayer & Friedman 2002). Although less evidence exists of a link between HRV and aspects of cognition, a similar pattern is emerging, suggesting that higher levels of baseline HRV and HRV withdrawal are associated with performance on self-regulation and EF tasks in children (e.g., Chapman et al. 2010, Marcovitch et al. 2010) and adults (e.g., Hansen et al. 2003, Kimhy et al. 2013). Taken together, these results suggest that higher resting HRV and HRV withdrawal are associated with more flexible and adaptive regulatory behavior and that lower resting HRV and lower HRV withdrawal are associated with hypervigilance and impaired prefrontal regulation of the response to emotional stimuli (Park & Thayer 2014, Thayer & Lane 2009).

Increasingly, evidence suggests that early adversity is associated with dysregulation of both PNS and SNS function, although most evidence comes from studies of forms of early adversity that are more extreme than differences in SES. Overall, the pattern is characterized by lower resting HRV and HRV withdrawal and, to a lesser degree, by increased sympathetic activity, consistent with heightened vigilance and prefrontal hypoactivity. More evidence exists on the role of the PNS, likely because nonintrusive measures of SNS function, such as measures of salivary α-amylase (sAA) and pre-ejection period (PEP), have only recently become more common in developmental studies (for a review, see Propper & Holochwost 2013). Effects of early adversity on the ANS have been documented as early as the prenatal period, as fetuses of mothers reporting higher levels of perceived stress have lower resting levels of HRV (Allister et al. 2001, DiPietro et al. 1996), and greater socioeconomic adversity during pregnancy is associated with heightened SNS reactivity across development to age five (Alkon et al. 2014). In addition, maternal depression and substance abuse during pregnancy is associated in infants with lower resting levels of HRV, HRV withdrawal, and elevated heart rate, which likely reflects a combination of PNS and SNS activity (e.g., Field et al. 1995, Schuetze et al. 2011). Consistent with the evidence reviewed above, differences in interactions with caregivers are also associated with differences in regulation of the ANS. Lower resting HRV in infants is associated with poorer parent–child joint communication (Porter 2003) and higher levels of parental marital conflict (Porter et al. 2003), and increased parental marital conflict is also associated with lower HRV withdrawal in response to maternal disengagement (e.g., Moore 2010). In addition, higher levels of sAA in response to challenge are associated with irregular profiles of attachment associated with early adversity (Oosterman et al. 2010).

Other studies extend the findings associating early adversity and dysregulation of ANS function and, like the pattern of results in studies of early adversity and cortisol, present a somewhat inconsistent pattern of results that highlights the need to consider the interaction between physiological profiles of reactivity and context. Although higher resting HRV and increased HRV withdrawal have been found to be associated with adaptive behavior, recent evidence suggests that this may not always be the case in children from lower SES backgrounds. Children from lower SES backgrounds who receive insensitive caregiving have higher levels of problem behavior, but only if they also have higher levels of resting HRV (Conradt et al. 2013). Similarly, children from lower SES backgrounds with higher HRV withdrawal at one month of age exhibit more behavioral dysregulation at age three, but only if they were exposed to higher levels of caregiver stress (Conradt et al. 2016). Higher HRV withdrawal in response to challenge tasks is also associated with poorer behavioral and academic outcomes in kindergartners, but only in the context of higher family adversity, whereas children with higher HRV withdrawal but with lower levels of family adversity have higher levels of educational engagement and academic competence (Obradovic et al. 2010). Similar patterns have been reported in studies of more extreme forms of early adversity. For example, Skowron and colleagues (2014) found that HRV withdrawal predicts better inhibitory control in children who had not experienced child maltreatment but that, in children who had experienced child maltreatment, better inhibitory control was instead predicted by HRV augmentation, with stronger effects occurring in tasks in which children were engaged with the maltreating caregiver. Taken together, these results are consistent with the theory of biological sensitivity to context (Ellis & Boyce 2008) and a recent extension of this theory, the adaptive calibration model (Del Giudice et al. 2011). Both models suggest that the stress response system interacts with environmental context such that high reactivity may be adaptive in more supportive environments but less adaptive in more negative and potentially threatening environments associated with early adversity. The adaptive calibration model describes a wider range of stress response profiles that potentially interact with the severity and duration of stressors related to early adversity, providing testable hypotheses for future studies.

Although less evidence exists on the effects of early adversity on the interaction between the PNS and SNS (Propper & Holochwost 2013), some researchers have suggested that more reactive and vigilant profiles associated with early adversity might be characterized, in some contexts, by SNS dominance and blunted PNS activity (e.g., Del Giudice et al. 2011). Some evidence suggests that a pattern of PNS activation and SNS inhibition may represent a profile of resilience (e.g., El-Sheikh et al. 2009). Response strategies to mild stressors may be dictated, first, by the evolutionarily newer PNS system, followed by a shift to the evolutionarily older SNS system if the PNS system is ineffective (Beauchaine et al. 2007). If this is the case, the ability of children from backgrounds of adversity to mount a PNS response to challenge may be limited by a less flexible PNS system, which could result in a greater relative reliance on SNS resources, imposing, in turn, greater allostatic load. Because research on this model is limited and comes mostly from studies of infants, it is necessarily speculative at this time. Future research on the effects of early adversity that incorporates independent measures of PNS and SNS function in the same participants will shed valuable light on this question (Propper & Holochwost 2013).

THE IMMUNE SYSTEM

As discussed above, early adversity is associated with a wide range of poor health outcomes across the lifespan, including both infectious and inflammation-related diseases (Irwin & Cole 2011, McEwen & Gianaros 2010). Importantly, adult behavior alone does not explain these patterns, and evidence suggests that early adversity leaves a biological residue (Chen & Miller 2013) that may operate independently of subsequent experience and behavior. For example, even in a sample of well-educated and affluent physicians, rates of coronary heart disease were more than twice as high at age 50 for those raised in lower SES households (Kittleson et al. 2006). Increasingly, evidence suggests that these enduring effects are likely mediated by the immune system and its interactions with the neural and stress regulation systems discussed above. Central to emerging hypotheses on the role of the immune system is the role of the HPA axis and SNS, as well as related brain systems, in the regulation of broad patterns of gene expression in immune cells.

Key to the function of the immune system is the activation of immune response genes that encode antibodies, as well as regulatory molecules such as cytokines. This activation is triggered by different types of internal signals (for a detailed review, see Irwin & Cole 2011). Two broad classes of internal signals have been found: extracellular pathogens (e.g., bacteria), which activate proinflammatory programming, and intracellular pathogens (e.g., viruses), which activate antiviral programming. Both responses come at an energetic cost to the organism.

More recently, the brain has emerged as a third class of stimulus that plays a vital role in the modulation of the immune response. This neural modulation is beneficial for adaptation and survival because it allows for the suppression of the effects of inflammation and sickness behavior when the broader environmental context presents more immediate threats. Neural suppression of the transcription of both proinflammatory and antiviral genetic programming occurs via multiple mechanisms. The first involves the release of glucocorticoids from the HPA axis, a mechanism that is protective against hyperinflammatory disease. The second involves the SNS, which simultaneously inhibits antiviral genes and activates proinflammatory genes via multiple pathways, including the production of proinflammatory cytokines, with a net effect of increased expression of proinflammatory immune response genes. This occurs even when glucocorticoid levels are stable or elevated, which appears to be the result of a functional desensitization of the GR (Pace et al. 2007) that is related to chronic stress and threat in animal models (e.g., Powell et al. 2011), as well as early adversity in humans (G.E. Miller et al. 2009). These cytokines also work within the brain, in part via receptors in the hippocampus and hypothalamus, to activate a broad array of sickness behaviors, including anhedonia and fatigue, reductions in exploratory and reward-seeking behavior, altered cognitive and motor function, sleep alterations, and reduced social functioning (e.g., Dantzer et al. 2008). Neuroimaging studies have found that this cytokine-induced pattern of sickness behaviors is associated with altered connectivity among the ACC, medial PFC, and amygdala and reduced ventral striatum activation to reward (e.g., Eisenberger et al. 2010, Harrison et al. 2009).

Reductions in glucocorticoid-mediated feedback inhibition have the effect of increasing proinflammatory gene expression, even at baseline levels. Allostatic theories (McEwen & Gianaros 2010) propose that physiological systems survive best if they are prepared to actively anticipate challenges and proactively alter their functioning in preparation, leading to the idea of a forward-looking immune system programmed by the environment. Thus, an environment characterized by chronic exposure to real or perceived threats to survival might program a more proinflammatory phenotype that is beneficial for shorter-term survival but confers adverse longer-term consequences for a range of health outcomes.

VULNERABILITY OF IMMUNE SYSTEM FUNCTION

Early adversity is also associated with altered immune system function at different stages of development. Increased levels of circulating biomarkers of inflammation, such as the cytokines C-reactive protein (CRP), interleukin-6 (IL-6), and tumor necrosis factor α (TNFα), provide a reliable index of systemic inflammation in studies of humans. Increased production of proinflammatory cytokines is found in newborns experiencing greater prenatal maternal stress (Wright et al. 2010) and in children from lower SES backgrounds (e.g., Azad et al. 2012, Broyles et al. 2012). This altered function may endure into adolescence and adulthood, as adolescents exposed to early family adversity show increasingly greater production of proinflammatory cytokines over time (Miller & Chen 2010). Furthermore, young adults from lower SES backgrounds show increased proinflammatory cytokine production compared to adults from higher SES backgrounds, even in the absence of differences in adult SES (G.E. Miller et al. 2009). In addition, early adversity is associated with higher rates of inflammation-related diseases typical of older age in adults in their thirties, with stronger effects when adversity occurred earlier in development (Ziol-Guest et al. 2012). Consistent with the mechanisms discussed above, several of these studies also found an association between early adversity and decreased sensitivity to glucocorticoids. One specific mechanism that appears to underlie chronic proinflammatory gene expression is sleep, as elevated levels of proinflammatory biomarkers have been consistently found in people suffering sleep disturbances (for a review, see Irwin et al. 2016). Disruptions of sleep are associated with both early adversity and chronic stress, and poor sleep habits have been linked to poor academic outcomes in children from lower SES backgrounds, with family stress and inconsistency in the home environment hypothesized to be moderating factors in this relationship (for a review, see Buckhalt 2011).

The neuroimmune network hypothesis of Nusslock & Miller (2016) builds on and integrates much of the evidence discussed above. This hypothesis notes the large overlap between health outcomes with a suspected inflammatory etiology and those associated with early adversity. The network hypothesis proposes that early adversity amplifies crosstalk between multiple systems in a manner that leads to chronic low-grade inflammation that contributes to this wide range of poor health outcomes. Given the evidence that early adversity may lead both to a more reactive, hyper-vigilant profile mediated by corticoamygdala circuitry and HPA and SNS mechanisms and to a proinflammatory phenotype, the neuroimmune network hypothesis posits that this combination of effects leads to increased bidirectional traffic between the brain and immune system, creating a positive feedback loop that heightens risk over time. The hypothesis further posits an additional bidirectional pathway involving the corticostriatal pathway, which supports reward processing. Given the evidence that early adversity is associated with blunted reward sensitivity and that this sensitivity is mediated in part by inflammatory cytokines (e.g., A.H. Miller et al. 2009), the hypothesis posits that a more proinflammatory phenotype leads to higher rates of high-risk and addictive behavior. Such high-risk behaviors (e.g., smoking, poor nutrition) in turn have proinflammatory effects (e.g., Kiecolt-Glaser 2010, Yanbaeva et al. 2007), thereby potentially creating another positive feedback loop. Finally, given the evidence that early adversity is associated with differences in PFC structure and function and emerging evidence that inflammation may also affect the structure, function, and connectivity of the PFC and other brain areas (e.g., Gianaros et al. 2012, Marsland et al. 2008), the model posits that these differences in self-regulation and inhibition of amygdala reactivity may further contribute to a self-perpetuating cycle driven by increased neuroimmune crosstalk. As Nusslock & Miller (2016) note, several aspects of this hypothesis are speculative but provide fruitful directions for future research. Although this is not part of the hypothesis and is also speculative, it is interesting to note that lower HRV has also been associated with higher levels of proinflammatory cytokines (for a review, see Thayer & Sternberg 2006), raising the possibility that an autonomic profile of SNS dominance and blunted PNS activity may also contribute to a proinflammatory phenotype and associated chronic low-grade inflammation.

CONCLUSION

The effects of early adversity are evident across numerous levels of analysis and at multiple levels of society, and the costs to society are great. The costs of growing up in poverty are estimated to be equivalent to almost 4% of gross domestic product, or approximately $500 billion per year, distributed across costs associated with increases in direct and indirect health expenditures and the values of life expectancy, economic output, and crime victimization (Holzer et al. 2008). A recent study estimates that the 20% of society that is most vulnerable to effects associated with early adversity incur as much as 80% of the costs to society associated with social welfare, health, and crime (Caspi et al. 2016). Thus, there is a degree of urgency in the need for a more mechanistic understanding of early adversity that can inform efforts to ameliorate these costly effects.

Neurobiological Targets for Intervention

Although the studies reviewed in this article represent great progress in understanding the relationships between early adversity and multiple integrated neurobiological systems, because they are correlational, they are necessarily limited in the degree to which causation can be inferred from them. However, studies that employ experimental designs provide the opportunity to build on correlational studies in ways that inform both theories regarding the causal pathways and policies that seek to ameliorate the costly effects of early adversity. Building on the work described above, translational researchers are designing, implementing, and assessing interventions that include consideration of the multiple integrated biological systems affected by adversity. A well-informed intervention should also target the proximal pathways through which adversity operates and incorporate these pathways into theory-of-change models (e.g., Fisher et al. 2016); consistent with the research above, evidence from experimental studies suggests that interventions addressing the caregiving environment may yield particularly high dividends. Some of these studies include one or more of the neurobiological systems described as outcome measures, providing valuable evidence on the potential for intervention to alter the adverse developmental trajectory of these vulnerable systems. In this section, we briefly highlight a subset of interventions targeting early adversity.

Consistent with our framework emphasizing the two sides of plasticity (Stevens & Neville 2006), we consider whether the same neural systems that are vulnerable in the face of early adversity might also, under different conditions, be capable of enhancement. We focus specifically on interventions that have included assessment of one or more of the integrated biological systems identified above and that specifically target an aspect of the early caregiving environment, thereby examining the second side of plasticity, namely the capacity for vulnerable subsystems to be modified for the better.

Several studies document the responsiveness of the neurobiological systems reviewed in this article to interventions targeting the early caregiving environment, ranging from adoption out of institutional rearing (Tottenham et al. 2010) to targeted interventions (Neville et al. 2013). As an example, in our own research, we have examined the effects of an 8-week, two-generation intervention for families of preschool children living in poverty. The program combined direct work with small groups of children on attention and self-regulation activities with small-group training for parents, providing tools and strategies for the home focused, in part, on reducing family stress. Children randomly assigned to receive the intervention showed an increase in the effects of selective attention on neural processing from before to after the training relative to children in both active and passive control groups, and parents randomly assigned to the intervention reported less parenting stress compared to parents from both control groups (Neville et al. 2013). In addition to underscoring the importance of targeting caregiving, this result also highlights the potential of two-generation interventions that simultaneously target attention and self-regulation in children and family stress in parents.

Stress is another neurobiological target for intervention. Increasingly, intervention studies are examining cortisol: One review reported that, of 19 studies incorporating cortisol into rigorous experimental designs, more than half were published after 2008 (Slopen et al. 2014). This review found that 18 of the 19 studies published found at least one significant change in cortisol with interventions, many of which targeted caregiving in some way. Importantly, all eight studies that included a comparison group from lower-risk backgrounds reported evidence that patterns of cortisol activity in intervention groups from higher-risk backgrounds changed with intervention to more closely resemble patterns of children from lower-risk backgrounds. Although there was inconsistency in how interventions affected cortisol, this pattern nonetheless illustrates the plasticity of the HPA system and suggests that interventions can alter the developmental trajectory of stress regulation systems in ways that may lead to better health outcomes. For example, in seminal studies of an intervention targeting stress in foster parents and preschool-aged foster children, Fisher and colleagues (Fisher & Stoolmiller 2008, Fisher et al. 2007) demonstrated that the intervention reduces stress in foster parents and normalizes diurnal cortisol patterns in foster children to levels more comparable with community controls relative to foster families who did not receive the intervention. Another study also found that a classroom-based program targeting self-regulation in kindergarten children had positive effects on multiple self-regulation and academic measures, as well as effects on cortisol specific to children from high-poverty schools, illustrating that classroom-based approaches targeting self-regulation can also impact stress physiology in children from backgrounds of adversity (Blair & Raver 2014).

Although considerably less evidence exists regarding the response of the ANS to intervention, one study suggests that this system exhibits considerable plasticity and also underscores the importance of caregiving, particularly early caregiving. McLaughlin and colleagues (2015) found that institutionalized children show blunted cortisol and SNS reactivity in response to psychosocial stressors compared to children randomly assigned to adoption into high-quality foster care. They also found that earlier age of placement into foster care is associated with normalization of cortisol reactivity, as well as greater HRV withdrawal during a social task, suggesting sensitive periods underlying the plasticity of these systems and some specificity with regard to the timing of caregiving changes and the development of more flexible PNS function. Although more study is necessary, this result demonstrates that the ANS may be amenable to early intervention.

Finally, some evidence suggests that the immune system is responsive to early interventions focused on the caregiving environment. Miller and colleagues (2014) demonstrated that African American adolescents from lower SES backgrounds who were randomly assigned as children to receive an intervention designed to strengthen parenting, family relationships, and youth competencies had lower levels of inflammation across six cytokines 8 years after receiving the intervention. These effects were mediated by improvements in parenting, again highlighting the importance of targeting the caregiving environment. The authors hypothesize that changes in parenting may have led children to adopt an adaptive shift and persist strategy. This strategy entails a combination of acceptance and endurance in the face of adversity and has been shown to moderate the relationships between SES and both glucocorticoid sensitivity and systemic inflammation in adolescents and their parents (Chen et al. 2015). The identification of adaptive psychosocial characteristics that can be targeted in interventions and that have the potential to mitigate the effects of early adversity via physiological and inflammatory processes represents a promising future direction of research in this area.

FUTURE DIRECTIONS

Although considerable progress has been made to understand the ways in which early adversity gets under the skin to affect multiple neurobiological systems, much important work remains. We close by briefly highlighting multiple ongoing and future directions in this research, many of which have been discussed by researchers whose work is the focus of this review. Although our review has emphasized the importance of caregiving, there are multiple additional influences on the development and plasticity of the systems discussed above. These include both genetic and epigenetic effects, as well as other environmental influences such as pollution, exposure to toxins, nutrition, and exercise, among many others. With regard to stress, it is particularly important to consider other psychosocial factors with implications for health, including the degree to which an individual feels control in life and, relatedly, subjective social status. It is also important to consider factors that confer resilience because, despite the profound effects reviewed in this article, a substantial proportion of children who experience early adversity avoid many of these poor outcomes. Research that identifies mediators or moderators that may confer vulnerability as well as resilience, as does some of the evidence on caregiving discussed above, is important in this regard.

Future research should also employ more longitudinal designs that include a greater consideration of interactions between early adversity and the developmental trajectories of different neurobiological systems in a life-course perspective. Employment of these designs involves careful consideration of both how and when adversity is measured, as well as differential contributions of different aspects of adversity at different points in development and the integration of measures of multiple neurobiological systems. This will, in turn, provide more specificity to inform the development of theoretically driven interventions and theory-based evaluations of the efficacy of interventions on targeted systems. We have highlighted interventions targeting the systems that are the focus of this review; however, other intervention approaches, including behavioral programs that target physical activity and social integration, as well as pharmacological and therapeutic programs, show promise in ameliorating the effects of early adversity (McEwen & Gianaros 2010). In addition, promising work in developing countries illustrates how evidence-based interventions can be designed in ways that address challenges to large-scale implementation (Neville et al. 2015).

Future work should also continue the ongoing focus on efforts to use scientific evidence to inform public policy. Central to these efforts is the need to continue to improve public as well as professional (e.g., education, health care) understanding of this research and the profound relationships between early adversity and neurobiological development. A good example is the work of the National Scientific Council on the Developing Child, the Center on the Developing Child, and the FrameWorks Institute in taking an evidence-based approach to the iterative development of metaphors to communicate complex scientific concepts to nonscientists; these metaphors have, in turn, been used successfully to promote a broader understanding of concepts such as brain architecture and toxic stress (Shonkoff & Bales 2011). It is crucial for scientists to be closely involved in their communities and to make efforts to share their work directly with the public when possible. Increased public understanding can potentially lead to greater public support for evidence-based public policies, such as investments in early education and caregiver support, that have the potential to more broadly address issues related to early adversity.

Finally, as we have tried to highlight in this review, progress in this area requires continued and increased consideration of findings from different disciplines, as well as interdisciplinary collaborations. It is increasingly evident that these collaborations should include neuroscientists, cognitive neuroscientists, social and developmental psychologists, geneticists, epidemiologists, prevention and intervention scientists, educators, economists, and policy makers. Such collaborative efforts will lead to more progress in understanding the complex interplay among the biological and environmental factors that underlie the broad and costly effects of early adversity, as well as the plasticity that provides hope for the amelioration of these effects.

DISCLOSURE STATEMENT

The authors are not aware of any affiliations, memberships, funding, or financial holdings that might be perceived as affecting the objectivity of this review.

ACKNOWLEDGMENTS

The authors would like to acknowledge the support of grants from the Department of Health and Human Services, the Administration for Children and Families (90YR0076), and the National Science Foundation (1539698) to E.P. and H.N.

LITERATURE CITED

Alkon A, Boyce WT, Tran L, Harley KG, Neuhaus J, Eskenazi B. 2014. Prenatal adversities and Latino children's autonomic nervous system reactivity trajectories from 6 months to 5 years of age. *PLOS ONE* 9:e86283

Allister L, Lester BM, Carr S, Liu J. 2001. The effects of maternal depression on fetal heart rate response to vibroacoustic stimulation. *Dev. Neuropsychol.* 20:639–51

Arnsten AF. 2009. Stress signalling pathways that impair prefrontal cortex structure and function. *Nat. Rev. Neurosci.* 10:410–22

Aron AR, Robbins TW, Poldrack RA. 2004. Inhibition and the right inferior frontal cortex. *Trends Cogn. Sci.* 8:170–77

Azad MB, Lissitsyn Y, Miller GE, Becker AB, HayGlass KT, Kozyrskyj AL. 2012. Influence of socioeconomic status trajectories on innate immune responsiveness in children. *PLOS ONE* 7:e38669

Badanes LS, Watamura SE, Hankin BL. 2011. Hypocortisolism as a potential marker of allostatic load in children: associations with family risk and internalizing disorders. *Dev. Psychopathol.* 23:881–96

Baydar N, Akcinar B. 2015. Ramifications of socioeconomic differences for three year old children and their families in Turkey. *Early Child. Res. Q.* 33:33–48

Beauchaine TP, Gatzke-Kopp L, Mead HK. 2007. Polyvagal theory and developmental psychopathology: emotion dysregulation and conduct problems from preschool to adolescence. *Biol. Psychol.* 74:174–84

Beauchaine TP, Thayer JF. 2015. Heart rate variability as a transdiagnostic biomarker of psychopathology. *Int. J. Psychophysiol.* 98:338–50

Berntson GG, Cacioppo JT, Quigley KS. 1993. Respiratory sinus arrhythmia: autonomic origins, physiological mechanisms, and psychophysiological implications. *Psychophysiology* 30:183–96

Blair C, Granger DA, Willoughby M, Mills-Koonce R, Cox M, et al. 2011. Salivary cortisol mediates effects of poverty and parenting on executive functions in early childhood. *Child Dev.* 82:1970–84

Blair C, Raver CC. 2012. Child development in the context of adversity: experiential canalization of brain and behavior. *Am. Psychol.* 67(4):309–18

Blair C, Raver CC. 2014. Closing the achievement gap through modification of neurocognitive and neuroendocrine function: results from a cluster randomized controlled trial of an innovative approach to the education of children in kindergarten. *PLOS ONE* 9:e112393

Blair C, Raver CC. 2015. School readiness and self-regulation: a developmental psychobiological approach. *Annu. Rev. Psychol.* 66:711–31

Bradbury B, Corak M, Waldfogel J, Washbrook E. 2015. *Too Many Children Left Behind: The US Achievement Gap in Comparative Perspective*. New York: Russell Sage Found.

Brito NH, Noble KG. 2014. Socioeconomic status and structural brain development. *Front. Neurosci.* 8:276

Brooks-Gunn J, Duncan GJ. 1997. The effects of poverty on children. *Future Child.* 7:55–71

Broyles ST, Staiano AE, Drazba KT, Gupta AK, Sothern M, Katzmarzyk PT. 2012. Elevated C-reactive protein in children from risky neighborhoods: evidence for a stress pathway linking neighborhoods and inflammation in children. *PLOS ONE* 7:e45419

Bruce J, Fisher PA, Pears KC, Levine S. 2009a. Morning cortisol levels in preschool-aged foster children: differential effects of maltreatment type. *Dev. Psychobiol.* 51:14–23

Bruce J, Gunnar MR, Pears KC, Fisher PA. 2013. Early adverse care, stress neurobiology, and prevention science: lessons learned. *Prev. Sci.* 14:247–56

Bruce J, McDermott JM, Fisher PA, Fox NA. 2009b. Using behavioral and electrophysiological measures to assess the effects of a preventive intervention: a preliminary study with preschool-aged foster children. *Prev. Sci.* 10:129–40

Buckhalt JA. 2011. Insufficient sleep and the socioeconomic status achievement gap. *Child Dev. Perspect.* 5:59–65

Cacioppo JT, Gardner WL, Berntson GG. 1999. The affect system has parallel and integrative processing components: Form follows function. *J. Personal. Soc. Psychol.* 76:839–55

Caspi A, Houts RM, Belsky DW, Harrington H, Hogan S, et al. 2016. Childhood forecasting of a small segment of the population with large economic burden. *Nat. Hum. Behav.* 1:0005

Chapman H, Woltering S, Lamm C, Lewis M. 2010. Hearts and minds: coordination of neurocognitive and cardiovascular regulation in children and adolescents. *Biol. Psychol.* 84:296–303

Chen E, Cohen S, Miller GE. 2010. How low socioeconomic status affects 2-year hormonal trajectories in children. *Psychol. Sci.* 21:31–37

Chen E, Hanson MD, Paterson LQ, Griffin MJ, Walker HA, Miller GE. 2006. Socioeconomic status and inflammatory processes in childhood asthma: the role of psychological stress. *J. Allergy Clin. Immunol.* 117:1014–20

Chen E, Matthews KA. 2003. Development of the cognitive appraisal and understanding of social events (CAUSE) videos. *Health Psychol.* 22(1):106–10

Chen E, McLean KC, Miller GE. 2015. Shift-and-persist strategies: associations with socioeconomic status and the regulation of inflammation among adolescents and their parents. *Psychosom. Med.* 77:371–82

Chen E, Miller GE. 2013. Socioeconomic status and health: mediating and moderating factors. *Annu. Rev. Clin. Psychol.* 9:723–49

Chen E, Paterson LQ. 2006. Neighborhood, family, and subjective socioeconomic status: How do they relate to adolescent health? *Health Psychol.* 25:704–14

Cicchetti D, Rogosch FA. 2001. The impact of child maltreatment and psychopathology on neuroendocrine functioning. *Dev. Psychopathol.* 13:783–804

Cicchetti D, Rogosch FA. 2009. Adaptive coping under conditions of extreme stress: multilevel influences on the determinants of resilience in maltreated children. *New Dir. Child Adolesc. Dev.* 2009(124):47–59

Conradt E, Beauchaine T, Abar B, Lagasse L, Shankaran S, et al. 2016. Early caregiving stress exposure moderates the relation between respiratory sinus arrhythmia reactivity at 1 month and biobehavioral outcomes at age 3. *Psychophysiology* 53:83–96

Conradt E, Measelle J, Ablow JC. 2013. Poverty, problem behavior, and promise: differential susceptibility among infants reared in poverty. *Psychol. Sci.* 24:235–42

D'Angiulli A, Herdman A, Stapells D, Hertzman C. 2008. Children's event-related potentials of auditory selective attention vary with their socioeconomic status. *Neuropsychology* 22:293–300

Dantzer R, O'Connor JC, Freund GG, Johnson RW, Kelley KW. 2008. From inflammation to sickness and depression: when the immune system subjugates the brain. *Nat. Rev. Neurosci.* 9:46–56

Del Giudice M, Ellis BJ, Shirtcliff EA. 2011. The adaptive calibration model of stress responsivity. *Neurosci. Biobehav. Rev.* 35:1562–92

Dillon DG, Holmes AJ, Birk JL, Brooks N, Lyons-Ruth K, Pizzagalli DA. 2009. Childhood adversity is associated with left basal ganglia dysfunction during reward anticipation in adulthood. *Biol. Psychiatry* 66:206–13

DiPietro JA, Hodgson DM, Costigan KA, Hilton SC, Johnson TR. 1996. Fetal neurobehavioral development. *Child Dev.* 67(5):2553–67

Dozier M, Manni M, Gordon MK, Peloso E, Gunnar MR, et al. 2006. Foster children's diurnal production of cortisol: an exploratory study. *Child Maltreat.* 11:189–97

Duc NHC. 2016. Developmental risk factors in Vietnamese preschool-age children: cross-sectional survey. *Pediatr. Int.* 58(1):14–21

Duncan G, Brooks-Gunn J, Klebanov P. 1994. Economic deprivation and early childhood development. *Child Dev.* 65:296–318

Eisenberger NI, Berkman ET, Inagaki TK, Rameson LT, Mashal NM, Irwin MR. 2010. Inflammation-induced anhedonia: Endotoxin reduces ventral striatum responses to reward. *Biol. Psychiatry* 68:748–54

Ellis B, Boyce W. 2008. Biological sensitivity to context. *Psychol. Sci.* 17:183–87

El-Sheikh M, Hinnant JB, Erath S. 2011. Developmental trajectories of delinquency symptoms in childhood: the role of marital conflict and autonomic nervous system activity. *J. Abnorm. Psychol.* 120:16–32

El-Sheikh M, Kouros CD, Erath S, Cummings EM, Keller P, Staton L. 2009. Marital conflict and children's externalizing behavior: pathways involving interactions between parasympathetic and sympathetic nervous system activity. *Monogr. Soc. Res. Child Dev.* 74:vii

Evans G. 2004. The environment of childhood poverty. *Am. Psychol.* 59:77–92

Evans GW, English K. 2002. The environment of poverty: multiple stressor exposure, psychophysiological stress, and socioemotional adjustment. *Child Dev.* 73:1238–48

Evans GW, Gonnella C, Marcynyszyn LA, Gentile L, Salpekar N. 2005. The role of chaos in poverty and children's socioemotional adjustment. *Psychol. Sci.* 16:560–65

Evans GW, Schamberg MA. 2009. Childhood poverty, chronic stress, and adult working memory. *PNAS* 106:6545–49

Farah M, Betancourt L, Shera D, Savage J, Giannetta J, et al. 2008. Environmental stimulation, parental nurturance and cognitive development in humans. *Dev. Sci.* 11:793–801

Farah M, Shera D, Savage J, Betancourt L, Giannetta J, et al. 2006. Childhood poverty: specific associations with neurocognitive development. *Brain Res.* 1110:166–74

Fernald LC, Kariger P, Hidrobo M, Gertler PJ. 2012. Socioeconomic gradients in child development in very young children: evidence from India, Indonesia, Peru, and Senegal. *PNAS* 109(Suppl. 2):17273–80

Fernald LC, Weber A, Galasso E, Ratsifandrihamanana L. 2011. Socioeconomic gradients and child development in a very low income population: evidence from Madagascar. *Dev. Sci.* 14(4):832–47

Field T, Pickens J, Fox NA, Nawrocki T, Gonzalez J. 1995. Vagal tone in infants of depressed mothers. *Dev. Psychopathol.* 7:227–31

Fisher PA, Beauchamp KG, Roos LE, Noll LK, Flannery J, Delker BC. 2016. The neurobiology of intervention and prevention in early adversity. *Annu. Rev. Clin. Psychol.* 12:331–57

Fisher PA, Stoolmiller M. 2008. Intervention effects on foster parent stress: associations with child cortisol levels. *Dev. Psychopathol.* 20:1003–21

Fisher PA, Stoolmiller M, Gunnar MR, Burraston BO. 2007. Effects of a therapeutic intervention for foster preschoolers on diurnal cortisol activity. *Psychoneuroendocrinology* 32:892–905

Gee DG, Gabard-Durnam LJ, Flannery J, Goff B, Humphreys KL, et al. 2013. Early developmental emergence of human amygdala–prefrontal connectivity after maternal deprivation. *PNAS* 110:15638–43

Gianaros P, Manuck SB, Sheu L, Votruba-Drzal E, Craig A, Hariri A. 2011. Parental education predicts corticostriatal functionality in adulthood. *Cereb. Cortex* 21:896–910

Gianaros PJ, Horenstein JA, Hariri AR, Sheu LK, Manuck SB, et al. 2008. Potential neural embedding of parental social standing. *Soc. Cogn. Affect. Neurosci.* 3(2):91–96

Gianaros PJ, Marsland AL, Sheu LK, Erickson KI, Verstynen TD. 2012. Inflammatory pathways link socioeconomic inequalities to white matter architecture. *Cereb. Cortex* 23(9):2058–71

Goodman E, Slap GB, Huang B. 2003. The public health impact of socioeconomic status on adolescent depression and obesity. *Am. J. Public Health* 93:1844–50

Graziano P, Derefinko K. 2013. Cardiac vagal control and children's adaptive functioning: a meta-analysis. *Biol. Psychol.* 94:22–37

Gunnar M, Quevedo K. 2007. The neurobiology of stress and development. *Annu. Rev. Psychol.* 58:145–73

Gunnar MR, Brodersen L, Nachmias M, Buss K, Rigatuso J. 1996. Stress reactivity and attachment security. *Dev. Psychobiol.* 29:191–204

Gunnar MR, Morison SJ, Chisholm K, Schuder M. 2001. Salivary cortisol levels in children adopted from Romanian orphanages. *Dev. Psychopathol.* 13:611–28

Gunnar MR, Vazquez DM. 2001. Low cortisol and a flattening of expected daytime rhythm: potential indices of risk in human development. *Dev. Psychopathol.* 13:515–38

Haber SN, Knutson B. 2010. The reward circuit: linking primate anatomy and human imaging. *Neuropsychopharmacology* 35:4–26

Hackman D, Farah M, Meaney M. 2010. Socioeconomic status and the brain: mechanistic insights from human and animal research. *Nat. Rev. Neurosci.* 11:651–59

Hamadani JD, Tofail F, Huda SN, Alam DS, Ridout DA, et al. 2014. Cognitive deficit and poverty in the first 5 years of childhood in Bangladesh. *Pediatrics* 134(4):e1001–8

Hampton Wray A, Stevens C, Pakulak E, Isbell E, Bell T, Neville H. 2017. Development of selective attention in preschool-age children from lower socioeconomic status backgrounds. *Dev. Cogn. Neurosci.* 26:101–11

Hansen AL, Johnsen BH, Thayer JF. 2003. Vagal influence on working memory and attention. *Int. J. Psychophysiol.* 48:263–74

Hanson JL, Chandra A, Wolfe BL, Pollak SD. 2011. Association between income and the hippocampus. *PLOS ONE* 6:e18712

Harrison NA, Brydon L, Walker C, Gray MA, Steptoe A, Critchley HD. 2009. Inflammation causes mood changes through alterations in subgenual cingulate activity and mesolimbic connectivity. *Biol. Psychiatry* 66:407–14

Heckman JJ. 2006. Skill formation and the economics of investing in disadvantaged children. *Science* 312:1900–2

Hertzman C, Boyce T. 2010. How experience gets under the skin to create gradients in developmental health. *Annu. Rev. Public Health* 31:329–47

Hoffmann R, Hu Y, De Gelder R, Menvielle G, Bopp M, Mackenbach JP. 2016. The impact of increasing income inequalities on educational inequalities in mortality: an analysis of six European countries. *Int. J. Equity Health* 15:103

Holzer HJ, Whitmore Schanzenbach D, Duncan GJ, Ludwig J. 2008. The economic costs of childhood poverty in the United States. *J. Child. Poverty* 14:41–61

Irwin MR, Cole SW. 2011. Reciprocal regulation of the neural and innate immune systems. *Nat. Rev. Immunol.* 11:625–32

Irwin MR, Olmstead R, Carroll JE. 2016. Sleep disturbance, sleep duration, and inflammation: a systematic review and meta-analysis of cohort studies and experimental sleep deprivation. *Biol. Psychiatry* 80:40–52

Jednoróg K, Altarelli I, Monzalvo K, Fluss J, Dubois J, et al. 2012. The influence of socioeconomic status on children's brain structure. *PLOS ONE* 7:e42486

Joëls M, Baram TZ. 2009. The neuro-symphony of stress. *Nat. Rev. Neurosci.* 10:459–66

Kiecolt-Glaser JK. 2010. Stress, food, and inflammation: psychoneuroimmunology and nutrition at the cutting edge. *Psychosom. Med.* 72:365–69

Kim P, Evans GW, Angstadt M, Ho SS, Sripada CS, et al. 2013. Effects of childhood poverty and chronic stress on emotion regulatory brain function in adulthood. *PNAS* 110:18442–47

Kimhy D, Crowley O, McKinley P, Burg M, Lachman M, et al. 2013. The association of cardiac vagal control and executive functioning: findings from the MIDUS study. *J. Psychiatric Res.* 47:628–35

Kishiyama MM, Boyce WT, Jimenez AM, Perry LM, Knight RT. 2009. Socioeconomic disparities affect prefrontal function in children. *J. Cogn. Neurosci.* 21(6):1106–15

Kittleson MM, Meoni LA, Wang N-Y, Chu AY, Ford DE, Klag MJ. 2006. Association of childhood socioeconomic status with subsequent coronary heart disease in physicians. *Arch. Intern. Med.* 166:2356–61

Koss KJ, Hostinar CE, Donzella B, Gunnar MR. 2014. Social deprivation and the HPA axis in early development. *Psychoneuroendocrinology* 50:1–13

Lipina S, Martelli M, Vuelta B, Colombo J. 2005. Performance on the A-not-B task of Argentinian infants from unsatisfied and satisfied basic needs homes. *Interam. J. Psychol.* 39:49–60

Lipina SJ, Posner MI. 2012. The impact of poverty on the development of brain networks. *Front. Hum. Neurosci.* 6:238

Liston C, McEwen BS, Casey BJ. 2009. Psychosocial stress reversibly disrupts prefrontal processing and attentional control. *PNAS* 106:912–17

Loman MM, Gunnar MR. 2010. Early experience and the development of stress reactivity and regulation in children. *Neurosci. Biobehav. Rev.* 34:867–76

Luby J, Belden A, Botteron K, Marrus N, Harms MP, et al. 2013. The effects of poverty on childhood brain development: the mediating effect of caregiving and stressful life events. *JAMA Pediatr.* 167:1135–42

Lupien SJ, King S, Meaney MJ, McEwen BS. 2001. Can poverty get under your skin? Basal cortisol levels and cognitive function in children from low and high socioeconomic status. *Dev. Psychopathol.* 13:653–76

Lupien SJ, McEwen BS, Gunnar MR, Heim C. 2009. Effects of stress throughout the lifespan on the brain, behaviour and cognition. *Nat. Rev. Neurosci.* 10:434–45

Maier SF, Amal J, Baratta MV, Paul E, Watkins LR. 2006. Behavioral control, the medial prefrontal cortex, and resilience. *Dialogues Clin. Neurosci.* 8(4):397–406

Marcovitch S, Leigh J, Calkins SD, Leerks EM, O'Brien M, Blankson AN. 2010. Moderate vagal withdrawal in 3.5-year-old children is associated with optimal performance on executive function tasks. *Dev. Psychobiol.* 52:603–8

Marmot M. 2015. *The Health Gap: The Challenge of an Unequal World*. London: Bloomsbury

Marsland AL, Gianaros PJ, Abramowitch SM, Manuck SB, Hariri AR. 2008. Interleukin-6 covaries inversely with hippocampal grey matter volume in middle-aged adults. *Biol. Psychiatry* 64:484–90

McDermott JM, Westerlund A, Zeanah CH, Nelson CA, Fox NA. 2012. Early adversity and neural correlates of executive function: implications for academic adjustment. *Dev. Cogn. Neurosci.* 2:S59–66

McEwen BS, Gianaros PJ. 2010. Central role of the brain in stress and adaptation: links to socioeconomic status, health, and disease. *Ann. N. Y. Acad. Sci.* 1186:190–222

McEwen BS, Stellar E. 1993. Stress and the individual: mechanisms leading to disease. *Arch. Intern. Med.* 153:2093–101

McLaughlin KA, Sheridan MA, Tibu F, Fox NA, Zeanah CH, Nelson CA. 2015. Causal effects of the early caregiving environment on development of stress response systems in children. *PNAS* 112:5637–42

McLoyd V. 1998. Socioeconomic disadvantage and child development. *Am. Psychol.* 53:185–204

Merikangas KR, He J-P, Burstein M, Swanson SA, Avenevoli S, et al. 2010. Lifetime prevalence of mental disorders in US adolescents: results from the National Comorbidity Survey Replication-Adolescent Supplement (NCS-A). *J. Am. Acad. Child Adolesc. Psychiatry* 49:980–89

Miller AH, Maletic V, Raison CL. 2009. Inflammation and its discontents: the role of cytokines in the pathophysiology of major depression. *Biol. Psychiatry* 65:732–41

Miller GE, Brody GH, Yu T, Chen E. 2014. A family-oriented psychosocial intervention reduces inflammation in low-SES African American youth. *PNAS* 111:11287–92

Miller GE, Chen E. 2010. Harsh family climate in early life presages the emergence of a proinflammatory phenotype in adolescence. *Psychol. Sci.* 21(6):848–56

Miller GE, Chen E, Fok AK, Walker H, Lim A, et al. 2009. Low early-life social class leaves a biological residue manifested by decreased glucocorticoid and increased proinflammatory signaling. *PNAS* 106:14716–21

Miller GE, Chen E, Parker KJ. 2011a. Psychological stress in childhood and susceptibility to the chronic diseases of aging: moving toward a model of behavioral and biological mechanisms. *Psychol. Bull.* 137:959–97

Miller GE, Chen E, Zhou ES. 2007. If it goes up, must it come down? Chronic stress and the hypothalamic-pituitary-adrenocortical axis in humans. *Psychol. Bull.* 133:25–45

Miller GE, Lachman ME, Chen E, Gruenewald TL, Karlamangla AS, Seeman TE. 2011b. Pathways to resilience: maternal nurturance as a buffer against the effects of childhood poverty on metabolic syndrome at midlife. *Psychol. Sci.* 22:1591–99

Moore GA. 2010. Parent conflict predicts infants' vagal regulation in social interaction. *Dev. Psychopathol.* 22:23–33

Mueller EM, Stemmler G, Wacker J. 2010. Single-trial electroencephalogram predicts cardiac acceleration: a time-lagged P-correlation approach for studying neurovisceral connectivity. *Neuroscience* 166:491–500

Neville H, Pakulak E, Stevens C. 2015. Family-based training to improve cognitive outcomes for children from lower socioeconomic status backgrounds: emerging themes and challenges. *Curr. Opin. Behav. Sci.* 4:166–70

Neville HJ, Stevens C, Pakulak E, Bell TA, Fanning J, et al. 2013. Family-based training program improves brain function, cognition, and behavior in lower socioeconomic status preschoolers. *PNAS* 110(9):12138–43

Noble K, McCandliss B, Farah M. 2007. Socioeconomic gradients predict individual differences in neurocognitive abilities. *Dev. Sci.* 10:464–80

Noble KG, Houston SM, Brito NH, Bartsch H, Kan E, et al. 2015. Family income, parental education and brain structure in children and adolescents. *Nat. Neurosci.* 18:773–78

Noble KG, Houston SM, Kan E, Sowell ER. 2012. Neural correlates of socioeconomic status in the developing human brain. *Dev. Sci.* 15:516–27

Noble KG, Norman MF, Farah MJ. 2005. Neurocognitive correlates of socioeconomic status in kindergarten children. *Dev. Sci.* 8:74–87

Nusslock R, Miller GE. 2016. Early-life adversity and physical and emotional health across the lifespan: a neuroimmune network hypothesis. *Biol. Psychiatry* 80:23–32

Obradovic J, Bush NR, Stamperdahl J, Adler NE, Boyce WT. 2010. Biological sensitivity to context: the interactive effects of stress reactivity and family adversity on socioemotional behavior and school readiness. *Child Dev.* 81:270–89

Oosterman M, De Schipper JC, Fisher P, Dozier M, Schuengel C. 2010. Autonomic reactivity in relation to attachment and early adversity among foster children. *Dev. Psychopathol.* 22:109–18

Pace TW, Hu F, Miller AH. 2007. Cytokine-effects on glucocorticoid receptor function: relevance to glucocorticoid resistance and the pathophysiology and treatment of major depression. *Brain Behav. Immun.* 21:9–19

Park G, Thayer JF. 2014. From the heart to the mind: Cardiac vagal tone modulates top-down and bottom-up visual perception and attention to emotional stimuli. *Front. Psychol.* 5:278

Phelps EA, LeDoux JE. 2005. Contributions of the amygdala to emotion processing: from animal models to human behavior. *Neuron* 48:175–87

Pollak SD, Vardi S, Putzer Bechner AM, Curtin JJ. 2005. Physically abused children's regulation of attention in response to hostility. *Child Dev.* 76:968–77

Porges SW. 1996. Physiological regulation in high-risk infants: a model for assessment and potential intervention. *Dev. Psychopathol.* 8:43–58

Porges SW. 2007. The polyvagal perspective. *Biol. Psychol.* 74:116–43

Porter CL. 2003. Coregulation in mother-infant dyads: links to infants' cardiac vagal tone. *Psychol. Rep.* 92:307–19

Porter CL, Wouden-Miller M, Silva SS, Porter AE. 2003. Marital harmony and conflict: links to infants' emotional regulation and cardiac vagal tone. *Infancy* 4:297–307

Powell ND, Mays JW, Bailey MT, Hanke ML, Sheridan JF. 2011. Immunogenic dendritic cells primed by social defeat enhance adaptive immunity to influenza A virus. *Brain Behav. Immun.* 25:46–52

Propper CB, Holochwost SJ. 2013. The influence of proximal risk on the early development of the autonomic nervous system. *Dev. Rev.* 33:151–67

Raizada RDS, Richards TL, Meltzoff A, Kuhl PK. 2008. Socioeconomic status predicts hemispheric specialisation of the left inferior frontal gyrus in young children. *NeuroImage* 40:1392–401

Rao H, Betancourt L, Giannetta JM, Brodsky NL, Korczykowski M, et al. 2010. Early prenatal care is important for hippocampal maturation: evidence from brain morphology in humans. *NeuroImage* 49:1144–50

Raver CC, Blair C, Willoughby M. 2013. Poverty as a predictor of 4-year-olds' executive function: new perspectives on models of differential susceptibility. *Dev. Psychol.* 49:292–304

Rubio-Codina M, Attanasio O, Meghir C, Varela N, Grantham-McGregor S. 2015. The socioeconomic gradient of child development: cross-sectional evidence from children 6–42 months in Bogota. *J. H. Resour.* 50(2):464–83

Saez E, Zucman G. 2016. Wealth inequality in the United States since 1913: evidence from capitalized income tax data. *Q. J. Econ.* 131:519–78

Sapolsky RM. 2004. Social status and health in humans and other animals. *Annu. Rev. Anthropol.* 33:393–418

Sarsour K, Sheridan M, Jutte D, Nuru-Jeter A, Hinshaw S, Boyce W. 2011. Family socioeconomic status and child executive functions: the roles of language, home environment, and single parenthood. *J. Int. Neuropsychol. Soc.* 17:120–32

Schady N, Behrman J, Araujo MC, Azuero R, Bernal R, et al. 2015. Wealth gradients in early childhood cognitive development in five Latin American countries. *J. Hum. Resour.* 50(2):446–63

Schickedanz A, Dreyer BP, Halfon N. 2015. Childhood poverty: understanding and preventing the adverse impacts of a most-prevalent risk to pediatric health and well-being. *Pediatr. Clin. North Am.* 62:1111–35

Schuetze P, Eiden RD, Colder CR, Gray TR, Huestis MA. 2011. Physiological regulation in cigarette exposed infants: an examination of potential moderators. *Neurotoxicol. Teratol.* 33:567–74

Sheridan MA, Sarsour K, Jutte D, D'Esposito M, Boyce WT. 2012. The impact of social disparity on prefrontal function in childhood. *PLOS ONE* 7:e35744

Shonkoff JP. 2012. Leveraging the biology of adversity to address the roots of disparities in health and development. *PNAS* 109:17302–7

Shonkoff JP, Bales SN. 2011. Science does not speak for itself: translating child development research for the public and its policymakers. *Child Dev.* 82:17–32

Shonkoff JP, Garner AS, Siegel BS, Dobbins MI, Earls MF, et al. 2012. The lifelong effects of early childhood adversity and toxic stress. *Pediatrics* 129:e232–46

Shook N, Pena P, Fazio RH, Sollers JJ III, Thayer JF. 2007. Friend or foe: heart rate variability and the negativity bias in learning about novel objects. *Psychophysiology* 44:S39

Skowron EA, Cipriano-Essel E, Gatzke-Kopp LM, Teti DM, Ammerman RT. 2014. Early adversity, RSA, and inhibitory control: evidence of children's neurobiological sensitivity to social context. *Dev. Psychobiol.* 56:964–78

Sloan RP, Huang M-H, Sidney S, Liu K, Williams OD, Seeman T. 2005. Socioeconomic status and health: Is parasympathetic nervous system activity an intervening mechanism? *Int. J. Epidemiol.* 34:309–15

Slopen N, McLaughlin KA, Shonkoff JP. 2014. Interventions to improve cortisol regulation in children: a systematic review. *Pediatrics* 133(2):312–26

Stevens C, Lauinger B, Neville H. 2009. Differences in the neural mechanisms of selective attention in children from different socioeconomic backgrounds: an event-related brain potential study. *Dev. Sci.* 12:634–46

Stevens C, Neville H. 2006. Neuroplasticity as a double-edged sword: deaf enhancements and dyslexic deficits in motion processing. *J. Cogn. Neurosci.* 18:701–4

Thayer JF, Åhs F, Fredrikson M, Sollers JJ, Wager TD. 2012. A meta-analysis of heart rate variability and neuroimaging studies: implications for heart rate variability as a marker of stress and health. *Neurosci. Biobehav. Rev.* 36:747–56

Thayer JF, Brosschot JF. 2005. Psychosomatics and psychopathology: looking up and down from the brain. *Psychoneuroendocrinology* 30:1050–58

Thayer JF, Friedman BH. 2002. Stop that! Inhibition, sensitization, and their neurovisceral concomitants. *Scand. J. Psychol.* 43:123–30

Thayer JF, Lane RD. 2007. The role of vagal function in the risk for cardiovascular disease and mortality. *Biol. Psychol.* 74:224–42

Thayer JF, Lane RD. 2009. Claude Bernard and the heart–brain connection: further elaboration of a model of neurovisceral integration. *Neurosci. Biobehav. Rev.* 33:81–88

Thayer JF, Sternberg E. 2006. Beyond heart rate variability. *Ann. N. Y. Acad. Sci.* 1088:361–72

Tottenham N, Hare T, Millner A, Gilhooly T, Zevin J, Casey B. 2011. Elevated amygdala response to faces following early deprivation. *Dev. Sci.* 14:190–204

Tottenham N, Hare TA, Quinn BT, McCarry TW, Nurse M, et al. 2010. Prolonged institutional rearing is associated with atypically large amygdala volume and difficulties in emotion regulation. *Dev. Sci.* 13:46–61

Tottenham N, Sheridan MA. 2010. A review of adversity, the amygdala and the hippocampus: a consideration of developmental timing. *Front. Hum. Neurosci.* 3:68

Tracy M, Zimmerman FJ, Galea S, McCauley E, Vander Stoep A. 2008. What explains the relation between family poverty and childhood depressive symptoms? *J. Psychiatric Res.* 42:1163–75

Ursache A, Blair C, Stifter C, Voegtline K. 2013. Emotional reactivity and regulation in infancy interact to predict executive functioning in early childhood. *Dev. Psychol.* 49:127–37

Ursache A, Noble KG. 2016. Neurocognitive development in socioeconomic context: multiple mechanisms and implications for measuring socioeconomic status. *Psychophysiology* 53:71–82

Ursache A, Noble KG, Blair C. 2015. Socioeconomic status, subjective social status, and perceived stress: associations with stress physiology and executive functioning. *Behav. Med.* 41:145–54

Wilkinson RG, Pickett K. 2009. *The Spirit Level: Why More Equal Societies Almost Always Do Better*. London: Allen Lane

Wright RJ, Visness CM, Calatroni A, Grayson MH, Gold DR, et al. 2010. Prenatal maternal stress and cord blood innate and adaptive cytokine responses in an inner-city cohort. *Am. J. Respir. Crit. Care Med.* 182:25–33

Yanbaeva DG, Dentener MA, Creutzberg EC, Wesseling G, Wouters EF. 2007. Systemic effects of smoking. *Chest J.* 131:1557–66

Ziol-Guest KM, Duncan GJ, Kalil A, Boyce WT. 2012. Early childhood poverty, immune-mediated disease processes, and adult productivity. *PNAS* 109:17289–93

The Prefrontal Cortex and Neurological Impairments of Active Thought

Tim Shallice[1,2] and Lisa Cipolotti[3,4]

[1] Institute of Cognitive Neuroscience, University College London, London WC1E 6BT, United Kingdom; email: t.shallice@ucl.ac.uk

[2] Cognitive Neuropsychology and Neuroimaging Lab, Scuola Internazionale Superiore di Studi Avanzati (SISSA), 34136 Trieste, Italy

[3] Neuropsychology Department, National Hospital for Neurology and Neurosurgery, London WC1N 3BG, United Kingdom; email: l.cipolotti@ucl.ac.uk

[4] Dipartimento di Psicologia, University of Palermo, 90133 Palermo, Italy

Annu. Rev. Psychol. 2018. 69:157–80

First published as a Review in Advance on August 16, 2017

The *Annual Review of Psychology* is online at psych.annualreviews.org

https://doi.org/10.1146/annurev-psych-010416-044123

Keywords

active thought, neuropsychology, prefrontal cortex, supervisory system, reasoning, lateralization of function

Abstract

This article reviews the effects of lesions to the frontal cortex on the ability to carry out active thought, namely, to reason, think flexibly, produce strategies, and formulate and realize plans. We discuss how and why relevant neuropsychological studies should be carried out. The relationships between active thought and both intelligence and language are considered. The following basic processes necessary for effective active thought are reviewed: concentration, set switching, inhibiting potentiated responses, and monitoring and checking. Different forms of active thought are then addressed: abstraction, deduction, reasoning in well-structured and ill-structured problem spaces, novel strategy generation, and planning. We conclude that neuropsychological findings are valuable for providing information on systems rather than networks, especially information concerning prefrontal lateralization of function. We present a synthesis of the respective roles of the left and right lateral prefrontal cortex in active thought.

Contents

INTRODUCTION

Overall Perspective

This review is concerned with what neuropsychological findings can tell us about the cognitive processes underlying active thinking. By active thinking, we refer to mental processes that allow us to confront situations where we do not respond routinely to the environment but, rather, effectively address problems that can be big or small. Active thinking entails a set of complex mental processes, for example, those involved in abstraction, deduction, and other forms of reasoning between alternative possibilities, switching lines of thought, selecting strategies, inhibiting obvious responses, and formulating and realizing plans. For example, organizing a dinner party would entail many active thinking processes, whereas daydreaming or implicit processes like priming would not be considered active thinking.

A number of well-known neuropsychological tests designed to assess prefrontal function require active thinking. Typical examples are tests such as Wisconsin Card-Sorting (switching lines of thought), Proverb Interpretation (abstraction), Stroop (inhibition), Tower of Hanoi (planning), and tests of fluid intelligence such as Progressive Matrices or Cattell Culture Fair (reasoning between alternative possibilities). Following frontal lobe lesions, performance on these tests is typically impaired. This suggests that the frontal lobes are critically involved in active thinking.

Impairments in active thinking are also exemplified by a number of frontal lobe syndromes that involve release of irrelevant environmentally triggered actions. Examples include the grasp reflex, where the patient whose palm is being stroked by a doctor grasps the doctor's fingers despite being repeatedly instructed not to (De Renzi & Barbieri 1992), or the somewhat analogous situation where the patient is instructed not to move their eyes to a distracting light but does so anyway (Paus et al. 1991). At a higher level, there is utilization behavior, originally described by Lhermitte (1983). In this case, the patient makes a standard afforded action to one of the objects surrounding him, such as dealing from a pack of cards, without being told to do so or, in the so-called incidental form, when explicitly told to do something else (Shallice et al. 1989). These examples highlight behaviors that occur when active thinking processes are absent or impaired through brain injury. Interestingly, these syndromes have been most frequently described in patients with lesions involving medial frontal areas (see De Renzi & Barbieri 1992).

Prefrontal functions are involved in many different cognitive domains. They have been well reviewed fairly recently by Szczepanski & Knight (2014). This review, therefore, focuses only on those cognitive domains we consider critical for active thinking. Thus, we discuss individual cognition rather than social cognition and ongoing reasoning rather than (long-term) memory, learning, motivation, and emotion.

Our review is structured in the following fashion. The Introduction considers why we have chosen neuropsychological evidence, out of the many cognitive neuroscience techniques available, to be used for the review of the cognitive processes underlying active thinking. We then address the methodological approaches adopted for the neuropsychological investigation of prefrontal functions. The second section briefly outlines our theoretical framework for active thinking, which is largely based on the Norman & Shallice (1986) supervisory system model of prefrontal cortex (PFC) functioning. We also consider the relationship between active thinking and potentially overlapping cognitive domains such as intelligence and language. The third section will deal with processes that are prerequisites for active thinking, namely concentration, set shifting, thought inhibition, and monitoring and checking. In the fourth section, we discuss different types of core active thinking processes, including abstraction, deduction, novel strategy selection, insight, and planning. The final section aims to produce an overall theoretical synthesis.

Why Neuropsychology?

As cognitive processes become more abstract and distant from sensory and motor processes, it becomes increasingly difficult to investigate them adequately using behavioral means alone. Thus, discussing theorists working on reasoning about syllogisms, Khemlani & Johnson-Laird (2012, p. 453) wrote, "Thirty-five years ago they had only heuristic accounts that explained biases and errors, and so the domain appeared to be an excellent test case for cognitive science. There are now 12 sorts of theories of syllogisms and monadic inferences, and so skeptics may well conclude that cognitive science has failed." A more powerful source of empirical findings seems to be required. Methodologies related to the brain are obvious candidates.

Within human cognitive neuroscience, there are two main classes of methodologies. The oldest class consists of those methodologies derived from lesion studies of neurological patients, which have recently been supplemented by transcranial magnetic stimulation (TMS) and, somewhat more conceptually distantly, by the study of the cognitive effects of individual differences in brain structure across the normal population. The second class consists of those methodologies where on-line measures are taken of brain processes while normal subjects carry out tasks; these methodologies include positron emission tomography (PET), functional magnetic resonance imaging (fMRI), electroencephalography (EEG), magnetoencephalography (MEG), and so on.

If one's aim is to provide accurate anatomical correspondences for known cognitive processes or to provide real-time information on processing, the second class is much to be preferred. Despite this clear advantage of the second class of methodology, the first class, especially neuropsychology, has complementary advantages for the development of cognitive theory. There are at least five reasons for this:

- If one takes cognitive theory to refer to models like classic box-and-arrow information-processing ones, then neuropsychological data can speak directly to cognitive theory. Appropriate inferences are derived from a set of simple assumptions, first formalized by Caramazza (1986). They are based on the idea of subtraction of components from an overall system. Of course, subtraction in reality is complicated by complex processes related to the recovery process (see Henson et al. 2016 for a good example). However, to a first approximation, subtraction is a plausible characterization of the effect of a brain lesion. So, this approach was much used in the heyday of cognitive neuropsychology. Moreover, the same set of assumptions can be used to relate such data to connectionist models, as well (Shallice & Cooper 2011). By contrast, methodologies of the second type require complex bridging assumptions, based on physics and physiology, to relate their data to cognitive theory.
- It is generally accepted that activation-based findings do not necessarily imply causal efficacy (see Gilaie-Dotan et al. 2015 for a particularly clear example). This possibility is of particular concern for lateralization of function. Thus, neuropsychological data show language functions to be strongly lateralized. Crossed aphasia is very rare. In a consecutive series of over 1,200 aphasics with unilateral lesions, only 4% had right-hemisphere lesions (Croquelois & Bogousslavsky 2011). However, neuroimaging studies of language processing often report bilateral activation patterns, although they are somewhat smaller in size in the right hemisphere (Jung-Beeman 2005). So, considering merely the presence or absence of activation may, in effect, hide real lateralization of function.
- Neuropsychological data provide additional sources of behavioral evidence that are not generally available from other cognitive neuroscience methods, namely, the nature of the responses and, in particular, the errors made. These can be very informative for specifying the function damaged. Below, we consider two examples, the concrete interpretation of proverbs and strategy-reflecting responses.
- When carrying out a cognitive neuroscience experiment on neurologically intact subjects, the investigators are entirely reliant on their own theoretical framework to set up the study. Neurological patients can produce behaviors that strikingly challenge theoretical preconceptions. Phineas Gage and HM are the most famous such cases, but there are many others. They facilitate serendipity.
- Some problem solving situations involve a single step change, where the subject makes a change in strategy in one trial. Examples are those involving insight (see the section titled From Lateral Transformations to Strategy Shifts). They cannot be effectively studied using standard activation-based methods that require summing over multiple trials because the critical situations cannot be reproduced; a repeat would no longer be novel. Instead, damage to the relevant systems may prevent strategy change occurring, thus allowing relevant investigation.

We therefore primarily address findings from neuropsychological studies and consider other methodologies where their findings help interpret the results of such studies. Of course, neuropsychological methods have their own limitations, which we discuss in the next section.

The Neuropsychological Approach to Frontal Functions

Researchers concerned with making inferences about normal cognitive function from neuropsychological data have used three main approaches: the single case study (including its close relation, the multiple single case study), the case series, and the group study. In the first approach, individual patients are selected for study depending on their theoretical interest. In the second and third approaches, all patients who fit the appropriate criteria are reported. In the second approach, each patient is treated as a separate test of relevant theories, whereas in the third approach, results are averaged across all patients in a group.

Historically, researchers have tended to favor one approach and reject others. In contrast, Shallice (2015) has argued that all three approaches are legitimate but have different potential problems and so are more powerful in combination. This statement needs to be qualified as far as prefrontal functions are concerned. Often, performance on paradigms sensitive to prefrontal lesions can have a large range in the normal population—consider, as an example, the Stroop test. Impairment, then, becomes more easily detected using group studies due to variance reduction with increased n.

In practice, the anatomically based group study, where the patient is allocated to a group according to their site of lesion, is the most widely used method for studying prefrontal functions. This type of study comes in two forms. In the more traditional approach, the anatomical regions are decided a priori. In the oldest such version, the classical approach, there is a simple comparison between patients with unilateral left and right frontal lesions. In a more refined approach (the Stuss-Alexander method), patients with frontal lesions are divided into those with left lateral, right lateral, superior medial, and inferior medial (including orbital) frontal lesions, this division being based partly on statistical grounds and partly on clinical ones (Stuss et al. 1998). In the modified Stuss-Alexander method, the two medial groups are combined.

The alternative approach (the critical lesion localization method) uses the range of performance produced by patients in a series. It determines whether there are patients with lesions in a particular region who perform worse than those with lesions elsewhere without specifying the region in advance. A package such as voxel-based lesion symptom mapping (VLSM)—now sometimes called lesion behavior mapping (Bates et al. 2003, Rorden & Karnath 2004)—is used.

Recently, Mah et al. (2014) have criticized existing methods of this type, which make the simplifying assumption that damage to any voxel is independent of that to any other voxel. Unfortunately, the assumption is flawed when applied to brain lesions caused by stroke. In this case, the arterial tree structure of the vascular system means that there will be a high correlation between damage to functionally critical and noncritical regions fed by the same artery. Mah et al. (2014) advocated a high-dimensional multivariate approach. However, to our knowledge, this approach has yet to be applied in an analysis of the effects of prefrontal lesions. Related criticisms may apply to brain tumors, but if they do, then the associated noncritical regions will not be the same as those for vascular damage. This makes replication, especially across etiology, very useful. This is also the case for a second problem—the existence of large silent regions due to insufficient patients for complete coverage.

In fact, for the purpose of drawing inferences about the separability of executive systems, the precise anatomical location of a critical area is not important. Performance on a given test requires many subprocesses. So, the inferential logic of cognitive neuropsychology depends on the relative performance of the patient across multiple tests. We adopt an analogous approach using groups. If the critical areas for one test do not overlap with those of another, then we take this as evidence that the two tests do not rely on the same set of subsystems. As we discuss in the section titled From Lateral Transformations to Strategy Shifts, two tests that appear to involve inhibition—the Stroop and the Hayling B Sentence Completion Test—lateralize differently in the PFC, and, therefore, the most critical processes for performing the two tests differ.

By contrast, lesions to an area can affect performance on more than one test. This, then, puts on the intellectual agenda the possibility that the resources required by test performance may overlap cognitively as well as anatomically. For example, Tsuchida & Fellows (2013) used VLSM on the performance of 45 frontal patients on three tests—task-switching, the Stroop, and a spatial search task. The authors found that similar left ventrolateral regions were critical for the first two tasks. A different, more medial region was critical for the spatial search task. The authors held that the existence of a common critical area for the first two tasks meant that "they are likely to be related to disruption of a single underlying process" (Tsuchida & Fellows 2013, p. 1797). We consider that this result provides suggestive evidence only.

Adopting a group study methodology is, however, beset with a host of methodological problems. Typically, patients differ widely in age and premorbid cognitive abilities. In addition, lesions vary greatly in etiology and size. Moreover, these two types of factors can interact in a complex fashion. Thus, Cipolotti et al. (2015b) examined two tests sensitive to prefrontal damage—Advanced Progressive Matrices and Stroop. Increasing age was found to exacerbate the effects of frontal damage, as measured using age-specific norms. This exacerbated age effect on executive performance in frontal patients was not ameliorated by proxies of cognitive reserve such as education or IQ (Macpherson et al. 2017). This suggests that any behavioral effect that a lesion has can only manifest itself when influenced by many strong confounding factors. Large samples of patients and well-matched subgroups are therefore required.

How, then, is one to proceed in practice? One approach is to limit the sample by, say, restricting selection to a particular type of etiology, such as vascular lesions. Thus, patients in subgroups should be better matched. In support of this view, Karnath & Steinbach (2011) argue that it is best to restrict patient samples to those suffering strokes and reject other etiologies, in particular, tumors. The authors suggest that the effects of tumors are too diffuse and not well localized. In fact, there are clear examples showing that postoperative tumors can give strong localization effects (for a particularly clear example, see Papagno et al. 2011). Moreover, if one was to include only patients with vascular lesions, collecting a large sample of frontal patients with well-matched subgroups for a new set of tests would, in practice, take much too long.

A common practice, therefore, is to mix different etiologies in the patient sample to obtain a large enough group. But are the effects of, say, strokes and tumors even roughly equivalent when affecting similar parts of the cortex? To answer this question, Cipolotti et al. (2015a) compared 100 frontal patients with four different types of etiology on four frontal executive tasks (Advanced Progressive Matrices, Stroop Color-Word Test, Letter Fluency-S, Trail-Making Test Part B). The four groups consisted of one vascular group and three with different types of tumor–high-grade gliomas, low-grade gliomas, and meningiomas. The groups did not differ significantly in size or location of lesion. Strong behavioral effects on performance of the frontal tests were found for age and premorbid cognitive abilities. However, only on one test—Trail-Making Part B—was a significant difference between etiologies obtained when age was partialed out in an analysis of covariance. Critically, the significance did not survive Bonferroni correction, as there was no reason to consider Trail-Making, which later research has shown to be not specific to frontal lesions (Chan et al. 2015), to be more susceptible to differences in etiology than the other three tests. We therefore conclude that it is acceptable practice to mix etiologies to overcome the great variability in the population under study.

We therefore include all types of neuropsychological methods in our review but concentrate on the a priori groups approach. We note the number of relevant patients, as the results of studies with small group sizes are especially likely to be biased by the idiosyncrasies of a few patients or by imperfect matching across subgroups.

BROAD-BRUSH ASPECTS OF ACTIVE THOUGHT

Dual System Brain-Based Models of Cognitive Control

Within the literature on reasoning, a variety of so-called dual system models have been put forward. Most of them differentiate between a fast, automatic, and unconscious mode of processing and a slow, deliberate, conscious one (Kahneman & Frederick 2002). In the reasoning field, the two are often called the products of system 1 and of system 2, respectively (Stanovich 1999).

Before the development of dual system models of reasoning, the Russian neuropsychologist Alexander Luria (1966) argued that neuropsychological evidence supports a theoretical framework in which the PFC contains a system for the programming, regulation, and verification of activity—adopting the terminology of the reasoning literature, a system 2. This prefrontal system implements its functioning by calling upon a more posterior system in the cortex—a system 1. A number of neuroscientists have adopted a related type of dual system model framework for conceptualizing PFC function in information processing terms (see Shallice 1982, Miller & Cohen 2001, Duncan 2010). In this review, we adopt Norman & Shallice's (1986) framework.

Contention scheduling—the system 1 of this framework—is the lower-level control system that can effect routine thought and action operations. It operates in a production-system fashion, including selecting action and thought schemas involving more posterior dedicated processing systems and connections (Cooper & Shallice 2000). The syndromes discussed in the Introduction as examples of nonactive thought, such as utilization behavior, represent contention scheduling operating in isolation.

If contention scheduling cannot cope with a nonroutine situation, a second, higher-level control system comes into play, the supervisory system, believed to be in the PFC. The supervisory system is responsible for the control mechanisms that modulate contention scheduling top down by boosting relevant action and thought schemas to allow novel goal-directed behavior. The supervisory system is loosely equivalent to the executive system or control processes in other theoretical frameworks. Where it differs is in being more specific about what it modulates and how. It is the key system involved in active thinking.

Another major brain-based model descending intellectually from Luria's ideas is the multiple demand network approach of Duncan (2010). Using neuroimaging, Duncan & Owen (2000) found that more difficult tasks in many different domains—such as perception, response selection, and working memory—activate the same set of regions, mainly in the frontal and parietal cortices, so-called multiple demand regions. These regions are held to have the function of programming other regions of the brain to carry out nonautomatic tasks. This is a similar function to that held to be carried out by a supervisory system. Duncan (2013, p. 41) also argues that "the fMRI literature contains little consensus on clear repeatable functional distinctions" between different regions within the multiple demand network. We address how the neuropsychological evidence relates to the two models and to equipotentiality below.

Active Thought and Intelligence

Duncan et al. (2000) also argued that the multiple demand regions are the seat of fluid intelligence, g. Thus, they made a major link to another cognitive domain, intelligence, and aimed to support g as a solid scientific concept.

The neuropsychological literature does not support the idea that a reduction in g is sufficient to explain frontal patients' executive impairments. Roca et al. (2010) showed that it is for some tests (e.g., Wisconsin Card-Sorting). However, for others, such as the Hayling B, both Roca et al. (2010) and Cipolotti and colleagues (2016) have demonstrated that frontal patients' impairment cannot be fully explained by reduced g. Similarly, impairments in other executive tests, such as Stroop and Proverb Interpretation, were shown to be not accounted for by an effect on g.

However, Duncan & Owen's (2000) claim about g related specifically to multiple demand regions. To test this claim, Woolgar et al. (2010) gave the Cattell Culture Fair IQ test to 80 patients with cortical lesions. The volume of lesions both in multiple demand regions and outside those regions was assessed. For the group as a whole, there was a significant correlation between the IQ score and multiple demand volume, and the result remained highly significant when total lesion volume was partialed out. However, for the 44 pure frontal patients, the correlation was no longer significant if non–multiple demand volume was partialed out. So, as far as the PFC is concerned, the theoretical claim was not strongly supported by evidence from neuropsychology.

Active Thought and Language

Thought and language processes are intertwined in numerous complex ways (Gentner & Goldin-Meadow 2003), but in the mature adult brain, how independently can active thought take place without language? One potential line of evidence comes from aphasia: Can aphasics reason? This has been investigated in quite a number of aphasic patients in whom relatively preserved reasoning has been shown (Varley 2014). However, studies have tended to be rather loose, relying on essentially clinical reports or on a fairly crude analysis of the processing problems of the patients. An exception is the study of Varley et al. (2005), where three patients with severe problems in comprehension and production of syntax were given a variety of arithmetic and calculation tasks. Two of the patients were near ceiling on some calculation tasks with quasisyntactic aspects, such as three-figure subtraction, including problems with negative answers. They also performed adequately, but not perfectly, on problems involving interpretation of brackets. Thus, it appeared that the understanding and execution of syntactic operations could be relatively preserved in arithmetic when such operations were severely impaired in language.

Grammatical encoding is, however, part of what Levelt (1989) characterized as the formulator stage of language production. It can be inferred from such studies that the formulator and articulator stages operate relatively specifically within the language domain as opposed to the thought domain. The key issue, therefore, relates to the so-called conceptualizer stage, which precedes them in language production. It produces what Levelt (1989) calls the preverbal message, which, in our approach, requires active thought. However, can active thought occur without the involvement of conceptualizer-stage processes?

A relatively little-known aphasia syndrome bears on this question. This syndrome, called dynamic aphasia, is a subtype of the clinical category of transcortical motor aphasia and was first described by Luria (1970). He described two patients who could answer questions but were incapable of narrative speech. In dynamic aphasia, the inner mechanics of the language system—the formulator and articulator stages—appear to operate relatively normally, but the patient says little, especially in spontaneous speech. For instance, patient ROH of Costello & Warrington (1989), when asked to describe his last holiday, produced, in 30 s, only "I'm . . ." Typically, in sentence generation tasks, the patient failed to produce a response or was extremely slow. However, some direct questions could be answered appropriately, and any sentence that was produced was lexically, syntactically, and morphologically correct. What appears to be impaired is the conceptualizer stage.

About 10 other patients of this type have been described as single cases. A massive influence on the performance of these patients is the range of alternatives that are potentially available to the speaker (Robinson et al. 1998). When this is high, the dynamic aphasia patient typically cannot respond. But when the situation allows only a very restricted set of possibilities, the patient typically produces a correct sentence. For instance, patient ANG of Robinson et al. (1998) was given a range of tasks that involved this contrast. Thus, when she was asked to produce a sentence including a common object, such as a telephone, that was shown as a picture, she scored 0/6. On the other hand, when presented with a simple scene to describe (e.g., a girl ice skating), she scored 34/34. When asked to produce a sentence including a single proper name (e.g., Hitler) she scored 26/28, saying, for instance, "Hitler is one of those wicked people that should never have been born." But given a single common word (e.g., sea), where the range of alternatives is greater, she scored only 14/28, saying, in this case, "No idea."

Related results were obtained at the same time by Thompson-Schill et al. (1998), using a task in which patients were asked to generate a verb given a noun. Nouns were divided into two groups according to the diversity of responses given by controls. Four patients with posterior left inferior frontal lesions had significantly more difficulty with high-selection (i.e., inconsistent) verbs than with low-selection verbs, compared with controls. Nine patients with lesions elsewhere in the frontal lobes did not have this problem.

ANG, too, had a left inferior frontal gyrus lesion. This localization of the main form of dynamic aphasia was supported by a group study. Robinson et al. (2010) found that a subgroup of 12 patients with lesions involving the left inferior frontal gyrus performed significantly worse than 35 patients with other frontal lesions and normal controls in generating a sentence from a high-frequency word but not in generating a sentence from low-frequency words, where there would be fewer selection requirements.

These findings all fit with the idea that the dynamic aphasic patient is impaired in constructing the preverbal message at the conceptualizer stage. This shows up behaviorally when the process is at all difficult, such as when there are many alternative possibilities. Is this a problem that affects active thought processes in situations where language is not required? Individual dynamic aphasic patients can apparently perform much better on reasoning tasks. For instance, patient CH (Robinson et al. 2005), a patient with dynamic aphasia similar to that of ANG, although somewhat less severe, performed in the high average range on the IQ test Advanced Progressive Matrices and in the superior range on WAIS Block Design. However, such a comparison involves many disparate cognitive components. It is not comparable to the Varley et al. (2005) study of syntactic aspects of arithmetic, where there was excellent matching between verbal and nonverbal tasks.

One type of task that requires active thought and has been studied in both verbal and nonverbal forms in the same patients is that of fluency—generation of items defined by a particular criterion. Phonemic fluency, i.e., generating as many words as possible in a fixed time beginning with a particular letter, has been extensively studied by neuropsychologists since the pioneering work of Brenda Milner (1964). This type of fluency is usually much impaired in dynamic aphasic patients. In Robinson et al.'s (2012) study, performance on this test was compared with that on seven other fluency tasks. In a sample of 40 frontal patients, out of the 11 who performed worse than any healthy control on phonemic fluency, 6 had left inferior frontal gyrus lesions, as one would expect if dynamic aphasia leads to poor phonemic fluency.

Patients with left lateral lesions in this sample did not generally have word production impairments. On a naming test, their scores were similar to those of right lateral lesion patients and not significantly different from those of normal controls. Yet, on phonemic fluency, they produced only just over 50% of the number of words that right lateral patients did. By contrast, on a task requiring them to produce as many designs as they could given certain constraints, they performed equally well as right lateral patients. Thus, CH, for instance, was well within the normal range. Even more surprising, the left lateral patients performed similarly to the right lateral patients in the ideational fluency task—e.g., "How many uses you can think of for a brick?" In comparison with right lateral lesion patients, their fluency deficit was restricted to verbal material. We assume that a phonemic fluency deficit, if word production processes are intact, is a sign of impairment in the production of the preverbal message by the conceptualizer stage. Thus, it would appear that this process, at least in part, is purely in the language domain and not basically reliant only on general active thought processes.

ESSENTIAL PREREQUISITES FOR ACTIVE THOUGHT

Volition and Concentration

In this section, we deal with the processes that might be considered the nuts and bolts of active thought. We start with the most basic prerequisites for active thought, volition and concentration. Clinically, syndromes such as apathy and akinetic mutism, the failure to initiate actions or speech (Cummings 1993), which represent the extreme loss of volition, have been associated with lesions to the medial PFC.

Formal neuropsychological testing supports the idea of a weakening of processes underlying volition in superior medial prefrontal lesions. In the so-called ROBBIA set of studies (Stuss & Alexander 2007, Shallice & Gillingham 2012), the Stuss-Alexander subdivision of the frontal cortices was adopted with approximately 40 frontal patients. These studies included simple reaction time, two versions of choice reaction time, task switching, and go-no-go. In none of these paradigms was the left or right lateral or the inferior medial group significantly slower than the normal controls. In all of them, however, the members of the superior medial group were significantly slower than normal subjects and, in most, significantly slower than the other patient groups. Moreover, the effects were large. Thus, in one task, the healthy control group took, on average, 607 ms, and three of the four frontal patient groups took from 533 to 643 ms, but the superior medial group took 821 ms. In addition, in the more difficult conditions, such as the switch condition in task switching, which is more difficult than the repeat condition, the superior medial group were disproportionately slowed.

Stuss et al. (1995, 2005) argued that the primary impairment of the superior medial group in these tasks is one of energization. They argued that, in the supervisory system model, contention scheduling operating alone would not be optimal in reaction time tasks. For instance, a selected schema would gradually lose activation over several seconds. Thus, for better performance, top-down boosting of lower-level action schemas would be needed. Energization, then, is seen as the process required to initiate supervisory system operations. This closely corresponds to a number of characterizations of the function of the anterior cingulate derived from functional imaging, such as those of Posner & DiGirolamo (1998) and Kerns et al. (2004). Energization may be seen as the material substrate of volition and the basis of concentration.

In this approach, impairments following superior medial lesions should be found much more widely, even on cognitively simple tasks. They are. Thus, MacPherson et al. (2010) investigated the performance of 55 frontal patients, subdivided into subgroups with medial, orbital, and lateral damage, on the Elevator Counting subtest (Manly et al. 1994). This test assesses the ability to sustain attention by presenting a long series of tones at a slow rate. Optimally, one simply counts the tones. The medial and left lateral groups were significantly impaired on the task compared to healthy controls, with the medial group making errors 13% of the time in comparison to the controls' 1.6% error rate. In contrast, the right lateral patients were not impaired.

Energization impairments could also account for certain medial frontal findings reported in some studies discussed above. In Robinson et al.'s (2012) fluency study, discussed in the previous section, the medial frontal group, unlike the lateral frontal groups, was impaired on all eight fluency tasks, so an energization account is more plausible than a purely cognitive one. Medial frontal lesions are also the predominant site for the grasp reflex and utilization behavior, discussed in the Introduction, where the task is simple and all that is required is to realize the will to carry it out. In lay terms, the superior medial region can be seen as the locus of the system producing volition and concentration.

Set Switching and Response Inhibition

A second prerequisite for active thought is flexibility. Classically, the best-known deficit following prefrontal lesions was, indeed, difficulty switching sets. This deficit leads to a consequent increase in perseveration, as in the Wisconsin Card-Sorting test, which loads heavily on the ability to switch from responding to one perceptual dimension to another (Milner 1963).

Such clinical tests are, however, complex and have multiple components, including discovery. Much cleaner are so-called task switching paradigms, in which two simple tasks that use the same stimuli are carried out repeatedly in a rapid random ordering. Three studies have used such paradigms with 35 or more frontal patients (Aron et al. 2004, Shallice et al. 2008, Tsuchida & Fellows 2013). All three studies showed left frontal patients to have either increased error rates early in learning (Shallice et al. 2008) or increased reaction times each time the task switched. Aron et al. (2004) suggested that what is impaired in these patients is top-down (supervisory) control of task set (action schema). Regarding the critical anatomical areas, a VLSM analysis carried out by Tsuchida & Fellows (2013) was in agreement with a meta-analysis of functional imaging studies carried out by Derrfuss et al. (2005), suggesting that the left inferior frontal junction is critical for task switching.

However, Aron et al. (2004) also reported increased error rates in task switching in patients with right ventrolateral lesions. They attributed this to impairment in response inhibition. However, no such effect was found by either Tsuchida & Fellows (2013) or Shallice et al. (2008). Aron et al. (2003) had previously used a standard response inhibition task from human experimental psychology, namely, the stop signal task, with the same 17 right frontal patients but, unfortunately, no other frontal group. For five right frontal subregions, the correlation between amount of damage to the subregion and poor performance on the task was examined. For three of the regions, the correlation was significant, but for one—the inferior frontal gyrus—it was very high. The authors argued that this was the critical region involved in response inhibition, with the other significant effects arising due to correlations between the amount of damage in a region and that in its neighbor.

Very different results were, however, obtained by Picton et al. (2007), who studied 43 frontal patients with another response inhibition task—go-no-go. They found that the critical areas for false alarms were left areas 6 and 8, areas Aron et al. (2003) did not investigate. The four patients with lesions in these areas made 30% false alarms. By comparison, the 13 patients with right ventrolateral lesions made only 12% false alarms, not significantly different from the controls (8%). Moreover, the effects found in Aron et al.'s (2004) right frontal patients did not replicate in the two other task switching studies. The neuropsychological evidence fits better overall with a different perspective from neuroimaging that suggests that the role of the right inferior PFC in such tasks is bottom-up attention rather than inhibition (Hampshire et al. 2010). When a stop signal occurs after the initiating stimulus, attention must then be switched to the new stimulus. This is not required in go-no-go tasks.

Active Monitoring and Checking

Error detection is an ubiquitous aspect of human active thought, especially when a new skill is being acquired. It begins with a mismatch between actuality and expectation, but this can be detected by a variety of means, some very subtle (Rizzo et al. 1995). Thus, monitoring and checking are basic processes late in the time course of active thought. Neuropsychologically, these processes have long been thought to be controlled by dorsolateral PFC systems (Petrides 1994).

Neuropsychological evidence suggests that they are at least partly lateralized to the right. Stuss et al. (2005) asked 38 frontal patients, divided into groups based on the four Stuss-Alexander anatomical regions, to carry out reaction time tests in which the stimulus was preceded by a warning signal that occurred randomly from 3 s to 7 s before. For the simple reaction time condition, controls responded 30 ms to 40 ms more rapidly to the long than to the short warning intervals—the so-called foreperiod effect. This is to be expected, as the conditional probability of the stimulus occurring in a particular interval increases with the foreperiod. Three of the four frontal patient groups behaved in an identical fashion. The one exception was the right lateral group, which was actually slower in the long foreperiod condition. By contrast, when the foreperiod was fixed over a block of trials, the right lateral group behaved normally. Stuss et al. (2005) argued that, in the variable foreperiod condition, the right lateral group failed to monitor the fact that no stimulus had occurred and so did not increase preparation. When monitoring was not required because the foreperiod was constant over a block, they behaved normally. Thus, active monitoring was held to occur in the right lateral frontal area.

Qualitatively similar results have been obtained by Vallesi et al. (2007b) in a TMS study in which stimulation of the right dorsolateral PFC was contrasted with stimulation of the left dorsolateral PFC and the right angular gyrus. In a more direct attempt to replicate the precise paradigm used by Stuss et al. (2005), Vallesi et al. (2007a) studied 58 patients with fairly focal tumors. They obtained a partial replication. Premotor patients and parietal patients had foreperiod effects of the order of 30–55 ms both before and after operation, the same as normal controls. Left prefrontal patients showed a reduced foreperiod effect of 15–25 ms both before and after operation. The right prefrontal patients, however, were completely normal before operation, with a foreperiod effect of 55 ms, but this was drastically reduced to 10 ms after operation.

A number of neuroimaging studies point to a similar conclusion with respect to the involvement of the right rather than left PFC. Thus, Fleck et al. (2006) found that the right lateral PFC was also more active in low-confidence judgements, where more monitoring was needed, than in high-confidence ones in both memory and perceptual tasks (see also Sharp et al. 2004, Chua et al. 2006, Yokoyama et al. 2010; for another neuropsychological example, see Reverberi et al. 2005; note that only Sharp et al. and Reverberi et al. find a specifically lateral localization within the right PFC). Overall, there is some support for the idea that lateral regions within the right PFC are the most critical for active monitoring processes.

Working Memory

The reader may be surprised that an obvious requirement for active thought that has not yet been mentioned is working memory. Working memory has been associated with the lateral PFC since the neurophysiological work of Fuster & Alexander (1971) and Goldman-Rakic (1988). However, these classic neurophysiological experiments typically involved a monkey holding one position in space for up to a minute. Human working memory tasks involve the subject making operations on the much greater contents of a short-term store.

When short-term memory tasks are given to patients with frontal lesions, they can exhibit no deficits if operations do not need to be carried out on the contents of the relevant short-term memory store. Thus, D'Esposito & Postle (1999) reviewed all the studies they could find that compared groups of patients with lateral frontal lesions with normal controls on tasks that only loaded on short-term store capacity and did not involve operations. There were eight such studies for digit span and four for spatial span; none showed a significant difference between the two groups. Thus, although working memory tasks can produce deficits in frontal patients, the impairment does not appear to be one of storage, but rather one of monitoring or manipulation, as argued by Petrides (1994). We discuss monitoring in the previous section. In the next section, we discuss how manipulation can take different forms, each associated with different prefrontal regions.

FORMS OF ACTIVE THOUGHT

Abstraction

A key human ability for much higher-level thinking is the ability to abstract. Goldstein (1936), having worked with soldiers with war wounds, particularly wounds affecting the frontal cortex, described them as having a loss of abstract attitude. Goldstein's concept abstract attitude was rather complex. However, it can be operationalized with a clinical test: the interpretation of proverbs. Murphy et al. (2013) tested 46 patients with frontal lesions, subdivided into groups with left lateral, right lateral, and medial lesions, using a proverb interpretation test (PIT) adapted from Delis et al. (2001). This test assesses the ability to interpret a statement in an abstract rather than a concrete sense. Thus, for "Rome was not built in a day," a generalized understanding is that any great achievement takes patience and time to complete. A concrete understanding may refer to the time it takes to complete buildings or infrastructure or even to establish the Roman Empire. Medial frontal patients were the only frontal subgroup significantly impaired on the PIT relative to healthy controls. However, their most frequent responses were partially correct ones (e.g., "Things take time, but you will get there in the end"), so an energization deficit seems plausible. However, of the errors made by the left lateral group, 45% were concrete, indicating an inability to produce an abstraction. By contrast, only 12% of right lateral errors and 8% of those made by healthy controls were concrete. McDonald et al. (2008) made the related finding that epileptic patients with a left frontal focus produced poorer abstraction responses on this test than those with a right frontal focus. The left lateral region seems to be critical for abstraction, at least in the verbal domain.

Neuropsychological studies have not yet produced a tighter localization of any abstraction process in the comprehension of so-called figurative language. Imaging studies are not entirely consistent, but the most common site is the left inferior frontal gyrus (e.g., Rapp et al. 2004; see also Papagno et al. 2009 for convergent TMS evidence). Shallice & Cooper (2013) have argued that the representation of abstract concepts requires a neural architecture that supports the construction of hierarchical structures and that this is carried out in the left inferior frontal gyrus.

Of course, abstraction also occurs in nonverbal domains. For instance, it is an important component process in carrying out nonverbal IQ tests, such as the Progressive Matrices or the Cattell Culture Fair. However, tackling these tests requires many other processes, as well, so they cannot easily be used to localize nonverbal abstraction. One study that begins to address this issue is that of Reverberi et al. (2005). They tested 40 frontal patients on the Brixton task (Burgess & Shallice 1996a), where subjects must abstract the rules of how a blue circle moves across successive cards, each containing a 2×5 array of circles. Left lateral patients were impaired even with good working memory, but this was not the case for the other frontal groups. Recently, Urbanski et al. (2016) used analogy tasks, which are somewhat simpler than g tests but require abstraction. Patients were requested to find an analogy between a source set and one of two candidate sets of colored letters of varying size. Using VLSM, the critical region for impairment was found to be the anterior lateral PFC, again on the left. However, only 27 patients were included in this study, so coverage of the frontal lobes was rather patchy.

Deduction

Induction is the process by which one produces a novel conclusion from the information currently available, prototypically in the articulation of a new scientific theory. Producing a novel abstraction, the process discussed in the previous section, is a key aspect of induction. The complement to induction within reasoning is deduction, where conclusions follow logically and certainly from the assumptions, or premises. Deduction is, however, somewhat difficult to isolate neuropsychologically, as tests typically involve multiple premises. So, in addition to language comprehension, it relies heavily on working memory. Although the effect of this factor can be mitigated by allowing premises to remain visible, it is difficult to eliminate completely.

With functional imaging, the complex stages of processing involved in deduction can be tracked over time. Thus, Reverberi et al. (2010) used a clever complex design to attempt to isolate the moment in time when subjects, following interpretation of premises, were making logical inferences. Activation increased particularly in left areas 44 and 45. This result is broadly consistent with earlier functional imaging studies of deduction (e.g., Goel et al. 2000). However, the complexity of this study would make converging neuropsychological data valuable. Yet lesions to the putatively critical areas typically produce aphasic problems, which interfere with the interpretation of individual premises. Probably one of the most extensive studies of classical deduction in frontal patients was conducted by Reverberi and colleagues (2009), who tested 36 frontal patients on their ability to process one-, two-, or three-premise syllogisms. However, aphasic patients were excluded, and this resulted in no patients having lesions overlapping the critical left areas 44 and 45. Notably, however, the performance of right lateral patients was indistinguishable from healthy controls, unlike that of left lateral and medial patients. Deduction, like abstraction, is a left frontal process, at least when the stimuli used are verbal.

Reasoning in Well-Structured and Less Well-Structured Problem Spaces

A well-structured problem space is one where, as in games like chess or puzzles like the Tower of Hanoi, the start position and goal are clearly specified. The consequences of selecting one from the finite set of alternatives available at any stage of problem solution are also well specified in advance. By contrast, a less well-structured problem space, more typical of real life, is a problem situation where at least one of these conditions does not hold, as in planning the cooking of a meal for guests.

Tower tasks involve moving balls on pegs to achieve a goal position in the minimum number of moves. They constitute a nonverbal well-structured domain and have been extensively investigated neuropsychologically. The two studies involving the most patients are a Tower of London study by Shallice (1982), with 61 patients, and a Tower of Hanoi study by Morris et al. (1997), with 59 patients. Both tasks included conflict situation trials in which, early in the solution, the subject must move a ball in the opposite direction of its eventual goal peg. The two studies used the classical group approach, and both found a selective impairment in left frontal patients. Of particular interest, in the Morris et al. (1997) study, the impairment was found only for conflict situation trials occurring relatively early in the testing period.

Tasks such as these require what Petrides (1994) called manipulation of working memory contents, which he localized in the dorsolateral PFC. In particular, these tasks involve, among other processes, updating the contents of working memory (Miyake & Friedman 2012). The two Tower studies discussed in the previous paragraph do not speak to the specific localization within the left frontal lobe. More recently, functional imaging studies of these tasks have generally supported Petrides' view (Kaller et al. 2011, Crescentini et al. 2012). Thus, processes that are different from those underlying verbal deduction are presumably involved.

If we return to the issue of less well-structured problem spaces, Goel et al. (2007) used tasks that either were explicitly spatial or could be mapped onto a spatial dimension through the use of ordinal scale comparisons, such as, "Mary is smarter than John. John is smarter than Michael. Mary is smarter than Michael. Does it follow?" For half of the problems, the conclusion did not follow. Of these, half again were indeterminate, e.g., "Sarah is prettier than Heather. Sarah is prettier than Diane. Diane is prettier than Heather." The problems were given to 18 frontal patients. Goel and colleagues (2007) found that, for the determinate problems, both valid and invalid (e.g., Michael is smarter than Mary), the left frontal group performed worse than either healthy controls or the right frontal group. However, for the indeterminate problems that were not well structured, it was the right frontal group that performed much worse than either of the other two groups, which did not differ.

Goel et al. (2007) used the mental models approach of Johnson-Laird (1983) and held that the indeterminate problems require the construction of at least two models for the alternative possibilities, as well as holding the information that one or the other can be correct. They further argued that the left frontal lobe is adept at constructing determinate and unambiguous representations, whereas the right frontal lobe is needed to maintain "fluid, indeterminate, vague and ambiguous representations" (Goel et al. 2007, p. 2249). The study of Goel et al. is rather small for strong theoretical conclusions, but, as we discuss in the next section, its results resonate with other findings.

From Lateral Transformations to Strategy Shifts

In a single case study of an architect who had had a right frontal meningioma removed, Goel & Grafman (2000) made a different, if related, contrast between the functions of the left and right PFC. Despite having an IQ of 125 and a maintained ability to carry out the basic skills of his profession, the patient was unable to operate effectively as an architect. Goel & Grafman (2000) argued that he had retained the ability to make what they called vertical transformations, namely, more detailed versions of the same idea. What he had lost was held to be the ability to make lateral transformations, where one moves from one idea to a different type of idea, which the authors held to be a function of the right frontal lobe.

Support for a similar idea comes from a rather surprising source. In an attempt to develop a task requiring cognitive inhibition, Burgess & Shallice (1996b) invented the Hayling Sentence Completion Test. In section B of this test, subjects are presented with a sentence frame, such as "The ship sank very close to the . . ." The task of the subject is to give a word unrelated to the completion of the sentence or to any word in the sentence. "Banana" would be an example of such a word. In an initial study of 91 patients, the Hayling B test proved to be highly sensitive to frontal lesions. Patients with anterior lesions produced more than double the error score of either posterior-lesioned patients or healthy controls. No significant lateralization effects were found.

This result looks like a difficulty with inhibition. However, it was noted that, after a few trials, healthy controls tended to develop a strategy of looking around the room to select an object or of making an association with their previous response. Their aim was to produce a word before the sentence frame was presented. They then no longer had to inhibit the completion; they merely had to check that their already generated word did not, by chance, relate to the sentence frame. Anterior-lesioned patients gave far fewer responses that fitted either of these two strategies than did posterior-lesioned patients or healthy controls. They did not generate an effective strategy to circumvent the difficulty of the task.

Three studies have indicated surprising right frontal involvement in this entirely verbal task. Roca et al. (2010) examined the extent to which g scores could explain frontal deficits in several tasks with 44 frontal patients. As discussed above, they found that, for five tasks, one of which was a much shortened version of the Hayling test, the frontal deficit could not be explained merely as a consequence of impairment in fluid IQ. Six patients performed particularly badly on this set of tasks. Five of them had right frontal lesions.

In another study using the full Hayling test, Volle et al. (2012) tested 45 patients with focal cortical lesions. They then used two critical lesion localization procedures. For both clinical measures of Hayling B, that of reaction time and that of errors, the critical lesion sites were in the right frontal lobe. For the more sensitive lesion localization procedure, the reaction time slowing localized to right lateral areas 45 and 47 and increased errors to right orbitofrontal area 11.

Robinson et al. (2015) gave the Hayling test to 90 focal frontal lesion patients and used the Stuss-Alexander grouping method. On the reaction time measure, it was the right lateral group that were grossly slow—performing more than four times worse than the healthy control group— while the left lateral group did not differ from controls. On the error measure, the right lateral group was, again, the only patient group that performed significantly worse than controls, with an error score more than three times as high as that of the control. Moreover, they made very few responses indicating use of an effective strategy. More specifically, the difference between the effects of left and right lesions lay, again, in the inferior lateral frontal cortex.

In a different, smaller set of right frontal patients, those with lateral lesions were compared on the Hayling test to those with orbitofrontal lesions. Right lateral patients were found to make many suppression errors, to produce very few strategy-connected words, and to require longer thinking times, all measures known to correlate with fewer strategy responses. In contrast, the orbitofrontal group performed normally. This supports the notion that it is the inferior right lateral cortex rather than the orbitofrontal cortex that is involved in strategy production (Cipolotti et al. 2015c).

A general inhibition problem is an implausible explanation of the right lateral impairment. Cipolotti et al. (2016) tested 30 frontal patients on both the Hayling task and the Stroop. The right frontal group performed much worse than the left frontal one on the Hayling task, but for the Stroop, there was an insignificant effect in the other direction.

By contrast, the notion that the right inferior lateral regions are critical for novel strategy production in problem solving has been supported by two studies, one employing functional imaging and the other cortical thickness differences across normal subjects. Both studies used problem solving tasks that involved an insightful lateral move to produce a novel strategy. One used Guilford's matchstick task (Goel & Vartanian 2005), and the other the so-called Nim or Subtraction game (Seyed-Allaei et al. 2017). Both found the critical area to be right area 47. Whether its role lies in the creation of a novel structure or plan or the realization of the inadequacy of an earlier strategy remains to be established.

Planning for Future Action

Reasoning needs to be implemented in action, often after a gap in time. Intentions need to be set up and then realized later. Typically, other tasks have to be carried out in the interval. Thus, planning for future action typically leads to a multitasking situation. Shallice & Burgess (1991) described three frontal patients who performed well on a wide range of clinical tests of frontal lobe function but were specifically impaired when given two tests of multitasking. Each of these tests—Six Elements and Multiple Errands—required patients to organize themselves to interleave a number of different tasks without cues as to when to switch, while obeying a set of simple rules written on a card in front of them. This study showed that multitasking was a separable frontal function. The one patient, AP, in whom the lesion could be well localized had a bilateral lesion of the frontopolar cortex (areas 10 and 11) (Shallice & Cooper 2011). Burgess et al. (2000) used another multitasking test, the Greenwich, which required three different tasks to be interleaved over 10 minutes. When memory was not impaired, poor overall performance was associated with lesions to the more polar and medial aspects of areas 8, 9, and 10. Area 10 appears to be critical. Roca et al. (2011) compared seven frontal patients with area-10 damage to eight patients without this damage. The patients with area-10 damage were more impaired in multitasking but less so on response inhibition and abstract reasoning.

That the temporal aspect of setting up and realizing intentions may indeed be the core deficit of the multitasking impairment is shown by a study by Volle et al. (2011). With the assistance of a stopwatch, 45 patients with focal lesions had to press a spacebar every 30 s while carrying out another task. The eight patients with area-10 lesions pressed the spacebar once every 48 s, in comparison with the rate of once every 32 s for the other patients. On control tasks not involving time, the area-10 patients were unimpaired.

Functional imaging studies, too, have given strong parallel evidence for the involvement of bilateral area 10 in multitasking and, in particular, in the generation and realization of intentions (Koechlin et al. 1999; Burgess et al. 2001, 2011).

THEORETICAL CONCLUSIONS

In this review, we have focused on neuropsychological group studies of what we termed active thought and on the localization of the principal processing components of a variety of tasks involving it. We have assumed that different localizations imply different computational functions. The most basic conclusion one can draw from the neuropsychological literature is that the PFC has a complex computational structure with a large set of subsystems combining to realize active thought. This is because impairments at the supervisory level differ qualitatively on at least some combinations of lateral versus medial, left versus right, anterior versus posterior prefrontal, and dorsal versus ventral.

In addition, most frontal tasks involve many components. Thus, the complexity of the neurocognitive architecture could well be greater than neuropsychological group studies alone currently indicate. This is because these pick out one or a very few critical regions. For instance, we have shown that right lateral frontal systems for novel strategy selection are important in carrying out the Hayling task. Yet Robinson et al. (2016) have recently described two patients with different types of difficulty completing the task, with one type of difficulty being clearly related to inhibition. Both had left frontal lesions! The task undoubtedly involves multiple systems relevant for active thought.

In this case, why are neuropsychological studies valuable? They clearly show that the affected systems are crucial. In addition, though, they complement functional imaging findings informatively with respect both to lateralization of function and to the role of networks or their constituent subsystems. Regarding lateralization of functions, one frequently obtains the impression from the imaging literature that the two frontal cortices have basically equivalent functions; activation is often bilateral. The neuropsychological literature provides a different perspective. The two lateral PFCs appear to have markedly different functions with respect to active thought.

There are a number of different ways in which these contrasting functions have been characterized. Thus, Stuss & Alexander (2007) and Shallice & Gillingham (2012) contrast task setting and setting up a program (left lateral frontal region) with active monitoring (right lateral frontal region). The latter is well supported by the currently reviewed studies, the former by the Morris et al. (1997) study of the Tower of Hanoi task. Goel and colleagues (2000, 2007), instead, made the contrast between vertical operations in a well-structured problem space (left) and lateral ones in an ill-structured space (right). This fits the results on deduction and Tower tasks (left) and Hayling tasks well.

Computationally, one can combine these two sets of contrasts. The left lateral region becomes the site where Duncan's serially operating program is realized; this fits, too, with the task switching studies. The program then runs on systems in premotor and posterior cortices. By contrast, the right lateral region would be where processes operate in parallel either separately, to detect any of a range of potential errors (active monitoring), or in combination, to produce a novel strategy. This would fit with the left lateral region having a much higher degree of internal inhibition than the right because, at each stage, the left lateral region selects, top down, one from a range of possible thought and action schemas.

Within the left lateral frontal lobe, the contrasting localizations of deduction (ventrolateral) and Tower task operations (dorsolateral) fit roughly with a Petrides-like anatomical perspective. Cognitively, the contrast supports the view that rule-based mental logic and mental model–based reasoning both exist but rely on anatomically different systems (Goel 2007). As far as mental model–based reasoning is concerned, Knauff (2013) has argued that the model itself is parietally located, and the existence of a qualitatively organized representation of objects in space in the right parietal lobe (Buiatti et al. 2011) supports this.

Regarding the contrast between the findings of neuropsychology and those of functional imaging on the role of networks or their constituent subsystems, imaging provides evidence on the network of systems involved in task execution. Focal lesion patients provide evidence more often, if the lesion is small, on single systems. From this perspective, Duncan & Owen's (2000) frontoparietal multiple demand network may be seen as composed of a variety of special-purpose subsystems that combine to realize, for instance, mental model–based reasoning in tests of fluid IQ.

The clearest example of this functional distinction between parts of the network is the contrast between lesions to lateral and superior medial frontal regions. Both contain parts of the multiple demand network. However, lesions affect the two regions differently across a range of neuropsychological tests, including reaction time, fluency, and reasoning tasks. In the current approach, the superior medial PFC energizes supervisory operations, but the lateral PFC implements them; the two regions have different functions.

The impaired performance on different tasks demonstrated by patients with lesions in the same region can also give rise to theoretical questions. Consider the left inferior frontal region. We argue that it is involved in constructing the preverbal message but also in the representation of abstraction. Both of these require hierarchically organized structures relating to language. But do they involve the same system? We will not know until it is investigated whether dissociations can exist between tasks involving the two regions.

Neuropsychological findings on active thought do not just show that certain brain systems are critical for task execution. They also complement findings from functional imaging in two different ways. First, rather than giving information on whole networks, they highlight the role of the systems of which these networks are composed. Second, rather than downplaying differential lateralization of function, they emphasize it. Whether they can also help answer the key question of how these supervisory subsystems interact remains to be seen.

SUMMARY POINTS

1. For active thought processes, neuropsychology provides valuable evidence on underlying functional subsystems and their lateralization.

2. For the medial PFC, the subsystems to which such evidence relates are critical for energizing supervisory processes.

3. For the left lateral PFC, these subsystems are critical for top-down schema activation, updating, deduction, and, more anteriorly, abstraction.

4. For the left ventrolateral PFC, these subsystems help to construct preverbal messages.

5. For the right lateral PFC, these subsystems underpin active monitoring and, more inferiorly, are critically involved in the production of novel strategies.

6. For the frontopolar PFC, these subsystems play a key role in the setting up and maintenance of intentions.

FUTURE ISSUES

1. For models of frontoparietal control networks, of which the multiple demand network is one, are the frontal components functionally different or functionally equivalent to the parietal components?

2. Does the left lateral PFC have stronger inhibition internal to the region than the right lateral PFC, as suggested above?

3. For some claimed processes (e.g., active monitoring) and even some tasks (e.g., Hayling B), there is a broad agreement across studies about which frontal lobe plays the more critical role, but there is disagreement over the specific parts of the lobe responsible. Is this due to variations across samples of patients tested or due to subtle differences in the cognitive processes employed to perform the particular version of the task used?

4. Abstraction and formation of a preverbal message both involve more anterior parts of the inferior left lateral frontal lobe. Do they have any processes in common? For instance, extrapolating from Hagoort's (2013) ideas on localization of so-called unification processes, could the region be required for the construction of multilevel structures (Shallice & Cooper 2013)?

5. Are impairments following lesions to the inferior lateral right frontal region in tasks like the stop task due to impairments to systems controlling response inhibition or to those controlling bottom-up attention?

6. What is the involvement of the right frontal region in novel strategy attainment tasks, such as Hayling B? Does this region contain systems that create a novel structure or plan, or systems that determine that the preceding strategy was inadequate and thus needs changing? Are there yet further possibilities?

DISCLOSURE STATEMENT

The authors are not aware of any affiliations, memberships, funding, or financial holdings that might be perceived as affecting the objectivity of this review.

ACKNOWLEDGMENTS

We would like to thank Edgar Chan for his comments on an earlier version of the paper and Sara Gharooni for her assistance in preparing the paper. L.C. is supported by the Biomedical Research Centre of the National Institute for Health Research and University College London Hospitals.

LITERATURE CITED

Aron AR, Fletcher PC, Bullmore ET, Sahakian BJ, Robbins TW. 2003. Stop-signal inhibition disrupted by damage to right inferior frontal gyrus in humans. *Nat. Neurosci.* 6(2):115–16

Aron AR, Monsell S, Sahakian BJ, Robbins TW. 2004. A componential analysis of task-switching deficits associated with lesions of left and right frontal cortex. *Brain* 127(7):1561–73

Bates E, Wilson SM, Saygin AP, Dick F, Sereno MI, et al. 2003. Voxel-based lesion–symptom mapping. *Nat. Neurosci.* 6(5):448–50

Buiatti T, Mussoni A, Toraldo A, Skrap M, Shallice T. 2011. Two qualitatively different impairments in making rotation operations. *Cortex* 47(2):166–79

Burgess PW, Gonen-Yaacovi G, Volle E. 2011. Functional neuroimaging studies of prospective memory: What have we learned so far? *Neuropsychologia* 49(8):2246–57

Burgess PW, Quayle A, Frith CD. 2001. Brain regions involved in prospective memory as determined by positive emission tomography. *Neuropsychologia* 39(6):545–55

Burgess PW, Shallice T. 1996a. Bizarre responses, rule detection and frontal lobe lesions. *Cortex* 32:241–59

Burgess PW, Shallice T. 1996b. Response suppression, initiation and strategy use following frontal lobe lesions. *Neuropsychologia* 34(4):263–72

Burgess PW, Veitch E, de Lacy Costello A, Shallice T. 2000. The cognitive and neuroanatomical correlates of multitasking. *Neuropsychologia* 38(6):848–63

Caramazza A. 1986. On drawing inferences about the structure of normal cognitive systems from the analysis of patterns of impaired performance: the case for single-patient studies. *Brain Cogn.* 5(1):41–66

Chan E, MacPherson SE, Robinson G, Turner M, Lecce F, et al. 2015. Limitations of the trail making test part-B in assessing frontal executive dysfunction. *J. Int. Neuropsychol. Soc.* 21(2):169–74

Chua EF, Schacter DL, Rand-Giovannetti E, Sperling RA. 2006. Understanding metamemory: neural correlates of the cognitive process and subjective level of confidence in recognition memory. *NeuroImage* 29(4):1150–60

Cipolotti L, Healy C, Chan E, Bolsover F, Lecce F, et al. 2015a. The impact of different aetiologies on the cognitive performance of frontal patients. *Neuropsychologia* 68:21–30

Cipolotti L, Healy C, Chan E, MacPherson SE, White M, et al. 2015b. The effect of age on cognitive performance of frontal patients. *Neuropsychologia* 75:233–41

Cipolotti L, Healy C, Spanò B, Lecce F, Biondo F, et al. 2015c. Strategy and suppression impairments after right lateral prefrontal and orbito-frontal lesions. *Brain* 139(2):e10

Cipolotti L, Spanò B, Healy C, Tudor-Sfetea C, Chan E, et al. 2016. Inhibition processes are dissociable and lateralized in human prefrontal cortex. *Neuropsychologia* 93:1–12

Cooper R, Shallice T. 2000. Contention scheduling and the control of routine activities. *Cogn. Neuropsychol.* 17(4):297–338

Costello AL, Warrington EK. 1989. Dynamic aphasia: the selective impairment of verbal planning. *Cortex* 25(1):103–14

Crescentini C, Seyed-Allaei S, Vallesi A, Shallice T. 2012. Two networks involved in producing and realizing plans. *Neuropsychologia* 50(7):1521–35

Croquelois A, Bogousslavsky J. 2011. Stroke aphasia: 1,500 consecutive cases. *Cerebrovasc. Dis.* 31(4):392–99

Cummings JL. 1993. Frontal-subcortical circuits and human behavior. *Arch. Neurol.* 50(8):873–80

De Renzi E, Barbieri C. 1992. The incidence of the grasp reflex following hemispheric lesion and its relation to frontal damage. *Brain* 115(1):293–313

Delis DC, Kaplan E, Kramer JH. 2001. *Delis-Kaplan Executive Function System (D-KEFS)*. San Antonio, TX: Psychol. Corp.

Derrfuss J, Brass M, Neumann J, von Cramon DY. 2005. Involvement of the inferior frontal junction in cognitive control: meta-analyses of switching and Stroop studies. *Hum. Brain Mapp.* 25(1):22–34

D'Esposito M, Postle BR. 1999. The dependence of span and delayed-response performance on prefrontal cortex. *Neuropsychologia* 37:1303–15

Duncan J. 2010. The multiple-demand (MD) system of the primate brain: mental programs for intelligent behaviour. *Trends Cogn. Sci.* 14(4):172–79

Duncan J. 2013. The structure of cognition: attentional episodes in mind and brain. *Neuron* 80(1):35–50

Duncan J, Owen AM. 2000. Common regions of the human frontal lobe recruited by diverse cognitive demands. *Trends Neurosci.* 23(10):475–83

Duncan J, Seitz RJ, Kolodny J, Bor D, Herzog H, et al. 2000. A neural basis for general intelligence. *Science* 289(5478):457–60

Fleck MS, Daselaar SM, Dobbins IG, Cabeza R. 2006. Role of prefrontal and anterior cingulate regions in decision-making processes shared by memory and nonmemory tasks. *Cereb. Cortex* 16(11):1623–30

Fuster JM, Alexander GE. 1971. Neuron activity related to short-term memory. *Science* 173:652–54

Gentner D, Goldin-Meadow S, eds. 2003. *Language in Mind: Advances in the Study of Language and Thought.* Cambridge, MA: MIT Press

Gilaie-Dotan S, Saygin AP, Lorenzi LJ, Rees G, Behrmann M. 2015. Ventral aspect of the visual form pathway is not critical for the perception of biological motion. *PNAS* 112(4):E361–70

Goel V. 2007. Anatomy of deductive reasoning. *Trends Cogn. Sci.* 11:435–41

Goel V, Buchel C, Frith C, Dolan RJ. 2000. Dissociation of mechanisms underlying syllogistic reasoning. *NeuroImage* 12:504–14

Goel V, Grafman J. 2000. Role of the right prefrontal cortex in ill-structured planning. *Cogn. Neuropsychol.* 17(5):415–36

Goel V, Tierney M, Sheesley L, Bartolo A, Vartanian O, Grafman J. 2007. Hemispheric specialization in human prefrontal cortex for resolving certain and uncertain inferences. *Cereb. Cortex* 17(10):2245–50

Goel V, Vartanian O. 2005. Dissociating the roles of right ventral lateral and dorsal lateral prefrontal cortex in generation and maintenance of hypotheses in set-shift problems. *Cereb. Cortex* 15:1170–77

Goldman-Rakic P. 1988. Topography of cognition: parallel distributed networks in primary association cortex. *Annu. Rev. Neurosci.* 11:137–56

Goldstein K. 1936. The significance of the frontal lobes for mental performances. *J. Neurol. Psychopathol.* 1:27–40

Hagoort P. 2013. MUC (memory, unification, control) and beyond. *Front. Psychol.* 4:416

Hampshire A, Chamberlain SR, Monti MM, Duncan J, Owen AM. 2010. The role of the right inferior frontal gyrus: inhibition and attentional control. *NeuroImage* 50(3):1313–19

Henson RN, Greve A, Cooper E, Gregori M, Simons JS, et al. 2016. The effects of hippocampal lesions on MRI measures of structural and functional connectivity. *Hippocampus* 26(11):1447–63

Johnson-Laird PN. 1983. *Mental Models: Towards a Cognitive Science of Language, Inference, and Consciousness.* Cambridge, MA: Harvard Univ. Press

Jung-Beeman M. 2005. Bilateral brain processes for comprehending natural language. *Trends Cogn. Sci.* 9(11):512–18

Kahneman D, Frederick S. 2002. Representativeness revisited: attribute substitution in intuitive judgment. In *Heuristics of Intuitive Judgement: Extensions and Applications*, ed. T Gilovich, D Griffin, D Kahneman, pp. 49–81. New York: Cambridge Univ. Press

Kaller CP, Rahm B, Spreer J, Weiller C, Unterrainer JM. 2011. Dissociable contributions of left and right dorsolateral prefrontal cortex in planning. *Cereb. Cortex* 21(2):307–17

Karnath HO, Steinbach JP. 2011. Do brain tumours allow valid conclusions on the localisation of human brain functions? Objections. *Cortex* 47(8):1004–6

Kerns JG, Cohen JD, MacDonald AW, Cho RY, Stenger VA, Carter CS. 2004. Anterior cingulate conflict monitoring and adjustments in control. *Science* 303(5660):1023–26

Khemlani S, Johnson-Laird PN. 2012. Theories of the syllogism: a meta-analysis. *Psychol. Bull.* 138(3):427–57

Knauff M. 2013. *Space to Reason: A Spatial Theory of Human Thought.* Cambridge, MA: MIT Press

Koechlin E, Basso G, Pietrini P, Panzer S, Grafman J. 1999. The role of the anterior prefrontal cortex in human cognition. *Nature* 399:148–51

Levelt WJM. 1989. *Speaking: From Intention to Articulation.* Cambridge, MA: MIT Press

Lhermitte F. 1983. "Utilization behavior" and its relation to lesions of the frontal lobes. *Brain* 106(2):237–55

Luria AR. 1966. *Human Brain and Psychological Processes.* New York: Harper & Row

Luria AR. 1970. *Traumatic Aphasia: Its Syndromes, Psychology and Treatment.* The Hague: Mouton

MacPherson SE, Healy C, Allerhand M, Spano B, Tudor-Sfetea C, et al. 2017. Cognitive reserve and cognitive performance of patients with focal frontal lesions. *Neuropsychologia* 96:19–28

MacPherson SE, Turner MS, Bozzali M, Cipolotti L, Shallice T. 2010. Frontal subregions mediating Elevator Counting task performance. *Neuropsychologia* 48(12):3679–82

Mah YH, Husain M, Rees G, Nachev P. 2014. Human brain lesion-deficit inference remapped. *Brain* 137(9):2522–31

Manly T, Robertson IH, Anderson V, Nimmo-Smith I. 1994. *The Test of Everyday Attention (TEA-CH)*. Bury St. Edmunds, UK: Thames Val. Test Co.

McDonald CR, Delis DC, Kramer JH, Tecoma ES, Iragui VJ. 2008. A componential analysis of proverb interpretation in patients with frontal lobe epilepsy and temporal lobe epilepsy: relationships with disease-related factors. *Clin. Neuropsychol.* 22(3):480–96

Miller EK, Cohen JD. 2001. An integrative theory of prefrontal cortex function. *Annu. Rev. Neurosci.* 24(1):167–202

Milner B. 1963. Effects of different brain lesions on card sorting: the role of the frontal lobes. *Arch. Neurol.* 9(1):90–100

Milner B. 1964. Some effects of frontal lobectomy in man. In *The Frontal Granular Cortex and Behavior*, ed. JM Warren, K Akert, pp. 313–34. New York: McGraw-Hill

Miyake A, Friedman NP. 2012. The nature and organisation of individual differences in executive functions: four general conclusions. *Curr. Dir. Psychol. Sci.* 21(1):8–14

Morris RG, Miotto EC, Feigenbaum JD, Bullock P, Polkey CE. 1997. Planning ability after frontal and temporal lobe lesions in humans: the effects of selection equivocation and working memory load. *Cogn. Neuropsychol.* 14(7):1007–27

Murphy P, Shallice T, Robinson G, MacPherson SE, Turner M, et al. 2013. Impairments in proverb interpretation following focal frontal lobe lesions. *Neuropsychologia* 51(11):2075–86

Norman DA, Shallice T. 1986. Attention to action. In *Consciousness and Self-Regulation: Advances in Research and Theory*, ed. RJ Davidson, GE Schwartz, D Shapiro, pp. 1–18. New York: Springer

Papagno C, Fogliata A, Catricala E, Miniussi C. 2009. The lexical processing of abstract and concrete nouns. *Brain Res.* 1263:78–86

Papagno C, Miracapillo C, Casarotti A, Romero Lauro LJ, Castellano A, et al. 2011. What is the role of the uncinate fasciculus? Surgical removal and proper name retrieval. *Brain* 134(2):405–14

Paus T, Kalina M, Patočková L, Angerova Y, Cerny R, et al. 1991. Medial versus lateral frontal lobe lesions and differential impairment of central-gaze fixation maintenance in man. *Brain* 114(5):2051–67

Petrides M. 1994. Frontal lobes and working memory: evidence from investigations of the effect of cortical excisions in nonhuman primates. In *Handbook of Neuropsychology*, Vol. 9, ed. F Boller, J Grafman, pp. 59–82. Amsterdam: Elsevier Sci.

Picton TW, Stuss DT, Alexander MP, Shallice T, Binns MA, Gillingham S. 2007. Effects of focal frontal lesions on response inhibition. *Cereb. Cortex* 17(4):826–38

Posner MI, DiGirolamo GJ. 1998. Conflict, target detection and cognitive control. In *The Attentive Brain*, ed. R Parasuraman, pp. 401–23. Cambridge, MA: MIT Press

Rapp AM, Leube DT, Erb M, Grodd W, Kircher TT. 2004. Neural correlates of metaphor processing. *Cogn. Brain Res.* 20(3):395–402

Reverberi C, Cherubini P, Frackowiak RS, Caltagirone C, Paulesu E, Macaluso E. 2010. Conditional and syllogistic deductive tasks dissociate functionally during premise integration. *Hum. Brain Mapp.* 31(9):1430–45

Reverberi C, Lavaroni A, Gigli GL, Skrap M, Shallice T. 2005. Specific impairments of rule induction in different frontal lobe subgroups. *Neuropsychologia* 43:460–72

Reverberi C, Shallice T, D'Agostini S, Skrap M, Bonatti LL. 2009. Cortical bases of elementary deductive reasoning: inference, memory, and metadeduction. *Neuropsychologia* 47(4):1107–16

Rizzo A, Ferrante D, Bagnara S. 1995. Handling human error. In *Expertise and Technology: Cognition and Human-Computer Cooperation*, ed. PC Hoc, E Cacciabue, pp. 195–212. Hillsdale, NJ: Lawrence Erlbaum

Robinson G, Blair J, Cipolotti L. 1998. Dynamic aphasia: an inability to select between competing verbal responses? *Brain* 121(1):77–89

Robinson G, Cipolotti L, Walker DG, Biggs V, Bozzali M, Shallice T. 2015. Verbal suppression and strategy use: a role for the right lateral prefrontal cortex? *Brain* 138(4):1084–96

Robinson G, Shallice T, Bozzali M, Cipolotti L. 2010. Conceptual proposition selection and the LIFG: neuropsychological evidence from a focal frontal group. *Neuropsychologia* 48(6):1652–63

Robinson G, Shallice T, Bozzali M, Cipolotti L. 2012. The differing roles of the frontal cortex in fluency tests. *Brain* 135(7):2202–14

Robinson G, Shallice T, Cipolotti L. 2005. A failure of high level verbal response selection in progressive dynamic aphasia. *Cogn. Neuropsychol.* 22(6):661–94

Robinson G, Walker DG, Biggs V, Shallice T. 2016. When does a strategy intervention overcome a failure of inhibition? Evidence from two left frontal brain tumour cases. *Cortex* 79:123–9

Roca M, Parr A, Thompson R, Woolgar A, Torralva T, et al. 2010. Executive function and fluid intelligence after frontal lobe lesions. *Brain* 133:234–47

Roca M, Torralva T, Gleichgerrcht E, Woolgar A, Thompson R, et al. 2011. The role of area 10 (BA10) in human multitasking and in social cognition: a lesion study. *Neuropsychologia* 49(13):3525–31

Rorden C, Karnath HO. 2004. Using human brain lesions to infer function: a relic from a past era in the fMRI age? *Nat. Rev. Neurosci.* 5(10):812–19

Seyed-Allaei S, Avanki ZN, Bahrami B, Shallice T. 2017. Major thought restructuring: the roles of the different prefrontal cortical regions. *J. Cogn. Neurosci.* 2:1–15

Shallice T. 1982. Specific impairments of planning. *Philos. Trans. R. Soc. B* 298(1089):199–209

Shallice T. 2015. Cognitive neuropsychology and its vicissitudes: the fate of Caramazza's axioms. *Cogn. Neuropsychol.* 32(7–8):385–411

Shallice T, Burgess PW. 1991. Deficits in strategy application following frontal lobe damage in man. *Brain* 114(2):727–41

Shallice T, Burgess PW, Schon F, Baxter DM. 1989. The origins of utilization behaviour. *Brain* 112(6):1587–98

Shallice T, Cooper RP. 2011. *The Organisation of Mind.* Oxford, UK: Oxford Univ. Press

Shallice T, Cooper RP. 2013. Is there a semantic system for abstract words? *Front. Hum. Neurosci.* 7:175

Shallice T, Gillingham SM. 2012. On neuropsychological studies of prefrontal cortex: the ROBBIA approach. In *Principles of Frontal Lobe Function*, ed. DT Stuss, RT Knight, pp. 475–89. Oxford, UK: Oxford Univ. Press

Shallice T, Stuss DT, Picton TW, Alexander MP, Gillingham S. 2008. Multiple effects of prefrontal lesions on task-switching. *Front. Hum. Neurosci.* 2:2

Sharp DJ, Scott SK, Wise RJ. 2004. Monitoring and the controlled processing of meaning: distinct prefrontal systems. *Cereb. Cortex* 14(1):1–10

Stanovich KE. 1999. *Who is Rational? Studies of Individual Differences in Reasoning.* Hove, UK: Psychol. Press

Stuss DT, Alexander MP. 2007. Is there a dysexecutive syndrome? *Philos. Trans. R. Soc. B* 362(1481):901–15

Stuss DT, Alexander MP, Hamer L, Palumbo C, Dempster R, et al. 1998. The effects of focal anterior and posterior brain lesions on verbal fluency. *J. Int. Neuropsychol. Soc.* 4(3):265–78

Stuss DT, Alexander MP, Shallice T, Picton TW, Binns MA, et al. 2005. Multiple frontal systems controlling response speed. *Neuropsychologia* 43(3):396–417

Stuss DT, Shallice T, Alexander MP, Picton TW. 1995. A multidisciplinary approach to anterior attentional functions. *Ann. N.Y. Acad. Sci.* 769(1):191–212

Szczepanski SM, Knight RT. 2014. Insights into human behavior from lesions to the prefrontal cortex. *Neuron* 83(5):1002–18

Thompson-Schill SL, Swick D, Farah MJ, D'Esposito M, Kan IP, Knight RT. 1998. Verb generation in patients with focal frontal lesions: a neuropsychological test of neuroimaging findings. *PNAS* 95(26):15855–60

Tsuchida A, Fellows LK. 2013. Are core component processes of executive function dissociable within the frontal lobes? Evidence from humans with focal prefrontal damage. *Cortex* 49(7):1790–800

Urbanski M, Bréchemier ML, Garcin B, Bendetowicz D, de Schotten MT, et al. 2016. Reasoning by analogy requires the left frontal pole: lesion-deficit mapping and clinical implications. *Brain* 139(6):1783–99

Vallesi A, Mussoni A, Mondani M, Budai R, Skrap M, Shallice T. 2007a. The neural basis of temporal preparation: insights from brain tumor patients. *Neuropsychologia* 45(12):2755–63

Vallesi A, Shallice T, Walsh V. 2007b. Role of the prefrontal cortex in the foreperiod effect: TMS evidence for dual mechanisms in temporal preparation. *Cereb. Cortex* 17(2):466–74

Varley R. 2014. Reason without much language. *Lang. Sci.* 46:232–44

Varley RA, Klessinger NJ, Romanowski CA, Siegal M. 2005. Agrammatic but numerate. *PNAS* 102(9):3519–24

Volle E, de Lacy Costello A, Coates LM, McGuire C, Towgood K, et al. 2012. Dissociation between verbal response initiation and suppression after prefrontal lesions. *Cereb. Cortex* 22:2428–40

Volle E, Gonen-Yaacova G, de Lacy Costello A, Gilbert SJ, Burgess PW. 2011. The role of rostral prefrontal cortex in prospective memory: a voxel-based lesion study. *Neuropsychologia* 49(8):2185–98

Woolgar A, Parr A, Cusack R, Thompson R, Nimmo-Smith I, et al. 2010. Fluid intelligence loss linked to restricted regions of damage within frontal and parietal cortex. *PNAS* 107(33):14899–902

Yokoyama O, Miura N, Watanabe J, Takemoto A, Uchida S, et al. 2010. Right frontopolar cortex activity correlates with reliability of retrospective rating of confidence in short-term recognition memory performance. *Neurosci. Res.* 68(3):199–206

Infant Statistical Learning

Jenny R. Saffran[1] and Natasha Z. Kirkham[2]

[1]Department of Psychology, University of Wisconsin–Madison, Madison, Wisconsin 53706;
email: jenny.saffran@wisc.edu

[2]Department of Psychological Sciences, Birkbeck, University of London, London WC1E 7HX,
United Kingdom; email: n.kirkham@bbk.ac.uk

Annu. Rev. Psychol. 2018. 69:181–203

First published as a Review in Advance on August
9, 2017

The *Annual Review of Psychology* is online at
psych.annualreviews.org

https://doi.org/10.1146/annurev-psych-122216-
011805

Keywords

statistical learning, infancy, cognitive development, language development,
sequence learning, perceptual development, multisensory

Abstract

Perception involves making sense of a dynamic, multimodal environment.
In the absence of mechanisms capable of exploiting the statistical patterns
in the natural world, infants would face an insurmountable computational
problem. Infant statistical learning mechanisms facilitate the detection of
structure. These abilities allow the infant to compute across elements in their
environmental input, extracting patterns for further processing and subsequent learning. In this selective review, we summarize findings that show
that statistical learning is both a broad and flexible mechanism (supporting learning from different modalities across many different content areas)
and input specific (shifting computations depending on the type of input
and goal of learning). We suggest that statistical learning not only provides
a framework for studying language development and object knowledge in
constrained laboratory settings, but also allows researchers to tackle real-
world problems, such as multilingualism, the role of ever-changing learning
environments, and differential developmental trajectories.

Contents

1. INTRODUCTION

How do learners discern the structure organizing their environments? This question has been at the center of intellectual debates since the founding of the field of psychology, providing impetus for the theories of Ivan Pavlov and B.F. Skinner. In the domain of linguistics, a similar question—how learners discern the structure of natural languages—led to the two dominant perspectives of the twentieth century: the structural linguistics of Leonard Bloomfield and Zellig Harris and the generative linguistics of Harris's most famous student, Noam Chomsky.

All theories agree that learners must have some way to ascertain which patterns are relevant to acquire and store and which are not. But what factors determine which patterns merit learning? This is where theoretical accounts diverge. Do the data themselves tell learners what matters and why? Or do learners receive guidance—via innate predispositions or knowledge—illuminating what to learn? As the structures to be learned become more abstract and less transparently mirrored in the input, the answers to these questions become less obvious. Similarly, as the number of possible patterns explodes combinatorially in complex input, it becomes less clear which patterns are tracked and why. As Gibson (1966) stressed, we need to understand the nature of the input before we can understand the nature of processing.

Statistical learning mechanisms have become prominent in cognitive and developmental science because they provide ways to test specific hypotheses about what is learned from any given set of input, and how. The term statistical learning originated in the machine learning literature and made contact with cognitive science through its application to problems in natural language processing and computer vision. In particular, connectionist models and other computational analyses of linguistic corpora demonstrated that, for suitably equipped learners, myriad statistical patterns are available in language input that could help learners to break the code of their native language. When creating models of human vision, it has become obvious that cortical-cell behavior is related to the statistics inherent in the natural environment (Field 1987).

1.1. Initial Evidence for Statistical Learning in Human Infants

The analyses described above made it clear that statistical patterns lurk in the natural world, including both the linguistic and visual environments. What remained unknown was whether human learners could take advantage of these patterns. In particular, the primary targets of interest for theories of unsupervised learning are infants, who have the most to learn and the least prior knowledge about how to allocate their efforts. Are infants statistical learners?

Several lines of research, beginning in the 1980s, have suggested that the answer is yes. For example, the developmental decline of sensitivity to non-native speech contrasts during the first year suggests that infants are sensitive to the distribution of individual speech sounds in their native language (e.g., Kuhl et al. 1992, Werker & Tees 1984). In the visual domain, researchers in infant cognition found that infants are sensitive to spatial relationships among repetitive events. For example, young infants can learn simple (two-location), predictable spatial sequences in the visual expectation paradigm, which uses anticipatory eye movements as the index of learning (Haith 1993). By 10 months of age, infants can use correlational structure to discover simple visual categories (Canfield & Haith 1991, Younger 1985, Younger & Cohen 1986). Although these studies were not designed to assess statistical learning mechanisms per se, they provide clear evidence that infants are sensitive to statistical regularities.

1.2. Infant Statistical Language Learning: Initial Evidence

One particular learning problem emerged as an important early test case for claims about infant statistical learning: word segmentation. Speech, even speech addressed to infants, is essentially continuous (except at utterance boundaries). Thus, in order to segment speech into words, infants must have some way to break the speech stream into word-like units. This problem captured researchers' interest for several related reasons. First, it is a very difficult problem to solve without knowing in advance what the words are, as evidenced by decades of research devoted to speech-to-text technology. Second, despite this difficulty, infants discover word forms in fluent speech sometime in the middle of the first year of postnatal life (e.g., Jusczyk & Aslin 1995). Finally, this is a problem that requires learning. Although there are certainly innate constraints that could be helpful (e.g., Seidl & Johnson 2006, Shukla et al. 2007), infants cannot know a priori which specific sounds are going to be words in their native languages.

The first infant study on word segmentation was published by Goodsitt et al. (1993). In this study, 7-month-olds heard utterances containing a target syllable preceded by two context syllables. The infants were sensitive to the statistical structure of the syllables that served as context for the target syllable. When the context syllables always occurred in the same order, infants were better able to detect the subsequent target syllable, supporting the hypothesis that infants can cluster syllables based on statistical patterns.

Subsequent studies by Saffran et al. (1996) assessed 8-month-olds' ability to track statistical patterns in continuous speech. The only cues available to chunk the speech into word-like units were the statistical regularities with which syllables co-occurred. After two minutes of exposure to the speech stream, infants could discriminate words from sequences of syllables spanning a word boundary (see Pelucchi et al. 2009b for related evidence using natural language stimuli). Importantly, these learning outcomes involved no instruction or explicit feedback, suggesting that statistical learning could be a mandatory response to structured input.

1.3. Infant Statistical Learning in Other Domains: Initial Evidence

A key question raised by these early studies concerns domain specificity. Are statistical learning abilities tailored specifically for a particular domain, like language? Or do they operate across multiple domains (e.g., music, vision, movement)? The first study to address this issue used a musical tone analog of the Saffran et al. (1996) task (Saffran et al. 1999). The results suggested that infants can successfully track nonlinguistic auditory statistics. Although these findings cannot tell us whether the same learning mechanisms subserve learning in both linguistic and nonlinguistic inputs, they are consistent with the view that statistical learning mechanisms are not tailored specifically for language.

Successive studies expanded these investigations to the visual modality. Fiser & Aslin (2001) demonstrated that adult statistical learning of shape conjunctions (i.e., scenes of arbitrary complex shapes presented simultaneously on a grid) was not only spontaneous but also rapid. Participants learned first-order and higher-order statistics from the spatial arrangement of the shapes in the scene without being instructed to do so. In other words, not only did they learn the immediate relationships between the shapes, they also detected broader probabilistic regularities. Subsequent studies investigated similar capacities in infants. Kirkham et al. (2002) presented 2-, 5-, and 8-month-olds with a visual analog of the original Saffran et al. (1996) paradigm. During test trials, each age group showed heightened looking time to a randomly ordered presentation of the same shapes, suggesting a sensitivity to statistics in the original temporal sequence. Subsequent studies revealed that infants are sensitive to many different statistical regularities in the visual domain across both temporal and spatial input, enabling them to extract patterns for further processing (Bulf et al. 2011, Fiser & Aslin 2002, Kirkham et al. 2007, Tummeltshammer & Kirkham 2013, Tummeltshammer et al. 2017, Wu et al. 2011).

1.4. Infant Statistical Language Learning

With these data in hand, one might ask whether statistical learning has any bearing on language learning. That is, if infants are able to track statistical regularities across myriad types of input, the original demonstrations of statistical language learning may have been unintentionally misleading in suggesting that statistical learning mechanisms subserve language development. As a case in point, consider the Saffran et al. (1996) study. In describing the results, the authors suggested that "our results raise the intriguing possibility that infants possess experience-dependent mechanisms that may be powerful enough to support not only word segmentation but also the acquisition of other aspects of language" (Saffran et al. 1996, p. 1928). Note, however, that the results of this study simply showed that infants could discriminate between high- and low-probability syllable sequences. Although this ability would certainly be useful for word segmentation, the study did not provide evidence for word segmentation per se.

To address this issue, Graf Estes et al. (2007) investigated whether the output of statistical tracking in fluent speech is actually word-like. They exposed 17-month-old infants to a stream of nonsense words, with only statistical cues to indicate word boundaries. Following exposure, the sound sequences were mapped to novel objects. Infants only acquired the words when the labels were statistically defined words in the fluent speech (for results using natural language stimuli, see Hay et al. 2011). When the labels spanned word boundaries in the fluent speech stream, infants failed to map them to novel objects. These results are consistent with the hypothesis that statistical learning mechanisms are harnessed in domain-relevant ways. In the case of the sequential statistics that characterize continuous speech, infants can exploit these regularities in the service of discovering candidate words in fluent speech (for related evidence in younger infants, see Erickson et al. 2014, Saffran 2001b, Shukla et al. 2011).

1.5. Infant Statistical Learning: Now What?

Over the past two decades, there has been an explosion of research in the area of infant statistical learning. The original Saffran et al. (1996) infant statistical learning study has been cited over 4,000 times (Google Scholar, accessed 2017, **https://scholar.google.com/scholar?hl=en&q= saffran+aslin+newport&btnG=&as_sdt=1%2C50&as_sdtp=**) and has been applied to myriad learning problems, ages, species, disorders, and implementations. Although scholars disagree about just how useful these mechanisms may be for solving specific problems (e.g., Johnson & Tyler 2010, Lidz & Gagliardi 2015), there appears to be consensus that infants are sensitive to statistical regularities in their environments.

In the remainder of this review, we ask: Now what? There is abundant evidence that infants are sensitive to statistical regularities and that this sensitivity reflects a robust form of incidental learning. The question we hope to address is what this sensitivity to statistical structure does for infants. To do so, we deconstruct statistical learning into the elements across which computations can occur and the statistics computed over those elements. We then turn to real-world problems where statistical learning approaches may provide novel explanations while raising new questions for future work. Finally, we take a step back and ask why we are statistical learners. The goal is to provide a selective review of the literature, organized in such a way as to motivate future research in this dynamic area.

2. STATISTICS OF WHAT? THE PRIMITIVES OVER WHICH STATISTICS ARE COMPUTED

One of the main arguments leveled by Chomsky against classic learning theory accounts of language acquisition is known as the argument from the poverty of the stimulus (e.g., Chomsky 1965). The crux of this argument lies in the availability of the right kinds of data in the input given the linguistic target to be acquired. Children receive restricted input both quantitatively (in terms of the number of utterances they are exposed to) and qualitatively (in terms of how well the data point to the structures to be acquired). More than 50 years later, debates over the innateness of specific linguistic devices still turn on arguments based on poverty of the stimulus (for a current discussion, see Han et al. 2016, Piantadosi & Kidd 2016). Developmental arguments that hinge on the input extend far beyond the problem of language acquisition. Indeed, since William James first described it as a "blooming, buzzing confusion" (James 1890, p. 488), the infant's complex and noisy multisensory environment has been viewed as an obstacle to learning, obscuring signals and making information less accessible.

From a statistical learning perspective, the stimulus remains problematic. We still ask whether the data support the types of inferences and abstractions that characterize mature knowledge systems. But the quantitative issues are quite different. The question is not whether there are sufficient data in the input. The problem, instead, is that there is too much data. There are vastly many statistics that could be computed over any set of input. This is the case, in part, because of the number of potential computations themselves—a topic which we address below. But the problem of the richness of the stimulus also resides in the nature of the input itself. There are so many potential elements to track. How do infants determine which primitives—the elements over which computations occur—to learn about?

Consider a problem like word segmentation. How do learners know which information to prioritize in their computations? Learners might track the probabilities of co-occurrence of features, phonemes, or syllables, all of which would be reasonable primitives over which to perform computations (e.g., Newport & Aslin 2004). But what about a cue like pitch contour? Pitch is integral to lexical structure in tonal languages like Mandarin or Hmong, and tones are discoverable via statistical information in adult speech (e.g., Gauthier et al. 2007). But pitch contours, however linguistically relevant, are likely irrelevant to word boundary detection, even in a tonal language. Indeed, even speakers of tonal languages find pitch contours difficult to use for word segmentation (Wang & Saffran 2014).

Similar issues arise when considering the primitives over which visual statistical learning operates. Is each visual feature dimension (e.g., color, shape, orientation) independent? Or are features bound together to create higher-order multidimensional units? And does this sensitivity to either single dimensions or feature chunks change across development? For example, both adults and infants track the statistics of human action sequences (Baldwin et al. 2008, Monroy et al. 2017, Stahl et al. 2014). One can imagine that, in this situation, the details of each visual element would not only be less important than the gestalt of the action being performed, but would also be a distraction from the task at hand.

Furthermore, consider the combination of auditory and visual stimuli. Some visual cues could be helpful insofar as they are correlated with auditory information (e.g., mouth movements) and vice versa (e.g., noting an intensification in sound as an object gets closer). But should learners track them? What about other visual cues, like eye blinks? These are not plausibly useful as cues to linguistic structure. But what is to keep language learners from tracking their statistics as well?

To some degree, this argument is absurd. Obviously, learners do not track the correlations between eye blinks and word boundaries. But why not? This is the problem of the richness of the stimulus. Learners are presumably constrained to consider some elements in their computations and not others. The interesting questions surround the determination of which types of units are tracked and why.

2.1. The Primitives that Enter into Infants' Computations

The question of primitives matters in any consideration of statistical learning because changing the units that are tracked can change the outcome of learning. This issue was explicitly addressed in a series of developmental studies of statistical learning in tone sequences. As described above, Saffran et al. (1999) demonstrated that similar learning outcomes occurred for continuous sequences of musical tones as for sequences of syllables. This result, however, raised the interesting question of primitives. Consider a tone sequence like AC#E, created to be analogous to a syllable sequence like "golabu." One can compute transitional probabilities between the individual tones (absolute pitches: AC#E), as one would between syllables. But tone sequences contain another primitive that is not present in syllable sequences: musical intervals (relative pitches: ascending major third followed by ascending minor third). These two types of information were confounded in the original study by Saffran et al. (1999), making it unclear which primitives infants tracked.

Subsequent studies revealed interesting developmental differences in the prioritization of musical primitives. Whereas 8-month-olds appear to be biased to track absolute pitches given continuous streams of tones, adults are biased to track relative pitches (Saffran & Griepentrog 2001). Both groups of participants in these studies heard the same sequence of tones in the input, but the groups appear to have learned different things because they tracked different primitives. These preferences for particular primitives can be shifted by altering the input such that absolute pitches are no longer informative, leading infants to track relative pitches (Saffran et al. 2005), or by making the input more musical, leading adults to track absolute pitches (Saffran 2003).

In the case of visual statistics, the issue of what constitutes a visual primitive rears its much-debated head (e.g., Edelman et al. 2002, Marr 1982). Is the learner attending to single feature dimensions individually in a multi-element scene or chunking these elements together and tracking across objects? In the early laboratory studies (e.g., Fiser & Aslin 2002, Kirkham et al. 2002), visual stimuli were created to be simple two-dimensional, unimodal elements, with the primitives being basic shapes or colors. Either the stimuli removed color from the equation (so that tracking occurred across monochrome individual shapes) or the shapes and colors were perfectly correlated. To determine which features infants were tracking, Kirkham et al. (2007) exposed 8- and 11-month-olds to a spatiotemporal sequence of identical shapes (i.e., the location of the shapes comprised the statistics). Only 11-month-olds showed evidence of learning; 8-month-olds required the shapes to be uniquely colored to pick up on the sequence. In other words, the younger infants needed more cues to the sequence to demonstrate learning. This finding suggested, for the first time, a developmental trajectory in sensitivity to specific visual statistics.

Using a different paradigm assessing infants' ability to track objects made up of multiple features, Kirkham and colleagues (2012) replicated this developmental trajectory; it was not until 10 months of age that infants could reliably unbind the features to track the informative ones. Further addressing the issue of binding across features, Turk-Browne et al. (2008) familiarized adults to a sequence of multifeatured objects and then tested them on objects either without their unique colors or without their shapes. Adults bound features together during learning, depressing their test performance when either of the features was removed. Although in comparable studies adults could easily track the statistics of monochrome shapes, the features presented during the learning phase are clearly important. Turk-Browne et al. (2008) interpreted their results to suggest that visual statistical learning not only depends on what has been encoded, but could actually provide cues as to what is an object.

Subsequent studies manipulated the stimuli to look at clusters of visual elements (e.g., objects). In a series of studies looking at expectations about object integrity based on feature co-occurrence, Wu et al. (2011) showed 9-month-olds a temporal sequence of colorful multipart objects, within which some parts co-occurred more often than others. The results revealed that infants were sensitive to the differential statistics of the parts within the objects, suggesting that the infants were computing relations not only between the objects, but also within them. Statistical tracking occurs across a variety of different primitives depending on the learning objective.

This pattern of results suggests several general points that should be considered in the study of statistical learning. First, primitives matter; some types of units may be prioritized over others by dint of both perceptual biases (e.g., infant tracking of absolute pitch) and experience (e.g., adult tracking of relative pitch). In addition, primitives matter when considering the learning goal (e.g., predictions about upcoming shapes versus expectations about how objects should behave). Second, the structure of the input matters; the prioritization of units can be shifted when supported by the input. When the sequence of tone words is continually transposed, as in the study by Saffran et al. (2005), the statistics of absolute pitches lose their value—they fail to predict structure. Under those circumstances, infants appear to increase the weight of relative pitches.

The third general point pertains to domain specificity. The specificity of the primitives is one way to construe domain specificity. On this view, whether the computations themselves are general is distinct from considerations of the input representations. It seems clear that different domains of knowledge place distinct demands on perception. Music and language are both auditory, but they make use of different perceptual primitives for the most part (with the exception of some aspects of prosody). Shapes, objects, and action sequences are all part of the visual environment, but the learner must track across increasingly broadly defined primitives. In other words, the learner must chunk multiple individual features (e.g., color, shape) together to fully represent a rich, dynamic, and complex sensory environment (e.g., a sequence of actions). Many of the distinctions between different domains arise from the use of different inputs. The computations themselves may be quite similar, just computed over different types of elements (e.g., Saffran 2008).

2.2. Experience as a Determinant of Primitives

The primitives that enter into statistical learning computations are affected by experience in a particular domain (e.g., Krogh et al. 2013). Some of the evidence to support this claim comes from comparisons between infants and adults, as in the studies on absolute versus relative pitch described in the previous section. Another example comes from a study by Thiessen (2010) examining the role of correlated cues in statistical learning. When adults were given a sequence of syllables paired with shapes, they were better able to learn the syllable statistics than when the shapes were not present. Infants, however, were equally good at tracking the syllable statistics whether the correlated shapes were present or not. Thiessen (2010) hypothesized that this pattern of results can be explained by differences in learners' prior experiences. Adults expect syllable strings to be paired with visual referents based on a lifetime of exposure to language, whereas 8-month-old infants do not yet have this expectation. To test this hypothesis, Thiessen (2010) tested adults on a tone sequence analog of the syllable task, reasoning that adults should not expect tone strings to be paired with shapes. Indeed, the presence of the referents did not improve learning, supporting the view that prior exposure shapes expectations in statistical learning.

A related example comes from the body of work on infant rule learning. This task, pioneered by Marcus and colleagues (1999), involved abstraction away from the specific sequences to which infants are exposed. Infants are better at this task in some domains than others (e.g., Marcus et al. 2007). Experience seems to mediate these effects. Learning is facilitated by the use of familiar rather than unfamiliar stimuli, such as animals rather than abstract shapes or upright faces rather than inverted faces (e.g., Bulf et al. 2015, Saffran et al. 2007). Experience can also inhibit learning. For example, younger infants are actually better than older infants at abstracting across tone sequences because older infants' knowledge of musical structure may inhibit some types of generalizations (Dawson & Gerken 2009). Even within-experiment manipulations can affect whether infants generalize in these tasks. Simply giving 7-month-old infants exposure to social agents who appear to be using tones communicatively leads infants to generalize beyond the tone sequences they have heard, something they do not do in the absence of this experience (Ferguson & Lew-Williams 2016).

As suggested by this last result, experience with the input can affect downstream learning. When learners are first exposed to a particular set of stimuli, some of the primitives may be opaque. An infant listening to a stream of speech initially has access only to statistics at the level of sounds (phonetic features, phonemes, syllables, etc.). Until she learns some of the words, statistics at the word level are invisible (e.g., Saffran & Wilson 2003, Sahni et al. 2010).

Experience with the input affects the primitives over which statistics are computed. This is because statistical learning is dynamic; the output of one learning experience can serve as the input to a new learning experience (Saffran 2008). Saffran & Wilson (2003) investigated this phenomenon by exposing 12-month-old infants to a fluent speech stream in which the words were organized according to a simple grammar. Infants were then tested on grammatical versus ungrammatical sentences, with both types of test items equated for the sequential probabilities of the syllables. Infants successfully discriminated between the test items, suggesting that they were able to solve the task at the level of word patterns rather than just the level of syllable patterns. Infants began the task by tracking syllables but ended up also tracking words.

The structure of the input drives statistical learning in other ways as well. The input can call attention to some dimensions of the stimuli, highlighting them downstream in learning. For example, infants who are primed with a list of two-syllable nonsense words separated by pauses are subsequently better at using statistical regularities to detect new two-syllable words than to detect three-syllable words in fluent speech, and vice versa (Lew-Williams & Saffran 2012). We find similar results with other types of phonological patterns: Exposure to items that follow one particular pattern facilitates detection of similar items in fluent speech with only statistical cues to word boundaries (Saffran & Thiessen 2003, Thiessen & Saffran 2007). Infants can also use specific experiences—such as exposure to adjacent regularities—to help bootstrap the acquisition of more complex nonadjacent regularities across a single experiment (Lany & Gómez 2008).

The structure of the input helps learners to determine which types of generalizations to draw from the available data. Gerken (2006) adapted the infant rule learning task described above such that the input supported both a broad generalization (ABA versus ABB) and a narrow generalization (AAdi versus AdiA). Infants generalized in the way that was the most consistent with the structure of the input. In a follow-up study, Gerken (2010) made a small change to the input by adding a few counterexamples to the narrow generalization at the end of exposure. Just three counterexamples were enough to shift infants toward the broader generalization, suggesting that infants' learning outcomes are updated on something close to a trial-by-trial basis.

3. WHICH STATISTICS DO LEARNERS TRACK?

These considerations of the primitives over which learning occurs lead us to the next major issue: the computations themselves. Which computations are occurring over these primitives? Do computations change across development and/or across primitives? Learners must be constrained to some degree in deciding which statistics to track (for discussions of the computational constraints required for optimal visual statistical learning in adults, see Fiser & Aslin 2005, Fiser et al. 2007). One way in which the learner can be constrained is by the eventual goal of learning. If the learner is trying to predict an upcoming event based on previous events, then the statistics will look different than if she is trying to bind across different modalities to form a coherent representation of a scene or display. However, in most infancy paradigms, there is no specified goal or outcome; the infant is placed in front of a display showing a series of events, and looking times and/or eye movements are measured. So what are the computations that are performed automatically? And do these computations change when a goal is specified?

3.1. Frequency, Transitional Probabilities, and Dependencies

The original work by Saffran et al. (1996) presented the elements of computation as transitional probabilities (i.e., one event in the stream is dependent upon others). These probabilities were higher within words (1.0) than between words (0.33). Additional studies across different domains followed suit. The transitional probabilities between syllables, shapes, objects, audiovisual events, and faces were similar to the original language studies, with within-event probabilities at 1.0 and between-event probabilities significantly lower (e.g., Bulf et al. 2011; Kirkham et al. 2002, 2007; Saffran et al. 1999; Wu et al. 2011).

Frequency counting as an alternative possible computation was ruled out quickly with frequency-controlled studies in both the auditory and the visual domain (Aslin et al. 1998, 2001).

By at least 8 months of age, infants appeared to be tracking transitional probabilities regardless of frequency of appearance. Subsequent studies examined this issue in more detail. Marcovitch & Lewkowicz (2009) extended the work of Kirkham et al. (2002) by presenting infants with sequences of shape pairs, defined independently by transitional probabilities and by frequency. Although 2-month-olds failed to show a sensitivity to either computation, 5- and 8-month-olds could track both frequency information and transitional probabilities.

Any given set of inputs contains myriad levels of statistical regularities. What information do infants use to determine which level(s) to track? Research on nonadjacent dependency learning has pointed to some of the key variables that influence this process. For example, given three-word strings, infants tend to learn the adjacent probabilities between those words. However, when the variability of the middle item is increased, infants shift to learn the nonadjacent pairs spanning the middle word (Gómez 2002). Adults learning similar structures are able to track both adjacent and nonadjacent relationships in the same sets of inputs (e.g., Romberg & Saffran 2013a). Interestingly, adults are more aware of the nonadjacent relationships than the adjacent relationships, suggesting that, at least for adults, explicit representations may influence some aspects of statistical learning.

3.2. Complexity and Maximizing Information Gathering

In the real world, input can be measured as more or less complex (i.e., information can have higher or lower levels of redundancy). Complexity has direct implications for which statistics will be attended to. Addyman & Mareschal (2013) ran a modified version of Kirkham et al.'s (2002) experiment, omitting the habituation phase and using looks away as the dependent measure. This dependent measure allowed for a subtler assessment of infant attention. The results suggested that, in temporally organized visual sequences, 5-month-olds are more sensitive to local repetitions than global statistics. Infants tended to look away during more repetitive portions of the sequence (e.g., during a patterned sequence versus a random sequence). In other words, when complexity was low, infants allocated less attention to the sequence.

These results have implications not only for discussions of which statistics are being computed, but also for thinking about how attention is deployed within these paradigms. Kidd and colleagues (2012, 2014) provided additional evidence suggesting differential attentional deployment as a function of complexity. In their experiments, infants observed visual and auditory episodes of varying complexity based on the predictability (or likelihood) of an upcoming event. In line with their predictions, infants were more likely to look away during episodes of either very low or very high complexity, preferring to allocate attention to events of intermediate complexity.

Learning itself is affected by complexity. In an eye-tracking study with 8-month-olds, three levels of predictability were embedded within one spatiotemporal sequence (Tummeltshammer & Kirkham 2013). Infants showed faster saccade (eye movement) latencies, more anticipation, and increased accuracy to items that were highly predictable relative to items that were either deterministic or unpredictable. In this case, learners may be maximizing information gathering by using likelihoods to constrain search (e.g., Dougherty et al. 2010, Gweon et al. 2010, Téglás et al. 2011, Yu et al. 2007). Because deterministic relations are unambiguous, they offer little information to the infant and, perhaps, little incentive to test possible outcomes with anticipatory looking. Low-probability relations have the most alternatives (and are perhaps most engaging for the infant), but the relevant hypotheses take longer to generate and test. Finally, high-probability relations offer the incentive to gain information but only a few alternatives to confirm or reject, making them a good target for an information-seeking infant with limited resources.

3.3. Issues of Input Specificity

In the visual domain, learners must track statistics not just temporally but also spatially. This differs from auditory input, in which the information to be learned is primarily arrayed in time, not space. In the original visual statistical learning paradigm with infants, Kirkham et al. (2002) presented each group of infants with a temporal sequence of shapes, looming one at a time from the middle of a screen. Results showed that infants were as capable in the visual domain as in the auditory domain, providing a clear analog to the Saffran et al. (1996) study. However, an important aspect of the ability to perceive the visual environment as coherent and intelligible is understanding objects' spatial locations and what their present locations might predict about future events. Acquisition of this type of knowledge is essential for motion perception and for the production of action sequences; one has to learn not only which actions are appropriate, but also where and when they should be performed. For example, if, while looking out the window of your house, you see your child walking up the path to the front door, you can reasonably predict that you will see her next in the doorway of your house. You can use this information to guide appropriate anticipatory behavior, such as moving to a location that provides a view of the door to greet your child as she comes inside. In other words, each visual event is temporally related both to the previous event and to the future event and occurs within a spatial context.

Indeed, by 8 months of age, infants can learn temporally ordered statistics that involve informative spatial relations (Kirkham et al. 2007, Sobel & Kirkham 2006, Tummeltshammer & Kirkham 2013) and predictable co-occurrences in multi-element scenes (Fiser & Aslin 2002). As mentioned above, 8-month-olds' success in Kirkham et al.'s (2007) spatiotemporal paradigm occurred only when the elements were easily differentiable (e.g., differently colored shapes, each bound to an individual location). This suggests an interesting developmental trajectory in the effect of stimulus type on tracking statistics and highlights the importance of stimuli in processing the input.

Visual streams containing both backward and forward conditional probabilities provide an interesting opportunity to evaluate input specificity. Whereas some statistics, such as frequency, do not contain any information about order or direction, conditional probabilities can differ when computed with respect to the forward direction (i.e., X followed by Y) or the backward direction (i.e., Y preceded by X). Research in the auditory domain has demonstrated that both infants and adults are sensitive to statistical regularities defined in the backward as well as the forward direction (Jones & Pashler 2007, Pelucchi et al. 2009a, Perruchet & Desaulty 2008). However, language is inherently temporal, which suggests a need to be receptive to temporal order. Sensitivity to backward and forward statistics could be modality specific rather than domain general. Indeed, when 8-month-olds were familiarized to either temporal or spatial visual displays, they did not encode the visual regularities in the same way across both temporal and spatial dimensions (Tummeltshammer et al. 2017). Infants computed the predictive direction only in the temporal condition, with chunking occurring in the spatial condition. These data are consistent with the view that the computations performed by learners are susceptible to the specifics of the input.

Modality constraints observed in some studies of statistical learning can be construed as perceptual biases that affect domain-general computational principles (Frost et al. 2015). Studies with adults suggest substantial modality effects (e.g., Conway & Christiansen 2005, Emberson et al. 2011, Saffran 2002). For example, Saffran (2001b) developed an artificial grammar learning task in which the presence of a statistical cue to syntactic phrase structure (predictive dependencies between elements of phrases) was manipulated across conditions. Adults, children, and infants were better able to learn the grammar when predictive dependencies were present (Saffran 2001a, Saffran et al. 2008). The same pattern of results was obtained when adults were trained on auditory non-linguistic sequences (computer alert sounds) and on spatial arrays of visual images (Saffran 2002).

However, when presented with sequences of visual images—organized like auditory information in time, but presented visually—the benefits afforded by the statistical regularity were not observed (Saffran 2002). These results are consistent with the modality effects on learning described above. Visual information, unlike auditory information, is typically less transient, with patterns organized in space rather than time. These differences appear to impact the outcome of statistical learning.

4. REAL-WORLD PROBLEMS

Researchers considering what statistical learning can do for learners have approached a number of important and interesting problems through this lens. These approaches have both suggested novel answers and raised new questions for researchers.

4.1. Multilingualism

Since the earliest discussions of the possible role of statistical learning in language development, questions about bilingual learners have come to the fore. If statistical regularities play a key role in such language learning processes as phonemic learning, word segmentation, and word learning, what happens in bilingual environments? Can learners track multiple sets of statistics simultaneously? If so, what cues do they use to help them determine which bits of input go with which language? Strikingly, infants in bilingual environments acquire language at roughly the same pace as their monolingual peers, despite having twice as much to learn—and half the amount of input (e.g., Byers-Heinlein & Fennell 2014, Costa & Sebastián-Gallés 2014, Hoff et al. 2012).

The first study to examine the problem of bilingual statistical learning placed adults in a simulated bilingual environment created by interleaving two artificial languages (Weiss et al. 2009). By design, the languages contained overlapping syllable inventories. In order to recover the correct underlying statistics from each language, learners needed to keep the two languages separate. As long as an indexical cue—speaker voice—was available to highlight the presence of two languages, learners successfully tracked the two systems independently.

In another study, Antovich & Graf Estes (2017) tested 14-month-old infants in a simulated bilingual exposure task in which two artificial language streams were interleaved. Again, an indexical cue was present to indicate to learners that multiple streams were present. In contrast to the results of Weiss et al. (2009), monolingual infants failed to demonstrate learning of dual interleaved speech streams. However, bilingual infants were able to track both sets of regularities. Also in contrast to the results of Weiss et al. (2009), the two languages did not overlap in their syllable inventories. It is thus unclear whether the bilingual infants treated the input as being drawn from two languages or whether they acquired one larger set of words. Regardless, these findings suggest that infants who have had more experience dealing with complex and highly variable sets of input—i.e., bilingual infants—are better able to cope with this rich set of experimental input than monolingual infants.

In these studies, indexical information—a change in speaker voice—helped to mark the presence of two distinct speech streams. In monolingual language input, however, infants must learn to collapse over speaker identity. That is, the pitch of a word does not change its meaning (at least in nontonal languages). This observation raises an interesting question for infant statistical language learning research: Do infants collapse statistics across speakers within a single language? A recent study by Graf Estes & Lew-Williams (2015) suggests that the answer hinges on variability. When infants were exposed to an artificial language spoken by eight different female voices, infants successfully tracked the sequential statistics in the input. However, when just two voices were present, infants failed to demonstrate learning, presumably because they did not collapse the statistics across the two voices. Taken with the previously discussed studies about simulated bilingual acquisition, these results raise important questions about the role of variability in statistical learning. The distribution of exemplars in memory has been argued to be highly sensitive to variability, helping to explain patterns of results across myriad statistical learning tasks (Thiessen & Pavlik 2013).

4.2. Individual Differences

Another area where statistical learning approaches have been gaining traction is the study of individual differences (e.g., Siegelman & Frost 2015, Siegelman et al. 2017). This issue is of interest both in terms of individual differences in learning in themselves and insofar as individual differences in learning help to explain variability in key outcomes, such as native language learning.

Much of the research in this area has focused on adults, to facilitate correlations between statistical learning results and measures of cognitive or academic achievement. For example, English-speaking adults who performed better at a visual statistical learning task showed higher levels of performance in the acquisition of the Hebrew writing system, which is highly patterned (Frost et al. 2013). Experience with Mandarin in the college classroom improved adults' performance on an auditory statistical language learning task (Potter et al. 2016). Skill at auditory statistical learning, but not visual statistical learning, appears to be related to musical skill (Vasuki et al. 2016).

Few studies have addressed individual differences in statistical learning in infancy. This is due at least in part to methodological constraints. Tasks like the head-turn preference procedure—used in many infant auditory learning studies—are not amenable to individual difference studies. They provide a single score for each infant—a difference score for looking on novel versus familiar trials. There is no evidence that the size of that difference is meaningful—that is, that an infant with a larger novelty preference learned more than an infant with a smaller novelty preference. Issues of direction of preference also complicate attempts to use preferential looking procedures to study individual differences. Unless there is a habituation component to the task, it is often not possible to make strong a priori predictions about the expected direction of preference.

Visual statistical learning tasks hold promise for studies of individual differences in infancy because they permit the collection of continuous measures that are clearly interpretable. For example, Shafto et al. (2012) used a reaction time measure in a visual anticipation task to assess statistical learning in 8.5-month-old infants. The results were correlated with the infants' vocabularies, as assessed by parental report. Indeed, infants' processing speed in sequential learning tasks predicts vocabulary size months later (Ellis et al. 2014). Studies with child learners suggest a similar pattern of results: 6- to 8-year-olds' visual statistical learning skills predict their level of performance on measures of native language syntax comprehension (Kidd & Arciuli 2016). Research investigating the relationship between visual attention in infancy (from a visual pattern prediction task) and later childhood behavior and temperament showed that mean fixation duration infancy was positively associated with effortful control and negatively associated with surgency, hyperactivity, and inattention in childhood (Papageorgiou et al. 2014).

4.3. Developmental Disabilities

A related approach to understanding individual differences involves comparisons between groups of infants or children who are known to be following different developmental trajectories. These studies ask whether relative strengths and weaknesses in statistical learning can help to explain the patterns of deficits observed in infants and children with developmental disabilities. The first study to take this approach concerned adolescents with specific language impairment (SLI)—weakness in native language skill relative to other academic and cognitive skills (Tomblin et al. 2007). Participants with grammatical language impairment performed worse than their typically developing peers on a serial reaction time task requiring detection of visual patterns. Similar findings emerged from a study of grade school–aged children with SLI tracking statistical patterns in a word segmentation task (Evans et al. 2009). Compared to a nonverbal IQ–matched comparison group, the children did poorly on the statistical language learning task. Interestingly, the children with SLI performed even worse on a version of the word segmentation task using tone sequences rather than syllables, suggesting, in line with the Tomblin et al. (2007) findings, that the children's learning challenges are not limited to linguistic materials.

A recent meta-analysis of the extant literature confirmed this general pattern: Children with SLI perform worse on statistical learning tasks than children who are typical language learners (Obeid et al. 2016). These findings are interesting given the potential links between statistical learning and native language acquisition. Similar conclusions were drawn by a study comparing children with developmental dyslexia (DD) and children with typical development (Gabay et al. 2015). Children with DD performed more poorly on linguistic and tone sequence statistical learning tasks than children in the comparison group. Moreover, performance on both the linguistic and nonlinguistic statistical learning tasks was correlated with reading measures. These data are consistent with the view that challenges in procedural learning underlie at least some aspects of DD (e.g., Lum et al. 2013).

It is not the case, though, that all developmental language learning deficits can be attributed to challenges in statistical learning. The same meta-analysis examined the extant literature on statistical learning in children and adolescents with autism spectrum disorders (ASD) (Obeid et al. 2016). Strikingly, the data across numerous studies suggest that autistic individuals do not show difficulties in statistical learning tasks. For example, Mayo & Eigsti (2012) tested autistic children with the same materials previously used by Evans et al. (2009) in their study of children with SLI. The autistic children showed the same pattern of performance as children with typical development. Thus, the tracking of sequential statistics does not, in itself, provide a way to differentiate between language disorders that may have quite different etiologies. That said, it is worth noting that the vast majority of studies investigating language learning in autistic children have sampled relatively high-functioning children (Obeid et al. 2016). Autistic children who show more language deficits may exhibit different patterns of functioning.

Using event-related electrophysiological methodology, Jeste et al. (2015) presented children with ASD with an oddball paradigm version of the Kirkham et al. (2002) test in which the sequence was infrequently interrupted by a deviant or unexpected stimulus. Results showed a positive association between visual statistical learning and both nonverbal IQ and social function in children with ASD. Children with high nonverbal IQ scores demonstrated a larger (more negative) response to the unexpected trials (i.e., the 10% of the trials during which a shape was followed by an unmatching shape), as quantified by the N1 component difference (see Vogel & Luck 2000 for a discussion of the N1 component). This was opposite to the response of the typically developing group, who showed a greater response to the expected trials, suggesting greater allocation of attention to unexpected events. This preliminary work suggests that there may be statistical learning processing differences between children with ASD and typically developing children.

It would be ideal to be able to test infants at risk for developmental disorders on these sorts of tasks. Doing so would allow researchers to disentangle the starting state—abilities to detect sequential regularities, for example—from the effects of experience in detecting sequential regularities. Diagnoses like SLI, DD, and ASD currently cannot be made in early infancy. However, other types of developmental disorders, such as genetic syndromes arising from deletions or point mutations (in which part of a chromosome or DNA sequence is lost during replication), are diagnosed in infancy and provide fascinating opportunities to examine early learning abilities. Williams syndrome (WS) is a genetic disorder that is associated with significant intellectual disabilities, although with relative sparing of language abilities. Cashon et al. (2016) tested a group of infants with WS on the Saffran et al. (1996) artificial language segmentation task. The data provide the first evidence that infants with developmental disorders can track sequential statistics. Understanding how these abilities are used—and how they are combined with detection of other types of regularities—may help us to understand the developmental trajectories characterizing children with different disorders and individual differences more generally (e.g., Thomas et al. 2009). For example, some evidence suggests that infants with WS are more reliant on prosodic cues than their typically developing peers, at least after the first year of postnatal life (Nazzi et al. 2003). More complex approaches to studying early learning, asking how infants integrate multiple sources of information rather than focusing on how infants track single cues, will be necessary to develop a deeper understanding of the emergence of these complex phenotypes.

4.4. Noise, Distraction, and Context

In the real world, the infant learner is faced by another set of problems: noise and distraction. The literature reviewed above has shown the infant to be a robust learner, sensitive to the statistics in the input across a wide variety of situations. However, in the real world, those statistics can be in a fierce competition for attention among other, equally enticing cues. Tummeltshammer & Kirkham (2013) asked whether attention to highly probabilistic events would shift with the addition of noise. In a paradigm looking at three different spatiotemporal probabilities, infants showed heightened learning of a highly predictable event (as opposed to deterministic or low-probability events). However, when noise was added to the paradigm (in the guise of a light going on and off in a separate area of the screen), despite absolute attention to the events being the same as in the previous condition, infants now showed better learning of the deterministic events. This suggests that sensitivity to input statistics is context dependent. A series of studies by Tummeltshammer and colleagues (2014a,b; 2017) have expanded upon the issue of context, showing that visual statistical learning is mediated by stimulus salience, source reliability, and mode of presentation.

5. WHY ARE WE STATISTICAL LEARNERS?

As we have described throughout this review, there is ample evidence that human infants, along with other learners, are sensitive to the statistical structure of their environment. We have also tried to highlight the ways in which statistical learning abilities serve infants well, given the structure of the environment into which they are born. At least some of these abilities are observed in other species (e.g., Abe & Watanabe 2011, Santolin et al. 2016, Toro & Trobalón 2005). Almost 50 years ago, Rescorla (1968) demonstrated that conditioning is actually dependent on more complicated factors than just contiguity of the pairing. Conditioning is affected by the base rate of unconditioned stimulus occurrence, against which a conditioned stimulus/unconditioned stimulus (CS/US) contiguity takes place. In other words, if a tone always occurs just before a shock is administered to a rat, but shocks also occur in absence of a tone, the CS/US pairing is not learned. If, later, the same number of tones is presented but the shocks only occur after the tone, then the animal learns, even though in both cases the rate of tone–shock pairings is identical. Thus, it is not the absolute frequency of the pairings that is important, but the general probabilistic relationship between the variables. Conditioning takes place only when the US has predictive value. Rescorla's (1968) work refuted the traditional belief that the CS/US pairing frequency was the crucial aspect of classical conditioning and showed that animals are sensitive, instead, to the statistics of each individual situation.

5.1. Relationships Between Statistical Learning and the Environment

To some extent, we can construe infants' learning abilities as well tailored to their environments. This way of thinking makes sense when considering the physical environment, which predates human evolution. The modality-specific constraints described above are a good example of tailoring: Learners appear to be better at tracking sequential statistics in auditory stimuli, which tend to be more temporally fleeting than stimuli in the visual environment. The latter are more temporally stable, with structures organized more in terms of space than of time. The degree to which our learning abilities reflect these differences may be due to modality constraints on learning and memory that are present prior to experience in these domains. Alternatively, infants' divergent early experiences with auditory and visual inputs, possibly dating to prenatal exposure, may have shaped modality-specific constraints on learning and memory. Regardless of the locus of the constraints, they are a good fit to the world.

Another way to think about the relationship between statistical learning and the world is to consider the idea that our learning abilities themselves may have played a role in shaping our environments. Consider the structure of natural languages. An enduring puzzle in the study of linguistics concerns cross-linguistic similarities. Although languages appear to be very different on their surface, much of the underlying structure of human languages is remarkably similar. Whereas some of these similarities likely reflect historical relationships, others seem unlikely to be explainable in those terms. Indeed, these considerations played a major role in the original positing of a language acquisition device containing innate knowledge about possible human languages.

Statistical learning accounts are not sophisticated enough to be able to account for many detailed aspects of language acquisition, especially some of the more complex linguistic structures that do not appear to be transparently mirrored in the input (e.g., Han et al. 2016). However, both experimental tasks and computational models have suggested specific ways in which constraints on statistical learning might have influenced the structure of natural languages (e.g., Christiansen & Chater 2008, Saffran 2001b, Smith et al. 2017). The general idea is that language structures that are more learnable, particularly by infants and young children, should be more prevalent in the languages of the world than structures that are more difficult to learn. Moreover, if the constraints on learning precede the structures that they have shaped, the same constraints on learning should be evident in learning nonlinguistic structures (e.g., Saffran 2002).

Although there is not a great deal of data to support this theoretical perspective, the extant studies are promising. For example, infants are better able to track phonotactic patterns—the statistics of phoneme co-occurrence conditioned by position within syllables and words—when the observed patterns mirror the types of regularities present in natural languages (Saffran & Thiessen 2003). Similarly, infants are better able to acquire linguistic phrase structure when it contains distributional regularities—within-phrase predictive elements—that mirror structures found in natural languages (Saffran et al. 2008). Similar constraints on learning appear given non-linguistic input designed to simulate language structures (C. Santolin & J.R. Saffran, unpublished manuscript; Thiessen 2011).

5.2. Memory and Prediction

Statistical learning mechanisms are well suited to our environments, and our environments, in turn, may have been shaped by our learning mechanisms—at least for structures that are culturally transmitted. In this section, we turn to an even more speculative question: Why do we track statistics in the first place?

One possibility is that the detection of statistical patterns is a result of the structure of memory (e.g., Perruchet & Vintner 1998, Thiessen & Pavlik 2013). For example, the iMinerva model proposed by Thiessen & Pavlik (2013) simulates a range of statistical learning phenomena using principles of long-term memory: activation, decay, integration, and abstraction. Thus, sensitivity to statistical regularities is due to the properties of memory and forgetting. Memory-based approaches to statistical learning permit the integration of multiple learning tasks that appear quite different on the surface but that may be explainable under the umbrella of memory considerations (e.g., Thiessen 2017). This leads nicely to another major question currently debated in visual statistical learning: Is this type of learning best thought of as chunking or statistical computation (see Perruchet & Pacton 2006)? One alternative interpretation for infants' seeming sensitivity to statistical distributions across visual input is that it is the outcome of a broader associative learning strategy (i.e., chunking; Miller 1956). This implies that co-occurring elements in a scene are extracted and stored as a structured chunk (Perruchet & Peereman 2004), allowing infants to recall regularities encountered in the environment without relying on sophisticated computational abilities [see the models PARSER (word segmentation; Perruchet & Vintner 1998) and TRACX (sequence segmentation and chunk extraction; French et al. 2011, Mareschal & French 2017)]. However, as noted by Perruchet and colleagues (Perruchet & Pacton 2006, Perruchet & Peereman 2004), statistical learning and chunking explanations may not be mutually exclusive, and, indeed, chunking may arise from an initial sensitivity to statistical regularities.

Another way to think about why we track statistics entails a shift in focus from learning statistics to using statistics (e.g., Hasson 2017). Statistical information sharpens predictions. To the extent that our brains and, by extension, our cognitive and linguistic systems are engaged in reduction of uncertainty, statistical information should be informative. Note that this way of framing the issues—around prediction—is neutral concerning the specific types of statistical information that are relevant; any type of information, from Bayesian priors to transitional probabilities to the weights in connectionist networks, could, in principle, help to tune predictions. By tuning predictions, learners have the opportunity to reduce errors to better anticipate outcomes.

Predictive contexts also provide the opportunity for learners to generate internal error signals, which may supplement bottom-up statistical information and facilitate learning. For example, consider the following simple predictive learning study by Romberg & Saffran (2013b). In one condition, infants saw a brief video repeatedly on the left side of the screen, and learned to saccade predictively to the left, anticipating the reward. After several such trials, the reward occurred on the right side of the screen. The question of interest was what infants would do on the next trial. Would they respond by anticipating on the left based on the overall statistical information (the reward was much more likely to occur on the left), or would they weight the error signal more highly and look to the right? Interestingly, the infants' behavior was unaffected by a single unexpected trial; they continued to predict the reward on the left. However, after a second unexpected trial, the infants updated their predictions and became less biased to the left side. Across the experiment, the evidence suggested that infants updated their predictions based on the evidence they observed, but not based on a single counterexample.

6. CONCLUSION

We began this review by placing theories of statistical learning firmly in the middle of the big question of how the structured environment is detected by infants. We have presented evidence to suggest that infants' sensitivity to statistical structure is not only broad, applied across modalities and domains, but also focused, attending to the specifics of the input and the varying goals of perception. We have suggested that statistical learning is part of a reciprocal determinism between the brain mechanisms and the environment, in which each helps shape the other, perhaps crucially related to the structure of human memory itself.

Normal perception is concerned with real-life events: dynamic multimodal scenes that involve language, objects, and action. For statistical learning to be of use, it must be a mechanism that is flexible enough to encompass all of these dimensions. For example, solely attending to the relationships between individual features in a sensory scene would eventually create a computational bottleneck that would strangle the system. Thus, the primitives of statistical computation matter, changing the outcome of learning. They are affected by experience and modified by perceptual biases. And what are the actual computations operating over these primitives? In the field of infant statistical learning, transitional probabilities, frequencies, redundancies, dependencies, and conditional probabilities (temporal and spatial) have all played a part in this discussion. Although the research continues, it is clear from the work to date that these computations depend on both the age of the infant (perhaps shifting from frequency counting or attention to local redundancies to transitional probabilities across the first year of life) and the specifics of the input. At present, numerous different implementations can account for the empirical findings. It is up to the field to generate experimental results that can tease them apart.

For statistical learning to be useful, it has to tell us something about real-world problems. And it does: It offers insights into issues specific to multilinguals and tackles problems of real-world chaos (e.g., noise and distraction). Recently, studies using statistical learning paradigms have begun to shine light on individual differences in perception and certain developmental disabilities.

In sum, statistical learning is a rich and robust learning mechanism allowing infants to find structure (and meaning) in the blooming, buzzing confusion. We recognize that we have only touched the surface of the field in this review. But we hope that we have raised issues and questions that will help to motivate the next generation of research on statistical learning.

DISCLOSURE STATEMENT

The authors are not aware of any affiliations, memberships, funding, or financial holdings that might be perceived as affecting the objectivity of this review.

ACKNOWLEDGMENTS

Preparation of this manuscript was supported by a grant from the National Institute of Child Health and Human Development (R37HD037466) to J.R.S. and by a Nuffield Foundation Grant (PSA68) and a British Academy Small Research Grant (SG-47879) to N.Z.K.

LITERATURE CITED

Abe K, Watanabe D. 2011. Songbirds possess the spontaneous ability to discriminate syntactic rules. *Nat. Neurosci.* 14(8):1067–74

Addyman C, Mareschal D. 2013. Local redundancy governs infants' spontaneous orienting to visual-temporal sequences. *Child Dev.* 84(4):1137–44

Antovich DM, Graf Estes K. 2017. Learning across languages: Bilingual experience supports dual language statistical word segmentation. *Dev. Sci.* In press

Aslin RN, Saffran JR, Newport EL. 1998. Computation of conditional probability statistics by 8-month-old infants. *Psychol. Sci.* 9(4):321–24

Aslin RN, Slemmer JA, Kirkham NZ, Johnson SP. 2001. *Statistical learning of visual shape sequences.* Presented at Biennial Meet. Soc. Res. Child Dev., Apr. 19–22, Minneapolis, MN

Baldwin D, Andersson A, Saffran J, Meyer M. 2008. Segmenting dynamic human action via statistical structure. *Cognition* 106(3):1382–407

Bulf H, Brenna V, Valenza E, Johnson SP, Turati C. 2015. Many faces, one rule: the role of perceptual expertise in infants' sequential rule learning. *Front. Psychol.* 6:1595

Bulf H, Johnson SP, Valenza E. 2011. Visual statistical learning in the newborn infant. *Cognition* 121(1):127–32

Byers-Heinlein K, Fennell CT. 2014. Perceptual narrowing in the context of increased variation: insights from bilingual infants. *Dev. Psychobiol.* 56(2):274–91

Canfield RL, Haith MM. 1991. Young infants' visual expectations for symmetric and asymmetric stimulus sequences. *Dev. Psychol.* 27:198–208

Cashon CH, Ha OR, Estes KG, Saffran JR, Mervis CB. 2016. Infants with Williams syndrome detect statistical regularities in continuous speech. *Cognition* 154:165–68

Chomsky N. 1965. *Aspects of the Theory of Syntax*. Cambridge, MA: MIT Press

Christiansen MH, Chater N. 2008. Language as shaped by the brain. *Behav. Brain Sci.* 31(05):489–509

Conway CM, Christiansen MH. 2005. Modality-constrained statistical learning of tactile, visual, and auditory sequences. *J. Exp. Psychol. Learn. Mem. Cogn.* 31(1):24–39

Costa A, Sebastián-Gallés N. 2014. How does the bilingual experience sculpt the brain? *Nat. Rev. Neurosci.* 15(5):336–45

Dawson C, Gerken L. 2009. From domain-generality to domain-sensitivity: 4-month-olds learn an abstract repetition rule in music that 7-month-olds do not. *Cognition* 111(3):378–82

Dougherty M, Thomas R, Lange N. 2010. Toward an integrative theory of hypothesis generation, probability judgment, and hypothesis testing. *Psychol. Learn. Motiv.* 52:299–342

Edelman S, Intrator N, Jacobson JS. 2002. Unsupervised learning of visual structure. *Proc. Int. Workshop Biol. Motiv. Comp. Vis., 2nd, Tübingen, Ger.*, pp. 629–42. Berlin: Springer

Ellis EM, Gonzalez MR, Deák GO. 2014. Visual prediction in infancy: What is the association with later vocabulary? *Lang. Learn. Dev.* 10(1):36–50

Emberson LL, Conway CM, Christiansen MH. 2011. Timing is everything: Changes in presentation rate have opposite effects on auditory and visual implicit statistical learning. *Q. J. Exp. Psychol.* 64(5):1021–40

Erickson L, Thiessen ET, Graf Estes K. 2014. Statistically coherent labels facilitate categorization in 8-month-olds. *J. Mem. Lang.* 72:49–58

Evans JL, Saffran JR, Robe-Torres K. 2009. Statistical learning in children with specific language impairment. *J. Speech Lang. Hear. Res.* 52(2):321–35

Ferguson B, Lew-Williams C. 2016. Communicative signals support abstract rule learning by 7-month-old infants. *Sci. Rep.* 6:25434

Field DJ. 1987. Relations between the statistics of natural images and the response properties of cortical cells. *J. Opt. Soc. Am. A* 4(12):2379–94

Fiser J, Aslin RN. 2001. Unsupervised statistical learning of higher-order spatial structures from visual scenes. *Psychol. Sci.* 12(6):499–504

Fiser J, Aslin RN. 2002. Statistical learning of new visual feature combinations by infants. *PNAS* 99(24):15822–26

Fiser J, Aslin RN. 2005. Encoding multielement scenes: statistical learning of visual feature hierarchies. *J. Exp. Psychol. Gene.* 134(4):521–37

Fiser J, Scholl BJ, Aslin RN. 2007. Perceived object trajectories during occlusion constrain visual statistical learning. *Psychon. Bull. Rev.* 14(1):173–78

French RM, Addyman C, Mareschal D. 2011. TRACX: a recognition-based connectionist framework for sequence segmentation and chunk extraction. *Psychol. Rev.* 118(4):614–36

Frost R, Armstrong BC, Siegelman N, Christiansen MH. 2015. Domain generality versus modality specificity: the paradox of statistical learning. *Trends Cogn. Sci.* 19(3):117–25

Frost R, Siegelman N, Narkiss A, Afek L. 2013. What predicts successful literacy acquisition in a second language? *Psychol. Sci.* 24(7):1243–52

Gabay Y, Thiessen ED, Holt LL. 2015. Impaired statistical learning in developmental dyslexia. *J. Speech Lang. Hear. Res.* 58(3):934–45

Gauthier B, Shi R, Xu Y. 2007. Learning phonetic categories by tracking movements. *Cognition* 103(1):80–106

Gerken L. 2006. Decisions, decisions: infant language learning when multiple generalizations are possible. *Cognition* 98(3):B67–74

Gerken L. 2010. Infants use rational decision criteria for choosing among models of their input. *Cognition* 115(2):362–66

Gibson JJ. 1966. *The Perception of the Visual World*. Boston: Houghton Mifflin

Gómez RL. 2002. Variability and detection of invariant structure. *Psychol. Sci.* 13(5):431–36

Goodsitt JV, Morgan JL, Kuhl PK. 1993. Perceptual strategies in prelingual speech segmentation. *J. Child Lang.* 20(2):229–52

Graf Estes K, Evans JL, Alibali MW, Saffran JR. 2007. Can infants map meaning to newly segmented words? Statistical segmentation and word learning. *Psychol. Sci.* 18(3):254–60

Graf Estes K, Lew-Williams C. 2015. Listening through voices: infant statistical word segmentation across multiple speakers. *Dev. Psychol.* 51(11):1517–28

Gweon H, Tenenbaum JB, Schulz LE. 2010. Infants consider both the sample and the sampling process in inductive generalization. *PNAS* 107(20):9066–71

Haith MM. 1993. Future-oriented processes in infancy: the case of visual expectations. In *Visual Perception and Cognition in Infancy*, ed. CE Granrud, pp. 235–64. Hillsdale, NJ: Erlbaum

Han CH, Musolino J, Lidz J. 2016. Endogenous sources of variation in language acquisition. *PNAS* 113(4):942–47

Hasson U. 2017. The neurobiology of uncertainty: implications for statistical learning. *Phil. Trans. R. Soc. B* 372(1711):20160048

Hay JF, Pelucchi B, Estes KG, Saffran JR. 2011. Linking sounds to meanings: infant statistical learning in a natural language. *Cogn. Psychol.* 63(2):93–106

Hoff E, Core C, Place S, Rumiche R, Senor M, Parra M. 2012. Dual language exposure and early bilingual development. *J. Child Lang.* 39:1–27

James W. 1890. *The Principles of Psychology*. Cambridge, MA: Harvard Univ. Press

Jeste SS, Kirkham N, Senturk D, Hasenstab K, Sugar C, et al. 2015. Electrophysiological evidence of heterogeneity in visual statistical learning in young children with ASD. *Dev. Sci.* 18(1):90–105

Johnson EK, Tyler MD. 2010. Testing the limits of statistical learning for word segmentation. *Dev. Sci.* 13(2):339–45

Jones J, Pashler H. 2007. Is the mind inherently forward looking? Comparing prediction and retrodiction. *Psychon. Bull. Rev.* 14(2):295–300

Jusczyk PW, Aslin RN. 1995. Infants' detection of the sound patterns of words in fluent speech. *Cogn. Psychol.* 29(1):1–23

Kidd E, Arciuli J. 2016. Individual differences in statistical learning predict children's comprehension of syntax. *Child Dev.* 87(1):184–93

Kidd C, Piantadosi ST, Aslin RN. 2012. The Goldilocks effect: Human infants allocate attention to visual sequences that are neither too simple nor too complex. *PLOS ONE* 7(5):e36399

Kidd C, Piantadosi ST, Aslin RN. 2014. The Goldilocks effect in infant auditory attention. *Child Dev.* 85(5):1795–804

Kirkham NZ, Richardson DC, Wu R, Johnson SP. 2012. The importance of "what": Infants use featural information to index events. *J. Exp. Child Psychol.* 113(3):430–39

Kirkham NZ, Slemmer JA, Johnson SP. 2002. Visual statistical learning in infancy: evidence for a domain general learning mechanism. *Cognition* 83(2):B35–42

Kirkham NZ, Slemmer JA, Richardson DC, Johnson SP. 2007. Location, location, location: development of spatiotemporal sequence learning in infancy. *Child Dev.* 78(5):1559–71

Krogh L, Vlach HA, Johnson SP. 2013. Statistical learning across development: flexible yet constrained. *Front. Psychol.* 3:598

Kuhl PK, Williams KA, Lacerda F, Stevens KN, Lindblom B. 1992. Linguistic experience alters phonetic perception in infants by 6 months of age. *Science* 255:606–8

Lany J, Gómez RL. 2008. Twelve-month-old infants benefit from prior experience in statistical learning. *Psychol. Sci.* 19(12):1247–52

Lew-Williams C, Saffran JR. 2012. All words are not created equal: Expectations about word length guide infant statistical learning. *Cognition* 122(2):241–46

Lidz J, Gagliardi A. 2015. How nature meets nurture: universal grammar and statistical learning. *Annu. Rev. Linguistics* 1:333–53

Lum JA, Ullman MT, Conti-Ramsden G. 2013. Procedural learning is impaired in dyslexia: evidence from a meta-analysis of serial reaction time studies. *Res. Dev. Disabil.* 34:3460–76

Marcovitch S, Lewkowicz DJ. 2009. Sequence learning in infancy: the independent contributions of conditional probability and pair frequency information. *Dev. Sci.* 12(6):1020–25

Marcus GF, Fernandes KJ, Johnson SP. 2007. Infant rule learning facilitated by speech. *Psychol. Sci.* 18(5):387–91

Marcus GF, Vijayan S, Rao SB, Vishton PM. 1999. Rule learning by seven-month-old infants. *Science* 283(5398):77–80

Mareschal D, French RM. 2017. TRACX2: a connectionist autoencoder using graded chunks to model infant visual statistical learning. *Phil. Trans. R. Soc. B* 372(1711):20160057

Marr D. 1982. *Vision*. San Francisco: WH Freeman & Co.

Mayo J, Eigsti IM. 2012. Brief report: a comparison of statistical learning in school-aged children with high functioning autism and typically developing peers. *J. Autism Dev. Disord.* 42(11):2476–85

Miller GA. 1956. The magical number seven, plus or minus two: some limits on our capacity for processing information. *Psychol. Rev.* 63(2):81–97

Monroy CD, Gerson SA, Hunnius S. 2017. Toddlers' action prediction: statistical learning of continuous action sequences. *J. Exp. Child Psychol.* 157:14–28

Nazzi T, Paterson S, Karmiloff-Smith A. 2003. Early word segmentation by infants and toddlers with Williams syndrome. *Infancy* 4(2):251–71

Newport EL, Aslin RN. 2004. Learning at a distance: 1. Statistical learning of non-adjacent dependencies. *Cogn. Psychol.* 48:127–62

Obeid R, Brooks PJ, Powers KL, Gillespie-Lynch K, Lum JA. 2016. Statistical learning in specific language impairment and autism spectrum disorder: a meta-analysis. *Front. Psychol.* 7:1245

Papageorgiou KA, Smith TJ, Wu R, Johnson MH, Kirkham NZ, Ronald A. 2014. Individual differences in infant fixation duration relate to attention and behavioral control in childhood. *Psychol. Sci.* 25(7):1371–79

Pelucchi B, Hay JF, Saffran JR. 2009a. Learning in reverse: Eight-month-old infants track backward transitional probabilities. *Cognition* 113(2):244–47

Pelucchi B, Hay JF, Saffran JR. 2009b. Statistical learning in a natural language by 8-month-old infants. *Child Dev.* 80(3):674–85

Perruchet P, Desaulty S. 2008. A role for backward transitional probabilities in word segmentation? *Mem. Cogn.* 36:1299–305

Perruchet P, Pacton S. 2006. Implicit learning and statistical learning: one phenomenon, two approaches. *Trends Cogn. Sci.* 10:233–38

Perruchet P, Peereman R. 2004. The exploitation of distributional information in syllable processing. *J. Neurolinguist.* 17:97–119

Perruchet P, Vintner A. 1998. PARSER: a model for word segmentation. *J. Mem. Lang.* 39:246–63

Piantadosi ST, Kidd C. 2016. Endogenous or exogenous? The data don't say. *PNAS* 113(20):E2764

Potter C, Wang T, Saffran JR. 2016. Second language experience facilitates statistical learning of novel linguistic materials. *Cogn. Sci.* 41(S4):913–27

Rescorla RA. 1968. Probability of shock in the presence and absence of CS in fear conditioning. *J. Comp. Physiol. Psychol.* 66(1):1–5

Romberg AR, Saffran JR. 2013a. All together now: concurrent learning of multiple structures in an artificial language. *Cogn. Sci.* 37(7):1290–320

Romberg AR, Saffran JR. 2013b. Expectancy learning from probabilistic input by infants. *Front. Psychol.* 3:610

Saffran JR. 2001a. The use of predictive dependencies in language learning. *J. Mem. Lang.* 44:493–515

Saffran JR. 2001b. Words in a sea of sounds: the output of statistical learning. *Cognition* 81:149–69

Saffran JR. 2002. Constraints on statistical language learning. *J. Mem. Lang.* 47(1):172–96

Saffran JR. 2003. Absolute pitch in infancy and adulthood: the role of tonal structure. *Dev. Sci.* 6(1):35–43

Saffran JR. 2008. What can statistical learning tell us about infant learning? In *Learning and the Infant Mind*, ed. A Needham, A Woodward, pp. 29–46. Oxford, UK: Oxford Univ. Press

Saffran JR, Aslin RN, Newport EL. 1996. Statistical learning by 8-month-old infants. *Science* 274:1926–28

Saffran JR, Griepentrog GJ. 2001. Absolute pitch in infant auditory learning: evidence for developmental reorganization. *Dev. Psychol.* 37(1):74–85

Saffran JR, Hauser M, Seibel R, Kapfhamer J, Tsao F, Cushman F. 2008. Grammatical pattern learning by human infants and cotton-top tamarin monkeys. *Cognition* 107(2):479–500

Saffran JR, Johnson EK, Aslin RN, Newport EL. 1999. Statistical learning of tone sequences by human infants and adults. *Cognition* 70(1):27–52

Saffran JR, Pollak SD, Seibel RL, Shkolnik A. 2007. Dog is a dog is a dog: Infant rule learning is not specific to language. *Cognition* 105(3):669–80

Saffran JR, Reeck K, Niebuhr A, Wilson D. 2005. Changing the tune: The structure of the input affects infants' use of absolute and relative pitch. *Dev. Sci.* 8(1):1–7

Saffran JR, Thiessen ED. 2003. Pattern induction by infant language learners. *Dev. Psychol.* 39(3):484–94

Saffran JR, Wilson DP. 2003. From syllables to syntax: multilevel statistical learning by 12-month-old infants. *Infancy* 4(2):273–84

Sahni SD, Seidenberg MS, Saffran JR. 2010. Connecting cues: Overlapping regularities support cue discovery in infancy. *Child Dev.* 81(3):727–36

Santolin C, Rosa-Salva O, Vallortigara G, Regolin L. 2016. Unsupervised statistical learning in newly hatched chicks. *Curr. Biol.* 26(23):R1218–20

Seidl A, Johnson EK. 2006. Infant word segmentation revisited: Edge alignment facilitates target extraction. *Dev. Sci.* 9(6):565–73

Shafto CL, Conway CM, Field SL, Houston DM. 2012. Visual sequence learning in infancy: domain-general and domain-specific associations with language. *Infancy* 17(3):247–71

Shukla M, Nespor M, Mehler J. 2007. An interaction between prosody and statistics in the segmentation of fluent speech. *Cogn. Psychol.* 54(1):1–32

Shukla M, White KS, Aslin RN. 2011. Prosody guides the rapid mapping of auditory word forms onto visual objects in 6-mo-old infants. *PNAS* 108(15):6038–43

Siegelman N, Bogaerts L, Christiansen MH, Frost R. 2017. Towards a theory of individual differences in statistical learning. *Phil. Trans. R. Soc. B* 372(1711):20160059

Siegelman N, Frost R. 2015. Statistical learning as an individual ability: theoretical perspectives and empirical evidence. *J. Mem. Lang.* 81:105–20

Smith K, Perfors A, Fehér O, Samara A, Swoboda K, Wonnacott E. 2017. Language learning, language use and the evolution of linguistic variation. *Phil. Trans. R. Soc. B* 372(1711):20160051

Sobel DM, Kirkham NZ. 2006. Blickets and babies: the development of causal reasoning in toddlers and infants. *Dev. Psychol.* 42:1103–15

Stahl AE, Romberg AR, Roseberry S, Golinkoff RM, Hirsh-Pasek K. 2014. Infants segment continuous events using transitional probabilities. *Child Dev.* 85(5):1821–26

Téglás E, Vul E, Girotto V, Gonzalez M, Tenenbaum JB, Bonatti LL. 2011. Pure reasoning in 12-month-old infants as probabilistic inference. *Science* 332(6033):1054–59

Thiessen ED. 2010. Effects of visual information on adults' and infants' auditory statistical learning. *Cogn. Sci.* 34(6):1093–106

Thiessen ED. 2011. Domain general constraints on statistical learning. *Child Dev.* 82(2):462–70

Thiessen ED. 2017. What's statistical about learning? Insights from modelling statistical learning as a set of memory processes. *Phil. Trans. R. Soc. B* 372(1711):20160056

Thiessen ED, Pavlik PI. 2013. iMinerva: a mathematical model of distributional statistical learning. *Cogn. Sci.* 37(2):310–43

Thiessen ED, Saffran JR. 2007. Learning to learn: infants' acquisition of stress-based strategies for word segmentation. *Lang. Learn. Dev.* 3(1):73–100

Thomas MS, Annaz D, Ansari D, Scerif G, Jarrold C, Karmiloff-Smith A. 2009. Using developmental trajectories to understand developmental disorders. *J. Speech Lang. Hear. Res.* 52(2):336–58

Tomblin JB, Mainela-Arnold E, Zhang X. 2007. Procedural learning in adolescents with and without specific language impairment. *Lang. Learn. Dev.* 3(4):269–93

Toro JM, Trobalón JB. 2005. Statistical computations over a speech stream in a rodent. *Atten. Percept. Psychophys.* 67(5):867–75

Tummeltshammer K, Amso D, French RM, Kirkham NZ. 2017. Across space and time: Infants learn from backward and forward visual statistics. *Dev. Sci.* In press

Tummeltshammer KS, Kirkham NZ. 2013. Learning to look: Probabilistic variation and noise guide infants' eye movements. *Dev. Sci.* 16(5):760–71

Tummeltshammer KS, Mareschal D, Kirkham NZ. 2014a. Infants' selective attention to reliable visual cues in the presence of salient distractors. *Child Dev.* 85(5):1981–94

Tummeltshammer KS, Wu R, Sobel DM, Kirkham NZ. 2014b. Infants track the reliability of potential informants. *Psychol. Sci.* 25(9):1730–38

Turk-Browne NB, Isola PJ, Scholl BJ, Treat TA. 2008. Multidimensional visual statistical learning. *J. Exp. Psychol. Learn. Mem. Cogn.* 34(2):399–407

Vasuki PRM, Sharma M, Demuth K, Arciuli J. 2016. Musicians' edge: a comparison of auditory processing, cognitive abilities and statistical learning. *Hear. Res.* 342:112–23

Vogel EK, Luck SJ. 2000. The visual N1 component as an index of a discrimination process. *Psychophysiology* 37(2):190–203

Wang T, Saffran JR. 2014. Statistical learning of a tonal language: the influence of bilingualism and previous linguistic experience. *Front. Psychol.* 5:953

Weiss DJ, Gerfen C, Mitchel AD. 2009. Speech segmentation in a simulated bilingual environment: a challenge for statistical learning? *Lang. Learn. Dev.* 5(1):30–49

Werker J, Tees RC. 1984. Cross-language speech perception: evidence for perceptual reorganization during the first year of life. *Infant Behav. Dev.* 7:49–63

Wu R, Gopnik A, Richardson DC, Kirkham NZ. 2011. Infants learn about objects from statistics and people. *Dev. Psychol.* 47(5):1220–29

Younger BA. 1985. The segregation of items into categories by ten-month-old infants. *Child Dev.* 54:858–67

Younger BA, Cohen LB. 1986. Developmental change in infants' perception of correlations among attributes. *Child Dev.* 57:803–15

Yu C, Smith LB, Klein KA, Shiffrin RM. 2007. Hypothesis testing and associative learning in cross-situational word learning: Are they one and the same? *Proc. Annu. Meet. Cogn. Sci. Soc., 29th, Nashville, TN*, pp. 737–42. Austin, TX: Cogn. Sci. Soc.

How Children Solve the Two Challenges of Cooperation

Felix Warneken

Department of Psychology, University of Michigan, Ann Arbor, Michigan 48109;
email: warneken@umich.edu

Annu. Rev. Psychol. 2018. 69:205–29

First published as a Review in Advance on
September 6, 2017

The *Annual Review of Psychology* is online at
psych.annualreviews.org

https://doi.org/10.1146/annurev-psych-122216-011813

Keywords

cooperation, fairness, development, evolution, chimpanzees

Abstract

In this review, I propose a new framework for the psychological origins of
human cooperation that harnesses evolutionary theories about the two major
problems posed by cooperation: generating and distributing benefits. Children develop skills foundational for identifying and creating opportunities
for cooperation with others early: Infants and toddlers already possess basic skills to help others and share resources. Yet mechanisms that solve the
free-rider problem—critical for sustaining cooperation as a viable strategy—
emerge later in development and are more sensitive to the influence of social
norms. I review empirical studies with children showing a dissociation in the
origins of and developmental change seen in these two sets of processes. In
addition, comparative studies of nonhuman apes also highlight important
differences between these skills: The ability to generate benefits has evolutionary roots that are shared between humans and nonhuman apes, whereas
there is little evidence that other apes exhibit comparable capacities for distributing benefits. I conclude by proposing ways in which this framework
can motivate new developmental, comparative, and cross-cultural research
about human cooperation.

Contents

INTRODUCTION

Cooperation is a defining feature of human social life. Humans share valuable resources, assist others who need help, and pool their efforts to yield outcomes beyond the capabilities of any one individual. Our species depends on cooperation more than any other primate, exhibiting levels of sophistication and flexibility in cooperation that are not seen elsewhere in the animal kingdom. How do these cooperative abilities emerge, especially given the fact that selfish motivations can often prevail over our cooperative tendencies? Developmental studies with children are a powerful tool to study the human condition, providing insight into the early origins of our social abilities, as well as how these abilities change over the lifespan. In addition, comparative studies with our closest primate relatives can determine which aspects of our cooperative capacities are unique to humans and which are shared with other apes and, thus, potentially evolutionarily ancient. Thus, integrating developmental and comparative approaches can shed light on the biological origins and social forces that shape human cooperation.

This article reviews the recent surge in research on the cooperative abilities of children and our ape cousins—as well as the limitations in these abilities. I propose a new framework that connects evolutionary models concerning the fitness benefits of cooperation with the proximate psychological mechanisms that implement these behaviors in the mind. I argue that, for individuals to become proficient cooperators, they must have two different sets of psychological skills to address two different challenges. The first set of abilities deals with the challenge of generating benefits through cooperation, whereas the second deals with distributing those benefits and stabilizing cooperation once it emerges. To date, little work has taken a synthetic view of both of these sets of skills (Calcott 2008). For example, there has been much empirical work on human abilities to create benefits—aiming to explain how human cooperation (including aspects such as our ability to feel empathy or to collaborate in teams) differs from that of other animals—without directly addressing the second challenge of how benefits will be distributed to make cooperation a viable option over the long term (Batson 2011, Hoffman 2000, Tomasello et al. 2005). Conversely, evolutionary models tend to target the second challenge and show how cooperation can be sustained when people reciprocate or punish selfishness to support cooperation, but these theories do not give much regard to the issue of how these benefits could be generated through cooperation in the first place (Nowak 2006).

The Two Challenges of Cooperation: Creating and Distributing Benefit

I propose that the two challenges of generating and distributing benefits are supported by two different sets of psychological capacities that can be dissociated in both ontogeny and phylogeny. Ontogenetically, the skills to generate benefit through cooperation arise early in development, whereas mechanisms to distribute benefit in a way that safeguards cooperation against defection are acquired later—and sometimes strongly depend on children's understanding of social norms that prescribe how cooperative benefits should be distributed. These norms increasingly guide children's own cooperation as they grow older and also shape their expectations about how others should interact with them. That is, children start out as cooperators who are focused on creating benefits and only begin to safeguard their cooperative tendencies against the exploitation of free-riders later on (see **Figure 1**). This distinction is also apparent phylogenetically, as humans and chimpanzees share the basic abilities to generate benefit, but humans have species-unique processes to distribute benefit that enable cooperative behaviors at a scale not found in our closest evolutionary relatives. It is, of course, important to emphasize the fact that several other factors

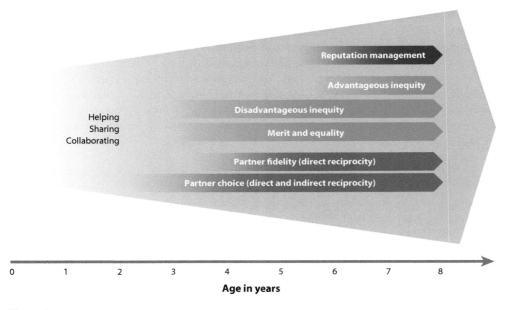

Figure 1

Developmental onset of abilities to generate benefits (*written in black*) and to distribute benefits (*written in white*).

may influence rates of cooperative behaviors in humans and other species. Like many other so- cial behaviors, children's cooperation may fluctuate depending on their mood, whether they are interacting with a familiar or unfamiliar person, or whether they are tested in a friendly environ- ment (Barragan & Dweck 2014, Carpenter et al. 2013). However, although context can play an important role, this proposal concerns the developmental onset of psychological capacities that can solve the challenge of distributing benefit and stabilize cooperation.

An alternative to the view I propose in this review is that both of these sets of skills are inte- grated from the beginning, emerging in the same timeframe. This view conjectures that children safeguard their cooperation against free-riding from the time they can first generate benefit, with decisions to cooperate already motivated by concerns about how the generated benefit can be recouped in some form, such as by benefiting kin, promoting reciprocity, or improving one's own reputation (Nowak 2006). This view is often assumed in evolutionary theories: Cooperative behaviors that are vulnerable to free-riding cannot be sustained, so the capacities to generate and distribute benefits must evolve in tandem (Calcott 2008). A similar view is often applied to the ontogenetic emergence of these skills. For example, young infants already possess several concepts that are critical for distributing benefits, such as identifying cooperative individuals, preferring them to uncooperative individuals (Hamlin et al. 2007, Kuhlmeier et al. 2003), and expecting to see equal resource divisions (Sloane et al. 2012). This work is often viewed as evidence that young children can solve the free-rider problem to some degree. However, I would argue that, just as hearing is not the same as talking, representing and evaluating the social world in this way does not mean that children already regulate their own actions based upon these principles. I show that, in terms of their actual cooperative behaviors, children exhibit a clear developmental lag between the two skill sets, and it is only during middle childhood that children integrate the two set of skills and become able to cooperate in ways that are sustainable in the long term. Children are thus initially rather naive and become more vigilant against free-riding and more proficient at negotiating the balance between their own and a partner's interests over the course of development.

To evaluate these hypotheses, I review the current empirical evidence concerning the develop- ment of the critical social-cognitive skills that underpin different forms of cooperation in children. I focus in particular on the age of emergence of different forms of altruistically and mutualistically motivated cooperation to assess whether the different mechanisms of generating benefit emerge earlier than the skills to distribute benefit, such as reciprocity and expectations about fairness. Finally, I examine what biological and social factors may influence this sequence of emergence. In particular, I argue that comparative evidence shows that basic skills for generating benefits have biological roots shared with great apes, whereas skills for distributing benefits are more sensitive to local cultural norms of behavior.

Integrating Psychological Mechanism and Ultimate Function

The question of the causes of cooperation (or any behavior) can be broken down into proximate questions about psychological mechanisms and ultimate questions about evolutionary function (Mayr 1961, Tinbergen 1963). Ultimate questions focus on the fitness consequences and evolu- tionary history of behaviors—why the behaviors exist—whereas proximate questions concern the implementation and development of these behaviors in the mind and brain—how the behaviors work. Cooperative behaviors, especially altruistically motivated behaviors, have long been puzzling because they appear to reduce an individual's evolutionary fitness. However, modern evolutionary theory has developed several accounts of how different forms of cooperation can evolve through natural selection (Nowak 2006, West et al. 2007). These models show how cooperative behaviors can, in fact, lead to fitness benefits, although sometimes in indirect and intricate ways; for instance, altruistically motivated behavior can be explained through the genetic relatedness with recipients or reciprocal relationships where current costs are outweighed by future benefits.

However, models focused on the ultimate function of cooperative behaviors do not tell us what psychological capacities individuals need to perform these behaviors. While there are multiple ways in which cooperation could evolve, proximate mechanisms put a constraint on what can actually emerge. For example, reciprocity may seem to be a straightforward solution to the problem of cooperation, but it is not viable if individuals cannot individuate others or do not know who did what to whom. Similarly, reputation and punishment may, in principle, be able to weed out uncooperative individuals, but not if individuals cannot represent third-party relations, cannot communicate to others what they saw, or lack the motivation to stand up for others. Thus, although it is critical to distinguish these different levels of analysis, it is equally important to understand their interrelationship—how proximate mechanisms can constrain or enable behaviors with different ultimate consequences. Following Calcott (2008), I propose that there are two distinct classes of proximate mechanisms that instantiate human cooperation: those for generating benefit and those for distributing benefit.

HOW CHILDREN LEARN TO GENERATE BENEFIT THROUGH COOPERATION

The first challenge for cooperation is creating benefits. How can individuals produce benefits that would be absent without cooperative action? Acts of mutualistic collaboration provide a good example. When individuals collaborate, they create benefits for the participating cooperators that they would not obtain if they had acted alone. From a mere payoff perspective, it is easy to explain why individuals would choose to engage in a collective act (such as hunting together rather than alone) that creates these mutualistic benefits. However, this presupposes that individuals have the ability to identify the added value that may result from this collective act. Furthermore, even if individuals recognize these added benefits, they have to find a way to actually accomplish the task by socially coordinating their behaviors with others. Thus, even though the emergence of mutualism appears fairly straightforward from an ultimate perspective, identifying such opportunities and executing the cooperative act successfully can be quite challenging in terms of the proximate mechanisms needed.

Other examples include altruistically motivated acts that are aimed at benefiting another individual rather than the self. These may come in various forms depending on the type of need an altruist has to detect and whether emotional support, practical help, or sharing of resources would be most appropriate. A lack of altruistic intervention could be due to limitations in detecting the need or to a lack of motivation. Such acts can be altruistically motivated (in that they are intended to help another individual) but not necessarily altruistic from an evolutionary perspective (in terms of fitness costs and benefits). Rather, they are best thought of as building blocks for behaviors, such as kin-directed helping or reciprocity, that depend on an initial act of altruism that (in real life if not in experiments) can later be recouped through indirect fitness benefits or additional interactions with that partner.

Helping and Comforting

Helping is one of the earliest manifestations of altruistic behaviors. In the second year of life, children begin to comfort others who are in distress or pain, lend a helping hand to someone who is struggling with a practical problem such as reaching for an object that is too far away, and offer helpful information with the simple act of pointing to an object a person is searching for. What is striking about children's helping is not only its early emergence but also the fact that children are able to help with a diverse set of problems, often in flexible ways. For example, when encountering someone in pain or distress, children can employ many different responses, including directly comforting the victim, helping to repair a broken toy, handing over their own toy, or seeking help from others (Eisenberg et al. 2015). Similarly, 18-month-olds are able to infer various types of action goals and flexibly offer the appropriate instrumental help by picking up objects that someone has dropped on the ground, helping put away objects by holding doors open, or applying a newly acquired technique for accessing the contents of a novel box when a clumsy adult fails to do so (Warneken 2016). In these situations, children know both when to help—differentiating between intentional and accidental outcomes—and how to help—by handing over and pointing to objects a person needs rather than those that are irrelevant (Hepach et al. 2016, Liszkowski et al. 2006). Control conditions rule out the possibility that children do this for unrelated reasons, such as stimulus enhancement, social interaction, or simple reestablishment of the original physical state (Hepach et al. 2017a, Warneken 2013, Warneken & Tomasello 2006). Taken together, these results show that children intelligently adapt their helping to facilitate the fulfillment of another person's action goal.

As children develop into sophisticated helpers, they require fewer cues to know when and how to act. One example of this development is children's response to other's emotions. Babies can already respond to an overt expression of distress, such as a face that is in pain or drenched in tears. By 18–24 months, children begin to take the situational context into account. They react appropriately when the situation calls for it, showing concern and helping when a victim loses her belongings to a destructive bully, even when the victim remains stoic and shows no overt facial expression to cue the child to their emotional distress (Vaish et al. 2009). Conversely, when 18-month-olds see an adult be upset over an event that could not actually have hurt the person, they show little sympathy for this "cry baby" (Chiarella & Poulin-Dubois 2013, Hepach et al. 2013).

Children make inferences based upon fairly minimal cues in instrumental helping and informing contexts, as well. Although verbal and nonverbal communication increase the likelihood that children will help, especially in cases where the problem is more opaque, they are often not necessary (Pettygrove et al. 2013, Svetlova et al. 2010). Indeed, by 2 years of age, children are able to help proactively in the absence of any eliciting cues—such as when a person does not realize that the objects she wanted to clean up had rolled off a table while she was turned away (Warneken 2013). This suggests that children are able to draw on situational cues to infer when help is needed. Young children can also help in anticipation of a problem. When a person is mistaken about the actual location of an object she is searching for, 18-month-olds direct her to the correct location before she looks in the wrong spot (Knudsen & Liszkowski 2012b). Similarly, they warn a person who is unaware that two buckets had been swapped and would thus likely reach into the wrong bucket, which holds an aversive object (Knudsen & Liszkowski 2012a). Thus, children can predict the person's action in light of her state of knowledge and intervene proactively. Finally, children can even correct a person's course of action and do what is actually helpful. That is, children do not blindly assist in completing any concrete action that another person pursues, but rather use their understanding of the person's ultimate action goal (e.g., ignoring a request for a cup with a hole and instead handing an intact cup; Martin & Olson 2013) or even their ignorance about the true state of the world (Buttelmann et al. 2009) to help appropriately.

Importantly, there is strong evidence that children's early helping behaviors are altruistically motivated, i.e., aimed at creating a benefit for others rather than a benefit for the self. Children often help spontaneously without solicitation from the recipient or a third party (Warneken 2016). They care about the needs of their peers as well as those of younger children, not just potential authority figures (Hamann et al. 2012, Hepach et al. 2017b, Kaneko & Hamazaki 1987). They help when their parents are not watching (Warneken 2013, Warneken & Tomasello 2013b) and even when the beneficiary is away (Hepach et al. 2017a). Moreover, in studies on instrumental and emotional helping, children still help even when they are neither rewarded nor praised. The offering of rewards does not elicit more helping in the immediate situation (Warneken et al. 2007) and can even undermine children's intrinsic motivation and reduce future helping (Warneken & Tomasello 2008). Last but not least, children seem to genuinely care about the other person's need as a goal in itself. One striking example comes from helping situations in which 2-year-olds show arousal (as measured by changes in pupil dilation) when they witness a person's goal remain unresolved because an object is out of reach or the person receives the wrong object. However, they are relieved when the person receives the appropriate help and attains the goal, regardless of whether they themselves or some other bystander provided the help (Hepach et al. 2012, 2016). Thus, children appear motivated to help another person achieve their goal for other reasons besides demonstrating their mastery of the situation or obtaining a reputation for goodwill.

Sharing Resources

Like children's tendency to help with practical and emotional problems, children's resource sharing emerges in the second year of life. When someone else is in need, 18-month-olds are willing to give up their own resources. For example, toddlers are willing to share food snacks when they have a bowl of crackers and the experimenter's bowl is empty (Brownell et al. 2013, Dunfield & Kuhlmeier 2013, Dunfield et al. 2011, Pettygrove et al. 2013), sacrifice some of their own toys so that a deprived experimenter can play as well (Warneken & Tomasello 2013a), and give up one of their own balloons when an experimenter has lost hers (Vaish et al. 2009). Importantly, these are instances of sharing in which children give up a resource, thus paying a real cost for sharing, rather than instances of sharing for mutual play or to initiate a social interaction.

For children to give up a valuable resource, cues of the recipient's needs are important, as they are with early helping. For example, children are more likely to share when the recipient provides more explicit behavioral and communicative cues about her desire for a resource. This is particularly true at younger ages. For example, 18-month-olds share toys and food only after the recipient makes her need explicit or even directly asks the child to share, including by palm-up gestures or stating, "I don't have any crackers." For 24-month-olds, much more subtle cues are sufficient. They typically share before a recipient makes a request and often immediately upon realizing that the other person ended up empty handed (Brownell et al. 2013, Dunfield & Kuhlmeier 2013, Dunfield et al. 2011, Pettygrove et al. 2013, Warneken & Tomasello 2013a). In these studies, the vast majority of toddlers share something, and the age differences are the spontaneity and speed, rather than the overall rate, of sharing. In sum, these studies show that children are willing to intervene even at their own cost, at least when the need for intervention is salient. Very young children appear to need more explicit cues about another's need of a resource, but, upon realizing the need, they are willing to share.

These studies with toddlers may also explain why sharing rates are initially low in studies using the dictator game. In this game, children are given a choice in how to divide up a resource between themselves and a passive recipient (who is often not present or known). In such dictator games, young children are mainly self-serving and give away little, if anything (see Ibbotson 2014 for an overview). By contrast, adults give, on average, 30% of their resources away (Engel 2011). However, in these cases, neither the circumstances nor the absent recipients evoke any signs of need, hunger, or urgency. This is often done deliberately to eliminate opportunities for reciprocity or reputational effects, a methodology that is appropriate for older children and adults but that limits the validity for young children. In other developmental studies, the situation is slightly more interactive, with two children sitting across from each other and the participant (the dictator) choosing between two predetermined options, e.g., one reward for the self and none for the other versus one reward for each (Graves & Graves 1978, Thompson et al. 1997). Although this task is more concrete than regular dictator games, several researchers have raised concerns about the task demands, as young children often fail comprehension checks, and small variations in task administration result in wide age variation, perhaps due to attentional demands (Burkart & Rueth 2013, House et al. 2012, Tomasello & Warneken 2008). These kinds of tasks are better suited for older children, especially to test for children's developing sense of fairness, but are not suitable to determine whether sharing is present in toddlers. These tasks elicit little sharing in young children, not necessarily because children lack altruistic sentiments, but rather because the tasks lack the core features that elicit it.

Mutualistic Collaboration

Young children not only act for others to achieve individual goals, they also act with others collaboratively. This collaboration encompasses social games and problem-solving tasks in which two individuals have to join forces because one person cannot retrieve a reward alone. For example, one person has to activate a mechanism on one side of an apparatus while the partner simultaneously manipulates the other side of the apparatus to retrieve a reward (Brownell & Carriger 1990). Other examples involve objects that are too large for one person to handle, such as when a wooden block bounces on a large trampoline that two people have to hold up (Warneken & Tomasello 2007, Warneken et al. 2006). From approximately 14 to 18 months of age, children begin to coordinate their actions successfully in such situations.

Children are not just responding to the other person's action and rigidly performing one role (like a dog playing fetch), but rather appear able to represent both roles as interconnected parts of a social activity. Children quickly learn how to interact in novel situations after very little experience and often only a single demonstration (Warneken et al. 2006). They also engage in role reversal, flexibly switching between two complementary actions, performing whatever role is necessary to successfully engage in the activity (Carpenter et al. 2005; Warneken et al. 2006, 2007). This indicates that they are able to represent the respective actions as part of an overarching action plan, rather than just executing their own individual act. This is also apparent from studies in which 14-month-olds are onlookers of an act between two collaborators: The infants form a representation of each individual's act not as an isolated means–end relationship but as an act that complements the partner's action (Henderson & Woodward 2011). With active experience, even 10-month-olds seem to form such an expectation (Henderson et al. 2013).

In addition, children do not just follow the partner's lead but actively participate; when an adult partner interrupts the joint activity, children often try to reengage the partner by communicating, offering the toy, or trying to help the partner with their role (Gräfenhain et al. 2009, Ross & Lollis 1987, Warneken et al. 2006). Children treat the other person not just as a social tool that they need to accomplish their own goal, but as an agent with intentions to either collaborate or not. For example, 21-month-olds try to reengage a collaborator who is unable to continue (by helping and informing) over someone who is unwilling to continue (Warneken et al. 2012). Thus, children respond not only to the behavioral outcome, but also to the partner's intention that leads to it.

Toddlers collaborate not only with adults, but also with peers. This result is noteworthy for at least two reasons. First, although interactions with adults are interesting in their own right and seem to constitute the first steps toward successful collaboration, these situations are highly structured by the adults. In contrast, children are left to their own devices during peer interactions, enabling researchers to assess their skill level independent of adult scaffolding. Second, this result provides insight into how children of similar status (as compared to the inherent hierarchy of adult–child interaction) negotiate how the interaction should unfold, and how resources should be distributed in mutualistic tasks in which two individuals work toward an otherwise unobtainable resource.

Peers begin to successfully coordinate their actions with each other during the second half of the second year of life (Brownell 2011, Eckerman & Peterman 2001). This includes coordinated attempts to initiate social interactions with peers, such as taking turns to act on an object (Eckerman et al. 1989), as well as synchronizing one's own action with that of a peer, as in the case of two children simultaneously pulling two handles protruding from a music box to make a puppet sing (Brownell et al. 2006). In tasks that require the temporal and spatial coordination of two actions, children younger than 2 years old often struggle, but during the third year of life, they become proficient at tasks such as pulling handles simultaneously or performing complementary roles, as when one child manipulates a lever so that another child can retrieve an object (Ashley & Tomasello 1998, Brownell & Carriger 1990, Brownell et al. 2006). Thus, children are capable of collaborating with each other without adult scaffolding but become successful in this collaboration slightly later than they are in collaboration with an adult partner.

HOW CHILDREN LEARN TO DISTRIBUTE BENEFIT

The previous section showed that children develop the basic skills to generate benefit early, in the second year of life. But the second challenge for cooperators is to find a way to distribute benefit that can sustain cooperation. This challenge is particularly apparent for cooperation among genetically unrelated individuals, where cooperation is threatened by free-riders who reap the benefits while paying fewer or no costs. For example, when individuals collaborate to create a collective good, free-riders are better off if they obtain the same benefit without contributing. Similarly, when two individuals interact repeatedly, a defector who receives more often than she gives to the other will be better off in the long term than a cooperator who always gives. Therefore, abilities to create benefit through cooperation must be complemented by mechanisms to guard against free-riders. When do children first begin to exhibit these behaviors in cooperative contexts?

Direct Reciprocity

How cooperation evolves in the face of free-riding is at the core of many game-theoretic and evolutionary models. Such models show that reciprocity is a powerful way to stabilize cooperation. Specifically, in direct reciprocity, two individuals exchange favors by acting in a manner that is contingent on how a partner has treated them and can be better off in the long term than if they had not cooperated at all. An important distinction for mechanisms of reciprocity is that between partner fidelity and partner choice (Baumard et al. 2013, Hammerstein 2003, Kuhlmeier et al. 2014). Partner fidelity concerns situations where two social partners interact repeatedly and make decisions about how to interact. Partner choice concerns situations in which individuals can, in addition, make choices about with whom to interact. Therefore, partner fidelity and partner choice likely tap into different psychological abilities.

Partner fidelity. At what age do children begin to cooperate differently depending on how a social partner has treated them in the past? The earliest instances of reciprocity in terms of partner fidelity have been found in 3.5-year-olds. Children shared more resources with a partner who had previously shared with them than with a defector who had never shared with them (Warneken & Tomasello 2013a). By contrast, 2.5-year-olds cooperated at the same level with both cooperators and defectors. Similar results were found in forced choice tasks, where 2.5-year-olds generally chose a prosocial option that provided a payoff to both actors rather than a selfish option that provided a reward only to themselves, regardless of whether an adult partner had acted prosocially or selfishly toward them before (Sebastian-Enesco et al. 2013). Studies with peers found that it was not until around 5.5 years of age (House et al. 2013a) that children began acting in a manner that is contingent on the choices of a peer partner; in some contexts, this development occurred even later, at 6–8 years of age (Dahlman et al. 2007). Therefore, the earliest age for which there is evidence that children look back on how their partner has treated them and adjust their cooperation accordingly is approximately 3.5 years and, in many cases, even older.

Another important aspect of reciprocity is the ability to look ahead, i.e., being able to anticipate whether a partner will likely reciprocate later—the so-called shadow of the future. Whereas 5-year-olds share more when they know the interaction will be iterated compared to a one-shot interaction, 3-year-olds share the same amount regardless (Kenward et al. 2015, Sebastian-Enesco & Warneken 2015). Similarly, when one of two children can obtain a valuable resource every other time, 5-year-olds spontaneously develop a strategy of turn taking so the beneficiary alternates across trials (Melis et al. 2016), whereas 3-year-olds do not. Thus, current evidence shows that contingent reciprocity in terms of partner fidelity does not emerge before middle childhood. Although young children already possess the skills to generate benefit through cooperation, they are not yet using contingent reciprocity to adjust how cooperative they should be toward a given individual.

Partner choice. Although young children do not yet adjust their level of cooperation contingent on an agent's cooperation, studies suggest that partner choice could emerge earlier in development: When children are forced to choose between two potential partners, they prefer to interact with cooperative over uncooperative individuals. In one study, 21-month-olds interacted with a clumsy adult who tried and failed to hand them objects and with an unwilling adult who had teased them with the toy. When both adults then simultaneously reached for the same object, children gave it to the nice rather than the mean adult (Dunfield & Kuhlmeier 2010). Similarly, 3.5-year-olds helped someone who had previously told them where to find a toy over someone who had withheld helpful information (Dunfield et al. 2013). Therefore, children direct their helping preferentially toward those with good intentions over those who prove to be downright mean.

These two studies provide some initial information about children's developing preferences in partner choice situations, but many open questions remain. So far, only helping behaviors have been studied, and nothing is known about partner choice when children have to sacrifice resources—unlike much of the work on partner fidelity, which has also focused on more costly sharing decisions. Moreover, there has been no work examining whether children are more likely to engage in a mutualistic collaboration with nice over mean individuals.

Indirect Reciprocity

In indirect reciprocity, cooperation can emerge in triads or larger groups where cooperators gain a good reputation and are treated more favorably by third parties. One important component of this development is attending to the third-party behaviors of others and preferentially choosing to interact with partners who cooperated with others. A second component is managing one's own reputation: taking into account how one's behavior will look in the eye of the beholder. These two components of indirect reciprocity both emerge later in development, with reputation management not coming online until middle or even late childhood.

Partner choice. There is clear evidence that young infants can evaluate how agents treat others, detecting and preferring cooperative agents who help others over those who are antisocial (Hamlin et al. 2007, Kuhlmeier et al. 2003). One important question is at what age children actually start to apply these social evaluations to choose with whom to cooperate. Several studies have combined social evaluation and cooperative partner choice by first introducing children to a nice and a mean adult and then having both adults reach for the same object to solicit help. In fact, these evaluations do not seem to drive cooperative choices until later in development, much later than the first emergence of helping, at 14–18 months. One study found that 17- and 22-month-olds helped indiscriminately, but 26-month-olds helped the nice over the mean adult, at least in the first trial (Dahl et al. 2013). Similarly, Vaish et al. (2010) found that 3-year-olds preferentially helped by giving a marble to a cooperative or a neutral adult over an antisocial adult (who had destroyed another person's belongings). This was apparent even when the antisocial person tried but failed to harm an individual, indicating that children assess the person's intentions, not just the outcome of their actions. Interestingly, when children then distributed a second marble, they mostly gave it to the antisocial agent. Thus, although children have a bias toward helping nice over mean individuals, they do not completely withhold help from uncooperative individuals and appear to countervail their initial choices.

Other studies have used resource distributions as a dependent measure. Kenward & Dahl (2011) found that, when 4.5-year-olds were asked to distribute three cookies between a mean and a nice puppet (who had previously helped or hindered a third puppet), they tended to give more to the nice puppet. However, these children also had a strong tendency to try to make things equal: They gave the same amount to both the mean and the nice puppet when there were even numbers of cookies to distribute (see Olson & Spelke 2008 for similar conclusions). Therefore, 4.5-year-olds bias their sharing to cooperative over uncooperative individuals only when forced to do so. In contrast, 3-year-olds share indiscriminately in the same situation. Taken together, these studies show that, over the course of development, children become more discriminating in their helping and sharing with cooperative over uncooperative individuals. Infants and toddlers up to 2 years old seem mostly indiscriminate in their cooperation; starting in the third year of life, children begin to bias their helping in forced choice situations and, between 3 and 4 years old, also begin to favor a cooperative over an uncooperative individual when allocating unequal resources.

Reputation management. The previous section examined how children evaluate others based on their behavior with third parties and whether they use those evaluations when choosing how to interact in cooperative contexts. But what about children's own cooperativeness when others observe them? At what age do children begin to care about their own reputation? To assess such observer effects, studies have manipulated several features of the situational context: the presence of peer recipients (who are affected by the cooperation), peer or adult observers (who are just watching), and subtle cues of being observed (such as pictures of eyes).

The earliest instances of reputation-based effects have been found in 5-year-olds in the presence of peer recipients who were affected by the child's decision. Specifically, Leimgruber et al. (2012) found that children exhibited more generosity when they were observed by the recipient sitting across from them than when visual access was blocked. Buhrmester et al. (1992) found that children between 5 and 13 years old shared more when deciding face-to-face than when deciding in private, at least with an acquaintance or disliked peers—when the recipient was a friend, privacy did not reduce sharing.

Other studies looked at the effect of uninvolved third-party observers who are not directly affected by the decision. In this case, 5-year-olds were significantly less likely to steal a sticker from an absent child when a peer was watching, but showed only a trend toward more helping

(Engelmann et al. 2012). When an observing peer could later give resources to the participant, 5-year-olds shared more with another child than they did when there was no observer (Engelmann et al. 2013). Other studies put an adult into the observer role. Findings varied quite dramatically in terms of the age of onset, finding observer effects at 5 (Fujii et al. 2015), 6–8 (Shaw et al. 2014), 7–8 (Froming et al. 1985), or 10 years old (Zarbatany et al. 1985). Indeed, there is no evidence that children younger than 5 years of age are influenced by such adult surveillance.

More indirect audience effects on children appear to emerge much later, if at all. For example, children are insensitive to whether others will later find out about their cooperative decisions, for example, because their decision will be publically written on a blackboard for everyone to see (Blake et al. 2015b, Zarbatany et al. 1985). When participants decided in a classroom setting with peers nearby, rather than being monitored directly, evidence indicated that these effects occur at 9–10 years of age at the earliest (Houser et al. 2012, Takagishi et al. 2015). Moreover, there is no evidence that subtle observational cues, such as pictures of eyes, influence children (Fujii et al. 2015, Vogt et al. 2014); in contrast, this effect may influence cooperation in adults, although to a limited degree (Northover et al. 2016). Thus, subtle cues of being observed do not appear to affect sharing in children at an age when the presence of an actual adult observer directly monitoring them influences their costly sharing.

Furthermore, it is important to note that many studies that do detect evidence that children manage their reputation actually involve an observer who, in principle, could directly respond to the child's concrete action in the moment (by scolding, being upset, etc.). Consequently, it is not necessarily required that children represent to themselves how other individuals will form an opinion of the child as a cooperative or uncooperative person, let alone share those insights with other group members. Cases where effects in terms of forming a public image could occur through reputation have rarely been tested, and current studies suggest that these effects emerge at approximately 7–10 years of age. This development seems to involve more complex processes, with children having to consider what image the public may form of them, coinciding with their explicit understanding of impression management (Aloise-Young 1993, Banerjee 2002, Hill & Pillow 2006). Together, this evidence shows that potential threats to reputation are not part of children's early repertoires, and reputational effects are based upon late-developing processes that require higher-level social-cognitive reasoning and, probably, much experience.

Principles of Fairness

A final critical mechanism in sustaining cooperation is fairness. A large body of work shows that adults use principles such as equality and equity (or merit) to decide how to distribute resources. Moreover, adults police others who violate these principles, judging unfair individuals negatively and even punishing them for being selfish to others. Although there is debate over the specific function of these principles, especially over whether they serve to uphold group standards or resolve conflicting interests between individuals, there is consensus that they play an important role in stabilizing cooperation. Therefore, it is essential to understand at what age these different mechanisms begin to influence children's cooperation.

Collaboration as the basis of equality and merit. The principles of equality and merit are first used when children actively collaborate with others. This can be seen in 3-year-old children. When they collaborate to obtain a common resource, such as by jointly pulling in a board with rewards, they usually split resources equally (Ulber et al. 2015, Warneken et al. 2011). Moreover, when a lucky child ends up with more resources than an unlucky partner, they correct the situation so that both end up with similar amounts (Hamann et al. 2011). Importantly, children equalize the outcome more often after collaboration than after either individual work or windfall gains, indicating that collaboration evokes a stronger sense of equality. Children appear to be intrinsically motivated to share in this way, as children who were offered a reward if they share after collaboration are subsequently less likely to continue sharing in an equal manner (Ulber et al. 2016). These behaviors occur spontaneously, even in the complete absence of any prompting from authority figures such as experimenters or parents.

The connection between collaboration and more equal outcome distributions has been consistently found in 3-year-olds (Hamann et al. 2011; Melis et al. 2013; Ulber et al. 2015, 2016; Warneken et al. 2011). By contrast, 2-year-olds tend to accept unequal outcomes even if they work together to acquire the rewards, as well as to share pooled resources in a more haphazard manner irrespective of how they have been obtained (Hamann et al. 2011, Ulber et al. 2015). Thus, although younger children already coordinate to retrieve resources, children's strategies for distribution of the resources based upon equality emerge only by approximately 3 years of age.

At the same age, children also share resources based upon merit. When one child has to work more than the other, 3-year-olds are more likely to give more rewards to the one who worked more (Hamann et al. 2014, Kanngiesser & Warneken 2012, Schäfer et al. 2015). An even starker contrast occurs when the partner does not contribute anything at all. Whereas 3-year-olds will share with a collaborator, they share very little with a free-rider who dares to request some of the spoils without participating in the work task (Baumard et al. 2011, Melis et al. 2013). This can be seen as evidence for an appreciation of a basic sense of merit in terms of ordinal equity, where someone who works more or more successfully receives relatively more. This is likely a precursor of proportional equity, where rewards are exactly proportional to the work input, a concept that obviously requires much more sophisticated quantitative reasoning. In fact, merit (or equity) may be the overarching principle, with equality being the outcome of merit-based decisions: Equal work deserves equal pay. It is thus possible that mutualistic collaboration may lay the foundation for children's fairness-based sharing.

Children's emerging sense of equality: inequity aversion. Over the course of childhood, equality-based sharing becomes more prominent, including in situations of windfall gains. Three types of phenomena highlight this pattern: children's sharing in dictator games, their responses to advantageous inequality, and their willingness to engage in third-party punishment. First, in dictator games, children become more likely with age to distribute resources equally when dividing them up and to opt for equal over unequal allocations in binary choice tasks (for overviews, see Gummerum et al. 2008, Ibbotson 2014, McAuliffe et al. 2017). Although children's increasing tendency to give more could be explained by a developing sense of generosity, it is striking that children often appear to give exactly half, which might indicate that they are aiming for equality.

The second line of work, testing children's advantageous inequity aversion, presents a similar developmental pattern. When children are confronted with an allocation that favors them over a peer, such as four candies for themselves and only one candy for a peer, and are then given a choice to either accept this allocation or reject it, younger children accept it without hesitation. However, by 7–8 years of age, children frequently reject these allocations, opting that no one should get anything if the alternative is that they themselves receive more than the peer (Blake & McAuliffe 2011). This suggests a strong sense of equality, where children are willing to sacrifice both their own and the partner's resources to avoid inequality—a behavior that cannot be explained by self-interest or generosity.

The third line of evidence comes from third-party punishment. In this case, research shows that school-aged children not only care about sharing in dyadic situations where resources are distributed between themselves and peers, but also care about how resources are being distributed between others when they have no direct stake in the outcomes. Starting at 6 years of age, children will pay a cost to intervene against a selfish peer who wants to keep all the resources rather than splitting them equally with another peer (Jordan et al. 2014, McAuliffe et al. 2015). This is another piece of evidence for the notion that children care about equality, enforcing it in others even when they themselves are not directly affected, and actually sacrifice their own resources to prevent inequality. Yet this more adult-like sense of equality emerges much later than children's earliest forms of helping, sharing, and collaboration.

HOW NONHUMAN APES GENERATE AND DISTRIBUTE BENEFIT

Children provide insights into the developmental origins of human cooperation, and nonhuman apes can provide further insights into the biological origins. First, nonhuman apes present a strong test of whether certain abilities and social practices are necessary for cooperative behaviors to emerge. There is no indication that nonhuman apes reward their offspring for good behavior or teach them social norms, and they would obviously not be able to give explanations even if they wanted to. They thus provide a natural experiment for how cooperation works in a cognitively sophisticated species that nonetheless lacks human socialization practices. Second, chimpanzees and bonobos are our two closest living relatives, so they can reveal which aspects of human cooperation rely on late-evolving human-unique traits and which aspects may have deeper evolutionary roots.

Helping and Sharing in Nonhuman Apes

There is clear evidence that chimpanzees engage in instrumental helping, use fairly sophisticated social-cognitive skills to identify when help is needed, and help flexibly in different kinds of situations. For example, chimpanzees help when a human or a conspecific fails to retrieve an object that is out of reach (Warneken et al. 2007, Warneken & Tomasello 2006). They even select the correct tool from a set of options, demonstrating that they know when to help and in what way (Yamamoto et al. 2012). Moreover, when a conspecific fails to pull in a rope that has a bag of food attached to it, they unhook the rope so the partner can pull it in (Melis et al. 2011), and they also unlock doors for conspecifics who try to access a neighboring room (Melis et al. 2008, Warneken et al. 2007; for similar results with bonobos, see Tan & Hare 2013). In these studies, subjects perform these acts selectively in experimental conditions where help is needed compared to matched control conditions in which these acts would not be helpful. Therefore, chimpanzees make inferences about the goal another individual is trying to achieve and try to help in a variety of ways. Importantly, chimpanzees also succeed in novel situations, ruling out the hypothesis that their helping is simply the outcome of previous rewards or training.

Chimpanzees also seem motivated by the other individual's problem, rather than obtaining a benefit for themselves. Concrete rewards such as being offered a piece of food are not necessary to elicit helping (Greenberg et al. 2010; House et al. 2014; Melis et al. 2008, 2011; Warneken & Tomasello 2006; Yamamoto et al. 2009, Yamamoto et al. 2012), nor do they increase the rate of helping (Warneken et al. 2007). Moreover, chimpanzees help even if direct reciprocation from a conspecific is not possible (Greenberg et al. 2010; House et al. 2014; Melis et al. 2008, 2011; Warneken & Tomasello 2006; Yamamoto et al. 2009, 2012). Chimpanzees are even willing to pay some opportunity and effort costs in order to help, as they will climb to a farther location to retrieve something for the recipient (Warneken et al. 2007, experiment 2) or leave an attractive activity behind to offer help (Melis et al. 2011, Warneken et al. 2007). Taken together, these studies show that the basic cognitive ability and motivation to help are present in other apes as well as in young children.

Apes create benefits not only through helping, but also through sharing, although to a more limited degree. Experiments and naturalistic observations converge on the finding that, although chimpanzees occasionally give up food that they have in their possession, they mostly do so in the form of passive rather than active food transfers, and often only after harassment (Boesch & Boesch 1989, Gilby 2006, Hockings et al. 2007, Tanaka & Yamamoto 2009, Ueno & Matsuzawa 2004). Therefore, chimpanzee sharing is rarely self-initiated and requires strong cues from the recipient. Studies with bonobos paint a slightly different picture. Although they are equally closely related to humans as are chimpanzees, they are more likely to share food with others than are chimpanzees. Bonobos are generally more socially tolerant and are willing to cofeed side by side rather than monopolizing the resource (Wobber et al. 2010). They even actively open a door so a conspecific can join them, especially if it is an unfamiliar individual (Hare & Kwetuenda 2010). However, this behavior occurs primarily in cases where they gain direct physical access to the partner, showing that a desire for unobstructed social and sexual play trumps their desire for food (Tan & Hare 2013). Thus, food sharing is not only a human attribute: It is also present in our closest evolutionary relatives, although to different degrees in chimpanzees and more tolerant bonobos.

Despite these commonalities between chimpanzees and young children, there are also important differences. One such difference concerns the cues that elicit helping and sharing behaviors across species. Whereas children help proactively—helping others who do not signal a need for help—chimpanzees only seem to help reactively in response to explicit goal cues. For example, they are far more likely to help when the recipient actively tries to pull in a bag or communicates toward the subject, rather than when the recipient remains passive (Melis et al. 2011). Similarly, chimpanzees virtually never offer a tool to a conspecific unless the recipient actively reaches for it (Yamamoto et al. 2009, 2012) and exhibit much lower rates of helping when recipients are not actively engaged in a task (such as trying to open or retrieve something) but are rather passively waiting (House et al. 2014). Along the same lines, sharing is rare in experiments in which chimpanzees passively wait for another chimpanzee subject to deliver food to them, even when it comes at no additional cost to the provider (Hamann et al. 2011, House et al. 2014, Jensen et al. 2006, Melis et al. 2011, Silk et al. 2005, Vonk et al. 2008, Yamamoto & Tanaka 2010). Thus, these studies on food sharing corroborate the notion that actively signaling need is a critical component for chimpanzee altruism. It is an open question whether the difference in proactive and reactive cooperation is best explained by a difference in the cognitive capacity to detect when help is needed or by a difference in motivation such that chimpanzees require more active solicitation to be nudged into action.

Mutualistic Collaboration in Nonhuman Apes

Chimpanzees and bonobos are able to coordinate efforts in mutualistic tasks, as well. Several studies have shown that chimpanzees succeed in collaborative tasks that one individual cannot solve alone. This has been demonstrated in variations of a simple but ingenious apparatus where a board with food is placed out of reach and two chimpanzees have to each pull one end of a long rope threaded around the board to move it closer and access the food. If one chimpanzee acts alone, they end up with a rope but no food (Hirata & Fuwa 2007).

Studies show that chimpanzees will wait for a partner to arrive so they can pull together (Hirata & Fuwa 2007; Hirata et al. 2010; Melis et al. 2006a,b), actively solicit help from a partner (Hirata & Fuwa 2007; but see Warneken et al. 2006), and open a door to let a chimpanzee enter from a waiting room (Melis et al. 2006a). They even remember their prior success with different collaborators and selectively open the door for skillful over unskillful partners (Melis et al. 2006a). Chimpanzees succeed in situations where they and their partner have to perform the same action at the same time, such as pulling ropes, but also when they have to perform two complementary actions in sequence, such as using two different tools on an apparatus (Melis & Tomasello 2013). Chimpanzees can even engage in a basic form of division of labor, keeping the tool they need and handing another tool to the partner (Melis & Tomasello 2013), and reversing roles when necessary (Fletcher et al. 2012).

Taken together, these results show that chimpanzees perceive their own and the partner's action as interconnected. They not only understand what they have to do but also what the other chimpanzee has to do. They can adjust their own actions to the actions of the partner and facilitate the partner's action in addition to their own. Chimpanzees are able to represent more than their own means–action sequence and integrate, at least on some level, the action that the partner has to perform and the ways in which each individual's actions are interrelated. Therefore, chimpanzees possess abilities that are critical to generating mutualistic benefit through collaboration.

Mechanisms for Distributing Benefits in Nonhuman Apes

Given these findings, one may expect that helping and collaboration should be widespread in chimpanzees. However, apes are actually quite limited in their ability to solve the other cooperation problem: how to distribute benefits. First, helping behaviors occur mainly in situations that are low cost, where any distribution of a concrete benefit (such as food) is not necessary. By contrast, when chimpanzees can obtain or keep a valuable resource, such as food, for themselves, selfishness trumps their altruistic tendencies. Second, sharing tasks that directly measure how they distribute benefit show that dominance and self-interest usually prevail. Bonobos appear more tolerant in this regard, although food sharing simply for the other individual's sake is rare. Third, chimpanzees succeed at collaboration tasks only when paired with a tolerant partner and often do not even bother to start working with a dominant individual who monopolizes the apparatus and the food. Moreover, even when working with a tolerant partner, chimpanzees succeed only when the food-distribution problem has already been solved for them: When they are in separate rooms or the food is spread apart on a long board, they collaborate. When they would have to haggle over a pile of food in the center, they fail (Melis et al. 2006b). Interestingly, this is less of an issue for the generally more tolerant bonobos, who collaborate even when food is clumped (Hare et al. 2007). This highlights that, in cases of potential mutualism, finding ways to distribute benefits is essential for cooperation to ensue.

There are many other striking differences in how humans and other apes distribute benefits from cooperation. There is evidence that chimpanzees form reciprocal relationships with others in their natural behaviors, preferentially cooperating with individuals with whom they uphold a long-term friendship (Gomes et al. 2009). However, these patterns can be regarded as forms of partner choice that operate over longer timescales and are supported by positive feelings toward the other [also called attitudinal reciprocity (Schino & Aureli 2010)] rather than as contingent reciprocity, as seen in human children. Whether chimpanzees can engage in contingent reciprocity based on a conspecific's prior behavior is less clear. Although some studies find that chimpanzees return a favor (Engelmann et al. 2015, Melis et al. 2008), chimpanzees do not seem to initiate future-directed reciprocity when they could choose to take turns at receiving a reward (Melis et al. 2016). These differences between humans and nonhuman apes are likely due to increased psychological demands, with contingent reciprocity requiring individuals to keep track of favors given and received, delay gratification, and anticipate future return benefits, all of which are psychological processes that are more taxing than partner choice. Even more taxing are cases of indirect reciprocity based on reputation. In fact, chimpanzees do not take into account how their own behavior is viewed in the eye of the beholder: They share or steal food from another chimpanzee whether a third party is watching or not (Engelmann et al. 2012) and do not intervene against uncooperative behavior when they are in the role of a third party (Riedl et al. 2012).

Lastly, apes do not appear to respond to or enforce fairness norms. Chimpanzees do not correct an unequal outcome after collaboration (Hamann et al. 2011), nor do they share more with a collaborator over a laggard (Melis et al. 2013), in contrast to 3-year-old children, who treat joint benefits differently from windfall gains and individual work. One issue under debate is whether chimpanzees show inequity aversion in instances when they refuse to engage in a token exchange with an experimenter who offers a conspecific a better deal (Bräuer et al. 2006, Brosnan & de Waal 2003). However, these instances would, at best, reflect disadvantageous inequity aversion. In contrast, there is no evidence that chimpanzees show advantageous inequity aversion, a more stringent criterion for a sense of fairness that emerges much later in humans (McAuliffe et al. 2017). This lack of concern for fairness principles is also apparent in their punishment decisions: Chimpanzees seek revenge against others who stole from them (Jensen et al. 2007), but not when they are an uninvolved third party witnessing one chimpanzee steal from another (Riedl et al. 2012). By contrast, at 3 years of age, children intervene against theft and other antisocial behaviors (Riedl et al. 2015, Vaish et al. 2011) and, at approximately 6 years of age, enact fairness norms against selfish individuals (McAuliffe et al. 2017). Therefore, a striking difference between the species appears in the adoption and enforcement of fairness norms—a way of regulating cooperative behaviors that is only found in humans.

CONCLUSION AND FUTURE DIRECTIONS

Overall, current developmental and comparative evidence suggests a major distinction between skills for generating benefits and skills for distributing benefits from cooperation. From early in life, children are able to generate benefits through acts of helping, sharing, and collaboration. Although these abilities become more sophisticated over the course of development, the core abilities to engage in altruistic and mutualistic cooperation emerge early and are already in place in the second year of life. Yet there is a different developmental trajectory for the complementary abilities to distribute benefits. These skills—such as contingent reciprocity, managing one's own reputation, and sharing based upon fairness norms—only emerge later in development, after children have gained some practice in cooperating with others (see **Figure 1**). This is apparent for both altruistically and mutualistically motivated behavior, supporting the hypothesis of a developmental lag between these two different sets of abilities. Comparative studies also support this dissociation. Children's abilities to generate benefits find many parallels in chimpanzees and bonobos, suggesting deep evolutionary roots that date back to at least the last common ancestor of humans and our primate cousins. By contrast, humans and other apes differ qualitatively in the mechanisms of distributing benefits, with future-directed reciprocity, fairness norms, and reputation building as likely candidates for human-unique ways of stabilizing and expanding cooperative behaviors. This distinction provides a new framework for current empirical evidence on children's developing cognition. Moreover, it points to outstanding questions about the origins of cooperation in development, the specificity versus universality of these processes across diverse cultural groups, and the ways in which human cooperation differs from that of other apes.

Developmental Origins

What explains the developmental emergence and dissociation of the different sets of abilities? Children develop the basic skills to generate benefit early. In the second year of life, children begin to help others in a variety of ways, based on their emerging ability to detect other's emotional needs, action goals, and knowledge states. They quickly develop more sophistication in knowing when and how to intervene, requiring less overt cues about when others are in trouble and when they should take action. Similarly, children also begin to successfully coordinate their actions with adults in the second year of life, probably facilitated by the adult's expertise. Shortly thereafter, children begin to collaborate successfully with peers, with major improvements in coordination during the third year of life. This experimental work is corroborated by observational studies of children in their naturalistic interactions, which have identified the second year of life as the age window during which children begin to help, share, and cooperate with parents, siblings, and peers (Brownell 2011, Dahl 2015, Dunn & Munn 1986, Eckerman & Peterman 2001, Hay et al. 1999, Howes & Farver 1987, Zahn-Waxler et al. 1992).

Even fairly young children can, therefore, solve the first challenge of cooperation with a behavioral repertoire that is flexible and intelligent, harnessing their increasingly sophisticated social-cognitive capacities and using them for cooperative ends. This evidence from children is complemented by evidence that nonhuman apes share many of the same skills. Overall, this suggests that these abilities may be based upon a biological predisposition and do not intrinsically require human-unique socialization practices to emerge. Socialization practices can, of course, build upon this foundation, but young children are neither purely selfish individuals nor motivational blank slates that have to be (re)programmed to cooperate with others (Melis & Warneken 2016, Warneken 2016). For example, as children gain more experience with cooperation and learn relevant social norms about such behavior, they expand the circle of individuals they cooperate with and learn new ways to respond in such contexts. Nonetheless, the groundwork for these behaviors is laid in early ontogeny.

Regarding the mechanisms of distributing benefits, this framework proposes that the first step for developmental research is to identify those strategies that support cooperation from an ultimate perspective (such as direct and indirect reciprocity), and the second step is to then elucidate the psychological mechanisms necessary for children to actually use such strategies in their cooperative behavior. One prediction from this framework is that mechanisms that serve important foundational functions across many diverse social behaviors—such as a preference for kin or familiar individuals over unfamiliar individuals—will likely apply earlier to cooperative contexts. That is, such mechanisms can be coopted for cooperative interactions or operate in this way simply by virtue of cooperation being a subclass of social behaviors. By contrast, strategies that are more specific and narrowly tailored to cooperative behaviors—even if they are deceptively simple rules, such as tit-for-tat—may emerge later. For example, instantiating reciprocal interactions may be nontrivial from a psychological perspective, as this requires the ability to delay gratification and, perhaps, the ability to represent future events, which children do not master before middle childhood (Atance 2008). Reputation-based reciprocity may emerge even later, after children develop the perspective-taking skills necessary to understand how others represent their behavior and how they may spread the word in a social group. Therefore, this framework can motivate specific predictions about the age of emergence of different strategies to distribute benefit, based upon the required psychological capacities.

Current empirical evidence supports this view (**Figure 1**). Infants and toddlers appear to be initially fairly indiscriminate in their cooperation, but then to gradually add more ways to safeguard their cooperation. This starts with the emergence of selective partner choice at approximately 2 to 3 years of age and then develops into contingent reciprocity between 3 and 4 years of age, such that children look back at how a given partner has cooperated with them and adjust their cooperation accordingly. However, it is not until 5 years of age that they look ahead and cooperate more when the partner can reciprocate in the future. Early cooperative behaviors are also not yet mediated by concerns of audience effects. The earliest age for which there is evidence of observer effects is

5 years, although this is only in very restricted contexts where the observer is literally in their face, and more prototypical audience and reputation effects do not occur until 7–8 years of age. Finally, the earliest forms of fairness concerns emerge in collaborative contexts at approximately 3 years of age, with responses to advantageous inequity aversion and costly third-party punishment being signs of a strong, impartial sense of fairness that develops later in childhood, at around school age.

Cultural Similarities and Differences

This distinction between early-emerging, biologically based abilities to generate benefits and later-emerging, socially shaped abilities to distribute benefits also provides new predictions about where we should observe cultural variation in developmental patterns. In particular, early-emerging skills to generate benefits through cooperation should be more universally present across cultural groups. Although local customs and parental practices may influence the specific expression and prevalence of cooperative behaviors (e.g., household chores, farming, caring for siblings), the basic capacity for flexible cooperation should be found in young children across populations. Existing studies support this prediction, showing that the basic cooperative capacities expressed in, e.g., helping and collaboration emerge in toddlerhood across diverse cultural groups (Callaghan et al. 2011, Drummond et al. 2015, Kärtner et al. 2010, Köster et al. 2016).

Conversely, the framework suggests that there should be greater variation in the abilities to distribute benefits across cultures. The ways in which children solve the second cooperation problem may be tied to their specific social ecology and cultural traditions, so some (but not all) of these skills will be more sensitive to such cultural inputs. For example, individuals across all populations generally have close ties to relatives, but also interact with nonrelatives on a regular basis, so strategies supporting kin selection and direct reciprocity should be more widely observed. However, other mechanisms—such as giving either egalitarian or merit-based norms greater weight—depend on social expectations, and norms may differ depending on the values of the social group. Similarly, moral norms vary widely in terms of obligations to favor an in-group versus those to be impartial, factors that could radically sway a child's decision of how to treat others and divide resources. In fact, research shows strikingly different developmental trajectories of fairness-based behaviors in egalitarian sharing (House et al. 2013b), ordinal versus proportional equity (Schäfer et al. 2015), and advantageous inequity aversion (Blake et al. 2015a) across different populations. Echoing the call for more research in diverse cultural groups, this framework specifically proposes that the extent of cross-cultural variation will differ for the two sets of skills for cooperation and why such variation would occur.

Evolution and Human Uniqueness

Finally, this proposal suggests a new path for comparative research about the evolution of the human mind. By studying cooperative behaviors in terms of the means to generate and distribute benefits, we can gain a deeper understanding about the presence or absence of cooperative behaviors in different species. Empirical research should specify what psychological mechanisms are required for a given cooperative activity with the goal of identifying which cognitive, motivational, or behavioral capacities may explain why a given species performs or fails to perform certain acts of cooperation.

An analysis of solutions to the free-rider problem that focuses on ultimate function may miss a critical proximate factor that explains differences between species. Certain animal species may lack a certain cooperative behavior not because of problems with distributing benefits and mitigating the free-rider problem, but rather because they are not sophisticated enough to perform benefit-creating acts that require them to assess when and how to cooperate. On the flip side, individuals from a certain species may possess the required abilities to generate benefits through cooperation (such as identifying need or coordinating joint efforts) but may not use them reliably across contexts because they have not found a general solution to the problem of how to distribute benefits and stabilize cooperation as a viable strategy. In experimental studies, it is possible to remove these constraints (such as by predividing the spoils of a collaborative activity). As such, experiments can sometimes reveal cooperative abilities that were previously thought to be absent based on naturalistic behaviors. This could explain why chimpanzees engage in cooperative behaviors such as helping and collaboration in controlled experiments even though these behaviors remain fragile and are not expressed at a similar scale as in humans. Over the course of human evolution, these same kinds of constraints needed to be lifted in order to generate robust cooperative tendencies in our species.

The framework developed in this review provides a new look at the question of how human cooperation may have evolved, putting the interrelationship between abilities to generate and to distribute benefits at the center of theoretical explanations and empirical inquiry. It suggests that, as new ways of distributing benefits emerged in human evolution, cooperative behaviors were strengthened and expanded, creating a positive feedback loop between mechanisms to generate and distribute benefits. Humans found novel ways to address the two challenges of cooperation, with more sophisticated psychological abilities and new social practices expanding the scope of cooperation and taking it to a level that is unparalleled in the animal kingdom.

DISCLOSURE STATEMENT

The author is not aware of any affiliations, memberships, funding, or financial holdings that might be perceived as affecting the objectivity of this review.

ACKNOWLEDGMENTS

I thank Alexandra Rosati for helpful comments on and discussion of an earlier version of this review. I received support from a Joy Foundation Fellowship at the Radcliffe Institute for Advanced Study and a National Science Foundation CAREER award.

LITERATURE CITED

Aloise-Young PA. 1993. The development of self-presentation: self-promotion in 6- to 10-year-old children. *Soc. Cogn.* 11(2):201–22

Ashley J, Tomasello M. 1998. Cooperative problem-solving and teaching in preschoolers. *Soc. Dev.* 7(2):143–63

Atance CM. 2008. Future thinking in young children. *Curr. Dir. Psychol. Sci.* 17(4):295–98

Banerjee R. 2002. Audience effects on self-presentation in childhood. *Soc. Dev.* 11(4):487–507

Barragan RC, Dweck CS. 2014. Rethinking natural altruism: Simple reciprocal interactions trigger children's benevolence. *PNAS* 111(48):17071–74

Batson CD. 2011. *Altruism in Humans.* Oxford, UK: Oxford Univ. Press

Baumard N, Andre JB, Sperber D. 2013. A mutualistic approach to morality: the evolution of fairness by partner choice. *Behav. Brain Sci.* 36(1):59–78

Baumard N, Mascaro O, Chevallier C. 2011. Preschoolers are able to take merit into account when distributing goods. *Dev. Psychol.* 48(2):492–98

Blake PR, McAuliffe K. 2011. "I had so much it didn't seem fair": Eight-year-olds reject two forms of inequity. *Cognition* 120(2):215–24

Blake PR, McAuliffe K, Corbit J, Callaghan TC, Barry O, et al. 2015a. The ontogeny of fairness in seven societies. *Nature* 528:258–62

Blake PR, Piovesan M, Montinari N, Warneken F, Gino F. 2015b. Prosocial norms in the classroom: the role of self-regulation in following norms of giving. *J. Econ. Behav. Organ.* 115:18–29

Boesch C, Boesch H. 1989. Hunting behavior of wild chimpanzees in the Tai national park. *Am. J. Phys. Anthropol.* 78:547–73

Bräuer J, Call J, Tomasello M. 2006. Are apes really inequity averse? *Proc. Biol. Sci.* 273(1605):3123–28

Brosnan SF, de Waal FBM. 2003. Monkeys reject unequal pay. *Nature* 425(6955):297–99

Brownell CA. 2011. Early developments in joint action. *Rev. Philos. Psychol.* 2(2):193–211

Brownell CA, Carriger MS. 1990. Changes in cooperation and self-other differentiation during the second year. *Child Dev.* 61(4):1164–74

Brownell CA, Iesue SS, Nichols SR, Svetlova M. 2013. Mine or yours? Development of sharing in toddlers in relation to ownership understanding. *Child Dev.* 84(3):906–20

Brownell CA, Ramani GB, Zerwas S. 2006. Becoming a social partner with peers: cooperation and social understanding in one- and two-year-olds. *Child Dev.* 77(4):803–21

Buhrmester D, Goldfarb J, Cantrell D. 1992. Self-presentation when sharing with friends and nonfriends. *J. Early Adolesc.* 12(1):61–79

Burkart JM, Rueth K. 2013. Preschool children fail primate prosocial game because of attentional task demands. *PLOS ONE* 8(7):e68440

Buttelmann D, Carpenter M, Tomasello M. 2009. Eighteen-month-old infants show false belief understanding in an active helping paradigm. *Cognition* 112:337–42

Calcott B. 2008. The other cooperation problem: generating benefit. *Biol. Philos.* 23:179–203

Callaghan T, Moll H, Rakoczy H, Warneken F, Liszkowski U, et al. 2011. Early social cognition in three cultural contexts. *Monogr. Soc. Res. Child Dev.* 76(2):vii–142

Carpenter M, Tomasello M, Striano T. 2005. Role reversal imitation and language in typically developing infants and children with autism. *Infancy* 8(3):253–78

Carpenter M, Uebel J, Tomasello M. 2013. Being mimicked increases prosocial behavior in 18-month-old infants. *Child Dev.* 84(5):1511–18

Chiarella SS, Poulin-Dubois D. 2013. Cry babies and pollyannas: Infants can detect unjustified emotional reactions. *Infancy* 18(s1):E81–96

Dahl A. 2015. The developing social context of infant helping in two US samples. *Child Dev.* 86(4):1080–93

Dahl A, Schuck RK, Campos JJ. 2013. Do young toddlers act on their social preferences? *Dev. Psychol.* 49(10):1964–70

Dahlman S, Ljungqvist P, Johannesson M. 2007. *Reciprocity in young children.* Work. Pap. 674, SSE/EFI Ser. Econ. Finance, Stockh. Sch. Econ.

Drummond J, Waugh WE, Hammond SI, Brownell CA. 2015. Prosocial behavior during infancy and early childhood: developmental patterns and cultural variations. *Int. Encycl. Soc. Behav. Sci.* 19:233–37

Dunfield KA, Kuhlmeier VA. 2010. Intention-mediated selective helping in infancy. *Psychol. Sci.* 21(4):523–27

Dunfield KA, Kuhlmeier VA. 2013. Classifying prosocial behavior: children's responses to instrumental need, emotional distress, and material desire. *Child Dev.* 84(5):1766–76

Dunfield KA, Kuhlmeier VA, Murphy L. 2013. Children's use of communicative intent in the selection of cooperative partners. *PLOS ONE* 8(4):e61804

Dunfield KA, Kuhlmeier VA, O'Connell L, Kelley E. 2011. Examining the diversity of prosocial behaviour: helping, sharing, and comforting in infancy. *Infancy* 16(3):227–47

Dunn J, Munn P. 1986. Siblings and the development of prosocial behaviour. *Int. J. Behav. Dev.* 9(3):265–84

Eckerman CO, Davis CC, Didow SM. 1989. Toddlers' emerging ways of achieving social coordinations with a peer. *Child Dev.* 60(2):440–53

Eckerman CO, Peterman K. 2001. Peers and infant social/communicative development. In *Blackwell Handbook of Infant Development*, ed. G Bremner, A Fogel, pp. 326–50. Hoboken, NJ: Wiley

Eisenberg N, Spinrad TL, Knafo-Noam A. 2015. Prosocial development. In *Handbook of Child Psychology and Developmental Science*, Vol. 3, ed. RM Lerner, ME Lamb, pp. 610–56. Hoboken, New Jersey: Wiley. 7th ed.

Engel C. 2011. Dictator games: a meta study. *Exp. Econ.* 14(4):583–610

Engelmann JM, Herrmann E, Tomasello M. 2012. Five-year-olds, but not chimpanzees, attempt to manage their reputations. *PLOS ONE* 7(10):e48433

Engelmann JM, Herrmann E, Tomasello M. 2015. Chimpanzees trust conspecifics to engage in low-cost reciprocity. *Proc. R. Soc. B* 282(1801):20142803

Engelmann JM, Over H, Herrmann E, Tomasello M. 2013. Young children care more about their reputation with ingroup members and potential reciprocators. *Dev. Sci.* 16(6):952–58

Fletcher G, Warneken F, Tomasello M. 2012. Differences in cognitive processes underlying the collaborative activities of children and chimpanzees. *Cogn. Dev.* 27(2):136–53

Froming WJ, Allen L, Jensen R. 1985. Altruism, role-taking, and self-awareness: the acquisition of norms governing altruistic behavior. *Child Dev.* 56(5):1223–28

Fujii T, Takagishi H, Koizumi M, Okada H. 2015. The effect of direct and indirect monitoring on generosity among preschoolers. *Sci. Rep.* 5:1–4

Gilby IC. 2006. Meat sharing among the Gombe chimpanzees: harassment and reciprocal exchange. *Anim. Behav.* 71:953–63

Gomes CM, Mundry R, Boesch C. 2009. Long-term reciprocation of grooming in wild West African chimpanzees. *Proc. Biol. Sci.* 276(1657):699–706

Gräfenhain M, Behne T, Carpenter M, Tomasello M. 2009. Young children's understanding of joint commitments. *Dev. Psychol.* 45(5):1430–43

Graves NB, Graves TD. 1978. The impact of modernization on the personality of a Polynesian people or, how to make an up-tight rivalrous Westerner out of an easy-going generous Pacific Islander. *Hum. Organ.* 37(2):115–35

Greenberg JR, Hamann K, Warneken F, Tomasello M. 2010. Chimpanzee helping in collaborative and noncollaborative contexts. *Anim. Behav.* 80(5):873–80

Gummerum M, Hanoch Y, Keller M. 2008. When child development meets economic game theory: an interdisciplinary approach to investigating social development. *Hum. Dev.* 51:235–61

Hamann K, Bender J, Tomasello M. 2014. Meritocratic sharing is based on collaboration in 3-year-olds. *Dev. Psychol.* 50(1):121–28

Hamann K, Warneken F, Greenberg JR, Tomasello M. 2011. Collaboration encourages equal sharing in children but not in chimpanzees. *Nature* 476(7360):328–31

Hamann K, Warneken F, Tomasello M. 2012. Children's developing commitments to joint goals. *Child Dev.* 83(1):137–45

Hamlin JK, Wynn K, Bloom P. 2007. Social evaluation by preverbal infants. *Nature* 450(7169):557–59

Hammerstein P. 2003. Why is reciprocity so rare in social animals? A Protestant appeal. In *Genetic and Cultural Evolution of Cooperation*, ed. P Hammerstein, pp. 83–93. Cambridge, MA: MIT Press

Hare B, Kwetuenda S. 2010. Bonobos voluntarily share their own food with others. *Curr. Biol.* 20(5):R230–31

Hare B, Melis AP, Woods V, Hastings S, Wrangham R. 2007. Tolerance allows bonobos to outperform chimpanzees on a cooperative task. *Curr. Biol.* 17(7):619–23

Hay DF, Castle J, Davies L, Demetriou H, Stimson CA. 1999. Prosocial action in very early childhood. *J. Child Psychol. Psychiatry* 40(6):905–16

Henderson AME, Wang Y, Matz LE, Woodward AL. 2013. Active experience shapes 10-month-old infants' understanding of collaborative goals. *Infancy* 18(1):10–39

Henderson AME, Woodward AL. 2011. "Let's work together": What do infants understand about collaborative goals? *Cognition* 121(1):12–21

Hepach R, Haberl K, Lambert S, Tomasello M. 2017a. Toddlers help anonymously. *Infancy* 22(1):130–45

Hepach R, Kante N, Tomasello M. 2017b. Toddlers help a peer. *Child Dev.* 88(5):1642–52

Hepach R, Vaish A, Grossmann T, Tomasello M. 2016. Young children want to see others get the help they need. *Child Dev.* 87(6):1703–14

Hepach R, Vaish A, Tomasello M. 2012. Young children are intrinsically motivated to see others helped. *Psychol. Sci.* 23(9):967–72

Hepach R, Vaish A, Tomasello M. 2013. Young children sympathize less in response to unjustified emotional distress. *Dev. Psych.* 49(6):1132–38

Hill V, Pillow BH. 2006. Children's understanding of reputations. *J. Genet. Psychol.* 167(2):137–57

Hirata S, Fuwa K. 2007. Chimpanzees (*Pan troglodytes*) learn to act with other individuals in a cooperative task. *Primates* 48(1):13–21

Hirata S, Morimura N, Fuwa K. 2010. Intentional communication and comprehension of the partner's role in experimental cooperative tasks. In *The Mind of the Chimpanzee: Ecological and Experimental Perspectives*, ed. EV Lonsdorf, SR Ross, T Matsuzawa, pp. 251–64. Chicago: Univ. Chicago Press

Hockings KJ, Humle T, Anderson JR, Biro D, Sousa C, et al. 2007. Chimpanzees share forbidden fruit. *PLOS ONE* 2(9):e886

Hoffman ML. 2000. *Empathy and Moral Development: Implications for Caring and Justice.* Cambridge, UK: Cambridge Univ. Press

House BR, Henrich J, Brosnan SF, Silk JB. 2012. The ontogeny of human prosociality: behavioral experiments with children aged 3 to 8. *Evol. Hum. Behav.* 33(4):291–308

House BR, Henrich J, Sarnecka B, Silk JB. 2013a. The development of contingent reciprocity in children. *Evol. Hum. Behav.* 34(2):86–93

House BR, Silk JB, Henrich J, Barrett HC, Scelza BA, et al. 2013b. Ontogeny of prosocial behavior across diverse societies. *PNAS* 110(36):14586–91

House BR, Silk JB, Lambeth SP, Schapiro SJ. 2014. Task design influences prosociality in captive chimpanzees (*Pan troglodytes*). *PLOS ONE* 9(9):e103422

Houser D, Montinari N, Piovesan M. 2012. Private and public decisions in social dilemmas: evidence from children's behavior. *PLOS ONE* 7(8):1–6

Howes C, Farver J. 1987. Toddlers' responses to the distress of their peers. *J. Appl. Dev. Psychol.* 8(4):441–52

Ibbotson P. 2014. Little dictators: a developmental meta-analysis of prosocial behavior. *Curr. Anthropol.* 55(6):814–21

Jensen K, Call J, Tomasello M. 2007. Chimpanzees are vengeful but not spiteful. *PNAS* 104(32):13046–50

Jensen K, Hare B, Call J, Tomasello M. 2006. What's in it for me? Self-regard precludes altruism and spite in chimpanzees. *Proc. R. Soc. Lond. B* 273:1013–21

Jordan JJ, McAuliffe K, Warneken F. 2014. Development of in-group favoritism in children's third-party punishment of selfishness. *PNAS* 111(35):12710–15

Kaneko R, Hamazaki T. 1987. Prosocial behavior manifestations of young children in an orphanage. *Psychologia* 30:235–42

Kanngiesser P, Warneken F. 2012. Young children consider merit when sharing resources with others. *PLOS ONE* 7(8):1–5

Kärtner J, Keller H, Chaudhary N. 2010. Cognitive and social influences on early prosocial behavior in two sociocultural contexts. *Dev. Psychol.* 46(4):905–14

Kenward B, Dahl M. 2011. Preschoolers distribute scarce resources according to the moral valence of recipients' previous actions. *Dev. Psychol.* 47(4):1054–64

Kenward B, Hellmer K, Winter LS, Eriksson M. 2015. Four-year-olds' strategic allocation of resources: attempts to elicit reciprocation correlate negatively with spontaneous helping. *Cognition* 136:1–8

Knudsen B, Liszkowski U. 2012a. 18-month-olds predict specific action mistakes through attribution of false belief, not ignorance, and intervene accordingly. *Infancy* 17(6):672–91

Knudsen B, Liszkowski U. 2012b. Eighteen- and 24-month-old infants correct others in anticipation of action mistakes. *Dev. Sci.* 15(1):113–22

Köster M, Cavalcante L, de Carvalho RVC, Dôgo Resende B, Kärtner J. 2016. Cultural influences on toddlers' prosocial behavior: how maternal task assignment relates to helping others. *Child Dev.* 87(6):1727–38

Kuhlmeier VA, Dunfield KA, O'Neill AC. 2014. Selectivity in early prosocial behavior. *Front. Psychol.* 5:836

Kuhlmeier VA, Wynn K, Bloom P. 2003. Attribution of dispositional states by 12-month-olds. *Psychol. Sci.* 14(5):402–8

Leimgruber KL, Shaw A, Santos LR, Olson KR. 2012. Young children are more generous when others are aware of their actions. *PLOS ONE* 7(10):e48292

Liszkowski U, Carpenter M, Striano T, Tomasello M. 2006. 12- and 18-month-olds point to provide information for others *J. Cogn. Dev.* 7(2):173–87

Martin A, Olson KR. 2013. When kids know better: paternalistic helping in 3-year-old children. *Dev. Psychol.* 49(11):2071–81

Mayr E. 1961. Cause and effect in biology. *Science* 134(3489):1501–6

McAuliffe K, Blake PR, Steinbeis N, Warneken F. 2017. The developmental foundations of human fairness. *Nat. Hum. Behav.* 1:42

McAuliffe K, Jordan JJ, Warneken F. 2015. Costly third-party punishment in young children. *Cognition* 134:1–10

Melis AP, Altrichter K, Tomasello M. 2013. Allocation of resources to collaborators and free-riders in 3-year-olds. *J. Exp. Child Psychol.* 114(2):364–70

Melis AP, Grocke P, Kalbitz J, Tomasello M. 2016. One for you, one for me: humans' unique turn-taking skills. *Psychol. Sci.* 27(7):987–96

Melis AP, Hare B, Tomasello M. 2006a. Chimpanzees recruit the best collaborators. *Science* 311:1297–300

Melis AP, Hare B, Tomasello M. 2006b. Engineering cooperation in chimpanzees: tolerance constraints on cooperation. *Anim. Behav.* 72(2):275–86

Melis AP, Hare B, Tomasello M. 2008. Do chimpanzees reciprocate received favours? *Anim. Behav.* 76(3):951–62

Melis AP, Tomasello M. 2013. Chimpanzees' (*Pan troglodytes*) strategic helping in a collaborative task. *Biol. Lett.* 9(2):20130009

Melis AP, Warneken F. 2016. The psychology of cooperation: insights from chimpanzees and children. *Evol. Anthropol.* 25(6):297–305

Melis AP, Warneken F, Jensen K, Schneider AC, Call J, Tomasello M. 2011. Chimpanzees help conspecifics obtain food and non-food items. *Proc. R. Soc. Lond. B* 278(1710):1405–13

Northover SB, Pedersen WC, Cohen AB, Andrews PW. 2016. Artificial surveillance cues do not increase generosity: two meta-analyses. *Evol. Hum. Behav.* 38(1):144–53

Nowak MA. 2006. Five rules for the evolution of cooperation. *Science* 314(5805):1560–63

Olson KR, Spelke ES. 2008. Foundations of cooperation in young children. *Cognition* 108(1):222–31

Pettygrove DM, Hammond SI, Karahuta EL, Waugh WE, Brownell CA. 2013. From cleaning up to helping out: parental socialization and children's early prosocial behavior. *Infant Behav. Dev.* 36(4):843–46

Riedl K, Jensen K, Call J, Tomasello M. 2012. No third-party punishment in chimpanzees. *PNAS* 109(37):14824–29

Riedl K, Jensen K, Tomasello M. 2015. Restorative justice in children. *Curr. Biol.* 25(13):1731–35

Ross HS, Lollis SP. 1987. Communication within infant social games. *Dev. Psychol.* 23(2):241–48

Schäfer M, Haun DBM, Tomasello M. 2015. Fair is not fair everywhere. *Psychol. Sci.* 26(8):1252–60

Schino G, Aureli F. 2010. Primate reciprocity and its cognitive requirements. *Evol. Anthropol.* 19:130–35

Sebastian-Enesco C, Hernandez-Lloreda MV, Colmenares F. 2013. Two-and-a-half-year-old children are prosocial even when their partners are not. *J. Exp. Child Psychol.* 116(2):186–98

Sebastian-Enesco C, Warneken F. 2015. The shadow of the future: 5-year-olds, but not 3-year-olds, adjust their sharing in anticipation of reciprocation. *J. Exp. Child Psychol.* 129:40–54

Shaw A, Piovesan M, Montinari N, Olson KR, Gino F, Norton MI. 2014. Children develop a veil of fairness. *J. Exp. Psychol. Gen.* 143(1):363–75

Silk JB, Brosnan SF, Vonk J, Henrich J, Povinelli DJ, et al. 2005. Chimpanzees are indifferent to the welfare of unrelated group members. *Nature* 437(7063):1357–59

Sloane S, Baillargeon R, Premack D. 2012. Do infants have a sense of fairness? *Psychol. Sci.* 23(2):196–204

Svetlova M, Nichols SR, Brownell CA. 2010. Toddlers' prosocial behavior: from instrumental to empathic to altruistic helping. *Child Dev.* 81(6):1814–27

Takagishi H, Fujii T, Koizumi M, Schug J, Nakamura F, Kameshima S. 2015. The development of the effect of peer monitoring on generosity differs among elementary school-age boys and girls. *Front. Psychol.* 6:1–6

Tan J, Hare B. 2013. Bonobos share with strangers. *PLOS ONE* 8(1):e51922

Tanaka M, Yamamoto S. 2009. Token transfer between mother and offspring chimpanzees (*Pan troglodytes*): mother-offspring interaction in a competitive situation. *Anim. Cogn.* 12(Suppl. 1):S19–26

Thompson C, Barresi J, Moore C. 1997. The development of future-oriented prudence and altruism in preschoolers. *Cogn. Dev.* 12:199–212

Tinbergen N. 1963. On aims and methods of ethology. *Z. Tierpsychol.* 20:410–33

Tomasello M, Carpenter M, Call J, Behne T, Moll H. 2005. Understanding and sharing intentions: the origins of cultural cognition. *Behav. Brain Sci.* 28:675–735

Tomasello M, Warneken F. 2008. Share and share alike. *Nature* 454:1057–58

Ueno A, Matsuzawa T. 2004. Food transfer between chimpanzee mothers and their infants. *Primates* 45(4):231–39

Ulber J, Hamann K, Tomasello M. 2015. How 18- and 24-month-old peers divide resources among themselves. *J. Exp. Child Psychol.* 140:228–44

Ulber J, Hamann K, Tomasello M. 2016. Extrinsic rewards diminish costly sharing in 3-year-olds. *Child Dev.* 87(4):1192–203

Vaish A, Carpenter M, Tomasello M. 2009. Sympathy through affective perspective taking and its relation to prosocial behavior in toddlers. *Dev. Psychol.* 45(2):534–43

Vaish A, Carpenter M, Tomasello M. 2010. Young children selectively avoid helping people with harmful intentions. *Child Dev.* 81(6):1661–69

Vaish A, Missana M, Tomasello M. 2011. Three-year-old children intervene in third-party moral transgressions. *Br. J. Dev. Psychol.* 29:124–30

Vogt S, Efferson C, Berger J, Fehr E. 2014. Eye spots do not increase altruism in children. *Evol. Hum. Behav.* 36(3):224–31

Vonk J, Brosnan SF, Silk JB, Henrich J, Richardson AS, et al. 2008. Chimpanzees do not take advantage of very low cost opportunities to deliver food to unrelated group members. *Anim. Behav.* 75:1757–70

Warneken F. 2013. Young children proactively remedy unnoticed accidents. *Cognition* 126(1):101–8

Warneken F. 2016. Insights into the biological foundation of human altruistic sentiments. *Curr. Opin. Psychol.* 7:51–56

Warneken F, Chen F, Tomasello M. 2006. Cooperative activities in young children and chimpanzees. *Child Dev.* 77(3):640–63

Warneken F, Gräfenhain M, Tomasello M. 2012. Collaborative partner or social tool? New evidence for young children's understanding of joint intentions in collaborative activities. *Dev. Sci.* 15(1):54–61

Warneken F, Hare B, Melis AP, Hanus D, Tomasello M. 2007. Spontaneous altruism by chimpanzees and young children. *PLOS Biol.* 5(7):1414–20

Warneken F, Lohse K, Melis AP, Tomasello M. 2011. Young children share the spoils after collaboration. *Psychol. Sci.* 22(2):267–73

Warneken F, Tomasello M. 2006. Altruistic helping in human infants and young chimpanzees. *Science* 311(5765):1301–3

Warneken F, Tomasello M. 2007. Helping and cooperation at 14 months of age. *Infancy* 11(3):271–94

Warneken F, Tomasello M. 2008. Extrinsic rewards undermine altruistic tendencies in 20-month-olds. *Dev. Psychol.* 44(6):1785–88

Warneken F, Tomasello M. 2013a. The emergence of contingent reciprocity in young children. *J. Exp. Child Psychol.* 116(2):338–50

Warneken F, Tomasello M. 2013b. Parental presence and encouragement do not influence helping in young children. *Infancy* 18(3):345–68

West SA, Griffin AS, Gardner A. 2007. Evolutionary explanations for cooperation. *Curr. Biol.* 17(16):R661–72

Wobber V, Hare B, Maboto J, Lipson S, Wrangham R, Ellison PT. 2010. Differential changes in steroid hormones before competition in bonobos and chimpanzees. *PNAS* 107(28):12457–62

Yamamoto S, Humle T, Tanaka M. 2009. Chimpanzees help each other upon request. *PLOS ONE* 4(10):1–7

Yamamoto S, Humle T, Tanaka M. 2012. Chimpanzees' flexible targeted helping based on an understanding of conspecifics' goals. *PNAS* 109(9):3588–92

Yamamoto S, Tanaka M. 2010. The influence of kin relationship and reciprocal context on chimpanzees' other-regarding preferences. *Anim. Behav.* 79:595–602

Zahn-Waxler C, Radke-Yarrow M, Wagner E, Chapman M. 1992. Developmental concern for others. *Dev. Psychol.* 28(1):126–36

Zarbatany L, Hartmann DP, Gelfand DM. 1985. Why does children's generosity increase with age: susceptibility to experimenter influence or altruism? *Child Dev.* 56(3):746–56

Linking Language and Cognition in Infancy

Danielle R. Perszyk[1] and Sandra R. Waxman[1,2]

[1] Department of Psychology, Northwestern University, Evanston, Illinois 60208;
email: drp@u.northwestern.edu, s-waxman@northwestern.edu

[2] Institute for Policy Research, Northwestern University, Evanston, Illinois 60208

Annu. Rev. Psychol. 2018. 69:231–50

First published as a Review in Advance on
September 6, 2017

The *Annual Review of Psychology* is online at
psych.annualreviews.org

https://doi.org/10.1146/annurev-psych-122216-011701

Keywords

infancy, language acquisition, conceptual development, categorization, developmental plasticity, developmental tuning

Abstract

Human language, a signature of our species, derives its power from its links to human cognition. For centuries, scholars have been captivated by this link between language and cognition. In this article, we shift this focus. Adopting a developmental lens, we review recent evidence that sheds light on the origin and developmental unfolding of the link between language and cognition in the first year of life. This evidence, which reveals the joint contributions of infants' innate capacities and their sensitivity to experience, highlights how a precocious link between language and cognition advances infants beyond their initial perceptual and conceptual capacities. The evidence also identifies the conceptual advantages this link brings to human infants. By tracing the emergence of a language–cognition link in infancy, this article reveals a dynamic developmental cascade in infants' first year, with each developmental advance providing a foundation for subsequent advances.

Contents

INTRODUCTION

Language is a hallmark of our species and our most powerful cultural and cognitive tool. The power of language derives not from the exquisite detail of its signals or the precision of its grammatical rules but from its intricate and inextricable link to human cognition. This link, unparalleled elsewhere in the animal kingdom, serves as the conduit through which we share with others the contents of our minds. It enables us to move beyond the exigencies of the here and now, to represent the past and the future, to build upon one another's knowledge and beliefs, and to consider different perspectives on the same phenomena. Through human language, we can essentially hijack one another's minds, working collectively to invent history and time, to promote religious beliefs and scientific theories, and to create literature and art.

George Miller (1990, p. 12), a father of the cognitive revolution in psychology, described this uniquely human link eloquently:

> Human language is the happy result of bringing together two systems that all higher organisms must have: a representational system and a communication system .... A representational system is necessary if an organism is going to move around purposefully in its environment; a communication system is necessary if an organism is going to interact with others of its own kind. Presumably, some of the historical disagreements over the importance of language for our understanding of human cognition arose because different protagonists identified language with different parts of this combination. It is certainly true that human beings are not the only animals capable of a complex representational intelligence, nor are they the only animals that communicate. But human beings do seem to be the only animals in which a single system serves both of these functions.

Questions concerning this relationship between human language and cognition have long captivated attention in all of the fields currently within the cognitive sciences (Fodor 1975, Gleitman & Papafragou 2005, Whorf 1956). Decades, if not centuries, of lively debate have illuminated several issues that lie at the intersection of human language and cognition, but, until recently, a more fundamental question has been left unaddressed: How do infants begin to forge a link between language and cognition in the first place? And what advantages, if any, do such links afford the developing infant mind?

In this article, our goal is to shed light on the developmental origins of this uniquely human link and to trace how it unfolds in infancy. Focusing primarily (but not exclusively) on the first year of life, we peel back the layers to reveal the foundation of this language–cognition interface. Shifting the focus to infants also shifts the questions under investigation. The question is no longer whether language and cognition are linked; instead, the questions are how this link begins, what initial capacities (if any) support infants as they first forge this link, how these capacities are then sculpted by the forces of maturation and experience, and how this precocious link advances infants' acquisition of knowledge.

Three Recurring Themes

Three interrelated themes central to the developmental sciences are woven together throughout this review (**Figure 1**). These themes, built on an assumption that human infants are endowed with an innate capacity to acquire human language (Chomsky 1986, Gleitman 1990, Pinker 1994), guide current investigations into how a language–cognition link unfolds and how this link fuels infants' acquisition of core cognitive capacities. The first theme concerns the joint contributions of maturation and experience. We examine how these twin engines of development guide infants to establish increasingly precise links between language and cognition. The second theme is the idea that human language and cognitive development are best characterized as a series of cascading effects that unfold over developmental time, with each point along the developmental continuum

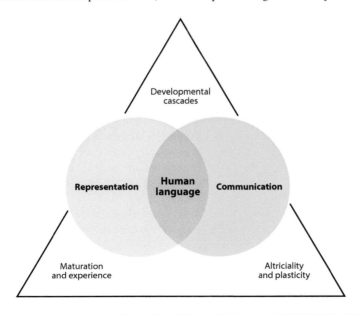

Figure 1

Human language occupies the intersection of our systems for representation and communication. Interactions between nature and nurture—reflected in the sculpting forces of maturation and experience and in the synergy between altriciality and plasticity—provide our foundation for language. Developmental cascades, in turn, characterize our acquisition of language.

setting constraints upon the next (Werker & Hensch 2015). The third theme, articulated below, highlights the importance of two other signatures of our species—our altricial status at birth and our exceptional developmental plasticity.

Human infants are altricial at birth, neurally and behaviorally immature even in comparison to our closest evolutionary relatives. For example, the human infant's brain at birth is less than 30% the size of an adult's, a ratio that is substantially lower than that observed in other primate species (DeSilva & Lesnik 2006). Moreover, infants of other species are endowed at birth with the behavioral tools that permit them to maintain proximity with their caregivers (e.g., an ability to cling to their caregivers or to locomote alongside them), but human infants have no such behavioral endowment. Notice that this altricial status brings with it a developmental imperative: It falls to human caregivers to maintain close contact with their infants and to do so for an extraordinarily protracted period. Human infants' exceptionally long period of dependency, paired with their innate cognitive and linguistic capacities (Carey 2009, Chomsky 1986, Spelke & Kinzler 2007) and their responsiveness to experience (Kuzawa & Bragg 2012, Werker & Hensch 2015), is "advantageous for a species whose major specialization is its capacity for learning and whose basic invention is culture" (Gleitman et al. 2011, p. 588). And, we add, these foundations of human development are also advantageous for a species whose signature is the link between language and cognition.

The Advantages of Adopting a Developmental Lens

Approaching the relationship between language and cognition using a developmental lens is especially compelling. Although an infant from a remote village in the Chaco rain forest and an infant from an urban Chicago neighborhood will each grow up amid objects and events that the other has never seen, immersed in daily practices that the other has not witnessed, and listening to language that the other cannot understand, there are strong convergences in their acquisition of fundamental conceptual and linguistic capacities (Schieffelin & Ochs 1986, Waxman & Lidz 2006). Within their first year, infants across the world's communities begin to acquire language. Also within their first year, infants establish categories of objects and events (e.g., DOG, BOTTLE; RUN, SLEEP) that capture commonalities among distinct individual objects or events. These early categories serve as a basis for learning and guide infants' expectations about objects and events that they have not yet witnessed. These categories, rudimentary at first, also develop in alignment with a small set of abstract concepts, including concepts as fundamental to human thought as objects, number, space, causation, and agency (Baillargeon et al. 2016, Carey 2009, Spelke 2017).

Importantly, these early linguistic and conceptual advances do not proceed independently. Instead, infant language and conceptual development are powerfully and implicitly linked (for reviews, see Ferguson & Waxman 2016a, Swingley 2012).

When we adopt a developmental lens, it becomes clear that this link unfolds dynamically, beginning in the first months of life. Uncovering this dynamic process—as well as the factors that drive it—has major implications for understanding the ontogenetic and phylogenetic origins of human language and cognition.

LANGUAGE EXERTS A HIDDEN POWER: THE EFFECTS OF LANGUAGE IN EARLY CONCEPTUAL DEVELOPMENT

In the words of ancient Greek poet Alcaeus, "Language exerts a hidden power, like the moon on the tides." Although he almost certainly could not have known it at the time, this is an especially apt description of the effects of language on infant cognition in the first year of life. Three lines of recent developmental work, each with its own theoretical framework, have shed new light on the ways in which language exerts this influence in infancy. These lines of research include investigations of the link between words and categories, core knowledge, and natural pedagogy.

Words as Invitations to Form Categories

Most research investigating the early development of a link between language and cognition in infants and young children has focused on word learning. This focus makes sense because word learning is an achievement that stands at the crossroads between linguistic and conceptual development. After all, to learn the meaning of a word, learners must identify a portion of the ongoing stream of speech (a problem for a communication system to solve), identify a referent for that word (a problem for a representational system to solve), and establish a mapping between the word and its referent. Moreover, the early word learning research focused primarily on object categories. This focus is apt because categories are fundamental building blocks of cognition. They exert far-reaching influence on virtually all aspects of learning and cognition across species and across development: When we identify two objects as members of the same category, we establish their equivalence at a certain level of representation, permitting us to identify new members of the category and to make inferences about nonobvious properties from one member of the category to another. This has tremendous consequences for subsequent learning; for example, by establishing a category DOG, we can learn from just one encounter with a single dog to avoid all dogs that bare their teeth (even ones we have not yet seen) instead of painfully and repeatedly requiring first-hand evidence from each individual dog that happens to bare its teeth. Object categories also support memory and reasoning, guiding our predictions about the likely behaviors and properties of objects—even objects we have yet to encounter and properties (e.g., an organism's DNA) that we have never observed (Gelman 2004, Medin & Ortony 1989, Waxman & Gelman 2009).

Roger Brown (1958), the father of the modern study of child language and a contemporary of George Miller, famously argued that words are invitations to form categories. When he articulated this point of view, Brown had preschool-aged children in mind. However, more recent developmental evidence reveals that, even before infants begin to speak, words invite them to form categories. The evidence for this claim comes from a robust behavioral paradigm, elegant in its simplicity. It is essentially an object categorization task with two phases. During the familiarization phase, infants view a series of discriminably different objects (e.g., dog, horse, duck) from a given object category (e.g., animal). Next, during the test phase, infants view two new objects—one a member of the now-familiar category (e.g., a cat) and the other a member of an entirely different category (e.g., an apple). The logic of this paradigm is straightforward: If infants detect the category-based commonalities among the familiarization objects, then they should distinguish the novel test image from the familiar; if they fail to detect these commonalities, then they should perform at chance levels (Aslin 2007, Colombo 2002, Golinkoff et al. 1987). Because this paradigm permits researchers to hold constant the objects infants view while systematically manipulating the amount and kind of auditory information that infants hear, designs like this have shed light not only on whether infants can form object categories, but also on how their capacity to do so is shaped by language.

The evidence reveals that, by 12 months of age, even before they produce more than a few words on their own, infants have established a principled link between object naming and object categorization. If each in a series of familiarization objects is introduced in conjunction with the same novel word embedded in a naming phrase (e.g., "Look at the blick!"), infants successfully form an object category, exhibiting a reliable preference for the novel test object (e.g., the apple rather than the cat). However, when precisely the same familiarization objects are presented under different auditory conditions, infants fail to form object categories. First, when the familiarization objects are introduced with phrases that include no novel word (e.g., "Look at that!"), 12-month-olds fail to form categories (Waxman & Markow 1995). Second, when different novel words are applied to each familiarization object (e.g., "Look at the blick!"; "Look at the toma!"; "Look at the modi!"), they fail to form categories (Ferguson et al. 2015, Waxman & Braun 2005, Waxman & Markow 1995, Xu 2002). Third, not all consistently applied signals promote categorization. Instead, this link is specific to language: When the familiarization objects are paired consistently with signals outside the linguistic domain (e.g., tone sequences), infants fail to form categories (Balaban & Waxman 1997, Fulkerson & Waxman 2007).

Thus, by their first birthday, infants successfully cull novel words from the ongoing stream of speech, track whether the same (or different) words have been applied to a set of objects, and expect that a series of distinct objects named consistently with the same word share commonalities.

This expectation cannot be reduced to a simple associative mechanism (Waxman & Gelman 2009). After all, although both tone sequences and naming phrases have been applied with the very same consistency to the very same sets of familiarization objects, only infants listening to language successfully form object categories. The claim in this case is not that an infant's ability to form an object category depends entirely on listening to language. This claim is clearly false: Even without listening to language, preverbal infants and nonhuman animals successfully form some object categories, although this typically requires a considerable number of learning trials (for reviews, see Mareschal & Quinn 2001, Smith et al. 2012). Instead, the claim is both measured and precise: For human infants, words are invitations to form categories. Naming a set of distinct objects with the same name (e.g., "Look at the blick!") effectively highlights commonalities among them, commonalities that go undetected in the absence of naming (e.g., "Look at that!") (Althaus & Plunkett 2016, Waxman & Markow 1995). This invitation is in place early enough to support infants' first forays into building a lexicon (Bergelson & Swingley 2012, Tincoff & Jusczyk 2012) and to support their acquisition of fundamental representations of kinds, relations, and individuals (Dewar & Xu 2007, Waxman & Lidz 2006, Yin & Csibra 2015).

But this link between words and object categories, expressed so clearly by 12 months of age, does not remain constant across development. Instead, it provides the foundation upon which infants will subsequently build the more precise links that are the hallmark of human language. Infants will discover not only distinct words (e.g., "dog" and "chasing"), but also distinct kinds of words (e.g., nouns and verbs); they will also discover that distinct kinds of words are linked to distinct kinds of underlying meaning (e.g., nouns and object categories; verbs and event categories or relations). Importantly, these more precise links do not emerge all at once; they unfold in a cascading fashion. For infants in their first year, any consistently applied novel word, whether it is presented as a noun, adjective, or verb (e.g., "Look at the blick!"; "Look at the blick one!"; "Watch it blick!"), highlights a wide range of commonalities, including those that underlie object categories (e.g., dog versus horse), object properties (e.g., red versus green; soft versus sharp), or relationships among objects (e.g., chasing versus fleeing). At roughly 13 months of age, however, infants begin to establish a more precise mapping; they first tease apart the nouns from the other grammatical forms and link them specifically to categories of objects (e.g., dog), but not to properties of objects or events (e.g., green, chasing) (Waxman 1999). Next, with a noun–category link in place, infants go on to establish precise links for the predicates, including adjectives and verbs. Evidence that this developmental cascade begins with infants' discovery of a noun–category link converges well with linguistic evidence that discovering the meaning of a predicate depends in part upon the nouns that they take as arguments (Gleitman et al. 2005, Klibanoff & Waxman 2000, Mintz & Gleitman 2002, Waxman & Lidz 2006).

From this perspective, then, the 12-month-olds' link between language and cognition serves as an engine that catalyzes subsequent language and conceptual development. Notice that, because these increasingly precise links unfold in a cascading fashion, the cognitive consequences of naming will evolve rapidly and systematically over the first 2 years of life, depending upon how far along an infant is in the developmental cascade.

But what does this increasingly precise link between language and cognition afford the infant? Recent evidence has shown that it unlocks representational capacities that distinguish human cognition from that of our evolutionary relatives.

Language and Systems of Core Knowledge

Human infants share basic representational capacities with nonhuman animals. In particular, there appear to be hardwired systems for representing objects, tracking numerosity, navigating in space, perceiving causation, and detecting agency (for reviews, see Baillargeon et al. 2016, Carey 2009, Spelke & Kinzler 2007). Several of these systems, in turn, appear to operate within encapsulated modules. That is, the output of a module or computation is encapsulated from information represented elsewhere in the cognitive system. For example, adult-like representations of number are composed of one module dedicated to approximating large ratios and another dedicated to tracking a small number of individuals (Feigenson et al. 2004). Similarly, representations of large-scale space and how to navigate within it are comprised of one module dedicated to orienting via the geometry of a landscape and another dedicated to orienting via particular landmarks (Lee et al. 2006). Distinct, encapsulated modules like these are the foundations of core knowledge, and they serve as building blocks for higher-order cognition. But if humans and nonhumans alike share these basic building blocks, then why do humans' representational capacities so far exceed those of other species? The key, as George Miller suggested, is that humans' representational systems are intertwined with their communication system—language.

More specifically, researchers working from the core knowledge perspective have proposed that it is language that permits humans to weave together otherwise encapsulated representations within core knowledge systems, and that this connection among representations (along with the combinatorial capacity it affords) is the gateway to higher-order, abstract representations (Carey 2009, Spelke 2017). Beginning in infancy, human language boosts the representational capacities of core knowledge by translating otherwise encapsulated representations into a shared language-like format. These shared representations scaffold subsequent conceptual advancements. There is especially compelling evidence for the role of language in augmenting our representations of object, number, and space. For instance, the object representations of prelinguistic infants and nonhuman animals are characterized by coarse-grained spatiotemporal criteria, including cohesion (objects move as bounded wholes), continuity (objects move on unobstructed paths), and contact (objects do not interact at a distance) (Aguiar & Baillargeon 1999, Spelke 1990). Learning words for objects and object kinds permits infants to represent objects in a more finely grained, conceptually rich format (for reviews, see Waxman & Gelman 2009, Xu 2007). Likewise, as mentioned above, the numerical representations of prelinguistic infants and nonhuman animals occur in two distinct modules, one that approximates ratios among large quantities and another that specifies exact quantity in small sets (with a limit that appears to be three) (Feigenson et al. 2004). However, with the acquisition of language (specifically, learning number words and aligning them with sets), it becomes possible for infants to combine these otherwise distinct representations and to represent numbers, small and large, with exactness (Condry & Spelke 2008).

Evidence from deaf individuals deprived of language input from birth goes one step further, suggesting that language is a causal force bridging otherwise distinct representations and representational formats. For example, deaf children born to hearing parents do not receive the richly structured linguistic input that their counterparts (hearing infants of hearing parents or deaf infants of deaf parents fluent in sign language) receive. In the absence of this linguistic input, deaf children of hearing parents create their own unique gestural system known as homesign. Remarkably, homesign exhibits many fundamental features of more fully developed languages (e.g., American Sign Language or English). However, a fuller and more richly structured linguistic system emerges only when homesign systems are shared among a community of signers (for a review, see Goldin-Meadow 2017). Without access to such a richly structured linguistic system—one that includes words for representing precise number and precise spatial relations—homesigners appear to have difficulty representing exact quantities larger than three (Spaepen et al. 2011) and representing abstract spatial relations (Pyers et al. 2010).

Thus, research from the perspective of core knowledge suggests that language knits together distinct representational modules within and across otherwise encapsulated knowledge systems. In this view, language is what makes it possible to form the discrete, symbolic, and abstract representations that characterize the human mind.

Language as a Component of Natural Pedagogy

Infants' language and cognitive development do not occur in a vacuum. Instead, a signature of human development is that infants and their caregivers interact in rich social-communicative contexts. From the first days of life, infant–caregiver interactions are reciprocally social, filled with face-to-face communication, turn taking, and other communicative cues (e.g., eye gaze, infant-directed intonation, pointing). Social exchanges like these, which are especially engaging for infants, are the stage upon which language and conceptual development unfold (for reviews, see Csibra & Gergely 2009, Kuhl 2007, Vouloumanos & Waxman 2014).

Csibra & Gergely (2009) have proposed a theory of natural pedagogy to capture the effects of this broader set of communicative cues in infancy. In their view, the power of language comes, at least in part, from its social-communicative status. In this account, the effects of language [and especially infant-directed speech (IDS)] are on par with the effects of other ostensive social-communicative cues, including eye gaze and pointing. From the perspective of natural pedagogy, human infants are prepared by evolution to favor ostensive information conveyed by a pedagogical partner, to interpret ostensive cues as referential, and to expect that these cues signal kind-relevant, generalizable information.

There is now considerable evidence not only that infants are sensitive to ostensive cues, but also that such cues boost infant learning beyond what they could glean from observation alone and, in this way, boost human infants' learning in ways that are unavailable to nonhuman species (for reviews, see Csibra & Gergely 2009, Csibra & Shamsudheen 2015). For example, infants use ostensive cues to learn about referential gaze (Senju & Csibra 2008, Senju et al. 2008), to make inferences about the identity and location of hidden objects (Moll & Tomasello 2004), and to learn from novel cues (Wu et al. 2014). Infants' attention to ostensive cues also guides their memory and learning. For instance, if a caregiver points to an object that then disappears, infants remember what the object looked like but not its precise location; in contrast, if a caregiver reaches for an object that then disappears, infants remember its location but not what it looked like (Yoon et al. 2008). Likewise, if a caregiver introduces an object with IDS, infants can better identify that object's category membership even in the presence of conflicting surface features; if the object is introduced without IDS, infants are more likely to be distracted by conflicting surface features and to have more difficulty focusing on object kind (Kovács et al. 2017).

Language stands out as an especially potent ostensive cue. In the first year of life, infants expect that language, but not nonlinguistic signals (e.g., coughs, laughs), is a medium through which we share knowledge, beliefs, and intentions (Martin et al. 2012; Vouloumanos et al. 2012, 2014). By 12 months of age, infants' neural responses to images of an object vary as functions of whether they know the object's name (Gliga et al. 2009). By 14 months of age, infants' expectations in the context of naming are quite abstract. In one experimental design, 14-month-olds observed an actor produce an unconventional act: She turned on a light using her head, rather than her hands. Infants were then invited to turn on the light themselves. The way that they did so varied as a function of whether the event was named. If the actor provided a label for her unconventional act ("I'm going to blick"), infants imitated her behavior precisely, turning on the light with their heads. However, if the actor provided no such label ("Look at this"), infants turned on the light in a more conventional fashion, using their hands (Chen & Waxman 2013, Gergely et al. 2002).

The theory of natural pedagogy thus offers a compelling description of infants' sensitivity to social-communicative cues and the consequences of these cues for streamlining learning. It also dovetails with decades of evidence that language supports infants' ability to form categories (Waxman & Gelman 2009, Waxman & Markow 1995).

However, over the course of the first 2 years of life, infants' responses to human language part company with their responses to other ostensive, communicative signals like eye gaze and pointing. Even before they can combine words on their own, infants discover that there are distinct kinds of words and phrases; they also pinpoint with increasing precision how distinct kinds of words map onto distinct kinds of meaning (Waxman & Gelman 2009). In contrast, infants' responses to eye gaze and pointing do not follow this developmental trajectory. Although eye gaze and pointing may direct an infants' attention to one object or event over another, neither of these signals has the precision to specify which aspect of the scene an infant should attend to. This kind of precision is a feature reserved for human language.

DEVELOPMENTAL ORIGINS OF THE LANGUAGE–COGNITION LINK

The evidence reviewed above showcases several different ways in which language does, indeed, exert a hidden power on infant cognition. But how do infants come to link language and cognition in the first place?

To address this question, researchers have sought to identify how, and how early, infants begin to link language and cognition: What capacities, perhaps innately endowed or evolutionarily specified, are available to infants in the first months of life and how are they shaped by maturation and experience? Research on this topic, itself in its infancy, has been inspired not only by theories of language and cognitive development, but also by elegant studies of perceptual development. Before describing the evidence for the developmental origins of the language–cognition link, we set the stage by describing how infants tune their perceptual systems to the auditory and visual signals of our species.

Tuning to the Signals of Our Species

Human infants are certainly born altricial, but they are just as certainly not born as blank slates. Instead, within hours of their birth, infants reveal strong perceptual preferences and perceptual discriminatory capacities. These early perceptual capacities—evident in auditory, visual, and cross-modal perception—start out broad at birth and are then rapidly tuned in response to infants' postnatal experience. There is wide agreement that this process of perceptual narrowing is a domain-general one: The same fundamental learning processes guide infants' tuning within and across modalities (for reviews, see Maurer & Werker 2014, Scott et al. 2007).

At birth, infants' perceptual preferences and capacities in the auditory domain are broad. Newborns equally prefer listening to human and nonhuman vocalizations over other sounds (Vouloumanos et al. 2010), and they can distinguish among sounds across human languages (Werker & Tees 1984) and nonhuman primate vocalizations (Friendly et al. 2013a). Within their first months, infants' broad preferences narrow specifically to human language (Vouloumanos et al. 2010). Similarly, within their first year, infants' perception of native language sounds becomes sharpened, while their perception of nonnative language and nonhuman primate sounds concomitantly decreases (Friendly et al. 2013a, Werker & Tees 1984).

Perceptual narrowing, evident in infant behavior and neural activity (Kuhl & Rivera-Gaxiola 2008, Shultz et al. 2014), has been documented not only in speech perception, but also in infants' face perception and intermodal perception (for a review, see Maurer & Werker 2014). Homing in on voices, faces, and the correspondences between familiar voices and faces results in the integration of multisensory systems (Bruderer et al. 2015, Lewkowicz & Ghazanfar 2009). Within and across diverse perceptual systems, infants' initially broad preferences and discriminatory capacities become increasingly specialized for processing certain signals, chief among them the voices and faces of members of their own communities. Tuning processes like these are advantageous for infants because they increase the signal value for communicative signals available in their communities. Moreover, perceptual narrowing within and across perceptual modalities proceeds with no conscious effort required from the learner (Kraus & Slater 2016). In essence, then, even before infants begin to speak, they establish increasingly precise, efficient, and integrated perceptual systems.

The phenomenon of perceptual narrowing showcases the dynamic interplay between infants' impressive perceptual abilities at birth and their responsivity to postnatal experience. Especially compelling evidence comes from exposure studies. There are two classes of such studies. Studies in the first class examine natural variation in exposure (to language or faces) to identify how it shapes infants' perception. For instance, a classic experiment by Werker & Tees (1984) demonstrated that the particular language to which infants are exposed shapes their sensitivity to the sounds of that language. Likewise, Bar-Haim et al. (2006), Kelly et al. (2005, 2007), and Quinn et al. (2002) showed that the particular faces to which infants are exposed shape their sensitivity to the features of those faces.

Studies in the second class have adopted an even more direct approach, systematically manipulating infants' exposure to various stimuli. For example, providing infants with exposure to nonnative phonemes (Maye et al. 2002), nonnative musical rhythms (Hannon & Trehub 2005), monkey vocalizations (Friendly et al. 2013b), monkey faces (Fair et al. 2012, Pascalis et al. 2005), or other-race faces (Heron-Delaney et al. 2011) enables them to make distinctions among these signals, even months after they had tuned their perception specifically to signals in their native environment. Studies that provide infants with prolonged exposure, typically throughout the developmental window in which perceptual narrowing would occur, reveal that this exposure can maintain a developmentally prior perceptual ability (Pascalis et al. 2005). Similarly, studies that provide infants with brief exposure, even for only a few minutes and at an age beyond which perceptual narrowing has occurred, reveal that this exposure can reinstate a developmentally prior perceptual ability (Fair et al. 2012). Whether prolonged or brief, however, exposure must occur at key developmental junctures that correspond to infants' sensitive periods (Doupe & Kuhl 1999, Werker & Hensch 2015).

This work highlights human infants' plasticity at the behavioral and neural levels. Yet experience is not the only factor that guides perceptual narrowing; the effects of experience are often tempered by infants' maturational status. Evidence for an interaction between experience and maturation comes from comparisons between full-term and preterm infants. Because preterm infants are born early, they are exposed to language and faces (outside the womb) earlier than are full-term infants of the same maturational age. Comparisons between full-term and preterm infants have been instrumental in disentangling the relative contributions of experience and maturation across several perceptual domains, and collectively, these comparisons paint a nuanced picture. Infants' tuning of some perceptual capacities depends upon their maturational status [e.g., rhythmic and phonemic perception (Peña et al. 2010, 2012), luminance contrast (Bosworth & Dobkins 2009)], but tuning of other categories emerges primarily in response to postnatal experience [e.g., phonotactic acquisition (Gonzalez-Gomez & Nazzi 2012), chromatic contrast (Bosworth & Dobkins 2009)]. These findings help explain how subtle differences in developmental timing may amplify later differences.

Although tuning processes are ubiquitous throughout the animal kingdom (Lorenz 1937), the degree of tuning in humans far surpasses that observed in other species (Zangenehpour et al. 2009). Ultimately, perceptual tuning is adaptive, ensuring that human infants increasingly direct their attention toward the signals of our species, especially those who serve as their communicative and pedagogical partners (Vouloumanos & Waxman 2014, Vouloumanos et al. 2009).

However, the evidence for perceptual tuning cannot, on its own, reveal how language becomes linked to cognition. Addressing this question requires us to move beyond a focus on perception alone to consider how infants come to link the language they hear with the objects and events they observe in the world.

Beyond Perception: Tuning a Link Between Language and Cognition

Crucially, acquiring a human language and conceptual system requires more than tuning to the signals of its speakers. The power of human language derives from its links to cognition. In a recent line of work, researchers sought to identify how early infants begin to link language and cognition and to trace how this link unfolds in the first months of life. The results reveal that, by 3 months of age, infants not only prefer to listen to the communicative signals of our species, but have also established a principled and surprisingly early link between these signals and the fundamental cognitive process of categorization. Using the categorization task described above (see the section titled Words as Invitations to Form Categories), Ferry et al. (2010) discovered that, for infants as young as 3 months of age, listening to language (but not tone sequences) boosts object categorization.

Moreover, in the first months of life, language is not the only signal that exerts this advantageous cognitive effect. For infants at 3 and 4 months of age, vocalizations of nonhuman primates (in this case, those of the blue-eyed Madagascar lemur, *Eulemur macaco flavifrons*) also facilitate object categorization (Ferry et al. 2013). Unlike the link to human language, infants' early link between nonhuman primate vocalizations and cognition is short-lived; by 6 months of age, infants have tuned the link specifically to language (Ferry et al. 2013). The developmental timing of this tuning roughly corresponds to infants' brain responses to human and nonhuman vocalizations in their first months of life (Shultz et al. 2014).

Together, these findings provide several developmental insights. First, a link between human vocalizations and object categorization, evident at 3 months of age, derives from a broader template that initially encompasses vocalizations of both humans and nonhuman primates. Second, this initially broad template cannot be derived solely on the basis of experience. Despite the fact that, by 3 months of age, infants have had rich exposure to language but virtually no exposure to lemur vocalizations, these vocalizations confer the same cognitive advantage. Third, the cognitive advantage of listening to lemur vocalizations cannot be attributed to low-level acoustic features such as signal complexity: Infants listening to backward speech [the same speech segment used by Ferry et al. (2010) but played backward] fail to form object categories at any age. This outcome converges with the neural evidence that forward speech is processed differently than backward speech in the infant brain from birth (Dehaene-Lambertz et al. 2002). Fourth, by 6 months of age, infants tune this initially broad link specifically to human vocalizations. In effect, then, they home in on precisely those signals (human language) that will ultimately constitute the foundations of meaning.

Finally, although we now know that language boosts cognition throughout infants' first year, the mechanism underlying the language–cognition link at 3 and 4 months of age is still unclear. Because infants at 3 and 4 months of age are unable to parse words from the sentences in which they are embedded (Bortfeld et al. 2005, Jusczyk & Aslin 1995, Seidl et al. 2015), it is unlikely that, at this age, words serve as invitations to form categories. What is more likely is that listening to language (and perhaps especially to IDS) engenders in young infants a kind of heightened arousal or attention to their surroundings, and that this promotes object categorization. This possibility converges well with cross-species ethological evidence indicating that certain privileged signals engage animals' attention (Owren et al. 2011, Vergne & Mathevon 2008). Perhaps, in very young infants, listening to language (like eye gaze) promotes learning by increasing arousal and attention, rather than by launching an explicit search for meaning. Before long, however, language will take off on its own unique developmental trajectory—one that allows infants to discover and generate precise kinds of meanings, in potentially infinite combinations, in a way that no other species can.

The evidence that infants have begun to link language and cognition in their first 6 months raises a new question: How do infants identify which signals in their environment to link to cognition in the first place?

Tuning the Language–Cognition Link: Developmental Mechanisms

Two recent series of studies have addressed this question, investigating the mechanisms by which infants establish and tune their precocious language–cognition link. Both series take as their methodological starting point the evidence concerning the influence of language and nonlinguistic signals (e.g., lemur vocalizations, backward speech, tone sequences) on infant object categorization (Balaban & Waxman 1997; Ferry et al. 2010, 2013; Fulkerson & Waxman 2007). Together, these studies suggest that there may be two distinct routes for tuning the language–cognition link in infants' first 6 months, one for tuning the initially privileged signals (human and nonhuman primate vocalizations) and another for establishing new links for signals that fall outside infants' initial template (tone sequences).

Tuning initially privileged signals: the effect of exposure.
Using an exposure paradigm inspired by those pioneered in the perceptual tuning literature, Perszyk & Waxman (2016) systematically manipulated infants' exposure to lemur vocalizations. Infants in the exposure condition listened to 2 minutes of lemur vocalizations, embedded in a soundtrack of instrumental music. Immediately after this period of passive exposure, infants were engaged in the categorization task. Merely exposing 6- and 7-month-olds to lemur vocalizations permitted them to reinstate the developmentally prior link between this signal and object categorization. Moreover, this was more than a fleeting phenomenon. Another group of infants listened to lemur vocalizations for 6 weeks, beginning at 4 months of age and lasting until they were 6 months of age. At 6 months, infants were brought into the lab to participate in the categorization task. Although at the time of their

lab visit these infants had not heard a lemur vocalization for days, they nonetheless successfully formed object categories. This reveals that merely exposing infants to lemur vocalizations—an initially privileged signal—has a robust and long-lasting effect. In contrast, exposing infants to backward speech had no effect on their success in the categorization task. This reveals that passive exposure to signals outside infants' initial template does not permit them to forge a new link to cognition.

Moreover, the effect of exposure appears to be constrained by infants' maturational status. To disentangle the effects of infants' experience listening to language and their maturational status, Perszyk et al. (2017) compared full-term and preterm infants' responses on the object categorization task while listening to language. Preterm infants showed precisely the same patterns as their full-term counterparts when they were matched for maturational age. This outcome converges with evidence from studies of speech perception (Peña et al. 2010, 2012), but takes the field one step further: Exposure is gated by maturation not only as infants tune to the signals of their language, but also as they link those signals to cognition.

These results illustrate that infants' experience with the signals in their ambient environment, together with their maturational state, guides them as they forge increasingly precise links between the sounds they hear and the core cognitive processes that will ultimately serve as foundations of meaning. Importantly, the effect of exposure is evident only for the signals in infants' earliest template: human and nonhuman primate vocalizations. Exposure alone does not permit infants to create, de novo, a link between cognition and an otherwise inert signal (e.g., backward speech or tone sequences).

This evidence also raises a new question. A hallmark of human communication is our remarkably flexible capacity to infuse otherwise nonlinguistic signals, like tone sequences (e.g., Morse code) and smoke signals, with communicative status. Does this flexible appropriation of new signals rest upon a fully developed system of language, or is it available to infants?

Establishing new links to cognition: the effect of social-communicative exchanges. There is now converging evidence that infants as young as 6 months of age can, in fact, forge a new link between a nonlinguistic signal and cognition, but only if the signal is embedded within a rich social-communicative exchange (Ferguson & Lew-Williams 2016, Ferguson & Waxman 2016b). For example, Ferguson & Waxman's (2016b) design takes as its starting point infants' object categorization while listening to tone sequences. Recall that tone sequences (like backward speech) consistently fail to promote object categorization throughout the first year (Balaban & Waxman 1997, Ferry et al. 2010, Fulkerson & Waxman 2007). Ferguson & Waxman systematically manipulated 6-month-old infants' exposure to tone sequences. By design, and in sharp contrast to the passive exposure phase in Perszyk & Waxman's (2016) paradigm, in this case the exposure phase was decidedly social and communicative. Before participating in the categorization task, infants watched a videotaped dialogue between two young women, one speaking in English and the other responding by beeping in sine-wave tone sequences (which were dubbed). Simply observing this 2-minute dialogue between the speaker and the beeper had a remarkable effect: 6-month-olds now successfully formed object categories while listening to tone sequences. Yet when the very same tone sequences were uncoupled from the social-communicative exchange, infants failed to form categories in the subsequent categorization task. Thus, infants as young as 6 months of age are sufficiently flexible to link an otherwise arbitrary signal to cognition, but they make this link only if the arbitrary signal is embedded within a rich social-communicative interchange. This outcome, which has now been documented for both object categorization and abstract rule learning (Ferguson & Lew-Williams 2016), converges with evidence for the power of communicative ostensive cues on infant cognition (see also Csibra & Gergely 2009).

Mechanisms of tuning the language–cognition link: two distinct routes. Considered together, these results suggest there are (at least) two routes by which young infants forge a connection between communicative signals and core cognitive capacities like categorization and abstract rule learning. For signals that are part of infants' initial template (e.g., human and nonhuman primate vocalizations), mere exposure is sufficient to either maintain or reinstate a developmentally prior link to cognition (Perszyk & Waxman 2016). In contrast, for signals that fall outside infants' initial template (e.g., tone sequences, backward speech), a different route is required: Infants link otherwise arbitrary signals to cognition only if they are embedded within a rich social-communicative interchange (Ferguson & Lew-Williams 2016, Ferguson & Waxman 2016b, May & Werker 2014, Namy & Waxman 1998, Woodward & Hoyne 1999).

FUTURE DIRECTIONS AND CONCLUSIONS

In this article, we have reviewed the developmental origins and unfolding of a link between language and infants' core cognitive capacities. A goal for future work will be to broaden the empirical and theoretical base and to bring the behavioral evidence into closer alignment with new evidence from evolutionary theory and developmental neuroscience. For example, how do infants' neural responses to the signals that are included in their initially broad template differ from those that are outside this initial template? How do infants' neural responses to these signals change as infants increasingly tune this link?

Bridging Infant Cognition and Evolutionary Theory

The possibility that infants have at their disposal two distinct routes for linking communicative signals and core cognitive capacities brings to mind recent neuroscientific claims that there are dual pathways underlying various communication systems. For example, Owren et al. (2011) and Ackermann et al. (2014) propose a dual pathway model for human acoustic communication, arguing that speech production engages two separate neuroanatomic channels. One channel, shared among primates, reflects subcortical mechanisms that support affective vocalizations (e.g., for nonhumans, warning or mating calls; for humans, affective intonation). A second channel, specific to humans, reflects cortical mechanisms that support articulate speech. Similarly, Senju & Johnson (2009) propose a dual pathway model of human eye gaze communication. They argue that a subcortical route, which may have served the evolutionary function of signaling social rank (Gobel et al. 2015), is augmented in humans by a more elaborate cortical route—a social brain network—which may serve the more precise, human-specific function of identifying communicative or pedagogical intent (Senju & Csibra 2008, Senju & Johnson 2009).

Although it is possible that these dual pathway models are related to the developmental evidence we have described in this review, this is, at best, speculative. Perhaps infants' initially broad link between cognition and communicative signals—including both human and nonhuman primate vocalizations—corresponds to an ancestral route that confers its cognitive advantage via primate-general affective and attentional neural systems. Perhaps infants' capacity to link new signals, including tone sequences, by embedding them within social-communicative dialogues corresponds to a human-specific route. This human-specific route may be built upon the ancestral route but may confer its cognitive advantage via more recently evolved neural systems. This possibility is related to documented parallels between human evolution and development for cortical expansion (Hill et al. 2010).

Bridging Infant Cognition and Developmental Neuroscience

Infants' neural responses to both language and objects have received considerable attention (e.g., Csibra et al. 2000; Grossmann et al. 2009; Kaufman et al. 2003, 2005; Kuhl & Rivera-Gaxiola 2008; Quinn et al. 2006; Southgate et al. 2008). More recently, developmental neuroscience has sought to identify neural signatures underlying the language–cognition interface in infants. Although this work is itself in its infancy, there are hints that infants' neural responses converge with the behavioral evidence documenting the effects of naming on cognition. For example, by 9–12 months of age, infants' neural responses to objects vary systematically as a function of whether they are named correctly (Friedrich & Friederici 2010, Parise & Csibra 2012). Gliga et al. (2009) provide more direct neural evidence for a link between naming and object representation: At 12 months of age, infants' neural responses to objects vary as a function of whether they know a name for the objects—even when they are viewing those objects in the absence of their names. This outcome precisely mirrors the behavioral evidence that naming objects (presented consistently during familiarization) influences infants' attention to new and as-yet unnamed objects (presented in silence during the test) (Waxman & Markow 1995).

Because the earliest neural evidence concerning the language–cognition link currently comes from infants at 9 months of age, this work cannot yet shed light on the neural processes underlying infants' earliest language–cognition links or how they unfold in the first 6 months. By harnessing the now considerable behavioral evidence to state-of-the-art techniques in developmental neuroscience, researchers may illuminate how infants' brain systems interact in their first months and how they are sculpted by experience. In our view, the most exciting frontiers will be those that bring the rich theoretical framework on speech processing—thus far proposed for adults (for review, see Giraud & Poeppel 2012)—to investigations of infant development. If the past is a prologue to the future, we suspect that focusing on cascading neural oscillatory activity (Goswami 2011, 2016) will be an ideal avenue for identifying the developmental origins and unfolding of the links between language and cognition in young infants.

SUMMARY

In this article, we have reviewed evidence that illuminates the developmental origins of infants' precocious language–cognition link, how it unfolds, and how it advances infants beyond their initial perceptual and conceptual capacities. The evidence reveals that even before infants can recognize the sound of their own names, links between language and cognition are in place. Infants' earliest link, evident by 3 months of age (Ferry et al. 2010), is part of a broader initial template that includes both human and nonhuman primate vocalizations. This indicates that human development is shaped not only by experience, but also by capacities inherent in the infant: Although 3-month-olds have acquired considerable exposure to human language and virtually no exposure to nonhuman primate vocalizations, both signals confer the same cognitive advantage. At 6 months of age, when infants have tuned this link specifically to human vocalizations (Ferry et al. 2013), they nonetheless remain sensitive to experience: Passive exposure to nonhuman primate vocalizations permits infants to maintain or reinstate a link between this signal and cognition (Perszyk & Waxman 2016). However, for signals that fall outside of infants' initial template (backward speech, tone sequences), passive exposure alone is insufficient to create a new link to cognition (Ferguson & Waxman 2016b, Perszyk & Waxman 2016). Instead, signals like these must be embedded within a social-communicative context (Ferguson & Waxman 2016b). Thus, there appear to be at least two routes by which infants can link signals to cognition in their first year of life. This combined evidence illustrates the joint contributions of infants' innate capacities and their sensitivity to experience, highlighting how a precocious link between language and cognition advances infants beyond their initial perceptual and conceptual capacities.

This early emerging link between language and cognition also makes possible a suite of conceptual and representational capacities that distinguish human cognition from that of our evolutionary relatives. In infants' first year, language takes the lead among the other ostensive cues, enabling infants to learn far more than they could from observation alone. Language also enables infants to weave together representations from otherwise distinct systems of knowledge. These links between language and cognition are the gateway to advancing core systems of knowledge and establishing the higher-order, abstract representations that are the signature of human cognition (Carey 2009, Spelke & Kinzler 2007).

Perhaps most importantly from a developmental vantage point, we have argued that the language–cognition link is not a steady state. The information an infant gleans from listening to language will vary as a function of their developmental status and the precision of their language–cognition link at that time. In their first months, simply listening to language boosts cognition (Csibra & Gergely 2009, Ferry et al. 2010). A few months later, the consequences of listening to language become considerably more nuanced and more powerful as infants discover increasingly precise links between language and concepts. A constellation of factors that are unique to human development—infants' prolonged period of dependency, exquisite sensitivity to experience, and powerful learning strategies—collectively spark a cascade of developmental change whose ultimate result is the acquisition of language and its unparalleled interface with cognition.

DISCLOSURE STATEMENT

The authors are not aware of any affiliations, memberships, funding, or financial holdings that might be perceived as affecting the objectivity of this review.

LITERATURE CITED

Ackermann H, Hage SR, Ziegler W. 2014. Brain mechanisms of acoustic communication in humans and nonhuman primates: an evolutionary perspective. *Behav. Brain Sci.* 37:529–604

Aguiar A, Baillargeon R. 1999. 2.5-month-old infants' reasoning about when objects should and should not be occluded. *Cogn. Psychol.* 39:116–57

Althaus N, Plunkett K. 2016. Categorization in infancy: Labeling induces a persisting focus on commonalities. *Dev. Sci.* 19(5):770–80

Aslin RN. 2007. What's in a look? *Dev. Sci.* 10(1):48–53

Baillargeon R, Scott RM, Bian L. 2016. Psychological reasoning in infancy. *Annu. Rev. Psychol.* 67:159–86

Balaban MT, Waxman SR. 1997. Do words facilitate object categorization in 9-month-old infants? *J. Exp. Child Psychol.* 64:3–26

Bar-Haim Y, Ziv T, Lamy D, Hodes RM. 2006. Nature and nurture in own-race face processing. *Psychol. Sci.* 17(2):159–63

Bergelson E, Swingley D. 2012. At 6–9 months, human infants know the meanings of many common nouns. *PNAS* 109(9):3253–58

Bortfeld H, Morgan JL, Golinkoff RM, Rathbun K. 2005. Mommy and me: Familiar names help launch babies into speech-stream segmentation. *Psychol. Sci.* 16(4):298–304

Bosworth RG, Dobkins KR. 2009. Chromatic and luminance contrast sensitivity in fullterm and preterm infants. *J. Vis.* 9(13):1–16

Brown R. 1958. *Words and Things: An Introduction to Language*. Glencoe, IL: Free Press

Bruderer AG, Danielson DK, Kandhadai P, Werker JF. 2015. Sensorimotor influences on speech perception in infancy. *PNAS* 112(44):13531–36

Carey S. 2009. *The Origin of Concepts*. Oxford, UK: Oxford Univ. Press

Chen ML, Waxman SR. 2013. "Shall we blick?" Novel words highlight actors' underlying intentions for 14-month-old infants. *Dev. Psychol.* 49(3):426–31

Chomsky N. 1986. *Knowledge of Language: Its Nature, Origin, and Use.* Santa Barbara, CA: Greenwood Publ. Group

Colombo J. 2002. Infant attention grows up: the emergence of a developmental cognitive neuroscience perspective. *Curr. Dir. Psychol. Sci.* 11(6):196–200

Condry KF, Spelke ES. 2008. The development of language and abstract concepts: the case of natural number. *J. Exp. Psychol. Gen.* 137(1):22–38

Csibra G, Davis G, Spratling MW, Johnson MH. 2000. Gamma oscillations and object processing in the infant brain. *Science* 290:1582–85

Csibra G, Gergely G. 2009. Natural pedagogy. *Trends Cogn. Sci.* 13(4):148–53

Csibra G, Shamsudheen R. 2015. Nonverbal generics: human infants interpret objects as symbols of object kinds. *Annu. Rev. Psychol.* 66:689–710

Dehaene-Lambertz G, Dehaene S, Hertz-Pannier L. 2002. Functional neuroimaging of speech perception in infants. *Science* 298(5600):2013–15

DeSilva J, Lesnik J. 2006. Chimpanzee neonatal brain size: implications for brain growth in *Homo erectus*. *J. Hum. Evol.* 51(2):207–12

Dewar K, Xu F. 2007. Do 9-month-old infants expect distinct words to refer to kinds? *Dev. Psychol.* 43(5):1227–38

Doupe AJ, Kuhl PK. 1999. Birdsong and human speech: common themes and mechanisms. *Annu. Rev. Neurosci.* 22:567–631

Fair J, Flom R, Jones J, Martin J. 2012. Perceptual learning: 12-month-olds' discrimination of monkey faces. *Child Dev.* 83(6):1996–2006

Feigenson L, Dehaene S, Spelke E. 2004. Core systems of number. *Trends Cogn. Sci.* 8(7):307–14

Ferguson B, Havy M, Waxman SR. 2015. The precision of 12-month-old infants' link between language and categorization predicts vocabulary size at 12 and 18 months. *Front. Psychol.* 6:1319

Ferguson B, Lew-Williams C. 2016. Communicative signals promote abstract rule learning by 7-month-old infants. *Sci. Rep.* 6:25434

Ferguson B, Waxman SR. 2016a. Linking language and categorization in infancy. *J. Child Lang.* 44(3):527–52

Ferguson B, Waxman SR. 2016b. What the [beep]? Six-month-olds link novel communicative signals to meaning. *Cognition* 146:185–89

Ferry AL, Hespos SJ, Waxman SR. 2010. Categorization in 3- and 4-month-old infants: an advantage of words over tones. *Child Dev.* 81(2):472–79

Ferry AL, Hespos SJ, Waxman SR. 2013. Nonhuman primate vocalizations support categorization in very young human infants. *PNAS* 110(38):15231–35

Fodor JA. 1975. *The Language of Thought.* Cambridge, MA: Harvard Univ. Press

Friedrich M, Friederici AD. 2010. Maturing brain mechanisms and developing behavioral language skills. *Brain Lang.* 114(2):66–71

Friendly RH, Rendall D, Trainor LJ. 2013a. Learning to differentiate individuals by their voices: infants' individuation of native- and foreign-species voices. *Dev. Psychobiol.* 56(2):228–37

Friendly RH, Rendall D, Trainor LJ. 2013b. Plasticity after perceptual narrowing for voice perception: reinstating the ability to discriminate monkeys by their voices at 12 months of age. *Front. Psychol.* 4:718

Fulkerson AL, Waxman SR. 2007. Words (but not tones) facilitate object categorization: evidence from 6- and 12-month-olds. *Cognition* 105(1):218–28

Gelman SA. 2004. Psychological essentialism in children. *Trends Cogn. Sci.* 8(9):404–9

Gergely G, Bekkering H, Király I. 2002. Developmental psychology: rational imitation in preverbal infants. *Nature* 415(6873):755–56

Giraud A-L, Poeppel D. 2012. Cortical oscillations and speech processing: emerging computational principles and operations. *Nat. Neurosci.* 15(4):511–17

Gleitman H, Gross J, Reisberg D. 2011. *Psychology.* New York: W.W. Norton. 8th ed.

Gleitman L, Papafragou A. 2005. Language and thought. In *Cambridge Handbook of Thinking and Reasoning,* Vol. 9, ed. K Holyoak, R Morrison, pp. 633–61. Cambridge, UK: Cambridge Univ. Press

Gleitman LR. 1990. The structural sources of verb meanings. *Lang. Acquis.* 1(1):3–55

Gleitman LR, Cassidy K, Nappa R, Papafragou A, Trueswell JC. 2005. Hard words. *Lang. Learn. Dev.* 1(1):23–64

Gliga T, Volein A, Csibra G. 2009. Verbal labels modulate perceptual object processing in 1-year-old infants. *J. Cogn. Neurosci.* 22(12):2781–89

Gobel MS, Kim HS, Richardson DC. 2015. The dual function of social gaze. *Cognition* 136:359–64

Goldin-Meadow S. 2017. What the hands can tell us about language emergence. *Psychon. Bull. Rev.* 24(1):213–18

Golinkoff RM, Hirsh-Pasek K, Cauley KM, Gordon L. 1987. The eyes have it: lexical and syntactic comprehension in a new paradigm. *J. Child Lang.* 14(1):23–45

Gonzalez-Gomez N, Nazzi T. 2012. Phonotactic acquisition in healthy preterm infants. *Dev. Sci.* 15(6):885–94

Goswami U. 2011. A temporal sampling framework for developmental dyslexia. *Trends Cogn. Sci.* 15(1):3–10

Goswami U. 2016. Educational neuroscience: neural structure-mapping and the promise of oscillations. *Curr. Opin. Behav. Sci.* 10:89–96

Grossmann T, Gliga T, Johnson MH, Mareschal D. 2009. The neural basis of perceptual category learning in human infants. *J. Cogn. Neurosci.* 21(12):2276–86

Hannon EE, Trehub SE. 2005. Tuning in to musical rhythms: Infants learn more readily than adults. *PNAS* 102(35):12639–43

Heron-Delaney M, Anzures G, Herbert JS, Quinn PC, Slater AM, et al. 2011. Perceptual training prevents the emergence of the other race effect during infancy. *PLOS ONE* 6(5):1–5

Hill J, Inder T, Neil J, Dierker D, Harwell J, Van Essen D. 2010. Similar patterns of cortical expansion during human development and evolution. *PNAS* 107(29):13135–40

Jusczyk PW, Aslin RN. 1995. Infants' detection of the sound patterns of words in fluent speech. *Cogn. Psychol.* 29:1–23

Kaufman J, Csibra G, Johnson MH. 2003. Representing occluded objects in the human infant brain. *Proc. R. Soc. Lond. B.* 270:S140–43

Kaufman J, Csibra G, Johnson MH. 2005. Oscillatory activity in the infant brain reflects object maintenance. *PNAS* 102(42):15271–74

Kelly DJ, Quinn PC, Slater AM, Lee K, Ge L, Pascalis O. 2007. The other-race effect develops during infancy: evidence of perceptual narrowing. *Psychol. Sci.* 18(12):1084–89

Kelly DJ, Quinn PC, Slater AM, Lee K, Gibson A, et al. 2005. Three-month-olds, but not newborns, prefer own-race faces. *Dev. Sci.* 8(6):F31–36

Klibanoff RS, Waxman SR. 2000. Basic level object categories support the acquisition of novel adjectives: evidence from preschool-aged children. *Child Dev.* 71(3):649–59

Kovács ÁM, Téglás EA, Gergely G, Csibra G. 2017. Seeing behind the surface: Communicative demonstration boosts category disambiguation in 12-month-olds. *Dev. Sci.* In press. **https://doi.org/10.1111/desc.12485**

Kraus N, Slater J. 2016. Beyond words: how humans communicate through sound. *Annu. Rev. Psychol.* 67:83–103

Kuhl P, Rivera-Gaxiola M. 2008. Neural substrates of language acquisition. *Annu. Rev. Neurosci.* 31:511–34

Kuhl PK. 2007. Is speech learning "gated" by the social brain? *Dev. Sci.* 10(1):110–20

Kuzawa C, Bragg J. 2012. Plasticity in human life history strategy. *Curr. Anthropol.* 53(6):S369–82

Lee SA, Shusterman A, Spelke ES. 2006. Reorientation and landmark-guided search by young children: evidence for two systems. *Psychol. Sci.* 17(7):577–82

Lewkowicz DJ, Ghazanfar AA. 2009. The emergence of multisensory systems through perceptual narrowing. *Trends Cogn. Sci.* 13(11):470–78

Lorenz K. 1937. On the formation of the concept of instinct. *Nat. Sci.* 25:289–300

Mareschal D, Quinn PC. 2001. Categorization in infancy. *Trends Cogn. Sci.* 5(10):443–50

Martin A, Onishi KH, Vouloumanos A. 2012. Understanding the abstract role of speech in communication at 12 months. *Cognition* 123:50–60

Maurer D, Werker JF. 2014. Perceptual narrowing during infancy: a comparison of language and faces. *Dev. Psychobiol.* 56(2):154–78

May L, Werker JF. 2014. Can a click be a word? Infants' learning of non-native words. *Infancy* 19(3):281–300

Maye J, Werker JF, Gerken LA. 2002. Infant sensitivity to distributional information can affect phonetic discrimination. *Cognition* 82:B101–11

Medin D, Ortony A. 1989. Psychological essentialism. In *Similarity and Analogical Reasoning*, ed. S Vosniadou, A Ortony, pp. 179–95. Cambridge, UK: Cambridge Univ. Press

Miller GA. 1990. The place of language in a scientific psychology. *Psychol. Sci.* 1(1):7–14

Mintz TH, Gleitman LR. 2002. Adjectives really do modify nouns: the incremental and restricted nature of early adjective acquisition. *Cognition* 84(3):267–93

Moll H, Tomasello M. 2004. 12- and 18-month-old infants follow gaze to spaces behind barriers. *Dev. Sci.* 7(1):1–9

Namy LL, Waxman SR. 1998. Words and gestures: infants' interpretations of different forms of symbolic reference. *Child Dev.* 69(2):295–308

Owren MJ, Amoss RT, Rendall D. 2011. Two organizing principles of vocal production: implications for nonhuman and human primates. *Am. J. Primatol.* 73(6):530–44

Parise E, Csibra G. 2012. Electrophysiological evidence for the understanding of maternal speech by 9-month-old infants. *Psychol. Sci.* 23(7):728–33

Pascalis O, Scott LS, Kelly DJ, Shannon RW, Nicholson E, et al. 2005. Plasticity of face processing in infancy. *PNAS* 102(14):5297–300

Peña M, Pittaluga E, Mehler J. 2010. Language acquisition in premature and full-term infants. *PNAS* 107(8):3823–28

Peña M, Werker JF, Dehaene-Lambertz G. 2012. Earlier speech exposure does not accelerate speech acquisition. *J. Neurosci.* 32(33):11159–63

Perszyk DR, Ferguson B, Waxman SR. 2017. Maturation constrains the effect of exposure in linking language and thought: evidence from healthy preterm infants. *Dev. Sci.* In press. **https://doi.org/10.1111/desc.12522**

Perszyk DR, Waxman SR. 2016. Listening to the calls of the wild: the role of experience in linking language and cognition in young infants. *Cognition* 153:175–81

Pinker S. 1994. *The Language Instinct*. New York: Harper Collins

Pyers JE, Shusterman A, Senghas A, Spelke ES, Emmorey K. 2010. Evidence from an emerging sign language reveals that language supports spatial cognition. *PNAS* 107(27):12116–20

Quinn PC, Westerlund A, Nelson CA. 2006. Neural markers of categorization in 6-month-old infants. *Psychol. Sci.* 17(1):59–66

Quinn PC, Yahr J, Kuhn A, Slater AM, Pascalis O. 2002. Representation of the gender of human faces by infants: a preference for female. *Perception* 31(9):1109–21

Schieffelin B, Ochs E. 1986. Language socialization. *Annu. Rev. Anthropol.* 15:163–91

Scott LS, Pascalis O, Nelson CA. 2007. A domain-general theory of the development of perceptual discrimination. *Curr. Dir. Psychol. Sci.* 16(4):197–201

Seidl A, Tincoff R, Baker C, Cristia A. 2015. Why the body comes first: effects of experimenter touch on infants' word finding. *Dev. Sci.* 18(1):155–64

Senju A, Csibra G. 2008. Gaze following in human infants depends on communicative signals. *Curr. Biol.* 18:668–71

Senju A, Csibra G, Johnson MH. 2008. Understanding the referential nature of looking: infants' preference for object-directed gaze. *Cognition* 108(2):303–19

Senju A, Johnson MH. 2009. The eye contact effect: mechanisms and development. *Trends Cogn. Sci.* 13(3):127–34

Shultz S, Vouloumanos A, Bennett RH, Pelphrey K. 2014. Neural specialization for speech in the first months of life. *Dev. Sci.* 17(5):766–74

Smith JD, Berg ME, Cook RG, Murphy MS, Crossley MJ, et al. 2012. Implicit and explicit categorization: a tale of four species. *Neurosci. Biobehav. Rev.* 36(10):2355–69

Southgate V, Csibra G, Kaufman J, Johnson MH. 2008. Distinct processing of objects and faces in the infant brain. *J. Cogn. Neurosci.* 20:741–49

Spaepen E, Coppola M, Spelke ES, Carey SE, Goldin-Meadow S. 2011. Number without a language model. *PNAS* 108(8):3163–68

Spelke ES. 1990. Principles of object perception. *Cogn. Sci.* 14:29–56

Spelke ES. 2017. Core knowledge, language, and number. *Lang. Learn. Dev.* 13(2):147–70

Spelke ES, Kinzler KD. 2007. Core knowledge. *Dev. Sci.* 10(1):89–96

Swingley D. 2012. Cognitive development in language acquisition. *Lang. Learn. Dev.* 8:1–3

Tincoff R, Jusczyk PW. 2012. Six-month-olds comprehend words that refer to parts of the body. *Infancy* 17(4):432–44

Vergne AL, Mathevon N. 2008. Crocodile egg sounds signal hatching time. *Curr. Biol.* 18(12):513–14

Vouloumanos A, Druhen MJ, Hauser MD, Huizink AT. 2009. Five-month-old infants' identification of the sources of vocalizations. *PNAS* 106(44):18867–72

Vouloumanos A, Hauser MD, Werker JF, Martin A. 2010. The tuning of human neonates' preference for speech. *Child Dev.* 81(2):517–27

Vouloumanos A, Martin A, Onishi KH. 2014. Do 6-month-olds understand that speech can communicate? *Dev. Sci.* 17(6):872–79

Vouloumanos A, Onishi KH, Pogue A. 2012. Twelve-month-old infants recognize that speech can communicate unobservable intentions. *PNAS* 109(32):12933–37

Vouloumanos A, Waxman SR. 2014. Listen up! Speech is for thinking during infancy. *Trends Cogn. Sci.* 18(12):642–46

Waxman SR. 1999. Specifying the scope of 13-month-olds' expectations for novel words. *Cognition* 70(3):B35–50

Waxman SR, Braun I. 2005. Consistent (but not variable) names as invitations to form object categories: new evidence from 12-month-old infants. *Cognition* 95(3):B59–68

Waxman SR, Gelman SA. 2009. Early word-learning entails reference, not merely associations. *Trends Cogn. Sci.* 13(6):258–63

Waxman SR, Lidz JL. 2006. Early word learning. In *Handbook of Child Psychology*, Vol. 2, ed. D Kuhn, R Siegler, pp. 299–335. Hoboken, NJ: Wiley. 6th ed.

Waxman SR, Markow DB. 1995. Words as invitations to form categories: evidence from 12- to 13-month-old infants. *Cogn. Psychol.* 29(3):257–302

Werker JF, Hensch TK. 2015. Critical periods in speech perception: new directions. *Annu. Rev. Psychol.* 66:173–96

Werker JF, Tees RC. 1984. Cross-language speech perception: evidence for perceptual reorganization during the first year of life. *Infant Behav. Dev.* 7:49–63

Whorf BL. 1956. *Language, Thought and Reality*. Cambridge, MA: MIT Press

Woodward AL, Hoyne KL. 1999. Infants' learning about words and sounds in relation to objects. *Child Dev.* 70(1):65–77

Wu R, Tummeltshammer KS, Gliga T, Kirkham NZ. 2014. Ostensive signals support learning from novel attention cues during infancy. *Front. Psychol.* 5:251

Xu F. 2002. The role of language in acquiring object kind concepts in infancy. *Cognition* 85(3):223–50

Xu F. 2007. Sortal concepts, object individuation, and language. *Trends Cogn. Sci.* 11(9):400–6

Yin J, Csibra G. 2015. Concept-based word learning in human infants. *Psychol. Sci.* 26(8):1316–24

Yoon JMD, Johnson MH, Csibra G. 2008. Communication-induced memory biases in preverbal infants. *PNAS* 105(36):13690–95

Zangenehpour S, Ghazanfar AA, Lewkowicz DJ, Zatorre RJ. 2009. Heterochrony and cross-species intersensory matching by infant vervet monkeys. *PLOS ONE* 4(1):e4302

Cognitive Foundations of Learning from Testimony

Paul L. Harris,[1] Melissa A. Koenig,[2]
Kathleen H. Corriveau,[3] and Vikram K. Jaswal[4]

[1]Graduate School of Education, Harvard University, Cambridge, Massachusetts 02138;
email: Paul_Harris@gse.harvard.edu

[2]Institute of Child Development, University of Minnesota, Minneapolis, Minnesota 55436;
email: mkoenig@umn.edu

[3]School of Education, Boston University, Boston, Massachusetts 02215; email: kcorriv@bu.edu

[4]Department of Psychology, University of Virginia, Charlottesville, Virginia 22904;
email: jaswal@virginia.edu

Annu. Rev. Psychol. 2018. 69:251–73

First published as a Review in Advance on August 9, 2017

The *Annual Review of Psychology* is online at
psych.annualreviews.org

https://doi.org/10.1146/annurev-psych-122216-011710

Keywords

testimony, trust, informants, appraisal, counterintuitive, unobservable

Abstract

Humans acquire much of their knowledge from the testimony of other people. An understanding of the way that information can be conveyed via gesture and vocalization is present in infancy. Thus, infants seek information from well-informed interlocutors, supply information to the ignorant, and make sense of communicative acts that they observe from a third-party perspective. This basic understanding is refined in the course of development. As they age, children's reasoning about testimony increasingly reflects an ability not just to detect imperfect or inaccurate claims but also to assess what inferences may or may not be drawn about informants given their particular situation. Children also attend to the broader characteristics of particular informants—their group membership, personality characteristics, and agreement or disagreement with other potential informants. When presented with unexpected or counterintuitive testimony, children are prone to set aside their own prior convictions, but they may sometimes defer to informants for inherently social reasons.

Contents

1. INTRODUCTION

> There is no species of reasoning more common, more useful, and even necessary to human life than that which is derived from testimony.
>
> —David Hume (1748, p. 119)

Any culture with access to a human language has access to human testimony, which stands alongside memory, perception, and inference as a primary and fundamental source of knowledge. The study of testimony raises a suite of conceptual, empirical, and normative questions about how knowledge is gained from testimony, especially in childhood. In this review, we first identify basic aspects of testimony: its scope and characteristic features, its limits, and the role of trust. Second, we underline the impact of testimony on cognitive development. Third, we analyze children's receptivity to testimony in both infancy and early childhood, arguing that infants possess a basic understanding of how testimony works and that preschoolers make a differentiated appraisal of their informants along several dimensions, some epistemic and some not. Fourth, we consider how children respond when testimony conflicts with what they observe or assume to be the case. Finally, we highlight promising directions for future research. Throughout this review, we recognize that the study of testimonial knowledge is an interdisciplinary endeavor and seek to connect the growing psychological literature with insights from other fields. At the same time, given the scope of recent research on testimony, we offer a selective rather than a comprehensive review.

1.1. What Is Testimony?

It is hard to overstate the amount of knowledge that children gain from others via testimony. Even apparently direct observation (e.g., seeing a Dalmatian dog, looking at a photograph of the planet Earth) has a hidden layer of testimonial input that we typically take for granted: Identifying the dog or the planet depends on our capacity to apply culturally acquired concepts (Gelman 2009, Harris & Koenig 2006). Moreover, the accumulation of cultural, scientific, and historical knowledge over time depends on the transmission of knowledge gained from testimony.

Philosophers traditionally characterize testimony as language-based exchanges that consist of "tellings generally" (Fricker 1995, p. 396) or "statements of someone's thoughts or belief" (Sosa 1991, p. 219). In recent reviews of the empirical literature, psychologists have generally followed this tradition, taking it as "uncontroversial that human beings often use language to make credible assertions and that listeners treat such testimony as reliable evidence for the truth of those assertions" (Harris & Koenig 2006, p. 505). This characterization of testimony includes religious and scientific claims, claims based on a speaker's first-hand experience, and claims deriving from a speaker's reflection or expertise.

All testimony requires some sort of medium—a means by which a speaker can relay a message to a listener. Although spoken statements are generally treated as the bread and butter of testimonial exchange, testimony extends well beyond spoken utterances. It includes written language (Robinson et al. 2013) as well as nonverbal communication (Harris & Lane 2014). Indeed, it can extend to conventional indicators such as maps and road signs (Corriveau & Harris 2015) and to commemorative artifacts such as tombstones and statues. It includes resources such as Wikipedia, where authorship is typically anonymous and collaborative, as well as legal cases, where the identity and credentials of a source are of paramount importance. In this review, we stay close to the standard usage of testimony by focusing primarily on verbal communication. Nevertheless, we probe the foundations of testimonial exchange by reviewing the preverbal communication patterns of infants, and we acknowledge that testimony can serve as an umbrella term to cover the various ways in which different media, verbal as well as nonverbal, serve to transmit knowledge and belief (Callanan 2006).

Consider Lackey's (2008) suggestion that problems in defining testimony are connected to at least two aspects of our concept of testimony. "On the one hand, we think of testimony as a source of knowledge or belief for hearers, regardless of a speaker's intention to be a source. On the other hand, we often think of testimony as involving the intention to communicate information to other people, regardless of the needs or interests of the hearers" (Lackey 2008, p. 19). To see the significance of the first point, consider the knowledge gained from overheard conversations or from posthumously published memoirs. Our conception of testimony includes such knowledge, i.e., knowledge that is gained from speakers who do not address a given individual or, indeed, anyone in particular. This is especially relevant for child listeners, who may not be directly addressed by speakers (Hart & Risley 1995) but who begin to interpret overheard exchanges from an early age (Akhtar et al. 2001, Harris & Lane 2014).

Lackey's second point bears on another central aspect of our concept of testimony. We allow that speakers may communicate their beliefs to others, regardless of whether any listener gains from it at all. For example, it seems natural to say that when religious believers talk to devoutly atheist listeners about their beliefs in miracles, their claims count as testimony (Harris & Koenig 2006). Similarly, when infants produce gestures or incomplete utterances and an interlocutor fails to understand them, these early acts of communication still count as testimony (Harris & Lane 2014, Liszkowski et al. 2008). By implication, our concept of testimony does not require the conjunction of a speaker's intention and a listener's epistemic gains, but allows for the disjunction of these features (Lackey 2008).

1.2. The Limits of Testimony

Are there limits to the types of knowledge that can be transmitted via testimony to others? Notions like testimony and testifying have long been associated with reports of experience, especially observational experience. In this way, testimony counts as an undisputed source of empirical knowledge. But what about other, less empirical, types of knowledge, such as knowledge of logic, math, morality, or God? Kant was sympathetic to testimony as a source of empirical knowledge, but rejected other categories of testimony, arguing that testimony always conveys some empirical content (as discussed in Gelfert 2006). Thus, we differentiate listeners who can only parrot what they have been told (e.g., regarding a mathematical theorem) from listeners who can understand for themselves, or demonstrate to others, how and why the theorem is true (Williams 1972). Similar concerns have been raised about testimony's capacity to directly transmit moral knowledge: We typically credit someone with knowing a moral principle under their own power not simply because they were told about it, but because they appreciate it for the right reasons (Jones 1999). Testimony might help us to recognize the full scope of a moral principle (Harris 2012) but might not help us see the significance of the principle itself. Such cases point to potential limits on the kinds of knowledge that can be gained from others via testimony.

1.3. Trust in Testimony

Much of the current research on learning from testimony treats testimony as a species of evidence, not unlike other impersonal forms of evidence on which knowledge and justified belief can be based. When testimony is understood in this way, decisions to accept it can be treated as probabilistic estimates about the truth of a claim based on the evidence, with speakers serving as more or less reliable vehicles of transmission (Shafto et al. 2012, Sobel & Kushnir 2013, Sperber et al. 2010). Although it is indeed true that testimony counts as evidence for learners, this strictly evidential picture leaves open questions about trust, how to characterize it, and the various roles it might play in children's acceptance of particular claims. In work on testimony, children have been shown to treat certain speakers as more reliable sources of information, but this evidential treatment seems different from the sense in which we might interpersonally trust others, taking them at their word without knowing very much about them or having evidence against them (Holton 1994, Marušić 2015).

By focusing on the evidentiary value of testimony, we neglect both its normative aspect, as expressed via speech acts with various practical aims, as well as the greater stock of reasons that children, and all agents, have to trust another person (Koenig & McMyler 2017). We also ignore central questions about the attitude of trust: Is it a propositional attitude, like belief (McMyler 2011, Marušić 2015)? Are there two types of trusting attitudes, one that is affective and one that is merely predictive (Faulkner 2011)? Or is trust a form of interpersonal reliance taken from a participant stance (Baier 1986, Holton 1994), a stance that motivates various decisions we make even in the teeth of negative evidence against the person who is trusted? Is it all of these things? In characterizing the foundations of testimonial learning, we seek to address how it is achieved not just by integrating prior beliefs with evidence, but also by invoking the social and interpersonal goals and values that make testimonial learning possible (Jaswal & Kondrad 2016).

2. TESTIMONY AND THE NATURE OF COGNITIVE DEVELOPMENT

According to one influential program of research on cognitive development, children everywhere are born into a world constrained by various physical, biological, and psychological regularities. Accordingly, a major agenda has been to work out how children grasp those universal regularities, to study, for example, how they come to grasp universal constraints on human existence imposed by the inevitability of death or the fallibility of beliefs. This line of research has often explored parallels between the scientist and the child in their search for causal regularities in the natural world (Gopnik & Wellman 2012).

Without denying the importance of this agenda, the study of children's learning from testimony highlights a neglected possibility, namely that children may come to conceptualize universal regularities not only on the basis of unmediated, observable evidence but also via the lens of the surrounding culture—a lens conveyed to them through the testimonial practices of their culture (Harris & Koenig 2006). For example, when they think about the universal constraints imposed by the inevitability of death or by the fallibility of beliefs, their developing ideas likely reflect assumptions conveyed to them via those testimonial practices. They will come to understand the biological inevitability of death, but they may also come to believe that there is an afterlife, whether in Heaven or among the Ancestors (Harris 2011); furthermore, even if they accept the fallibility of human beliefs, they may come to believe in the infallibility of God's beliefs (Heiphetz et al. 2016).

Indeed, recent evidence highlights the possibility that the very assumption that there are natural causal regularities constraining what can possibly happen in the world is an assumption that can be affected by testimonial practices. Children who have not received a religious education doubt that violations of ordinary causal constraints can ever happen. By contrast, children who have received a religious education within a Christian or an Islamic tradition are more likely to believe that miracles can occur (Corriveau et al. 2015, Davoodi et al. 2016). By implication, many children arrive at a view of the world in which the laws of nature can be overridden by divine or supernatural forces.

Because children learn from testimony and not just from the observation and interpretation of universal regularities, we also need to consider the cognitive impact of variation in the testimonial practices that they encounter. For example, we know that the frequency and complexity of the language input that young children receive vary sharply with the socioeconomic status of their parents (Hart & Risley 1995), with the level of their parents' formal education (Huttenlocher et al. 2007), and with their access to literacy (Levine et al. 2012). Such variation in language input is a cause for concern among educators because it is plausibly associated with marked variation in vocabulary size and reading skill. However, variation in the quantity of language input is also accompanied by variation in the style of input. To take one example, parents differ in the extent to which they use conversation either as a practical tool to get things done via the frequent issuing of instructions and imperatives or, alternatively, as an epistemic tool for exploration and information exchange about phenomena displaced from the time and place of the conversation (Hart & Risley 1995, Rowe 2012). Emerging evidence suggests that these stylistic features of language input impact children's working model of how information can be gathered, not via first-hand observation, but via the testimony of others. For example, children who are exposed more often to conversation as an epistemic tool ask more questions of their adult interlocutors (Kurkul & Corriveau 2017, Tizard & Hughes 1984).

As noted in Section 1, philosophical approaches to testimony have concentrated on the spoken word. Yet the written word is clearly a distinctive source of testimony in both the secular and the spiritual domains. It is also distinctive because it provides a powerful conduit for testimony that traverses history and geography in ways that are rarely possible for oral testimony. Recent findings highlight three other notable features of written testimony. First, soon after they have acquired the ability to decode simple written words, young children are more inclined to trust written over oral messages. For example, when supplied with conflicting names for unfamiliar creatures or conflicting instructions about how to act on an unfamiliar apparatus, young readers favor information conveyed via written as opposed to oral testimony (Robinson et al. 2013)—a bias not seen in prereaders. Apparently, the written word rapidly assumes an authority over the spoken word in the minds of young children.

Second, analyses of the linguistic complexity of different media, especially written versus oral media, highlight dramatic variation in vocabulary breadth. Weizman & Snow (2001) report that mothers produced only a small percentage of rare word types—fewer than 2% of all word types—when speaking to their 5-year-olds across a variety of settings. By contrast, mothers' rare word production tripled when they read aloud to their children from information-oriented books.

Moreover, compared to children's books, newspapers and popular magazines include more than double the number of rare words (Cunningham & Stanovich 1998).

Third, written testimony, especially expository text, is distinctive in its frequent reliance not just on rare vocabulary items but also on a special repertoire of language forms and functions that co-occur across academic texts in various disciplines, including the use of discourse connectives (e.g., "although" or "in other words") and conceptual anaphors (e.g., "The evaporation of water occurs due to rising temperatures. This process...”). Comprehending these linguistic features of academic texts calls for skills not captured by standard measures of vocabulary (Uccelli et al. 2015). By implication, learning from written texts calls for and likely nurtures (Levine et al. 2012) a distinctive set of discourse processing skills.

In sum, a focus on the way that children learn from testimony encourages researchers to think of children not only as constructing an objective or universally valid conception of the world but also as steeping themselves in the culturally inflected views of their community or civilization—as conveyed to them via oral as well as written testimony (Harris 2012).

3. INFANTS UNDERSTAND HOW TESTIMONY WORKS

Much recent work on testimony has examined children's learning from testimony in the preschool period and later (Mills 2013). Before discussing those findings in subsequent sections, we first consider the foundations of such learning. We begin by reviewing infants' sensitivity to affective signals and then consider their grasp of how information can be exchanged via gesture and vocalization.

3.1. Affective Signals

Sorce et al. (1985) showed that 14-month-olds could be guided by their mother's facial expressions of emotion. When approaching an apparent cliff, infants saw their mothers silently express either negative or positive affect. Infants were more likely to traverse the cliff if their mother signaled positive affect. Subsequent research has revealed three notable parameters of such social referencing, as it came to be called. First, infants construe emotional signals not simply as encouraging or discouraging their ongoing actions but rather as an affective commentary on an aspect of the immediate environment highlighted by the gaze of the signaler. Thus, infants (aged 12 and 18 months) adjusted their behavior toward a toy when an adult expressed positive or negative affect while looking at it but not when the adult's view of the toy was blocked (Moses et al. 2001). In addition, when two toys were simultaneously present, infants adjusted their behavior selectively— i.e., with respect to the toy that the adult was gazing at when emoting. Moreover, if a mother had signaled her affect toward a novel stimulus, for example a stranger, her infant continued to use that signal to calibrate his or her approach to the stranger even when the mother turned her attention elsewhere (De Rosnay et al. 2006). Thus, infants monitor the attention of an adult to figure out the target of his or her emotional signals, and they adjust their behavior toward that target accordingly. Absent a plausible target, no adjustment is made. But if a target is identified, infants continue to regulate their behavior toward it even when the adult no longer provides relevant signals. In sum, infants can identify the target of affective testimony, remember its valence, and act appropriately toward the target thereafter.

Second, affective signals have an impact only within certain limits. Tamis-Lemonda et al. (2008) found that, when 18-month-olds were uncertain about a situation, they heeded emotional signals, but they did not otherwise. For example, faced with a steep slope, positive maternal affect did not encourage infants to descend. Conversely, faced with a gentle slope, negative maternal affect did not discourage them from descending. But faced with difficult-to-evaluate, intermediate slopes, maternal affect had a marked effect. Positive maternal affect prompted infants to descend and negative maternal affect led them to stop or retreat. Kim & Kwak (2011) obtained similar results in a study of toy exploration by 12- and 16-month-olds. An adult's emotional signals had little impact on infants' reactions to unambiguously attractive or repellant toys but did moderate their reactions toward more ambiguous toys. Indeed, in the case of the ambiguous toys, infants were more likely to seek guidance by looking toward an adult.

Third, infants are discriminating about whose affective signals they are guided by. Given that infants often turn to an attachment figure when experiencing anxiety, we might expect them to prioritize a familiar caregiver when seeking affective guidance. However, Kim & Kwak (2011) noticed that infants looked more at the experimenter than at their mother when faced with a novel toy. Infants appeared to treat the experimenter as the local expert, implying that they sought information about the nature of the toy rather than emotional reassurance in the wake of anxiety. Support for this conclusion emerged in a series of studies in which 12-month-olds met two experimenters, only one of whom displayed expertise in playing with various toy sets (Stenberg 2013). When subsequently presented with an ambiguous mechanical dinosaur, infants were more likely to seek and accept affective guidance, whether positive or negative, from the expert as compared to the nonexpert. Infants also evaluate the reliability of an informant's affective signals. Thus, 14-month-olds were unlikely to follow the gaze of an adult who expressed positive reactions when looking into containers that turned out to be empty; similarly, infants ranging from 13 to 16 months old were unlikely to faithfully imitate an adult whose affective signals had proven unreliable (Poulin-Dubois & Brosseau-Liard 2016).

In summary, these studies of social referencing show that 1-year-olds look to adults for an emotional commentary on situations that evoke uncertainty; they approach situations that receive a positive commentary but retreat from situations that receive a negative commentary. Infants are selective about whose commentary they seek and accept. They look to an apparently well-informed stranger rather than their mother, an expert rather than a nonexpert, and a reliable emoter rather than an unreliable one. Yet such learning from affective signals is restricted; infants seek and rely on guidance about ambiguous situations or objects visible in the immediate environment. As discussed in the next section, other preverbal signals convey information that goes beyond the immediate environment.

3.2. Gesture and Vocalization

When a caregiver points, the infant often follows suit and vice versa. One construal of such reciprocity is that pointing is a gesture par excellence for establishing joint attention. Yet pointing can also serve another function—the transmission of information about a target, including an invisible target. The findings of Behne et al. (2012) are illustrative. Infants of 12 months watched as the experimenter concealed an object in one hand and then, sliding each hand under a box, prevented infants from inferring which particular box she had left the object in. However, when she then pointed at the correct box, infants used that gesture to guide their search. Indeed, when one adult played the role of seeker by covering her eyes while a second adult hid the object, some infants helpfully responded to the seeker's queries by pointing to the correct box. These findings suggest that, even at 12 months of age, infants have a rich and bidirectional understanding of pointing as a source of testimony—rich because they realize that pointing can convey information about hidden objects in addition to visible ones and bidirectional because they appreciate that, via pointing, they can both receive and transmit information about such hidden objects.

Strong evidence of infants' bidirectional conception of pointing was obtained by Krehm et al. (2014). Infants of 9 and 11 months old first watched as an adult exhibited a preference for manipulating one of two objects. In a subsequent test phase, the two objects were placed out of the adult's reach and she pointed to the one she preferred—as if requesting that it be handed to her. Both age groups expressed more surprise (i.e., stared longer) when a second adult handed over her nonpreferred object rather than the one she had pointed to. This differential looking pattern was not shown if the requester produced a noncommunicative hand gesture—a closed fist rather than a point—or if the second adult covered her eyes during the requester's point. Martin et al. (2012) obtained similar results when the requester indicated her desired object not by pointing but by saying "koba"—a word that was meaningless for the 12-month-olds being tested but that, in the context, could be taken to imply a request for the preferred object. Again, control conditions confirmed that infants were selective in assuming that a communicative act had occurred. They did not display selective looking if the requester coughed rather than spoke or produced an affective vocalization ("Oooh!") rather than a lexical item. Finally, Vouloumanos et al. (2012) obtained similar results when one adult communicated a request for help in stacking a ring on an out-of-reach funnel by saying "koba" to an interlocutor. Again, infants' looking times implied that they expected the interlocutor to understand the request and respond appropriately—they looked only briefly when the interlocutor stacked the ring but stared for longer if she did not respond as intended. Taken together, these studies show that 12-month-olds are intelligent third-party observers and interpreters of nonverbal testimony. They realize that someone can produce a point or a lexical item (but not a cough or an "Oooh!") to indicate which object or action is wanted, and they expect an interlocutor to understand and comply with such requests.

Do infants understand more straightforwardly informative assertions as well as requests? More specifically, do they understand that an informant may communicate with an interlocutor to update or guide the interlocutor rather than to make a request? Song et al. (2008) had 18-month-olds watch two adults. The seeker placed a ball in a box and then briefly left. In her absence, a second adult moved the ball to a cup but either told the returning seeker about the ball's new location ("The ball is in the cup!") or said something less informative ("I like the cup."). Infants' looking times indicated that they were surprised when the seeker who was told its new location looked for the ball in its original location (i.e., the box) and, conversely, when the seeker who was told something uninformative looked in its new location. Fusaro & Harris (2013) showed that 18-month-olds also grasp that head gestures can be informative. When one adult enquired about the location of an object by pointing to each of two boxes and asking, "Is it in here?," a second adult replied with a nod in one case and a shake of the head in the other. If then prompted to search, infants selected the correct box as inferred from the adults' exchange. In summary, 18-month-olds realize that a point, a verbal utterance, or a head gesture can transmit information from one person to another.

Granted that infants can make sense of such communicative acts when they observe them from a third-party or bystander perspective, how far do they spontaneously engage in such acts to either seek or provide information? Begus & Southgate (2012) concluded that 16-month-olds use the pointing gesture not simply to call attention to an object of interest but also to seek information about it. When shown various objects, they were likely to point at them if an accompanying adult seemed potentially well informed but pointed less often if the adult was poorly informed, as indexed by prior misnaming of familiar objects. These findings are fully consistent with research on preschoolers, who also spurn inaccurate informants (Harris & Corriveau 2011, Koenig & Harris 2005). Further evidence of spontaneous information seeking in the second year is reported by Chouinard (2007). Parents of children ranging from 12 to 23 months old recorded their children's "questions" in the home. Questions did not need to be explicit to warrant recording. For example, if a toddler picked up a novel object, held it toward a parent, and said "Uh?," it was treated as question meaning, roughly, "What's this?" Analysis confirmed that the majority of children's "questions" (80%) sought information rather than, for example, practical help or attention.

Most were requests for a name, but information about locations and activities was also sought, especially by older toddlers. Finally, toddlers are better at processing solicited, as compared to unsolicited, information. Thus, Begus et al. (2014) found that 16-month-olds were more accurate at reproducing actions demonstrated on novel objects that they had pointed at, as compared to novel objects that they had ignored. In summary, infants spontaneously adopt an interrogative stance in the second year. They use gestures and vocalizations to solicit information, especially from apparently knowledgeable interlocutors. Moreover, if they have sought information, rather than being given it unsolicited, they are more likely or better able to process it effectively.

As emphasized above, as third-party observers, infants display an understanding of the way that an informed individual can alert or update someone who is less informed. Given infants' understanding of dialogic communication, we can reasonably expect infants to supply information unbidden, especially when they know something that an interlocutor does not. Indeed, when 18-month-olds saw an adult place an object in one of several containers and then saw a second adult transfer it to a new container, they spontaneously helped the first adult to relocate the object by pointing at the new container, but only if she had been absent during the transfer (Knudsen & Liszkowski 2012). Similarly, when an object slid to the floor and an adult expressed puzzlement, 12-month-olds were more likely to point to it if the adult had not seen it slide to the floor than if the adult had seen it slide but seemed puzzled as to how it came to do so (Liszkowski et al. 2008). Thus, infants' points are not reflexive responses to expressions of puzzlement. Rather, infants point to inform someone when their expressions of puzzlement signal ignorance of an object's current location.

In summary, infants of 12–18 months are capable not just of convergent attention on a common object, as routinely emphasized in research on joint attention, but also of contributing to a convergence of knowledge. They grasp that a divergence of knowledge between two people can be transformed into a convergence if missing information is appropriately conveyed from one interlocutor to the other. Simply stated, infants understand the basic elements of testimony (Harris & Lane 2014). In the role of third-party observer, infants expect interlocutors to respond appropriately to requests and assertions. In the role of informant, they proffer specific information to the ignorant or mistaken. In the role of questioner, they direct interrogative gestures and vocalizations to other people, especially to those unimpeached by prior inaccuracy.

4. CHILDREN'S REASONING ABOUT INFORMANTS

As Hume was right to stress, testimonial learning gives us the opportunity to study a common and important "species of reasoning" (Hume 1748, p. 119). Indeed, the research reviewed above suggests that key aspects of this reasoning process emerge early: Infants are sensitive to informant reliability—they pay less heed to those who have proven inaccurate or ignorant and show an interest in the conditions that explain a speaker's error or anomalous statement (Henderson et al. 2015, Koenig & Echols 2003). Further insight into this reasoning process has come from research presenting children with various kinds of imperfect speakers. Importantly, children do not give one singular response to such sources. Rather, children's distinct and specific patterns of response suggest that they reason about the particular factors—of the informant or the situation—that might limit or undermine trustworthiness. For example, when presented with a speaker who inaccurately named objects but who clearly looked inside two boxes, 4- and 5-year-olds doubted her subsequent labeling claims but accepted her claims about where objects were hidden (Brosseau-Liard & Birch 2011). Conversely, when a speaker's visual access to information was held fixed, but the conceptual significance of her errors varied, they treated her categorical errors as a more serious breach than transient, factual errors (Kondrad & Jaswal 2012, Stephens & Koenig 2015; see also Einav &

Robinson 2010). Preschool-aged readers treat an informant with access to printed information as reliable but no longer trust that informant when his or her access to print is removed (Einav et al. 2013). Children's nuanced rejection of informants reflects their sensitivity to the conditions under which accuracy is achieved. From infancy, children not only discern the truth or falsity of a report, but also show an interest in how informants obtained their information.

Granted that no informant will prove either omniscient or fully ignorant, how do children respond to the inevitable gaps in a speaker's knowledge? Although they reject claims made by ignorant speakers (Sabbagh & Shafman 2009), they are more positively disposed to speakers whose earlier professions of ignorance are later followed by claims to know something. They expect a professedly ignorant speaker to profess more ignorance, but they take seriously her new and unmarked claims, accepting them at rates no different than previously accurate speakers (Kushnir & Koenig 2017). Thus, professions of ignorance, when kept distinct from the other things that the speaker knows, are not treated by children as penalties against a speaker. Such findings are consistent with other evidence that young children adopt an open-minded view of the relationship between a speaker's state of ignorance and her later behavior (Friedman & Petrashek 2009), continually adjusting their trust based on an informant's ongoing accuracy (Ronfard & Lane 2017).

In appraising an informant, the monitoring of accuracy will not be enough. Informants can provide accurate but insufficient information, and children are alert to misleading omissions. For example, if they know that a toy has multiple functions and witness a teacher's incomplete instruction, they mistrust her (Gweon et al. 2014). Conversely, they are prone to assume that a teacher has been exhaustive in the absence of counterevidence. For example, if they encounter an apparently knowledgeable teacher who demonstrates a single function of a novel toy, then they infer that it has no additional functions (Bonawitz et al. 2011, Shneidman et al. 2016). Such research sheds light on the conditions under which a speaker's nonexhaustive statements might or might not be penalized, not simply against standards of accuracy but also against standards of informativeness or relevance (Wilson & Sperber 2002).

Overall, young children appreciate several distinct ways in which speakers can be imperfect and realize that not all of them signal risks of misinformation. Their interpretive sensitivity is especially evident when they treat the same behaviors as grounds for doubting an informant in certain contexts but not others. As discussed above, when the situation constrains or limits an inaccurate speaker's access to information, children take that limited access into account in their interpretation of the speaker. When a speaker's anomalous claims are explicable in terms of her playful actions (Henderson et al. 2015), children interpret and excuse them. When a speaker admits to her ignorance, it signals that she does not present a general risk of misinformation (Kushnir & Koenig 2017). When an informant omits information, it may or may not be condoned. Thus, children's testimonial reasoning reflects an ability not just to detect false statements, bad intentions, or the withholding of information, but also to assess what such behaviors signify about the informant given her particular situation. By implication, when children reason about testimony, they are making inferences at two levels simultaneously. They are reasoning about particular claims in light of the information that is available to the informant and also making—or withholding—inferences about the informant's (trustworthy) character.

5. APPRAISAL OF AN INFORMANT'S SOCIAL STANDING AND PERSONALITY

The research described above highlights young children's emerging ability to use various types of epistemic cues to evaluate a speaker's claims and future credibility. Yet children often hear claims that cannot be evaluated via either experience or logic. For example, when told about the existence of invisible or absent referents (Ganea & Harris 2013, Harris et al. 2006) or past and future events (Corriveau et al. 2009c), children cannot easily check those claims. They will encounter instances where verification is possible, but lack the requisite expertise (e.g., to check the evidence for speciation). They will also encounter instances where the claims in question amount to cultural assumptions rather than verifiable assertions. Under these circumstances, it might be useful to the children to evaluate the social standing of an informant. In this section, we highlight children's use of three types of social information: social relationships, personality characteristics, and informant consensus.

Preschool children prefer to learn new information from their mother rather than a stranger (Corriveau et al. 2009b) and from a familiar rather than an unfamiliar teacher (Corriveau & Harris 2009). They are more likely to seek or endorse information provided by individuals belonging to the same social group as themselves, as indexed by their race (Chen et al. 2013), minimal group status (Hetherington et al. 2014), age (Jaswal & Neely 2006), accent (Corriveau et al. 2013b), or gender (Shutts et al. 2010). They also favor informants who enjoy greater influence or appeal within any given group, as indexed by their strength-based dominance (Bernard et al. 2016), prestige (Chudek et al. 2012), or physical attractiveness (Bascandziev & Harris 2016). Privileging information from familiar informants, from members of their in-group, and from those with higher status is likely to facilitate the transmission of local and pertinent cultural information (Boyd & Richerson 1985).

Children also consider the personality characteristics of an informant. They prefer to learn from an informant who has been attributed prosocial, as opposed to antisocial, intentions (Landrum et al. 2013, Mascaro & Sperber 2009). Similarly, they prefer to learn from an informant who is described positively by a third party—as kind rather than mean, smart rather than not smart, and honest rather than dishonest. Moreover, such selectivity becomes more pronounced with age (Lane et al. 2013). One possible interpretation of these findings is that children are prone to halo effects—they favor informants with any type of positive trait. However, children are actually more selective. When Hermes et al. (2015) presented children with a choice between individuals who had each displayed a positive trait—either superior expertise in naming or superior strength—children were likely to seek help from the former in a task calling for knowledge and from the latter in a task calling for strength. Moreover, this selective pattern was only found among children who could correctly answer trait questions (e.g., "Who is smarter?" and "Who is stronger?"), providing strong evidence that children's trait attributions mediated their selective help seeking.

Children assess not only the individual characteristics of informants but also agreement among informants; they are receptive to claims endorsed by a consensus (Chen et al. 2013; Corriveau & Harris 2010; Corriveau et al. 2009a, 2013a; DiYanni et al. 2015; Morgan et al. 2015a). Arguably, children use consensus information to make an inference about the likely truth of a given claim; unanimity could provide children with especially persuasive evidence for its truth. Alternatively, children might defer to a consensus in the face of social pressure (Jaswal & Kondrad 2016). If so, children should publicly defer to a consensus but make a different judgment in private. Some research supports this conclusion, with children altering their judgment depending on the presence or absence of the experimenter (Corriveau et al. 2013a) or of the consensus (Corriveau & Harris 2010). Such respectful deference might lead to local adjustments in children's overt pronouncements but would not entail a genuine change of judgment (see also Koenig & Woodward 2010). It might also vary by culture. Indeed, children of East Asian descent appear to be more influenced by consensus information than children of European American descent (Corriveau & Harris 2010, Corriveau et al. 2013a, DiYanni et al. 2015).

In summary, young children, like adults, have several ways of evaluating their informants. They can use testimony to appraise the informants themselves, especially with respect to their history of accuracy or bias. But they also appraise their informants more broadly in terms of their group status, their personality traits, and their agreement—or lack of agreement—with other informants. In future research, it will be important to study how children respond when these lines of appraisal point in different directions. Castelain et al. (2015) reported an interesting study along these lines. They found that 4- to 6-year-olds from traditional Mayan communities favored speakers who cited perceptual reasons ("P because I saw that p") over speakers who cited circular reasons ("P because p"). These same children also favored socially dominant over socially subordinate speakers. However, when these two cues were put into conflict, children treated a sound argument from a socially subordinate speaker as better than a circular argument from a dominant speaker. By implication, well before they reach school age, young children show an appreciation for sufficiently good reasons or arguments as considerations that weigh in their evaluation of informants' claims. Moreover, even in nonegalitarian communities, such as traditional Mayan communities, that preserve strong social hierarchies between adults and children, children's evaluations of arguments can override source-based cues like dominance when sufficiently good arguments are produced.

6. TESTIMONY AND PRIOR KNOWLEDGE

Much of the information conveyed through testimony is likely to be neutral with respect to what the recipient already knows. For example, when a teacher explains that the process by which plants transform light into energy is called photosynthesis, this label may be news to many students, but it probably does not conflict with any information or conceptual framework that they already have. If the information comes from a speaker they view as credible (see Section 4) and if other important prerequisites for learning are in place (e.g., attention, motivation, memory), this new fact is likely to be incorporated into their knowledge base.

There are, however, situations where someone's claim may be surprising in light of what a listener already believes. For example, testimony that the Earth is round conflicts with the naive intuition (based on personal experience) that it is flat. Understanding how children navigate such conflicts—the circumstances under which they retain their existing beliefs versus those under which they give them up in favor of the claim conveyed through testimony—has been the subject of much recent research (Lane & Harris 2014). This is an important issue philosophically because beliefs formed on the basis of first-hand experience seem like they should be more salient, immediate, and reliable than beliefs formed on the basis of testimony [e.g., Hume 1748, Locke 1975 (1689)]. It is also an important issue practically because imparting unexpected or counterintuitive knowledge is an important part of education in many domains, particularly science (e.g., Shtulman 2017).

Children often weight unexpected testimony more heavily than their existing beliefs, but their deference has limits. Children's receptivity can be influenced by a number of factors, including the strength of those existing beliefs, characteristics of the speaker, and individual differences in how willing and able children are to ignore the claim in question. Children may also be receptive to unexpected testimony for social rather than epistemic reasons.

Toddlers and even infants balk when they hear a speaker produce a claim that is blatantly false. For example, if a speaker calls a cup a shoe, infants will stare at the speaker (Koenig & Echols 2003), and toddlers will often produce an explicit denial: "No" (Pea 1982). More generally, children are not routinely gullible (Lane & Harris 2014, Woolley & Ghossainy 2013). Nevertheless, if speakers make a claim that is unexpected but somewhat plausible given the available evidence, children are quite receptive (Bernard et al. 2015). A simple but powerful demonstration of this receptivity comes from a study on category induction. In Gelman & Markman's (1986) study, 4-year-olds were shown three line drawings—for example, a tropical fish, a dolphin, and a shark. The experimenter explained that the fish stayed underwater to breathe whereas the dolphin popped above the water to breathe and asked children how the shark breathed. Crucially, the experimenter referred to the shark either as a dolphin (a label that was consistent with its appearance) or as a fish (a label that was unexpected given its appearance). Children tended to make the inference that matched the label given, even when that was perceptually unexpected: If the shark was referred to as a dolphin, they inferred that it popped above the water to breathe; if it was referred to as a fish, they inferred that it stayed underwater. Children occasionally commented when the label was discrepant from the target's appearance by, for example, noting that the shark was a "funny-looking" fish (e.g., Gelman & Coley 1991). But most of the time, they simply accepted the label the experimenter provided and treated the target like a member of the named category.

That said, children are not always deferential to such unexpected categorizations. There is some evidence, for example, that older children may be less deferential than younger ones. In a variant of Gelman & Markman's (1986) procedure, Jaswal (2004) showed 3- and 4-year-olds specially designed hybrid animals and objects—for example, a dog-like animal that had some features of a cat (e.g., a long tail and tabby cat coloring). When children heard this hybrid dog referred to neutrally (as "this one"), they overwhelmingly inferred that it shared characteristics with other dogs—a reasonable inference given its appearance. But when another group of children heard the same hybrid referred to as a "cat," 3-year-olds tended to infer that it shared characteristics with other cats, whereas 4-year-olds were ambivalent. In many cases, the older children spontaneously rejected the label ("No, it's not a cat"). A plausible explanation for the age difference is that, as children gain experience—in this case, as they encounter more cats and dogs—they become more confident of the boundaries of those categories and, thereby, more skeptical of testimony that conflicts with their intuitions about them.

In addition to age, the strength of children's prior beliefs and the culture in which they are raised can influence how they respond to unexpected information. In a study by Chan & Tardif (2013), kindergartners and second graders in the United States and Hong Kong were asked to identify several objects. Some were perceptually ambiguous (e.g., an object that looked like it could be either a button or a wheel), so that children were expected to have only weak intuitions about their identities. Indeed, about half of the children tended to refer to these objects with the label of one of the possible categories, and half with the label of the other. When a teacher referred to the ambiguous objects using labels opposite to the ones a particular child had used earlier, most children, irrespective of age and culture, tended to accept them, even though the labels did not match what children had said earlier.

Children were also asked to identify objects that were prototypical members of their category (e.g., a prototypical button), and almost all named them accordingly. When the teacher referred to these objects using counterintuitive labels, children were not uniformly deferential. Instead, an interaction between age and culture emerged: Kindergartners in the United States accepted the teacher's labels, but kindergartners in Hong Kong and second graders in both cultures were less likely to do so. Chan & Tardif (2013) proposed that children who could recognize that they had strong intuitions about the identities of the prototypical items were resistant to the counterintuitive labels. This metacognitive recognition was derived from experience and, in the case of the kindergarteners in Hong Kong, from an educational system that emphasizes early self-reliance and autonomy.

Children's receptiveness to unexpected testimony can also depend on the quality of their relationship with the speaker (Corriveau et al. 2009b), as well as online cues to the speaker's competence and confidence. For example, 4-year-olds in Jaswal's (2004) study involving hybrids tended to be skeptics about unexpected labels, but they could be turned into believers if the speaker simply acknowledged that the testimony was going to seem surprising (e.g., "You're not going to believe this, but this is actually a cat"). This statement signaled that the speaker's use of an unexpected label was intentional and, perhaps, that she had some special knowledge about the thing being named (see also Jaswal 2006). Conversely, Jaswal & Malone (2007) showed that 3-year-olds, who tended to be believers about unexpected labels, could be turned into skeptics if the speaker simply said "I think" as she was offering them a label, thereby conveying uncertainty.

The examples given so far in this section have focused on children's responses to testimony that conflicts with their expectations about the name of the category to which something belongs. Yet in order to learn a conventional vocabulary, children have to be receptive to information from other people: The only way to learn that a table is called a table, for example, is by being willing to accept that this is its name. Other domains of knowledge seem less reliant on information from other people. For example, some of children's expectations about the behavior of physical objects (e.g., that solid objects cannot move from one location to another without crossing the intervening space) are in place early in infancy (Spelke et al. 1992). These expectations are reinforced continuously in daily life; exceptions are likely to be quite rare. One might therefore predict that intuitions about the physical world would be relatively immune to testimony that challenges them. In fact, however, children are sometimes willing to entertain unexpected testimony even when it conflicts with an event they have just seen.

For example, in Ma & Ganea (2010), preschoolers watched as an adult hid a toy in one location and then heard the same adult claim it was somewhere else. Most 3-year-olds looked where the adult said it was, whereas most 4- and 5-year-olds looked where they had seen it hidden, consistent with findings, described above, that younger children are more receptive to unexpected information than older children. Interestingly, if the 3-year-olds first had experience of finding the hidden object without any conflicting testimony, they tended to ignore the adult when she claimed, on a later trial, that the toy was not where they had seen it hidden, presumably because the initial experience allowed them to build up confidence in the accuracy of their own expectations in this particular setting (see also Jaswal 2010).

Even when testimony describes objects that behave in ways that violate well-entrenched principles of naive physics, like gravity, young children are sometimes receptive. For example, in Lane & Harris (2015), 3- to 8-year-olds heard a speaker claim that a metal object called a "pleak" could float above a table and were asked to decide how certain they were about this claim. Children at all ages were, on average, ambivalent, suggesting that even the oldest children entertained the possibility that objects can behave in unexpected ways—not inconceivable given that there are exceptions to principles of naive physics (e.g., a remote control can apparently activate another object at a distance). Admittedly, 3- and 4-year-olds were more likely than older children to accept that the speaker's counterintuitive claim was true, but baseline measures showed that their pre-existing intuitions were less firm.

Children's early receptivity to counterintuitive testimony may originate from an adaptive, domain-general bias to trust that other people will treat them in helpful (or at least benign) ways (Baier 1986, Jaswal et al. 2010). This bias to believe testimony is likely to become stronger with experience because most of what children (and adults) are told is likely to be true or, at least, to reflect what speakers believe to be true. Children are novices in many of the domains that they encounter, so accepting claims by default could be adaptive, saving them, as listeners, from having to engage in the time-consuming and sometimes impossible task of verifying everything that they are told. Indeed, there is some evidence that, when adults are provided a piece of testimony, they accept it as true by default; they can unaccept it, but this requires cognitive effort (Gilbert 1991). This leads to the interesting prediction that individual differences in inhibitory control—the ability to inhibit a prepotent response—could be related to how credulous children are to unexpected testimony.

Jaswal et al. (2014) investigated this possibility in a study with 2.5- to 3.5-year-olds. Children were invited to find and eat Goldfish crackers. In each trial, they watched as a cracker was dropped into one of three intertwined tubes and indicated into which of three opaque cups the cracker had landed. Children's initial indication was almost always correct, but before they learned that this was the case, an adult confederate claimed that the cracker had landed in a different (incorrect) cup. Children were then asked to indicate a second time where the cracker had landed. There was enormous variability in how children responded to the adult's unexpected testimony. About 40% acquiesced on most or all trials, and 60% resisted on most or all trials. Consistent with the hypothesis that not believing requires more cognitive effort than believing, resistant children performed more accurately than acquiescent children on a separate, computerized spatial conflict task designed to measure inhibitory control.

Although the ability to inhibit a prepotent response may be related to the likelihood that children respond skeptically to misleading testimony (but see Heyman et al. 2013), there are circumstances under which children with more advanced executive functioning skills (of which inhibitory control is one) can benefit from unexpected testimony. In Bascandziev et al.'s (2016) experiment, for example, toddlers who scored higher on some measures of executive functioning were better able to take advantage of an experimenter's counterintuitive (and accurate) testimony about the physical world than toddlers who scored lower.

Being receptive to testimony obviously provides a way to obtain information from other people, but it can also be a means of engaging socially with other people (Jaswal & Kondrad 2016). That is, children may sometimes seem receptive to unexpected testimony not because they believe it but because the speaker is someone with whom they would like to affiliate. In some of the studies reviewed above, attempts were made to demonstrate the relative unimportance of such social goals by, for example, establishing that children were willing to pass the information on to another person outside the earshot of the original speaker (e.g., Chan & Tardif 2013, Jaswal et al. 2009). However, there is no doubt that children's endorsement of a given claim can be influenced by social factors. As noted in the previous section, children are especially prone to publicly endorse the unexpected claims of a consensus even if they demur in private.

7. FUTURE DIRECTIONS

Research on children's learning from testimony has progressed in two distinct directions. First, in the wake of early empirical findings, investigators have conducted an intense analysis of so-called selective trust—the tendency of children and, indeed, infants to favor the claims of one informant over another, especially in light of their differential history of reliability. Second, investigators have explored the key conceptual point that there is much about the world that children cannot observe first hand. Thus, it is appropriate for them to consult other people about this vast, unobservable terrain. We conclude with brief comments about the future directions of these two endeavors.

Some commentators have pointed out the limited ecological validity of the standard paradigm for studying selective trust. In everyday life, children are rarely confronted with two informants whose profile is equivalent in all but one respect, such as prior accuracy, or with two informants who produce circumscribed but conflicting claims. In future research on selective trust, it will be helpful to make three changes. First, children can be presented with informants who differ along more than one dimension to assess the relative impact of each dimension on children's trust over the course of development (e.g., Corriveau & Harris 2009, Corriveau et al. 2013b, Hermes et al. 2015, Hetherington et al. 2014). Second, we can ask how far children trust a single informant with a known profile. As discussed in Section 6, children tend to accept claims, even counterintuitive claims, made by one informant when no competing claim is made (Jaswal & Kondrad 2016). Nevertheless, children's encoding of a claim made by a single unreliable informant may be liable to weaken over time (Sabbagh & Shafman 2009). By implication, we should ask not just about children's immediate uptake or endorsement, but also about their longer-term consolidation of claims made by different informants—for example, those who have proven reliable as compared to those who have not or those who belong to the recipient's in-group as compared to those who do not. Third, research on selective trust has focused on the transmission of circumscribed claims—such as the name of a novel object—in the context of a one-shot, one-way testimonial delivery. But life outside of the laboratory is more complicated. It can involve claims—such as the existence of God or the universality of death—that are deeper than the names of objects. Moreover, rather than a brief, one-shot exchange, it can involve successive encounters, as children repeatedly hear about topics that puzzle or worry them. Finally, it may involve a dialog between children and their informants, rather than a one-way pronouncement by an informant. Indeed, children are not acquiescent and passive recipients of testimony; they also seek to remedy their ignorance or confusion by asking questions, sometimes in the context of an extended passage of intellectual search in which they pose multiple questions (Tizard & Hughes 1984).

Initially, children's questions tend to be of the what and where variety, but, by about 30 months old, as many as one-quarter of the questions asked by children in Western, middle-class communities are how and why questions intended to elicit explanatory responses (Chouinard 2007). Children often ask questions when they encounter something anomalous. Thus, a question like "Why doesn't the butter stay on top (of hot toast)?" is presumably motivated by the observation that most objects do not sink into each other. Such questions imply an expectation that dialog can help to make sense of apparent anomalies (Harris 2012). Indeed, after a satisfactory explanation, children are likely to acknowledge their agreement or pose a follow-up question on the same topic. Absent a satisfactory explanation, they may reiterate their initial question or offer an explanation of their own (Frazier et al. 2009, Kurkul & Corriveau 2017). Moreover, preschoolers differentiate between informative explanations (e.g., "It rains because the clouds fill with water and get too heavy") and quasicircular ones (e.g., "It rains because water falls from the sky and gets us wet") (Corriveau & Kurkul 2014), showing superior memory for informative explanations (Frazier et al. 2016). Finally, they are sometimes prepared to challenge explanations that run counter to what they know (Harris 2012). In sum, research on testimony would benefit from a focus on everyday, explanatory dialog between children and their informants (e.g., Luce et al. 2013). Indeed, as noted in Section 2, there may be potent cumulative effects at work in the context of such dialog. Some children may be increasingly engaged and supported in reflective dialog, whereas others may be increasingly discouraged. Arguably, such divergent engagement and support lead children to different assumptions about the benefits and social acceptability of seeking, discussing, or challenging explanations from others (Reifen Tagar et al. 2014).

Turning to the second direction of research—testimony about the unobservable—findings highlight an intriguing paradox (Harris et al. 2006). Young children justify their belief in the existence of various unobservable entities—some drawn from the scientific domain and some from the religious domain—in a similar fashion. They invoke the known characteristics of the various entities, characteristics that they presumably learned about via testimony. For example, they justify their belief in the existence of germs by noting that they can make you sick; they justify their belief in the existence of God by noting that God has the power of a Creator. However, despite this parallel in the way that children justify their claims about scientific and religious entities, they express greater confidence in the existence of scientific entities (Harris & Corriveau 2014). Findings in adults highlight a similar pattern (Shtulman 2013).

The explanation of these findings is likely to have broad implications for the study of testimony, especially concerning unobservable phenomena. Two different lines of explanation seem feasible. First, the differential confidence displayed in scientific as compared to religious entities may reflect the pattern of testimony surrounding each type of entity. Affirmations with respect to scientific phenomena, such as germs, are often matter-of-fact and widely accepted. Affirmations with respect to religious phenomena, such as the afterlife, may be exhortative and contested. On this view, the differentiation between religious and scientific entities is due to the fact that children and adults register the sociolinguistic differences in the pattern of testimony surrounding phenomena in these two domains. Second, the alternative possibility is that, despite the parallels in their patterns of explanation, children and adults have some deep-seated sense that there is a distinction between the grounds for scientific, as compared to spiritual, belief, and they bring that ontological intuition to the various testimonial claims that they encounter. Research in communities that differ in the relative standing of science and religion should help to resolve this debate.

8. CONCLUSIONS

Research on testimony is young—it began just over a decade ago. Yet we are optimistic about its long-term future for several reasons. First, philosophical analysis dating back to the Scottish Enlightenment has long identified testimony as an important source of knowledge. Despite that conceptual warrant, psychologists have been slow to focus on testimony. This hesitation has been especially evident in developmental psychology, where, following in the footsteps of Rousseau and Piaget, investigators have tended to romanticize the child's cognitive autonomy and to dismiss children's receptivity to other people's assertions as mere verbalism. Given the emerging connections between philosophical analyses of trust in testimony and empirical research on children's competence (see Sections 1 and 4), we are confident that the importance of children's learning from testimony can no longer be underestimated.

Second, empirical work on children's learning from testimony has led to a keener appreciation of its considerable scope. For example, Harris & Koenig (2006) deliberately followed philosophical precedent by focusing on verbal testimony. Yet, as set out in Section 3, children's learning from oral testimony is preceded and likely supported by an earlier capacity to learn from information conveyed via nonverbal gestures. In addition, recent evidence indicates that children who can read invest more trust in written than in spoken messages (Robinson et al. 2013). We anticipate that future work on testimony will continue to push beyond standard usage of that term.

Third, there is increasing recognition of the importance of learning from others, not just in the human species or in our primate cousins (Whiten 2017) but in a range of other species, from whales to sticklebacks and from birds to bees (Whiten et al. 2017). Yet learning from the verbal testimony of others is a uniquely human competence, one that is absent among primates, despite their skills at tool construction and cultural transmission. Thus, we anticipate increasing attention, both in biology and psychology, to the contribution that is made by testimony in comparison to other potent mechanisms of social learning, such as imitation (Morgan et al. 2015b).

Finally, we are optimistic given the range and intensity of current empirical research on testimony. Reviewing it has been an enjoyable challenge.

SUMMARY POINTS

1. Research on testimony has underlined how children learn not just from their own first-hand observation but also from the credible assertions of other people.

2. In learning from others' testimony, children steep themselves in the culturally inflected views of their community or civilization.

3. Preverbal infants understand how testimony works: They grasp that information can be communicated by gesture or vocalization from one interlocutor to another.

4. Children reason about an informant's claims, drawing inferences about the trustworthiness of the claim and the person making it.

5. Children also appraise their informants more broadly in terms of their group status, their personality traits, and their agreement—or lack of agreement—with other informants.

6. Credible testimony can lead children to set aside or revise their initial intuitions in a variety of cognitive domains.

7. Future research is likely to expand our concept of testimony but also sharpen our understanding of the extent to which learning from testimony is a distinctively human form of cultural learning.

DISCLOSURE STATEMENT

The authors are not aware of any affiliations, memberships, funding, or financial holdings that might be perceived as affecting the objectivity of this review.

LITERATURE CITED

Akhtar N, Jipson J, Callanan MA. 2001. Learning words through overhearing. *Child Dev.* 72:416–30

Baier A. 1986. Trust and antitrust. *Ethics* 96:231–60

Bascandziev I, Harris PL. 2016. The beautiful and the accurate: Are children's selective trust decisions biased? *J. Exp. Child Psychol.* 152:92–105

Bascandziev I, Powell LJ, Harris PL, Carey S. 2016. A role for executive functions in explanatory understanding of the physical world. *Cogn. Dev.* 39:71–85

Begus K, Gliga T, Southgate V. 2014. Infants learn what they want to learn: Responding to infant pointing leads to superior learning. *PLOS ONE* 9:e108817

Begus K, Southgate V. 2012. Infant pointing serves an interrogative function. *Dev. Sci.* 15:611–17

Behne T, Liszkowski U, Carpenter M, Tomasello M. 2012. Twelve-month-olds' comprehension and production of pointing. *Br. J. Dev. Psychol.* 30:359–75

Bernard S, Castelain T, Mercier H, Kaufmann L, Van der Henst J, Clément F. 2016. The boss is always right: Preschoolers endorse the testimony of a dominant over that of a subordinate. *J. Exp. Child Psychol.* 152:307–17

Bernard S, Harris PL, Terrier N, Clément F. 2015. Children weigh the number of informants and perceptual uncertainty when identifying objects. *J. Exp. Child Psychol.* 36:70–81

Bonawitz E, Shafto P, Gweon H, Goodman ND, Spelke E, Schulz L. 2011. The double-edged sword of pedagogy: Instruction limits spontaneous exploration and discovery. *Cognition* 120:322–30

Boyd R, Richerson PJ. 1985. *Culture and the Evolutionary Process.* Chicago: Univ. Chicago Press

Brosseau-Liard PE, Birch SA. 2011. Epistemic states and traits: Preschoolers appreciate the differential informativeness of situation-specific and person-specific cues to knowledge. *Child Dev.* 82:1788–96

Callanan MA. 2006. Cognitive development, culture, and conversation: comments on Harris and Koenig's "Truth in testimony: how children learn about science and religion." *Child Dev.* 77:525–30

Castelain T, Bernard S, der Henst V, Mercier H. 2015. The influence of power and reason on young Maya children's endorsement of testimony. *Dev. Sci.* 19:957–66

Chan CC, Tardif T. 2013. Knowing better: the role of prior knowledge and culture in trust in testimony. *Dev. Psychol.* 49:591–601

Chen EE, Corriveau KH, Harris PL. 2013. Children trust a consensus composed of outgroup members—but do not retain that trust. *Child Dev.* 84:269–82

Chouinard MM. 2007. Children's questions: a mechanism for cognitive development. *Monogr. Soc. Res. Child Dev.* 72:1–129

Chudek M, Heller S, Birch S, Henrich J. 2012. Prestige-biased cultural learning: Bystander's differential attention to potential models influences children's learning. *Evol. Hum. Behav.* 33:46–56

Corriveau KH, Chen EE, Harris PL. 2015. Judgments about fact and fiction by children from religious and non-religious backgrounds. *Cogn. Sci.* 39:353–82

Corriveau KH, Fusaro M, Harris PL. 2009a. Going with the flow: Preschoolers prefer non-dissenters as informants. *Psychol. Sci.* 20:372–77

Corriveau KH, Harris PL. 2009. Choosing your informant: weighing familiarity and recent accuracy. *Dev. Sci.* 12:426–37

Corriveau KH, Harris PL. 2010. Preschoolers (sometimes) defer to the majority in making simple perceptual judgments. *Dev. Psychol.* 46:437–45

Corriveau KH, Harris PL. 2015. Children's developing realization that some stories are true: links to the understanding of beliefs and signs. *Cogn. Dev.* 34:76–87

Corriveau KH, Harris PL, Meins E, Fernyhough C, Arnott B, et al. 2009b. Young children's trust in their mother's claims: longitudinal links with attachment security in infancy. *Child Dev.* 80:750–61

Corriveau KH, Kim AL, Schwalen C, Harris PL. 2009c. Abraham Lincoln and Harry Potter: children's differentiation between historical and fantasy characters. *Cognition* 112:213–25

Corriveau KH, Kim E, Song G, Harris PL. 2013a. Young children's deference to a consensus varies by culture and judgment setting. *J. Cogn. Cult.* 13:367–81

Corriveau KH, Kinzler K, Harris PL. 2013b. Accuracy trumps accent in children's endorsement of object labels. *Dev. Psychol.* 49:470–79

Corriveau KH, Kurkul KE. 2014. "Why does rain fall?"; Children prefer to learn from an informant who uses noncircular explanations. *Child Dev.* 85:1827–35

Cunningham AE, Stanovich KE. 1998. What reading does for the mind. *Am. Educ.* 22:8–15

Davoodi T, Corriveau KH, Harris PL. 2016. Distinguishing between realistic and fantastical figures in Iran. *Dev. Psychol.* 52:221–31

De Rosnay M, Cooper PJ, Tsigaras N, Murray L. 2006. Transmission of social anxiety from mother to infant: an experimental study using a social referencing paradigm. *Behav. Res. Ther.* 44:1165–75

DiYanni CJ, Corriveau KH, Kurkul K, Nasrini J, Nini D. 2015. The role of consensus and culture in children's imitation of inefficient actions. *J. Exp. Child Psychol.* 137:99–110

Einav S, Robinson EJ. 2010. Children's sensitivity to error magnitude when evaluating informants. *Cogn. Dev.* 25:218–32

Einav S, Robinson EJ, Fox A. 2013. Take it as read: origins of trust in knowledge gained from print. *J. Exp. Child Psychol.* 114:262–74

Faulkner P. 2011. *Knowledge on Trust.* Oxford, UK: Oxford Univ. Press

Frazier BN, Gelman SA, Wellman HM. 2009. Preschoolers' search for explanatory information within adult-child conversation. *Child Dev.* 80:1592–611

Frazier BN, Gelman SA, Wellman HM. 2016. Young children prefer and remember satisfying explanations. *J. Cogn. Dev.* 17:718–36

Fricker E. 1995. Telling and trusting: reductionism and anti-reductionism in the epistemology of testimony. *Mind* 104:393–411

Friedman O, Petrashek AR. 2009. Children do not follow the rule "ignorance means getting it wrong." *J. Exp. Child Psychol.* 102:114–21

Fusaro M, Harris PL. 2013. Dax gets the nod: Toddlers detect and use social cues to evaluate testimony. *Dev. Psychol.* 49:514–22

Ganea PA, Harris PL. 2013. Early limits on the verbal updating of an object's location. *J. Exp. Child Psychol.* 114:89–101

Gelfert A. 2006. Kant on testimony. *Br. J. Hist. Philos.* 14:627–52

Gelman SA. 2009. Learning from others: children's construction of concepts. *Annu. Rev. Psychol.* 60:115–40

Gelman SA, Coley JD. 1991. Language and categorization: the acquisition of natural kind terms. In *Perspectives on Language and Thought: Interrelations in Development*, ed. SA Gelman, JP Byrnes, pp. 146–96. Cambridge, UK: Cambridge Univ. Press

Gelman SA, Markman EM. 1986. Categories and induction in young children. *Cognition* 23:183–209

Gilbert D. 1991. How mental systems believe. *Am. Psychol.* 46:107–19

Gopnik A, Wellman HM. 2012. Reconstructing constructivism; causal models, Bayesian learning mechanisms, and the theory theory. *Psychol. Bull.* 138:1085–108

Gweon H, Pelton H, Konopka JA, Schulz LE. 2014. Signs of omission: Children selectively explore when teachers are under-informative. *Cognition* 132:335–41

Harris PL. 2011. Death in Spain, Madagascar, and beyond. In *Children's Understanding of Death*, ed. V Talwar, PL Harris, M Schleifer, pp. 19–40. Cambridge, UK: Cambridge Univ. Press

Harris PL. 2012. *Trusting What You're Told: How Children Learn from Others*. Cambridge, MA: Harvard Univ. Press

Harris PL, Corriveau KH. 2011. Young children's selective trust in informants. *Philos. Trans. R. Soc. B* 366:1179–90

Harris PL, Corriveau KH. 2014. Learning from testimony about religion and science. In *Trust and Skepticism: Children's Selective Learning from Testimony*, ed. E Robinson, S Einav, pp. 28–41. Hove, UK: Psychol. Press

Harris PL, Koenig MA. 2006. Trust in testimony: how children learn about science and religion. *Child Dev.* 77:505–24

Harris PL, Lane JD. 2014. Infants understand how testimony works. *Topoi Int. Rev. Philos.* 33:443–58

Harris PL, Pasquini ES, Duke S, Asscher JJ, Pons F. 2006. Germs and angels: the role of testimony in young children's ontology. *Dev. Sci.* 9:76–96

Hart B, Risley TR. 1995. *Meaningful Differences in Everyday Experience of Young American Children*. Baltimore, MD: Paul H Brookes Publ.

Heiphetz L, Lane JD, Waytz A, Young LL. 2016. How children and adults represent God's mind. *Cogn. Sci.* 40:121–44

Henderson AM, Graham SA, Schell V. 2015. 24-month-olds' selective learning is not an all-or-none phenomenon. *PLOS ONE* 10(6):e0131215

Hermes J, Behne T, Rakoczy H. 2015. The role of trait reasoning in young children's selective trust. *Dev. Psychol.* 51:1574–87

Hetherington C, Hendrickson C, Koenig MA. 2014. Reducing an in-group bias in preschool children: the impact of moral behavior. *Dev. Sci.* 17:1042–49

Heyman GD, Sritanyaratana L, Vanderbilt KE. 2013. Young children's trust in overtly misleading advice. *Cogn. Sci.* 37:646–67

Holton R. 1994. Deciding to trust, coming to believe. *Aust. J. Philos.* 72:63–76

Hume D. 1748. *Philosophical Essays Concerning Human Understanding*. New York: Georg Olms Verl.

Huttenlocher J, Vasilyeva M, Waterfall HR, Vevea JL, Hedges LV. 2007. The varieties of speech to young children. *Dev. Psychol.* 43:1062–83

Jaswal VK. 2004. Don't believe everything you hear: preschoolers' sensitivity to speaker intent in category induction. *Child Dev.* 75:1871–85

Jaswal VK. 2006. Preschoolers favor the creator's label when reasoning about an artifact's function. *Cognition* 99:B83–92

Jaswal VK. 2010. Believing what you're told: young children's trust in unexpected testimony about the physical world. *Cogn. Psychol.* 61:248–72

Jaswal VK, Croft AC, Setia AR, Cole CA. 2010. Young children have a specific, highly robust bias to trust testimony. *Psychol. Sci.* 21:1541–47

Jaswal VK, Kondrad RL. 2016. Why children are not always epistemically vigilant: cognitive limits and social considerations. *Child Dev. Perspect.* 10:240–44

Jaswal VK, Lima OK, Small JE. 2009. Compliance, conversion and category induction. *J. Exp. Child Psychol.* 102:182–95

Jaswal VK, Malone LS. 2007. Turning believers into skeptics: 3-year-olds' sensitivity to cues to speaker credibility. *J. Cogn. Dev.* 8:263–83

Jaswal VK, Neely LA. 2006. Adults don't always know best: Preschoolers use past reliability over age when learning new words. *Psychol. Sci.* 17:757–58

Jaswal VK, Pérez-Edgar K, Kondrad RL, Palmquist CM, Cole CA, Cole CE. 2014. Can't stop believing: inhibitory control and resistance to misleading testimony. *Dev. Sci.* 176:965–76

Jones K. 1999. Second-hand moral knowledge. *J. Philos.* 96:55–78

Kim G, Kwak K. 2011. Uncertainty matters: impact of stimulus ambiguity on infant social referencing. *Infant Child Dev.* 20:449–63

Knudsen B, Liszkowski U. 2012. Eighteen and 24-month-old infants correct others in anticipation of action mistakes. *Dev. Sci.* 15:113–22

Koenig MA, Echols CH. 2003. Infants' understanding of false labeling events: the referential roles of words and the speakers who use them. *Cognition* 87:179–208

Koenig MA, Harris PL. 2005. Preschoolers mistrust ignorant and inaccurate speakers. *Child Dev.* 76:1261–77

Koenig MA, McMyler B. 2017. Testimonial knowledge: understanding the evidential, uncovering the interpersonal. In *The Routledge Handbook of Social Epistemology*, ed. M Fricker, P Graham, D Henderson, N Pederson, J Wyatt. New York: Routledge Publ. In press

Koenig MA, Woodward AW. 2010. Sensitivity of 24-month-olds to the prior inaccuracy of the source: possible mechanisms. *Dev. Psychol.* 46:815–26

Kondrad RL, Jaswal VK. 2012. Explaining the errors away: Young children forgive understandable semantic mistakes. *Cogn. Dev.* 27:126–35

Krehm M, Onishi KH, Vouloumanos A. 2014. Infants under 12 months understand that pointing is communicative. *J. Cogn. Dev.* 15:527–38

Kurkul K, Corriveau KH. 2017. Question, explanation, follow-up: a mechanism for learning from others? *Child Dev.* In press

Kushnir T, Koenig MA. 2017. What I don't know won't hurt you: the relation between professed ignorance and later knowledge claims. *Dev. Psychol.* 53:826–35

Lackey J. 2008. *Learning from Words: Testimony as a Source of Knowledge.* Oxford, UK: Oxford Univ. Press

Landrum AR, Mills CM, Johnston AM. 2013. When do children trust the expert? Benevolence information influences children's trust more than expertise. *Dev. Sci.* 16:622–38

Lane JD, Harris PL. 2014. Confronting, representing, and believing counterintuitive concepts: navigating the natural and the supernatural. *Perspect. Psychol. Sci.* 9:144–60

Lane JD, Harris PL. 2015. The role of intuition and informants' expertise in children's epistemic trust. *Child Dev.* 86:919–26

Lane JD, Wellman HM, Gelman SA. 2013. Informants' traits weigh heavily in young children's trust in testimony and in their epistemic inferences. *Child Dev.* 84:1253–68

Levine RA, Levine SE, Schnell-Anzola B, Rowe ML, Dexter E. 2012. *Literacy and Mothering: How Women's Schooling Changes the Lives of the World's Children.* Oxford, UK: Oxford Univ. Press

Liszkowski U, Carpenter M, Tomasello M. 2008. Twelve-month-olds communicate helpfully and appropriately for knowledgeable and ignorant partners. *Cognition* 108:732–39

Locke J. 1975 (1689). *An Essay Concerning Human Understanding.* Oxford, UK: Oxford Univ. Press

Luce MR, Callanan MA, Smilovic S. 2013. Links between parents' epistemological stance and children's evidence talk. *Dev. Psychol.* 49:454–61

Ma L, Ganea PA. 2010. Dealing with conflicting information: young children's reliance on what they see versus what they are told. *Dev. Sci.* 13:151–60

Martin A, Onishi KH, Vouloumanos A. 2012. Understanding the abstract role of speech in communication at 12 months. *Cognition* 123:50–60

Marušić B. 2015. *Evidence and Agency.* Oxford, UK: Oxford Univ. Press

Mascaro O, Sperber D. 2009. The moral, epistemic, and mindreading components of children's vigilance towards deception. *Cognition* 112:367–80

McMyler B. 2011. *Testimony, Trust and Authority.* Oxford, UK: Oxford Univ. Press

Mills CM. 2013. Knowing when to doubt: developing a critical stance when learning from others. *Dev. Psychol.* 49:404–18

Morgan TJH, Laland KN, Harris PL. 2015a. The development of adaptive conformity in young children: effects of uncertainty and consensus. *Dev. Sci.* 18:511–24

Morgan TJH, Uomini NT, Rendell LE, Chouinard-Thuly L, Street SE, et al. 2015b. Experimental evidence for the co-evolution of hominin tool-making teaching and language. *Nat. Commun.* 6:6029

Moses LJ, Baldwin DA, Rosicky JG, Tidball G. 2001. Evidence for referential understanding in the emotions domain at twelve and eighteen months. *Child Dev.* 72:718–35

Pea RD. 1982. Origins of verbal logic: spontaneous denials by two- and three-year-olds. *J. Child Lang.* 9:597–626

Poulin-Dubois D, Brosseau-Liard P. 2016. The developmental origins of selective social learning. *Curr. Dir. Psychol. Sci.* 25:60–64

Reifen Tagar M, Federico CM, Lyons KE, Ludeke S, Koenig MA. 2014. Heralding the authoritarian? Orientation toward authority in early childhood. *Psychol. Sci.* 25:883–92

Robinson EJ, Einav S, Fox A. 2013. Reading to learn: prereaders' and early readers' trust in text as a source of knowledge. *Dev. Psychol.* 49:505–13

Ronfard S, Lane JD. 2017. Preschoolers continually adjust their epistemic trust based on an informant's ongoing accuracy. *Child Dev.* In press

Rowe ML. 2012. A longitudinal investigation of the role of quantity and quality of child-directed speech in vocabulary development. *Child Dev.* 83:17–74

Sabbagh MA, Shafman D. 2009. How children block learning from ignorant speakers. *Cognition* 112:415–22

Shafto P, Eaves B, Navarro DJ, Perfors A. 2012. Epistemic trust: modeling children's reasoning about others' knowledge and intent. *Dev. Sci.* 15:436–47

Shneidman L, Gweon H, Schulz LE, Woodward AL. 2016. Learning from others and spontaneous exploration: a cross-cultural investigation. *Child Dev.* 87:723–35

Shtulman A. 2013. Epistemic similarities between students' scientific and supernatural beliefs. *J. Educ. Psychol.* 105:199–212

Shtulman A. 2017. *Scienceblind: Why Our Intuitive Theories About the World Are So Often Wrong*. New York: Basic Books

Shutts K, Banaji MR, Spelke ES. 2010. Social categories guide young children's preferences for novel objects. *Dev. Sci.* 13:599–610

Sobel DM, Kushnir T. 2013. Knowledge matters: how children evaluate the reliability of testimony as a process of rational inference. *Psychol. Rev.* 120:779–97

Song H-J, Onishi KH, Baillargeon R, Fisher C. 2008. Can an agent's false belief be corrected by an appropriate communication? Psychological reasoning in 18-month-old infants. *Cognition* 109:295–315

Sorce JF, Emde RN, Campos J, Klinnert MD. 1985. Maternal emotional signaling: its effect on the visual cliff behavior of 1-year-olds. *Dev. Psychol.* 21:195–200

Sosa E. 1991. Testimony and coherence. In *Knowledge in Perspective: Selected Essays in Epistemology*, pp. 215–22. Cambridge, UK: Cambridge Univ. Press

Spelke ES, Breinlinger K, Macomber J, Jacobson K. 1992. Origins of knowledge. *Psychol. Rev.* 99:605–32

Sperber D, Clément F, Heintz C, Mascaro O, Mercier H, et al. 2010. Epistemic vigilance. *Mind Lang.* 25:359–93

Stenberg G. 2013. Do 12-month-old infants trust a competent adult? *Infancy* 18:873–904

Stephens EC, Koenig MA. 2015. Varieties of testimony: children's selective learning in semantic versus episodic domains. *Cognition* 137:182–88

Tamis-LeMonda CS, Adolph KE, Lobo SA, Karasik LB, Ishak S, et al. 2008. When infants take mothers' advice: 18-month-olds integrate perceptual and social information to guide motor action. *Dev. Psychol.* 44:734–46

Tizard B, Hughes M. 1984. *Young Children Learning*. London: Fontana

Uccelli P, Phillips Galloway E, Barr CD, Meneses A, Dobbs CL. 2015. Beyond vocabulary: Core Academic Language Skills (CALS) that support text comprehension. *Read. Res. Q.* 50:337–56

Vouloumanos A, Onishi KH, Pogue A. 2012. Twelve-month-old infants recognize that speech can communicate unobservable intentions. *PNAS* 109:12933–37

Weizman ZO, Snow CE. 2001. Lexical input as related to children's vocabulary acquisition: effects of sophisticated exposure and support for meaning. *Dev. Psychol.* 37:265–79

Whiten A. 2017. Social learning and culture in child and chimpanzee. *Annu. Rev. Psychol.* 68:129–54

Whiten A, Ayala F, Feldman MD, Laland KN. 2017. The extension of biology through culture. *PNAS* 114(30):7775–81

Williams BAO. 1972. Knowledge and reasons. In *Problems in the Theory of Knowledge/Problèmes de la Théorie de la Connaissance*, ed. GH Von Wright, pp. 1–11. Berlin: Springer

Wilson D, Sperber D. 2002. Truthfulness and relevance. *Mind* 111:583–632

Woolley JE, Ghossainy M. 2013. Revisiting the fantasy–reality distinction: children as naïve skeptics. *Child Dev.* 84:1496–510

Gender Stereotypes

Naomi Ellemers

Faculty of Social Sciences, Utrecht University, 3508 TC Utrecht, Netherlands;
email: N.ellemers@uu.nl

Annu. Rev. Psychol. 2018. 69:275–98

First published as a Review in Advance on
September 27, 2017

The *Annual Review of Psychology* is online at
psych.annualreviews.org

https://doi.org/10.1146/annurev-psych-122216-011719

Keywords

gender, stereotyping, implicit bias, objectification, communication, backlash effects

Abstract

There are many differences between men and women. To some extent, these are captured in the stereotypical images of these groups. Stereotypes about the way men and women think and behave are widely shared, suggesting a kernel of truth. However, stereotypical expectations not only reflect existing differences, but also impact the way men and women define themselves and are treated by others. This article reviews evidence on the nature and content of gender stereotypes and considers how these relate to gender differences in important life outcomes. Empirical studies show that gender stereotypes affect the way people attend to, interpret, and remember information about themselves and others. Considering the cognitive and motivational functions of gender stereotypes helps us understand their impact on implicit beliefs and communications about men and women. Knowledge of the literature on this subject can benefit the fair judgment of individuals in situations where gender stereotypes are likely to play a role.

Contents

1. DIFFERENT PEOPLE OR DIFFERENT WORLDS?

"Women are from Venus, men are from Mars" is a phrase that is often used to explain observed differences in the way women and men think, feel, and act. It conveys the inevitability of such differences by suggesting that men and women originate from planets that are millions of miles apart, implying that they are as inherently different as they would be if they were separate species.

There is no denying that there are differences between men and women in many life domains. The question, however, is to what extent these differences reflect the way men and women essentially *are*, and to what extent they result from how we *think* men and women differ from each other because of gender stereotypes. Identifying the nature and content of gender stereotypes clarifies the fact that they not only describe typical differences between men and women, but also prescribe what men and women should be and how they should behave in different life domains.

Even if men and women display similar characteristics, preferences, and ambitions, the different views and stereotypical expectations that we have of them place them in different worlds. Considering the origins and the implications of gender stereotypes helps us understand how these relate to gender differences in society. The research reviewed in this article reveals how gender stereotypes contribute to the development and perpetuation of such differences by leading people to treat men and women differently.

2. THE NATURE OF GENDER STEREOTYPES

Stereotypes reflect general expectations about members of particular social groups. However, even if there is an overall difference between these groups, not all individual exemplars in these groups will necessarily differ from each other. For instance, on average, men are taller than women, but we all know individual men and women for whom this is not true or for whom the difference is even reversed. Yet the stereotypical perception that a particular feature characterizes membership of a specific group typically leads people to overemphasize differences between groups and underestimate variations within groups.

The tendency to perceive individuals as representatives of different social groups has been documented for a variety of groups in a range of contexts. Research has also revealed that the impact of such social categorization on the assignment of traits and features to members of particular groups can be quite fluid depending on the situation and the contrast with relevant comparison groups that seems most salient (Oakes et al. 1994). For instance, psychologists may seem quite creative when compared to physicists but appear much less creative when compared to artists. Additionally, there are many situations in which psychologists are not even evaluated as representatives of their profession simply because their qualifications are not relevant (e.g., in a sports contest) or not visible (e.g., when walking in the street).

However, such stereotype fluidity and context dependence are much less likely to emerge in relation to gender categorizations and gender stereotypes. Gender is considered a primary feature in person perception. Children and adults immediately and implicitly cluster unknown individuals by their gender, even when this categorization is not relevant to the situation and has no informational benefits (e.g., Bennett et al. 2000, Ito & Urland 2003). Furthermore, even though we all know examples of gender bending, gender continues to be seen as a binary categorization, in which we tend to compare men to women and women to men, anchoring any differences in terms of a contrast between them. Thus, gender categorizations are immediately detected, are chronically salient, seem relatively fixed, and are easily polarized. This contributes to the formation and persistence of gender stereotypes and reinforces perceptions of differences between men and women.

2.1. A Kernel of Truth?

Gender stereotypes reflect the primary importance we attach to task performance when judging men and to social relationships when considering women. Assertiveness and performance are seen as indicators of greater agency in men, and warmth and care for others are viewed as signs of greater communality in women (e.g., Kite et al. 2008). Differences in the emphasis placed on agency versus care are, indeed, visible in the way men and women behave and the life choices they make. Action tendencies and overconfidence in men result in more risky choices (e.g., in sexual behavior, alcohol and drug use, gambling, driving; Byrnes et al. 1999), whereas women are more cautious in these domains. Men and women also tend to work in different occupations and take on different caretaking roles. Social survey and census data show that, across 30 industrialized countries, there is a clear segregation according to gender in occupational roles: Certain occupations (such as policing) are dominated by men, whereas other occupations (such as nursing) are dominated by women (Jarman et al. 2012). Women across different countries and cultures spend more time on household activities than men do, regardless of their employment status. In 2015, an average difference of 50 minutes per day in the time spent on housework was observed between the male and female members of couples living in the United States (Bur. Labor Stat. 2016). Furthermore, even though both men and women are willing to incur personal costs to help others, they typically do this in different ways. For instance, men are more likely to engage in emergency rescues (displaying agency), whereas women are more inclined to volunteer for the Peace Corps (indicating communality) (Becker & Eagly 2004).

These observations of how men and women behave seem easily explained by referring to inherent biological differences between them (see also Ellemers 2014). Indeed, the larger physical strength of men and the ability of women to bear children predispose them for different types of activities and relate to testosterone and oxytocin levels, which can also impact behavior. Accordingly, these gender differences are often seen as deeply rooted in evolution and hard-wired in the brain, reflecting the different roles and survival values of agentic versus caring behaviors for men and women living in hunter-gatherer societies. However, this account does not adequately represent current scientific insights.

For instance, recent evidence suggests that the division of gender roles in hunter-gatherer societies is much more egalitarian than is often assumed (Dyble et al. 2015). Furthermore, there is no one-to-one relationship between specific hormones and specific behaviors. For instance, although testosterone tends to be seen as a precursor of aggressive behavior, it can also elicit prosocial behavior and care (Van Honk et al. 2011). Hormonal changes not only depend on gender but are also triggered by important life events and situational experiences. Indeed, men and women show equal increases in oxytocin levels 6 months after the birth of their first child, which helps them accommodate the caring demands of the new situation (Gordon et al. 2010). Furthermore, there is no evidence that the brains of men and women are wired differently. Magnetic scans of over 1,400 human brains could not establish reliable differences in the nature and volume of the tissue (gray matter, cortex) or connectivity between areas in male and female brains (Joel et al. 2015; see also Fine 2013). Similarly, a review of hundreds of studies on cognitive performance (e.g., math ability), personality and social behaviors (e.g., leadership), and psychological well-being (e.g., academic self-esteem) reveals more similarities than differences between men and women (Hyde 2014). In fact, the studies cited above generally observe larger differences among individual women and individual men than between men and women as groups, providing evidence against the impact of biology as the main factor in creating behavioral gender differences.

Thus, if there is a kernel of truth underlying gender stereotypes, it is a tiny kernel and does not account for the far-reaching inferences we often make about essential differences between men and women (Bussey & Bandura 1999). Instead, research indicates that gender differences develop over the life span, due to the way boys and girls are raised and educated. In this process, biological differences set the stage for shared beliefs about the characteristic traits and abilities of women and men. But research evidence strongly indicates that the different societal roles and power positions of men as economic providers and women as homemakers—rather than biological distinctions between them—emphasize and enlarge initial differences. Social roles—over and above gender—have been found to impact hormonal regulation, self-regulation, and social regulation, which ultimately elicit different thoughts, feelings, and behaviors in men and women (Eagly & Wood 2013).

2.2. Helpful or Harmful?

Stereotypes in general and gender stereotypes in particular may be helpful when there is a need to make quick estimates of how unknown individuals are likely to behave or when trying to understand how large groups of people generally differ from each other. However, these very same functions make stereotypes much less helpful in estimating the exact potential or evaluating the defining characteristics of specific individuals. Yet this is what we often do when we rely on group-based expectations instead of judging individuals by their own merits. Gender stereotypes exaggerate the perceived implications of categorizing people by their gender and offer an oversimplified view of reality. They reinforce perceived boundaries between women and men and seemingly justify the symbolic and social implications of gender for role differentiation and social inequality. The broad awareness of gender stereotypes has far-reaching implications for those who rely on stereotypical expectations to evaluate others, as well as those who are exposed to these judgments. Gender stereotypes are shared by women and men, and their implications affect stereotype users and targets of both genders.

If we take the perspective of stereotype users, there is overwhelming research evidence that gender-stereotypical expectations influence the way we judge the abilities of women and men. That is, both male and female evaluators tend to perceive and value the same performance differently depending on the gender of the individual who displayed this performance. This is evident from experimental studies where identical information about individual achievements is ascribed to either a woman or a man. Similar conclusions emerge from real-life observations, where diverging evaluations of men and women are traced back to objective performance criteria.

In educational contexts, gender stereotyping causes female students to be seen as less talented than male students in all areas of science (Leslie et al. 2015). For instance, in biology, male students are seen to excel even when their female classmates actually have higher grades (Grunspan et al. 2016). Experimental studies further reveal that an identical CV and application letter results in different perceived competence levels and job offers depending on whether the applicant is identified as John or Jennifer (Moss-Racusin et al. 2012). Imaginary differences in perceived skill have also been documented in the evaluation of creative products, such as the design of a house, depending on whether it carried the name of a male or female architect (Proudfoot et al. 2015).

Gender stereotypes not only influence the perceived potential of men and women when they are being selected for future careers, but also impact how the work actually performed by men and women is rated and valued. This was revealed in an experimental study where evaluations of teacher behaviors (e.g., promptness) during an online course were rated nearly a full point higher (at 4.35 instead of 3.55 on a five-point scale) when the instructor was identified by a male name instead of a female name (MacNell et al. 2015). These evaluative differences prompted by gender stereotypes can have important consequences for the career development and income levels of men and women, which can accumulate into substantial gender inequalities in the course of a life span. This has been documented many times, for instance, in census data comparing the wages of men and women entering the labor market with equal qualifications and employed in similar job types (Buffington et al. 2016).

Throughout their careers, women are less likely than men to be selected for promotions and prestigious positions. For instance, female professors of management were less likely than male professors to be awarded an endowed chair, even when there was no difference in their objective performance (academic publications, citations), nor in their personal circumstances at work (years into career, discipline) or at home (children) (Treviño et al. 2015). That this reflects a broader tendency to undervalue the professional performance of women is clearly visible in a meta-analysis of almost 100 empirical studies conducted among 378,850 employees in different industries (Joshi et al. 2015). Even considering the fact that the work performance of women tends to be evaluated less favorably than the performance of men, observed gender differences in rewards (salary, bonuses, promotions) are almost 14 times larger than these performance ratings would indicate.

These differences have been documented most extensively and most clearly in educational and work contexts, where reliance on gender stereotypes can be tested against objective performance differences. However, mirroring higher expectations of men in general ability and task performance domains, we see that women are evaluated more favorably than men in terms of warmth, empathy, and altruism—even when this is unfounded. For instance, in many countries, fathers have no or very limited access to parental leave and are less likely to be granted custody of their children after divorce, based on the assumption that men attach less importance to parenthood than women do or are less well equipped to take care of children than women are.

2.3. Can We Avoid Gender Stereotypes?

In light of the visible evidence that men as well as women can and do care for family members and friends and that women as well as men can display high levels of performance and ambition, it would seem silly to maintain that warmth typifies (all) women and competence characterizes (all) men.

Indeed, at present, many people would be reluctant to explicitly make such claims. Nevertheless, their private convictions and implicit beliefs still often rely on these stereotypical associations—without them realizing that this is the case. For instance, in computerized reaction time tasks, people more quickly and effortlessly connect names and faces of women to various aspects of family life, whereas names and faces of men come more easily to mind when thinking about professional careers (Greenwald & Banaji 1995). Indeed, across different cultures and contexts, even those who are reluctant to claim that women are less competent (i.e., do not endorse hostile sexist views) may still believe that women are particularly sensitive and need to be protected by men (so-called benevolent sexism; Glick et al. 2000).

People find it difficult to recognize that these more subtle and implicit beliefs may also reflect stereotypical views of women and men (Barreto & Ellemers 2015). Yet the gender stereotypes implicitly endorsed in this way can overrule more explicitly stated intentions to treat men and women equally. For instance, the admiration for stereotypical qualities of women that characterizes endorsement of benevolent sexist views is associated with acceptance of domestic violence against women (Glick et al. 2002) and a desire to restrict their rights to regulate pregnancy and reproduction (Huang et al. 2016). In couples that implicitly endorse gender stereotypes in this way, the needs of the male partner for intimacy are prioritized over the achievement ambitions of the female partner (Hammond & Overall 2015). In task contexts, benevolent and implicit—rather than more hostile and explicit—references to gender stereotypes cause women to downplay their achievements and ambitions and to emphasize their interpersonal skills (Barreto et al. 2010).

The power of implicit beliefs is also visible among parents, even those who claim that they show no difference in how they raise boys and girls. Those who implicitly make gender stereotypical associations are more likely to behave differently toward their sons than their daughters, for instance, when disciplining them (Endendijk et al. 2014). Thus, from a very early age, children are implicitly taught about gender stereotypes and reproduce them in their own beliefs and behaviors. For instance, the implicit assumption that math is not for girls is already observed among girls at age nine. This assumption becomes stronger in adolescence and better predicts academic achievement and enrollment preferences than girls' explicit views about gender and math (Steffens et al. 2010). Thus, even though explicit attitudes toward men and women have become more egalitarian over the years—and, in many countries, legislation is in place to enforce equal treatment—at the implicit level, gender stereotypes continue to shape our judgments and behaviors.

2.4. Gendered Expectations

Across different domains, gender stereotypes implicitly impact the expectations we have about the qualities, priorities, and needs of individual men and women, as well as the standards to which we hold them (see **Table 1**). The implicit impact of gender stereotypes is clearly visible in research revealing that relational criteria dominate the way we regard and evaluate women. Indeed, men as well as women are inclined to evaluate women primarily in terms of their appearance, rather than their accomplishments, whereas they do not evaluate men in this way (Fredrickson & Roberts 1997). As a result, looks dominate our judgment of the general worth of women, even in contexts where they should be irrelevant. This was the case for Ann Hopkins, a consultant who had clearly established her professional credentials and earning power. However, she was rated unfit for partnership in her firm because her behavior, make-up, and dress style were considered insufficiently feminine (see also Fiske et al. 1991). Research has revealed that this case represents a more systematic pattern in how women of different races and occupations are evaluated, which emerges regardless of how familiar or attractive they are. Unfortunately, women are perceived as less competent and are even considered less fully human when evaluators focus on their appearance

Table 1 Gender stereotypes and gendered expectations

Gender stereotypes	Male	Female
Stereotypical domain	Agency	Communality
Relevant behavior	Individual task performance	Care for others
Anticipated priorities	Work	Family
Perceived qualities	Competence	Warmth
Neglected needs	Interpersonal connection	Professional achievement

(Cikara et al. 2011). Such objectification effects do not diminish the perceived qualities of men, even when they are evaluated in terms of their appearance (Heflick et al. 2011).

Gender stereotypes also implicitly affect the way we search for romantic partners and the qualities we seek in them. When describing their ideal partner, men claim that they are attracted to women who are as intelligent as or more intelligent than they are. However, when actually interacting with a specific individual, they indicate being less romantically interested in women who seem to outsmart them (Park et al. 2015). Even if men do value a romantic partner who is assertive and independently minded, women tend to assume that men will be more attracted to them when they behave in a deferential, accommodating, and agreeable way (Hornsey et al. 2015). Thus, even for those who explicitly indicate that gender stereotypes should not matter, stereotypical preferences and beliefs implicitly shape the way men and women try to appear attractive and engage in romantic and work relationships.

Finally, parenthood also causes us to perceive men and women differently, with gender stereotypes implicitly guiding our judgment. When women become parents, we tend to assume that caring for their children will be their first priority and should make them less committed and ambitious at work. However, when men become fathers, this does not impact negatively on their perceived suitability as workers. These implicit expectations—even if unwarranted—impact the job and career opportunities that women and men receive. A survey of over 40,000 employees in 36 countries revealed that men and women reported similar issues in combining work and family roles (Lyness & Judiesch 2014). Yet managers see these issues as more of a problem for women than for men. For instance, in a study in which job applications were rated, mothers were approximately two times less likely to be recommended for the job than women without children, despite the fact that their stated qualifications were identical (Correll et al. 2007). Indeed, the lower perceived competence of mothers, in particular, causes them to be considered less suitable for promotion at work (Heilman & Okimoto 2008). Thus, different studies have revealed that professional women are seen as less competent after they become mothers, whereas this is not the case for men who become fathers. As a consequence, people are generally less willing to hire, promote, or educate working mothers than working fathers or workers without children (Cuddy et al. 2004).

Women are not the only ones to suffer from implicit gender stereotypes; men do as well, albeit in different ways. Men are underrepresented in occupational and family roles that emphasize communality and care, and gender stereotypes implicitly prevent their interest and inclusion in such roles (Croft et al. 2015). Yet the implicit assumption that relationships with others and interpersonal vulnerability are less relevant for men can have debilitating effects over time. These effects were illustrated in a meta-analysis of 78 samples surveying nearly 20,000 research participants. This survey revealed that men who were prompted by the masculine stereotype to be self-reliant and exert power over women suffered social costs, regardless of their race, age, or sexual orientation. They displayed all manner of unfavorable outcomes indicating negative social functioning and impaired mental health, including depression, loneliness, and substance abuse (Wong et al. 2017).

3. MAKING SENSE OF THE WORLD

We use stereotypes to make sense of the world. Our stereotypical expectations activate specific brain areas that help us identify, interpret, and remember the things we see, hear, and learn about others (Amodio 2014). By determining what captures our attention, what information seems valuable, and what should be remembered, stereotypes generally form a very strong and powerful filter through which we process objective information about men and women (e.g., Fiske & Taylor 2013). For the reasons discussed above, gender stereotypes perform all of these functions even more consistently and pervasively than stereotypes about other groups. This makes stereotypes resilient to change because information revealing that they no longer form an adequate shorthand to characterize the group is likely to be ignored, discounted, or forgotten (Wigboldus et al. 2003).

3.1. Cognitive Functions

Competence and warmth are basic dimensions in human perception. Research has found that they are primary features we assess when evaluating unknown others and are universally applicable dimensions that help us compare different groups in society. We use these dimensions to predict the most likely behavior of others, inferring their abilities from competence judgments and their intentions from perceived warmth (Fiske et al. 2002). The perception that men as a group are more competent and women as a group are more warm thus elicits the expectation that the abilities of men are likely to be superior to those of women and the intentions of women to be more benevolent than those of men. As indicated above, these stereotypical expectations may come to dominate the views we have of individual women and men, as they influence the way we respond to and process more specific information that might help us refine our judgment.

Individuals who clearly violate stereotypical expectations capture our attention, and stereotype-inconsistent information can dominate our judgment, as detailed in Section 3.3. However, in any situation where information about specific individuals is scarce or ambiguous, we tend to favor information that confirms the stereotype. For instance, we are more likely to attend to information that matches our stereotypical expectations. Event-related potentials in the brain (P600, a peak in electrical brain activity elicited by linguistic errors and anomalies) indicate that it is easier for people to capture and understand information about unknown others that is consistent with the gender stereotype (she is a nurse) than counter-stereotypical information (she is a mechanic) (Canal et al. 2015).

The impact that this has on people's judgments of others was demonstrated in a study where participants received equal amounts of information about the achievements and fame of men and women. Yet when asked to assess unknown men and women, participants relied on general gender stereotypical expectations to assign more fame to men than to women, instead of benefiting from the concrete information they had just received (Banaji & Greenwald 1995). At the same time, research participants were probably unaware of their failure to attend to information that was inconsistent with the gender stereotype, as this failure occurred irrespective of whether they explicitly agreed with gender stereotypes.

When processing information, we tend to consider observations that match our stereotypical expectations as more veridical, reliable, and informative than counter-stereotypical observations. This has been documented quite extensively in the attributions that are made for identical achievements of women and men in education or work (Swim & Sanna 1996). Performance successes or failures that seem to match stereotypical expectations are seen as accurately reflecting individual talents and abilities. However, accomplishments that are not in line with the stereotype tend to be discounted. These are attributed to external circumstances (e.g., help from others) or temporary conditions (e.g., an easy assignment, exceptional effort, or cheating). For instance, mathematics teachers saw high test results of boys in the class as indicative of their ability for logical reasoning, whereas identical achievements of girls were ascribed to exceptional effort. Conversely, performance failures of boys were seen as indicating lack of effort, whereas they were considered diagnostic of lack of ability for logical reasoning in girls (Tiedemann 2000).

Similar mechanisms also make it less likely for women to get credited for their contribution to a team result or joint performance. For instance, in a series of experiments in which people were asked to evaluate the work of a mixed-sex dyad, the contribution of the woman in the dyad was devalued. That is, women were seen as being less likely than men to have contributed to or influenced the work that had been carried out by the dyad (Heilman & Haynes 2005). This has important implications for many work contexts where people work together as a team or have to share credit for joint performance or achievement of group targets.

Finally, stereotypes facilitate the recall of information that is stereotype consistent over stereotype-inconsistent information. Stereotypes are used as a memory retrieval cue, even for things that people remember about their own past behavior. This was revealed in research where high school students were asked about the marks they had received for different school subjects. Two studies showed that the recall of actual school results was biased by gender stereotypes. Female students who endorsed gender stereotypes consistently underestimated the marks that they had actually received for math and overestimated their school marks in language and arts subjects. Likewise, men who endorsed gender stereotypes recalled their math grades to be higher than they actually had been (Chatard et al. 2007). Judgments that are made about others are also impacted by the selective recall of achievements that match gender-stereotypical expectations, as seemed to be the case in a study of the remuneration of male and female executives of listed firms in the United Kingdom (Kulich et al. 2011). This study determined that the high performance and achievements of male executives were taken into account to determine their bonuses, whereas the performance of female executives seemed to be forgotten when decisions about bonus affordance were made.

All these different mechanisms work together, as gender stereotypes are used to attend to, organize, and store information about individual men and women. Because privilege is given to information that matches stereotypical expectations, the threshold for noticing, valuing, and retaining counter-stereotypical information is higher than that for information that matches gender stereotypes (see **Figure 1**).

3.2. Communication

In the case of groups about which many people have little to no knowledge, such as homeless people or migrants from faraway countries, it is relatively easy to understand why we rely on stereotypes to predict and understand the behaviors of individual group members. When we have no detailed knowledge of the group, lack first-hand experience with individual group members, and have little concrete evidence of their intentions and abilities, it makes sense to infer expectations about individuals from characteristics of the group. It also makes sense not to discard these group-based expectations on the basis of a single diverging experience, especially when the group is seen as a potential source of threat. It is better to be safe than sorry. But all these valid considerations fall away in the case of gender stereotypes. Most of us have intense and intimate connections with members of both gender groups, and interactions are mostly positive instead of aggressive (Radke et al. 2016). Plenty of information is available about the concrete qualities, desires, and achievements of individual men and women, and it is clear that men and women are not all the same. How, then, is it possible that group-based expectations materialize from all these individual experiences, and how are gender stereotypes communicated?

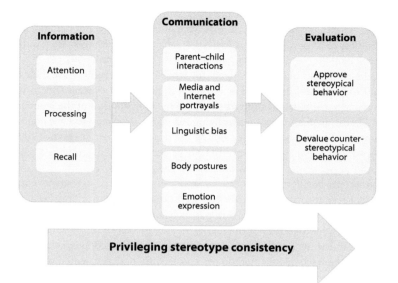

Figure 1

Privileging stereotype consistency in how people deal with information, communicate with each other, and evaluate others.

This communication mostly happens implicitly, through the way we speak about and portray the activities, desires, and achievements of men and women. For instance, in the way they raise and educate their children, parents may implicitly teach them what (in)appropriate behaviors for women and men are. Even parents who may consciously avoid buying gender-specific toys and claim they treat their sons and daughters equally communicate these implicit expectations, for instance, when reading a picture book with their children. They convey what they consider to be appropriate behaviors and activities for boys and girls by making more positive comments about images of children engaging in gender-stereotypical activities (Endendijk et al. 2014).

Media representations also reinforce stereotypical expectations of men and women, for instance, by primarily showing men in expert roles and women in caregiving roles in advertisements, TV series, and news programs or by printing photographs portraying the face and upper torso of men while providing full-body images of women, which facilitates the tendency to evaluate women on the basis of their dress style and body shape (Matthews 2007). Likewise, media coverage of public figures focuses on the achievements of men, for instance, in sports or politics, while addressing the appearance or personal relationships of women. This happened, for instance, at the Wimbledon tennis tournament of 2016, when news reports elaborated on Serena Williams' tennis dress instead of her stellar play. Information provided on the Internet also conveys and reinforces gender stereotypes. For instance, Google was criticized because its image search algorithms almost exclusively come up with gender stereotypical representations for various occupations (such as doctors versus nurses) (Cohn 2015). These media and Internet portrayals are not without consequences. In fact, one review of research revealed that, over time, the gender stereotypes implicitly conveyed in this way impact the beliefs that girls develop about gender roles, their bodies, and sexual relationships (Ward & Harrison 2005). An experimental study further found that undergraduate students who were induced to play a video game as a sexualized female character showed diminished self-efficacy as a result of this experience (Behm-Morawitz & Mastro 2009).

The verbal accounts we provide and receive about the behaviors of others and ourselves also implicitly convey and reinforce gender-stereotypical expectations. The words we choose to describe specific achievements reflect the stereotypical attributions we tend to make. Experimental research shows that we use more abstract terms (such as adjectives) to describe behavior that matches stereotypical expectations. Conversely, when these same behaviors are displayed by someone for whom they are counter-stereotypical, more concrete terms (such as action verbs) are used (Maass 1999). To the person receiving such verbal messages (e.g., "he is smart" versus "she did well on the test"), the more abstract terms implicitly communicate a stable disposition or characteristic property of what the person is, whereas more concrete terms are seen to convey the situational and temporary nature of what the person does (Wigboldus et al. 2000). Such communications implicitly maintain gender stereotypes as an adequate representation of the group, even when recounting examples of counter-stereotypical behaviors.

Such linguistic biases can have far-reaching implications, as was revealed, for instance, by an analysis of 1,244 recommendation letters from 54 countries, submitted to support the grant applications of postdoctoral researchers in the geosciences. Across the board, female applicants were significantly less likely to be described as "excellent" by those who were trying to support them, regardless of whether the recommendations were made by men or women (Dutt et al. 2016). Likewise, recommendation letters for applicants for an academic faculty position were more likely to contain "standout" (excellent, outstanding, exceptional, unmatched) and "ability" (talent, genius, brilliant, gifted) words for male candidates, whereas "grindstone" words (hardworking, conscientious, dependable, thorough, dedicated) were chosen more often to praise the abilities and achievements of female candidates (Schmader et al. 2007). To perform well in many professional jobs and roles, both talent and dedication are needed. Yet evaluators may be implicitly prompted to prioritize perceived talent over demonstrated dedication, for instance, by the language used to ask for their judgments, as was revealed by an examination of 2,823 applications for an early career grant from the Dutch National Science Foundation. Female applicants received lower ratings than male applicants on forms containing gendered evaluation labels and were less likely to have their applications awarded, even though there was no difference in the perceived quality of the proposals they submitted (Van der Lee & Ellemers 2015).

Non-verbal communications, particularly body posture, may also implicitly convey and reinforce gender stereotypes. In public situations, men and women tend to adopt different body postures, with men displaying more expansive and open postures (arms and legs spread up or out, taking up physical space), whereas women are more likely to show closed and contractive postures (crossed arms and legs, squeezing in) (Cashdan 1998). Male and female dress styles (pants versus skirts), the differential body size of men and women, and childhood socialization about proper demeanor for girls and boys all contribute to these differences. The implicit activation of gender stereotypes also leads women to adopt more contractive body postures (De Lemus et al. 2012).

However, open and expansive body postures also relate to dominance and high power, whereas closed and contractive body postures indicate submission and low power. Such postures convey information to others but also affect the way people perceive and present themselves (Carney et al. 2010), as was illustrated by a study where participants were asked to take on specific body postures while preparing for a mock job interview. In this study, men and women who had adopted an expansive (versus contractive) posture before the start of the interview were perceived by others as more captivating and enthusiastic during the interview and were considered more hirable by their evaluators. In fact, their body language, rather than their verbal presentation, dominated these ratings (Cuddy et al. 2015b). Thus, the body postures typically shown by women—which are reinforced when gender stereotypes are implicitly activated—signal submissiveness and low power to others as well as to themselves. This makes them behave less confidently and causes them to be considered less competent in a work context, unwittingly enacting gender stereotypes.

Finally, the emotions expressed by men and women also communicate and reinforce gender-stereotypical expectations. Research suggests that men and women tend to have similar emotional experiences. However, the way they communicate about their emotions is different, with men expressing all negative emotions as anger—an emotion related to action and agency—and women more likely to indicate sadness—which is associated with lack of control over the situation (Plant et al. 2000). Likewise, gender stereotypes guide the way we recognize and label emotions expressed by others. Research shows that parents reading a picture book implicitly teach their children to label emotions in gender-stereotypical ways by referring to gender-neutral drawings of a sad child as female, while assuming that an angry child is male (Van der Pol et al. 2015). Thus, the ways we express, interpret, and communicate about emotional experiences are modified by gender stereotypes.

3.3. Stereotype Disconfirmation

Individuals who clearly disconfirm stereotypical expectations tend to be devalued. We decide that they are not representative for their gender group rather than revising stereotypical expectations. This happens, for instance, for women working in male-dominated jobs, who are seen as unfeminine (Badgett & Folbre 2003), and for professional women, who are seen as members of a specific subtype of women that is high in competence but low in warmth—just like men (Fiske et al. 2002). At the same time, flamboyant gay men are seen as low in competence and high in warmth—just like women (Clausell & Fiske 2005).

Gender stereotypes thus not only capture how we expect men and women to behave, but also communicate how we think they *should* behave (Prentice & Carranza 2002). Indeed, women who behave in line with the stereotype are evaluated more positively than women who seem to challenge gender-stereotypical expectations (Eagly & Mladinic 1994). In fact, men and women agree that gender-stereotypical views indicate both that men are more competent than women and that they *ought* to be more competent. Likewise, these views convey the idea not only that women tend to be more communal and warm than men, but also that this is the way they *should* be (Ramos et al. 2017). Thus, gender stereotypes also provide people with shifting standards against which the qualities and achievements of men and women are evaluated (Biernat & Manis 1994). As a result, men who behave modestly in a professional context violate expectations of the masculine stereotype and are disliked because they are seen as weak and insecure (Moss-Racusin et al. 2010). Conversely, women who display agentic behavior (by being competent, ambitious, and competitive) seem insufficiently nice and are disliked and devalued as a result (Rudman & Phelan 2008).

This places women in leadership roles in a difficult position because, in different countries across the world, the type of behavior that is required for professional success seems incompatible with how women are expected to behave on the basis of their gender (Schein et al. 1996). Indeed, women in supervisory roles are less likely to elicit threat responses and competitiveness in their male subordinates when they show their leadership in a feminine way by being an efficient project manager, rather than displaying ambition and asserting their authority (Netchaeva et al. 2015, Williams & Tiedens 2016).

The incompatible requirements for female leadership also play out more implicitly, for instance, in preferences for voice pitch. Women, on average, have higher-pitched voices than men. However, both men and women prefer male and female leaders with lower voices (Klofstad et al. 2012), even in stereotypically feminine domains (Anderson & Klofstad 2012). Having a deep voice apparently helps people to be successful in leadership roles. For instance, analysis of natural speech performed by almost 800 chief executive officers (CEOs) at public companies revealed that those with deeper voices managed larger companies, made more money, and held longer tenure (Mayew et al. 2013). For women, however, there is a cost to lowering their voices to be more effective leaders. Even though women tend to be perceived as more dominant when they have lower voices (Borkowska & Pawlowski 2011), they are also considered less attractive by men (Feinberg et al. 2008).

When professional and life roles do not fit gender stereotypical expectations, this inconsistency impacts perceived self-efficacy and restricts life choices for both women and men. The female stereotype restricts the professional choices of women, as beliefs about the characteristic behaviors of a good mother or a good worker dominate work–family decisions (Williams et al. 2016). These beliefs overrule rational arguments and clear business cases documenting the benefits of equal treatment of men and women. For instance, when women start earning more money than their husbands, they increase (rather than decrease) the amount of time they invest in household work, presumably to avoid violating stereotypical expectations of a good wife (Bittman et al. 2003). In other contexts, too, women provide unpaid care to comply with stereotypical norms—not because they are intrinsically motivated to do so—which makes them less available for paid work and causes them economic disadvantage (Folbre 2012).

Likewise, the male stereotype discourages men from taking on caring roles in the family because others do not value these roles in men. Experimental research reveals that fathers who give up employment and sacrifice financial security to care for their children are devalued, whereas mothers who make identical choices are highly approved (Riggs 1997). In reality, stay-at-home and employed fathers do not differ from each other in terms of the masculine and feminine features that characterize them; they only have different attitudes toward the division of gender roles (Fischer & Anderson 2012). Yet a series of studies has indicated that men and women express less liking for stay-at-home fathers than for employed fathers and also think that stay-at-home fathers are not regarded very highly by others (Brescoll & Uhlmann 2005).

4. RESILIENCE TO CHANGE

Due to their prescriptive nature—elucidated above—gender stereotypes are not neutral a priori expectations. Instead, they prescribe what a good group member is like and, thus, tap into the very basic desire of individuals to be respected and included as a proper and good group member (Ellemers & Jetten 2013). The easiest way to achieve this goal is to embrace and enact behaviors and preferences that are prototypical for the group. Thus, gender stereotypes motivate men and women to adapt their self-views, behavioral expressions, and life choices to what seems appropriate for their group and in this sense function as self-fulfilling prophecies (Ridgeway & Smith-Lovin 1999).

Gender stereotypes help us to perform well in domains that seem gender appropriate and prevent us from excelling in counter-stereotypical domains, such as mathematics for women and social sensitivity for men (Koenig & Eagly 2005). The undermining effects of stereotype threat (versus stereotype lift) have been documented in many domains, ranging from academic to sports performance. Different mechanisms have been found to contribute to this, and these mechanisms occur at least partly outside of people's awareness (Schmader et al. 2008). Physiological stress at the prospect of having to perform in a counter-stereotypical domain impairs the ability of individuals to process information in the prefrontal cortex. Furthermore, under these circumstances, individuals are prevented from fully attending to the task because part of their brain is occupied with monitoring their performance (Krendl et al. 2008) or social acceptance (Ståhl et al. 2012b). Finally, extra effort is needed to suppress negative thoughts and emotions. All these mechanisms take up cognitive resources needed to perform well on the task (Schmader & Johns 2003). Even though individuals may be motivated to invest the additional effort needed to compensate for these cognitive and emotional demands, they are unable to keep this up, causing their performance to suffer over time (Ståhl et al. 2012a).

4.1. The Motivation to Be a Good Group Member

The impairment of people's performance in counter-stereotypical domains may seem a purely cognitive problem, but it is also driven by motivational concerns. That is, all these debilitating effects of gender stereotypes on task performance emerge most strongly for individuals who attach high importance to their gender identity and desire to behave as a good group member (Schmader 2002). Indeed, individuals who are strongly identified with their gender group find it highly threatening to be seen as a nonprototypical group member (Schmitt & Branscombe 2001). As a result, men entering a stereotypically masculine occupation (e.g., marine commando recruits, surgical trainees) were found to be less motivated and more likely to abandon their professional ambitions when they considered themselves to be less masculine than their coworkers (Peters et al. 2015). Likewise, lack of fit of women's occupational choices with the gender stereotype makes individuals less committed and ambitious at work (Peters et al. 2012). Thus, the motivation to be a good group member and accommodate gendered expectations places individuals in a self-defeating cycle, causing them to underperform, lose their self-confidence, and indicate lack of engagement in domains that do not match the stereotype (Derks et al. 2007).

4.2. The Motivation to Believe the World Is Just

Motivational processes not only make individuals conform to gender stereotypes, but also make people believe in these stereotypes as accurately indicating the abilities and motives of individual women and men. That is, even if we can see that men and women have different social roles and outcomes as a group, we strongly believe that this is the result of individual differences in preferences and abilities or reflects biological differences, as indicated above. This illusion of meritocracy is so strong that it prevents us from seeking, processing, or accepting evidence indicating that differences in societal outcomes may stem from gender stereotyping (Barreto & Ellemers 2015). As long as people perceive gender-stereotypical task preferences and life choices—including their own—as individual choices, they can maintain the conviction that men and women have equal opportunities and can make counter-stereotypical choices if they want to do so. Indeed, a study of stay-at-home mothers established that individuals who viewed their current situation as resulting from personal choice were less inclined to perceive workplace barriers to be related to gender (Stephens & Levine 2011). In general, the belief that social differences stem from individual choices masks the possibility that members of different groups are not treated equally and discourages attempts at relieving such inequality. Instead, it perpetuates the conviction that gender stereotypes offer a veridical and accurate picture of what men and women are and the societal roles they freely choose to fulfill.

The motivation to see the world as a just place where everyone receives the outcomes they deserve also makes people ascribe more valued features to groups that already have high status (Ridgeway 2001). Thus, we see that gender stereotypes are slightly adapted across situations, so that the male stereotype consistently represents characteristics that are the most valued in that context. For instance, it was found that the degree to which individualism versus collectivism is nationally valued predicts the likelihood that individualism versus collectivism is associated with the stereotype of men (Cuddy et al. 2015a).

4.3. The Motivation to Act Effectively

Finally, stereotypes motivate people to accommodate to existing expectations because challenging the status quo is incompatible with the behavior prescribed by the stereotype, particularly for women. On the one hand, the stereotype implies that women are expected to care for and help each other instead of trying to stand out. This does not match the requirements of many work and life contexts, where individuals are expected to compete with each other for the best opportunities or outcomes. In these contexts, the ambition and competitive behavior that is considered quite acceptable or even desirable for men is seen as inappropriate and unfeminine when displayed by women (Faniko et al. 2016). This poses an invisible hurdle for women who try to get ahead or improve their situation.

When, on the other hand, women express resentment at unequal outcomes or point out that they are disadvantaged by gender-stereotypical expectations, they are seen as complainers (Kaiser & Miller 2001). As long as the pervasive impact of gender stereotypes is not acknowledged, those who speak up are disliked for acting inappropriately, even by other women (Garcia et al. 2010). Indeed, for men, expressions of anger can instill respect and enhance their perceived standing. For women, expressing anger reduces their perceived competence, results in lower wages, and undermines their status in the workplace (Brescoll & Uhlmann 2008). These social costs of expressing anger have far-reaching implications, as they also prevent women from contesting current gender inequalities by engaging in collective action—for which the expression of anger is an important requirement (Radke et al. 2016).

These different motivational mechanisms all implicitly contribute to the reproduction of stereotypes and maintenance of the status quo. The motivations to justify, explain, and reproduce gender stereotypes work slightly differently depending on whether the individual is afforded privilege or disadvantage as a result (see **Figure 2**). In the next sections, I elaborate on each of these perspectives in turn.

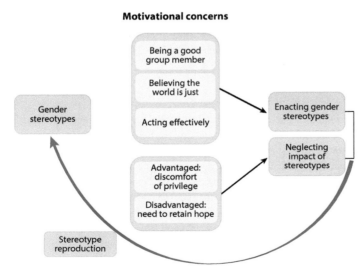

Figure 2

Motivational mechanisms that contribute to the reproduction of gender stereotypes.

4.4. The Discomfort of Privilege

Most individuals find themselves, at least sometimes, in situations where gender stereotypes would give them the benefit of the doubt. This is the case, for instance, for men who seek career advancement at work or for women who hope to be awarded custody of their children after divorce. At the same time, the awareness that stereotypes can be a source of advantage for them causes people discomfort. It is much more satisfying to maintain the conviction that one's successes in life reflect personal character (leadership ability) or individual effort (time invested in childcare). Believing that there is a contingency between individual merit and societal outcomes protects people from feeling guilt about any undeserved privilege they might enjoy and from shame at being unable to provide similar opportunities for others.

The discomfort of privilege has been documented in empirical research. The awareness that groups have unequal chances in society raises emotional responses indicating a focus on prevention and resistance toward reparation measures among those who benefit from current arrangements (Ellemers et al. 2010). Other studies have documented increases in blood pressure and heart rate when individuals are confronted with the possibility that their group will lose its privileged position. For instance, men showed a cardiovascular threat response when they were asked to discuss gender inequality and changing gender relations in society with women (Scheepers et al. 2009).

The reluctance to acknowledge unwarranted privilege also explains why group-based differences tend to be downplayed and denied—particularly by those who benefit from these differences. This tendency is visible, for instance, in responses to empirical evidence that gender stereotypes play a role in explaining the underrepresentation of women in science, technology, engineering, and mathematics (STEM) fields. Studies consistently show that men are more reluctant than women to accept the validity of data showing this role, especially when they work in STEM fields themselves (Handley et al. 2015, Moss-Racusin et al. 2015). These results resonate with the more general phenomenon that feelings of collective guilt at having enjoyed group-based privilege induce denial more easily than inviting compensation efforts, especially among individuals who are strongly identified with their group. In fact, experimental studies have revealed that men may act out against women when the privilege of their group is called into question. For instance, a set of studies established that highly identified men who think that the legitimacy, value, or distinctiveness of their male identity is under threat are more inclined to harass women by exposing them to pornographic images (Maass et al. 2003).

4.5. The Need to Retain Hope

It may seem obvious that those who benefit from group-based differences are motivated to retain them. However, those who suffer disadvantage due to their group membership also contribute to maintaining the status quo. Why would this be the case? Individuals who have the ambition to carve out their own life choices would be discouraged by realizing that gender stereotypes will limit their options and curb their ambitions. For them, it is threatening to accept that the mere reality of their gender—which they cannot change—would determine important outcomes in life, regardless of their individual achievements or the personal sacrifices they are willing to make.

This is why even those who may be disadvantaged by gender-stereotypical thinking resist the notion that gender stereotypes impact the way they are evaluated by others: Not acknowledging group-based disadvantage offers them a way to retain their hope. For instance, women prefer not to seek evidence that gender stereotypes may reduce their chances of being offered an attractive job (Stroebe et al. 2010). Indeed, countering the common belief that people easily claim discrimination to mask personal failures, evidence from several studies reveals that there is a general reluctance to make such claims, which are psychologically and socially costly (for a review, see Barreto et al.

2008). Thinking of gender discrimination in the past motivates men to display their best abilities. However, it was found to reduce women's perceived chances of individual success in the present, undermine their ability to perform well, and prevent them from taking advantage of opportunities offered (Barreto et al. 2004).

Women who are successful in masculine job types and functions often claim that they were not held back by their gender, and others willingly accept the validity of these claims. Yet these women (labeled queen bees) tend to demonstrate their suitability for such jobs by emphasizing how different they are from other women. Thus, their strategy to avoid being held back by gender stereotypes leads them to put down other women who make different life choices. This has been documented in studies for a variety of job types and work contexts, ranging from academia to the police force (Derks et al. 2016, Faniko et al. 2017). Although this may be a viable strategy for individuals to maintain hope that success is feasible in a masculine work environment, it also reinforces the notion that stereotypically masculine properties and behaviors are more important at work.

A different strategy is followed by those who emphasize the added value of gender-stereotypical contributions to enhance advancement opportunities for women. This has been documented in research on the glass cliff effect (Ryan & Haslam 2007), where women are selected for positions of leadership due to their allegedly superior social emotional skills. Although this may seem a productive way to induce more gender equity, research has revealed that it also places women in very risky positions, where they lack the necessary material resources and interpersonal support to do well (Ellemers et al. 2012).

The common thread connecting these different strategies is that they help individuals retain hope that they will not be restricted by gender stereotypes in reaching important life goals and outcomes. Yet, to the extent that this causes them to neglect the impact of gendered expectations on the way they formulate their ambitions and are viewed by others, these strategies also lead them to reproduce the very stereotypes they try to escape (Ellemers & Barreto 2015). Again, these mechanisms that contribute to maintaining the status quo have been documented most extensively for women who seek advancement in male-dominated professions or job types. But they are likely to be just as valid for men trying to function in female-dominated contexts. In general, when individuals aiming to disconfirm the validity of gendered expectations are not seen as proper group members by themselves or by others, stereotypical expectations of the gender group will not change. Moreover, if gendered abilities or achievements do not contribute to success in counter-stereotypical domains, then the ambitions of other individuals are curbed. As long as people fail to recognize that gender stereotypes—rather than individual merits and choices—lie at the root of such differences, change is very unlikely.

5. HOW WE CAN BENEFIT FROM THIS KNOWLEDGE

Gender stereotypes not only affect the way we perceive others and the opportunities we afford them, but also impact our conceptions of self, the demeanor we see as desirable, the life ambitions we consider appropriate, and the outcomes we value. These effects may harm our resolve to engage with domains we find personally valuable, undermine our ability to perform well, and impair our life outcomes. Paradoxically, then, the firm belief that gender stereotypes accurately reflect the achievements and priorities of most men and women prevents individuals from displaying their unique abilities and acting in line with their personal preferences.

How can we benefit from the knowledge gained about the origins, nature, and functions of gender stereotypes? To begin with, it is important to realize that they contain a kernel of truth that is tiny but self-fulfilling, because gendered expectations have a strong impact on the way we perceive and enact gender differences. Gender stereotypes reflect gendered role relations in society: Only when substantial numbers of men and women can be observed in a broader range of roles will our stereotypical associations change. This change can be achieved in different ways:

1. Acknowledge the pervasive nature and the cognitive and motivational functions of gender stereotypes. This constitutes an important step in combating their negative side effects. Accepting that we are all subject to gendered expectations and that these may bias our judgments of specific individuals makes it possible to identify and correct for such biases. Indeed, because gender stereotypes are so ubiquitous and implicit, we cannot rely on explicit intentions to consider individual merit alone. Outsourcing the responsibility for equal treatment to a diversity office can reduce vigilance against implicit bias and invite unequal treatment (Kaiser et al. 2013).

2. Lift the burden of proof from those who may be disadvantaged. This makes us less dependent on their ability to recognize unequal treatment and their willingness to complain. In fact, the identification of whether and how gender stereotypes may bias individual evaluations and result in unequal opportunities is more powerful and effective when it is done by those who are advantaged (Drury & Kaiser 2014). For instance, fathers who take an equal part in household duties cause their daughters to express counter-stereotypical preferences and ambitions (Croft et al. 2014).

3. Educate people about the descriptive and prescriptive nature of stereotypes. Knowledge of the pervasiveness and implicit effects of stereotypes releases people from the conviction that all gender differences are biologically determined and hard-wired. Such knowledge enables them to recognize the implicit effects that gender stereotypes may have for themselves and others. Sharing these experiences helps them to develop concrete strategies to deal with gendered expectations (Williams & Dempsey 2014).

4. Support employees in reconciling stereotypical male and female role expectations regarding work and family demands. Male and female workers experience stress when work and family roles seem incompatible. However, when supervisors at work acknowledge both types of demands and facilitate the possibility of combining work and family roles, this benefits the work satisfaction, work performance, and indicators of physical health of men and women over time (Van Steenbergen & Ellemers 2009).

5. Reconsider and re-evaluate the nature of different social roles and job types. The unidimensional distinction between masculine roles that rely mainly on competition and achievement and feminine roles that require empathy and care does not do justice to contemporary requirements in social interactions or in the workplace. People cannot function well in the modern workplace without emotional intelligence and interpersonal skills. Likewise, a broader range of task abilities and achievements is needed for families to function well in a globalized and digitalized world. The inclusion of a larger variety of individuals with a more diverse set of skills and abilities will benefit individual as well as collective outcomes. Clarifying how different functions and job types require masculine as well as feminine skill sets raises the interest of both men and women in performing in these roles (Diekman et al. 2017).

Gender stereotypes prevent women and men from equally sharing the care for children and family members and from equally benefiting from the interpersonal connections made through these activities. Gender stereotypes prevent women with successful careers from finding a romantic partner and men without employment from feeling valued. They cause us to underestimate the emotional burden of care functions for women and the physical burden of strenuous labor for men. This is not only costly for the individuals involved but also for society, as it impacts the psychological and physical well-being of individuals, the resilience of families, and the long-term availability and contributions of workers in the labor market. We are only human and have to accept that we are subject to stereotypical thinking and gendered expectations. Accepting our fallibility in this way, rather than denying that gender stereotypes play a role while implicitly reproducing them, makes it easier to correct for any undesired outcomes that may result.

DISCLOSURE STATEMENT

The author is not aware of any affiliations, memberships, funding, or financial holdings that might be perceived as affecting the objectivity of this review.

LITERATURE CITED

Amodio D. 2014. The neuroscience of prejudice and stereotyping. *Nat. Rev. Neurosci.* 15:670–82

Anderson RC, Klofstad CA. 2012. Preference for leaders with masculine voices holds in the case of feminine leadership roles. *PLOS ONE* 7(12):e51216

Badgett MVL, Folbre N. 2003. Job gendering: occupational choice and the labor market. *Ind. Relat.* 42:270–98

Banaji MR, Greenwald AG. 1995. Implicit gender stereotyping in judgments of fame. *J. Personal. Soc. Psychol.* 68:181–98

Barreto M, Ellemers N. 2015. Detecting and experiencing prejudice: new answers to old questions. *Adv. Exp. Soc. Psychol.* 52:139–219

Barreto M, Ellemers N, Cihangir S, Stroebe K. 2008. The self-fulfilling effects of contemporary sexism: how it affects women's well-being and behavior. In *The Glass Ceiling in the 21st Century: Understanding Barriers to Gender Inequality*, ed. M Barreto, M Ryan, M Schmitt, pp. 99–123. Washington, DC: Am. Psychol. Assoc.

Barreto M, Ellemers N, Palacios M. 2004. The backlash of token mobility: the impact of past group experiences on individual ambition and effort. *Personal. Soc. Psychol. Bull.* 30:1433–45

Barreto M, Ellemers N, Piebinga L, Moya M. 2010. How nice of us and how dumb of me: the effect of exposure to benevolent sexism on women's task and relational self-descriptions. *Sex Roles* 62:532–44

Becker SW, Eagly AH. 2004. The heroism of women and men. *Am. Psychol.* 59:163–78

Behm-Morawitz E, Mastro D. 2009. The effects of the sexualization of female video game characters on gender stereotyping and female self-concept. *Sex Roles* 61:808–23

Bennett M, Sani F, Hopkins N, Agostini L, Malucchi L. 2000. Children's gender categorization: an investigation of automatic processing. *Br. J. Dev. Psychol.* 18:97–102

Biernat M, Manis M. 1994. Shifting standards and stereotype-based judgments. *J. Personal. Soc. Psychol.* 66:5–20

Bittman M, England P, Sayer L, Folbre N, Matheson G. 2003. When does gender trump money? Bargaining and time in household work. *Am. J. Sociol.* 109:186–214

Borkowska B, Pawlowski B. 2011. Female voice frequency in the context of dominance and attractiveness perception. *Anim. Behav.* 82:55–59

Brescoll VL, Uhlmann EL. 2005. Attitudes toward traditional and nontraditional parents. *Psychol. Women Q.* 29:436–45

Brescoll VL, Uhlmann EL. 2008. Can angry women get ahead? Status conferral, gender, and expression of emotion in the workplace. *Psychol. Sci.* 19:268–75

Buffington C, Cerf B, Jones C, Weinberg BA. 2016. STEM training and early career outcomes of female and male graduate students: evidence from UMETRICS data linked to the 2010 Census. *Am. Econ. Rev.* 106:333–38

Bur. Labor Stat. 2016. *Charts by topic: household activities*. Am. Time Use Surv. Rep., Bur. Labor Stat., US Dep. Labor, Washington, DC

Bussey K, Bandura A. 1999. Social cognitive theory of gender development and differentiation. *Psychol. Rev.* 106:676–713

Byrnes JP, Miller DC, Schafer WD. 1999. Gender differences in risk taking: a meta-analysis. *Psychol. Bull.* 125:367–83

Canal P, Garnham A, Oakhill J. 2015. Beyond gender stereotypes in language comprehension: self sex-role descriptions affect the brain's potentials associated with agreement processing. *Front. Psychol.* 6:1953

Carney DR, Cuddy AJC, Yap AJ. 2010. Power posing: Brief nonverbal displays affect neuroendocrine levels and risk tolerance. *Psychol. Sci.* 21:1363–68

Cashdan E. 1998. Smiles, speech, and body posture: how women and men display sociometric status and power. *J. Nonverbal Behav.* 22:209–28

Chatard A, Guimond S, Selimbegovic L. 2007. "How good are you in math?" The effect of gender stereotypes on students' recollection of their school marks. *J. Exp. Soc. Psychol.* 43:1017–24

Cikara M, Eberhardt JL, Fiske ST. 2011. From agents to objects: sexist attitudes and neural responses to sexualized targets. *J. Cogn. Neurosci.* 23:540–51

Clausell E, Fiske ST. 2005. When do subgroup parts add up to the stereotypic whole? Mixed stereotype content for gay male subgroups explains overall ratings. *Soc. Cogn.* 23:161–81

Cohn E. 2015. Google image search has a gender bias problem. *Huffington Post*, Apr. 10. **https://www.huffingtonpost.com/2015/04/10/google-image-gender-bias_n_7036414.html**

Correll SJ, Benard S, Paik I. 2007. Getting a job: Is there a motherhood penalty? *Am. J. Sociol.* 112:483–99

Croft A, Schmader T, Block K. 2015. An underexamined inequality: cultural and psychological barriers to men's engagement with communal roles. *Personal. Soc. Psychol. Rev.* 19:343–70

Croft A, Schmader T, Block K, Baron AS. 2014. The second shift reflected in the second generation: Do parents' gender roles at home predict children's aspirations? *Psychol. Sci.* 25:1418–28

Cuddy AJ, Wolf EB, Glick P, Crotty S, Chong J, Norton MI. 2015a. Men as cultural ideals: Cultural values moderate gender stereotype content. *J. Personal. Soc. Psychol.* 109:622–35

Cuddy AJC, Fiske ST, Glick P. 2004. When professionals become mothers, warmth doesn't cut the ice. *J. Soc. Issues* 60:701–18

Cuddy AJC, Wilmuth CA, Yap AJ, Carney DR. 2015b. Preparatory power posing affects nonverbal presence and job interview performance. *J. Appl. Psychol.* 100:1286–95

De Lemus S, Spears R, Moya M. 2012. The power of a smile to move you: complementary submissiveness in women's posture as a function of gender salience and facial expression. *Personal. Soc. Psychol. Bull.* 38:1480–94

Derks B, Van Laar C, Ellemers N. 2007. The beneficial effects of social identity protection on the performance motivation of members of devalued groups. *Soc. Issues Policy Rev.* 1:217–56

Derks B, Van Laar C, Ellemers N. 2016. The queen bee phenomenon: why women leaders distance themselves from junior women. *Leadersh. Q.* 27:456–69

Diekman AB, Steinberg M, Brown ER, Belanger AL, Clark EK. 2017. A goal congruity model of role entry, engagement, and exit: understanding communal goal processes in STEM gender gaps. *Personal. Soc. Psychol. Rev.* 21:142–75

Drury BJ, Kaiser CR. 2014. Allies against sexism: the role of men in confronting sexism. *J. Soc. Issues* 70:637–52

Dutt K, Pfaff DL, Bernstein AF, Dillard JS, Block CJ. 2016. Gender differences in recommendation letters for postdoctoral fellowships in geoscience. *Nat. Geosci.* 9:805–8

Dyble M, Salali GD, Chaudhary N, Page A, Smith D, et al. 2015. Sex equality can explain the unique social structure of hunter-gatherer bands. *Science* 348:796–98

Eagly AH, Mladinic A. 1994. Are people prejudiced against women? Some answers from research on attitudes, gender stereotypes, and judgments of competence. *Eur. Rev. Soc. Psychol.* 5:1–35

Eagly AH, Wood W. 2013. The nature-nurture debates: 25 years of challenges in understanding the psychology of gender. *Perspect. Psychol. Sci.* 8:340–57

Ellemers N. 2014. Women at work: how organizational features impact career development. *Policy Insights Behav. Brain Sci.* 1:46–54

Ellemers N, Barreto M. 2015. Modern discrimination: how perpetrators and targets interactively perpetuate social disadvantage. *Curr. Opin. Behav. Sci.* 3:142–46

Ellemers N, Jetten J. 2013. The many ways to be marginal in a group. *Personal. Soc. Psychol. Rev.* 17:3–21

Ellemers N, Rink F, Derks B, Ryan M. 2012. Women in high places: when and why promoting women into top positions can harm them individually or as a group (and how to prevent this). *Res. Organ. Behav.* 32:163–87

Ellemers N, Scheepers D, Popa A. 2010. Something to gain or something to lose? Affirmative action and regulatory focus emotions. *Group Process. Intergroup Relat.* 13:201–13

Endendijk JJ, Groeneveld MG, Mesman J, Van der Pol LD, Van Berkel SR, et al. 2014. Boys don't play with dolls: mothers' and fathers' gender talk during picture book reading. *Parent. Sci. Pract.* 14:141–61

Faniko K, Ellemers N, Derks B. 2016. Queen bees and alpha males: Are successful women more competitive than successful men? *Eur. J. Soc. Psychol.* 46:903–13

Faniko K, Ellemers N, Derks B, Lorenzi-Cioldi F. 2017. Nothing changes, really: why women who break through the glass ceiling end up reinforcing it. *Personal. Soc. Psychol. Bull.* 43:638–51

Feinberg DR, DeBruine LM, Jones BC, Perrett DI. 2008. The role of femininity and averageness of voice pitch in aesthetic judgments of women's voices. *Perception* 37:615–23

Fine C. 2013. Neurosexism in functional neuroimaging: from scanner to pseudo-science to psyche. In *The SAGE Handbook of Gender and Psychology*, ed. MK Ryan, NR Branscombe, pp. 45–60. London: Sage

Fischer J, Anderson VN. 2012. Gender role attitudes and characteristics of stay-at-home and employed fathers. *Psychol. Men Masc.* 13:16–31

Fiske ST, Bersoff DN, Borgida E, Deaux K, Heilman ME. 1991. Social science research on trial: use of sex stereotyping research in Price Waterhouse v. Hopkins. *Am. Psychol.* 46:1049–60

Fiske ST, Cuddy AC, Glick P, Xu J. 2002. A model of (often mixed) stereotype content: Competence and warmth respectively follow from perceived status and competition. *J. Personal. Soc. Psychol.* 82:878–902

Fiske ST, Taylor SK. 2013. *Social Cognition: From Brains to Culture*. London: Sage

Folbre N. 2012. Should women care less? Intrinsic motivation and gender inequality. *Br. J. Ind. Relat.* 50:597–619

Fredrickson B, Roberts TA. 1997. Objectification theory: toward understanding women's lived experiences and mental health risks. *Psychol. Women Q.* 21:173–206

Garcia D, Schmitt MT, Branscombe NR, Ellemers N. 2010. Women's reactions to ingroup members who protest discriminatory treatment: the importance of beliefs about inequality and response appropriateness. *Eur. J. Soc. Psychol.* 40:733–45

Glick P, Fiske ST, Mladinic A, Saiz J, Abrams D, et al. 2000. Beyond prejudice as simple antipathy: hostile and benevolent sexism across cultures. *J. Personal. Soc. Psychol.* 79:763–75

Glick P, Sakalli-Ugurlu N, Ferreira MC, Souza MA. 2002. Ambivalent sexism and attitudes toward wife abuse in Turkey and Brazil. *Psychol. Women Q.* 26:292–97

Gordon I, Zagoory-Sharon O, Leckman JF, Feldman R. 2010. Oxytocin and the development of parenting in humans. *Biol. Psychiatry* 68:377–82

Greenwald AG, Banaji MR. 1995. Implicit social cognition: attitudes, self-esteem, and stereotypes. *Psychol. Rev.* 102:4–27

Grunspan DZ, Eddy SL, Brownell SE, Wiggins BL, Crowe AJ, Goodreau SM. 2016. Males under-estimate academic performance of their female peers in undergraduate biology classrooms. *PLOS ONE* 11:e0148405

Hammond MD, Overall NC. 2015. Benevolent sexism and support of romantic partner's goals: undermining women's competence while fulfilling men's intimacy needs. *Personal. Soc. Psychol. Bull.* 41:1180–94

Handley IM, Brown ER, Moss-Racusin CA, Smith JA. 2015. Quality of evidence revealing subtle gender biases in science is in the eye of the beholder. *PNAS* 112:13201–6

Heflick N, Goldenberg J, Cooper D, Puvia E. 2011. From women to objects: appearance focus, target gender, and perceptions of warmth, morality and competence. *J. Exp. Soc. Psychol.* 47:572–81

Heilman ME, Haynes MC. 2005. No credit where credit is due: attributional rationalization of women's success in male-female teams. *J. Appl. Psychol.* 90:905–16

Heilman ME, Okimoto T. 2008. Motherhood: a potential source of bias in employment decisions. *J. Appl. Psychol.* 93:189–98

Hornsey MJ, Wellauer R, McIntyre JC, Barlow FK. 2015. A critical test of the assumption that men prefer conformist women and women prefer nonconformist men. *Personal. Soc. Psychol. Bull.* 41:755–68

Huang Y, Davies PG, Sibley CG, Osborne D. 2016. Benevolent sexism, attitudes toward motherhood, and reproductive rights: a multi-study longitudinal examination of abortion attitudes. *Personal. Soc. Psychol. Bull.* 42:970–84

Hyde J. 2014. Gender similarities and differences. *Annu. Rev. Psychol.* 65:373–98

Ito TA, Urland GR. 2003. Race and gender on the brain: electrocortical measures of attention to the race and gender of multiply categorizable individuals. *J. Personal. Soc. Psychol.* 85:616–26

Jarman J, Blackburn RM, Racko G. 2012. The dimensions of occupational gender segregation in industrial countries. *Sociology* 46:1003–19

Joel D, Berman Z, Tavor I, Wexler N, Gaber O, et al. 2015. Sex beyond the genitalia: the human brain mosaic. *PNAS* 112:15468–73

Joshi A, Son J, Roh H. 2015. When can women close the gap? A meta-analytic test of sex differences in performance and rewards. *Acad. Manag. J.* 58:1516–45

Kaiser CR, Major B, Jurcevic I, Dover TL, Brady LM, Shapiro JR. 2013. Presumed fair: ironic effects of organizational diversity structures. *J. Personal. Soc. Psychol.* 104:504–19

Kaiser CR, Miller CT. 2001. Stop complaining! The social costs of making attributions to discrimination. *Personal. Soc. Psychol. Bull.* 27:254–63

Kite ME, Deaux K, Haines EL. 2008. Gender stereotypes. In *Psychology of Women: A Handbook of Issues and Theories*, Vol. 2, ed. FL Denmark, MA Paludi, pp. 205–36. New York: Praeger

Klofstad CA, Anderson RC, Peters S. 2012. Sounds like a winner: Voice pitch influences perception of leadership capacity in both men and women. *Proc. R. Soc. Lond. B* 279:2698–704

Koenig AM, Eagly AH. 2005. Stereotype threat in men on a test of social sensitivity. *Sex Roles* 52:489–96

Krendl AC, Richeson JA, Kelley WM, Heatherton TF. 2008. The negative consequences of threat: a functional magnetic resonance imaging investigation of the neural mechanisms underlying women's underperformance in math. *Psychol. Sci.* 19:168–75

Kulich C, Trojanowski G, Ryan MK, Haslam SA, Renneboog LDR. 2011. Who gets the carrot and who gets the stick? Evidence of gender disparities in executive remuneration. *Strateg. Manag. J.* 32:301–21

Leslie S-J, Cimpian A, Meyer M, Freeland E. 2015. Expectations of brilliance underlie gender distributions across academic disciplines. *Science* 347:262–65

Lyness KS, Judiesch MK. 2014. Gender egalitarianism and work-life balance for managers: a multisource perspective in 36 countries. *Appl. Psychol. Int. Rev.* 63:96–129

Maass A. 1999. Linguistic intergroup bias: stereotype perpetuation through language. *Adv. Exp. Soc. Psychol.* 31:79–121

Maass A, Cadinu M, Guarnieri G, Grasselli A. 2003. Sexual harassment under social identity threat: the computer harassment paradigm. *J. Personal. Soc. Psychol.* 85:853–70

MacNell L, Driscoll A, Hunt AN. 2015. What's in a name: exposing gender bias in student ratings of teaching. *Innov. High. Educ.* 40:291–303

Matthews JL. 2007. Hidden sexism: facial prominence and its connections to gender and occupational status in popular print media. *Sex Roles* 57:515–25

Mayew WJ, Parsons CA, Venkatachalam M. 2013. Voice pitch and the labor market success of male chief executive officers. *Evol. Hum. Behav.* 34:243–48

Moss-Racusin CA, Dovidio JF, Brescoll VL, Graham MJ, Handelsman J. 2012. Science faculty's subtle gender biases favor male students. *PNAS* 109:16474–79

Moss-Racusin CA, Molenda AK, Cramer CR. 2015. Can evidence impact attitudes? Public reactions to evidence of gender bias in STEM fields. *Psychol. Women Q.* 39:194–209

Moss-Racusin CA, Phelan JE, Rudman LA. 2010. When men break the gender rules: status incongruity and backlash against modest men. *Psychol. Men Masc.* 11:140–51

Netchaeva E, Kouchaki M, Sheppard LD. 2015. A man's (precarious) place: men's experienced threat and self-assertive reactions to female superiors. *Personal. Soc. Psychol. Bull.* 41:1247–59

Oakes PJ, Haslam SA, Turner JC. 1994. *Stereotyping and Social Reality*. Oxford, UK: Blackwell

Park LE, Young AF, Eastwick PW. 2015. (Psychological) distance makes the heart grow fonder: effects of psychological distance and relative intelligence on men's attraction to women. *Personal. Soc. Psychol. Bull.* 41:1459–73

Peters K, Ryan MK, Haslam SA. 2015. Marines, medics, and machismo: Lack of fit with masculine occupational stereotypes discourages men's participation. *Br. J. Soc. Psychol.* 106:635–55

Peters K, Ryan M, Haslam SA, Fernandes H. 2012. To belong or not to belong: evidence that women's occupational disidentification is promoted by lack of fit with masculine occupational prototypes. *J. Personal. Psychol.* 11:148–58

Plant TA, Hyde JS, Keltner D, Devine PC. 2000. The gender stereotyping of emotion. *Psychol. Women Q.* 24:81–92

Prentice DA, Carranza E. 2002. What women and men should be, shouldn't be, are allowed to be, and don't have to be: the contents of prescriptive gender stereotypes. *Psychol. Women Q.* 57:269–81

Proudfoot D, Kay AC, Koval CZ. 2015. A gender bias in the attribution of creativity: archival and experimental evidence for the perceived association between masculinity and creative thinking. *Psychol. Sci.* 26:1751–61

Radke HRM, Hornsey MJ, Barlow FK. 2016. Barriers to women engaging in collective action to overcome sexism. *Am. Psychol.* 71:863–74

Ramos MR, Barreto M, Ellemers N, Moya M, Ferreira L. 2017. What hostile and benevolent sexism communicate about men's and women's warmth and competence. *Group Process. Intergroup Relat.* In press

Ridgeway CL. 2001. Gender, status, and leadership. *J. Soc. Issues* 57:637–55

Ridgeway CL, Smith-Lovin L. 1999. The gender system and interaction. *Annu. Rev. Sociol.* 25:191–216

Riggs JM. 1997. Mandates for mothers and fathers: perceptions of breadwinners and care givers. *Sex Roles* 37:565–80

Rudman LA, Phelan JE. 2008. Backlash effects for disconfirming gender stereotypes in organizations. *Res. Organ. Behav.* 28:61–79

Ryan MK, Haslam SA. 2007. The glass cliff: exploring the dynamics surrounding the appointment of women to precarious leadership positions. *Acad. Manag. Rev.* 32:549–72

Scheepers D, Ellemers N, Sintemaartensdijk N. 2009. Suffering from the possibility of status loss: physiological responses to social identity threat in high status groups. *Eur. J. Soc. Psychol.* 39:1075–92

Schein VE, Mueller R, Lituchy T, Liu J. 1996. Think manager—think male: a global phenomenon? *J. Organ. Behav.* 17:33–41

Schmader T. 2002. Gender identification moderates stereotype threat effects on women's math performance. *J. Exp. Soc. Psychol.* 38:194–201

Schmader T, Johns M. 2003. Converging evidence that stereotype threat reduces working memory capacity. *J. Personal. Soc. Psychol.* 85:440–52

Schmader T, Johns M, Forbes C. 2008. An integrated process model of stereotype threat effects on performance. *Psychol. Rev.* 115:336–56

Schmader T, Whitehead J, Wysocki VH. 2007. A linguistic comparison of letters of recommendation for male and female chemistry and biochemistry job applicants. *Sex Roles* 57:509–14

Schmitt MT, Branscombe NR. 2001. The good, the bad, and the manly: threats to one's prototypicality and evaluations of fellow in-group members. *J. Exp. Soc. Psychol.* 37:510–17

Ståhl T, Van Laar C, Ellemers N. 2012a. How stereotype threat affects cognitive performance under a prevention focus: Initial cognitive mobilization is followed by depletion. *J. Personal. Soc. Psychol.* 102: 1239–51

Ståhl T, Van Laar C, Ellemers N, Derks B. 2012b. Searching for acceptance: Prejudice expectations direct attention towards social acceptance cues when under a promotion focus. *Group Process. Intergroup Relat.* 15:523–38

Steffens MC, Jelenec P, Noack P. 2010. On the leaky math pipeline: comparing implicit math-gender stereotypes and math withdrawal in female and male children and adolescents. *J. Educ. Psychol.* 102:947–63

Stephens NM, Levine CS. 2011. Opting out or denying discrimination? How the framework of free choice in American society influences perceptions of gender inequality. *Psychol. Sci.* 22:1231–36

Stroebe K, Barreto M, Ellemers N. 2010. Experiencing discrimination: how members of disadvantaged groups can be helped to cope with discrimination. *Soc. Issues Policy Rev.* 4:181–213

Swim JK, Sanna LJ. 1996. He's skilled, she's lucky: a meta-analysis of observers' attributions for women's and men's successes and failure. *Personal. Soc. Psychol. Bull.* 22:509–19

Tiedemann J. 2000. Gender-related beliefs of teachers in elementary school mathematics. *Educ. Stud. Math.* 41:191–207

Treviño LJ, Gomez-Mejia LR, Balkin DB, Mixon FG. 2015. Meritocracies or masculinities? The differential allocation of named professorships by gender in the academy. *J. Manag.* **https://doi.org/10.1177/0149206315599216**

Van der Lee R, Ellemers N. 2015. Gender contributes to personal research funding success in the Netherlands. *PNAS* 112:12349–53

Van der Pol LD, Groeneveld MG, Van Berkel SR, Endendijk JE, Hallers-Haalboom ET, et al. 2015. Fathers' and mothers' emotion talk with their girls and boys from toddlerhood to preschool age. *Emotion* 15:854–64

Van Honk J, Terburg D, Bos PA. 2011. Further notes on testosterone as a social hormone. *Trends Cogn. Sci.* 15:291–92

Van Steenbergen E, Ellemers N. 2009. Is managing the work–family interface worthwhile? Benefits for employee health and performance. *J. Organ. Behav.* 30:617–42

Ward LM, Harrison K. 2005. The impact of media use on girls' beliefs about gender roles, their bodies, and sexual relationships: a research synthesis. In *Featuring Females: Feminist Analyses of Media*, ed. E Cole, JH Daniel, pp. 3–23. Washington, DC: Am. Psychol. Assoc.

Wigboldus DHJ, Dijksterhuis A, Van Knippenberg A. 2003. When stereotypes get in the way: Stereotypes obstruct stereotype-inconsistent trait inferences. *J. Personal. Soc. Psychol.* 84:470–84

Wigboldus DHJ, Semin GR, Spears R. 2000. How do we communicate stereotypes? Linguistic bases and inferential consequences. *J. Personal. Soc. Psychol.* 78:5–18

Williams JC, Berdahl JL, Vandello JA. 2016. Beyond work-life "integration." *Annu. Rev. Psychol.* 67:515–39

Williams JC, Dempsey R. 2014. *What Works for Women at Work: Four Patterns Working Women Need to Know.* New York: NYU Press

Williams MJ, Tiedens LZ. 2016. The subtle suspension of backlash: a meta-analysis of penalties for women's implicit and explicit dominance behavior. *Psychol. Bull.* 142:165–97

Wong YJ, Ho M-HR, Wang S-Y, Miller ISK. 2017. Meta-analyses of the relationship between conformity to masculine norms and mental health-related outcomes. *J. Couns. Psychol.* 64:80–93

Attitudes and Attitude Change

Dolores Albarracin and Sharon Shavitt

Department of Psychology and Department of Business Administration,
University of Illinois at Urbana-Champaign, Champaign, Illinois 61822;
email: dalbarra@illinois.edu, shavitt@illinois.edu

Annu. Rev. Psychol. 2018. 69:299–327

First published as a Review in Advance on August 25, 2017

The *Annual Review of Psychology* is online at psych.annualreviews.org

https://doi.org/10.1146/annurev-psych-122216-011911

Keywords

attitude, persuasion, evaluative judgment, opinion, belief, goal, culture

Abstract

This review covers research on attitudes and attitude change published between 2010 and 2017. We characterize this period as one of significant progress toward an understanding of how attitudes form and change in three critical contexts. The first context is the person, as attitudes change in connection to values, general goals, language, emotions, and human development. The second context is social relationships, which link attitude change to the communicator of persuasive messages, social media, and culture. The third context is sociohistorical and highlights the influence of unique events, including sociopolitical, economic, and climatic occurrences. In conclusion, many important recent findings reflect the fact that holism, with a focus on situating attitudes within their personal, social, and historical contexts, has become the zeitgeist of attitude research during this period.

Contents

THE MEANING OF AND INTEREST IN ATTITUDES

The study of attitudes is the study of evaluations, and it has been part of social psychology since that field first emerged with Thomas & Znaniecki's (1918–1920) *The Polish Peasant in Europe and America*. The term attitude was initially used by Jung (1923) in his writing about psychological types to describe a readiness to respond, a definition later incorporated by Allport (1935). However, as there are no guarantees that, for example, liking a political candidate will yield support for that candidate at the polls, overt behavioral responses are no longer part of the definition of attitudes. Rather, the attitude–behavior relationship is best seen an empirical question outside the definition of attitude, a definition that simply focuses on the evaluative nature of attitudes as favor or disfavor.

Attitudes have a subject matter (referred to as the object or target), which can be an object, a person, or an abstract idea. Attitudes are thus relevant to many disciplines, including marketing (e.g., attitudes toward products), advertising (e.g., attitudes toward advertisements), political behavior (e.g., attitudes toward political candidates, parties, or voting), and health (e.g., attitudes toward protective behaviors, new medications, or the health system). Attitudes toward other people are studied in the domain of interpersonal liking, attitudes toward the self in the domain of self-esteem, and attitudes toward abstract ideas in the domain of values. Attitudes can be specific, or they can generalize across objects, with people holding attitudes that are either generally positive or generally negative (Hepler & Albarracín 2013). The contemporary representation of a hater comes to mind when we consider general attitudes, which are dispositional evaluations irrespective of the object.

Attitudes can be measured by simply asking respondents to report their attitudes or by inferring attitudes from spontaneous evaluative reactions to the presentation of the attitude object (see Ehret et al. 2015). Indirect measures of attitudes, referred to as implicit measures, are designed to assess automatic evaluations that may be dissociated from the explicit, self-report measures but may still predict behavior in some contexts (e.g., Sheets et al. 2011, Stanley et al. 2011). Although the introduction of implicit measures has probably been the most notable change in attitude research over the past two decades, interest in attitudes has remained fairly stable over time. A search for research on attitudes in the *Journal of Personality and Social Psychology* since its first publication shows ongoing interest. Specifically, in an analysis of one issue in every five years since the journal's inception, a count of articles whose abstracts mention attitude, persuasion, belief, opinion, or evaluative judgments reveals that such articles comprise a fairly steady 20% of publications. As shown in **Figure 1**, there is sustained and long-standing scholarship in this area over the course of no less than six decades.

Covering the vast field of attitudes within the space constraints of this review is a challenge. We therefore make important choices, focusing on the literature published between 2010 and 2017,

Attitude: a person's evaluation of an object on a favorable to unfavorable continuum

Value: attitude toward an abstract entity

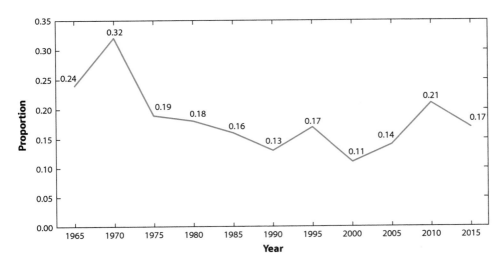

Figure 1

Proportion of articles in the *Journal of Personality and Social Psychology* whose abstracts mention attitude, persuasion, belief, opinion, or evaluative judgment.

to continue where coverage ended in a previous *Annual Review of Psychology* article on attitudes and attitude change (Bohner & Dickel 2011). We performed several systematic PsycINFO searches, using attitude change as a keyword to search all psychological outlets and attitude as a keyword to search social psychological outlets. We also conducted more targeted PsycINFO searches for attitude and value, attitude and goal, attitude and emotion, attitude and metaphor, attitude and language, attitude and source, and attitude and network. For areas with multidisciplinary appeal, we searched Google Scholar and included other behavioral science outlets (e.g., in consumer behavior). This review is intended to identify contributions about generational and developmental effects on attitudes, historical effects on attitudes, and the cultural context of attitudes. Regrettably, space constraints prohibit us from covering some important areas, including the vast literatures on prejudice and on evolutionary influences on cognition and motivation, even though they sometimes address attitudes and attitude change. We are confident that other reviews will fill these gaps.

ATTITUDE CHANGE

On our optimistic days, we assume that our children will enjoy cleaning their rooms and that American citizens will support the right candidate and actually vote on election day. Likewise, public policy makers continue to search for the optimal fear appeal to curb smoking, scientists hope for representatives' understanding and approval of research funding, and fundraisers seek ways of increasing philanthropy and support for valuable causes. In other words, we all hope for the right attitudes and count on attitude change and behavior in a myriad of socially relevant areas. But what can we say about how much attitudes actually change?

One approach to addressing this question is conceptual: The degree of attitude change depends on whether one adopts a theoretical conceptualization of attitudes as being crystallized in memory, as in-the-moment evaluations, or as hybrid structures. When attitudes are defined as a fixed memory, stored permanently for later retrieval when the opportunity and the need arise, change is difficult to explain. When attitudes are defined as constructed based on temporary considerations, such as the perceiver's mood at a particular time (Schuldt et al. 2011), attitudes are always changing.

Attitude change: movement from one evaluative category to another (e.g., favor to disfavor)

Most likely, attitudes are partly memory based and partly constructed on the fly (Albarracin et al. 2005), which would be consistent with a contemporary understanding of information processing as a neural network in which activation patterns stem from situational constraints as well as chronic connection weights (see Calanchini & Sherman 2013, van Bavel et al. 2012). This hybrid model allows for attitude stability as well as change.

The second approach to degree of change is to answer the question asked by policy makers and other stakeholders: If we measure attitudes at two points in time, how much of a difference will we notice? All studies of attitude change are relevant to this question, with meta-analyses providing appropriate estimates of average change in response to communications or interventions. Recent research includes experiments designed to produce attitude change in the laboratory, as well as interventions conducted in the field. The area of intergroup attitudes provides examples of how much change we can expect. In laboratory studies, even simply imagining intergroup contact appears to shift evaluations (Miles & Crisp 2014). A synthesis of research in which participants were asked to imagine contact with an outgroup member revealed $d = 0.36$ for explicit attitudes (U3 $= 64\%$) and $d = 0.31$ for implicit attitudes (U3 $= 62\%$) (Miles & Crisp 2014). These results reveal that 14% of participants who imagined outgroup contact were likely to have more positive explicit attitudes than those who did not imagine. Correspondingly, 12% of participants who imagined outgroup contact were likely to have more positive implicit attitudes than those who did not imagine.

A meta-analysis by Lemmer & Wagner (2015) focused on field interventions to reduce intergroup conflict that introduced contact between two ethnic groups. This meta-analysis revealed that, immediately after contact, approximately 61% of the participants in the interventions had positive intergroup attitudes, versus 50% of those participants not having contact ($d = 0.28$, U3 $= 61\%$). Diversity training, often implemented in organizational settings, has similar effects on attitudes ($d = 0.23$, U3 $= 59\%$; Kalinoski et al. 2013). In conclusion, some attitude change is possible even in domains that are traditionally resistant to change.

Many programs designed for the real world pursue changes in behavior and often do not measure changes in attitudes. However, a recent meta-analysis (Tyson et al. 2014) assessed attitude change in response to interventions to reduce risky sexual behavior both immediately after the intervention and following a delay. Regardless of the time of assessment, the effect of the interventions was $d = 0.257$, which implies that 60% of the recipients experienced change following the intervention, versus 50% in the absence of an intervention. Another meta-analysis (Steinmetz et al. 2016) was conducted to measure the average effect of interventions designed on the basis of the theory of planned behavior (Ajzen & Madden 1986) and yielded similar conclusions. The domains of these programs varied greatly. Of the interventions, 33% targeted physical activity, 19% nutrition, 16% work or study issues (e.g., ergonomic behaviors, stress management), 11% alcohol and drug use, 8% adherence to medical regimens, 7% driving behavior, 4% sexual behavior, and 2% hygiene. On average, these programs were associated with a $d = 0.24$ for attitude change, an effect size that can be visualized by thinking that 59% of intervention recipients were likely to have more positive attitudes relative to 50% of the nonrecipients.

Research conducted in the laboratory can often obtain stronger effects than field studies for several reasons, including better control of distraction and reduced random error. During the past few years, a synthesis of experimental research on fear appeals was conducted to demonstrate the extent to which fear could lead to attitude, intention, and behavior change (Tannenbaum et al. 2015). In this synthesis, the researchers compared messages designed to induce a high level of fear in such diverse areas as health, financial decisions, and driving safety. The results for attitudes showed an average change of $d = 0.20$ (U3 $= 57\%$).

All in all, attitude change based on interventions or messages delivered at a particular time hovers around $d = 0.22$, which is a small effect. However, this change may, in some cases, be quite durable, as beliefs and attitudes have been known to persist despite attempts at correction (for a recent treatment of these issues, see Chan et al. 2017). Motivated cognition suggests that attitudes and beliefs that are consistent with other values are likely to persist. Defensive cognitive processes can be recruited to protect the attitudes and beliefs, particularly when accuracy motivation is low (Hart et al. 2009), and people set high thresholds of evidence to refute cherished points of view (Hart et al. 2009). Belief persistence, however, obeys other mechanisms, as well. For example, Ecker and colleagues (2014) introduced the belief that the suspect of a crime scenario was an Australian Aboriginal. The degree of later correction of this information, however, was unrelated to prejudice, suggesting the involvement of nonmotivational processes. Moreover, initial beliefs persist more when people generate reasons why the initial information is true but correspondingly less when they generate reasons why alternate scenarios might be true (Chan et al. 2017). A mental model of reasoning (Chan et al. 2017) details how people construct a web of mental models from which they derive causal conclusions. New information tends to produce new or extended models of explanation without leading people to discard key information not explained by the new model (Chan et al. 2017). Therefore, effective corrections must provide a causal alternative to fully explain mental models. For example, effective corrections of climate change denial must account for random variability in temperature in addition to introducing fossil fuel burning as the explanation for systematic temperature increases (Jamieson & Hardy 2014).

Attitudes are of particular concern in the area of climate change, where scholars and practitioners are investigating the potential for reducing climate change denial. Recent research has wrestled with the irony of strong extant climatological evidence accompanied by public disbelief and denial (Mercier 2016, Mercier & Sperber 2011). Naturally, cultural representations can be slow to align with scientific evidence, but progress has been made in other areas, including public acceptance of the health dangers of smoking (Ranney & Clark 2016). An apparent roadblock to aligning attitudes with scientific evidence is difficulties in teaching audiences about the mechanisms of global warming. In a series of experiments (Ranney & Clark 2016), participants were instructed about climate change mechanisms and completed measures of knowledge and beliefs before and after the instruction. Effects on knowledge were easy to obtain in most areas and were also large following instruction about climate change mechanisms (Ranney & Clark 2016). Belief change was also quite large, with 99% of the participants accepting climate change postinstruction relative to 50% preinstruction (Ranney & Clark 2016, experiment 2; U3 = 99). Of course, this is a relatively simple belief change, as opposed to the aforementioned attempts at changing more complex intergroup attitudes or health behaviors.

A sustained interest in the study of implicit attitudes has generated fascinating demonstrations of the effects of unique and historic events. The election of Barack Obama to the US presidency was such an event and provided the perfect natural experiment for the study of implicit racial attitudes as a function of media display of a Black person occupying a high-status position (Roos et al. 2013). This work was conducted in the United States and in Canada, assuming differential media coverage and, therefore, differential attitude change following the 2008 election (Roos et al. 2013). Implicit attitudes were measured using evaluative priming, a procedure that connects spontaneous activation of positive versus negative concepts to a stimulus—in this case, Black and White faces. Our calculation of the degree of change the authors observed in the United States reveals $d = 0.55$ and Cohen's U3 = 71%. This sizable effect implies that US implicit attitudes toward Blacks were 21% more positive after the election than before it.

Changes in implicit attitudes are promising, although still not an assurance of changes in behavior. In particular, a meta-analysis of implicit attitudes as predictors of behavior revealed an average correlation r of 0.15 or 0.12 for racial and intergroup attitudes (Oswald et al. 2015). These attitudes were measured using the implicit association test (Greenwald et al. 2015), developed and refined in prior decades with the goal of circumventing social desirability concerns and the common reluctance to express prejudicial attitudes. Although earlier estimates of these associations were only moderately higher ($r = 0.24$ and $r = 0.20$ for racial and intergroup attitudes, respectively; Greenwald et al. 2009), the recent low associations suggest minimally consequential changes, at least with the current measurement instruments (Oswald et al. 2015; see also Greenwald et al. 2015). Cameron et al. (2012), Galdi et al. (2012), and Meissner & Rothermund (2013) provide analyses of other implicit measures.

TOWARD A HOLISTIC UNDERSTANDING OF ATTITUDES

The longstanding research interest in attitudes has uncovered many details about the cognitive and motivational processes of attitude formation, attitude change, attitude–behavior correspondence, and persuasion. A careful look at the most recent work brings to light some qualitative changes in the scientific agenda in recent years, i.e., a shift from a focus on microprocesses to a more holistic, contemporary understanding of attitudes as they exist in three fundamental contexts: (*a*) the person as a whole, in relation to values, broad goals, language, emotions, other attitudes, and the lifespan; (*b*) the social context, including communicators, as well as social media and social networks; and (*c*) the broad context, particularly the sociohistorical context, in relation to the generational, cultural, and historical backdrop of attitudes.

The Person as Context

The first context is that of the person as a whole. In this section, we consider the powerful role of a person's values, general goals, emotions, linguistic processes, evaluative processes, life span and developmental aspects, and temporal and spatial context in shaping their attitudes and persuasion processes.

The context of values. Attitude scholars have traditionally had an interest in values, defined as attitudes toward abstract entities. For instance, a person with universalist values probably has a favorable attitude toward policies that foster equality; a person with security values is likely to favor policies that assure safety and stability in their environment. These values exist within a motivational structure that often links values to support for particular policies (e.g., Schwartz et al. 2012), although the influence of values is often tempered by other considerations. Over the past several years, interest in values has burgeoned.

A series of recent experiments (Wolsko et al. 2016) has provided a compelling demonstration of how linking a specific advocacy to broad values can shift attitudes toward a policy. When it comes to environmental attitudes, liberals see damage to the environment as an injustice, which easily connects with liberals' preoccupation with harm and care. Media messages about environmental issues advocate these values, which leaves these communications in a situation of preaching to the choir while neglecting the unconverted (Feinberg & Willer 2013, Wolsko et al. 2016). Wolsko and colleagues (2016) designed a series of studies crossing liberal and conservative ideologies with environmental messages that appealed to either individualizing or binding morals. Individualizing values include concern about caring, nurturing, and protecting vulnerable individuals from harm. For instance, a statement of individualizing values might be, "Show your love for all of humanity and the world in which we live by helping to care for our vulnerable natural environment" (Wolsko et al. 2016, p. 9). Binding values involve ingroup loyalty, authority, respect, and purity or sanctity.

For instance, a statement of binding values might be, "Show you love your country by joining the fight to protect the purity of America's natural environment" (Wolsko et al. 2016, p. 9).

The results from four experiments converged on the conclusion that liberals had equally strong intentions toward conservation regardless of the type of appeal they received. In contrast, conservatives had stronger intentions after receiving the binding message than after receiving either the individualizing message or a control message. Attitudes toward climate change were also measured by asking participants to rate statements such as, "The seriousness of climate change is exaggerated." As with intentions, the attitudes of liberals were similarly in favor of policies to counter climate change in the individualizing, binding, and control conditions alike. The attitudes of conservatives, however, were more positive in the binding condition than in the individualizing or control conditions.

Within the spectrum of conservative ideology, the influence of values on attitudes appears to interact with prevailing social norms. Research conducted by Oyamot et al. (2012) considered this possibility in a large experiment conducted via a phone survey of a diverse US sample. Authoritarian upbringing was gauged by endorsement of respect and obedience (versus independence and self-reliance). Attitudes toward immigrants were measured with reports of feelings toward legal immigrants, which correlated negatively with authoritarian upbringing. Furthermore, participants were informed that Americans' feelings were generally positive, mixed, or negative toward immigrants— a manipulation of social norms. The effects of these norms on attitudes depended not only on authoritarian upbringing but also on participants' current level of humanitarian values, measured with items such as, "Those who are unable to provide for their basic needs should be helped by others." Among participants reporting a more authoritarian upbringing, those with more humanitarian values exposed to the mixed norm reported more liking for immigrants than in the other conditions. Participants with authoritarian upbringing, however, reported more dislike for immigrants when exposed to the negative norm. Overall, then, humanitarian values attenuated xenophobic attitudes when the norm was mixed but increased xenophobia when the norm was negative.

Just as certain values modulate the impact of conservative social norms, values can also govern the impact of conservative advocacies. In particular, egalitarian values are often invoked to oppose affirmative action policies that recommend paying attention to traditionally underrepresented groups in educational and work settings. Therefore, invoking these values can increase the persuasiveness of communications condemning affirmative action. Research conducted by Blakenship et al. (2012) has shown that general messages about the value of equality were more successful at decreasing support for affirmative action than were messages directly attacking affirmative action. Furthermore, when values were easily accessible from memory, highlighting them had little effect. However, when values were not easily accessible, bringing them to mind decreased acceptance of affirmative action policies (Blankenship et al. 2015).

Both self-interest values and moral values can legitimize attitudes and make it subjectively appropriate to act on those attitudes (Miller & Effron 2010). One basis for this legitimacy is the personal relevance of an issue. For example, gay marriage is personally relevant to gays and lesbians who are likely to experience direct consequences from the policy. In addition, moral values can legitimize action independently of material self-interest (Effron & Miller 2012). In line with a moral legitimacy effect, participants reported feeling more comfortable taking action on policies that were not materially relevant to them (e.g., pro-choice issues for males) when they moralized the issue (Effron & Miller 2012).

Even though moral values and material self-interest can both guide attitudes, the relative weight of each interest type can be impacted by temporal distance. A persuasive message presented to non-White college students announced a reduction of financial aid for minority students (Hunt et al. 2010). The students were told that reduction would either take effect immediately or be

Norm: shared societal or situational expectations that can shape attitudes and guide behavior

implemented a year later, thus varying temporal distance to be either short or long. Self-interest was measured as financial strain, and values were measured as social dominance orientation. According to construal level theory (Wakslak et al. 2007), psychological distance alters the basis for decisions. When considering imminent decisions, concrete, material considerations receive more weight. In contrast, when considering delayed situations, abstract considerations receive more weight. As predicted, when the policy was to be effective immediately, material self-interest was the primary motivation for opposing the policy. However, when the policy was less imminent, political values were the primary driver of the opposition.

General action goal: effortful end state that can be satisfied by various cognitive and physical behavioral means

Abstract values are appropriate guides for attitudes in a number of contexts. Research conducted in Brazil, New Zealand, and South Africa provided a unique demonstration of the value-to-attitude pathways, as well as the fact that attitudes act as partial mediators of the influence of values on behavior (Milfont et al. 2010). Across countries, self-interest values predicted negative attitudes toward environmental issues, whereas altruistic values predicted favorable attitudes toward environmental issues. These attitudes had a moderate association with environmental behavior, an association that included the indirect effect of altruistic (but not self-interest) values. Overall, then, this work is another demonstration that attitudes are embedded within a network of values that must be taken into account to understand the influence of attitudes on behavior.

The context of goals. Attitudes can be brought to mind in the service of action goals, as in the case when considering a behavioral goal reminds us of what we like and dislike about the execution and outcomes of the behavior. General action and inaction goals are a particular type of overly general goal that have received research attention in the past few years. General action has been defined as motor or cognitive output, and general inaction has been defined as the lack of action (Albarracín & Handley 2011, Albarracín et al. 2008). The action end of the action–inaction continuum comprises intense or frequent motor and cognitive behavior, whereas the inaction end comprises neither motor nor cognitive behavior (e.g., non-REM sleep). The action end includes important, well-planned, effortful behaviors such as acquiring knowledge, as well as seemingly undemanding behaviors such as eating when food is present. General action and general inaction can be set to guide people toward activity or inactivity end-states, respectively, which are, in turn, achieved by temporarily accessible or chronically available behavioral means. These action and inaction goals have important implications for attitude activation and change.

In research conducted by Albarracín & Handley (2011), experimental participants primed with general action or inaction goals reported prior attitudes toward a topic after being (versus not being) forewarned that they would receive a message about a topic. The role of general goals becomes clear in association with the more specific goals people have in the moment (Albarracín & Handley 2011). Therefore, when people activate a general action goal in the context of processing a persuasive communication, the general action goal may be fulfilled by the specific goal of thinking about prior attitudes. Thus, prior attitudes are likely to become more accessible and, in turn, block the influence of the message.

Albarracín & Handley (2011) tested various aspects of the influence of general action goals on attitude accessibility and change. Participants previously primed with action (e.g., go), control (e.g., pear), or inaction (e.g., rest) words completed measures of attitudes toward gun control or euthanasia after they had or had not been forewarned that they would receive a persuasive message about either gun control or euthanasia. Findings indicated that attitudes that were relevant to the message were reported faster in action than in inaction goal conditions, whereas irrelevant attitudes were not affected. Further studies showed less attitude change when forewarned participants were primed with action than when they were primed with inaction and that action goals generally decreased elaborative processing of the persuasive message. Unfortunately, some of these experiments had low statistical power, an issue that has been linked to false positives only in recent years (Simmons et al. 2011). Therefore, further research in this area is important to, first, identify strong manipulations and, then, implement designs that maximize statistical power.

Research on attitudes has also uncovered broad evaluative responses toward action and inaction. All else equal, people appear to evaluate action more favorably than inaction. Words like action are evaluated to be more positive than words of inaction, even when the inaction word is one with pleasant connotations, such as calm (McCulloch et al. 2012). It may, therefore, be adaptive for social groups to instill favorable attitudes toward action, leading to action being positive by default. This pattern, however, is associated with Christian beliefs, suggesting that part of the action positivity effect derives from the overgeneralization of an ethic in which work is virtuous and inactivity is sinful.

Even though unspecified action is generally perceived to be positive, a switch in norms may lead perceivers to refocus and reevaluate action and inaction. When action is described as positive within a particular investment firm, participants who make financial decisions regret losing after not investing more than losing after investing (Feldman & Albarracín 2016). In contrast, when inaction is described as positive within a particular investment firm, participants who make financial decisions regret losing after investing more than losing after not investing (Feldman & Albarracín 2016). Therefore, despite an overall favoring of action, people are highly sensitive to normative information and can shift their evaluations according to the context.

The context of language. Another area receiving considerable attention concerns linguistic processes that affect attitude formation as well as attitude–behavior correspondence. The use of metaphors and their impact on attitudes is one important focus of investigation. For instance, reading about the police as either guardians or warriors led to, respectively, more and less liking for the police (Thibodeau et al. 2017). These effects were due to metaphors operating as an explanatory device rather than simply activating semantic concepts with different evaluative implications.

Interestingly, the use of metaphors is apparently dependent on the degree of psychological distance (Liberman & Trope 1998) of the object or situation being explained. Given that metaphors are used in explanation of abstract rather than concrete concepts, greater psychological distance from a concept should increase the likelihood of using metaphors for explanation. Furthermore, people may actively seek metaphors more often to understand psychologically distant concepts than psychologically close concepts (Jia & Smith 2013). The metaphor that an influx of immigrants is analogous to physical contamination of the body leads to negative attitudes toward immigration. However, this metaphorical impact is stronger when people think about immigration a year in the future than when they think about immigration a day in the future (Jia & Smith 2013).

Recent research has also shed new light on the role of self-talk, or inner speech, in attitude formation, as well as its role as a precursor of behavioral performance. The majority of adults report engaging in an ongoing internal dialogue, or self-talk, generally covertly. People may repeat sentences (e.g., "You/I can do it!" "Stay focused!") if they believe this speech will motivate them (Dolcos & Albarracin 2014). The structure of this talk, particularly the effects of the use of the first or second person in self-talk as well as the role of self-posed questions, is beginning to be the subject of research. When people face challenges or when their past behavior has yielded undesirable outcomes, the self splits into a speaker and a receiver, leading to addressing the self in the second person (Zell et al. 2012a). This form of second-person self-talk is supposedly beneficial for self-regulation because it resembles the form of external control experienced by children (Dolcos & Albarracin 2014, Zell et al. 2012a). Therefore, such self-talk is probably a natural way of controlling behavior later in life (Dolcos & Albarracin 2014, Zell et al. 2012b).

In research conducted by Dolcos & Albarracin (2014), participants were randomly assigned to one of two experimental groups (i.e., You or I self-talk conditions) or to a control group. Participants were then given the opportunity to choose to work on anagrams and received instructions to prepare for the task by writing self-directed advice. Participants in the control condition completed the anagrams without this type of preparation. As the researchers predicted, participants who prepared for the anagram task using sentences beginning with "You" performed better on the task than participants who wrote sentences beginning with "I" or participants in the control condition. More importantly for this review, attitudes followed the pattern of behavioral performance and were mediators of the effect of the second-person self-talk. These results imply that, even though second-person self-talk is more commanding that first-person self-talk, the impact of the second person still resembles that of intrinsic motivation. Research on self-talk has also been conducted in the area of social anxiety (Kross et al. 2014) and promises to generate important insights in the years to come.

How people use verbs has been another focus of attention in the area of attitudes, particularly with respect to the use of past and present and their influence on attitude–behavior correspondence. For example, if people recount a past experience drinking alcohol, does using the present or the past tense affect reliance on past behavior as a basis for intentions to drink again in the future? Carrera and colleagues (2012) sought answers to this very question. In their work, participants wrote a description about alcohol drinking using either the simple past or the present tense. They also reported their attitudes toward drinking and their intentions to drink again in the future, as well as the frequency of past alcohol drinking. Consistent with the possibility that the past involves greater psychological distance than the present, attitudes predicted intentions better when drinking was described in the past tense than when it was described in the present tense. In contrast, past behavior predicted intentions better when drinking was described in the present tense than when it was described in the past tense.

The context of emotions. Even though emotions are relevant to many attitude domains (see Clore & Schnall 2005), they appear to be particularly relevant to political attitudes of various types. For example, during times of war, presidential approval, an attitude toward the president's performance, can depend on the specific emotions of anger and anxiety (Lambert et al. 2010). The term "rally around the flag" describes political situations in which an external threat enhances support for an otherwise unappreciated right-leaning president. In Argentina, General Galtieri was president toward the end of a drawn-out military dictatorship responsible for international isolation, 30,000 missing people, and a large number of political prisoners. When he went to war against the United Kingdom, however, his approval rating soared, and supportive citizens filled May Square in Buenos Aires. Likewise, in the United States, George W. Bush enjoyed a similar trajectory when his approval ratings moved from 39% to 90% following the attacks on September 11, 2001. According to Lambert and colleagues (2010), the impact of 9/11 on attitudes toward Bush was mediated by corresponding increases in anger and anxiety. In an experimental presentation of 9/11 footage years after the event, participants' retrospective approval of Bush was higher after the 9/11 video than after a control video, and these attitudes were mediated by the specific emotions of anger and anxiety, whereas more general negative emotions had no influence (Lambert et al. 2010).

Emotion regulation strategies can also exert an impact on political attitudes. Intergroup attitudes in the Israeli–Palestinian conflict were investigated, in the area of emotional regulation, by Halperin et al. (2013). In their first study, Halperin et al. (2013) asked half of their participants to apply a cognitive reappraisal technique as they viewed an upcoming presentation. Specifically, they were taught to respond to the presentation as if they were scientists, thinking analytically

Self-talk:
self-directed inner speech, often designed to control behavior

in a cold, dispassionate way. After this manipulation, all participants watched an anger-inducing multimedia presentation about Israel's disengagement from the Gaza Strip and subsequent Palestinian aggression. The cognitive reappraisal technique was effective at reducing anger toward Palestinians, anger that, in turn, correlated negatively with support for conciliatory policies and positively with support for aggressive policies. Although the study had a relatively small sample ($d = 0.65$, $N = 39$), similar findings were obtained in a second experiment with measures of anger and attitudes obtained 5 months after the manipulation of cognitive reappraisal (Halperin et al. 2013).

General or dispositional attitude: attitudes that characterize the person as evaluating most objects positively, neutrally, or negatively

The context of other attitudes and evaluative processes. As researchers have opened their eyes to broad attitude patterns, it has become apparent that people's attitudes can be similar across different objects. In particular, shared affective traits can provide information about attitudes regardless of whether the object is President Trump, a new movie, or a toaster. Recent research has investigated this possibility in a series of studies and an independent replication and extension. In this work, Hepler & Albarracín (2013) investigated tendencies to generally like or dislike stimuli, defined as systematic variation in attitude valence as a function of individuals. These dispositional attitudes were measured by having participants evaluate a large number of stimuli to gauge central tendencies. From an initial set of 200 evaluations, findings yielded a final scale of 16 items about diverse objects such as taxidermy, cold showers, soccer, and politics, rated on scales from 1 (unfavorable) to 7 (favorable). This scale had high internal consistency, as well as high test-retest reliability, and exhibited good convergent and divergent validity. In particular, dispositional attitudes should be related to other traits associated with positive or negative affect (e.g., extraversion, optimism) and, indeed, were. However, all of these personality measures accounted for only about 20% of the variance in general attitudes, hinting at the uniqueness of dispositional attitudes.

General or dispositional attitudes are also useful because they can predict unknown attitudes, including attitudes toward completely novel objects. Two of the studies reported by Hepler & Albarracín (2013) obtained measures of dispositional attitudes, other traits, and attitudes toward a never-encountered microwave described in an advertisement. Reported attitudes toward the new product were consistently predicted by dispositional attitudes above and beyond all other individual difference measures (e.g., behavioral activation, optimism, trait negative affect, trait positive affect, agreeableness, need for cognition, need for closure, and more). Therefore, people who generally liked objects also liked a newly presented object, whereas people who generally disliked objects disliked it.

An intriguing implication of dispositional attitudes is that they should be expected to also broadly predict behavior, a possibility examined by Hepler & Albarracin (2014; for a replication, see Eschleman et al. 2015). Over two experiments, participants reported their dispositional attitudes as well as their time spent on a number of daily behaviors, such as personal care, education, working, and traveling. Dispositional attitudes correlated with the number of behaviors reported, but this was the case for both more and less effortful behaviors. Thus, dispositional attitudes appeared to predict behavior on the high-effort, active end as well as the low-effort, inactive end. Apparently, then, dispositional attitudes do not predict only active behavior but rather goal engagement, including sleeping, more generally.

Individual differences in evaluations have also been described as valence weighting. The valence weighting bias (Pietri et al. 2013) has been studied with a paradigm in which participants learn about beans of varying shapes and patterns of speckles that produce either positive or negative outcomes when selected. After participants learn about the beans, they are presented with new beans that resemble previous positive or negative beans. Thus, when a novel bean has characteristics resembling both a positive and negative bean, a participant who weighs negative information more heavily should classify that bean as negative, whereas a participant who weighs positive information more heavily should classify that bean as positive. Rocklage & Fazio (2014) used this same paradigm to obtain participant measures of valence weighting. Similar to the conclusions of Hepler & Albarracin's studies, this individual difference measure predicted approach and avoidance behavior toward objects in a novel environment. Also, participants with a negative-valence-weighting bias were more likely than those with a positive-valence-weighting bias to change attitudes in response to negative but false information about an object.

The context of time and space. Above, we discuss the impact of psychological distance on attitudes in the context of language and emotion. Beyond these areas, the effects of construing objects up close and at a distance have also been the subject of research on what factors influence attitudes. According to construal level theory (Liberman & Trope 1998), people construe psychologically proximal objects more concretely. Based on this premise, Ledgerwood et al. (2010) hypothesized and confirmed that attitudes toward proximal objects were influenced by social information, such as the preferences of romantic partners. In contrast, attitudes toward more distant objects were less influenced by social normative considerations and, in one of the experiments, were influenced by values. Some of these experiments were statistically underpowered (less than 80% power), implying that the probability of both false negatives (power is the confidence with which the null hypothesis may be rejected) and false positives is potentially high. However, the findings illustrate an important aspect of the broader picture of attitude bases.

The context of development. The developmental stage and childhood socialization of the individual is another fundamental context within which attitudes are shaped and reshaped. Recent research has investigated a variety of developmental and life-stage factors that predispose individuals to particular attitudes and ideologies.

Shifts in specific attitudes across the life span. Developmental shifts are observable in attitudes toward several specific topic areas. For instance, music preferences are subject to a variety of developmental shifts across the life span (Bonneville-Roussy et al. 2013), and these shifts shed light on the contextual factors that shape personal tastes. Adolescent audiences are more passionately engaged with music, regarding it as more important than do older adults and enjoying it in more contexts. Moreover, data from an Internet survey sample of a quarter million respondents showed marked and consistent age trends in musical preferences (Bonneville-Roussy et al. 2013). Specifically, preferences for mellow, unpretentious, and sophisticated music increased throughout the life span, whereas preferences for music that is intense and more contemporary was highest in adolescents and declined in later years. This latter finding not only gives hope to parents of teenage death metal fans but also supports the notion that the personality traits and psychosocial goals that characterize each stage of life give rise to distinct musical tastes. For example, intense music is perceived as "aggressive, tense, and antiestablishment" (Bonneville-Roussy et al. 2013, p. 12; see also Rentfrow et al. 2011), which may be more resonant with the needs of adolescents struggling with issues of identity development and autonomy. Consistent with this possibility, research also points to age-specific preferences for particular types of media content (for a review, see Valkenburg et al. 2016). Anyone who has ever spent an evening observing ticket buyers at the multiplex will not be surprised to learn that younger adults show a stronger preference for arousing, frightening, and even violent media content compared to middle-aged and older adults, who, in turn, show stronger preferences for calmer, more uplifting, and more meaningful media content (e.g., Mares & Sun 2010).

Beyond the realm of individual tastes, developmental shifts in self-focused attitude domains have been important subjects of investigation. For instance, attitudes toward the self (i.e., self-esteem) show age-related shifts that follow a quadratic trend across the life span, climbing from adolescence until middle age (approximately 50–60 years) and then decreasing in old age, largely due to declines in health and socioeconomic status (Orth et al. 2010, 2012). Moreover, self-esteem has a significant influence on personal experiences across all major life domains (Orth et al. 2012). Attitudes toward one's own aging have also been investigated (Miche et al. 2014) and are shaped by a variety of life-stage and health factors. Finally, researchers have examined the relationship between age and job attitudes, finding a positive relationship between age and overall job satisfaction (for a meta-analysis, see Ng & Feldman 2010).

Materialism:
a belief or ideology emphasizing the importance of pursuing financial success, material riches, and high status through consumer choices

Developmental antecedents of attitudinal systems. Using data from a two-wave national survey of early child development, in which parents of 1-month-old infants were interviewed and the children were surveyed 18 years later, Fraley et al. (2012) examined how early caregiving environments help to shape conservative versus liberal political ideologies in late adolescence. Parents who endorsed more authoritarian attitudes regarding parenting when their children were infants tended to raise children who were more ideologically conservative. Additional data on the sample's temperament in early childhood (age 4.5) suggested that children who showed early signs of a fearful temperament or had deficits in inhibitory control tended to become conservative by age 18, whereas children who showed high levels of activity and restlessness in early childhood tended to become liberal as young adults. These findings support a motivated social cognition perspective that casts conservatism as a motivated response to anxiety and fear and liberalism as a response to restlessness and undercontrolled ego-related functions.

Another form of ideology, materialism, has also been a focus of developmental research. Twenge & Kasser (2013) examined societal factors that influence the development of materialistic values. Their analysis pointed to middle childhood as a particularly important time in the development of late-adolescent materialism. Those who, during this life stage, experienced high levels of societal instability and disconnection (indexed by societal rates of unemployment and divorce) tended to become more materialistic 10 years later, as young adults. Similarly, those exposed to high levels of social modeling of consumerist practices (as indexed by societal advertising spending) in late childhood were also more likely to become materialistic as young adults. Fortunately, a study of 12–18 year olds suggested that parental and peer influences during childhood can mitigate the development of materialistic attitudes in adolescents (Chaplin & John 2010). By contributing to the growth of self-esteem in adolescents, parents and peers can decrease the tendency to look to material goods as ways to build positive self-views.

Developmental shifts in processing. According to socioemotional selectivity theory (Carstensen 2006) motivational shifts across the life span affect the selective processing of information. In contrast to younger people, who are motivated to pursue goals of acquiring knowledge and broadening horizons, older adults, as they grow to appreciate the fragility of life, increasingly prioritize present-focused goals of emotional satisfaction and meaning. This change in goals leads to a shift toward positive information in information processing as people age, a phenomenon referred to as the age-related positivity effect (e.g., Reed et al. 2014). A recent meta-analysis confirmed that, when information processing is unconstrained and people are allowed to allocate their attention spontaneously, older people are significantly more likely to attend to and recall positive than negative information, whereas the opposite pattern is seen among younger adults (Reed et al. 2014). This shift can be associated with a variety of effects in persuasion contexts, such as age differences in responses to gain- and loss-framed messages (e.g., Mikels et al. 2016, Notthoff & Carstensen 2014).

The Social Context

Sleeper effect: delayed persuasion of a message when presentation by a noncredible communicator serves as a discounting cue

Social inputs comprise a key contextual influence on attitudes. Therefore, understanding the role played by the views of others, whether message communicators, friends and network members, or social media inputs, continues to be a significant focus of attitude research.

The communicator. Persuasive communications entail an implicit or explicit interaction with the source of the message, a factor that has been of interest to researchers since the field of persuasion began. Recent findings underscore the importance of this relationship, for instance, by showing that the persuasiveness of messages can be enhanced by an alignment between a communicator's and an audience's power state (Dubois et al. 2016). Specifically, high-power communicators tend to generate messages that prioritize competence information, which is more persuasive to high-power audiences, whereas low-power communicators tend to generate messages with greater warmth, which is more persuasive to low-power audiences.

Recent research has also enhanced understanding of the processes surrounding source credibility, such as the sleeper effect. Classically, the sleeper effect involves an increase in persuasion following a delay after a message is presented by a noncredible source. For instance, recipients of political communications may discount a message from a political opponent because they do not perceive the source of the message as credible. Over time, however, the recipients may recall the message but not its noncredible source and, thus, become more persuaded than they were immediately after the message presentation (Kumkale & Albarracín 2004). The conditions for this effect have been well elucidated meta-analytically (Kumkale & Albarracín 2004), but the definition of the effect has typically been circumscribed to these situations.

In contrast to this classic scholarship, recent research has uncovered a different type of sleeper effect involving the communicator instead of the message itself. In the traditional sleeper effect, the influence of an otherwise effective message remains dormant because it has been discounted as coming from a noncredible source. However, it is conceivable that a favorable impression of a communicator may exert a delayed influence if it remains dormant after being discounted because of weak arguments (Albarracin et al. 2017). In a series of experiments, participants were induced to form impressions of communicators (e.g., political candidates) who provided noncompelling arguments. As predicted, under these conditions, the source's credibility had a delayed effect on the influence of the message; this effect occurred for various topics and delay lengths.

This novel type of sleeper effect is likely to take place in political campaign contexts, as well as other contexts in which evaluating the communicator is paramount. This novel finding confirms that message recipients can process information about the communicator in as much depth as information about the arguments. As is well known, sources and other cues to persuasion can have multiple roles—they can be processed as peripheral cues or processed in more detail (Wegener et al. 2010). This assumption of multiple roles in current versions of the elaboration likelihood model (Wegener et al. 2010) as well as the unimodel (Kruglanski & Gigerenzer 2011) highlights how most information can be processed either elaborately or nonelaborately. One recent demonstration of this possibility entailed an analysis of the attitude–behavior relationship. Specifically, attitudes formed on the basis of extensive information about a source, which supposedly elicits high levels of processing, were more persistent and predictive of behavior than attitudes formed on the basis of brief information about the source (Pierro et al. 2012). As persistence and impact on behavior are frequent consequences of high levels of elaboration (Barden & Tormala 2014, Howe & Krosnick 2017), this work shows once more that communicators can be the target of much attention and thinking (for other research on the effects of concentrating on the communication source, see Clark & Evans 2014, Clark et al. 2013).

Social media and social networks. With the advent of smart phones and the popularization of online platforms, the study of media effects has moved into the territory of emerging media. Some of this work has achieved considerable methodological sophistication, as in longitudinal studies conducted in naturalistic conditions. For example, the effects of violent video game use on aggressive behavior (von Salisch et al. 2011) were studied using cross-lagged models in Germany. This study showed that children's aggressiveness predicted subsequent violent media use but that violent media use did not predict aggressiveness. Thus, the effects of violent video game use on aggressive attitudes are, at best, weak.

Buzz marketing, which leverages word of mouth from popular opinion leaders to change attitudes within a social network, offers substantial promise for persuasion and has received considerable scholarly attention (e.g., Berger 2014). The potential of buzz marketing is illustrated by a study of the effects of a health-promotion campaign developed and delivered through a partnership between the University of Nebraska and the Centers for Disease Control, which involved recruiting teenagers as buzz agents. The campaign ran between 2007 and 2013 and showed promising effects (Struthers & Wang 2016). Remarkably, 66% of buzz agents improved their attitude toward physical activity, 63% improved their attitude toward consumption of fruit, and 51% improved their attitude toward consumption of vegetables, with corresponding changes in behavior in all areas. In addition to the teenagers who acted as agents of change, other teens who liked the campaign changed attitudes more than those who did not like the campaign. Although this evidence does not imply that the campaign changed attitudes overall, it did change the attitudes of the teenagers who liked the campaign.

A similar campaign that included social media was designed to decrease comments expressing body dissatisfaction (fat talk) on college campuses (Garnett et al. 2014). The campaign was implemented in two New England universities. The campaign activities included hosting events about fat talk, teaching students how to promote positive body conversations, and encouraging students to sign an online pledge to end fat talk. One of the central messages was "Friends Don't Let Friends Fat Talk," and the organizers of the campaign recommended that this message be displayed online and in physical locations on the campuses. The campaign had a small effect on body dissatisfaction, defined as a negative attitude toward one's own body. In addition, actual reductions in negative self-talk were observed for students who remembered being exposed to the campaign, although the study was, overall, underpowered.

Network effects on attitudes have received some attention because of observed similarities in behavior among people who are socially connected. On the one hand, friends are likely similar because people develop relationships with similar others through a process of social selection. On the other hand, friends may become similar through their interactions with others, through a process of social influence. In the first case, the similarity precedes friendship; in the second, similarity follows friendship. In a longitudinal study of this issue (de Klepper et al. 2010), the attitudes toward discipline among students of the Royal Naval Academy of the Netherlands were followed over time, along with their friendship patterns. Findings indicated that similarity in attitudes toward discipline was due to influence rather than selection. Naval students had attitudes similar to those of their friends because they had become friends with others who had then influenced them.

The influence of members of an individual's social network is also apparent in work on how activating social goals can influence attitudes. Women's romantic goals, for example, can make them distance themselves from pursuing careers in science, technology, engineering, and math

(STEM) fields (Park et al. 2011). Merely viewing images or overhearing conversations related to romantic relationships yielded less positive attitudes toward STEM fields, but this pattern was apparent only among women. Looking at the problem using a within-subject paradigm, women felt more desirable and engaged in more romantic activities on days when they pursued romantic goals. Unfortunately, however, on those same days, women pursued fewer math-related activities. This effect of romantic goals also appeared to persist over time, with romantic goals from the previous day making women less invested in math on the following day. Although these findings are discouraging for policy makers trying to increase representation of women in STEM fields, women's STEM presence may increase through the use of ingroup STEM experts promoting STEM fields to other women. In particular, these programs lead to more positive implicit and explicit attitudes toward STEM, as well as commitment to pursue STEM careers, among women (Stout et al. 2011).

The social functions of attitudes are an intriguing topic, and recent research has shed light on a broad set of interpersonal motives associated with attitudes. One such function is the feeling of familiarity experienced by people who share similar negative attitudes (Weaver & Bosson 2011). Apparently, sharing a negative attitude is sufficient to increase feelings of familiarity (Weaver & Bosson 2011), probably because expressing negative attitudes to strangers is counternormative in US culture. Another important social function involves attitudinal ambivalence as a way of smoothing over interpersonal differences (Pillaud et al. 2013). In particular, people express more ambivalence when issues are socially controversial, and experimentally increasing topic controversy leads individuals to manifest more ambivalence (Pillaud et al. 2013). Therefore, attitudes both influence relations with others and can be strategically altered for self-presentation purposes. Even in online contexts, communicating one's attitudes can serve a range of functions (including impression management, social bonding, and emotion regulation; Berger 2014).

The Historical Context

Achieving a holistic, contextualized understanding of attitudes requires consideration of the generational, historical, and cultural shifts that give rise to individual evaluations.

Generational context. Generational differences in attitudes generally arise from and are reflective of broad sociocultural changes that occur at specific time periods (Donnelly et al. 2016, Twenge & Kasser 2013, Twenge et al. 2016a). That is, generational differences reflect the impact of the larger cultural context on the individual. How different are the attitudes of people born into, say, the Millennial generation (born 1980–1994) from those of members of Generation X (GenXers; born 1965–1979) or Baby Boomers (born 1946–1964)? Although these types of questions have frequently been addressed through one-time polling comparisons (e.g., Nteta & Greenlee 2013), such cross-sectional comparisons across generations at a given point in time are problematic because they confound cohort, age, and historical influences.

Twenge and colleagues (e.g., Donnelly et al. 2016, Twenge & Kasser 2013, Twenge et al. 2016a) have addressed this question by carefully analyzing multiple large-scale surveys of social attitudes. For instance, in a study of political ideology using age–period–cohort analysis (Yang & Land 2013) on three large-scale and nationally representative surveys, Twenge et al. (2016b) separated the effects of the ages of the respondents from those of their cohort and historical time period. The results uncovered trends toward both greater conservatism and increased political polarization among the Millennial generation. Millennial twelfth graders and entering college students appear to be more politically polarized than Baby Boomers and GenXers were at the same age. Specifically, more twelfth graders in the 2010s identified as either strong Democrats or

Culture: a shared meaning system and common values held among people who share a geographic region, language, or historical period

Millennial: a member of the generation born between 1980 and 1994; their attitudes and ideologies have been the subject of extensive study

Cohort: a group born into the same generation

strong Republicans than did those in earlier decades. At the same time, more Millennials identified as being politically conservative than did either GenXers or Baby Boomers at the same age, and a smaller proportion identified as Democrats than did Boomers.

However, ideological attitudes are not the complete story. The trend toward greater self-identification as conservatives among Millennials exists alongside their increasingly liberal and tolerant attitudes regarding religious nonbelievers, nontraditional gender roles, and same-sex marriage (for a review, see, e.g., Donnelly et al. 2016) and their decreased beliefs in God or religion (Twenge et al. 2016a). This result illustrates that attitudes toward specific issues and topics do not necessarily define or track overall party identification in a consistent way. The characteristics that define ideological attitudes are themselves dynamic and shaped by their sociocultural context—as a result, what was defined as conservative in 1970 does not necessarily correspond to what that word currently means. For instance, Millennials and GenXers have mostly continued the social trends begun by prior cohorts toward more egalitarian attitudes about gender roles, with greater support for working mothers and nonworking fathers compared to previous generations (Donnelly et al. 2016). Taken together, these results suggest that some nuance is required when summarizing generational differences in political attitudes.

Much stronger claims have been made about generational shifts in attitudes toward the self, community, work, and materialistic lifestyles. Characterizing the Millennial cohort as "Generation Me," Twenge (2014) reviewed evidence that Millennials are more self-focused and individualistic, endorsing more favorable attitudes and values regarding money, fame, and social image while showing less community feeling than previous cohorts. Millennials are less likely than previous cohorts to report empathic concern or to take others' perspectives, being less likely to agree that "I often have tender, concerned feelings for people less fortunate than me" or "I sometimes try to understand my friends better by imagining how things look from their perspective" (Konrath et al. 2011).

Moreover, GenXer and Millennial respondents appear to have more materialistic attitudes compared to the Boomer generation (Twenge & Kasser 2013). They also appear to have less favorable attitudes regarding the importance of work and less willingness to work hard compared to Boomers (Twenge & Kasser 2013). Specifically, in a national survey of twelfth graders, among GenXer and Millennial respondents, desires for expensive material purchases (e.g., a new car every 2–3 years, a vacation house, a recreational vehicle) have steadily increased relative to those of youth in the 1970's. At the same time, the attitudes of twelfth graders toward the centrality of work appear to have declined, as measured by agreement with such items as, "I want to do my best in my job, even if this sometimes means working overtime." These patterns suggest that, among younger generations, material desires may have exceeded willingness to work to fulfill them. Note, however, that the evidence for shifts in materialism may depend upon how materialism is assessed (see Trzesniewski & Donnellan 2010) and that several studies show no generational differences in work ethic endorsement (see Zabel et al. 2016).

Climatic and historical events as context. Major climatic and social occurrences of the past decade have enabled psychologists to study the effects of naturalistic events on attitudes. Studying the effects of hurricanes on political and social attitudes is a creative instance of this approach (e.g., Levy et al. 2010, Rudman et al. 2013). For instance, in Rudman et al.'s (2013) work, New Jersey residents were surveyed before and after Hurricanes Irene and Sandy to determine support for politicians who try to combat or deny climate change. Implicit attitudes toward a Green politician were negative before both hurricanes but became positive afterwards. These patterns were most pronounced for participants who had been personally affected by the hurricanes.

The impact of the 2007–2008 global financial crisis on political attitudes was investigated in a large panel study in New Zealand (Milojev et al. 2015). As was the case in most of the rest of the world, the crisis greatly impacted New Zealand's economy, producing a 3.4% decrease in the gross domestic product and a 3-to-7% increase in unemployment. According to system justification theory (Jost & Banaji 1994), people at an economic or social disadvantage need to perceive the system as being just, a dynamic that helps to explain conservatism in underprivileged groups. Consistent with this possibility, New Zealanders of lower socioeconomic status showed an increase in political conservatism following the financial crisis. Attitudes, then, can depend not only on climatic but also on economic factors outside of the individual's control.

The impact of political events on attitudes was illustrated above when we discussed the emotional concomitants of the rally around the flag effect (Lambert et al. 2010). Other unique historical events have presented ideal opportunities to study the potent changes induced by such events. One such case involved the longstanding political and legal system of segregation in place in South Africa between 1948 and 1994. Intergroup attitudes were surveyed at various points over a 37-year period (1973–2009), allowing Mynhardt (2013) to investigate historical changes associated with these events. The ambitious study involved measures of attitudes toward English-speaking Whites, Afrikaans-speaking Whites, Indians, "coloureds," and Blacks. Notably, over the period of study, English-speaking Whites' attitudes toward their own group became less positive ($d = 0.29$), whereas the English-speaking Whites' attitudes toward Indians, Afrikaans-speaking Whites, and coloureds became more favorable. Despite these promising changes, the attitudes of English-speaking Whites toward Blacks became more negative ($d = 0.70$) during the entire period, including post-Apartheid. Furthermore, during the period of consolidation and social transformation (2000–2008), the favorability of their attitudes toward Blacks continued to plummet. The attitudes of Blacks were also interesting, showing an initial liking for English-speaking Whites and a negative turn in attitudes toward Afrikaans-speaking Whites following racial discord in the 1970s.

The impact of the presidential candidacy and election of Barack Obama, analyzed above, appears to have affected White Americans' attitudes towards Black Americans. In analyses of election surveys from 1992 to 2008, in which US representative samples of White respondents rated Blacks on scales from "stupid" to "intelligent" and from "lazy" to "hardworking," Whites' beliefs in Blacks' intelligence and work ethic became stronger and less prejudicial, although Whites continued to be perceived more positively than Blacks (Welch & Sigelman 2011). These attitudinal shifts have been described as the Obama effect and show how ethnic diversity among those who hold powerful positions can revolutionize social attitudes.

Culture as context. The sociocultural context influences attitudinal processes in a number of ways, as a rapidly growing body of research demonstrates. For instance, cultural factors can influence information processing strategies (Briley et al. 2014), shaping thinking styles (Lalwani & Shavitt 2013, Nisbett et al. 2001), general goals (Torelli & Shavitt 2010, Yang et al. 2015), and the role of feelings and metacognitive experiences in decision making (Hong & Chang 2015).

Western and non-Western cultural contexts. Most work in this area focuses on the distinctions between independent and interdependent self-construals, individualistic and collectivistic cultural backgrounds and orientations, or Western and non-Western cultural contexts. For instance, Hong & Chang (2015) showed that an independent versus interdependent self-construal (either measured or primed) strengthens the influence of incidental affect on evaluations, whereas an interdependent self-construal strengthens the reliance on reasons. Moreover, independents (interdependents) value a selected option more highly when they use a feeling-based (reason-based) strategy in choosing, presumably because the independent self seeks to enhance its own personal satisfaction whereas the interdependent self is concerned with justifying its preferences to others.

As a result of the broad influences of culture on attitude formation and change, cultural factors are often described as moderators of attitudinal processes (see Albarracin et al. 2005). Attitude scholars acknowledge cultural effects on established processes, but their influence is cast as a boundary condition. Until recently, cross-cultural theorizing has not generally been applied in an effort to expand attitudinal theorizing. However, many of the definitional and theoretical assumptions in the attitudes literature reflect primarily Western philosophical commitments. Furthermore, much of the extant knowledge about persuasion phenomena has emerged from a traditional approach to attitudes and social cognition, in which the defining feature is the focus on the individual. In this Western, person-centric model, the focus is on the development and expression of personal preferences and making one's decisions based on these preferences. This approach, as developed in the West, may offer an incomplete account of the nature and function of evaluative processes in non-Western contexts. It is worth considering the extent to which these premises apply to attitudes in non-Western cultural contexts. How do attitudes function in contexts where maintaining relationships, fulfilling expected social roles, and being normatively appropriate are often more important than forming and expressing distinct personal preferences?

Several studies have suggested that attitudes function differently in non-Western cultures. For example, Indian employees are more likely than Americans to make choices based upon what is expected by authority figures, irrespective of their own personal preferences (Savani et al. 2012). An analysis of survey data tapping concern for the environment from 48 countries (Eom et al. 2016) showed that, for nations that are less individualistic, personal attitudes are less predictive of environmental behavior intentions. A follow-up experiment showed that, although environmental attitudes are a strong predictor of pro-environmental product choices in the United States, they are not in Japan, where, instead social norms predict choices (Eom et al. 2016).

Most attitude theories assume, for instance, that personal preferences and choices rooted in those preferences are foundational and are, therefore, the key to achieving persuasion outcomes. However, in non-Western contexts, where a normative-contextual model applies (Riemer et al. 2014), normative pressures, structured through cultural practices, shape attitudes. Parents direct their children's attention to normative aspects of events ("What were the children doing?") rather than to their own personal emotional responses ("Did you like it?") (Wang 2013), and other societal structures reinforce the emphasis on norms and relationships (Markus & Conner 2013).

In other words, in many cultures, the emphasis is on awareness of social expectations, norms, and obligations and integration of these factors into one's preferences (e.g., Gelfand et al. 2011, Li et al. 2017, Miller et al. 2011). Chiu et al. (2010) point out that, in such contexts, intersubjective perceptions (people's perceptions of the normative consensus) can better explain choices than can personal beliefs and values. Rather than holding unique personal preferences that set the self apart, individuals hold attitudes that help them to conform and to validate shared social norms (Boer & Fischer 2013), serving to affirm and deepen relationships with others. Moreover, Easterners, as compared to Westerners, tend to have a more difficult time choosing at all, and this indecisiveness is tied to dialectical thinking (Ng & Hynie 2014), a belief system that tolerates contradictory information (Spencer-Rodgers et al. 2010) and emphasizes interconnections and holistic relationships. In contrast, Westerners prefer action, and their intolerance of contradiction leads to oppositional attitudes toward the concepts of action and inaction, which appear contradictory, whereas people from dialectical East Asian societies express more balanced and moderate views about action and inaction (Zell et al. 2012a) and other targets (see Johnson et al. 2011). Indeed, in Western contexts, having stable and internally consistent attitudes is fundamentally important to guiding action, and ambivalent attitudes are, therefore, undesirable (Riemer et al. 2014). As a result, among Westerners, having ambivalent attitudes is aversive, and such attitudes

Person-centric model: traditional Western view of attitudes, defined by a focus on the individual and the development and expression of personal preferences are more likely than univalent attitudes to change, whereas this is not the case among Easterners (Ng et al. 2012).

East Asian philosophy emphasizes the idea that everything needs to be evaluated in its context (Nisbett et al. 2001). This principle leads to an enhanced tendency to see interconnections between elements of a larger whole, for instance, between a parent brand (e.g., McDonald's) and a new brand extension launched by the brand that is not an obvious fit (e.g., McDonald's salads). Holistic (versus analytic) thinkers can be more favorable toward distant brand extensions for functional products because they are more likely to find symbolic relationships among such products (Monga & John 2010). Similarly, whereas consumers in general tend to judge a product's quality based on its price, having a holistic thinking style strengthens this perceived price–quality relationship (Lalwani & Shavitt 2013). Specifically, consumers who adopt a holistic rather than an analytic thinking style are more likely to use a product's price to evaluate its quality because of their tendency to see interrelations between price and other product elements (Lalwani & Shavitt 2013).

Research points to differences in the functions of attitudes, as well. In Western contexts, personal attitudes often serve a self-expressive function, as preferences are strategically formed and expressed to convey desired individual identities (e.g., Berger 2014). In contrast, in non-Western contexts, harmony and social cohesion are more persuasive (e.g., Han & Shavitt 1994), and attitudes function to enhance relational embeddedness (Riemer et al. 2014) and to express values of conformity and tradition that support social norms (Boer & Fischer 2013). In such contexts, self-expression, as an assertion of individuality, is less motivating, and self-expressive acts are less prevalent (e.g., Chu & Kim 2011, Kim & Sherman 2007). In line with this pattern, an analysis of online customer reviews posted in China (on **https://www.amazon.cn**) and the United States (on **https://www.amazon.com**) revealed that Chinese reviews were less self-expressive than American reviews in that they were less likely to provide their personal opinions about products and contained fewer recommendations to others (Lai et al. 2013).

Taken together, then, a growing body of research suggests cultural differences in the structure, functions, and characteristics of attitudes. Traditional attitude theorizing has tended to view attitudes as intrapersonal entities tuned to the pursuit of individual goals—a person-centric model. There are significant opportunities to broaden attitude theorizing to address the distinct normative-contextual aspects of attitudes in non-Western cultures (Riemer et al. 2014).

Horizontal and vertical cultural contexts. In addition to the broad distinction between individualistic, independent cultures and collectivistic, interdependent ones, recent research has also addressed the influence of other important dimensions of culture on attitudes and persuasion processes (for a review, see Shavitt et al. 2017). For instance, cultures vary in their propensity to emphasize hierarchy, a distinction within the individualism–collectivism continuum that is captured by cultures or orientations that are horizontal (valuing equality) versus vertical (emphasizing hierarchy; Triandis & Gelfand 1998). In vertical-individualist societies, such as the United States and Great Britain, an individualistic form of hierarchy, where gaining personal status is linked to the individual self and people seek opportunities to stand out and to impress others, is emphasized. In contrast, in horizontal-individualist societies, such as Denmark, Norway, and Australia, the focus is on expressing uniqueness, self-reliance, and self-expression rather than improving personal status. In vertical-collectivist societies, such as South Korea, China, and India, the emphasis is on fulfilling duties, prioritizing ingroup goals over personal goals, and complying with authority figures. Finally, in horizontal-collectivist societies, such as Brazil and some other Latin American contexts, the emphasis is on interdependence, benevolence, and sociability, not hierarchy (Torelli & Shavitt 2010; for a review, see Shavitt & Cho 2016). Differences in orientation along the

---

Individualism:
cultural value system emphasizing the importance of self-reliance and independence and the pursuit of personal goals over the ingroup's goals

Collectivism:
cultural value system emphasizing pursuit of group goals, harmony, interdependence with others, and maintenance of strong relationships

horizontal–vertical continuum have also been shown within countries among ethnic and cultural groups. For instance, Hispanic Americans tend to score higher than European Americans in horizontal collectivism and lower in vertical individualism (Torelli & Shavitt 2010, Torelli et al. 2015).

This horizontal versus vertical cultural distinction is reflected in the content of persuasive appeals and in attitudinal patterns. For instance, an analysis of the content of over 1,200 magazine advertisements in five countries (Denmark, South Korea, Poland, Russia, and the United States) revealed that advertisements in vertical cultures (e.g., the United States and South Korea) put more emphasis on status, luxury, and prestige than do ads in horizontal cultures (e.g., Denmark) (Shavitt et al. 2011). For example, in vertical cultures, advertisements are more likely to use prestigious endorsers identified as Ivy League graduates or to label brands as "award-winning." On the other hand, uniqueness appeals are more prevalent in horizontal individualist cultures (e.g., Denmark) than in countries that fall into vertical cultural categories. For instance, such advertisements may highlight how the advertised brand expresses consumers' personal style.

Similarly, consumers tend to prefer brands and advertisements that resonate with these horizontal and vertical cultural orientations (Torelli & Shavitt 2010, Torelli et al. 2012). For example, having a horizontal collectivistic orientation predicts liking a brand that conveys self-transcendence values in its advertising (e.g., "Supporting humanitarian programs in developing countries because we care about building a better world.") and predicts an affinity for brands that embody concerns for the welfare of others. Having a vertical collectivistic orientation predicts liking a brand that conveys conservation values (e.g., "The status quo in luxury watches. A tradition of classic designs and impeccable workmanship for 115 years."). Having a vertical individualistic orientation predicts liking brands that symbolize status and prestige and advertisements that convey self-enhancement (e.g., "An exceptional piece of adornment that conveys your status and signifies your exquisite taste."), whereas having a horizontal individualistic orientation predicts liking a brand that conveys openness (e.g., "A travel companion to help you live an exciting life full of adventures waiting around every corner.") (Torelli & Shavitt 2010, Torelli et al. 2012). Moreover, these relations emerge across cultural groups. For example, Brazilians, who score relatively high in horizontal collectivistic orientation (compared to European Americans, Canadians, and East Asians), tend to prefer brands that symbolize prosocial values more than do individuals in other cultural groups. Norwegians, who score relatively low in vertical individualistic orientation, tend to prefer brands that symbolize status and prestige values less than do individuals in the other groups. A multilevel analysis further indicated that vertical individualistic and horizontal collectivistic cultural orientations partially mediate cultural group–level differences in liking for these respective types of brands (Torelli & Shavitt 2010, study 3). Evidence also suggests that distinct mindsets can be triggered when concepts relevant to each cultural orientation are cued, influencing the processing of information about an object (Torelli & Shavitt 2010).

CONCLUSION

Our review highlights the sizeable and long-standing research interest in attitudes and attitude change. Research between 2010 and 2017 has elucidated many details regarding the cognitive and motivational processes of attitude formation, attitude change, and attitude–behavior correspondence. That said, this period of attitude research has been characterized by significant shifts. Our focus on contextual factors in this review encapsulates a key qualitative change in recent years in the scientific research agenda on attitudes—a shift from a focus on microprocesses to a more holistic, contemporary understanding of attitudes as they exist in three fundamental contexts: the person as a whole, the social context, and the broad sociohistorical context. This contextual focus on the person as a whole links attitude change to individual values, general goals, language, emotions, and developmental and life span influences. The focus on the social context links attitude change to the individual's interactions with communicators, social networks, and social media. The focus on the broad sociohistorical context recognizes the impact of historically significant climatic, political, and economic events, as well as the fundamental impact of culture on the characteristics and functions of attitudes.

For decades, particularly during the 1980s and 1990s, research on attitude change was primarily focused on information processing—a label applying a computer processing metaphor, assumed to operate across situations and topics. The period of research covered in the previous *Annual Review of Psychology* article on attitudes and attitude change was characterized as one of integrative theorizing (Bohner & Dickel 2011), as efforts to integrate cognitive process models and explicit and implicit attitudes were a primary concern. In the current period (2010–2017), a new contextualism has added nuance to our understanding of attitudes, bringing with it more attention to the substantive content of attitudes. Rather than seeking integration, this approach offers an enhanced understanding of distinctions between attitudinal domains. After years of leaving attitude objects out of the conversation, attitude change research now increasingly concerns itself with shifts in specific attitude clusters (e.g., attitudes toward political issues, music, jobs and work, community, climate change, materialistic goals, status brands, authority figures, and even the concepts of action or inaction) and what these shifts reveal about the contexts in which these attitudes were formed. As future research continues to mine the influence of the personal, social, and sociohistorical contexts, we look forward to a more situated understanding of attitude formation and change.

SUMMARY POINTS

1. The degree of attitude change generally observed in published research tends to be modest, at about one third of a standard deviation.

2. Linking a specific advocacy to broad values can shape attitudes toward a policy in line with the values. Values influence behavior by mediating influences on attitudes more specifically connected to the behavior.

3. Attitudes are easier to remember and more difficult to change when action goals are activated.

4. Second-person self-talk can induce positive attitudes toward a task.

5. Emotional regulation can reduce negative attitudes.

6. Developmental shifts are observable in attitudes toward many topic areas, from music and media to the self. The roots of political and materialistic ideologies can be traced to early childhood experiences.

7. The attitudes of the Millennial generation differ from those of prior generations in being more conservative fiscally and politically, liberal socially (e.g., support for egalitarian gender roles and same-sex marriage), individualistic, self-focused, and materialistic.

8. Attitude theorizing, as developed in the West, offers an incomplete account of how attitudes function and are structured in non-Western cultures, where normative processes play a stronger role in shaping attitudes and their functions.

FUTURE ISSUES

1. It is important to maintain a common terminology to facilitate tracking attitude research. Currently, some of the work on attitudes uses terms such as "evaluative judgments" or "values" instead of "attitudes."

2. We are only beginning to understand patterns of delayed attitude change, and these patterns deserve future attention.

3. Attitudes must be studied within social networks and in relation to historic and other environmental events.

4. Attitude change strategies must be systematically tested across cultures.

5. Analyses of generational or developmental influences on attitudes must disentangle the influences of age, historical time period, and cohort.

6. To expand attitude theorizing across cultural regions, the distinct characteristics and functions of attitudes in non-Western cultures deserve attention.

7. Although most attitude research is properly statistically powered, some areas are not and require increased methodological rigor.

8. Psychological research on attitudes would benefit from greater attention to public policy considerations and applied issues.

DISCLOSURE STATEMENT

The authors are not aware of any affiliations, memberships, funding, or financial holdings that might be perceived as affecting the objectivity of this review.

LITERATURE CITED

Ajzen I, Madden TJ. 1986. Prediction of goal-directed behavior: attitudes, intentions, and perceived behavioral control. *J. Exp. Soc. Psychol.* 22(5):453–74

Albarracín D, Handley IM. 2011. The time for doing is not the time for change: effects of general action and inaction goals on attitude retrieval and attitude change. *J. Personal. Soc. Psychol.* 100(6):983–98

Albarracín D, Handley IM, Noguchi K, McCulloch KC, Li H, et al. 2008. Increasing and decreasing motor and cognitive output: a model of general action and inaction goals. *J. Personal. Soc. Psychol.* 95(3):510–23

Albarracin D, Kumkale GT, Del Vento PP. 2017. How people can become persuaded by weak messages presented by credible communicators: Not all sleeper effects are created equal. *J. Exp. Soc. Psychol.* 68:171–80

Albarracin D, Zanna MP, Johnson BT, Kumkale GT. 2005. Attitudes: introduction and scope. In *The Handbook of Attitudes*, ed. D Albarracin, BT Johnson, MP Zanna, pp. 3–19. Hove, UK: Psychol. Press

Allport GW. 1935. Attitudes. In *A Handbook of Social Psychology*, ed. C Murchison, pp. 798–844. Worcester, MA: Clark Univ. Press

Barden J, Tormala ZL. 2014. Elaboration and attitude strength: the new meta-cognitive perspective. *Soc. Personal. Psychol. Compass* 8(1):17–29

Berger J. 2014. Word of mouth and interpersonal communication: a review and directions for future research. *J. Consum. Psychol.* 24(4):586–607

Blankenship KL, Wegener DT, Murray RA. 2012. Circumventing resistance: using values to indirectly change attitudes. *J. Personal. Soc. Psychol.* 103(4):606–21

Blankenship KL, Wegener DT, Murray RA. 2015. Values, inter-attitudinal structure, and attitude change: Value accessibility can increase a related attitude's resistance to change. *Personal. Soc. Psychol. Bull.* 41(12):1739–50

Boer D, Fischer R. 2013. How and when do personal values guide our attitudes and sociality? Explaining cross-cultural variability in attitude-value linkages. *Psychol. Bull.* 139(5):1113–47

Bohner G, Dickel N. 2011. Attitudes and attitude change. *Annu. Rev. Psychol.* 62:391–417

Bonneville-Roussy A, Rentfrow PJ, Xu MK, Potter J. 2013. Music through the ages: trends in musical engagement and preferences from adolescence through middle adulthood. *J. Personal. Soc. Psychol.* 105(4):703–17

Briley D, Wyer RS, Li E. 2014. A dynamic view of cultural influence: a review. *J. Consum. Psychol.* 24(4):557–71

Calanchini J, Sherman JW. 2013. Implicit attitudes reflect associative, non-associative, and non-attitudinal processes. *Soc. Personal. Psychol. Compass* 7(9):654–67

Cameron CD, Brown-Iannuzzi JL, Payne BK. 2012. Sequential priming measures of implicit social cognition: a meta-analysis of associations with behavior and explicit attitudes. *Personal. Soc. Psychol. Rev.* 16(4):330–50

Carrera P, Muñoz D, Caballero A, Fernández I, Albarracín D. 2012. The present projects past behavior into the future while the past projects attitudes into the future: how verb tense moderates predictors of drinking intentions. *J. Exp. Soc. Psychol.* 48(5):1196–200

Carstensen LL. 2006. The influence of a sense of time on human development. *Science* 312:1913–16

Chan MS, Jones CR, Albarracin D. 2017. Countering false beliefs: an analysis of the evidence and recommendations of best practices for the retraction and correction of scientific misinformation. In *The Oxford Handbook of the Science of Science Communication*, ed. KH Jamieson, D Kahan, DA Scheufele, pp. 331–39. Oxford, UK: Oxford Univ. Press

Chaplin LN, John DR. 2010. Interpersonal influences on adolescent materialism: a new look at the role of parents and peers. *J. Consum. Psychol.* 20(2):176–84

Chiu C-Y, Gelfand MJ, Yamagishi T, Shteynberg G, Wan C. 2010. Intersubjective culture: the role of intersubjective perceptions in cross-cultural research. *Perspect. Psychol. Sci.* 5(4):482–93

Chu SC, Kim Y. 2011. Determinants of consumer engagement in electronic word-of-mouth (eWOM) in social networking sites. *Int. J. Advert.* 30(1):47–75

Clark JK, Evans AT. 2014. Source credibility and persuasion: the role of message position in self-validation. *Personal. Soc. Psychol. Bull.* 40(8):1024–36

Clark JK, Wegener DT, Sawicki V, Petty RE, Briñol P. 2013. Evaluating the message or the messenger? Implications for self-validation in persuasion. *Personal. Soc. Psychol. Bull.* 39(12):1571–84

Clore GL, Schnall S. 2005. The influence of affect on attitude. In *The Handbook of Attitudes*, ed. D Albarracin, BT Johnson, MP Zanna, pp. 437–90. Hove, UK: Psychol. Press

de Klepper M, Sleebos E, van de Bunt G, Agneessens F. 2010. Similarity in friendship networks: selection or influence? The effect of constraining contexts and non-visible individual attributes. *Soc. Netw.* 32(1):82–90

Dolcos S, Albarracin D. 2014. The inner speech of behavioral regulation: intentions and task performance strengthen when you talk to yourself as a You. *Eur. J. Soc. Psychol.* 44(6):636–42

Donnelly K, Twenge JM, Clark MA, Shaikh SK, Beiler-May A, Carter NT. 2016. Attitudes toward women's work and family roles in the United States, 1976–2013. *Psychol. Women Q.* 40(1):361684315590774

Dubois D, Rucker DD, Galinsky AD. 2016. Dynamics of communicator and audience power: the persuasiveness of competence versus warmth. *J. Consum. Res.* 43(1):68–85

Ecker UKH, Lewandowsky S, Fenton O, Martin K. 2014. Do people keep believing because they want to? Preexisting attitudes and the continued influence of misinformation. *Mem. Cogn.* 42(2):292–304

Effron DA, Miller DT. 2012. How the moralization of issues grants social legitimacy to act on one's attitudes. *Personal. Soc. Psychol. Bull.* 38(5):690–701

Ehret PJ, Monroe BM, Read SJ. 2015. Modeling the dynamics of evaluation: a multilevel neural network implementation of the iterative reprocessing model. *Personal. Soc. Psychol. Rev.* 19(2):148–76

Eom K, Kim HS, Sherman DK, Ishii K. 2016. Cultural variability in the link between environmental concern and support for environmental action. *Psychol. Sci.* 27(10):1–9

Eschleman KJ, Bowling NA, Judge TA. 2015. The dispositional basis of attitudes: a replication and extension of Hepler and Albarracín 2013. *J. Personal. Soc. Psychol.* 108(5):e1–15

Feinberg M, Willer R. 2013. The moral roots of environmental attitudes. *Psychol. Sci.* 24(1):56–62

Feldman G, Albarracín D. 2016. Norm theory and the action-effect: the role of social norms in regret following action and inaction. *J. Exp. Soc. Psychol.* 69:111–20

Fraley RC, Griffin BN, Belsky J, Roisman GI. 2012. Developmental antecedents of political ideology: a longitudinal investigation from birth to age 18 years. *Psychol. Sci.* 23(11):1425–31

Galdi S, Gawronski B, Arcuri L, Friese M. 2012. Selective exposure in decided and undecided individuals. *Personal. Soc. Psychol. Bull.* 38(5):559–69

Garnett BR, Buelow R, Franko DL, Becker C, Rodgers RF, Austin SB. 2014. The importance of campaign saliency as a predictor of attitude and behavior change: a pilot evaluation of social marketing campaign Fat Talk Free Week. *Health Commun.* 29(10):984–95

Gelfand MJ, Raver JL, Nishii L, Leslie LM, Lun J, et al. 2011. Differences between tight and loose cultures: a 33-nation study. *Science* 332(6033):1100–4

Greenwald AG, Banaji MR, Nosek BA. 2015. Statistically small effects of the implicit association test can have societally large effects. *J. Personal. Soc. Psychol.* 108(4):553–61

Greenwald AG, Poehlman TA, Uhlmann EL, Banaji MR. 2009. Understanding and using the implicit association test: III. Meta-analysis of predictive validity. *J. Personal. Soc. Psychol.* 97(1):17–41

Halperin E, Porat R, Tamir M, Gross JJ. 2013. Can emotion regulation change political attitudes in intractable conflicts? From the laboratory to the field. *Psychol. Sci.* 24(1):106–11

Han S-P, Shavitt S. 1994. Persuasion and culture: advertising appeals in individualistic and collectivistic societies. *J. Exp. Soc. Psychol.* 30(4):326–50

Hart W, Albarracín D, Eagly AH, Brechan I, Lindberg MJ, Merrill L. 2009. Feeling validated versus being correct: a meta-analysis of selective exposure to information. *Psychol. Bull.* 135(4):555–88

Hepler J, Albarracín D. 2013. Attitudes without objects: evidence for a dispositional attitude, its measurement, and its consequences. *J. Personal. Soc. Psychol.* 104(6):1060–76

Hepler J, Albarracin D. 2014. Liking more means doing more: Dispositional attitudes predict patterns of general action. *Soc. Psychol.* 45(5):391–98

Hong J, Chang HH. 2015. "I" follow my heart and "we" rely on reasons: the impact of self-construal on reliance on feelings versus reasons in decision making. *J. Consum. Res.* 41(April):1392–411

Howe LC, Krosnick JA. 2017. Attitude strength. *Annu. Rev. Psychol.* 68:327–51

Hunt CV, Kim A, Borgida E, Chaiken S. 2010. Revisiting the self-interest versus values debate: the role of temporal perspective. *J. Exp. Soc. Psychol.* 46(6):1155–58

Jamieson KH, Hardy BW. 2014. Leveraging scientific credibility about Arctic sea ice trends in a polarized political environment. *PNAS* 111(Suppl.):13598–605

Jia L, Smith ER. 2013. Distance makes the metaphor grow stronger: a psychological distance model of metaphor use. *J. Exp. Soc. Psychol.* 49(3):492–97

Johnson TP, Shavitt S, Holbrook AL. 2011. Survey response styles across cultures. In *Cross-Cultural Research Methods in Psychology*, ed. D Matsumoto, F van de Vijver, pp. 130–75. Oxford, UK: Oxford Univ. Press

Jost JT, Banaji MR. 1994. The role of stereotyping in system-justification and the production of false consciousness. *Br. J. Soc. Psychol.* 33(1):1–27

Jung CG. 1923. *Psychological Types, or the Psychology of Individuation*. Zürich: Rascher Verl.

Kalinoski ZT, Steele-Johnson D, Peyton EJ, Leas KA, Steinke J, Bowling NA. 2013. A meta-analytic evaluation of diversity training outcomes. *J. Organ. Behav.* 34(8):1076–104

Kim HS, Sherman DK. 2007. "Express yourself": culture and the effect of self-expression on choice. *J. Personal. Soc. Psychol.* 92(1):1–11

Konrath SH, O'Brien EH, Hsing C. 2011. Changes in dispositional empathy in American college students over time: a meta-analysis. *Personal. Soc. Psychol. Rev.* 15(2):180–98

Kross E, Bruehlman-Senecal E, Park J, Burson A, Dougherty A, et al. 2014. Self-talk as a regulatory mechanism: How you do it matters. *J. Personal. Soc. Psychol.* 106(2):304–24

Kruglanski AW, Gigerenzer G. 2011. Intuitive and deliberate judgments are based on common principles. *Psychol. Rev.* 118(1):97–109

Kumkale GT, Albarracín D. 2004. The sleeper effect in persuasion: a meta-analytic review. *Psychol. Bull.* 130(1):143–72

Lai J, He P, Chou H-M, Zhou L. 2013. Impact of national culture on online consumer review behavior. *Glob. J. Bus. Res.* 7(1):109–15

Lalwani AK, Shavitt S. 2013. You get what you pay for? Self-construal influences price-quality judgments. *J. Consum. Res.* 40(2):255–67

Lambert AJ, Scherer LD, Schott JP, Olson KR, Andrews RK, et al. 2010. Rally effects, threat, and attitude change: an integrative approach to understanding the role of emotion. *J. Personal. Soc. Psychol.* 98(6):886–903

Ledgerwood A, Trope Y, Chaiken S. 2010. Flexibility now, consistency later: Psychological distance and construal shape evaluative responding. *J. Personal. Soc. Psychol.* 99(1):32–51

Lemmer G, Wagner U. 2015. Can we really reduce ethnic prejudice outside the lab? A meta-analysis of direct and indirect contact interventions. *Eur. J. Soc. Psychol.* 45(2):152–68

Levy SR, Freitas AL, Mendoza-Denton R, Kugelmass H, Rosenthal L. 2010. When sociopolitical events strike cultural beliefs: divergent impact of Hurricane Katrina on African Americans' and European Americans' endorsement of the Protestant work ethic. *Basic Appl. Soc. Psychol.* 32(3):207–16

Li R, Gordon S, Gelfand MJ. 2017. Tightness-looseness: a new framework to understand consumer behavior. *J. Consum. Psychol.* 27(3):377–91

Liberman N, Trope Y. 1998. The role of feasibility and desirability considerations in near and distant future decisions: a test of temporal construal theory. *J. Personal. Soc. Psychol.* 75(1):5–18

Mares ML, Sun Y. 2010. The multiple meanings of age for television content preferences. *Hum. Commun. Res.* 36(3):372–96

Markus HR, Conner A. 2013. *Clash!: How to Thrive in a Multicultural World.* New York: Plume

McCulloch KC, Li H, Hong S, Albarracin D. 2012. Naïve definitions of action and inaction: the continuum, spread, and valence of behaviors. *Eur. J. Soc. Psychol.* 42(2):227–34

Meissner F, Rothermund K. 2013. Estimating the contributions of associations and recoding in the implicit association test: the ReAL model for the IAT. *J. Personal. Soc. Psychol.* 104(1):45–69

Mercier H. 2016. The argumentative theory: predictions and empirical evidence. *Trends Cogn. Sci.* 20(9):689–700

Mercier H, Sperber D. 2011. Why do humans reason? Arguments for an argumentative theory. *Behav. Brain Sci.* 34(2):57–111

Miche M, Elsässer VC, Schilling OK, Wahl H-W. 2014. Attitude toward own aging in midlife and early old age over a 12-year period: examination of measurement equivalence and developmental trajectories. *Psychol. Aging* 29(3):588–600

Mikels JA, Shuster MM, Thai ST, Smith-Ray R, Waugh CE, et al. 2016. Messages that matter: age differences in affective responses to framed health messages. *Psychol. Aging* 31(4):409–14

Miles E, Crisp RJ. 2014. A meta-analytic test of the imagined contact hypothesis. *Group Process. Intergroup Relat.* 17(1):3–26

Milfont TL, Duckitt J, Wagner C. 2010. A cross-cultural test of the value-attitude-behavior hierarchy. *J. Appl. Soc. Psychol.* 40(11):2791–813

Miller DT, Effron DA. 2010. Psychological license: when it is needed and how it functions. *Adv. Exp. Soc. Psychol.* 43(C):115–55

Miller JG, Das R, Chakravarthy S. 2011. Culture and the role of choice in agency. *J. Personal. Soc. Psychol.* 101(1):46–61

Milojev P, Greaves L, Osborne D, Sibley CG. 2015. Stability and change in political conservatism following the global financial crisis. *Personal. Soc. Psychol. Bull.* 41(1):127–39

Monga AB, John DR. 2010. What makes brands elastic? The influence of brand concept and styles of thinking on brand extension evaluation. *J. Mark.* 74(3):80–92

Mynhardt JC. 2013. Intergroup attitude change in South Africa: a thirty-seven year longitudinal study. *J. Psychol. Afr.* 23(4):549–60

Ng AH, Hynie M. 2014. Cultural differences in indecisiveness: the role of naïve dialecticism. *Personal. Individ. Differ.* 70:45–50

Ng AH, Hynie M, MacDonald TK. 2012. Culture moderates the pliability of ambivalent attitudes. *J. Cross-Cult. Psychol.* 43(8):1313–24

Ng T, Feldman D. 2010. The relationships of age with job attitudes: a meta-analysis. *Pers. Psychol.* 63(3):677–718

Nisbett RE, Peng K, Choi I, Norenzayan A. 2001. Culture and systems of thought: holistic versus analytic cognition. *Psychol. Rev.* 108(2):291–310

Notthoff N, Carstensen LL. 2014. Positive messaging promotes walking in older adults. *Psychol. Aging* 29(2):329–41

Nteta TM, Greenlee JS. 2013. A change is gonna come: generational membership and White racial attitudes in the 21st century. *Polit. Psychol.* 34(6):877–97

Orth U, Robins RW, Widaman KF. 2012. Life-span development of self-esteem and its effects on important life outcomes. *J. Personal. Soc. Psychol.* 102(6):1271–88

Orth U, Trzesniewski KH, Robins RW. 2010. Self-esteem development from young adulthood to old age: a cohort-sequential longitudinal study. *J. Personal. Soc. Psychol.* 98(4):645–58

Oswald FL, Mitchell G, Blanton H, Jaccard J, Tetlock PE. 2015. Using the IAT to predict ethnic and racial discrimination: small effect sizes of unknown societal significance. *J. Personal. Soc. Psychol.* 108(4):562–71

Oyamot CM, Fisher EL, Deason G, Borgida E. 2012. Attitudes toward immigrants: the interactive role of the authoritarian predisposition, social norms, and humanitarian values. *J. Exp. Soc. Psychol.* 48(1):97–105

Park LE, Young AF, Troisi JD, Pinkus RT. 2011. Effects of everyday romantic goal pursuit on women's attitudes toward math and science. *Personal. Soc. Psychol. Bull.* 37(9):1259–73

Pierro A, Mannetti L, Kruglanski AW, Klein K, Orehek E. 2012. Persistence of attitude change and attitude-behavior correspondence based on extensive processing of source information. *Eur. J. Soc. Psychol.* 42(1):103–11

Pietri ES, Fazio RH, Shook NJ. 2013. Weighting positive versus negative: the fundamental nature of valence asymmetry. *J. Personal.* 81(2):196–208

Pillaud V, Cavazza N, Butera F. 2013. The social value of being ambivalent: self-presentational concerns in the expression of attitudinal ambivalence. *Personal. Soc. Psychol. Bull.* 39(9):1139–51

Ranney MA, Clark D. 2016. Climate change conceptual change: Scientific information can transform attitudes. *Top. Cogn. Sci.* 8(1):49–75

Reed AE, Chan L, Mikels JA. 2014. Meta-analysis of the age-related positivity effect: age differences in preferences for positive over negative information. *Psychol. Aging* 29(1):1–15

Rentfrow PJ, Goldberg LR, Levitin DJ. 2011. The structure of musical preferences: a five-factor model. *J. Personal. Soc. Psychol.* 100(6):1139–57

Riemer H, Shavitt S, Koo M, Markus HR. 2014. Preferences don't have to be personal: expanding attitude theorizing with a cross-cultural perspective. *Psychol. Rev.* 121(4):619–48

Rocklage MD, Fazio RH. 2014. Individual differences in valence weighting: when, how, and why they matter. *J. Exp. Soc. Psychol.* 50(1):144–57

Roos LE, Lebrecht S, Tanaka JW, Tarr MJ. 2013. Can singular examples change implicit attitudes in the real-world? *Front. Psychol.* 4(Sept.):1–14

Rudman LA, McLean MC, Bunzl M. 2013. When truth is personally inconvenient, attitudes change: the impact of extreme weather on implicit support for Green politicians and explicit climate-change beliefs. *Psychol. Sci.* 24(11):2290–96

Savani K, Morris MW, Naidu NVR. 2012. Deference in Indians' decision making: introjected goals or injunctive norms? *J. Personal. Soc. Psychol.* 102(4):685–99

Schuldt JP, Konrath SH, Schwarz N. 2011. "Global warming" or "climate change"? *Public Opin. Q.* 75(1):115–24

Schwartz SH, Cieciuch J, Vecchione M, Davidov E, Fischer R, et al. 2012. Refining the theory of basic individual values. *J. Personal. Soc. Psychol.* 103(4):663–88

Shavitt S, Cho H. 2016. Culture and consumer behavior: the role of horizontal and vertical cultural factors. *Curr. Opin. Psychol.* 8:149–54

Shavitt S, Cho H, Barnes A. 2017. Culture and Consumer Behavior. In *Handbook of Cultural Psychology*, ed. S Kitayama, D Cohen. New York: Guilford Press. 2nd ed. In press

Shavitt S, Johnson TP, Zhang J. 2011. Horizontal and vertical cultural differences in the content of advertising appeals. *J. Int. Consum. Mark.* 23:297–310

Sheets P, Domke DS, Greenwald AG. 2011. God and country: the partisan psychology of the presidency, religion, and nation. *Polit. Psychol.* 32(3):459–84

Simmons JP, Nelson LD, Simonsohn U. 2011. False-positive psychology: Undisclosed flexibility in data collection and analysis allows presenting anything as significant. *Psychol. Sci.* 22(11):1359–66

Spencer-Rodgers J, Williams MJ, Peng K. 2010. Cultural differences in expectations of change and tolerance for contradiction: a decade of empirical research. *Personal. Soc. Psychol. Rev.* 14(3):296–312

Stanley DA, Sokol-Hessner P, Banaji MR, Phelps EA. 2011. Implicit race attitudes predict trustworthiness judgments and economic trust decisions. *PNAS* 108(19):7710–15

Steinmetz H, Knappstein M, Ajzen I, Schmidt P, Kabst R. 2016. How effective are behavior change interventions based on the theory of planned behavior? A three-level meta-analysis. *Z. Psychol.* 224(3):216–233

Stout JG, Dasgupta N, Hunsinger M, McManus MA. 2011. STEMing the tide: using ingroup experts to inoculate women's self-concept in science, technology, engineering, and mathematics (STEM). *J. Personal. Soc. Psychol.* 100(2):255–70

Struthers A, Wang M. 2016. Buzz agents in a teen-driven social marketing campaign: Positive campaign attitude leads to positive changes in health outcomes. *Soc. Mark. Q.* 22(3):218–35

Tannenbaum MB, Hepler J, Zimmerman RS, Saul L, Jacobs S, et al. 2015. Appealing to fear: a meta-analysis of fear appeal effectiveness and theories. *Psychiatr. Bull.* 141(6):1178–204

Thibodeau PH, Crow L, Flusberg SJ. 2017. The metaphor police: a case study of the role of metaphor in explanation. *Psychon. Bull. Rev.* 24(5):1375–86

Thomas WI, Znaniecki F. 1918–1920. *The Polish Peasant in Europe and America*. Boston: Gorham Press

Torelli CJ, Özsomer A, Carvalho SW, Keh HT, Maehle N. 2012. Brand concepts as representations of human values: Do cultural congruity and compatibility between values matter? *J. Mark.* 76(July):92–108

Torelli CJ, Shavitt S. 2010. Culture and concepts of power. *J. Personal. Soc. Psychol.* 99(4):703–23

Torelli CJ, Shavitt S, Cho YI, Holbrook AL, Johnson TP, Weiner S. 2015. Justice or compassion? Cultural differences in power norms affect consumer satisfaction with power-holders. *Int. Mark. Rev.* 324(3):279–306

Triandis HC, Gelfand MJ. 1998. Converging measurement of horizontal and vertical individualism and collectivism. *J. Personal. Soc. Psychol.* 74(1):118–28

Trzesniewski KH, Donnellan MB. 2010. Rethinking "Generation Me": a study of cohort effects from 1976–2006. *Perspect. Psychol. Sci.* 5(1):58–75

Twenge JM. 2014. *Generation Me—Revised and Updated: Why Today's Young Americans Are More Confident, Assertive, Entitled—and More Miserable than Ever Before*. New York: Atria Books

Twenge JM, Honeycutt N, Prislin R, Sherman RA. 2016a. More polarized but more Independent: political party identification and ideological self-categorization among US adults, college students, and late adolescents, 1970–2015. *Personal. Soc. Psychol. Bull.* 42(10):1364–83

Twenge JM, Kasser T. 2013. Generational changes in materialism and work centrality, 1976–2007: associations with temporal changes in societal insecurity and materialistic role modeling. *Personal. Soc. Psychol. Bull.* 39(7):883–97

Twenge JM, Sherman RA, Exline JJ, Grubbs JB. 2016b. Declines in American adults' religious participation and beliefs, 1972–2014. *SAGE Open* 6(1):2158244016638133

Tyson M, Covey J, Rosenthal HES. 2014. Theory of planned behavior interventions for reducing heterosexual risk behaviors: a meta-analysis. *Health Psychol.* 33(12):1454–67

Valkenburg PM, Peter J, Walther JB. 2016. Media effects: theory and research. *Annu. Rev. Psychol.* 67(1):315–38

van Bavel JJ, Xiao YJ, Cunningham WA. 2012. Evaluation is a dynamic process: moving beyond dual system models. *Soc. Personal. Psychol. Compass.* 6:438–54

von Salisch M, Vogelgesang J, Kristen A, Oppl C. 2011. Preference for violent electronic games and aggressive behavior among children: the beginning of the downward spiral? *Media Psychol.* 14(3):233–58

Wakslak C, Liberman N, Trope Y. 2007. Construal levels and psychological distance: effects on representation, prediction, evaluation, and behavior. *J. Consum. Psychol.* 17(2):83–95

Wang Q. 2013. Chinese socialization and emotion talk between mothers and children in native and immigrant Chinese families. *Asian Am. J. Psychol.* 4(3):185–92

Weaver JR, Bosson JK. 2011. I feel like I know you: sharing negative attitudes of others promotes feelings of familiarity. *Personal. Soc. Psychol. Bull.* 37(4):481–91

Wegener DT, Petty RE, Blankenship KL, Detweiler-Bedell B. 2010. Elaboration and numerical anchoring: implications of attitude theories for consumer judgment and decision making. *J. Consum. Psychol.* 20(1):5–16

Welch S, Sigelman L. 2011. The "Obama Effect" and White racial attitudes. *Ann. Am. Acad. Polit. Soc. Sci.* 634(Feb.):207–20

Wolsko C, Ariceaga H, Seiden J. 2016. Red, white, and blue enough to be green: effects of moral framing on climate change attitudes and conservation behaviors. *J. Exp. Soc. Psychol.* 65:7–19

Yang H, Stamatogiannakis A, Chattopadhyay A. 2015. Pursuing attainment versus maintenance goals: the interplay of self-construal and goal type on consumer motivation. *J. Consum. Res.* 42(1):93–108

Yang Y, Land KC. 2013. *Age-Period-Cohort Analysis: New Models, Methods, and Empirical Applications.* Boca Raton, FL: CRC Press

Zabel KL, Biermeier-Hanson BBJ, Baltes BB, Early BJ, Shepard A. 2016. Generational differences in work ethic: fact or fiction? *J. Bus. Psychol.* 32(3):301–15

Zell E, Su R, Li H, Ho M-HR, Hong S, et al. 2012a. Cultural differences in attitudes toward action and inaction: the role of dialecticism. *Soc. Psychol. Personal. Sci.* 4(5):521–28

Zell E, Warriner AB, Albarracín D. 2012b. Splitting of the mind: when the you I talk to is me and needs commands. *Soc. Psychol. Personal. Sci.* 3(5):549–55

RELATED RESOURCES

Banaji MR, Greenwald AG. 2016. *Blindspot: Hidden Biases of Good People.* New York: Bantam

Brock TC, Green MC. 2005. *Persuasion: Psychological Insights and Perspectives.* Newcastle upon Tyne, UK: Sage. 2nd ed.

Mercier H, Sperber D. 2017. *The Enigma of Reason.* Cambridge, MA: Harvard Univ. Press

Sloman S, Fernbach P. 2017. *The Knowledge Illusion: Why We Never Think Alone.* New York: Riverhead Books

Persuasion, Influence, and Value: Perspectives from Communication and Social Neuroscience

Emily Falk[1,2,3] and Christin Scholz[1]

[1]Annenberg School for Communication, University of Pennsylvania, Philadelphia, Pennsylvania 19104; email: falk@asc.upenn.edu, christin.scholz@asc.upenn.edu

[2]Department of Psychology, University of Pennsylvania, Philadelphia, Pennsylvania 19104

[3]Marketing Department, The Wharton School, University of Pennsylvania, Philadelphia, Pennsylvania 19104

Annu. Rev. Psychol. 2018. 69:329–56

First published as a Review in Advance on September 27, 2017

The *Annual Review of Psychology* is online at psych.annualreviews.org

https://doi.org/10.1146/annurev-psych-122216-011821

Keywords

persuasion, social influence, communication, value, neuroscience, fMRI

Abstract

Opportunities to persuade and be persuaded are ubiquitous. What determines whether influence spreads and takes hold? This review provides an overview of evidence for the central role of subjective valuation in persuasion and social influence for both propagators and receivers of influence. We first review evidence that decisions to communicate information are determined by the subjective value a communicator expects to gain from sharing. We next review evidence that the effects of social influence and persuasion on receivers, in turn, arise from changes in the receiver's subjective valuation of objects, ideas, and behaviors. We then review evidence that self-related and social considerations are two key inputs to the value calculation in both communicators and receivers. Finally, we highlight biological coupling between communicators and receivers as a mechanism through which perceptions of value can be transmitted.

Contents

1. INTRODUCTION

People's preferences and behaviors are strongly influenced by others. A daughter encourages her parent to stop smoking. A coach shares an inspirational news article to raise team morale. A person, let's call her Emily, is more likely to take the stairs to her fifth-floor office if she is with her sporty colleague, let's call her Christin, than if she is with colleagues who prefer the elevator. Knowing that Emily respects Christin's healthy lifestyle would also increase Christin's willingness to actively encourage Emily because she can expect Emily to think more positively of her and respond with appreciation rather than rejection. In parallel, knowing that Christin likes taking the stairs might make the personal health and social benefits of stair taking more salient to Emily than the ease of taking the elevator.

In this review, we argue that the diverse set of thought processes that determine what information communicators share (e.g., facts about smoking, an inspirational news article, encouragement to take the stairs) and whether receivers are influenced (e.g., to quit smoking, to train harder for a sport, to take the stairs) do so via a common pathway, namely subjective value maximization. Valuation involves explicitly and implicitly weighing perceived costs and benefits to derive the value of choices or actions and has been conceptualized as a motivating force for action (Bartra et al. 2013, Levy & Glimcher 2012). In other words, people make choices to maximize the value they expect from their actions. In this review, we examine the role of this broad class of value calculations in decisions to share information (Section 2.1) and susceptibility to influence in information receivers (Section 2.2). Among multiple person-level, social, and environmental factors,

---

Subjective value: a person- and situation-specific estimate of choice value (c) from the weighted average of differently valued choice-relevant dimensions (d):
$SV(c) = \Sigma \, weight_d \times value_d$

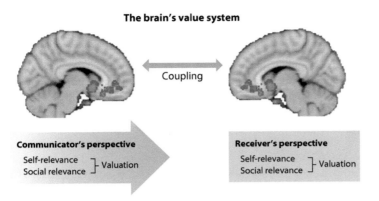

The brain's value system

Coupling

Communicator's perspective

Self-relevance ⎱ Valuation
Social relevance ⎰

Receiver's perspective

Self-relevance ⎱ Valuation
Social relevance ⎰

Figure 1

Overview of persuasion and social influence from the perspectives of communicators and receivers. The brain image depicts the ventral striatum and parts of ventromedial prefrontal cortex from an automated meta-analysis of studies that involve the term "value." Figure made using **http://neurosynth.org**.

we highlight self-relevance (Section 3.1) and social relevance (Section 3.2) as inputs to the value computation and neural coupling (Section 4) as a process through which subjective value may be transmitted between communicators and receivers (see **Figure 1**).

Our argument is grounded in social science research on active forms of persuasion (e.g., trying to convince a loved one to quit smoking or being persuaded by a public service announcement; for a review, see Albarracin & Shavitt 2018), more passive forms of social influence (e.g., taking the stairs because others are doing it; for a review, see Cialdini & Goldstein 2004) and interpersonal contagion (e.g., sharing an inspiring news article; for a review, see Berger 2014). Core aspects of prior theories in each of these domains have implicitly focused on people's attempts to maximize subjective value when making decisions about sharing information or being influenced. We highlight these elements and explicitly conceptualize each as a form of a more general class of value-based decision making. This conceptualization creates a bridge across prior theories, as well as a concrete link to the previously disconnected literature on neuroscientific underpinnings of subjective valuation, which has served as a guiding force in understanding a more general set of choices and actions in other domains.

Recent findings in neuroscience provide insights into how the brain calculates and represents subjective value in service of decision making (see Bartra et al. 2013, Clithero & Rangel 2014, Levy & Glimcher 2012). This neural perspective suggests that brain systems that calculate subjective value represent a final common pathway or common currency through which different decision alternatives (e.g., sharing one piece of information or another, taking the stairs or the elevator) can be reconciled, prioritized, and realized in behavior and preferences (Bartra et al. 2013, Kable & Glimcher 2009). As such, conceptualizing persuasion and social influence in terms of value-based decision making complements and extends prior theorizing in fruitful ways.

There are several other advantages to linking psychological and economic models of persuasion, social influence, and successful communication more broadly to neural models of value-based decision making. First, neural models offer a specific way to quantify the relationship between inputs to the subjective value calculation and the resulting decisions and actions. For example, expectancy value models of behavior change (Fishbein & Ajzen 2011) suggest that the overall probability of choosing a particular option is determined by the average value of the expected consequences of each choice weighted by its likelihood of occurrence. For instance, Emily will be more likely to take the stairs if she believes that positive outcomes, such as bonding with Christin

Persuasion: changes in preferences or behaviors in information receivers conforming to active attempts by a communicator to encourage such changes

Social influence: changes in preferences or behaviors resulting from passive observation of others' actions, inferences about others' perspectives, and broader social norms

Value-based decision making: choice selection based on the extent to which each option is positively or negatively valued

or positive downstream health effects, are highly probable results of taking the stairs. In contrast, she will be unlikely to take the stairs if she expects the result to be arriving late and sweaty at a meeting on the fifth floor.

Given the wide range of dimensions that inform the expected costs and benefits of a decision, it can be difficult for individuals to self-report on the exact processes that lead to their choices. Neuroimaging provides a method of simultaneously measuring and quantifying a wide range of possible input dimensions to the subjective value calculation and, thereby, provides a different perspective on decision making processes. Measurement occurs in real time, as people are exposed to different information, and without requiring the participant to consciously reflect on the processes that are contributing to his or her decisions, preferences, or actions. Therefore, this neural evidence is agnostic to whether or not the processes in question are consciously accessible to the participant (Lieberman 2007); this is important because, as with many fundamental processes (Krumpal 2011, Wilson & Nisbett 1978, Wilson & Schooler 1991), motivations to share (Barasch & Berger 2014) and to update attitudes and behaviors in response to persuasion and social influence (Cialdini & Goldstein 2004) often occur automatically, outside of conscious awareness. Within this context, we refer to communicators who may intentionally seek to persuade (e.g., by trying to convince a parent to quit smoking), may share without explicitly identifying persuasion as a motive (e.g., by sending an inspirational news article), or may influence others indirectly through actions (e.g., by turning toward the door to the stairs out of habit without thinking about influencing a colleague). In parallel, we refer to receivers who may or may not be consciously aware of the communicator's influence on them (e.g., actively considering the merits of an argument versus following a colleague up the stairs without explicitly thinking about it).

2. THE ROLE OF VALUATION IN COMMUNICATION, PERSUASION, AND SOCIAL INFLUENCE

Decisions both to communicate and to conform to the influence of others centrally involve subjective valuation. Within the brain, activity within the ventromedial prefrontal cortex (VMPFC) and ventral striatum (VS) integrates multiple different inputs from other parts of the brain into a common value signal. This signal offers a means for comparison between different choices on a common scale, which informs corresponding actions (see **Figure 1**). Importantly, this common value signal is not specific to one category of stimuli or choices and scales reliably with how much a person values a wide range of stimuli, including both primary (e.g., food, sex) and secondary (e.g., financial) rewards (Bartra et al. 2013, Chib et al. 2009, Levy & Glimcher 2012, McNamee et al. 2013). By putting the universe of inputs on a common scale, the brain can make choices about which alternatives are subjectively more valuable in a given context (e.g., whether to take the stairs or the elevator, whether to eat an apple or a chocolate bar, whether to share or not share a piece of information).

The value signal also accounts for past experiences to guide future behavior through the process of reinforcement learning. To do so, the brain computes a reward prediction error (Schultz 2006), tracking the difference between a person's expected outcome (e.g., reward) and the actual outcomes of actions. When an action produces higher than expected rewards, it is seen as more valuable and reinforced, whereas when an action produces less reward (or more punishment or conflict) than expected, it is devalued; these changes in value also correspondingly guide future action. A similar principle guides social learning from the behaviors and outcomes observed in others. In both cases, choices with higher than expected (experienced or observed) rewards are more likely to be chosen in the future, whereas choices with lower than expected (experienced or observed) rewards are less likely to be chosen in the future.

One form of reward that may be especially relevant in the communication context comes from anticipated and received social approval. Because social connection is fundamental to human

Reinforcement learning: changes in the choice likelihood of a particular option based on expected rewards and punishments experienced through past behavior

Social learning: changes in the choice likelihood of a particular option based on observed behaviors, rewards, and punishments experienced by others

survival (Baumeister & Leary 1995, Lieberman & Eisenberger 2009), it makes sense that the brain would reinforce successful communication strategies and conformity to group norms as ends in themselves. This should be especially true to the extent that particular communication strategies and conformity result in better coordination and stronger bonds between people (i.e., conforming helps me fit in with my friends). Within this framework, we conceptualize decisions to share information as attempts to maximize the expected value to the communicator, with particular attention paid to anticipated social rewards. The expected value of sharing could be informed by the communicator's own past experiences with information sharing or by the communicator's observations of the consequences when others share. In parallel, we conceptualize both persuasion and social influence as inputs to value-based decision making in receivers; the actions and recommendations of others provide broader information about the value of ideas, objects, and behaviors to the receiver (i.e., if my friend likes it, it may have value to me), in addition to the social value of conformity and social connection described above.

As reviewed in greater detail below, core theories of persuasion, social influence, and behavior change have incorporated ideas about subjective valuation and value maximization under different names, highlighting, among others, beliefs about the consequences of behavior for oneself or self-interest (Darke & Chaiken 2005, Fishbein & Ajzen 2011, Johnson et al. 2004, O'Keefe 2012). In parallel, neural systems that are key to computing subjective value are robustly observed across studies of sharing, persuasion, and social influence. Decisions to share information, as well as successfully persuading or influencing others, involve increased activity in the brain's value system (Baek et al. 2017, Falk et al. 2013, Scholz et al. 2017b), and some have argued that humans may find intrinsic reward or positive value in sharing information with others (Falk et al. 2013, Tamir & Mitchell 2012). On the receiving end, social influence from peers (Campbell-Meiklejohn et al. 2010; Cascio et al. 2015; Klucharev et al. 2009, 2011; Nook & Zaki 2015; Welborn et al. 2016; Zaki et al. 2011) and media (Chua et al. 2011; Falk et al. 2012a, 2013, 2016) changes the value that receivers ascribe to objects and actions.

Consistent with social learning theory (Bandura 2001) and theories of embodied social cognition (Semin & Cacioppo 2008), recent evidence also suggests that synchronization between communicators and receivers is a key component of successful persuasion and social influence, beyond the brain activity observed in either party alone (Scholz et al. 2017b, Stephens et al. 2010). Social learning, or using social information to update one's own preferences and actions, is an efficient mode of learning (Bandura 2001), with conformity to group norms as a central, valued commodity that promotes approaching positive social outcomes (Cialdini & Goldstein 2004) and avoiding negative social sanctions (Fehr & Fischbacher 2004). Likewise, conformity and mirroring of others can promote positive relationships with others (Cacioppo & Cacioppo 2012), in part by activating social-cognitive and value systems in the person being mirrored (Cacioppo et al. 2014).

2.1. The Communicator's Perspective

People share when they believe that information is valuable to the receiver (Barasch & Berger 2014, Berger & Milkman 2012, Reeck et al. 2016), valuable to the way that others will see them (Lampel & Bhalla 2007), or valuable to the relationship between the sharer and receiver (Clark & Kashima 2007). Berger (2014) argues that sharing is motivated by five key factors: impression management, emotion regulation, information acquisition, social bonding, and persuasion of others. Each of these motives can be conceptualized as being valuable to the sharer, as these motivations correspond to central human goals of holding a positive image of the self and maintaining positive social relationships (Baumeister & Leary 1995, Mezulis et al. 2004, Taylor 2006, Taylor & Brown 1988).

Conformity: changes in receivers' preferences or behavior to align with those of others due to persuasion or social influence

Information sharing: transmission of information from communicators to receivers with the implicit (social influence) or explicit (persuasion) goal of exerting influence

Neural evidence also suggests that sharing recruits the value system and may offer a parsimonious way of quantifying and comparing various motives. In this view, opportunities to fulfill one or multiple motivations associated with sharing could each increase the value of sharing information, either alone or in concert. These inputs could be weighed using the same context-dependent neural machinery (Cox & Kable 2014) that compares value in other domains (e.g., purchase decisions, mate selection) and increases the value signal associated with sharing a given piece of information, rather than sharing other information or not sharing at all. Empirical evidence supports this view. For example, the ideas that end up being shared most successfully are those that increase activity in the brain's value system when potential sharers are first exposed to them (Baek et al. 2017, Falk et al. 2013, Scholz et al. 2017a). More broadly, participants are willing to pay more money to share information than to answer trivia, and the act of sharing also increases activity in the brain's value system (Tamir et al. 2015).

2.2. The Receiver's Perspective

Theory and evidence support a key role for valuation in the receivers being socially influenced or persuaded. When incoming information changes the receiver's perceived value of ideas and actions, the receiver is more likely to update their views or behaviors to be consistent with the message based on that value signal. For example, expectancy value theories of persuasion and behavior change suggest that people's expectations of what will happen if they act and their evaluation of the expected outcome determine, in part, whether and what action is taken (Fishbein & Ajzen 2011). Studies of argument quality similarly suggest that people are persuaded less by facts and more by subjective value: "[T]he persuasive impact of argument quality, as it has been operationalized, is much less about logic than it is about valence. That is, persuasion is more about suggesting good rather than bad *consequences* (valence) for the message recipient than it is about creating impeccably logical—a.k.a. truthful or likely—arguments" (Johnson et al. 2004, p. 216). O'Keefe (2012) further highlights the fact that a wide range of message effects that have traditionally been studied separately (e.g., gain versus loss frames, individualistic versus collectivistic frames, prevention- versus promotion-focused appeals, fear appeals) all draw a connection between taking a specific action and a subjectively valuable outcome or consequence (consequence-based arguments). At their core, these theories align with subjective expected utility models, which are central to a broad set of economic theories (Samuelson 1937, Savage 1954, Von Neumann & Morgenstern 1944). Likewise, behavioral and neuroeconomic theories of decision making assume that actors make decisions to maximize subjective value (Camerer et al. 2005, Levy & Glimcher 2012).

As such, conceptualizing persuasion in terms of value to the actor bridges psychological, economic, and neuroscientific perspectives on persuasion, influence, and behavior change. In particular, although psychologists typically do not assume that people know their preferences, nor that these preferences are stable, theories in both psychology and economics have considered ways in which people assign value to ideas and act accordingly, with psychologists perhaps placing greater emphasis on contextual factors (e.g., social norms, framing, attributes of the communicator, self-relevance in a specific context) as inputs to the value computation. In other words, the value assigned to a particular choice or action is subjective and takes into account a wide range of features that depend on the individual and social context. Likewise, neural evidence highlights a key role for valuation in conformity to social influence induced by perceived social norms and by persuasive messaging and offers a specific and quantifiable signal tracking the process.

2.2.1. Social influence and value in the brain. Neural evidence supports the idea that conforming to social influence implicates the brain's value system. First, one set of studies points to the

involvement of the brain's value system in tracking divergence versus consensus with group opinion; some evidence suggests that, rather than tracking the value of the stimulus in isolation, the brain initially tracks convergence and divergence with group opinion as an end in itself. In these studies, a participant's brain activity is monitored during exposure to information about others' preference ratings, which either agree or disagree with an earlier rating made by the participant. Studies arguing for this first perspective suggest that activity is typically higher in the value system during consensus with others' opinions than when participant opinions diverge from the group (but see Cascio et al. 2015). For example, in one early study, Klucharev and colleagues (2009) argued that social influence exerted by learning normative information (in this case, the preferences of others) encourages and reinforces certain preferences and behaviors while discouraging others. Their core argument is that conformity to social norms (i.e., updating ratings to align with group norms) is driven by valuation processes that are similar to the type of reinforcement learning that guides motivated behaviors more generally. In this study, participants rated the attractiveness of female faces and then received feedback about peer perceptions of the same faces. Later, the participants rerated the attractiveness of the faces. The team focused on brain systems known to track value within the brain's VS and the complementary capacity to detect conflict within parts of the medial frontal cortex. When participants' beliefs about the attractiveness of female faces deviated from the (experimentally manipulated) opinions of others, such deviations from the social norm correspondingly produced decreases in brain regions tracking value and increases in brain regions tracking conflict (Klucharev et al. 2009). The magnitude of this signal was associated with participants updating their own ratings of facial attractiveness to conform to peer norms. In a second sample, the authors showed that the effects were stronger when participants believed that the group ratings were made by other people, compared to when participants believed ratings were made by a computer, suggesting that conformity may be a form of reinforced social learning. In their example focused on facial attractiveness, deviations from the social norm triggered a prediction error tracking the difference between a person's expected outcome (i.e., alignment with social norms may lead to social rewards) and actual outcomes (i.e., misalignment with the group) and caused participants to update their valuation of the faces.

Other teams have also found evidence consistent with the idea that the brain monitors social cues that indicate alignment and misalignment with group opinions during peer feedback and have tracked these neural signals within brain systems associated with conflict monitoring and value (Berns et al. 2005, Cascio et al. 2015, Tomlin et al. 2013). For example, agreement (versus disagreement) with expert opinions about music was associated with increased activity in the brain's valuation system within the VS (Campbell-Meiklejohn et al. 2010). Likewise, agreement (versus disagreement) with peer opinions about food was associated with increased activity in the brain's value system within the VMPFC (Nook & Zaki 2015). By contrast, nonconformity to peer opinions has been associated with increased activity in brain regions implicated in salience, arousal, and conflict monitoring (Berns et al. 2005, Tomlin et al. 2013), which the authors interpreted to indicate the saliency or negative arousal produced by going against peer opinions. This account also fits with the broader argument that conformity is first triggered by detecting divergence from group opinion and arises as a result of learning in which alignment with group norms and values is reinforced and deviations produce conflict signals.

A brain stimulation study offered further evidence for a causal role played by the conflict monitoring component of reinforcement learning in conformity (Klucharev et al. 2011). In an experiment similar to the team's earlier functional magnetic resonance imaging (fMRI) study of conformity, participants rated the attractiveness of female faces before learning about peer perceptions of the same faces; however, in this study, one group of participants made their initial ratings and received peer feedback while undergoing brain stimulation [transcranial magnetic stimulation (TMS)] to decrease activity within part of the posterior medial frontal cortex implicated in conflict detection. Other participants completed the task under TMS within a control region or under sham stimulation that did not alter brain activity but involved procedures similar to those of the other groups. When participants later provided their final face ratings, those whose neural conflict monitoring activity was downregulated during peer feedback showed significantly lower rates of conformity to peer feedback compared to the control and sham stimulation groups. Consistent with an account of conformity that emphasizes monitoring for potential conflicts with social referents, this study provides stronger causal evidence for the role of conflict detection, and reinforcement learning more broadly, in conformity.

A complementary study using pharmacology also suggests that modulating neurochemicals, such as dopamine, involved in reinforcement learning within the brain's value system can alter people's tendency to conform. In this study, methylphenidate, an indirect dopamine agonist, increased the value of conformity and the resulting tendency for subjects to conform to the judgments of others (Campbell-Meiklejohn et al. 2012).

A second group of studies have examined brain activity following social influence, typically as participants rerate stimuli following exposure to others' opinions. In these studies, greater activity in the value system tracks stimuli that were more positively (versus negatively) rated by peers, and this activity may more closely parallel participants' final valuation of the stimulus itself, rather than the social value of fitting in. This relationship has been found for stimuli such as abstract symbols (Mason et al. 2009), faces (Zaki et al. 2011), celebrity-endorsed consumer products (Klucharev et al. 2008), and foods (Nook & Zaki 2015).

Nook & Zaki (2015) found results consistent with the idea that the value system tracks alignment with group opinions during initial exposure to social feedback (i.e., greater value-related activity for agreement than disagreement during feedback) and valence of group opinions during final ratings (i.e., greater value-related activity for stimuli rated more highly by the group); they examined brain activity both during initial exposure to peer feedback about food preferences and during participants' subsequent ratings of foods. Disentangling the valence of peer opinions from the value of consensus during initial peer feedback, they found that, during initial exposure to peer opinions, activity in the value system was greatest when participant opinions aligned with peer opinions and was relatively lower when peer ratings were either higher or lower than the participant's. In later ratings, however, they observed higher behavioral ratings, as well as greater activity within the VMPFC, in response to foods that peers had earlier rated higher versus those that peers had rated lower.

This is not universally the case, with studies by Cascio et al. (2015) and Welborn et al. (2016) reporting greater (rather than less) activity in parts of the value system during exposure to divergent peer opinions; notably, both of these studies focused on adolescents, raising the question of whether there may be developmental changes in the relationship between activity in the value system and social influence. More broadly, questions remain about the extent to which value-related activity tracks the value of conformity (i.e., aligning with the group opinion), the valence of the group opinion (i.e., increasing for stimuli that are more highly valued by the group), or an interaction that accounts for these factors in addition to a participant's starting or final valuation. In addition, different parts of the value system (e.g., the VS, the VMPFC) are highlighted in different investigations. As such, additional research is needed to understand the temporal dynamics of these effects and the conditions under which different parts of the value system are most influential. Critically, studies have differentially focused on brain activity during initial preference ratings, peer feedback, and final preference ratings and have not consistently ordered participant preference ratings and feedback relative to one another. In addition, these phases have been grouped together differently across studies (e.g., grouping preference ratings and peer feedback together before the scan versus grouping peer feedback and final ratings together during the scan versus delivering peer influence during the scan and collecting final ratings after). Despite these methodological differences, common patterns across these studies are consistent with the idea that, in adults, the brain's value system tracks deviations and promotes conformity when social norm feedback is initially presented (i.e., during a learning phase) and may subsequently track the updated value of the stimulus (i.e., liking the stimulus after the participant's attitude is changed to reflect the norm).

Complementing the within-subject effects described above, several of these studies have found that the magnitude of reaction within key regions of interest also tracks with individual differences in sensitivity to social influence (Cascio et al. 2015, Klucharev et al. 2009, Nook & Zaki 2015, Welborn et al. 2016). Additional studies in teens have also found evidence for links between susceptibility to social influence and sensitivity within the value system (Chein et al. 2011) and brain systems tracking conflict and distress as a result of social exclusion (Falk et al. 2014).

2.2.2. Persuasion and value in the brain. One key component of the brain's valuation system, the VMPFC, is consistently implicated in studies of persuasive messaging, such that brain activity in the VMPFC in response to persuasive messages has been associated with subsequent message-consistent behavior change. These findings are robust across messages about smoking (Falk et al. 2011), physical activity (Falk et al. 2015), and sunscreen use (Falk et al. 2010). For example, in one early study conducted in sunny Los Angeles, participants were scanned using fMRI during exposure to messages about the need to wear sunscreen every day. Activity in the VMPFC during exposure to the health messages was associated with increased message-consistent behavior change (i.e., increasing sunscreen use) one week later. Vezich and colleagues (2016) replicated these findings and extended them in several important ways. First, the team showed that the association between VMPFC activity during sunscreen message exposure and subsequent behavior change was particularly strong for messages highlighting message value in terms of reasons why one should use sunscreen (versus how to use sunscreen). Second, activity in the VMPFC was greater for gain-framed messages than for loss-framed messages. Furthermore, activity within the VMPFC during gain- but not loss-framed messages was predictive of subsequent message-consistent behavior change. The response in the VMPFC to gain-framed messages is consistent with theories of persuasion that emphasize the idea that perceived positive consequences for the message receiver are a key path to persuasion (Fishbein & Ajzen 2011, Johnson et al. 2004, O'Keefe 2012) and also align with psychological and behavioral economic theories suggesting that messages highlighting positive consequences (i.e., gain-framed messages) are particularly effective in encouraging prevention behaviors such as wearing sunscreen (Rothman et al. 2006).

In a study complementing these findings, Falk and colleagues (2015) sought to determine whether interventions could experimentally alter message value to the receiver and, thus, activity in the value system and whether this would, in turn, produce greater behavior change. To do so, the team used self-affirmation, a technique that is known to decrease defensiveness and increase receptivity to health messaging (for a review, see Cohen & Sherman 2014). In results that are consistent with the central role of value in persuasion, participants who were self-affirmed prior to receiving physical activity messages showed greater activity in the VMPFC during exposure to the messages and also went on to change their behavior more over the following month.

Building on this work, Cooper and colleagues (2017) sought to determine whether connectivity between the VMPFC and VS (i.e., key brain regions implicated in valuation) would predict behavior change. They found that participants who showed greater connectivity between the VMPFC and VS during exposure to the physical activity messages also became less sedentary in the following month. Conceptually related results were also observed in smokers exposed to graphic warning messages related to the social and health consequences of smoking. In that context, connectivity within the value system during negative, smoking-relevant images (versus neutral control images) predicted changes in smoking behavior (Cooper et al. 2017).

Together, these results highlight the role of neural valuation in persuasion and subsequent behavior change. Indeed, a parsimonious explanation for the wide range of message characteristics, study samples, and topics that link activity in the brain's value system with message-consistent behavior change is that subjective valuation acts as a final common pathway to persuasion, as in other forms of decision making. This aligns with the view that multiple types of message effects can be unified as consequence-based arguments (O'Keefe 2012), where affecting perceived consequences (and, thus, the subjective value of decision alternatives) is key to successful influence and behavior change (Fishbein & Ajzen 2011).

Moving beyond individual decisions to the effects of persuasive communications at scale, activity within the value system in relatively small groups of people is also associated with behaviors in large-scale populations. For example, Falk and colleagues (2012a) examined brain responses to televised antismoking ad campaigns in a group of 28 smokers and, independently, assessed the success of those same ads in increasing the number of calls to smoking quitlines within large-scale populations. In this case, average brain activity in the value system within the 28 smokers who watched ads from the different campaigns inside the fMRI scanner correctly predicted the campaigns' relative effectiveness in increasing quitline calls in larger populations when the ads were aired at scale. Similar results were observed in a study linking brain activity in the VMPFC in a small group of smokers to click-through rates in a statewide email campaign attempting to motivate smokers to quit smoking (Falk et al. 2016). Activity in the VS and VMPFC during exposure to health-related content has also been linked to large-scale sharing (n = 117,611 Internet shares) of the same health news articles on the *New York Times* website (Scholz et al. 2017a).

Outside of the health domain, responses in the brain's value system in a group of 27 participants tracked with large-scale music sales (Berns et al. 2010). Specifically, increased activity within the VS while the participants listened to songs was directly associated with the later population-level popularity of the songs. By contrast, participants' self-reports of liking of and familiarity with the songs did not predict the population-level sales. Likewise, in a study linking consumer ratings and biological responses to large-scale effectiveness of advertisements (Venkatraman et al. 2015), neural responses in the VS were more tightly coupled with real-world outcomes than a range of other self-report and biological indicators. Consistent with the interpretation that positive value drives these effects, both self-reported positive arousal and activity in the VS from 28 people during exposure to photographs of potential recipients of microloans predicted the population-level success of those photos in garnering actual loans based on an Internet database consisting of 13,500 loan requests (Genevsky & Knutson 2015). Extending this logic to a cheaper and more portable neuroimaging technology, brain responses collected with an electroencephalogram (EEG) during exposure to movie trailers were significantly associated with objectively tracked box office ticket sales (Boksem & Smidts 2015). Specifically, EEG signals that are believed to originate in the medial prefrontal cortex (MPFC) (beta oscillations) were associated with population-level box office sales, above and beyond participants' self-reported ratings of movie trailers (Boksem & Smidts 2015). Taken together, these results suggest that there is enough commonality across individuals in which persuasive communications increase activity in the brain's value system that neural activity in small groups is associated with large-scale outcomes across populations. In addition, across these studies, brain activity has predicted variance in behavioral outcomes that differs from what is predicted using other methods, such as self-report of intentions.

2.3. Open Questions About the Role of the Value System in Persuasion and Social Influence

Value maximization is at the core of theories of persuasion and social influence across the social sciences. Underscoring this perspective, decisions to share information, being socially influenced by information about others' preferences, and being persuaded by explicit arguments all centrally involve the brain's value system such that increased activity in the value system (in communicators) promotes sharing information and (in receivers) being influenced by that information. Several open questions remain, however, about the exact nature of the value system's involvement in different parts of the persuasion and influence process and about the circumstances under which different components of the value system (e.g., the VS, the VMPFC) are most relevant. In addition, future research that takes a more nuanced view of subregions of the value system known to track valence (i.e., increase with positively valued stimuli, decrease with negatively valued stimuli) versus salience or the absolute value evaluations (i.e., increase with both extremely positive and negative stimuli) will be informative in understanding receptivity and resistance to influence.

3. SELECTED INPUTS TO THE VALUE COMPUTATION

What factors increase or decrease subjective value? Social science theories highlight numerous antecedents to persuasion, social influence, and behavior change. Likewise, the brain's value system is anatomically and functionally coupled with multiple other brain regions and networks that serve a wide range of functions. As described above, these connections might be important factors in determining value during persuasion and social influence by contributing to the signal produced by the brain's valuation system. We highlight two inputs to subjective valuation—self-relevance and social relevance—that are common across theories of persuasion, social influence, and behavior change and that are especially important to the neural computation of value in information communicators and receivers (Scholz & Falk 2017).

3.1. The Value of Self-Relevance

Most studies of value-based decision making implicitly or explicitly focus on the value to oneself rather than the value of an object to some other target. Self-relevance and self-interest also play a central role in several major theories of persuasion, social influence, and behavior change. Complementing and extending these views, neuroscientists have linked activity in brain systems encoding self-relevance to valuation, persuasion, and behavior change.

Neural activity associated with self-related processing, for instance, when participants are judging whether a personality trait describes them or not, is frequently localized in clusters within the MPFC and precuneus/posterior cingulate cortex (PC/PCC) (Murray et al. 2012). Neuroimaging research suggests that computations of self-relevance and value are highly intertwined (D'Argembeau et al. 2012, Enzi et al. 2009, Heatherton et al. 2006, Northoff & Hayes 2011). Specifically, functionally similar regions of the VMPFC are active in response to judgments of self-relevance (Denny et al. 2012, Falk et al. 2010, Murray et al. 2012, Northoff et al. 2006) and valuation (Bartra et al. 2013, Levy & Glimcher 2012). Paralleling links between self-relevance and value in the brain, psychologists have shown biases in the judgment of self-relevance and value, which include positive illusions, positivity biases, and self-serving attributions (Mezulis et al. 2004, Taylor & Brown 1988). On average, self-related entities are judged to be disproportionately valuable and things or concepts perceived to be valuable are readily attributed to the self. Perhaps due in part to its strong connections to valuation, self-relevance is a key consideration for both communicators, in evaluating whether to share information, and receivers, in determining whether they are persuaded. This is also reflected in studies within psychology and communication that show that self-relevance influences how deeply arguments are processed (Johnson & Eagly 1989). In addition, consequences to the self (i.e., self-interest) influence whether people view arguments positively or negatively (Darke & Chaiken 2005).

3.1.1. The communicator's perspective. From the communicator's perspective, the expected consequences to the self impact the value of sharing a piece of information. Sharing information can make an individual look smart, friendly, or helpful but could similarly harm sharers by making them appear ignorant or tactless. More generally, the promotion and maintenance of a positive self-image are a central human motive (Mezulis et al. 2004), which can be effectively served by communicating with and influencing others, for instance, through self-enhancement, or the sharing of information that highlights desirable qualities of the sharer (Berger 2014, Cappella et al. 2015). In other words, the extent to which sharing a piece of information allows the sharer to present themselves in a positive light is one key input to the calculation of information-sharing value.

Existing work in communication and social neuroscience supports this idea. Generally, the extent to which information is perceived to be self-relevant (Botha & Reyneke 2013) and in line with the sharer's existing beliefs (Cappella et al. 2015) affects whether and how intensively people engage with content. Furthermore, self-relevant content is more likely to be shared, and consumers are more likely to exaggerate the benefits of self-relevant content (Chung & Darke 2006). Additionally, activity in brain regions implicated in self-relevance increases in response to ideas that communicators report wanting to share with others and ideas that are subsequently shared with enthusiasm (Falk et al. 2012b, 2013). For instance, in one study (Falk et al. 2012b), participants first learned about new TV show ideas while undergoing fMRI. Afterwards, they were recorded on video while talking about each show idea with the intention of sharing it with another person. When scanned participants showed greater brain activity in regions associated with self-related processing (including the MPFC and PC/PCC), their later descriptions of those shows were more enthusiastic.

One often-cited reason (e.g., Berger 2014) for self-related information tending to be associated with high information-sharing value is that sharing self-related information fulfills self-enhancement and self-presentational goals (Lee & Ma 2012, De Angelis et al. 2012, Wien & Olsen 2014). For instance, sharing research findings about a new fitness method might make a sharer look intelligent as well as health-conscious. To the extent that these qualities are in line with how the sharer wants to be viewed, this increases the value of sharing the information. Generally, topics that are self-relevant tend to be discussed most frequently (Dunbar et al. 1997, Landis & Burtt 1924, Naaman et al. 2010). For example, in an analysis of Twitter data, Naaman and colleagues (2010) describe 80% of their sample as "Meformers," that is, users who primarily share information about themselves.

Recent neuroscientific work has further demonstrated a relationship between neural activity in brain regions associated with valuation and the act of sharing self-related information (Tamir & Mitchell 2012), adding support to the idea that sharing self-related information has value to the sharer. Specifically, in a series of behavioral and neuroimaging experiments, neural activity in both regions associated with self-related thought and valuation was more active when participants disclosed their own beliefs and opinions than when they considered those of others. In addition, when participants were given the choice to answer either questions about themselves for a small reward or questions about facts or the thoughts of others for a slightly higher monetary reimbursement, they were willing to forgo an average of 17% in potential earnings for the opportunity to self-disclose (Tamir & Mitchell 2012). In sum, self-disclosure might be inherently valuable to communicators and engages neural systems similar to those engaged by monetary rewards.

3.1.2. The receiver's perspective. Self-relevance and self-interest are key elements in several major theories of persuasion, social influence, and behavior change. For example, both the elaboration likelihood model of persuasion (Petty & Cacioppo 1986) and the heuristic systematic model (Chaiken 1980) argue that people are motivated to reflect more deeply on self-relevant information and that this elaboration can, in turn, result in more durable attitude change. Studies in these traditions find robust evidence that, when more self-relevant outcomes are at stake, people scrutinize the message more, and, thus, stronger arguments show stronger persuasive effects (Johnson & Eagly 1989). Additional work has found that self-interest directly affects information processing and persuasion, such that people are more favorable toward ideas and actions that favor their self-interest (Darke & Chaiken 2005).

In the health domain, a core element of the health belief model of behavior change is an individual's perception of their personal susceptibility to certain health risks and diseases as consequences of health behaviors (Rosenstock 1990, Rosenstock et al. 1988), suggesting a core role for self-focused considerations. Furthermore, various models of behavior change, among them the reasoned action approach (Fishbein & Ajzen 2011) and social cognitive theory (Bandura 2001), emphasize the concept of self-efficacy or perceived behavioral control, which captures a receiver's perception of their ability and opportunity to carry out a specific behavior (Fishbein & Ajzen 2011).

Evidence from neuroimaging also points to a role for self-relevance in the effects of messages on receivers. Early studies in the brain-as-predictor tradition (Berkman & Falk 2013) within the field of persuasion have often focused on aspects of the VMPFC involved in both valuation and judgments of self-relevance. As described above, several studies have shown that neural reactivity in the VMPFC to persuasive messaging scales with subsequent, message-consistent behavior change in a variety of contexts. However, as mentioned above, both self-related and value-related processing are frequently colocalized within neighboring regions in the MPFC, which causes ambiguity regarding the correct psychological interpretation of the observed activity (Poldrack 2006). More recent work has begun to examine both pathways simultaneously. For instance, Cooper and colleagues (2015) examined both overlapping and nonoverlapping regions of interest associated with self-related and value-related thought within the MPFC while participants were exposed to antismoking advertisements. Increased activity in a unique cluster associated with self-related processing and, separately, activity in a unique cluster associated with positive valuation were significantly associated with subsequent reductions in smoking, suggesting the involvement of both processes.

One study reviewed above, in which Vezich and colleagues (2016) tested whether activity in the VMPFC in response to persuasive messages was associated with sunscreen behavior change, argued that VMPFC activity may represent integration of the message's value into the receiver's self-concept. In one set of analyses, the authors tested whether activity in the VMPFC was more strongly associated with behavior change for current sunscreen users or for nonusers. If the former were true, this would indicate that the VMPFC may index existing predispositions to agree with messages. By contrast, for nonusers, changing behavior in response to persuasive messages may involve incorporating message concepts into the self-concept. Vezich and colleagues (2016) showed that activity in the VMPFC was more strongly associated with behavior change for participants who were not already heavy sunscreen users. The authors thus argued that activity in the VMPFC likely tracks positive valuation of arguments and potential integration with a message receiver's self-concept (rather than simply a predisposition to value or identify with the messages).

Other studies have also examined activity across broader sets of brain regions implicated in self-relevance and value processing. For instance, when participants were first exposed to abstracts of *New York Times* articles about health, average activity across nonoverlapping regions within the VMPFC and VS chosen for their role in valuation, and within the MPFC and PC/PCC chosen for their role in self-related processing, scaled with their intention to read the full text of each article (Baek et al. 2017). Taken together, these studies suggest that both self-related thought and valuation are relevant to the impact of persuasion on receivers.

In addition to this correlational evidence, the effects of self-related processing on both brain activity in the VMPFC and downstream behavior change have also been shown in experimental studies that manipulated the self-relevance of messages to their receivers through techniques such as tailoring and self-affirmation. Specifically, one neuroimaging study manipulated the self-relatedness of antismoking messages through tailoring so that, in high-tailored blocks, participants received messages written to directly address their personal smoking habits (e.g., number of cigarettes per day), whereas, in low-tailored blocks, they received less extensively tailored messages and, in generic blocks, untailored, factual statements about smoking. Contrasting both high- and low-tailored blocks against generic blocks showed increased activity in areas within the brain's self-system, including the MPFC and PC/PCC. The same was observed when contrasting high- and low-tailored blocks (Chua et al. 2011). The same research group used independent neuroimaging tasks to identify overlapping regions that are more active during exposure to tailored than to untailored messages, as well as during a self-localizer task that contrasts judgments about the self to judgments about valence. Neural responses to tailored antismoking messages within this conjunctive mask that responded to both tailoring and self-relevance significantly predicted smoking cessation at a 4-month follow-up measurement (Chua et al. 2011). These neural results are in line with a larger body of work on the effects of tailoring that demonstrates that messages that are tailored to specific individuals' traits and values can also increase persuasiveness and behavior change (Kreuter et al. 1999, Strecher et al. 2005), as well as research that highlights the idea that messages of specific self-interest positively bias information processing and attitude judgments (Darke & Chaiken 2005).

Approaching the problem of self-relevance from another angle, self-affirmation interventions increase receivers' willingness to accept otherwise threatening information, for instance, about the negative health outcomes of a behavior, as self-relevant and can increase the effectiveness of persuasive messages (Cohen & Sherman 2014). This result is achieved by reminding message recipients of their broader values, which go beyond the element of their self-image that is attacked by the message (e.g., being a smoker). In an fMRI study of sedentary adults, those who were affirmed prior to receiving health messages about the risks of not getting enough physical activity showed greater activity in brain regions associated with processing self-relevance and value compared to an unaffirmed control group. In turn, this increased activity within the VMPFC was associated with greater message-consistent increases in physical activity (Falk et al. 2016). Together, these studies suggest that manipulations that increase self-relevance may, in turn, increase the value of the message to the receiver and facilitate persuasion. As such, both neural and behavioral evidence highlight the importance of self-relevance in determining message value and persuasive impact.

The work described above is agnostic to the fact that different pieces of information are relevant to the self for different reasons (e.g., because they relate to a core value or a current, short-term project one is involved in). Construal-level theory of psychological distance argues that people use themselves as a reference when determining how close (or relevant) information is, such that the reference point for psychological distance "is the self in the here and now, and the different ways in which an object might be removed from that point—in time, in space, in social distance, and in hypotheticality—constitute different distance dimensions" (Trope & Liberman 2010, p. 440), which are related to one another and affect preferences and behaviors through similar cognitive pathways. Similarly, in the brain, these core proximal dimensions of self-representation overlap within the MPFC (Tamir & Mitchell 2011), suggesting that different ways of making messages psychologically closer to the self might each similarly affect the value signal, which, in turn, leads to persuasion and behavior change. In sum, evidence from psychological and neuroscientific studies suggests that various forms of self-relevance (e.g., tailoring arguments to specific receivers, highlighting proximal consequences, including testimonials from socially proximal sources who are similar to the receiver) may affect persuasion, preferences, and action through similar underlying pathways.

3.2. Social Relevance and Value Processing

Returning to one of our core arguments regarding the neural bases of successful communication, social belonging is a critical feature of human society that has supported the survival of the human race for thousands of years (Baumeister & Leary 1995). Several studies have demonstrated links between social outcomes and valuation. Indeed, the same brain regions that encode nonsocial rewards and punishments are also sensitive to social rewards and punishments such as approval and rejection by others (Bhanji & Delgado 2014, Fareri & Delgado 2014, Lieberman & Eisenberger 2009). As such, in addition to self-related thought, considerations of the impact of sharing information on others and, crucially, on one's social relationships with others are relevant to determining the value of information sharing (Berger 2014), as well as to being receptive to persuasion and social influence (Cialdini & Goldstein 2004, Fishbein & Ajzen 2011). That is, sharers need to consider their receivers' current mindsets to estimate their potential responses to shared information and to determine the impact of sharing on a conversation or relationship. Similarly, receivers need to evaluate the intentions and opinions of sharers to contextualize shared information and devise appropriate responses. Others' preferences can influence receivers not only by providing information about what is valued by others (and, thus, might be valuable to the receiver) but also by providing opportunities for social acceptance through conformity (Cialdini & Goldstein 2004).

The cognitive process of considering the mental states of others is often called theory of mind or mentalizing (Frith & Frith 2006, Schurz et al. 2014). Neurally, a broad set of regions, including the temporoparietal junction (TPJ), temporal lobes, and dorsomedial prefrontal cortex, are consistently functionally associated with mentalizing (Dufour et al. 2013). In the following sections, we review evidence for the involvement of mentalizing in both communicators deciding to share and receivers being influenced.

3.2.1. The communicator's perspective. To effectively transmit information or further a persuasive attempt, communicators need to consider the characteristics, knowledge, beliefs, and current mental states of potential message receivers. These factors can have implications for the expected social outcomes of sharing and, thus, impact information-sharing value. Neuroscientific evidence supports the idea that information-sharing value in communicators is partly driven by thoughts about the mental states of receivers. For example, people showed greater activity in the brain's mentalizing system when they considered whether to share *New York Times* health articles with others compared to when they made other types of decisions (i.e., decisions to read the articles themselves and decisions about the articles' contents) (Baek et al. 2017). The same study further identified a positive relationship between activity in neural regions associated with mentalizing and self-reported intentions to share health news information with others. Together, these results indicate that brain regions implicated in mentalizing are more engaged in the social context of sharing than in other contexts and scale with preferences to share certain types of information over others.

Psychological (Traxler & Gernsbacher 1993) and neural (Dietvorst et al. 2009) evidence also indicates that taking the perspective of others can increase the effectiveness of communication and that successful persuaders activate brain regions that support understanding others' minds more than do unsuccessful persuaders (Dietvorst et al. 2009, Falk et al. 2013). For instance, Dietvorst and colleagues (2009) studied mentalizing in salespeople, who need to understand the mindsets of their customers in order to devise effective sales pitches. More successful salespeople tended to be stronger self-reported mentalizers and showed more neural activity in a set of brain regions associated with mentalizing, including the TPJ and MPFC.

Based on a communicator's considerations of the mental states of their receivers, the communicator can adjust their sharing strategies to anticipate and mold expected audience responses. This can serve to improve persuasive attempts and maximize impact on receivers or to manage an interaction or broader relationship between sharers and receivers. This type of audience sensitivity is often called audience tuning. Existing empirical work has demonstrated the frequent occurrence of audience tuning in communicators (Barasch & Berger 2014, Clark & Murphy 1982). For instance, across several experiments, Barasch & Berger (2014) showed that participants systematically adjusted their information-sharing behavior depending on the audience characteristics, such as the number of people receiving their messages. For example, during broadcasting (or sharing with many others), participants avoided sharing content that could have reflected negatively on themselves, and during narrowcasting (or sharing with one specific other), participants were more inclined to share content that might be useful to the receiver. Audience characteristics can also affect persuasion and social influence indirectly by altering communicator motivations. Specifically, based on further self-reports, Barasch & Berger (2014) concluded that the effects of audience characteristics were driven by sharer focus; sharers tended to be more self-focused and concerned about motives like self-enhancement during broadcasting, leading to high sharing value for information that reflected positively on the communicator, and more other-focused during narrowcasting, resulting in more helpful sharing.

A neuroimaging study on the same phenomenon revealed that brain regions associated with mentalizing were, in fact, more active during both narrow- and broadcasting when each type of sharing was compared to a control condition in which participants identified the main topic of the article, suggesting that people are not exclusively self-focused during either type of sharing interaction (Scholz et al. 2016). A direct comparison of narrow- and broadcasting (Scholz et al. 2016), however, suggested more intensive mentalizing activity during narrowcasting, dovetailing with the findings regarding other-focused sharing reported by Barasch & Berger (2014). Thus, these findings suggest that sharers take into account the current context, as well as the thoughts and potential reactions of their audience, in deciding what to share and how to do it.

In sum, these findings suggest two important conclusions. First, mentalizing is an important component of the cognitive architecture of sharing decisions across contexts. Second, contextual characteristics like audience size might affect sharing value indirectly by altering the relative weight of sharer motives (e.g., to self-enhance or manage social relationships), which are used to judge information-sharing value.

3.2.2. The receiver's perspective.
Social factors also strongly shape the degree to which receivers are influenced. Receivers consider the potential mental states, including motives, expertise, and opinions, of communicators in determining whether they are persuaded (Wilson & Sherrell 1993) and may also consider implications for their relationship with the communicator (DeWall 2010). The importance of social considerations for the targets of persuasive attempts is evident in work within the fields of communication science and economics, as well as the social psychological and neuroscientific literatures.

Many studies have demonstrated that social motives such as affiliation are strong drivers toward compliance and conformity. Cialdini & Goldstein (2004) provide an overview of this work and argue that conformity in receivers is partly driven by the desire for social approval and to promote bonding. When receivers agree with communicators, more harmonious, amicable interactions and relationships ensue. The prospect of positive relational outcomes, in turn, increases the value of compliance and conformity to receivers, somewhat independently of the value of the target belief or behavior. Consistent with this argument, motivation to connect with others has been associated with greater mirroring of a confederate's behavior, an effect that is heightened when earlier attempts to affiliate are hindered by an unfriendly confederate (Lakin & Chartrand 2003). Likewise, people who wrote about being excluded (relative to those who wrote about inclusion or a neutral topic) were more likely to form attitudes on a new policy that were consistent with an anticipated discussion partner's attitudes (DeWall 2010). In other words, behavioral and attitudinal conformity may offer a means to connect with potential social ties, and this motive may be enhanced when other bonds are threatened.

In addition, neural evidence reveals a central role of social relevance in conformity. For instance, when adolescent participants were exposed to feedback suggesting that others' ratings of mobile game applications differed from their own, greater activity in the mentalizing system was associated with a greater likelihood of updating recommendations to conform to group feedback (Cascio et al. 2015). Welborn and colleagues (2016) also highlight a central role of the brain's mentalizing system in conformity in adolescents. During a prescan survey, a group of 16- to 18-year-old participants made ratings of artwork and then received feedback for each piece that consisted of parental opinions, feedback that consisted of peer opinions, or no feedback in the control condition. Critically, the research team focused on neural activity in situations when parental and peer opinions diverged from the participant's. In addition to activity within the value system (in the VMPFC), the authors found evidence for increased activity in several brain regions implicated in mentalizing (e.g., the bilateral TPJ, the precuneus) and cognitive control [e.g., the right ventrolateral prefrontal cortex (rVLPFC)] during social influence from both parents and peers. Further, activity in some of these regions (including the VMPFC, rTPJ, and rVLPFC) scaled with the participants' susceptibility to peer influence. The authors interpreted these findings as indicating that mentalizing and cognitive control resources may help to make sense of others' opinions and then override one's own existing opinions in favor of the social norm. These findings are aligned with theories of influence that place strong emphasis on social norms (Cialdini & Goldstein 2004, Rimal & Lapinski 2015) and suggest that norms are shaped both by external social forces and by internal perceptions of value in individuals (Rimal & Lapinski 2015). Likewise, the copresence of activity within brain systems tracking the mental states of others as well as value provides an interesting additional perspective on classic theories of behavior change that give central roles to both social and self-focused dimensions in determining people's intentions to behave in specific ways (Fishbein & Ajzen 2011, Rimal & Lapinski 2015).

3.3. Open Questions About Inputs to the Value Calculation

Two key inputs to the brain's value computation in both communicators and receivers are the self-relevance and the social relevance of the information. Opportunities to increase positive self-views, to increase bonding, and to increase social status each promote sharing. Likewise, to the extent that information increases positive expectations for the self, illustrates positive outcomes achieved by others, or promises to promote social bonding with a communicator, it also increases the value of conformity in receivers. Additional research is needed to understand the relative weight of these and other considerations across situations, as well as to understand how these considerations interact with individual differences to determine whether information is shared and whether it influences the receiver.

4. BIOLOGICAL COUPLING AS AN INDEX OF SUCCESSFUL COMMUNICATION AND INFLUENCE

In the preceding sections, we have presented evidence that activity in the brain's value system in both communicators and receivers is associated with social influence and persuasion. Connecting the literatures on social influence and persuasion in communicators and receivers, we argue that this is not a coincidence. Beyond the processes in either party alone, the degree of synchrony between speakers and listeners is one hallmark of successful communication.

Synchronization of psychological and biological processes in communicators and receivers may facilitate successful communication, social learning, and relationship maintenance (Burgoon et al. 2007; Cacioppo & Cacioppo 2012; Cappella 1996, 1997). These effects of synchronization have been observed across multiple modalities, including synchronization of nonverbal signals (Cappella 1996, Lakin & Chartrand 2003, Richardson & Dale 2005), language patterns (Branigan et al. 2000, Gonzales et al. 2009, Niederhoffer & Pennebaker 2002), and brain activity of speakers and listeners (Hasson et al. 2012, Silbert et al. 2014, Stephens et al. 2010). Social learning theory emphasizes mirroring as a way to learn not only specific actions, but also the social normative context surrounding those actions in society (Bandura 2001). Neuroscientists have also argued that mirror neurons, which fire both when an actor performs and when an actor observes the same action, provide an efficient path to understanding others and to learning and adopting actions (for a review, see Iacoboni 2009). More broadly, this embodied view of social cognition suggests that biological systems that promote mimicry allow us to understand, and in some cases feel the effects of or conform to, the experiences, thoughts, and emotions of others (Hatfield et al. 1993, Semin & Caccioppo 2008), which, in turn, can promote joint coordination of action (Semin & Caccioppo 2008) and bonding (Caccioppo & Caccioppo 2012). Indeed, even in the absence of a goal to persuade, brain regions involved in mentalizing and value show increased activity when receivers are synchronized with a communicator (Caccioppo et al. 2014); in this way, synchrony may be one indicator of successful communication, which, in turn, may increase the expected value of continued communication and social interaction and prime neural resources for understanding others' minds and interacting effectively (Spunt et al. 2015).

4.1. Communication Between Pairs

In the domain of successful communication, Stephens and colleagues (2010) demonstrated evidence of speaker–listener coupling in several brain regions involved in value, self-relevance, and mentalizing, including the MPFC, striatum, posterior cingulate, and TPJ. Importantly, the degree of synchrony between speakers' and listeners' brains was associated with successful communication, defined in terms of the listener's comprehension of the speaker's story. Furthermore, in some of the brain regions that showed this coupling (MPFC, striatum, dorsolateral prefrontal cortex), listeners' brains actually anticipated (i.e., preceded) the speakers' corresponding activity, and the degree of this anticipatory coupling was also associated with successful communication. Stephens and colleagues (2010) also showed that these effects are specific to the process of successful communication—speaker–listener pairs that did not share the same language (i.e., speaker speaks Russian, listener does not) did not show the same results. This work highlights the possibility that successfully creating shared understanding of information relates to synchronization of speakers' and listeners' brains. The demonstration of anticipatory coupling complements and extends theories of social cognition that emphasize the fact that communicators and receivers do not merely synchronize arbitrarily, but rather use coupling as a means to understand one another's needs and coordinate or coregulate one another's behaviors (Semin & Caccioppo 2008).

The processes of synchronization and coupling may be driven by biological processes and conscious or unconscious motivations in a communicator, a receiver, or both (Semin & Cacioppo 2008). As reviewed above, there is value to both communicators and receivers in being in sync with one another, and in the real world, communication processes are often bidirectional. Conformity and synchronization between communicators and receivers may promote bonding (Cialdini & Goldstein 2004) by allowing dyads to understand one another and to coregulate behavior to coordinate complex tasks (Semin & Cacioppo 2008). In line with this view, synchrony between pairs may be reinforced not only in the brain of the person conforming, but also in that of the person being mirrored (Cacioppo et al. 2014). Cacioppo and colleagues (2014) randomly assigned communicators to experience differing degrees of synchrony with their nonverbal communication signals. Communicators not only liked receivers more when they evidenced greater synchrony, but also showed increased brain activity in regions implicated in mentalizing and value processing when receivers synchronized with them. This aligns with the view, presented above, that coupling may be reinforced and perpetuated by value maximization in both the communicator and receiver.

Scholz and colleagues (2017) examined neural coupling as a possible pathway to social influence. The team measured brain activity in a first set of participants as they read news article headlines and summaries, which they subsequently communicated to others in the form of social media posts. A second group of participants were then exposed to the same article headlines and the commentaries from the first group. Both groups rated the articles, allowing a quantification of the degree of preference correlation between communicators and receivers. At the neural level, the team found correlated brain activity in regions of interest implicated in valuation, self-relevance, and mentalizing between sharers and receivers. This effect was selective to communicating pairs, such that no such effect was observed for randomly paired, noncommunicating participants in the two groups. Furthermore, the degree of correlated activity within these brain networks was also associated with the degree of correlation between speaker and listener preferences.

4.2. Synchrony Across Audiences

In addition to direct coupling of brain responses in communicators and receivers, mass media may also serve as a vehicle to bring an audience into sync, thereby capturing the collective mind. Early neuroscience research on intersubject correlation demonstrated that there is a significant amount of similarity in the way that different people's brains respond to natural stimuli like movies (Hasson et al. 2004). More recent research also demonstrates similarity in the functional connectivity patterns as people listened to stories, such that similarity of neural responses was associated with greater narrative comprehension (Simony et al. 2016). Applying this to testing whether effective mass communications may exert their effects by capturing the collective mind of an audience, Schmälzle and colleagues (2015) examined brain responses to strong and weak political speeches. They found that stronger (i.e., more effective versus less effective) political speeches elicited greater intersubject correlation in the medial-frontal cortex among an audience of listeners (Schmälzle et al. 2015). They suggested that more powerful or persuasive media take hold of audiences more collectively and drive synchronization not only in brain regions implicated in auditory and language processing, but also in higher-order systems that help make sense of the message. In a study complementing these results, Dmochowski and colleagues (2014) showed that synchrony of neural responses originating in the MPFC also predicted the degree of audience engagement during the pilot episode of a television show and during Super Bowl ads (Dmochowski et al. 2014). Such a process of collective audience engagement is consistent with the idea that cultures align around common values (Schwartz 2006), which are, in part, influenced by collective exposure to media (e.g., Gerbner 1998). The ability to study how audiences respond collectively to stimuli offers the potential for a finer-grained analysis of which elements of a communication context bring audiences most readily into and out of sync with one another and to tie these dynamics to downstream effects on an audience's ideas, preferences, and behaviors.

4.3. Open Questions Relevant to Biological Synchrony and Communication

Synchronization of responses between communicators and receivers promotes successful communication and social influence, but additional research is needed to identify the factors that promote synchrony between communicators and receivers and the extent to which biological synchrony causes successful communication outcomes and vice versa. Importantly, this synchrony seems to occur across communication contexts but may be influenced by communicators, receivers, their combination, or an external force such as media. Theories of embodied cognition argue that synchrony allows one actor to simulate the experience of the other and to anticipate and coordinate action, but this is an area of active debate and research. In the context of persuasion and social influence, this type of coupling may facilitate the spread of specific value signals and, thus, preferences and behaviors, which may be mutually reinforced by the value of coordinating and remaining in sync with valued referents. Future research is needed to test this proposition and to document the neural mechanisms involved.

5. FUTURE DIRECTIONS

With a few notable exceptions, reviewed above, existing research on the neuroscience of persuasion and social influence has primarily focused on individuals in isolation or in asynchronous communication between dyads. In parallel, in examining those individuals' brains, research in this domain has focused primarily on average activity within specific regions of interest. Finally, as with much social and neuroscientific research, the populations studied have tended toward Western, educated samples. Growing bodies of research, however, suggest that incorporating information about broader social networks and brain network dynamics during tasks and examining a broader set of study populations may substantially expand our understanding of and the precision of forecasts derived from brain data. Within each of these areas, additional research is also needed to determine the extent to which conscious awareness of the process in question alters the brain and the behavioral dynamics at play.

5.1. Social Networks and the Brain

A few studies have examined individual differences in social network position as it relates to the neural processes involved in successful communication. For example, teens who connected more otherwise unconnected friends in their social network (i.e., information brokers) showed greater activity within brain systems associated with mentalizing during decisions about what to recommend to others (O'Donnell et al. 2017). Further research is needed to document the links between the properties of a person's social network and their brain's response to the possibility of sharing ideas and being influenced. Initial studies document the role of the brain's value system in processes that are relevant to successful communication, such as tracking popularity within a social network (Zerubavel et al. 2015). As such, integrating social network and neuroscience data will facilitate more nuanced consideration of the different pathways through which ideas spread, as well as links to a range of related social, cognitive, and affective processes (Schmälzle et al. 2017). For example, extant research on the neural bases of sharing has not distinguished between independent sharing events spurred by a single mass broadcast and sharing that occurs through deep chains (i.e., structural virality; Goel et al. 2015); future research may determine whether the underlying psychology and neuroscience of sharing differ in these contexts. Future research can also elucidate the extent to which sharer characteristics, receiver characteristics, or interactions between them are most important for determining the likelihood of influence (see also Scholz & Falk 2017).

5.2. Brain Network Dynamics Supporting Social Influence and Persuasion

Studies building on an emerging literature in network neuroscience (Bullmore & Bassett 2011) have also begun to examine how broader network dynamics in the brain might relate to susceptibility to social influence (Cooper et al. 2017). For example, Wasylyshyn and colleagues (2017) found that teens who showed more global coupling between key brain regions implicated in mentalizing and the rest of the brain during social exclusion also showed greater susceptibility to peer influence on their later driving decisions. These types of studies may also help clarify when and how specific regions of interest are most important; for example, in the current review, we have focused heavily on the brain's value system, and on the VS and VMPFC in particular. Although these regions are clearly implicated in both successful communication and susceptibility to influence, some studies have found more robust evidence for one or for the other, and additional research is needed to clarify the roles of each, as well as their relationships to other brain systems in support of communication and influence.

5.3. Cultural and Environmental Determinants

Additional research is also needed to determine the extent to which the findings described above apply across cultures, socioeconomic circumstances, and developmental stages. For example, value, self, and social processes may be given relatively different weights according to cultural background, environmental constraints, and developmental stage. Preliminary evidence suggests that social influence may operate differently in the brain depending on cultural variables such as socioeconomic background (Cascio et al. 2017), and the brain systems most relevant to social influence may differ between adolescents and adults. Finally, additional research is needed to understand when and how culture (Chiao et al. 2016, Han et al. 2013) influences the neural bases of persuasion, social influence, and communication more broadly. Likewise, understanding how these processes might vary in cross-cultural or intergroup communication settings is also critical.

5.4. Implicit and Explicit Motivations

Although, as we have argued, one strength of neural models of social influence and persuasion is that they are agnostic to whether the processes are consciously accessible to participants, there may be distinctions between conscious and unconscious processes related to persuasion and social influence from the perspective of communicators (Cacioppo et al. 2014, Scholz et al. 2017b) and receivers (Gawronski & Bodenhausen 2011) in terms of the antecedents of the value calculation or other dimensions that could be modeled in the brain. Future research is needed to unpack the ways in which the degree of persuasive intent in communicators or conscious awareness of susceptibility in receivers alters the value computation and communication process.

6. CONCLUSION

From the perspective of both communicators and receivers, successful communication and social influence involve positive valuation of ideas, driven, in part, by self- and social relevance. These processes are associated with both the communicator's decisions to share and the influence on receivers; in addition, emerging research suggests that biological coupling between sharers and receivers may facilitate successful communication. Conceptualizing persuasion and social influence under the umbrella of a more general class of value-based decisions offers a framework to link prior social science theories with emerging research in neuroscience, which, in turn, may provide new theoretical insight (e.g., about the antecedents and dynamics of the implementation of this process), as well as practical advantages in improving our ability to model and predict specific outcomes.

SUMMARY POINTS

1. Decision processes within the realm of persuasion and social influence (e.g., decisions to share information or to be influenced) can be effectively conceptualized as forms of a more general class of value-based decision making.

2. Value-based decision making involves explicitly and implicitly weighing perceived costs and benefits to arrive at the value of specific choices or actions. Highly valued options are more likely to be pursued.

3. In communicators, the brain's value system tracks the value of sharing information and is implicated in sharing decisions.

4. In receivers, the brain's value system tracks the value of incoming information about the opinions and behaviors of others relative to one's own and is implicated in conforming to persuasion and social influence.

5. Self-relevance is one key source of value that influences decisions to share information and to conform to social influence and persuasive attempts. Neural signatures related to self-related processing are positively associated with both information sharing and reception.

6. Social relevance is a second factor that influences the value of decisions to share information and to conform to social influence and persuasive attempts. Neural signatures related to considering the mental states of others are positively associated with both information sharing and reception.

7. Communicator–receiver synchrony in key brain regions related to valuation, self-related thought, and social processing may underpin successful persuasion, social influence, and communication more broadly.

DISCLOSURE STATEMENT

The authors are not aware of any affiliations, memberships, funding, or financial holdings that might be perceived as affecting the objectivity of this review.

ACKNOWLEDGMENTS

This work was supported in part by National Institutes of Health grant 1DP2DA03515601 (New Innovator Award to E.F.), the Army Research Laboratory under Cooperative Agreement number W911NF-10-2-0022, National Institutes of Health/National Cancer Institute grant 1R01CA180015–01 (to E.F.), and a DARPA Young Faculty Award (YFA-D14AP00048 to E.F.), and by generous support from HopeLab. Thanks go to Shelley Taylor, Matthew Lieberman, Joseph Cappella, Joseph Kable, and the Penn Communication Neuroscience Lab for insightful feedback.

LITERATURE CITED

Albarracin D, Shavitt S. 2018. Attitudes and attitude change. *Annu. Rev. Psychol.* 69. In press

Baek EC, Scholz C, O'Donnell MB, Falk EB. 2017. The value of sharing information: a neural account of information transmission. *Psychol. Sci.* 28(7):851–61

Bandura A. 2001. Social cognitive theory: an agentic perspective. *Annu. Rev. Psychol.* 52:1–26

Barasch A, Berger J. 2014. Broadcasting and narrowcasting: how audience size affects what people share. *J. Mark. Res.* 51(3):286–99

Bartra O, McGuire JT, Kable JW. 2013. The valuation system: a coordinate-based meta-analysis of BOLD fMRI experiments examining neural correlates of subjective value. *NeuroImage* 76:412–27

Baumeister RF, Leary MR. 1995. The need to belong: desire for interpersonal attachments as a fundamental human motivation. *Psychol. Bull.* 117(3):497–529

Berger J. 2014. Word of mouth and interpersonal communication: a review and directions for future research. *J. Consum. Psychol.* 24(4):586–607

Berger J, Milkman KL. 2012. What makes online content viral? *J. Mark. Res.* 49(2):192–205

Berkman ET, Falk EB. 2013. Beyond brain mapping: using neural measures to predict real-world outcomes. *Curr. Dir. Psychol. Sci.* 22(1):45–50

Berns GS, Capra CM, Moore S, Noussair C. 2010. Neural mechanisms of the influence of popularity on adolescent ratings of music. *NeuroImage* 49:2687–96

Berns GS, Chappelow J, Zink CF, Pagnoni G, Martin-Skurski ME, Richards J. 2005. Neurobiological correlates of social conformity and independence during mental rotation. *Biol. Psychiatry* 58(3):245–53

Bhanji JP, Delgado MR. 2014. The social brain and reward: social information processing in the human striatum. *WIREs Cogn. Sci.* 5(1):61–73

Boksem MAS, Smidts A. 2015. Brain responses to movie trailers predict individual preferences for movies and their population-wide commercial success. *J. Mark. Res.* 52(4):482–92

Botha E, Reyneke M. 2013. To share or not to share: the role of content and emotion in viral marketing. *J. Public Aff.* 13(2):160–71

Branigan HP, Pickering MJ, Cleland AA. 2000. Syntactic co-ordination in dialogue. *Cognition* 75(2):B13–25

Bullmore ET, Bassett DS. 2011. Brain graphs: graphical models of the human brain connectome. *Annu. Rev. Clin. Psychol.* 7:113–40

Burgoon JK, Stern LA, Dillman L. 2007. *Interpersonal Adaptation: Dyadic Interaction Patterns*. Cambridge, UK: Cambridge Univ. Press

Cacioppo S, Cacioppo JT. 2012. Decoding the invisible forces of social connections. *Front. Integr. Neurosci.* 6:51

Cacioppo S, Zhou H, Monteleone G, Majka EA, Quinn KA, et al. 2014. You are in sync with me: neural correlates of interpersonal synchrony with a partner. *Neuroscience* 277:842–58

Camerer C, Loewenstein G, Prelec D. 2005. Neuroeconomics: how neuroscience can inform economics. *J. Econ. Lit.* 43(1):9–64

Campbell-Meiklejohn DK, Bach DR, Roepstorff A, Dolan RJ, Frith CD. 2010. How the opinion of others affects our valuation of objects. *Curr. Biol.* 20(13):1165–70

Campbell-Meiklejohn DK, Simonsen A, Jensen M, Wohlert V, Gjerløff T, et al. 2012. Modulation of social influence by methylphenidate. *Neuropsychopharmacology* 37:1517–25

Cappella JN. 1996. Why biological explanations? *J. Commun.* 46:4–7

Cappella JN. 1997. Behavioral and judged coordination in adult informal social interactions: vocal and kinesic indicators. *J. Personal. Soc. Psychol.* 72(1):119–31

Cappella JN, Kim HS, Albarracín D. 2015. Selection and transmission processes for information in the emerging media environment: psychological motives and message characteristics. *Media Psychol.* 18:396–424

Cascio CN, O'Donnell MB, Bayer J, Tinney FJ, Falk EB. 2015. Neural correlates of susceptibility to group opinions in online word-of-mouth recommendations. *J. Mark. Res.* 52(4):559–75

Cascio CN, O'Donnell MB, Simons-Morton BG, Bingham CR, Falk EB. 2017. Cultural context moderates neural pathways to social influence. *Cult. Brain* 5(1):50–70

Chaiken S. 1980. Heuristic versus systematic information processing and the use of source versus message cues in persuasion. *J. Personal. Soc. Psychol.* 39(5):752–66

Chein J, Albert D, O'Brien L, Uckert K, Steinberg L. 2011. Peers increase adolescent risk taking by enhancing activity in the brain's reward circuitry. *Dev. Sci.* 14(2):F1–10

Chiao J, Li S-C, Turner R. 2016. *The Oxford Handbook of Cultural Neuroscience.* Oxford, UK: Oxford Univ. Press

Chib VS, Rangel A, Shimojo S, O'Doherty JP. 2009. Evidence for a common representation of decision values for dissimilar goods in human ventromedial prefrontal cortex. *J. Neurosci.* 29(39):12315–20

Chua HF, Ho SS, Jasinska AJ, Polk TA, Welsh RC, et al. 2011. Self-related neural response to tailored smoking-cessation messages predicts quitting. *Nat. Neurosci.* 14(4):426–27

Chung CMY, Darke PR. 2006. The consumer as advocate: self-relevance, culture, and word-of-mouth. *Mark. Lett.* 17(4):269–79

Cialdini RB, Goldstein NJ. 2004. Social influence: compliance and conformity. *Annu. Rev. Psychol.* 55:591–621

Clark AE, Kashima Y. 2007. Stereotypes help people connect with others in the community: a situated functional analysis of the stereotype consistency bias in communication. *J. Personal. Soc. Psychol.* 93(6):1028–39

Clark HH, Murphy GL. 1982. Audience design in meaning and reference. *Adv. Psychol.* 9:287–99

Clithero JA, Rangel A. 2014. Informatic parcellation of the network involved in the computation of subjective value. *Soc. Cogn. Affect. Neurosci.* 9(9):1289–302

Cohen GL, Sherman DK. 2014. The psychology of change: self-affirmation and social psychological intervention. *Annu. Rev. Psychol.* 65:333–71

Cooper N, Bassett DS, Falk EB. 2017. Coherent activity between brain regions that code for value is linked to the malleability of human behavior. *Sci. Rep.* 7:43250

Cooper N, Tompson S, O'Donnell MB, Falk EB. 2015. Brain activity in self- and value-related regions in response to online antismoking messages predicts behavior change. *J. Media Psychol.* 27(3):93–109

Cox KM, Kable JW. 2014. BOLD subjective value signals exhibit robust range adaptation. *J. Neurosci.* 34(49):16533–43

D'Argembeau A, Jedidi H, Balteau E, Bahri M, Phillips C, Salmon E. 2012. Valuing one's self: medial prefrontal involvement in epistemic and emotive investments in self-views. *Cereb. Cortex* 22(3):659–67

Darke PR, Chaiken S. 2005. The pursuit of self-interest: self-interest bias in attitude judgment and persuasion. *J. Personal. Soc. Psychol.* 89(6):864–83

De Angelis M, Bonezzi A, Peluso AM, Rucker DD, Costabile M. 2012. On braggarts and gossips: a self-enhancement account of word-of-mouth generation and transmission. *J. Mark. Res.* 49(4):551–63

Denny BT, Kober H, Wager TD, Ochsner KN. 2012. A meta-analysis of functional neuroimaging studies of self- and other judgments reveals a spatial gradient for mentalizing in medial prefrontal cortex. *J. Cogn. Neurosci.* 24(8):1742–52

DeWall CN. 2010. Forming a basis for acceptance: Excluded people form attitudes to agree with potential affiliates. *Soc. Influence* 5(4):245–60

Dietvorst RC, Verbeke WJMI, Bagozzi RP, Yoon C, Smits M, van der Lugt A. 2009. A sales force-specific theory-of-mind scale: tests of its validity by classical methods and functional magnetic resonance imaging. *J. Mark. Res.* 46(5):653–68

Dmochowski JP, Bezdek MA, Abelson BP, Johnson JS, Schumacher EH, Parra LC. 2014. Audience preferences are predicted by temporal reliability of neural processing. *Nat. Commun.* 5:4567

Dufour N, Redcay E, Young L, Mavros PL, Moran JM, et al. 2013. Similar brain activation during false belief tasks in a large sample of adults with and without autism. *PLOS ONE* 8(9):e75468

Dunbar RIM, Marriott A, Duncan NDC. 1997. Human conversational behavior. *Hum. Nat.* 8(3):231–46

Enzi B, de Greck M, Prösch U, Tempelmann C, Northoff G. 2009. Is our self nothing but reward? Neuronal overlap and distinction between reward and personal relevance and its relation to human personality. *PLOS ONE* 4(12):e8429

Falk EB, Berkman ET, Lieberman MD. 2012a. From neural responses to population behavior: Neural focus group predicts population-level media effects. *Psychol. Sci.* 23(5):439–45

Falk EB, Berkman ET, Mann T, Harrison B, Lieberman MD. 2010. Predicting persuasion-induced behavior change from the brain. *J. Neurosci.* 30(25):8421–24

Falk EB, Berkman ET, Whalen D, Lieberman MD. 2011. Neural activity during health messaging predicts reductions in smoking above and beyond self-report. *Health Psychol.* 30(2):177–85

Falk EB, Cascio CN, O'Donnell MB, Carp J, Tinney FJ Jr., et al. 2014. Neural responses to exclusion predict susceptibility to social influence. *J. Adolesc. Health* 54(5 Suppl.):S22–31

Falk EB, Morelli SA, Welborn BL, Dambacher K, Lieberman MD. 2013. Creating buzz: the neural correlates of effective message propagation. *Psychol. Sci.* 24(7):1234–42

Falk EB, O'Donnell MB, Cascio CN, Tinney F, Kang Y, et al. 2015. Self-affirmation alters the brain's response to health messages and subsequent behavior change. *PNAS* 112(7):1977–82

Falk EB, O'Donnell MB, Lieberman MD. 2012b. Getting the word out: neural correlates of enthusiastic message propagation. *Front. Hum. Neurosci.* 6:313

Falk EB, O'Donnell MB, Tompson S, Gonzalez R, Cin SD, et al. 2016. Functional brain imaging predicts public health campaign success. *Soc. Cogn. Affect. Neurosci.* 11(2):204–14

Fareri DS, Delgado MR. 2014. Social rewards and social networks in the human brain. *Neuroscientist* 20(4):387–402

Fehr E, Fischbacher U. 2004. Social norms and human cooperation. *Trends Cogn. Sci.* 8:185–90

Fishbein M, Ajzen I. 2011. *Predicting and Changing Behavior: The Reasoned Action Approach*. Abingdon, UK: Taylor & Francis

Frith CD, Frith U. 2006. The neural basis of mentalizing. *Neuron* 50(4):531–34

Gawronski B, Bodenhausen GV. 2011. The associative-propositional evaluation model. *Adv. Exp. Soc. Psychol.* 44:59–127

Genevsky A, Knutson B. 2015. Neural affective mechanisms predict market-level microlending. *Psychol. Sci.* 26(9):1411–22

Gerbner G. 1998. Cultivation analysis: an overview. *Mass Commun. Soc.* 1(3–4):175–94

Goel S, Anderson A, Hofman J, Watts DJ. 2015. The structural virality of online diffusion. *Manag. Sci.* 62(1):180–96

Gonzales AL, Hancock JT, Pennebaker JW. 2009. Language style matching as a predictor of social dynamics in small groups. *Commun. Res.* 37(1):3–19

Han S, Northoff G, Vogeley K, Wexler BE, Kitayama S, Varnum MEW. 2013. A cultural neuroscience approach to the biosocial nature of the human brain. *Annu. Rev. Psychol.* 64:335–59

Hasson U, Ghazanfar AA, Galantucci B, Garrod S, Keysers C. 2012. Brain-to-brain coupling: a mechanism for creating and sharing a social world. *Trends Cogn. Sci.* 16(2):114–21

Hasson U, Nir Y, Levy I, Fuhrmann G, Malach R. 2004. Intersubject synchronization of cortical activity during natural vision. *Science* 303(5664):1634–40

Hatfield E, Cacioppo JT, Rapson RL. 1993. Emotional contagion. *Curr. Dir. Psychol. Sci.* 2(3):96–99

Heatherton TF, Wyland CL, Macrae CN, Demos KE, Denny BT, Kelley WM. 2006. Medial prefrontal activity differentiates self from close others. *Soc. Cogn. Affect. Neurosci.* 1:18–25

Iacoboni M. 2009. Imitation, empathy, and mirror neurons. *Annu. Rev. Psychol.* 60:653–70

Johnson BT, Eagly AH. 1989. Effects of involvement on persuasion: a meta-analysis. *Psychol. Bull.* 106(2):290–314

Johnson BT, Smith-McLallen A, Killeya LA, Levin KD. 2004. Truth or consequences: overcoming resistance to persuasion with positive thinking. In *Resistance and Persuasion*, ed. ES Knowles, JA Linn, pp. 215–33. Mahwah, NJ: Lawrence Erlbaum Assoc.

Kable JW, Glimcher PW. 2009. The neurobiology of decision: consensus and controversy. *Neuron* 63(6):733–45

Klucharev V, Hytönen K, Rijpkema M, Smidts A, Fernández G. 2009. Reinforcement learning signal predicts social conformity. *Neuron* 61(1):140–51

Klucharev V, Munneke MAM, Smidts A, Fernández G. 2011. Downregulation of the posterior medial frontal cortex prevents social conformity. *J. Neurosci.* 31(33):11934–40

Klucharev V, Smidts A, Fernandez G. 2008. Brain mechanisms of persuasion: how "expert power" modulates memory and attitudes. *Soc. Cogn. Affect. Neurosci.* 3:353–66

Kreuter MW, Strecher VJ, Glassman B. 1999. One size does not fit all: the case for tailoring print materials. *Ann. Behav. Med.* 21(4):276–83

Krumpal I. 2011. Determinants of social desirability bias in sensitive surveys: a literature review. *Qual. Quant.* 47(4):2025–47

Lakin JL, Chartrand TL. 2003. Using nonconscious behavioral mimicry to create affiliation and rapport. *Psychol. Sci.* 14(4):334–39

Lampel J, Bhalla A. 2007. The role of status seeking in online communities: giving the gift of experience. *J. Comput. Mediat. Commun.* 12(2):434–55

Landis MH, Burtt HE. 1924. A study of conversations. *J. Comp. Psychol.* 4(1):81–89

Lee CS, Ma L. 2012. News sharing in social media: the effect of gratifications and prior experience. *Comput. Hum. Behav.* 28(2):331–39

Levy DJ, Glimcher PW. 2012. The root of all value: a neural common currency for choice. *Curr. Opin. Neurobiol.* 22(6):1027–38

Lieberman MD. 2007. Social cognitive neuroscience: a review of core processes. *Annu. Rev. Psychol.* 58:259–89

Lieberman MD, Eisenberger NI. 2009. Neuroscience: pains and pleasures of social life. *Science* 323(5916):890–91

Mason MF, Dyer RG, Norton MI. 2009. Neural mechanisms of social influence. *Organ. Behav. Hum. Decis. Process.* 110:152–59

McNamee D, Rangel A, O'Doherty JP. 2013. Category-dependent and category-independent goal-value codes in human ventromedial prefrontal cortex. *Nat. Neurosci.* 16(4):479–85

Mezulis AH, Abramson LY, Hyde JS, Hankin BL. 2004. Is there a universal positivity bias in attributions? A meta-analytic review of individual, developmental, and cultural differences in the self-serving attributional bias. *Psychol. Bull.* 130(5):711–47

Murray RJ, Schaer M, Debbané M. 2012. Degrees of separation: a quantitative neuroimaging meta-analysis investigating self-specificity and shared neural activation between self- and other-reflection. *Neurosci. Biobehav. Rev.* 36(3):1043–59

Naaman M, Boase J, Lai C-H. 2010. Is it really about me? Message content in social awareness streams. *Proc. ACM Conf. Comput. Supp. Coop. Work, Savannah, GA*, pp. 189–92. New York: ACM

Niederhoffer KG, Pennebaker JW. 2002. Linguistic style matching in social interaction. *J. Lang. Soc. Psychol.* 21(4):337–60

Nook EC, Zaki J. 2015. Social norms shift behavioral and neural responses to foods. *J. Cogn. Neurosci.* 27(7):1412–26

Northoff G, Hayes DJ. 2011. Is our self nothing but reward? *Biol. Psychiatry* 69(11):1019–25

Northoff G, Heinzel A, de Greck M, Bermpohl F, Dobrowolny H, Panksepp J. 2006. Self-referential processing in our brain: a meta-analysis of imaging studies on the self. *NeuroImage* 31(1):440–57

O'Donnell MB, Bayer JB, Cascio CN, Falk EB. 2017. Neural bases of recommendations differ according to social network structure. *Soc. Cogn. Affect. Neurosci.* 12(1):61–69

O'Keefe DJ. 2012. The relative persuasiveness of different forms of arguments-from-consequences. *Commun. Yearbook* 36:109–35

Petty RE, Cacioppo JT. 1986. The elaboration likelihood model of persuasion. *Adv. Exp. Soc. Psychol.* 19:123–205

Poldrack RA. 2006. Can cognitive processes be inferred from neuroimaging data? *Trends Cogn. Sci.* 10(2):59–63

Reeck C, Ames DR, Ochsner KN. 2016. The social regulation of emotion: an integrative, cross-disciplinary model. *Trends Cogn. Sci.* 20(1):47–63

Richardson DC, Dale R. 2005. Looking to understand: the coupling between speakers' and listeners' eye movements and its relationship to discourse comprehension. *Cogn. Sci.* 29(6):1045–60

Rimal RN, Lapinski MK. 2015. A re-explication of social norms, ten years later. *Commun. Theory* 25(4):393–409

Rosenstock IM. 1990. The health belief model: explaining health behavior through expectancies. In *Health Behavior and Health Education: Theory, Research, and Practice*, ed. K Glanz, FM Lewis, BK Rimer, pp. 39–62. San Francisco: Jossey-Bass

Rosenstock IM, Strecher VJ, Becker MH. 1988. Social learning theory and the health belief model. *Health Educ. Behav.* 15(2):175–83

Rothman AJ, Bartels RD, Wlaschin J, Salovey P. 2006. The strategic use of gain- and loss-framed messages to promote healthy behavior: how theory can inform practice. *J. Commun.* 56(s1):S202–20

Samuelson PA. 1937. A note on measurement of utility. *Rev. Econ. Stud.* 4(2):155–61

Savage LJ. 1954. *The Foundations of Statistics*. New York: Wiley

Schmälzle R, Häcker FEK, Honey CJ, Hasson U. 2015. Engaged listeners: shared neural processing of powerful political speeches. *Soc. Cogn. Affect. Neurosci.* 10(8):1137–43

Schmälzle R, O'Donnell MB, Garcia JO, Cascio CN, Bayer J, et al. 2017. Brain connectivity dynamics during social interaction reflect social network structure. *PNAS* 114(20):5153–58

Scholz C, Baek EC, O'Donnell MB, Falk EB. 2016. *Sharing for the (social) self and others: neural mechanisms driving broad- and narrowcasting*. Presented at Annu. Meet. Int. Commun. Assoc., Fukuoka, Jpn.

Scholz C, Baek EC, O'Donnell MB, Kim HS, Cappella JN, Falk EB. 2017a. A neural model of information virality. *PNAS* 114(11):2881–86

Scholz C, Dore BP, Baek EC, O'Donnell MB, Falk EB. 2017b. *A neural propagation system: neurocognitive and preference synchrony in information sharers and their receivers*. Presented at Annu. Meet. Int. Commun. Assoc., San Diego

Scholz C, Falk EB. 2017. The neuroscience of information sharing. In *Handbook of Communication in the Networked Age*, ed. S González-Bailón, B Foucault Welles. Oxford, UK: Oxford Univ. Press. In press

Schultz W. 2006. Behavioral theories and the neurophysiology of reward. *Annu. Rev. Psychol.* 57:87–115

Schurz M, Radua J, Aichhorn M, Richlan F, Perner J. 2014. Fractionating theory of mind: a meta-analysis of functional brain imaging studies. *Neurosci. Biobehav. Rev.* 42:9–34

Schwartz S. 2006. A theory of cultural value orientations: explication and applications. *Comp. Sociol.* 5(2):137–82

Semin GR, Cacioppo JT. 2008. Grounding social cognition: synchronization, entrainment, and coordination. In *Embodied Grounding: Social, Cognitive, Affective, and Neuroscientific Approaches*, ed. GR Semin, ER Smith, pp. 119–47. Cambridge, UK: Cambridge Univ. Press

Silbert LJ, Honey CJ, Simony E, Poeppel D, Hasson U. 2014. Coupled neural systems underlie the production and comprehension of naturalistic narrative speech. *PNAS* 111(43):E4687–96

Simony E, Honey CJ, Chen J, Lositsky O, Yeshurun Y, et al. 2016. Dynamic reconfiguration of the default mode network during narrative comprehension. *Nat. Commun.* 7:12141

Spunt RP, Meyer ML, Lieberman MD. 2015. The default mode of human brain function primes the intentional stance. *J. Cogn. Neurosci.* 27(6):1116–24

Stephens GJ, Silbert LJ, Hasson U. 2010. Speaker-listener neural coupling underlies successful communication. *PNAS* 107:14425–30

Strecher VJ, Marcus A, Bishop K, Fleisher L, Stengle W, et al. 2005. A randomized controlled trial of multiple tailored messages for smoking cessation among callers to the cancer information service. *J. Health Commun.* 10(Suppl. 1):105–18

Tamir DI, Mitchell JP. 2011. The default network distinguishes construals of proximal versus distal events. *J. Cogn. Neurosci.* 23(10):2945–55

Tamir DI, Mitchell JP. 2012. Disclosing information about the self is intrinsically rewarding. *PNAS* 109(21):8038–43

Tamir DI, Zaki J, Mitchell JP. 2015. Informing others is associated with behavioral and neural signatures of value. *J. Exp. Psychol. Gen.* 144(6):1114–23

Taylor SE. 2006. Tend and befriend. *Curr. Dir. Psychol. Sci.* 15(6):273–77

Taylor SE, Brown JD. 1988. Illusion and well-being: a social psychological perspective on mental health. *Psychol. Bull.* 103(2):193–210

Tomlin D, Nedic A, Prentice DA, Holmes P, Cohen JD. 2013. The neural substrates of social influence on decision making. *PLOS ONE* 8(1):e52630

Traxler MJ, Gernsbacher MA. 1993. Improving written communication through perspective-taking. *Lang. Cogn. Process.* 8(3):311–34

Trope Y, Liberman N. 2010. Construal-level theory of psychological distance. *Psychol. Rev.* 117(2):440–63

Venkatraman V, Dimoka A, Pavlou PA, Vo K, Hampton W, et al. 2015. Predicting advertising success beyond traditional measures: new insights from neurophysiological methods and market response modeling. *J. Mark. Res.* 52(4):436–52

Vezich IS, Katzman PL, Ames DL, Falk EB, Lieberman MD. 2016. Modulating the neural bases of persuasion: why/how, gain/loss, and users/non-users. *Soc. Cogn. Affect. Neurosci.* 12(2):283–97

Von Neumann J, Morgenstern O. 1944. *Theory of Games and Economic Behavior.* Princeton, NJ: Princeton Univ. Press

Wasylyshyn N, Hemenway B, Garcia JO, Cascio CN, O'Donnell MB, et al. 2017. Global brain dynamics during social exclusion predict subsequent behavioral conformity. arXiv:1710.00869 [q-bio.NC]

Welborn BL, Lieberman MD, Goldenberg D, Fuligni AJ, Galván A, Telzer EH. 2016. Neural mechanisms of social influence in adolescence. *Soc. Cogn. Affect. Neurosci.* 11(1):100–9

Wien AH, Olsen SO. 2014. Understanding the relationship between individualism and word of mouth: a self-enhancement explanation. *Psychol. Mark.* 31(6):416–25

Wilson EJ, Sherrell DL. 1993. Source effects in communication and persuasion research: a meta-analysis of effect size. *J. Acad. Mark. Sci.* 21(2):101–12

Wilson TD, Nisbett RE. 1978. The accuracy of verbal reports about the effects of stimuli on evaluations and behavior. *Soc. Psychol.* 41(2):118–31

Wilson TD, Schooler JW. 1991. Thinking too much: Introspection can reduce the quality of preferences and decisions. *J. Personal. Soc. Psychol.* 60(2):181–92

Zaki J, Schirmer J, Mitchell JP. 2011. Social influence modulates the neural computation of value. *Psychol. Sci.* 22(7):894–900

Zerubavel N, Bearman PS, Weber J, Ochsner KN. 2015. Neural mechanisms tracking popularity in real-world social networks. *PNAS* 112(49):15072–77

Social Mobilization

Todd Rogers,[1] Noah J. Goldstein,[2] and Craig R. Fox[2]

[1]John F. Kennedy School of Government, Harvard University, Cambridge, Massachusetts 02138; email: Todd_Rogers@hks.harvard.edu

[2]Anderson School of Management, University of California, Los Angeles, California 90095; email: noah.goldstein@anderson.ucla.edu, cfox@anderson.ucla.edu

Annu. Rev. Psychol. 2018. 69:357–81

First published as a Review in Advance on September 25, 2017

The *Annual Review of Psychology* is online at psych.annualreviews.org

https://doi.org/10.1146/annurev-psych-122414-033718

Keywords

social influence, collective action, charitable giving, voter mobilization, environmental behavior, field experiments

Abstract

This article reviews research from several behavioral disciplines to derive strategies for prompting people to perform behaviors that are individually costly and provide negligible individual or social benefits but are meaningful when performed by a large number of individuals. Whereas the term social influence encompasses all the ways in which people influence other people, social mobilization refers specifically to principles that can be used to influence a large number of individuals to participate in such activities. The motivational force of social mobilization is amplified by the fact that others benefit from the encouraged behaviors, and its overall impact is enhanced by the fact that people are embedded within social networks. This article may be useful to those interested in the provision of public goods, collective action, and prosocial behavior, and we give special attention to field experiments on election participation, environmentally sustainable behaviors, and charitable giving.

Contents

INTRODUCTION

In 2011, 10,000 Egyptian citizens joined a protest in Tahrir Square to topple a corrupt government. Attending this event put each citizen's life in serious jeopardy, with a credible risk of retaliation and imprisonment. Yet one could reasonably argue that the consequent overthrow of the Egyptian government was not affected by any typical participant: Any one of those brave Egyptians could have stayed home without significantly affecting the outcome.

In 2016, over 138 million US citizens voted in the US Presidential election. These citizens spent millions of hours in total performing this behavior, rather than engaging in leisure or other productive activities. None of those individual voters had a meaningful impact on the election outcome.

In 2007, 281,000 car buyers paid more than $22,000 each for a Toyota Prius, the first fuel-efficient hybrid car that was a breakout mainstream success. Many of these purchasers were motivated to reduce their carbon footprints. In reviewing the car, Edmunds noted that it was "less powerful and agile" than its peer midsize sedan, and Kelley Blue Book highlighted concerns about the expected long-term ownership costs compared to its peers (https://www.edmunds.com/toyota/prius/2007/). Yet any single car buyer purchasing a Prius instead of a much-less-efficient vehicle would result in no detectable effect on Earth's changing climate.

A well-functioning civil society requires a large number of citizens to regularly act in ways that traditional economics characterizes as irrational. People must take actions for which the cost outweighs the benefit to them and that only help the collective if many people participate. In this article, we review psychological factors that can be leveraged to prompt a large number of people to engage in these kinds of behaviors. We define "social mobilization" as the effort to marshal many people to perform behaviors that impose a net cost on each individual who complies and provide negligible collective benefit unless performed by a large number of individuals. Examples include civic engagement behaviors like voting or volunteering, environmentally sustainable behaviors like conservation or recycling, and charitable contributions of time and money.

Collective action is a topic that has interested a range of social scientists for decades.[1] In particular, economists have long recognized that rational self-interested individuals should not contribute to the achievement of common goals or to public goods that can be consumed by

---

[1]There have been a variety of excellent reviews on related topics across disciplines. These include psychological perspectives on social dilemmas (Dawes 1980, Weber et al. 2004), psychological perspectives on prosocial behavior (Keltner et al. 2014, Penner et al. 2005), a sociological perspective on collective identity and social movements (Polletta & Jasper 2001), political science and economic perspectives on the logic and evolution of collective action (Ostrom 1998, 2014), an evolutionary perspective on cooperation (Kraft-Todd et al. 2015), and an experimental economics perspective on the provision of public goods (Chaudhuri 2011). Though related, the perspectives of each of these reviews differ quite substantially from that of this review.

others at no additional cost and from which others cannot be readily excluded (Samuelson 1954). Mancur Olson (1965) articulated this zero contribution thesis in his classic book *Logic of Collective Action*. He wrote that "unless there is coercion or some other special device to make individuals act in their common interest, rational, self-interested individuals will not act to achieve their common or group's interests" (Olson 1965, p. 2; quoted in Ostrom 2014, p. 235). Of course, people commonly violate this thesis, as illustrated by the three anecdotes that opened this review. Our focus is on how to develop interventions that can prompt many individuals to exhibit such other-benefiting behaviors.

In experimental economics, collective action is commonly modeled using a public goods game (or related *n*-player prisoner's dilemma) in which each player chooses (usually privately) how much of their personal resources to contribute to a public pool of money. This pool is multiplied by a number greater than one and less than the total number of players, and the payoff of this public good is divided evenly among all players, even those who did not choose to contribute. Rational choice theory predicts that all players will free ride by contributing nothing because they have an individual incentive to do so no matter how much others contribute (this is the Nash equilibrium). Nevertheless, laboratory experiments frequently observe high levels of contribution in these games, especially when participants expect others to cooperate (for a recent review, see Chaudhuri 2011).

In this review, we focus on the psychology of collective action, with a particular focus on interventions that social mobilizers can develop and administer to effectively prompt many individuals to take personally costly actions that benefit the collective. Several notes concerning the scope of this topic are in order. First, our definition requires that the immediate individual costs of acting exceed the immediate individual benefits, so that taking action entails some measure of self-sacrifice or exposure to possible negative consequences. We therefore exclude tactics such as coercion or compensation that provide a material incentive for people to take action. Moreover, by focusing on costly actions, we look beyond mere attitudinal persuasion (e.g., Petty & Cacioppo 2012) or interpersonal compliance and conformity (e.g., Cialdini & Goldstein 2004).

Second, social mobilization involves prompting people to perform behaviors that primarily benefit a group of other people; the meaning and purpose of social mobilization are fundamentally social. Thus, the other-benefiting nature of social mobilization can amplify the effectiveness of some influence principles (e.g., adherence to social norms, public commitments, and social accountability). Where available, we discuss direct evidence for this amplification phenomenon, and where this evidence is not available, we appeal to indirect evidence. This focus on motivating other-benefiting behaviors also brings to the fore some insights that have been underappreciated in the social influence literature. For instance, we focus on the many ways in which social connectedness (and the digital social networks that have emerged to facilitate it) can amplify efforts to mobilize people to perform other-benefiting behaviors. In so doing, we deemphasize influence principles that primarily prompt self-benefiting behaviors (e.g., scarcity and authority).

Third, social mobilization as we define it focuses on situations in which individual action is practically meaningless and public benefits only emerge when many people perform the behavior. Thus, we exclude situations where a small subset of individuals have disproportionate influence over collective outcomes or make a disproportionate sacrifice, as with giving large philanthropic contributions, donating an organ to a known recipient, or volunteering for a dangerous military operation.

A basic psychological motive underlying many of the social mobilization principles that we discuss is people's fundamental need to belong or feel socially connected to others. Humans have a natural tendency to seek and maintain social connectedness (Baumeister & Leary 1995, McClelland 1985). This desire for social esteem, some argue, is the origin of self-esteem: Self-esteem functions as a way to monitor and manage one's social belonging. Self-esteem, these researchers argue, has evolved to ensure that people exert effort to maintain or improve their social standing (Leary & Baumeister 2000). Consistent with this argument's assertion of the primacy of social belonging, the threat of social rejection is highly aversive, causing neural reactions similar to those involved in physical pain (MacDonald & Leary 2005). In short, humans have a fundamental need to feel that they are socially connected with others. Because of this, strategies that harness social principles to prompt other-benefiting behaviors can be especially mobilizing.

We organize behavioral principles for social mobilization into five intervention elements that have proven to be potent in the behavioral literature. As a convenient mnemonic, the first letter of each principle forms the acronym PANIC. Social mobilization efforts tend to be more effective when they are (*a*) personal, i.e., they involve more personal and personalized interactions between people who can relate to one another; (*b*) accountable, i.e., they make people's behavior observable to others, so that they feel that action or inaction could have consequences for their reputations and social standing; (*c*) normative, i.e., they convey what relevant people think others should do or what relevant people actually do; (*d*) identity relevant, i.e., they align behaviors with the ways in which people actually see themselves or would like to see themselves; and (*e*) connected, i.e., they leverage the structure of people's networks of relationships and the platforms that maintain those networks. **Table 1** lists and defines social mobilization strategies associated with each of these five principles.

Table 1 Summary of social mobilization principles discussed in this review

Personal	**Social mobilization efforts tend to be more effective when they involve more personal and personalized interactions between people who can relate to one another.**
Personal interactions	In-person face-to-face authentic mobilization efforts are more effective than scripted, purely verbal, or written mobilization efforts.
Personalized potential beneficiaries	Social mobilization efforts are more effective when beneficiaries are identified or determined in advance.
Synchrony	Coordinated behaviors between participants can enhance social bonds and collective identities, rendering social mobilization efforts more effective.
Accountable	**Social mobilization efforts tend to be more effective when reputation-relevant behavior is observable to others.**
Social observability	People are more likely to engage in other-benefiting behaviors when they are led to expect that their behaviors will be observable to others.
Postbehavior signaling opportunities	People are more likely to engage in other-benefiting behaviors when they expect that others will observe evidence of their behaviors after the fact.
Observability cues	Environmental cues that are associated with being observed (e.g., photographs of eyes) can promote other-benefiting behaviors.
Normative	**Social mobilization efforts tend to be more effective when they convey what relevant people think others should do as well as what relevant people actually do.**
Injunctive norm salience	Reminding people of shared values and beliefs concerning how the group expects them to behave can enhance mobilization efforts.
Norm of reciprocity	Providing people with unconditional favors, gifts, or other-benefiting sacrifices can make people feel obliged to repay these gestures through participation in social mobilization activities.
Beneficial descriptive norms	Evidence of the pervasiveness of behaviors can amplify the effectiveness of social mobilization efforts, especially when the behaviors are performed by others who are similar to or in similar contexts as the people being targeted.

(Continued)

Table 1   (*Continued*)

Identity relevant	**Social mobilization efforts tend to be more effective when they align behaviors with the ways people actually see themselves or would like to see themselves.**
Symbolic identity displays	When people display behaviors that are representative of a particular group identity, they tend to feel more connected to that group and more willing to engage in mobilization activities.
Identity–behavior associations	Associating a behavior with a desirable identity can turn performing the behavior into an opportunity to affirm that the desirable identity is self-relevant.
Identity labeling	Reinforcing the idea that people possess other-benefiting identities can increase the behaviors associated with those identities.
Foot-in-the-door	Small, initial requests for other-benefiting behaviors can promote other-benefiting identities and lead people to be open to larger, related requests.
Self-prediction	People tend to believe that they will perform other-benefiting behaviors that they might not actually perform, but people's desire to behave consistently with what they say can make self-predictions self-fulfilling.
Hypocrisy avoidance	When people become aware that their behaviors have been inconsistent with a desirable identity, they can be especially likely to subsequently perform identity-consistent behavior.
Connected	**Social mobilization efforts tend to be more effective when they leverage the structure of people's networks of relationships and the platforms that maintain those networks.**
Close connections among individuals	Directing social mobilization efforts at people who are well-connected to other individuals can lead to positive spillover effects such that mobilization propagates from the target to other individuals.
Influential individuals within social networks	Focusing appeals on people who have many strong and embedded connections in a social network can help propagate mobilization appeals through simple contagion.
Observability within networks	Making behaviors more visible to other members of a social network can amplify propagation of behaviors across social networks.
Communities on the periphery of a larger social network	When contagion depends on redundant messages from similar people, social mobilization may be enhanced by targeting communities of individuals on the periphery of a larger network.

In this review, we cite the most compelling available field evidence from across various behavioral sciences to illustrate and explain each principle, with particular focus on more recent research. The principles share an underlying emphasis on social concerns and needs, and some of the evidence we marshal could speak to multiple social mobilization principles. We note these connections throughout. We afford special attention to research in three relevant domains that have received substantial attention in recent years: electoral participation, environmental conservation, and charitable giving. The behaviors that are central to these domains exemplify a key aspect of social mobilization in that they offer potentially substantial collective benefits while imposing individual costs. Because our definition of social mobilization emphasizes active interventions in field settings (as opposed to the laboratory), we pay particular attention to interventions that have been investigated in experimental field research, which has flourished in recent years.

Before proceeding, we hasten to note that social mobilization tactics rely on causes that people find compelling. People's willingness to engage in these behaviors may be moderated or mediated by moral emotions such as moral outrage or existential guilt (Montada & Schneider 1989), other-focused emotions such as empathic anger (Batson et al. 2007), or self-conscious emotions such as pride and shame (Tracy et al. 2007). We surmise that most of the social mobilization principles that we review operate, in part, through the emotions they evoke. Because there has been scant field experimentation on the direct role of emotions in social mobilization, they are not a central focus in this review (for a sociological perspective on emotions in social movements, see Jasper 2011).

We turn next to a more detailed characterization of our key principles of social mobilization and their application across various domains.

PERSONAL

The first principle of social mobilization is that the more personal and personalized an interaction is, the more impact it will tend to have on subsequent behaviors. This principle suggests that social mobilization will be more effective when interactions are made more person-to-person (rather than impersonal), involve personalizing the beneficiaries of behaviors, and structure actions so people feel synchronized and connected with others. A recent meta-analysis of cooperation in social dilemma games (Balliet 2010) supports our emphasis on personal interaction. It found that face-to-face discussion before the games began was associated with greater rates of cooperation than situations in which there was no discussion, especially for larger groups. The first contemporary randomized field experiment studying voter mobilization techniques examined the impact of different levels of personal interaction, finding that the more personal the communication, the more effective it was (Gerber & Green 2000). This conclusion generally held up over more than 100 get-out-the-vote (GOTV) randomized field experiments reviewed by Green and colleagues (2013). Being encouraged to vote by a canvasser at one's door tends to be about 150% as effective at increasing turnout as being encouraged over the phone by a volunteer caller communicating conversationally (as opposed to communicating in a highly scripted way). Meanwhile, conversational volunteer callers tend to be three times as effective as more scripted live commercial callers, and live commercial callers tend to be seven times as effective as GOTV mailers.

Newer modalities of communication generate effects consistent with the notion that the more personal interactions are the more effective they are at mobilizing individuals. Standard encouragements sent through bulk email have no positive impact on turnout (Green et al. 2013, Nickerson 2007). Personalized messages sent by email from people who are personally acquainted with the recipient tend to be relatively more effective, reflecting the power of social connectedness, as discussed in the section titled Connected (T.C. Davenport, unpublished manuscript). Standard encouragements delivered through automated robocalls have no impact on turnout, whereas standard encouragements delivered through live calls have a relatively sizable impact. Standard messages sent through text messages can have a slight positive impact on turnout, but they appear to have become less effective as they have become more widely used (Malhotra et al. 2011). This decay of treatment effect from text messaging over time may result from the increasing use of personal text messages, making each marginal text message relatively less notable and, perhaps, less likely to capture attention.

Personal interactions have also been shown to be potent at increasing recycling behavior: Face-to-face solicitation of recycling pledges increased pledges and subsequent recycling substantially more than impersonal solicitation (Reams & Ray 1993). More personal appeals make a difference in charitable giving, as well. For instance, one field experiment found that Salvation Army volunteers solicited more donations from customers exiting a store when the volunteer made eye contact with the passersby and engaged them verbally, compared to when they avoided eye contact or other forms of engagement (Andreoni et al. 2011; see also Dolinski et al. 2001).

There are several reasons that appeals involving more personal interactions are more potent than appeals involving less personal interactions. First, more personal interactions undoubtedly garner more attention than less personal interactions. For example, people surely pay more attention to a message when it is delivered face-to-face than when it is delivered through the mail. Second, when people are asked in face-to-face interactions to perform other-benefiting behaviors, they tend to believe that—and even overestimate the extent to which—others will interpret their performance of the behaviors as indications that they are good people (Flynn & Lake 2008). Third, partly because of this heightened perception of the social costs of declining to perform a behavior, personal interactions may be especially likely to elicit pledges to perform other-benefiting behaviors. Pledges to perform future behaviors are often more than just cheap talk because they can increase the likelihood that people actually follow through on those behaviors, as discussed in more depth in the section titled Identity Relevant. For example, the vast majority of people pledge to vote when asked, and being asked increases actual voting relative to not being asked (Nickerson & Rogers 2010, Sherman 1980). Fourth, personal interactions may make pledges especially potent because people may grow concerned that they could encounter the elicitor in the future and, thus, may be prompted to report whether they actually performed the pledged behavior (Rogers et al. 2016). This accountability process is discussed in more detail in the section titled Accountable. Fifth, more personal interactions likely foster deeper personal connections than less personal interactions (see Drolet & Morris 2000). Deeper social connections engage people's empathy and their fundamental desire for acceptance, both of which tend to increase motivation to behave in socially desirable ways (Baumeister & Leary 1995). Sixth, more personal interactions create opportunities to notice similarities between oneself and another person, and perceived social similarity increases people's likelihoods of complying with requests (Cialdini & Goldstein 2004, Gehlbach et al. 2016).

Although some of the aforementioned factors are relevant to multiple forms of social influence, we assert that personal interactions can be especially potent in the context of social mobilization. People may be uncomfortable exerting personal social influence on others due to the perception that the goal of such influence is personal gain—thus, it may feel selfish. However, when personal social influence serves other-benefiting purposes, people may be more willing to engage in it. For instance, people may be more comfortable asking friends and acquaintances for contributions to a fundraiser to help children with cancer than for contributions to help cover their own medical expenses. Relatedly, when soliciting for other-benefiting behaviors, people may make stronger personal appeals and be more forceful than when requesting benefits for themselves. For instance, women tend to negotiate more effectively and more assertively when they are doing so on behalf of others rather than of themselves (Amanatullah & Morris 2010).

In addition to personalizing interactions, social mobilization may be aided by personalizing the potential beneficiaries of interventions (see Slovic et al. 2007). Mother Teresa described this idea about personalized potential beneficiaries by saying: "If I look at the mass I will never act. If I look at one, I will." Research on the identifiable victim effect reports that people are more motivated to help identified than statistical victims and that identification is stronger when more information is provided about the individual (e.g., a picture, name, and age) (Kogut & Ritov 2005). Other work finds that merely determining a victim (or beneficiary) in advance, rather than leaving this to be determined, increases people's willingness to donate in both lab and field studies, even when no identifying personal information has been provided (Small & Loewenstein 2003). Further research has pointed to the role of emotions in the identifiable victim effect. In one small study (Genevsky et al. 2013), participants donated more money to orphans who were more identifiable (depicted in photographs rather than silhouettes), and this effect was mediated by self-rated positive arousal. Similarly, Grant and colleagues (2007) found that those working for a fundraising call center worked harder and raised more money when they had an opportunity to meet briefly with a beneficiary of the fundraising (as opposed to reading a letter from a beneficiary or having no exposure to a beneficiary). Finally, there is also evidence of an identified impact effect, whereby providing tangible details about the effect of a potential donor's contribution—a way of personalizing the impact of the donation on the beneficiary—increases charitable giving (Cryder et al. 2013).

Another strategy for social mobilization that is related to personalization involves increasing feelings of synchrony. Participants in marches, protests, and other civic actions often perform behaviors such as marching, holding up signs, singing, or chanting in unison. Perceived similarity among those participating in such events—such as similarity in perceived identity (e.g., women) or even clothing (e.g., wearing a knitted pink hat)—can foster social bonds among them (see Cialdini & Goldstein 2004). These social bonds can be further enhanced when participants engage in these behaviors in synchrony (see Chartrand & Lakin 2013). Public gatherings that involve synchronized chants, protests, and marches effectively personalize the group, blurring the psychological boundaries between the self and others who were previously merely strangers (Páez et al. 2015, Paladino et al. 2010). By strengthening participants' social bonds and sense of identity (see the section titled Identity Relevant), feelings of synchrony likely also prompt individual participants to perform other-benefiting behaviors that are valued by the other participants.

ACCOUNTABLE

When behaviors are observable to others, people are more likely to perform reputation-enhancing behaviors and avoid reputation-damaging ones. Because other-benefiting behaviors tend to be reputation enhancing (Nowak & Sigmund 1998), the accountability that comes from one's behavior being observed is a powerful principle for social mobilization. This motivation can be particularly powerful when the direct beneficiaries of the behaviors are the observers themselves, although it also affects behavior when the observers are not the direct beneficiaries (see Kraft-Todd et al. 2015). Although the direct beneficiaries of other-benefiting behaviors may reciprocate (see the section titled Normative), even others who are not direct beneficiaries often reward those who perform other-benefiting behaviors (indirect reciprocity) (Nowak & Sigmund 1998). Whether a behavior is construed to be reputation enhancing or reputation damaging may vary by person and situation (Ariely et al. 2009). For this reason, observability's impact on behavior depends on people's beliefs about others' preferences and expectations (Lerner & Tetlock 1999).

In addition to the broad strategy of harnessing people's behavioral responsiveness to social accountability (social observability), there are three narrower, complementary strategies for social mobilization: signaling opportunities, observability cues, and observability avoidance. Social observability entails increasing people's expectations that their behaviors will be observable to others. Observability interventions are increasingly possible today given the availability of ever-improving personalized data.

Gerber and colleagues (2010) examined the impact on voter turnout of a single GOTV mailer that created up to three levels of social observability concerning whether recipients voted. The first level involved informing the recipients that, after the election, a third party (the researcher) would examine whether the recipients voted. The second level, added to the previous level, was the claim that, after the election, recipients' cohabitants would be informed of whether the recipients voted. Finally, the third level, added to the other two levels, was the claim that recipients' neighbors would also be informed of whether the recipients voted. Voting behavior increased as the GOTV mailer involved more potential observers. The condition that induced the greatest level of social observability (in which people's neighbors were involved) resulted in a treatment effect that was an order of magnitude larger than a typical GOTV mailing. These social observability effects were undoubtedly the result of some combination of people's desires to avert the reputational damage of observers knowing that they did not vote and their desires to gain the reputation boost of observers knowing that they did vote. The original study occurred in a relatively low-turnout election, and the main findings have since been replicated in relatively high-turnout elections, as well (Rogers et al. 2017). The social observability GOTV strategy has subsequently been operationalized in a range of less invasive ways. For example, communicating that people who vote will be added to a Civic Honor Roll (Panagopoulos 2013) or that names of those who vote will be published in the local newspaper (Panagopoulos 2010) have been shown to generate sizable turnout increases. Consistent with work showing that bad outcomes have greater impact on behavior than good ones (i.e., negativity bias; see Baumeister et al. 2001), publicizing the fact that people have not voted has proven to be more potent than publicizing the fact that they have voted (Gerber et al. 2010)—suggesting that shame motivates turnout more than does pride.

Social observability has also been harnessed to increase environmentally friendly behaviors and charitable giving. For example, Delmas & Lessem (2014) found that delivering private energy feedback and social comparison data to people living in residence halls was ineffective at reducing their energy consumption, but making energy use information public resulted in a 20% reduction in consumption (see also Yoeli et al. 2013). Likewise, Schwartz and colleagues (2013) found that residents who were sent mailings informing them that their energy use was being studied by researchers consumed less energy than members of a control group who were not told that they were being studied. Similar effects have been found at the organizational level, as well. For example, prominently publishing a list of companies that have failed to comply with environmental regulations had a larger effect on compliance than fines and penalties (Foulon et al. 2002). There may be additional pressure to comply when those who would directly benefit from people's prosocial actions are observing the actions (e.g., Alpizar et al. 2008) or when the solicitor of the action might have reason to judge a lack of contribution as being due to prejudice (Norton et al. 2012). Although increasing the social observability of a behavior may increase the number of people who perform it, increasing social observability can also create social welfare costs. People dislike some observability interventions, and research has shown that, under some conditions, people are willing to forego compensation in order to avoid situations in which their behavior will be observed (DellaVigna et al. 2012). Those engaged in social mobilization must balance the consequences of these strategies.

Another way to harness social observability is to create postbehavior signaling opportunities that allow people to show others that they performed a behavior and, thus, increase the reputation enhancement from performing a behavior. This suggests that one reason to vote could be to be seen by others as having voted. The prominence of "I Voted" stickers (or "I Voted" buttons on Facebook) may reflect this phenomenon. In fact, Rogers et al. (2016) found that simply alerting people at the top of a GOTV mailing that they may be called after the election and asked about their voting experience increased their likelihoods of voting. Similarly, DellaVigna and colleagues (2017) found that alerting people before an election that they would be asked in person after the election if they voted appeared to increase turnout. As the authors put it, some people appear to "vote to tell others." In a related survey, respondents reported being asked an average of five times after an election whether they voted; thus, people typically have quite a few opportunities to tell others that they voted or to try to justify why they did not.

Voting to tell others that one voted may contribute to the sizable effect on turnout of having festivals at polling places on Election Day (Addonizio et al. 2007): The more observers present when one votes, the more observers whose impressions of a person can be enhanced by the person's voting (in addition, the presence of a large number of voters signals a social norm, as we discuss in the section titled Normative). The motivating power of signaling that one voted could also help explain why voting rates fell in small communities in Switzerland when voters were given the option to vote by mail rather than in person (Funk 2010). When people vote in person, they can signal that they are voters to observers who are voting as well.

Postbehavior signaling opportunities can also increase charitable giving. For instance, Harbaugh (1998) finds that the prestige of giving is a motive for alumni of a law school to contribute to their alma mater, as a large proportion of individuals strategically donate just enough money to enter a higher publicly acknowledged giving category. In field and lab experiments, the likelihood and amount of charitable giving increases when the opportunity for postbehavior public recognition is offered. This effect appears to be driven by a desire to improve one's reputation rather than an effort to induce others to donate as well (Karlan & McConnell 2014). In the environmental domain, the distinctive and recognizable design of the Toyota Prius, the first mainstream hybrid automobile, allowed individuals who purchased it to conspicuously display their environmentally friendly choice to others. In many communities, this purchase decision was seen as other benefiting and, therefore, was likely to be reputation enhancing (Griskevicius et al. 2010).

Mere observability cues can sometimes trigger behavioral responses similar to actual social observability. For example, several studies have found that the subtle visual presence of eye images can motivate people to perform reputation-enhancing behaviors. Bateson and colleagues (2006) found that placing a picture of eyes on the wall above a communal coffee and tea station increased contributions to the station's beverage fund. Similarly, Haley & Fessler (2005) found that placing an image that resembled eyes on the screens of participants' computers increased giving during a subsequent dictator game, and Krupka & Croson (2016) found that people were more likely to donate to their public library when the solicitation included three dots forming the shape of an upside-down triangle, which also resembles a face, compared to three dots arranged as a right-side-up triangle. Panagopoulos (2014) found that adding images of eyes to a GOTV mailer increased its impact on turnout, as well. These findings may suggest that the presence of eye images can induce a feeling akin to being socially observed, prompting people to behave as if they were actually being observed.

Finally, we note that people are sometimes willing to incur costs to reduce the observability associated with other-benefiting behaviors that they do not intend to perform or would rather not perform (Dana et al. 2006). For example, people exhibit observability avoidance when they avoid store exits at which Salvation Army volunteers are stationed (Andreoni et al. 2011) and avoid answering their own doors when they know canvassers will be asking for donations (DellaVigna et al. 2012). In an election participation study, people were so affected by the prospect of others knowing that they did not vote that they intentionally did not answer their doors to respond to a face-to-face survey for which they would have been compensated (DellaVigna et al. 2017). Observability avoidance likely results in people not performing other-benefiting behaviors that they might have performed if exit from observability were not an option. Thus, reducing opportunities to avoid observability may increase other-benefiting behaviors (Hirschman 1970).

NORMATIVE

Another powerful social mobilization principle is that leveraging normative information can strongly affect other-benefiting behaviors. Norm information can be categorized as descriptive or injunctive (see Cialdini & Trost 1998). Injunctive norms refer to expectations about what behaviors are commonly approved of or disapproved of in a community (i.e., what ought to be done), whereas descriptive norms refer to beliefs about what behaviors are commonly performed in a given situation (i.e., what is done). Both kinds of norms can be enlisted for social mobilization.

Increasing injunctive norm salience can be an effective strategy for social mobilization. For many behaviors—especially other-benefiting ones—there are widely shared injunctive norms. The ideas that one should recycle and that one should not litter are examples. Another widely held injunctive norm is that citizens should vote. Formal models of why people vote incorporate the sense of civic duty to vote as a core rationale, and this variable is especially predictive of who will vote and who will not (A. Blais and C.H. Achen, unpublished manuscript). Surprisingly, interventions that have attempted to increase the salience of the injunctive norm to vote have tended to have minimal impact on turnout (Gerber & Green 2000), perhaps due to the already high salience of the norm as elections approach and the near ubiquity of the belief. Similarly, interventions that have tried to reinforce individuals' civic duty to conserve natural resources have also tended to have minimal impact, likely for similar reasons (Nolan et al. 2008).

However, when commonly approved behavior is ambiguous, communicating injunctive norms can strongly influence behavior. For example, consider the behavior of taking samples of petrified wood from the Petrified Forest National Park in the United States. To many, it is not clear whether this behavior is considered acceptable. Consequently, exposing park visitors to a sign conveying an injunctive norm that one should not take petrified wood appears to reduce wood theft (Cialdini et al. 2006). Another example is the use of free plastic bags at grocery stores. To many, it may be ambiguous whether using these free bags (versus reusable shopping bags) is the right thing to do. Thus, exposing shoppers to a sign conveying an injunctive norm urging them to minimize their use of the plastic bags reduced the number of bags taken (de Groot et al. 2013). Interventions that increase injunctive norm salience can be especially effective when they help people understand the meaning and rationale behind an injunctive norm. For example, Asensio & Delmas (2015) found that connecting residents' energy usage with the amount of pollution they were responsible for emitting each month (alongside the health impact on the community, like increases in childhood asthma and cancer) caused residents to reduce their energy usage. Interventions that increase injunctive norm salience may be especially potent in the context of social mobilization because injunctive norms tend to serve other-benefiting purposes, and society tends to cultivate these norms for collective purposes.

One especially potent injunctive norm is that we should reciprocate kind gestures from others. The injunctive norm of reciprocity, which obliges people to repay others when they have been helped, is one of the strongest and most pervasive injunctive norms across human cultures (Gouldner 1960). Some charitable organizations make use of reciprocity by accompanying donation requests with unsolicited gifts. For instance, the Disabled American Veterans' success rate nearly doubled when they included in their mailers an unsolicited gift of individualized address labels (Smolowe 1990). Although much of the research done on this topic has examined reciprocity as a function of one party doing a direct favor for (or providing a gift to) another, Goldstein and colleagues (2011) showed that individuals could be mobilized to conserve environmental resources via a sense of reciprocity even when those individuals were not the beneficiary of the favor. This research found that hotel guests were more likely to reuse their towels when the hotel reported that it had already made an unconditional donation to an environmental charity on their behalf and then asked the guests to return the favor (reciprocity by proxy) compared to when it promised to make a donation on behalf of guests only if the guests reused their towels (incentive by proxy, which is the basis of many real-world cause-related marketing appeals).

Whereas injunctive norms convey what behaviors others think are acceptable and expect, descriptive norms convey what others typically actually do. People tend to conform to descriptive social norms, particularly when they feel uncertain about what kind of behavior is correct in a given situation (see Cialdini & Goldstein 2004). Economists have examined a closely related phenomenon. Laboratory experiments using anonymous public goods games show that around half of participants are conditional cooperators who contribute more to a public good when they expect others to contribute more, whereas less than one third free ride on others' contributions (Fischbacher et al. 2001), and that people update their beliefs about others' behavior from their experience of it and then adjust their own behaviors accordingly (Fischbacher & Gächter 2010). A field experiment of student contributions to scholarship funds similarly documents a significant positive correlation between students' expectations about the contribution rates of others and their own willingness to contribute (Frey & Meier 2004).

Descriptive norms may be especially powerful because they appear to influence behavior through automatic channels as opposed to more deliberative ones (Jacobson et al. 2011). Additionally, people tend to underestimate the mobilizing power of descriptive norms on their own behavior, which may contribute to the effectiveness of interventions conveying descriptive norm information. For example, Nolan et al. (2008) found that California homeowners predicted that, among four possible factors, descriptive norms would be the factor least likely to influence energy conservation behaviors. A subsequent field experiment found that descriptive norm information was, in fact, the most potent of the factors at changing energy conservation behaviors (for a related finding, see Schultz et al. 2015).

Interventions that highlight beneficial descriptive norms tend to change behavior by making already-known descriptive norms salient, making previously unknown descriptive norms known, or correcting misperceptions about descriptive norms (see Miller & Prentice 2016). This descriptive information can be presented in a variety of formats, including the raw number of people engaging in the desired behavior (Gerber & Rogers 2009), the percentage of people engaging in the behavior (Goldstein et al. 2008), the average amount that a group of people engages in the behavior (Schultz et al. 2007), lists of individuals who have already engaged in the behavior (Reingen 1982), and firsthand observations of the frequency of the behavior in one's own environment (Berger & Heath 2008, Cialdini et al. 1990). Field experiments that have manipulated descriptive norms have found that they influence behavior in a number of domains, including soliciting blood donations (Reingen 1982), encouraging towel reuse in hotels (Goldstein et al. 2008), increasing motivation to vote (Gerber & Rogers 2009), and affecting charitable giving (Frey & Meier 2004). Beneficial descriptive norms may be especially useful for increasing other-benefiting behaviors because they often convey an invitation to work with others toward a common cause—for example, urging people to "join others" in reusing their towels (e.g., Goldstein et al. 2008)—and such cues tend to instill motivation toward that cause in individuals (Carr & Walton 2014).

A central question when developing descriptive norm interventions is whose norms should be communicated. Similarity-aligned descriptive norms tend to be most effective. These are the norms of reference groups with which people feel similar and are also related to the principle discussed in the next section, titled Identity Relevant. People are more likely to conform to a given descriptive norm if they share a social identity with the reference group associated with that norm (e.g., Goldstein & Cialdini 2007). For example, public radio listeners calling into a fundraising drive donated more when they learned that someone matching their own gender had just made a relatively large donation (Shang et al. 2008). The more strongly people positively identify with a social group, the more they will tend to conform to the descriptive norms of that group (see Swann & Bosson 2010). The inverse is also true: as people want to disassociate themselves from a given social group (e.g., an undesirable outgroup) their behaviors will tend to deviate from the norms of that group (Berger & Heath 2008). Consistent with the work discussed above in the section titled Accountable, people's behavior deviates even more strongly from the norms of undesirable groups when it is observable to others (White & Dahl 2006). A key implication of these findings is that social mobilization interventions leveraging descriptive norms must take into account people's perceived similarity to and affinity for potential reference groups.

Another dimension of similarity-aligned descriptive norms is whether people view the reference group as physically proximate to themselves. Goldstein et al. (2008) argued that people may be especially likely to follow the normative behavior of reference groups that are or have been physically proximate to them relative to those that are or have been more distant. They found that hotel guests were more likely to reuse their towels when the descriptive norm for towel reuse referred to the behavior of other guests who had previously stayed in their exact room compared to other relevant reference groups (e.g., all other hotel guests, similar-gender hotel guests, or fellow citizens). Of course, in many cases, physically proximate reference groups are also personally important reference groups with which people closely identify. For example, Martin (2012) reported that British citizens were more likely to pay their taxes when they received a letter urging them to pay that mentioned the proportion of citizens from their particular town complying, compared to when they received compliance information about more global reference groups in their postcode or the country as a whole (for a related finding in energy consumption, see Loock et al. 2012; for related findings in charitable giving, see Agerström et al. 2016; Kessler & Milkman 2017, experiment 2).

Just as people's behavior tends to conform to beneficial descriptive norms, it also tends to conform to counterproductive descriptive norms. For this reason, social mobilization interventions should selectively normalize desired behavior and marginalize undesired behavior. Communicating descriptive norms about undesired behavior can backfire. For example, Cialdini and colleagues (2006) found that signage at a national park highlighting the fact that many people had previously stolen petrified wood from the park appeared to encourage the very theft the park aimed to prevent. Similarly, Gerber & Rogers (2009) found that informing people that voter turnout would be relatively low reduced people's motivation to vote compared to informing them that turnout would be relatively high. Interestingly, changing beliefs about expected turnout did not change people's beliefs about an election's closeness or importance or their likelihood of casting a pivotal vote. A subsequent GOTV field experiment targeting Latino citizens underscored the importance of selective descriptive norms, showing that adding to a GOTV mailer the phrase "Only 20% of registered young Latinos voted in 2006" decreased actual turnout relative to the same GOTV mailer without the phrase (Keane & Nickerson 2015).

Selective descriptive norms are especially important when social mobilization interventions communicate descriptive norms as statistical averages. For example, Schultz et al. (2007) provided residents with personalized energy use feedback that included the descriptive norm in the form of the average energy use of their neighborhood. As expected, those who consumed more energy than average subsequently reduced their energy consumption; however, those who consumed less energy than average subsequently increased their energy consumption. However, researchers found that the lower-than-average energy users could be prevented from backsliding if they were also provided with injunctive norm information. Adding an explicit injunctive message (a smiley face emoticon) conveying that their low energy consumption was approved of by the message senders (and presumably society more generally) neutralized the negative effect of providing descriptive norm information to lower-than-average energy users. Opower, an organization that partners with utilities to provide communications that include personalized electricity use feedback and descriptive norms to residents, has leveraged both the descriptive and injunctive elements of the Schultz et al. (2007) work to great effect on a massive scale. The organization's scaled intervention meaningfully reduces energy usage (Allcott 2011, Ayres et al. 2013) and is remarkably persistent, even after it discontinues administration of its intervention (Allcott & Rogers 2014; for similar results in water conservation, see Ferraro & Price 2013).

In addition to providing the descriptive norm about average energy use, Opower's intervention also provides a descriptive norm about the energy use of the top 20% of most-efficient neighbors. This aspirational reference group of exceptionally energy-efficient neighbors likely reduces the possible backfire effect among those who are more energy efficient than their average neighbor but less energy efficient than the top 20% of their most-efficient neighbors. However, it is not clear that descriptive norm interventions need to include both the average and the aspirational reference groups to be successful. For instance, Meeker and colleagues (2016) substantially reduced doctors' unwarranted prescription of antibiotics by presenting both personalized feedback about their inappropriate prescription rate and the inappropriate prescription rates of the best 10%

of physicians in their clinics. That said, we note that communicating the descriptive norms of exceptional performers can sometimes backfire because this information can discourage those who perceive the aspirational norm as unattainable, which can lead to counterproductive quitting (Rogers & Feller 2016; see also Delmas et al. 2017).

Finally, descriptive and injunctive norms should be aligned when possible. For example, Cialdini (2003) reports achieving a 25% advantage in recycling tonnage using public service announcements showing many individuals recycling and disapproving of a lone individual who does not. However, when alignment is not possible, mobilization campaigns may choose to emphasize one norm over another depending on other features of the campaign; for example, White & Simpson (2013) found that, when grass recycling campaigns appealed to the collective self (e.g., we), both norms were equally effective, but when they appealed to the individual self (e.g., you), descriptive norms were more effective.

IDENTITY RELEVANT

Social mobilization efforts can be enhanced by leveraging the intimate connection between people's identities and their behavior. People hold many competing identities. One person may be a US citizen, father, son, husband, vegetarian, student, Marine Corps veteran, moral person, and Philadelphian. Each of these identities carries with it different behavioral tendencies (see Swann & Bosson 2010). In any specific moment, each identity is more or less accessible and, thus, has more or less influence on behavior. We discuss five strategies for making an identity associated with performing specific other-benefiting behaviors more accessible in key moments and increasing the personal importance of a given identity.

Broadly speaking, there are two identity types: social identities and self-identities. As briefly discussed in the section titled Normative, social identities encompass people's perceptions and beliefs about social groups with which they have an emotional identification. According to social identity theory (Tajfel & Turner 1979), individuals' self-concepts are strongly influenced by the social groups and categories to which they perceive themselves as belonging. The influence of social group identification on behavior depends both on the strength of a person's identification with the social group and on the social identity's salience at the moment a behavior is to be performed.

Once a particular social identity has been made salient, people are more likely to behave consistently with what they believe to be the prototypical group behavior or with what they believe to be in the group's interests. Social identities can be especially mobilizing when the identity group is threatened or when people feel that the status differential between the identity group and the group in power is illegitimate (van Zomeren et al. 2008). Thus, social mobilization campaigns will tend to be more motivating when they highlight a sense of threat to a given identity, unjust treatment toward those who share that identity, status differences between those who share that identity and those in power, and illegitimacy of those in power. A good example is the 2017 Women's March in Washington, DC, in which millions of women (and men and children) rallied around the world the day after the inauguration of Donald Trump as President of the United States. Reasons that protesters cited for their participation included the unjust threat to women's rights (i.e., privacy, contraception, health care, etc.) and their status and respect in the world by the words and stated policies of the new President, and the belief that the new President may have come to power illegitimately (due to alleged interference by Russia and the unusual intervention of the Director of the US Federal Bureau of Investigation).

The example of the Women's March suggests that an effective strategy for harnessing shared identity is to create symbolic identity displays that allow participants to feel more strongly connected with others in their group. This could then increase other-benefiting behaviors that are aligned with that social identity (Páez et al. 2015). Because people's possessions are often extensions of their identities (Belk 1988), apparel can be a useful form for these symbolic identity displays to take. Examples of symbolic apparel include the pink hats worn at the Women's March, the identical T-shirts worn by volunteers of various causes, the ash cross rubbed on the foreheads of Christians on Ash Wednesday, and the colored rubber bracelets worn by those who have donated to and are concerned about a given cause. This strategy complements that of creating postbehavior signaling opportunities, described in the section titled Accountable, as well as that of creating opportunities for synchrony, described in the section titled Personal. However, in addition to creating opportunities to enhance people's reputations and increase perceptions of closeness with others, these symbolic identity displays serve as opportunities to make salient and amplify people's shared identities and increase the likelihood of performing behaviors associated with those identities or benefiting relevant groups.

Thus far (in both this section and the section titled Normative), we have focused mostly on strategies that harness social identities. In addition, strategies leveraging self-identities can be equally potent. Self-identities entail how people perceive themselves, including people's knowledge or perceptions about their own traits, attributes, and values. Social mobilization efforts based on self-identity typically harness people's natural motivation to see themselves in a positive light (Leary 2007) and behave in a manner that is consistent with their favorable self-identities and previous statements and behaviors (for a review, see Cialdini 2008). We illustrate next how these insights can be applied in the context of social mobilization.

One social mobilization strategy involving identity is to associate an other-benefiting behavior with a desirable identity. Nurturing identity–behavior associations entails associating a behavior with a desirable identity, thereby turning performance of the behavior into an opportunity to affirm a desirable identity. For instance, Bryan and colleagues (2011) found that voter turnout was higher after people answered a series of election-related questions as part of an online survey the night before an election when the questions contained noun-identity language ("be a voter") compared to when they contained verb-action language ("to vote"). "Be a voter" language implies that one can claim a desirable identity ("a voter") as self-relevant by performing the behavior (casting a vote) (see also Bryan et al. 2016, Gerber et al. 2016).

Another social mobilization strategy harnessing identity is known as identity labeling. Identity labeling involves explicitly asserting and affirming that a person possesses a value, trait, attitude, belief, or other label that they have previously demonstrated, and then making a request for which compliance is consistent with that label. This strategy tends to work because individuals for whom a desired identity is asserted want to live up to the positive attributes, values, or beliefs associated with that identity—even in private, when target individuals do not believe that the labeler would be aware of their behavior. For instance, in the charitable giving domain, appeals to one's identity as a past donor or member of a community can render fundraising appeals more effective. Kessler & Milkman (2017) reported that lapsed donors to the American Red Cross were more likely to donate again when solicitation mailings sent to them included an additional line reminding them of the date of their previous gift.

Identity labels can also be aspirational. For instance, in one field experiment (Tybout & Yalch 1980, p. 409), after participants completed a survey about an upcoming election, experimenters briefly reviewed the responses and verbally labeled randomly assigned participants as being "above-average citizen[s] . . . who [are] very likely to vote" or as being "average citizen[s] . . . with an average likelihood of voting." Affirming that people possessed this identity increased turnout. Importantly, we note that 81% of all participants in this study voted, so that the "above average" label was likely credible to those who received it, and such labels would probably not be credible if administered to a population who rarely if ever voted. In order for an identity label to be effective, it must be credible to its recipient (LeBoeuf et al. 2010). That said, given the increasing availability and quality of commercial data detailing people's past behaviors, personalized labeling interventions may be increasingly practical in the years to come.

People's motivation to behave consistently with their identities can be leveraged to enhance social mobilization efforts in several ways. The foot-in-the-door strategy aims to motivate people to engage in a given target behavior by first asking them to perform a smaller, related behavior at an earlier point in time and then later making the larger target request (Freedman & Fraser 1966; see Burger 1999 for a review and meta-analysis). The underlying mechanism for this effect is believed to be a self-perception process whereby people infer traits, attributes, attitudes, and beliefs about their identity based on the initial, smaller behavior they first perform. Target individuals are then motivated to act consistently with this newly strengthened (or at least more salient) identity (Cialdini et al. 1995). In the social mobilization sphere, the ultimate goal is often to motivate citizens to engage in relatively difficult, time-consuming, or costly actions, where the psychological barrier to initial participation is fairly high. The foot-in-the-door strategy can increase engagement in such behaviors by lowering the psychological barrier to entry, so to speak, and then leading target individuals to perform increasingly costly actions that accord with the newly established identity. In the domain of environmental conservation, for example, Scott (1977) found that participants were more willing to engage in tedious manual labor as part of a recycling campaign if they had been asked two weeks earlier to put a small sign in their window saying "CONSERVE RESOURCES—RECYCLE."

The attributions that people are likely to make about why they are engaging in an initial behavior (i.e., their self-identity) are critical to the success of foot-in-the-door interventions. The more costly (i.e., active, effortful, uncompensated) the initial action, the more invested people become in the subsequent behavior because people tend to interpret their effort as signifying the strength of their commitment to the underlying identity and cause (for a review, see Cialdini 2008). These findings create an interesting dilemma for those involved in social mobilization campaigns: The very factors that increase the likelihood that people will engage in the initial behaviors—making those behaviors effortless, costless, or passive or offering a strong social or monetary incentive—may reduce target individuals' subsequent commitment to the cause. Thus, social mobilizers must balance the percentage of people who engage in the initial behavior with the likelihood that they will internalize that initial behavior and see the issue as important to them and worthy of future action.

Another strategy for harnessing self-identity and consistency involves having people explicitly predict their future behavior. Because of the importance of self-consistency, asking people to make self-predictions about whether they will perform a behavior in the future can make them more likely to perform that behavior (Greenwald et al. 1987, Morwitz et al. 1993). Because people are especially prone to believing that they will perform other-benefiting behaviors in the future (Milkman et al. 2009), self-prediction may be especially potent for social mobilization efforts. Several field studies have shown that asking people to self-predict if they will vote can increase turnout (Greenwald et al. 1987, Nickerson & Rogers 2010). Although the likely impact of self-prediction on election participation is small (Smith et al. 2003), this intervention is inexpensive and tends to have a positive incremental effect (Nickerson & Rogers 2010). Similarly, researchers have found that self-predictions about recycling behavior can increase actual recycling (Werner et al. 1995) and that asking prospective blood donors whether they can be counted on to show up to an appointment can decrease no-show rates (Lipsitz et al. 1989). As discussed in the section titled Accountable, self-predictions tend to be especially potent when they are made in front of others because others may hold one responsible for the accuracy of one's predictions (Pallak & Cummings 1976). Self-predictions are also more potent when they are relatively specific. For example, hotel guests were more likely to reuse their towels when they were asked to make a specific commitment about towel reuse to help the environment, compared to when they were asked to make a more general commitment to help the environment (Baca-Motes et al. 2013).

Because holding a self-identity that one is a hypocrite can be unpleasant, framing a behavior as an opportunity for hypocrisy avoidance can be a powerful social mobilization strategy. For example, Dickerson and colleagues (1992) approached swimmers on their way to the locker room after a swim. One group of swimmers was asked if they always make their showers as short as possible (most admitted that they did not), whereas a second group was asked to publicly advocate that people take shorter showers by signing their names to a flyer on the topic (most agreed); a third group received both interventions (in that order). Participants who were asked both questions proceeded to take the shortest showers, presumably because this action allowed participants to restore their favorable self-identity as a nonhypocrite. Relatedly, Kantola and colleagues (1984) found that households that were high consumers of electricity were especially likely to reduce energy consumption when they were reminded of the discrepancy between their high consumption and the fact that they had previously indicated on a survey that they felt that it was their duty to save electricity. Taken together, these findings suggest that a hypocrisy-avoidance strategy can aid in social mobilization; however, as Schultz (2014) notes, in order to succeed, such a strategy requires that individuals value these goals in the first place.

CONNECTED

The final principle of social mobilization is as much an amplifier of the others as it is a distinct principle. The ways in which information and influence are propagated from individual to individual in a social network can play a critical role in mobilizing people to perform other-benefiting behaviors, as influence spreads beyond those who are directly targeted. We discuss four strategies for harnessing social connectedness to amplify social mobilization efforts.

The first strategy is to leverage close connections among individuals. One experiment suggests that being directly encouraged to vote by someone one knows can be more effective than being encouraged to vote by a stranger (Nickerson 2007). Likewise, GOTV door-to-door canvassing not only increases turnout among targeted individuals, but also indirectly increases turnout among those who live with the targeted individuals (Nickerson 2008). Similar within-household spillovers arise for student absenteeism–reduction interventions. When one sibling in a household is targeted, the effect spills over to other siblings within the household, as well (Rogers & Feller 2017).

A second strategy for exploiting connectedness is to target influential individuals within social networks. How personally connected two individuals feel affects the influence they exert on each other. People with whom an individual has a strong tie, such as kin and close friends, tend to provide the individual with more information, advice, and emotional and instrumental support than those with weak ties, such as casual acquaintances (Coleman 1988, Contractor & DeChurch 2014). Thus, strong ties offer more opportunity for influencing people than weak ties do. This suggests that an effective intervention strategy is to target individuals who have many strong ties in a given network. For instance, Paluck and colleagues (2016) found that antibullying interventions were most effective when they targeted students with whom many other students reported spending time. In the conservation behavior context, block leaders designated to promote residential curbside recycling programs were more successful at inducing recycling behaviors when they had closer connections with their neighbors (Everett & Peirce 1992), and people tended to influence their friends' littering and recycling behaviors in a high school community (Long et al. 2014).

Identifying and targeting influential individuals are facilitated by the ubiquity of online networks. For instance, a field experiment examined the decisions of 1.3 million Facebook users regarding whether or not to adopt a commercial application that allowed users to share movie information and opinions (Aral & Walker 2014). The program sent automated notifications about a focal user's actions on the application to a randomized subset of that focal user's Facebook friends, and the researchers then examined the impact of this manipulation on subsequent adoption of the application. The researchers found that certain measures of tie strength between two people (whether the online friends attended the same college, shared other institutional affiliations, or lived in the same town) predicted greater influence from the focal individual. Moreover, the more ties a focal person shared with a target person (the more embedded the connection), the more influential the focal person tended to be on the target. A related experiment using similar methodology (Aral & Walker 2012) found that characteristics of the focal user (e.g., gender) were more important than characteristics of targets in predicting the spread of adoption of the application and that these influential focal individuals tended to naturally cluster together in networks. This finding suggests that mobilization efforts can be especially effective when they target influential people with influential friends.

A third strategy for amplifying social mobilization efforts is to enhance observability within networks. Individuals often learn about the relative attractiveness of options by observing the behaviors of others (i.e., descriptive norms), and literature in economics shows that this can lead to information cascades that cause groups of individuals in networks to make the same (correct or incorrect) choice (Bikhchandani et al. 1998). Such herding behavior has been documented in laboratory experiments (Anderson & Holt 1997) and may contribute to emergent collective actions such as increasing participation in dangerous protests (e.g., Lohmann 1994). Indeed, one study found that the number of protests on a given day during the Arab Spring of 2010–2011 could be predicted by coordination in the (highly visible) use of Twitter hashtags (i.e., the more intense use of a smaller number of hashtags) the previous day in the region, which presumably reflected the intensity of interest in protest activity (Steinert-Threlkeld et al. 2015).

For a behavior to spread within a network (Christakis & Fowler 2009; but see also Lyons 2011), those with whom a person is connected must be able to learn that the person performed the behavior. For example, the spread of residential solar power systems through communities appears to be affected by whether neighbors can observe the rooftop installations (Graziano & Gillingham 2015). Social media can amplify social mobilization by making indicators of behaviors more observable to others within people's networks. In one study, Facebook users were randomly assigned to one of two treatment arms or an untreated control group (Bond et al. 2012). Those assigned to what we term the simple encouragement group received encouragements to vote and an opportunity to click on an "I Voted" button to be displayed to others. Those in what we term the social connectedness group were administered the same treatment and also saw the profile pictures of up to six of their Facebook friends who had already clicked on the "I Voted" button. Whereas the behavior of those in the simple encouragement group was indistinguishable from that of those in the control, those in the social connectedness group were more likely to click the "I Voted" button and to actually vote. Intriguingly, about half of the effect on actual voting spilled over to those Facebook friends with whom these people communicated most frequently. Given that people typically had many such close friends, the total treatment effect was larger on close friends of treated individuals than it was on the treated individuals themselves. This study illustrates the fact that social mobilization can be amplified when the behavior of targeted individuals is communicated to people with whom targets are socially connected, especially those with whom targets have strong ties. We note that nearly 20% of people offered the chance to click the "I Voted" button actually clicked it, an extremely high rate for an online behavior. Because individuals had no economic incentive to express that they had voted, this presumably reflects the motivation to be seen by others as the kind of person who votes. Such a button is one of many ways social networks can create signaling opportunities (as discussed in the section titled Accountable). Many people signaling to their friends that they had voted gave rise to a similarity-aligned descriptive social norm (as discussed in the section titled Normative), which presumably mobilized more people to vote and click the "I Voted" button, creating a virtuous cycle.

Although some behaviors can spread through one person exposing a target individual to the behavior or message, many social behaviors require that multiple people expose a target individual (especially when target individuals see those people as similar to themselves; see Centola 2011). For such behaviors, it may be especially effective to target communities on the periphery of larger social networks, as illustrated by an online study (Centola 2010) in which participants were randomly assigned to a position within a social network for sharing health-related information. Participants were assigned to either a network in which people were interconnected within dense neighborhoods that were less strongly connected to each other (clustered lattice network) or a network containing the same number of total connections that were spread randomly throughout the network (random network). The clustered lattice network offered more opportunities for participants to receive the same signal from multiple unconnected individuals and exhibited faster overall spread of the health behaviors—perhaps by increasing the credibility of the information or signaling wider prevalence of the behavior throughout the larger social network. These findings suggest that, for some behaviors, social mobilizers can be more effective if they target clustered networks on the periphery of larger networks rather than focusing on influencers with many isolated connections in casual contact networks. Participation in protests may rely on this form of contagion. In this process, people receive multiple signals from moderate activists, many of whom are on the periphery of people's networks. These moderate activists' behavior may be more informative of general interest in the protest activities than signals coming from individuals who might be considered core to the domain and activities, such as professional organizers or media sources. Indeed, an analysis of Twitter activity during the Arab Spring (2010–2011) that linked geotagged Twitter activity with protests found that regional coordination of Twitter hashtags predicted more protests the following day if that coordination came from individuals on the periphery of the networks (those with relatively few followers) than if it came from more central and core individuals (those with relatively many followers) (Steinert-Threlkeld 2017).

In sum, whereas some of the research on social networks (as described above) points to the power of targeting influential members who are often central to networks, this research highlights the importance of also targeting communities on the periphery of a larger social network. Although more research is needed to better understand the circumstances under which each strategy is most effective, there is evidence that targeting both types of connections can foster mobilization of different social behaviors.

CONCLUSION

This review began with descriptions of three widely performed other-benefiting behaviors. Any particular Egyptian protester in 2011 could have stayed safe at home, and their government would have toppled anyway. Any particular US citizen could have saved half an hour or more by skipping voting in 2016, and Donald Trump would still have been elected President. And any particular early model Prius owner could have saved thousands of dollars by purchasing a better-performing, less-fuel-efficient car, and the course of global climate change would have been unaffected.

Yet a large number of individuals performed each of these behaviors. In this review, we have explored how insights from behavioral science research can be used to develop interventions that mobilize a large number of people to perform behaviors that are costly and practically meaningless when performed by any one person. Throughout, we have underscored the centrality of social dimensions to human motivations to help others, exploring the interplay between social concerns and social mobilization. Most people have powerful psychological needs to belong, to be well regarded by others, and to see themselves as positive contributors to relevant social groups. Such needs make most people especially responsive to social mobilization interventions that are particularly personal, entail social accountability, harness positive social norms, are identity relevant, and leverage social networks. This review has described how interventions designed to mobilize people to perform other-benefiting behaviors can create those conditions and has reviewed many new field applications of these ideas. We look forward to an increasing number of field experiments on social mobilization in the years to come and the novel theoretical insights that will emerge from such work.

DISCLOSURE STATEMENT

The authors are not aware of any affiliations, memberships, funding, or financial holdings that might be perceived as affecting the objectivity of this review.

ACKNOWLEDGMENTS

We thank David Tannenbaum, Job Krijnen, Jake Fisher, Barbara Lawrence, and the editor of the *Annual Review of Psychology*, Susan Fiske, for a number of very helpful comments on this work. We also thank Tim Cummings, Jessica Lasky-Fink, Julia Merlin, Anna Valuev, and Mary Yeh for assistance in preparing this manuscript.

LITERATURE CITED

Addonizio EM, Green DP, Glaser JM. 2007. Putting the party back into politics: an experiment testing whether election day festivals increase voter turnout. *PS Polit. Sci. Polit.* 40(4):721–27

Agerström J, Carlsson R, Nicklasson L, Guntell L. 2016. Using descriptive social norms to increase charitable giving: the power of local norms. *J. Econ. Psychol.* 52:147–53

Allcott H. 2011. Social norms and energy conservation. *J. Public Econ.* 95(9):1082–95

Allcott H, Rogers T. 2014. The short-run and long-run effects of behavioral interventions: experimental evidence from energy conservation. *Am. Econ. Rev.* 104(10):3003–37

Alpizar F, Carlsson F, Johansson-Stenman O. 2008. Anonymity, reciprocity, and conformity: evidence from voluntary contributions to a national park in Costa Rica. *J. Public Econ.* 92(5):1047–60

Amanatullah ET, Morris MW. 2010. Negotiating gender roles: Gender differences in assertive negotiating are mediated by women's fear of backlash and attenuated when negotiating on behalf of others. *J. Personal. Soc. Psychol.* 98(2):256–67

Anderson LR, Holt CA. 1997. Information cascades in the laboratory. *Am. Econ. Rev.* 87(5):847–62

Andreoni J, Rao JM, Trachtman H. 2011. *Avoiding the ask: a field experiment on altruism, empathy, and charitable giving*. NBER Work. Pap. w17648

Aral S, Walker D. 2012. Identifying influential and susceptible members of social networks. *Science* 337(6092):337–41

Aral S, Walker D. 2014. Tie strength, embeddedness, and social influence: a large-scale networked experiment. *Manag. Sci.* 60(6):1352–70

Ariely D, Bracha A, Meier S. 2009. Doing good or doing well? Image motivation and monetary incentives in behaving prosocially. *Am. Econ. Rev.* 99(1):544–55

Asensio OI, Delmas MA. 2015. Nonprice incentives and energy conservation. *PNAS* 112(6):E510–15

Ayres I, Raseman S, Shih A. 2013. Evidence from two large field experiments that peer comparison feedback can reduce residential energy usage. *J. Law Econ. Organ.* 29(5):992–1022

Baca-Motes K, Brown A, Gneezy A, Keenan EA, Nelson LD. 2013. Commitment and behavior change: evidence from the field. *J. Consum. Res.* 39(5):1070–84

Balliet D. 2010. Communication and cooperation in social dilemmas: a meta-analytic review. *J. Confl. Resolut.* 54(1):39–57

Bateson M, Nettle D, Roberts G. 2006. Cues of being watched enhance cooperation in a real-world setting. *Biol. Lett.* 2(3):412–14

Batson CD, Kennedy CL, Nord L, Stocks EL, Fleming DA, et al. 2007. Anger at unfairness: Is it moral outrage? *Eur. J. Soc. Psychol.* 37:1272–85

Baumeister RF, Bratslavsky E, Finkenauer C, Vohs KD. 2001. Bad is stronger than good. *Rev. Gen. Psychol.* 5(4):323–70

Baumeister RF, Leary MR. 1995. The need to belong: desire for interpersonal attachments as a fundamental human motivation. *Psychol. Bull.* 117(3):497–529

Belk RW. 1988. Possessions and the extended self. *J. Consum. Res.* 15(2):139–68

Berger J, Heath C. 2008. Who drives divergence? Identity signaling, outgroup dissimilarity, and the abandonment of cultural tastes. *J. Personal. Soc. Psychol.* 95(3):593–607

Bikhchandani S, Hirshleifer D, Welch I. 1998. Learning from the behavior of others: confirmity, fads, and informational cascades. *J. Econ. Perspect.* 12(3):151–70

Bond RM, Fariss CJ, Jones JJ, Kramer AD, Marlow C, et al. 2012. A 61-million-person experiment in social influence and political mobilization. *Nature* 489:295–98

Bryan CJ, Walton GM, Dweck CS. 2016. Psychologically authentic versus inauthentic replication attempts. *PNAS* 113(43):E6549–50

Bryan CJ, Walton GM, Rogers T, Dweck CS. 2011. Motivating voter turnout by invoking the self. *PNAS* 108(31):12653–56

Burger JM. 1999. The foot-in-the-door compliance procedure: a multiple-process analysis and review. *Personal. Soc. Psychol. Rev.* 3(4):303–25

Carr PB, Walton GM. 2014. Cues of working together fuel intrinsic motivation. *J. Exp. Soc. Psychol.* 53:169–84

Centola D. 2010. The spread of behavior in an online social network experiment. *Science* 329(5996):1194–97

Centola D. 2011. An experimental study of homophily in the adoption of health behavior. *Science* 334(6060):1269–72

Chartrand TL, Lakin JL. 2013. The antecedents and consequences of human behavioral mimicry. *Annu. Rev. Psychol.* 64:285–308

Chaudhuri A. 2011. Sustaining cooperation in laboratory public goods experiments: a selective survey of the literature. *Exp. Econ.* 14(1):47–83

Christakis NA, Fowler JH. 2009. *Connected: The Surprising Power of Our Social Networks and How They Shape Our Lives.* Boston: Back Bay Books

Cialdini RB. 2003. Crafting normative messages to protect the environment. *Curr. Dir. Psychol. Sci.* 12(4):105–9

Cialdini RB. 2008. *Influence: Science and Practice.* Boston: Allyn & Bacon. 5th ed.

Cialdini RB, Demaine LJ, Sagarin BJ, Barrett DW, Rhoads K, Winter PL. 2006. Managing social norms for persuasive impact. *Soc. Influ.* 1(1):3–15

Cialdini RB, Goldstein NJ. 2004. Social influence: compliance and conformity. *Annu. Rev. Psychol.* 55:591–621

Cialdini RB, Reno RR, Kallgren CA. 1990. A focus theory of normative conduct: recycling the concept of norms to reduce littering in public places. *J. Personal. Soc. Psychol.* 58(6):1015–26

Cialdini RB, Trost MR. 1998. Social influence: social norms, conformity, and compliance. In *The Handbook of Social Psychology*, ed. DT Gilbert, ST Fiske, G Lindzey, pp. 151–92. Boston: McGraw-Hill. 4th ed.

Cialdini RB, Trost MR, Newsom JT. 1995. Preference for consistency: the development of a valid measure and the discovery of surprising behavioral implications. *J. Personal. Soc. Psychol.* 69(2):318–28

Coleman JS. 1988. Social capital in the creation of human capital. *Am. J. Sociol.* 94:S95–120

Contractor NS, DeChurch LA. 2014. Integrating social networks and human social motives to achieve social influence at scale. *PNAS* 111(Suppl. 4):13650–57

Cryder CE, Loewenstein G, Scheines R. 2013. The donor is in the details. *Organ. Behav. Hum. Decis. Process.* 120(1):15–23

Dana J, Cain DM, Dawes RM. 2006. What you don't know won't hurt me: costly (but quiet) exit in dictator games. *Organ. Behav. Hum. Decis. Process.* 100(2):193–201

Dawes RM. 1980. Social dilemmas. *Annu. Rev. Psychol.* 31:169–93

de Groot JIM, Abrahamse W, Jones K. 2013. Persuasive normative messages: the influence of injunctive and personal norms on using free plastic bags. *Sustainability* 5(5):1829–44

DellaVigna S, List J, Malmendier U. 2012. Testing for altruism and social pressure in charitable giving. *Q. J. Econ.* 127(1):1–56

DellaVigna S, List JA, Malmendier U, Rao G. 2017. Voting to tell others. *Rev. Econ. Stud.* 84(1):143–81

Delmas MA, Lessem N. 2014. Saving power to conserve your reputation? The effectiveness of private versus public information. *J. Environ. Econ. Manag.* 67(3):353–70

Delmas MA, Vezich SI, Goldstein NJ. 2017. *Better than average or worse than the best? Unpacking peer influences in residential energy use feedback.* Work. Pap., Inst. Environ. Sustain., Univ. Calif. Los Angeles

Dickerson CA, Thibodeau R, Aronson E, Miller D. 1992. Using cognitive dissonance to encourage water conservation. *J. Appl. Soc. Psychol.* 22(11):841–54

Dolinski D, Nawrat M, Rudak I. 2001. Dialogue involvement as a social influence technique. *Personal. Soc. Psychol. Bull.* 27(11):1395–406

Drolet AL, Morris MW. 2000. Rapport in conflict resolution: accounting for how face-to-face contact fosters mutual cooperation in mixed-motive conflicts. *J. Exp. Soc. Psychol.* 36(1):26–50

Everett JW, Peirce JJ. 1992. Social networks, socioeconomic status, and environmental collective action: residential curbside block leader recycling. *J. Environ. Syst.* 21(1):65–84

Ferraro PJ, Price MK. 2013. Using nonpecuniary strategies to influence behavior: evidence from a large-scale field experiment. *Rev. Econ. Stat.* 95(1):64–73

Fischbacher U, Gächter S. 2010. Social preferences, beliefs, and the dynamics of free riding in public goods experiments. *Am. Econ. Rev.* 100(1):541–56

Fischbacher U, Gächter S, Fehr E. 2001. Are people conditionally cooperative? Evidence from a public goods experiment. *Econ. Lett.* 71(3):397–404

Flynn FJ, Lake VK. 2008. If you need help, just ask: underestimating compliance with direct requests for help. *J. Personal. Soc. Psychol.* 95(1):128–43

Foulon J, Lanoie P, Laplante B. 2002. Incentives for pollution control: regulation or information? *J. Environ. Econ. Manag.* 44(1):169–87

Freedman JL, Fraser SC. 1966. Compliance without pressure: the foot-in-the-door technique. *J. Personal. Soc. Psychol.* 4(2):195–202

Frey BS, Meier S. 2004. Social comparisons and pro-social behavior: testing "conditional cooperation" in a field experiment. *Am. Econ. Rev.* 94(5):1717–22

Funk P. 2010. Social incentives and voter turnout: evidence from the Swiss mail ballot system. *J. Eur. Econ. Assoc.* 8(5):1077–103

Gehlbach H, Brinkworth ME, King AM, Hsu LM, McIntyre J, Rogers T. 2016. Creating birds of similar feathers: leveraging similarity to improve teacher-student relationships and academic achievement. *J. Educ. Psychol.* 108(3):342–52

Genevsky A, Västfjäll D, Slovic P, Knutson B. 2013. Neural underpinnings of the identifiable victim effect: Affect shifts preferences for giving. *J. Neurosci.* 33(43):17188–96

Gerber A, Green D. 2000. The effects of canvassing, telephone calls, and direct mail on voter turnout: a field experiment. *Am. Polit. Sci. Rev.* 94(3):653–63

Gerber AS, Green DP, Larimer CW. 2010. An experiment testing the relative effectiveness of encouraging voter participation by inducing feelings of pride or shame. *Polit. Behav.* 32(3):409–22

Gerber AS, Huber GA, Biggers DR, Hendry DJ. 2016. A field experiment shows that subtle linguistic cues might not affect voter behavior. *PNAS* 113(26):7112–17

Gerber AS, Rogers T. 2009. Descriptive social norms and motivation to vote: Everybody's voting and so should you. *J. Polit.* 71(1):178–91

Goldstein NJ, Cialdini RB. 2007. The spyglass self: a model of vicarious self-perception. *J. Personal. Soc. Psychol.* 92(3):402–17

Goldstein NJ, Cialdini RB, Griskevicius V. 2008. A room with a viewpoint: using social norms to motivate environmental conservation in hotels. *J. Consum. Res.* 35(3):472–82

Goldstein NJ, Griskevicius V, Cialdini RB. 2011. Reciprocity by proxy: a novel influence strategy for stimulating cooperation. *Adm. Sci. Q.* 56(3):441–73

Gouldner AW. 1960. The norm of reciprocity: a preliminary statement. *Am. Sociol. Rev.* 25(2):161–78

Grant AM, Campbell EM, Chen G, Cottone K, Lapedis D, Lee K. 2007. Impact and the art of motivation maintenance: the effects of contact with beneficiaries on persistence behavior. *Organ. Behav. Hum. Decis. Process.* 103(1):53–67

Graziano M, Gillingham K. 2015. Spatial patterns of solar photovoltaic system adoption: the influence of neighbors and the built environment. *J. Econ. Geogr.* 15(4):815–39

Green DP, McGrath MC, Aronow PM. 2013. Field experiments and the study of voter turnout. *J. Elections Public Opin. Parties* 23(1):27–48

Greenwald AG, Carnot CG, Beach R, Young B. 1987. Increasing voting behavior by asking people if they expect to vote. *J. Appl. Psychol.* 72(2):315–18

Griskevicius V, Tybur JM, Van den Bergh B. 2010. Going green to be seen: status, reputation, and conspicuous conservation. *J. Personal. Soc. Psychol.* 98(3):392–404

Haley KJ, Fessler DM. 2005. Nobody's watching? Subtle cues affect generosity in an anonymous economic game. *Evol. Hum. Behav.* 26(3):245–56

Harbaugh WT. 1998. The prestige motive for making charitable transfers. *Am. Econ. Rev.* 88(2):277–82

Hirschman AO. 1970. *Exit, Voice, and Loyalty: Responses to Decline in Firms, Organizations, and States.* Cambridge, MA: Harvard Univ. Press

Jacobson RP, Mortensen CR, Cialdini RB. 2011. Bodies obliged and unbound: differentiated response tendencies for injunctive and descriptive social norms. *J. Personal. Soc. Psychol.* 100(3):433–48

Jasper JM. 2011. Emotions and social movements: twenty years of theory and research. *Annu. Rev. Sociol.* 37:285–303

Kantola SJ, Syme GJ, Campbell NA. 1984. Cognitive dissonance and energy conservation. *J. Appl. Psychol.* 69(3):416–21

Karlan D, McConnell MA. 2014. Hey look at me: the effect of giving circles on giving. *J. Econ. Behav. Organ.* 106:402–12

Keane LD, Nickerson DW. 2015. When reports depress rather than inspire: a field experiment using age cohorts as reference groups. *J. Polit. Mark.* 14(4):381–90

Keltner D, Kogan A, Piff PK, Saturn SR. 2014. The sociocultural appraisals, values, and emotions (SAVE) framework of prosociality: core processes from gene to meme. *Annu. Rev. Psychol.* 65:425–60

Kessler JB, Milkman KL. 2017. Identity in charitable giving. *Manag. Sci.* In press

Kogut T, Ritov I. 2005. The "identified victim" effect: an identified group, or just a single individual? *J. Behav. Decis. Mak.* 18(3):157–67

Kraft-Todd G, Yoeli E, Bhanot S, Rand D. 2015. Promoting cooperation in the field. *Curr. Opin. Behav. Sci.* 3:96–101

Krupka EL, Croson RT. 2016. The differential impact of social norms cues on charitable contributions. *J. Econ. Behav. Organ.* 128:149–58

Leary MR. 2007. Motivational and emotional aspects of the self. *Annu. Rev. Psychol.* 58:317–44

Leary MR, Baumeister RF. 2000. The nature and function of self-esteem: sociometer theory. *Adv. Exp. Soc. Psychol.* 32:1–62

LeBoeuf RA, Shafir E, Bayuk JB. 2010. The conflicting choices of alternating selves. *Organ. Behav. Hum. Decis. Process.* 111(1):48–61

Lerner JS, Tetlock PE. 1999. Accounting for the effects of accountability. *Psychol. Bull.* 125(2):255–75

Lipsitz A, Kallmeyer K, Ferguson M, Abas A. 1989. Counting on blood donors: increasing the impact of reminder calls. *J. Appl. Soc. Psychol.* 19(13):1057–67

Lohmann S. 1994. The dynamics of informational cascades: the Monday demonstrations in Leipzig, East Germany, 1989–91. *World Polit.* 47(1):42–101

Long J, Harré N, Atkinson QD. 2014. Understanding change in recycling and littering behavior across a school social network. *Am. J. Community Psychol.* 53(3–4):462–74

Loock C, Landwehr J, Staake T, Fleisch E, Pentland A. 2012. *The influence of reference frame and population density on the effectiveness of social normative feedback on electricity consumption.* Presented at Int. Conf. Inf. Syst., Dec. 16–19. Orlando, FL

Lyons R. 2011. The spread of evidence-poor medicine via flawed social-network analysis. *Stat. Polit. Policy* 2(1). **https://doi.org/10.2202/2151-7509.1024**

MacDonald G, Leary MR. 2005. Why does social exclusion hurt? The relationship between social and physical pain. *Psychol. Bull.* 131(2):202–23

Malhotra N, Michelson MR, Rogers T, Valenzuela AA. 2011. Text messages as mobilization tools: the conditional effect of habitual voting and election salience. *Am. Polit. Res.* 39(4):664–81

Martin S. 2012. 98% of HBR readers love this article. *Harvard Business Review*, Oct. **https://hbr.org/2012/10/98-of-hbr-readers-love-this-article**

McClelland DC. 1985. *Human Motivation*. Glenview, IL: Scott Foresman

Meeker D, Linder JA, Fox CR, Friedberg MW, Persell SD, et al. 2016. Effect of behavioral interventions on inappropriate antibiotic prescribing among primary care practices: a randomized clinical trial. *JAMA* 315(6):562–70

Milkman KL, Rogers T, Bazerman MH. 2009. Highbrow films gather dust: time-inconsistent preferences and online DVD rentals. *Manag. Sci.* 55(6):1047–59

Miller DT, Prentice DA. 2016. Changing norms to change behavior. *Annu. Rev. Psychol.* 67:339–61

Montada L, Schneider A. 1989. Justice and emotional reactions to the disadvantaged. *Soc. Justice Res.* 3(4):313–44

Morwitz VG, Johnson E, Schmittlein D. 1993. Does measuring intent change behavior? *J. Consum. Res.* 20(1):46–61

Nickerson DW. 2007. Does email boost turnout? *Q. J. Polit. Sci.* 2(4):369–80

Nickerson DW. 2008. Is voting contagious? Evidence from two field experiments. *Am. Polit. Sci. Rev.* 102(1):49–57

Nickerson DW, Rogers T. 2010. Do you have a voting plan? Implementation intentions, voter turnout, and organic plan making. *Psychol. Sci.* 21(2):194–99

Nolan JM, Schultz PW, Cialdini RB, Goldstein NJ, Griskevicius V. 2008. Normative social influence is underdetected. *Personal. Soc. Psychol. Bull.* 34(7):913–23

Norton MI, Dunn EW, Carney DR, Ariely D. 2012. The persuasive "power" of stigma? *Organ. Behav. Hum. Decis. Process.* 117(2):261–68

Nowak MA, Sigmund K. 1998. Evolution of indirect reciprocity by image scoring. *Nature* 393(6685):573–77

Olson M. 1965. *Logic of Collective Action: Public Goods and the Theory of Groups.* Cambridge, MA: Harvard Univ. Press

Ostrom E. 1998. A behavioral approach to the rational choice theory of collective action: presidential address, American Political Science Association, 1997. *Am. Polit. Sci. Rev.* 92(1):1–22

Ostrom E. 2014. Collective action and the evolution of social norms. *J. Nat. Resourc. Policy Res.* 6(4):235–52

Páez D, Rimé B, Basabe N, Wlodarczyk A, Zumeta L. 2015. Psychosocial effects of perceived emotional synchrony in collective gatherings. *J. Personal. Soc. Psychol.* 108(5):711–29

Pallak MS, Cummings W. 1976. Commitment and voluntary energy conservation. *Personal. Soc. Psychol. Bull.* 2(1):27–30

Paluck EL, Shepherd H, Aronow PM. 2016. Changing climates of conflict: a social network experiment in 56 schools. *PNAS* 113(3):566–71

Panagopoulos C. 2010. Affect, social pressure and prosocial motivation: field experimental evidence of the mobilizing effects of pride, shame and publicizing voting behavior. *Polit. Behav.* 32(3):369–86

Panagopoulos C. 2013. Positive social pressure and prosocial motivation: evidence from a large-scale field experiment on voter mobilization. *Polit. Psychol.* 34(2):265–75

Panagopoulos C. 2014. I've got my eyes on you: implicit social-pressure cues and prosocial behavior. *Polit. Psychol.* 35(1):23–33

Penner LA, Dovidio JF, Piliavin JA, Schroeder DA. 2005. Prosocial behavior: multilevel perspectives. *Annu. Rev. Psychol.* 56:365–92

Petty R, Caccioppo J. 2012. *Communication and Persuasion: Central and Peripheral Routes to Attitude Change.* New York: Springer

Polletta F, Jasper JM. 2001. Collective identity and social movements. *Annu. Rev. Sociol.* 27:283–305

Reams MA, Ray BH. 1993. The effects of three prompting methods on recycling participation rates: a field study. *J. Environ. Syst.* 22:371–79

Reingen PH. 1982. Test of a list procedure for inducing compliance with a request to donate money. *J. Appl. Psychol.* 67(1):110–18

Rogers T, Feller A. 2016. Discouraged by peer excellence: exposure to exemplary peer performance causes quitting. *Psychol. Sci.* 27(3):365–74

Rogers T, Feller A. 2017. *Intervening through influential third parties: reducing student absences at scale via parents.* Work. Pap., John F. Kennedy Sch. Gov., Harvard Univ., Cambridge, MA

Rogers T, Green DP, Ternovski J, Young CF. 2017. Social pressure and voting: a field experiment conducted in a high-salience election. *Elect. Stud.* 46:87–100

Rogers T, Ternovski J, Yoeli E. 2016. Potential follow-up increases private contributions to public goods. *PNAS* 113(19):5218–20

Samuelson PA. 1954. The pure theory of public expenditure. *Rev. Econ. Stat.* 36(4):387–89

Schultz PW. 2014. Strategies for promoting proenvironmental behavior. *Eur. Psychol.* 19(2):107–17

Schultz PW, Estrada M, Schmitt J, Sokoloski R, Silva-Send N. 2015. Using in-home displays to provide smart meter feedback about household electricity consumption: a randomized control trial comparing kilowatts, cost, and social norms. *Energy* 90(1):351–58

Schultz PW, Nolan JM, Cialdini RB, Goldstein NJ, Griskevicius V. 2007. The constructive, destructive, and reconstructive power of social norms. *Psychol. Sci.* 18(5):429–34

Schwartz D, Fischhoff B, Krishnamurti T, Sowell F. 2013. The Hawthorne effect and energy awareness. *PNAS* 110(38):15242–46

Scott CA. 1977. Modifying socially-conscious behavior: the foot-in-the-door technique. *J. Consum. Res.* 4(3):156–64

Shang J, Reed A, Croson R. 2008. Identity congruency effects on donations. *J. Mark. Res.* 45(3):351–61

Sherman SJ. 1980. On the self-erasing nature of errors of prediction. *J. Personal. Soc. Psychol.* 39(2):211–21

Slovic P, Finucane ML, Peters E, MacGregor DG. 2007. The affect heuristic. *Eur. J. Oper. Res.* 177(3):1333–52

Small DA, Loewenstein G. 2003. Helping a victim or helping the victim: altruism and identifiability. *J. Risk Uncertain.* 26(1):5–16

Smith JK, Gerber AS, Orlich A. 2003. Self-prophecy effects and voter turnout: an experimental replication. *Polit. Psychol.* 24(3):593–604

Smolowe J. 1990. Contents require immediate attention. *Time Magazine* 64, Nov. 26

Steinert-Threlkeld ZC. 2017. Spontaneous collective action: peripheral mobilization during the Arab Spring. *Am. Polit. Sci. Rev.* 111(2):379–403

Steinert-Threlkeld ZC, Mocanu D, Vespignani V, Fowler J. 2015. Online social networks and offline protest. *EPJ Data Sci.* 4:19

Swann WB, Bosson JK. 2010. Self and identity. In *Handbook of Social Psychology*, ed. DT Gilbert, ST Fiske, G Lindzey, pp. 589–628. Hoboken, NJ: Wiley

Tajfel H, Turner JC. 1979. An integrative theory of intergroup conflict. In *The Social Psychology of Intergroup Relations*, ed. WG Austin, S Worchel, pp. 33–37. Monterey, CA: Brooks/Cole

Tracy JL, Robins RW, Tangney JP, eds. 2007. *The Self-Conscious Emotions: Theory and Research*. New York: Guilford Press

Tybout AM, Yalch RF. 1980. The effect of experience: a matter of salience? *J. Consum. Res.* 6(4):406–13

van Zomeren M, Postmes T, Spears R. 2008. Toward an integrative social identity model of collective action: a quantitative research synthesis of three socio-psychological perspectives. *Psychol. Bull.* 134(4):504–35

Weber JM, Kopelman S, Messick DM. 2004. A conceptual review of decision making in social dilemmas: applying a logic of appropriateness. *Personal. Soc. Psychol. Rev.* 8(3):281–307

Werner CM, Turner J, Shipman K, Twitchell FS, Dickson BR, et al. 1995. Commitment, behavior, and attitude change: an analysis of voluntary recycling. *J. Environ. Psychol.* 15(3):197–208

White K, Dahl DW. 2006. To be or not be? The influence of dissociative reference groups on consumer preferences. *J. Consum. Psychol.* 16(4):404–14

White K, Simpson B. 2013. When do (and don't) normative appeals influence sustainable consumer behaviors? *J. Mark.* 77(2):78–95

Yoeli E, Hoffman M, Rand DG, Nowak MA. 2013. Powering up with indirect reciprocity in a large-scale field experiment. *PNAS* 110(Suppl. 2):10424–29

Developmental Origins of Chronic Physical Aggression: A Bio-Psycho-Social Model for the Next Generation of Preventive Interventions

Richard E. Tremblay,[1] Frank Vitaro,[2] and Sylvana M. Côté[3,4]

[1]Department of Pediatrics and Department of Psychology, University of Montreal, Montreal QC H3T 1J4, Canada; email: richard.ernest.tremblay@umontreal.ca

[2]School of Psychoeducation, University of Montreal, Montreal QC H3T 1J4, Canada; email: frank.vitaro@umontreal.ca

[3]Department of Social and Preventive Medicine, University of Montreal, Montreal QC H3T 1J4, Canada; email: sylvana.cote.1@umontreal.ca

[4]INSERM U1219, University of Bordeaux, 33400 Talence, France

Annu. Rev. Psychol. 2018. 69:383–407

First published as a Review in Advance on October 16, 2017

The *Annual Review of Psychology* is online at psych.annualreviews.org

https://doi.org/10.1146/annurev-psych-010416-044030

Keywords

physical aggression, development, prevention, genetics, epigenetics, intergenerational

Abstract

This review describes a bio-psycho-social approach to understanding and preventing the development of chronic physical aggression. The debate on the developmental origins of aggression has historically opposed genetic and environmental mechanisms. Recent studies have shown that the frequency of physical aggression peaks in early childhood and then decreases until old age. Molecular genetic studies and twin studies have confirmed important genetic influences. However, recent epigenetic studies have highlighted the important role of environments in gene expression and brain development. These studies suggest that interrelated bio-psycho-social channels involved in the development of chronic physical aggression are generally the product of an intergenerational transmission process occurring through assortative mating, genetic inheritance, and the inheritance of physical and social environmental conditions that handicap brain functioning and support the use of physical aggression to solve problems. Given these intergenerational mechanisms and physical aggression onset in infancy, it appears clear that preventive interventions should start early in pregnancy, at the latest.

Contents

1. INTRODUCTION

The study of physical aggression among humans includes a very large spectrum of topics, from the study of wars between countries to that of biting among toddlers in childcare centers. The causes and consequences of physical aggression among humans and animals are studied by a wide variety of specialists, such as anthropologists, biologists, criminologists, ethologists, historians, psychologists, neurologists, philosophers, psychiatrists, and surgeons.

2. THE LONG-STANDING NATURE–NURTURE DEBATE

The focus of this review is recent research into the developmental origins of chronic physical aggression by humans. However, to understand recent research questions and answers in a given research area, it is always useful to keep in mind its long-term history.

As illustrated by the story of Cain and Abel in the Bible, the topic of aggression among humans is probably as old as humanity, and questions concerning the developmental origins of aggression were investigated by many philosophers from ancient Greece to modern times. Not surprisingly, one central issue over the centuries has been the nature–nurture origin of aggression. For example, Aristotle, in his book *Politics*, concluded that humans grow from irrational to rational behavior because "anger and will and desire are implanted in a child from their very birth, but reason and understanding develop as they grow older" (Aristotle 1943, p. 405). Some 800 years later, Augustin of Thagase and Hippo (Saint Augustine) played a major role in developing the idea of original sin based, in part, on his observations of young children's aggressive behavior [Augustine 1960 (397–401 AD)]. This line of reasoning was reiterated 1,200 years after Augustine by the British philosopher Thomas Hobbes. He noted, "Unless you give infants everything they want, they cry and get angry, they even beat their own parents," and concluded that aggressive adults were simply behaving like children [Hobbes 1998 (1647), p. 11]. However, a century later, Jean-Jacques Rousseau [1979 (1762), p. 5], one of the most influential philosophers of the Enlightenment and still a reference for many education specialists, strongly stated the nurture hypothesis in the first phrase of his famous book on the education of children: "God makes all things good; man meddles with them and they become evil." He also summarized the research agenda for many developmental psychologists, sociologists, and criminologists over the past century: "There is no original sin in the human heart, the how and why of the entrance of every vice can be traced" [Rousseau 1979 (1762), p. 56].

One of the best illustrations of the modern nature–nurture clash concerning the development of aggression is found in two books published approximately half a century ago. The first was *On Aggression* by the ethologist Konrad Lorenz (1966), originally written in German; the second was *Aggression: A Social Learning Perspective* by the psychologist Albert Bandura (1973). Lorenz's book was based on his observations of animal behavior and concluded that humans, like all other animals, inherited an aggressive instinct, which could lead to the destruction of humanity. Bandura's book was based on studies of children in a laboratory situation, where they were shown to spontaneously imitate an adult hitting a Bobo doll. Bandura, 200 years after Rousseau, reached a similar conclusion: "People are not born with preformed repertories of aggressive behaviors; they must learn them in one way or another" (Bandura 1973, p. 61). It is probably fair to say that most psychologists trained during the last 30 years of the twentieth century were convinced that humans learn to aggress from their environment, and most biologists trained during that period were convinced that humans, like other animals, instinctively use aggression.

To understand this long-standing philosophical and scientific debate, it is important to note that the term learn to aggress is used here to mean that, if a child never saw a human physically aggress another, this child would not be able to aggress even if he needed to do so to defend himself. The above quotations from Rousseau and Bandura appear to have that meaning. Those who argue that there is a genetic-instinctual basis to physical aggression generally do not deny that there are also learning components. It seems obvious that, for aggression, as for other physical skills that have a strong genetic-instinctual basis (eating, running, jumping, smelling, tasting, etc.), there is much that an individual must learn to use that skill effectively. This may be the reason why play fighting is common during the early development of cats, dogs, monkeys, and humans (Palagi et al. 2016, Parent & Meaney 2008).

At the end of the twentieth century, large-scale longitudinal studies were planned specifically to investigate the developmental mechanisms by which children learn to aggress from their environment. Many of these studies were driven partly by the hypothesis that children were becoming more aggressive because of violence on television (Eron et al. 1963, Huesmann et al. 1984). A few studies by psychologists during the 1930s had either observed young children's physical aggression (Murphy 1937) or questioned parents on their children's expression of anger (Goodenough 1931), but no studies had done long-term follow-ups from early childhood to adolescence to try to address the nature–nurture issue. In fact, to our knowledge, even biologists and psychologists who studied aggression in mammals, such as rats, mice, and primates, had not done developmental studies to unravel the developmental origins of aggression, probably because it appeared obvious to them that aggression is an adaptive mechanism needed for a species to survive, as it appeared obvious to social psychologists and sociologists that humans learn to aggress from their environment.

3. DEVELOPMENTAL TRAJECTORIES OF PHYSICAL AGGRESSION FROM EARLY CHILDHOOD TO OLD AGE

The first prospective longitudinal studies with yearly assessments of physical aggression from childhood to adolescence reported surprising results from a social learning perspective, especially regarding the negative influence of television violence on children's aggression (Eron et al. 1963, Huesmann et al. 1984). If observing physical aggression on television made children more physically violent, we would expect that children's physical aggression would increase with age because the exposure to violence on television increases with age. However, results from longitudinal studies in North Carolina (Cairns et al. 1989) and Canada (Nagin & Tremblay 1999) showed, surprisingly, a substantial decrease in the frequency of instances of physical aggression from school entry to adolescence. To rule out the hypothesis that one particular group of children were increasing their frequency of aggression with age whereas most others decreased their frequency of aggression, developmental trajectory analyses of the data were made to identify differences in developmental trajectories. Results showed that no significant group of children went from a low frequency of physical aggression during childhood to a high frequency during adolescence. Those who frequently aggressed in adolescence were those who frequently aggressed during childhood. These results from a Canadian longitudinal study were replicated with longitudinal studies in Italy, New Zealand, and the United States (e.g., Broidy et al. 2003, Di Giunta et al. 2010).

The developmental trajectories of physical aggression during elementary school years and adolescence suggest that, if children learn to aggress from their environment, then this must happen before school entry. Thus, longitudinal studies of physical aggression were initiated with birth cohorts. Results from these studies showed (see **Figure 1**) that physical aggression is often initiated during the first year of life (e.g., Hay et al. 2014, Naerde et al. 2014, Tremblay et al. 1999), substantially increases in frequency with physical growth up to 3–4 years of age, and then starts decreasing (Campbell et al. 2006, Côté et al. 2006, Dearing et al. 2015, Naerde et al. 2014).

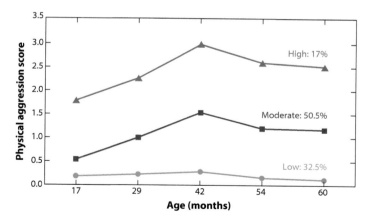

Figure 1

Developmental trajectories of physical aggression from 17 to 60 months old. Figure adapted with permission from Côté et al. (2007a).

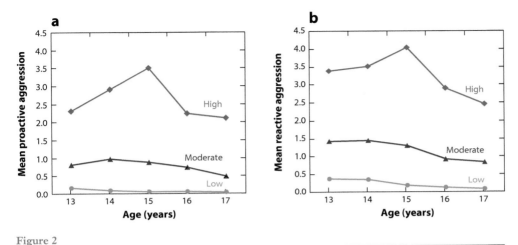

Figure 2

Trajectories of (*a*) proactive aggression and (*b*) reactive aggression from 13 to 17 years old.

These longitudinal studies of physical aggression during adolescence and early adulthood showed that the frequency of instances of physical aggression continues to decline with age for the majority of children. However, among the most physically aggressive individuals, there is often a slight increase during mid-adolescence, followed by a decline (Lacourse et al. 2002, van Lier et al. 2009; see **Figure 2**). Few studies have monitored the development of physical aggression from adolescence through adulthood with longitudinal studies. The best data comes from court records of a sample of male juvenile delinquents living in Boston in 1940 (Sampson & Laub 2003). The results showed a clear decline in arrests for violent crimes from early adulthood to old age. Similar results were obtained for physical aggression among couples from cross-sectional and short-term longitudinal studies (Bookwala et al. 2005, O'Leary & Woodin 2005, Suitor et al. 1990, Vickerman & Margolin 2008).

Thus, research on the development of physical aggression from infancy to old age indicates that (*a*) humans start to physically aggress before the end of their first year after birth, and (*b*) the frequency of physical aggression reaches a peak during the first 3–4 years after birth and then decreases until old age. A small group of individuals, mainly males, tend to use physical aggression more frequently than others throughout life, and they are more likely to increase the frequency of their physical aggression during mid-adolescence. Thus, from a learning perspective, one of the most important challenges for a young human is to learn not to physically aggress others.

4. BIO-PSYCHO-SOCIAL MECHANISMS THAT SUPPORT CHRONIC PHYSICAL AGGRESSION

To identify the mechanisms that support the developmental trajectories of physical aggression described above, we need studies that go beyond the mere description of these developmental trajectories. The fact that humans start to use physical aggression before they reach their first birthday suggests that they do not need to observe physical aggression by other humans to initiate physical aggression themselves. It also suggests that there is, indeed, a strong genetic-instinctual basis to human use of physical aggression. To understand the extent to which the different developmental trajectories of physical aggression are determined by genetic and environmental mechanisms, we need genetically informative research designs. However, to understand the bio-psycho-social mechanisms that are triggered by genes and by environments at different periods during development, we also need designs that assess the different developmental pathways from conception to adulthood. These pathways may include neurophysiological as well as psychological and social processes. As we discuss below, this will require hard work by future generations of scholars.

4.1. Studies of Sex Differences

It has long been common knowledge that human males use physical aggression more often than human females. Sexual dimorphism is, indeed, one of the most robust findings from studies on aggression (Daly & Wilson 1990, Quetelet 1833). Men are found to use aggression more than females when studies focus on direct forms of aggression (e.g., physical or verbal aggression) and when the target of the aggression is an individual not known to the perpetrator. Conversely, females are found to use aggression more often than males when studies focus on indirect forms of aggression (e.g., psychological or social aggression) and when the target of the aggression is an individual known to the perpetrator (Archer 2000, Archer & Côté 2005).

However, the developmental origins of these sex differences in aggression have been studied only recently with large population samples of children. For example, with a large sample of Canadian children from 2 to 8 years of age (Côté et al. 2007b), significant differences were observed in the proportions of boys and girls who followed the highest and the lowest developmental trajectories of physical aggression, based on parent reports (see **Figure 3**). More boys than girls (53.6% versus 46.4%) were on the high physical aggression trajectory, whereas more girls than boys (57.2% versus 42.7%) were on the low physical aggression trajectory. The reverse was observed for indirect aggression (e.g., when the individual is mad at someone, they get others to dislike that person): More girls than boys (57.6% versus 42.3%) were on a high indirect aggression trajectory. With another large population sample and a different statistical approach, Baillargeon et al. (2007) reported that 5% of 17-month-old boys used physical aggression on a frequent basis compared to 1% of girls the same age, and the magnitude of the difference was the same one year later. Finally, in a comparison of six large longitudinal studies from Canada, New Zealand, and the United States, Broidy et al. (2003) reported similar sex differences based on teacher reports from school entry to adolescence.

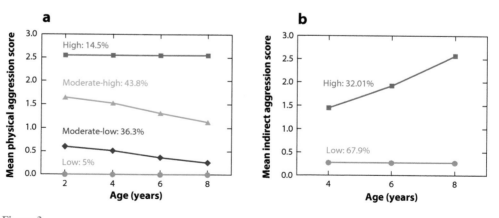

Figure 3

Developmental trajectories of (*a*) physical aggression between 2 and 8 years old and (*b*) indirect aggression between 4 and 8 years old. Figure adapted with permission from Côté et al. 2007b.

4.2. Twin Studies

One frequently used and genetically informative type of study involves comparing the frequency of aggressive behavior within and between pairs of monozygotic (MZ) and dizygotic (DZ) twins raised together. The basic logic behind these studies is that genetic mechanisms are likely to play an important role if MZ twins are more similar than DZ twins in their propensity to use physical aggression because MZ twins share the same genes, whereas DZ twins share only half of their genes, like non-twin brothers and sisters. Twin studies with elementary school children, adolescents, and adults have, indeed, shown that there is a relatively strong genetic component to the use of physical aggression (Brendgen et al. 2005, 2008; Burt 2009; Hicks et al. 2004; Rhee & Waldman 2002; Tuvblad et al. 2009). Not surprisingly, twin studies also indicate that genetic effects are probably mediated by brain development. For example, with a sample of twins in which continuity in proactive aggression (i.e., a type of predatory aggressive behavior) was shown to be influenced by genetic factors (Tuvblad et al. 2009), associations were found between the frequency of aggression, fear conditioning deficits (Gao et al. 2015), and a number of brain morphology characteristics related to the fronto-limbic-striatal circuit, such as cortical thickness in frontal regions (Yang et al. 2016).

To what extent are these genetic determinants of physical aggression active during early childhood? To address this question, a study of twins was initiated at birth and the frequency of physical aggressions was reported by parents at 20, 36, and 50 months (Dionne et al. 2003). At 20 months, the heritability of physical aggression was compared to the heritability of language development. Interestingly, the strength of the genetic influences on individual differences was higher for physical aggression (58%) than for expressive vocabulary (39%), whereas the strength of the shared environmental influence was high for expressive vocabulary (51%) but nil (0%) for physical aggression. Further analyses of the data on the development of physical aggression using the same twin sample indicated important genetic effects that changed over time (Lacourse et al. 2014). The contribution of genetic factors to the variance in frequency of physical aggression at 20 months was 60% and decreased to 50% at 50 months, whereas new genetic effects appeared at 36 and 50 months. Two separate sets of uncorrelated genetic factors accounted for the variation in initial level and growth rate. Results did not indicate any environmental effects (shared or nonshared) on the initial level of physical aggression (at 20 months) or on its stability and its growth rate from 20 to 50 months. Thus, during early childhood, when physical aggression is on the rise, genetic factors explain a substantial part of individual differences in the frequency of aggression (as seen in **Figure 1**). The fact that the genes involved appear to change on a yearly basis is not surprising considering that early childhood is a developmental period with accelerated growth of key instruments for the use and control of aggression, such as limbs and muscles, as well as neurological control over cognitive and emotional development.

Similar estimates of genetic effects were obtained from a larger longitudinal study with older twins (at 3, 7, and 10 years of age) using an assessment of aggressive behavior that was not limited to physical aggression (Hudziak et al. 2003). The developmental analyses from this study identified a similar dynamic process where genetic effects at 3 years old interacted with new genetic contributions at 7 years old. Interestingly, the important contribution of nonshared environmental factors was specific to a given age.

Although these two twin studies assessed different aspects of aggressive behavior (physical and nonphysical) by children from 20 months to 12 years old, they both support the hypothesis that the stability of aggressive behavior is influenced by both genetic and environmental factors from infancy to early adolescence. The larger study of children between 3 and 12 years of age had sufficient power to show that genetic effects were larger for boys and shared environmental effects were larger for girls. It remains to be tested if this is true specifically for physical aggression, but developmental analyses of physical aggression during early childhood have shown that girls learn more quickly than boys to use alternatives to physical aggression and to replace physical aggression with indirect aggression (Baillargeon et al. 2007, Côté et al. 2006, Hay et al. 2011).

4.3. Molecular Genetic Studies

Molecular genetic studies of animals and humans have identified numerous genes involved in aggressive behavior. For example, a recent comparison of three genetic mouse models (Malki et al. 2014) identified a network of 14 genes associated with aggression-related behavior. Another mouse study (Yu et al. 2014) identified periods during development when the brain is particularly sensitive to the effects of dopamine and serotonin on aggressive behavior. Research in humans has similarly shown that various genes involved in serotonin and dopamine metabolism, for example, the *monoamine oxidase A* (*MAOA*), *dopamine receptor 2* (*DRD2*), and *serotonin transporter* (*5-HTT* or *SLC6A4*) genes (Belsky & Pluess 2013, Caspi et al. 2002, Pavlov et al. 2012), are associated with aggression in both humans and other animals. However, the genes that play a role in the development of aggressive behavior are not the same at different developmental periods, as the twin studies summarized above indicated. For example, Pingault et al. (2013a) modeled the age-dependent contribution of the *MAOA* gene to the development of physical aggression between 6 and 12 years of age and found that its influence appears to emerge over time. Using the same sample assessed during late adolescence and early adulthood, Ouellet-Morin et al. (2016) showed that the genetic moderation of adverse family environment by the *MAOA* gene, with reference to aggression and other forms of antisocial behavior, may be active only at certain levels of family adversity and varies according to the different antisocial outcomes that are being assessed.

Thus, molecular genetic studies with animals and humans have shown that numerous brain-related genes play an important role in the developmental trajectories of aggression. However, the genes involved vary with age and interact with the environment in which the individuals live.

4.4. Environmental Effects on Gene Expression (Epigenetics)

The study of environmental impacts on gene expression (epigenetics) and human aggressive behavior began only a decade ago. The basic point to remember concerning genetic influences and epigenetics is that genes can be turned on and off by environmental events through chemical signals, and genes can have effects only if they are turned on (Szyf 2009). Thousands of studies have shown that environments can play important roles in the development of behaviors and diseases by programming gene expression at different points during development. The study that led us to use epigenetic research to understand the development of chronic physical aggression was a mouse study where frequency of maternal licking at birth was shown to have a long-term impact on the offspring's ability to cope with stress through DNA methylation of the *glucocorticoid receptor* gene (Weaver et al. 2004).

It will take a few years before we have data on human behavior development and epigenetics as good as those provided by the mouse studies (Meaney & Szyf 2005), but numerous studies have shown that the epigenetic mechanisms observed in the mouse model probably apply to humans from the prenatal period onwards. For example, a recent study showed associations between placental methylation and the newborn reactive–poorly regulated profile, a well-known neurobehavioral profile (Paquette et al. 2015).

One of the key advantages of epigenetic research is that it provides a tool to study intergenerational transmission of behavior and health problems. The basic hypothesis is that parents' behavior from conception onwards can impact offspring brain development, behavior, and health through its impact on the offspring's gene expression programming. This type of gene–environment interplay is well illustrated in the study of maternal mouse licking at birth, mentioned above. Parental behaviors in humans probably have epigenetic impacts on their offspring throughout development, and these epigenetic effects on brain development are likely to start early on during pregnancy (Glover 2011). One example of this mechanism is the putative impact of maternal mental health on offspring development. Numerous studies have shown associations between maternal mental health and children's behavior problems (e.g., Côté et al. 2007a, Herba et al. 2013). One of the underlying mechanisms of this link, besides genetic transmission, may be epigenetic impacts of maternal neuroendocrine functioning and behavior on offspring's brain development during pregnancy. For instance, Braithwaite et al. (2015) showed that maternal depression during pregnancy is associated with increased DNA methylation of 2-month-old male offspring's glucocorticoid receptor gene promotor region, which plays a critical role in the ability to respond to stress. Maternal depression during pregnancy was also associated with 2-month-old female and male brain-derived neurotrophic factor gene promotor, which plays an essential role in neurodevelopment.

The long-term epigenetic effects of maternal smoking during pregnancy are another good example of intergenerational effects of parental behavior on offspring's development. With a variety of research designs, researchers have associated smoking during pregnancy with many behavior problems in offspring, including chronic physical aggression during early childhood (Dolan et al. 2016, Gaysina et al. 2013, Huijbregts et al. 2008). In a UK longitudinal study of 800 newborn children (Richmond et al. 2015), epigenetic analyses of umbilical cord blood showed an association between maternal smoking during pregnancy and DNA methylation in seven gene regions. The duration and intensity of smoking during pregnancy also led to a dose-dependent response. The children were followed throughout development and blood samples were taken again at 7 and 17 years of age. The longitudinal analysis revealed that some methylation sites were persistently perturbed, whereas others showed reversibility. The investigators then focused on the methylation sites that were perturbed from birth to 17 years of age. Controlling for postnatal smoke exposure from mothers and fathers, they found that a critical window of exposure during pregnancy made the major contribution to the long-term perturbed DNA methylation sites.

The first epigenetic study on human chronic physical aggression (Provençal et al. 2013) compared DNA methylation in cytokines and their regulators in T cells and monocytes between Canadian boys who were on a chronic and a normal physical aggression trajectory from kindergarten to adolescence (Nagin & Tremblay 1999). Results provided evidence for an association between male physical aggression and differential DNA methylation in cytokines and their regulators in T cells and monocytes. A second study (Provençal et al. 2014), comparing the same two groups of boys (chronic aggression trajectory versus normal trajectory), used an epigenome-wide approach and identified 448 distinct gene promoters that were differentially methylated in the two groups. An identical study with females (Guillemin et al. 2014) showed that, for both males and females, the methylation of 31 gene promoters was associated with physical aggression.

Two further studies with the same sample of males focused on the association among chronic physical aggression, brain functioning, and DNA methylation. The first study (Booij et al. 2010) used positron emission tomography to compare brain serotonin synthesis in males on a high physical aggression trajectory with that of males on a low physical aggression trajectory. Results showed that males on the high-aggression trajectory had lower brain serotonin synthesis in the orbitofrontal cortex. The second study (Wang et al. 2012) hypothesized that this lower brain serotonin synthesis was associated with DNA methylation of critical genes in the serotonin pathway and detectable in peripheral white blood cells. Higher levels of methylation were, indeed, observed in T cells and monocytes for the high-aggression group, who also showed lower brain serotonin synthesis.

Finally, Checknita et al. (2015) examined the association between the serotonergic system's *MAOA promoter* gene methylation and antisocial behavior during adulthood. The males from Wang et al.'s (2012) study who were on the normal trajectory from childhood to adolescence were compared to prisoners with an antisocial personality diagnosis. Results showed that *MAOA promoter* gene hypermethylation was associated with the antisocial personality disorder diagnosis, supporting the hypothesis that this hypermethylation is the mechanism that explains why impulsive aggression and antisocial behavior are associated with serotonergic system dysregulation.

4.5. Environmental Effects on the Brain and Aggressive Behavior

The epigenetic studies described above have shown that the environment can impact the development of aggressive behavior through its impact on gene expression, which, in turn, impacts brain development and eventually behavior. But the impact of the environment on behavior can be directly mediated by the brain. The clearest studies come from observations of animal behavior because they enable a more extensive control of the environment and more precise measurements of brain functioning and behavior. A useful recent example is a rat study that tested the hypothesis that chronic passive exposure to aggressive behavior can lead to aggressive behavior in the individual exposed. Suzuki & Lucas (2015) randomly exposed 72 rats to aggressive behavior for either 1 day or 23 days. Results showed that those who were exposed for 23 days had reduced dopamine density in the bilateral nucleus accumbens shell and increased amygdaloid receptor densities (serotonin). These effects on brain functioning interacted to lead to high levels of aggression. Thus, being forced to observe physical aggressions for long periods of time has an impact on brain functioning (dopamine–serotonin interactions) that can lead to high levels of aggression. However, this does not mean that a newborn rat needs to observe aggression to learn to aggress. Aggression, like mating, is a goal-directed innate social behavior associated with brain-regulated emotions and motivations and that can be measured in mice and flies as well as humans (Anderson 2016).

Numerous studies of school-age children have shown that aggression is associated with characteristics of the social environment (e.g., Anderson et al. 2010, Huesmann et al. 2017). In a large population sample study of the earliest social environment, the family, results showed that the best predictors of a high physical aggression trajectory between 17 and 42 months old were the following: young siblings, mothers with high levels of antisocial behavior before the end of high school, mothers who started having children at an early age, mothers who smoked during pregnancy, mothers with coercive parenting behavior, families with low income, and dysfunctional families (Tremblay et al. 2004).

However, few social environmental studies of aggression control for genetic effects on physical aggression or on social environmental variables that are correlated with physical aggression. Studies of genetically identical (MZ) twins are one of the best research designs to control for genetic effects while testing for environmental effects in human children. With a longitudinal study of 223 MZ twin pairs in Canada, Vitaro et al. (2011) examined whether having an aggressive friend increases one's aggression. This was done by testing if the difference in aggression between members of an MZ twin pair increased from kindergarten to first grade when one member of a pair had the more highly aggressive friend in kindergarten than the other. Results for both boys and girls showed that within-pair differences in friends' aggression among pairs of MZ twins in kindergarten significantly predicted increased within-pair differences in aggression the following year (first grade). These results clearly show that children's use of aggression can be influenced through their close friendships even when we control for genetic effects. However, in a follow-up study that used the same sample of MZ twins and a similar control for genetic influences, Vitaro et al. (2016) found no effect of friends' aggression from middle childhood to early adolescence, possibly because older children, as compared to younger children, increasingly select their social environment in tune with their genetic dispositions (through a process known as a gene–environment correlation).

The same investigators also found that, although social experiences (such as friends' aggression) do not always predict changes in children's behavior, they may nevertheless operate to trigger the genetic liability for aggression. First, in two separate studies, they found that the genetic component associated with physical aggression was stronger when children had aggressive friends than when they had nonaggressive friends (Brendgen et al. 2008, van Lier et al. 2007). They also found that genetic influences were moderated by social experiences at the group level, such as classroom norms toward aggression. As expected, results confirmed that genetic factors did influence children's aggressive behavior, but that the genetic effects on aggression were attenuated or exacerbated depending on whether classroom norms were unfavorable or favorable to aggression, respectively, thus confirming that peer group norms impact genetic effects (Brendgen et al. 2013, Vitaro et al. 2015).

These peer group effects on the development of children's aggressive or antisocial behavior have been hotly debated as childcare has become a norm in Western societies (e.g., Belsky & Steinberg 1978). Data from a US longitudinal study specifically designed to investigate the effects of childcare did show that children who attended childcare for long periods of time were more likely to be disruptive during their elementary school years (Belsky et al. 2007). However, other longitudinal studies that also followed large random samples of children until the end of elementary school did not find these negative impacts (e.g., Zachrisson et al. 2013). Indeed, one population-based longitudinal study in Canada found that early initiation of childcare for children of mothers with low education helped these children learn not to physically aggress between 17 and 60 months (Côté et al. 2007a). Another study with the same sample compared the development of physical aggression, opposition, shyness, and social withdrawal between 6 and 12 years of age for children who went to childcare and those who did not (home care). **Figure 4** shows that, during their kindergarten year (age 6 years), the children who had not been in childcare were rated by teachers as less physically aggressive and less oppositional than those who had been in childcare. However, the difference between the two groups for both physical aggression and opposition disappeared by the second year in school (age 7 years). It is important to note that the reverse phenomenon was observed for teacher ratings of shyness and withdrawal. These results highlight the fact that, throughout development, humans adapt their social behavior to social group norms, but that this process takes time.

As with the twin studies discussed above, this does not mean that the social behavior of the children is totally explained by the group norms. The genetic and environmental effects can be observed when the research design is appropriate. An interesting example of this is a molecular genetic study (Belsky & Pluess 2013) using the same data as the US childcare study by Belsky et al. (2007). Results showed that the *dopamine receptor D4* (*DRD4*) gene moderated the effect of childcare quality on teacher-reported social skills (e.g., "makes friends easily," "controls temper when arguing with other children," "asks permission before using someone else's property"), but only in kindergarten and first grade. Interestingly, this time period is exactly the same school entry period in which significant differences in social behavior were observed between children with and without childcare experience in the Canadian study described in **Figure 3** (Pingault et al. 2015). These results highlight the fact that longitudinal studies need to differentiate transition periods from stable social environment periods.

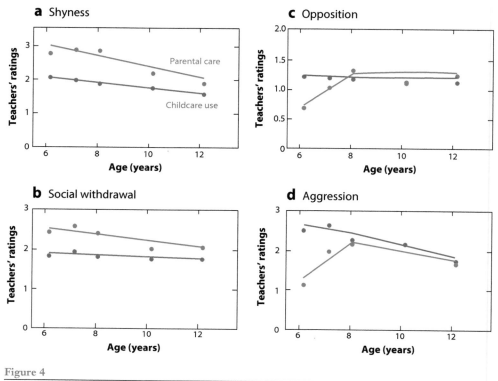

a Shyness

c Opposition

b Social withdrawal

d Aggression

Figure 4

Developmental trajectories of behavior problems from 6 to 12 years old according to early childcare use.
(*a*) Shyness. (*b*) Social withdrawal. (*c*) Opposition. (*d*) Aggression. Figure adapted with permission from
Pingault et al. (2015).

Finally, it is important to briefly mention a completely different and very recent line of research
on the interplay between the environment and the brain that has been labeled the gut-brain
hypotheses. The human gut microbiome is a bacterial environment shown to have important
impacts on the brain and on behavior. It has been linked to physical health problems but also
to anxiety, depression, alcoholism, and aggression. Recent studies with animals have shown that
the gut microbiome is important from the prenatal period to adulthood and that changing the
bacterial environment of the gut can have significant and sex-specific impacts on social behavior,
including aggression (e.g., Bailey & Coe 1999, Robertson et al. 2017, Sylvia et al. 2017).

4.6. Intergenerational Transmission: Numerous Interrelated
Bio-Psycho-Social Channels

Intergenerational research on antisocial behavior, especially on the bio-psycho-social mechanisms
involved, has been relatively limited. Longitudinal studies have shown that children of parents who
were convicted of criminal behavior are more at risk of being themselves convicted of criminal
behavior during adolescence and adulthood (see Farrington et al. 2017, Theobald et al. 2016).
Adoption studies have also shown that children of parents with a criminal history are less at risk
of criminal behavior when adopted by parents without a criminal record (Mednick et al. 1984). A
Canadian longitudinal study on the early development of chronic physical aggression highlighted
the fact that this association between the antisocial behavior of parents and that of children starts

very early in life (Tremblay et al. 2004). The study showed that maternal reports of antisocial behavior during their own adolescence predicted the chronic physical aggression of their child between 17 and 42 months old. This study further showed that the mothers of children who became chronically aggressive were, at the child's birth, more likely to be among the youngest and poorest, to be separated from the father, to have not completed high school, to have smoked during pregnancy, and to have had postpartum depression. This network of associations illustrates well the fact that the intergenerational transmission of behavior problems occurs through numerous interrelated bio-psycho-social channels. The child inherits a mix of their parent's genes, and their mother's smoking, stress, poverty, and depression during pregnancy impact the fetus' brain development through epigenetic mechanisms. From the postnatal period onwards, the physical and social environments created by a poor, young, depressed woman with low education, behavior problems, and coercive parenting in a dysfunctional family clearly fail to provide the care and education needed by the brain of a young child to learn to control their emotions and behavior. On the contrary, they may exacerbate further the expression of the child's genetic liability and contribute further epigenetic effects of their own.

However, the problems do not start with conception. We often forget that assortative mating (mating with someone who has similar characteristics) is one of the initial mechanisms that lead to the numerous interrelated bio-psycho-social channels that impact human development from pregnancy onwards. In a recent large (N = 707,263) population study in Sweden, Nordsletten et al. (2016) showed that there was more assortative mating for mental illnesses than for physical illnesses. The odds that a male with a psychiatric diagnosis had a mate with a psychiatric diagnosis was OR 2.24 (CI,2.21–2.27; P < 0.001), and the odds that a female with a psychiatric diagnosis had a mate with a diagnosis was OR 2.11(CI,2.08–2.14; P < 0.001). The correlation among mates in terms of diagnosis was 0.45 for attention deficit/hyperactivity disorder, which is strongly associated with chronic physical aggression from early childhood onwards (Carbonneau et al. 2016, Pingault et al. 2013b). It is important to emphasize that assortative mating brings together, for the reproduction of the next generation, mates that have similar histories, not only for physical and mental health problems but also for education, ability to self-control, and values on numerous crucial issues for children's development, such as nutrition, discipline, lifestyle, and respect for others (Domingue et al. 2014, Frisell et al. 2012, Grant et al. 2007, Kandler et al. 2012, Keller et al. 2013, Tognetti et al. 2014, Zietsch et al. 2011).

Figure 5 illustrates the complex network of interrelated genetic, epigenetic, neuropsychological, and social factors that are involved in the transmission of chronic physical aggression from one generation to another. This perspective is in line with the suggestion by the Nobel Prize winner and ethologist Nikolaas Tinbergen (1963) that behavior needs to be explained from four perspectives: the historical and survival value of the behavior in past generations as well as the development of the behavior within an individual's life and the proximal causal factors.

From the left to the right of **Figure 5**, we follow the intergenerational process with two lines of ancestors transmitting their genetic, economic, educational, cultural, health, and lifestyle characteristics to a male and a female who become parents of a child. The developmental changes in this child's DNA expression, brain, and behavior are shown to be determined by their intergenerational inheritance but also by the environments in which they will grow and interact. The uniqueness of this individual is largely determined by the genetic, economic, educational, cultural, health, and lifestyle characteristics they received from their ancestors through their parents but also by the unique environment in which they grow up.

To understand this complex process, it is useful to consider the developmental differences between MZ twins, DZ twins, and singleton siblings living with their parents or adopted by unrelated adults (e.g., Kendler et al. 2015, McAdams et al. 2015). Members of twin pairs, whether

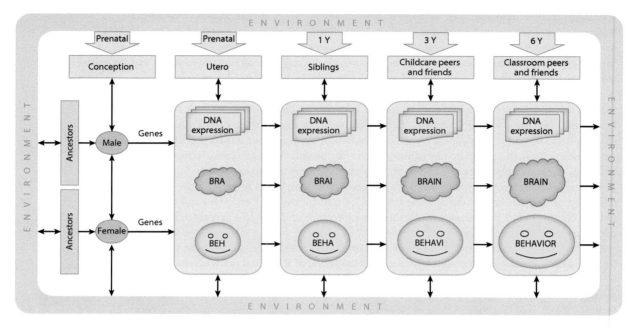

Figure 5

Network of interrelated intergenerational, genetic, epigenetic, neuropsychological, and social factors involved in the development of chronic physical aggression.

MZ or DZ, have the same ancestors and parents. When we consider DZ twins, we see that, with time, they become as different as ordinary siblings, but, because they share half of their genes, they become much more similar than adopted children living with the same parents. When we consider MZ twins, we see that, with time, they become much more similar than DZ twins and normal singleton siblings because they share the same genes. These comparisons highlight the power of genes. However, there is a limit to the power of genes, as can be seen from the fact that differences between MZ twins will increase with time because of the power of the environment, which impacts not only how they perceive the world and behave but also when their genes are expressed and, thus, how their brain functions and how they behave.

5. CAN CHRONIC PHYSICAL AGGRESSION BE PREVENTED?

Although understanding the development of physical aggression is, by itself, interesting, the aim of these studies is usually to provide information that will help prevent the development of chronic physical aggression problems and possibly reduce physical aggressions among humans. The numerous mechanisms involved in the development of chronic physical aggression described above suggest that we need to target many risk and protective factors. These include parents' behavior problems, family functioning, peer interactions, childcare, and school environments, as well as biological mechanisms related to brain functioning. However, one of the main findings of these studies is that humans start to use physical aggression during early childhood, and the children who are on a high physical aggression trajectory at that time are more likely to maintain higher frequencies of physical aggression into adulthood. This, of course, suggests that early childhood interventions are more likely to prevent chronic aggression problems than later interventions. This is clearly not a new idea. Erasmus [1529 (1985), p. 321] summarized it well in his essay on education: "We should be especially careful with our children during their first years. For at this stage their behavior is guided by instinct more than by reason, so that they are inclined equally to good and evil—more to the latter perhaps—and it is always easier to forget good habits than to unlearn bad ones." However, the idea that physical aggression and other antisocial behaviors are learned from the environment mainly during adolescence led both the Surgeon General of the United States (Surg. Gen. US 2001) and the World Health Organization (WHO 2002, p. 31) to conclude that violent behavior starts during adolescence and that these violent adolescents neither were highly aggressive during childhood nor had behavior problems during early childhood. The result of these beliefs is that most experiments to prevent aggressive or antisocial behaviors target preadolescents and adolescents. In this section, we focus on the few studies that have targeted young children, starting with interventions during pregnancy.

5.1. Prevention Initiated During Pregnancy

The best known experimental intervention targeting pregnant women at high risk of having children with chronic antisocial behavior is the Elmira project in the United States (Eckenrode et al. 2010, Olds et al. 1986). The pregnant women were young, unmarried, and poor. Nurses visited the women once a month between the twenty-fourth week of pregnancy and the child's second birthday, giving support to the mothers in three areas of their life: (*a*) personal development, including education, workforce integration, and family planning; (*b*) health-related behavior, including smoking prevention and adequate nutrition for the mother and child; and (*c*) competent care of the child and maternal sensitivity. The nurses also helped link mother and child with community services. Results showed that the intervention reduced child abuse and neglect and maternal delinquency (Olds et al. 1986, 2007) and showed, at the 19-year follow-up, a significant reduction of arrests for the female offspring (Eckenrode et al. 2010). The latter finding is an especially important and encouraging result because female offspring will become the mothers of the next generation.

A more recent pregnancy experiment was carried out in a poor neighborhood of Dublin, Ireland (Doyle & PFL Eval. Team 2016). The study randomly allocated 230 pregnant women to a high- and a low-support program. The high-support program included home visits up to school entry at 4 or 5 years of age and a parenting support program. Results after 5 years showed significant differences between the two groups of children in numerous developmental outcomes, such as overall cognitive development, language development, attention, hyperactivity, motor skills, social competence, autonomy, and amount of hospital services used from birth to school entry. Surprisingly, however, there were no significant impacts on children's aggression, oppositional defiance, anxiety, and prosocial and respectful behavior, as assessed by teachers. One would expect that, if the wide-ranging positive impacts are maintained in the long run, they will reduce the likelihood of aggressive antisocial behavior by favoring social acceptance from normative peers and improved academic performance.

5.2. Prevention Initiated During Early Childhood

Children's cognitive abilities and parents' disciplinary skills have been the focus of most prevention programs during the preschool period. Head Start programs for socially disadvantaged children aged 3–5 years in the United States were shown to improve academic success in the short term and to prevent arrests and court referrals in the long term (Garces et al. 2002). The best known of these programs is the High-Scope Perry Preschool project, which targeted African American children age 3–4 years with parents with a low IQ. The 2-year program included a daily preschool program aimed at increasing cognitive abilities and weekly home visits. Several long-term assessments up to age 40 showed that children who participated in the program were more likely to be employed, more likely to earn higher annual incomes, more likely to have graduated from high school, and less likely to have been arrested compared to the children who were part of the control group (Schweinhart et al. 1993). A study of the mechanisms that could explain these important long-term results concluded that the preschool program had impacts on the social skills of the children rather than on the targeted cognitive skills (Heckman et al. 2013).

Several parent training programs have been tested for preschool-aged children (e.g., Patterson 1982, Sanders et al. 2000). One of these programs for parents of preschoolers with behavior problems included components that also targeted the child and the teacher. A randomized control trial of its impact was made with a sample of 159 4- to 7-year-old children with oppositional defiant disorder (Webster-Stratton et al. 2001). The children were assigned to one of the following conditions: the parent program only; the child program only; the parent and teacher programs; the child and teacher programs; and the child, parent, and teacher programs. The five conditions were compared to a waiting-list control condition. At the end of a 6-month intervention period, children in the three conditions with the child program showed more prosocial skills with peers than the children in the control condition. No difference between treatment and control was observed for children in the two conditions without the child program. Similarly, parents in the three parent program conditions manifested less negative and more positive parenting and reported fewer child behavior problems than parents in the control condition and parents in the two conditions without parent training. Finally, children's behavior problems at school were reduced for those whose teacher participated in the teacher program relative to the control children. Overall, the conditions that included all three programs produced the best results after 6 months. At a 2-year follow-up, teachers reported an equal proportion of children with behavior problems across all five treatment conditions (i.e., around 50%). However, parents in the condition that included both the parent and teacher programs reported fewer cases of behaviorally disordered children relative to only one other condition, the parent-program-only condition, suggesting that more than one component may be necessary to achieve optimal results (see also Gardner et al. 2006). In an 8- to 12-year follow-up study of the children in the parent training condition, Webster-Stratton and her colleagues (2011) found that the majority maintained their postintervention progress, although one out of four reported major delinquent acts or had contact with the justice system.

5.3. Prevention Initiated During the Elementary School Period

Multitarget, multicomponent programs for preventing conduct problems in at-risk children have also been assessed during the elementary school years. For example, the Fast Track program (Conduct Probl. Prev. Res. Group 1992, 2004) had six components: (*a*) group parent training; (*b*) home visits; (*c*) group-based social skills training with the children; (*d*) peer-pairing, in which a target child and a no-risk peer participated in guided play sessions; (*e*) academic tutoring; and (*f*) teacher support. The program was implemented in four sites in the United States and targeted a large sample of children age 7 who scored above the ninetieth percentile on the aggressive–disruptive scale of the Child Behavior Checklist. The program was initially set to last until the end of elementary school but was eventually extended to tenth grade. After the first three years, the evaluation results were, at best, moderate, with effect sizes varying between 0.2 and 0.5 on teacher ratings of disruptive behavior. After five years (by age 11 or fifth grade), 37% of the randomly assigned Fast Track children had no conduct problem dysfunction, compared to 27% of control children (Conduct Probl. Prev. Res. Group 2002). Evaluations in late adolescence showed that the children in the prevention group were significantly better off with respect to important outcomes, such as Diagnostic and Statistical Manual of Mental Disorders diagnoses for conduct disorder, criminal offenses, and interpersonal violence, compared to their counterparts in the control group, although the effect sizes remained moderate (Conduct Probl. Prev. Res. Group 2010). Finally, by age 25, 69% of the participants in the control group manifested at least one externalized, internalized, or substance-related problem, compared to 59% in the experimental group. Interestingly and importantly, mediation analyses showed that about one third of Fast Track's impact on later crime outcomes was accounted for by improvements in social and self-regulation skills during childhood (ages 6–11), such as prosocial behavior, emotion regulation, and problem solving (Sorensen et al. 2016).

A less intensive and shorter program was tested experimentally in Canada at approximately the same time and targeted kindergarten boys from schools in low socioeconomic areas who were among the most aggressive and hyperactive. The 2-year program (between 7 and 9 years of age) included a home-based parent training component and a school-based social-cognitive skills training component. Notably, the social-cognitive component was delivered at school in a small-group format that included one or two target boys and three or four prosocial peers. In comparison to the control group, boys who participated in the intervention were found to have less self-reported delinquency and substance use throughout adolescence (Castellanos-Ryan et al. 2013, Lacourse et al. 2002, Tremblay et al. 1995, Vitaro et al. 2001) and to have fewer criminal records by 24 years of age (Boisjoli et al. 2007). In addition, the intervention reduced property crime by age 28 but did not seem to impact violent crimes (Vitaro et al. 2013).

The experimental preventive interventions reviewed above show important short-, medium-, and long-term effects. But we must admit that we are far from having the impact we would like to have on the lives of these unfortunate children and parents that suffer from their behavior problems and create much suffering around them. How can we push forward to better understand the onset of these behavior problems and the means to change the life-course of these unfortunate people?

Long-term interventions that aim for long-term impacts will, of course, always appear to lag behind the advancement of knowledge when they are eventually published. For example, the preventive interventions described above did not include genetic, epigenetic, or brain imaging assessments because they were all initiated before the advancement of knowledge in these areas. We clearly need a new generation of preventive experiments that will make use of the recent knowledge on chronic aggression development to plan the interventions and to assess the long-term impacts. For example, to have significant long-term impacts, we will most likely need to tailor interventions with babies to their genetic, epigenetic, and neuroendocrine profiles, in the same way we tried to tailor the past interventions to the differences in behavior profiles and profiles of the family needs. We may also need to adopt a developmentally sensitive approach that includes the notion of stepwise continuous prevention for the extreme cases of individuals who do not revert to normative behavior during a given developmental period (Vitaro & Tremblay 2016). The next section gives examples of prevention experiments that would help achieve these aims.

5.4. Toward Integrated Bio-Psycho-Social Prevention Trials

We suggest that the intergenerational nature of physical and mental health problems highlighted above (**Figure 5**) is key in planning future prevention experiments and that this should lead to prevention experiments that start during early pregnancy at the latest. Parents who have had behavior problems carry with them pervasive high-risk environmental conditions (e.g., low education, low income, poor neighborhoods, and risky lifestyle choices such as use of tobacco, alcohol and drugs and unhealthy nutrition), which impact childhood and adulthood psychopathology through many interrelated channels, including impacts on the children's DNA methylation. Interventions that do not start close to conception could not impact the many causal pathways that are already present during fetal life. Bovet (1951) already suggested using this intergenerational perspective in the first World Health Organization report, which happened to be on juvenile delinquency. Epigenetic research has now provided access to one of the important mechanisms by which the intergenerational problems are transmitted. If brain development is compromised through epigenetic effects during pregnancy, and if the child's parents also lack self-control, then it is easy to understand that the child will lack the cognitive and environmental support needed to develop the self-control that is essential to learning effective alternatives to physical aggression.

From this perspective, mothers are likely to have the greatest impact on early gene expression because their lifestyle during pregnancy has direct biological impacts on the child's development. Epigenetic effects during pregnancy suggest that we need to fundamentally revisit our thinking concerning early prevention of chronic physical aggression because, although male children are much more severely affected, pregnant women need to be our prime target to prevent a new generation of males and females with chronic physical aggression and similar intergenerational physical and mental health problems. This epigenetic perspective suggests that successful prevention of many physical and mental health problems may be easier to achieve by ameliorating the pre- and early postnatal environment, rather than by chasing bad genes (Bernet et al. 2007, Gluckman et al. 2008) or trying to change individuals' environments once they clearly have physical or mental health problems. Finally, we emphasize the fact that mothers, fathers, and children should not be blamed for the genes and the environment they inherit at conception and onwards. These families need to receive intensive and long-lasting support to break the intergenerational cycle of chronic behavior problems.

Intergenerational prevention trials should be initiated by enrolling in longitudinal and experimental studies large samples of young primiparous pregnant women with low levels of education. Intensive preventive interventions should be randomly allocated, especially to pregnant women with a history of antisocial behavior problems and their spouses, specifically targeting their lifestyle during pregnancy (i.e., smoking, drinking, drugs, spousal abuse) and their parental care and family life from birth onwards. Judging by the results of past experiments with these families (Boisjoli et al. 2007, Conduct Probl. Prev. Res. Group, 2005, Doyle & PFL Eval. Team 2016, Eckenrode et al. 2010), it is likely that supportive interventions maintained until the children are young adults will have the strongest impacts. Data collection would include genetic and repeated epigenetic information on parents and children and parenting behavior, as well as brain imaging and cognitive, health, and behavior development of the children. Longitudinal and experimental studies such as these will assess the short- and long-term impacts of the preventive interventions, but they will also advance knowledge on the causal mechanisms involved in the development of problem behaviors. The identification of these mechanisms will, in turn, help researchers design the following generation of interventions.

We believe that we will substantially advance our understanding of the mechanisms that lead to chronic physical aggression if, in these longitudinal and experimental studies, we regularly monitor the changes in epigenetic profiles, brain structure, brain functioning, cognition, and language, as well as changes in social-emotional behavior from birth onwards. This monitoring should, of course, include the changes in the children's environmental factors, such as parenting practices, family functioning, peer relationships, and social environments.

6. CONCLUSIONS

The aim of this review was to describe a bio-psycho-social approach to understanding and preventing the development of chronic physical aggression. We first highlighted the fact that, from a long-term historical perspective, the debate on the developmental origins of aggression opposed those who supported a genetic mechanism (nature) to those who supported an environmental mechanism (nurture). We then presented recent longitudinal studies that show that human physical aggression starts at the end of the first year of life, reaches a peak in frequency before entry into kindergarten, and then decreases in frequency until old age. The appearance of physical aggression during the first year of life suggests that a human's very first acts of physical aggression are spontaneous reactions to anger (nature), rather than imitations of physical aggression in their environment (nurture). The very high frequency of physical aggression during early childhood and its decline throughout life also indicate that there are important brain maturation processes that are involved in the development of the ability to control physical aggression and that the environment plays an important role in learning alternatives to the use of physical aggression to solve problems. Molecular genetic studies with animals and humans, as well as twin studies, have confirmed important genetic influences on the use of physical aggression. However, more recently, epigenetic studies have highlighted the important role environments play, from conception onwards, in the expression of genes that impact brain development and behavior. From the present state of knowledge, we can conclude that the development of chronic physical aggression is generally influenced by genetic and environmental factors through numerous interrelated bio-psycho-social channels from conception onwards. The general mechanism that can be hypothesized from the recent bio-psycho-social studies is that the interrelated bio-psycho-social factors involved in the development of chronic physical aggression are generally the product of an intergenerational transmission process through assortative mating, genetic inheritance, and inheritance of physical and social environmental conditions that handicap brain development and support the tendency to use physical aggression as a means of solving problems.

Given these intergenerational mechanisms and the onset of physical aggression in infancy, it appears clear that preventive interventions should start early in pregnancy at the latest and continue throughout childhood and adolescence. In many cases, it may take more than one generation to break the intergenerational transmission. To our knowledge, no experimental preventive intervention with pregnant women has, to this day, specifically targeted risk for chronic physical aggression.

We suggest that the life-long beneficial impacts of preventive interventions with families of children at high risk of chronic physical aggression will be obtained only if intensive interventions are initiated early in pregnancy and maintained throughout the children's development. Based on results from previous studies (Eckenrode et al. 2010) and the key role of maternal health and lifestyle in brain development during fetal life and early childhood, we hypothesize that the effects of these very early preventive interventions will be greater for girls and that these effects will have a still greater impact on the next generation of boys and girls.

DISCLOSURE STATEMENT

The authors are not aware of any affiliations, memberships, funding, or financial holdings that might be perceived as affecting the objectivity of this review.

LITERATURE CITED

Anderson CA, Shibuya A, Ihori N, Swing EL, Bushman BJ, et al. 2010. Violent video game effects on aggression, empathy, and prosocial behavior in Eastern and Western countries: a meta-analytic review. *Psychol. Bull.* 136:151–73

Anderson DJ. 2016. Circuit modules linking internal states and social behaviour in flies and mice. *Nat. Rev. Neurosci.* 17:692–704

Archer J. 2000. Sex differences in aggression between heterosexual partners: a meta-analytic review. *Psychol. Bull.* 126:651–80

Archer J, Côté S. 2005. Sex differences in aggressive behavior: a developmental and evolutionary perspective. In *Developmental Origins of Aggression*, ed. RE Tremblay, WW Hartup, J Archer, pp. 425–43. New York: Guilford Press

Aristotle. 1943. Politics. In *Aristotle: On Man and the Universe*, transl. B Jowett. New York: Walter J Black Roslyn

Augustine. 1960 (397–401 AD). *Confessions*. New York: Doubleday

Bailey MT, Coe CL. 1999. Maternal separation disrupts the integrity of the intestinal microflora in infant rhesus monkeys. *Dev. Psychobiol.* 35:146–55

Baillargeon RH, Zoccolillo M, Keenan K, Côté S, Perusse D, et al. 2007. Gender differences in physical aggression: a prospective population-based survey of children before and after 2 years of age. *Dev. Psychol.* 43:13–26

Bandura A. 1973. *Aggression: A Social Learning Analysis*. New York: Holt

Belsky J, Pluess M. 2013. Genetic moderation of early child-care effects on social functioning across childhood: a developmental analysis. *Child Dev.* 84:1209–25

Belsky J, Steinberg LD. 1978. The effects of day care: a critical review. *Child Dev.* 49:929–49

Belsky J, Vandell DL, Burchinal M, Clarke-Stewart KA, McCartney K, et al. 2007. Are there long-term effects of early child care? *Child Dev.* 78:681–701

Bernet W, Vnencak-Jones CL, Farahany N, Montgomery SA. 2007. Bad nature, bad nurture, and testimony regarding MAOA and SLC6A4 genotyping at murder trials. *J. Forensic Sci.* 52:1362–71

Boisjoli R, Vitaro F, Lacourse E, Barker ED, Tremblay RE. 2007. Impact and clinical significance of a preventive intervention for disruptive boys: 15-year follow-up. *Br. J. Psychiatry* 191:415–19

Booij L, Tremblay RE, Leyton M, Séguin JR, Vitaro F, et al. 2010. Brain serotonin synthesis in adult males characterized by physical aggression during childhood: a 21-year longitudinal study. *PLOS ONE* 5:e11255

Bookwala J, Sobin J, Zdaniuk B. 2005. Gender and aggression in marital relationships: a life-span perspective. *Sex Roles* 52:797–806

Bovet L. 1951. *Psychiatric Aspects of Juvenile Delinquency*. Geneva: World Health Organ.

Braithwaite EC, Kundakovic M, Ramchandani PG, Murphy SE, Champagne FA. 2015. Maternal prenatal depressive symptoms predict infant NR3C1 1F and BDNF IV DNA methylation. *Epigenetics* 10:408–17

Brendgen M, Boivin M, Vitaro F, Bukowski WM, Dionne G, et al. 2008. Linkages between children's and their friends' social and physical aggression: evidence for a gene-environment interaction. *Child Dev.* 79:13–29

Brendgen M, Dionne G, Girard A, Boivin M, Vitaro F, et al. 2005. Examining genetic and environmental effects on social aggression: a study of 6-year-old twins. *Child Dev.* 76:930–46

Brendgen M, Girard A, Vitaro F, Dionne G, Boivin M. 2013. Do peer group norms moderate the expression of genetic risk for aggression? *J. Crim. Justice* 41:324–30

Broidy LM, Nagin DS, Tremblay RE, Bates JE, Brame B, et al. 2003. Developmental trajectories of childhood disruptive behaviors and adolescent delinquency: a six site, cross national study. *Dev. Psychol.* 39:222–45

Burt SA. 2009. Are there meaningful etiological differences within antisocial behavior? Results of a meta-analysis. *Clin. Psychol. Rev.* 29:163–78

Cairns RB, Cairns BD, Neckerman HJ, Ferguson LL, Gariépy JL. 1989. Growth and aggression: I. Childhood to early adolescence. *Dev. Psychol.* 25:320–30

Campbell SB, Spieker S, Burchinal M, Poe MD, NICHD Early Child Care Res. Netw. 2006. Trajectories of aggression from toddlerhood to age 9 predict academic and social functioning through age 12. *J. Child Psychol. Psychiatry* 47:791–800

Carbonneau R, Boivin M, Brendgen M, Nagin D, Tremblay RE. 2016. Comorbid development of disruptive behaviors from age $1^1/_2$ to 5 years in a population birth-cohort and association with school adjustment in first grade. *J. Abnorm. Child Psychol.* 44:677–90

Caspi A, McClay J, Moffitt TE, Mill J, Martin J, et al. 2002. Role of genotype in the cycle of violence in maltreated children. *Science* 297:851–54

Castellanos-Ryan N, Séguin JR, Vitaro F, Parent S, Tremblay RE. 2013. Impact of a 2-year multimodal intervention for disruptive 6-year-olds on substance use in adolescence: randomised controlled trial. *Br. J. Psychiatry* 203:188–95

Checknita D, Maussion G, Labonté B, Comai S, Tremblay RE, et al. 2015. Monoamine oxidase A gene promoter methylation and transcriptional downregulation in an offender population with antisocial personality disorder. *Br. J. Psychiatry* 206:216–22

Conduct Probl. Prev. Res. Group. 1992. A developmental and clinical model for the prevention of conduct disorder: the Fast Track program. *Dev. Psychopathol.* 4:509–27

Conduct Probl. Prev. Res. Group. 2002. Evaluation of the first 3 years of the Fast Track prevention trial with children at high risk for adolescent conduct problems. *J. Abnorm. Child Psychol.* 30:19–35

Conduct Probl. Prev. Res. Group. 2004. The effects of the Fast Track program on serious problem outcomes at the end of elementary school. *J. Clin. Child Adolesc. Psychol.* 33:650–61

Conduct Probl. Prev. Res. Group. 2005. *The Long-Term Prevention of Serious Conduct Disorder, Interpersonal Violence, and Violent Crime.* University Park, PA: Pa. State Univ.

Conduct Probl. Prev. Res. Group. 2010. The effects of a multiyear universal social-emotional learning program: the role of student and school characteristics. *J. Consult. Clin. Psychol.* 78:156–68

Côté SM, Boivin M, Nagin DS, Japel C, Xu Q, et al. 2007a. The role of maternal education and non-maternal care services in the prevention of children's physical aggression. *Arch. Gen. Psychiatry* 64:1305–12

Côté SM, Vaillancourt T, Barker ED, Nagin D, Tremblay RE. 2007b. The joint development of physical and indirect aggression: predictors of continuity and change during childhood. *Dev. Psychopathol.* 19:37–55

Côté SM, Vaillancourt T, LeBlanc JC, Nagin DS, Tremblay RE. 2006. The development of physical aggression from toddlerhood to pre-adolescence: a nation wide longitudinal study of Canadian children. *J. Abnorm. Child Psychol.* 34:71–85

Daly M, Wilson M. 1990. Killing the competition: female/female and male/male homicide. *Hum. Nat.* 1:81–107

Dearing E, Zachrisson HD, Naerde A. 2015. Age of entry into early childhood education and care as a predictor of aggression: faint and fading associations for young Norwegian children. *Psychol. Sci.* 26:1595–607

Di Giunta L, Pastorelli C, Eisenberg N, Gerbino M, Castellani V, et al. 2010. Developmental trajectories of physical aggression: prediction of overt and covert antisocial behaviors from self- and mothers' reports. *Eur. Child Adolesc. Psychiatry* 19:873–82

Dionne G, Tremblay RE, Boivin M, Laplante D, Pérusse D. 2003. Physical aggression and expressive vocabulary in 19-month-old twins. *Dev. Psychol.* 39:261–73

Dolan CV, Geels L, Vink JM, van Beijsterveldt CEM, Neale MC, et al. 2016. Testing causal effects of maternal smoking during pregnancy on offspring's externalizing and internalizing behavior. *Behav. Genet.* 46:378–88

Domingue BW, Fletcher J, Conley D, Boardman JD. 2014. Genetic and educational assortative mating among US adults. *PNAS* 111:7996–8000

Doyle O, PFL Eval. Team. 2016. *Preparing for Life early childhood intervention final report: Did Preparing for Life improve children's school readiness?* Work. Pap., Geary Inst., Univ. Coll. Dublin

Eckenrode J, Campa M, Luckey DW, Henderson CR, Cole R, et al. 2010. Long-term effects of prenatal and infancy nurse home visitation on the life course of youths: 19-year follow-up of a randomized trial. *Arch. Pediatr. Adolesc. Med.* 164:9–15

Erasmus of Rotterdam. 1529 (1985). A declamation on the subject of early liberal education for children. In *Collected Works of Erasmus: Literary and Educational Writings*, ed. GK Sowards, pp. 297–346. Toronto: Univ. Toronto Press

Eron LD, Walder LO, Toigo R, Lefkowitz MM. 1963. Social class, parental punishment for aggression, and child aggression. *Child Dev.* 34:849–67

Farrington DP, Ttofi MM, Crago RV. 2017. Intergenerational transmission of convictions for different types of offenses. *Vict. Offenders* 12:1–20

Frisell T, Pawitan Y, Langstrom N, Lichtenstein P. 2012. Heritability, assortative mating and gender differences in violent crime: results from a total population sample using twin, adoption, and sibling models. *Behav. Genet.* 42:3–18

Gao Y, Tuvblad C, Schell A, Baker L, Raine A. 2015. Skin conductance fear conditioning impairments and aggression: a longitudinal study. *Psychophysiology* 52:288–95

Garces E, Thomas D, Currie J. 2002. Longer-term effects of Head Start. *Am. Econ. Rev.* 92:999–1012

Gardner F, Burton J, Klimes I. 2006. Randomised controlled trial of a parenting intervention in the voluntary sector for reducing child conduct problems: outcomes and mechanisms of change. *J. Child Psychol. Psychiatry* 47:1123–32

Gaysina D, Fergusson DM, Leve LD, Horwood J, Reiss D, et al. 2013. Maternal smoking during pregnancy and offspring conduct problems: evidence from 3 independent genetically-sensitive research designs. *JAMA Psychiatry* 70:956–63

Glover V. 2011. Prenatal stress and the origins of psychopathology: an evolutionary perspective. *J. Child Psychol. Psychiatry* 52:356–67

Gluckman PD, Hanson MA, Cooper C, Thornburg KL. 2008. Effect of in utero and early-life conditions on adult health and disease. *N. Engl. J. Med.* 359:61–73

Goodenough FL. 1931. *Anger in Young Children*. Westport, CT: Greenwood Press

Grant JD, Heath AC, Bucholz KK, Madden PAF, Agrawal A, et al. 2007. Spousal concordance for alcohol dependence: evidence for assortative mating or spousal interaction effects? *Alcohol. Clin. Exp. Res.* 31:717–28

Guillemin C, Provençal N, Suderman M, Côté SM, Vitaro F, et al. 2014. DNA methylation signature of childhood chronic physical aggression in T cells of both men and women. *PLOS ONE* 9:e86822

Hay DF, Nash A, Caplan M, Swartzentruber J, Ishikawa F, et al. 2011. The emergence of gender differences in physical aggression in the context of conflict between young peers. *Br. J. Dev. Psychol.* 29:158–75

Hay DF, Waters CS, Perra O, Swift N, Kairis V, et al. 2014. Precursors to aggression are evident by 6 months of age. *Dev. Sci.* 17:471–80

Heckman J, Pinto R, Savelyev P. 2013. Understanding the mechanisms through which an influential early childhood program boosted adult outcomes. *Am. Econ. Rev.* 103:2052–86

Herba CM, Tremblay RE, Boivin M, Liu XC, Mongeau C, et al. 2013. Maternal depressive symptoms and children's emotional problems: Can early child care help children of depressed mothers? *JAMA Psychiatry* 70:830–38

Hicks BM, Krueger RF, Iacono WG, McGue M, Patrick CJ. 2004. Family transmission and heritability of externalizing disorders: a twin-family study. *Arch. Gen. Psychiatry* 61:922–28

Hobbes T. 1998 (1647). *On the Citizen*. New York: Cambridge Univ. Press

Hudziak JJ, van Beijsterveldt CEM, Bartels M, Rietveld MJH, Rettew DC, et al. 2003. Individual differences in aggression: genetic analyses by age, gender, and informant in 3-, 7-, and 10-year-old Dutch twins. *Behav. Genet.* 33:575–89

Huesmann LR, Dubow EF, Boxer P, Landau SF, Gvirsman SD, et al. 2017. Children's exposure to violent political conflict stimulates aggression at peers by increasing emotional distress, aggressive script rehearsal, and normative beliefs favoring aggression. *Dev. Psychopathol.* 29:39–50

Huesmann LR, Lagerspetz K, Eron LD. 1984. Intervening variables in the TV violence–aggression relation: evidence from two countries. *Dev. Psychol.* 20:746–75

Huijbregts SCJ, Séguin JR, Zoccolillo M, Boivin M, Tremblay RE. 2008. Maternal prenatal smoking, parental antisocial behavior, and early childhood physical aggression. *Dev. Psychopathol.* 20:437–53

Kandler C, Bleidorn W, Riemann R. 2012. Left or right? Sources of political orientation: the roles of genetic factors, cultural transmission, assortative mating, and personality. *J. Personal. Soc. Psychol.* 102:633–45

Keller MC, Garver-Apgar CE, Wright MJ, Martin NG, Corley RP, et al. 2013. The genetic correlation between height and IQ: shared genes or assortative mating? *PLOS Genet.* 9:e1003451

Kendler KS, Turkheimer E, Ohlsson H, Sundquist J, Sundquist K. 2015. Family environment and the malleability of cognitive ability: a Swedish national home-reared and adopted-away cosibling control study. *PNAS* 112:4612–17

Lacourse E, Boivin M, Brendgen M, Petitclerc A, Girard A, et al. 2014. A longitudinal twin study of physical aggression in early childhood: evidence for a developmentally dynamic genome. *Psychol. Med.* 44:2617–27

Lacourse E, Côté S, Nagin DS, Vitaro F, Brendgen M, et al. 2002. A longitudinal-experimental approach to testing theories of antisocial behavior development. *Dev. Psychopathol.* 14:909–24

Lorenz K. 1966. *On Aggression*. New York: Harcourt Brace World

Malki K, Pain O, Du Rietz E, Tosto MG, Paya-Cano J, et al. 2014. Genes and gene networks implicated in aggression related behaviour. *Neurogenetics* 15:255–66

McAdams TA, Rijsdijk FV, Neiderhiser JM, Narusyte J, Shaw DS, et al. 2015. The relationship between parental depressive symptoms and offspring psychopathology: evidence from a children-of-twins study and an adoption study. *Psychol. Med.* 45:2583–94

Meaney MJ, Szyf M. 2005. Environmental programming of stress responses through DNA methylation: life at the interface between a dynamic environment and a fixed genome. *Dialogues Clin. Neurosci.* 7:103–23

Mednick SA, Gabrielli WF Jr., Hutchings B. 1984. Genetic influences in criminal convictions: evidence from an adoption cohort. *Science* 224:891–94

Murphy LB. 1937. *Social Behavior and Child Personality*. New York: Columbia Univ. Press

Naerde A, Ogden T, Janson H, Zachrisson HD. 2014. Normative development of physical aggression from 8 to 26 months. *Dev. Psychol.* 50:1710–20

Nagin D, Tremblay RE. 1999. Trajectories of boys' physical aggression, opposition, and hyperactivity on the path to physically violent and nonviolent juvenile delinquency. *Child Dev.* 70:1181–96

Nordsletten AE, Larsson H, Crowley JJ, Almqvist C, Lichtenstein P, et al. 2016. Patterns of nonrandom mating within and across 11 major psychiatric disorders. *JAMA Psychiatry* 73:354–61

Olds D, Henderson CR, Chamberlin R, Talelbaum R. 1986. Preventing child abuse and neglect: a randomized trial of nurse home visitation. *Pediatrics* 78:65–78

Olds DL, Sadler L, Kitzman H. 2007. Programs for parents of infants and toddlers: recent evidence from randomized trials. *J. Child Psychol. Psychiatry* 48:355–91

O'Leary KD, Woodin EM. 2005. Partner aggression and problem drinking across the lifespan: How much do they decline? *Clin. Psychol. Rev.* 25:877–94

Ouellet-Morin I, Côté SM, Vitaro F, Hébert M, Carbonneau R, et al. 2016. Effects of the MAOA gene and levels of exposure to violence on antisocial outcomes. *Br. J. Psychiatry* 208:42–48

Palagi E, Burghardt GM, Smuts B, Cordoni G, Dall'Olio S, et al. 2016. Rough-and-tumble play as a window on animal communication. *Biol. Rev.* 91:311–27

Paquette AG, Lester BM, Lesseur C, Armstrong DA, Guerin DJ, et al. 2015. Placental epigenetic patterning of glucocorticoid response genes is associated with infant neurodevelopment. *Epigenomics* 7:767–79

Parent CI, Meaney MJ. 2008. The influence of natural variations in maternal care on play fighting in the rat. *Dev. Psychobiol.* 50:767–76

Patterson GR. 1982. *A Social Learning Approach to Family Intervention*, Volume 3: *Coercive Family Process*. Eugene, OR: Castalia

Pavlov KA, Chistiakov DA, Chekhonin VP. 2012. Genetic determinants of aggression and impulsivity in humans. *J. Appl. Genet.* 53:61–82

Pingault J-B, Côté SM, Booij L, Ouellet-Morin I, Castellanos-Ryan N, et al. 2013a. Age-dependent effect of the MAOA gene on childhood physical aggression. *Mol. Psychiatry* 18:1151–52

Pingault J-B, Côté SM, Lacourse E, Galéra C, Vitaro F, et al. 2013b. Childhood hyperactivity, physical aggression and criminality: a 19-year prospective population-based study. *PLOS ONE* 8:1–7

Pingault J-B, Tremblay RE, Vitaro F, Japel C, Boivin M, et al. 2015. Early nonparental care and social behavior in elementary school: support for a social group adaptation hypothesis. *Child Dev.* 86:1469–88

Provençal N, Suderman MJ, Caramaschi D, Wang DS, Hallett M, et al. 2013. Differential DNA methylation regions in cytokine and transcription factor genomic loci associate with childhood physical aggression. *PLOS ONE* 8:e71691

Provençal N, Suderman MJ, Guillemin C, Vitaro F, Côté SM, et al. 2014. Association of childhood chronic physical aggression with a DNA methylation signature in adult human T cells. *PLOS ONE* 9:e89839

Quetelet A. 1833. *Research on the Propensity for Crime at Different Ages*. Brussels: M. Hayez

Rhee SH, Waldman ID. 2002. Genetic and environmental influences on antisocial behavior: a meta-analysis of twin and adoption studies. *Psychol. Bull.* 128:490–529

Richmond RC, Simpkin AJ, Woodward G, Gaunt TR, Lyttleton O, et al. 2015. Prenatal exposure to maternal smoking and offspring DNA methylation across the lifecourse: findings from the Avon Longitudinal Study of Parents and Children (ALSPAC). *Hum. Mol. Genet.* 24:2201–17

Robertson RC, Seira Oriach C, Murphy K, Moloney GM, Cryan JF, et al. 2017. Omega-3 polyunsaturated fatty acids critically regulate behaviour and gut microbiota development in adolescence and adulthood. *Brain Behav. Immun.* 59:21–37

Rousseau J-J. 1979 (1762). *Emile or On Education.* New York: Basic Books

Sampson RJ, Laub JH. 2003. Life-course desisters? Trajectories of crime among delinquent boys followed to age 70. *Criminology* 41:555–92

Sanders MR, Markie-Dadds C, Tully LA, Bor W. 2000. The Triple P-positive parenting program: a comparison of enhanced, standard, and self-directed behavioral family intervention for parents of children with early onset conduct problems. *J. Consult. Clin. Psychol.* 68:624–40

Schweinhart LL, Barnes HV, Weikart DP. 1993. *Significant Benefits: The High/Scope Perry School Study Through Age 27.* Ypsilanti, MI: High/Scope Press

Sorensen LC, Dodge KA, Conduct Probl. Prev. Res. Group. 2016. How does the Fast Track intervention prevent adverse outcomes in young adulthood? *Child Dev.* 87:429–45

Suitor JJ, Pillemer K, Straus MA. 1990. Marital violence in a life course perspective. In *Physical Violence in American Families: Risk Factors and Adaptations to Violence in 8,145 Families,* ed. MA Straus, RJ Gelles, pp. 305–17. New Brunswick, NJ: Transaction

Surg. Gen. US. 2001. *Youth Violence: A Report of the Surgeon General.* Washington, DC: Health Hum. Serv.

Suzuki H, Lucas LR. 2015. Neurochemical correlates of accumbal dopamine D-2 and amygdaloid 5-HT1B receptor densities on observational learning of aggression. *Cogn. Affect. Behav. Neurosci.* 15:460–74. Erratum. 2015. *Cogn. Affect. Behav. Neurosci.* 15:721

Sylvia KE, Jewell CP, Rendon NM, St John EA, Demas GE. 2017. Sex-specific modulation of the gut microbiome and behavior in Siberian hamsters. *Brain Behav. Immun.* 60:51–62

Szyf M. 2009. Implications of a life-long dynamic epigenome. *Epigenomics* 1:9–12

Theobald D, Farrington DP, Ttofi MM, Crago RV. 2016. Risk factors for dating violence versus cohabiting violence: results from the third generation of the Cambridge Study in Delinquent Development. *Crim. Behav. Mental Health* 26:229–39

Tinbergen N. 1963. On aims and methods of ethology. *Z. Tierpsychol.* 20:410–33

Tognetti A, Berticat C, Raymond M, Faurie C. 2014. Assortative mating based on cooperativeness and generosity. *J. Evol. Biol.* 27:975–81

Tremblay RE, Japel C, Pérusse D, McDuff P, Boivin M, et al. 1999. The search for the age of "onset" of physical aggression: Rousseau and Bandura revisited. *Crim. Behav. Mental Health* 9:8–23

Tremblay RE, Nagin D, Séguin JR, Zoccolillo M, Zelazo PD, et al. 2004. Physical aggression during early childhood: trajectories and predictors. *Pediatrics* 114:e43–50

Tremblay RE, Pagani-Kurtz L, Mâsse LC, Vitaro F, Pihl RO. 1995. A bimodal preventive intervention for disruptive kindergarten boys: its impact through mid-adolescence. *J. Consult. Clin. Psychol.* 63:560–68

Tuvblad C, Raine A, Zheng M, Baker LA. 2009. Genetic and environmental stability differs in reactive and proactive aggression. *Aggress. Behav.* 35:437–52

van Lier P, Boivin M, Dionne G, Vitaro F, Brendgen M, et al. 2007. Kindergarten children's genetic vulnerabilities interact with friends' aggression to promote children's own aggression. *J. Am. Acad. Child Adolesc. Psychiatry* 46:1080–87

van Lier PAC, Vitaro F, Barker ED, Koot HM, Tremblay RE. 2009. Developmental links between trajectories of physical violence, vandalism, theft, and alcohol-drug use from childhood to adolescence. *J. Abnorm. Child Psychol.* 37:481–92

Vickerman KA, Margolin G. 2008. Trajectories of physical and emotional marital aggression in midlife couples. *Violence Vict.* 23:18–34

Vitaro F, Brendgen M, Boivin M, Cantin S, Dionne G, et al. 2011. A monozygotic twin difference study of friends' aggression and children's adjustment problems. *Child Dev.* 82:617–32

Vitaro F, Brendgen M, Giguère C-É, Tremblay RE. 2013. Early prevention of life-course personal and property violence: a 19-year follow-up of the Montreal Longitudinal-Experimental Study (MLES). *J. Exp. Criminol.* 9:411–27

Vitaro F, Brendgen M, Girard A, Boivin M, Dionne G, et al. 2015. The expression of genetic risk for aggressive and non-aggressive antisocial behavior is moderated by peer group norms. *J. Youth Adolesc.* 44:1379–95

Vitaro F, Brendgen M, Girard A, Dionne G, Tremblay RE, et al. 2016. Links between friends' physical aggression and adolescents' physical aggression: What happens if gene-environment correlations are controlled? *Int. J. Behav. Dev.* 40:234–42

Vitaro F, Brendgen M, Tremblay RE. 2001. Preventive intervention: assessing its effects on the trajectories of delinquency and testing for mediational processes. *Appl. Dev. Sci.* 5:201–13

Vitaro F, Tremblay RE. 2016. Developmental targeted prevention of conduct disorder and their related consequences. In *Oxford Research Encyclopedias: Criminology and Criminal Justice*, ed. H Pontell, pp. 3–28. Oxford, UK: Oxford Univ. Press

Wang D, Szyf M, Benkelfat C, Provençal N, Caramaschi D, et al. 2012. Peripheral SLC6A4 DNA methylation is associated with in vivo measures of human brain serotonin synthesis and childhood physical aggression. *PLOS ONE* 7:e39501

Weaver ICG, Cervoni N, Champagne FA, D'Alessio AC, Sharma S, et al. 2004. Epigenetic programming by maternal behavior. *Nat. Neurosci.* 7:847–54

Webster-Stratton C, Mihalic S, Fagan A, Arnold D, Taylor T, et al. 2001. *Blueprints for Violence Prevention*, Volume 11: *The Incredible Years: Parent, Teacher, and Child Training Series*. Boulder, CO: Cent. Study Prev. Violence

Webster-Stratton C, Rinaldi J, Reid JM. 2011. Long-term outcomes of Incredible Years parenting program: predictors of adolescent adjustment. *Child Adolesc. Mental Health* 16:38–46

WHO (World Health Organ.). 2002. *World Report on Violence and Health*. Geneva: WHO

Yang Y, Joshi SH, Jahanshad N, Thompson PM, Baker LA. 2016. Neural correlates of proactive and reactive aggression in adolescent twins. *Aggress. Behav.* 43(3):230–40

Yu Q, Teixeira CM, Mahadevia D, Huang Y, Balsam D, et al. 2014. Dopamine and serotonin signaling during two sensitive developmental periods differentially impact adult aggressive and affective behaviors in mice. *Mol. Psychiatry* 19:688–98

Zachrisson HD, Dearing E, Lekhal R, Toppelberg CO. 2013. Little evidence that time in child care causes externalizing problems during early childhood in Norway. *Child Dev.* 84:1152–70

Zietsch BP, Verweij KJH, Heath AC, Martin NG. 2011. Variation in human mate choice: simultaneously investigating heritability, parental influence, sexual imprinting, and assortative mating. *Am. Nat.* 177:605–16

Improving Student Outcomes in Higher Education: The Science of Targeted Intervention

Judith M. Harackiewicz and Stacy J. Priniski

Department of Psychology, University of Wisconsin–Madison, Madison, Wisconsin 53706;
email: jmharack@wisc.edu, spriniski@wisc.edu

Annu. Rev. Psychol. 2018. 69:409–35

First published as a Review in Advance on
September 20, 2017

The *Annual Review of Psychology* is online at
psych.annualreviews.org

https://doi.org/10.1146/annurev-psych-122216-
011725

Keywords

intervention, achievement gaps, belonging, utility value, values affirmation

Abstract

Many theoretically based interventions have been developed over the past two decades to improve educational outcomes in higher education. Based in social-psychological and motivation theories, well-crafted interventions have proven remarkably effective because they target specific educational problems and the processes that underlie them. In this review, we evaluate the current state of the literature on targeted interventions in higher education with an eye to emerging theoretical and conceptual questions about intervention science. We review three types of interventions, which focus on the value students perceive in academic tasks, their framing of academic challenges, and their personal values, respectively. We consider interventions that (*a*) target academic outcomes (e.g., grades, major or career plans, course taking, retention) in higher education, as well as the pipeline to college, and (*b*) have been evaluated in at least two studies. Finally, we discuss implications for intervention science moving forward.

Contents

INTRODUCTION

Many theoretically based interventions have been developed over the past two decades to improve educational outcomes in higher education, and there has been great interest and excitement about the potential of these brief and cost-effective interventions to address important societal issues (Wilson 2011). Researchers have found that targeted interventions can have powerful and long-lasting effects when they address specific motivational processes at crucial time points in the educational process. Some have called these targeted interventions motivation interventions (Lazowski & Hulleman 2016) or social-psychological interventions (Wilson 2006, Yeager & Walton 2011), reflecting their theoretical grounding. Walton (2014) has referred to them as wise interventions because they are theoretically precise and address basic psychological processes that can interfere with optimal academic functioning. Indeed, these three labels all capture a critical feature of targeted interventions—a basis in theory that identifies the most powerful levers of change in academic settings. The theories that underlie these interventions take into account the context, the person, and person × context interactions to address real-world problems and are thus inherently social psychological. We refer to these social-psychological interventions as targeted because they target a specific problem, the psychological process underlying the problem, the students who should benefit from intervention, and the specific academic outcomes that should reveal those benefits.

Targeted interventions address specific educational problems, such as closing achievement gaps for underrepresented racial/ethnic minority (URM) students; promoting science, technology, engineering, and mathematics (STEM) career pursuit among women; increasing interest and engagement in gateway science courses; or helping first-year students cope with the college transition. With a well-defined problem, interventions can target the psychological processes most

Figure 1

Conceptual model of targeted interventions.

relevant to the problem. Students can struggle in college or lose motivation in fields of study for many reasons. They may lack a strong preparatory background for college or financial resources, and we would not expect social-psychological interventions to address these structural factors. However, students may also struggle for more psychological reasons: They may lack interest in certain topics and become disengaged in classes, or they may lack confidence in their abilities. They may experience identity threat in certain fields and wonder if an academic discipline is right for them, or they may doubt whether they belong in college. They may experience a cultural mismatch between institutional norms and their own values. All of these psychological processes are critical for academic outcomes, and all can be targeted by social-psychological interventions.

In addition to identifying the specific problem targeted by an intervention, it is important to consider the implications for measurement of academic outcomes. Some interventions focus on promoting motivation and performance in particular courses, where measures would thus be course specific, such as engagement, interest, and course grades. Others focus on promoting motivation in a field or broader domain, such as STEM fields or engineering, in which case the outcome measures would be field specific, such as course taking, retention in those fields, or interest in a discipline. Many interventions are even more general, targeting academic adjustment and performance in college, in which case the outcome measures would be college general, such as college adjustment and fit, overall grade point average (GPA), and graduation rate. The primary outcomes targeted by an intervention serve as a measure of intervention efficacy, but they can also trigger positive recursive processes that drive longer-term impacts. For example, if a student gets a good grade in a critical gateway science course, they may become more interested in the field, take more science courses, and eventually pursue a STEM career. **Figure 1** shows our conceptual model.

THREE TYPES OF INTERVENTIONS

In this review, we consider a wide range of targeted interventions that have been tested in higher education and distinguish between three types of intervention: those that focus on how students perceive value in academic tasks (task value interventions), those that change the way students frame academic challenges (framing interventions), and those that focus on students' personal values (personal values interventions). These interventions are all student-centered and share some core features: All convey some information hypothesized to affect a psychological process and engage the student in a process of active reflection that often involves conversation or writing. There are important differences, however, in their domain specificity and the behaviors, thought processes, and academic outcomes they target. In short, the primary difference is in where they focus students' attention and reflection.

Task value interventions focus on the task at hand, which can be defined as a specific topic in a class or a field of study, but the emphasis is always on academic content. These interventions communicate the value or importance of the content, either by providing examples of the relevance or usefulness of academic tasks for personal goals or by encouraging students to think about task value for themselves through writing exercises. For example, in a utility-value intervention (a type of task value intervention) implemented in a college biology class, students wrote about how course topics were relevant to their own lives or useful for themselves or others (Harackiewicz et al. 2016a). In a communal utility-value intervention, Brown et al. (2015) provided students with information about how biomedical research could address communal goals (helping others, working with others). Such task value interventions focus on how students perceive their coursework or fields of study, which can then be connected with personal goals through a process of reflection. Because of their task specificity, these interventions may be most relevant for stimulating engagement and performance in specific courses or promoting interest in particular fields.

Framing interventions focus on the challenges that students may face during academic transitions and help students cope with adversity by framing challenges as common and improvable. They include a broad range of interventions designed to address a variety of common concerns, such as doubts about belonging, doubts about ability, or group-specific challenges (e.g., coming to college as a URM student), by helping students adopt a more adaptive outlook or mindset. For example, Walton & Cohen's (2007) social belonging intervention provided statistics and quotes from more senior students illustrating the fact that challenges of adjustment to college are common and can be overcome. These interventions focus on influencing how students think about challenges, whereas task value interventions focus on the task at hand. Framing interventions may be most relevant for promoting adjustment during critical academic transitions, such as the transition to college, and for academic performance at a general level across courses or domains.

Personal values interventions focus on students' core values. Like framing interventions, these interventions center on the student, but they work more indirectly by reinforcing personal values rather than the academic tasks at hand. For example, in their seminal values affirmation intervention with middle school students, Cohen and colleagues (2006) asked students to choose their most important values from a list and then write about why those values were important to them. The same intervention has been used in college physics classes (Miyake et al. 2010). These values are broad (e.g., friends and family, independence, sense of humor), and writing about them reinforces a student's sense of identity and self-worth, providing a buffer against threats so that they can cope with adversity in college. As such, this may be the most general of the three types of intervention considered in this review, and personal values interventions may be particularly relevant for promoting academic adjustment and performance at a general level, across courses or domains and over time.

SCOPE OF REVIEW

In this review, we consider interventions that (*a*) target academic outcomes (e.g., grades, major or career plans, course taking, retention) in higher education, as well as the pipeline to college, and (*b*) have been evaluated in at least two studies.[1] Those that meet our criteria are summarized in **Tables 1–3**. Many of the interventions covered in this review have also been tested in middle school or high school contexts, but because we focus on interventions that target educational issues in college, we focus our review on experimental studies conducted in college and university settings

---

[1] Several other promising interventions have not (yet) been tested in multiple studies and are therefore not included: Acee & Weinstein's (2010) and Yeager and colleagues' (2014) task value interventions; Landau and colleagues' (2014), Jamieson and colleagues' (2016), and Browman & Destin's (2016) framing interventions; and Kizilcec and colleagues' (2017) intervention, which is a hybrid of task value and personal values interventions. In addition, two studies in our review also contain tests of interventions not (yet) tested in multiple studies: Yeager and colleagues' (2016) critical feedback and cultural fit interventions and Walton and colleagues' (2015) affirmation training intervention are not included in this review.

Table 1 Summary of task value interventions in higher education

Study	Problem	Context and sample	Intervention	Primary findings
Task value interventions				
Course specific				
Hulleman et al. (2010, study 2)[a]	Promoting engagement for low performers	One section of introductory psychology at a public university ($n = 318$)	**Utility value:** two writing assignments, completed as homework	Increased interest in the course and intention to major in psychology for students with low initial exam grades
Hulleman et al. (2017, study 2)[a]	Promoting engagement for low performers	Two sections of introductory psychology at a public university ($n = 357$)	**Utility value:** two writing assignments, completed as an online homework activity	Increased interest in the field of psychology and final exam performance for all students and particularly for students with low initial exam scores, especially men
Harackiewicz et al. (2016a)[b]	Racial and social class achievement gaps	Eight sections of introductory biology for STEM majors at a public university ($n = 1{,}040$)	**Utility value:** three writing assignments, completed as homework	Increased course performance for all students and particularly for first-generation underrepresented minority students, as well as students with low prior GPAs and students with high motivation to help others
Canning et al. (2018)[a]	Promoting persistence in STEM	Majority students in three sections of introductory biology for STEM majors at a public university ($n = 577$)	**Utility value:** one to three writing assignments, completed as homework	Increased course performance, enrollment in another biology course, and STEM major persistence
Field specific				
Brown et al. (2015, studies 1–3)	Promoting interest in biomedical research careers	Three laboratory studies with undergraduates from public universities ($n = 55, 140, 160$); studies 1 and 2 took place at a Hispanic-serving institution	**Utility value:** an article read by students describing how a faculty's biomedical research project could help others	Increased interest in pursuing a career in biomedical research
Harackiewicz et al. (2012) and Rozek et al. (2017)	Promoting STEM motivation	High school students and their parents from the longitudinal Wisconsin Study of Families and Work and a five-year follow-up ($n = 181$ families)	**Utility value:** two brochures and a website sent to parents in their teens' tenth- and eleventh-grade years, highlighting the usefulness of STEM courses and strategies for talking about STEM courses with their teens	Increased STEM course taking among the teens in high school, increased math and science scores on ACT college preparatory exam; indirectly increased college STEM course taking, career aspirations, and likelihood of declaring a STEM major in college through the high school STEM outcomes

[a]Measured a combination of course-specific, field-specific, and college-general outcomes.
[b]Tested interventions from two different categories.
Abbreviations: GPA, grade point average; STEM, science, technology, engineering, and mathematics.

and discuss studies from other contexts only if they were critical in the development of interventions tested in higher education contexts (e.g., Cohen et al. 2006, Hulleman & Harackiewicz 2009) or if the intervention was implemented in high school with a follow-up in college (e.g., Harackiewicz et al. 2012, Yeager et al. 2016).

The intervention studies we review are diverse. They range in scope from small-scale field studies, with interventions administered in labs or single classes, to large-scale field trials. Some interventions were integrated into classes, but others were administered outside of classes, in prematriculation activities, special orientation projects, or laboratory studies. We focus on the context and sample for the research, the educational problem targeted, the specific intervention tested, and the outcome measures assessed, examining whether targeted

Table 2 Summary of framing interventions in higher education

Study	Problem	Context and sample	Intervention	Primary findings
Framing interventions				
Field specific				
Walton et al. (2015)	Gender gap in engineering	First-year engineering students at a public university; activities were completed one on one or in small groups in engineering classrooms, as a research study ($n = 228$)	**Social belonging:** reading materials framing belonging concerns in the engineering program, saying-is-believing essay	Increased first-year engineering GPAs for women in male-dominated engineering majors
College general				
Wilson & Linville (1982, 1985)	Promoting performance for first-year students	Three laboratory studies with first-year undergraduates who reported being concerned about their first-semester grades ($n = 31; 37; 36$)	**Attributional reframing:** booklet and video framing GPA concerns, saying-is-believing essay	Increased overall GPAs in the semester after the intervention was implemented, especially for men
Walton & Cohen (2007, study 2; 2011)	Racial achievement gap	First-year students (second semester) at a selective private university, in a laboratory setting ($n = 37; 92$)	**Social belonging:** reading materials framing belonging concerns, saying-is-believing essay and video	Increased overall GPAs in the semester after the intervention was implemented (Walton & Cohen 2007) and through senior year (Walton & Cohen 2011) for African American students
Yeager et al. (2016, study 1)	Promoting persistence in college	High school seniors from five urban charter schools who had been admitted to two- or four-year colleges (primarily African American and FG students); activities completed online in high school computer labs in May of their senior year ($n = 584$)	**Social belonging:** reading materials framing belonging concerns, saying-is-believing essays **Mindset:** reading materials framing intelligence, saying-is-believing essays **Combined:** both interventions, received one week apart	Social belonging: increased percentage of students who stayed enrolled full-time through their first year of college Mindset: no effect Combined: increased college persistence to the same degree as social belonging alone

(Continued)

Table 2   (*Continued*)

Study	Problem	Context and sample	Intervention	Primary findings
College general				
Yeager et al. (2016, study 2)	Racial persistence gap	Incoming students at a public university; activities completed as part of prematriculation tasks online in the summer before college ($n = 7{,}335$)	**Social belonging:** reading materials framing belonging concerns, saying-is-believing essays **Mindset:** reading materials framing intelligence, saying-is-believing essays **Combined:** shortened versions of both interventions, received in one session	Social belonging: increased percentage of underrepresented (FG and URM) students who stayed enrolled full-time through their first year of college Mindset: increased college persistence among underrepresented students to the same degree as social belonging alone Combined: increased college persistence among underrepresented students to the same degree as either intervention alone
Yeager et al. (2016, study 3)	Racial achievement gap	Incoming students at a selective private university; activities completed as part of prematriculation tasks online in the summer before college ($n = 1{,}592$)	**Social belonging:** reading materials framing belonging concerns, saying-is-believing essays	Increased first-year GPAs for underrepresented (FG and URM) students
Stephens et al. (2014, 2015)	Social class achievement gap	First-year students at a selective private university; activities completed as part of a research study in the first month of the semester ($n = 168$) Two-year follow-up laboratory study ($n = 133$)	**Difference education:** a discussion panel framing diverse backgrounds and adjustment to college, saying-is-believing video	Increased first-year GPAs for FG college students; increased psychosocial adjustment during the first year of college for all students Improved coping in stressful situations for FG students two years later
Aronson et al. (2002)	Racial achievement gap	Undergraduates at a selective private university; activities completed in small-group laboratory sessions ($n = 79$)	**Mindset:** video framing intelligence, saying-is-believing essays	Increased overall GPAs for the quarter after the intervention for all students, especially for African American students

Abbreviations: FG, first-generation; GPA, grade point average; URM, underrepresented racial minority.

outcomes are course or field specific (e.g., course grades, STEM grades) or college general (e.g., overall GPA), as well as longer-term effects, such as course taking over time or career choices.

Our goal is to assess the state of the intervention research literature, with an eye to theoretical and conceptual questions about intervention science more generally. What makes these interventions so powerful? How replicable are the effects obtained to date? When possible, we evaluate evidence for targeted intervention processes, i.e., whether the researchers identified processes that help us understand how the intervention works and whether they tested for mediation

Table 3 Summary of values affirmation interventions in higher education

Study	Problem	Context and sample	Intervention	Primary findings
Values affirmation interventions				
Course specific				
Miyake et al. (2010)	Gender gap in physics	Two sections of introductory physics for STEM majors at a public university ($n = 399$)	**Values affirmation:** students wrote about their most important values, once as an in-class practice writing exercise and once as an online homework assignment	Increased performance for women on course exams and a standardized physics test
Harackiewicz et al. (2014a)[a]	Social class achievement gap in biology	Three sections of introductory biology for STEM majors at a public university ($n = 798$)	**Values affirmation:** twice during the semester, students wrote about their most important values as an in-class practice writing exercise	Increased course performance, enrollment in another biology course, and overall semester GPAs for first-generation college students
Harackiewicz et al. (2016a)[b]	Social class achievement gap in biology	Eight sections of introductory biology for STEM majors at a public university ($n = 1,040$)	**Values affirmation:** twice during the semester, students wrote about their most important values as an in-class practice writing exercise **Utility value: see Table 1**	No effect
College general				
Layous et al. (2017)	Promoting performance for students with low belonging	First- and second-year undergraduates at a public university; activities completed in small groups in a laboratory setting ($n = 105$)	**Values affirmation:** students ranked a list of values and wrote about their most important value	Increased overall GPAs for all students and particularly for students with low sense of belonging and for men
Brady et al. (2016)	Racial achievement gap for Latino students	First- and second-year undergraduates; activities completed in a laboratory setting Follow-up two years later ($n = 183$)	**Values affirmation:** students ranked a list of values and wrote about their most important value	Increased postintervention GPAs for Latino students; decreased postintervention GPAs for White students
Tibbetts et al. (2016a)	Social class achievement gap	Three-year follow-up of an intervention completed in three sections of introductory biology for STEM majors at a public university ($n = 788$)	**Values affirmation:** twice during the semester, students wrote about their most important values as an in-class practice writing exercise	Increased postintervention GPAs for first-generation college students

[a]Measured a combination of course-specific, field-specific, and college-general outcomes.
[b]Tested interventions from two different categories.
Abbreviation: STEM, science, technology, engineering, and mathematics.

	Task value	Framing	Personal values
Course specific e.g., engagement, interest, course grades	Utility-value intervention (4)	X	Values affirmation intervention (3)
Field specific e.g., course taking, interest in field, career choices	Communal utility-value intervention (3) Parent utility-value intervention (2)	Social belonging intervention (1)	X
School general e.g., enrollment rates, retention, overall GPA	X	Attributional reframing (3) Mindset intervention (3) Difference education intervention (2) Social belonging intervention (5)	Values affirmation intervention (3)

Figure 2

Targeted interventions in higher education can be divided into three types (task value, framing, and personal values) targeting outcomes at three levels (course specific, field specific, and school general). This figure summarizes the interventions that have been tested in each category of this classification system, as well as the number of experimental studies conducted (in parentheses).

of intervention effects. In addition, we consider whether intervention effects extended across contexts or over time through recursive processes. **Figure 2** shows our classification system, the specific interventions tested, and the number of experimental studies evaluated in each category.

TASK VALUE INTERVENTIONS

Of the task value interventions reviewed in this article, the utility-value intervention is supported by the highest number of randomized controlled trials (Harackiewicz et al. 2016b, Tibbetts et al. 2016b). This intervention is grounded in Eccles and colleagues' (Eccles et al. 1983, Eccles & Wigfield 2002) expectancy value model, which posits that the most proximal predictors of achievement and achievement-related choices (e.g., which courses to take, how hard to study for an exam) are students' expectations that they can succeed and the extent to which they value the task or topic. Thus, the students who are most likely to struggle in a given course are those with low expectations of success (due to either a history of poor performance or a lack of confidence) and those who do not see the value in what they are learning. The hypothesis driving the utility-value intervention is that if educators can help their students find value in the course material, this will give students a reason, and thus the motivation, to engage with the material and ultimately improve their performance. Specifically, the intervention targets utility value, the value perceived in a task or topic as a result of its usefulness for achieving short- or long-term goals. For example, students might perceive utility value in a physiology course because they can use what they learn to make their workouts safer and more effective.

There are two basic strategies by which educators can promote perceptions of value: They can tell students that course topics are useful and important (i.e., educators communicate value directly), or they can task their students with discovering that value for themselves (i.e., students generate value), most often through a writing exercise in which students relate course topics to their own lives (Canning & Harackiewicz 2015, Durik et al. 2015, Gaspard et al. 2015). Both strategies were tested first with several laboratory studies and then in the field, although self-generated utility-value interventions are more common in the field (for a review, see Harackiewicz & Hulleman 2010, Harackiewicz et al. 2014b). Because these interventions target value in particular content, most are course-level interventions. However, it is important to note that engaging students with the content of a course also engages them with the content of that field. This is one avenue by which these seemingly granular, content-focused interventions could have far-reaching consequences, such as impacting students' educational and career choices.

Course-Specific Task Value Interventions

The course-specific task value interventions tested to date have been self-generated utility-value interventions. In a prototypical self-generated utility-value intervention, students complete a series of course writing assignments in which they choose a topic covered in the current unit of the course and either discuss the relevance and utility value of the topic (the intervention condition) or summarize the topic (the control condition). This intervention provides students opportunities to make concrete connections between what they are learning and things that they care about, fostering perceptions of value as well as engagement with the course content. The first field test of this intervention was in high school science classes (Hulleman & Harackiewicz 2009). The utility-value intervention was particularly effective for students with low expectations of success, improving their grades in the science course and increasing their interest in science more broadly. Since this initial high school study, the intervention has been tested in a variety of college courses, with promising results.

Hulleman et al. (2010) administered a utility-value intervention twice during the second half of the semester in one large section of a college introductory psychology course. Among students who performed poorly on early exams, the utility-value intervention increased interest in the field of psychology, as well as intention to major in psychology. Furthermore, Hulleman and colleagues found that the mechanism driving these effects was the targeted process of perceived utility value. In other words, for students who were initially struggling, the intervention increased perceptions of value for the material they were learning, which, in turn, increased their interest in the field and their intention to major in psychology.

Another study, conducted in two large sections of an introductory psychology course, found that the utility-value intervention increased final exam scores and interest in psychology for all students on average and for students who performed poorly on initial exams in particular (Hulleman et al. 2017). In addition, they found that the utility-value intervention had the strongest positive effects for the students who were most at risk in this context, males who performed poorly on initial exams. They examined intervention mechanisms and found that, for students with low grades on early exams, the intervention increased their confidence (i.e., performance expectations) and that this confidence, in turn, explained higher final exam grades.

Hulleman and colleagues' (2010, 2017) work in large introductory psychology courses demonstrates that the utility-value intervention can be effective for struggling students, including groups of students who tend to underperform. This raises the possibility that the utility-value intervention can address achievement gaps. Harackiewicz and colleagues (2016a) tested this possibility with a large-scale field trial in eight sections of an introductory biology course for STEM majors (over four semesters). Their approach was novel in two ways. First, they used an intersectional analysis to examine achievement gaps for first-generation (FG) college students (i.e., those for whom neither parent has a four-year college degree) and URM students, as well as students at the intersection of these groups, who are both FG and URM (FG-URM). Second, they examined students' motivational profiles to understand the characteristics of different groups that might influence their receptivity to the intervention.

Harackiewicz and colleagues (2016a) found that FG-URM students had a unique motivational profile: They were least confident about their background in biology and were uncertain about their belonging in college more generally. However, they were also highly motivated to perform well in the course and to use their education to give back to society and help others, especially their families and communities. Harackiewicz and colleagues hypothesized that the utility-value intervention might give FG-URM students opportunities to connect course material to their positive motivations (i.e., their desire to use their education to help others), which could make the intervention particularly powerful for this group. Indeed, the intervention increased grades for all students on average and for FG-URM students in particular, reducing the achievement gap between FG-URM and majority students by 61%. Interestingly, the intervention was also effective for students with low prior GPAs (above and beyond the FG-URM intervention effect), replicating prior work by Hulleman and colleagues (2010), and for any students with higher levels of helping motives (not just FG-URM students).

Harackiewicz and colleagues (2016a) examined intervention mechanisms and found that the intervention effect for FG-URM students was mediated by engagement. Students in the utility-value condition, and FG-URM students in particular, wrote longer essays, indicating that they engaged more with the material than did students in the control condition. This engagement, in turn, explained increases in course performance. To explore how this played out in the content of the essays, Harackiewicz and colleagues analyzed the essays using text analysis (Pennebaker et al. 2007). Utility-value essays contained more personal pronouns and more words related to social relationships, especially family, which is concordant with FG-URM students' desire to give back to their families and communities. Furthermore, these essays contained more words indicative of cognitive engagement and insight. This is consistent with experimental work showing that task value interventions increase engagement and conceptual change (Johnson & Sinatra 2013). Beigman Klebanov and colleagues (2017) analyzed these same essays using natural language processing techniques. They found that utility-value writing was characterized by argumentative and narrative elements, suggesting that students were both providing personal narratives and building arguments and claims (e.g., about why biology is valuable). Together, these analyses reveal some of the ways that writing about utility value can increase engagement and promote learning.

Canning and colleagues (2018) tested the utility-value intervention in three sections of an introductory biology class for STEM majors but varied the number of utility-value assignments (from zero to three) to examine the effects of intervention dosage on performance. They also followed students to see whether they enrolled in the second course in the biology sequence and whether they abandoned plans to major in STEM (93% of students entered the course with plans to major in a STEM field), as measures of STEM persistence. They found that students who received at least one utility-value assignment earned higher grades in the course, were more likely to enroll in the second biology course, and were less likely to abandon their STEM major. However, students assigned the maximum dosage (three assignments) earned the highest grades and were most likely to take the next biology course, suggesting that students benefited from multiple doses of the intervention. Moreover, the intervention's positive effect on continuation to the second course (a distal outcome) was mediated by grades in the first course. In other words, students who performed better as a result of the utility-value intervention were more likely to take another biology course, suggesting one mechanism by which a course-specific intervention can influence field-specific outcomes through recursive processes.

Field-Specific Task Value Interventions

Many studies of course-specific task value interventions also found effects on field-level outcomes, such as interest in the field (Hulleman et al. 2017), intention to major in the field (Hulleman et al. 2010), retention in a STEM major, or course taking in a field (Canning et al. 2018). In addition, some task value interventions targeted field-level outcomes directly. Brown and colleagues (2015) developed an intervention designed to promote interest in biomedical careers by helping students perceive the value of biomedical research for achieving communal (i.e., helping-oriented) goals. They communicated utility value directly by giving students an article that described how a research project could help others. Across three laboratory studies, they found that the communal utility-value intervention increased students' interest in pursuing a career in biomedical research, relative to a control group, and that these effects were mediated by the perceived communal value of biomedical research (Brown et al. 2015).

In an experimental field study, Harackiewicz and colleagues (2012) tested a directly communicated utility-value intervention to help parents of high school students see the value of math and science course taking and share that value with their teens. They hypothesized that giving parents tools (two brochures and a website) to help them talk about the importance of math and science would influences their teens' perceptions of value and elective course choices. Indeed, teens whose parents received the utility-value intervention took, on average, an extra semester of math or science in their last two years of high school, relative to a control group whose parents did not receive the intervention.

A five-year follow-up of these students found that the intervention had also increased students' math and science scores on college preparatory exams (i.e., the ACT) by 12 percentile points (Rozek et al. 2017). Importantly, these short-term outcomes (course taking and ACT scores in high school) had long-term consequences. Rozek and colleagues found indirect effects of the intervention such that students whose parents had received the utility-value intervention took more math and science courses in high school and earned higher ACT scores, and that these targeted high school outcomes were predictive of students' college STEM course taking, majors, and career aspirations. Thus, even when an intervention is not expected to directly influence long-term outcomes—this intervention targeted parental involvement and high school course taking—short-term intervention effects can initiate recursive processes that impact students' long-term trajectories.

Task Value Interventions: Summary and Discussion

Together, these studies show that task value interventions can be a powerful tool for engaging students in thinking and writing about the why of learning, giving them a platform for exploring how their coursework can help them achieve important personal goals. A consistent pattern of results has emerged across a variety of contexts and modes of intervention delivery; these interventions have proven most effective for students who struggle in courses. However, there is also evidence of main effects in almost all of these studies; in other words, some utility-value interventions have had positive effects for all students on average (Harackiewicz et al. 2012, 2016a; Brown et al. 2015; Canning et al. 2018; Hulleman et al. 2017), and it will be important to clarify when and why task value interventions should work for all students versus only for those who struggle (Schwartz et al. 2016). Careful attention has been paid in these studies to targeted motivational processes in these studies, with evidence for mediation of intervention effects by the targeted process of perceived utility value and other processes such as positive expectancies and engagement. Finally, the results of Canning et al. (2018) and Rozek et al. (2017) document some recursive effects from the targeted outcomes (course grades and high school course taking) to more distal outcomes, illuminating important pathways for the long-term effects of utility-value interventions.

Perhaps unsurprisingly given the theoretical grounding of these interventions, they most often focus on single courses or particular fields. Indeed, we did not find any task value interventions targeting college-general outcomes (e.g., cumulative GPA). However, the evidence indicates that task value interventions can increase motivation at the field level both directly, in a single-session laboratory study (Brown et al. 2015) and a semester-long biology course (Canning et al. 2018), and indirectly, over a span of five years, by promoting STEM course taking and test performance in high school (Rozek et al. 2017). Furthermore, recent work (Brown et al. 2015, Harackiewicz et al. 2016a) suggests connecting specifically to helping-oriented goals might be a powerful intervention technique (Thoman et al. 2015, 2017). In fact, Yeager and colleagues (2014) and Paunesku et al. (2015) have developed a task value intervention for high school students that focuses students on self-transcendent (helping-oriented) goals for learning. Like other task value interventions, the purpose intervention has shown positive effects on grades for low-performing students. Although there have not been enough studies testing the purpose intervention at the college level for inclusion in this review, initial work is promising. In sum, current research suggests that task value interventions can have broad implications for educational trajectories.

FRAMING INTERVENTIONS

Framing interventions include a diverse set of interventions to counteract the maladaptive ways students might interpret challenges. Drawing on attribution theory (Weiner 1974, Ross & Nisbett 2011), these interventions tap into processes by which students make sense of their academic experiences. For example, a student who receives bad grades in their first semester might attribute their poor performance to a lack of intelligence (a maladaptive attribution) or to the steep learning curve of adjusting to college, which they will overcome in time (an adaptive attribution). Thus, framing interventions target common maladaptive beliefs by providing students with alternate frames. Two messages are key: that challenge is a normal or natural experience (i.e., not exclusively attributable to an individual's own shortcomings) and that students can exercise control over their academic outcomes through personal growth (i.e., challenges can be overcome with effort). These messages are particularly important in the transition to college for underrepresented students (e.g., URM students, FG students, women in STEM) who may experience adversity as evidence that the college environment is unwelcoming or even discriminatory, posing major threats to their sense of belonging (Walton 2014). Therefore, almost all of the studies in this category are college-general interventions targeting students' framing of challenge in the transition to college.

Early work by Wilson & Linville (1982, 1985) tested an intervention using this attributional approach. They showed struggling first-year students statistics and interviews indicating that most students' grades were lower than anticipated their first semester but improved over time. Some participants also wrote an essay explaining to high school students how initial low grades were attributable to temporary factors (e.g., not knowing how to take college exams). Such saying-is-believing exercises are designed to increase internalization of the intervention message by having students convey it in their own words (often through writing) to benefit students who will face similar challenges in the future (Aronson 1999). Across three studies, the intervention improved students' performance on GRE problems immediately after the intervention and improved students' college GPAs in the following semester, although both effects were stronger for men than for women (Wilson & Linville 1985). These strategies have informed the design of interventions in more recent work. In fact, a research group in Canada has implemented a very similar treatment protocol, called attributional retraining (AR), with introductory psychology students (for a review, see Perry & Hamm 2017, Perry et al. 2014),[2] and all the interventions reviewed below draw, at least in part, on the methods developed by Wilson & Linville.

---

[2]There are many studies of AR (see, e.g., Hall et al. 2007, Haynes et al. 2006, Perry et al. 2010), but we do not include these studies in our review because they employ different methodology. AR treatment interventions have been studied with longitudinal quasi-experimental designs with treatment not randomized at the student level, whereas all the studies included in our review conducted randomization at the student level.

College-General Framing Interventions

Our review identified three types of framing interventions that were tested at the college-general level and met our inclusion criteria. These interventions include social belonging interventions, difference education interventions, and mindset interventions.

Social belonging interventions. The seminal work on the social belonging intervention was conducted by Walton & Cohen (2007, 2011) to address achievement gaps for African American students at a selective college. Second-semester students read statistics and quotes from more senior students indicating that most students worry about whether they belong in college during their first year but that these concerns lessen over time. Participants then wrote an essay about why that would be the case, using examples from their own experiences, and recorded a video testimonial for future students. Control activities were similar but focused on adjusting to the physical environment in college (e.g., the architecture, weather). This intervention improved African American students' GPAs the semester after the intervention (Walton & Cohen 2007) as well as their overall GPAs, measured at a postgraduation follow-up (Walton & Cohen 2011). Daily diary measures collected in the week after the intervention revealed that, for African Americans in the intervention condition, experiences of adversity no longer influenced their sense of belonging, and this decoupling process mediated the intervention effects on GPA (Walton & Cohen 2011). In addition, Walton & Cohen found that African American students in the intervention condition reported engaging in more adaptive academic behaviors (e.g., emailing professors, spending more time studying) in the week following the intervention (Walton & Cohen 2007) and reported higher levels of a sense of belonging, health, and well-being in the postgraduation survey (Walton & Cohen 2011).

Yeager and colleagues (2016) adapted this social belonging intervention so that it could be delivered online and tested at scale to address three different goals: to increase rates of college enrollment among charter high school students (study 1), to address persistence gaps for disadvantaged (URM and FG) students at a public flagship university (study 2), and to address performance gaps for disadvantaged students at a highly selective private university (study 3). In all three studies, the intervention materials conveyed the same messages as Walton & Cohen's (2007) belonging intervention, but the student quotes were customized for each context. The intervention delivered during senior year at charter high schools increased the percentage of students who stayed enrolled full-time through their first year of college (32% in the control group versus 45% in the intervention group), and this effect was mediated by a measure of students' social and academic involvement behaviors on campus (e.g., living on campus, using academic support services).

In studies 2 and 3, the intervention was delivered as part of the online orientation process in the summer before college. In study 2, the intervention increased the percentage of disadvantaged students who stayed enrolled full-time through their first year of college (69% in the control group versus 73% in the intervention group). This effect was mediated by a survey measure of social and academic involvement. In study 3, the intervention increased first-year GPA among disadvantaged students, as well as these students' social and academic involvement behaviors (e.g., having a mentor, using academic support services). Together, these studies demonstrate that the social belonging intervention can be adapted to target students' framing of belonging concerns across a variety of contexts, with impressive results (Yeager et al. 2016).

Difference education interventions. Stephens and colleagues (2014) developed the difference education intervention to provide a more adaptive frame for FG college students in the transition to college. These students are less likely to have the procedural knowledge needed to take advantage of campus resources and less likely to feel a sense of belonging or fit in the college environment due to a cultural mismatch between their values and institutional norms (Stephens et al. 2012). In the difference education intervention (Stephens et al. 2014), first-year students attended a one-hour panel in which a diverse group of students discussed how their backgrounds were sources of both challenge and strength and described strategies they used to navigate challenges and become a successful student. Participants then recorded a video testimonial for future students. Control participants attended a similar panel, but the panelists did not discuss their backgrounds. All students in the intervention condition reported more academic and social engagement at the end of the first year of college, and FG students in the intervention condition earned higher first-year GPAs than FG students in the control condition, an effect that was mediated by their increased use of campus resources (e.g., emailing professors, attending office hours). In a follow-up study two years later, students from the difference education intervention condition mentioned more aspects of their background in a speech about their college experience, indicating that they retained the intervention message and were more comfortable talking about the role of background. In addition, FG students from the intervention condition showed higher levels of anabolic balance reactivity, a measure of physiological striving, compared to FG students from the control condition. Stephens and colleagues (2015) concluded that the difference education intervention initiated recursive processes that helped FG students view their backgrounds as a source of strength and cope more effectively with stressful tasks.

Mindset interventions. Mindset interventions are based on Dweck's (1999) work on lay theories of intelligence, wherein a maladaptive theory would be that intelligence cannot be changed (a fixed mindset), whereas an adaptive theory would be that intelligence is malleable and can be increased with effort (a growth mindset). The prototypical mindset intervention is an eight-week program to teach middle school students about brain plasticity and how they could develop their intelligence by exercising their brain like a muscle (e.g., Blackwell et al. 2007). Whereas this method is not practical in college contexts, a few studies have tried to distill this message into a briefer intervention for college students.

Aronson and colleagues (2002) developed an intervention to combat stereotype threat, with the idea that the stereotype that African Americans have a fixed lack of intelligence could be rendered powerless if one holds the belief that intelligence is malleable. The mindset intervention, delivered in a laboratory setting, involved a brief video explaining how researchers have found that the brain can grow and develop new neuronal connections and a saying-is-believing exercise. This intervention closed gaps between African American and White students' GPAs in the semester after the intervention, and this effect was mediated by students' growth mindset beliefs.

Yeager and colleagues (2016) also tested mindset interventions in studies 1 and 2 of their social belonging research, described above. Participants read an article summarizing the scientific research supporting the idea that intelligence is malleable and then wrote an essay expressing this message to future students who might be struggling in school. In both studies, some students were randomly assigned to receive both the social belonging intervention and the mindset intervention, which allowed a test of combined intervention. In study 1, the mindset intervention had no effect on college enrollment, and the combined intervention was no more effective than the social belonging intervention alone. In study 2, all three interventions increased enrollment among disadvantaged students; there were no differences in the effectiveness of the mindset intervention, the social belonging intervention, and the combined intervention.

Field-Specific Framing Interventions

Only one study has adapted a framing intervention to address a field-specific problem: Walton and colleagues (2015) adapted Walton and Cohen's (2007) original social belonging intervention (a college-general intervention) to address the gender achievement gap in an engineering program. First-semester engineering students in the intervention condition were given statistics and quotes from senior engineering students and wrote a letter to a future engineering student conveying the intervention messages in their own words. Women in male-dominated engineering majors (e.g., mechanical engineering) who received the social belonging intervention earned higher first-year engineering GPAs, perceived adversity as more manageable, had more friendships with their male colleagues, and, by the second semester, were more confident that they could succeed in the field, compared to women in the control group.

Framing Interventions: Summary and Discussion

The framing interventions reviewed above target an impressive number of educational problems, but they share a common goal: improving students' academic experiences by providing adaptive frames for common challenges, from belonging concerns, to beliefs about performance and intelligence, to cultural mismatch. They can have far-reaching benefits for students' academic adjustment and long-term outcomes. Across a variety of contexts and modes of intervention delivery, the pattern of results indicates that these interventions have improved important academic outcomes for students adjusting to college. The targeted populations have varied from students struggling in school (Wilson & Linville 1982) to African American students (Aronson et al. 2002), first-generation students (Stephens et al. 2014), women in engineering (Walton et al. 2015), and disadvantaged students in general (Yeager et al. 2016), and this impressive diversity suggests the great potential of the framing approach for a number of educational problems.

However, as with task value interventions, there is also some evidence of positive effects for all students on average (Stephens et al. 2014, 2015; Yeager et al. 2016), and it will be important to clarify when and why framing interventions work for all students. Some results are more consistent than they first appear, once the problem is clearly defined. For example, Yeager et al. (2016) noted that almost all students in their study 1 were either URM or FG students and, thus, predicted a main effect for the belonging and mindset interventions. Other findings are inconsistent; Yeager et al. (2016, study 1) failed to find an effect of the mindset intervention, and Stephens et al. (2014) found a main effect of the difference education intervention that specifically targeted FG students. Overall, however, the consistency of findings is impressive, and we anticipate that the pattern of results will become increasingly clear as more work is done to replicate these findings within the same contexts (Wilson & Linville 1985, Walton & Cohen 2011) and between contexts (Yeager et al. 2016).

Exploration of targeted processes in these studies has focused less on the specific cognitive processes hypothesized to drive intervention effects (with the exception of Aronson et al. 2002) and more on the academic behaviors that students report in academic transitions. These behaviors are typically assessed with surveys and represent adaptive behaviors such as emailing professors, making friends, and attending office hours. Such measures capture an approach orientation consistent with a positive framing of challenge, but they vary widely across studies. It will be important to standardize such measures so that results can be compared across studies. However, the mediation analyses reported by Stephens et al. (2014) and Yeager et al. (2016) clearly suggest that such measures are key to understanding how framing interventions work in college transitions. Less attention has been paid to recursive processes in the framing studies reviewed above, in part because these studies are more recent, with less opportunity for follow-up over time. However, there is some evidence that physical health processes may be implicated over time (Walton & Cohen 2011, Stephens et al. 2015), and this is a promising direction. Surprisingly, scant attention has been paid to the content and style of students' writing in these interventions, and this might be a missed opportunity for extending the study of these intervention dynamics. Continued exploration of targeted and recursive processes over time will be essential for understanding how framing interventions work to improve student outcomes.

PERSONAL VALUES INTERVENTIONS

The values affirmation intervention is based in self-affirmation theory (Steele 1988), which argues that individuals are motivated to maintain an overall sense of self-integrity. If a student experiences identity threat in an important academic domain (e.g., a woman taking a physics test), then their self-integrity is called into question. Self-affirmation interventions give people an opportunity to reflect on sources of self-worth in other domains. Writing about personal values affirms self-integrity on a broader level and thereby diminishes the negative impact of identity threats in a particular situation. This intervention is not specific to threats in particular domains and has been implemented in a variety of contexts (e.g., health, relationships, sports; see Cohen & Sherman 2014 for a review).

Cohen and colleagues (2006, 2009) were the first to implement this intervention in an academic context. They found that, when three cohorts of seventh graders completed a values affirmation exercise in class, African American students performed better and had higher overall GPAs for the term than African American students in the control group, and that their GPAs in core courses remained higher over two years, especially among those with lower initial GPAs. They argued that early improvements in performance initiated recursive processes that disrupted the negative performance trajectory observed in the control condition. Indeed, the intervention effects on GPA in year 2 (distal outcome) were mediated by GPA in year 1 (targeted outcome). These effects have been replicated in several middle school studies (e.g., Bowen et al. 2013, Sherman et al. 2013, Borman et al. 2016), and more recent work at the middle school level has focused on understanding the mediators, moderators, and boundary conditions for these effects. For example, Shnabel and colleagues (2013) examined the values affirmation essays from the original Cohen studies (Cohen et al. 2006) and found that all students wrote more about social belonging in the values affirmation condition, and that this improved grades for African American students. Thus, recent work provides strong evidence that values affirmation can have both immediate and long-term benefits for underrepresented students, but it is also important to note that there have been some failures to replicate these findings in middle school contexts (Dee 2015, Protzko & Aronson 2016, Hanselman et al. 2017).

Course-Specific Values Affirmation Interventions

Miyake and colleagues (2010) conducted the first test of a values affirmation intervention in college to address gender gaps in an introductory physics course. To make the values affirmation exercise fit seamlessly in a college science course, the instructor told students that the exercise was a chance to practice their writing skills. It was implemented as an in-class activity in the first week of the semester and as an online homework assignment in the fourth week (just prior to the first midterm exam). Thus, in contrast to the social belonging or difference education interventions, the values affirmation intervention was fully integrated into the class and presented as a course assignment. It improved women's exam grades and scores on a standardized physics exam, reducing achievement gaps between women and men in the course.

Harackiewicz and colleagues (2014a) implemented the values affirmation intervention in an introductory biology course for STEM majors, using the same basic methods as Miyake et al. (2010). However, this intervention was targeted for a different problem, the social class achievement gap between FG and continuing-generation (CG) students. FG students in the intervention condition earned higher grades in the biology course as well as higher overall GPAs that semester, reducing the social class achievement gap. In addition, FG students in the intervention condition were more likely to enroll in the next course in the biology sequence. This effect was mediated by course grades: The intervention improved FG students' grades in the biology course, which, in turn, increased their likelihood of continuing in biology. Together, these two studies suggest that the values affirmation intervention can be integrated into college science classes with positive effects.

In the Harackiewicz et al. (2016a) utility-value intervention study, discussed above, the researchers also tested a values affirmation intervention crossed with the utility-value intervention in a 2 × 2 design. The values affirmation intervention was implemented exactly as it was by Harackiewicz et al. (2014a), but the positive effect for FG students was not replicated, and there were no significant interactions with the utility-value intervention. The researchers discussed a number of factors that might have accounted for this nonreplication, most notably that the social class achievement gap was larger in the semester that the Harackiewicz et al. (2014a) study was conducted. Indeed, previous research suggests that values affirmation is more effective when achievement gaps are larger (Hanselman et al. 2014). Another possibility is that the addition of the utility-value intervention (which involved three more writing assignments) dampened the effects of the values affirmation intervention. This analysis suggests that it may not work to combine different types of writing interventions in a single semester. Although the values affirmation intervention can have powerful effects, it is sensitive to contextual and sample differences in ways that we do not yet fully understand. More research is needed to identify factors that moderate the effectiveness of the values affirmation intervention in college contexts.

College-General Values Affirmation Interventions

Self-affirmation interventions are designed to combat identity threats on a broad level. When groups are threatened by stereotypes about intelligence or ability, their identity threat is not limited to a single course. Therefore, it is not surprising that interventions implemented in a single course can have downstream college-general effects (e.g., on overall GPA), as was the case in Cohen et al.'s (2009) original study and Harackiewicz and colleagues' (2014a) study in college biology. However, the interventions we review in this section target college-general effects as the primary outcomes. Furthermore, like much of the more recent work on values affirmation interventions in middle school contexts, each of these studies has a particular focus on the moderators and mediators of intervention effects.

Whereas other work focused on demographic moderators, such as gender, social class, or race, Layous and colleagues (2017) examined psychological moderators of values affirmation intervention effects. They noted a common theme for all the groups that have benefited from values affirmation: threats to a sense of belonging. Thus, in a sample of primarily White undergraduates, Layous and colleagues administered the values affirmation exercise in a laboratory setting and tested whether the intervention would be effective for students with a low sense of belonging. They found no effects of the intervention on a math test administered immediately after the intervention. However, when they examined students' grades over two semesters, they found that the values affirmation intervention improved GPAs for all students on average compared to the control condition, and that this effect was stronger for men and for students with low levels of belonging.

Brady and colleagues (2016) implemented the values affirmation intervention in a laboratory study and then followed students over time. They found a positive effect on postintervention GPAs for Latino students at a two-year follow-up, but the effect was negative for White students. In the fourth semester after the intervention, participants returned to the lab and completed a stressful academic task (making a list of everything they had to get done before the end of the semester), after which they were given a blank piece of paper to write about whatever was on their mind. Brady and colleagues analyzed these essays and found that Latino students who had received a values affirmation intervention two years earlier showed spontaneous self-affirmations in their writing. In other words, they focused on personal values and positive sources of worth. Furthermore, Latino students from the affirmation condition reported more confidence in their ability to cope with all the tasks they needed to complete, compared to those in the control condition. Brady and colleagues tested whether these spontaneous self-affirmations mediated the effects of the intervention on confidence and GPA. They found that among Latino students, the intervention increased their tendency to self-affirm, which improved their confidence in their coping ability, leading to better grades that semester. These results provide insight into the recursive processes through which the values affirmation intervention influenced academic performance over a two-year period.

Tibbetts and colleagues (2016a) conducted a follow-up study of the Harackiewicz et al. (2014a) sample and found that the values affirmation intervention improved FG students' overall postintervention GPAs over the course of three years. They used text analyses to investigate the mechanisms of these long-term effects. Their analysis was grounded in cultural mismatch theory (Stephens et al. 2012), which states that, although everyone holds both independent and interdependent values to some degree, FG students face a mismatch because university culture places more emphasis on independence, whereas FG students have more interdependent backgrounds. Therefore, Tibbetts and colleagues coded for both independent and interdependent writing. They found that the effects of the values affirmation intervention on course grades, academic belonging, and overall GPA three years later were all mediated by independent themes. In other words, for FG students, writing about independence in their values affirmation essays led to higher grades in the biology course, higher levels of academic belonging, and higher GPAs over a three-year period. Although most FG students who wrote about independence also wrote about interdependent themes (95%), it was affirming their independent values (which match the academic context) that proved most beneficial in this context.

Values Affirmation Interventions: Summary and Discussion

Like the framing intervention studies, the values affirmation intervention studies reviewed above targeted an impressive number of educational problems, from gender gaps in a physics course (Miyake et al. 2010) and the social class achievement gap in a biology course (Harackiewicz et al. 2014a) to performance among students with low belonging (Layous et al. 2017). However, the number of tests of values affirmation in college contexts is small, and the results have not been consistent (e.g., Harackiewicz et al. 2016a). This inconsistency highlights the urgency for researchers to demonstrate how this intervention works in college contexts and for whom. Recent studies have provided insights into the psychological moderators of values affirmation interventions (Layous et al. 2017), as well as the proximal and distal mediators of intervention effects. Work by Tibbetts and colleagues (2016a) demonstrated that the content of the values affirmation essays can provide important clues about their proximal mechanisms, revealing that, for FG students experiencing identity threat due to a cultural mismatch, the benefits of the intervention were mediated by themes of independence. Finally, Brady and colleagues' (2016) work illuminated a more distal mechanism, that values affirmation interventions can improve long-term outcomes through recursive processes involving students' propensity to self-affirm under threat.

Values affirmation interventions were first tested in middle schools, administered by teachers in small classes. In contrast, introductory college classes are large and impersonal, and it may be difficult to administer a personal writing exercise in this context. However, it is not clear that the implementation of the intervention needs to be the same across contexts. Indeed, some of the work at the college level has been implemented in laboratory settings, rather than classrooms, with positive results (Brady et al. 2016, Layous et al. 2017). Given the recent work showing that the content of values affirmation essays works differently for middle school minority students and FG college students (Shnabel et al. 2013, Tibbetts et al. 2016a), it is clear that more work is needed to understand how values affirmation works in different contexts and for different groups.

IMPLICATIONS FOR INTERVENTION SCIENCE

The studies reviewed above reveal the power of a targeted approach to intervention research in higher education. The interventions evaluated in these studies were grounded in theory and developed through laboratory research and small-scale field studies, culminating in the field trials considered in this review. As we survey the progress to date, it seems clear that intervention scientists have made great strides over the past 15 years. The interventions are well crafted and the research methods are rigorous, with careful attention paid to intervention mechanisms and recursive processes.

Conducting randomized controlled field trials is a complicated process. It requires close collaboration with teaching faculty or university administrators, first to adapt the intervention for the particular context and student population and then to implement interventions in courses or academic advising contexts. Well-powered studies require large samples (especially if the intervention is targeted to help underrepresented minority groups) such that these studies can take years to run. The current body of intervention research in higher education spans a wide array of problems, ranging from achievement gaps in college courses, to promoting STEM career pursuit, to facilitating transitions to college for underrepresented students. However, these studies represent the first wave of a new science, and there were too few studies in any category of our classification system to permit a more quantitative review. In fact, the impressive range of problems targeted by these interventions proved to be a limitation for our review—there were very few studies targeting the same problems with comparable measures. Although there was strong empirical support for each of the three types of intervention in general, more research is needed to address critical questions of replication and generalizability of findings.

Replication and Beyond

Given that the interventions reviewed above are contextually specific interventions, how should we conceptualize the question of replication? In some ways, the interventions literature represents an ideal case for thinking about the replication issues currently facing the field—hypotheses are straightforward and well specified (and often preregistered), and the studies are typically well powered, but direct replication is almost never possible. What kind of precision should we expect, and how should we think about conceptual replications and extension of interventions to different populations? How should we interpret nonreplications?

Our review reveals impressive patterns of consistent findings for each type of intervention but also reveals some inconsistencies across studies and some failures to replicate findings. We would not expect each intervention to be equally effective across every implementation, of course; in fact, the pattern of inconsistent findings may help identify areas for future research and qualify conclusions until we have more data in hand. In the case of task value interventions, for example, there was a consistent pattern of findings that the interventions had positive effects for students who struggle in classes [with some internal replications across sections of courses or semesters (e.g., Harackiewicz et al. 2016a)], but there are inconsistencies in the mediators between studies (e.g., perceived values, expectancies, engagement) that raise important questions about intervention mechanisms. In the case of framing interventions, there was a consistent pattern of findings that framing interventions promoted positive outcomes in academic transitions, but some evidence of nonreplication of growth mindset effects (Yeager et al. 2016, study 2). More critically, no two studies in the framing category examined the exact same problem, making it difficult to assess the question of direct replication [however, some studies had internal replications with multiple cohorts (e.g., Walton & Cohen 2011)].

We found more evidence of nonreplication for values affirmation, in part because the foundational studies were conducted earlier (Cohen et al. 2006, Miyake et al. 2010), allowing more time for replication studies to emerge. Indeed, future reviews may contend with more nonreplications of task value and framing interventions, and we expect that the field of intervention science will be all the better for it. As is the case with values affirmation, each replication and nonreplication can tell us something about the intervention, its mechanisms, and the conditions under which it is most effectively implemented. For example, replication studies in middle school have revealed that intervention effects may be moderated by context (Hanselman et al. 2014) and by timing of implementation (Cook et al. 2012).

In addition to questions about the replicability of intervention effects, it is important to think about the generalizability of the mechanism. For example, values affirmation interventions were successfully implemented to address achievement gaps for underrepresented minority students in middle school, then for women in college physics, and then for FG students in college biology classes. Should we expect the intervention to work the same way in all three cases? If a social belonging intervention works for African American students in a selective university, will it work the same way for women in engineering programs or for underrepresented students starting college at their state university? And if a utility-value intervention promotes interest and performance for struggling students in a psychology class, will we expect this to work in the same way that utility-value interventions help minority students perform better in college biology classes?

On the one hand, the theories behind these interventions provide hypotheses about general mechanisms that should apply across contexts and populations. For example, if struggling students in psychology and minority students in biology both fail to see any value in what they are learning, a utility-value intervention might work for both groups. On the other hand, our application of theory needs to be more context dependent; we might implement the intervention differently or invoke different mechanisms for how the intervention works in particular contexts. In the Harackiewicz et al. (2016a) study, FG minority students believed that biology was valuable (the vast majority had biology-related majors), but they benefited from the utility-value intervention because it allowed them to connect course content to their helping goals. This particular mechanism is likely not generalizable to all populations. These questions become even more complicated when considering recursive processes, which interact with natural processes in the environment (e.g., performing well in a biology course may catch the attention of faculty, who invite the student to join their lab, which increases the likelihood that the student will pursue a career in that field, etc.), and are thus context dependent, at least to some degree. Thus, our theories will need to be informed and revised by what we learn from testing interventions in multiple contexts. Moving forward, it will be important to consider these issues as we design and evaluate intervention research.

Implementation: How and Where?

There are four ways that these interventions have been implemented in randomized controlled trials: (*a*) in laboratory sessions, with assessment of academic outcomes (e.g., Aronson et al. 2002, Brown et al. 2015); (*b*) in orientation or advising sessions outside of class (Stephens et al. 2014, Walton et al. 2015); (*c*) in preorientation activities, included as part of the prematriculation process (Yeager et al. 2016); or (*d*) in classes, integrated into the class structure (e.g., Harackiewicz et al. 2016a, Miyake et al. 2010). There are methodological trade-offs associated with each mode of delivery. Lab studies offer the greatest control and opportunity for in-depth assessment of targeted processes. For example, Brady and colleagues (2016) were able to explore self-affirmation and recursive processes by bringing participants back into the lab two years after participating in a laboratory-based values affirmation study. Similarly, Stephens et al. (2015) were able to collect physiological data to examine recursive processes two years after a differences education intervention. However, any time participants are brought back to the lab for follow-up, researchers must contend with attrition and problems of self-selection that undercut the power of randomization at the original point of implementation. Selection bias may also apply when students are recruited for advising or orientation sessions scheduled outside of classes. Although randomization within these contexts allows evaluation of treatment effects within the sample, the generalizability of the studies is unclear. In these cases, it is imperative that researchers describe recruitment procedures and characterize their sample relative to the targeted population. The inclusion of campus-wide control groups (e.g., Walton & Cohen 2011, Stephens et al. 2014) can be helpful in this process.

When interventions are embedded in prematriculation activities or incorporated into class curricula, samples are more representative of the targeted population, with fewer concerns about selection bias. However, it is essential to track whether all students complete prematriculation and required course assignments to evaluate treatment compliance and fidelity (O'Donnell 2008, Hulleman & Cordray 2009). Implementation in these contexts requires close collaboration with course instructors or deans to ensure that materials are appropriate for the context and that randomization is carried out properly. Moreover, when working in these contexts, it is important to design control conditions that are plausible, i.e., that have pedagogical value (in the case of course-based interventions) or make sense as prematriculation orientation activities. For example, in control conditions of the utility-value intervention study in biology classes (Harackiewicz et al. 2016a), students were asked to write essays summarizing course material, whereas students in the intervention condition were asked to summarize information and then explain the relevance and utility value of that information. Thus, the intervention had pedagogical value for all students, which could justify its inclusion in curricula. The major disadvantage of these approaches is that it is much more difficult to examine targeted processes. There are limited opportunities to administer questionnaires, let alone measure physiological data. Even when possible, there are risks: The more that data collection is added to the course or orientation, the more that it will be experienced as a research study, reducing the authenticity and potential generalizability of the findings.

Thus, all delivery methods have benefits and disadvantages. Intervention scientists must consider the goals of their study. A study that aims to test process questions is perhaps best conducted in the laboratory. However, a study that aims to test how the intervention works in the field will need to be embedded in the educational context (i.e., the course, prematriculation activities, orientation, or advising sessions, depending on the intervention). Indeed, there is an important interplay between laboratory and context-embedded studies: Interventions tested in the lab are scaled up for field tests, which then suggest additional process questions to be tested in the lab, so that the intervention can be refined. For example, after their analyses of values affirmation essays from field studies, Shnabel et al. (2013) and Tibbetts et al. (2016a) returned to the lab to manipulate writing themes to test their field-driven hypotheses.

Implementation: Who and Why?

In the range of intervention studies reviewed above, researchers have targeted different groups of students in different contexts—women in physics classes and engineering programs, African American students at a selective university, students who struggle on early exams in psychology classes, etc.—as well as broader groups of students. For example, Yeager et al. (2016) targeted disadvantaged students, defined differently in each of three studies, based on historical achievement data in each context: In study 1, all participants were either URM or FG students; in study 2, the disadvantaged group included all African American, Latino, and FG students; in study 3, the disadvantaged group included all African American, Latino, Native, Pacific Islander, and FG students. Harackiewicz et al. (2012) targeted all parents and teens with their directly communicated utility-value intervention. Other researchers targeted narrower groups of students at the intersection of two dimensions—i.e., low-performing males in psychology classes (Hulleman et al. 2017) and FG-URM students in biology classes (Harackiewicz et al. 2016a). The dizzying array of populations targeted in the studies reviewed above indicates how differently problems have been conceptualized and how difficult it is to compare results across studies.

Given that targeted interventions focus on specific educational problems for particular groups of students, it is important to consider the individual characteristics that may predispose students to benefit from a given intervention. For example, framing and values affirmation interventions have proven to alleviate belonging concerns, thus promoting academic performance for underrepresented students (e.g., African American students in college, women in physics) and students with a low sense of belonging. Utility-value interventions have been powerful in improving performance for students who struggle in a class and for students with strong helping motives by increasing their engagement with course content and helping them to connect the material to their own lives and goals. In order to implement an intervention with maximum effectiveness, it is important to consider the specific processes that social-psychological interventions target and how those processes vary across different populations.

If interventions target a general process, such as belonging concerns in the transition to college, it may be theoretically consistent to target all disadvantaged students in that context. With other interventions, however, hypotheses may be more specific. We recommend that researchers (continue to) conduct pilot work and use focus groups (e.g., Walton et al. 2015) to assess the problem, population, and context. This process has two major benefits. First, baseline assessment and focus groups can help identify which type of intervention might be appropriate in a given context and which groups might be most responsive that intervention (e.g., Harackiewicz et al. 2016a). Second, a deeper understanding of the context will provide insight into the ways in which intervention materials can be customized to be most resonant with students. When assessing students' motivational profiles, it is important to remember that students' identities overlap and intersect, with implications for intervention. For example, an intervention that benefits women may not benefit FG students, and FG women may have a unique set of needs that would not be well addressed by either interventions for women or interventions for FG students (Cole 2009).

In addition to the intersectionality of demographic categories (e.g., race and gender), it may be fruitful to consider overlap between demographic categories and psychological variables. Layous and colleagues' (2017) work suggests that values affirmation interventions can be effective for any student with belonging concerns. Does this fully explain the benefits of values affirmation for underrepresented minorities or FG students? Likewise, interventions that target achievement gaps may be working primarily through benefits for low performers or through other characteristics of the group. For example, Yeager and colleagues' (2016) definition of disadvantaged students as groups with a history of poor performance raises the interesting possibility that the positive effects of social belonging interventions could be indicative of positive effects for poor performers more generally.

As a final note, we think it will be important in future work to conduct more fine-grained analyses of intervention mechanisms for different groups. Much of the work in this review investigates mechanism in terms of psychological processes or behaviors affected by the intervention, and this work is crucial. However, there is another, more proximal layer of mechanism that has been gaining attention in recent work. Nearly all of the interventions in this review involve some amount of writing, and text analysis of students' essays may offer new insights into how different groups internalize intervention messages and what types of writing interventions have the greatest benefits for students. Indeed, work by Harackiewicz and colleagues (2016a), Beigman Klebanov and colleagues (2017), Shnabel and colleagues (2013), and Tibbetts and colleagues (2016a) demonstrates that these words, direct from students' pens or keyboards, can reveal underlying intervention mechanisms.

In sum, our review suggests that targeted interventions can be powerful in improving student outcomes in higher education. However, there are many theoretical and methodological issues to address as we continue to build a toolbox of interventions that target critical problems in education. We recommend that researchers and practitioners proceed with cautious optimism and continue the arduous but crucial work of understanding how, when, and for whom motivational interventions can improve educational outcomes.

DISCLOSURE STATEMENT

The authors are not aware of any affiliations, memberships, funding, or financial holdings that might be perceived as affecting the objectivity of this review.

ACKNOWLEDGMENTS

We thank Jilana Boston, Cameron Hecht, and Yoi Tibbetts for helpful comments on earlier versions of this manuscript. This research was supported by the National Institutes of Health (grant R01GM102703). This research was also supported by the the Institute of Education Sciences, US Department of Education, through award R305B15003 to the University of Wisconsin–Madison. The opinions expressed are those of the authors and do not represent the views of the US Department of Education or the National Institutes of Health.

LITERATURE CITED

Acee TW, Weinstein CE. 2010. Effects of a value-reappraisal intervention on statistics students' motivation and performance. *J. Exp. Educ.* 78:487–512

Aronson E. 1999. The power of self-persuasion. *Am. Psychol.* 54:875–84

Aronson J, Fried CB, Good C. 2002. Reducing the effects of stereotype threat on African American college students by shaping theories of intelligence. *J. Exp. Soc. Psychol.* 38:113–25

Beigman Klebanov B, Burstein J, Harackiewicz JM, Priniski SJ, Mulholland M. 2017. Reflective writing about the utility value of science as a tool for increasing STEM motivation and retention—can AI help scale up? *Int. J. Artif. Intell. Educ.* In press

Blackwell LS, Trzesniewski KH, Dweck CS. 2007. Implicit theories of intelligence predict achievement across an adolescent transition: a longitudinal study and an intervention. *Child Dev.* 78:246–63

Borman GD, Grigg J, Hanselman P. 2016. An effort to close achievement gaps at scale through self-affirmation. *Educ. Eval. Policy Anal.* 38:21–42

Bowen NK, Wegmann KM, Webber KC. 2013. Enhancing a brief writing intervention to combat stereotype threat among middle-school students. *J. Educ. Psychol.* 105:427–35

Brady ST, Reeves SL, Garcia J, Purdie-Vaughns V, Cook JE, et al. 2016. The psychology of the affirmed learner: spontaneous self-affirmation in the face of stress. *J. Educ. Psychol.* 108:353–73

Browman AS, Destin M. 2016. The effects of a warm or chilly climate toward socioeconomic diversity on academic motivation and self-concept. *Personal. Soc. Psychol. Bull.* 42:172–87

Brown E, Smith J, Thoman D, Allen J, Muragishi G. 2015. From bench to bedside: a communal utility value intervention to enhance students' biomedical science motivation. *J. Educ. Psychol.* 107:1116–35

Canning EA, Harackiewicz JM. 2015. Teach it, don't preach it: the differential effects of directly-communicated and self-generated utility-value information. *Motiv. Sci.* 1:47–71

Canning EA, Harackiewicz JM, Priniski SP, Hecht CA, Tibbetts Y, Hyde JS. 2018. Improving performance and retention in introductory biology with a utility-value intervention. *J. Educ. Psychol.* In press

Cohen GL, Garcia J, Apfel N, Master A. 2006. Reducing the racial achievement gap: a social-psychological intervention. *Science* 313:1307–10

Cohen GL, Garcia J, Purdie-Vaughns V, Apfel N, Brzustoski P. 2009. Recursive processes in self-affirmation: intervening to close the minority achievement gap. *Science* 324:400–3

Cohen GL, Sherman DK. 2014. The psychology of change: self-affirmation and social psychological intervention. *Annu. Rev. Psychol.* 65:333–71

Cole ER. 2009. Intersectionality and research in psychology. *Am. Psychol.* 64:170–80

Cook JE, Purdie-Vaughns V, Garcia J, Cohen GL. 2012. Chronic threat and contingent belonging: protective benefits of values affirmation on identity development. *J. Personal. Soc. Psychol.* 102:479–96

Dee TS. 2015. Social identity and achievement gaps: evidence from an affirmation intervention. *J. Res. Educ. Eff.* 8:149–68

Durik AM, Hulleman CS, Harackiewicz JM. 2015. One size fits some: Instructional enhancements to promote interest don't work the same for everyone. In *Interest in Mathematics and Science Learning*, ed. KA Renninger, M Nieswandt, S Hidi, pp. 49–62. Washington, DC: Am. Educ. Res. Assoc.

Dweck CS. 1999. *Self-Theories: Their Role in Motivation, Personality, and Development*. Philadelphia: Psychol. Press

Eccles J, Adler T, Futterman R, Goff S, Kaczala C, Meece J. 1983. Expectations, values and academic behaviors. In *Perspective on Achievement and Achievement Motivation*, ed. JT Spence, pp. 75–146. San Francisco: W. H. Freeman

Eccles JS, Wigfield A. 2002. Motivational beliefs, values, and goals. *Annu. Rev. Psychol.* 53:109–32

Gaspard H, Dicke A-L, Flunger B, Brisson BM, Häfner I, et al. 2015. Fostering adolescents' value beliefs for mathematics with a relevance intervention in the classroom. *Dev. Psychol.* 51:1226–40

Hall NC, Perry RP, Goetz T, Ruthig JC, Stupnisky RH, Newall NE. 2007. Attributional retraining and elaborative learning: improving academic development through writing-based interventions. *Learn. Individ. Differ.* 17:280–90

Hanselman P, Bruch SK, Gamoran A, Borman GD. 2014. Threat in context: school moderation of the impact of social identity threat on racial/ethnic achievement gaps. *Sociol. Educ.* 87:106–24

Hanselman P, Rozek CS, Grigg J, Borman GD. 2017. New evidence on self-affirmation effects and theorized sources of heterogeneity from large-scale replications. *J. Educ. Psychol.* 109:405–24

Harackiewicz JM, Canning EA, Tibbetts Y, Giffen CJ, Blair SS, et al. 2014a. Closing the social class achievement gap for first-generation students in undergraduate biology. *J. Educ. Psychol.* 106:375–89

Harackiewicz JM, Canning EA, Tibbetts Y, Priniski SJ, Hyde JS. 2016a. Closing achievement gaps with a utility-value intervention: disentangling race and social class. *J. Personal. Soc. Psychol.* 111:745–65

Harackiewicz JM, Hulleman CS. 2010. The importance of interest: the role of achievement goals and task values in promoting the development of interest. *Soc. Personal. Psychol. Compass* 4:42–52

Harackiewicz JM, Rozek CS, Hulleman CS, Hyde JS. 2012. Helping parents to motivate adolescents in mathematics and science: an experimental test of a utility-value intervention. *Psychol. Sci.* 23:899–906

Harackiewicz JM, Smith JL, Priniski SJ. 2016b. Interest matters: the importance of promoting interest in education. *Policy Insights Behav. Brain Sci.* 3:220–27

Harackiewicz JM, Tibbetts Y, Canning EA, Hyde JS. 2014b. Harnessing values to promote motivation in education. In *Advances in Motivation and Achievement*, ed. SA Karabenick, TC Urden, pp. 71–105. Bingley, UK: Emerald Group Publ. Ltd.

Haynes TL, Ruthig JC, Perry RP, Stupnisky RH, Hall NC. 2006. Reducing the academic risks of over-optimism: the longitudinal effects of attributional retraining on cognition and achievement. *Res. High. Educ.* 47:755–79

Hulleman CS, Cordray DS. 2009. Moving from the lab to the field: the role of fidelity and achieved intervention strength. *J. Res. Educ. Eff.* 2:88–110

Hulleman CS, Godes O, Hendricks BL, Harackiewicz JM. 2010. Enhancing interest and performance with a utility value intervention. *J. Educ. Psychol.* 102:880–95

Hulleman CS, Harackiewicz JM. 2009. Promoting interest and performance in high school science classes. *Science* 326:1410–12

Hulleman CS, Kosovich JJ, Barron KE, Daniel DB. 2017. Making connections: replicating and extending the utility value intervention in the classroom. *J. Educ. Psychol.* 109:387–404

Jamieson JP, Peters BJ, Greenwood EJ, Altose AJ. 2016. Reappraising stress arousal improves performance and reduces evaluation anxiety in classroom exam situations. *Soc. Psychol. Personal. Sci.* 7:579–87

Johnson ML, Sinatra GM. 2013. Use of task-value instructional inductions for facilitating engagement and conceptual change. *Contemp. Educ. Psychol.* 38:51–63

Kizilcec RF, Saltarelli AJ, Reich J, Cohen GL. 2017. Closing global achievement gaps in MOOCs: Brief interventions address social identity threat at scale. *Science* 355:251–52

Landau MJ, Oyserman D, Keefer LA, Smith GC. 2014. The college journey and academic engagement: how metaphor use enhances identity-based motivation. *J. Personal. Soc. Psychol.* 106:679–98

Layous K, Davis EM, Garcia J, Purdie-Vaughns V, Cook JE, et al. 2017. Feeling left out, but affirmed: protecting against the negative effects of low belonging in college. *J. Exp. Soc. Psychol.* 69:227–31

Lazowski RA, Hulleman CS. 2016. Motivation interventions in education: a meta-analytic review. *Rev. Educ. Res.* 86:602–40

Miyake A, Kost-Smith LE, Finkelstein ND, Pollock SJ, Cohen GL, et al. 2010. Reducing the gender achievement gap in college science: a classroom study of values affirmation. *Science* 330:1234–37

O'Donnell CL. 2008. Defining, conceptualizing, and measuring fidelity of implementation and its relationship to outcomes in K-12 curriculum intervention research. *Rev. Educ. Res.* 78:33–84

Paunesku D, Walton GM, Romero C, Smith EN, Yeager DS, Dweck CS. 2015. Mind-set interventions are a scalable treatment for academic underachievement. *Psychol. Sci.* 26:784–93

Perry RP, Chipperfield JG, Hladkyj S, Pekrun R, Hamm JM. 2014. Attribution-based treatment interventions in some achievement settings. *Adv. Motiv. Achiev.* 18:1–35

Perry RP, Hamm JM. 2017. An attribution perspective on competence and motivation: theory and treatment interventions. In *Handbook of Competence and Motivation: Theory and Application*, ed. AJ Elliot, CS Dweck, DS Yeager, pp. 61–84. New York: Guilford Press. 2nd ed.

Perry RP, Stupnisky RH, Hall NC, Chipperfield JG, Weiner B. 2010. Bad starts and better finishes: attributional retraining and initial performance in competitive achievement settings. *J. Soc. Clin. Psychol.* 29:668–700

Pennebaker JW, Booth RJ, Francis ME. 2007. Linguistic inquiry and word count: LIWC. *Software.* **http://liwc.wpengine.com/**

Protzko J, Aronson J. 2016. Context moderates affirmation effects on the ethnic achievement gap. *Soc. Psychol. Personal. Sci.* 7:500–7

Ross L, Nisbett RE. 2011. *The Person and the Situation: Perspectives of Social Psychology.* London: Pinter & Martin

Rozek CS, Svoboda RC, Harackiewicz JM, Hulleman CS, Hyde JS. 2017. Utility-value intervention with parents increases students' STEM preparation and career pursuit. *PNAS* 114:909–14

Schwartz DL, Cheng KM, Salehi S, Wieman C. 2016. The half empty question for socio-cognitive interventions. *J. Educ. Psychol.* 108:297–404

Sherman DK, Hartson KA, Binning KR, Purdie-Vaughns V, Garcia J, et al. 2013. Deflecting the trajectory and changing the narrative: how self-affirmation affects academic performance and motivation under identity threat. *J. Personal. Soc. Psychol.* 104:591–618

Shnabel N, Purdie-Vaughns V, Cook JE, Garcia J, Cohen GL. 2013. Demystifying values-affirmation interventions: Writing about social belonging is a key to buffering against identity threat. *Personal. Soc. Psychol. B* 39:663–76

Steele CM. 1988. The psychology of self-affirmation: sustaining the integrity of the self. *Adv. Exp. Soc. Psychol.* 21:261–302

Stephens NM, Fryberg SA, Markus HR, Johnson CS, Covarrubias R. 2012. Unseen disadvantage: how American universities' focus on independence undermines the academic performance of first-generation college students. *J. Personal. Soc. Psychol.* 102:1178–97

Stephens NM, Hamedani MG, Destin M. 2014. Closing the social-class achievement gap: A difference-education intervention improves first-generation students' academic performance and all students' college transition. *Psychol. Sci.* 25:943–53

Stephens NM, Townsend SS, Hamedani MG, Destin M, Manzo V. 2015. A difference-education intervention equips first-generation college students to thrive in the face of stressful college situations. *Psychol. Sci.* 26:1556–66

Thoman DB, Brown ER, Mason AZ, Harmsen AG, Smith JL. 2015. The role of altruistic values in motivating underrepresented minority students for biomedicine. *BioScience* 65:183–88

Thoman DB, Muragishi GA, Smith JL. 2017. Research microcultures as socialization contexts for underrepresented science students. *Psychol. Sci.* 28:760–73

Tibbetts Y, Harackiewicz JM, Canning EA, Boston JS, Priniski SJ, et al. 2016a. Affirming independence: exploring mechanisms underlying a values affirmation intervention for first-generation students. *J. Personal. Soc. Psychol.* 110:635–59

Tibbetts Y, Harackiewicz JM, Priniski SJ, Canning EA. 2016b. Broadening participation in the life sciences with social-psychological interventions. *CBE Life Sci. Educ.* 15:es4

Walton GM. 2014. The new science of wise psychological interventions. *Curr. Dir. Psychol. Sci.* 23:73–82

Walton GM, Cohen GL. 2007. A question of belonging: race, social fit, and achievement. *J. Personal. Soc. Psychol.* 92:82–96

Walton GM, Cohen GL. 2011. A brief social-belonging intervention improves academic and health outcomes among minority students. *Science* 331:1447–51

Walton GM, Logel C, Peach JM, Spencer SJ, Zanna MP. 2015. Two brief interventions to mitigate a "chilly climate" transform women's experience, relationships, and achievement in engineering. *J. Educ. Psychol.* 107:468–85

Weiner B. 1974. *Achievement Motivation and Attribution Theory*. Morristown, NJ: General Learning Press

Wilson TD. 2006. The power of social psychological interventions. *Science* 313:1251–52

Wilson TD. 2011. *Redirect: The Surprising New Science of Psychological Change*. New York: Little, Brown

Wilson TD, Linville PW. 1982. Improving the academic performance of college freshmen: attribution therapy revisited. *J. Personal. Soc. Psychol.* 42:367–76

Wilson TD, Linville PW. 1985. Improving the performance of college freshmen with attributional techniques. *J. Personal. Soc. Psychol.* 49:287–93

Yeager DS, Henderson MD, Paunesku D, Walton GM, D'Mello S, et al. 2014. Boring but important: A self-transcendent purpose for learning fosters academic self-regulation. *J. Personal. Soc. Psychol.* 107:559–80

Yeager DS, Walton GM. 2011. Social-psychological interventions in education: They're not magic. *Rev. Educ. Res.* 81:267–301

Yeager DS, Walton GM, Brady ST, Akcinar EN, Paunesku D, et al. 2016. Teaching a lay theory before college narrows achievement gaps at scale. *PNAS* 113:E3341–48

Why Social Relationships Are Important for Physical Health: A Systems Approach to Understanding and Modifying Risk and Protection

Julianne Holt-Lunstad

Departments of Psychology and Neuroscience, Brigham Young University, Provo, Utah 84602; email: Julianne_holt-lunstad@byu.edu

Annu. Rev. Psychol. 2018. 69:437–58

First published as a Review in Advance on October 16, 2017

The *Annual Review of Psychology* is online at psych.annualreviews.org

https://doi.org/10.1146/annurev-psych-122216-011902

Keywords

social relationships, social connection, social isolation, loneliness, social network, social ecological model

Abstract

Social relationships are adaptive and crucial for survival. This review presents existing evidence indicating that our social connections to others have powerful influences on health and longevity and that lacking social connection qualifies as a risk factor for premature mortality. A systems perspective is presented as a framework by which to move social connection into the realm of public health. Individuals, and health-relevant biological processes, exist within larger social contexts including the family, neighborhood and community, and society and culture. Applying the social ecological model, this review highlights the interrelationships of individuals within groups in terms of understanding both the causal mechanisms by which social connection influences physical health and the ways in which this influence can inform potential intervention strategies. A systems approach also helps identify gaps in our current understanding that may guide future research.

Contents

INTRODUCTION AND OVERVIEW

Humans are social animals. Across a number of social species, there is evidence that being part of a group is adaptive for survival. For example, being part of a group can provide protection from predators (Ioannou et al. 2012) and from the elements (Black et al. 2016), as well as increased access to resources such as food (Beauchamp 2014, Pays et al. 2013). Humans are one of the most vulnerable species at birth, relying on others for nearly all aspects of survival—a human infant would simply die if left alone. Although water, food, and shelter are key to survival, it is also clear that humans would not survive without the care and nurturance of others. Throughout the lifespan, social connections continue to play a vital role (Fagundes et al. 2011, Hawkley & Capitanio 2015).

From this perspective, it has been argued that social connection may be viewed as a biological need directly tied to survival. Much as thirst drives one to consume water, loneliness may be a biologically adaptive response motivating one to reconnect socially (Cacioppo et al. 2014). Neuro-science also supports the notion of social connection as being adaptive—we use more metabolic resources when coping with threat alone than when we are in the presence of others (Coan & Sbarra 2015, Coan et al. 2006), and social pain shares neural mechanisms with physical pain (Eisenberger 2012). Both of these points suggest the biological manifestation of motivational cues to maintain close social ties.

Indeed, across several different measurement approaches, evidence indicates that those who are more socially connected live longer (Holt-Lunstad et al. 2010). Epidemiological research has examined this prospectively in large community samples by measuring social connection in indi-viduals and then following these individuals over time, often over decades, to determine if social connection predicted survival or time to death. Since the seminal review done by House and colleagues (1988), which included five prospective studies, the body of evidence has grown expo-nentially to now include hundreds of studies, millions of participants, and broader measurement approaches. Several recent published reviews and meta-analyses also synthesize the relevant data, including the protective effect of social relationships (broadly defined; Holt-Lunstad et al. 2010), social contact frequency (Shor & Roelfs 2015), and family ties (Shor et al. 2013), whereas others demonstrate the risk associated with lacking social connection via loneliness and social isolation (Holt-Lunstad et al. 2015), divorce (Sbarra et al. 2011, Shor et al. 2012a), being single (Roelfs et al. 2011), and widowhood (Shor et al. 2012b). Taken together, we now have robust evidence indicating that being socially connected has a powerful influence on longevity, such that having more and better relationships is associated with protection and, conversely, that having fewer and poorer relationships is associated with risk. When benchmarked against other leading risk factors for mortality, the magnitude of this effect is equivalent to or exceeds that of obesity (Holt-Lunstad et al. 2010, 2015).

One fundamentally important question remains—what exactly is a social relationship? This question has been an area of inquiry and debate for decades among relationship scientists. Because the term relationship is commonly used by scientists and laypeople alike, it is often used with the assumption that the meaning is obvious (Reis et al. 2000). A defining characteristic of a social relationship is that there is interaction between the relationship partners and that this interaction exerts mutual influence over behavior (Berschied & Reis 1998). Although interaction is a necessary feature of relationships, it is not sufficient for all types of relationships. Close relationships include this hallmark feature of influence over behavior, but this influence occurs over extended periods of time, are emotionally laden, and are characterized by idiosyncratic representations of others (Berschied & Reis 1998). Thus, it is clear that the very nature of social relationships is complex and necessitates a nuanced approach with consideration of multiple factors.

As the scientific community continues to elucidate the relationship between social relationships and physical health, it is vital to view relationships from an interdisciplinary and multilevel perspective. Therefore, this review proposes the potential utility of a systems approach when evaluating the link between social relationships and physical health. This review focuses primarily on physical health and longevity; however, a systems approach may be applied to social and mental health outcomes, as well. The systems approach views each individual as existing within a network of four separate yet embedded dimensions: the individual, the family and close relationships, the community, and the society. This approach does not sacrifice individual consideration, but rather places each individual within a broader context. The broader consideration of influences from relationship, community, and society aids in our understanding of social connection as a protective factor (or social disconnection as a risk factor) and could be applied to efforts aimed at developing effective interventions and preventative efforts.

This review first provides a background description of social systems and how they fit with current measurement approaches. Next, to emphasize the need to consider a systems approach in advancing social connection into the realm of public health, the evidence that multifactorial risk factors are both common and appropriate in public health is highlighted. The bulk of this review then places the existing literature on the association between social relationships and health into a systems framework to (*a*) better understand underlying causes and (*b*) identify gaps in our approaches to developing effective preventative and intervention efforts. In conclusion, gaps in the existing literature are presented to articulate future directions.

SOCIAL SYSTEMS

The field of psychology generally approaches scientific inquiry at the level of the individual, and the study of social relationships is no exception. This approach has garnered important insights into the factors that influence affect, cognitions, behaviors, individual differences, etc. However, this individualistic approach represents only one of many levels that can be utilized to understand the complex ways in which social connection influences physical health.

From a systems approach, the aim is "to classify systems according to the way the parts are organized or interrelated, and ... to describe typical patterns of behavior for the different classes of systems as defined" (Vetere 1987, pp. 18–19). Simply stated, a system is a set of interrelated or interacting elements. Thus, a systems theory approach to social relationships organizes the complex myriad of conceptualizations into a hierarchy of levels of influence. These relationships are open systems in which information, energy, and materials are exchanged between nested levels, or systems, within the environment. A systems perspective of social relationships acknowledges the following four concepts: First, each individual encompasses hierarchically organized biological and behavior systems, which are influenced by the individual's social relationships, and these systems are in place from conception. Second, each relationship has an ecological niche, which includes social and physical environmental systems. Third, each relationship's ecological niche is embedded in a larger societal and cultural system. Fourth, over time, these systems evolve and influence each other (Reis et al. 2000). Importantly, this perspective recognizes not only the influence of relationships at multiple levels (micro to macro), but also their embeddedness within each other, resulting in mutual influence.

How Does a Social Systems Approach Fit Within Current Measurement Approaches?

Social connection has been used as an umbrella term to represent the multiple ways in which individuals connect to others emotionally, behaviorally, and physically. Current measurement approaches include three broad categorizations that assess very different aspects of social relationships: structural, functional, and qualitative indicators of social connection (Holt-Lunstad et al. 2017; see **Figure 1**). Structural indicators of connection are typically quantitative in nature, assessing the number or diversity of social relationships or roles or frequency of social contact. In essence, structural measures attempt to capture the existence of relationships and their influence in one's life. Functional indicators, on the other hand, attempt to capture the actual or perceived availability of the kinds of aid and resources that relationships may provide. Thus, functional

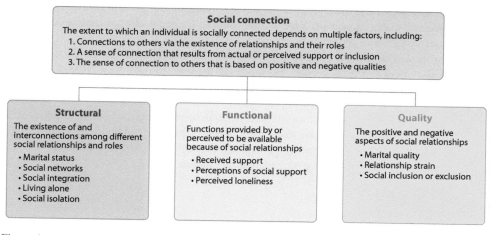

Figure 1

Social connection as a multifactorial construct including structural, functional, and quality components.

measures go beyond evaluating the presence or absence of others to assess what they may do or provide in the relationship. The bulk of the epidemiological literature has focused primarily on structural and functional measurement approaches. A growing body of evidence further indicates that the quality, or positive and negative aspects, of these relationships is also important to a complete evaluation of social connection. As argued elsewhere (see Holt-Lunstad et al. 2017), all three of these components are important to consider in assessing health and mortality risk.

Most current measurement approaches do not explicitly target one level (individual, family, community, society); however, some appear to align more with specific levels than with others. For instance, measurement of functional support, particularly perceived support or loneliness, may be viewed as an individual-level assessment given its reliance on an individual's personal perceived reality. Measures of relationship quality may fall more squarely within the realm of the relationship or family level because this quality relates to a specific relationship, whereas structural measures such as social integration or network size may align more with network- or community-level assessments. However, we can extrapolate how each may be influenced by other levels. For instance, one's individual perception may be based on expectations set in early familial experiences or societal norms, and self-reports of relationship quality and network size may be influenced by individual personality characteristics and social sensitivity. It is also important to note that most current measurement approaches do not explicitly measure across levels, which is a considerable limitation.

A major setback for advancing social connections into the broader field of public health has been the lack of consistency in measurement approaches. Given the diversity of measures of social connection, there exists a lack of clarity on what exactly the problem is in which we should intervene. For example, should we be focused on reducing loneliness, increasing social support, reducing relationship distress, or providing assistance in the home? Another setback is the fact that most large-scale research opts for a short assessment (e.g., of marital status or living arrangements) to maximize feasibility. However, binary measures have been found to be less predictive of mortality risk than more complex measures (Holt-Lunstad et al. 2010). In cases where longer, more thorough assessment is utilized, these assessments often target only one component of social relationships (e.g., perceived social support or loneliness), making it difficult to compare findings across studies. It should be noted that, despite relative differences in predictive utility, functional, structural, and quality measures have all significantly predicted risk (Holt-Lunstad et al. 2010). However, there are low correlations between these measures, indicating that they are measuring distinct constructs and that each needs to be considered. Measurement approaches that are multidimensional, such as complex social integration, may consider multiple levels given that they include structural and functional components—although quality is less represented in these approaches (Holt-Lunstad et al. 2010, Robles et al. 2014). Importantly, multidimensional approaches have been shown to be the strongest predictor of mortality risk (Holt-Lunstad et al. 2010). Thus, it is important to recognize that most current assessment approaches may not adequately capture the different levels of social influence that may affect health via different pathways. Taking a systems approach to measurement could potentially increase the predictability of risk and improve screening.

SYSTEMS APPROACH TO UNDERSTANDING RISK AND PROTECTION

In order to better understand the impact of social connection on physical health, individual-level outcomes need to be examined within the broader context that created them. As psychologists, we can take cues from population health, which utilizes a more comprehensive approach to examining health risk over the lifespan. The ecological model, already embraced by population health, is an ideal way to include the added benefits of a broader perspective without sacrificing the detail-oriented precision of a levels approach. The Institute of Medicine has defined the ecological model

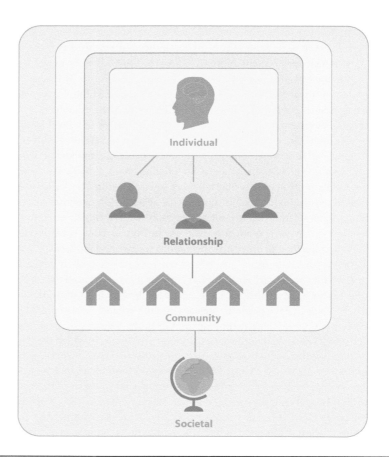

Figure 2

Social ecological model.

as "a model of health that emphasizes the linkages and relationships among multiple factors (or determinants) affecting health" (Inst. Med. 2003, p. 32). If the evidence supports elevating social connection to a public health priority, then it would serve us well to apply the existing evidence using this model to move the field forward.

In the United States, the Centers for Disease Control and Prevention (CDC) uses the social ecological model to examine the causes and potential prevention strategies of risk factors such as violence (CDC 2015). This four-level model takes into account the complex interactions between factors at the individual, relationship, community, and society levels. **Figure 2** draws upon this model, and the overlapping shapes illustrate how factors at one level are embedded within or influence factors at another level. Given the fact that social disconnection (e.g., isolation, loneliness, poor-quality relationships) is a significant risk factor for premature mortality, each of these levels could be similarly applied to examining causal factors and prevention strategies.

Social Connection as a Risk or Protective Factor

Risk factors have been defined as variables that increase the probability of an undesirable outcome (e.g., death), whereas protective factors increase the probability of a desired outcome (e.g., survival) (Kraemer et al. 1997). Social connections significantly predict health for either good or bad; thus, they may be viewed as both a risk and a protective factor. The evidence linking social relationships to health includes clear examples of both processes (e.g., lacking companionship and relationship conflict are associated with risk, whereas social integration and social support are protective). The mortality risk from being socially disconnected, whether it be from isolation or loneliness, also appears to be linear—existing across the continuum from those who are extremely isolated to those who are moderately and mildly isolated (Tanskanen & Anttila 2016). Furthermore, combined data from four nationally representative studies found strong dose–response associations between social integration and lower risk for physiological dysregulation in both early and later life (Yang et al. 2016). Being more socially connected is protective, whereas less social connection is associated with risk.

In order to establish social connection as a risk or protective factor, it is also critical to establish temporal precedence—lacking social connection should precede poor health. Indeed, prospective studies are ideal for testing the temporal precedence. The studies included in the meta-analyses discussed above (e.g., Holt-Lunstad et al. 2010, Roelfs et al. 2011, Shor & Roelfs 2015, Shor et al. 2012a) were prospective in nature and controlled for initial health status, establishing the temporal precedence and ruling out reverse causality. Thus, we have clear and robust evidence that the degree to which one is socially connected predicts levels of risk for or protection from morbidity and mortality.

Can we claim, however, that social connection causally influences risk or protection? To establish causation, experimentation involving manipulation of the proposed causal agent is viewed as the gold standard. In humans, we cannot randomly assign individuals to be isolated or in a poor-quality relationship, resulting in difficulty claiming causal influence. However, similar challenges were faced for other public health risk factors, such as smoking, yet we are all familiar with the claim that smoking causes cancer. Indeed, causal claims in public health apply the criteria of probabilistic causation rather than that of necessary and sufficient causation (Parascandola & Weed 2001, Parascandola et al. 2006). For example, obesity increases the risk of heart disease in a probabilistic manner, but not all those who are obese will develop heart disease. Applying probabilistic causation, evidence that social isolation increases the risk of mortality in a predictive and dose-response manner bolsters claims of causal risk and protection.

Multiply Determined Risk Factors

Similar to the influence of other health risk factors (e.g., hypertension, obesity, smoking, cholesterol levels), the influence of social relationships is complex and multifactorial (Stampfer et al. 2004). What does it mean for a risk factor to be multifactorial? Simply put, it means that there is no single putative causal factor. A prime example of a multifactorial risk factor is obesity, which has been targeted as a top priority for public health interventions because it has been associated with an increased risk for type 2 diabetes, cardiovascular disease, cancer, and all-cause mortality (Flegal et al. 2013). Within this initiative, physical activity, nutrition, and obesity are interrelated constructs, each independently linked to risk and protection (Dietz & Gortmaker 2016, Lombard et al. 2009, Plotnikoff et al. 2015). Poor nutrition and lack of physical activity are both behaviors linked to obesity, but they also work in conjunction with biological predispositions and environmental factors. For example, poor nutrition is impacted by genetics and early life experience, which can both result in physiological changes that increase obesity. In addition, physiological determinants are joined by socioeconomic influences. Large portion sizes, saturated and trans fat intake, refined carbohydrate consumption, and highly available fast food are more likely within certain socioeconomic contexts, such as food deserts (Ebbeling et al. 2002). Therefore, there are multiple factors to consider, and there is no single mechanism on which to intervene.

Social connection (or lack thereof) is likewise multiply determined (see **Figure 1**). Within a systems approach, the field can further explore the extent to which individual, family, community, and societal factors within each level influence the structure, function, and quality of social connections. Because social (dis)connection is multiply determined, to address social connection within the realm of public health, modifiable risk factors and viable targets for intervention must be identified.

SYSTEMS APPROACH TO UNDERSTANDING CAUSAL MECHANISMS

In order to address the public health relevance of social connection, the field could benefit from applying a systems approach. Using the social ecological model, the following sections identify and describe potential causal pathways at the individual, family, community, and society levels that significantly influence risk or protection. The major conceptual approaches and supporting evidence are summarized for each level, and a brief description of how it is or may be influenced by other levels is provided. It is important to note that such descriptions do not represent exhaustive reviews, but rather are illustrative examples. Furthermore, level-based descriptions are merely for organization's sake and do not imply that each level is independent of other levels.

Individual-Level Factors

Within an individual, there are biological, cognitive, psychological, and personality characteristics that may increase the likelihood that one is socially connected or, conversely, isolated. Of course, even these individual factors are themselves intertwined and exert mutual influence.

Given that social connection has a strong link to survival, evidence points to the possibility that (via biological mechanisms) we are wired to desire and to be rewarded by connection and, conversely, to feel discomfort when we lack these connections. Reviews of data indicate biological indicators of social sensitivity, including genetic factors (Way & Lieberman 2010) and inflammatory processes (Eisenberger et al. 2017). For example, studies of gene association suggest that variation within genes that affect brain functioning (specifically serotonin and opioid transportation) influence the degree to which individuals are emotionally responsive to their social environment. Research has also suggested potential neurochemical mechanisms that support social bonding and affiliative behavior, such as oxytocin (Ross & Young 2009). Although this evidence is more developed within the animal model literature, evidence in humans is emerging. According to the "brain opioid theory of attachment," endogenous opioids (e.g., μ-opioids) are triggered by social experiences to mediate the reward associated with social bonding and affiliation (Loseth et al. 2014, Machin & Dunbar 2011). It is important to note that even genetic markers of social sensitivity are influenced by the larger social environment (Mitchell et al. 2013), suggesting that these biological (microlevel) processes are interacting within the larger context of macrolevel factors.

Social cognition describes the way the brain processes social information. Being able to infer the intentions, thoughts, and feelings of those around us is critical to engaging in our social world. Neuroscience evidence suggests that we may have both common and dedicated systems for social processing and that there may be evidence of self–other overlap (Beckes et al. 2013). According to the "social baseline theory," the brain expects social relationships that include interdependence, shared goals, and attention. If these expectations are not met, the brain will perceive that fewer resources are available. This results in increased physiological and cognitive effort, which can be accompanied by acute and chronic distress (Coan & Sbarra 2015). This suggests that the brain is designed to expect social relationships as the baseline, or the normal operating state. Furthermore, social insults such as rejection produce the same pattern of brain activation as physical pain, thereby alerting the individual to damages in social connections (Eisenberger et al. 2003). These findings, when taken cumulatively, could suggest that individual differences at the cognitive level impact perception and actual experience of social interactions, connection, and disconnection.

Psychological factors including both states and disorders (e.g., stress, depression, and anxiety) can also provide important insight, as both are associated with social withdrawal and impairments (Craske & Stein 2016, Ditzen & Heinrichs 2014). Social conditions such as rejection and interpersonal stress can also increase the risk of depression, suggesting that the associations between social conditions and health are complex and may share common mechanisms (Slavich & Irwin 2014). Our relationships are also closely tied to perceptions of stress. The stress buffering effect of social support is perhaps one of the most widely researched influences of social relationships on health. Indeed, many recent reviews summarize the processes, conditions, and biological mechanisms by which this effect operates (Ditzen & Heinrichs 2014, Hostinar 2015, Hostinar & Gunnar 2015). Recent research also indicates that our social relationships can be a source of stress influencing health (Oliveira et al. 2016). Regardless of the direction, it is clear that social relationships influence health via stress processes and that early experiences, developmental factors, and differences in genetically influenced biological systems can moderate this effect (Ditzen & Heinrichs 2014, Hennessy et al. 2009, Uchino 2009).

Personality, by definition, is a set of enduring traits distinct to an individual. Certainly, such characteristics could have profound effects on the degree to which individuals engage socially and the quality of those relationships. These characteristics would include temperament and individual differences. Some psychologists argue that there are five basic personality dimensions (the so-called Big Five): extraversion, agreeableness, openness, conscientiousness, and neuroticism. When evaluating social connection from the perspective of the Big Five approach, studies have found that the traits of extraversion and neuroticism are important correlates of loneliness (Asendorpf & van Aken 2003). In addition, loneliness covaries in a linear fashion with emotional stability, surgency, agreeableness, conscientiousness, shyness, and sociability (Cacioppo et al. 2006). There is also evidence that hostile individuals find social support stressful and do not benefit from intimacy in daily life (Vella et al. 2008).

Overall, when we consider the myriad of factors at the individual level, we also need to consider their influence on structural, functional, and quality aspects of social connections. We need not limit our consideration to the measurement approaches that are perhaps most closely associated with the individual (perceptions of loneliness and perceptions of support). As an illustrative example, an individual-level personality characteristic, openness to new experience, may influence the degree to which one forms new relationships that, in turn, may influence the size and diversity of one's social network. Systematically applying each of the individual-level factors across the domains of social connection further points out areas where the field has strong evidence and areas where we have gaps in the literature.

Relationship-Level Factors

When examining factors beyond the individual level, psychologists and relationship scientists may consider dyads (e.g., romantic partner, caregiver) but often stop short of considering the larger familial context. Close relationships, such as those with a romantic partner, family members, and even close friends, may influence an array of experiences and a host of behaviors. Research in the area of close relationships (i.e., couple, caregiver, or familial relationships) is most closely tied to the relationship level. Within the close relationships literature, attachment, early childhood experiences, and social control have been the most widely used conceptual approaches. Thus, these are highlighted as illustrative examples.

Attachment. Attachment processes may be relevant to understanding how parent–child relationships and adult romantic relationships may influence health and well-being. First proposed nearly 50 years ago, attachment theory asserts that we have a biologically based, innate tendency to form bonds with an attachment figure as an adaptive means to protect us from harm and to regulate distress (Bowlby 1969). Attachment processes were originally proposed to involve infant–caregiver bonds but are now thought to continue to play an important role in maintaining relationships throughout the lifespan, with the primary attachment figure shifting to a romantic partner in adulthood (Mikulincer & Shaver 2007).

Attachment has been linked to health-relevant processes (physiology, affective states, health behavior, and health outcomes; for reviews, see Pietromonaco et al. 2013, Robles & Kane 2014). The attachment system was initially thought to primarily act on emotion regulation by reducing threat and increasing feelings of security, thereby blunting physiological reactivity (Diamond & Hicks 2004); however, additional pathways and interactions between these pathways have been noted. For example, the social-cognitive and emotion regulatory functions associated with attachment provide increased energy to the brain, in turn influencing eating behavior and health (Robles & Kane 2014). Despite the growing body of evidence linking attachment to a variety of health-relevant processes, additional data is needed linking attachment to chronic disease-related clinical endpoints (Robles & Kane 2014). Although attachment processes are clearly dyadic, attachment style can be viewed as an individual difference characteristic—again underscoring the importance of the embeddedness across social system levels.

Early childhood experiences. More recently, a growing body of research has suggested that early childhood may be a sensitive period, and experiences during this time may have long-term influences on health-relevant biology. For example, the National Child Development Study in the United Kingdom found that social isolation in children aged 7–11 predicted higher midlife rates of C-reactive protein—a reliable marker of inflammation associated with coronary heart disease (CHD), depression, and type 2 diabetes (Lacey et al. 2014). Similarly, parental separation (i.e., divorce) during childhood predicted inflammation as an adult (Lacey et al. 2013). Indeed, despite heterogeneity in measurement approaches, childhood adversity appears to have consistent effects on the risk for CHD (Appleton et al. 2016). Early childhood adversity, whether it occurs via neglect or threat, has also been shown to influence neural development (McLaughlin et al. 2014). Moreover, the growing body of work on early childhood experiences suggests the importance of considering gene–environment interactions from a developmental perspective (Lemery-Chalfant et al. 2013, Lovely et al. 2017). For example, evidence suggests that children with a particular gene variant may be more sensitive to their early childhood environment than children without that variant (Berry et al. 2014). Together, these data suggest the importance of the early social environment and the potential need for early interventions.

Social control. Close relationships, including friendships and romantic and familial relationships, can also exert tremendous influence over health-relevant behaviors and self-regulation. Any attempt to influence a relationship partner, whether it is direct (e.g., by requesting, urging, or demanding) or indirect (e.g., by motivating, inspiring, or supporting), would be defined as social control (Lewis & Rook 1999). Meta-analytic data examining social control on health behaviors and psychological responses (well-being and affect responses) indicate that social control generally improved health behaviors and psychological well-being (Craddock et al. 2015). However, social control strategy (positive or negative) was a moderator of these findings—indicating that positive social control (e.g., logic, positive reinforcement, modeling) was associated with improved health behaviors and well-being, whereas negative social control (e.g., disapproval, pressure, restriction) was associated with decreased well-being and health behaviors (Craddock et al. 2015). Of course, these results may occur through both conscious and unconscious processes (for reviews, see Fitzsimons & Finkel 2010, Fitzsimons & vanDellen 2015) resulting from individual-, community-, and society-level factors.

Direct influence on physiology. Friendship and familial ties may also have direct influences on health-relevant physiology (Robles & Kiecolt-Glaser 2003, Uchino 2006). Of course, it is often difficult to disentangle interpersonal processes to distinguish the relationship influence from the individual's perception of the relationship (individual-level influence). Dyadic approaches and analytic strategies, which model actor and partner effects, suggest the importance of considering both relationship partners. Partner effects have been found on a variety of health-relevant physiological processes including cardiovascular, endocrine, and immune function (Robles & Kiecolt-Glaser 2003). In an innovative study examining the role of social connection on fibrinogen levels (a biomarker of inflammation and cardiovascular risk), ratings of social connection completed by a person's friends and family were more predictive than the person's own ratings of perceived connection (Kim et al. 2016). These data suggest that the relationship has objective influence that is just as, if not more, important for health risk than individual perceptions.

Many other functional, structural, and relationship quality dimensions may also be important to consider. For example, there is a burgeoning area of research on the influence of partner responsiveness on not only relationship outcomes, but also health-relevant physiology (Slatcher et al. 2015) and health behaviors (Derrick et al. 2013). There is also evidence that structural indicators of relationship status, such as marital status (Manzoli et al. 2007), as well as marital quality (Robles et al. 2014), are also strong predictors of longevity. To fully grasp the causal influence of social relationships on health, these and other relationship-level factors will need to be considered.

Community-Level Factors

Although one's social network usually encompasses close relationships with family members, it also extends to larger social contexts such as one's entire social network, neighborhood, or community. It is important to evaluate this broad perspective of social influence, as even distant connections within this social network can impact health. Christakis & Fowler (2007, 2008, 2013) conducted a series of studies examining the powerful influence of social networks. Using large-scale data sets, they were able to identify clustering of a variety of health-related outcomes of interest. For example, in one study, they examined the interconnections of relationships within the social networks of 12,067 people over the course of several decades and found that one's body mass index (BMI) was highly related to the BMIs of one's friends (Christakis & Fowler 2007). In other words, there was clustering of obesity within social networks. These data showed that a person's likelihood of becoming obese was significantly increased if they had a friend, spouse, or sibling that was obese—thus, obesity spread through social network ties. This clustering has been found among at least 15 different health-relevant behaviors (e.g., smoking, sleep, obesity, heavy drinking) and affective states (e.g., happiness, loneliness, depression) (Christakis & Fowler 2013). More specifically, these studies have found that the effect extends to three degrees of influence—i.e., to the friends of our friend's friends (Christakis & Fowler 2007, 2008, 2013). There are some health-related factors (health screening and sexual orientation), however, that do not spread via social network ties. This influence, or spread, may be due to individuals choosing to associate with others who are similar (homophily), sharing an environmental context, or being directly influenced by their contacts (induction). The three degrees of influence have also been demonstrated in a large-scale analysis of over 40 million Twitter responses (Bliss et al. 2011), suggesting the potential impact of online social networks.

Characteristics of one's community or neighborhood environment can also favorably or adversely influence health beyond the impact of individual-level characteristics (Baum et al. 2016). Public health is increasingly recognizing the importance of the characteristics of the built environment, including walkable areas, traffic, and recreational facilities, that influence a variety of health-related outcomes (Malambo et al. 2016). For instance, older adults in high-crime neighborhoods report feeling trapped, making social participation difficult—thus, neighborhood factors may contribute to social isolation (Portacolone et al. 2017). Those in disadvantaged neighborhoods are less likely to enjoy the health advantages associated with strong social networks (Wen et al. 2005). Of course, the influences of social class on neighborhood racial and ethnic composition and neighborhood resources such as community centers may all be important factors to consider. Neighborhood characteristics have received wide attention, but characteristics of other settings should be further investigated to clarify the link between social network impact, environmental context, and health.

Community-level characteristics may also include educational, clinical and health care, and workplace settings. Importantly, these community settings are social contexts (i.e., settings where social relationships may develop or where social interaction occurs) as well as normative contexts (i.e., settings providing informal or formal rules about the appropriateness of social relationships or interactions). Educational settings can shape social experiences, attitudes, and information from childhood through early adulthood, and perhaps beyond. Although exposure to health care settings is typically infrequent, the health care setting is highly influential in setting the stage for what is considered important for health. Furthermore, workplace settings are where individuals spend a significant portion of almost every day, making this setting highly influential due to chronic exposure.

Society-Level Factors

Society-level factors help create a climate in which social connection may be encouraged or inhibited. These factors include social and cultural norms that influence health-related behaviors, such as physical activity and eating patterns (Ball et al. 2010, Templeton et al. 2016). For instance, messages that convey normative lifestyle expectations and desirability may be communicated via television, movies, books, or newspapers (Berkowitz 2004). Of course, we need to acknowledge that these social messages do not always promote healthy lifestyles (e.g., physical activity) and can also shape societal norms that may promote risky behaviors (e.g., smoking, alcohol and drug abuse).

Societal norms also influence the level of social participation viewed as acceptable or desirable. For example, there is cultural variation in norms that value independence and interdependence. Western cultures such as that of the United States place a high value on personal independence. This may be reflected in demographic trends indicating that there are more people in the United States living alone now than ever before, and fewer people are getting married and having children (Vespa et al. 2013). Among older adults in the United States, the socially desirable living arrangement is independent living. Indeed, in a nationally representative sample of adults over the age of 60, 90% indicated that they intended to stay in their current home (AARP 2012). These trends, taken together with an increasing aging population, suggest that older adults will have fewer social and familial resources to draw upon in old age (Rook 2009). Thus, societies that value independence, and communities that support it, may be doing so at the detriment of long-term health.

Of course, society-level factors may be influenced by factors at other levels. Indeed, there is evidence to suggest that genetic variation and neural activation (individual-level factors) may influence cultural differences. For example, a review of cross-national data reveals robust correlations between variants in genes with social sensitivity alleles and the degree to which each population is characterized by individualism or collectivism (Way & Lieberman 2010). Likewise, meta-analytic data has demonstrated that cultural differences in brain activity related to social and nonsocial processing are mediated by distinct neural networks—such that individuals from Western cultures demonstrate greater activation in brain regions associated with self- and emotion regulation, whereas those from Eastern cultures, which value collectivism more highly, show greater activation in regions associated with social cognitive processing (Han & Ma 2014).

Independent, Additive, and Synergistic Effects of Component Social Factors

Most research focuses on only one component of social connection, and, thus, we have a vast literature establishing these components in a variety of populations. However, we have less data in which these different components have been measured within the same sample. By doing so, we can examine the relative influence of each component independent of the others, and perhaps more importantly, we can directly test for additive and synergistic effects of these social connection components. Although there are currently not enough of these studies to examine meta-analytically, there are a few studies that can provide preliminary insight. For instance, when researchers examined the influence of loneliness and social network size on immune response, both were significant predictors, but the poorest immune response was found among individuals who both were high in loneliness and had a small social network (i.e., were isolated) (Pressman et al. 2005); however, in another study with mortality as an outcome, no synergistic effect was found (Tanskanen & Anttila 2016). Additional studies have measured both social isolation or social network size and loneliness in the same sample; however, most only tested for independent effects and not for synergistic effects. Of course, these findings have important implications for research, risk assessment, and, ultimately, the development of effective interventions.

DEVELOPING EFFECTIVE INTERVENTIONS

In the realm of public health, it is important to determine risk for the purposes of predicting and identifying those who are most vulnerable to potential poor health, as well as the factors that can be modified to reduce that risk. Despite strong epidemiological and experimental evidence establishing a direct influence of social connection on health, the major challenge has been developing effective interventions. Early work suggested that medical patient participation in peer support groups could significantly increase survival (Spiegel et al. 1989). For instance, in the landmark study by Spiegel et al. (1989), metastatic breast cancer patients who participated in support groups in addition to receiving standard care lived twice as long as patients who only received standard care. However, attempts to replicate this study have led to debate, as subsequent interventions have been less effective (Boesen & Johansen 2008, Kissane & Li 2008).

There are now multiple reviews of the intervention literature, including evaluations of social support interventions (Hogan et al. 2002) and interventions aimed specifically at reducing loneliness (Cacioppo et al. 2015) and isolation (Franck et al. 2016, Gardiner et al. 2017) among older adults. These reviews indicate a variety of implementation strategies, including individual and group interventions and peer-led and professionally delivered interventions, as well as differing social foci (e.g., perceptions of support, network size, social skills) and presenting problems (e.g., cancer, substance abuse, loneliness). These reviews also reveal varying levels of effectiveness among existing interventions, with some being successful and some unsuccessful. Despite robust evidence of the influence of social connections on health, when we attempt to intervene to reduce risk, there is no clear indication of what works best for whom.

Examining the characteristics of the intervention studies highlights several important limitations of the existing literature that may explain why interventions fail. For example, most interventions intervene too late—when the health condition is advanced (at the tertiary level). Many do not take relationship quality into account. Some may be intervening to increase social contact or interaction or the receipt of resources without regard to more subjective aspects of social connections, such as perceived support and relationship quality. Most interventions, due to logistical constraints, are limited to acute treatments, when the time course of the influence of relationships is likely chronic. Importantly, most interventions have been at the individual level and have not utilized existing close relationships or community.

Multilevel (Systems) Approach to Prevention and Interventions

There appears to be a disconnect between implementation efforts and the science that established the importance of social connections. When taking a social ecological approach to addressing social connection (or lack thereof), we need to consider intervening upon the potential causal mechanisms across these levels and to recognize that these levels are embedded within each other and may influence each other. Examples of how interventions have been or could be applied across social system levels highlight the need for additional efforts in this area.

Potential Interventions Across Social Systems

At the individual level, intervention strategies have included those aimed at reducing perceptions of loneliness (Cacioppo et al. 2015, Masi et al. 2011). Although there are a variety of approaches, one review determined that interventions that address maladaptive thinking via cognitive behavioral therapy were associated with the greatest success (Cacioppo et al. 2015). Despite this success, it should be noted that these effects were relatively small. Furthermore, among interventions dealing with individual-level contributory factors, most have targeted cognitive and psychological factors, with few interventions specifically targeting biological or personality factors. Certainly, some factors may be more modifiable than others, but advancements in biologically based treatments suggest potential for intervention.

Prevention efforts should also be considered. We know from other behavioral and lifestyle risk factors (e.g., smoking, obesity) that individual-based interventions have not had as much success as preventative efforts and interventions aimed at the societal and population level. It is difficult and costly to design interventions that reach every individual; thus, interventions at the individual level tend to target those at highest risk (i.e., isolated older adults or chronically ill patients; see **Figure 3**). Individual-based interventions rarely capture others along the risk trajectory and miss the opportunity to prevent risk. Unfortunately, very little systematic research has been aimed at evaluating the efficacy of preventative efforts in the realm of social connection. Prevention strategies may be designed to promote attitudes, beliefs, and behaviors that ultimately prevent isolation and loneliness (Saito et al. 2012).

At the relationship or family level, prevention and intervention strategies may include parenting or family-focused prevention programs and mentoring and peer programs designed to reduce conflict, foster social skills, and promote healthy relationships. Current intervention approaches aimed at reducing social isolation have often utilized one-on-one strategies such as befriending (Mead et al. 2010) or mentoring (Dickens et al. 2011). Although these approaches may be aimed at creating relationships, the use of strangers or hired personnel may have limited impact relative to approaches that include existing relationships (e.g., friends or family). Furthermore, approaches that target couples and families may increase in efficacy when attention is paid to the quality of

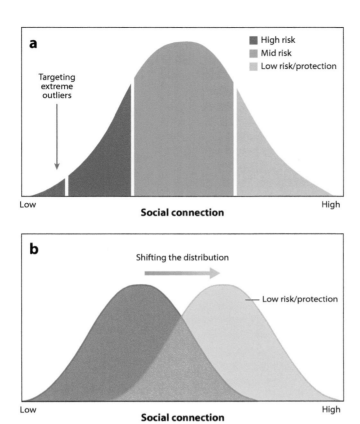

Figure 3

Conceptual representations of social connection and potential influence of prevention and intervention efforts at individual and population levels. (*a*) Individual-level interventions typically only target those on the extreme low end. (*b*) Population-based interventions may shift the distribution.

these relationships (Martire et al. 2010, Robles et al. 2014), as increasing contact with one's spouse or family may have unintended negative effects if conflict or strain is present.

At the community level, prevention and intervention strategies may be designed to influence the social and physical environments. This might include improving opportunities in neighborhoods, as well as improving the social climate, processes, and policies within school, workplace, and health care settings. One community-based intervention, the Blue Zones Project (**https://www.bluezonesproject.com/**), is based on factors identified to be characteristic among rare longevity hotspots around the world—where a disproportionate segment of the population live well into their 90s, 100s, and beyond. They identified nine factors that contribute to longer, healthier, and happier lives—three of which are social (i.e., family first, right tribe, belong). The Blue Zone Project includes multiple social components among its guiding principles of longevity in hopes of transforming several US cities into healthier and happier communities. Other community-based interventions include anti-bullying programs within schools (Lee et al. 2015) and buddy benches (**http://buddybench.org/**) to promote social inclusion. Communities are building infrastructure to make cities more walkable and safe. Hospitals and clinics can provide early assessments to refer high-risk individuals to community resources. Nonetheless, clear data demonstrating the effectiveness of these interventions in increasing both social connectedness and physical health outcomes are still needed; in some cases, the interventions have been shown to be less effective than expected (Hatzenbuehler et al. 2017, Oishi et al. 2015), suggesting that greater refinement is needed.

At the society level, we can consider normative, structural, institutional, and policy approaches. For example, strategies may target social and cultural norms that place a higher value on independence than on connection. Normative messaging can be effectively used in mass media campaigns, as well as in subtle messaging in the mainstream media, such as television shows and movies (Schultz et al. 2007). Other large societal factors to consider include the health, economic, educational, and social policies that help to promote social equality and minimize inequalities between groups. Family-friendly policies, such as guaranteed (or paid) parental leave to encourage connection at critical periods and tax incentives for living with or near an aging parent or providing direct care, may be instituted. Governments or national and international health organizations may establish consensus reports that establish guidelines and recommendations for social activity, similar to recommendations on how much physical activity one should get per week. Regardless of the exact approach, interventions should be evidence based and subject to periodic review and revision based on emerging evidence over time. Whereas individual-level interventions target only those at highest risk, society-level interventions have the capability to shift the entire population (see **Figure 3**).

Of course, intervention approaches need not be targeted specifically at one level. A recent innovative intervention approach suggests that we can target individuals within a social network that can have profound effects at the population level. For example, in a public health (nutrition) intervention that included 5,773 individuals within 32 villages in Honduras, it was found that targeting influential individuals within a social network was associated with increased behavioral change in the social network more generally relative to targeting individuals who were randomly chosen (Kim et al. 2015). These results suggest that, by utilizing such approaches, we may be able to capitalize on the distributive properties of social networks, thereby utilizing fewer resources and more effectively intervening in the population.

As is the case with other multiply determined risk factors for mortality, some levels may be more modifiable than others. Although social norms may be difficult and slow to change, attitudes toward smoking are a prime indicator that it can be done. The CDC (2016) estimates that 15.1% of US adults currently smoke, whereas in 1965, the smoking rate was 42.4% (US Dep. Health Hum. Serv. 2014). Attitudes toward smoking have mirrored this dramatic shift; in 1966, only 40% of Americans recognized smoking as a major cause of cancer, compared to 71% in 2001 (Cummings & Proctor 2014). We can see how rates of smoking have shifted over time as normative attitudes have changed. This shift can also be illustrated using smoking rates that differ across countries, with the accompanying different cultural views of smoking. It is not difficult to see parallels in the social norms and trends that may be contributing to the increases in social isolation and loneliness seen across many nations. Could a shift in our social norms and attitudes from independence toward interdependence and connection lead to a reduction in health risks similar to the shifts seen in the case of smoking?

CONCLUSION AND FUTURE DIRECTIONS

We now have substantial evidence that social connection has a protective effect on health and longevity and, conversely, that lacking connection is linked to risk. A systems approach provides a framework to advance our understanding of the mechanisms linking social connection to health risk, develop effective strategies for reducing risk, and take into account future developments.

A systems approach can potentially provide a substantially broader impact on public health than individual-based interventions. As depicted in **Figure 3**, most individual-based interventions only target those deemed at high risk, i.e., those at the extreme end of the risk continuum. This approach adopts the "theory of bad apples" rather than the "theory of continuous improvement" (Berwick 1989). Although these theories were originally applied to productivity in workplace settings, they can be and have been applied to improvements in public health. The "bad apples" approach seeks out precise tools to identify statistical outliers. Those at the extreme end are identified and labeled as deficient and in need of fixing to eliminate the problem. Although we should not ignore those on the extreme end of the risk continuum, exclusively focusing on this group has important limitations. First, it assumes that there is a dichotomous threshold effect of risk, meaning that below a certain threshold one is at risk, and above it one is not. However, the cumulative data do not support this (Holt-Lunstad et al. 2010). Rather, it is imperative that we recognize that there is a continuous dose-response risk trajectory (Yang et al. 2016) and that we do not focus attention and efforts entirely on one extreme end. Second, this approach may contribute to stigmatizing the lack of social connection. Stigmatization may lead to defensive responses to assessment tools (e.g., individuals denying that there is a problem) and potential exacerbation of the problem. Indeed, there is considerable social stigma associated with loneliness, such that, in one study, individuals labeled lonely were viewed as less likable, less attractive, and less preferred as a friend (Lau & Gruen 1992). In contrast, an approach of continuous improvement would promote the idea that we can all benefit from establishing and maintaining healthy social relationships. Finally, and perhaps most importantly, focusing efforts on the extreme end of the risk continuum ignores a significant portion of the population. Instead, interventions aimed at the community and society levels that reach the entire risk spectrum may result in population-level shifts—thereby effecting a greater degree of change in risk (see **Figure 3**).

Social trends in most Western cultures suggest that individuals are becoming more socially disconnected (McPherson et al. 2006, Perissinotto et al. 2012, Pew Res. Cent. 2009). Widespread use of technology (Pew Res. Cent. 2015) as a primary means of connecting socially has important implications. Future research must consider the mechanisms by which technology may influence social connection for both good and bad and how technology can be utilized as a tool to improve assessment and intervention. Whereas previous assessment attempts, particularly those that are population based, were designed with brevity in mind, we now have the capability to use big data to identify those who may be at greatest risk (Bates et al. 2014). Just as advertisers use big data to identify and advertise specific products to target customers, we can use the myriad of sensors (e.g., audio, visual, physiological responses, activity, location) already included in existing devices, both wearable and within the environment, to identify those at risk (e.g., those who do not leave the house, have not spoken with others, or are distressed), as well as to nudge individuals to make corrections. Technology is also increasingly used as an intervention tool, but a review of existing data suggests that careful attention is needed to address nuances in what will be effective for different people (Chen & Schulz 2016). Of course, technology is ever changing, and at an exponentially rapid pace; thus, we are on the verge of having the ability to make larger changes than ever before. The capabilities to assess and intervene in a multifactorial and social ecological manner are within our reach.

DISCLOSURE STATEMENT

The author is not aware of any affiliations, memberships, funding, or financial holdings that might be perceived as affecting the objectivity of this review.

LITERATURE CITED

AARP. 2012. The United States of Aging survey. Rep., AARP, Washington, DC. http://www.aarp.org/content/dam/aarp/livable-communities/learn/research/the-united-states-of-aging-survey-2012-aarp.pdf

Asendorpf JB, van Aken MAG. 2003. Personality–relationship transaction in adolescence: core versus surface personality characteristics. *J. Personal.* 71:629–66

Appleton AA, Holdsworth E, Ryan M, Tracy M. 2016. Measuring childhood adversity in life course cardiovascular research: a systematic review. *Psychosom. Med.* 79(4):434–40

Ball K, Jeffery RW, Abbott G, McNaughton SA, Crawford D. 2010. Is healthy behavior contagious: associations of social norms with physical activity and healthy eating. *Int. J. Behav. Nutr. Phys. Act.* 7:86

Bates DW, Saria S, Ohno-Machado L, Shah A, Escobar G. 2014. Big data in health care: using analytics to identify and manage high-risk and high-cost patients. *Health Aff.* 33:1123–31

Baum S, Kendall E, Parekh S. 2016. Self-assessed health status and neighborhood context. *J. Prev. Interv. Community* 44:283–95

Beauchamp G. 2014. *Social Predation: How Group Living Helps Predators and Prey*. Amsterdam: Elsevier

Beckes L, Coan JA, Hasselmo K. 2013. Familiarity promotes the blurring of self and other in the neural representation of threat. *Soc. Cogn. Affect. Neurosci.* 8:670–77

Berkowitz AD. 2004. An overview of the social norms approach. In *Changing the Culture of College Drinking*, ed. L Lederman, L Stewart, pp. 193–214. Cresskill, NJ: Hampton Press

Berry D, McCartney K, Petrill S, Deater-Deckard K, Blair C. 2014. Gene-environment interaction between DRD4 7-repeat VNTR and early child-care experiences predicts self-regulation abilities in prekindergarten. *Dev. Psychobiol.* 56:373–91

Berscheid E, Reis HT. 1998. Attraction and close relationships. In *The Handbook of Social Psychology*, Vol. 2, ed. DT Gilbert, ST Fiske, G Lindzey, pp. 193–281. New York: McGraw-Hill. 4th ed.

Berwick DM. 1989. Continuous improvement as an ideal in health care. *N. Engl. J. Med.* 320:53–56

Black C, Collen B, Johnston D, Hart T. 2016. Why huddle? Ecological drivers of chick aggregations in gentoo penguins, *Pygoscelis papua*, across latitudes. *PLOS ONE* 11:e0145676

Bliss CA, Kloumann IM, Harris KD, Danforth CM, Dodds PS. 2011. Twitter reciprocal reply networks exhibit assortativity with respect to happiness. arXiv:1112.1010 [cs.SI]

Boesen EH, Johansen C. 2008. Impact of psychotherapy on cancer survival: time to move on? *Curr. Opin. Oncol.* 20:372–77

Bowlby J. 1969. *Attachment and Loss: Volume 1. Attachment*. New York: Basic Books

Cacioppo JT, Cacioppo S, Boomsma DI. 2014. Evolutionary mechanisms for loneliness. *Cogn. Emot.* 28:3–21

Cacioppo S, Grippo AJ, London S, Goossens L, Cacioppo JT. 2015. Loneliness: clinical import and interventions. *Perspect. Psychol. Sci.* 10:238–49

Cacioppo JT, Hawley LC, Ernst JM, Burlson M, Berntson GG, et al. 2006. Loneliness within a nomological net: an evolutionary perspective. *J. Res. Personal.* 40:1054–85

CDC (Cent. Dis. Control). 2015. *The social-ecological model: a framework for prevention*. Rep., Div. Violence Prev., Nat. Cent. Inj. Prev. Control, Cent. Dis. Control, Atlanta, GA. **https://www.cdc.gov/violenceprevention/overview/social-ecologicalmodel.html**

CDC (Cent. Dis. Control Prev.). 2016. Cigarette smoking among adults—United States, 2005–2015. *Morb. Mortal. Wkly. Rep.* 65(44):1205–11

Chen YR, Schulz PJ. 2016. The effect of information communication technology interventions on reducing social isolation in the elderly: a systematic review. *J. Med. Internet Res.* 18:e18

Christakis NA, Fowler JH. 2007. The spread of obesity in a large social network over 32 years. *N. Engl. J. Med.* 357:370–79

Christakis NA, Fowler JH. 2008. The collective dynamics of smoking in a large social network. *N. Engl. J. Med.* 358:2249–58

Christakis NA, Fowler JH. 2013. Social contagion theory: examining dynamic social networks and human behavior. *Stat. Med.* 32:556–77

Coan JA, Sbarra DA. 2015. Social baseline theory: the social regulation of risk and effort. *Curr. Opin. Psychol.* 1:87–91

Coan JA, Schaefer HS, Davidson RJ. 2006. Lending a hand: social regulation of the neural response to threat. *Psychol. Sci.* 17:1032–39

Craddock E, vanDellen MR, Novak SA, Ranby KW. 2015. Influence in relationships: a meta-analysis on health-related social control. *Basic Appl. Soc. Psychol.* 37(2):118–30

Craske MG, Stein MB. 2016. Anxiety. *Lancet* 388:3048–59

Cummings KM, Proctor RN. 2014. The changing public image of smoking in the United States: 1964–2014. *Cancer Epidemiol. Biomark. Prev.* 23(1):32–36

Derrick JL, Leonard KE, Homish GG. 2013. Perceived partner responsiveness predicts decreases in smoking during the first nine years of marriage. *Nicotine Tob. Res.* 15:1528–36

Diamond LM, Hicks AM. 2004. Psychobiological perspectives on attachment: implications for health over the lifespan. In *Adult Attachment: Theory, Research, and Clinical Implications*, ed. WS Rholes, JA Simpson, pp. 240–263. New York: Guilford Press

Dickens AP, Richards SH, Hawton A, Taylor RS, Greaves CJ, et al. 2011. An evaluation of the effectiveness of a community mentoring service for socially isolated older people: a controlled trial. *BMC Public Health* 11:218

Dietz WH, Gortmaker SL. 2016. New strategies to prioritize nutrition, physical activity, and obesity interventions. *Am. J. Prev. Med.* 51(5):e145–50

Ditzen B, Heinrichs M. 2014. Psychobiology of social support: the social dimension of stress buffering. *Restor. Neurol. Neurosci.* 32:149–62

Ebbeling CB, Pawlak DB, Ludwig DS. 2002. Childhood obesity: public-health crisis, common sense cure. *Lancet* 360:473–82

Eisenberger NI. 2012. The pain of social disconnection: examining the shared neural underpinnings of physical and social pain. *Nat. Rev. Neurosci.* 13:421–34

Eisenberger NI, Lieberman MD, Williams KD. 2003. Does rejection hurt? An FMRI study of social exclusion. *Science* 302:290–92

Eisenberger NI, Moieni M, Inagaki TK, Muscatell KA, Irwin MR. 2017. In sickness and in health: the co-regulation of inflammation and social behavior. *Neuropsychopharmacology* 42:242–53

Fagundes CP, Bennett JM, Derry HM, Kiecolt-Glaser JK. 2011. Relationships and inflammation across the lifespan: social developmental pathways to disease. *Soc. Personal. Psychol. Compass* 5:891–903

Fitzsimons GM, Finkel EM. 2010. Interpersonal influences on self-regulation. *Curr. Dir. Psychol. Sci.* 19:101–5

Fitzsimons GM, vanDellen MR. 2015. Goal pursuit in close relationships. In *Handbook of Personality and Social Psychology: Interpersonal Relations and Group Processes*, ed. JA Simpson, JF Dovidio, pp. 273–96. Washington, DC: Am. Psychol. Assoc.

Flegal KM, Kit BK, Orpana H, Graubard BI. 2013. Association of all-cause mortality with overweight and obesity using standard body mass index categories: a systematic review and meta-analysis. *JAMA* 309:71–82

Franck L, Molyneux N, Parkinson L. 2016. Systematic review of interventions addressing social isolation and depression in aged care clients. *Qual. Life Res.* 25:1395–407

Gardiner C, Geldenhuys G, Gott M. 2017. Interventions to reduce social isolation and loneliness among older people: an integrative review. *Health Soc. Care Community*. In press

Han S, Ma Y. 2014. Cultural differences in human brain activity: a quantitative meta-analysis. *NeuroImage* 99:293–300

Hatzenbuehler ML, Flores JE, Cavanaugh JE, Onwuachi-Willig A, Ramirez MR. 2017. Anti-bullying policies and disparities in bullying: a state-level analysis. *Am. J. Prev. Med.* 53(2):184–91

Hawkley LC, Capitanio JP. 2015. Perceived social isolation, evolutionary fitness and health outcomes: a lifespan approach. *Philos. Trans. R. Soc. Lond. B* 370(1669):20140114

Hennessy MB, Kaiser S, Sachser N. 2009. Social buffering of the stress response: diversity, mechanisms, and functions. *Front. Neuroendocrinol.* 30:470–82

Hogan BE, Linden W, Najarian B. 2002. Social support interventions: Do they work? *Clin. Psychol. Rev.* 22:383–442

Holt-Lunstad J, Robles T, Sbarra D. 2017. Advancing social connection as a public health priority. *Am. Psychol.* 72(6):517–30

Holt-Lunstad J, Smith TB, Baker M, Harris T, Stephenson D. 2015. Loneliness and social isolation as risk factors for mortality: a meta-analytic review. *Perspect. Psychol. Sci.* 10:227–37

Holt-Lunstad J, Smith TB, Layton JB. 2010. Social relationships and mortality risk: a meta-analytic review. *PLOS Med.* 7:e1000316

Hostinar CE. 2015. Recent developments in the study of social relationships, stress responses, and physical health. *Curr. Opin. Psychol.* 5:90–95

Hostinar CE, Gunnar MR. 2015. Social support can buffer against stress and shape brain activity. *AJOB Neurosci.* 6:34–42

House JS, Landis KR, Umberson D. 1988. Social relationships and health. *Science* 241:540–45

Inst. Med. 2003. *Who Will Keep the Public Healthy? Educating Public Health Professionals for the 21st Century.* Washington, DC: Natl. Acad. Press

Ioannou CC, Guttal V, Couzin ID. 2012. Predatory fish select for coordinated collective motion in virtual prey. *Science* 337:1212–15

Kim DA, Benjamin EJ, Fowler JH, Christakis NA. 2016. Social connectedness is associated with fibrinogen level in a human social network. *Proc. Biol. Sci.* 283(1837):20160958

Kim DA, Hwong AR, Stafford D, Hughes DA, O'Malley AJ, et al. 2015. Social network targeting to maximise population behaviour change: a cluster randomised controlled trial. *Lancet* 386:145–53

Kissane D, Li Y. 2008. Effects of supportive-expressive group therapy on survival of patients with metastatic breast cancer: a randomized prospective trial. *Cancer* 112:443–44

Kraemer HC, Kazdin AE, Offord DR, Kessler RC, Jensen PS, Kupfer DJ. 1997. Coming to terms with the terms of risk. *Arch. Gen. Psychiatry* 54(4):337–43

Lacey RE, Kumari M, Bartley M. 2014. Social isolation in childhood and adult inflammation: evidence from the National Child Development Study. *Psychoneuroendocrinology* 50:85–94

Lacey RE, Kumari M, McMunn A. 2013. Parental separation in childhood and adult inflammation: the importance of material and psychosocial pathways. *Psychoneuroendocrinology* 38:2476–84

Lau S, Gruen GE. 1992. The social stigma of loneliness: effect of target person's and perceiver's sex. *Personal. Soc. Psychol. Bull.* 18(2):182–89

Lee S, Kim CJ, Kim DH. 2015. A meta-analysis of the effect of school-based anti-bullying programs. *J. Child Health Care* 19:136–53

Lemery-Chalfant K, Kao K, Swann G, Goldsmith HH. 2013. Childhood temperament: passive gene-environment correlation, gene-environment interaction, and the hidden importance of the family environment. *Dev. Psychopathol.* 25:51–63

Lewis MA, Rook KS. 1999. Social control in personal relationships: impact on health behaviors and psychological distress. *Health Psychol.* 18:63–71

Lombard CB, Deeks AA, Teede HJ. 2009. A systematic review of interventions aimed at the prevention of weight gain in adults. *Public Health Nutr.* 12(11):2236–46

Loseth GE, Ellingsen DM, Leknes S. 2014. State-dependent μ-opioid modulation of social motivation. *Front. Behav. Neurosci.* 8:430

Lovely C, Rampersad M, Fernandes Y, Eberhart J. 2017. Gene-environment interactions in development and disease. *Wiley Interdiscip. Rev. Dev. Biol.* 6:e247

Machin AJ, Dunbar R. 2011. The brain opioid theory of social attachment: a review of the evidence. *Behavior* 148:985–1025

Malambo P, Kengne AP, De Villiers A, Lambert EV, Puoane T. 2016. Built environment, selected risk factors and major cardiovascular disease outcomes: a systematic review. *PLOS ONE* 11:e0166846

Manzoli L, Villari P, Pirone GM, Boccia A. 2007. Marital status and mortality in the elderly: a systematic review and meta-analysis. *Soc. Sci. Med.* 64:77–94

Martire LM, Schulz R, Helgeson VS, Small BJ, Saghafi EM. 2010. Review and meta-analysis of couple-oriented interventions for chronic illness. *Ann. Behav. Med.* 40:325–42

Masi CM, Chen HY, Hawkley LC, Cacioppo JT. 2011. A meta-analysis of interventions to reduce loneliness. *Personal. Soc. Psychol. Rev.* 15:219–66

McLaughlin KA, Sheridan MA, Lambert HK. 2014. Childhood adversity and neural development: deprivation and threat as distinct dimensions of early experience. *Neurosci. Biobehav. Rev.* 47:578–91

McPherson M, Smith-Lovin L, Brashears ME. 2006. Social isolation in America: changes in core discussion networks over two decades. *Am. Sociol. Rev.* 71(3):353–75

Mead N, Lester H, Chew-Graham C, Gask L, Bower P. 2010. Effects of befriending on depressive symptoms and distress: systematic review and meta-analysis. *Br. J. Psychiatry* 196:96–101

Mikulincer M, Shaver PR. 2007. *Attachment in Adulthood: Structure, Dynamics, and Change*. New York: Guilford Press

Mitchell C, McLanahan S, Brooks-Gunn J, Garfinkel I, Hobcraft J, Notterman D. 2013. Genetic differential sensitivity to social environments: implications for research. *Am. J. Public Health* 103(Suppl. 1): S102–10

Oishi S, Saeki M, Axt J. 2015. Are people living in walkable areas healthier and more satisfied with life? *Appl. Psychol. Health Well-Being* 7:365–86

Oliveira BS, Zunzunegui MV, Quinlan J, Fahmi H, Tu MT, Guerra RO. 2016. Systematic review of the association between chronic social stress and telomere length: a life course perspective. *Ageing Res. Rev.* 26:37–52

Parascandola M, Weed DL. 2001. Causation in epidemiology. *J. Epidemiol. Community Health* 55:905–12

Parascandola M, Weed DL, Dasgupta A. 2006. Two Surgeon General's reports on smoking and cancer: a historical investigation of the practice of causal inference. *Emerg. Themes Epidemiol.* 3:1

Pays O, Beauchamp G, Carter AJ, Goldizen AW. 2013. Foraging in groups allows collective predator detection in a mammal species without alarm calls. *Behav. Ecol.* 24(5):1229–36

Perissinotto CM, Stijacic Cenzer I, Covinsky KE. 2012. Loneliness in older persons: a predictor of functional decline and death. *Arch. Intern. Med.* 172(14):1078–83

Pew Res. Cent. 2009. Social isolation and new technology. *Pew Research Center*, Nov. 4

Pew Res. Cent. 2015. US Smartphone use in 2015. *Pew Research Center*, April 1

Pietromonaco PR, Uchino B, Dunkel Schetter C. 2013. Close relationship processes and health: implications of attachment theory for health and disease. *Health Psychol.* 32:499–513

Plotnikoff RC, Costigan SA, Williams RL, Hutchesson MJ, Kennedy SG, et al. 2015. Effectiveness of interventions targeting physical activity, nutrition and healthy weight for university and college students: a systematic review and meta-analysis. *Int. J. Behav. Nutr. Phys. Act.* 12:45

Portacolone E, Perissinotto C, Yeh JC, Greysen SR. 2017. "I feel trapped": the tension between personal and structural factors of social isolation and the desire for social integration among older residents of a high-crime neighborhood. *Gerontologist.* In press

Pressman SD, Cohen S, Miller GE, Barkin A, Rabin BS, Treanor JJ. 2005. Loneliness, social network size, and immune response to influenza vaccination in college freshmen. *Health Psychol.* 24:297–306

Reis HT, Collins AW, Berschied E. 2000. The relationship context of human behavior and development. *Psychol. Bull.* 126:844–72

Robles TF, Kane HS. 2014. The attachment system and physiology in adulthood: normative processes, individual differences, and implications for health. *J. Personal.* 82:515–27

Robles TF, Kiecolt-Glaser JK. 2003. The physiology of marriage: pathways to health. *Physiol. Behav.* 79:409–16

Robles TF, Slatcher RB, Trombello JM, McGinn MM. 2014. Marital quality and health: a meta-analytic review. *Psychol. Bull.* 140:140–87

Roelfs DJ, Shor E, Kalish R, Yogev T. 2011. The rising relative risk of mortality for singles: meta-analysis and meta-regression. *Am. J. Epidemiol.* 174:379–89

Rook KS. 2009. Gaps in social support resources in later life: an adaptational challenge in need of further research. *J. Soc. Pers. Relatsh.* 26(1):103–12

Ross HE, Young LJ. 2009. Oxytocin and the neural mechanisms regulating social cognition and affiliative behavior. *Front. Neuroendocrinol.* 30:534–47

Saito T, Kai I, Takizawa A. 2012. Effects of a program to prevent social isolation on loneliness, depression, and subjective well-being of older adults: a randomized trial among older migrants in Japan. *Arch. Gerontol. Geriatr.* 55:539–47

Sbarra DA, Law RW, Portley RM. 2011. Divorce and death: a meta-analysis and research agenda for clinical, social, and health psychology. *Perspect. Psychol. Sci.* 6:454–74

Schultz PW, Nolan JM, Cialdini RB, Goldstein NJ, Griskevicius V. 2007. The constructive, destructive, and reconstructive power of social norms. *Psychol. Sci.* 18:429–34

Shor E, Roelfs DJ. 2015. Social contact frequency and all-cause mortality: a meta-analysis and meta-regression. *Soc. Sci. Med.* 128:76–86

Shor E, Roelfs DJ, Bugyi P, Schwartz JE. 2012a. Meta-analysis of marital dissolution and mortality: reevaluating the intersection of gender and age. *Soc. Sci. Med.* 75:46–59

Shor E, Roelfs DJ, Curreli M, Clemow L, Burg MM, Schwartz JE. 2012b. Widowhood and mortality: a meta-analysis and meta-regression. *Demography* 49:575–606

Shor E, Roelfs DJ, Yogev T. 2013. The strength of family ties: a meta-analysis and meta-regression of self-reported social support and mortality. *Soc. Netw.* 35:626–38

Slatcher RB, Selcuk E, Ong AD. 2015. Perceived partner responsiveness predicts diurnal cortisol profiles 10 years later. *Psychol. Sci.* 26:972–82

Slavich GM, Irwin MR. 2014. From stress to inflammation and major depressive disorder: a social signal transduction theory of depression. *Psychol. Bull.* 140:774–815

Spiegel D, Bloom JR, Kraemer HC, Gottheil E. 1989. Effect of psychosocial treatment on survival of patients with metastatic breast cancer. *Lancet* 2:888–91

Stampfer MJ, Ridker PM, Dzau VJ. 2004. Risk factor criteria. *Circulation* 109:IV3–5

Tanskanen J, Anttila T. 2016. A prospective study of social isolation, loneliness, and mortality in Finland. *Am. J. Public Health* 106:2042–48

Templeton EM, Stanton MV, Zaki J. 2016. Social norms shift preferences for healthy and unhealthy foods. *PLOS ONE* 11:e0166286

Uchino BN. 2006. Social support and health: a review of physiological processes potentially underlying links to disease outcomes. *J. Behav. Med.* 29:377–87

Uchino BN. 2009. What a lifespan approach might tell us about why distinct measures of social support have differential links to physical health. *J. Soc. Personal. Relatsh.* 26:53–62

US Dep. Health Hum. Serv. 2014. *The Health Consequences of Smoking—50 Years of Progress: A Report of the Surgeon General.* Atlanta, GA: US Dep. Health Hum. Serv.

Vella EJ, Kamarck TW, Shiffman S. 2008. Hostility moderates the effects of social support and intimacy on blood pressure in daily social interactions. *Health Psychol.* 27: S155–62

Vespa J, Lewis JM, Kreider RM. 2013. *America's families and living arrangements: 2012.* Curr. Pop. Rep. P20-570, US Census Bur., Washington, DC

Vetere A. 1987. General system theory and the family: a critical evaluation. In *Ecological Studies of Family Life*, ed. A Vetere, A Gale, pp. 18–33. Chichester, UK: Wiley

Way BM, Lieberman MD. 2010. Is there a genetic contribution to cultural differences? Collectivism, individualism and genetic markers of social sensitivity. *Soc. Cogn. Affect. Neurosci.* 5:203–11

Wen M, Cagney KA, Christakis NA. 2005. Effect of specific aspects of community social environment on the mortality of individuals diagnosed with serious illness. *Soc. Sci. Med.* 61:1119–34

Yang YC, Boen C, Gerken K, Li T, Schorpp K, Harris KM. 2016. Social relationships and physiological determinants of longevity across the human life span. *PNAS* 113(3):578–83

Principles and Challenges of Applying Epigenetic Epidemiology to Psychology

Meaghan J. Jones,[1,2] Sarah R. Moore,[1,2] and Michael S. Kobor[1,2,3]

[1] Centre for Molecular Medicine and Therapeutics, British Columbia Children's Hospital, Vancouver, British Columbia V6H 3N1, Canada; email: mjones@cmmt.ubc.ca, smoore@cmmt.ubc.ca, msk@cmmt.ubc.ca

[2] Department of Medical Genetics, University of British Columbia, Vancouver, British Columbia V6H 3N1, Canada

[3] Human Early Learning Partnership, University of British Columbia, Vancouver, British Columbia V6T 1Z3, Canada

Annu. Rev. Psychol. 2018. 69:459–85

First published as a Review in Advance on October 16, 2017

The *Annual Review of Psychology* is online at psych.annualreviews.org

https://doi.org/10.1146/annurev-psych-122414-033653

Keywords

DNA methylation, epigenetics, study design, psychology, methods

Abstract

The interplay of genetically driven biological processes and environmental factors is a key driver of research questions spanning multiple areas of psychology. A nascent area of research focuses on the utility of epigenetic marks in capturing this intersection of genes and environment, as epigenetic mechanisms are both tightly linked to the genome and environmentally responsive. Advances over the past 10 years have allowed large-scale assessment of one epigenetic mark in particular, DNA methylation, in human populations, and the examination of DNA methylation is becoming increasingly common in psychological studies. In this review, we briefly outline some principles of epigenetics, focusing on highlighting important considerations unique to DNA methylation studies to guide psychologists in incorporating DNA methylation into a project. We discuss study design and biological and analytical considerations and conclude by discussing interpretability of epigenetic findings and how these important factors are currently being applied across areas of psychology.

Contents

THE EMERGING INTERSECTION OF EPIGENETICS AND PSYCHOLOGY

At the crux of psychological research is the question of how genetic predisposition and salient experiences together mold human behavior and psychological development. Epigenetic marks, a set of modifications to DNA and its packaging that can influence gene expression but do not alter genomic sequence, are hypothesized to mediate this interplay of genetic variation and experience, offering a potential avenue for investigating this fundamental question of how we become who we are. Consequently, the scientific community and the public alike have become interested in the role of epigenetics in developmental and psychological processes.

In contrast to DNA sequence, which is set at conception and is, for the most part, static across the lifespan, epigenetic marks undergo dramatic changes during the natural course of development. Variations in the epigenome, defined as the combination of epigenetic marks across the genome, begin with the fundamental role the epigenome plays in cellular differentiation during embryogenesis, leading to distinct epigenetic profiles in particular cells and tissues. Although some epigenetic marks, especially those involved in determining cell fate, are highly stable, many continue to change over the life course in response to external cues from the surrounding environment. Moreover, epigenetic marks also appear to be a mechanistic overlay to the genome, molding genetically guided developmental plasticity processes in response to key signals. Epigenetic marks may thus provide a molecular basis for (*a*) the enduring effects of early life exposures via biological embedding and (*b*) the convergence of genetic and environmental variation in the manifestation of phenotypes (Boyce & Kobor 2015, Hertzman 1999, Meaney & Ferguson-Smith 2010). Given this role of epigenetic marks in orchestrating a delicate balance between persistence and plasticity across development, the study of these marks has become a prominent theme in health, clinical, and developmental psychology and related fields like behavioral neuroscience.

The growing interest in epigenetic processes as compelling developmental mechanisms is amplified by the increasing affordability of epigenetic technology, particularly in terms of one specific epigenetic modification, DNA methylation (DNAm). The number of large-scale projects incorporating DNAm has grown rapidly, yielding unprecedented opportunities for interrogation of DNAm in human populations. Rather than covering the theoretical reasons to investigate epigenetics, the purpose of this article is to contextualize existing epigenetic research in psychology in terms of the current available technologies and methodological advances. The unique aspects of DNAm biology that make it so fascinating also translate to a complex set of methodological considerations. Thus, after presenting a brief overview of epigenetics in general and DNAm in particular, we dive deeply into the world of epigenetic methodology before commenting on where current psychology research stands and how it can improve.

DNA METHYLATION: AN ACCESSIBLE EPIGENETIC MARK FOR HUMAN PSYCHOLOGICAL STUDIES

Epigenetics refers to modifications of DNA and DNA packaging that alter the accessibility of DNA and potentially regulate gene expression without changing the sequence of DNA itself. DNAm is the most highly studied epigenetic mark in human population studies, but other epigenetic factors include noncoding RNAs, histone variants, and histone tail modifications (Henikoff & Greally 2016). Together, these modifications are coordinated to regulate access to DNA by a variety of factors that control gene expression and cellular phenotype. DNAm is the most commonly studied in human populations for two major reasons: It is easily quantifiable, and it is relatively stable and, thus, does not require complex processing of samples after collection. Other epigenetic marks are more difficult to study, as they require special handling of samples or large amounts of sample.

One of the main roles of DNAm is in cellular differentiation. As stem cells divide and gradually differentiate into specific terminal cell types, DNAm patterns become increasingly cell type specific. This pattern of specification, which explains how cells with the same genetic sequence, such as neurons and white blood cells, have very different functions, was originally hypothesized by Waddington (1959). Landscapes of DNAm are, thus, highly divergent between cell types, with cells from similar lineages showing more similar DNAm profiles (Christensen et al. 2009, Ziller et al. 2013). Thus, in contrast to genetic information, DNAm is highly tissue specific. This trajectory of differentiation is reflected in widespread changes in DNAm over human development and suggests the possibility of windows of opportunity during which DNAm is changeable and particularly sensitive to environmental insults (**Figure 1**).

Notably, like gene expression and other traits, DNAm is also heavily influenced by genetic variation (Gutierrez Arcelus et al. 2013). Thus, the genome and environment together can sculpt

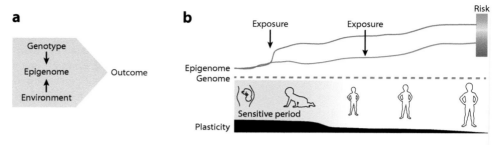

Figure 1

Conceptual outline of how DNA methylation can function as a mechanism of biological embedding. (*a*) The epigenome is sculpted by both the genome and the environment, and, together, these three factors can influence health and behavior outcomes over developmental time. (*b*) Example of how the epigenome could be altered during sensitive periods and result in risk. The blue individual and red individual have slightly different genomes (*dotted line*), and their epigenomes (*solid lines*) begin to diverge early in development due to genetic and environmental differences. During a sensitive period of heightened plasticity (*orange box*), the red individual is exposed to a particular environmental effect (*black arrows*), which alters their epigenome. Later in life, when the blue individual is exposed to the same environment, their epigenome is not altered, as they are out of the sensitive period.

DNAm across the lifespan, which is part of the reason why DNAm is such a compelling potential mechanism of biological embedding.

Biology of DNA Methylation

In humans and other vertebrates, DNA becomes methylated primarily on cytosine (C) nucleotides that are followed by guanine (G) nucleotides, which, in sequence, are referred to as CpGs. Methyl groups can also be found on cytosines in other contexts (non-CpG DNAm; see **Figure 2a**), although at much lower levels (Guo et al. 2013, Ziller et al. 2011). Critical enzymes called DNA methyltransferases (DNMTs) are responsible for the deposition of methyl groups at CpGs in DNA (Bestor 2000, Christensen et al. 2009). Because CpGs are palindromic in the double-stranded DNA, methyl groups are added symmetrically (**Figure 2a**). DNAm deposition can be de novo, when a completely unmethylated CpG becomes symmetrically methylated, but it is also required during cell division to ensure replication of DNAm patterns across generations of cells. When a cell divides, the newly replicated DNA strand contains only unmethylated CpGs, so DNMTs are required to recognize that a CpG is asymmetrically methylated and methylate the new daughter strand. Different DNMTs are responsible for each of these functions.

Together, these enzymes are responsible for DNAm being heritable from cell to cell during division. When cells divide, the action of DNMTs ensures that the epigenetic pattern from the mother cell is faithfully replicated in the daughter. Important aspects of epigenetic programming, such as cell lineage markers, are thus maintained across cell divisions. Interestingly, these mechanisms also allow for the cell-to-cell transmission of epigenetic patterns associated with the cell's past exposures —they create a form of cellular memory that can be passed along to daughter cells. It is these patterns that can be detected in studies examining associations between current DNAm and exposures or events in the past.

For many years, methylated cytosine was considered to be the most important modification to DNA involved in cellular memory, but recent research has shed light on other modifications, including 5-hydroxymethylation (hmC), which occurs in the same CpG context (Wu & Zhang 2014). The role of hmC is unclear, but it is present in the mammalian brain at levels 5–10 times

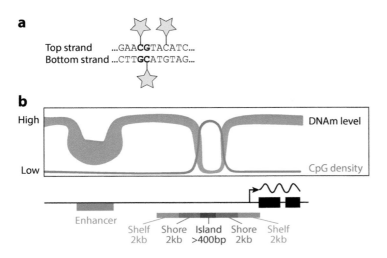

Figure 2

Locations of DNA methylation (DNAm) by genetic sequence and genomic region. (*a*) Methyl cytosine (indicated by a star) is present symmetrically on both DNAm strands at CpG dinucleotides (*left*) but on only a single strand if present at other cytosines (*right*). (*b*) Schematic of gene region with enhancer (*light blue*), transcription start site (*arrow*), and exons (*black rectangles*). The CpG island with shores and shelves is indicated below, with typical region sizes shown. Above is a schema of average CpG density (*blue line*) and typical DNAm level (*gray line*; thicker indicates more variability).

higher than in any other tissue (Ficz et al. 2011, Jin et al. 2011, Song et al. 2013, Wen et al. 2014). Importantly, many common methods of measuring DNAm do not differentiate methylcytosine from hydroxymethylcytosine, so it is critical to consider the presence of hydroxymethylcytosine when interpreting results from these types of assays (Stewart et al. 2015, Yu et al. 2012).

Locations of DNA Methylation

DNAm is not present uniformly across the genome, partly because of the relative scarcity of CpGs compared to other nucleotide combinations. Methylated cytosines, which are primarily observed in CpGs, are vulnerable to mutation into thymines, so it is hypothesized that they have been replaced by thymines over evolutionary time and thus are now found at lower than expected levels (Antequera 2003). Areas of comparatively high CpG content have been termed CpG islands; these islands tend to be unmethylated compared to nonisland CpGs and are found associated with approximately 70% of known gene promoters (Illingworth & Bird 2009, Weber et al. 2007). Flanking these regions of high CpG density and low DNAm are CpG island shores, which are usually defined as 2-kilobase regions on either side of the island (**Figure 2b**) (Irizarry et al. 2009). Shores tend to be more variable and more highly methylated than CpG islands and, thus, are more often of interest in population epigenetic studies. Beyond the shores are shelves, which cover an additional 2 kilobases flanking the shores. In total, there are approximately 28 million CpGs in the genome, but less than 10% are found in CpG islands. Because nonisland CpGs tend to be methylated, 60–80% of CpGs in the genome are methylated, and many are in repetitive sequences (Smith & Meissner 2013). The position of a CpG relative to a gene or other genomic feature is fundamental to its role in regulation of gene expression and will be discussed at length in the section titled Relationship Between DNA Methylation and Gene Expression.

DNA Methylation Technologies

DNAm can be measured in a number of different ways. In particular, the ability to make quantitative measurements, affordability, and scalability differ greatly between some of these methods and are important considerations for psychology studies (for reviews, see Bock 2012, Rivera & Ren 2013). There are two broad categories of methods to assess DNAm: pull-down based and bisulfite based. Pull-down-based methods rely on immobilized antibodies or proteins that recognize and bind to methylated cytosines, resulting in a pull down of methylated DNA, which is then sequenced to identify the regions where DNAm was found. Although these are less specific and less quantitative than the bisulfite methods discussed below, they are unbiased and can be powerful for exploratory purposes.

The other, more common, method of measuring DNAm is to use sodium bisulfite to convert DNAm information into differences in genetic sequence information, which can be easily quantified using well-established sequencing tools. Treatment with sodium bisulfite converts unmethylated cytosines into thymine (T), whereas methylated cytosines are protected and remain intact. Comparing the number of CpGs remaining to the number that converted to TpGs (thymine–guanine pairs) provides a quantitative measure of the proportion of DNA molecules methylated at that CpG position.

Within the four most common bisulfite sequencing methods, the main distinguishing feature is the number of CpGs that can be assessed. Small numbers of neighboring CpGs (tens to hundreds) can be quantified using technologies like pyrosequencing. Moderate numbers can be measured using targeted panels of up to a few thousand CpGs on a next-generation sequencer (Taylor et al. 2007). Both of these techniques are best used when the targeted genomic region(s) are known and limited, for example, when there is a small set of candidate genes. For a broader picture of DNAm in the cell and for discovery of novel genomic regions associated with a particular phenotype or condition, it is necessary to use a technique like large-scale sequencing or a microarray. Sequencing can be performed on the whole genome, but the relatively small number of CpGs, combined with the high cost of sequencing, means that this method is costly and bioinformatically challenging unless sequencing is targeted to CpG-containing regions using a technique like reduced representation bisulfite sequencing (RRBS) or CaptureSeq (Gu et al. 2011; Libertini et al. 2016a,b; Ziller et al. 2013, 2016).

The most common method for measuring DNAm is the commercially available microarray. These arrays hybridize bisulfite-treated DNA to immobilized probes that recognize specific regions of the genome and stain them with fluorescent labels to quantify methylated versus unmethylated DNA. Because microarrays are limited in the number of sites they can assess, they lack the true genome-wide measurements of whole-genome bisulfite sequencing, but their relatively low cost, their high reproducibility and reliability, and the plethora of existing data make them extremely attractive.

The primary source of DNAm microarrays is Illumina (based in San Diego, California); it began its production with the GoldenGate array in 2007, which measured approximately 1,500 CpGs (Bibikova et al. 2006). Since then, Illumina has released three new arrays, each larger than the previous one. The 27k, with approximately 27,000 CpGs, was released in 2009; the 450k, with approximately 480,000 CpGs, was released in 2011; and the newest model, the EPIC array, with approximately 860,000 CpGs, was released in 2016 (Bibikova et al. 2009, 2011; Moran et al. 2016). It should be noted that even the EPIC array is not truly epigenome wide, as it still covers less than 5% of CpGs present across the genome. Between 2007 and the present, methods and strategies for analyzing the data being generated by these arrays have been published, tested, and refined, as is discussed in detail in the following sections.

CONSIDERATIONS: STUDY DESIGN

The approach to incorporating DNAm should be informed by both the unique characteristics of DNAm data and the specific research question. In this section, we discuss a few key areas of study design specific to DNAm that are relevant to considerations of sample size, planned analyses, and inferences that can be made from DNAm findings.

Candidate Genes Versus Epigenome-Wide Studies

Early DNAm studies, particularly those conducted before the advent of genome-wide DNAm techniques, examined specific candidate genes hypothesized to be associated with the variable of interest. These methods have waned in recent years in favor of more global approaches, particularly microarrays, due to the increased affordability and information content of these approaches. Candidate and epigenome-wide approaches, however, are not mutually exclusive.

For researchers making use of epigenome-wide strategies but interested in particular candidate genes, DNAm for an a priori set of candidates may be selected from the array data for hypothesis-driven analyses. Data for these candidate genes would be isolated from and assessed separately from the remainder of the DNAm array data; whole epigenome discovery can then proceed after candidate analysis has been completed.

Analyzing candidates separately from the remainder of the whole genome data has the advantage of lower penalties for multiple testing. To take advantage of this multiple test correction benefit without adversely biasing or skewing the analysis, it is essential that the list of candidate genes be determined in advance. Previous studies on a variable of interest that examined DNAm, gene expression, or even genotyping are an excellent start, but it is also worthwhile to hypothesize and investigate potential molecular mechanisms implicated by basic research. The number of candidate genes identified can be flexible, but multiple test penalties should be considered, as should the total number and position of CpGs assigned to the gene of interest available on the array. For example, if gene A, which may be involved in the variable of interest, has 2,000 CpGs present on the array, then this will significantly degrade the benefits of reducing the number of tests. In these cases, and where sample sizes limit power, it may be beneficial to select a few CpGs from important regulatory regions, such as transcription factor binding sites or enhancers, rather than testing all gene-associated CpGs.

It is also important to note that there are substantial advantages to epigenome-wide DNAm analysis aside from the opportunities for discovery of novel associations. With array DNAm data, it is possible to identify other important biological variables that may not have been measured. These include (*a*) ethnic group, using methylated sites that are highly predictive of ancestry (Rahmani et al. 2016); (*b*) relative proportion of cell types in each sample (if quantified in a heterogeneous tissue), based on methylation of a few hundred reference CpGs (Esposito et al. 2016, Guintivano et al. 2013, Houseman et al. 2012); and (*c*) genetic relatedness of samples from individuals, using the single nucleotide polymorphisms (SNPs) present on the DNAm arrays. As discussed in the section titled Considerations: Biological, these variables are important for properly controlling DNAm analyses, and, thus, the ability to extract them from array data is a significant bonus.

Effect Size

An important consideration when embarking on a study involving DNAm is that the effect sizes will likely be quite small. Effect sizes in DNAm studies are partly constrained by how and where DNAm is measured. For example, in a single cell, a particular CpG is present only twice (once on each member of a chromosome pair), so the DNA can be 0%, 50%, or 100% methylated. When assessing a participant's DNA sample, however, hundreds or millions of cells are measured at the same time. Thus, a change in DNAm at a small subset of cells will, by necessity, be reflected as a small but dimensional change in overall DNAm of the whole biological sample. Small effects can also be attributed to the nature of methylation at the regions in the methylome that are commonly targeted. CpG islands and promoters typically have very low DNAm levels; thus, they have a low dynamic range over which they could exhibit DNAm changes.

The typical effect sizes, including those of DNAm findings that have been extensively validated, generally do not exceed 10% in terms of the mean difference in proportion of methylated DNA strands between groups of individuals (Breton et al. 2017). The mean difference is often referred to as a delta beta, typically calculated as the mean difference between groups or the range in a certain interval for continuous variables. For instance, replicated associations between smoking exposure and DNAm both in adults and in infants exposed in utero typically range in effect size from 1% to 10% (Gao et al. 2015, Joubert et al. 2016). DNAm differences for the broader, noisier, or less objective exposures (e.g., socioeconomic status) common in psychology are expected to be comparable or even smaller. Researchers must therefore carefully consider the variability in a targeted region and assume small effect sizes to design studies with adequate power (see the section titled Verification, Validation, and Replication).

In addition, combining the small effect sizes with possible technological or biological variation means that it can be difficult to distinguish true signals from noise. One often-recommended method that decreases the likelihood of false positives is establishing an a priori threshold to consider a finding biologically significant. An arbitrary delta beta of 5% (meaning that 5% of DNA tested gained or lost DNAm at that locus) is common. However, many findings in exploratory studies linking DNAm to exposures in psychology do not meet this threshold, and smaller effect sizes (approximately 2%) have been extensively validated in large cohorts and shown to have downstream effects on gene expression (Breton et al. 2017).

Central Versus Surrogate Tissues

In the context of human studies, the tissue specificity of DNAm creates a significant challenge for the use of surrogate tissues in cases where the primary tissue of choice is not available. This is particularly relevant to psychological studies, where, in many cases, DNAm within the brain might be of ultimate interest but samples of the brain can only be collected postmortem. Postmortem tissues have been useful in many studies, but for studies of living participants, accessible peripheral tissues, such as saliva, buccal epithelial cells collected from a cheek swab, or blood collected by venipuncture or a finger prick, are the only viable options (Davies 2009, Lowe et al. 2013).

The challenge for studies that use peripheral tissues as surrogates is determining whether DNAm differences associated with phenotypes in the surrogate tissue are reflecting parallel changes in the tissue of interest. For many studies focused on behavior, it is thus imperative to rigorously ascertain the extent to which peripheral epigenetic patterns reflect those in the brain. Recent studies on the concordance between central and surrogate tissues have shown mixed patterns, in which some sites are highly concordant across tissues but others are discordant (Davies et al. 2012, Farré et al. 2015, Hannon et al. 2015). Some reports have suggested that the most concordant sites between tissues are more likely to be genetically regulated (Edgar et al. 2017a, Hannon et al. 2015). A few of these studies have created resources that allow patterns of DNAm at specific CpGs of interest to be compared between blood and brain, including BeCON (**https://redgar598.shinyapps.io/BECon/**), a recently published resource from our group (Edgar et al. 2017a, Hannon et al. 2015). These are excellent resources for determining whether findings in blood can be expected to be similar in the brain. Parallel efforts for other tissues such as saliva and cheek swab will be key to future research.

In other cases, accessible biological samples such as blood may, in fact, be extremely informative, with DNAm in these tissues more directly reflecting the exposure of interest. In particular, for studies assessing the stress response and its effects on inflammation, blood is, in fact, the correct primary tissue (Kim et al. 2016, Ligthart et al. 2016). In these situations, identifying functional associations between exposures and DNAm is more likely because the effect is being observed in the tissue of interest.

Timing of Biological Sampling

The inferences that can be made from a DNAm finding depend on the time point at which measurement of DNAm occurred in the course of a study design. For this discussion, it is helpful to distinguish between studies targeting DNAm as an outcome of an exposure, as a predictor of a psychological condition, or as a mediator (i.e., a potential mechanism bridging an earlier exposure to a behavioral outcome).

In developmental research, DNAm is commonly assessed as an outcome of an earlier environmental exposure. Despite the apparent temporal precedence of exposures before DNAm measurement, without longitudinal repeated measures, the inferences drawn in this case must be primarily correlational. DNAm patterns at one time point, accompanied by either recollected measurements of an early exposure or an exposure that was measured in a sample followed prospectively, will not necessarily reflect a pattern attributable to the exposure of interest because environments are often highly confounded. To infer causality, DNAm should be measured a minimum of once before the exposure and once after (if the exposure is postnatal).

In the case of studies with a focus on DNAm as a predictor of future psychological conditions, assessing DNAm at multiple time points may not be as critical, depending on the hypothesis being tested. If DNAm patterns are hypothesized to be a biomarker of risk for developing a disorder at a later time point, it is adequate to obtain one snapshot of DNAm measured at a time point that precedes the typical onset of the disorder. Obtaining two time points of DNAm still offers an advantage, however, if there is interest in biological changes that may accompany the transition to a psychological disorder. Comparing DNAm pre- and post-disease onset with two time points could identify such a pattern (although whether DNAm plays a causal role would still be unclear).

In psychological science, assessment of statistical mediators is commonplace. Many studies conceptualize DNAm as a biological mechanism that links environmental exposures to subsequent outcomes. It is important to note that time ordering is necessary for statistical mediation analysis to distinguish a mediator from a merely confounding influence and is still not sufficient for causal inference (MacKinnon et al. 2000). As mentioned above, DNAm may reflect stable a priori differences and may be attributable to inherent differences between an exposed and unexposed group. Thus, the preferable design to support a mediation model would be assessment of DNAm at both a pre-exposure time point and a time point between exposure and the outcome. Moreover, random assignment of an exposure obtained, for example, through a randomized controlled trial in intervention research is the only means of estimating a true causal effect of an exposure on DNAm, and this randomization must be done in the context of an adequately powered study. Unless a mediator, in this case DNAm, is also randomly assigned, estimating its causal effect on a psychological disorder is not possible.

Finally, although it is ideal to collect more than one time point of DNAm data, it is clearly a costly endeavor. Researchers have to weigh the trade-off between a larger sample size and a larger number of time points of DNAm; their decision will depend on the larger research question and strategy. Regardless of the design selected, it is important for researchers to acknowledge the limitations of their study and to approach mechanistic interpretations cautiously.

CONSIDERATIONS: BIOLOGICAL

Once study-specific decisions such as sample size, study type, and tissue have been made, it is important to consider some unique biological properties of DNAm data and how they will influence data collection and analysis. Because DNAm plays an important role in development and differentiation and has a close relationship with genetic variation, these factors can affect DNAm study results adversely if they are not incorporated into study design and analysis.

Sex

Psychological conditions or behaviors can often be sex specific, resulting in substantial interest on the part of researchers in identifying sex-specific DNAm patterns. Sex chromosome composition is a major driver of genome-wide DNAm patterns, rendering these analyses highly interesting. DNAm is involved in the inactivation of one of the two X chromosomes in females. The silent X chromosome is tightly packaged and heavily methylated, resulting in a highly differential pattern of X chromosome methylation between males and females. Because of this important difference, the X and Y chromosomes should be analyzed separately from the autosomes, as they require different normalization and analysis strategies (Cotton et al. 2015).

Beyond the X chromosome, sex in general is also a determinant of DNAm pattern on the autosomes. The mechanism by which these sex-specific differences arise is unknown but likely reflects the many physiological and developmental differences between males and females. This sex-specific variation, then, is of particular interest to researchers looking for DNAm patterns associated with sex-specific psychological conditions or phenotypes. Incorporating sex into analyses by, first, attempting to balance sex between groups; second, including it as a covariate; and, possibly, third, including it as a moderator in downstream analyses, is critical for DNAm studies.

Genetic Variation and Ethnicity

DNAm is associated with ethnic backgrounds due to shared genetic ancestry as well as cultural and environmental commonalities. The relationship between DNAm and genetic variation is complex, but there are specific sites of DNAm that are highly associated with nearby genetic variants such as SNPs, referred to as methylation quantitative trait loci (mQTLs) (Banovich et al. 2014, Fraser et al. 2012, Gutierrez Arcelus et al. 2013, Hannon et al. 2016, van Dongen et al. 2016). mQTLs may be tissue and developmental stage specific and may vary widely across a population, even within an ethnic group (Teh et al. 2014). Genetic variation is only one of several means by which ethnicity is related to DNAm. Cell type differences, diet, lifestyle, or habitat, as demonstrated by the examples below, also contribute to ethnicity-driven patterns in DNAm. Researchers can attempt to account for these factors by controlling for ethnicity in DNAm studies.

Recent work has isolated genetic effects from environmental and cultural influences on DNAm. One study assessed DNA sequence and epigenomic variation in two African populations with different current habitats, as well as historically different lifestyles (hunter-gatherers versus farmers) (Fagny et al. 2015). Both current habitat and historical circumstances had impacts on variation in DNAm: Variation was accounted for by historical population differences corresponding with nearby genetic variation. The functions of genomic regions implicated in historical ancestry related to developmental processes, whereas current habitats implicated genomic areas with cellular and immune functions. Similarly, in a study of individuals from diverse Hispanic backgrounds, self-identified ethnicity and genetically determined ancestry each accounted for common as well as distinct variation in the methylome. Self-identified ethnicity but not ancestry overlapped with prenatal exposure to smoking, suggesting that culturally identified ethnic groups reflect exposures that may not be accounted for if only genetic ancestry is considered (Galanter et al. 2017).

Age

DNAm is not stable over the lifetime; rather, it has been shown to change with age, in some cases becoming more variable over time and in others demonstrating tight associations with chronological age. This was first observed in identical twins, where young twins were epigenetically highly similar, but older twins became more and more different (Fraga et al. 2005). This observation prompted the epigenetic drift hypothesis, in which environmental and stochastic changes over the lifespan are embedded into the genome and contribute to increasing diversity over time (Teschendorff et al. 2013b).

In addition to the interindividual divergence in DNAm patterns, there are common age-related patterns in DNAm changes that occur across individuals. All tissues examined to date have shown an overall decrease in DNAm with age, although some sites gain DNAm (Bell et al. 2012, Bjornsson et al. 2004, Boks et al. 2009, Florath et al. 2014, Hannum et al. 2013, Horvath et al. 2012, Johansson et al. 2013, Lister et al. 2013, Weidner et al. 2014). Changes in DNAm with age have been extensively reviewed (for further information, see Issa 2014, Teschendorff et al. 2013b, Zampieri et al. 2015).

The associations between DNAm and age are important to consider when beginning a study that will measure DNAm across participants. If the study sample includes a wide range of ages, it is important to attempt to balance ages across groups and to control for chronological age in analyses. Another age-related epigenetic phenomenon, the epigenetic clock, is discussed in the section titled Epigenetic Age.

CONSIDERATIONS: ANALYSIS

The biological and study design considerations described above can result in challenges for DNAm analysis. The effect sizes of some of these variables, particularly ethnicity, age, and sex, on DNAm can be larger than the effect sizes observed for an exposure or condition of interest in psychological studies. Thus, it is particularly important to check for and statistically correct confounders, as they can easily overwhelm true signal and inflate false positives. Conversely, the statistical noise associated with these variables can mask subtle associations with variables of interest even when they are not confounded with it, resulting in an inflation of false negatives. It is recommended that, in any study where age, sex, and ethnicity are not either uniform or balanced across groups, these variables be, at minimum, included as covariates in analyses.

In addition to the need to control confounding variables, DNAm data has unique characteristics that influence its analysis. DNAm data is often presented as a beta value approximating percent methylation. Because most assays measure DNAm across thousands or millions of cells, the beta value represents the average level of DNAm across all of these cells. Beta values are biologically meaningful but can be statistically problematic, as they have low variances at methylation values near 0 or 1. For that reason, statistical analysis is often performed on M values—log transformed methylation values—but results are typically reported as the more biologically relevant beta values (Du et al. 2010).

Types of Genome-Wide DNA Methylation Analyses

As DNAm studies have become more frequent, analysis methods have been designed to take advantage of the opportunities of this particular data type. DNAm data analysis has borrowed methods from both gene expression research and genome-wide association studies, and early studies primarily used epigenome-wide association studies along with assessments of global DNAm that measured mean DNAm or DNAm at repetitive elements in the genome (Baccarelli et al. 2010, Bollati et al. 2009, Rakyan et al. 2011). These analyses are still popular but are now complemented by more complex methods.

Analyses often include an association study identifying specific CpGs or groups of CpGs that are associated with a specific variable of interest. Methods used in this type of analysis include multiple linear regression or correlation analyses. Recent advanced methods have assessed more complex groupings of CpGs; these methods fall into two main categories based on whether they group CpGs in physical neighborhoods or by similarities in DNAm pattern. The former includes methods like DMRcate and Bumphunter, which incorporate the genomic location information for CpGs to identify regions of differential DNAm (Jaffe et al. 2012, Peters et al. 2015). These region-based methods are powerful but require caution for two reasons: First, in cases where variables have small effect sizes, these methods can show bias toward less variable, more CpG-dense regions. Second, many of these methods do not take into account the possibility that multiple functional elements may underlie a cluster of CpGs, which may result in erroneously grouping CpGs that are not functionally related to one another. The other category discovers CpGs with similar DNAm patterns regardless of genomic location, as methylation of CpGs at disparate locations may be functionally related due to the folding and packaging of chromatin. These methods include weighted gene correlated network analysis and functional epigenomic modules (Jiao et al. 2014, Langfelder & Horvath 2008).

In addition to associations, recent work has focused on DNAm variability as a potential marker. These assays determine whether interindividual variability, either at specific probes or across the epigenome, is different between groups. Higher variability has been associated with depression in discordant twins, as well as with type 1 diabetes (Dempster et al. 2014, Paul et al. 2016); however the consequences of altered variability in DNAm are still poorly understood.

DNA Methylation Data Processing

Raw DNAm data must be extensively processed prior to analysis. To monitor the effectiveness of these steps, DNAm data is often assessed using principal components analysis (PCA), a strategy to reduce many variables to a set of independent components that account for maximal variability in the data. By condensing the data from thousands of probes to a manageable number of principal components, statistical associations between these components and technical and biological variables can be observed to confirm that data processing steps are performed correctly (**Figure 3**). In **Figure 3**, which uses cheek swab samples, PCA indicates the relative strengths of associations with technical (batch) and biological (sex, ethnicity, age, and cell type) variables. This and the following sections will outline the steps involved in reducing these confounders. Below, we discuss each stage of data processing and refer back to **Figure 3** to highlight how successful data correction is confirmed.

The initial preprocessing steps deal with technical variables inherent in the DNAm microarray, outlined in **Table 1** (Bibikova et al. 2011, Fortin et al. 2016). First, detailed examinations of the genomic regions assessed on the DNAm arrays have shown that a subset of probes on the array are technically unreliable, and lists of such probes that should be excluded from analysis have been published (Y.-A. Chen et al. 2014, Pidsley et al. 2016, Price et al. 2013). Second, many CpGs present on the array are invariable across samples, particularly within a tissue. An empirically determined set of these invariant CpGs has been identified and can be removed from analysis to minimize multiple hypothesis testing (Edgar et al. 2017b). Third, DNAm data can show batch effects, an issue common to microarrays and sequencing platforms. Batch effects can be detected and corrected, if found, using methods such as ComBat or sva (Leek et al. 2012, Teschendorff

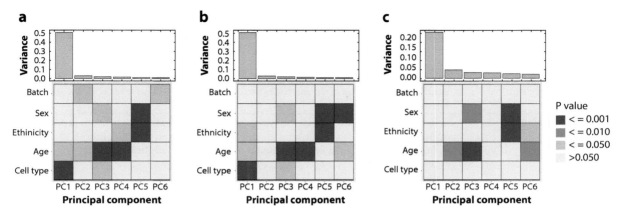

Figure 3

Principal components analysis of DNA methylation (DNAm) data indicating association of technical and biological variables with principal components. The DNAm data were derived from cheek swabs, which can include both buccal epithelia and white blood cells, so the relative proportions of buccal epithelia were calculated using the reference-based methods described in the section titled Cell Type Differences. In each case, the top bar plot indicates the proportion of variance explained by each of the top six principal components, and the bottom heat map indicates the p-value of analysis of variance (ANOVA) (for batch, sex, ethnicity, and age) or Spearman correlation (for cell type). (*a*) Raw data shows strong associations with each variable, with cell type responsible for approximately 50% of the variance. (*b*) After correction for batch, no principal components are still associated with technical batch, but 50% of variance is now associated with cell type. (*c*) After correction for cell type, the top principal component has less variance (approximately 20%) and is no longer associated with cell type. Associations with age, sex, and ethnicity remain strong and should be corrected for either prior to or during analysis.

et al. 2011). In **Figure 3*b***, we demonstrate the use of PCA to assess the success of batch correction, showing that variability due to the technical batch effect has been removed.

Cell Type Differences

As described above, DNAm plays an important role in the development and differentiation of specific cell types. Stem cells exhibit specific DNAm and gene expression patterns, which are further resolved as the cells differentiate (Álvarez-Errico et al. 2014, L. Chen et al. 2014). This results in terminally differentiated cell types with highly cell type–specific DNAm patterns (Guintivano et al. 2013, Reinius et al. 2012). In fact, cell type within a tissue is the second-biggest contributor to DNAm variation, after tissue type (Farré et al. 2015). The example in **Figure 3** shows the extent to which cell type proportions are associated with DNAm profiles, as more than 50% of the variance in the data is due to interindividual differences in buccal cell proportions (shown in **Figure 3*a,b*** but corrected in **Figure 3*c***). If this data had been analyzed without correcting for cell types, it would be unclear whether any significant findings were due to true DNAm differences between groups or simply to differences in cell composition.

In the brain, for example, neurons and glia show very different DNAm profiles (Guintivano et al. 2013, Lister et al. 2013). This means that, if two samples with different proportions of neurons are compared, then the differences between the samples will primarily reflect those differences in cell type, rather than any underlying condition or phenotype. It is thus important to consider tissue sampling across participants to minimize interindividual differences in cell counts. Cell counts are often not collected when tissues are stored due to labor intensiveness and cost, but, fortunately, it is possible to predict underlying cell type differences for brain tissue, as well as for some of the

Table 1 Steps in data cleaning and processing for DNA methylation data from Illumina microarray platforms

Step	Description	Common tools
1. Raw data	Data is generated from the scanner and extracted as IDAT files	Illumina scanner software
2. Background subtraction, color correction	Basic normalization removes background signal and equalizes the intensities of the two colors used on the arrays	Illumina Genome Studio or Minfi R package (Aryee et al. 2014)
3. Probe filtering	Probes that are unreliable or unnecessary are removed. These can include: ■ Probes with high within-sample variability or insufficient signal ■ Probes that are known to hybridize to multiple sites in the genome ■ Probes found in repetitive regions ■ Probes on the X and Y chromosomes (see the section titled Sex) ■ Probes with little or no interindividual variability (optional)	Additional annotations (Y.-A. Chen et al. 2014, Edgar et al. 2017b, Price et al. 2013)
4. Normalization	Normalization equalizes the ranges of the two probe types on the array	BMIQ, wateRmelon R package, Minfi R package (Aryee et al. 2014, Pidsley et al. 2013, Teschendorff et al. 2013a)
5. Batch correction	Batch correction removes any effects of the batch, including chip, plate, or row	ComBat function in sva R package (Teschendorff et al. 2011)
6. Final data	At this point, data can be analyzed or corrected for known confounders (e.g., cell type, sex, ethnicity)	See Jones et al. (2015b)

more common surrogate tissues: saliva, blood, and cheek swab (Guintivano et al. 2013, Houseman et al. 2012, Smith et al. 2015).

These methods are referred to as reference-based methods because they rely on reference profiles created from isolated cell types to infer the likely underlying cell composition (Houseman et al. 2012). Reference-based methods are limited, however, by the requirement for reference profiles for each component cell type, which means that they often cannot predict proportions for very infrequently occurring cell types or for tissues in which it is difficult to isolate cell types. The references may also be developmental stage specific, which could influence the accuracy of the predictions at different ages. To circumvent some of these limitations, reference-free methods correct for the effects of cell composition without actually predicting the cell counts (Houseman et al. 2012, 2014; Lam et al. 2012; Zou et al. 2014). However, it is much more difficult to assess the performance of these measures in reducing interindividual variability. The use of reference-based methods that predict cell types versus methods that correct for interindividual variability without using cell type references is still highly debated (Hattab et al. 2017; McGregor et al. 2016, 2017). Because excellent and well-characterized reference profiles for adult blood, brain, and saliva exist, these profiles are reliable and recommended for use in DNAm studies (Guintivano et al. 2013, Houseman et al. 2012, Smith et al. 2015). However, it has been shown that adult blood references do not work well on cord blood, for example, so for other tissues or developmental stages, it is important to consider both reference-based and reference-free methods (Yousefi et al. 2015).

In both cases, the method incorporates information on interindividual variability due to cell type, either directly, as in reference-based methods, or indirectly, as in non-reference-based methods, with the goal of controlling for this important type of variation (Jones et al. 2015b).

Adding further complications, the differences in cell type can themselves be related to the phenotype, as has occurred in a number of studies (Esposito et al. 2016, Jones et al. 2013, Liu et al. 2013). In those cases, the cell type differences are an important and interesting finding to be discussed, but they must be carefully controlled for if the goal is to find DNAm changes that are independent of cell type (Paul et al. 2016).

Verification, Validation, and Replication

Another consideration for DNAm studies is the sheer magnitude of measurements—bisulfite sequencing may record millions of CpGs, the 450k array measures over 480,000 sites, and the Illumina EPIC array measures over 850,000 sites. With this number of tests, it is essential to correct for multiple comparisons to avoid false positives, but typical methods can be overly conservative. Stringent multiple test correction, like Bonferroni $p < 0.05$, would require a nominal p-value less than 5×10^{-8}, so more often, a false discovery rate (FDR)–based method like Benjamini-Hochberg correction is used (Benjamini & Hochberg 1995). This method also has limitations, particularly the fact that the corrected p-value is based on the underlying distribution of nominal p-values, which can be complex to resolve across experiments if the underlying distributions are different. Partly for these reasons, some researchers are now using a very low nominal p-value (approximately 1×10^{-6}) or a higher FDR (approximately 0.1) and adding a second measure of biological feasibility, such as variability or range, to reduce the number of hits (Esposito et al. 2016, Ladd-Acosta et al. 2014, Lam et al. 2012). However, this loosening of statistical stringency makes verification, validation, and, especially, replication of DNAm findings particularly important.

In this context, verification refers to measuring DNAm through another method—often pyrosequencing of hits from array technology. This method occasionally has the added benefit of measuring new CpGs in the genome that are not on the array, adding new associations with the variable of interest. Validation refers to measuring the same relationship between the variable of interest and the hit in samples reserved from the initial study. Replication entails repeating the same analysis on completely independent samples (Michels et al. 2013).

Thus, when designing studies, it is important to budget and reserve samples to verify findings by another method, to either reserve a subset of samples for validation or recruit additional participants for that purpose, and to examine the literature closely for appropriate cohorts for replication. One important consideration, especially for replication in an independent data set, is the idea that methylation in the replication should be assessed in the same tissue and age range as in the original study, and the variables of interest should be assessed by common measurement. It might be challenging to replicate a finding discovered in blood samples in a cohort with cheek swabs, for example. Differences in tissue type or variable measurement can reduce the likelihood of replication.

Within the psychology landscape, reproducibility of results has become an issue at the forefront of discussion (see Open Sci. Collab. 2015). The risk for false positives is substantial for expensive methylation studies due to typically limited sample sizes, small effects, and, in the case of array-based data, the measurement of hundreds of thousands of data points. Collaborations and the development of research consortia can build the funding and resources required for larger sample sizes and concomitant replications.

As more DNAm data sets are generated, there are sufficient numbers of published findings to allow the application of meta-analysis. A number of consortia have been organized to combine cohort data with the goal of creating larger studies in which to validate and extend prior findings. Recently, a large meta-analysis validated previous findings, outlined above, on the connection between DNAm at genes in the aryl hydrocarbon receptor repressor (AHRR) pathway and prenatal exposure to cigarette smoke, and also discovered previously unknown associations

(Joubert et al. 2016). In the near future, meta-analyses will undoubtedly become more prevalent, which will help to confirm reliable results.

Data Access

Microarray, sequencing, and other types of data are frequently deposited to online repositories, and, indeed, upon acceptance of a manuscript, many biomedical journals require that such data be deposited so that it can be publicly accessed. It is in the best interests of researchers and funders alike that this deidentified data be shared widely, as it allows for effective replication of studies. Making use of this data for replication comes with its own challenges but is hugely advantageous to the field as a whole. Public access to data can be a sensitive issue, as participant data collected as part of a study can often be proprietary and personal, with associated ethical issues. It is thus important to verify that proper consent is in place when biological samples are collected to ensure that data can be anonymized and shared with the broader community. In cases where specific types of data cannot be shared, it is beneficial for researchers to be open to collaborations with others who may request specific analyses or reanalyses of data.

IMPLICATIONS OF DNA METHYLATION FINDINGS

Perhaps the most intriguing aspect of epigenetic studies in psychological science is the possibility of identifying biological mechanisms accounting for the effects of environmental exposures correlated with human behavior. However, it is important to approach epigenetic findings with caution and to resist the allure of jumping to mechanistic interpretations. At the present stage of human research, correlations between psychological conditions or environmental exposures are, indeed, correlational and do not necessarily imply a causal mechanism. Currently, associative epigenetic signatures are best understood as potential biomarkers until further investigation of molecular mechanisms discovers underlying functional effects.

The distinction between a DNAm finding being a biomarker versus a causal mechanism is one of the fundamental questions in epigenetics today and involves asking whether there is sufficient evidence to infer whether differences observed are cause or consequence (Ladd-Acosta 2015). It is important to note that determining actual causality in any association study is very challenging (see the section titled Timing of Biological Sampling). Mendelian randomization is one method that has been proposed to assess causality without the burden of longitudinal measurement. It uses genotype as a fixed variable from which to test causality but is possible only in cases where there is a known genetic variant that is uniquely associated with the variable of interest (Relton & Davey Smith 2012), an assumption that is rarely met with psychological phenotypes.

Without causal study designs or Mendelian randomization, it is still possible to make hypotheses as to whether an association between DNAm and a variable of interest might be functional or not and to target identified sites in downstream molecular experiments. The uncertainty of these interpretations should be presented, however, and mechanistic language should be limited in this presentation. Evidence that a psychological DNAm finding in a surrogate tissue such as blood or cheek swabs exhibits a similar relationship in brain tissue would be encouraging for future research. Also, prior evidence that DNAm at the region of interest is associated with gene expression changes or conformational changes to DNA would also increase confidence that further work might uncover a mechanism.

In cases where such evidence is not available, associations between DNAm and a variable of interest can still be relevant as biomarkers. These biomarkers can be used for identification purposes and can be particularly useful if they are marks of an exposure or event that can have future health relevance. In that case, these marks could inform targeted interventions or lifestyle changes to alter future risk.

In both cases, signatures of DNAm that are associated with an environmental exposure, health, or behavior offer translational avenues. For associations for which evidence of mechanistic involvement is available, understanding the actual molecular mechanism is important for identifying novel therapeutics or treatments. Biomarkers can also be used to stratify populations for more targeted interventions or as early markers of intervention effectiveness (for an excellent review of the challenges of interpreting epigenetic findings, see Lappalainen & Greally 2017).

Relationship Between DNA Methylation and Gene Expression

When analysis is completed and specific CpGs or groups of CpGs have been identified as being associated with a variable of interest, one potential next step is assessing whether the DNAm differences observed alter gene expression. This is not required, as DNAm associations can be valuable even if gene expression does not change, but is one way to assess possible outcomes. Although measuring RNA in addition to DNAm is ideal, RNA is often not collected, as it is more difficult to stabilize during biological sampling. It is possible to infer potential influences on gene expression from DNAm patterns, but this has two related complications. The first is determining how (or whether) to assign CpGs to a specific gene, and the second is determining what possible effects on gene expression the DNAm change might have; these effects depend on both the direction of the DNAm change and the specific location and function of the CpG.

Mapping CpGs to a specific gene is more difficult than it might appear, as CpGs might be found within or near a single gene or near multiple genes. Many systems have been created to annotate CpGs, particularly those on the 450k array, to specific genes, and these can vary widely (Y.-A. Chen et al. 2014; Edgar et al. 2017a; Farré et al. 2015; Price et al. 2013, 2016). It is also important to note that, in some cases, CpGs may not be annotated to a gene at all. This does not mean that the differential DNAm of that CpG has no outcome; instead, it is possible that it is involved in a relationship that has not yet been mapped.

Once the CpGs of interest have been mapped to genes, it is possible to hypothesize how the observed change might influence expression of those genes based on the type of genomic feature in which the change is observed. In general, genomic features like DNase hypersensitive sites, enhancers, and transcription factor binding sites are indicators that there might be an association with gene expression. A University of California, Santa Cruz website (**http://genome.ucsc.edu/cgi-bin/hgGateway**) is an excellent resource, as it has a useful visual interface; includes data from large-scale mapping projects like ENCODE, Roadmap Epigenome, and the 1,000 Genomes Project; and can be customized with user-generated data (Bernstein et al. 2010, Diehl & Boyle 2016, Meyer et al. 2013, Sloan et al. 2016). Generally, promoter CpG island–associated DNAm is weakly but negatively associated with gene expression, whereas gene body DNAm is weakly but positively associated (Gutierrez Arcelus et al. 2013, Schübeler 2015, Wagner et al. 2014). Other genomic features, like enhancers and insulators, have less clear trends (Kozlenkov et al. 2014, Ziller et al. 2013). Hypotheses regarding gene expression changes should be tempered, however, as there are many exceptions to these rules, and other underlying genomic features might influence expression in a gene-specific manner (Gutierrez Arcelus et al. 2013).

Finally, it is essential to examine the tissue-specific expression of any associated genes to determine whether and when genes are expressed. In some cases, DNAm differences may be found at genes that are not expressed in a particular tissue or are only expressed under specific conditions. DNAm patterns have been shown to prime cells for future responses and, in some cases, predict condition-specific gene expression, so it is important to investigate these issues (Lam et al. 2012).

Epigenetic Age

In addition to the above-described assessment of specific CpGs or groups of CpGs to a variable of interest, a recently developed tool provides an alternative use of DNAm data. Researchers had previously observed that DNAm levels were associated with chronological age, but in recent years, specific epigenetic clocks—patterns of DNAm that accurately predict chronological age across a population—have been published (Florath et al. 2014, Hannum et al. 2013, Horvath 2013, Weidner et al. 2014; for a review, see Jones et al. 2015a). Thus, in contrast to the epigenome-wide and candidate gene studies described above, an analysis of epigenetic age is calculated based on a specific set of CpGs, which are highly informative of age.

It has been hypothesized that these clocks represent a measurement of biological age, and, indeed, studies have shown that deviations of epigenetic age—that is, higher epigenetic age compared to chronological age—is associated with a variety of health conditions (Horvath & Levine 2015; Horvath et al. 2015, 2016; Levine et al. 2015; Marioni et al. 2015). Given the general interest in psychology in the lasting impacts of stress on the aging process, the use of epigenetic clocks for determining age acceleration has become particularly useful for testing hypotheses on the mechanistic links between psychological stressors and age-related disease. For instance, age acceleration has been predicted by cumulative lifetime stress, trauma, and harsh parenting (for a review, see Zannas et al. 2015), and these effects can be counteracted by supportive environments (Brody et al. 2016a,b; Miller & Sadeh 2014).

Epigenetic Inheritance Across Generations

A particularly intriguing feature of epigenetics in the developmental origins of health is the idea of epigenetic inheritance across generations. As mentioned above, DNAm is heritable from cell to cell (i.e., within one organism's lifespan), creating a memory of DNAm that reflects past exposures. The idea that this could be extended to human generations, i.e., that epigenetic changes can be inherited from parent to child, is very compelling and, simultaneously, complex.

The idea of inheritance across generations has been divided into two categories: intra- and inter- or transgenerational epigenetic inheritance (Miska & Ferguson-Smith 2016). The theory of intragenerational inheritance involves the idea that, during pregnancy, child DNAm patterns are altered by exposure to the maternal in utero environment, which is a product of the mother's lifetime exposures. These effects may plausibly be observed up to two generations after the exposure, as the germ cells of the exposed child, which will go on to make the next generation, are also exposed. True transgenerational inheritance requires transmission of epigenetic marks themselves to the next generation in the absence of the exposure. Transgenerational inheritance thus requires evidence of three-generation transmission through the female line, as the offspring of the third generation is the first to not directly encounter the in utero exposure. These distinctions have been covered in detail in an excellent review (van Otterdijk & Michels 2016). Correct usage of these definitions is essential to accurately describe how environmental influences propagate across generations. To date, there is evidence for intragenerational transmission of many environmental exposures but no true evidence of transgenerational inheritance in humans (Heard & Martienssen 2014, Joubert et al. 2016, Radtke et al. 2011).

APPLICATION TO CURRENT AREAS OF PSYCHOLOGY

Now that we have outlined the methodological and conceptual considerations in DNAm studies, we provide an overview of some existing issues in the psychology literature, in which epigenetic analysis has become popular. We outline a few examples, reflecting on how the issues raised above have been addressed (or unaddressed) to date. We note that the intention in highlighting some examples is not to single out particular studies but merely to elaborate on methodological advancements, as the understanding of the issues discussed above has grown rapidly in the past few years.

Developmental Studies

The designs and goals of developmental studies incorporating DNAm are wide ranging, but tissue type and time ordering of sample collection are particularly relevant issues. Out of necessity, many studies assess DNAm in a common surrogate tissue, blood, years after an early environmental exposure. Far from being a limitation, in studies focused on the biological embedding of stress, blood is actually the tissue of interest. Specifically, psychological exposures are theorized to add wear and tear on the body, accelerating the physiological processes of aging that may, indeed, affect inflammatory and immunological processes via DNAm mechanisms; thus, these effects are most relevantly studied in blood (Miller et al. 2009, Zannas et al. 2015). For example, in a study assessing the effects of extreme social deprivation, Esposito et al. (2016) reported DNAm findings as well as cell type composition of peripheral blood mononuclear cells as outcomes given the hypothesized importance of inflammatory systems.

In contrast, the majority of studies in psychology assess DNAm in peripheral tissues, with the primary interest being the brain. For instance, many human studies have sought to explore the link between DNAm at the glucocorticoid receptor gene *NR3C1* in peripheral tissue and early life exposures following animal work reporting DNAm changes in brain tissue (Turecki & Meaney 2016, Pan et al. 2014, Weaver et al. 2004). Methylation at this promoter has low variability across individuals, yielding very small observed effects and uncertainty around whether these effects are consistent in brain tissue, although some work has found consistent patterns in a small cohort of hippocampal samples of suicide victims who experienced early childhood abuse (McGowan et al. 2009). Because bioinformatic methods for correction for interindividual differences in cell type (i.e., hippocampal neurons or glia) were not available in this early work, replication with correction is required.

In addition, developmental studies are typically longitudinal, as time ordering is critical to making inferences about potentially enduring effects of early exposures. Much of the earliest DNAm work in development relied on precollected data and incorporated DNAm analysis of collected samples after the fact at later developmental stages (e.g., Essex et al. 2013). As covered above, the best-case scenario for making a causal inference would be to assess DNAm both pre- and post-exposure, to the extent that exposures are temporally discrete. One candidate DNAm study focusing on promoters of the oxytocin receptor gene and brain-derived neurotrophic factor promoters assessed DNAm at these sites in blood pre- and post-exposure to the Trier social stress test (Unternaehrer et al. 2012). The authors found a change in methylation at the oxytocin receptor; however, pre- and post-stress differences in DNAm were no longer significant after adjustment for blood cell counts. This study thus also highlights the importance of accounting for cell composition when attempting to elucidate the causal effects of exposures. As collection of biological samples becomes more commonplace, the assessment of DNAm changes pre– and post–social exposures in longitudinal contexts is an intriguing possibility for future work.

Candidate Gene Studies

Candidate gene studies in psychology focus on DNAm within one gene or a small number of genes of interest, often in peripheral tissues. The candidate approach is applied in several domains of psychology research but commonly encompasses neurodevelopmental hypotheses specific to the biological effects of one of several popular candidates related to neurotransmitter or neuropeptide function (e.g., *5-HTTLPR, OXTR, MAOA*). The neuroimaging epigenetic literature, for instance, almost entirely focuses on these candidates, including *NR3C1*, as discussed above (Nikolova & Hariri 2015). However, one study to date has applied whole epigenome analysis with neuroimaging (Chen et al. 2015).

There are a few noteworthy methodological limitations of the current candidate gene literature. First, there has largely been a focus on candidate gene promoters, which, as mentioned above, tend to exhibit minimal variability, as most promoters are typically unmethylated. Second, strategies such as taking an average or a principal component of multiple CpGs in an effort to collapse DNAm measurements into one methylation variable for further analysis are commonplace. This strategy might be problematic, as groups of CpGs could overlap with different types of functional regions, so collapsing a group together risks removing important functional information. Third, with most candidate studies, the absence of genome-wide data and, typically, lack of cell counts or cell sorting mean that DNAm is quantified across more than a single cell type without the ability to correct for cell type proportions. As the major driver of variation in DNAm is cell type (see above), these results could easily be seriously confounded. There are ways around these drawbacks, however; for example, one study targeted a known functional intronic region and grouped CpGs according to spatial proximity to binding sites for analysis, and findings were replicated in a subsample that accounted for cell type proportions (Klengel et al. 2013).

Psychological Disorders

Brain tissue is of primary interest in the manifestation of psychological disorders, and the epigenetics psychiatric literature has the advantage of brain biobanks available for cases and controls with various psychiatric conditions. For instance, an epigenome-wide study of CpG-rich regions in prefrontal cortex tissues obtained from individuals diagnosed with schizophrenia, individuals diagnosed with bipolar disorder, and controls identified epigenetic modifications involved in neuronal development and metabolism (Hannon et al. 2016, Mill et al. 2008). We note that cell type was not controlled for, as is typical of many studies in this area, and, thus, the association could be driven by cell type differences.

Given the potential link between the historical interaction of genetic factors and exposures and DNAm patterns, another possibility is to use DNAm as a predictor or marker of risk for psychiatric disorders. In a recent article applying epigenome-wide analysis to DNAm in peripheral blood in men, early-life stress in the form of separation from families was not found to relate to DNAm (Khulan et al. 2014). However, later psychological follow-ups revealed that epigenetic signatures predicted the onset of depressive symptoms 5–10 years following sample collection. Although cell type was also not accounted for in this study and, thus, it should be interpreted with caution, it does showcase the potential of DNAm patterns and their possible reflection of earlier interplay of genetic and environmental risk as predictors of psychological outcomes.

CONCLUDING REMARKS

Epigenetics offers an exciting avenue for inquiries into the origin and development of psychological health and human disease. The prominent role of DNAm in early cell differentiation and plasticity makes it an intriguing molecular mechanism for the biological embedding of early experiences but, paradoxically, also introduces the major caveat of its variability being strongly driven by genetic sequence and cell type. To move the study of DNAm in psychological and developmental processes forward, careful attention to these and other idiosyncratic characteristics of DNAm is critical for study design and interpretation. We hope this review will be useful in guiding researchers in incorporating this promising approach into the study of biological underpinnings in psychological science.

DISCLOSURE STATEMENT

The authors are not aware of any affiliations, memberships, funding, or financial holdings that might be perceived as affecting the objectivity of this review.

ACKNOWLEDGMENTS

We would like to thank Drs. Suzanne Vrshek-Schallhorn, Greg Miller, Elizabeth Conradt, and Jenny Tung for their input and recommendations.

LITERATURE CITED

Álvarez-Errico D, Vento-Tormo R, Sieweke M, Ballestar E. 2014. Epigenetic control of myeloid cell differentiation, identity and function. *Nat. Rev. Immunol.* 15(1):7–17

Antequera F. 2003. Structure, function and evolution of CpG island promoters. *Cell Mol. Life Sci.* 60(8):1647–58

Aryee MJ, Jaffe AE, Corrada-Bravo H, Ladd-Acosta C, Feinberg AP, et al. 2014. Minfi: a flexible and comprehensive Bioconductor package for the analysis of Infinium DNA methylation microarrays. *Bioinformatics* 30(10):1363–69

Baccarelli A, Tarantini L, Wright RO, Bollati V, Litonjua AA, et al. 2010. Repetitive element DNA methylation and circulating endothelial and inflammation markers in the VA normative aging study. *Epigenetics* 5(3):222–28

Banovich NE, Lan X, McVicker G, van de Geijn B, Degner JF, et al. 2014. Methylation QTLs are associated with coordinated changes in transcription factor binding, histone modifications, and gene expression levels. *PLOS Genet.* 10(9):e1004663

Bell JT, Tsai P-C, Yang T-P, Pidsley R, Nisbet J, et al. 2012. Epigenome-wide scans identify differentially methylated regions for age and age-related phenotypes in a healthy ageing population. *PLOS Genet.* 8(4):189–200

Benjamini Y, Hochberg Y. 1995. Controlling the false discovery rate: a practical and powerful approach to multiple testing. *J. R. Stat. Soc. Ser. B* 57(1):289–300

Bernstein BE, Stamatoyannopoulos JA, Costello JF, Ren B, Milosavljevic A, et al. 2010. The NIH Roadmap Epigenomics Mapping Consortium. *Nat. Biotechnol.* 28(10):1045–48

Bestor TH. 2000. The DNA methyltransferases of mammals. *Hum. Mol. Genet.* 9(16):2395–402

Bibikova M, Barnes B, Tsan C, Ho V, Klotzle B, et al. 2011. High density DNA methylation array with single CpG site resolution. *Genomics* 98(4):288–95

Bibikova M, Le J, Barnes B, Saedinia-Melnyk S, Zhou L, et al. 2009. Genome-wide DNA methylation profiling using Infinium® assay. *Epigenomics* 1(1):177–200

Bibikova M, Lin Z, Zhou L, Chudin E, Garcia EW, et al. 2006. High-throughput DNA methylation profiling using universal bead arrays. *Genome Res.* 16(3):383–93

Bjornsson HT, Fallin MD, Feinberg AP. 2004. An integrated epigenetic and genetic approach to common human disease. *Trends Genet.* 20(8):350–58

Bock C. 2012. Analysing and interpreting DNA methylation data. *Nat. Rev. Genet.* 13(10):705–19

Boks MP, Derks EM, Weisenberger DJ, Strengman E, Janson E, et al. 2009. The relationship of DNA methylation with age, gender and genotype in twins and healthy controls. *PLOS ONE* 4(8):e6767

Bollati V, Schwartz J, Wright R, Litonjua A, Tarantini L, et al. 2009. Decline in genomic DNA methylation through aging in a cohort of elderly subjects. *Mech. Ageing Dev.* 130(4):234–39

Boyce WT, Kobor MS. 2015. Development and the epigenome: the "synapse" of gene-environment interplay. *Dev. Sci.* 18(1):1–23

Breton CV, Marsit CJ, Faustman E, Nadeau K, Goodrich JM, et al. 2017. Small-magnitude effect sizes in epigenetic end points are important in children's environmental health studies: the Children's Environmental Health and Disease Prevention Research Center's Epigenetics Working Group. *Environ. Health Perspect.* 125(4):511–26

Brody GH, Miller GE, Yu T, Beach SRH, Chen E. 2016a. Supportive family environments ameliorate the link between racial discrimination and epigenetic aging: a replication across two longitudinal cohorts. *Psychol. Sci.* 27(4):530–41

Brody GH, Yu T, Chen E, Beach SRH, Miller GE. 2016b. Family-centered prevention ameliorates the longitudinal association between risky family processes and epigenetic aging. *J. Child Psychol. Psychiatry* 57(5):566–74

Chen L, Kostadima M, Martens JHA, Canu G, Garcia SP, et al. 2014. Transcriptional diversity during lineage commitment of human blood progenitors. *Science* 345(6204):1251033

Chen L, Pan H, Tuan TA, Teh AL, MacIsaac JL, et al. 2015. Brain-derived neurotrophic factor (BDNF) Val66Met polymorphism influences the association of the methylome with maternal anxiety and neonatal brain volumes. *Dev. Psychopathol.* 27(1):137–50

Chen Y-A, Lemire M, Choufani S, Butcher DT, Grafodatskaya D, et al. 2014. Discovery of cross-reactive probes and polymorphic CpGs in the Illumina Infinium HumanMethylation450 microarray. *Epigenetics* 8(2):203–9

Christensen BC, Houseman EA, Marsit CJ, Zheng S, Wrensch MR, et al. 2009. Aging and environmental exposures alter tissue-specific DNA methylation dependent upon CpG island context. *PLOS Genet.* 5(8):e1000602

Cotton AM, Price EM, Jones MJ, Balaton BP, Kobor MS, Brown CJ. 2015. Landscape of DNA methylation on the X chromosome reflects CpG density, functional chromatin state and X-chromosome inactivation. *Hum. Mol. Genet.* 24(6):1528–39

Davies M. 2009. To what extent is blood a reasonable surrogate for brain in gene expression studies: estimation from mouse hippocampus and spleen. *Front. Neurosci.* 3:54

Davies MN, Volta M, Pidsley R, Lunnon K, Dixit A, et al. 2012. Functional annotation of the human brain methylome identifies tissue-specific epigenetic variation across brain and blood. *Genome Biol.* 13(6):R43

Dempster EL, Wong CCY, Lester KJ, Burrage J, Gregory AM, et al. 2014. Genome-wide methylomic analysis of monozygotic twins discordant for adolescent depression. *Biol. Psychiatry* 76(12):977–83

Diehl AG, Boyle AP. 2016. Deciphering ENCODE. *Trends Genet.* 32(4):238–49

Du P, Zhang X, Huang C-C, Jafari N, Kibbe WA, et al. 2010. Comparison of Beta-value and M-value methods for quantifying methylation levels by microarray analysis. *BMC Bioinform.* 11(1):587

Edgar RD, Jones MJ, Meaney MJ, Turecki G, Kobor MS. 2017a. BECon: a tool for interpreting DNA methylation findings from blood in the context of brain. *Transl. Psychiatry* 7:e1187

Edgar RD, Jones MJ, Robinson WP, Kobor MS. 2017b. An empirically driven data reduction method on the human 450K methylation array to remove tissue specific non-variable CpGs. *Clin. Epigenet.* 9:11

Esposito EA, Jones MJ, Doom JR, MacIsaac JL, Gunnar MR, Kobor MS. 2016. Differential DNA methylation in peripheral blood mononuclear cells in adolescents exposed to significant early but not later childhood adversity. *Dev. Psychopathol.* 28(4):1385–99

Essex MJ, Boyce WT, Hertzman C, Lam LL, Armstrong JM, et al. 2013. Epigenetic vestiges of early developmental adversity: childhood stress exposure and DNA methylation in adolescence. *Child Dev.* 84(1):58–75

Fagny M, Patin E, MacIsaac JL, Rotival M, Flutre T, et al. 2015. The epigenomic landscape of African rainforest hunter-gatherers and farmers. *Nat. Commun.* 6:10047

Farré P, Jones MJ, Meaney MJ, Emberly E, Turecki G, Kobor MS. 2015. Concordant and discordant DNA methylation signatures of aging in human blood and brain. *Epigenet. Chromatin* 8:19

Ficz G, Branco MR, Seisenberger S, Santos F, Krueger F, et al. 2011. Dynamic regulation of 5-hydroxymethylcytosine in mouse ES cells and during differentiation. *Nature* 473(7347):398–402

Florath I, Butterbach K, Müller H, Bewerunge-Hudler M, Brenner H. 2014. Cross-sectional and longitudinal changes in DNA methylation with age: an epigenome-wide analysis revealing over 60 novel age-associated CpG sites. *Hum. Mol. Genet.* 23(5):1186–201

Fortin J-P, Triche TJ, Hansen KD. 2016. Preprocessing, normalization and integration of the Illumina HumanMethylationEPIC array with minfi. *Bioinformatics* 33(4):558–60

Fraga MF, Ballestar E, Paz MF, Ropero S, Setien F, et al. 2005. Epigenetic differences arise during the lifetime of monozygotic twins. *PNAS* 102(30):10604–9

Fraser HB, Lam LL, Neumann SM, Kobor MS. 2012. Population-specificity of human DNA methylation. *Genome Biol.* 13(2):R8

Galanter JM, Gignoux CR, Oh SS, Torgerson D, Pino-Yanes M, et al. 2017. Differential methylation between ethnic sub-groups reflects the effect of genetic ancestry and environmental exposures. *eLife* 6:e20532

Gao X, Jia M, Zhang Y, Breitling LP, Brenner H. 2015. DNA methylation changes of whole blood cells in response to active smoking exposure in adults: a systematic review of DNA methylation studies. *Clin. Epigenet.* 7:113

Gu H, Smith ZD, Bock C, Boyle P, Gnirke A, Meissner A. 2011. Preparation of reduced representation bisulfite sequencing libraries for genome-scale DNA methylation profiling. *Nat. Protoc.* 6(4):468–81

Guintivano J, Aryee MJ, Kaminsky ZA. 2013. A cell epigenotype specific model for the correction of brain cellular heterogeneity bias and its application to age, brain region and major depression. *Epigenetics* 8(3):290–302

Guo JU, Su Y, Shin JH, Shin J, Li H, et al. 2013. Distribution, recognition and regulation of non-CpG methylation in the adult mammalian brain. *Nat. Neurosci.* 17(2):215–22

Gutierrez Arcelus M, Lappalainen T, Montgomery SB, Buil A, Ongen H, et al. 2013. Passive and active DNA methylation and the interplay with genetic variation in gene regulation. *eLife* 2:e00523

Hannon E, Lunnon K, Schalkwyk L, Mill J. 2015. Interindividual methylomic variation across blood, cortex, and cerebellum: implications for epigenetic studies of neurological and neuropsychiatric phenotypes. *Epigenetics* 10(11):1024–32

Hannon E, Spiers H, Viana J, Pidsley R, Burrage J, et al. 2016. Methylation QTLs in the developing brain and their enrichment in schizophrenia risk loci. *Nat. Neurosci.* 19(1):48–54

Hannum G, Guinney J, Zhao L, Zhang L, Hughes G, et al. 2013. Genome-wide methylation profiles reveal quantitative views of human aging rates. *Mol. Cell* 49(2):359–67

Hattab MW, Shabalin AA, Clark SL, Zhao M, Kumar G, et al. 2017. Correcting for cell-type effects in DNA methylation studies: Reference-based method outperforms latent variable approaches in empirical studies. *Genome Biol.* 18:24

Heard E, Martienssen RA. 2014. Transgenerational epigenetic inheritance: myths and mechanisms. *Cell* 157(1):95–109

Henikoff S, Greally JM. 2016. Epigenetics, cellular memory and gene regulation. *Curr. Biol.* 26(14):R644–48

Hertzman C. 1999. The biological embedding of early experience and its effects on health in adulthood. *Ann. N. Y. Acad. Sci.* 896:85–95

Horvath S. 2013. DNA methylation age of human tissues and cell types. *Genome Biol.* 14(10):R115

Horvath S, Garagnani P, Bacalini MG, Pirazzini C, Salvioli S, et al. 2015. Accelerated epigenetic aging in Down syndrome. *Aging Cell* 14(3):491–95

Horvath S, Gurven M, Levine ME, Trumble BC, Kaplan H, et al. 2016. An epigenetic clock analysis of race/ethnicity, sex, and coronary heart disease. *Genome Biol.* 17(1):171

Horvath S, Levine AJ. 2015. HIV-1 infection accelerates age according to the epigenetic clock. *J. Infect. Dis.* 212(10):1563–73

Horvath S, Zhang Y, Langfelder P, Kahn RS, Boks MP, et al. 2012. Aging effects on DNA methylation modules in human brain and blood tissue. *Genome Biol.* 13(10):R97

Houseman EA, Accomando WP, Koestler DC, Christensen BC, Marsit CJ, et al. 2012. DNA methylation arrays as surrogate measures of cell mixture distribution. *BMC Bioinform.* 13:86

Houseman EA, Molitor J, Marsit CJ. 2014. Reference-free cell mixture adjustments in analysis of DNA methylation data. *Bioinformatics* 30(10):1431–39

Illingworth RS, Bird AP. 2009. CpG islands—"a rough guide". *FEBS Lett.* 583(11):1713–20

Irizarry RA, Ladd-Acosta C, Wen B, Wu Z, Montano C, et al. 2009. The human colon cancer methylome shows similar hypo- and hypermethylation at conserved tissue-specific CpG island shores. *Nat Genet.* 41(2):178–86

Issa J-P. 2014. Aging and epigenetic drift: a vicious cycle. *J. Clin. Invest.* 124(1):24–29

Jaffe AE, Murakami P, Lee H, Leek JT, Fallin MD, et al. 2012. Bump hunting to identify differentially methylated regions in epigenetic epidemiology studies. *Int. J. Epidemiol.* 41(1):200–9

Jiao Y, Widschwendter M, Teschendorff AE. 2014. A systems-level integrative framework for genome-wide DNA methylation and gene expression data identifies differential gene expression modules under epigenetic control. *Bioinformatics* 30(16):2360–66

Jin SG, Wu X, Li AX, Pfeifer GP. 2011. Genomic mapping of 5-hydroxymethylcytosine in the human brain. *Nucleic Acids Res.* 39(12):5015–24

Johansson A, Enroth S, Gyllensten U. 2013. Continuous aging of the human DNA methylome throughout the human lifespan. *PLOS ONE* 8(6):e67378

Jones MJ, Farré P, McEwen LM, MacIsaac JL, Watt K, et al. 2013. Distinct DNA methylation patterns of cognitive impairment and trisomy 21 in Down syndrome. *BMC Med. Genom.* 6:58

Jones MJ, Goodman SJ, Kobor MS. 2015a. DNA methylation and healthy human aging. *Aging Cell.* 14(6):924–32

Jones MJ, Islam SA, Edgar RD, Kobor MS. 2015b. Adjusting for cell type composition in DNA methylation data using a regression-based approach. *Methods Mol. Biol.* 1589:99–106

Joubert BR, Felix JF, Yousefi P, Bakulski KM, Just AC, et al. 2016. DNA methylation in newborns and maternal smoking in pregnancy: genome-wide consortium meta-analysis. *Am. J. Hum. Genet.* 98(4):680–96

Khulan B, Manning JR, Dunbar DR, Seckl JR, Raikkonen K, et al. 2014. Epigenomic profiling of men exposed to early-life stress reveals DNA methylation differences in association with current mental state. *Transl. Psychiatry* 4:e448

Kim D, Kubzansky LD, Baccarelli A, Sparrow D, Spiro A, et al. 2016. Psychological factors and DNA methylation of genes related to immune/inflammatory system markers: the VA Normative Aging Study. *BMJ Open* 6(1):e009790

Klengel T, Mehta D, Anacker C, Rex-Haffner M, Pruessner JC, et al. 2013. Allele-specific FKBP5 DNA demethylation mediates gene-childhood trauma interactions. *Nat. Neurosci.* 16(1):33–41

Kozlenkov A, Roussos P, Timashpolsky A, Barbu M, Rudchenko S, et al. 2014. Differences in DNA methylation between human neuronal and glial cells are concentrated in enhancers and non-CpG sites. *Nucleic Acids Res.* 42(1):109–27

Ladd-Acosta C. 2015. Epigenetic signatures as biomarkers of exposure. *Curr. Environ. Health Rep.* 2(2):117–25

Ladd-Acosta C, Hansen KD, Briem E, Fallin MD, Kaufmann WE, Feinberg AP. 2014. Common DNA methylation alterations in multiple brain regions in autism. *Mol. Psychiatry* 19(8):862–71

Lam LL, Emberly E, Fraser HB, Neumann SM, Chen E, et al. 2012. Factors underlying variable DNA methylation in a human community cohort. *PNAS* 109(Suppl. 2):17253–60

Langfelder P, Horvath S. 2008. WGCNA: an R package for weighted correlation network analysis. *BMC Bioinform.* 9:559

Lappalainen T, Greally JM. 2017. Associating cellular epigenetic models with human phenotypes. *Nat. Rev. Genet.* 18:441–51

Leek JT, Johnson WE, Parker HS, Jaffe AE, Storey JD. 2012. The sva package for removing batch effects and other unwanted variation in high-throughput experiments. *Bioinformatics* 28(6):882–83

Levine ME, Lu AT, Bennett DA, Horvath S. 2015. Epigenetic age of the pre-frontal cortex is associated with neuritic plaques, amyloid load, and Alzheimer's disease related cognitive functioning. *Aging* 7(12):1198–211

Libertini E, Heath SC, Hamoudi RA, Gut M, Ziller MJ, et al. 2016a. Information recovery from low coverage whole-genome bisulfite sequencing. *Nat. Commun.* 7:11306

Libertini E, Heath SC, Hamoudi RA, Gut M, Ziller MJ, et al. 2016b. Saturation analysis for whole-genome bisulfite sequencing data. *Nat. Biotechnol.* 34:691–93

Ligthart S, Marzi C, Aslibekyan S, Mendelson MM, Conneely KN, et al. 2016. DNA methylation signatures of chronic low-grade inflammation are associated with complex diseases. *Genome Biol.* 17(1):255

Lister R, Mukamel EA, Nery JR, Urich M, Puddifoot CA, et al. 2013. Global epigenomic reconfiguration during mammalian brain development. *Science* 341(6146):1237905

Liu Y, Aryee MJ, Padyukov L, Fallin MD, Hesselberg E, et al. 2013. Epigenome-wide association data implicate DNA methylation as an intermediary of genetic risk in rheumatoid arthritis. *Nat. Biotechnol.* 31(2):142–47

Lowe R, Gemma C, Beyan H, Hawa MI, Bazeos A, et al. 2013. Buccals are likely to be a more informative surrogate tissue than blood for epigenome-wide association studies. *Epigenetics* 8(4):445–54

MacKinnon DP, Krull JL, Lockwood CM. 2000. Equivalence of the mediation, confounding and suppression effect. *Prev. Sci.* 1(4):173–81

Marioni RE, Shah S, McRae AF, Chen BH, Colicino E, et al. 2015. DNA methylation age of blood predicts all-cause mortality in later life. *Genome Biol.* 16(1):25

McGowan PO, Sasaki A, D'Alessio AC, Dymov S, Labonté B, et al. 2009. Epigenetic regulation of the glucocorticoid receptor in human brain associates with childhood abuse. *Nat. Neurosci.* 12(3):342–48

McGregor K, Bernatsky S, Colmegna I, Hudson M, Pastinen T, et al. 2016. An evaluation of methods correcting for cell-type heterogeneity in DNA methylation studies. *Genome Biol.* 17:84

McGregor K, Labbe A, Greenwood CMT. 2017. Response to: correcting for cell-type effects in DNA methylation studies: Reference-based method outperforms latent variable approaches in empirical studies. *Genome Biol.* 18:25

Meaney MJ, Ferguson-Smith AC. 2010. Epigenetic regulation of the neural transcriptome: the meaning of the marks. *Nat. Neurosci.* 13(11):1313–18

Meyer LR, Zweig AS, Hinrichs AS, Karolchik D, Kuhn RM, et al. 2013. The UCSC Genome Browser database: extensions and updates 2013. *Nucleic Acids Res.* 41:D64–69

Michels KB, Binder AM, Dedeurwaerder S, Epstein CB, Greally JM, et al. 2013. Recommendations for the design and analysis of epigenome-wide association studies. *Nat. Methods* 10(10):949–55

Mill J, Tang T, Kaminsky Z, Khare T, Yazdanpanah S, et al. 2008. Epigenomic profiling reveals DNA-methylation changes associated with major psychosis. *Am. J. Hum. Genet.* 82(3):696–711

Miller GE, Chen E, Fok AK, Walker H, Lim A, et al. 2009. Low early-life social class leaves a biological residue manifested by decreased glucocorticoid and increased proinflammatory signaling. *PNAS* 106(34):14716–21

Miller MW, Sadeh N. 2014. Traumatic stress, oxidative stress and post-traumatic stress disorder: neurodegeneration and the accelerated-aging hypothesis. *Mol. Psychiatry* 19(11):1156–62

Miska EA, Ferguson-Smith AC. 2016. Transgenerational inheritance: nodels and mechanisms of non-DNA sequence-based inheritance. *Science* 354(6308):59–63

Moran S, Arribas C, Esteller M. 2016. Validation of a DNA methylation microarray for 850,000 CpG sites of the human genome enriched in enhancer sequences. *Epigenomics* 8(3):389–99

Nikolova YS, Hariri AR. 2015. Can we observe epigenetic effects on human brain function? *Trends Cogn. Sci.* 19(7):366–73

Open Sci. Collab. 2015. Estimating the reproducibility of psychological science. *Science* 349(6251):aac4716

Pan P, Fleming AS, Lawson D, Jenkins JM, McGowan PO. 2014. Within- and between-litter maternal care alter behavior and gene regulation in female offspring. *Behav. Neurosci.* 128(6):736–48

Paul DS, Teschendorff AE, Dang MAN, Lowe R, Hawa MI, et al. 2016. Increased DNA methylation variability in type 1 diabetes across three immune effector cell types. *Nat. Commun.* 7:13555

Peters TJ, Buckley MJ, Statham AL, Pidsley R, Samaras K, et al. 2015. De novo identification of differentially methylated regions in the human genome. *Epigenet. Chromatin* 8:6

Pidsley R, Wong CCY, Volta M, Lunnon K, Mill J, Schalkwyk LC. 2013. A data-driven approach to preprocessing Illumina 450K methylation array data. *BMC Genom.* 14:293

Pidsley R, Zotenko E, Peters TJ. 2016. Critical evaluation of the Illumina MethylationEPIC BeadChip microarray for whole-genome DNA methylation profiling. *Genome Biol.* 17(1):208

Price EM, Penaherrera MS, Portales-Casamar E, Pavlidis P, Van Allen MI, et al. 2016. Profiling placental and fetal DNA methylation in human neural tube defects. *Epigenet. Chromatin* 9:6

Price ME, Cotton AM, Lam LL, Farré P, Emberly E, et al. 2013. Additional annotation enhances potential for biologically-relevant analysis of the Illumina Infinium HumanMethylation450 BeadChip array. *Epigenet. Chromatin* 6(1):4

Radtke KM, Ruf M, Gunter HM, Dohrmann K, Schauer M, et al. 2011. Transgenerational impact of intimate partner violence on methylation in the promoter of the glucocorticoid receptor. *Transl. Psychiatry* 1(7):e21

Rahmani E, Shenhav L, Schweiger R, Yousefi P, Huen K, et al. 2016. Genome-wide methylation data mirror ancestry information. *Epigenet. Chromatin* 10:1

Rakyan VK, Down TA, Balding DJ, Beck S. 2011. Epigenome-wide association studies for common human diseases. *Nat. Rev. Genet.* 12(8):529–41

Reinius LE, Acevedo N, Joerink M, Pershagen G, Dahlen S-E, et al. 2012. Differential DNA methylation in purified human blood cells: implications for cell lineage and studies on disease susceptibility. *PLOS ONE* 7(7):e41361

Relton CL, Davey Smith G. 2012. Two-step epigenetic Mendelian randomization: a strategy for establishing the causal role of epigenetic processes in pathways to disease. *Int. J. Epidemiol.* 41(1):161–76

Rivera CM, Ren B. 2013. Mapping human epigenomes. *Cell* 155(1):39–55

Schübeler D. 2015. Function and information content of DNA methylation. *Nature* 517(7534):321–26

Sloan CA, Chan ET, Davidson JM, Malladi VS, Strattan JS, et al. 2016. ENCODE data at the ENCODE portal. *Nucleic Acids Res.* 44(D1):D726–32

Smith AK, Kilaru V, Klengel T, Mercer KB, Bradley B, et al. 2015. DNA extracted from saliva for methylation studies of psychiatric traits: evidence tissue specificity and relatedness to brain. *Am. J. Med. Genet. B* 168B(1):36–44

Smith ZD, Meissner A. 2013. DNA methylation: roles in mammalian development. *Nat. Rev. Genet.* 14(3):204–20

Song C-X, Szulwach KE, Dai Q, Fu Y, Mao S-Q, et al. 2013. Genome-wide profiling of 5-formylcytosine reveals its roles in epigenetic priming. *Cell* 153(3):678–91

Stewart SK, Morris TJ, Guilhamon P, Bulstrode H, Bachman M, et al. 2015. oxBS-450K: a method for analysing hydroxymethylation using 450K BeadChips. *Methods* 72:9–15

Taylor KH, Kramer RS, Davis JW, Guo J, Duff DJ, et al. 2007. Ultradeep bisulfite sequencing analysis of DNA methylation patterns in multiple gene promoters by 454 sequencing. *Cancer Res.* 67(18):8511–18

Teh AL, Pan H, Chen L, Ong M-L, Dogra S, et al. 2014. The effect of genotype and in utero environment on interindividual variation in neonate DNA methylomes. *Genome Res.* 24(7):1064–74

Teschendorff AE, Marabita F, Lechner M, Bartlett T, Tegner J, et al. 2013a. A beta-mixture quantile normalization method for correcting probe design bias in Illumina Infinium 450 k DNA methylation data. *Bioinformatics* 29(2):189–96

Teschendorff AE, West J, Beck S. 2013b. Age-associated epigenetic drift: implications, and a case of epigenetic thrift? *Hum. Mol. Genet.* 22(R1):R7–15

Teschendorff AE, Zhuang J, Widschwendter M. 2011. Independent surrogate variable analysis to deconvolve confounding factors in large-scale microarray profiling studies. *Bioinformatics* 27(11):1496–505

Turecki G, Meaney MJ. 2016. Effects of the social environment and stress on glucocorticoid receptor gene methylation: a systematic review. *Biol. Psychiatry* 79(2):87–96

Unternaehrer E, Luers P, Mill J, Dempster E, Meyer AH, et al. 2012. Dynamic changes in DNA methylation of stress-associated genes (OXTR, BDNF) after acute psychosocial stress. *Transl. Psychiatry* 2:e150

van Dongen J, Nivard MG, Willemsen G, Hottenga J-J, Helmer Q, et al. 2016. Genetic and environmental influences interact with age and sex in shaping the human methylome. *Nat. Commun.* 7:11115

van Otterdijk SD, Michels KB. 2016. Transgenerational epigenetic inheritance in mammals: How good is the evidence? *FASEB J.* 30(7):2457–65

Waddington CH. 1959. Canalization of development and genetic assimilation of acquired characters. *Nature* 183(4676):1654–55

Wagner JR, Busche S, Ge B, Kwan T, Pastinen T, Blanchette M. 2014. The relationship between DNA methylation, genetic and expression inter-individual variation in untransformed human fibroblasts. *Genome Biol.* 15(2):R37

Weaver ICG, Cervoni N, Champagne FA, D'Alessio AC, Sharma S, et al. 2004. Epigenetic programming by maternal behavior. *Nat. Neurosci.* 7(8):847–54

Weber M, Hellmann I, Stadler MB, Ramos L, Pääbo S, et al. 2007. Distribution, silencing potential and evolutionary impact of promoter DNA methylation in the human genome. *Nat. Genet.* 39(4):457–66

Weidner CI, Lin Q, Koch CM, Eisele L, Beier F, et al. 2014. Aging of blood can be tracked by DNA methylation changes at just three CpG sites. *Genome Biol.* 15(2):R24

Wen L, Li X, Yan L, Tan Y, Li R, et al. 2014. Whole-genome analysis of 5-hydroxymethylcytosine and 5-methylcytosine at base resolution in the human brain. *Genome Biol.* 15(3):R49

Wu H, Zhang Y. 2014. Reversing DNA methylation: mechanisms, genomics, and biological functions. *Cell* 156(1–2):45–68

Yousefi P, Huen K, Quach H, Motwani G, Hubbard A, et al. 2015. Estimation of blood cellular heterogeneity in newborns and children for epigenome-wide association studies. *Environ. Mol. Mutagen.* 56(9):751–58

Yu M, Hon GC, Szulwach KE, Song C-X, Jin P, et al. 2012. Tet-assisted bisulfite sequencing of 5-hydroxymethylcytosine. *Nat. Protoc.* 7(12):2159–70

Zampieri M, Ciccarone F, Calabrese R, Franceschi C, Bürkle A, Caiafa P. 2015. Reconfiguration of DNA methylation in aging. *Mech. Ageing Dev.* 151:60–70

Zannas AS, Provençal N, Binder EB. 2015. Epigenetics of posttraumatic stress disorder: current evidence, challenges, and future directions. *Biol. Psychiatry* 78(5):327–35

Ziller MJ, Gu H, Müller F, Donaghey J, Tsai LTY, et al. 2013. Charting a dynamic DNA methylation landscape of the human genome. *Nature* 500(7463):477–81

Ziller MJ, Müller F, Liao J, Zhang Y, Gu H, et al. 2011. Genomic distribution and inter-sample variation of non-CpG methylation across human cell types. *PLoS Genet.* 7:e1002389

Ziller MJ, Stamenova EK, Gu H, Gnirke A, Meissner A. 2016. Targeted bisulfite sequencing of the dynamic DNA methylome. *Epigenet. Chromatin* 9:55

Zou J, Lippert C, Heckerman D, Aryee M, Listgarten J. 2014. Epigenome-wide association studies without the need for cell-type composition. *Nat. Methods* 11(3):309–11

Psychology, Science, and Knowledge Construction: Broadening Perspectives from the Replication Crisis

Patrick E. Shrout[1] and Joseph L. Rodgers[2]

[1]Department of Psychology, New York University, New York, New York 10003;
email: pat.shrout@nyu.edu

[2]Department of Psychology and Human Development, Peabody College, Vanderbilt University,
Nashville, Tennessee 37205; email: joseph.l.rodgers@vanderbilt.edu

Annu. Rev. Psychol. 2018. 69:487–510

The *Annual Review of Psychology* is online at
psych.annualreviews.org

https://doi.org/10.1146/annurev-psych-122216-011845

Keywords

statistics, methodology, replication

Abstract

Psychology advances knowledge by testing statistical hypotheses using empirical observations and data. The expectation is that most statistically significant findings can be replicated in new data and in new laboratories, but in practice many findings have replicated less often than expected, leading to claims of a replication crisis. We review recent methodological literature on questionable research practices, meta-analysis, and power analysis to explain the apparently high rates of failure to replicate. Psychologists can improve research practices to advance knowledge in ways that improve replicability. We recommend that researchers adopt open science conventions of preregistration and full disclosure and that replication efforts be based on multiple studies rather than on a single replication attempt. We call for more sophisticated power analyses, careful consideration of the various influences on effect sizes, and more complete disclosure of nonsignificant as well as statistically significant findings.

Contents

INTRODUCTION

In the past decade, articles in both the scientific and popular press have described a supposed crisis in science—particularly in psychological science. These articles claim that there are many findings that do not replicate in new studies and that researchers have adopted practices that will lead to false conclusions. In response to the crisis, scores of articles have been written that diagnose the problem, evaluate its impact, and suggest solutions. This burgeoning literature prompted us to write this article in the *Annual Review of Psychology*.

We review what we consider to be the most important points in the literature and make special efforts to include perspectives from clinical, cognitive, health, organizational, developmental, and social psychology, as well as neuroscience. We argue that the sense of crisis in the past decade has produced important insights and conventions, notably the emphasis on open science, whereby predictions, analysis plans, data, and supplemental material are made available to the broad scientific community. We also argue, however, that confusion about some statistical procedures and misinterpretation of important methodological issues have led some commentators to conclude that the state of our science is worse than it is. The events of the past decade may even signal natural and positive growth within psychological research and methods.[1]

Our chapter works through a series of nine questions: (*a*) Why do people say there is now a crisis? (*b*) How did scientific conventions for evaluating evidence evolve? (*c*) What are the specific problems with scientific practices in psychology? (*d*) What procedural steps have been taken to address these problems? (*e*) How can statistical theory help address the problems? (*f*) How can psychological theory help inform effect size variation? (*g*) How can replicable findings become more common in psychology? (*h*) Do new norms and procedures cause collateral damage to some scientists and disciplines? (*i*) What is the take-home message about how psychological science can speed knowledge construction?

OVERVIEW: WHY DO PEOPLE SAY THERE IS A CRISIS?

People who believe that there is a crisis point to three sets of events as evidence. The first involved scientific fraud by psychological scientists, including the highly publicized case of social psychologist Diederik Stapel (Bhattacharjee 2013), as well as less publicized cases such as those of cognitive psychologist Marc Hauser and social psychologist Lawrence Sanna (Wade 2010). The second, related set of events was the publication of articles by a series of authors (Ioannidis 2005, Kerr 1998, Simmons et al. 2011, Vul et al. 2009) criticizing questionable research practices (QRPs) that result in grossly inflated false positive error rates in the psychological literature. The third set of events involved the effort by the Open Science Collaboration to replicate 100 results that were systematically sampled from three top-tier journals in psychology: (*a*) Only 36% of the replication efforts yielded significant findings, (*b*) 32% of the original findings were no longer significant when combined with the new data, (*c*) effect sizes in the replication studies were about half the size of those in the original studies, and (*d*) failures to replicate were related to features of the original study (e.g., replication failures were more common in social than in cognitive psychological studies and in studies reporting surprising rather than intuitive findings). These events reverberated throughout the psychological and broader scientific communities, and special sessions on replication, QRPs, and open science at national meetings of major societies attracted standing-room-only crowds. In fact, concerns over research ethics, QRPs, reproducibility of reported analyses, and replication of empirical findings go far beyond the boundaries of the field of psychology (Dickersin & Rennie 2012, Ioannidis 2005), although our treatment in this article focuses on our own field.

These concerns have led to many articles by scientists and methodologists whose very attention to replication has reinforced the sense of crisis. Some authors were explicitly negative about the state of our science (Coyne 2016, Schmidt & Oh 2016), whereas others suggested new methods, norms, and explanations for the disturbing events just reviewed. Many of these articles implied that the null hypothesis statistical test (NHST) traditions of the twentieth century were susceptible to implicit and even explicit attempts to deceive reviewers, editors, and readers about the strength of the evidence presented in empirical articles. Given that current research may not be optimally advancing knowledge, journal editors published statements that set standards designed to improve the integrity of published findings.

Still other articles have taken a more sanguine view about science and the current sense of crisis (e.g., Maxwell et al. 2015, Stroebe 2016). These treatments have reinterpreted QRPs and

---

[1]Readers can find both overlapping and also relatively different perspectives on many of the issues we treat in the review in this volume by Nelson et al. (2018).

the replication crisis as unfortunate but relatively natural features of the scientific enterprise, ones that must be policed and sanctioned but that are hardly worth the disciplinary panic that has ensued. Methodologists within this perspective have formally analyzed apparently surprising replication results and concluded that they are neither surprising nor difficult to interpret.

ORIGINS: HOW DID SCIENTIFIC CONVENTIONS FOR EVALUATING EVIDENCE EVOLVE?

Beginning with the establishment of Wilhelm Wundt's psychology laboratory in 1879, knowledge construction in psychology has been associated with the scientific method. Basic textbooks in psychology are packed with findings based on empirical evidence, which is itself typically embedded in a scaffold of psychological theory that fills gaps in the evidence and suggests new avenues of research. Theories are typically developed inductively from empirical patterns but then provide deductive special cases that can be further evaluated to enhance knowledge construction.

In his seminal work *A System of Logic*, Mill [2008 (1843)] defined the philosophical basis for the true experiment as the method of differences. He posited that, when two groups were exactly equivalent in all respects except that one received a treatment, any posttreatment differences were logically emergent from the treatment. The problem for Mill and for subsequent laboratory and natural scientists was how to make groups exactly equal pretreatment. For 75 years following Mill's work, equating was achieved using systematic designs that mechanically equated on obvious confounding factors (Box 1978, pp. 144–45).

As an agricultural scientist, Fisher was concerned about natural variation that obscured inferences made by direct observations. His insight (e.g., Fisher 1925) was to use random assignment to exactly equate groups across replications so that the effect of a treatment could be explicitly studied. His logical expansion of Mill's method [combined with work by Neyman & Pearson (1928, 1933)] became NHST, which requires scientists to work within a falsification context: How likely are the data under a null hypothesis in which the scientists' theories are incorrect? If the data are unusual under the null hypothesis, we reject the null hypothesis, whereas if the data are not unusual, then the null hypothesis is not rejected.

Fisher proposed defining "unusual" as less than or equal to 1 in 20 ($\alpha = 0.05$), although he had no intention for $\alpha = 0.05$ to become an industry standard: "If one in twenty does not seem high enough odds, we may ... draw the line at one in fifty (the 2 per cent point), or one in a hundred (the 1 per cent point)" (Fisher 1925, p. 504). Setting α allows tuning for the necessary trade-off between Type I and Type II errors, though modern researchers seldom consider using this tuning potential. Obviously, if replicable results were the only research goal, setting α lower (say, $\alpha = 0.001$) would reduce Type I errors. The result would be fewer Type I errors but increased Type II errors and reduced power if the study design were held constant.

Fisher was a scientist studying agricultural yield—for example, attempting to optimize the effect of fertilizer and planting practices. He naturally used replication across individual plants, plots, elevation levels, and rainfall to study variation in crop yield. To be clear, Fisher's original concern was never with the question of whether the original finding replicates. Rather, he viewed replication as a logical mechanism to achieve the goal, originally stated by Mill, of equating two groups prior to treatment—the equating occurred probabilistically across replications.

We believe that Fisher would bring similar concerns to evaluating the current replication crisis. Likely, he would simply suggest that when results do not replicate, science is proceeding as it should in a self-correcting manner. Similarly, when results do replicate, continued caution and scrutiny are still appropriate. However, Fisher and his colleagues were concerned with logical and statistical issues rather than fraud, deceit, and carelessness.

CONCERNS: WHAT ARE THE SPECIFIC PROBLEMS WITH SCIENTIFIC PRACTICES IN PSYCHOLOGY?

Among the factors that diminish accumulation of knowledge, outright fraud is the most serious, but it also appears to be low in prevalence. We do not devote much of this review to the prevention of outright fraud, as there are legal and professional tools available to do this. However, we note that a colleague who inexplicably violates the trust of the scientific enterprise primes the fear that we must be suspicious of others. The overgeneralization of such suspicions can be pernicious.

Fraud aside, several authors have written about ways in which researchers systematically increase Type I error rates and overstate the magnitude of effects. Researchers have identified a set of QRPs that are likely to lead to scientific claims that are false or too strong. These practices are often encouraged in a motivational environment where hiring, tenure, promotion, and grants are heavily influenced by numbers of publications in top-tier journals (Nosek et al. 2012). These journals aim to publish important, novel, and theoretically motivated findings that have a compelling narrative.

Kerr (1998) described a pattern of formulating hypotheses after research results are known (HARKing), in which the research appears more confirmatory than it actually was. For example, suppose a study yields few statistically significant results, but one significant result was an unanticipated interaction. A skeptical view would consider the interaction to be likely due to sampling variation, and a correction for multiple analyses of the data might show that the result is not unusual. However, suppose that the author finds a literature that would have actually predicted the interaction and then writes the introduction to suggest that the study was designed to test this specific interaction. Even a skeptic might be convinced that the evidence was compelling. Kerr invites the skeptic to think again.

HARKing confuses exploratory and confirmatory studies and presents results from the former as though they were the latter. Exploratory studies are an important component of most research programs and can lead to discoveries of interesting associations, complicated multivariate structures, and rare but important occurrences (Ledgerwood et al. 2017). Statistical methods for data exploration are well known (Tukey 1977), and advances in machine learning and other exploratory data mining tools are extending the reach and power of exploration (e.g., McArdle & Ritschard 2014). However, insights from exploration should be confirmed in new data: "Exploratory data analysis is detective in character. Confirmatory data analysis is judicial or quasi-judicial in character" (Tukey 1977, p. 3). NHST is designed to control false positive rates for confirmatory studies under the assumption that hypotheses and analytic procedures are defined ahead of time. HARKed results typically violate the assumption of full disclosure.[2]

Vul et al. (2009) described a pattern of reporting functional magnetic resonance imaging (fMRI) results that also mixed exploratory analysis and confirmatory claims. They noted that many fMRI studies reported extremely high correlations (>0.8) between brain activation and individual differences and speculated that at least some of the high correlations were due to initial exploration and identification of brain regions of interest that were subsequently treated as if they were known. Vul et al. (2009) showed that, if the same data were used to find promising associations and then to test those associations, biased correlation estimates and inflated Type I error rates would result.

Simmons et al. (2011) described ways in which an investigator motivated to obtain publishable findings might report a result with a higher Type I error rate than the nominal test statistic

---

[2]Investigators who make an unexpected finding as they explore data and then disclose that many tests were used to uncover the finding can use the modern multiple comparison methods of Benjamini & Hochberg (1995) to reduce the likelihood of false discovery.

suggests. The key QRPs they highlighted were (*a*) using more than one dependent variable that reflects the outcome of interest, (*b*) carrying out interim data analysis during the data collection and stopping the study when a desired finding becomes significant, (*c*) carrying out multiple analyses with different covariates as ancillary variables, and (*d*) dropping groups or levels to focus on a larger effect in a subset of the data. These QRPs can lead to grossly inflated Type I error rates, even without HARKing unexpected findings.

In addition to QRPs that introduce uncontrolled increases in Type I error or inflation of estimated effect sizes, statistical errors can lead to additional bias. Bakker & Wicherts (2011) checked 281 articles and found statistical errors in 18% of them. Although these errors might have simply added white noise to the literature, the authors found that the vast majority made the results more apparently significant and thereby more reportable in journal articles.

False positive results are not the only kinds of errors that are important to address in psychology. One historically important QRP is to carry out studies with inadequate statistical power to test interesting effects. For example, Rossi (1990) reported that, in a survey of published studies, average power to detect what Cohen (1988) called a medium effect (e.g., $d = 0.50$) was 57%. There is no evidence that this high Type II error rate has improved in the 25 years since the Rossi report. The problem of high false negative rates is compounded by the habit of some recent researchers to conclude that an effect is absent if a test is nonsignificant. Confidence bounds around parameter estimates are infrequently used to characterize nonsignificant findings as either informative about a small or absent effect or indicative of an inconclusive study design (Cumming 2014).

PRACTICAL RESPONSES: WHAT PROCEDURAL STEPS HAVE BEEN TAKEN TO ADDRESS THESE PROBLEMS?

The reported low replication rate in the Open Science Collaboration studies, as well as extensive discussions of QRPs, has led to constructive suggestions for improving scientific procedures in psychology. One useful thread of discussion concerns the definition and meaning of replication. A direct or exact replication is a new study that employs the same procedure, materials, measures, and study population as the original study. The sample size need not be the same in an exact replication; indeed, a power analysis will usually suggest a larger sample (Brandt et al. 2014). A systematic replication is a direct replication in which some ancillary features, such as the order of the presentation of stimuli, are different from the original. A conceptual replication is intentionally different from a direct replication and is designed to assess generalizability, as well as veracity, of a result. It may involve a similar but not identical intervention, alternate measures of the outcome, or samples from a distinctly different population or era (Fabrigar & Wegener 2016, Ledgerwood et al. 2017). The distinctions between exact, systematic, and conceptual replications represent a continuum.

All types of replication are informative—the question is which gets priority. When a conceptually replicated effect is statistically significant, it shows that the phenomenon is more general (Stroebe 2016). However, if the effect does not replicate, the investigator does not know if the original finding is suspect or if it does not extend to other measures, procedures, or contexts (Fabrigar & Wegener 2016).

Other commentaries have suggested that we rethink the twentieth-century assumption that individual scientists can be trusted to report the relevant results and theorizing that led to the studies. Instead of trust, the theme of the new norms is openness. In 2013, Brian Nosek led a group that established the Center for Open Science and the Open Science Framework (OSF), a nonprofit organization that facilitates the sharing of study plans, materials, and documents. The OSF promotes scientific quality by facilitating a sequence of steps: (*a*) Preregister confirmatory hypotheses before data are collected, including outcomes and analyses; (*b*) preregister study design, including procedures, measures, and planned sample size; (*c*) make data and analysis syntax available so that others can reproduce the results. The OSF provides a pragmatic infrastructure for implementing the suggested norms (Nosek et al. 2015), building on a tradition of preregistration in health studies (De Angelis et al. 2005).

Preregistering hypotheses makes it possible to rule out HARKing and also guards against many of the QRPs identified by Simmons et al. (2011) and others (Nosek & Lakens 2014, Wagenmakers et al. 2012). Requiring explanation of the sample size rationale both encourages formal power analyses and guards against investigators stopping the study when desired results are obtained. Providing the original data used to make scientific claims guards against incorrect inferences that are based on misspecified statistical analyses. In our opinion, the preregistration movement and the OSF support for it have been the most important outcomes of the replication crisis.

A number of other contributions to the replication literature have emphasized traditional approaches to strong science. Some have recommended increased sample sizes (Button et al. 2013, Francis 2012a, Maxwell et al. 2015, Perugini 2014), and some have even suggested specific target sample sizes of approximately 90 per group (Vazire 2016). Others have advocated for increased attention to measurement error (Asendorpf et al. 2013) and to the quality of peer review (Coyne 2016, Nosek & Bar-Anan 2012) and for flexibility regarding the traditional significance level of $p < 0.05$ (Vazire 2016). Among the most controversial suggestions is that a cadre of researchers should act to identify other researchers whose results seem to replicate with lower frequency than the norm (Francis 2012c, Simonsohn 2013).

Editors of various journals have been processing these recommendations and have issued statements about accountability and quality control mechanisms For example, *Psychological Science* instituted badges to mark articles that implement the new norms of preregistration, open access to materials, and open access to data (Kidwell et al. 2016). We discuss these editorial steps further in the final section of this article.

STATISTICAL RESPONSES: HOW CAN STATISTICAL THEORY HELP ADDRESS THE PROBLEMS?

While editors and leaders pondered policies to improve the quality of psychological research, quantitative psychologists and statisticians studied the formal logic and mathematics of the replication process. In this section, we review four aspects of this work: (*a*) the use of refined power analysis for replication studies, (*b*) the role of meta-analysis in understanding replication variation, (*c*) the promise of Bayesian analysis for understanding replication variation, and (*d*) the use of resampling methods.

Planning Power for a Replication Study

When the Open Science Collaboration planned the replication studies of 100 sampled findings, they reported that the new studies had 0.92 power on average. These calculations were undoubtedly based on the effect sizes of the original reports. The sample sizes of the replication studies were typically larger than in the original report, with a median sample size more than 25% larger than the original (Open Sci. Collab. 2015). Even with larger samples, those replication studies were likely underpowered. McShane & Böckenholt (2014) noted that any meta-analysis reveals effect size heterogeneity; different studies report different effect sizes. This heterogeneity may be due to changes in setting, procedures, and subject characteristics. When the variability is taken into account in the power analysis, the replication sample needs to be larger, often considerably so.

Maxwell et al. (2015) came to the same conclusion but added concerns about statistical bias and estimation variation in the effect estimate. The typical power analysis for a close replication is a conditional power analysis, which treats the effect size as known and fixed. Maxwell et al. (2015) argued that the correct analysis takes into account the uncertainty of the effect size distribution. Describing the possible range of effect sizes is challenging because of publication bias (Francis 2012b) as well as the sampling variation of any estimate of an effect size. To illustrate publication bias, suppose that a study is theoretically justified, the hypothesis is preregistered, and the analysis is planned and properly executed, but that statistical power is only 50%. A lucky investigator would obtain a sample effect size that is randomly larger than the population value and would therefore publish, whereas an unlucky investigator would obtain an effect size that is smaller and nonsignificant due to sampling fluctuations alone. The latter result would historically not be published, and so the published effects would be biased relative to the sampling distribution. Publication bias accounts for at least part of the observation that effect sizes in the Open Science Collaboration replication studies were about half the size of the original studies (Open Sci. Collab. 2015).

In addition to publication bias, there is sampling variation in the reported effect size. This variation is larger as the sample size of the original study gets smaller. What is often not appreciated is that the impact on power of a small effect size change is not linear. **Figure 1** shows the sample size that is needed to obtain 95%, 90%, and 80% power for a range of effect sizes, measured as Cohen's d. This figure shows that, if one reduces an effect size from 0.8 to 0.7, then the required total sample size for 95% power increases by 26 (from 84 to 110); if the effect size is reduced from 0.4 to 0.3, then the sample size increases by 252 (from 328 to 580). The change in required n is even more dramatic if the effect size is reduced from 0.3 to 0.2. Taking the midpoint of a

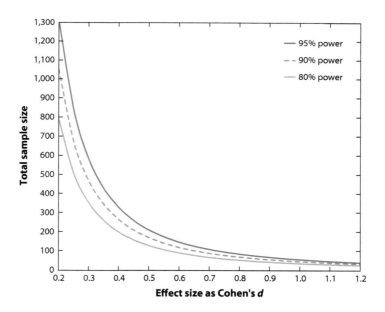

Figure 1

Power analysis showing the total sample size needed to achieve 95%, 90%, and 80% power for a two-group t test as a function of assumed effect size in Cohen's d metric. Power is calculated assuming equal sample sizes in both groups and a two-tailed test with $\alpha = 0.05$. Note that small differences in effect sizes in the $d = 0.2$–0.6 range have large effects on required sample size.

range of possible effect sizes is likely to lead in the long run to an underpowered study because of this nonlinear pattern. A correction for sampling variation involves computing power from the lower bound of a confidence interval on the effect size, as Maxwell et al. (2015) demonstrated. A number of statisticians have studied, from a frequentist perspective, the problem of describing the distribution of the unknown effect size to obtain an optimal predictive power estimate (Anderson & Maxwell 2017, McShane & Böckenholt 2014, Perugini et al. 2014, Taylor & Muller 1996). A promising alternate approach is to take a Bayesian perspective, which we discuss below.

Even if an appropriate power analysis is carried out and the replication study is properly powered, Maxwell et al. (2015) pointed out that it is often not possible to strongly infer that there is no effect. The replication study can produce results that are consistent with some effect size of interest, as well as results consistent with absolutely no effect. To make a strong claim that there is no meaningful effect from a frequentist perspective, the replication study must be designed as an equivalence study (Rogers et al. 1993, Seaman & Serlin 1998). Equivalence studies are used to show that a generic drug has the same effectiveness as the original patented drug. They require specifying an effect interval around the null value that is considered to be virtually (if not exactly) null and then showing that the new data are only consistent with effect sizes in the null-equivalent interval. To make a strong equivalence statement, the sample size typically needs to be very large. Maxwell et al. (2015) provided an illustration where the required sample sizes were between 1,000 and 10,000 per group, depending on how sure the scientist wants to be that no small effect is present. Given those requirements, Maxwell et al. (2015) recommended that psychologists cease their focus on single replications and instead use multiple studies to obtain a range of new effect sizes. As multiple studies are completed and reported, the focus can shift to estimating effect size distributions, rather than binary decisions.

Maxwell et al. (2015) reinterpreted the Open Science Collaboration's finding that only 36 of 100 replication efforts were significant as fully consistent with methodological expectations. Although a successful replication rate of 36% was surprising to many, Maxwell et al. (2015) demonstrated that the finding does not signal a crisis. Instead, we need to focus on understanding distributions of effect sizes rather than on trying to obtain closure on whether an effect is true or false from a single study. The shift in focus from testing of hypotheses to estimation of effects makes meta-analysis and Bayesian methods particularly useful, as we discuss next.

Meta-Analysis of Multiple Replications

Meta-analytic techniques provide key tools for analyzing and interpreting distributions of effects from replication studies. From a meta-analytic perspective, finding that two studies have different outcomes is not a problem. Rather, it is a common result as evidence accumulates (Schmidt & Oh 2016). Many authors addressing statistical issues related to replication have noted that meta-analysis is an important analytic tool (e.g., Braver et al. 2014, Cumming 2014, Fabrigar & Wegener 2016, Maxwell et al. 2015, McShane et al. 2016).

Meta-analysis allows not only estimation of the average and variation of effect sizes but also substantive exploration of factors that moderate the size of the effects. In the context of meta-analysis, the original study now has status weighted according to its sample size (as do the other studies), and the unnatural focus on the single original study is avoided. Treating study results from multiple studies as random effects, generating effect size distributions rather than assumed fixed values, has often been advised (see, for example, Borenstein et al. 2009). However, an important caveat is that traditional random effect models require more than a few replications. Many statisticians would recommend 20 or more studies to obtain stable variation estimates, but Bayesian methods, described below, may be used with a smaller number when an appropriate prior distribution can be specified.

An important future direction for meta-analysis is the consideration of the population of situations and studies that are characterized by the average effect size estimates. McShane et al. (2016) considered how selection effects can lead to misleading conclusions about overall effects. Bonett (2009) considered an alternative to a random effect model that does not require envisioning a meaningful superpopulation of effects. Replication projects (Simons et al. 2014, reviewed in detail below) provide a meaningful framework for considering effect estimates obtained across independent labs to be samples from a population of replications; they also avoid the file drawer problem, whereby nonsignificant findings are not reported publically. Special efforts must be taken to assure that meta-analysis is not carelessly used to summarize findings that are biased by p-hacking (Braver et al. 2014). The application of sophisticated meta-analytic methods to data from coordinated preregistered studies of specific effects has great promise for knowledge production in psychology.

In addition to meta-analysis of studies, there is a literature on meta-analysis of individual data (Stewart & Parmar 1993), also called integrative data analysis (Curran & Hussong 2009). This approach is worth considering when individual data from studies are available and when there are few replications that can be combined with the original study. If the studies can be considered comparable, then the combined sample will have more power than the original study, and the precision of the combined estimates will increase. This approach also allows flexibility in examining the impact of different statistical models and adjustments. If individual data are available for a large number of studies, then the multilevel model can include random effects for the treatment.

The Promise of Bayesian Analysis

Although most modern treatments of psychological statistics are frequentist rather than Bayesian, the original methods in statistics were firmly Bayesian; the publication of Bayes' Theorem (posthumously) in 1761 and subsequent contributions from Laplace are often identified as the beginning of the field of statistics (see Fisher 1958, Stigler 1986). It was more than 150 years later that Fisher, Neyman, and Pearson developed the components of the frequentist school of statistics, which, once blended, became NHST. Despite early skepticism, their methods were ultimately so influential that Bayesian thinking virtually disappeared for several decades, until a revival began in the 1950s (see Zabell 1989). Fisher was dismissive of the Bayesian perspective early in his career, but became ever more appreciative of inverse probability theory (Aldrich 2008).

Inverse probability refers to evaluating the probability of a hypothesis given the data. In contrast, frequentist NHST procedures evaluate the probability of the data given the null hypothesis. Even frequentists believe the Bayesian to be the more natural scientific formulation (e.g., Cohen 1994, Maxwell et al. 2015) and to be ideally suited to addressing issues of replication. At a conceptual level, a Bayesian blends prior knowledge (a prior distribution) with the data to arrive at revised knowledge (a posterior distribution). Specifically, a Bayesian takes past results, combines them with one or more efforts to replicate those results, and arrives at an updated opinion. The explicit incorporation of emerging data into scientific assessment and interpretation of phenomena is one reason that the Bayesian approach is both useful and appealing (Kruschke & Liddell 2017).

Another advantage of the Bayesian approach for replication is the way that it directly deals with the plausibility of the null hypothesis. Gallistel (2009, p. 439) noted, "Conventional statistical analysis cannot support [the null hypothesis]; Bayesian analysis can." In the frequentist school, the null is either rejected or not rejected. Bayesian methods support a more formal approach to direct evaluation of the null hypothesis. Wagenmakers et al. (2016) provided a clear explanation of how the Bayes factor—the ratio of the probability of the null hypothesis to the probability of a competing hypothesis—can quantify evidence for the absence of an effect relative to a hypothesized effect. When the Bayes factor is greater than 1.0, the null hypothesis is more likely, given the data, than the alternative. When the Bayes factor is less than 1.0, the alternative is more likely.

Bayesian statisticians have developed new methodology to study replication efforts. Verhagen & Wagenmakers (2014) developed a null and alternative hypothesis framework explicitly directed to test whether the effect in the new data is similar to what was found in the initial study or whether the new effect is absent. Of additional note is that Verhagen & Wagenmakers (2014) used a bootstrap to obtain a Bayesian posterior distribution, and they also compared their method to the partial Bayes factor, based on a cross-validation methodology in a Bayesian context.

The promise of Bayesian analysis is especially appreciated by researchers who are interested in estimation, such as interval estimation and meta-analysis (Kruschke & Liddell 2017, Scheibehenne et al. 2016). Bayesian estimation of the posterior distribution of parameter values given new data is informative and can be estimated using numerical methods that are becoming widely available (see, e.g., Kruschke 2015). The posterior distribution can be graphed, and the likelihood of the different values (given the data) can be assessed. The interval where the values are most likely is called the highest density interval or the credible interval. Although it is sometimes compared to frequentist confidence intervals, this interval contains richer information about the likelihood of various values than confidence intervals. When Bayesian methods are used in meta-analysis, both between-study and within-study variations contribute to the overall posterior distribution. Kruschke & Liddell (2017) demonstrated how meta-analysis forest plots can be modified to show more information about the posterior distributions within and between studies.

Resampling Methods

Resampling methods (e.g., Beasley & Rodgers 2009, Efron 1979) and cross-validation (for a detailed treatment, see Efron & Gong 1983) are useful statistical tools to bring to the study of replication results. Both methods are based on a replication perspective. Resampling methods test hypotheses using the data to build empirical sampling distributions, rather than theoretical sampling distributions. Cross-validation approaches use multiple samples within a single study; the first sample (the estimation or training sample) is used to identify models in an approximately exploratory context, whereas the second sample (often the calibration sample) is used to further investigate hypotheses in a confirmatory sense. However, resampling methods usually consider the research context where the data were collected to be fixed, and, thus, that source of variation is ignored by these methods.

BLENDING PSYCHOLOGY WITH STATISTICS: HOW CAN PSYCHOLOGICAL THEORY HELP INFORM EFFECT SIZE VARIATION?

The statistical responses to the replication crisis emphasize the fact that effect size values needed for power analyses come from distributions of effect sizes. Meta-analyses can show how much variation there is in these distributions but cannot necessarily distinguish between the sources of variation—effect heterogeneity (McShane & Böckenholt 2014) or estimation variability (Maxwell et al. 2015). Even if meta-analyses are not available to inform a researcher about how much variation to expect, it is important to recognize that variation is likely to exist. One way to think about this variation is to use psychological theory to anticipate factors that might moderate the effect of central interest.

Modeling Effect Variation

To illustrate how one can conceive of effect variation, consider a loud sound right behind you, such as a firecracker or a gunshot. It would be a rare person who would not jump, and we speculate that the effect of this sonic intervention would be in the order of $d = 2$ or larger. However, it is possible to think of circumstances where the effect would be attenuated or enhanced. We consider four classes of such moderating factors: (*a*) the strength of the intervention, (*b*) the choice of outcome, (*c*) characteristics of the participants, and (*d*) the setting and context of the study (see also Asendorpf et al. 2013).

Intervention strength. The intervention can vary in intensity and purity. In the case of the firecracker, its size and location would be associated with the intensity of the sound. In some instances, a single intervention ends up having a distribution of effect sizes because replications of stimuli involve different words, phrases, pictures, or confederates, and each instance of the stimulus has a possibly different intervention effect. When the stimuli or delivery mechanisms of interventions are sampled, they must be considered random effects in the analysis (Westfall et al. 2015).

Outcome. Interventions can have impacts on a range of outcomes. For example, the loud popping sound would affect skin response, blinking response, and the neural networks that process the sensation. An intervention for depression might reduce symptoms as reflected in either brief psychological screening measures or extensive psychiatric diagnostic protocols (Tackett et al. 2017). Often, investigators choose an outcome that is easily or affordably assessed even if it might be less affected by the intervention.

Participant characteristics. The characteristics of the participants can have important moderating effects on interventions. Someone with auditory impairment would not react to a gunshot as much as someone with normal hearing. A veteran with posttraumatic stress disorder might have an enhanced reaction. Moderation of effects by participant characteristics is common. Relationship researchers, for example, can show that daily partner criticism has a larger effect on people with attachment anxiety relative to persons who are securely attached (Overall et al. 2014). Psychopathology research has studied so-called personalized medicine, where a patient's genetic profile is often related to responsiveness to a pharmacologic intervention (Ozomaro et al. 2013).

Study setting and context. Studies may have effects that vary because of features of the laboratory settings, such as sound isolation, lighting, color scheme, and temperature. An important setting feature is whether the experiment is carried out in a controlled lab or in an uncontrolled home setting using online technology. Another feature of the setting is the expertise of the research group; a replication study carried out by an experienced research team might obtain a different result than one by an undergraduate class (Bench et al. 2017). Related to setting are the broader social context and whether that context is likely to moderate the outcome. Van Bavel et al. (2016) showed that contextual sensitivity was an important predictor of whether the replication result matched the original result.

Equation 1 represents a formal specification of the effect size in a specific study, which we represent as Δ, with subscripts for intervention type (i), outcome (k), participant type (p), and setting factors (s), which can modify the effect in a specific circumstance:

$$\Delta_{ikps} = \mu + \xi_i + \theta_k + \pi_p + \eta_s + \xi\theta_{ik} + \xi\pi_{ip} + +\xi\eta_{is} + \cdots + \pi\eta_{ps} + \varepsilon_{ikps}. \qquad 1.$$

This equation represents effect variation as main effects of the type of modifier and as two-way interactions of those effects, but one can model an even longer list of higher interaction terms. Equation 1 is inspired by generalizability theory (Cronbach et al. 1972), which describes various sources of variance of measurements in an extension of classical test theory. Consistent with this approach, we assume a universe of persons, settings, and constructs to describe an average effect size, and μ describes that average (mean). We define the other terms as random effects that can increase or decrease the size of the intervention effect as a function of intervention type (ξ_i), outcome specification (θ_k), participant type (π_p), setting or context (η_s), or their interactions. All the distributions of the random effects are assumed to be centered at zero. We also assume that all factors are independent, insofar as each can be specified separately in an experimental design. Finally, we add a residual term (ε_{ikps}) to represent a portion of a study effect that is real but transient in time, sample, and context. If researchers design a study without attending to these effect modifiers, then the expected variance of Δ_{ikps} is the sum of the variances of all the effect modifier factors. The expected value of the effect in a specific study is μ plus the specific values of ξ, θ, π, and η, which correspond to the intervention, outcome, sample, and setting choices, respectively.

Equation 1 represents effect heterogeneity rather than sampling variation in the estimated effect. It can be used to represent the effect variation that occurs when a new study design moves from an exact or close replication to a conceptual replication. In an exact replication, investigators attempt to restrict all the moderating factors to be the same. In a conceptual replication, investigators might vary the implementation of the intervention, the primary outcome measure, the characteristics of the participants, and the setting where the study takes place (Brandt et al. 2014, Fabrigar & Wegener 2016). If care is not taken to consider the possible moderating factors, then the study might be implemented with an essentially arbitrary design regarding effect moderators.

Predicting Where the Effect Is Greatest

Rather than studying an intervention in an arbitrarily chosen but convenient design, consider a design where the investigator carefully specifies a combination of (*a*) intervention, (*b*) outcome, (*c*) participant type, and (*d*) study setting or context and where there is a theoretically based sweet spot for the effect. The ideal occurs when the effect is as large as our hypothetical firecracker effect. As a number of authors have argued in recent years (Edwards & Berry 2010, Fiedler 2017, Stroebe 2016), psychological theories can provide fertile ground for making predictions about mechanisms and contexts where large effects will occur. Theory can become proactive, in that it can be used to develop more nuanced theoretical propositions and more effective interventions.

However, we are not proposing that researchers find a constrained set of conditions where an effect is large and then make unqualified claims about the generality of the effect (Meiser 2011). Instead, we recommend that the effect space represented by Equation 1 be used to create a prototype effect and that generalizations be tested by explicitly changing the sources of effect variation in a series of conceptual replications. The program of research that examines boundaries and effect moderators will require larger sample sizes when the effect is diminished by a moderator or diluted by variation in subject or intervention characteristics. Considering the factors that can make intervention effects larger or smaller is particularly important when scientific findings are used as a basis for applications to clinical, health, or organizational psychology. In prevention science, for example, universal interventions such as education or training programs are administered to a large number of people with the knowledge that the average effect is small but that the exposure makes the intervention worthwhile. In contrast, targeted interventions might be limited to persons with risk factors such as obesity or smoking history. In that limited group, the average effect size might be quite large, justifying the focus on the special group. In the latter case, it might not be necessary for the initial researcher to show that the specific intervention is applicable to a broad population (see, for example, Offord et al. 1998).

When researchers think vaguely about the effect size and ignore features of their design that are likely to dilute the effect, their study can regress to the average effect, such as the value of $d = 0.41$ obtained from meta-analyses of all studies in a field (Richard et al. 2003). If a researcher plans a generic study design for a generic outcome, as in this case, the required sample size to obtain appropriate power may be 155 per group (LeBel et al. 2017). Such sample sizes make controlled laboratory studies difficult and may push investigators to use online testing with participants of variable quality (Paolacci & Chandler 2014). The shift from a setting that provides precision to one that leads to more noise might lead to effects that are even smaller than the average (for related points, see Finkel et al. 2017).

When effect heterogeneity is considered explicitly, it is possible to form a principled answer to the often-asked question: Is it better to carry out one study with $N = 400$ or ten studies, each with $N = 40$? If effect heterogeneity is considered likely, then many smaller studies done at different times and in collaboration with other labs will be more informative about the heterogeneity than a single large study, although the smaller studies will individually be less precise.

As noted above, Maxwell et al. (2015) explained that the relationship between effect size and power is nonlinear (see **Figure 1**). If subfields of psychology begin to accumulate information about effect sizes, as represented by Equation 1, researchers can specify a design where effects can be reliably observed. One problem with designing a study using the sweet spot and then finding a significant result in a relatively small sample is that skeptics will complain that the result is either a fluke or a product of HARKing or other QRPs. To address this skeptical concern, the researcher who uses principled theory to predict an effect (large or otherwise) should preregister that theoretical thinking.

BROADER SOLUTIONS: HOW CAN REPLICATIONS BECOME MORE COMMON IN PSYCHOLOGY?

More than forty years ago, Greenwald (1976) laid out his policies as incoming editor of the *Journal of Personality and Social Psychology* (JPSP): "There may be a crisis in personality and social psychology, associated with the difficulty often experienced by researchers in attempting to replicate published work" (Greenwald 1976, p. 2). Obviously, references to the urgency of the recent crisis are overstated. Greenwald recommended that authors provide evidence that a finding can be reproduced when exactly the same procedures are applied and also when a conceptually related hypothesis is tested. His suggestions led to the multiple study tradition in JPSP, designed to lead naturally to replication and the reduction in published Type I errors. As prescient as Greenwald was, the field did not yet understand that replication studies should be reported regardless of whether the new result was statistically significant. Often, there was a naive expectation that all of the reported studies should have results that were statistically significant.

Several authors noted that obtaining a series of significant findings when the underlying effect size is medium or small and power is limited is highly unlikely (Francis 2012c, Schimmack 2012, Simonsohn 2013). Although some attribute these unlikely events to QRPs on the part of the authors, the explanation cannot usually be known with any certainty. Reviewers and journal editors in the past might have suggested that nonsignificant results or studies be removed from the report to clarify the story. Whatever the reason, a pattern of four or five significant results related to an effect that is not very large in studies with small to medium power does not build confidence that the result will replicate in other laboratories. As Schimmack (2012) noted, replication results that are too consistently significant may lead, ironically, to disbelief.

In recent years, replication studies carried out in independent laboratories have been emphasized. One noteworthy model of a program to promote close replications is the Registered Replication Report (RRR) mechanism initiated by the Association for Psychological Science (Simons et al. 2014). These reports are the culmination of collaborative research carried out by multiple independent research teams to examine a specific research finding through multiple replication studies. The collaborative project is proposed and approved before the replication studies are carried out. The journal commits to publish a well-prepared RRR report regardless of findings. Once the RRR is accepted, the lead scientist develops a protocol and invites participation from a number of independent research groups. This protocol is sent to the original scientist for comment and review. The goal is to make the replication process constructive rather than antagonistic. When the multiple studies have been completed, a meta-analysis of the results is prepared that allows readers to form a conclusion about the size of the hypothesized effect, as well as the degree of effect heterogeneity.

At the time of this writing, five RRR reports have been published. We review two of these. One team (Alogna et al. 2014) replicated a study by Schooler & Engstler-Schooler (1990) that documented a so-called verbal overshadowing effect on visual memories. The original study found that, when subjects provided a verbal description of a target person seen on a video, they were 25% less likely to identify that target person in a subsequent identification test than subjects in a control condition. In the RRR project, two waves of studies were done. The first apparently misrepresented the original procedure, and so we focus on the second (RRR2). The RRR2 protocol was specific, requiring that subjects be White undergraduates and that they come to a lab room to participate. There were 22 research groups from 8 countries participating in RRR2, and sample sizes ranged from 33 to 83, with a median of 52. The aggregated results were analyzed using a random effect meta-analysis. Although only 8 out of the 22 studies (36%) found significant results as individual studies, the aggregated effect (0.16) was statistically significant (95% CI: 0.12, 0.20), and 100% of the results were in the predicted direction. The report concluded that the RRR2 studies "provide clear evidence for verbal overshadowing" (Alogna et al. 2014, p. 571). The estimated effect size was reduced by the RRR2 effort, and the precision of the estimate was much improved.

None of the other four RRR projects provided clear support for the original finding. For example, an RRR report by Hagger & Chatzisarantis (2016) examined ego depletion effects using a protocol carried out on computers by Sripada et al. (2014). Ego depletion occurs when finite self-control resources are used up by initial demands and subsequent self-control is hindered by the depletion of those limited resources. The RRR project involved 23 laboratories in 11 countries and a total of 2,141 respondents. Only 2 of the 23 studies were significant in the predicted direction, and one study yielded a significant result in the opposite direction. Based on a random effect meta-analysis, the average effect size was 0.04 (95% CI: −0.07, 0.15). Not only did the interval include zero, the upper bound was far from the effect size of the original study. The authors of the RRR concluded, "Results from the current multilab registered replication of the ego-depletion effect provide evidence that, if there is any effect, it is close to zero" (Hagger & Chatzisarantis 2016, p. 558).

The RRRs provide a model of how to generate close replications across labs. We believe that findings will be more likely to hold in such rigorous tests if they are first replicated in the original lab. Perhaps the best way to provide an exact replication is for the original investigators to build the replication into the original report (as in cross-validation). For example, if investigators have to make analytic decisions, such as refining measures or determining the most appropriate covariates, before carrying out a confirmatory analysis, they could randomly split the sample into a training sample and a confirmatory sample. The second sample would be set aside until the analytic decisions were made and then used to provide an exact replication of the initial analysis. The effect sizes in the second analysis will typically be smaller than in the first, and this provides important information about effect sizes for later research.

Neuroscientists often provide exact replications of their findings, either with new experiments on the same subjects (Overath et al. 2015) or with replications with new participants (Ding et al. 2016). Moreover, within-subject results are often shown in neuroscience journals at the individual level and support evaluation of whether an effect is found in literally every subject (Ding et al. 2016). For example, Overath et al. (2015) reported fMRI measurements of specific regions of the superior temporal sulcus (STS) that were more responsive to auditory stimuli composed of packages (quilts) of 960-ms segments of human speech than to packages of 30-ms segments. The longer segments contained sound that could be identified as speech, whereas the shorter segments were too short to be identified. No similar association to segment variation was found in early auditory cortex responsiveness. Findings were replicated on different days for up to four repeat fMRI sessions for the 15 subjects. These sessions included different control conditions, but the condition on STS variation with segment length was repeated each time. Although the authors did not report effect size in standardized measures, their figures show that the effect was very large ($d > 2.5$ to compare the 30-ms and 960-ms conditions). Effects of this size are apparent in graphical representations, as well as through formal statistical analysis. The participants are not sampled from a known population, and their representativeness cannot be assured, but the effect was found for all the participants, suggesting that it would likely replicate in other laboratories.

Ledgerwood & Sherman (2012) encouraged researchers in all areas of psychology to avoid making claims based on a single study. They reminded researchers that careful documentation of a scientific finding is akin to the strategy of the tortoise rather than that of the hare in the race to produce scientific knowledge. If an interesting result has a medium, rather than a large, effect size, it will take many more subjects and additional studies to establish that result. When the researcher finds that the interesting finding goes away with repeated replications, there may be no publication to reward the researcher for the effort. Although the failure to establish a predicted effect may slow the career of the individual scientist, the suppression of reports that turn out to be Type I errors may speed up the accumulation of knowledge in the field as a whole. Meanwhile, the strategy, discussed in the previous section, of identifying the set of circumstances where an intervention can produce a large effect and can be documented with a relatively small sample may help mark progress even for the individual scientist.

A novel strategy for testing researchers' favorite hypotheses before publication was reported by Schweinsberg et al. (2016). Called the Pipeline Project, this group reported results from a prepublication independent replication (PPIR) effort to test 10 hypotheses that were being examined (in the pipeline) by the Uhlmann lab. These focused on person-centered morality (six hypotheses), morality and markets (two hypotheses), and reputation management (two hypotheses). Rather than the Uhlmann lab publishing their findings and then inviting replications by others, the PPIR approach established the effects before initial publication with the help of 25 independent labs, which collected data on more than 5 of the 10 target hypotheses. The results were reported as a meta-analysis of the replication studies using both frequentist and Bayesian methods (Verhagen & Wagenmakers 2014). Six of the original study results had unqualified support from the replication, two others had qualified support, and two others were inconsistent with the PPIR results. Bayesian analyses quantified the evidence for the alternative hypothesis relative to the null hypothesis rather than simply providing a binary score card. This crowdsourcing approach to replication prior to publication is a promising new direction. Similar collaborative work is being done by the Many Labs project (Ebersole et al. 2016, Klein et al. 2014).

UNINTENDED SIDE EFFECTS: DO NEW NORMS AND PROCEDURES RESULT IN COLLATERAL DAMAGE TO SOME SCIENTISTS?

As calls have been made to change the way science is conducted in psychology by preregistering designs and analyses and increasing sample sizes, some authors have noted what might be called collateral damage. The three types of damage that have been identified are (*a*) slowing and ultimate reduction of new findings and phenomena, (*b*) penalizing different subfields with the imposition of one-size-fits-all norms, and (*c*) discouraging young scientists from staying in the field because of the higher bar for publication and professional advancement.

Finkel et al. (2015, 2017) argued that the new conventions and norms overemphasize reducing false positive errors at the expense of allowing false negative errors. In the effort to minimize reports of findings that do not replicate, the norms can discourage discovery, innovation, and astute observation. Preregistration and other efforts that minimize HARKing may decrease reports of legitimate insights that occur when examining data. The new norms suggest that such new data-driven exploratory findings should be checked using independent data from a new confirmatory study, but Finkel et al. (2015, 2017) pointed out that obtaining new data in fields such as relationship science, health psychology, or neuroscience (among others) might take years rather than months. They also argued that the current emphasis is on being skeptical about a purported interesting finding rather than about a report that an interesting prediction was not found. Baumeister (2016) even suggested that neglect of discovery in psychology will lead to the field becoming boring.

Although the issues of replication in science go well beyond psychology (Dickersin & Rennie 2012, Ioannidis 2005), many of the advances in open science have come from psychological scientists. Especially active have been those in social psychology, which has been singled out as having lower rates of replication (Open Sci. Collab. 2015). The norms for sample size, multiple close replications of a finding, preregistration, data sharing, and material sharing have received particular attention from social psychologists and from methodologists who do no empirical research themselves. Finkel et al. (2015) made a compelling argument that these norms should not be rigidly applied to all psychology subfields. Rules of thumb for minimum sample size do not take into account the time and expense of data collection, the statistical power afforded by well-specified longitudinal models, or effect size variability across different subareas. Finkel et al. (2015) also argue that sharing original data of video recordings may not be possible and that sharing all research materials in longitudinal studies would place an extreme burden on investigators. These concerns are not limited to relationship science. Similar concerns could apply to studies of motor development (e.g., Adolph et al. 2012), clinical science (e.g., Tackett et al. 2017), and neuroscience (e.g., Overath et al. 2015). If the suggestions and norms become calcified rules and regulations, progress in some areas of psychology could be diminished.

The shifting publication rules and extra effort needed to document designs and data before making them public or open have led to concerns about the pipeline of graduate students, postdocs, and untenured junior faculty (Baumeister 2016). Even if we agree that new procedures lead to fewer false positive claims, they may also suppress discovery of true positive results, and they take longer to implement—particular problems for graduate students, postdocs, and junior faculty. Finkel et al. (2017) argued that researcher resources should be considered a fixed quantity; thus, larger sample size requirements will necessarily result in fewer new studies and publications. Search and promotion committees at institutions need to recognize the costs of increased documentation and sample sizes and account for these when making hiring or promotion decisions.

CONCLUDING COMMENTS: WHAT IS THE TAKE-HOME MESSAGE ABOUT HOW PSYCHOLOGICAL SCIENCE CAN SPEED KNOWLEDGE CONSTRUCTION?

The most recent replication crisis has led to a number of important insights and practices for psychological sciences. First, just because a finding has been claimed on the basis of a statistical test (NHST or Bayesian) does not mean that a new study will obtain the same result. Second, multiple replication studies of important findings advance knowledge by affirming findings, identifying boundary conditions, or showing legitimate lack of replication. Third, openness with regard to the documentation of the development of ideas, the exploration of preliminary data, the analysis of confirmatory data, and the data themselves will help allay concerns about fraud, QRPs, and human error. Fourth, the community of scientists should support one another and the scientific enterprise by providing (*a*) resources for open preregistration of ideas, research plans and data; (*b*) new statistical methodology for gaining insights from existing data and for planning new informative data collection; and (*c*) collaborative crowdsourcing resources for replicating important scientific claims. Fifth, treating the dialectical relationship between exploratory and confirmatory research honestly and seriously can further the goals of identifying legitimate and meaningful knowledge production. In short, the replication crisis can be reframed as a mandate from the research community to engage in methodologically sound, ethically driven research in which probabilistic decisions are made explicitly and respected by an open research process.

To promote consistent and high-quality research, a number of groups have made lists of best practice guidelines (Asendorpf et al. 2013, Brandt et al. 2014, Fiedler 2017, Munafò et al. 2017, Nosek et al. 2015, Open Sci. Collab. 2017), and themes from these lists have been emphasized by journal editors (Brown et al. 2014, Giner-Sorolla 2016, Kawakami 2015, Lindsay 2015, Vazire 2016). We have collected a large number of these recommendations in **Table 1**, organized into sections related to (*a*) initial steps, (*b*) conduct of the study and analysis, (*c*) preparation of the scientific report, and (*d*) open science. The last section includes archiving data, analysis scripts, and materials, but implied in all sections is the widely endorsed emphasis on openness.

We are especially impressed by the resources that are being provided by the Center for Open Science through the OSF to facilitate openness in phases of scientific discovery and empirical confirmation. Some researchers were initially concerned that establishing norms of preregistration would stifle creativity and exploration, but the OSF has adapted its resources to make it possible to archive different types of plans and ideas and to control the degree to which these notes and plans are made public. OSF provides a virtual laboratory notebook where scientists can make lasting notes in ink (not pencil) about what ideas they are pursuing, the kinds of data required, and the requisite steps necessary to achieve their scientific goals. If the researcher is undecided about which measure to use or does not know if a procedure borrowed from one research context will work in a novel context, these reflections can be noted in the OSF for private use initially and for public disclosure after research progress has been made. To some researchers, this recording may seem obsessive and time consuming; nevertheless, we endorse this systematic and thoughtful approach, and we expect that many journals will adopt the standards that are emerging from the OSF (Nosek et al. 2015).

Table 1 explicitly encourages systematic thinking, whether the research is in an exploratory, confirmatory, or mixed mode. In the left-hand column, we list recommended activities, and in the right-hand column, we indicate whether the recommendation is relevant to confirmatory or exploratory research modes; we were struck by how often the recommendation is relevant for both confirmatory and exploratory research. The "Initial steps" heading emphasizes planning, in terms of research goals, study design, attention to reliable measurement, and setting acceptable Type I

Table 1 Recommendations for research practices designed to speed knowledge construction in psychology and to reduce concerns about replication success in both exploratory (E) and confirmatory (C) studies

Recommendation	Study type
Initial steps	
Articulate goals of research	E, C
Consider power-enhancing designs	E, C
Set Type I error rate for multiple tests	C
Address measurement error	E, C
Provide detailed power analysis	C
Set data collection start and stop rules	C
Preregister hypotheses	C
Preregister designs	E, C
Preregister materials	E, C
Preregister necessary exploratory steps	E, C
Preregister confirmatory analyses	C
Conduct of study and analysis	
Set aside data for confirmation	E, C
Report confidence and credibility intervals	E, C
Avoid binary statistical decisions	E, C
Justify restrictions on the sample	E, C
Enumerate possible effect modifiers	E, C
Model effect variation	E, C
Scientific report	
Report all confirmatory preregistered results	C
Report exploratory analyses	E, C
Be flexible about $p < 0.05$	E, C
Report negative findings	E, C
Disclose ad hoc decisions	E, C
Model causal process	C
Direct replication and cross-validate	C
Report log of all analyses done in online appendix	E, C
Open science	
Share primary data	E, C
Share analysis syntax	E, C
Provide relevant research materials	E, C
Collaborate to replicate	E, C
Add disclosure statement to reports	E, C
Use open-source software	E, C

error rates. In this phase, important decisions must be made, in confirmatory studies, about whether it is possible to find a constellation of intervention methods, outcome measurements, participant characteristics, time frames, and study settings that illustrate the prototype of the effect with a large effect size. Alternatively, decisions might be made to explore the generality of an effect already established under specific conditions. These decisions, as well as those about whether the study design involves within- or between-person effects and assessments about the range of likely effect sizes, have important implications for an appropriate power analysis. As these decisions are made, we recommend that they be registered (or revised) within the OSF system.

Once data are collected and available, analyses that are both exploratory and confirmatory will be carried out. If the data are plentiful, it is ideal to randomly set aside a portion of the data for a confirmation study in a cross-validation. Even with a confirmatory study, decisions often need to be made about which data are retained or set aside because of quality concerns, and whether certain items or measures display expected validity patterns. These decisions should be systematic, but researchers should avoid rules based on simple binary significance tests (e.g., Shrout & Yip-Bannicq 2017) and instead use confidence or credible intervals, recognizing that data are sometimes precise and sometimes indeterminate. A thorough analysis of both confirmatory and exploratory data evaluates whether associations and patterns are consistent across important subsets of the sample, such as males and females.

The actions under the "Open science" heading of **Table 1** emphasize full disclosure of all results, whether tests are statistically significant or not, and all ancillary analyses. If validation data are set aside, the replication results should be reported regardless of whether they support or conflict with the original claim. Even when a true effect is present, it is unlikely that objective replications will lead to tidy results (Schimmack 2012), and the presentation of all data allows other researchers a better understanding of the likely effect variation. One of the benefits of the recent replication publications is that editors and reviewers now expect more complicated reports. Another benefit of science in the twenty-first century is that many details can be archived in online supplements (see Nosek & Bar-Anan 2012 for one vision of the future).

Related to creating complete reports of planned and exploratory analyses and results is the archiving of original data, analysis syntax, descriptions of relevant measures, and descriptions of protocols. Many experts recommend that, when possible, analysis syntax for open-source software systems be used, rather than expensive commercial programs that are not always available to interested researchers. These materials can be archived in the OSF system.

Recommendations in **Table 1** and in similar lists should not be applied as general and rigid rules for psychological research. In particular, the practice of automatic rejection of studies because sample sizes are judged to be too small using a heuristic rule is the opposite of the thoughtful and critical practices that we hope are emerging from the replication storms of 2011–2016. That having been said, a careful consideration of effect sizes as distributions rather than as fixed points will often necessitate larger sample sizes in years to come.

Some commentators have indicted psychological science for too many false claims and shoddy practices. Our view is that recent attention to replication in particular and knowledge generation more generally has led to remarkable and positive effects. This attention has generally sharpened our methodological efforts, opened laboratory settings for unprecedented and positive scrutiny, created expansive collaborative efforts and new methodological tools to combine results across studies, and allowed thoughtful exchange across disciplinary boundaries that has moved psychological practice and research substantially forward. The future of psychological science is bright.

DISCLOSURE STATEMENT

The authors are not aware of any affiliations, memberships, funding, or financial holdings that might be perceived as affecting the objectivity of this review.

ACKNOWLEDGMENTS

The authors thank those who gave comments on earlier versions of this review, including participants in the Quantitative Methods Colloquium at Vanderbilt University, Couples Lab at New York University, Research Center for Group Dynamics at the University of Michigan, and the following individuals: Corina Berli, William Brady, Barry Cohen, Paul Eastwick, John Kruschke, Alison Ledgerwood, Uli Schimmack, Barbara Spellman, Gertrude Stadler, Rugile Tuskeviciute, Jay Van Bavel, Julian Wills, and Marika Yip-Bannicq.

LITERATURE CITED

Adolph KE, Cole WG, Komati M, Garciaguirre JS, Badaly D, et al. 2012. How do you learn to walk? Thousands of steps and dozens of falls per day. *Psychol. Sci.* 23(11):1387–94

Aldrich J. 2008. R. A. Fisher on Bayes and Bayes' theorem. *Bayesian Anal.* 3(1):161–70

Alogna VK, Attaya MK, Aucoin P, Bahník Š, Birch S, et al. 2014. Registered replication report. *Perspect. Psychol. Sci.* 9(5):556–78

Anderson SF, Maxwell SE. 2017. Addressing the "replication crisis": using original studies to design replication studies with appropriate statistical power. *Multivar. Behav. Res.* 52:305–24

Asendorpf JB, Conner M, de Fruyt F, de Houwer J, Denissen JJA, et al. 2013. Recommendations for increasing replicability in psychology. *Eur. J. Personal.* 27(2):108–19

Bakker M, Wicherts JM. 2011. The (mis)reporting of statistical results in psychology journals. *Behav. Res. Methods* 43(3):666–78

Baumeister. 2016. Charting the future of social psychology. *J. Exp. Soc. Psychol.* 66:153–58

Beasley WH, Rodgers JL. 2009. Resampling theory. In *Handbook of Quantitative Methods in Psychology*, ed. R Millsap, A Maydeu-Olivares, pp. 362–86. Thousand Oaks, CA: Sage

Bench SW, Rivera GN, Schlegel RJ, Hicks JA, Lench HC. 2017. Does expertise matter in replication? An examination of the reproducibility project: psychology. *J. Exp. Soc. Psychol.* 68:181–84

Benjamini Y, Hochberg Y. 1995. Controlling the false discovery rate: a practical and powerful approach to multiple testing. *J. R. Stat. Soc. Ser. B* 57(1):289–300

Bhattacharjee Y. 2013. The mind of a con man. *The New York Times Magazine*, Apr. 28

Bonett DG. 2009. Meta-analytic interval estimation for standardized and unstandardized mean differences. *Psychol. Methods* 14(3):225–38

Borenstein M, Hedges LV, Higgins JPT, Rothstein HR. 2009. *Introduction to Meta-Analysis*. Hoboken, NJ: Wiley

Box JF. 1978. *R. A. Fisher: The Life of a Scientist*. Hoboken, NJ: Wiley

Brandt MJ, IJzerman H, Dijksterhuis A, Farach FJ, Geller J, et al. 2014. The replication recipe: What makes for a convincing replication? *J. Exp. Soc. Psychol.* 50:217–24

Braver SL, Thoemmes FJ, Rosenthal R. 2014. Continuously cumulating meta-analysis and replicability. *Perspect. Psychol. Sci.* 9(3):333–42

Brown SD, Furrow D, Hill DF, Gable JC, Porter LP, Jacobs WJ. 2014. A duty to describe. *Perspect. Psychol. Sci.* 9(6):626–40

Button KS, Ioannidis JPA, Mokrysz C, Nosek BA, Flint J, et al. 2013. Power failure: why small sample size undermines the reliability of neuroscience. *Nat. Rev. Neurosci.* 14(5):365–76

Cohen J. 1988. *Statistical Power Analysis for the Behavioral Sciences*. Abingdon, UK: Routledge. 2nd ed.

Cohen J. 1994. The Earth is round (p < 0.05). *Am. Psychol.* 49(12):997–1003

Coyne JC. 2016. Replication initiatives will not salvage the trustworthiness of psychology. *BMC Psychol.* 4(1):28

Cronbach LJ, Gleser GC, Nanda H, Rajaratnam N. 1972. *The Dependability of Behavioral Measurements*. Hoboken, NJ: Wiley

Cumming G. 2014. The new statistics. *Psychol. Sci.* 25(1):7–29

Curran PJ, Hussong AM. 2009. Integrative data analysis. *Psychol. Methods* 14(2):81–100

De Angelis CD, Drazen JM, Frizelle FA, Haug C, Hoey J, et al. 2005. Is this clinical trial fully registered? A statement from the International Committee of Medical Journal Editors. *N. Engl. J. Med.* 352(23):2436–38

Dickersin K, Rennie D. 2012. The evolution of trial registries and their use to assess the clinical trial enterprise. *JAMA* 307(17):1861–64

Ding N, Melloni L, Zhang H, Tian X, Poeppel D. 2016. Cortical tracking of hierarchical linguistic structures in connected speech. *Nat. Neurosci.* 19(1):158–64

Ebersole CR, Atherton OE, Belanger AL, Skulborstad HM, Allen JM, et al. 2016. Many Labs 3: evaluating participant pool quality across the academic semester via replication. *J. Exp. Soc. Psychol.* 67:68–82

Edwards J, Berry J. 2010. The presence of something or the absence of nothing: increasing theoretical precision in management research. *Organ. Res. Methods* 13(4):668–89

Efron B. 1979. Bootstrap methods: another look at the jackknife. *Ann. Stat.* 7(1):1–26

Efron B, Gong G. 1983. A leisurely look at the bootstrap, jackknife, and cross-validation. *Am. Stat.* 37:36–48

Fabrigar LR, Wegener DT. 2016. Conceptualizing and evaluating the replication of research results. *J. Exp. Soc. Psychol.* 66:68–80

Fiedler K. 2017. What constitutes strong psychological science? The (neglected) role of diagnosticity and a priori theorizing. *Perspect. Psychol. Sci.* 12(1):46–61

Finkel EJ, Eastwick PW, Reis HT. 2015. Best research practices in psychology: illustrating epistemological and pragmatic considerations with the case of relationship science. *J. Personal. Soc. Psychol.* 108(2):275–97

Finkel EJ, Eastwick PW, Reis HT. 2017. Replicability and other features of a high-quality science: toward a balanced and empirical approach. *J. Personal. Soc. Psychol.* 113(2):244–53

Fisher RA. 1925. *Statistical Methods for Research Workers*. Edinburgh, Scotl.: Oliver & Boyd

Fisher RA. 1958. The nature of probability. *Centen. Rev. Arts Sci.* 2:261–74

Francis G. 2012a. The psychology of replication and replication in psychology. *Perspect. Psychol. Sci.* 7(6):585–94

Francis G. 2012b. Publication bias and the failure of replication in experimental psychology. *Psychon. Bull. Rev.* 19(6):975–91

Francis G. 2012c. Too good to be true: publication bias in two prominent studies from experimental psychology. *Psychon. Bull. Rev.* 19(2):151–56

Gallistel CR. 2009. The importance of proving the null. *Psychol. Rev.* 116(2):439–53

Giner-Sorolla R. 2016. Approaching a fair deal for significance and other concerns. *J. Exp. Soc. Psychol.* 65:1–6

Greenwald AG. 1976. An editorial. *J. Personal. Soc. Psychol.* 33(1):1–7

Hagger MS, Chatzisarantis NLD. 2016. A multilab preregistered replication of the ego-depletion effect. *Perspect. Psychol. Sci.* 11(4):546–73

Ioannidis JPA. 2005. Why most published research findings are false. *PLOS Med.* 2(8):e124

Kawakami K. 2015. Editorial. *J. Personal. Soc. Psychol.* 108(1):58–59

Kerr N. 1998. HARKing: hypothesizing after the results are known. *Personal. Soc. Psychol. Rev.* 2(3):196–217

Kidwell MC, Lazarević LB, Baranski E, Hardwicke TE, Piechowski S, et al. 2016. Badges to acknowledge open practices: a simple, low-cost, effective method for increasing transparency. *PLOS Biol.* 14(5):e1002456

Klein RA, Ratliff KA, Vianello M, Adams RB, Bahník S, et al. 2014. Investigating variation in replicability: a "many labs" replication project. *Soc. Psychol.* 45(3):142–52

Kruschke JK. 2015. *Doing Bayesian Data Analysis: A Tutorial with R, JAGS and Stan*. Burlington, MA: Academic. 2nd ed.

Kruschke JK, Liddell TM. 2017. The Bayesian new statistics: hypothesis testing, estimation, meta-analysis, and power analysis from a Bayesian perspective. *Psychon. Bull. Rev.* 24:1–29

LeBel EP, Campbell L, Loving TJ. 2017. Benefits of open and high-powered research outweigh costs. *J. Personal. Soc. Psychol.* 113(2):254–61

Ledgerwood A, Sherman JW. 2012. Short, sweet, and problematic? The rise of the short report in psychological science. *Perspect. Psychol. Sci.* 7(1):60–66

Ledgerwood A, Soderberg C, Sparks J. 2017. Designing a study to maximize informational value. In *Toward a More Perfect Psychology: Improving Trust, Accuracy, and Transparency*, ed. MC Makel, JA Plucker, pp. 33–58. Washington, DC: Am. Psychol. Assoc.

Lindsay DS. 2015. Replication in psychological science. *Psychol. Sci.* 26(12):1827–32

Maxwell SE, Lau MY, Howard GS. 2015. Is psychology suffering from a replication crisis? What does "failure to replicate" really mean? *Am. Psychol.* 70(6):487–98

McArdle JJ, Ritschard G. 2014. *Contemporary Issues in Exploratory Data Mining in the Behavioral Sciences.* Abingdon, UK: Routledge

McShane B, Böckenholt U. 2014. You cannot step into the same river twice: when power analyses are optimistic. *Perspect. Psychol. Sci.* 9(6):612–25

McShane BB, Böckenholt U, Hansen KT. 2016. Adjusting for publication bias in meta-analysis. *Perspect. Psychol. Sci.* 11(5):730–49

Meiser T. 2011. Much pain, little gain? Paradigm-specific models and methods in experimental psychology. *Perspect. Psychol. Sci.* 6(2):183–91

Mill JS. 2008 (1843). *A System of Logic.* London: Longmans, Green

Munafò MR, Nosek BA, Bishop DVM, Button KS, Chambers CD, et al. 2017. A manifesto for reproducible science. *Nat. Hum. Behav.* 1(1):21

Nelson LD, Simmons J, Simonsohn U. 2018. Psychology's renaissance. *Annu. Rev. Psychol.* 69. In press

Neyman J, Pearson ES. 1928. On the use and interpretation of certain test criteria for purposes of statistical inference: part I. *Biometrika* 20A(1/2):175–240

Neyman J, Pearson ES. 1933. On the problem of the most efficient tests of statistical hypotheses. *Philos. Trans. R. Soc. Math. Phys. Eng. Sci.* 231:289–337

Nosek BA, Alter G, Banks GC, Borsboom D, Bowman SD, et al. 2015. Promoting an open research culture. *Science* 348(6242):1422–25

Nosek BA, Bar-Anan Y. 2012. Scientific utopia: I. Opening scientific communication. *Psychol. Inq.* 23(3):217–43

Nosek BA, Lakens DD. 2014. Registered reports: a method to increase the credibility of published results. *Soc. Psychol.* 45(3):137–41

Nosek BA, Spies J, Motyl M. 2012. Scientific utopia: II. Restructuring incentives and practices to promote truth over publishability. *Perspect. Psychol. Sci.* 7(6):615–31

Offord DR, Kraemer HC, Kazdin AE, Jensen PS, Harrington R. 1998. Lowering the burden of suffering from child psychiatric disorder: trade-offs among clinical, targeted, and universal interventions. *J. Am. Acad. Child Adolesc. Psychiatry* 37(7):686–94

Open Sci. Collab. 2015. Estimating the reproducibility of psychological science. *Science* 349(6251):aac4716

Open Sci. Collab. 2017. Maximizing the reproducibility of your research. In *Psychological Science Under Scrutiny: Recent Challenges and Proposed Solutions*, ed. SO Lilienfeld, ID Waldman, pp. 3–21. New York: Wiley

Overall NC, Girme YU, Lemay J, Edward P, Hammond MD. 2014. Attachment anxiety and reactions to relationship threat: the benefits and costs of inducing guilt in romantic partners. *J. Personal. Soc. Psychol.* 106(2):235–56

Overath T, McDermott JH, Zarate JM, Poeppel D. 2015. The cortical analysis of speech-specific temporal structure revealed by responses to sound quilts. *Nat. Neurosci.* 18(6):903–11

Ozomaro U, Wahlestedt C, Nemeroff CB. 2013. Personalized medicine in psychiatry: problems and promises. *BMC Med.* 11(1):132

Paolacci G, Chandler J. 2014. Inside the Turk: understanding Mechanical Turk as a participant pool. *Curr. Dir. Psychol. Sci.* 23(3):184–88

Perugini M, Gallucci M, Costantini G. 2014. Safeguard power as a protection against imprecise power estimates. *Perspect. Psychol. Sci.* 9(3):319–32

Richard FD, Bond CF, Stokes-Zoota JJ. 2003. One hundred years of social psychology quantitatively described. *Rev. Gen. Psychol.* 7(4):331–63

Rogers JL, Howard KI, Vessey JT. 1993. Using significance tests to evaluate equivalence between two experimental groups. *Psychol. Bull.* 113(3):553–65

Rossi JS. 1990. Statistical power of psychological research. *J. Consult. Clin. Psychol.* 58(5):646–56

Scheibehenne B, Jamil T, Wagenmakers E. 2016. Bayesian evidence synthesis can reconcile seemingly inconsistent results. *Psychol. Sci.* 27(7):1043–46

Schimmack U. 2012. The ironic effect of significant results on the credibility of multiple-study articles. *Psychol. Methods* 17(4):551–66

Schmidt FL, Oh I. 2016. The crisis of confidence in research findings in psychology: Is lack of replication the real problem? Or is it something else? *Arch. Sci. Psychol.* 4(1):32–37

Schooler JW, Engstler-Schooler TY. 1990. Verbal overshadowing of visual memories: Some things are better left unsaid. *Cogn. Psychol.* 22(1):36–71

Schweinsberg M, Madan N, Vianello M, Sommer SA, Jordan J, et al. 2016. The pipeline project: pre-publication independent replications of a single laboratory's research pipeline. *J. Exp. Soc. Psychol.* 66:55–67

Seaman MA, Serlin RC. 1998. Equivalence confidence intervals for two-group comparisons of means. *Psychol. Methods* 3(4):403–11

Shrout PE, Yip-Bannicq M. 2017. Inferences about competing measures based on patterns of binary significance tests are questionable. *Psychol. Methods* 22(1):84–93

Simmons J, Nelson L, Simonsohn U. 2011. False-positive psychology: Undisclosed flexibility in data collection and analysis allows presenting anything as significant. *Psychol. Sci.* 22(11):1359–66

Simons DJ, Holcombe AO, Spellman BA. 2014. An introduction to registered replication reports at *Perspectives on Psychological Science. Perspect. Psychol. Sci.* 9(5):552–55

Simonsohn U. 2013. Just post it: the lesson from two cases of fabricated data detected by statistics alone. *Psychol. Sci.* 24(10):1875–88

Sripada C, Kessler D, Jonides J. 2014. Methylphenidate blocks effort-induced depletion of regulatory control in healthy volunteers. *Psychol. Sci.* 25(6):1227–34

Stewart LA, Parmar MKB. 1993. Meta-analysis of the literature or of individual patient data: Is there a difference? *Lancet* 341(8842):418–22

Stigler SM. 1986. *The History of Statistics: The Measurement of Uncertainty Before 1900.* Cambridge, MA: Harvard Univ. Press

Stroebe W. 2016. Are most published social psychological findings false? *J. Exp. Soc. Psychol.* 66:134–44

Tackett JL, Lilienfeld SO, Johnson SL, Krueger RF, Miller JD, et al. 2017. It's time to broaden the replicability conversation: thoughts for and from clinical psychological science. *Perspect. Psychol. Sci.* 12(5):742–56

Taylor DJ, Muller KE. 1996. Bias in linear model power and sample size calculation due to estimating noncentrality. *Commun. Stat. Theory Methods* 25(7):1595–610

Tukey JW. 1977. *Exploratory Data Analysis.* Reading, MA: Addison-Wesley

Van Bavel JJ, Mende-Siedlecki P, Brady WJ, Reinero DA. 2016. Contextual sensitivity in scientific reproducibility. *PNAS* 113(23):6454–59

Vazire S. 2016. Editorial. *Soc. Psychol. Personal. Sci.* 7(1):3–7

Verhagen J, Wagenmakers E. 2014. Bayesian tests to quantify the result of a replication attempt. *J. Exp. Psychol. Gen.* 143(4):1457–75

Vul E, Harris C, Winkielman P, Pashler H. 2009. Puzzlingly high correlations in fMRI studies of emotion, personality, and social cognition. *Perspect. Psychol. Sci.* 4(3):274–90

Wade N. 2010. Inquiry on Harvard lab threatens ripple effect. *The New York Times*, Aug. 12

Wagenmakers E, Verhagen J, Ly A. 2016. How to quantify the evidence for the absence of a correlation. *Behav. Res. Methods* 48(2):413–26

Wagenmakers E, Wetzels R, Borsboom D, van der Maas HLJ, Kievit RA. 2012. An agenda for purely confirmatory research. *Perspect. Psychol. Sci.* 7(6):632–38

Westfall J, Judd CM, Kenny DA. 2015. Replicating studies in which samples of participants respond to samples of stimuli. *Perspect. Psychol. Sci.* 10(3):390–99

Zabell S. 1989. R. A. Fisher on the history of inverse probability. *Stat. Sci.* 4(3):247–56

Psychology's Renaissance

Leif D. Nelson,[1] Joseph Simmons,[2]
and Uri Simonsohn[2]

[1]Haas School of Business, University of California, Berkeley, California 94720;
email: Leif_Nelson@haas.berkeley.edu

[2]The Wharton School, University of Pennsylvania, Philadelphia, Pennsylvania 19104;
email: jsimmo@upenn.edu, urisohn@gmail.com

Annu. Rev. Psychol. 2018. 69:511–34

First published as a Review in Advance on October 25, 2017

The *Annual Review of Psychology* is online at
psych.annualreviews.org

https://doi.org/10.1146/annurev-psych-122216-011836

Keywords

p-hacking, publication bias, renaissance, methodology, false positives,
preregistration

Abstract

In 2010–2012, a few largely coincidental events led experimental psychologists to realize that their approach to collecting, analyzing, and reporting data made it too easy to publish false-positive findings. This sparked a period of methodological reflection that we review here and call Psychology's Renaissance. We begin by describing how psychologists' concerns with publication bias shifted from worrying about file-drawered studies to worrying about *p*-hacked analyses. We then review the methodological changes that psychologists have proposed and, in some cases, embraced. In describing how the renaissance has unfolded, we attempt to describe different points of view fairly but not neutrally, so as to identify the most promising paths forward. In so doing, we champion disclosure and preregistration, express skepticism about most statistical solutions to publication bias, take positions on the analysis and interpretation of replication failures, and contend that meta-analytical thinking *increases* the prevalence of false positives. Our general thesis is that the scientific practices of experimental psychologists have improved dramatically.

Contents

INTRODUCTION

If a team of research psychologists were to emerge today from a 7-year hibernation, they would not recognize their field. Authors voluntarily posting their data. Top journals routinely publishing replication attempts, both failures and successes. Hundreds of researchers preregistering their studies. Crowded methods symposia at many conferences. Enormous increases in sample sizes. Some top journals requiring the full disclosure of measures, conditions, exclusions, and the rules for determining sample sizes. Several multilab replication efforts accepted for publication before any data were collected. Overall, an unprecedented focus on replicability. What on earth just happened?

Many have been referring to this period as psychology's "replication crisis." This makes no sense. We do not call the rain that follows a long drought a water crisis. We do not call sustained growth following a recession an economic crisis. Experimental psychologists spent several decades relying on methods of data collection and analysis that make it too easy to publish false-positive, nonreplicable results. During that time, it was impossible to distinguish between findings that are true and replicable and those that are false and not replicable. *That* period, when we were unaware of the problem and thus did nothing about it, constituted the real replication crisis.

That crisis appears to be ending. Researchers now understand that the old ways of collecting and analyzing data produce results that are not diagnostic of truth and that a new, more enlightened approach is needed. Thousands of psychologists have embraced this notion. The improvements to our field have been dramatic. This is psychology's *renaissance*.

THE RENAISSANCE BEGINS: 2010–2012

Psychology's renaissance began when, in 2010–2012, a series of events drove psychological scientists into a spiral of methodological introspection. In this section, we review the events that, in our view, were the most consequential.

1. Social psychology's most prestigious journal, the *Journal of Personality and Social Psychology*, published an article by Daryl Bem (2011) in which he presented nine experiments supporting a transparently outlandish claim—that people can be influenced by an unforeseeable future event. For example, in his study 8, Bem found that participants were better able to recall words that they were later randomly assigned to rehearse. The reaction to this article was one of widespread disbelief, both inside (e.g., Wagenmakers et al. 2011) and outside (e.g., Carey 2011b) of academia; not surprisingly, these results did not replicate (Galak et al. 2012).[1] Bem's article prompted psychologists to start wondering how such a well-respected and well-intentioned scientist could have amassed a large body of evidence for an obviously false hypothesis.

2. Diederik Stapel, one of social psychology's most prominent and prolific contributors, confessed to decades of data fabrication. He eventually retracted dozens of articles. Predictably, this attracted attention from psychologists, non–psychological scientists, and the media (see, e.g., Achenbach 2011, Carey 2011a). Almost simultaneously, two other psychologists—Lawrence Sanna at the University of Michigan and Dirk Smeesters at Erasmus University Rotterdam—were discovered to have been authors on multiple articles containing fabricated results (see Simonsohn 2013). Stapel, Smeesters, and Sanna were separately investigated for academic misconduct, and all three resigned from their tenured positions. Importantly, the investigation into Stapel's work uncovered problematic methodological practices even in studies that were not fabricated.[2] As did the publication of Bem's (2011) article, these events prompted many psychologists to re-evaluate how the field conducts research.

3. In 2011, we wrote "False-Positive Psychology" (Simmons et al. 2011), an article reporting the surprisingly severe consequences of selectively reporting data and analyses, a practice that we later called *p-hacking*. In that article, we showed that conducting multiple analyses on the same data set and then reporting only the one(s) that obtained statistical significance (e.g., analyzing multiple measures but reporting only one) can dramatically increase the likelihood of publishing a false-positive finding. Independently and nearly simultaneously, John et al. (2012) documented that a large fraction of psychological researchers admitted engaging in precisely the forms of *p*-hacking that we had considered; for example, about 65% of respondents indicated that they had dropped a dependent variable when reporting a study. Identifying these realities—that researchers engage in *p*-hacking and that *p*-hacking makes it trivially easy to accumulate significant evidence for a false hypothesis—opened psychologists' eyes to the fact that many published findings, and even whole literatures, could be false positive.

4. Doyen et al. (2012) reported a failure to replicate one of the most famous findings in social psychology, that priming people with elderly stereotypes made them walk more slowly (Bargh et al. 1996). This prompted a lively and widely publicized debate, which, in turn, prompted Nobel Prize winner Daniel Kahneman to write a widely circulated email calling for researchers to resolve the debate by conducting systematic replications. (We have archived

---

[1] Bem did not identify flaws in the replication study; instead he conducted a meta-analysis with 90 studies that he interpreted as corroborating his findings (Bem et al. 2016). The meta-analysis is available on the online platform F1000Research.

[2] For example, the report from the three Dutch university committees investigating Stapel said, "The following situation also occurred. A known measuring instrument consists of six items. The article referred to this instrument but the dataset showed that only four items had been included; two items were omitted without mention. In yet another experiment, again with the same measuring instrument, the same happened, but now with two different items omitted, again without mention. The only explanation for this behavior is that it is meant to obtain confirmation of the research hypotheses" (Levelt et al. 2012, p. 50). We have archived a copy of the report at **https://osf.io/eup6d/**.

some of these exchanges at **https://osf.io/eygvz/**.) Perhaps not coincidentally, replication attempts soon became much more common.

5. In 2011, psychologist Brian Nosek began organizing several collaborative replication efforts, in which multiple independent labs attempted to replicate previously published research (Open Sci. Collab. 2012). He and Jeffrey Spies also worked to develop an online platform, the Open Science Framework (OSF), which was originally released in 2012; it allowed researchers to more transparently record, share, and report their work. This effort culminated, in 2013, in their launch of the Center for Open Science, a nonprofit organization that has heavily influenced the movement toward better research practices in psychology.

P-HACKING EXPLAINS AN OLD PARADOX

Psychologists have long been aware of two seemingly contradictory problems with the published literature. On the one hand, the overwhelming majority of published findings are statistically significant (Fanelli 2012, Greenwald 1975, Sterling 1959). On the other hand, the overwhelming majority of published studies are underpowered and, thus, theoretically unlikely to obtain results that are statistically significant (Chase & Chase 1976, Cohen 1962, Sedlmeier & Gigerenzer 1989). The sample sizes of experiments meant that most studies should have been failing, but the published record suggested almost uniform success.[3]

There is an old, popular, and simple explanation for this paradox. Experiments that work are sent to a journal, whereas experiments that fail are sent to the file drawer (Rosenthal 1979). We believe that this "file-drawer explanation" is incorrect. Most failed studies are not *missing*. They are published in our journals, masquerading as successes.

The file-drawer explanation becomes transparently implausible once its assumptions are made explicit. It assumes that researchers conduct a study and perform one (predetermined) statistical analysis. If the analysis is significant, then they publish it. If it is not significant, then the researchers give up and start over. This is not a realistic depiction of researcher behavior. Researchers would not so quickly give up on their chances for publication, nor would they abandon the beliefs that led them to run the study, just because the first analysis they ran was not statistically significant. They would instead explore the data further, examining, for example, whether outliers were interfering with the effect, whether the effect was significant within a subset of participants or trials, or whether it emerged when the dependent variable was coded differently. Pre-2011 researchers did occasionally file-drawer a study, although they did not do so when the study failed, but rather when *p*-hacking did. Thus, whereas our file drawers are sprinkled with failed *studies* that we did not publish, they are overflowing with failed *analyses* of the studies that we did publish.

Prior to 2011, even psychologists writing about publication bias and statistical power had ignored the fact that *p*-hacking occurs, let alone the fact that it is a first-order problem for the validity of psychological research. Psychology suffered from *p*-hacking neglect.[4] For example, in the article that introduced the term "file-drawer problem," Rosenthal (1979, p. 638, emphasis

---

[3]In a satirical piece, Brian A. Nosek, under the pseudonym Ariana K. Bones, proposed a precognition explanation: Researchers are able to predict which studies will produce an unlucky result and, thus, they know not to run these studies (Bones 2012).

[4]Methodologists in other fields had brought up the problem we now know as *p*-hacking (Cole 1957, Ioannidis 2005, Leamer 1983, Phillips 2004). However, perhaps because they did not demonstrate that this was a problem worth worrying about or because they did not propose concrete and practical solutions to prevent it (i.e., they did not demonstrate that this was a solvable problem), their concerns did not have perceivable consequences on how research was conducted and reported in their fields.

added) wrote, "The extreme view ... is that the journals are filled with the 5% of the *studies* that show Type I errors, while the file drawers back at the lab are filled with the [other] 95% of the *studies*." Similarly, Greenwald (1975, table 1), in his seminal (and excellent) "Consequences of prejudice against the null hypothesis," considered four things researchers may do upon obtaining a nonsignificant result: (*a*) submitting the null finding for publication, (*b*) conducting an exact replication, (*c*) conducting a modified replication, or (*d*) giving up. His list excludes conducting additional analyses of the same data.

Vul et al. (2009), in their article about "voodoo correlations," represent an interesting partial exception to *p*-hacking neglect.[5] Focusing on fMRI research, they discussed the influence of choosing to report only the analyses of voxels that were statistically significant. However, the exception is only partial because Vul et al. suggested that the problem did not apply to psychological research more generally. For example, they wrote, "We suspect that the problems brought to light here are ones that most editors and reviewers of studies using purely behavioral measures would usually be quite sensitive to" (Vul et al. 2009, p. 285).[6]

Over the years, researchers repeatedly documented the fact that psychologists were running dramatically underpowered studies (e.g., Chase & Chase 1976, Cohen 1962), and they repeatedly called for sample sizes to be increased to levels that simple math revealed to be necessary. Eventually, Sedlmeier & Gigerenzer (1989) decided to see whether any of these articles had been successful in getting researchers to increase their sample sizes. They concluded that they were not; sample sizes had remained inadequately low. They speculated that this was in part because researchers overestimate the statistical power of small samples and, thus, the statistical power of their own small-sampled studies (citing, interestingly, Tversky & Kahneman 1971).[7] But this explanation is necessarily incomplete. How could researchers possibly maintain wrong beliefs about required sample sizes in the face of years of feedback from experience? It might make sense for new graduate students to erroneously think 12 participants per cell will be a sufficiently large sample size to test a counterintuitive attenuated interaction hypothesis, but it would not make sense for a full professor to maintain this belief after running hundreds of experiments that should have failed. It is one thing for a very young child to believe that 12 peas are enough for dinner and quite another for a chronically starving adult to do so.

P-hacking provides the real solution to the paradox. *P*-hacking is the only honest and practical way to *consistently* get underpowered studies to be statistically significant. Researchers did not learn from experience to increase their sample sizes precisely because their underpowered studies *were not failing*.[8] *P*-hacking allowed researchers to think, "I know that Jacob Cohen keeps saying that we need to increase our sample sizes, but most of my studies work; he must be talking about other people. They should really get their act together."

---

[5] Their article became well known with the title referencing "voodoo correlations," but shortly before publication, they replaced "voodoo" with "puzzlingly high."

[6] Fiedler (2011), in his article "Voodoo Correlations Are Everywhere," appears at first glance to extend Vul et al.'s (2009) conclusions to all psychological research. However, he actually makes a completely different point, expressing the concern that researchers may systematically design studies that are expected to generate larger effects (e.g., building in moderators that inflate effects). Fiedler's article was, therefore, about increasing generalizability rather than reducing false positives. Even his subsection on "Biases from the analyses" (Fiedler 2011, p. 166) exclusively pertained to decisions made *before* data collection.

[7] Sedlmeier & Gigerenzer (1989) also speculated that underpowered studies persisted because psychologists first learned about Fisher's approach to inference, which did not include discussions of statistical power, and only later learned about Neyman-Pearson's approach, which did include discussions of statistical power (see Sedlmeier & Gigerenzer 1989, p. 314, last paragraph). This explanation seems sufficiently implausible to us to be relegated to a footnote.

[8] For readers enamored with the peas analogy, *p*-hacking is like eating a seven-course meal after you eat the peas. Believing that $n = 12$ is enough is like attributing your satiety to the peas.

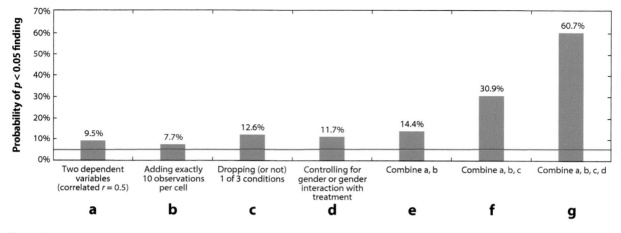

Figure 1

Probability that a study obtains statistical significance ($p < 0.05$) as a function of the types of p-hacking a researcher is willing to engage in (originally reported in Simmons et al. 2011, table 1). The figure is based on 15,000 simulated studies. The baseline study was a two-condition between-subjects design with 20 observations per cell drawn from the same normal distribution (thus, under the null hypothesis of no difference between conditions). The y axis depicts the share of studies for which at least one attempted analysis was significant. Results were obtained by (*a*) conducting three t-tests, one on each of two dependent variables and a third on the average of these two variables; (*b*) conducting one t-test after collecting 20 observations per cell and another after collecting an additional 10 observations per cell; (*c*) conducting t-tests for each of the three possible pairings of conditions and an ordinary least squares regression for the linear trend of all three conditions (coding: low $= -1$, medium $= 0$, high $= 1$); and (*d*) conducting a t-test, an analysis of covariance with a gender main effect, and an analysis of covariance with a gender interaction (each observation was assigned a 50% probability of being female). For bar *d*, we report a significant effect if the effect of the condition was significant in any of these analyses or if the gender $\times$ condition interaction was significant. The R code to reproduce these results can be found at **https://osf.io/a67ft/**.

In "False-Positive Psychology" (Simmons et al. 2011), we demonstrated that p-hacking represents a major threat to the validity of *all* empirical research that relies on hypothesis testing. Specifically, we showed how acceptable levels of p-hacking could raise false-positive rates to unacceptable levels (e.g., from 5% to 61%; see **Figure 1**). Furthermore, by moderately p-hacking two real experiments, we demonstrated how easy it is to obtain statistically significant evidence for a transparently false hypothesis: that listening to a song can change a person's age. It is now clear that, with enough analytic flexibility, p-hacking can turn any false hypothesis into one that has statistically significant support.[9]

It is tempting to take comfort in the fact that psychology publications usually contain more than one experiment (see, e.g., Stroebe 2016, section 1.6.1). Even if a single *study's* false-positive rate is as high as 61%, the odds of getting four false positives for a single *article* (in the predicted direction) is nevertheless quite low: $(0.61/2)^4 = 0.8\%$. However, this framing of the problem assumes two things—one that is never true and one that is sometimes not true. The first assumption is that researchers publish every study. They do not. If a researcher is willing to file-drawer even a small number of studies, a false-positive four-study article becomes easy enough to produce [Pashler & Harris (2012, argument 2, p. 533) provide an excellent discussion of this issue]. Framed differently, to find four experiments worth of significant evidence for a false (directional)

---

[9]The effect of p-hacking on Bayesian hypothesis testing and on both frequentist and Bayesian confidence intervals is just as severe (see Simonsohn 2014).

hypothesis, researchers need to run 160 studies if they do not p-hack but only 13 if they do.[10] The other assumption is that 61% represents some sort of upper bound, when, in fact, that estimate is likely to be conservative, particularly if researchers are able to flexibly contort the hypotheses to fit the data that they observe (Kerr 1998). In truth, it is not that hard to get a study's false-positive rate to be very close to 100%, in which case even a multistudy article's false-positive rate will be close to 100%.

Irrespective of these details, it is a mathematical fact that p-hacking makes it dramatically easier to generate false-positive findings, so much so that, for decades, p-hacking enabled researchers to achieve the otherwise mathematically impossible feat of getting most of their underpowered studies to be significant. P-hacking has long been the biggest threat to the integrity of our discipline.

FALSE POSITIVES ARE BAD, WE DO NOT KNOW HOW MANY THERE ARE, AND THAT DOES NOT MATTER

False positives are bad. Publishing them can cause scientists to spend precious resources chasing down false leads, policy makers to enact potentially harmful or ineffective policies, and funding agencies to allocate their resources away from hypotheses that are actually true. When false positives populate our literatures, we can no longer distinguish between what is true and what is false, undermining the very goal of science.

It is sometimes argued that any policy that reduces false positives will necessarily increase false negatives (e.g., Fiedler et al. 2012). However, because studying false positives diverts resources and attention away from the study of true hypotheses, the reduction of false positives can actually decrease false negatives. For instance, psychologists who realize that they should not study precognition because it is a false positive may instead discover true effects that would not have been discovered otherwise.

The need to prevent the publication of false positives is not controversial. What are controversial are the questions of whether the existing literature contains a large number of false-positive findings and, thus, how much of that literature should be believed. Some researchers believe that p-hacking and false positives are common, whereas others believe that they are relatively rare.

The evidence in favor of the commonness of false positives comes in two forms. First, as outlined in the previous section, it is extremely unlikely for researchers to have succeeded for so long in getting so many underpowered studies to be statistically significant without engaging in p-hacking; because p-hacking makes it nearly as easy to publish a false-positive as a true-positive finding, it seems reasonable to assume that many published findings are false positives. Second, systematic attempts to replicate existing findings have not been overwhelmingly successful (see, e.g., Alogna et al. 2014, Cheung et al. 2016, Open Sci. Collab. 2015, Wagenmakers et al. 2016).

The counterargument tends to come in two forms. One consists of dismissing failures to replicate as either poorly executed or misguided, an argument that we discuss in more detail in the section titled Replications. The other is grounded in the belief that researchers are well intentioned and that p-hacking is not. According to this view, asserting that researchers engage in p-hacking is tantamount to asserting that researchers are unethical. For example, in an editorial about these issues, Luce et al. (2012, p. iii) wrote, "we are concerned that the present tenor of the discussions and the structure of the solutions may produce an environment that presumes abuse."

---

[10]If the false-positive rate is 5% (1 in 20), one needs an average of 80 attempts to get four that are $p < .05$ in either direction and 160 attempts to get four in the predicted direction. If the false-positive rate is 61%, these numbers are 6.6 and 13.1, respectively.

Along the same lines, Fiedler & Schwarz (2016) criticized John et al.'s (2012) survey assessing the prevalence of questionable research practices on the grounds that the survey did not sufficiently distinguish between selective reporting that was well intentioned and selective reporting that was ill intentioned.

As we see it, both sides of this debate agree that the vast majority of researchers are honest and well intentioned. The disagreement is, instead, about whether honest and well-intentioned researchers will engage in p-hacking. As (honest and well-intentioned) researchers who p-hacked for many years, we strongly believe that they do.

P-hacking is a pervasive problem precisely because researchers usually do not realize that they are doing it or appreciate that what they are doing is consequential (Vazire 2015). It is not something that malevolent researchers engage in while laughing maniacally; it is something that benevolent researchers engage in while trying to understand their otherwise imperfect results. P-hacking is the byproduct of the very human tendency to justify actions that produce desirable outcomes (Kunda 1990, Mahoney 1979). To suspect that researchers p-hack is merely to suspect that they are human.

Fortunately, at the end of the day, this debate surrounding the prevalence of false positives is irrelevant. Whether one believes that false positives are common or rare, we can all agree that we should embrace research methods that prevent the publication of false positives. Thus, we do not need to agree on the prevalence of false positives, but only on the fact that the methods we used for many decades did not adequately defend against them.

To illustrate this point, imagine a surgeon who chooses at random which of a patient's diseased fingers to amputate. After the procedure, observers could consider whether the surgeon had amputated the correct or incorrect finger, but that consideration is obviously irrelevant for determining whether the surgeon should adopt a different, less error-prone method going forward. Like the surgeon, regardless of what happened previously, we should embrace the method that is demonstrably more likely to increase our chances of getting things right in the future.

Accordingly, in the following sections, we focus not on the question of whether false positives are common or rare, but on what we can do to prevent and correct them.

PREVENTING P-HACKING IN FUTURE RESEARCH

In this section, we discuss two policies to reduce p-hacking: disclosure and preregistration.

Disclosure

The most straightforward way to prevent researchers from selectively reporting their methods and analyses is to require them to report less selectively. At the bare minimum, this means requiring authors to disclose all of their measures, manipulations, and exclusions, as well as how they determined their sample sizes (Simmons et al. 2011). This allows reviewers to better diagnose whether authors' results are likely to have been obtained by p-hacking.

Although requiring scientists to report what they actually did in their studies should be uncontroversial, most journals have refrained from adopting this requirement. Still, important progress has been made. As editor, Eric Eich (2014) labored for months to implement these disclosure requirements at *Psychological Science*, and his successor, Stephen Lindsay (2015), extended them. Simine Vazire (2016) implemented similar requirements at *Social Psychological and Personality Science*.

Even journals that do not require authors to disclose all of their important methodological details have seen an uptick in authors' propensity to fully disclose their methods, both because of an increase in voluntary disclosure[11] and because many reviewers now demand it, often including the following text in their reviews (see **http://osf.io/hadz3**): "I request that the authors add a statement to the paper confirming whether, for all experiments, they have reported all measures, conditions, data exclusions, and how they determined their sample sizes. The authors should, of course, add any additional text to ensure the statement is accurate. This is the standard reviewer disclosure request endorsed by the Center for Open Science. I include it in every review." Disclosure is slowly becoming the norm, although it is not yet a ubiquitous requirement.

Preregistration

Whereas disclosure represents the bare minimum defense against *p*-hacking, proper preregistration represents the cure. Preregistrations are time-stamped plans for data analysis written before any data are analyzed. Preregistrations identify, in advance, which analyses are confirmatory and which are exploratory (Wagenmakers et al. 2012), greatly reducing the prevalence and influence of *p*-hacking (Bakker et al. 2012, van't Veer & Giner-Sorolla 2016).

One concern often raised about preregistrations is that they may hinder exploration. For example, Association for Psychological Science president Goldin-Meadow (2016) wrote, "[I] fear that preregistration will stifle discovery. Science isn't just about testing hypotheses—it's also about discovering hypotheses.... Aren't we supposed to let the data guide us in our exploration? How can we make new discoveries if our studies need to be catalogued before they are run?"

Overcoming this concern requires realizing that preregistrations do not tie researchers' hands, but merely uncover readers' eyes. Preregistering does not preclude exploration, but it does communicate to readers that it occurred. Preregistering allows readers to discriminate between confirmatory analyses, which provide valid *p*-values and trustworthy results, and exploratory analyses, which provide invalid *p*-values and tentative results (Moore 2016). Preregistration allows confirmatory results to be given the full credit that they deserve.

As we recently wrote (Simmons et al. 2017), preregistration has two key advantages over disclosure. First, it gives researchers the freedom to conduct analyses that could, if disclosed afterwards, seem suspicious, such as excluding participants who failed an attention check or running an unusual statistical test. Similarly, preregistration allows researchers to add observations to a study. For example, a researcher could specify a plan to add 100 observations if the key analysis is not significant after collecting the first 100 (see also Lakens 2014). Second, preregistration is the only way for authors to convincingly demonstrate that their key analyses were not *p*-hacked.

Psychologists currently have two main options for preregistration: AsPredicted (**http://AsPredicted.org**) and the OSF (**http://osf.io**). On AsPredicted, researchers preregister by completing a standardized form containing eight short questions. The platform then generates an easy-to-read one-page PDF (for an example, see **https://Aspredicted.org/nfj4s.pdf**), which can be shared anonymously during the review process and made public if and when the authors are ready to do so. On the OSF, researchers with accounts can collaborate, share, and archive files. These files are stored as elements within projects. Individual elements within a project can be locked and time stamped, registered, and used as study preregistrations if researchers provide the appropriate information or if they select a preregistration template (for step-by-step instructions, see **https://osf.io/sgrk6/**; for the set of templates, see **https://osf.io/zab38/**).

---

[11]We have suggested that authors include a standardized disclosure statement in their articles: "We report how we determined our sample size, all data exclusions (if any), all manipulations, and all measures in the study" (Simmons et al. 2012).

Although very few published studies in psychology have been preregistered, this is likely attributable to the considerable lag between study design and study publication. Indeed, there is ample evidence that preregistration is starting to catch on. AsPredicted was launched in December 2015. In its first 14 months, 1,631 different people completed an AsPredicted preregistration. We expect that in 3–5 years, published preregistered experimental psychology studies will be common.

ADDRESSING *P*-HACKING IN PAST RESEARCH

In this section, we discuss the two main approaches that researchers take to identify which published findings are true positives and which are false positives: attempts to replicate individual studies and statistical analyses of collections of studies.

Replications

To a scientist, a true effect is one that replicates under specifiable conditions (K12 Reader 2012, Popper 1963). Not surprisingly, widespread concern about the truth of existing effects has generated a surge of interest in replicating studies under the conditions originally specified. Accordingly, there have been discussions of how to increase the frequency of replications (Asendorpf et al. 2013, Koole & Lakens 2012), discussions of how to properly design replications (Brandt et al. 2014, Schmidt 2009), special issues dedicated to replications (Nosek & Lakens 2013, Pashler & Wagenmakers 2012), multilab replication efforts (Ebersole et al. 2016, Klein et al. 2014), and the creation of registered replication reports (Simons et al. 2014). Indeed, of CurateScience.org's database of over 1,000 attempts to replicate psychological studies (which we have archived at **http://web.archive.org/web/20170227214829/http://curatescience.org/**), approximately 96% of them have been conducted since 2011 (E.P. LeBel, personal communication).

Instead of reviewing this impressive body of largely unrelated studies, in this section, we discuss issues pertaining to the interpretation and analysis of replication results.

How to interpret failures to replicate. Just as it is impossible to bathe in the same river twice, it is impossible to run the same study twice. This unfortunate fact generates the same debate almost every time a failure to replicate becomes public, with some arguing that the replication casts doubt on the veracity of the original finding and others attributing the failure to substantive differences between the replication and the original (or to poor execution of the replication attempt). How should such debates be productively resolved?

Some of the debates are about differences in design. For example, the Open Science Collaboration (Open Sci. Collab. 2015) made painstaking efforts to precisely replicate the procedures from 100 published psychology studies. Nevertheless, some differences inevitably occurred and have been the subject of intense debate regarding how consequential they may be (Anderson et al. 2016, Gilbert et al. 2016, Inbar 2016, Van Bavel et al. 2016).

Even when the original design and the replication design are strictly identical, people may debate whether they are psychologically identical. For example, Doyen et al. (2012) failed to replicate the seminal study by Bargh et al. (1996), in which US participants primed with words associated with the elderly were reported to have walked more slowly when exiting the experiment. Stroebe & Strack (2014, p. 62), citing differences in the times and locations of the studies, wrote, "it is also possible that the concept of 'walking slowly' is not a central part of the stereotype of [the] elderly in Belgium some 20 years later." Similarly, when a registered replication report (Wagenmakers et al. 2016) failed to replicate Strack et al.'s (1988) finding that participants evaluate cartoons as funnier when biting a pencil in a way that makes them smile, Strack (2016, p. 929) responded that "despite the [similar] obtained ratings of funniness [M = 4.73 in original, M = 4.59 in replication], it must be asked if Gary Larson's The Far Side cartoons [used in these studies] that were iconic for the zeitgeist of the 1980s instantiated similar psychological conditions 30 years later."

Whose responsibility is it to empirically test whether differences between the original and the replication are responsible for a replication failure? Answers to this question fall on a continuum between two extremes. One extreme treats every hypothesized moderator as consequential until proven otherwise (e.g., assuming that only US participants stereotype the elderly as slow walkers unless data falsify this hypothesis). The other extreme treats every hypothesized moderator as inconsequential until proven otherwise (e.g., assuming that Belgians also stereotype the elderly as slow walkers unless data falsify this hypothesis). For instance, Simons (2014, p. 77) writes, "When researchers posit a moderator explanation for discrepant results, they make a testable claim. . . . They then can conduct a confirmatory study to manipulate that moderator and demonstrate that they can reproduce the effect and make it vanish. In fact, they have a responsibility to do so."

We propose a middle ground, whereby the burden of proof is on the researcher espousing the least plausible claim. If an original study manipulated hunger by having participants fast for 8 hours, whereas a failed replication manipulated hunger by having participants fast for 8 minutes, then the burden of proof is on the replicator to show that the failure persists when hunger is more effectively manipulated. On the other hand, if original researchers attribute a failure to replicate their research to the fact that the replication was conducted on a different day of the week, then the burden of proof is on them to show that the day-of-the-week moderator is relevant. Although original and replication researchers often disagree about the plausibility of hypothesized moderators, neutral observers often agree. Thus, neutral observers often agree on who has the burden of proof.

Sometimes, the plausibility of an original author's explanation for a replication failure can be assessed by conducting additional analyses on existing data (Simonsohn 2016b). For example, Carney et al. (2015, table 2, row 2) suggested that Ranehill et al. (2015) may have failed to replicate their power poses effect because Ranehill et al.'s Swiss participants, unlike Carney et al.'s (2010) US participants, may not have associated the same poses with power. This explanation predicts that the power manipulation should not have worked in the replication. However, in the Swiss replication, "results showed a significant effect of power posing on self-reported feelings of power," (Ranehill et al. 2015, p. 653) indicating that the power poses manipulation was, in fact, successful in Switzerland. To be clear, not all of Carney et al.'s (2015) hypothesized moderators are ruled out by this particular analysis. Our purpose is simply to illustrate how new analyses of existing data can be used to assess the plausibility of hypothesized moderators.

Regardless of who has the burden of proof, it is absolutely essential for those who are not convinced by a failure to replicate to make testable claims about the circumstance(s) under which the effect is expected to replicate and, therefore, the circumstances under which a failure to replicate would be informative. For example, to move the debate forward, if Strack (2016) believes that The Far Side cartoons are no longer sensitive to smile-inducing manipulations, he would need to specify a precise set of procedures for choosing stimuli that will produce the effect. If critics of a replication cannot specify conditions under which the effect is expected to replicate, then they are not making a scientific claim (Lakatos 1970).

What is a failure to replicate? In the previous section, we discussed how failures to replicate should be interpreted. But how do we even know when a replication attempt has failed? This question is harder to answer than it appears.

Replications have traditionally been deemed failures when the effect described by the original study is not statistically significant in the replication. This approach has two obvious flaws. First, a replication attempt could be nonsignificant simply because its sample size is too small (Asendorpf et al. 2013, Patil et al. 2016, Valentine et al. 2011, Verhagen & Wagenmakers 2014). Second, a replication attempt could be significant even if the effect size is categorically smaller than in the original. For example, imagine that an original study produces a significant effect size of $d = 0.80$ with 20 observations per cell, and a replication produces a significant effect size of $d = 0.01$ with 20 *million* observations per cell. Despite the statistically significant effect in the replication, it is clear that the original study could not have detected such a small effect. It thus seems odd to treat the replication as successful (Simonsohn 2015c).

An alternative approach is to examine whether the replication effect size is significantly different from the original effect size. This approach similarly suffers from two major problems. First, when original effects are barely significant (e.g., $p = 0.049$), replications with nearly infinite sample sizes may not be significantly different from the original, even if the true effect size is exactly zero (Asendorpf et al. 2013, Simonsohn 2015c). This means that replications of p-hacked false-positive findings are particularly unlikely to fail, as such findings tend to have p-values that are barely significant (Simonsohn et al. 2014a). Second, if the original and replication studies are both highly powered, a statistically significant difference may not be meaningful. For instance, if an original study found an effect size of $\hat{d} = 0.53$ and a replication found a significantly different effect size of $\hat{d} = 0.51$, it would be bizarre to conclude that the replication had failed.[12]

Other approaches to comparing original and replication results are also unsatisfactory. The Reproducibility Project (Open Sci. Collab. 2015) relied on a few different tests to assess how many of 100 replication attempts were failures. One such test examined whether the original study's effect size estimate was within the confidence interval of the replication. However, this approach ignores the uncertainty around the original study's effect size estimate and, consequently, inflates failure rates, making psychology seem *less* replicable than it is. Critical of the Reproducibility Project's conclusion, Gilbert et al. (2016) reanalyzed their data and tested whether the replication's effect size estimate was within the confidence interval of the original. However, this approach ignores the uncertainty around the replication's effect size estimate and, consequently, deflates failure rates, making psychology seem *more* replicable than it is (for a detailed discussion, see Simonsohn 2016a).

All of these approaches lack two critical features. First, they fail to account for the fact that replication attempts may be *inconclusive*, rather than definitive successes or failures (Etz & Vandekerckhove 2016, Simonsohn 2015c, Verhagen & Wagenmakers 2014). Second, they fail to test whether the effect size observed in the replication is small enough for us to call it a failure. To accomplish this, one must define what "small enough" means. One approach is to define "small enough" in absolute terms. For example, one could test whether the replication study allows one to reject an effect size of $|d| \geq 0.10$ (see, e.g., Greenwald 1975; Serlin & Lapsley 1985, 1992). This approach requires replication sample sizes to be very large, as one needs approximately 1,500 observations per cell to have an 80% chance to reject $d \geq 0.10$ if the true effect size is zero. A more practical definition of "small enough" incorporates a relative assessment of size. Two approaches have been proposed along these lines. One is a Bayesian approach that tests whether the replication is more consistent with there being no effect or with the conclusions from the original study, given an assumed prior (Verhagen & Wagenmakers 2014).[13] The other assesses whether the effect size

---

[12]Patil et al. (2016) propose concluding that a replication has failed when its point estimate lies outside of the "prediction interval" of the original study. This is mathematically equivalent to testing whether the standardized point estimates of the original and replication studies are significantly different from each other.

[13]The default Bayesian t-test (Rouder et al. 2009) could also be used to assess whether a replication has failed. It tests whether the results are more consistent with the null or with a default hypothesis. Unfortunately, when one uses the default hypothesis

observed in the replication would have been detectable with the sample size used in the original.[14] This second approach leads to easy-to-interpret results and requires replicators to run 2.5 times the sample size of the original to have an 80% chance of concluding that the replication has failed if the true effect is zero (Simonsohn 2015c).[15]

Returning to the Reproducibility Project, only 36 of its 100 replication attempts obtained a significant result (Open Sci. Collab. 2015). Many observers, including those in the popular press, interpreted this as meaning that the rest had failed. For example, an article in *The New York Times* indicated that "More than 60 of the studies did not hold up" (Carey 2015). However, once we apply a better test of failure to replicate that allows for replications to be categorized as inconclusive, the interpretation differs. Again, 36% were conclusive successes; however, among the remaining 64%, only 25% were conclusive failures, and 49% were inconclusive, i.e., neither failures nor successes (Simonsohn 2016a; for similar results using the Bayesian approach to evaluating replications, see Etz & Vandekerckhove 2016). This high share of inconclusive results reflects the fact that many of the 100 replications were underpowered, with samples smaller than 2.5 times the sample sizes of the original studies.

Analyzing a Collection of Studies

Whereas replications aim to elucidate whether *individual* studies contain evidence, they cannot easily elucidate whether *collections* of studies contain evidence. To accomplish this, researchers have resorted to statistical reanalyses of existing data. Some of these approaches are designed to tell us whether a collection of studies contains any evidence of selective reporting; others are designed to tell us whether a collection of studies contains any evidence of the effect of interest after controlling for selective reporting. We discuss each of these approaches in turn.

Have the results we observed been selectively reported? Researchers have used tools such as the funnel plot (Egger et al. 1997) and the excessive significance test (Francis 2012, Ioannidis & Trikalinos 2007, Schimmack 2012) to assess the likelihood that a literature (or individual article) is missing at least one nonsignificant result. This approach suffers from at least two shortcomings. First, it does not seek to answer a question that needs to be answered. We already know that researchers do not report 100% of their nonsignificant studies and analyses. Some researchers have reported some null findings, but none have reported all of them. Second, and even more important, knowing that a literature contains selective reporting tells us nothing about whether the effects in that literature are actually true (Morey 2013, Simonsohn 2012). Thus, this approach is unable to answer the question we are actually interested in: Does the literature contain evidence once you correct for selective reporting?

After controlling for selective reporting, do the data suggest the effect exists? Trim-and-fill is the most common approach for correcting for selective reporting in a collection of studies (Duval & Tweedie 2000). This technique aims to create an unbiased set of studies by removing some seemingly biased studies from the set (trimming) and replacing them with fictitious studies

---

that proponents of the test have advocated for, the test classifies even highly significant small-to-moderate effects as accepting the null. It is prejudiced against small effects (Simonsohn 2015b).

[14]Simonsohn (2015c) has specifically proposed testing whether the original study would have had 33% power to detect the effect size observed in the replication.

[15]There are Bayesian approaches to these types of tests as well. Kruschke (2013) provides an approach that adopts an absolute definition of "small enough."

that are seemingly missing from the set (filling). Unfortunately, trim-and-fill vastly undercorrects for selective reporting. For example, when the true effect size is zero ($d = 0$) and selective reporting inflates the estimate to $\hat{d} = 0.72$, trim-and-fill corrects the estimate to $\hat{d} = 0.66$, thus producing an effect size estimate that is nearly as biased as it would have been without the correction (Simonsohn et al. 2014b, figure 2).[16]

A different approach for correcting for selective reporting is p-curve analysis (Simonsohn et al. 2014a). P-curve is the distribution of statistically significant p-values from a set of studies.[17] We can think of p-curve as the histogram of significant p-values (what share are 0.01s, what share are 0.02s, etc.), although p-curve analysis treats p-values as continuous. P-curve's shape can be used to diagnose whether a literature contains replicable effects. True effects of any size ($d \neq 0$), studied with samples of any size, generate right-skewed p-curves (more very significant than barely significant p-values). Truly nonexistent effects ($d = 0$), studied with samples of any size, generate flat p-curves (just as many very significant as barely significant p-values). Thus, significantly right-skewed p-curves tell us that a literature contains at least some effects that are expected to replicate, and significantly flat p-curves tell us that a literature's studies are not expected to replicate. (Nonsignificant p-curves are inconclusive.) Although p-curve analysis performs much better than other methods that aim to correct for publication bias, it is not infallible.[18] Like all other methods, p-curve analysis may lead to inaccurate results when the analyzed collection of studies includes some that are fraudulent, erroneously reported, or ambitiously p-hacked (e.g., seeking $p < 0.01$ instead of $p < 0.05$).[19] P-curve analysis may also be inaccurate if p-curvers incorrectly choose p-values from individual studies or if they select which studies to analyze after looking at the results (see Footnote 17).[20]

Simmons & Simonsohn (2017) provide an example of p-curve analysis that illustrates its ability to diagnose the replicability of effects. As mentioned above, Ranehill et al. (2015) failed to replicate Carney et al.'s (2010) effects of power poses on behavioral and hormonal outcomes. However, they did replicate Carney et al.'s effects of power poses on feelings of power (the manipulation check). Carney et al. (2015) responded to Ranehill et al. by identifying 33 articles purporting to show that power poses do affect downstream outcomes or feelings of power. Simmons and Simonsohn (2017) p-curved those articles, and the p-curve results matched those of the replication. Although a p-curve of studies analyzing self-reported feelings of power was directionally right skewed (suggesting the presence of replicable effects), the p-curve of studies analyzing downstream outcomes was significantly flat (suggesting the absence of replicable effects).

---

[16]PET-PEESE (Stanley & Doucouliagos 2014) is an alternative but less popular tool. It performs poorly both in the presence of selective reporting (Gervais 2015) and in its absence (Simonsohn 2017). Psychologists should not use PET-PEESE.

[17]These p-values must come from an analysis that tested the original authors' hypothesis of interest, be statistically independent of each other, and be expected to have a uniform distribution under the null; we provide detailed guidelines on how to select p-values in ways that ensure that these statistical requirements are met (Simonsohn et al. 2014a, figure 4).

[18]P-curve analysis can also be used to estimate effect size correcting for publication bias (Simonsohn et al. 2014b).

[19]Ulrich & Miller (2015) first pointed out the problem with ambitious p-hacking. In "Better P-curves" (Simonsohn et al. 2015), we modified p-curve analysis to make it more robust.

[20]Some critics have claimed that p-curve analysis is distorted in the presence of effect size heterogeneity, that is, when different studies included in p-curve investigate effects of different sizes (McShane et al. 2016, van Aert et al. 2016). However, p-curve is actually robust to heterogeneity (see, e.g., Simonsohn et al. 2014a, figure 2; Simonsohn et al. 2014b, supplement 2). The different perspectives arise because of how the critics define the question of interest. P-curve estimates the average true effect of the studies that are included in the analyses, which is the result that we believe to be of interest. The critics would like p-curve to estimate the average effect of all studies that could ever be attempted, a result that we do not believe to be of interest. In any case, for any method to achieve the critics' objective, researchers would need to design and attempt their studies at random, which they do not.

INNOCENT ERRORS AND (NOT-SO-INNOCENT) FRAUD

Although p-hacking is arguably the biggest threat to the validity of published research, it is not the only threat. Results can also be false positive because of unintentional errors or fraud. In this section, we review efforts to address these important problems.

Unintentional Errors

Many parts of the publication process are susceptible to human error, including data entry and analysis, the copying of results from statistical software into manuscripts, and the copyediting process. Most errors are impossible for readers and reviewers to detect without having access to the raw data, making it impossible to assess their prevalence. However, some errors are visible to those who are looking for them. For example, one article with more than 600 Google Scholar citations contains the line, "…showing an increase in expected willingness to help when payment level increased from low to medium, $F(1, 607) = 3.48, p < 0.001$." That phrase includes all the information needed to detect the reporting error, as the p-value associated with $F(1, 607) = 3.48$ is not $p < 0.001$, but rather $p = 0.063$. It is clear that there is an error with the F-value, p-value, or both.[21]

To see how common it is for research articles to contain these types of errors, Bakker & Wicherts (2011) checked the internal consistency of 4,077 test results reported in various psychology journals. They found that 54% of articles contained at least one error, and 12% had at least one error that altered the statistical significance of a reported result.[22] In a separate effort, Brown & Heathers (2016) developed the granularity-related inconsistency of means (GRIM) test, which checks whether reported means of integer data (e.g., Likert scales) are consistent with reported sample sizes. For instance, if an article's sample size is $n = 10$, the mean of a Likert scale variable could include up to one decimal; thus, for example, 2.32 is not a possible mean when $n = 10$. Applying the GRIM test to a small sample of 71 articles, Brown & Heathers (2016) found that more than 50% had at least one error.

Although some researcher errors are slight and inconsequential, others are more serious and may invalidate the researchers' conclusions or expose deeper problems with the researchers' methods and analyses. For example, seemingly inconsequential errors detected by applying the GRIM test to a set of four articles by the same author led to the discovery of potentially more serious errors in unrelated articles by that author (see van der Zee et al. 2017).

Perhaps the simplest solution to this problem is to require authors to post their data and materials. Because even the most well-intentioned researcher is bound to make an occasional mistake, it makes sense to allow those mistakes to be identified and corrected. Public data posting not only allows others to verify the accuracy of the analyses, but also incentivizes authors to more carefully avoid errors (Miguel et al. 2014, Wicherts & Bakker 2012). We started posting data, code, and original materials for our own research a few years ago; it is sobering how often these actions lead us to catch errors shortly before we submit our manuscripts. Our own "False-Positive Psychology" article (Simmons et al. 2011) had a (fortunately inconsequential) error that was discovered, 5 years after publication, by a careful reader relying on our posted materials.[23]

---

[21]Every test result in this article is incorrect; our best guess is that the reported F-values are actually t-values. For instance, the quoted $F(1, 607) = 3.48$ should have been reported as $t(607) = 3.48$.

[22]Similar analyses and results are reported by Berle & Starcevic (2007), García-Berthou & Alcaraz (2004), and Nuijten et al. (2016).

[23]The error was discovered by Aurélien Allard; the updated R code to reproduce the simulations in the article explains the nature of the error (**https://osf.io/a67ft/**). **Figure 1** reports the corrected results.

The OSF has dramatically facilitated the posting of raw data and materials. Moreover, the journal *Psychological Science*, under the editorship of Eric Eich (2014) and in collaboration with the Center for Open Science, has introduced a badge system that places a small icon on the first page of articles that have made their data and materials publicly accessible. Kidwell et al. (2016) report that, before the badge system began (in 2014), authors publishing in *Psychological Science* were just as unlikely to make their data publicly available as were authors publishing in other leading journals (about 3% of authors did so). By the following year, authors publishing in *Psychological Science* were posting their data almost 40% of the time, whereas the other journals saw no increase at all.

Fraud

Many see fraud as the asteroid collision of social science, locally catastrophic but so rare that prevention is hardly relevant. Suspicions of fraud in, and the accompanying retractions of, articles published by Stapel, Smeesters, Sanna, Chiou, Förster, LaCour, and others suggest that this view of fraud may be naive. Discussions of fraud typically focus on two questions: How common is it and how can we stop it?[24]

Estimating the frequency of fraud is very difficult. Some blatantly detectable fraud is prevented by vigilant coauthors, reviewers, or editors and, thus, not typically observed by the rest of the field. The fraud that gets through those filters might be noticed by a very small share of readers. Of those readers, a very small number might ever make their concerns known. And of those concerns, fewer still will eventually be made public, as bringing forward concerns of fraud imposes reputational risks, enormous time commitments, and no tangible reward. This is merely to say that, for every case of fraud that is identified, there are almost certainly many more that are not. Even restricting the prevalence estimate to publicly identified cases, it is increasingly clear that fraud is frequent enough to require more than a passing consideration. To our knowledge, there is no perfect or excellent solution. We discuss three imperfect ones, from least to most promising.

Do not worry about it. Section 8.10 of the American Psychological Association code of ethics simply states, "psychologists do not fabricate data" (**http://web.archive.org/web/20160803035613/http://www.apa.org/ethics/code/manual-updates.aspx**). That statement clarifies the aspirations of the APA but not how it aims to detect or adjudicate violations of the ethical code. The status quo is to simply not worry about these violations. Although this has the benefits of being socially agreeable (e.g., suggesting that we assume that everyone is honest) and easy to implement, it is a dangerous and untenable approach.

Make data public. The APA code of ethics also states (in Section 8.14) that "after research results are published, psychologists do not withhold the data on which their conclusions are based." This is a good start to preventing fraud. As some have argued (Miguel et al. 2014, Simonsohn 2013, Wicherts 2011), the sharing of data serves the dual function of encouraging researchers to be accurate and honest and providing readers with the tools to detect errors and fraud. Requesting data from another researcher—particularly for the stated justification of suspecting fraud—is socially taxing. Furthermore, although the APA prescribes the sharing of data, there is no enforcement mechanism. We have heard many stories from other researchers who were told that the requested

---

[24]For information on Chiou's retracted article, see **http://datacolada.org/1**; for information on one of Förster's retracted articles, see **http://datacolada.org/21**. We refer to the other retracted articles in other sections of this review.

data were coming soon (but then never arrive), were impossible to share, had been lost, or were legally impounded. We have personally been denied data explicitly because the authors wished to avoid criticism; the authors wrote bluntly, "no data for you." The APA already says that data should be available upon request, but in practice, they are not (see e.g., Wicherts et al. 2006, 2011). Indeed, psychologists' reluctance to share data has been systematically documented (Wicherts et al. 2006). It seems insincere to equate being a psychologist with being a data sharer (as the APA does in the above quote) and to then fail to require psychologists to post their data.

Make studies auditable. Data-sharing policies would not have been enough to stop Mike LaCour from publishing a (since retracted) article in *Science* based on apparently fraudulent data (LaCour & Green 2014). The sequence that led to the development of the project and the publication of the article illustrates just how hard fraud is to detect and how destructive it can be. LaCour, a graduate student, approached Green, a renowned professor, with an early set of data. Green was skeptical and requested a replication, and LaCour delivered it; at that point, Green, a famously skeptical methodologist, was persuaded to coauthor the article. Although methodological expertise, a replication, the peer review process, and data sharing did not detect the apparent fraud, an audit of the study did. When a pair of graduate students were attempting a replication and needed more details than were included in the published article, they contacted the survey firm that had supposedly collected the data. The firm had never heard of LaCour and did not have the capacity to collect the type of data that LaCour had claimed to have obtained from them. It was not some sophisticated procedure that led to the retraction (none of those were sufficient), but rather something akin to the type of basic fact checking that journalists routinely do (Singal 2015; D. Broockman, J. Kalla, and P. Aronow, unpublished manuscript, **https://web.archive.org/web/https://stanford.edu/~dbroock/broockman_kalla_aronow_lg_irregularities.pdf**).

The US Internal Revenue Service does not audit all taxpayers, but all taxpayers are expected to file taxes as if they will be audited. We think that researchers should similarly behave as if they will be audited. For example, journals could require authors to provide information on exactly when (i.e., specific dates and times), exactly where, and by whom the data were collected. Journals could then do the routine fact checking that newspapers do. As it currently stands, if *The New York Times* writes an article about a publication in *Science*, only the former does any fact checking.

OTHER ATTEMPTS AT REFORM

In this review, we have focused on methodological reforms designed to diagnose or decrease the publication of false positives. However, not all of the methodological reforms proposed in recent years will, or even attempt to, accomplish this. In this section, we briefly discuss two such categories of reform: an emphasis on meta-analysis and a de-emphasis on *p*-values.

Meta-Analyses

The acknowledged fallibility of individual studies has inspired some researchers to advocate for considering aggregations of many studies instead (Braver et al. 2014, Stanley & Spence 2014, Tuk et al. 2015). We can characterize this perspective as advocating for meta-analytic thinking (Cumming 2014). Meta-analytic thinking has its benefits. It allows inferences to be based on larger and potentially more diverse samples, promotes collaboration among scientists, and incentivizes more systematic research programs. Nevertheless, meta-analytic thinking not only fails to solve the problems of *p*-hacking, reporting errors, and fraud, it dramatically exacerbates them. In our view, meta-analytic thinking would make the false-positives problem worse, not better (for other concerns about meta-analysis, see Sharpe 1997, Ueno et al. 2016).

What is so problematic about meta-analytical thinking? To answer this question, it is useful to distinguish between meta-analyses that aggregate studies across versus within articles. When aggregating studies across articles, the main goal is to compute an overall average effect. In fields like medicine, different research teams will sometimes conduct functionally identical studies of the same effect; in these cases, the average result is a more precise answer to the question everyone is asking (e.g., what is the average effect of Prozac on depression?). In psychology, however, different research teams study different effects; in these cases, the average result is a more precise answer to a question nobody is asking (e.g., what is the average effect of all possible psychological interventions that could ever be attempted on depression?). Indeed, meta-analyses in psychology typically estimate a parameter that does not exist (Simonsohn 2015a).

Leaving the meaningfulness of the question aside, there is the issue of the credibility of the answer. Meta-analysts are further from data collection than are the original researchers. That distance, in combination with the sheer number of studies included in meta-analyses, makes it infeasible for the meta-analyst (and for reviewers and readers of the meta-analysis) to assess the quality of the original data. For example, the meta-analyst cannot assess if an original result was caused by errors of data collection or analysis or if it was a product of a methodological detail that was not divulged by the original authors. Even assessing the quality of the original design is often infeasible given the number of studies involved (e.g., the presence of confounds or demand effects). Furthermore, the harder a meta-analyst works to avoid publication bias by including unpublished work, the more the quality control problem is amplified by the addition of content that has either never been reviewed or been reviewed and rejected. All of these factors are especially consequential given that errors in original studies are not random—they are usually biased in the direction of finding statistical significance—and thus do not cancel out across studies. The end result of a meta-analysis is as strong as the weakest link; if there is *some* garbage in, then there is *only* garbage out.

On the surface, aggregating studies *within* articles would seem to solve some of these problems, but, in fact, it makes some of those problems much more severe. Currently, the expectation is that, even in multistudy articles, an individual study must be judged on its own merits. Thus, if one study is deemed to be problematic, it need not affect what one infers about the others. When we evaluate evidence by relying on the statistical aggregation of all studies in an article, a single problematic study will contaminate the inferences of the remainder. Thus, a multistudy article may hinge on the impact of a single flawed study that carries all other studies through the meta-analytic filter.

If someone is presented with four cups of juice and one cup of poison, they can drink safely by avoiding the poisoned cup. However, if all five cups are poured into a single pitcher, they are going to get sick. Similarly, if one out of five studies is poorly done or obviously p-hacked, that study can be easily and safely ignored. However, if it is combined with the other studies into one analysis, it will taint them all (and that taint is likely to go unnoticed). In addition, combining many studies into one analysis can dramatically exacerbate the consequences of p-hacking. Consider a researcher who minimally p-hacks by simply choosing the best of three uncorrelated dependent variables. If they conduct one study, the false-positive rate increases to just 7.3%. However, if the same researcher were to apply the same behavior across 10 studies and then meta-analyze them, then the false-positive rate increases to a staggering 83% (Vosgerau et al. 2017).[25]

Thus, meta-analysis does not solve the problems the field faces; it exacerbates them.

---

[25] These calculations assume a directional prediction submitted to a two-sided test and, thus, a 2.5% false-positive rate without p-hacking.

P-Value Bashing

When, during the Lyndon Johnson administration,[26] Bakan (1966) wrote an article in opposition to the use of p-values in psychology, he raised complaints that will sound familiar to readers today: "the null hypothesis is generally false anyway" (p. 425), "papers in which significance has not been obtained are not submitted" (p. 427), "this wrongness is based on the commonly held belief that the p value is a 'measure' of degree of confidence" (p. 430), "we would be much better off if we were to attempt to estimate the magnitude of the parameters in the population" (p. 436), and, "In terms of a statistical approach which is an alternative, the various methods associated with the theorem of Bayes...may be appropriate" (p. 436). Strikingly, Bakan (1966, p. 423) opens this 50-year-old article by saying, "what will be said in this paper is hardly original. It is, in a certain sense, what 'everybody knows.'" We may accurately call these arguments the "old statistics critiques."

These old statistics critiques and the counterarguments put forward by those espousing the continued use of p-values have been rehashed by every generation of psychological researchers. Psychology's renaissance did not interfere with this tradition. Cumming (2014) has recently argued for point estimation and confidence intervals to be used over p-values, Kruschke (2013) for Bayesian estimation over p-values, and Wagenmakers et al. (2011) for Bayes factors over p-values.

Despite their repeated republication, the influence of the old statistics critiques on actual practice has not been significant. Like researchers in Bakan's era, researchers in our era rely heavily on p-values. Why is this the case?

We think it is because there is actually no compelling reason to abandon the use of p-values. It is true that p-values are imperfect, but, for the types of questions that most psychologists are interested in answering, they are no more imperfect than confidence intervals, effect sizes, or Bayesian approaches. The biggest problem with p-values is that they can be mindlessly relied upon; however, when effect size estimates, confidence intervals, or Bayesian results are mindlessly relied upon, the results are at least as problematic. It is not the statistic that causes the problem, it is the mindlessness. We suspect some readers will strongly disagree with our position (both today and 50 years from today), but they probably will not disagree with the fact that these alternative approaches do not address the fundamental problem that psychology's renaissance has concerned itself with: conducting research in ways that make false positives less likely.

CONCLUSION

Roughly seven years ago, our field realized that the credibility of our discipline hinged on changing the way we collect and analyze data. And the field has responded. Practices that promise to increase the integrity of our discipline—e.g., replications, disclosure, preregistration—are orders of magnitude more common than they were just a short time ago. Although they are not yet common enough, it is clear that the Middle Ages are behind us, and the Enlightenment is just around the corner.

DISCLOSURE STATEMENT

The authors are not aware of any affiliations, memberships, funding, or financial holdings that might be perceived as affecting the objectivity of this review.

---

[26]For our European friends, think Charles de Gaulle.

LITERATURE CITED

Achenbach J. 2011. Diederik Stapel: the lying Dutchman. *The Washington Post Blog*, Nov. 1. **http://web.archive.org/web/20170418235730/https://www.washingtonpost.com/blogs/achenblog/post/diederik-stapel-the-lying-dutchman/2011/11/01/gIQA86XOdM_blog.html**

Alogna VK, Attaya MK, Aucoin P, Bahník Š, Birch S, et al. 2014. Registered replication report: Schooler and Engstler-Schooler (1990). *Perspect. Psychol. Sci.* 9:556–78

Anderson CJ, Bahník Š, Barnett-Cowan M, Bosco FA, Chandler J, et al. 2016. Response to comment on "Estimating the reproducibility of psychological science." *Science* 351:1037

Asendorpf JB, Conner M, De Fruyt F, De Houwer J, Denissen JJ, et al. 2013. Recommendations for increasing replicability in psychology. *Eur. J. Personal.* 27:108–19

Bakan D. 1966. The test of significance in psychological research. *Psychol. Bull.* 66:423–37

Bakker M, van Dijk A, Wicherts JM. 2012. The rules of the game called psychological science. *Perspect. Psychol. Sci.* 7:543–54

Bakker M, Wicherts JM. 2011. The (mis)reporting of statistical results in psychology journals. *Behav. Res. Methods* 43:666–78

Bargh JA, Chen M, Burrows L. 1996. Automaticity of social behavior: direct effects of trait construct and stereotype activation on action. *J. Personal. Soc. Psychol.* 71:230–44

Bem D, Tressoldi PE, Rabeyron T, Duggan M. 2016. Feeling the future: a meta-analysis of 90 experiments on the anomalous anticipation of random future events. *F1000Res.* 4:1188

Bem DJ. 2011. Feeling the future: experimental evidence for anomalous retroactive influences on cognition and affect. *J. Personal. Soc. Psychol.* 100:407–25

Berle D, Starcevic V. 2007. Inconsistencies between reported test statistics and *p*-values in two psychiatry journals. *Int. J. Methods Psychiatric Res.* 16:202–7

Bones AK. 2012. We knew the future all along. *Perspect. Psychol. Sci.* 7:307–9

Brandt MJ, IJzerman H, Dijksterhuis A, Farach FJ, Geller J, et al. 2014. The replication recipe: What makes for a convincing replication? *J. Exp. Soc. Psychol.* 50:217–24

Braver SL, Thoemmes FJ, Rosenthal R. 2014. Continuously cumulating meta-analysis and replicability. *Perspect. Psychol. Sci.* 9:333–42

Brown NJ, Heathers JA. 2016. The GRIM test: A simple technique detects numerous anomalies in the reporting of results in psychology. *Soc. Psychol. Personal. Sci.* 8(4):363–69

Carey B. 2011a. Fraud case seen as a red flag for psychology research. *The New York Times*, Nov. 2

Carey B. 2011b. Journal's paper on ESP expected to prompt outrage. *The New York Times*, Jan. 5

Carey B. 2015. Many psychology findings not as strong as claimed, study says. *The New York Times*, Aug. 27. **https://web.archive.org/web/20170714054021/https://www.nytimes.com/2015/08/28/science/many-social-science-findings-not-as-strong-as-claimed-study-says.html**

Carney DR, Cuddy AJ, Yap AJ. 2010. Power posing: Brief nonverbal displays affect neuroendocrine levels and risk tolerance. *Psychol. Sci.* 21:1363–68

Carney DR, Cuddy AJ, Yap AJ. 2015. Review and summary of research on the embodied effects of expansive (versus contractive) nonverbal displays. *Psychol. Sci.* 26:657–63

Chase LJ, Chase RB. 1976. A statistical power analysis of applied psychological research. *J. Appl. Psychol.* 61:234–37

Cheung I, Campbell L, LeBel EP. 2016. Registered replication report: Study 1 from Finkel, Rusbult, Kumashiro, & Hannon 2002. *Perspect. Psychol. Sci.* 11:750–64

Cohen J. 1962. The statistical power of abnormal-social psychological research: a review. *J. Abnorm. Soc. Psychol.* 65:145–53

Cole LC. 1957. Biological clock in the unicorn. *Science* 125:874–76

Cumming G. 2014. The new statistics: why and how. *Psychol. Sci.* 25:7–29

Doyen S, Klein O, Pichon CL, Cleeremans A. 2012. Behavioral priming: It's all in the mind, but whose mind? *PLOS ONE* 7:e29081

Duval S, Tweedie R. 2000. Trim and fill: a simple funnel-plot–based method of testing and adjusting for publication bias in meta-analysis. *Biometrics* 56:455–63

Ebersole CR, Atherton OE, Belanger AL, Skulborstad HM, Allen JM, et al. 2016. Many Labs 3: evaluating participant pool quality across the academic semester via replication. *J. Exp. Soc. Psychol.* 67:68–82

Egger M, Smith GD, Schneider M, Minder C. 1997. Bias in meta-analysis detected by a simple, graphical test. *BMJ* 315:629–34

Eich E. 2014. Business not as usual. *Psychol. Sci.* 25:3–6

Etz A, Vandekerckhove J. 2016. A Bayesian perspective on the reproducibility project: psychology. *PLOS ONE* 11:e0149794

Fanelli D. 2012. Negative results are disappearing from most disciplines and countries. *Scientometrics* 90:891–904

Fiedler K. 2011. Voodoo correlations are everywhere—not only in neuroscience. *Perspect. Psychol. Sci.* 6:163–71

Fiedler K, Kutzner F, Krueger JI. 2012. The long way from α-error control to validity proper: problems with a short-sighted false-positive debate. *Perspect. Psychol. Sci.* 7:661–69

Fiedler K, Schwarz N. 2016. Questionable research practices revisited. *Soc. Psychol. Personal. Sci.* 7:45–52

Francis G. 2012. Too good to be true: publication bias in two prominent studies from experimental psychology. *Psychon. Bull. Rev.* 19(2):151–56

Galak J, LeBoeuf RA, Nelson LD, Simmons JP. 2012. Correcting the past: failures to replicate ψ. *J. Personal. Soc. Psychol.* 103:933–48

García-Berthou E, Alcaraz C. 2004. Incongruence between test statistics and P values in medical papers. *BMC Med. Res. Methodol.* 4:13

Gervais W. 2015. Putting PET-PEESE to the test. *Will Gervais Blog*, June 25. **https://web.archive.org/web/20170326200626/http://willgervais.com/blog/2015/6/25/putting-pet-peese-to-the-test-1**

Gilbert DT, King G, Pettigrew S, Wilson TD. 2016. Comment on "Estimating the reproducibility of psychological science." *Science* 351:1037

Goldin-Meadow S. 2016. Why preregistration makes me nervous. *Association for Psychological Science Observer*, Sept. **https://web.archive.org/web/20170227180244/http://www.psychologicalscience.org/observer/why-preregistration-makes-me-nervous**

Greenwald AG. 1975. Consequences of prejudice against the null hypothesis. *Psychol. Bull.* 82:1–20

Inbar Y. 2016. Association between contextual dependence and replicability in psychology may be spurious. *PNAS* 113(43):E4933–34

Ioannidis JPA. 2005. Why most published research findings are false. *PLOS Med.* 2:696–701

Ioannidis JPA, Trikalinos TA. 2007. An exploratory test for an excess of significant findings. *Clin. Trials* 4:245–53

John L, Loewenstein GF, Prelec D. 2012. Measuring the prevalence of questionable research practices with incentives for truth-telling. *Psychol. Sci.* 23:524–32

K12 Reader. 2012. The scientific method. In *2nd Grade Reading Comprehension Worksheets*. **http://www.k12reader.com/worksheet/the-scientific-method/view**

Kerr NL. 1998. HARKing: hypothesizing after the results are known. *Personal. Soc. Psychol. Rev.* 2:196–217

Kidwell MC, Lazarević LB, Baranski E, Hardwicke TE, Piechowski S, et al. 2016. Badges to acknowledge open practices: a simple, low-cost, effective method for increasing transparency. *PLOS Biol.* 14:e1002456

Klein RA, Ratliff K, Vianello M, Reginald B, Adams J, Bahnik S, et al. 2014. *Investigating variation in replicability: a "Many Labs" replication project*. Open Sci. Found. Proj., Cent. Open Sci./Va. Commonwealth Univ., Charlottesville, VA/Richmond, VA

Koole SL, Lakens D. 2012. Rewarding replications: a sure and simple way to improve psychological science. *Perspect. Psychol. Sci.* 7:608–14

Kruschke JK. 2013. Bayesian estimation supersedes the t test. *J. Exp. Psychol. Gen.* 142:573–603

Kunda Z. 1990. The case for motivated reasoning. *Psychol. Bull.* 108:480–98

LaCour MJ, Green DP. 2014. When contact changes minds: an experiment on transmission of support for gay equality. *Science* 346:1366–69

Lakatos I. 1970. Falsification and the methodology of scientific research programmes. In *Criticism and the Growth of Knowledge*, ed. I Lakatos, A Musgrave, pp. 170–96. Cambridge, UK: Cambridge Univ. Press

Lakens D. 2014. Performing high-powered studies efficiently with sequential analyses. *Eur. J. Soc. Psychol.* 44:701–10

Leamer EE. 1983. Let's take the con out of econometrics. *Am. Econ. Rev.* 73(1):31–43

Levelt WJ, Drenth P, Noort E. 2012. *Flawed science: the fraudulent research practices of social psychologist Diederik Stapel*. Rep., Tilburg Univ./Univ. Amsterdam/Univ. Groningen, Tilburg, Neth./Amsterdam/Groningen, Neth.

Lindsay DS. 2015. Replication in psychological science. *Psychol. Sci.* 26:1827–32

Luce MF, McGill A, Peracchio L. 2012. *Promoting an Environment of Scientific Integrity: Individual and Community Responsibilities*. Oxford, UK: Oxford Univ. Press

Mahoney MJ. 1979. Review paper: psychology of the scientist: an evaluative review. *Soc. Stud. Sci.* 9:349–75

McShane BB, Böckenholt U, Hansen KT. 2016. Adjusting for publication bias in meta-analysis: an evaluation of selection methods and some cautionary notes. *Perspect. Psychol. Sci.* 11:730–49

Miguel E, Camerer CF, Casey K, Cohen J, Esterling K, et al. 2014. Promoting transparency in social science research. *Science* 343:30–31

Moore DA. 2016. Preregister if you want to. *Am. Psychol.* 71:238–39

Morey RD. 2013. The consistency test does not—and cannot—deliver what is advertised: a comment on Francis 2013. *J. Math. Psychol.* 57:180–83

Nosek BA, Lakens DE. 2013. Call for proposals: special issue of *Social Psychology* on "replications of important results in social psychology." *Soc. Psychol.* 44:59–60

Nuijten MB, Hartgerink CH, van Assen MA, Epskamp S, Wicherts JM. 2016. The prevalence of statistical reporting errors in psychology (1985–2013). *Behav. Res. Methods* 48:1205–26

Open Sci. Collab. 2012. An open, large-scale, collaborative effort to estimate the reproducibility of psychological science. *Perspect. Psychol. Sci.* 7:657–60

Open Sci. Collab. 2015. Estimating the reproducibility of psychological science. *Science* 349(6251):aac4716

Pashler H, Harris CR. 2012. Is the replicability crisis overblown? Three arguments examined. *Perspect. Psychol. Sci.* 7:531–36

Pashler H, Wagenmakers EJ. 2012. Editors' introduction to the special section on replicability in psychological science: a crisis of confidence? *Perspect. Psychol. Sci.* 7:528–30

Patil P, Peng RD, Leek JT. 2016. What should researchers expect when they replicate studies? A statistical view of replicability in psychological science. *Perspect. Psychol. Sci.* 11:539–44

Phillips CV. 2004. Publication bias in situ. *BMC Med. Res. Methodol.* 4:20

Popper KR. 1963. *Conjectures and Refutations: The Growth of Scientific Knowledge*. New York: Basic Books

Ranehill E, Dreber A, Johannesson M, Leiberg S, Sul S, Weber RA. 2015. Assessing the robustness of power posing: no effect on hormones and risk tolerance in a large sample of men and women. *Psychol. Sci.* 26(5):653–56

Rosenthal R. 1979. The "file drawer problem" and tolerance for null results. *Psychol. Bull.* 86:638–41

Rouder JN, Speckman PL, Sun D, Morey RD, Iverson G. 2009. Bayesian t tests for accepting and rejecting the null hypothesis. *Psychon. Bull. Rev.* 16:225–37

Schimmack U. 2012. The ironic effect of significant results on the credibility of multiple-study articles. *Psychol. Methods* 17:551–66

Schmidt S. 2009. Shall we really do it again? The powerful concept of replication is neglected in the social sciences. *Rev. Gen. Psychol.* 13:90–100

Sedlmeier P, Gigerenzer G. 1989. Do studies of statistical power have an effect on the power of studies? *Psychol. Bull.* 105:309–16

Serlin RC, Lapsley DK. 1985. Rationality in psychological research: the good-enough principle. *Am. Psychol.* 40:73–83

Serlin RC, Lapsley DK. 1992. Rational appraisal of psychological research and the good-enough principle. In *A Handbook for Data Analysis in the Behavioral Sciences: Methodological Issues*, ed. G Keren, C Lewis, 199–228. Mahwah, NJ: Lawrence Erlbaum Assoc.

Sharpe D. 1997. Of apples and oranges, file drawers and garbage: why validity issues in meta-analysis will not go away. *Clin. Psychol. Rev.* 17:881–901

Simmons JP, Nelson LD, Simonsohn U. 2011. False-positive psychology: Undisclosed flexibility in data collection and analysis allows presenting anything as significant. *Psychol. Sci.* 22:1359–66

Simmons JP, Nelson LD, Simonsohn U. 2012. A 21 word solution. *Dialogue* 26(2):4–7

Simmons JP, Nelson LD, Simonsohn U. 2017. False-positive citations. *Perspect. Psychol. Sci.* In press

Simmons JP, Simonsohn U. 2017. Power posing: p-curving the evidence. *Psychol. Sci.* 28(5):687–93

Simons DJ. 2014. The value of direct replication. *Perspect. Psychol. Sci.* 9:76–80

Simons DJ, Holcombe AO, Spellman BA. 2014. An introduction to registered replication reports at *Perspectives on Psychological Science*. *Perspect. Psychol. Sci.* 9:552–55

Simonsohn U. 2012. It does not follow: evaluating the one-off publication bias critiques by Francis (2012a, 2012b, 2012c, 2012d, 2012e, in press). *Perspect. Psychol. Sci.* 7:597–99

Simonsohn U. 2013. Just post it: the lesson from two cases of fabricated data detected by statistics alone. *Psychol. Sci.* 24:1875–88

Simonsohn U. 2014. [13] Posterior-hacking. *Data Colada*, Jan. 13. **https://web.archive.org/web/ http://datacolada.org/13**

Simonsohn U. 2015a. [33] The effect size does not exist. *Data Colada*, Feb. 9. **https://web.archive.org/web/ http://datacolada.org/33**

Simonsohn U. 2015b. [35] The default Bayesian test is prejudiced against small effects. *Data Colada*, Apr. 9. **https://web.archive.org/web/http://datacolada.org/35**

Simonsohn U. 2015c. Small telescopes: detectability and the evaluation of replication results. *Psychol. Sci.* 26:559–69

Simonsohn U. 2016a. [47] Evaluating replications: 40% full ≠ 60% empty. *Data Colada*, March 3. **https://web. archive.org/web/http://datacolada.org/47**

Simonsohn U. 2016b. Each reader decides if a replication counts: reply to Schwarz and Clore 2016. *Psychol. Sci.* 27:1410–12

Simonsohn U. 2017. [59] PET-PEESE is not like homeopathy. *Data Colada*, Apr. 12. **https://web.archive. org/web/http://datacolada.org/59**

Simonsohn U, Nelson LD, Simmons JP. 2014a. P-curve: a key to the file drawer. *J. Exp. Psychol. Gen.* 143:534–47

Simonsohn U, Nelson LD, Simmons JP. 2014b. P-curve and effect size: correcting for publication bias using only significant results. *Perspect. Psychol. Sci.* 9:666–81

Simonsohn U, Simmons JP, Nelson LD. 2015. Better p-curves: making p-curve analysis more robust to errors, fraud, and ambitions p-hacking, a reply to Ulrich and Miller (2015). *J. Exp. Psychol. Gen.* 144:1146–52

Singal J. 2015. The case of the amazing gay-marriage data: how a graduate student reluctantly uncovered a huge scientific fraud. *New York Magazine*, May 29

Stanley DJ, Spence JR. 2014. Expectations for replications: Are yours realistic? *Perspect. Psychol. Sci.* 9:305–18

Stanley T, Doucouliagos H. 2014. Meta-regression approximations to reduce publication selection bias. *Res. Synth. Methods* 5:60–78

Sterling TD. 1959. Publication decisions and their possible effects on inferences drawn from tests of significance—or vice versa. *J. Am. Stat. Assoc.* 54(285):30–34

Strack F. 2016. Reflection on the smiling registered replication report. *Perspect. Psychol. Sci.* 11(6):929–30

Strack F, Martin L, Stepper S. 1988. Inhibiting and facilitating conditions of the human smile: a nonobtrusive test of the facial feedback hypothesis. *J. Personal. Soc. Psychol.* 54:768–77

Stroebe W. 2016. Are most published social psychological findings false? *J. Exp. Soc. Psychol.* 66:134–44

Stroebe W, Strack F. 2014. The alleged crisis and the illusion of exact replication. *Perspect. Psychol. Sci.* 9:59–71

Tuk MA, Zhang K, Sweldens S. 2015. The propagation of self-control: Self-control in one domain simultaneously improves self-control in other domains. *J. Exp. Psychol. Gen.* 144(3):639–54

Tversky A, Kahneman D. 1971. Belief in the law of small numbers. *Psychol. Bull.* 76:105–10

Ueno T, Fastrich GM, Murayama K. 2016. Meta-analysis to integrate effect sizes within an article: possible misuse and Type I error inflation. *Am. Psychol. Assoc.* 145(5):643–54

Ulrich R, Miller J. 2015. P-hacking by post hoc selection with multiple opportunities: detectability by skewness test? Comment on Simonsohn, Nelson, and Simmons (2014). *J. Exp. Psychol. Gen.* 144:1137–45

Valentine JC, Biglan A, Boruch RF, Castro FG, Collins LM, et al. 2011. Replication in prevention science. *Prev. Sci.* 12:103–17

van Aert RC, Wicherts JM, van Assen MA. 2016. Conducting meta-analyses based on p values: reservations and recommendations for applying p-uniform and p-curve. *Perspect. Psychol. Sci.* 11:713–29

Van Bavel JJ, Mende-Siedlecki P, Brady WJ, Reinero DA. 2016. Contextual sensitivity in scientific reproducibility. *PNAS* 113(23):6454–59

van der Zee T, Anaya J, Brown NJL. 2017. Statistical heartburn: an attempt to digest four pizza publications from the Cornell Food and Brand Lab. *PeerJ Preprints* 5:e2748v1

van't Veer AE, Giner-Sorolla R. 2016. Pre-registration in social psychology—a discussion and suggested template. *J. Exp. Soc. Psychol.* 67:2–12

Vazire S. 2015. This is what *p*-hacking looks like. *Sometimes I'm Wrong*, Feb. **https://web.archive.org/web/http://sometimesimwrong.typepad.com/wrong/2015/02/this-is-what-p-hacking-looks-like.html**

Vazire S. 2016. Editorial. *Soc. Psychol. Personal. Sci.* 7:3–7

Verhagen J, Wagenmakers EJ. 2014. A Bayesian test to quantify the success or failure of a replication attempt. *J. Exp. Psychol. Gen.* 143:1457–75

Vosgerau J, Simonsohn U, Nelson LD, Simmons JP. 2017. *Don't do internal meta-analysis: it makes false-positives easier to produce and harder to correct.* Open Sci. Found. Proj., Cent. Open Sci., Charlottesville, VA

Vul E, Harris CR, Winkielman P, Pashler H. 2009. Puzzlingly high correlations in fMRI studies of emotion, personality, and social cognition. *Perspect. Psychol. Sci.* 4:274–90

Wagenmakers EJ, Beek T, Dijkhoff L, Gronau QF, Acosta A, et al. 2016. Registered replication report: Strack, Martin, & Stepper 1988. *Perspect. Psychol. Sci.* 11(6):917–28

Wagenmakers EJ, Wetzels R, Borsboom D, van der Maas HL. 2011. Why psychologists must change the way they analyze their data: the case of psi: comment on Bem 2011. *J. Personal. Soc. Psychol.* 100(3):426–32

Wagenmakers EJ, Wetzels R, Borsboom D, van der Maas HL, Kievit RA. 2012. An agenda for purely confirmatory research. *Perspect. Psychol. Sci.* 7:632–38

Wicherts JM. 2011. Psychology must learn a lesson from fraud case. *Nature* 480:7

Wicherts JM, Bakker M. 2012. Publish (your data) or (let the data) perish! Why not publish your data too? *Intelligence* 40:73–76

Wicherts JM, Bakker M, Molenaar D. 2011. Willingness to share research data is related to the strength of the evidence and the quality of reporting of statistical results. *PLOS ONE* 6:e26828

Wicherts JM, Borsboom D, Kats J, Molenaar D. 2006. The poor availability of psychological research data for reanalysis. *Am. Psychol.* 61:726–28

Cumulative Indexes

Contributing Authors, Volumes 59–69

Kang SK, 66:547–74
Kaplan RM, 64:471–98
Kassam KS, 66:799–823
Kasser T, 67:489–514
Keen R, 62:1–21
Keith N, 66:661–87
Kelley K, 59:536–63
Kelloway EK, 60:671–92
Kelso E, 66:277–94
Keltner D, 65:425–60
Kenny DA, 68:601–25
Kern ML, 65:719–42
Kilduff M, 64:527–47
Kim HS, 65:487–514
Kingdom FAA, 59:143–66
Kirkham NZ, 69:181–203
Kish-Gephart JJ, 65:635–60
Kitayama S, 62:419–49;
  64:335–59
Klein WMP, 68:573–600
Knapen T, 69:77–103
Knobe J, 63:81–99
Kobor MS, 69:459–85
Koenig MA, 69:251–73
Kogan A, 65:425–60
Koob GF, 59:29–53
Kopp CB, 62:165–87
Kornell N, 64:417–44
Kounios J, 65:71–93
Kraiger K, 60:451–74
Kramer AF, 66:769–97
Kraus N, 67:83–103
Krosnick JA, 68:327–51
Kurzban R, 66:575–99
Kutas M, 62:621–47

L

Lagnado D, 66:223–47
Lakin JL, 64:285–308
Langdon R, 62:271–98
Le Moal M, 59:29–53
Lee HS, 64:445–69
Lent RW, 67:541–65
Lerner JS, 66:799–823
Leuner B, 61:111–40
Leventhal EA, 59:477–505
Leventhal H, 59:477–505
Levin HS, 65:301–31
Levine EL, 63:397–425
Levitin DJ, 69:51–75
Lewis RL, 59:193–224

Li X, 65:301–31
Li Y, 66:799–823
Lievens F, 59:419–50
Liu Z, 66:631–59
Loewenstein G, 59:647–72
Loftus EF, 68:1–18
Logel C, 67:415–37
London J, 69:51–75
Lord RG, 61:543–68
Loughnan S, 65:399–423
Lowenstein AE, 62:483–500
Lustig CA, 59:193–224

M

Macey WH, 64:361–88
MacKenzie SB, 63:539–69
MacKinnon DP, 62:299–329
Magnuson K, 68:413–34
Maguire EA, 67:51–82
Maher CP, 61:599–622
Mahon BZ, 60:27–51
Maier MA, 65:95–120
Manuck SB, 65:41–70
Mar RA, 62:103–34
Markus HR, 65:611–34
Martin CL, 61:353–81
Masicampo EJ, 62:331–61
Mason W, 66:877–902
Masten AS, 63:227–57
Mather M, 67:213–38
Matthews KA, 62:501–30
Matzel LD, 64:169–200
Maxwell SE, 59:536–63
Mayer JD, 59:507–36
McAdams DP, 61:517–42
McArdle JJ, 60:577–605
McCaffery JM, 65:41–70
McDermott JM, 65:235–65
McGaugh JL, 66:1–24
McIntosh AR, 64:499–525
McKay R, 62:271–98
McLemore KA, 64:309–33
Meaney MJ, 61:439–66
Mechoulam R, 64:21–47
Meck WH, 65:743–71
Medin DL, 66:249–75
Mehler J, 61:191–218
Mende-Siedlecki P, 66:519–45
Mermelstein RJ, 60:229–55
Metcalfe J, 68:465–89
Milad MR, 63:129–51

Miller DT, 67:339–61
Miller GE, 60:501–24
Miller MI, 66:853–76
Mills KL, 65:187–207
Mišic B, 64:499–525
Monin B, 67:363–85
Moore KS, 59:193–224
Moore SR, 69:459–85
Moore T, 68:47–72
Moors A, 67:263–87
Mori S, 66:853–76
Morris MW, 66:631–59
Morris R, 59:451–75
Morris RGM, 61:49–79
Morrison C, 59:55–92
Moscovitch M, 67:105–34
Mukamel R, 63:511–37
Mullen E, 67:363–85
Mulliken GH, 61:169–90
Munafò MR, 67:567–85

N

Nadel L, 67:105–34
Nader K, 61:141–67
Nagayama Hall GC,
  60:525–48
Napier JL, 60:307–37
Narayan AJ, 63:227–57
Nee D, 59:193–224
Nelson LD, 69:511–34
Nesbit JC, 61:653–78
Neville H, 69:131–56
Nichols S, 63:81–99
Niedenthal PM, 63:259–85
Norenzayan A, 67:465–88
Northoff G, 64:335–59
Norton ES, 63:427–52
Norton MI, 60:475–99

O

O'Doherty JP, 68:73–100
Ogle CM, 61:325–51
Oishi S, 65:581–609
ojalehto bl, 66:249–75
Olivola CY, 66:519–45
Olson BD, 61:517–42
Oppenheimer DM, 66:277–94
Owen AM, 64:109–33
Oxenham AJ, 69:27–50
Oyserman D, 68:435–63

P

Pakulak E, 69:131–56
Palmer SE, 64:77–107
Paluck EL, 60:339–67
Park DC, 60:173–96
Parker LA, 64:21–47
Parker SK, 65:661–91
Pauli WM, 68:73–100
Pennington BF, 60:283–306
Perszyk DR, 69:231–50
Peter J, 67:315–38
Pettersson E, 65:515–40
Pettigrew TF, 67:1–21
Phillips DA, 62:483–500
Phillips LA, 59:477–505
Phillips LT, 65:611–34
Piff PK, 65:425–60
Pine DS, 66:459–86
Pittman TS, 59:361–85
Ployhart RE, 65:693–717
Podsakoff NP, 63:539–69
Podsakoff PM, 63:539–69
Poldrack RA, 67:587–612
Postle BR, 66:115–42
Powers A, 67:239–61
Prakash RS, 66:769–97
Pratte MS, 63:483–509
Preacher KJ, 66:825–52
Prentice DA, 67:339–61
Price DD, 59:565–90
Priniski SJ, 69:409–35
Proctor RW, 61:623–51

Q

Qiu A, 66:853–76
Quas JA, 61:325–51
Quirk GJ, 63:129–51

R

Rabinowitz AR, 65:301–31
Ratcliff R, 67:641–66
Rausch JR, 59:536–63
Rauschecker AM, 63:31–53
Raver CC, 66:711–31
Recanzone GH, 59:119–42
Redden JP, 69:1–25
Ressler K, 67:239–61
Reuter-Lorenz P, 60:173–96
Richeson JA, 67:439–63

Rick S, 59:647–72
Rilling JK, 62:23–48
Rissman J, 63:101–28
Robbins P, 63:81–99
Robbins TW, 67:23–50
Roberts RD, 59:507–36
Rodgers JL, 69:487–510
Roediger HL III, 59:225–54
Rogers T, 69:357–81
Rosati AG, 66:321–47
Rothman AJ, 68:573–600
Rousseau DM, 67:667–92
Rubin KH, 60:141–71
Ruble DN, 61:353–81
Rünger D, 67:289–314
Ryan AM, 65:693–717

S

Sackett PR, 59:419–50
Saffran JR, 69:181–203
Salmon DP, 60:257–82
Salthouse T, 63:201–26
Sammartino J, 64:77–107
Samuel AG, 62:49–72
Sanchez JI, 63:397–425
Sandler I, 62:299–329
Sanfey AG, 62:23–48
Santos LR, 66:321–47
Saribay SA, 59:329–60
Sarkissian H, 63:81–99
Sasaki JY, 65:487–514
Sasaki Y, 66:197–221
Saturn SR, 65:425–60
Schloss KB, 64:77–107
Schmidt AM, 61:543–68
Schneider B, 64:361–88
Schoenfelder EN,
  62:299–329
Scholz C, 69:329–56
Schooler JW, 66:487–518
Schyns PG, 68:269–97
Scott RM, 67:159–86
Seyfarth RM, 63:153–77
Shadish WR, 60:607–29
Shallice T, 69:157–80
Shamsudheen R, 66:689–710
Shanks DR, 61:273–301
Sharma S, 67:239–61
Shavitt S, 69:299–327
Shaywitz BA, 59:451–75
Shaywitz SE, 59:451–75

Sheeran P, 68:573–600
Sherman DK, 65:333–71
Shevell SK, 59:143–66
Shi J, 65:209–33
Shrout PE, 69:487–510
Shukla M, 66:349–79
Siegler RS, 68:187–213
Simmons J, 69:511–34
Simonsohn U, 69:511–34
Simpson JA, 68:383–411
Slater J, 67:83–103
Sloman SA, 66:223–47
Smallwood J, 66:487–518
Sobel N, 61:219–41
Sommers SR, 67:439–63
Sommers T, 63:81–99
Spencer SJ, 67:415–37
Sporer AK, 60:229–55
Sporns O, 67:613–40
Staudinger UM, 62:215–41
Stephens NM, 65:611–34
Sternberg RJ, 65:1–16
Sterzer P, 69:77–103
Stevens C, 69:131–56
Stone AA, 64:471–98
Sue S, 60:525–48
Sunstein CR, 67:713–37
Sutter ML, 59:119–42

T

Tasselli S, 64:527–47
Teki S, 65:743–71
Thau S, 60:717–41
Thompson LL, 61:491–515
Tipsord JM, 62:189–214
Todorov A, 66:519–45
Tomasello M, 64:231–55
Tong F, 63:483–509
Tooby J, 64:201–29
Tremblay RE, 69:383–407
Treviño LK, 65:635–60
Trickett EJ, 60:395–419
Tsai KM, 66:411–31
Turk-Browne NB, 62:73–101
Turkheimer E, 65:515–40

U

Uleman JS, 59:329–60
Uskul AK, 62:419–49

V

Vaish A, 64:231–55
Valdesolo P, 66:799–823
Valkenburg PM, 67:315–38
van IJzendoorn MH, 66:381–409
Vandello JA, 67:515–39
Varnum MEW, 64:335–59
Vitaro F, 69:383–407
Vogeley K, 64:335–59
Vohs KD, 62:331–61
Voss MW, 66:769–97
Votruba-Drzal E, 68:413–34
Vu KL, 61:623–51

W

Wagenmakers E, 67:641–66
Wagner AD, 63:101–28
Wagner LM, 67:387–413
Walther JB, 67:315–38

Walumbwa FO, 60:421–49
Wanberg CR, 63:369–96
Wandell BA, 63:31–53
Wang J, 61:491–515
Wang M, 65:209–33
Wang S, 61:49–79
Ward J, 64:49–75
Warneken F, 69:205–29
Watanabe T, 66:197–221
Waxman SR, 69:231–50
Weber TJ, 60:421–49
Weinman J, 59:477–505
Welsh DP, 60:631–52
Werker JF, 66:173–96
West SA, 66:575–99
Westfall J, 68:601–25
Wexler BE, 64:335–59
Whiten A, 68:129–54
Whitney D, 69:105–29
Williams JC, 67:515–39
Winne PH, 61:653–78

Winocur G, 67:105–34
Wolchik SA, 62:299–329
Wolf M, 63:427–52
Wood J, 61:303–24
Wood W, 67:289–314

Y

Yamanashi Leib A, 69:105–29
Yarkoni T, 67:587–612
Yeatman JD, 63:31–53
Yeshurun Y, 61:219–41
Yousafzai AK, 66:433–57

Z

Zajdel M, 68:545–71
Zane N, 60:525–48
Zhang T, 61:439–66
Zirnsak M, 68:47–72

Article Titles, Volumes 59–69

Social Psychology

Organizational Psychology or Organizational Behavior

Action Errors, Error Management, and Learning in Organizations	M Frese, N Keith	66:661–87

Work Motivation

Self-Regulation at Work	RG Lord, JM Diefendorff, AM Schmidt, RJ Hall	61:543–68

Leadership

Leadership: Current Theories, Research, and Future Directions	BJ Avolio, FO Walumbwa, TJ Weber	60:421–49

Cognition in Organizations

Cognition in Organizations	GP Hodgkinson, MP Healey	59:387–417
Personnel Selection	PR Sackett, F Lievens	59:419–50
Creativity	BA Hennessey, TM Amabile	61:569–98
Heuristic Decision Making	G Gigerenzer, W Gaissmaier	62:451–82

Work Attitudes (Job Satisfaction, Commitment, Identification)

The Intersection of Work and Family Life: The Role of Affect	LT Eby, CP Maher, MM Butts	61:599–622
Job Attitudes	TA Judge, JD Kammeyer-Mueller	63:341–67
The Individual Experience of Unemployment	CR Wanberg	63:369–96

Organizational Climate/Culture

Organizational Climate and Culture	B Schneider, MG Ehrhart, WH Macey	64:361–88
(Un)Ethical Behavior in Organizations	LK Treviño, NA den Nieuwenboer, JJ Kish-Gephart	65:635–60
Beyond Work-Life "Integration"	JC Williams, JL Berdahl, JA Vandello	67:515–39

Job/Work Design

Beyond Motivation: Job and Work Design for Development, Health, Ambidexterity, and More	SK Parker	65:661–91

Industrial Psychology/Human Resource Management

Employee Recruitment	JA Breaugh	64:389–416